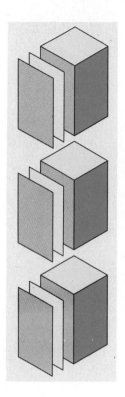

PASCAL
THE SOFTWARE
FUNDAMENTALS
OF COMPUTER SCIENCE

Richard A. Meyers
New York Institute of Technology

PRENTICE HALL
Englewood Cliffs, NJ 07632

Library of Congress Cataloging-in-Publication Data

Meyers, Richard A.
    Pascal : the software fundamentals of computer science / Richard
A. Meyers.
        p.   cm.
    Includes index.
    ISBN 0-13-725623-X
    1. Pascal (Computer program language)   I. Title.
QA76.73.P25M49 1992
005.13'3--dc20   91-28477
                                                      CIP

Acquisitions Editor/Editor-in-Chief: Marcia Horton
Production Editor: Bayani Mendoza de Leon
Marketing Manager: Gary June
Designers: Diana Andrews/Rosemarie Paccione
Cover Designer: Suzanne Behnke
Cover Illustrator: © Andrew Lange, Illustration and Design
Prepress Buyer: Linda Behrens
Manufacturing Buyer: Dave Dickey
Supplements Editor: Alice Dworkin
Editorial Assistant: Diana Penha

The author and publisher of this book have used their best efforts in preparing this book. These
efforts include the development, research, and testing of the theories and programs to determine
their effectiveness. The author and publisher make no warranty of any kind, expressed or
implied, with regard to these programs or the documentation contained in this book. The author
and publisher shall not be liable in any event for incidental or consequential damages in
connection with, or arising out of, the furnishing, performance, or use of these programs.

 © 1992 by Prentice-Hall, Inc.
A Simon & Schuster Company
Englewood Cliffs, NJ 07632

All rights reserved. No part of this book may be
reproduced, in any form or by any means,
without permission in writing from the publisher.

Printed in the United States of America
10 9 8 7 6 5 4 3 2 1

ISBN 0-13-725623-X

Prentice-Hall International (UK) Limited, *London*
Prentice-Hall of Australia Pty. Limited, *Sydney*
Prentice-Hall Canada Inc., *Toronto*
Prentice-Hall Hispanoamericana, S.A., *Mexico*
Prentice-Hall of India Private Limited, *New Delhi*
Prentice-Hall of Japan, Inc., *Tokyo*
Simon & Schuster Asia Pte. Ltd., *Singapore*
Editora Prentice-Hall do Brasil, Ltda., *Rio de Janeiro*

TRADEMARK INFORMATION

PC-DOS is a trademark of International
Business Machines Corporation

MS-DOS is a trademark of Microsoft
Corporation

UCSD is a trademark of the Regents
of University of California

Turbo Pascal is a trademark
of Borland International, Inc.

VAX is a registered trademark of
Digital Equipment Corporation

Macintosh is a registered trademark
of Apple Computer, Inc.

IBM is a registered trademark of
International Business Machines
Corporation

This book is dedicated to Beth,
my wife and my best friend

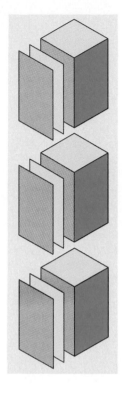

CONTENTS

2

INTRODUCTION TO PROGRAMMING 34

3

PROGRAM DEVELOPMENT 76

4

PROCEDURES   113

5

DECISION–MAKING   158

6

LOOPING

7

MORE BOOLEAN EXPRESSIONS AND INTRODUCTION TO ARRAYS 263

8

FUNCTIONS, BOOLEAN VARIABLES, AND ENUMERATED TYPES 314

9

TEXT FILES AND MORE STRING PROCESSING   361

10

MORE ONE–DIMENSIONAL ARRAYS   409

11

MULTIDIMENSIONAL ARRAYS

459

12

RECORDS AND ARRAYS OF RECORDS   507

13

DATA ABSTRACTION   551

14

SETS AND STRINGS   605

15

RECURSION   659

16

BINARY FILES AND POINTERS 713

17

LINKED LISTS WITH POINTERS 757

18

BINARY TREES 805

A

RESERVED WORDS AND STANDARD IDENTIFIERS   854

B

TABLE OF OPERATORS   856

C

HIERARCHY OF OPERATOR APPLICATIONS   858

D

TABLE OF STANDARD FUNCTIONS   859

E

TABLE OF STANDARD PROCEDURES   861

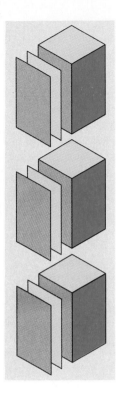

PREFACE

Advice to the Student

Welcome to the world of computer science in general and to this text in particular. In the course you are about to start, the text is one of the three resources that you will use. The other two resources are the classroom meetings and the sessions on the computer.

To get the most out of the course, use all three resources wisely. Prepare yourself by doing the assigned reading in advance of each class meeting. Then if you have a question, you will either have it answered in the lecture, or you can ask it at the appropriate time in the class meeting.

You are best prepared to start a programming project by going over both your lecture notes and the reading material from the text. In the first weeks of the course, you may want to have the text or the lecture notes in front of you while you familiarize yourself with the computer. As you become more proficient interacting with the computer, you should plan your projects *completely* before sitting down in front of the terminal. The more convinced you are that your program is correct and that it will run properly once it has been keyed in, the more fruitful your programming sessions will be.

Finally, do not forget that the key to becoming proficient in developing software is practice and plenty of it. Do as many of the short exercises at the end of each section of the text as you can, for most of them are geared toward helping you improve your software development skills. Also, give yourself plenty of time to do the machine projects. That way, if (when) problems arise, you will have time to analyze them and learn from your mistakes at a leisurely pace. You will, on the other hand, learn far less if you find yourself fixing or planning a project haphazardly the night before it is due.

The Purposes

A reference book of software engineering practices

Any text, whether it is a preschool reader or a treatise on the latest developments in particle physics, is written with a purpose in mind. This text's primary purpose is to serve as the main reading material for an introductory course in computer science at the college level (the CS1 course). It can, with additional outside reading, be adopted as the main text to cover the topics recommended by the ACM (Association for Computing Machinery) for the CS2 course.

The book fulfills a number of secondary purposes, all of which reflect the spirit of the ACM recommendations. It can be a reference handbook of current software engineering practices. These include the following:

1. Always writing modular code with good, clean interfaces.
2. Using abstraction in the software development process.
3. Testing a proposed software design thoroughly both from the top down and from the bottom up.
4. Accumulating an ever-growing "toolbox" of known algorithms that can be recycled and used to solve new problems.
5. Employing efficiency analysis on a proposed algorithm when necessary.
6. Writing source code documentation that is correct and informative.
7. Ensuring that one's source code is readable with consistent semantics for all variables and processes.

A reference book of the Pascal language

In many colleges, the language of instruction in courses beyond CS1 and CS2 is also Pascal. *Pascal: The Software Fundamentals of Computer Science* can, therefore, serve as a reference to the complete syntax and semantic usage of the constructs of Pascal in a more advanced CS course. A student can refer to it if he or she needs to clarify some point about the language not covered in the text of the more advanced course.

The Means

The means of fulfilling the primary purposes are also the ends of the secondary purposes, particularly those dealing with the software engineering practices. Let us talk a bit more about each of these practices we have listed.

I. *Modularity.* This topic is universally recognized as important. Like most other texts, this text also introduces procedures early. Procedural abstraction is used throughout, and all case studies are developed top–down, one block at a time. Starting with Chapter 4, most software development exercises at the end of the chapter are complex enough to require procedural abstraction for their solutions.

The importance of coding clean interfaces, developing small blocks of code, and writing adequate documentation for each module is stressed. In addition, we present many proven algorithms given in pseudocode form. These algorithms, with slight modifications, can be "plugged in" to the statement part of a modularized procedure or function. Therefore, they work as logical modules useful in solving part of a problem for which the relevant algorithm represents an appropriate solution.

II. *Abstraction*. This topic is covered at all levels of software development. On the simplest level, we use phrases such as *Ch is a digit* or *Int lies between 1 and 100* to represent a boolean expression not yet implemented. A proven algorithm represents a specific, yet modifiable, sequence of statements that return a known effect or result. The algorithms developed are initially described in the abstract and made more concrete with each refinement. Procedural abstraction is shown as a way to describe an involved process with a descriptive phrase that includes parameters. Data abstraction is introduced in Chapter 13 and used extensively throughout the remainder of the text to describe an involved process with a descriptive phrase that includes parameters.

The technique of going from the abstract to the concrete is also presented on all levels. Clearly, a precise boolean expression rather than the phrase *Int lies between 1 and 100* is required for the computer to act on the expressed condition. The text is full of examples where the abstract descriptions of the proven algorithms are the starting point for coding the nitty-gritty details of a block's statement. Every procedure called as an abstract process is developed with the idea that its abstract purpose must be met. Although the student is rightly discouraged from tampering with the operations of an abstract unit in a client program, the means for developing and testing each unit are thoroughly discussed.

III. *Testing*. The text stresses the need for testing source code at all stages of its development. We support the notion that testing should start with the first pseudocode description of the main block, and that the logic of a program should be thoroughly tested before it is compiled. The main tool to apply this testing is the predicate calculus, presented in a nonmathematical and hence nonthreatening way.

The idea of the program state is central to this approach. Pseudocode is, for the most part, not refined further until it is proven that the sequence of statements being described returns the desired program state. Any abstract description that needs to be refined further is described in terms of an initially known program state (preconditions) that should return a well-specified program state (postconditions). The refined description is tested using descriptive assertions to confirm that the required program state is indeed achieved.

Bottom–up testing is also covered, mostly in terms of making up test data for a desk trace or for a program that is already on line. The emphasis is on choosing sufficient data to show that the machine does (or will do) what is expected in all cases. Thus, we stress the importance of choosing data in such a way that each path in a program is tested. The student is encouraged to think of possible exceptional cases so he or she can choose data to test these exceptions.

IV. *The toolbox of proven algorithms*. Starting with the Chapter 3 material, we present *and prove* over 50 reusable algorithms. A compendium of these algorithms is given in Appendix G. The algorithms represent solutions to a very extensive taxonomy of problems dealing with input/output operations, procedural abstraction, decision making, looping, file processing, array processing, record-type and set-type processing, recursion, dynamic-variable processing, and data abstraction.

A tool kit is only as good as the craftsperson who uses it, so it is important to know which algorithm is useful for which problem. Students will get the most out of Appendix G by first learning to classify the kind of algorithm required to solve a given problem. Through study and practice, the student learns to determine whether a loop or a decision algorithm will solve the problem, whether or not a structured variable is needed, and so forth. A natural extension to this skill is learning how to determine which proven algorithm (if any) is the most appropriate one to use.

V. *Efficiency*. Although we do not emphasize big-Oh analysis throughout the text, we present it in Chapter 10 and refer to it as a conceptual tool. There is no heavy premium placed on the mathematics involved in finding an algorithm's big-Oh. In Chapter 15, for example, we implement a function to find the Nth Fibonacci number using an algorithm with a big-Oh exponentially dependent on N's value. The result of this analysis is cited, but the mathematical proof is not covered. The text does, however, derive a recursive procedure using the same algorithm in such a way that the efficiency is vastly improved.

VI. *Documentation*. Every procedure, when its header is first coded (either as a stub or as a fully coded procedure), comes complete with documentation on all formal parameter variables. A formalism is given for documenting each parameter using the words *in* and *out*. The meaning of the value taken on by each parameter (*in*, *out* or both) makes up the rest of the formalism. In the interest of saving space, *Pascal* does not follow up on this formalism for all examples. The spirit, however, is carried out, for every formal parameter is mentioned by name and purpose in a procedure's documentation. The meaning represented by each formal parameter value either as a precondition, a postcondition, or both is also a part of the less formalized documentation.

Every declared variable is documented with a sidebar comment. In this case, the documentation consists of a short phrase describing the variable's purpose. From the source code and the documentation, it is easy to infer whether or not the variable is fulfilling its documented purpose. Hence, documentation can also be used to describe the required criteria that must be achieved when a block's statement is tested for semantic consistency.

Finally, where appropriate, the text includes sidebar comments in the statement part of a block. Although Pascal is a sufficiently clear language that the code should speak for itself, we have included documentation to clarify any statements that might be misread or misunderstood. Sidebar comments are also given when we think the topic under discussion is still sufficiently new to the student that it requires further clarification.

VII. *Good semantics*. Semantic consistency is emphasized throughout the text. In Chapter 3, the point is made that a variable is expected to change its value but not its meaning over the scope of a block's statements. The "nonthreatening approach" to the predicate calculus bypasses the mathematical rigidity in favor of making assertions in terms of the implied semantics of the source code instructions. A loop invariant, for example, can be seen as a description of the purpose served by the variable over the scope of some looping process. The verification tools are thus given more as a means to check the semantics of a proposed design rather than as a rigorous mathematical process to ensure program correctness.

An Overview of the Contents

Our order of presentation of the material is generally traditional. In Chapter 1, the student follows a cookbook explanation to compile and run a program and is shown how the computer sets up the data areas to carry out the process. In Chapter 2, besides the usual presentation of the read in, display, and assignment statements, there is a section on file variables that is useful to students either using batch mode or PCs. The standard boolean type is not presented in this chapter, for we feel at this point the topic is very premature. Chapter 3 introduces the idea of the program state as well as the technique(s) of testing as part of the development process. Strings are given as a defined data type (using the reserved word TYPE) so the student is not stuck with single-character processing for the first half of the text.

All aspects of procedural abstraction are presented in Chapter 4. In Chapter 5, both the IF. . THEN. . ELSE construct and the CASE. . OF construct is given. The three looping constructs of Pascal are likewise presented in one chapter, namely Chapter 6. We have thus chosen to modularize the three skills of developing programs top-down using procedural abstraction, developing code that requires decision statements, and developing code that requires loop statements in one chapter apiece. In all three chapters, we follow through with the Chapter 3 material on verification, particularly in the development of case studies and the presentation of proven algorithms. Many proven algorithms given in Chapter 6 are cited throughout the remainder of the text.

The discussion of the reserved words AND, OR, NOT, and IN is delayed until Chapter 7 so that the student can thoroughly learn the skills of developing decision and loop statements using simple boolean expressions. Arrays are introduced, using only integer subscripts with this initial presentation. The student thus learns the convenience of using arrays in programs that require a large number of scalar variables all of the same type.

In Chapter 8, boolean variables are introduced where the student learns to use them to flag events in one part of a program so that they can control events in another part of the program. Programmer-defined enumerated types are likewise presented for the first time in this chapter. Because all scalar types will have been presented at this stage, the final new topic in Chapter 8 covers the abstraction and implementation of programmer-declared functions.

The subject matter of Chapter 9 is text files. The two standard functions eof and eoln are seen for the first time in this chapter. Much of the material is traditional, although it does depart a bit from the discussion of standard Pascal text files in its coverage of the ways different dialects open an external file to a file variable. There is also some additional material on string processing that can be applied mainly to read-in and display statements.

In Chapter 10, we resume the discussion of one-dimensional arrays, this time showing their usage where the subscripts have semantic content. Sorting, searching, and algorithm efficiency complete the remainder of the chapter's topics. Chapter 11 is a traditional chapter on multidimensional arrays. The examples given include subscripting of integer, char and enumerated types. Chapter 12 covers records for the first time. The bulk of the chapter deals with arrays of records.

Chapter 12 can be covered after the material in the first eight chapters is finished and reading has been assigned from Section 1 of Chapter 9 and Sections 2 and 4 from Chapter 10. This reading matter covers all topics recommended by the ACM for the CS1 Curriculum.

All material from Chapter 13 onward consists strictly of advanced topics. Chapter 13 is about data abstraction, using complex numbers, queues, and stacks as examples. We apply the FORWARD directive to separate the headers for each operation from their statements, thus conveying the spirit behind the implementation of separately compiled units within the limiting confines of standard Pascal.

The coverage of sets in Chapter 14 is traditional. The rest of the chapter completes the coverage of strings started in Chapter 3 and resumed in Chapter 9. The presentation builds on the Chapter 13 material, for a portable string unit is given as an ADT. The operations of the unit include the usual operations for string types that are implemented in the different Pascal dialects.

Chapter 15 is about recursion. The proven algorithms presented in this chapter give the student a firm foundation for developing recursive processes top-down. The technique of drawing trees to show the history of a program's run-time stack is covered, so that the student can do a desk trace on recursive algorithms.

Chapter 16 covers binary files and introduces pointers. The get and put procedures are not discussed because most dialects of Pascal for PCs do not include them. Virtually all syntax rules that apply to pointers are given in this chapter. The student can then read an undiluted discussion on the difficult topic of linked structures in the final two chapters without having to also learn about pointer syntax.

Linear linked lists make up the topics of Chapter 17. We depart from the usual form of presentation by first implementing some node primitive operations that can be included in the operations for all ADTs (queue, stack, and order list) requiring a linear list as the fundamental structure. Our purpose here is twofold: (1) Memory management is dealt with at the lowest possible level of implementation, and (2) inheritance, a property of object-oriented programming, is implied without being specifically discussed.

Chapter 18, the concluding chapter, is about binary trees. As with Chapter 17, node primitives are first introduced. Only after these have been coded are the topics that deal with the implementation and usage of binary search trees and expression trees covered.

Pedagogy

The text contains many pedagogical features that both clarify the material and give the student practice in using it. These include the following:

      I.   *Over 200 figures.* We use these figures to show

- syntax diagrams whenever a new construct is introduced
- top–down structure charts of many of the case studies
- desk tracing of source code (including trees for recursive algorithms)
- data structure charts for

    1. arrays
    2. arrays of records
    3. hierarchical records
    4. dynamic structures such as queues, stacks, and trees

II. *Proven algorithms*. They are presented at appropriate points in the text and reproduced in Appendix G. Each algorithm in the appendix contains

- a page reference where it was first introduced and proven
- a brief description of the kind of problem it solves
- a pseudocode description of the algorithm

III. *Numbered Program Design Rules*. They are likewise presented throughout the text and compiled in Appendix H. These rules aid the student in

- Avoiding common syntax errors
- Avoiding common semantic errors
- Testing a program or an algorithm's design
- Writing code that is easily read and understood

IV. *Program testing hints at the end of each chapter*. Testing is defined here in the broadest possible sense. Some hints are given to help the student write clearer code; hence, these hints imply testing one's code for clarity. Other hints show examples of coding and/or logic patterns that should be avoided. Most of the examples of bad code are not contrived; they are real errors committed by real students. In any case, the student uses these examples to test that his or her code does not emulate them. Hints are given on how to choose values either for desk tracing or on-line testing. These hints, particularly those given at the end of Chapters 5 and 6, must *not be glossed over* simply because they are part of the end-of-chapter subject matter.

V. *Three or four paragraphs of review at the end of each chapter*. These paragraphs mention all new terms introduced in the chapter.

VI. Exercises at the end of each section in each chapter. Between 40 to 50 exercises are given per chapter. All exercises are of the short-answer type, categorized as follows:

(a) *Test Your Understanding*. These are true or false, fill-ins, or one-phrase-answer type exercises dealing with the theoretical content of the section's topics.

(b) *Practice Your Analysis Skills*. Source code is presented and the student is asked either to desk trace the code or to give a brief explanation of what the code does.

(c) *Sharpen Your Implementation Skills*. These exercises ask the student to write source code, sometimes as little as a one-line statement, other times as much as a procedure requiring two or three auxiliary procedures.

(d) *Learn More About Your System*. In these exercises, the student conducts experiments to find out more about the properties of his or her computer.

Answers to about 40% of these four classes of exercises are given in Appendix J.

VII. *Between 15 and 20 short-answer exercises at the end of each chapter*. These exercises, which rarely require more than one sentence for an answer, are similar to the Test-Your-Understanding type of exercise given at the end of each section. The answers to about 40% of these exercises are also given in Appendix J.

VIII. *An average of 12 programming projects at the end of each chapter*. The projects are categorized as *Easy, Medium,* and *Difficult*. An easy project usually requires simple modifications of the programs and/or algorithms given in the chapter. A medium project requires a bit more original thought but, given sufficient time, the individual student should be able to do it. A difficult project, particularly those from Chapter 7 onward, is best assigned as a group project. It is possible, however, to assign some of them to individual students, although many of them are quite demanding.

Supplements

In addition to the text, the following supplements are available from Prentice-Hall:

1. A computerized test-item file containing well over 1000 true or false, multiple-choice, and short-answer questions to help the instructor design objective-type tests and quizzes.
2. A program disk that contains all complete programs presented in the text. The programs are coded in Turbo Pascal. Additional programs that drive the procedure and function examples are also included on the disk.
3. A supplementary text dealing solely with the Turbo Pascal dialect.
4. A program disk containing the source code to about half of the end-of-chapter projects.
5. An instructor's manual. This manual contains (a) transparency masters to about 100 figures in the text, (b) lecture notes to complement the subject matter of each chapter, (c) questions that start with the phrase, "Write a program, procedure, function, or source code fragment to . ." that are suitable for in-class exams, (d) a suggested methodology for grading these kinds of tests, and (e) the answers to the remaining end-of-section and end-of-chapter objective exercises.

Acknowledgments

This book could not have been written without the help of many people to whom I must express my deepest appreciation. The following professors provided reviews that were often enlightening, sometimes quite brutal, but, above all, always sincere: Shirley Beil, Normandale Community College; Sidney H. Brounstein, Montgomery College; Michael Covington, University of Georgia; Eileen Entin; Henry Etlinger, Rochester Institute of Technology; Frank T. Gergelyi, New Jersey Institute of Technology; Michael G. Gonzales, Gurjnedd-Mercy College; Dale Grovesnor, Iowa State University; Barbara Harris, DeVry Institute of Technology; William J. Joel, Marist College; Leon Levine, University of California at Los Angeles; John Lowther, Michigan Institute of Technology; and Keith B. Olson, Montana College of Mineral Science and Technology.

I am indebted to countless students of the CS5652 and CS5653 courses at New York Institute of Technology who suffered through various stages and revisions of the manuscript. Special thanks go to Christian Perez, a very talented young man, who prepared and tested all the software on the program disk.

There are also those in Prentice Hall to whom I owe a great deal. Ray Mullaney, the Development Editor, provided two very talented people, Shelly Langman during the earlier stages and Sylvia Dovner during the later stages, who helped me shape the text into a pedagogically sound product. Bayani Mendoza de Leon, the Production Editor, showed incredible patience during the many hours I spent in his office going over some of the finer points of the manuscript. Most of all I am indebted to the Acquisitions Editor, Marcia Horton, and her assistant, Diana Penha. For the three long years I have known them, they were unwaveringly upbeat and supportive during the many mood swings I underwent in bringing this work to fruition.

Last but not least, I must thank my wife Beth for giving up so many lost weekends, evenings, and summer vacations while I spent countless hours on the word processor creating and revising the manuscript.

Richard A. Meyers

C H A P T E R 1

COMPUTERS AND PROGRAMS

OBJECTIVES

After reading and studying the contents of this chapter, you should be able to

- Explain the difference between hardware and software

- Describe the purpose of each hardware component in a computer system

- Explain how a computer uses coded data for processing

- Describe and discuss the way various computer languages differ

- Use your system to edit, compile, and run a Pascal program

- Define many of the terms that make up the parts of a Pascal program

WITHOUT A DOUBT, you have been touched by the so-called "computer revolution." You have probably received computerized form letters in the mail, bills that a computer has generated, bank statements that have been made up with the help of a computer, and so forth. Although you may have been a recipient of the products generated by computers, you may know very little about the actual machines responsible for these products.

In this chapter, you will learn about the two systems associated with computers. The hardware system makes up the physical devices, and the software system makes up an instruction set that causes these devices to work. After reading the chapter, you should realize that the computer is not some all-powerful machine that has an innate intelligence of its own. In fact, the computer knows nothing and comprehends nothing; it simply carries out the instructions given.

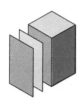

1.1 Hardware

The computer is an electronic machine that can carry out millions of instructions in a matter of seconds. *Programming* refers to the act of planning a set of instructions for the machine to carry out such that it produces some specified end result. The material of this text is mainly about programming. Before you start learning programming, though, you should first know something about the physical make-up of the computer.

A computer system

Even though you are not required to know all the electronic details, it is important that you know the purpose of each "black box" device that makes up the *hardware system* of the computer.

> **Hardware:** the physical components of a computer

> **Hardware system:** a set of hardware devices connected together in such a way that they make up a functioning computer capable of carrying out instructions.

Figure 1.1 is a diagram of a typical computer hardware system. The figure shows you that the system has five devices, namely, the input device(s), the output device(s), the CPU (central processing unit), primary memory, and secondary memory. The figure also shows that data appear to flow sometimes into a device, sometimes out of a device, and sometimes in and out of a device. Let us examine the purpose of each of these hardware devices.

> **Data:** information that has been prepared for and is processed by a computer.

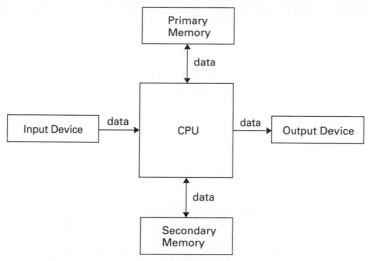

FIGURE 1.1 The hardware system of a typical computer.

The input device with which you will be working is the *keyboard* (see Figure 1.2). The output devices you will use are a *monitor* (Figure 1.3), a device that displays readable characters on a screen, or a *printer* (Figure 1.4), a device that displays characters on paper, thus producing a permanent copy of the processed data.

Input device: a hardware device that accepts data for the computer to process.

Output device: a hardware device that presents the results of the processed data.

FIGURE 1.2 A keyboard.

FIGURE 1.3 A monitor.

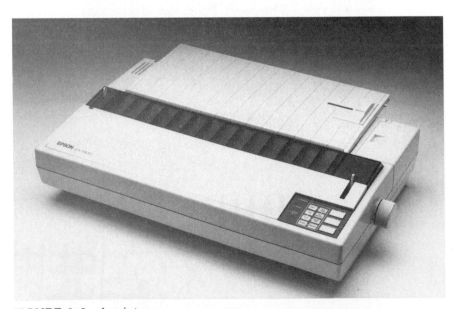

FIGURE 1.4 A printer.

The terminal

If you will be working on a *multiuser system* (Figure 1.5), you will communicate with the computer by means of a *terminal* (Figure 1.6). A multiuser system is *time-shared,* but you will usually feel that you are the only person using the computer, even though there may be many users at any given time. You will have this experience because the allocation of time for each user over any given second is broken up into milliseconds or even microseconds. Thus, you will be connected to the system's resources many times in just 1 second.

> **Multiuser system:** a computer system capable of servicing more than one user at any given time.

> **Terminal:** a work space consisting of an input device and an output device that are connected to the rest of the system.

> **Time-sharing:** the scheduled allocation of a computer's resources to each individual user.

Personal computers

Perhaps you will be working instead on a *personal computer*. When you use a personal computer (see Figure 1.7), you will communicate with it from the single *dedicated* terminal that is set up to the rest of the system. As you are the sole user of the computer for each session you have at the machine, there is no time-sharing involved.

> **Personal computer:** a computer that is meant to be used by only one individual at any given time.

FIGURE 1.5 A computer that can service more than one user.

FIGURE 1.6 Some computer terminals.

FIGURE 1.7 A personal computer.

Data
representation

During a session on the machine, data are entered by pressing the proper keys on the keyboard. The data entered from the keyboard are processed by the machine. The results of the processed data are then displayed as readable symbols by the output device. The symbols you see on the keys of a keyboard represent letters, numbers, and special characters that you can read. Likewise, the symbols displayed on the screen or seen on a computer-generated text are human-readable.

The computer does not directly process these symbols. Instead, it processes a coded representation of the value of a given symbol as a sequence of 0s and 1s. Any single representative 0 or 1 in a coded sequence is known as a *bit*. A sequence of eight of these bits, strung together to represent a readable character (such as the letter "A"), is known as a *byte*. One byte is a sufficient number of 0s and 1s to represent any character on the keyboard, but more than 1 byte is used to represent the value of numbers. The required number of bytes to represent a numeric value will vary from system to system, but all systems will use at least 2 bytes to represent any given number.

Highs and lows

The physical representation of a 0 or 1 is an actual voltage value that can be stored in an electronic device. When a voltage value is "high," that is, it takes on a value greater than a given threshold, such as 2.8 volts, it physically represents a 1. A voltage value of less than another threshold, such as 0.5 volt, represents a 0. Any value lying between these two voltages indicates that one or more pieces of the system hardware are malfunctioning. Such a malfunction is known as a *hardware fault*. If a fault is discovered in the computer, the faulty device must be replaced before the computer can again function properly.

Primary memory

When you sit down at the computer for a session, the data you use or generate are continuously being read from and written into *primary memory* as a result of your interaction with the computer. In order for any data to be processed, they must first be written into primary memory. This memory stores data values and the instructions that inform the machine how these values should be manipulated. The device(s) itself used to implement primary memory is electronic. (See Figure 1.8.)

Primary memory: the part of the computer that holds data that are used or meant to be used over the course of a single user–machine session.

You can visualize a primary memory device as something that contains a sequence of locations, known as *addresses*. Each address, which is an actual physical location that stores a fixed number of 0s and 1s, is represented by an integer value in the *binary system* of counting. This integer value is the means by which the computer stores a data value into or fetches a data value from a specified memory location.

Binary system: a system for representing numbers using only the symbols 0 and 1.

Figure 1.9 shows an example of how a computer stores information in primary memory. The address we see as 14322 is represented internally by the sequence 0011011111110010, mind-numbing to us humans, but easily read by the machine. The sequence of 0s and 1s stored in this location, 0000001100010001, represents the integer value 785. The values stored in the three sequential addresses

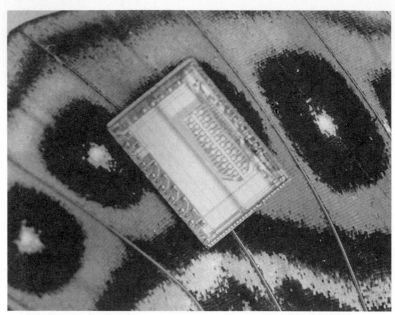

FIGURE 1.8 A primary memory device superimposed on a butterfly's wing.

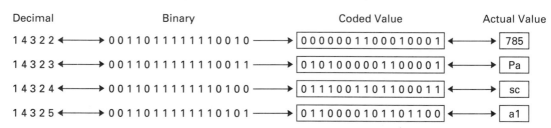

Decimal	Binary	Coded Value	Actual Value
1 4 3 2 2 ⟷	0 0 1 1 0 1 1 1 1 1 1 1 0 0 1 0 ⟶	0 0 0 0 0 0 1 1 0 0 0 1 0 0 0 1 ⟷	785
1 4 3 2 3 ⟷	0 0 1 1 0 1 1 1 1 1 1 1 0 0 1 1 ⟶	0 1 0 1 0 0 0 0 0 1 1 0 0 0 0 1 ⟷	Pa
1 4 3 2 4 ⟷	0 0 1 1 0 1 1 1 1 1 1 1 0 1 0 0 ⟶	0 1 1 1 0 0 1 1 0 1 1 0 0 0 1 1 ⟷	sc
1 4 3 2 5 ⟷	0 0 1 1 0 1 1 1 1 1 1 1 0 1 0 1 ⟶	0 1 1 0 0 0 0 1 0 1 1 0 1 1 0 0 ⟷	a1

FIGURE 1.9 An example of main memory storage.

14323 through 14325 have a combination of 0s and 1s in them that, when strung together, can represent the word "Pascal".

Volatile memory   Much of a computer's primary memory is *volatile,* or temporary. The values stored in the volatile part of primary memory are expected to change quite often during the course of session between you and the machine. When you are finished with a given session at the computer, these values are destroyed. The data stored and manipulated in volatile memory are not automatically restored when you again sit down for another session.

Secondary memory   Besides having primary memory, every computer is capable of reading from and writing into *secondary memory* that is *nonvolatile*. The contents of secondary memory are saved, even after a given session with the machine is finished. Data stored on secondary memory devices can be retrieved at some later session. Two such devices, the 5.25-inch and 3.5-inch *floppy disks* shown in Figure 1.10, are easily inserted and removed from the computer. They are used extensively as secondary storage devices with the personal computer.

FIGURE 1.10 Two kinds of floppy disks.

> **Secondary memory:** memory that is used over the course of more than one session with the machine.

When you use a floppy disk, you connect it to the rest of the system by inserting it into a *floppy disk port* on the computer (see Figure 1.11).

Most personal computers also have a *hard disk* that comes as part of the system (see Figure 1.12). This device cannot be removed from the system as easily as a

FIGURE 1.11 Inserting a floppy disk.

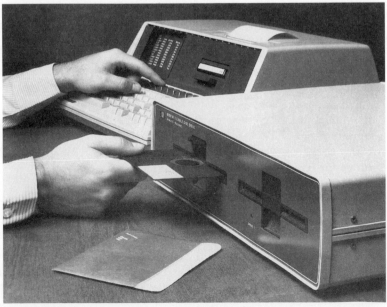

FIGURE 1.12 A hard disk for a personal computer.

floppy disk. Nevertheless, it still constitutes secondary memory, for any data stored in it are not destroyed when the machine is turned off.

Secondary memory on multiuser systems

The device for secondary memory on a multiuser system is likewise a hard disk (see Figure 1.13). A hard disk for a multiuser system stores many different users' accounts on it, so it is physically much larger than the hard disk in a personal computer. If you plan to work on a multiuser system, you will be given an account and allowed a certain amount of "disk space." The amount of disk space you get depends upon your agreement with the people who supervise the operation of the machine you are using.

The central processing unit

The instructions for the *CPU* to carry out are stored in primary memory. When the computer executes a program, the CPU determines, instruction by instruction, what actions must be carried out. Typical actions might be the reading in of values from the keyboard, the display of values on the output device, the arithmetic manipulation of two or more numbers, the logical manipulation (e.g., comparision) of two or more values, and so forth. If you look back at Figure 1.1, you will see that every data item that is read, processed, or displayed must pass through the CPU in order for its value(s) to cause some effect.

> **Central processing unit (CPU):** the part of the computer that actually carries out the instructions as read from primary memory.

Files

For most of your sessions on the computer, you will be using one or more *files*. In this text, you will work with two kinds of files, *program files* and *data files*. A program file consists of a series of instructions for the computer to follow. You will learn how to create a program file in Section 1.3. A file that simply stores data

FIGURE 1.13 A hard disk for a multiuser system.

to be processed or which have been processed is known as a data file. It is possible for the computer to create a data file by carrying out the instructions written in a program file.

File: a collection of data stored on a disk.

EXERCISES

Test Your Understanding

1. Name the five components of a computer hardware system and state the purpose of each.

2. What are the two differences between primary memory and secondary memory?

3. True or false? A computer processes data as literal character and numeric values. Explain your answer.

4. Name two types of files and state the difference between the two types.

1.2 Programming Languages

A computer is useful because it can execute *programs*. It is capable of executing programs because the instructions given to it are written in a *programming language*. In this section, wc classify the different programming languages and present a brief history of their development.

Computer program: a sequence of instructions that the machine carries out to produce an end result.

> **Programming language:** a set of symbols, words, and rules used to instruct the computer.

Machine language

Back in the late 1940s when the computer was first invented, all programs were written in *machine language*. Even today, all programs are ultimately executed in the particular computer's own machine language. A machine language program looks like a never-ending sequence of 0s and 1s. Although incomprehensible to us, this sequence of bits and bytes represents specific data values, addresses, and instructions that the computer can carry out to produce some understandable end result.

> **Machine language:** the actual language in which the computer carries out the instructions of a program.

Assembly language

The original programmers soon realized that it was time-consuming and error-prone to write programs in machine language. To make their work simpler, people started devising *assembly languages*. A program written in an assembly language is much easier to devise and read, for the mnemonic words of the language, such as ADD, SUB, and MOVE, freed the programmer from having to deal with all those 0s and 1s.

> **Assembly language:** a language that uses mnemonics to represent specific operations or specific internal components of a particular machine.

Any program written in a language other than the machine language of 0s and 1s is ultimately still executed in machine language. An assembly-language program, therefore, had to be translated into machine language before it could be executed. This task was (and is) carried out by the particular computing machine's *assembler*.

> **Assembler:** a program that translates assembly language into machine language.

High-level languages

Although assembly languages made the task of writing a program easier, they were dependent upon the particular machine being used. Moreover, it was necessary for the programmer to know something about the internal structure of the given machine. In the mid-1950s, a group of scientists at IBM addressed this problem directly and developed the first widely accepted *high-level language,* FORTRAN (an abbreviation for FORmula TRANslator). This language, an updated version of which is still in use today, was machine-independent.

> **High-level language:** a programming language where the programmer does not require knowledge of the actual computing machine to write a program in the language.

A program written in a high-level language, of which there are over 200 in use today, is also easier to read than a program written in assembly language. The words and symbols that make up a high-level language still must be computer-readable and hence represent a code by which we instruct the computer. For this reason, we often say a given program is *coded* in a given high-level language. We call such a program the *source program,* and an entire program or part of a program written in a high-level language is known as *source code*.

Source program: a program written in a high-level language.

As with assembly-language programs, source programs need to be translated into machine language. This act is done by another program called the *compiler*. The maching-language version of any source program is known as an *object program,* and the actual machine-language code is known as *object code*.

Compiler: the program that translates source code into object code.

Object program: the machine-language version of a source program.

Each programming language requires its own compiler to translate source code into object code. You will require a Pascal-language compiler to successfully code and execute the programs we present as exercises in this text. If you are going to work on a multiuser system, the necessary Pascal compiler will be included as part of the *system software*.

Software: any computer program or set of computer programs.

System software: a set of programs dedicated to a particular computer system that facilitates the use of the computer.

If you plan to use a personal computer to code your programs, you will need to buy one of the commercially available *program development systems* for the Pascal language and install it as part of your own system's software. The software of the program development system is given to you on a floppy disk, and the system is sold with supporting printed information that lets you know how to use it.

Program development system: a set of programs dedicated to developing source programs in a given programming language.

The Pascal language

The Pascal language was developed and standardized by Professor Nicholas Wirth in the early part of the 1970s. He created Pascal as an academic language so that computer-science students might have a simple yet powerful vehicle to learn good programming techniques. This language is the one most used at present in introductory college-level programming and computer-science courses.

Dialects

Although there is an ANSI (American National Standards Institute) Pascal language that is considered standard in the United States, many *dialects* of Pascal exist. As examples, we have VAX Pascal, Turbo Pascal, UCSD Pascal, Waterloo Pascal, Lightspeed Pascal, MacIntosh Pascal, and still others. All these dialects are very similar to each other, but they also have certain non-ANSI standard features.

Dialect: a different version of a high-level language.

We can distinguish the minor differences in appearance between the same program written in different dialects, but a compiler for one given dialect cannot make these adjustments. The rules for any one dialect must be satisfied *completely* in order for the compiler to change the source program into a workable object program. It is, therefore, unrealistic to expect a program written in one dialect to work successfully with a compiler for another dialect.

Strings: an example where dialects differ

We will do our best to adhere to ANSI Pascal throughout the text, but sometimes we will present certain nonstandard features if they are particularly important. For example, each Pascal dialect has its own rules for handling *strings*. The operations (reading in values, displaying values, deleting some characters, and so forth) are virtually the same, but the rules for implementing them differ slightly from dialect to dialect.

> **Strings:** a way to represent a sequence of characters as a word, a name, or some other meaningful ordered combination of individual characters.

Is it correct to minimize the differences between the way the different dialects process strings? If you want to make the machine properly execute a program you have coded in a given dialect, our answer is a resounding "No!" You must never forget that the rules of grammar for source code written in a particular dialect must be strictly followed. However, once you use the correct code to satisfy these specific rules, the actual operations performed will be virtually the same from dialect to dialect.

EXERCISES

Test Your Understanding

1. True or false? The computer directly carries out the instructions given to it in a high-level language.

2. What is the difference between a program that is assembled and one that is compiled?

3. Is there one universal Pascal language? Explain.

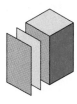

1.3 Programs and Programming

In this section, you will *edit* your first Pascal program. Then you will compile and execute the program. Finally, you will see some of the ways you can cause the computer to return incorrect results during the course of the program *run*.

This first session with the computer is designed for you to become familiar with your system's *editor* and to use a program whose source code has already been planned. It is only when you start the material of the next chapter that you will begin to learn the skills of *programming*.

> **Editing:** the act of entering the source code program from the keyboard into the computer.

> **Editor:** an interactive program that enables a user to create or modify a data file or a program file.

Program run: a single execution of a compiled program.

Programming: the act of planning, coding, and testing a computer program.

Operating systems

Every computer has an *operating system*. Typically, an operating system contains programs that allow you to (1) create a source program and an object program; (2) use the input, output, and memory devices properly; (3) set aside sufficient primary memory for the computer to run a program; (4) set up sufficient time for a given program to run to completion; and (5) allow a given user to be connected to the system from a terminal.

Operating system (OS): a set of programs that manages the computer's resources.

The first three operations are carried out on both multiuser and personal computer systems, but the final two operations are necessary only for multiuser systems. Regardless of what machine you are using, you will instruct the computer to carry out a given operating-system program using a command that belongs to the system's *command language*.

Command language: a given operating system's language.

Different systems have different command languages. Many personal computers use DOS, a command language that stands for *disk operating system*. A given command in this operating system is called a "DOS command." The Digital Equipment Corporation's VAX computer uses a language called DCL (DEC Command Language). A given command using this operating system is known as a "DCL command."

Log-on

If you are working on a multiuser system, you will need to *log on* to the computer system at a terminal. When you have logged on to the system, the terminal at which you are seated is connected to the system's CPU. Also, you are able to create and manipulate the contents of any files you may have on your own disk space. In order to log on to the system, you must follow a series of steps called *log-on protocol*. If you do not follow the correct steps in the correct order, the system will not be connected to your terminal.

Logging on: the act of connecting a terminal to a user's account and to the facilities of the computer system.

Log-on protocol: the necessary steps required for a user to log on.

There are certain keystrokes belonging to log-on protocol that every user must follow. If you have a multiuser system, your instructor will give you all the necessary details about log-on protocol for your system. In order for you to gain access to the files in your particular account, you must enter a unique combination of keystrokes known as a *password*. If you enter an incorrect password, you will not be given access to your files nor, indeed, will you gain access to the rest of the system.

The bootstrap
program

If you are using a personal computer, you need not worry about log-on proto-col, for you are working with a dedicated machine. Nonetheless, you must follow the proper steps to make the computer available for your personal use. When you follow these steps, the machine will first execute its *bootstrap program*. If you are using DOS, you can bootstrap your computer simply by turning it on and pressing the "Enter" key twice. Some systems are set up to bootstrap by simply having the user turn on the computer.

Bootstrap program: the program that initially makes the computer's facili-ties available to the user.

Editing and Running Your First Program

You are about to edit, compile, and run your first program. We can likewise say you are about to create a source program, then an object program, then execute a run of the object program. We will assume that you are working on an *interactive system*. We are thus assuming that you can edit, compile, and run the program from a termi-nal by direct interaction with the machine.

Interactive system: a system where the user and the machine can commu-nicate back and forth.

A command-driven process

If you are on a multiuser system, the chances are that the machine will carry out these actions when you type in the correct sequence of system commands. Un-less you enter the proper commands in the proper order, your attempts to edit, com-pile, and run a program will be unsuccessful. This process of making up a program is said to be *command-driven*.

Command-driven: a process that is interactively carried out when the user enters the proper sequence of system commands.

A menu-driven process

If you are working on a personal computer, you will need software to help you develop programs in the Pascal language. Once you have entered a command that transfers control to this Pascal development system, the rest of the process will probably be *menu-driven*. In this case, the computer will start the process by dis-playing a *menu* from which you must choose a given action. (See Figure 1.14.)

Menu-driven: a process that is carried out when the user selects an action or sequence of actions from a displayed menu or series of displayed menus.

Menu: a display of the choice of actions available to the user at any given time.

Editing

We are going to have you edit, compile, and run a program named `FindAreaOfCircle`. Before you can compile and run a program, you must first edit its source-code version, using the system's editor. If you are using a command-driven system, you will type in a command such as

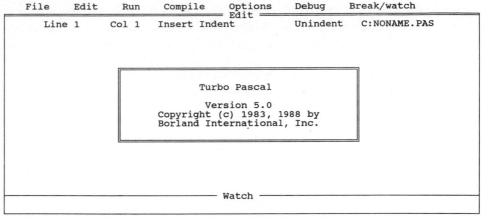

```
━━━━━━━━━━━━━━━━━━━━━━━ Edit ━━━━━━━━━━━━━━━━━━━━━━━
  Line 1      Col 1    Insert Indent              Unindent    C:NONAME.PAS



                      Turbo Pascal

                      Version 5.0
                Copyright (c) 1983, 1988 by
                Borland International, Inc.




━━━━━━━━━━━━━━━━━━━━━━━ Watch ━━━━━━━━━━━━━━━━━━━━━━━
```

F1-Help F5-Zoom F6-Switch F7-Trace F8-Step F9-Make F10-Menu

FIGURE 1.14   The main menu of Turbo Pascal 5.0.

edit FindAreaOfCircle.pas

The ".pas" sequence of characters indicates that you are editing a program written in Pascal source code.

If you are using a menu-driven system, you will select the item on the main menu (see Figure 1.14) labeled EDIT, then press "Enter". The system will then ask you for a filename, and you must type in FindAreaOfCircle, the name of the program. Then, when you press the "Enter" key, you will be ready to edit the program. If you find that you cannot edit a program following either of these two procedures, we suggest that you either consult your instructor or read your system's manual for further details.

Regardless of the system you are using, you edit the source-code version of a Pascal program by entering in text. For this exercise, you should enter the text that follows as Example 1.1.

Example 1.1

```pascal
PROGRAM FindAreaOfCircle(input,output);
  {The computer calculates and displays the area of a circle.}
CONST
  Pi = 3.1416;    {constant holds the defined value}
VAR
  Radius,         {radius of circle whose area is found}
  Area:           {calculated area of the circle}
            real;
BEGIN
  writeln('Hello, welcome to your first program.');
  writeln('This program finds and displays the area of a circle.');
  write('First, enter the radius:  ');
  readln(Radius);
```

```
Area:= Pi * sqr(Radius); {set Area to Pi times square of Radius}
writeln('The area of the circle is ',Area)
END.
```

After you have typed in the text and checked that *everything* has been entered exactly as shown, you have finished the editing process and your program is ready for *compilation*. If you are using a command-driven system, you must exit the editor program with the proper command. Your instructor will give you the necessary details. If you are using a menu-driven system, you simply return to the main menu, for you are now ready to specify the next action.

Compilation: changing a source-code program into an object code program using the source-code compiler.

On a command-driven system, the compiler program is called when you type in a command such as

```
pascal FindAreaOfCircle
```

Be sure to include the proper command and the filename. This particular command instructs the computer to use the system's Pascal compiler to change the source code into object code. If you are working with a menu-driven system, all you need do is select the COMPILE action and press the "Enter" key.

Did the computer carry out the compilation operation successfully? If so, it did not display any error messages, indicating there was nothing wrong with the *syntax* of your source code. If the compilation was unsuccessful, the computer displayed one or more *syntax error messages*. If you did get some error messages, you must go back and edit the program. Make sure that the source code you have edited agrees exactly with the text of the program given as Example 1.1. After you have fixed the errors, try once more to compile the program. You will know the syntax of the program is correct if the machine does not issue error messages when you attempt to compile the program.

Syntax: rules specifying the way the words and symbols of a programming language can be put together.

Syntax error: part of a source program that violates one or more of the syntax rules of the language.

Syntax error message: message issued by the system when an attempt is made to compile a source-code program with a syntax error(s) in it.

If you are working on a multiuser system and your source code compiles without an error, you are still not quite ready to run the program. You must first link the object code using a command such as

```
link FindAreaOfCircle
```

This linking operation allows the program access to a library of executable routines. Typical executable routines found in the library are those that carry out a display on some output device, those that read in data from some input device, and so forth. The program `FindAreaOfCircle` uses routines both to read in values from the keyboard and to carry out display. Usually, a multiuser system requires that you link a compiled object program to create an executable program. On virtually all development systems for personal computers, the linking operation is automatic.

Running the program

Once a program has been compiled and linked (multiuser system) or just compiled (single-user system), it is ready to be run. If you are using a command-driven process, you can run the program that you have just finished linking by entering the command

```
run FindAreaOfCircle
```

If you are using a menu-driven process, simply return to the main menu, select RUN, and press "Enter".

Now run the program. After the machine asks you for a radius, enter a numeric value (it can contain a decimal point), and press the "Enter" key. The computer will then display the area of the circle whose radius is the value you entered. Run the program a few more times with different values. Note that the same process is carried out for each different value read in as a radius. The results of each run differ, producing different values for the area, but each value displayed is the correct one for the radius entered.

time errors

Now that you have run the program `FindAreaOfCircle` successfully a number of times, try to make the program fail. All you have to do is type in a character such as the letter "A" rather than a numeric value, then press the "Enter" key. Rather than displaying the area of a circle with radius A (whatever that means), the computer will display an error message indicating that it cannot process the value you entered.

This type of error is known as a *run-time error*. Many programmers refer to such an error as a *program crash*. A run-time error occurs when some unforeseen event happens that the computer is incapable of processing. The unforeseen event in this case was that you entered data that did not represent a numeric value.

Run-time error: an error that happens during the course of a program run due to an event that makes further processing impossible.

Semantic errors

It is also possible to write a program that appears to run successfully only to have the machine produce incorrect results. You can, for example, delete the characters "Pi" and "*" on the next-to-last line of the program, then compile and run it again. The computer will display the area of a square, and the number you entered represents the square's length. The purpose of the program, however, is to find and display the area of a circle. Thus, the version of the program you just created has an error in it. This type of error is called a *semantic error,* or *logical error,* because the computer carried out an action that led to an incorrect final result. A semantic error may sometimes lead to a program crash and sometimes it may not. What happens depends upon the nature of the error.

Semantic error: an error in a program that causes an incorrect result even though the program compiles properly.

Correcting source code

If a program has errors in it, they must be found and corrected. When you find and correct the errors in a program, you are *debugging* it.

When you debug a program, you must *first find the error*, and only then should you change the offending source code. It is easy to find the syntax errors in a program, for the compiler will give you error messages. Other errors may be a bit more difficult to find. We will remind you again and again throughout the course of the text that the first stage in the debugging process is to find the offending code.

Debugging: the act of finding and correcting errors in source code.

It is very unwise to change incorrect code in the hope that the error will somehow be caught and simply "go away." Before you fix any errors in your code, you should know the cause of the error so that you can fix it properly. A good deal of this text deals with the technique of developing programs in such a way that the errors that do occur can be easily found and corrected.

Regardless of what type of error may occur, once you find it, you must go back and edit the source program again. You need not create a whole new program from scratch, you can simply edit the old program by fixing that part of the code that is incorrect.

EXERCISES

Test Your Understanding

1. Name at least three purposes of an operating system.

2. What is a command language? Why is this language necessary if you want to program in Pascal source code?

3. Name at least two programs that must be run before the computer can carry tions written in source code.

4. List the three ways a source program can be identified as incorrect.

5. True or false? There are some errors in a program that can be fixed without the need to change the source code.

Learn More About Your System

6. You are to get further practice with the editor by modifying the program FindAreaOfCircle so the computer will instead find and display the area of a square. The modifications require that you make the following changes:
   (a) Change every appearance of the word circle to the word square.
   (b) Delete the third and fourth lines of the program completely.
   (c) Change the word radius to the word side at every point in the text. This change should be made on both uppercase and lowercase occurrences of the word.
   (d) Delete the word Pi and the star (*) on the next-to-last line.
   (e) Change the character sequence enclosed by braces on the next-to-last line to read set Area to the square of the Side.

   Once you have made the changes, run the program, thus verifying that the source code is correct for this modified, hence different, program.

1.4 Components of a Pascal Program

Now that you have run your first program, you may want to know just what it caused the machine to do. It is too early to give you all the information yet, but in this section, we present a brief overview of the components of a Pascal program. We also briefly discuss the *semantic rules* that apply to these components. Refer back to this section often, for we give you many terms we will be using throughout the rest of the text.

> **Semantic rules:**   rules that give meaning to the set of instructions in a programming language.

Objects and processes

A Pascal program describes a *process* that produces a desired and meaningful result. When you read source code, you should be able to determine the actions the computer carries out from the source-code description. Therefore, you should be able to determine whether the process described actually leads to a correct result.

All processes require *objects* that hold data values as a result of processing or that are needed for processing. Every program that you write will consist of both objects and processes.

> **Process:**   a coded instruction or group of instructions that the computer carries out to produce some result.

> **Object:**   a location or a set of locations where a value(s) is stored. This value(s) can then be referred to in some process.

The Five Components of a Program

The components of a Pascal program are as follows:

1. reserved words
2. identifiers
3. literals
4. expressions
5. special symbols

Let us look at some examples of each of these five components as they apply to the program FindAreaOfCircle:

1. Reserved Words

> **Reserved word:**   a word that has a special meaning and cannot be used for any purpose other than that meaning.

The program FindAreaOfCircle has a total of five reserved words in it, namely, PROGRAM, CONST, VAR, BEGIN, and END. Some of Pascal's reserved words are associated with objects, and some are associated with processes. The word PRO-GRAM, for example, indicates that the remaining text makes up the source code of a Pascal program. This word is thus associated with a process we call a "program." As you read on, you will see that the reserved words CONST and VAR are associated with the program's objects, and that the words BEGIN and END are associated with the program's process.

2. Identifiers

Identifier: a representative name of an object or a process.

The program given as Example 1.1 contains the following identifiers: FindAreaOfCircle, writeln, write, readln, sqr, input, output, Pi, Radius, Area, and real. The first five identifiers are names for processes, and the last six identifiers are names for objects.

Standard processes

We already know that the identifier FindAreaOfCircle names a process that makes up a program. This particular process is programmer-defined. The other four processes, write, writeln, sqr, and readln are *standard processes*. The processes write, writeln, and readln can be classified as standard *procedures,* whereas the process sqr is a reference to a standard *function.*

Standard process: a process that is predefined for a given Pascal dialect.

Procedure: a process that is a subroutine or subprogram.

Function: a process that is a subroutine that returns a single value.

Certain processes are standard to all dialects. The 4 standard processes given in Example 1.1 have the same meaning in all dialects. The first two procedures, write and writeln, instruct the computer to display text, the function sqr returns the *square* of its argument, and the procedure readln instructs the computer to read in a value(s) from a line of text.

Standard objects

The two objects input and output are likewise *standard objects* (which have the same meaning in all dialects), while the other three objects, Pi, Radius, and Area, are programmer-declared. The first object, input, is used when the computer will read in data entered from the keyboard. The second object, output, is used if the machine is to display values on the output device.

Standard object.   a named object whose purpose is predefined for the given Pascal dialect.

Named constants

The third identifier Pi represents a *named constant.*

Constant: a quantity that does not change throughout the course of a program run.

Named Constant: a constant that can be referenced by identifier.

We know that Pi is a constant because its defined value of 3.1416 follows the reserved word CONST. All identifiers associated with this reserved word are defined constants. At the start of the program run, the value for Pi is fixed. If a reference is made to this value, as in the next-to-last line of the program, the computer substitutes the defined value in place of the identifier *reference*.

Reference: the use of an identifier in the source code.

Variables and types

The other two named objects, Radius and Area, are *variables*. We know these two objects are variables because they are associated with the reserved word VAR. A variable must be of a given *type*, but it can take on different values for each program run. The Pascal language also has some predefined *standard types* that can be referenced by identifier.

Variable: an object whose value may differ from one run to the next, and/or whose value may change throughout the course of a given program run.

Type: a variable or expression with a fixed appearance, such as that of an integer numeric, a real numeric, or a character, and a predefined set of possible operations.

Standard type: a type that has a predefined identifier in a given Pascal dialect. The four types real, integer, char (character), and boolean are standard types for all dialects of Pascal.

The value taken on by any given variable may change during the course of a program run. Likewise, it may differ in value from one run to the next. Its type, however, cannot change over the course of the run, nor can it differ from one run to the next.

The word real, as used in the program, specifies the type given to the variables Radius and Area. This word is also a standard identifier. Any associated variable of this type is seen as having a real number value that can have a decimal fraction as part of its value.

3. Literals (or "literal values") The program also contains many *anonymous constants,* all but one of them representing string values. Typical literals seen in the program were string values such as 'Hello, welcome to your first program.' and 'The area of the circle is '. The program also contained one real literal, namely 3.1416. This value was used to give a value to the named constant Pi. We often refer to anonymous string constants and anonymous numeric constants as "string literals" and "numeric literals."

Anonymous constant: a constant not referenced by identifier.

Literal: an anonymous constant.

4. Expressions (also "expression values")

Expression: a value formed by applying defined operations to values taken on by literals, named constants, and variables.

All string literals in Example 1.1 that are associated with the `write` and `writeln` processes make up expressions that are displayed at run time. Besides containing string expressions, the program also contained the numeric expressions `Pi * sqr(Radius)`, as seen on the next-to-last line of the program, and `Area`, as seen on the last line. Neither of these values represented numeric literals, for they were expressions formed using references to the values taken on by variables.

The value of the expression on the next-to-last line is found by making a reference to the named constant `Pi`, applying the multiplication operator (represented by a star), evaluating the standard Pascal function `sqr` (whose value is found by taking the square of the value of `Radius`), using the two symbols that form a left and a right pair of parentheses, and making a reference to the value taken on by the variable `Radius`. This combination of references and symbols evaluates to a real numeric value, hence a *real expression*. The expression itself represents the geometric formula you learned as, "Pi times the square of the Radius."

5. Special symbols

Special symbol: a character symbol or two symbols treated as a single symbol that is used to fulfill a particular purpose.

The program `FindAreaOfCircle` has many special symbols. Among them are the following: `{ } ( ) : ; , ' := ` and `.` (a period). The purpose of each symbol depends upon the context in which it is used. You will learn about the use of some of these symbols in the next section of this chapter.

EXERCISES

Test Your Understanding

1. What is the difference between an object and a process?

2. What is a standard object? What is a standard process?

3. List the reserved words found in the program `FindAreaOfCircle`.

4. List the identifiers for the standard processes referenced in the program `FindAreaOf-Circle`.

5. What is the difference between a variable and a constant?

6. Give an example of a named constant and an example of an anonymous constant from the program `FindAreaOfCircle`.

7. True or false? A named constant can be used to form part of an expression but an anonymous constant can never be used.

8. True or false? The value of a numeric literal can never be represented by a named constant.

9. Match the items of column A with those of column B.

Column A	Column B
reserved word	writeln
identifier	semicolon
literal	'The area of the circle is '
numeric expression	END
special symbol	Pi * sqr(Radius)

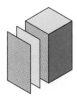

1.5 The Structure of a Pascal Program

A Pascal program, you will recall, is a coded process. Any process, as coded in Pascal, is divided into three parts. Each of these parts instructs the computer to do something. In this section, we define the three parts of a process and use Example 1.1 to show how the computer carries out the instructions for each part.

Three parts of a process

The program given as Example 1.1 is a coded process. Any coded process in the Pascal language can be broken up into three parts: (1) the header, (2) the declarations, and (3) the executable statements. Let us look at how the computer carries out the instructions represented by each part.

The *header* for the program given in the example is found on the first line of of the program's text. The reserved word PROGRAM indicates that the header will be followed by a sequence of code that makes up the rest of the program.

Header: the first part of a process. This part specifies the kind of process (e.g. PROGRAM), the identifier name of the process and the process interface(s).

Interface: a hardware or software implementation by which two different parts of a computer system or computer program can exchange data.

Computer execution of the header instruction

In Example 1.1, the program is named FindAreaOfCircle. The header also contains a list of files. In Pascal, the input device is represented as the standard input file, and the default output device is represented as the standard output file. When we see these two file identifiers listed in the program header, we expect the computer to read in values from the keyboard and use the default output device for display purposes. These actions will be carried out in the statement part of the program.

The computer carries out the implied instructions of the program header by setting up an interface between the program file and any data files listed in the header. Figure 1.15 shows the *data area* of the program after the computer has set up the interface from the header of Example 1.1.

Data area: the configuration of data at any given time during the execution of a program, procedure, or function. This configuration is most easily represented as a figure showing values and interfaces.

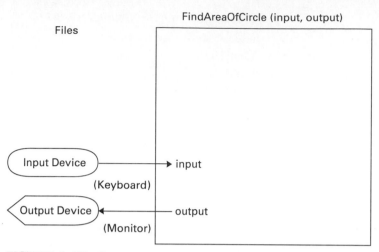

FIGURE 1.15 Data area set up by the program header of `FindAreaOfCircle`.

Declarations

    The *declarations* part of a process contains the nonstandard objects and processes that are to be referenced in the statement part. This part can be further subdivided into constant definitions, variable declarations and procedure/function declarations. None of these subparts is required; they are all optional.

> **Declarations:** the second part of a process. This part establishes identifiers to the objects and/or processes that are referenced in the statement part.

Meaning of the declarations in Example 1.1

    The reserved word CONST in a Pascal program indicates that the identifiers that follow will be used to name constants. We can say that this reserved word states that some constant definitions will make up part of the declarations section. In our example, we defined one constant, `Pi`, which can then be referenced in the statement part as the constant value `3.1416`.

    The constant definitions section ended with the reserved word VAR. This word starts the variable declarations section. In Example 1.1, the `real` variables `Radius` and `Area` were declared. Hence, they can be referenced in the statement part of the program. They are not given any values; they are expected to take on values by the actions in the statement part of the program.

Computer execution of declarations

    Example 1.1 had no declared procedures or functions, so the declarations part of the program ended with the variable declarations section. When the computer executes the instructions implied by the constant definitions and variable declarations, it sets up memory to store the values given to these objects.

    The data area after the computer sets up memory for the constant `Pi` and the variables `Radius` and `Area` is shown by Figure 1.16. The interface set up by the program header is still present, and three more objects have been created.

The statement part

    The executable statement part (simply called the *statement part*) of any process is delimited by the reserved words BEGIN and END. We can say these words are *delimiters* for the statement part of a process. The source code between the

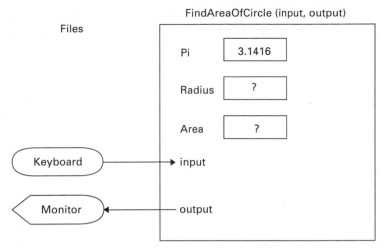

FindAreaOfCircle (input, output)

Files

Pi   3.1416

Radius   ?

Area   ?

Keyboard ──────→ input

Monitor ◄────── output

FIGURE 1.16   Complete data area set up by `FindAreaOfCircle`.

words BEGIN and END consists of *statements*, actions that the machine carries out using references to the objects and processes that have been defined or declared.

> **Delimiter:**   a symbol or reserved word used to establish the beginning and/or end of a portion of source code.

> **Statement:**   an instruction to the computer that is carried out in the statement part of the process. Each statement must have an implied or actual reference to one of the objects that belong to the process.

Semicolons

There are six lines between the reserved words BEGIN and END, where each line consists of a single statement. The semicolon, which appears after all but the last statement, is necessary to separate each statement. Indeed, if you look at other parts of the program, you will see the semicolon is found in many places. It is used, in many different contexts, to separate small parts of a program from each other.

A compound statement

Although the statement part of the program `FindAreaOfCircle` contains six different statements, we can say that these six statements make up the single *main statement* of the program. This single statement, which actually consists of a sequence of six statements, is an example of a *compound statement*. Every process that contains more than one statement can also be seen as consisting of a single compound statement.

> **Compound statement:**   a sequence of statements, delimited by the reserved words BEGIN and END, that are executed one after the other.

The Statements of `FindAreaOfCircle`

Let us now look at the effect of each of the statements that make up the compound statement of the program `FindAreaOfCircle`.

When the computer executes the first two statements of the program we named `FindAreaOfCircle`, it produces the following two-line display:

```
Hello, welcome to your first program.
This program finds and displays the area of a circle.
```

The computer makes a reference to the standard procedure `writeln` and uses the interface to the output device (the implied reference to the standard `output` file) to carry out the display.

When the third statement is carried out, the computer displays the line

```
First, enter the radius:
```

When the computer executes the `readln(Radius)` statement, it makes a reference to the standard procedure `readln`, thus making an implied reference to the standard `input` file to carry out the statement. After the user enters a number such as `6.32`, the computer changes the value of `Radius` from an unknown quantity to the value `6.32`.

Next the machine executes the *assignment statement* whose code is `Area:=Pi * sqr(Radius)`. This statement changes the value of `Area` from an unknown number to the value of the expression on the right-hand side of the *assignment operator* (the special symbol `:=`).

> **Assignment statement:** a statement that, when carried out, has the computer set the value of the expression on the right-hand side of the assignment operator to the variable on the left-hand side of the operator.
>
> **Assignment operator:** the special symbol used in forming an assignment statement.

A picture of the data area

The data area after the assignment statement has been carried out is shown in Figure 1.17. We have assumed that the value read in was `6.32`, as cited in our example. If a different value were read in, the two values of `Radius` and `Area` would be different. The objects in the data area itself, however, would be exactly the same. Moreover, because `Pi` is a constant, it will always have the same value, regardless.

The final statement

The final statement, as run on a Turbo 4.0 system using our sample input, produces the display

```
The area of the circle is 1.2548304384E+02
```

The computer carried out this statement by calling the standard procedure `writeln`. The string literal `'The area of the circle is '` is one of the specified display values. The rest of the display is given by the value of the expression assigned to the variable `Area`. The rules of syntax for `writeln` specify that this display is carried out in scientific notation.

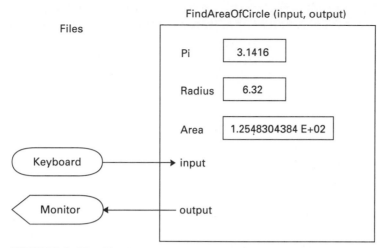

FIGURE 1.17 Final data area of `FindAreaOfCircle`.

Documentation

You may wonder about the parts of the program delimited by the braces that are also shaded in blue. We have said nothing yet about these parts. Indeed, we seem to have skipped over them entirely. We could do so because these special symbols delimited *comments*. Comments make up the *documentation* part of a program.

> **Comment:** source-code text delimited in such a way that the computer ignores it.

> **Documentation:** any kind of comment, used to clarify something about the program.

Our usage of comments

The comment on the second line of Example 1.1 describes the purpose of the program. It is good practice to make a comment about each process you code. We intend to follow this convention with all the source code we derive in this text. Note that we have also put comments beside all object declarations. We will likewise follow the convention of using *sidebar comments* to describe the purpose fulfilled by each constant or variable in a given process.

> **Sidebar comment:** a comment placed beside a line of compilable source code.

Finally, we used a sidebar comment to describe the quantity represented by the expression `Pi * sqr(Radius)`. From time to time, you may want to write a sidebar comment to clarify the meaning of some statement. Use these comments sparingly, however. You need not belabor the obvious. Too many sidebar comments in the statement part will make your code appear cluttered and thus less understandable.

Other Special Symbols, in Brief

You use a comma to separate identifiers and expressions from each other as part of some list. You will find that there are many ways you can code an identifier or expression list in a program. One use for the equal sign is to define the value of a named constant object. There is one other very important use for this special symbol. You always use a colon when you name variables in your source program. You will likewise use this symbol with variables in another context. Finally, you must put a period at the end of all Pascal programs. In this context, the period indicates the end of the program. You can also use a period to form real literals and to form part of another special symbol.

EXERCISES

Test Your Understanding

1. True or false? A program is a process.

2. Name the three parts of a coded process.

3. What reserved word is used with constant definitions?

4. What reserved word is used with variable declarations?

5. What is a compound statement? How is it delimited?

6. What does an assignment statement do?

7. Why do programmers use comments in their source code?

8. How are comments delimited?

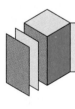

REVIEW AND EXERCISES

The physical components of a computer are known as *hardware*. A computer's *hardware system* is made up of some black boxes, each fulfilling a specific purpose. A typical system has five of these components, namely (1) an *input device*(s), (2) an *output device*(s), (3) *primary memory*, (4) *secondary memory*, and (5) the *CPU*.

The input device receives *data* from the *terminal* for processing. The output device, also part of a terminal, displays the results of the processed data. Primary memory, which is *volatile*, is internal memory stored on an electronic device(s). Most of the contents of this memory are destroyed when the machine is turned off. The contents written into secondary memory, consisting of removable *floppy disks* or an internal *hard disk*, can be saved and used for more than one session on the machine. The *central processing unit* carries out the actual data processing and is the central manager of the computer's hardware resources.

All *computer programs* are written in a *programming language*. The lowest level of a programming language is *machine language*. A program written in machine language is *coded* using only 0s and 1s. All programs, in order to run, must ultimately be translated into the particular computer's machine language.

A language at a somewhat higher level is an *assembly language* that uses *mnemonic* names for certain instructions and/or parts of the machine. A program written in assembly language, more readable than a program written in machine language, must be translated into machine language by an *assembler* program before it can run.

A *high-level language,* such as *Pascal,* allows the programmer to write *source code* that is independent of the particular characteristics of a given machine. Any program written in a high-level language requires a *compiler* for that language, a program that translates the source code into machine language *object code*.

A computer program written in a high-level language is developed using part or all of the programs in a given *software system*. A software system is a system of programs written with some purpose in mind. Every computer, for example, has its own *operating system,* a set of programs to manage the machine's resources. On *multiuser systems,* it is quite common to develop a program using some of the *operating system*'s *commands*. This process of program development is called *command-driven*. On a *personal computer system,* a *software development system* generally has to be *installed* to enable a user to develop the software in a given high-level language. Once the system is installed, the process of developing software is generally *menu-driven*.

The initial user–machine action in program development is *editing* using the system's *editor* program. Once the source code is edited, it must be *compiled*. If there are *syntax errors* (grammar errors) in the program, the computer will issue *syntax error messages* when compilation is attempted. All syntax errors must be fixed using the editor. Eventually, the edited source program will compile into an object program with no syntax errors in it.

If the program is developed on a multiuser system, the compiled object program must be *linked* to get an executable version of the program. Once an executable version of the program has been created, it is *run*. Sometimes a given program may not run to completion because of some unforeseen event that cannot be processed. When processing is aborted in this manner, the program is said to *crash* due to a *run-time error*.

In other cases, the program may run to completion but produce incorrect results. Should this event occur, the program has one or more *semantic* (also *logic*) *errors* in it. Whether a program crashes or yields incorrect results, the semantic errors are fixed by first finding them, then going back to the editor and modifying the offending lines of source code. This process of isolating and fixing errors is known as *debugging* a program.

Any Pascal source program contains *objects* and carries out *processes*. An object is a location where one or more values are stored, and a process is a sequence of actions carried out by the computer. Any given object or process in a Pascal program is named by *identifier* so that it can be *referenced* in the *statement part* of the program. Each *dialect* of Pascal has its own *standard objects* and *standard processes*. A standard object or process can be referenced without having to be defined or declared as part of the program.

A Pascal program contains *reserved words,* each of which can be used for only one given purpose, *identifiers,* which are names for objects and processes, *literals,* which are unnamed constant values, *expressions,* which are values formed from literals, references to objects, and/or one or more pre-defined operations, and *special symbols,* each of which consists of a single or double character that represents some given purpose.

Every Pascal program is structured in such a way that it can be divided into three sections. The first section, the *program header,* represents an *interface* between the *program* and any *data files* required for the program to run. Two of these data files might be the hardware system's input device and its output device.

The second section is the *declarations* section. This section contains the non-standard identifiers, which can be *constants, variables,* or processes that are referenced in the statement part of the program. A constant represents an object whose value is initially fixed and does not change over the course of the program. Its value can be referenced in the statement part of the program. A variable is an object whose value is not initially fixed. It is given a value from the statement part of the program. This value, once read in or *assigned,* can be referenced in the statement part of the program and may or may not change over the course of a program run.

The last section contains the statements (executable statements) of the program. All statements use or change one or more values of the objects that make up the program. The statement part is *delimited* by the reserved words BEGIN and END and consists of a sequence of statements, each separated by a semicolon. This sequence can be, and is, envisioned as a single *compound statement* that is executed in sequence, beginning with the statement following the reserved word BEGIN and ending with the statement preceding the reserved word END.

Documentation is an important part of a Pascal program. A program's documentation consists of *comments,* delimited by braces, which set apart portions of the program that the machine skips over. Either too much documentation or too little documentation makes a program difficult to read.

EXERCISES

Short Answers   Fill in the appropriate word(s) or answer *true* or *false* for each of the following:

1. A location for a data value or a set of data values is known as a(n) _____ .

2. True or false? A process can include other processes.

3. The part of memory that is destroyed when the machine is turned off is known as _____ memory.

4. A(n) _____ represents a name for an object or a process.

5. The practice of using _____ makes it easier for one programmer to understand another programmer's _____ _____ .

6. The program that translates human-readable language into machine language for a given high-level language is called its _____ .

7. An error detected by the machine during compilation is known as a(n) _____ error.

8. The hardware part of a system that consists of a monitor and a keyboard is known as a computer _____ .

9. The hardware part of the computer that does virtually all the processing is known as its _____ .

10. True or false? Once a program compiles correctly, it will run correctly.

11. An alternative version of a given programming language is known as a(n) _____ of the language.

12. A physical location on the actual machine where a data value is stored is known as a(n) _____ .

13. A(n) _____ _____ employs time-sharing software as part of the system.

14. The machine language for a computer is represented as a coded sequence of _____ s and _____ s.

15. The _____ _____ is the part of the program that represents a(n) _____ between the program itself and any external files.

16. The _____ section of a program contains the names of objects and processes that may be referenced in the statement part of a program.

17. The rules that give meaning to the set of instructions in a programming language make up its _____ rules.

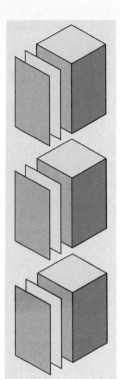

C H A P T E R 2

INTRODUCTION TO PROGRAMMING

OBJECTIVES

After reading and studying the contents of this chapter, you should be able to

- Read and use a syntax diagram in the construction of source code

- Code values representing numeric expressions or string literals

- Code statements that display values of coded expressions

- Define and use constants in a source program

- Declare and use variables in a source program

- Code statements that read values into variables from the keyboard

- Code statements that assign values to variables

- Trace the actions carried out by a sequence of statements

- Code statements that read values from or write values to text files

YOU ARE ABOUT TO WRITE your own Pascal programs. In this chapter, you will learn how to write code that instructs the machine to set aside memory for variables and constants. You will also learn to write code that instructs the computer to reference the values of constants. Likewise, you will learn how to reference and/or change the values of variables. Therefore, you will be interacting with the computer as a programmer, in addition to interacting with it as a program user.

Before you start this chapter, we should point out that program instructions do nothing by themselves. It is the computer that carries out instructions that "do things." You must never forget this fact. If you look at the objectives again, you will see that we have chosen words where instructions appear to be "doing" the actions. We have adopted this convention of imprecision for the sake of simplicity of expression.

2.1 Program Syntax

A source program will compile only if it has no syntax errors in it. In this section, you will learn how to use syntax diagrams to check if your source program obeys the syntax rules. In addition, you will learn how to write programs that display the values of literal expressions.

Syntax diagrams

Figure 2.1 shows the *syntax diagram* that must be satisfied in order for a Pascal source program to compile successfully.

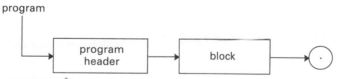

FIGURE 2.1   Syntax of a program.

Syntax diagrams invariably contain symbols connected by arrows. The symbols enclose some specific item belonging to Pascal syntax that must be placed at the given point in the source code. The arrows indicate the next part of code that must follow. The arrows of Figure 2.1 show you that a program must start with something called a *program header,* which is followed by something called a *block*. Then all programs must end with a period.

The meaning of the enclosing symbols

Syntax diagram: a pictorial diagram illustrating how to construct the source code for a Pascal program or a part of a Pascal program.

Any rectangle in a syntax diagram encloses a reference to another syntax diagram. Figure 2.1 shows that you must write code that satisfies the syntax rules for a program header and a block in order for the source program to compile. Any circle in a syntax diagram encloses a special symbol. Figure 2.1 further indicates that all programs must end with the period, one of Pascal's special symbols.

Program header syntax

The syntax diagram for a program header is shown in Figure 2.2. We use an oval to enclose any reserved word. The first identifier following the reserved word PROGRAM is the name of the program. The identifiers enclosed by parentheses make up the program's *file parameter list*. These identifiers represent the files that the machine will use when it carries out the statements of the program.

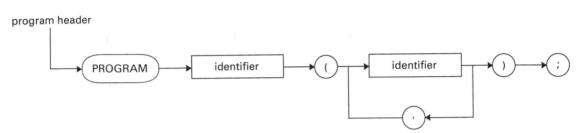

FIGURE 2.2 Syntax of a program header.

We coded the program header in Example 1.1 as PROGRAM FindAreaOfCircle(input,output);, where the semicolon separated the header from the block and the comma separated the input file from the output file. Note how the arrows in the syntax diagram show that it is possible for more than one identifier to be in the file parameter list.

Coding conventions

The Pascal compiler is case-insensitive to the uppercase and lowercase letters of reserved words and identifiers. The reserved word PROGRAM, for example, can just as easily be coded as Program, program, or even PrOgRaM. This property of Pascal allows us to choose a convention in coding reserved words and identifiers.

We choose to highlight all reserved words by coding them as *UPPERCASE* characters. We are furthermore going to code the first character of any non-standard identifier as an uppercase letter. If the identifier is a sequence of characters representing two or more words, we will use an uppercase letter for the first letter of each word. Thus, you have seen us name the program FindAreaOfCircle. Finally, we will use all lowercase letters when we reference standard identifiers. For example, we will always refer to the standard file identifiers in source code as input and output.

Input/output file parameters

The Pascal language is set up such that the CPU communicates with any *peripheral device* through a file parameter. The standard identifier input represents the file parameter used to read values from the keyboard. Likewise, the standard identifier output is the file parameter for the output device. If values are read in from the keyboard, most dialects require that the identifier input be in the file parameter list. Likewise, if values will be displayed, you should write the standard identifier output in the file parameter list.

Peripheral device: any input device, output device, or secondary memory storage device.

Identifier syntax   All identifiers must begin with a letter, either uppercase or lowercase, followed by a sequence of letters, digits, or letters and digits. From this requirement, we see that the following represent valid identifiers:

```
writeln
PrintName
integer
Version2
```

On the other hand, none of these can be valid identifiers:

```
3Bears
Forty-Niners
File.5
```

`3Bears` is invalid because it begins with a digit. `Forty-Niners` and `File.5` are invalid because they contain at least one character that is not a letter or a digit.

A block   A satisfactory syntax diagram for a block is shown in Figure 2.3. Note how the reserved words `BEGIN` and `END` delimit the sequence of statements that make up the block. The statements can then refer by identifier to the objects and processes of the block. They can also refer to any standard identifiers without their having to be declared. Although not every block requires definitions and declarations, it should always have at least one statement. If the program is to execute more than one action, moreover, it will have a compound statement. This statement, as we indicated in Chapter 1, is a sequence delimited by the reserved words `BEGIN` and `END`.

Sample program   When the computer executes the program coded as Example 2.1, it will display the one-line message

FIGURE 2.3 Syntax (incomplete) of a block.

block

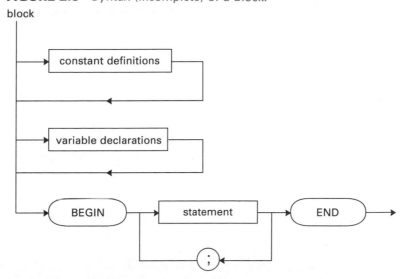

```
                                      Hi there!

             The program will compile and run because it satisfies all required syntax rules.
```

Example 2.1

```
PROGRAM GreetOne(output);
   {When this program is executed, the machine will display the string
   literal 'Hi there!' as a line of text on the output device.}
   BEGIN
       writeln('Hi there!')
   END.
```

Checking its
syntax

    The program header of GreetOne begins with the reserved word PRO-
GRAM and ends with the semicolon. The identifier GreetOne represents this program's name, and the file parameter output indicates the computer will produce
display when the program is run. The second and third lines, as seen by the delimiters in braces, enclose a comment. Because the compiler ignores all comments, the
text between the braces does not have to follow any syntax diagrams. We wrote such
a long comment simply to illustrate that you can write a comment extending over
more than one line of source code. The statement that actually produced the display
is found on the fifth line, between the reserved words BEGIN and END. Finally the
text of the program ends with the period as a special symbol.

Using blanks

    The compiler simply skips blank spaces and blank lines as long as no syntax
rules are violated. You should place blank lines and spaces in your program to help
make it more readable. For example, if GreetOne were coded as PROGRAM
GreetOne(output);BEGIN writeln('Hi there!')END., it will still
compile, but it would be far more difficult to read.

    Be very careful with reserved words, identifiers, and blanks. If the compiler
encounters BE GIN in your source code, it will not recognize the reserved word
BEGIN. If this reserved word is expected at the place where BE GIN is coded, the
machine will issue a compilation error message. Likewise, do not code an identifier
such as Greet One, for an attempt at compilation will also lead to a syntax error
message. Remember that a blank character cannot be used in forming an identifier.

    It is also important that you include blank characters where they are re-
quired. For example, a blank character is required to separate the reserved word
PROGRAM from the identifier representing the program's name. An attempt to compile a "header" coded as PROGRAMGreetOne(output); will result in a compilation error message.

    Aside from these few requirements, you are free to use or not use blanks as
you see fit. Thus, the compiler sees each of these coded program headers as equally
valid:

```
                    PROGRAM GreetOne    (output);
                    PROGRAM    GreetOne    (output);
                    PROGRAM GreetOne(output);
```

Display
statements

    The Pascal language has two standard writeln and write procedures that produce display. A procedure, when referenced by identifier in the statement part of a program, carries out the referenced process.

The procedure `writeln` is the name of a process to display a complete line of text. When this statement is executed, the next display statement will produce display on a new line. The `write` procedure names a process to display part of line of text. The next display statement after a `write` statement continues the display on the same line.

Display statement parameters

The `write` procedure and usually the `writeln` procedure has an actual parameter list. An actual parameter list is always delimited by a pair of parentheses. The items that make up the parameter list of a `write` or `writeln` statement will be expressions whose values are to be displayed. All expressions in a parameter list of either display statement are separated by commas.

> **Actual parameter list**: variables or expressions used or manipulated by the actions of the associated procedure.

A few short examples

Let us write two programs that will display the following literal expressions:

> 5   4   3   2   1   0 Blast off!

The program shown as Example 2.2 uses a single `writeln` statement where the parameter list contains six numeric literal expressions and a string literal expression. Note that the computer displays the expressions according to the order in which they are coded in the parameter list.

Example 2.2

```
PROGRAM Countdown(output);
   {The text of a countdown is displayed.}
   BEGIN
     writeln(5, 4, 3, 2, 1, 0, ' Blast off!')
   END.
```

The `write` statement labeled as {*1*} in Example 2.3 produces the first three numbers of the line display. The second `write` statement, labeled as {*2*} displays the three remaining numeric literals. The line display is completed when the computer carries out the `writeln` statement of line {*3*}.

Example 2.3

```
PROGRAM IICountdown(output);
   {Another version of the countdown program, using two write statements
   and a writeln statement.}
   BEGIN
{1}  write(5, 4, 3);
{2}  write(2, 1, 0);
{3}  writeln(' Blast off!')
   END.
```

It is possible to break up any of the sequences in `IICountdown` and still have the computer produce the same display. If we want to code `write` statements with only one parameter, we could break the code of line {1} in Example 2.3 into the following three statements and still get the same display:

```
write(5);
write(4);
write(3);
```

PROGRAM DESIGN RULE 2.1

When you use a sequence of `write` statements to display a line of text, make sure to end the line display with a `writeln` statement.

The final writeln

If you choose to code a display sequence using `write` statements, it is important that you end the sequence with a `writeln` statement. This statement effectively "returns the carriage" so the machine can start a new line of display. Be sure to follow this practice, for there is only a finite number of characters that can be displayed on a single line.

Some machines automatically wrap around display to the next line if there are too many characters. Other systems will crash at run time when the number of characters exceeds the maximum line length that the computer can display. Regardless of how your system behaves, it is good programming practice to "return the carriage" at the appropriate times.

*Default field
sizes*

If you run the program `Countdown` using Turbo Pascal, you may be puzzled because your display instead will look like

```
543210 Blast off!
```

The reason for this display is that the default *field size* for displaying an *integer* value in Turbo Pascal is 1. If the source code does not specify a field size for a given parameter, the system default field size is used. Each dialect has its own default field size for numeric expressions. On the machine we used (VAX 11-780), the default field size was 10, and so we got all those leading blanks.

Field size: the number of characters reserved for a right-justified display of an expression. A display is right-justified when its last character is the rightmost reserved position.

*String literals
and the
apostrophe*

Both sample programs you have seen displayed string literals. The syntax diagram for a string literal is shown in Figure 2.4. The diagram includes a double apostrophe (' ') as a special symbol. This symbol is required when an apostrophe makes up part of the literal's value. Suppose, for example, you want to code a statement

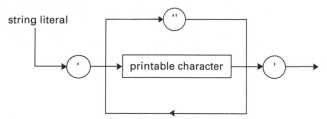

string literal

FIGURE 2.4 Syntax of a string literal.

that displays the line

$$\text{I'm tired, cold and hungry.}$$

Because the apostrophe is used as a delimiter for a string literal, the statement `writeln('I'm tired, cold and hungry.')` will not work. You can get around this difficulty by using a double apostrophe to represent the required apostrophe. Thus, the statement you need is coded as `writeln('I''m tired, cold and hungry.')`.

EXERCISES

Test Your Understanding

1. Indicate which of the following are valid identifiers:
   (a) RoyGBiv   **(b)** SangriLa2   **(c)** Roy G Biv   **(d)** begin
   (e) R-2-D-2   **(f)** integer   **(g)** C3PO   **(h)** output

2. Indicate which of the following are reserved words, which are standard identifiers, which can be user-defined identifiers, and which do not qualify as any of the three:
   (a) Backgammon   **(b)** writeln   **(c)** END   **(d)** AColor
   (e) 132   **(f)** PROGRAM   **(g)** C3P1   **(h)** Plan.1

Practice Your Analysis Skills

3. Correct the syntax errors in the following program:

```
PROGRAMGreet(output);
  BEGIN
    write('Hi there,');
    writeln(Guy)
    write('How are you,';
    writeln('Guy?'
  END.
```

4. What will be displayed by the following programs?

```
PROGRAM ShowSumAndDiff(output);
  BEGIN
    writeln('The sum of 3 and 5 is ',3 + 5);
    writeln('The difference between 3 and 5 is ', 3 - 5)
  END.
```

```
PROGRAM Friendly(output);
   BEGIN
      writeln('Hello there, my name is Roy G. Biv.');
      write('My age is ');
      writeln(75);
      writeln('I''m a very bright fellow.')
   END.
```

(Note: The exact display may differ from one machine to the next.)

Learn More About Your System

5. Run the program of Exercise 3 as it stands to see the syntax error messages your compiler generates. Write down the syntax error messages as you correct the code. You can use them for future reference.

2.2 Numeric Operators and Expressions

This section will show you how to form and display the values of simple numeric expressions. You will also learn how to specify the field size of the expressions you want the computer to display.

Numeric operators

Table 2.1 shows the numeric operators used in Standard Pascal. Some examples of numeric expressions are as follows:

Expression	Value
5 + 3 − 2	6
5 * 3 − 2	13
5 * (3 − 2)	5

TABLE 2.1 Numeric Operators of Standard Pascal

Operator	Operation
*	Multiplication
/	Real division
DIV	Integer division
MOD	Integer remainder
+	Addition
−	Subtraction

Operator hierarchy

We humans are given the luxury of forming numeric expressions like the one shown in Figure 2.5. Because of keyboard entry limitations, you cannot use underscores and superscripts to code numeric expressions. Any complicated expression you want to code must be done on one line using the rules suggested by Table 2.2. This table shows the order in which the different arithmetic operators are applied on

$$5.5 + \frac{3.82 - 2.15}{7.13 - 2.22}$$

FIGURE 2.5 An arithmetic expression.

TABLE 2.2 Showing Hierarchy of Applying Arithmetic Operators

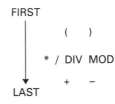

FIRST

( )

* / DIV MOD

+ –

LAST

an expression. When you use the table, you find that the desired expression of Figure 2.5 codes to the following single line of text:

$$5.5 + (3.82 - 2.15)/(7.13 - 2.22)$$

Operators on the same level

Table 2.2 does not show that two operators of the same order (e.g., multiplication and division) are applied from left to right. Thus, the expression 8/2*4 evaluates to be 16 (not 1) because the first expression to be evaluated is 8/2. An equivalent arithmetic expression looks like

$$\frac{8}{2} \cdot 4$$

If you want to code a statement where the computer displays the quotient formed when 8 is divided by the product of 2 and 4, the statement you must code is `writeln(8/(4*2))`.

A model for evaluating expressions

Let us give you a simple model for evaluating a numeric expression. We will assume that the machine requires several passes to complete an evaluation, and that it evaluates the highest operators in the hierarchy with each pass. After the final pass, a single number remains as the value of the expression.

Using our model, the expression 6*4 - 4*3 + 16/8 is evaluated as

Expression To Be Evaluated	Explanation
6 * 4 − 4 * 3 + 16/8	Original expression
24 − 12 + 2	* and / applied
14	+ and − applied

Suppose, instead, we took the same operators and numbers, but inserted a single matched pair of parentheses to form 6*(4 - 4*3 + 16)/8. With this expression, the evaluation sequence is described by

Expression To Be Evaluated	Explanation
6 * (4 − 4 * 3 + 16)/8	Original expression
6 * (4 − 12 + 16)/8	Apply * inside parentheses
6* (8)/8	Apply + and − inside parentheses
6*8/8	Now remove parentheses
6	Finally, apply * and /

Numeric types

There are two standard numeric types in Pascal, real and integer. A real numeric type is represented as a whole number with a decimal fraction, and an integer type is represented as a whole number. The machine internally represents these types differently. Likewise, you must code an integer literal differently from a real literal. You have already seen how to code integer literals, but it is possible to code real literals in one of two ways.

PROGRAM DESIGN RULE 2.2

Code any real literal with at least one digit before the decimal point.

Coding real literals

You can write real numeric literals either in fixed-point or floating-point notation. If you want to write a real literal as a simple decimal value, you would use fixed-point notation. Thus, the number that we call "seventy-five point three-six" can be written as 75.36. Standard Pascal, furthermore, requires that any real literal has at least one digit before the decimal point. Hence, the value of a real number equal to a decimal fraction such as 782/1000 must be coded as 0.782. If you write this value as .782, the machine will issue an error message when it attempts to compile your code.

You can also code real literals in floating-point notation, a format similar to that used with pocket calculators. The following shows some examples using this form:

Pascal Literal	Number Represented	Another Representation
6.625E−10	6.625×10^{-10}	0.0000000006625
3E+12	3.00×10^{12}	3,000,000,000,000
5.08E+03	5.08×10^3	5080

The numeric value before the character "E" represents a literal numeric value, just as before. The character "E" means that the number is multiplied by some power of 10. The integer value following this character represents the power of 10 the first number is multiplied by.

Division operations

When one integer expression is divided by another, two separate results are possible, namely an integer quotient or an integer remainder. The Pascal operators DIV (quotient) and MOD (remainder) are reserved words used as operators to obtain one of the two values resulting from integer division. These two operators can only be applied on expressions for which both operands are of type integer. The numeric result returned is also of type integer.

The third operator to perform division is the familiar slash. The value returned, regardless of the operand types, will always be of type real. Although the expression 4/2 does divide evenly as an integer, the machine nonetheless returns the quotient as the real value 2.0. The following table illustrates how the computer applies these operations to some expressions:

Expression	Value	Result's Type
12 DIV (4 + 2))	2	Integer
12 MOD (4 + 2))	0	Integer
12/(4 + 2))	2.0	Real
12/4 + 2	5.0	Real

Formatting Display

Integer display   The program of Example 2.4, whose run is shown below the program text, displays a two-line table, indicating the sum and difference of 782 and 513 on the first line of the table, and the sum and difference of 9182 and 9175 on the second line. Note that all four numeric expressions in the source code are followed by a colon. The integer value that follows the colon specifies a field size for the expression to be displayed. This value must be an expression of type integer, and it is used to reserve spaces for the associated display parameter. The display produced will differ according to the parameter's type.

Example 2.4

```
PROGRAM SmallTable(output);
  {The computer displays a table of four integer calculations.}
  BEGIN
      writeln(782 + 512: 10,  782 - 512: 10);
      writeln(9182 + 9175: 10,  9182 - 9175: 10)
  END.
```

```
     1294      270
    18357        7
```

When the parameter is of type integer, the field size expression represents the intended number of spaces between the last character of the previous display and the last digit of the integer value to be displayed. We call this display convention *right-justification*. If there is an insufficient number of spaces to produce a right-justified display for the given value, the computer will still display the true value of the associated expression.

Let us study some more examples to clarify how this mechanism works. We use the character '@' as a parameter of each `writeln` statement in order to highlight the way the machine applies the field-size expressions:

Statement	Displayed
`writeln('@',3 + 2: 1, '@');`	`@5@`
`writeln('@',3 + 2: 5, '@');`	`@    3@`
{1} `writeln('@',10*12: 1, '@');`	`@120@`
`writeln('@',10*12: 7, '@');`	`@    120@`
{2} `writeln('@',10*12: (3*3 + 2), '@');`	`@        120@`
{3} `writeln('I am ',39: 1,' years old.');`	`I am 39 years old.`

Note how statement {1} indicates that, regardless of the field size specified, the computer will always display the correct value of the numeric display parameter. Statement {2} indicates that the machine does not require an integer literal as a field-size expression, for any integer expression will do. Finally, the statement we have labeled as {3} shows you the best way to code a statement where numeric and string values must be displayed on one line. You simply reserve the minimum field size for the numeric display (i.e., 1) and write a leading blank and a trailing blank character as part of the string expression on either side of the numeric expression.

Two specification expressions are possible with real numbers. The first expression specifies the field size for the display. The second expression, which we will discuss shortly, represents the decimal precision for a fixed-point display. If no field size is specified, a default value (which differs from system to system) is assumed, and the real number is displayed as a floating-point literal. Regardless of the field size specified, the computer will count one space for a signed number. If the number is positive, this space is displayed as a leading blank. If the number is negative, the blank is replaced by a minus sign.

Any number expressed in floating-point notation consists of two parts, the *characteristic* and the *exponent*. The characteristic part is the real number value to the left of the character "E". The exponent part is the integer value expressing the power of 10 for the given real literal. When the machine displays a floating-point number, the exponent is always shown as a signed two-digit integer, regardless of its value. If you specify a small field size, the machine will round off some of the numbers that make up the characteristic part of the real expression. The machine will never, however, display a characteristic as an integer value.

The following shows how field size is applied when floating point display is specified:

Statement	Display
`writeln('@',3.1416:10,'@');`	`@ 3.142E+00@`
`writeln('@',-785.2132:9,'@');`	`@-7.85E+02@`
`writeln('@',0.0000009876:8,'@');`	`@ 9.9E-07@`
`writeln('@',3.1416:2,'@');`	`@ 3.1E+00@`

You can display real numeric expressions accurate to a given number of places with a precision specifier. This option works only on real numeric types, and only if you first specify a field size. The integer value for this second expression (following a second colon) specifies the number of decimal places to be displayed. When you specify an insufficient field size, the machine will accommodate by expanding the field size to allow for the specified precision.

Examples

Statement	Display
`writeln('@',3.14159:6:4,'@');`	`@3.1416@`
`{1} writeln('@',3.14159:1:4,'@');`	`@3.1416@`
`{2} writeln('@',3.14159:9:4,'@');`	`@   3.1416@`
`{3} writeln('@',3.14159E+00:9:4,'@');`	`@   3.1416@`
`writeln('@',3.14159:9:3,'@');`	`@   3.142 @`
`writeln('@',3.14159:6:2,'@');`	`@   3.14@`

Statement {1} in the table of examples indicates that even if an inadequate field size is expressed, the machine still uses the necessary six spaces to display the value accurate to four places. Statement {2} shows how right-justification is incorporated with real expressions. Statement {3} shows us that the computer treats a real literal the same way, regardless of how its value is expressed. The other examples show that the machine rounds off the display accurate to the specified number of places.

Field size with
string literals

Only a field-size specification has meaning for string expressions. If the value of the field-size expression is greater than the number of characters in the string, the machine right-justifies the display. When no field size is specified, the string is displayed as is. If the field size specified is less than the number of characters, most systems will truncate the display according to the number of characters specified. The following illustrates the rules:

Statement	Display
`writeln('@','Able was I','@');`	`@Able was I@`
`writeln('@','Able was I':15,'@')`	`@     Able was I@`
`writeln('@','Able was I':1,'@');`	`@A@`

Skipping lines

There may be times when you want the computer to display a blank line. The machine accomplishes this action by executing a *writeln* statement with no display parameters. You should make sure, however, that the statement is not preceded by any *write* statements with parameters. Otherwise the statement behaves as a simple carriage return. We can illustrate both instances with the sequence.

```
write('We have effectively not hit a carriage return.');
writeln;
writeln('The previous writeln returned the carriage.');
writeln;
writeln('The previous writeln displayed a blank line.');
```

where the display carried out when the computer executes the sequence is

```
We have effectively not hit a carriage return.
The previous writeln returned the carriage.

The previous writeln displayed a blank line.
```

EXERCISES

Test Your Understanding

1. What does the integer expression following the first colon of a `write` statement parameter specify?

2. What does the integer expression following the second colon of a `write` statement parameter specify?

3. Briefly explain the difference between a `write` and a `writeln` statement.

Practice Your Analysis Skills

4. Evaluate the following Pascal expressions:
   - **(a)** `15 - 10/5`
   - **(b)** `(15 - 10)/5`
   - **(c)** `78 DIV 32 + 78 MOD 32`
   - **(d)** `2*3 + 4/2 - (6 + 2)/8`
   - **(e)** `(14 + 15 + 16)/3/15`
   - **(f)** `(34*17)/(17*2)`
   - **(g)** `34*17/17*2`
   - **(h)** `15 MOD 5 + 16 MOD 8 - 7 MOD 2`
   - **(i)** `(14 DIV 2 - 2)/8`
   - **(j)** `35 DIV 5 MOD 5`
   - **(k)** `36/9*4`
   - **(l)** `36/(9*4)`

5. Which of the following expressions represent legitimate numbers recognizable by a Pascal compiler?
   - **(a)** `3.0E5`
   - **(b)** `34.82E-05`
   - **(c)** `16E5.2`
   - **(d)** `79.0081`
   - **(e)** `9368.14E-02`
   - **(f)** `3.0E`
   - **(g)** `.5831E+06`

6. How would a line of display appear for each of the following:
   - **(a)** `writeln(4:3,170:2,45.893:4:2);`
   - **(b)** `writeln(4:1,' ',170:1,' ',45.893:1:2);`
   - **(c)** `write('***':35);`
     `write(' COMMENT ');`
     `writeln('***');`
   - **(d)** `writeln('The answer is ',3.78:4:2);`
   - **(e)** `writeln('The answer is ', 3.78);`

Learn More About Your System

7. Code a program to have the computer carry out of the display statements in Exercise 6. You can use this program to check your answers for the exercise.

2.3 Constants and Variables

In this section, you will learn how to write programs using named variables and constants. Variables are particularly useful, for the machine can use them to process different values with each program run.

Syntax for defining constants

If your program requires constants, you can define them by writing code that satisfies the syntax diagram of Figure 2.6. The reserved word CONST indicates that some constant definitions will follow, the identifier represents the name of a given

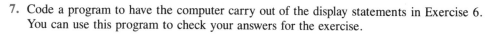

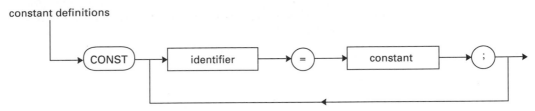

constant definitions

FIGURE 2.6   Syntax for constant definitions section.

constant, and the value of each constant must satisfy the syntax for the appearance of a real, integer, or string literal. Furthermore, all constants must be defined before the statement part of the block.

Example 2.5 is a fragment of code showing correct syntax for the constant definitions part of a block. Note that a constant can take on a string value like ALine, a real value like C or Pi, or an integer value like Octal. The value given to a constant can be used as often as required, but it cannot change over the course of a program run.

Example 2.5

```
CONST
  ALine =   = '_____';
  C = 3E+08;        {velocity of light in meters per second}
  Pi = 3.1416;      {ratio of circumference over radius}
  Octal = 8;        {radix value in octal number system}
```

Variable declarations   A variable can take on different values during the course of a program run. Figure 2.7 shows the syntax diagram for the variable declarations section of a block. Each identifier represents the name by which the variable is referenced in the statement part of the block. The type box, which is usually coded as a reference to an identifer, specifies the type of variable declared. Often these types are standard Pascal types such as real or integer. The variable declarations section for a block is always coded directly after the constant definitions section.

An example   The program shown as Example 2.6 will compile because all syntax rules are satisfied. When the machine runs this program, it will set aside memory for two constants and two variables, then execute an *empty statement*. An empty statement is a Pascal statement that does nothing. The machine will use the values at these locations only if we insert statements that refer to them by identifier between the re-

FIGURE 2.7   Syntax for variable declarations section.

variable declarations

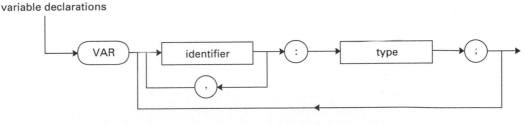

served words BEGIN and END. The words BEGIN and END will then delimit a program statement that carries out some actions.

Example 2.6

```
PROGRAM MakeMemory(input,output);
   {Program to show how machine allocates memory to objects.}
   CONST                      {constant definitions section}
      Pi = 3.1416;            {a real constant}
      Octal = 8;              {an integer constant}
   VAR                        {variable declarations section}
      ANumber: integer;       {an integer variable}
      Radius: real;           {a real variable}
   BEGIN
      {block's statements}
   END.
```

Memory allocation

Figure 2.8 shows the *memory allocation* for the four nonstandard objects of Example 2.6. The arrows show how the machine can use and/or change the values of these objects in the statement part of the program. Note that the values of constants never change, but that the values of the variables can (and should) change over the course of the program run. Furthermore, note that no initial values are given to the variables.

Memory allocation: the process where the computer sets aside primary memory required to carry out the instructions of a program.

The type char

The identifier char defines a standard type that can take on a single character value. Example 2.7 shows a declarations section where the computer will allocate memory for two variables named Ch and Letter, both of type char. Variables of this type can take on values such as '2' or 'A' because they are literal expressions for a single character. Being of type char, neither Ch nor Letter can take on an integer value such as 2 or 785. (Note that '2' represents the value of a char literal, and 2 represents the value of an integer literal.)

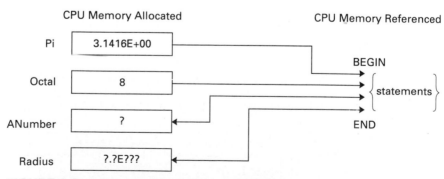

FIGURE 2.8 Memory allocation of Example 2.6.

Example 2.7

```
VAR
  Ch,
  Letter: char;    {two variables of type char are declared}
  Int1,
  Int2:  integer; {two variables of type integer are declared}
```

The comma and the colon

Example 2.7 also shows that `Int1` and `Int2` are of type `integer`. Look carefully at how we have used the commas, semicolons, and colons. You must use a comma in the variable declarations section of a block to separate two variables of the same type. Use a colon after the last variable in the list to indicate the end of the list of variables belonging to the given type. Finally, separate variable lists of different types with a semicolon.

Reading In Values From The Keyboard

One of the ways a variable(s) can take on a value(s) is to have the value(s) read in from the keyboard. This action(s) is carried out when the computer executes a `read` or a `readln` statement.

read, readln statements

The syntax diagram for a successful execution of a `read` or a `readln` statement is shown in Figure 2.9. When either of these standard procedures is executed, the computer reads in values from the keyboard. The parameter list contains references to variables whose values are read in. When either statement is encountered, the computer pauses for the user to enter as many literal values as there are parameters.

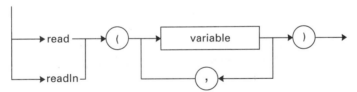

FIGURE 2.9 Syntax of a `read` or `readln` statement.

The literal values the computer reads in are assigned variable by variable to the parameter variables in the list. All characters entered must satisfy the syntax for the type literal of the variable being read in. If a character sequence does not represent a literal of the expected type, the machine will halt and issue a run-time error message.

Reading numeric values

If the computer is reading in a numeric value, it skips over any leading blanks or blank lines, expecting the first character to be a digit. If the first nonblank character read in is not a digit, the program will crash. If, instead, the computer encounters a digit, it keeps reading until the stream of characters representing the numeric literal is finished. The computer then sets the literal value to the corresponding parameter in the `read` or `readln` statement.

Suppose that two *integer* variables, `Int1` and `Int2` and a `real` variable, `Re1`, have been declared. Let us see how the statement `readln(Int1,Re1,Int2)` is applied to the following keyboard events. We have used "<eoln>" to represent a carriage return and braces (which are not part of the input sequence) to label a particular input:

```
{1}   73   98.56   54<eoln>
{2}   73   98.56<eoln>
      54<eoln>
{3}   73   98.56   54 SPQR<eoln>
{4}   73.1   98.56   54<eoln>
{5}   D73   98.56   54<eoln>
```

1. The computer reads in 73 to `Int1`, 98.56 to `Re1`, and 54 to `Int2`.
2. The same result as event {1}. In this case, however, after reading in the value to `Re1`, the machine skips over <eoln> before it reads in 54 to `Int2`.
3. The same values are read in as before. The values of the remaining characters after the 4 are ignored, for the `readln` (*read* a *line*) operation is executed.
4. This sequence will cause a crash because 73.1 represents a `real` numeric value, not the expected `integer` value.
5. Here, the crash will occur as soon as the first character is read in, even though all the remaining characters represent a good sequence.

How `readln` *works*

When the computer executes a `readln` statement, it inspects the characters entered until one of two run-time events occurs:

1. An incorrect sequence has been entered and the program has crashed.
2. A correct sequence has been entered and all values read in.

When values have been read in successfully, the computer ignores all remaining characters before <eoln>. It will execute any subsequent `read` or `readln` statements by inspecting the character sequence on the next line.

In what follows, the computer executes the `readln` statements for the input sequence shown by setting `Int1`'s value to 73 and `Re1`'s value to 98.45. The remaining characters (i.e., 6 and 2) on the first line are ignored because `readln` is executed. The value of 45 is thus read into `Int2` from the next line.

```
readln(Int1,Re1);
readln(Int2);

73   98.45   62<eoln>
     45<eoln>
```

How `read` *works*

When the computer executes a `read` statement, it sets values to the variables in the actual parameter list up to and including the last character used in setting a value to the last parameter. The remaining characters on the input line are candidates for values of the parameters in the next `read` or `readln` statement.

With the previous input sequence, the computer carries out the two statements that follow by first reading in 73 to `Int1` and 98.45 to `Re1`. It will then look for characters on the same line to carry out the `readln` statement. Hence, in this case, `Int2` is set to the value 62. The following line of the input sequence makes up candidate values for the next `read` or `readln` statement encountered in the program run.

$$read(Int1,Re1);$$
$$readln(Int2);$$

Reading char values

The `read` or `readln` statements can likewise read in values to variables of type `char`. In this case, however, no blank values or "`<eoln>`" characters are skipped over. If the character entered is either a blank or `<eoln>` when the statement `read(Ch)` is executed, the computer sets `Ch` to a blank character. Thus, every character entered, regardless of its appearance, is a candidate for reading in a value to a variable of type `char`.

The following shows a particular entry sequence of three keystrokes, and three `readln` statements with parameters of types `char`. The symbol ⊔ is used to represent a blank character.

$$T ⊔ 1<eoln>$$

```
{1} readln(Ch1,Ch2);
{2} readln(Ch1,Ch1,Ch1);
{3} readln(Ch1,Ch2,Ch1,Ch1);
```

For the given sequence of input characters, the three statements are carried out as follows:

1. 'T' is read into `Ch1` and '⊔' is read into `Ch2`.
2. 'T' is read into `Ch1`, then '⊔' is read into `Ch1`. The final value '1' is read into `Ch1`, which is the value taken on by `Ch1` after the `readln` statement is completed.
3. 'T' is read into `Ch1`, '⊔' is read into `Ch2`, then '1' is read into `Ch1`. Finally, the `<eoln>` character is read into `Ch1`, so that the final value taken on by `Ch1` is '⊔'. You should note that because `<eoln>` was read in, the next input line is *skipped over* in its entirety due to the action of `readln`.

Two Coded Programs

Now let us apply some of the material we have presented to code two short programs.

Example Problem 2.1

The problem statement

Let us write a program similar to that of Example 1.1. In this case, however, we want the user to enter a value indicating the radius of the circle and have the machine display its circumference. We require a constant to represent the value of Pi and a variable to hold a value read in for the radius of the circle. A typical run of the program might look like the following:

```
Enter radius:   7.95
The circumference is 49.9514
```

All text showing user-machine interactions will have the user's responses marked in blue. The solution to the problem is given as the program `FindCircumference`.

```
PROGRAM FindCircumference(input,output);
  {The computer displays the circumference of a circle whose radius is
  specified by the user.}
  CONST
    Pi = 3.1416;   {the value of Pi}
  VAR
    Radius: real;   {the radius of the circle}
  BEGIN
    write('Enter radius: ');
    readln(Radius);
    writeln('The circumference is ',2 * Pi * Radius:6:4)
  END. ◆
```

Displaying prompts

Improper keyboard entry will cause difficulties in the form of a run-time crash or having incorrect values read in. You can help the user know what is required by coding a `write` statement to display a message indicating the expected type of input. The informed user, upon reading the message, should enter meaningful characters. This hint is called a *prompt*, and it is coded as an *antibugging* measure.

Antibugging: the act of including statements in the source code to prevent the occurrence of run-time errors.

In `FindCircumference`, the statement `write('Enter radius: ');` was coded to display a prompting message.

PROGRAM DESIGN RULE 2.3

Always precede a series of `read` statements or a single `readln` statement with a `write` or `writeln` statement that describes the input expected by both format and type.

Most systems will allow the prompt to be coded as a `write` statement with a string literal as the prompting message. The prompt statement is then followed by a `readln` statement whose parameter list contains the identifier(s) of the variable(s) whose value(s) is to be read in.

Anonymous vs. named constants

The program `FindCircumference` contained six constant values, only one of which was named. The string constants `'Enter radius:    '` and `'The circumference is '` represented anonymous constants whose values were used in the program run. Likewise, the three integer literals 2, 6, and 4 were also anonymous constants.

Sometimes it is better to code a named constant and other times it is better to use an anonymous constant. Your decision of how to code a given constant will be made easier if you follow these suggestions:

1. Define a constant by an identifier if you plan to reference its value quite often in the rest of the source code.
2. Define a constant if it has a special meaning (e.g., 3.1416).
3. Generally, avoid cluttering the block with named constants that represent the values of prompting messages used in just one statement.

Example Problem 2.2

The problem statement

Suppose our computer is connected to a video game system. If the game player has scored above a certain number of points, the system calls a program to congratulate the user as follows:

The game player is asked to enter three letters indicating the initials of his or her name. Then he or she is prompted to enter the number of points scored. The computer echoes (displays back) the user's initials and the score, truncated to the nearest thousand, as a two-line message of congratulations. A sample run of the program is as follows:

```
Enter three initials of your name:   RGB
Enter the number of points scored:   12562
Congratulations, RGB.
You scored over 12,000 points in our game.
```

Let us write the code for this program.

Variables and constants needed

We need three variables of type char to represent the user's initials. The computer should echo these values at the appropriate time. We also need a variable of type integer to store the user's score. Finally, we define the constant Thousand, using its value in the coded expression Score DIV Thousand. The source code solution to the problem is shown as the program CongratulatePlayer.

```
PROGRAM CongratulatePlayer(input,output);
   {The computer displays a congratulatory message to the user on a
   video game well-played.}
```

```
CONST
   Thousand = 1000;      {used in applying the DIV operation to Score}
VAR
   Ch1, Ch2, Ch3: char;  {the player's initials}
   Score: integer;       {the player's score}
BEGIN
   write('Enter three initials of your name:   ');
   readln(Ch1,Ch2,Ch3);
   write('Enter the number of points scored:   ');
   readln(Score);
   writeln('Congratulations, ',Ch1,Ch2,Ch3,'.');
   write('You scored over ',Score DIV Thousand:1);
   writeln(',000 points in our game.')
END. ◆
```

EXERCISES

Test Your Understanding

1. Can a value of a constant be read from keyboard input? Explain.

2. Assume a Pascal program has constants defined and variables declared. In what order would the following words appear in the source code: (1) BEGIN, (2) CONST, (3) END, (4) PROGRAM, (5) VAR?

Practice Your Analysis Skills

3. We want the computer to execute the statement readln(Re1,Re2), where Re1 and Re2 are of type real. Indicate whether the machine will assign two values, crash the program, or pause for more input for each of the following inputs (ignore labels and leading blanks):

   (a)   17.28   15.13<eoln>
   (b)   16.205E+12   .75
   (c)   3.0E-09   91.3333333
   (d)   15<eoln>
   (e)   30E.12   65
   (f)   18   18<eoln>
   (g)   73.8-30E-01   Will this work?<eoln>
   (h)   73.8   -30E-01   Will this work?<eoln>
   (i)   Will this work?   73.8   -30E-01<eoln>

4. Answer the same question as in Exercise 3, where now the statement to be executed is readln(Ch1,Ch2) and Ch1 and Ch2 are of type char:

   (a)   JJ<eoln>
   (b)   X<eoln>
   (c)   <eoln>
   (d)   154<eoln>
   (e)   .;22<eoln>
   (f)   5 9<eoln>

5. Indicate the values assigned to Ch1 and Ch2 from Exercise 4.

2.4 The Assignment Statement

The assignment statement sets a value to a variable as an internal process. In this section, you will learn how to use the assignment statement on the three variable types you have studied.

Assignment statement syntax

A value can be assigned to any given variable using the assignment statement. Figure 2.10 is the syntax diagram for this statement. When the computer executes an assignment statement, it sets the value of the expression on the right-hand side of the assignment operator (: =) to the variable on the left-hand side of the operator.

assignment statement

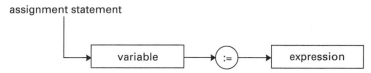

FIGURE 2.10 Syntax for an assignment statement.

Integer assignments

Suppose the variables Int1 and Int2, both of type integer, have been declared. They are to be assigned values through the execution of a sequence of assignment statements. The following shows the values these two variables will take on as a result of the sequence of statements that begins on the third line:

Statement	Result		
initially	Int1	⟷	?
initially	Int2	⟷	?
Int1:= 0;	Int1	⟷	0
Int2:= 7;	Int2	⟷	7
Int1:= Int2 DIV 2;	Int1	⟷	3
Int2:= Int2 + 1	Int2	⟷	8

The double-pointing arrow we use replaces the phrase ". . . contains the value. . . ." Note how the expression of the third statement (Int1:= Int2 DIV 2;) uses the value assigned to Int2 to change Int1's value. Int2's value is again referenced in the final statement, this time on both sides of the assignment operator. Here, the final value of Int2 is changed because the action of the statement effectively adds 1 to the original value of Int2.

Assignments to real variables

Suppose the values given to Int1 and Int2 at the end of the previous sequence can still be referenced. Suppose further that two variables, Re1 and Re2, both of type real, have been declared. The following shows how the computer carries out the assignment sequence beginning on the third line to these two real variables.

Statement	Result
initially	Int1 $\longleftrightarrow$ 3, Int2 $\longleftrightarrow$ 8
initially	Re1 $\longleftrightarrow$?, Re2 $\longleftrightarrow$?
Re1:= Int2 + 1;	Re1 $\longleftrightarrow$ 9.00E+00
Re2:= Int1/(Re1 + 1);	Re2 $\longleftrightarrow$ 0.30E+00
Re1:= Re1 + Re2;	Re1 $\longleftrightarrow$ 9.30E+00

Note that the first statement demonstrates that a `real` variable can be assigned a value using the value of an `integer` expression. This assignment shows that real variables are *assignment-compatible* with integer expressions.

The reserve case is not true, for an `integer` variable cannot be assigned the value of a `real` expression.

Assignment-compatible: if a given expression can be assigned to a variable without a syntax error, we say the expression is assignment-compatible with the variable.

char assignments

Suppose, we have also declared three variables, Ch1, Ch2, and Ch3, all of type `char`. Let us further suppose that the value for Ch1 was read in as the character 'R'. We then have the following:

Statement	Result
initially	Ch1 $\longleftrightarrow$ 'R' Ch2 $\longleftrightarrow$? Ch3 $\longleftrightarrow$?
Ch2:= Ch1;	Ch2 $\longleftrightarrow$ 'R'
Ch3:= 'J';	Ch3 $\longleftrightarrow$ 'J'
Ch1:= Ch3;	Ch1 $\longleftrightarrow$ 'J'
Ch2:= '9';	Ch2 $\longleftrightarrow$ '9'

Note that the last value is the char literal '9' and not the `integer` literal 9. A literal of type `char` is enclosed by apostrophes, but a literal of type `integer` has no association with this special symbol. For the moment, the only two `char` expressions we can code are literals and values taken on by variables. We will show you other ways to code `char` expressions in Section 3.3 of the next chapter.

The assignment rule

An assignment is executed only if the variable and expression are assignment-compatible. You cannot, for example, assign a `char` expression to an `integer` variable. Likewise, a `real` value cannot be assigned to an `integer` variable. The variable and expression should agree by type. The one exception to this rule is that an integer expression can be assigned to a real variable.

From the assignment rule, we find that the following attempted assignments will result in syntax-error messages:

Statement	Result
Ch1:= 2;	SYNTAX ERROR, expression is integer value
Ch1:= 2 + 3;	SYNTAX ERROR, expression is integer value
Int1:= Re1 + 1;	SYNTAX ERROR, expression is real value
Int2:= 6/3;	SYNTAX ERROR, expression is real value

It is impossible to crash a program if an attempt is made to assign an incompatible expression to a variable, because the compiler will pick up the incorrect assignment as a syntax error and issue an error message.

Example Problem 2.3

The problem statement

Let us write a program to find the sum of nine input integers. The program should also find and display the subtotal of the first three and the first six numbers. A typical run of the program might look like:

```
Enter three integer values for group 1:   70   90   85
Subtotal 1:   245
Enter three integer values for group 2:   60   73   46
Subtotal 2:   424
Enter three integer values for group 3:   53   97   81
Subtotal 3:   655
```

The solution

This program is a little more difficult to code, so we should think things through a bit more carefully. It is easy to get the first part of the program coded, for the computer reads in three `integer` values and then displays the sum of these values. Thus, a candidate sequence for processing the first set of values might be coded as

```
write('Enter group 1:   ');
readln(Int1,Int2,Int3);
Sum:= Int1 + Int2 + Int3;
writeln('Subtotal 1:   ',Sum:1);
```

We see from this sequence that we will need at least four variables to carry out the desired actions. With further thought, we realize that no more variables are necessary. The values read into `Int1`, `Int2`, and `Int3` outlive their usefulness once they are used to assign a value to Sum. We can, therefore, use these same variables to store the values of the other two groups. How, then, do we find and display a new subtotal?

When we give it a bit more thought, we see that we do not need another variable to represent the new sum. The machine can simply assign a new value to the variable Sum, using an expression to represent the sum of the old subtotal and the

three new values read. Thus, the new assignment to Sum codes to Sum:=
Sum + Int1 + Int2 + Int3.

The solution to the problem posed is coded as the program ShowSubTotal.

```
PROGRAM ShowSubTotals(input,output);
   {The user enters three sets of three integer values, and the computer
   finds and displays the subtotal after each set has been entered.}
   VAR
      Int1,       {first value in group}
      Int2,       {second value in group}
      Int3,       {third value in group}
      Sum:        {running subtotal for the groups}
                  integer;
   BEGIN
      write('Enter three integer values for group 1:   ');
      readln(Int1,Int2,Int3);
      Sum:= Int1 + Int2 + Int3;
      writeln('Subtotal 1:   ',Sum:1);
      write('Enter three integer values for group 2:   ');
      readln(Int1,Int2,Int3);
      Sum:= Sum + Int1 + Int2 + Int3;
      writeln('Subtotal 2:   ',Sum:1);
      write('Enter three integer values for group 3:   ');
      readln(Int1,Int2,Int3);
      Sum:= Sum + Int1 + Int2 + Int3;
      writeln('Subtotal 3:   ',Sum:1)
   END.
```

Desk tracing a program

Let us take the values of the sample data and apply them to the program we just coded. We will see if the values taken on by the variables using this sample data return the desired results. We thus study the program's actions using the techniques of *desk tracing*. You can never prove a program is correct with a single desk trace, for each trace is done on only one set of data. You can, however, show that a program is incorrect if the trace indicates it will produce an undesirable end result.

> **Desk tracing:** a technique used in program testing where data values are picked and then the actions carried out using these values are hand-traced according to the program statements.

A sample desk trace

Before the first sequence of integers are entered, the values taken on by the four variables are unknown. This situation is described by the following picture:

$$\text{Sum ? \qquad Int1 ? \qquad Int2 ? \qquad Int3 ?}$$

After the first three values are read in, the picture changes to

$$\text{Sum ? \qquad Int1 70 \qquad Int2 90 \qquad Int3 85}$$

Then when the machine executes the first assignment statement on the variable Sum, we get the picture

Sum 245   Int1 70   Int2 90   Int3 85

Following this assignment operation, the computer displays the value taken on by Sum.

When the second set of integers are entered, the picture changes to

Sum 245   Int1 60   Int2 73   Int3 46

The value taken on by Sum according to the action of the second assignment statement is the value of the expression Sum + Int1 + Int2 + Int3. When this assignment is carried out, the picture changes to

Sum 424   Int1 60   Int2 73   Int3 46

This value, representing the subtotal of the six integer values entered is then properly displayed.

The third set of values entered gives us the following picture:

Sum 424   Int1 53   Int2 97   Int3 81

The machine then carries out the final assignment statement, giving us the picture

Sum 655   Int1 53   Int2 97   Int3 81

This value, representing the total of the nine integers, is then displayed.

Some Comments on Coding Style

We conclude this section with a brief discussion on coding style. Remember that a human being, in addition to the computer, should be able to read source code. If you follow the suggestions in the forthcoming discussion, you will help ensure that your source code is easy to understand.

PROGRAM DESIGN RULE 2.4

Make all identifiers self-documenting.

Identifier names   If you look back at all the programs we coded, you will see that we chose a name for each identifier that implied something about its purpose. In the last example, we gave the Sum to the variable that stored the subtotal results. Int1 stored the first value read into each group, Int2 the second value read in, and Int3 the third value. In other programs, we used names such as Score, Pi, FindAreaOf-Circle, and so forth. When you choose meaningful identifier names, your source code will be easy to understand and hence modify, if necessary.

You are free to lay out variable declarations any way you want as long as the syntax rules are satisfied. You should strive, however, for a layout that is easy to read. As candidates that are all quite readable, we have the following:

```
{1}    VAR
           Int1: integer;
           Int2: integer;
           Re: real;


{2}    VAR
           Int1, Int2: integer;
           Re: real;


{3}    VAR
           Int1,
           Int2: integer;
           Re: real;


{4}    VAR
           Int1, {first integer variable}
           Int2: {second integer variable}
                 integer;
           Re:   {a real variable}
                 real;
```

Our preference is the last one because: (1) the rest of the line for each variable can be used for a sidebar comment, (2) the comments can be lined up easily, and (3) the identifiers for each type end with some white space as a natural separator between types.

"Unreadable code"

It is possible for the following version of the program ShowSubTotals to compile without errors because all syntax rules are satisfied:

```
program showsubtotals(input,output); var int1,int2,int3,sum: integer;
begin write('Enter three integer values for group 1:  ');
readln(int1,int2,int3); sum:= int1 + int2 + int3;
writeln('Subtotal 1:   ',sum:1);
write('Enter three integer values for group 2:  ');
readln(int1,int2,int3); sum:= sum + int1 + int2 + int3;
writeln('Subtotal 2:   ',sum:1);
write('Enter three integer values for group 3:  ');
readln(Int1,Int2,Int3); sum:= sum + int1 + int2 + int3;
writeln('Subtotal 3:   ',sum:1) end.
```

However, it is certainly not easy to read.

We have adopted certain layout conventions in this text. Your instructor may want you to use different conventions. Perhaps he or she will let you use whatever you feel most comfortable with. Regardless of what convention you follow, be consistent throughout. The basic idea is to make code readable to another person and not just the compiler.

In this text, we use the following conventions:

1. We put the program header on one line.
2. We put the reserved word CONST on one line.
3. We indent code associated with the word CONST.
4. We define only one constant identifier per line.
5. We unindent at the end of the constants definition section.
6. We put the reserved word VAR on one line.
7. We indent code associated with the word VAR.
8. We usually declare only one variable per line.
9. We unindent at the end of the variables declaration section.
10. We indent code associated with the reserved words BEGIN and END.
11. We put the words BEGIN and END on separate lines.
12. We line up the word END with the associated word BEGIN.
13. We usually put only one statement per line.

EXERCISES

Test Your Understanding

1. What is the required relationship between the variable and the expression for an assignment statement to work?

Practice Your Analysis Skills

2. Suppose Int1 and Int2 are declared as variables of type integer, Re is declared as a variable of type real, and Ch is declared as type char. Write down the display when the following sequence is carried out:

```
Int1:= 5;
Int2:= 7;
writeln(Int1*Int2:1);
Int2:= Int2 MOD Int1;
writeln(Int2:1);
Ch:= 'h';
writeln(Ch);
Re:= Int1/Int2;
writeln(' The result is ',Re:4:2)
```

3. Given the same declarations of Exercise 2, indicate which of the following will not compile:
   (a) Int1:= Int1/Int2;
   (b) Re1:= Int1/Int2;
   (c) Ch:= Ch + 1;
   (d) Re:= Int1 + Int2;

(e) `Re:= Int1 DIV Int2;`
(f) `Int1:= Re;`

4. Desk trace the values taken on by the variables if the following nine integer values were input for the run of `ShowSubTotals`:

$$
\begin{array}{rrr}
75 & 89 & 76 \\
43 & 56 & 81 \\
-10 & 43 & -15
\end{array}
$$

Sharpen Your Implementaton Skills

5. Write a program with variable declarations and reserved words so that the sequence of statements in Exercise 1 is actually carried out.

6. Write a program where the computer reads in two `real` values. It stores their product and then displays this result. Next, it reads in two more `real` values. It subtracts the product of these two numbers from the first product and stores this result. Then it displays the value stored.

2.5 Peripheral Units And Files

Suppose you are on a system that uses a *batch mode*. In this case, the data to be processed comes from a separate file whose contents are read at run time. You may need to store the results of a program in another file as text. Perhaps, instead, you are using a personal computer and are experiencing difficulty getting the display on the screen to be shown on the printer. The subject matter of this section deals with these input/output considerations.

Batch mode: the means by which data is entered and programs are executed without any intermediary interaction of the user with the computer.

Writing A Program For Batch Mode

If you are using a system where programs are run in batch mode, your program will need to read in data from one file containing text and write out data to another file containing text. You should therefore be able to write code that enables the CPU to get data from and send data to these text files.

The method we give you for achieving these actions is simplistic, but it will work with most multiuser systems. If the method outlined does not work for your system, your instructor will give you the necessary steps to enable you to write programs that work on your system.

Secondary storage devices and files

The computer can read data from and write data to secondary storage devices. The information contained in these devices is stored in data files. We are assuming that your instructor has given you an assignment where the data to be processed are stored in a file named `Prog1Data`. We are further assuming that he/she wants you to write the results of the processed data into another file named `Prog1Res`.

To use the two files in secondary storage, both file names must be found in the file parameter list. We are assuming that any values taken on by variables and constants can be displayed on the output device with which you are working. The only thing we are assuming you cannot do is write code where the computer reads values from the keyboard and processes them in a program.

Example Problem 2.4

*The problem
statement*

You have been assigned to write a program DoCalculations where the computer is to read in two real values from the file Prog1Dat. It should then calculate and store the sum and product of these values in the file Prog1Res.

*Coding the
header*

In order to fulfill these requirements for file interaction, you must code the program header where the two file names are in the file parameter list, PROGRAM DoCalculations (output, Prog1Dat, Prog1Res) ; ,

*Text file
variables*

Next, you will have to set up the files in such a way that the machine can read values from Prog1Dat and write values into Prog1Res. First, you must put the two names in the variable declarations section of the program. These names then serve to be identifiers for two file variables, files that the computer can access by identifier reference. Both files contain human-readable text, so they can be declared as type text, the standard Pascal type for human-readable files. The declarations section for the program is thus given as the code:

```
VAR
   Prog1Dat,      {file containing the data}
   ProgRes1:      {file containing the results of the run}
                  text;
   Re1,           {first real value read in from Prog1Dat}
   Re2,           {second real value read in from Prog1Dat}
   Sum,           {used to hold the sum of Re1 and Re2}
   Prod:          {used to hold the product of Re1 and Re2}
                  real;
```

*File-preparation
statements*

Next, you will need to code two statements in the program, one to prepare the file Prog1Dat for reading, and the other to prepare the file Prog1Res for writing. You can code these two statements as calls to the standard Pascal procedures reset and rewrite, using the respective file names as parameters. The file Prog1Dat is the parameter for reset, and the file Prog1Res is the parameter for rewrite.

These statements must be coded first to allow access to both files. Therefore, you must start the statement part of the program with the code that follows:

```
BEGIN
   reset(Prog1Dat);     {now Prog1Dat can be read from}
   rewrite(Prog1Res);   {now Prog1Res can be written into}
   {rest of statements}
END.
```

If values are read from an external file, the first parameter in the parameter list of a read or a readln statement is the file's representative name (in this case, its actual name). A line of text containing the values for Re1 and Re2 are thus read into these variables with the coded statement readln(Prog1Dat, Re1, Re2).

Likewise, the first parameter in a parameter list of the write or writeln statement is the file's representative name. If you want the computer to write a line of text into Prog1Res showing the values of Re1 and Re2 accurate to five places, you would code a statement such as writeln(Prog1Res, 'The values read were ', Re1: 7: 5, ' and ', Re2: 7: 5);. The coded solution to Example Problem 2.4 is shown below. When the program is run, all text sent to the file ProgRes1 is also shown on the output device.

```
PROGRAM DoCalculations(output, Prog1Dat, Prog1Res);
  {The computer reads two real values from the file Prog1Dat, then
  writes the sum and product of these values into Prog1Res. It also displays
  all values on the screen.}
VAR
  Prog1Dat,    {file containing the data}
  ProgRes1:    {file containing the results of the run}
               text;
  Re1,         {first real value read from Prog1Dat}
  Re2,         {second real value read from Prog1Dat}
  Sum,         {used to hold the sum of Re1 and Re2}
  Prod:        {used to hold the product of Re1 and Re2}
               real;
BEGIN
  {prepare files:}
  reset(Prog1Dat);
  rewrite(Prog1Res);
  {read values:}
  readln(Prog1Dat, Re1, Re2);
  {do calculations}
  Sum:= Re1 + Re2;
  Prod:= Re1 * Re2;
  {display all values:}
  writeln('The values read were ', Re1: 7: 5, ' and ', Re2: 7: 5);
  writeln('The sum of the values is ', Sum: 7: 5);
  writeln('The product of the values is ', Prod: 7: 5);
  {write all values into Prog1Res:}
  writeln(Prog1Res, 'The values read were ', Re1: 7: 5, ' and ', Re2: 7: 5);
  writeln(Prog1Res, 'The sum of the values is ', Sum: 7: 5);
  writeln(Prog1Res, 'The product of the values is ', Prod: 7: 5)
END. ◆
```

Text Files Parameters

Peripheral units

When the contents of a text file are to be read into main memory or values from main memory are to be written into secondary memory, the associated file's name must appear as the first parameter in a `read` or `write` statement. The parameters that follow are those used as if the machine were interacting with a keyboard or display device.

In Pascal, any peripheral unit from which text can be read or to which text can be written is treated as a file. The computer can communicate with one of these peripheral units as long as the proper software has been coded to create the interface. When no file parameter is expressed, the computer sends the values in the list of expressions to the output device as the default file. The interface is taken care of by default. If, for example, you want a screen display such as "Hi there!" to be carried out, you would simply code `writeln('Hi there!)`.

What happens, then, if you explicitly mention the output device as a file parameter with the coded statement `writeln(output, 'Hi There!')`? Nothing different, for you are still instructing the machine to send the same string literal for display on the output device. In this case, however, you are not using the default mechanism.

PCs and printers

On a personal computer, the output device is usually the screen, and the printer is seen as another peripheral unit. You will probably need to use the printer to get a copy of the run of your program. Therefore, you will need to know the name of the file your system uses for the printer. On many systems, you can simply use this name as the first parameter of a `write` or `writeln` statement to get the printer to respond.

Setting up an interface

Unfortunately, some systems may require that you include additional code for the computer to set up the interface. For example, in Turbo Pascal, you need to set up an interface by coding USES `printer;` directly after the program header. This code allows you to interface the CPU with the `lst` file, the name Turbo Pascal gives to the printer. If, for example, you want a program to make the machine display "Hi there!" on both the screen and the printer, you would have to code the program shown as Example 2.8.

Example 2.8

```
PROGRAM GreetOnBoth(lst,output);
   {A program that runs on Turbo 4.0 and later versions of Turbo Pascal.
   The computer displays "Hi there!" on both screen and printer.}
   USES
      printer;   {allows for interface between CPU and printer}
   BEGIN
      writeln(lst, 'Hi there!');       {display on the screen}
      writeln(lst, 'Hi there!');       {display on the printer}
   END.
```

Other systems may have a different name for the printer or require different code for setting up the interface between the CPU and printer. If you are using a PC with some other Pascal development system, consult the system's documentation. Although different identifiers and/or reserved words may be required, the basic concept we presented is still the same. You just need to find out the few keywords and/or identifiers that are necessary for your system's CPU to interface with its printer.

EXERCISES

Test Your Understanding

1. What is a text file? Can a source code program be considered a text file?

Practice Your Analysis Skills

2. Suppose the contents of the file Prog1Dat contained the following literal values:

   8.10   6.00

   Desk trace the actions carried out by the computer for these values.

Learn More About Your System

3. If you are a personal computer user, run Example 2.8 on your computer. If you do not have Turbo Pascal, read your system's documentation so you can code the program that will work like Example 2.8.

Program Testing Hints

All parts of a Pascal program, big or small, must satisfy the relevant syntax diagrams before the program compiles without errors. If there are syntax errors, the system will not compile the source program. Computers also have practical limitations that become evident at run time when a program either crashes or produces absurd results. In this section, we present some examples of different compilation errors and run-time errors you may encounter. We also give you some hints on how to prevent them or fix them.

Example 2.9

Misspelling a reserved word

```
PROGRAN Ex1(output);    {CONTAINS AN ERROR}
   {Illustrating a misspelled reserved word.}
   BEGIN
     writeln('Hello world');
   END.
```

When we attempted to compile the source code of Example 2.9, our particular compiler (VAX 11-780 Pascal) gave us the following error message:

```
00001        0    0   PROGRAN Ex1(output);
                    1
(1) Syntax: PROGRAM or MODULE expected
PASCAL completed with 1 diagnostic
```

Note that the compiler will not correct spelling errors.

More than one error message

Sometimes a single syntax error will cause a series of error messages. The next example shows what might happen in this case.

Example 2.10

```
PROGRAM Ex2(output);  {CONTAINS AN ERROR}
  COMST   {misspelled reserved word}
    Sum = 'The sum is ';
    Difference = 'The difference is ';
  BEGIN
    writeln(Sum, 7 + 5:1);
    writeln(Difference, 7 - 5:1)
  END.
```

When we attempted to compile Example 2.10, we got the following error messages:

```
00002          0   0     COMST   {misspelled reserved word}
                                  1
(1) Syntax:   BEGIN or declaration expected
00004          0   0     Difference = 'The difference is ';
                                  1
(1)  Syntax: BEGIN or declaration expected
00006          0   1     writeln(Sum, 7 + 5:1);
                                              1
(1)  Undeclared identifier SUM
00007          0   1     writeln(Diff, 7 - 5:1);
                                              1
(1)  Undeclared identifier DIFF
PASCAL completed with 4 diagnostics
```

Note that the compiler cannot recognize a nearly correct reserved word. The first error caused other error messages to be displayed. The last three error messages were also caused by the single misspelled reserved word. All four error messages will be eliminated when the word COMST is replaced by CONST.

PROGRAM DESIGN RULE 2.5

Correct the earlier syntax errors first.

An error-correcting hint

Now you see that one syntax error can lead to a number of syntax error messages. Given enough undeclared identifiers, missing semicolons, unterminated character strings (a missing string delimiter), and other errors, a simple 10-line program can easily generate a list of some 20-odd error messages. You should not be discouraged by all these messages. Just correct the earliest errors first. Some systems, such as Turbo Pascal, force you to follow this rule regardless. This particular compiler requires that you correct one syntax error at a time.

maxint Every system has a standard constant `maxint`. This defined number represents the highest integer value that can be expressed without returning strange results or error messages. The value of `maxint` depends upon the system you will be using. For example, VAX Pascal's `maxint` is equal to `2147483647`. Other systems may have a different value for this important constant. You should always be careful that the integer expressions you code will not exceed your system's value for `maxint`. When the computer attempts to evaluate too large an expression at run time, it may crash the program or generate absurd numbers. What actually happens depends upon the system.

buffer overflow The computer uses a buffer for all peripheral units. This memory location is capable of holding only a finite number of characters at any given time. The characters held are eventually sent to the associated peripheral device. When the computer executes a statement such as `write(1:20)`, for example, it fills the buffer of the `output` file up with 20 characters, 19 of which are blanks. If the following statement is `writeln`, the contents are sent to the display device, and the `output` buffer is emptied to allow space for the next line of text.

Buffer: primary memory used to interface the CPU with a peripheral unit.

PROGRAM DESIGN RULE 2.6

Learn how your system handles `write` and `writeln` statements for every data type.

On some systems, it is mandatory that you code a `writeln` statement to prevent the buffer from taking on too many characters. For example, VAX Pascal allows a maximum of 133 characters to be stored in the `output` buffer. Given this fact, when the machine attempts to execute the statement `writeln(1:40, 2:40, 3:40, 4:40)`, it will crash with an error message whose text is "record length exceeded by 27 characters".

Other systems will continue to display characters, using a format where the text continues automatically onto the next line. In Turbo Pascal, a `writeln` statement causes the machine to start a new line. Without the statement, the characters simply wrap around to the next line, and there is no buffer overflow message.

Pascal statements dealing with peripheral units differ greatly from system to system. Therefore, you should keep Program Design Rule 2.6 in mind as you learn about each new data type.

Commenting out statements Suppose you have written a program that causes some error you cannot seem to fix. You may not be able to fix the error but might still want to know if the rest of the program is good. You feel completely stuck, for you cannot deal with this offending statement unless you remove it from the block. If you do not want to delete it, you can simply comment it out as we have done with the second statement in the following sequence:

```
writeln('CIRCLE AREA = ',AreaCircle:4:2);
{writeln('RECTANGLE AREA = , AreaRect:4:2);}
writeln('SQUARE AREA = ',AreaSquare:4:2);
```

The computer will not compile this second (erroneous) statement.

Initializing
variables

A named constant takes on a defined value as soon as the program run is initiated. The first statement of the program, therefore, can use its value in an expression. No statement, however, can change its fixed value.

When a variable is declared, its initial value is unknown. It must take on a value before it can be used in an expression. If a reference is made to its value before it is read in or assigned, the machine will produce unpredictable results.

The initial statement in Example 2.11 attempts to assign a new value to Pi. The second statement makes a reference to an unassigned value for Radius. Both statements are wrong. The first statement will cause a syntax error. The second one will often cause a run-time crash, but some systems will issue a warning message at compilation time.

Example 2-11

```
PROGRAM MisuseTwo(input,output);
  CONST
    Pi = 3.14;
  VAR
    Radius, Area: real;
  BEGIN
    Pi:= 3.14159;                   {INCORRECT ASSIGNMENT}
    Area:= Pi * Radius * Radius     {REFERENCE TO UNASSIGNED VALUE}
  END.
```

EXERCISES

Test Your
Understanding

1. What does the identifier maxint represent?

Practice Your
Analysis Skills

2. Find the syntax errors in the following program:

```
PROGRAM DivAndMod(output);
  VAR
    Int1, Int2: integer;

  BEGIN
    write('Enter two integers:   )'
    READLN(Int1,Imt2);
    writeln('Their integer quotient is ',Int1 DIV Int2:1,'.');
```

```
      wirtlen('Their integer remainder is ,IntMOD Int2:1,'.')
  END.
```

Learn More About Your System

3. Edit and compile `DivAndMod` exactly as shown. Record the error messages and correct only the first error. Recompile again and record the error messages as before. Again, correct only the first error. Continue this process until you have a program that is correct. Note how the computer issues error messages in the context of the overall source program.

4. Compile, link, and run the following program:

```
PROGRAM UsingMaxint(output);

  BEGIN
    writeln('The highest integer is ',maxint:1);
    writeln('A higher number is ',maxint + 1:1);
     writeln('A very high number is ',maxint*maxint*maxint:1)
  END.
```

If the second statement caused a crash, comment it out, and run the program again.

REVIEW AND EXERCISES

A *syntax diagram* represents a pictorial description of the syntax rules for coding a given part of a program. In order for a program to compile, the source code must be written such that it satisfies all necessary syntax diagrams. The standard Pascal `write` and `writeln` statements are used to display the values taken on by the expressions in their *parameter lists*. These expressions can represent arithmetic values or string values.

The values for any *named constants* are found in the *constant definitions section* of a *block*. A named constant's value can be referenced but never changed. Program *variables* are declared in the *variable declarations section*. They can take on values either by the action of the standard `read` or `readln` procedures or by means of an *assignment* operation. Once a variable takes on a given value, it can be *referenced* to form part of an expression.

In Pascal, the computer communicates with all *peripheral units* as files. Every system has a special *file name* for any input or output device it uses. If you want to read values from a file that is not the *default input device,* you must write code to set up an *interface* to the file or device, then use the associated file name as the first parameter in any `read` or `readln` statement. Likewise, if you want to send the values of expressions to a file other than the *default output device,* you must write code to set up an interface, then use the associated file name as the first parameter in any `write` or `writeln` statement.

EXERCISES

Short Answers

1. In order to compile, every Pascal program must have the reserved words ____ _____ , and _____ .

2. True or false? Sometimes reserved words can be used as identifiers.

3. Explain briefly why comments are important.

4. True or false? The MOD and DIV operators can only be applied to integer expressions.

5. What value is returned by the expression 8/4? Is it real or integer?

6. Match the word(s) or symbol in Column A with the associated word(s) or symbol in Column B:

Column A	Column B
standard process	arithmetic operator
reserved word	assignment operator
data type	integer.
arithmetic expression	'Hi there!'
:=	writeln
statement separator	VAR
literal expression	;
MOD	7 DIV 2

7. True or false? An integer expression can be assigned to a real variable.

8. Briefly explain why you should not use a reference to a variable in an expression unless it has had a value assigned to it.

9. The standard identifier input is required if the program has any _____ or _____ statements in it.

10. Is output a reserved word, an identifier for a process, or an identifier for an object?

11. True or false? A constant identifier cannot appear on the left-hand side of the assignment operator.

12. True or false? A constant identifier cannot be a parameter of the read statement.

13. What is a prompt? How is it used?

14. Write down the exact appearance of the output for the following statement:

```
writeln(7.8951:4:2,' ',152:8,' ',7.91E-02:3:1,' ',87.55:3);
```

15. What does the standard identifier maxint represent?

Easy Projects

16. Write a program that outputs the following pattern:

```
*******
*******
*******
*******
*******
```

17. Write a program that outputs the following pattern:

```
         *
        * *
       * * *
      * * * *
       * * *
        * *
         *
```

18. Write a program that asks the user to input a radius, then displays the volume of a sphere with this radius. Define the constant Pi as 3.1416. (Volume of sphere = $\frac{4}{3}$ Pi · r^3.) Code the program so that the display appears as

```
Enter radius:     7.2285
The volume of the sphere is 1186.5756
```

19. Friendly Savings and Loan Association gives a fixed interest rate of 8% per year. Write a program that first asks the user to input an initial principal. The program then calculates the interest earned and the new principal at the end of the year. It then displays these values. Code the program so that a typical interaction looks like

```
Enter initial investment in dollars:   1000.00
After one year, you will have earned $80.00 in interest payments.
Your initial investment will have grown to $1080.00.
```

Medium Projects

20. Write a program to display the results of the calculations:

(a) $\dfrac{11 + 24}{2}$

(b) $\dfrac{(2)(6)}{5} - 0.1$

(c) $1.0374 + \dfrac{3.82 + 14.7}{2.10}$

(d) $\dfrac{8^2}{9}$

Use anonymous constants. Write the program to make the display appear as

```
Answers:
        (a)  17.50
        (b)  2.30
        (c)  9.86
        (d)  7.11
```

21. Write a program to display the same calculations as Exercise 5, but this time the display should look like

```
Answers:
        (a)  17.5000
        (b)  2.3
        (c)  9.8564
        (d)  7.111111111E+00
```

22. The formula to convert a temperature expressed in degrees Fahrenheit to the same temperature expressed in degrees Centigrade is

$$°Cent = 0.555 \, °Fahren - 32.$$

A temperature expressed in degrees Centigrade is expressed in degrees Kelvin as

$$°Kelvin = °Cent + 273.16$$

Write a program where the user enters a Fahrenheit temperature, and the computer finds and displays the equivalent Centigrade and Kelvin temperatures. The statement part of the program should not contain any anonymous numeric constants; it should only have references to constants that have already been defined.

23. Write a program where the user inputs two positive integer values. The output should show the values along with their sum and difference in the following form:

```
Input the two numbers:   9756   2375
            9756                9756
           +2375               -2375
           -----               -----
           12131                7381
```

Allow ten spaces between the two sets of calculations.

Difficult Projects

24. The officers of Friendly Savings and Loan (the bank with guaranteed 8% interest) want you to write a program so the user can see how his or her principal and interest grows after the first, second, and third years for a given starting principal. A typical run is as follows:

```
Enter starting principal:   100
    YEAR            INTEREST            PRINCIPAL
    ----            --------            ---------
     0                0.00               100.00
     1                8.00               108.00
     2                8.64               116.64
     3                9.33               125.97
```

Allow a field size of 15 spaces between the headings. Write the code for the program.

25. The surface area of a cuboid object is given by $S = 2(LW + LH + WH)$ and its volume by $V = LWH$, where L, W, and H are the respective lengths, widths, and heights. Use these two formulas to display a table of length, width, height, surface area, and volume for two sets of values that the user enters. The display should be in tabular form and carried out only after the user has entered the two sets of values. A typical run is as follows:

```
Enter first set of dimensions:   5   3   2
Enter second set of dimensions:  7   4   3
    OBJ #    LENGTH    WIDTH    HEIGHT       AREA      VOLUME
    -----    ------    -----    ------       ----      ------
      1        5         3         2          56         30
      2        7         4         3         120         84
```

You can simplify the problem by having the user enter integer values for the three dimensions.

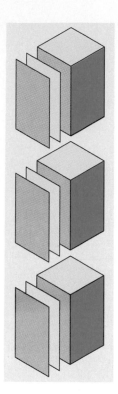

C H A P T E R 3

PROGRAM DEVELOPMENT

OBJECTIVES

After reading and studying the contents of this chapter, you should be able to:

- Use pseudocode as a tool in developing programs

- Use the method of successive refinements to develop programs

- Apply good testing techniques as part of the development process

- Reuse certain accepted algorithms to solve different coding problems

- Use a select group of standard Pascal functions to code expressions

- Use string variables in simple input/output applications.

BY NOW, you have had some practice in writing source code. As yet, however, you have not applied any formal techniques in finding the correct source code for a coding problem. In this chapter, you will learn a formalism you can apply to solve any kind of coding problem.

The formalism can be given in four short sentences: Describe the sequence of actions carried out by the computer. Test the description to see that it represents a correct solution to the problem. Refine the initial description by giving a more specific description for each of the described actions. Prove and further refine each of the refinements. Eventually, the program will have been described and refined to a sufficient degree that it can be coded.

3.1 Techniques of Program Development

In this section, you will learn about some of the tools you can use to develop source code. You will also learn the importance of stating the problem clearly enough so that you can apply the tools effectively on the problem statement.

The problem statement

The programs you will write and study in this text are *applications programs*. The applications program whose code you desire must satisfy the problem statement. This statement should unambiguously specify the nature of any "raw" (input) data that must be processed and the nature of the returned (output) data. Recall, for example, a paraphrase of the problem statement for Example Problem 2.3: "Write a program to find and display the total of nine input integers. The integers are to be read in groups of three, and the subtotal after each of the three groups is entered should be displayed."

> **Applications program**: any program written to solve a specific kind of problem applicable in areas such as business, engineering, word processing, and so forth. None of these applications directly relate to computer science.

This statement is clear and unambiguous. If, however, the problem is stated unclearly, you will not know exactly how to write a problem that you can call "correct." Suppose for example, the problem were stated as: "Write a program to find and display the subtotals of three groups of integers." This problem is not easy to solve because the details are not clear. How many integers make up a "group"? Where or how do we get the values of these integers? Before you can solve the problem to the satisfaction of the client who posed it, you must ask questions such as these lest you solve the wrong problem.

Feasibility

Sometimes a problem can be stated clearly, yet lack a logical solution. Suppose, for example, somebody asks you to write a program that counts the number of times 0 can be subtracted from 5 before the accumulated difference is also 0. We can write a program to attempt this solution, but the machine will not be able to return a satisfactory result because no *feasible* solution exists.

Feasibility: the property of a problem statement that makes it possible to have a solution.

Perhaps a solution is not practically feasible. In order to be practically feasible, the program must work within the hardware and software limitations of the machine. Every computer, for example, is limited by the size of maxint and by the number of bits of data it can store in primary memory at any given time. If either of these limits is exceeded at run time, the machine will return unpredictable, hence undesirable, results.

Algorithms   Every problem that has a solution follows an algorithm.

Algorithm: a finite sequence of prescribed actions that leads to the problem's solution.

The definition shows us that an algorithm has the following properties:

I. *Finiteness.* There is a measurable point at which we can say, "There are no more steps to be done. The problem is solved."

II. *Orderedness.* The first step in the sequence is followed by a second step. The second step leads to a third step, and so forth.

III. *Unambiguousness.* This property does not mean that choices are never made as part of the sequence. Most algorithms have steps in which one action is done in preference to another. In order for a preferred action to be done, however, one or more conditions must have been determined earlier in the sequence. These conditions must be stated in such a way that there is no doubt about the next action to be taken.

The Method of Successive Refinements

Algorithms, descriptions, and programs
Regardless of the size or complexity of a coding problem, you can develop the source code for its solution using a simple, yet very effective, method. This method, outlined in the following discussion, is a powerful tool you can apply to solve any problem whose solution is described as an algorithm.

When the machine runs a Pascal program, it carries out a sequence of actions whose description is enclosed by the reserved words BEGIN and END. This sequence is finite, ordered, and unambiguous. It is also a description of actions that the computer carries out. Therefore, we can say that any correctly coded Pascal program describes the algorithm that solves the problem.

The first draft
Suppose you have been given a problem to solve. If you have determined that a feasible solution exists, you should have a general idea of what actions you want the machine to execute. You can describe these actions as your initial first draft toward the coded solution to the problem. Because a source program is a description of a sequence of machine-generated actions, this method should work if you follow through correctly in the development process.

Let us say you have come up with an initial description of a solution to a coding problem. This initial description, although lacking in details, should have one overriding characteristic: *It describes the solution correctly*. If, upon further consideration, you find that you have not described a correct process, abandon it. Do not try to refine it further, for you will be refining a process that leads to an incorrect solution.

Refinements
If you have determined that the initial description of the process is correct, you can start work on the first refinement. Perhaps the solution you initially described listed five actions that are executed in sequence. You need to refine each of these actions. The first action may refine to a sequence described by perhaps three actions. These three actions that represent a refinement have a similar characteristic to that of the initial description, namely, *they must correctly describe the result of the action being refined*. If you find the refinement is incorrect, you must likewise abandon it and come up with a correct refinement. When you develop a program in this manner, you are employing the method of *successive refinements*.

> **Successive refinements:** a method of solution development where the actions to be carried out are described in general terms, then slowly refined and tested in such a way that the details continue to describe a correct solution. The description becomes more specific with each refinement.

An example
Let us apply this method to find a solution to Example Problem 2.3. We will start with an initial description that we will continue to refine. Our initial description might be as follows:

> *read in 3 input integers and display their sum*
> *read in 3 input integers and display the sum of all 6 integers*
> *read in 3 input integers and display the sum of all 9 integers*

We can refine the first described action using

> *read in values for Int1, Int2 and Int3*
> *Sum ← Int1 + Int2 + Int3*
> *display the value of Sum*

The second and third described actions are refined using

> *read in values for Int1, Int2 and Int3*
> *Sum ← Sum + Int1 + Int2 + Int3*
> *display the value of Sum*

(The pseudocode we use for an assignment statement has a left-pointing arrow to indicate that a new value has just been given to the associated variable.)
Note that we could have described the assignment statement for the second and third actions as

$$Sum \leftarrow Int1 + Int2 + Int3$$

Further consideration, however, would show that this assignment is incorrect, for the value taken on by Sum would represent the sum of only the last three values read in. Once we confirm this action is incorrect, we would stop the refinement process and fix our erroneous description. When we are satisfied with the new description, we can refine the actions further until the refinements look very close to actual source code.

Testing Techniques

There is more than one method you can use to test the proposed design of a program. Three of the most widely used techniques are *desk tracing, assertion testing,* and *on-line testing.*

Desk tracing.   We have already discussed this technique in Chapter 2. When you use this method, you make up sample data, then walk through the algorithm with it to see if you get the desired end result. A desk trace, however, can only prove that an algorithm is "correct" for one set of data, but is useful for finding and eliminating any obvious errors in your proposed algorithm.

Assertion testing.   Assertion testing will help you determine if a proposed algorithm is logically correct. In order to apply this method, you need to start the test with a description of the initial *program state*. An *assertion* indicating the change in the program state is then made for each step of the algorithm's description. The algorithm is shown to be logically correct if the program state, after the last step is carried out, describes the condition(s) required for a correct solution.

> **Program state:**   a description made at a specified point in the execution sequence of the program that describes (1) the condition(s) taken on by values of the program variables and (2) the characteristics of any display that has occurred.

> **Assertion:**   a description of the effect(s) a given step in an algorithm has on the program state.

An example of assertion testing

Let us apply assertion testing on Example Problem 2.3 from Chapter 2. Recall that this problem required nine integers values to be entered in 3 groups of 3 integers. After each group, a subtotal of all integers read in was to be displayed.

After the first three integer values are read in, we can assert that the variables Int1, Int2, and Int3 hold the values of the first group of 3 input integers. When the sum of these values is assigned to Sum, we can then assert that the value taken on by Sum represents the sum of the first 3 input integers. When Sum is then displayed, we then assert that the sum of the first 3 integers read in has been displayed.

After three more values are read into Int1, Int2, and Int3, we can state that the values taken on by these variables represent the values of the fourth, fifth and sixth integers that were entered. After the assignment Sum is made, we can say that the value it takes on represents the total of the first 6 integers. When the computer displays this value, more of the desired solution, namely the display of the subtotal of 6 integers read in, is carried out correctly.

The values taken on by Int1, Int2, and Int3 as a result of the third `readln` statement represent the seventh, eighth and ninth integers that were input. When these three integers are added to Sum, Sum's value now represents the sum of the 9 integers read in. When this value is displayed, the final action to be carried out is done correctly. Thus, the final program state where 3 subtotals are found and displayed is achieved. Hence, the code of Example Problem 2.3 is logically correct.

A critique of assertion testing

Overall, assertion testing is a very good way to test your code. It forces you to think about why you chose the variables and processes you did. It can be applied just as readily to test parts of a program as it can to test the entire program as a whole. In contrast to the desk-trace method, it also tests that your code will work for more than just one set of data. When you are ready to enter your program into the computer, you will therefore be more confident that you have found a correct solution. For all of these reasons, we plan to use assertion testing extensively as a tool in the program development process.

Unfortunately, if you have overlooked some conditions, assertion testing cannot guarantee a correct program. Suppose, for example, in the problem we have just tested, at run time the user keys in a sequence of characters that do not represent integer values. The program will, of course, crash. Clearly, the assertions we made in our tests did not account for this run time event! Our tests are still correct, however, as long as the user only enters integer values—events that are considered "normal" for this particular program.

On-Line Testing. You can only apply on-line testing once you have a runnable object program. Using this method, you make up data values to be processed by the actual program. You then examine the processed results to see if they were what you expected. This method, as with the desk tracing method, cannot tell you if a program is correct, but it can let you know if a program is incorrect.

Choosing data for on-line testing is a definite skill. Your goal in this case is to find ways to show that a solution is incorrect. Therefore, you want to choose enough values to test a program thoroughly, if not *exhaustively*. When you test a program exhaustively, you use enough data to ensure that every circumstance that can occur at run time has been tested. This goal may be impossible to achieve in practice, but it can be theoretically realized. The subject matter of this text includes methods you can apply in choosing data that theoretically exhaust all possibilities.

The importance of testing

Figure 3.1 summarizes the actions to follow in developing a program. Note how important it is to test the proposed solution at each step in the development process. Indeed, many tests are done within any given step of the same process. Each refinement, for example, should be tested before you go on to the next refinement. This process may be repeated many times before you are ready to write code. In like manner, once a program is running, more than one set of test data should be used before you can say you have coded a "good" program.

Maintenance

Sometimes it is necessary to do *maintenance* work on your program. Further work may be required either because some subtle bug was discovered or because the program must be upgraded. In either case, much of the existing source code is left unchanged or modified very little. You may need to analyze quite a bit of code, though, in order to determine where to put the changes and how best to implement them. Therefore, it is important for you to write programs that you can easily understand.

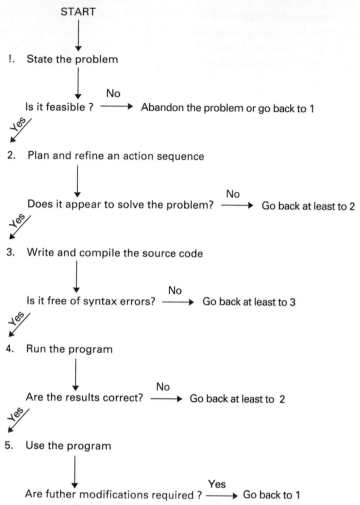

FIGURE 3.1 Steps in program development.

Maintenance: the act of modifying an existing program either to correct an error that has been found or to incorporate additional features that the user has requested.

A final note on human/machine interactions

Try to spend as much time away from the computer planning and checking the logic of your program as you do actually seated at a terminal. Ideally, you should view editing as something separate from the development process. *Do not get into the habit of composing your program at the terminal.* Even if you do write a solution that "works," it might be planned so poorly that it is difficult both to understand and to modify.

If your program has errors in it, it is usually better that you get a printout of the source program and do the debugging work away from the machine. You can make an exception to this practice if you are correcting simple syntax errors. If, however, you find yourself working on the same small piece of code for over an hour, chances are you would do better working away from the machine. The more you experiment on a portion of the code with the hope that it will work, the more you will find yourself losing an intellectual grasp of what you should be writing to fix the bug. Log off and think instead.

EXERCISES

Test Your Understanding

1. What are the three methods for testing a program? At which part of the development process can each method be employed?

2. List the three properties of an algorithm.

3. Describe the method of successive refinements.

Practice Your Analysis Skills

4. Apply a sequence of assertions to Example Problem 2.2. Your sequence should indicate:
   (a) what the values taken on by Ch1, Ch2, and Ch3 represent
   (b) what the value taken on by Score represents
   (c) how these values are used to produce a measurable effect

Sharpen Your Implementation Skills

5. Modify Example Problem 2.2 so that the computer displays the value of a given score that is in excess of so many hundreds of points.

3.2 Using Pseudocode

In this section, you will see many examples of pseudocode. Some examples will describe the solution to a specific problem. Others will describe a general algorithm that you can categorize as one that solves a class of problems.

> **Pseudocode:** an informal description of a program or part of a program where each part of the description has its actual correspondence as source code.

Example Problem 3.1

The problem statement

Let us develop and write a program to do the following: The user inputs three character values. The values are then displayed in reverse order. A typical run of this program looks like

```
Input three characters, then press <Enter>:  QBY
The characters reversed are YBQ
```

The initial description

We can describe the process we want the computer to carry out as

read in values for Ch1, Ch2, and Ch3
display Ch3, Ch2, Ch1

The description is one where three values are read in as the first action, then displayed in reverse order as the second action. Therefore, it describes a correct solution to the problem statement. The description further tells us that we need to declare three variables to solve the problem. It also tells us we need to code a `readln` procedure with Ch1, Ch2, and Ch3 as parameters. Likewise, we need to code a `writeln` procedure to display the values in the reverse order of Ch1, Ch2, and Ch3. We may need to use more variables or processes to solve the problem, but we will not know until we make further refinements.

When you describe a solution using pseudocode, the required variables, constants, and processes will become evident as the description unfolds. Often, you will not know all the variables you need or all the processes you require until you have refined the description to the point where you are ready to write it as source code.

Refinements

If we want the user to input values, he or she has to be told that these three values are characters. Thus, the first action described refines to

> *display prompt*
> *read in values for Ch1, Ch2, Ch3*

We now know that a call to the `write` procedure is required to display a prompting message. The second action can be refined to

> *display explanantory string, Ch3, Ch2, Ch1*

This description indicates we need a string constant as a formal parameter for the `writeln` statement.

Writing source code

We can write both of these refinements as source code. The first sequence we refined codes to

```
write('Enter three characters, then press <Enter>:   ');
readln(Ch1, Ch2, Ch3);
```

and the second piece of pseudocode becomes the coded statement

```
writeln('The characters reversed are ', Ch3, Ch2, Ch1)
```

The code for the program is as follows:

```
PROGRAM ReverseThree(input,output);
   {The user inputs three characters that are displayed in reverse.}
   VAR
      Ch1,   {first char value input}
      Ch2,   {second char value input}
      Ch3:   {third char value input}
         char;
```

```
BEGIN
   write('Enter three characters, then press <Enter>:    ');
   readln(Ch1, Ch2, Ch3);
   writeln('The characters reversed are ', Ch3, Ch2, Ch1)
END. ◆
```

Categorized
algorithms

Algorithms than can be categorized are very useful program development tools. If you find that one of these general-purpose algorithms characterizes the problem you want to solve, you have an initial description of the solution to your problem. You can then apply successive refinements on the ready-made algorithm to get a coded solution to the specific problem you need to solve.

A general algorithm that describes the very specific problem we just solved is given by the pseudocode description of Algorithm 3.1.

Algorithm 3.1

Read, display
expression(s):
a categorized
algorithm

{Algorithm to read in values, then use them for display:}
   read in values
   display the results, using these values in expressions
{end algorithm}

We use comments and numbering to formalize this description as an algorithm that we can categorize. We applied the first action of the algorithm on our specific problem when values were read into Ch1, Ch2, and Ch3. The second action corresponded to having the values displayed in the order Ch3, Ch2, and Ch1.

We used this algorithm on a number of other programs. As an example, the code that solved Example Problem 2.1 can be described by

read in value for Radius
display the value of the expression 2*Pi*Radius

Note that this description pointed out the need to define a value for the constant Pi in the constant definitions part of the program block.

Example Problem 3.2

Problem
statement

Let us write a program where the user inputs a number to represent the side of a square. The computer finds and stores its area, then displays the value stored. A typical run of the program might look like

Solution
description and
code

```
Input length of side:  7.82
The square's area is 61.15
```

The solution to the problem is described by

> *read in value for Side*
> *Area ← Side * Side*
> *display value of Area*

and the code is as follows:

```
PROGRAM SolveSquare(input,output);
  {A value representing the side of a square is input. The square's
  area is found and displayed.}
  VAR
    Side,   {representing the length of the side}
    Area:   {representing the square's area}
            real;

  BEGIN
    write('Input length of side:  ');
    readln(Side);
    Area:= Side * Side;
    writeln('The square''s area is ',Area:4:2)
  END.  ◆
```

The code for this program fits the pseudocode description of Algorithm 3.2.

Algorithm 3.2

Read, process, display: another versatile algorithm

> *{Algorithm to read, process, display:}*
> *read in value or values*
> *process the value or values*
> *display the result or results*
> *{end algorithm}*

This algorithm, which we call *read, process, display,* is even more versatile than the *read, display* algorithm (Algorithm 3.1). Many programs have solutions that satisfy this description. Indeed, this algorithm can be applied as one of the steps to solve part of a problem. We used it three times in sequence on Example Problem 2.3, as the following description shows:

read in values of Int1, Int2, Int3	*{1}*	*read*
Sum ← Int1 + Int2 + Int3		*process*
display value of Sum		*display*
read in values of Int1, Int2, Int3	*{2}*	*read*
Sum ← Sum + Int1 + Int2 + Int3		*process*
display value of Sum		*display*
read in values of Int1, Int2, Int3	*{3}*	*read*
Sum ← Sum + Int1 + Int2 + Int3		*process*
display value of Sum		*display*

The keyin
algorithm

We have applied an algorithm we can call *keyin* in many of our examples. We describe it as Algorithm 3.3 with the pseudocode.

Algorithm 3.3

> *{The Keyin algorithm:}*
> *display prompt string*
> *read in a value or set of values on an input line*
> *{end algorithm}*

Some examples of code we have written using this algorithm are

```
write('Enter radius:   ');        {Examples 1.1 and 2.6}
readln(Radius);

write('Enter three initials of your name:   ');     {Example 2.7}
readln(Ch1,Ch2,Ch3);

write('Enter the number of points scored:   ');     {Example 2.7}
readln(Score);
```

We can describe each of these sequences with a reference to the *keyin* algorithm by

> *keyin Radius*
>
> *keyin Ch1, Ch2, Ch3*
>
> *keyin Score*

EXERCISES

Test Your Understanding

1. Why is it useful to categorize algorithms?

2. What two standard Pascal statements are implied by the sequence of actions we describe as *keyin*?

Practice Your Analysis Skills

3. The following sequence of code represents the statement for a program named FindVolume. What algorithm does it use?

```
{a} write('Input the length, width and height:   ');
    readln(Length,Width,Height);
{b} Volume:= Length*Width*Height;
{c} writeln('The volume is ',Volume 4:2);
```

4. Describe each of the labeled sequences of Exercise 3 in terms of the algorithms *keyin*, *assign*, or *display*. Any description should include the variables or expressions involved.

5. Write the rest of the program for Exercise 3.

6. Write code that satisfies the following descriptions:
   (a) keyin Int1, Re1
   (b) display explanatory string, product of Int1 and Int2

3.3 Strings and Standard Functions

In this section you will learn how to define and use strings, a type that is not a part of standard Pascal. Virtually all systems, however, have the capabilities of processing string variables. You will also learn some of standard Pascal's functions, thus enabling you to code more expressions

> **String variable:**   a variable type that represents a group of characters put together in some meaningful sequence.

Strings

People, users of computers and programs, read and write characters in groups as "words." Therefore, it is useful to have a variable type to represent a word. We can represent a word using a string variable. A string variable, like the other variables you have seen, can take on a value either as the result of an assignment operation or as the result of having its value read in from the keyboard.

String types

If you want to write statements that use string variables, you will need to define them as another type. You must code a definition because there is no standard string type defined for Pascal. Virtually all systems will allow you to use strings, even though each system has its own syntax rules for defining a data type to represent a string. For example, a string type defined in Turbo Pascal requires that you use the Turbo Pascal reserved word STRING. The syntax diagram that needs to be satisfied in this dialect is shown in Figure 3.2.

Turbo Pascal string definition

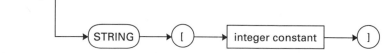

FIGURE 3.2   Defining a string type in Turbo Pascal.

To declare two string variables in Turbo Pascal, then, you would code

```
VAR
     String1,
     String2:  STRING[10];
```

It is important to note that the word STRING is a reserved word in Turbo Pascal and not in ANSI Pascal.

Once the variables have been declared, operations such as the following are allowed:

```
String1:= 'Mac';
String2:= '132876553';
String1:= 'Jack Jones';
```

Note that all expressions have 10 or less characters in them. The following assignment is illegal because there are too many characters in the string expression:

```
String2:= 'Joseph Conrad';      {ERRONEOUS CODE}
```

Type definitions

The declarations for `String1` and `String2` used anonymous types, because the type `STRING[10]` does not satisfy the syntax diagram for an identifier. It is possible, however, to name types in the type definitions section of a block. The TYPE definitions are found after the CONST definitions but before the VAR declarations. You use a TYPE definition to name a type for an associated variable(s) to be declared in the VAR declarations section.

> **Named type:** a data type that has an identifier reference.

> **Anonymous type:** a data type that does not have an identifier reference.

Figure 3.3 shows the syntax diagram for the TYPE definitions section. The word TYPE is a reserved word of standard Pascal. All subsequent types are defined according to other syntax diagrams.

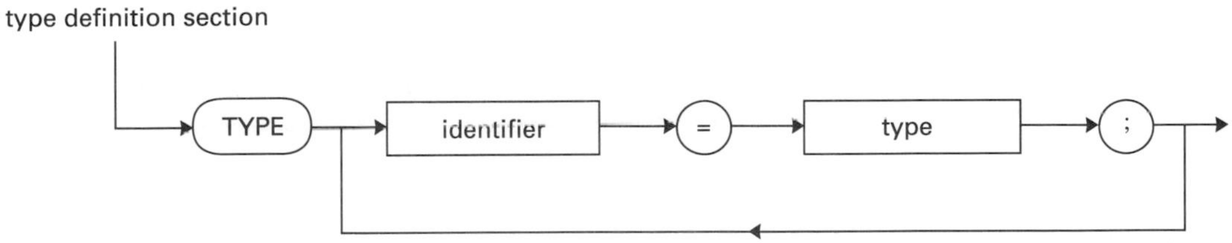

type definition section

FIGURE 3.3 Syntax diagram for TYPE definitions section of a block.

You can use a defined type in the following manner:

```
TYPE
    String10 = STRING[10];
VAR
    String1, String2: String10;
```

`String1` and `String2` are still string variables that can contain up to 10 characters, but now they belong to a named type.

*Dialects and
strings*

If you are using VAX Pascal, you would have to define a string type as `VARYING [SomeLength] OF char`, where `SomeLength` is a defined or anonymous integer constant. The syntax diagram for defining a string type in VAX Pascal is shown in Figure 3.4. To define a string type capable of holding up to 10 characters using VAX Pascal, you need to code

```
TYPE
    String10 = VARYING [10] OF char;
```

Once the type is defined, the two variables String1 and String2 can be declared just as before.

VAX Pascal string definition

FIGURE 3.4   Defining a string type in VAX Pascal.

Other dialects may require a different syntax. When a variable is declared to be of some defined string type, its value can be read and/or displayed using the readln and writeln procedures. These operations are possible regardless of the Pascal dialect in which the variable was declared. It is usually better to define any string type by name. Then the variable declarations look the same in all dialects, and the same read/write operations can be applied in all dialects.

Reading in values to strings   If a readln operation is applied to a string variable, the computer reads in the literal sequence of characters to the variable. Consider the following statements as they are applied to the given input:

```
readln(Name1);
readln(Name2);

Johnnie<eoln>
Joey<eoln>
```

Assuming no leading blanks, the computer sets the string literal 'Johnnie' to the string variable Name1 and the string literal 'Joey' to the string variable Name2.

It is possible to read in values for more than one string variable on any given line of input. However, the code required to accomplish this action is well beyond your present scope of understanding. For now, you should only write code to read in one value to one string variable using the readln statement.

Example Problem 3.3

The problem statement   Let us write a program to simulate the behavior of the philanthropist Charles C. Charles as he greets a guest at one of his many fund-raising parties. He will first introduce himself, then ask the guest's name. He will then repeat the guest's name with proper salutations. An example of the program run, simulating an interaction of Charles with William W. Williams is as follows:

```
Good evening, my name is Charles C. Charles.
May I know your good name?
William W. Williams
I'm very glad to meet you, William W. Williams.
```

The solution description

The solution can be described by the actions

> *display opening greeting using Charles' name*
> *keyin GuestName*
> *display greeting to guest using GuestName*

We see from the description that we need a constant to represent Charles' name and a variable to hold the value of GuestName. How many characters should we allow to be read in to this variable? Let us say that perhaps 50 characters will allow for the longest names. Having taken this consideration into account, we arrive at the code as shown:

```
PROGRAM GreetAGuest(input,output);
  {This program simulates an interaction between the host Charles C.
  Charles and a guest at one of his parties.}
  CONST
    HostsName = 'Charles C. Charles';
    MaxLength = 50;    {maximum length of characters allowed in string}
  TYPE
    NameType = STRING[MaxLength];   {Turbo Pascal dialect}
  VAR
    GuestName: NameType;
  BEGIN
    writeln('Good evening, my name is ',HostsName,'.');
    writeln('May I know your good name?');
    readln(GuestName);
    writeln('I"m very glad to meet you, ',GuestName,'.')
  END. ◆
```

Some Standard Functions

Pascal has its own library of functions, each of which is named by a standard identifier. Any given *function* is called by making a reference to its identifier. The function call itself must have an *argument* that is an expression of a given type. Any function call uses the value of this argument to return a value that can be used in forming some other expression.

Function: a process that uses an argument(s) to return a single value.

Argument: a parameter of a function call.

In Example 1.1, we used a call to the standard function `sqr` to form the expression coded as `Pi * sqr (Radius)`. This function call told the computer to return the *square* of the argument as a real numeric value. The value returned was then used to form an expression.

Syntax rules   A call to a standard Pascal function satisfies the syntax diagram of Figure 3.5. The identifier references one of the standard Pascal functions, and the expression parameter is the *argument* of the referenced function.

function call

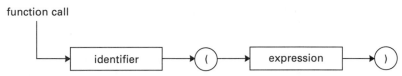

FIGURE 3.5   Syntax diagram for a call to a standard function.

Syntax checks   The compiler first checks to see if the function's identifier references a known function. Then it checks to see if the argument for the function is of the expected type. Finally, it checks to see if the value returned is used to form an expression whose syntax is correct. If any of the three checks indicates a syntax error, the compiler issues an error message.

Some standard functions   Table 3.1 shows some of the functions that belong to standard Pascal. The first column in the table represents the name of the given function. The second column gives a brief description of what the function does. The third column specifies the type of argument expected, and the fourth column indicates the value type the function returns. Let us look at the way we can form expressions with each of these functions. A complete list of the standard Pascal functions is given in Appendix D.

`sqr`, `sqrt`, *and* `abs`   The `sqr` function returns the value of the square of the argument. The same numeric type as the argument is returned. The `sqrt` function, as its identifier suggests, returns the square root of a real or integer *nonnegative* argument. The value returned is always of type `real`, even though the argument may be an `integer` that is a perfect square. The `sqrt` function must have an argument that is nonnega-

TABLE 3-1   Some Standard Functions of Pascal

Name	Value Returned	Argument Type	Result Type
abs	Absolute value of argument	Numeric	Same as argument
sqr	Square of the argument	Numeric	Same as argument
sqrt	Square root of the argument	Numeric	real
pred	Predecessor of the argument	Char	char
succ	Successor of the argument	Char	char
chr	Character whose value is the numeric representation of the argument	Integer	char
ord	Numeric code of the argument	Char	integer

tive because the square root of a negative number does not return a real value. Therefore, a coded statement such as `writeln(sqrt(7-16))` will cause a runtime crash. If, however, you code the statement as `writeln(sqrt(abs(7-16)))`, the computer will display the numeric literal 3.0000000E+00, because the square root of the *absolute value* of −9 is returned.

Nesting functions

Example 3.1 is a program that uses nested functions. In this example, the computer evaluates the expression for the hypotenuse by finding the values of `sqr(Side1)` and `sqr(Side2)` first. Once it has summed the two squares, it can then find the square root of the sum. The inner functions are evaluated first because the value of the argument for the outer function call depends on the values returned for the inner function calls.

Example 3.1

```
PROGRAM FindHypotenuse(input,output);
  {The hypotenuse of a right triangle is found, given values read into
  the sides.}
  VAR
    Side1,          {one of triangle's legs}
    Side2,          {other of triangle's legs}
    Hypotenuse:     {triangle's hypotenuse}
                    real;
  BEGIN
    write('Input the two sides of a right-triangle:  ');
    readln(Side1, Side2);
    Hypotenuse:= sqrt(sqr(Side1) + sqr(Side2));
    writeln('The length of the hypotenuse is ',Hypotenuse:4:2)
  END.
```

```
Input the two sides of a right triangle:  8.75  6.22
The length of the hypotenuse is 10.74
```

Machine representation of char *literals*

Each char literal is internally coded as a byte, a sequence of eight 0s and 1s, that is used in the machine-language version of a program. There are two coding schemes in wide use today, namely, ASCII (American Standard Coded Information Interchange) and EBCDIC (Extended Binary Coded Decimal Interchange Code), which are used to represent char literals in machine language. On systems that use the ASCII code, for example, the literal value of 'A' is represented by 01000001.

This sequence of bits also represents a unique number in the *binary system* of counting. Any number that can be represented in one system of counting has a unique representation in any other number system. The binary number representing the literal 'A' also represents the decimal number 65 in our *decimal system* of counting. Thus, we can say that the literal char value 'A' represents the decimal numeric value 65 when this number is coded as a binary number in ASCII.

The ord *and* chr *functions*

The standard ord function uses this correspondence to return the integer value in the decimal system that represents the coded value of the char argument. The standard chr function likewise returns the char value corresponding to the coded decimal value of the integer argument. Thus, the function call ord('A') returns the value 65, and the function call chr(65) returns the value 'A'.

Changing cases

It is interesting to note that the call chr(ord('A')) returns the literal 'A' because chr and ord are inverse functions. If you refer to Appendix A, you will see that the value of the integer expression ord('a') − ord('A') is the same value as that of the integer expression ord('b') − ord('B'), which is equal to the value of ord('c') − ord('C'), and so forth. The characters of the ASCII *collating sequence* were deliberately set up that way so that programmers can easily write code to change a lowercase char value to its corresponding uppercase letter.

> **Collating sequence:** the numeric order in which the char literals for a given system are coded in machine language.

The code to change a lowercase letter to uppercase is written as follows:

```
Letter:= chr(ord(Letter) + ord('A') − ord('a'));
```

Suppose, for example, the value taken on by Letter is 'g'. The last two terms of the chr argument can then be expressed by the equivalent integer value ord('G') − ord('g'). When the arithmetic is applied on the argument of chr, we get the expression chr(ord('G')).

Analogous code can be written to change an uppercase literal to its corresponding lowercase value (see Exercise 4).

pred *and* succ *functions*

Because there is a collating sequence, we also have two functions that respectively return the *pred*ecessor and *succ*essor of a char argument. For example, pred('C') returns 'B' and succ('C') returns 'D'.

Example Problem 3.4

Let us write a program that paraphrases two lines of the song "As easy as ABC." Two characters are read in, each representing the first character to be displayed in the revised two lines. The computer finds the value of the following two characters to be displayed for each line. Then it displays the two lines of the song. For the sake of simplicity, we will assume the user has a machine with the ASCII collating sequence. A typical run is as follows:

```
Input first character for first line:  1
Input first character for second line: X
It's easy as 123.
It's simple as XYZ.
```

The initial description

Let us use Ch11, Ch12, and Ch13 to represent char values associated with the first line. Ch21, Ch22, and Ch23 will be values associated with the second line. We can then describe the solution by

$$\textit{keyin Ch11}$$
$$\textit{keyin Ch21}$$
$$\textit{compute values for Ch12, Ch13, Ch22, and Ch23}$$
$$\textit{display line using values of Ch11, Ch12, and Ch13}$$
$$\textit{display line using values of Ch21, Ch22, and Ch23}$$

The description represents a correct solution to the problem, for we see that two values are entered, four more values are found, and then the values associated with the respective lines are displayed. Thus, we can go on to our refinements.

A refinement
    We can refine the line that computes the other values for display with the description

$$Ch12 \leftarrow succ(Ch11)$$
$$Ch13 \leftarrow succ(Ch12)$$
$$Ch22 \leftarrow succ(Ch21)$$
$$Ch23 \leftarrow succ(Ch22)$$

The rest of the initial description is trivial enough that we need no further refinements. The coded solution to the problem is as follows:

```
PROGRAM RewriteSong(input,output);
   {The user rewrites two lines of the song "Easy as ABC" by entering
   the first character to be displayed for the two revised lines.}
   VAR
      Ch11, Ch12, Ch13,     {char values for the first revised line}
      Ch21, Ch22, Ch23:     {char values for the second revised line}
                            char;
   BEGIN
      write('Input first character for first line:  ');
      readln(Ch11);
      write('Input first character for second line:  ');
      readln(Ch21);
      Ch12:= succ(Ch11);
      Ch13:= succ(Ch12);
      Ch22:= succ(Ch21);
      Ch23:= succ(Ch22);
      writeln('It''s easy as ', Ch11,Ch12,Ch13, '.');
      writeln('It''s simple as ', Ch21,Ch22,Ch23, '.')
   END.  ◆
```

EXERCISES

Test Your Understanding

1. Why is it necessary to define a string variable?

2. What do the expressions succ('s') and pred('k') evaluate to?

3. Explain why the inner functions of a coded expression must be evaluated before the outer function can be evaluated.

4. Write code to change an uppercase letter to its corresponding lowercase value.

5. Modify the program RewriteSong so that the user enters the last character to be displayed in each line. The first and second characters are then found before the display is carried out.

6. Edit and run the program RewriteSong such that the first values entered are 'Y' and '9'. Can you explain the results returned when the program is run?

Learn More About Your System

3.4 Top–Down Design

In this section, you will use *top–down design* to develop source code. All of the problems which are solved in the design process are integrated in such a way that they represent the solution to the overall problem. You will also learn how to draw and use *structure charts*. Finally, you will learn about the importance of writing a program with good *source-code semantics*.

> **Top–down design:** a method of program development in which the main problem is divided into subproblems that are individually solved. Each of these subproblems can be subdivided further, if necessary.

> **Structure chart:** a pictorial representation showing the breakdown of the main problem into the subproblems that make up a coded solution.

> **Source–code semantics:** a term used to describe the meaning given to each identifier and each statement found in a source program.

Program semantics

Every named constant and variable that belongs to a program block should represent a quantity that has only one meaning over the scope of the block. The value represented by a named constant will not change, but the value represented by a variable is expected to change. Its meaning, however, should not change.

If a variable's meaning does not change, we say it is *semantically consistent*. If all variables in a program are semantically consistent, the program is easy to read, maintain, and debug. A program with semantically inconsistent variables is poorly written even if it appears to solve the problem.

An example

The variables Int1, Int2, Int3, and Sum as coded in Example Problem 2.3 are semantically consistent. If you refer back to the source code for the program, you will see that our documentation is actually a description of the semantics given to each of the four variables. Note that regardless of which group of numbers was the most recent one read in, the value taken on by Int1 represented the first number of the group, the value of Int2 represented the second number, and that of Int3 represented the third number. Likewise, when Sum was assigned its new value after each group was read in, it represented the subtotal of all integer values that had been read in.

Income tax preparation

The process of preparing the IRS 1040 income tax form follows a standard algorithm, regardless of who is filling out the tax form. The algorithm can be described as follows:

1. Write down the initial gross income as the total of salary, tips, and wages earned.
2. Write down the number of exemptions claimed.
3. Calculate an initial value for taxable gross income using the initial gross income, the number of claimed exemptions, and the rate for each exemption claimed.
4. Revise the gross income and taxable gross income using values found from filling out the different tax schedules.
5. Calculate the tax using the value of the taxable gross income and the tax rate.

CASE STUDY 3.1

The problem statement

Write a program that helps the user with his or her income tax preparation. The user draws a basic salary, has a number of claimed exemptions, and must fill out Schedules B, D, and A. The first two schedules represent income earned on dividend payments and income earned on capital gains. Schedule A represents taxable deductions that are claimed. A fixed tax rate, regardless of the value of taxable gross income, is applied to the taxable gross income to obtain a value of the tax that must be paid.

The input values that must be read into the program are (1) the user's salary, (2) the number of claimed exemptions, and (3) the results of the three schedules. The output values for display are (1) the total gross income earned before taxes, (2) the amount of gross income subject to tax, (3) the amount of tax, and (4) the net income earned after taxcs. A typical run of the program is as follows:

```
Welcome to Tax Helper, the easy and carefree way to do
your taxes.  Enter all values in dollar amounts when
prompted.  If you have suffered a capital loss, enter
a negative value.  All other entries are positive.

Enter salary:  40000.00
Enter number of claimed exemptions: 3
Enter dividend income:  1500.00
Enter capital gains (+) or losses (-):  6500.00
Enter total of itemized deductions:  10000.00

Gross income ........  $48000.00
Taxable gross income .  $32000.00
Tax .................  $ 8000.00
Net income ..........  $40000.00
```

Each claimed exemption lowers the taxable gross income by $2000, and the tax rate is fixed at 25% of the taxable gross income.

*The initial
description*

We can describe the problem's solution initially with the pseudocode

> *display instructions*
> *keyin GI, NoOfExemptions {salary represents initial GI}*
> *calculate initial TGI using values of GI and NumberOfExemptions*
> *adjust TGI and GI according to the different schedules*
> *calculate Tax*
> *display the values of the expressions GI, TGI, Tax, GI-Tax*

You can turn back to the description of the initial algorithm for calculating income tax to confirm that we have described a correct solution to the problem. This initial draft shows we need to declare four variables, namely, GI, TGI, Tax, and NumberOfExemptions. The first three variables are of type real and the last variable is of type integer. The value of the expression GI-Tax represents the net income earned.

Note that the values taken on by the variables GI and TGI will change throughout the course of the program run. Yet, these two variables remain semantically consistent over the course of the run. The initial value assigned to GI represents the value of the gross income before it was adjusted according to the different schedules. The initial value assigned to TGI represents an analogous value. The final values taken on by GI and TGI represents the gross income and taxable gross income, respectively, after these initial values have been adjusted according to all the different schedules.

*A structure
chart*

The structure chart shown in Figure 3.6 describes the action and data flow involved in solving the problem. Each box encloses an action that belonged to our initial description of the program solution. From the chart, we can see that

FIGURE 3.6 Structure of DoTaxes through first level of planning.

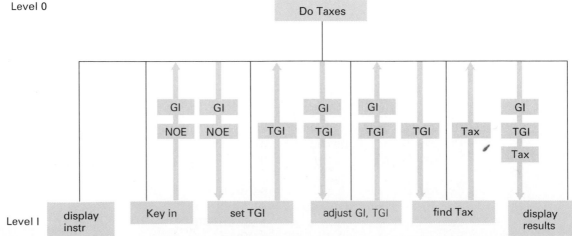

1. display instructions requires no variables
2. the action of *keyin* assigns values to GI (initial) and NoOfExemptions (abbreviated to "NOE")
3. *set TGI* uses *GI* and *NOE* to return a value to *TGI*
4. *adjust GI, TGI* changes the values of *GI* and *TGI*
5. *find Tax* uses the value of *TGI* to find a value for *Tax*
6. *display* uses the values of *GI*, *TGI*, and *Tax* for display purposes

Refinements

We can refine actions {3} through {6} to get the following:

{3} *TGI ← GI − NOE*ExemptionRate*
{4} *adjust GI, TGI from Schedule B*
    adjust GI, TGI from Schedule D
    adjust TGI from Schedule A
{5} *Tax ← TGI*TaxRate*
{6} *display a line showing value of GI*
    display a line showing value of TGI
    display a line showing value of Tax
    display a line showing value of GI − Tax

These refinements show us we need to define two constants, one to represent the value of a given exemption, and the other to represent the tax rate. It shows us that we also need to make further refinements to represent Schedule B, Schedule D, and Schedule A processing. The sample program run indicates that these schedules are figured in the order we have described, so it looks like the refinements are correct descriptions of what must be coded.

Refining the schedule adjustments

To adjust the GI and TGI from Schedule B, we need the following:

keyin Dividends
GI ← GI + Dividends
TGI ← TGI + Dividends

The actions to adjust GI and TGI for capital gains or losses (Schedule D) can be described by the sequence

keyin CapGains
GI ← GI + CapGains
TGI ← TGI + CapGains

where it is understood that a negative value assigned to CapGains represents an overall capital loss.

Finally, the deductions on a taxpayer's TGI (Schedule A) are handled by the sequence

keyin Deductions
TGI ← TGI − Deductions

These refinements show us we need to declare three more variables, namely, Dividends, CapGains, and Deductions, all of type real.

Assertion testing the final refinements

When the sequence of the last refinements are substituted in the proper place, that is, after the initial TGI is found and before the Tax is found, the values taken on by GI and TGI should represent their final processed values. If they do not, we have described an incorrect sequence. We can check to see if they indeed represent these values by describing what their values represent after each action of the refined sequence is completed.

From the described actions, we can make the following statements:

1.   The values taken on by GI and TGI after the value of Dividend has been added to each variable represent the values of GI and TGI after the Schedule B adjustments have been accounted for.

2.   The value taken on by GI and TGI after the value of CapGains has been added to each variable represents the values of GI and TGI after the Schedule B and D adjustments have been accounted for.

3.   The value taken on by TGI after the value of Deductions has been subtracted from this variable represents the value of TGI after the Schedule B, D, and A adjustments have been accounted for.

The third statement, the final action of the refined sequence, proves that both variables represent the final desired state. Therefore, the refinements we described lead to a correct solution.

We point out that each of the three statements describes part of the program state (as it relates to the two variables GI and TGI) once an action has been carried out. Each statement is, therefore, an assertion. We also point out that nothing is said in any assertion about *actual* values taken on by the two variables, but plenty is said about the meaning given to the values that they have taken on. Finally, and most importantly, all these assertions are possible because the two variables are semantically consistent throughout the course of the program run. Each new assignment represented an adjustment to the same two represented quantities.

The source code for the program is as follows. We give more "complete" names to the variables to help make the program more readable.

```
PROGRAM DoTaxes(input,output);
   {This program calculates and displays a user's income, gross income,
   and net income according to values read in.}
   CONST
      TaxRate = 0.25;                {25% rate for all(!)}
      ExemptionRate = 2000.00;   {$2000.00 for each claimed exemption}
   VAR
      NoOfExemptions:        {number of claimed exemptions}
                             integer;
      GrossIncome,           {accumulates a value for gross income}
      TaxableGrossIncome,    {accumulates a value for taxable gross income}
      Tax,                   {amount of tax bill}
      Dividends,             {total dividend income}
```

```
      CapGains,              {total net capital gains}
      Deductions:            {total of claimed deductions}
                             real;
   BEGIN
      {display instructions:}
      writeln('Welcome to Tax Helper, the easy and carefree way to do ');
      writeln('your taxes.  Enter all values in dollar amounts when ');
      writeln('prompted.  If you have suffered a capital loss, enter ');
      writeln('a negative value.  All other entries are positive.');
      {first keyin:}
      write('Enter salary:   ');
      readln(GrossIncome);
      write('Enter number of claimed exemptions:   ');
      readln(NoOfExemptions);
      {set initial TaxableGrossIncome:}
      TaxableGrossIncome:= GrossIncome - NoOfExemptions*ExemptionRate;
      {do Schedule B:}
      write('Enter dividend income:   ');
      readln(Dividends);
      GrossIncome:= GrossIncome + Dividends;
      TaxableGrossIncome:= TaxableGrossIncome + Dividends;
      {do Schedule D:}
      write('Enter capital gains (+) or losses (-):   ');
      readln(CapGains);
      GrossIncome:= GrossIncome + CapGains;
      TaxableGrossIncome:= TaxableGrossIncome + CapGains;
      {do Schedule A:}
      write('Enter total of itemized deductions:   ');
      readln(Deductions);
      TaxableGrossIncome:= TaxableGrossIncome - Deductions;
      {find tax:}
      Tax:= TaxableGrossIncome * TaxRate;
      {display results:}
      writeln('Gross income ........   $',GrossIncome:4:2);
      writeln('Taxable gross income .   $',TaxableGrossIncome:4:2:);
      writeln('Tax .................   $',Tax:4:2);
      writeln('Net income ..........   $',GrossIncome - Tax:4:2:)
   END.
```

Structure chart for the program

The structure chart for the overall program is shown as Figure 3.7. It has three levels to represent the three levels of refinement we needed to arrive at the final program solution. Note that each new level of refinement might uncover the need to declare more variables for the solution of the problem. As far as any actions on Level I were concerned, the variables Dividend, CapGains, and Deductions had no meaning or apparent purpose. It was only when we refined our actions down to a second level that we found we needed to declare those three variables. ◆

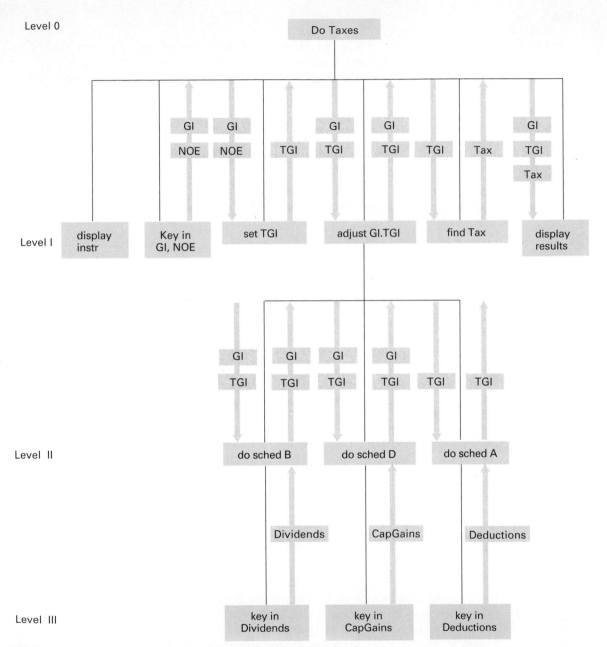

Level 0

Level I

Level II

Level III

FIGURE 3.7 Structure of overall program of DoTaxes.

EXERCISES

Test Your Understanding

1. True or false? All required variables are known after the initial description to a solution.

Practice Your Analysis Skills

2. Would the following sequence (assume prompts can be inserted where required) produce correct results if it replaces the sequence between the comments {do schedule B} and {find tax: }?

   ```
   readln(Dividends); readln(CapGains); readln(Deductions);
   GrossIncome:= GrossIncome + Dividends + CapGains;
   TaxableGrossIncome:= TaxableGrossIncome
                           + Dividends + CapsGains - Deductions;
   ```

   If you answered yes, prove your answer by assertion testing.

Sharpen Your Implementation Skills

   Other schedules might be necessary if our client's financial activities include (1) one or more sources of interest income, (2) profits or losses from some personal corporation, and (3) income from royalties. Each of these sources of income is taxable where (1) it belongs as part of Schedule B, (2) it belongs to an entirely new Schedule C, and (3) it belongs to an entirely new Schedule E.

3. Develop the necessary actions to modify Schedule B processing for interest income. Assume the interest income for all interest-bearing activities is available as one figure.

4. Develop the necessary actions to incorporate Schedule C processing in the program DoTaxes.

5. Do the same for handling royalties income. This kind of income belongs to Schedule E.

6. Write the program, putting the necessary modifications in their proper places.

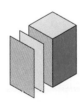

Program Testing Hints

In this section, we show you some of the ways you can misuse string variables and standard functions. Avoid writing this kind of code. We also present an example where a variable is semantically inconsistent. You should likewise avoid planning algorithms that use a variable for more than one purpose.

Assignment errors

Remember that the sqrt function will always return a real value, even if the argument is a perfect square. Likewise, it is useful to know that a char value is assignment-compatible with a string variable, but a string value is not assignment-compatible with a char variable, even if it contains only one char value. Suppose, then, we have the declarations

```
TYPE
   String10 = STRING[10];   {Turbo Pascal dialect}
VAR
   AString: String10;
   Ch: char;
   Int: integer;
   Re: real;
```

Given these declarations, the first two of the following statements will not compile, but the last two will:

```
Ch:= AString;        {ERRONEOUS  STATEMENT}
Int:= sqrt(Re);      {ERRONEOUS  STATEMENT}
AString:= Ch;
Re:= sqrt(Int);
```

String length
bugs

You should be aware that when you define and declare a string variable, you are setting a limit to the number of characters that it can take on as a value. Suppose, for example, we have

```
CONST
  MaxLength = 20;
TYPE
  String20 = STRING[MaxLength];     {Turbo Pascal dialect}
VAR
  AString: String20;
```

Let us take, for example, the following code, where, below it, we have shown an input string when the code is executed:

```
write('Input a string:   ');
readlN(AString);
```

```
Input a string:  Let'sCrashAgainLikeWeDidLastLog-On
```

Many systems will crash when more than 20 characters are entered. Other systems might truncate the string at 20 characters, thereby, resulting in the assignment AString ↔ 'Let'sCrashAgainLikeW'.

Length
considerations

Allot as many characters as necessary for your string variables. How many characters represent "necessity"? Given that the normal input line is allowed a maximum of 80 characters, if you define String80 using String80 = STRING[80], you will guarantee that a statement such as readln(AString) will not crash the program. However, do not be so liberal that you hide the semantics given to the declared variable. If you want a string variable to represent a single word, you would specify a length considerably less than 80 characters. Perhaps the longest word you might encounter would have 20 characters.

Reading in two
or more string
values

For now, avoid any attempt at code to read in more than one string value on a given input line. Suppose the variables AName and BName, strings capable of holding 10 characters, are applied in a readln statement to the input line shown below the statement:

```
readln(AName, BName);
Fred Ginger<eoln>
```

Most systems will return AName ↔ 'Fred Ginge' and BName ↔ 'r', where

the first 10 characters on the line are assigned to AName and the remaining character
is assigned to BName.

Use any declared variable for *only one purpose*. Suppose, for example, you
need a variable to store the sum of two input values. Given these requirements, the
following declarations and statements are easy to understand:

```
VAR
   Int1,    {first integer value read in}
   Int2,    {second integer value read in}
   Sum:     {sum of the two values}
            integer;

write('Input two integers:   ');
readln(Int1, Int2);
Sum:= Int1 + Int2;
```

As the documentation indicates, the two variables Int1 and Int2 are used to store
two values that are read in, and the variable Sum is used to hold their sum.

It is in fact still acceptable to code

```
VAR
   Int,    {last integer value read in}
   Sum:    {sum of integer values read in}
           integer;

Sum:= 0;
write('Input an integer:   );
readln(Int);
Sum:= Sum + Int;
write('Input another:   ');
readln(Int);
Sum:= Sum + Int;
```

Int is used strictly as a means of storing a single value that is read in, and Sum is
used strictly to sum the values that have been read in. Note that the initial value
given to Sum indicates that no values have been read in or summed at that point in
the execution sequence of the program.

PROGRAM DESIGN RULE 3.1

Write code that is semantically consistent.

You can make your code hard to read, however, if you use the same variable
to fulfill more than one purpose. By all means avoid writing code such as

```
write('Input two integers:   ');
readln(Int1,Int2);
Int1:= Int1 + Int2;     {BAD!! Int1 IS SERVING TWO DISTINCT PURPOSES!}
```

This example uses `Int1` both to store the value of an integer read in and to set a sum of the two integer values. This kind of code is difficult for another programmer to decipher. Just as a variable's type does not change over a program block, its semantics also should not.

EXERCISES

Practice Your Analysis Skills

1. Each of the following segments of source code may or may not fulfill the stated purpose of the "problem statement." If the source code is incorrect, make the necessary changes so that the segment satisfies the problem statement. You can assume that any obvious variable identifiers have been declared:

   (a) Problem statement: Write a segment of code that assigns the product of three user-input integers to a variable named `Product`.

   ```
   readln(Int1, Int2, Int3);
   Prod:= Prod*Int1*Int2*Int3;
   ```

   (b) Problem statement: Write a statement that adds the value of a given variable `Int` to the variable `Sum`.

   ```
   Sum:= Int;
   ```

   (c) Problem statement: Write a segment that assigns the arithmetic average of three user-input integers to the real variable `Ave`.

   ```
   readln(Int1, Int2, Int3);
   Ave:= Int1+Int2+Int3/3;
   ```

   (d) Problem statement: Write a segment that reads values for a first, middle, and last name. Assume no single name string has more than 20 characters in it. Set up the code so that the statement sequence neither causes a crash nor results in incorrect assignment values.

   ```
   write('Input full name:   ');
   readln(First,Middle,Last);
   ```

REVIEW AND EXERCISES

Once a program has been determined as *feasible,* its code is developed through repeated *description, testing,* and *refinement.* The program's actions are described using *pseudocode.* Only one criterion is required for valid pseudocode: the computer can carry out the actions being described. The pseudocode description is tested for correctness and then refined. The refinements are tested and then further refined. This process, the method of *successive refinements,* is the way a program can be developed from a general description to a specific solution.

Sometimes, you may recognize a particular problem as applicable to a given algorithm that has been both described and categorized. If you can recognize such a pattern, you can use the algorithm description as the first draft to a solution. The problem can then be solved by refining this first draft.

Assertion testing and *desk tracing* are two of the ways a description can be tested. Assertion testing is more reliable, for it can be applied to general cases. Desk tracing, however, is an easy way to identify an incorrect description. *On-line testing* is a third way, but it can only be done with a working program.

The Pascal language has a number of *standard functions.* Each standard function in Pascal has a single operand of a given (standard) type and it returns a result whose value is also a standard type. The value returned by a function represents the value of an expression and should be used in that context.

You can also define your own *string types* in the different dialects of Pascal. The standard read and write processes work on string types for all dialects. Once you have defined a string type that works in your dialect, you can use any of these processes in your programs. At this stage, it is best to read in a value for only one string variable per line. You can, however, write statements that will display the value of more than one string on a given line.

When a program is designed *top–down,* the overall program is divided up into subprograms, all of which need to be refined and coded. *Structure charts* are a useful aid in this design process, for you can use it to show *data flow* between each of the subprograms. The structure chart can use a data flow picture that shows the way the different subprograms use and change the values given to the program variables.

The value of a variable may change, but it is used properly only if it fulfills a single defined purpose in the program. When a program variable takes on a new value in a subprogram, it represents an event that has a meaning. If you can describe the meaning of this event as it relates to the variable's purpose, you have described an *assertion* that is both valid and useful. You can use assertions such as these to prove that a program is correct.

EXERCISES

Short Answers

1. True or false? An integer expression can be assigned to a real variable.

2. The technique of planning the broad steps of a program, then slowly filling in the coding details is known as the method of _____ _____ .

3. The values of pred('G') and succ('x') are _____ and _____ .

4. Why does a sequence such as the following represent bad coding practice?

```
write('Enter the two factors:   ');
readln(Int1, Int2);
Int1:= Int1 * Int2;
```

5. What modifications would you make on the coded sequence of Exercise 4 such that better code would result?

6. Your program does not compile due to a syntax-error message whose text is "TYPE MISMATCH". What kind of statement probably caused the error?

7. Suppose the char variable Ch1 has taken on the value 'y'. What will be the value taken on by Ch2 given the statement:

$$Ch2:= chr(ord(Ch1) + ord('A') - ord('a'))$$

8. Suppose Ch1 has taken on the value '5'. What will be displayed by the following statement?

$$writeln(10*(ord(Ch1) - ord('0'))$$

9. Indicate which of the following operators or standard functions will return a real value, which will return an integer value, and which will not return a numeric value when used to form an expression:

$$+ \quad DIV \quad / \quad chr \quad sqrt \quad sqr \quad * \quad ord$$

10. From Exercise 9, which requires a nonnumeric operand for it to work?

11. True or false? The following segment violates some of the syntax rules of standard Pascal:

```
TYPE
  Int = integer;
VAR
  Int1: Int;
```

12. Repeat Exercise 11 for

```
TYPE
  Int = integer;
{other code}
  BEGIN
    Int:= 7;
    {other code}
  END.
```

13. What value is returned to the variable Ch in

$$Ch:= pred(pred(pred('J')));$$

14. True or false? If STRING[10] represents valid syntax, the following code will cause a syntax error:

```
TYPE
  StringType = STRING[10];
VAR
  AString: StringType;
```

```
                   AString:= 'Vickery Brownestone';
```

Why did you answer as you did?

15. True or false? The following coded fragment will cause a syntax error:

```
VAR
    Int1, Int2: integer;

Int1:= 9;
Int2:= sqrt(Int1);
```

Explain your answer.

16. Is it possible for a value to be read into a variable and then later assign a new value to this variable using an assignment operation? If so, does this necessarily represent good coding? Why or why not?

Easy Projects

17. Write a program where the computer gets the name of two users (input) and then introduces one user to the other. Typically, you might have

```
What is your name?  John Jones
What is your name?  Jack Jackson
John Jones meet Jack Jackson.
```

18. Write a program where the computer finds and displays the sum and average of four input integers. Use exactly five variables to do this problem. A typical program run would look like

```
Input four integers:  75  82  36  84
Their sum is  227.
Their average is 69.25.
```

19. The neighborhood fruit market is selling fruits at the following prices: apples at 25¢ per apple, grapes at 70¢ per bunch, and oranges at $3 per dozen. Write a program whose run simulates the activity of the fruit market. The user first inputs how many of each fruit is desired. Then the computer displays the total bill. A typical run might look like

```
How many apples?  6
How many bunches of grapes?  2
How many oranges?  8
Your total bill is $4.90
```

Define constants where they are appropriate.

20. Hero's formula for the area of a triangle is given by

$$\text{Area} = \sqrt{S \cdot (S - A) \cdot (S - B) \cdot (S - C)}$$

where the formula for the semiperimeter S is given by

$$S = \tfrac{1}{2}(A + B + C)$$

Write a program that requests the three sides of a triangle from the user. The computer then finds and displays the area of the triangle accurate to two decimal places. A typical run is as follows:

```
Input length of the three sides:   78.43   93.86   45.55
The area of the triangle is 1780.27
```

Medium Projects

21. Redo Exercise 18 such that the same end result is returned, but this time do it using only two, or at most three, variables (correctly!). Write your program so that a typical run might look like

```
Input an integer:   75
Input an integer:   82
Input an integer:   36
Input an integer:   84
Their sum is 277.
Their average is 69.25.
```

22. Write a program where the computer first prompts the user for two integers. Once the values are input, the computer displays the sum, difference, product, real quotient, and two integer quotients on separate lines. Do this problem using only two variables. A typical run would look like

```
Input two integers:   46   8
The sum of the two is 54.
The difference between the two is 38.
The product of the two is 368.
The real quotient of the two is 5.75000E+00.
The integer quotient of the two is 5.
```

23. Redo Exercise 22, but this time use a variable to first hold the result of each calculation. Use the values assigned to each of these variables for the display.

24. Write a program where the use enters three characters. The computer then displays the six possible ways these three characters can be ordered.

25. Write a program where the machine requests the number of half-dollar pieces, the number of quarters, the number of dimes, the number of nickels and the number of pennies a person has. Once the values are entered, the computer then displays the dollar amount of the change. Write your program so that the statement part uses references to constant identifiers such as HalfWeight. This method is preferred over the use of anonymous constant expressions such as 50.

Difficult Projects

26. Suppose instead of the scenario presented in Exercise 19, the prices for the fruits differ from day to day. In this case, before the user orders fruit, he or she must find out the cost of the fruit. Thus, for example, the first few lines of interaction might look like:

```
Cost of one apple (cents):   25
Cost of bunch of grapes (cents):   70
Cost of one dozen oranges (dollars):   3.00
How many . . .
```

Write a program similar to the one of Exercise 19, except this program takes the varying cost of fruit into account. The user keys in the cost for the day after each prompt is displayed.

27. A baseball player's batting average is found by applying the formula

$$BA = Hits/(At\ bats)$$

where a hit is a single, double, triple, or home run. The ballplayer's slugging average is given by the formula

$$SA = (Singles + 2 \times Doubles + 3 \times Triples + 4 \times Home\ runs)/(At\ bats)$$

Write a program where the number of times a player has been at bat and the number of singles, doubles, triples, and home runs are entered. The computer then calculates and displays the batting and slugging averages. A typical run might look like

```
Input at bats:   553
Input singles:   79
Input doubles:   38
Input triples:   9
Input home runs:   22

Batting average   =   0.268
Slugging average   =   0.488
```

28. Standard Pascal has two trigonometric functions, sin and cos, that return the sine and cosine of the argument when it is expressed in radians. Recall that 1 radian is approximately 57.2958 degrees. Recall that the trigonometric identities for the four functions that do not belong to the standard identifiers of Pascal are expressed by

```
tan(X) = sin(X)/cos(X)
cot(X) = cos(X)/sin(X)
csc(X) = 1/sin(X)
sec(X) = 1/cos(X)
```

Write a program where the computer requests the value of an angle (in degrees). Once the user enters a value, the computer displays the values of the six trigonometric functions for the given angle. A typical run should look like

```
Input an angle (in degrees):   73.2
sin(73.2 degrees) = 0.957
cos(73.2 degrees) = 0.289
tan(73.2 degrees) = 3.312
cot(73.2 degrees) = 0.302
csc(73.2 degrees) = 1.045
sec(73.2 degrees) = 3.460
```

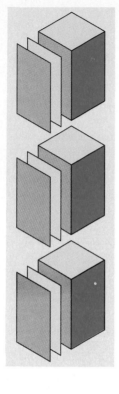

C H A P T E R 4

PROCEDURES

OBJECTIVES

After you have read and studied the material in this chapter, you should be able to

- **Explain how the parameter-passing mechanism works with procedures**

- **Desk trace a program that use procedures with parameters**

- **Design programs using procedural abstraction**

- **Use preconditions and postconditions to design procedures**

- **Correct code that uses variables improperly in the statement part of a procedure**

AT THE END OF THE PREVIOUS CHAPTER, you learned about the method of top-down design. In this chapter, you will learn how to write procedures, subprograms that are written to make the method of top-down design easier to implement. If you use procedures, your program will be easier to develop and read. Hence, it will also be easier to modify and maintain.

When you develop a program that uses a procedure(s), you write the procedure call first as one of the statements of the program. When you write this statement, you know the program state just before the procedure is called and the program state returned by the procedure's mechanism. At this stage of development, however, you do not know the details of the mechanism that changes the program state.

The mechanism to achieve the change in the program state is a sequence of statements. If you know the before and after states, you know what is required of the statements to get from the old state to the new state. You then fill in these details by describing the procedure's statements. If you have described a correct sequence, the desired program state is returned. The final step is to code the procedure, with its correct sequence of statements, as part of the program.

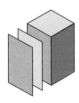

4.1   Procedures and Top-Down Design

In this section, you will learn the syntax rules for writing a procedure call in the statement part of a block and for declaring a procedure in the declarations part of a block. You will also learn how to plan and code a program using procedures. When you use procedures, you make it easier to apply the technique of top-down design. We introduce you to this new technique by developing and coding the case study of the previous chapter, this time using procedures rather than one long compound statement.

Procedural Abstraction

Procedures enable you to break down the details of a large program into an integrated set of smaller subprograms. If procedures are used, none of the required details that make the program correct are different from the details that make up a one-statement solution. The details of the single compound statement, however, are subdivided and hidden in a way that makes the program easier to plan and code.

Procedural abstraction

A statement which makes a reference to the identifier readln or the identifier writeln is a *procedure call*. When you write a procedure call, you know the effect(s) it will have on the program state. With a call to readln, for example, a value(s) will be read in to the variable(s) that make up the parameter list. With a call to writeln, the value(s) of the expression(s) will be displayed. In both instances, you do not know how the machine carries out these actions, but you do know the end result(s). This method of writing source code describes a technique used in top-down design known as *procedural abstraction*.

Procedure call: a statement where the computer executes a process that has been predeclared. A procedure call consists of an identifier reference to the process and an actual parameter list.

Actual parameter list: the list of variables and/or expressions that make up part of a procedure call.

Procedural abstraction: the separation of the details of a procedure's actions or statements from the effects it produces.

Programmer-declared procedures

The implementation details of the standard procedures of Pascal will always remain hidden from you. You do not know and should not have to know anything about these details. You can, however, use the method of procedural abstraction to write calls to your own procedures in the statement part of a program. In this case, because the procedures are your own invention, you must also handle the coding details that fulfill their intended purpose(s). You can, however, hide these details from the statement part of the block that called the procedure.

Using procedural abstraction

If we use procedural abstraction on Case Study 3.1, we might describe the sequence of statements to be executed as follows:

ShowInstructions
GetInitialIncome(GrossIncome, TaxableGrossIncome)
DoSchedules(GrossIncome, TaxableGrossIncome)
*Tax ← TaxableGrossIncome * TaxRate*
ShowResults(GrossIncome, TaxableGrossIncome, Tax, GrossIncome − Tax)

This pseudocode describes the statement part of the *main block* of the program we are going to rewrite. The 5 main block statements for this example consist of 4 procedure calls, 3 of which have an actual parameter list, and an assignment statement. Each one of the procedure calls, as well as the assignment statement, changes the program state. The program state before any one statement is executed describes the *preconditions* required for the statement to execute properly. The program state after any one statement is carried out describes the *postconditions* returned by the statement. The correct use of procedural abstraction requires that you know both the preconditions and the postconditions for any procedure call you intend to code.

Main block: the single block of code that makes up a program. When procedures are used, each procedure of the main block also contains a block of code.

Preconditions: a term, often used to describe the requirements for the proper execution of procedure call, that describes the requirements of the program state for a given statement to return a correct postcondition.

Postcondition: a term, often used to describe the effect(s) of a properly executed procedure call, that describes the new program state just after the given statement has been executed.

A procedure's preconditions and postconditions let you know (1) if the block statement you are developing describes a correct process and (2) the goal state that must be achieved when you develop the code for the abstracted procedure. When a procedure has an actual parameter list, as delimited by the parentheses in our pseudocode description, the variables and expressions of the list must be incorporated to imply either the preconditions, the postconditions, or both.

Using preconditions and postconditions

Let us look at the preconditions and postconditions for each of the 5 statements that make up the main block of DoTaxes. The procedure ShowInstructions has no preconditions, but the postcondition is that instructions have been displayed letting the user know the correct input for the program. The postconditions on GetInitialIncomes is that values have been assigned to the variables GrossIncome, representing the user's salary as read in from the keyboard, and TaxableGrossIncome, representing the user's salary less the deductions for dependents. This latter quantity is also read in from the keyboard. These two conditions are the preconditions of the procedure DoSchedules. The postconditions are that the values of GrossIncome and TaxableGrossIncome have been adjusted according to the Schedules B, D and A.

The precondition of the assignment statement is that a value has been assigned to TaxableGrossIncome as calculated from the base salary and all the schedules. The postcondition for this statement is that the value of the expression TaxableGrossIncome * TaxRate has been assigned to Tax. The preconditions for the procedure ShowResults are that the variables GrossIncome, TaxableGrossIncome, and Tax have taken on their final values. The postcondition for ShowResults is that these 3 values along with the value of the expression GrossIncome - Tax have been displayed.

Main block objects and process

It is interesting to note what the description of the main block tells us the program requires for its correct execution. First of all, only 3 variables are needed, namely, GrossIncome, TaxableGrossIncome, and Tax. A constant, TaxRate, must be defined. Finally 4 procedures must be declared, so the main block can call them.

When we code the main block, the other variables we used in the case study of the previous chapter will not be declared. They are necessary for the correct execution of the program, but they will be declared only in those blocks that require them. When you use procedural abstraction, you will find that far fewer *global variables* are necessary. We will define the constant ExemptionRate as a *global constant*, however, even though no reference from the main block is made to it. We shall explain our reasons for this practice in the discussion that follows.

Global variable: a variable declared in the main block of a program.

Global constant: a constant defined in the main block of a program.

Procedure Syntax and Semantics

So far, we have described the main block's statement for the program DoTaxes. We have said that it is only necessary to declare 3 variables in the main block. We have also said, however, that it is necessary to declare 4 procedures in the main block. We have not, as yet, written any source code, for we have not discussed the syntax rules for calling a procedure and declaring procedures. Now we will present these rules and then derive the source code for the program DoTaxes.

Calling a procedure

The syntax diagram to call a procedure is shown in Figure 4.1. The identifier represents the procedure's name and is a reference to a declared procedure. The variables and expressions enclosed by the parentheses make up the procedure call's actual parameter list. Note that all procedure calls described in the pseudocode of the main block statement of the program DoTaxes represent actual statements that satisfy the syntax required to make a procedure call.

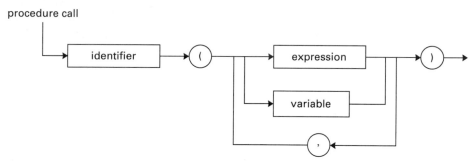

FIGURE 4.1 Syntax diagram for a procedure call.

A procedure's declaration

A procedure is a process. You may recall from Chapter 1 that a process requires a header, perhaps some declarations, and a (compound) statement. The declarations and compound statement make up the block part of a procedure, so that you can say a procedure consists of a header and a block. Figure 4.2 shows the syntax diagram for a procedure declaration.

Recall that a header is a software device that creates an interface. In the case of a procedure, the interface is between the actual parameters of the procedure and

FIGURE 4.2 Syntax diagram for a procedure declaration.

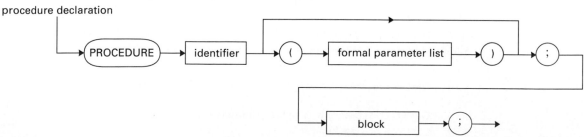

the *formal parameters* of the procedure header. These formal parameters make up the procedure's *formal parameter list*.

> **Formal parameter:** a variable found in the formal parameter list of a procedure declaration.

> **Formal parameter list:** the list of variables and their associated types that correspond to the variables and expressions of an actual parameter list as found in a matching procedure call.

Layout rules for a procedure declaration

You can declare a procedure as a process belonging to any given block. You should always place any procedure declaration after the variable declarations section of the block. The final part of a block consists of its compound statement, as delimited by the reserved words BEGIN and END. Any procedure declared in a program's main block must therefore be placed before the statement part of the program.

The syntax diagram for a formal parameter list is shown in Figure 4.3. Each formal parameter has a correspondence with an actual parameter. This correspondence between actual parameters and formal parameters sets up an internal mechanism known as *parameter passing*. There are two mechanims for parameter passing. One mechanism is associated strictly with some preconditions of the procedure. The other mechanism is always associated with some postconditions.

formal parameter list

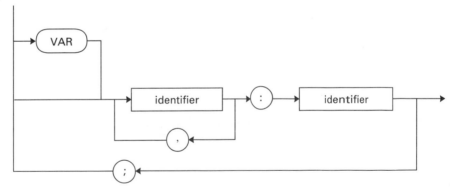

FIGURE 4.3 Syntax diagram for a formal parameter list.

Formal parameter list

An identifier before a colon which is not preceded by the reserved word VAR represents a *call by value*. When this mechanism is used, the identifier represents the name for a variable whose value can be referenced over the statement part of the procedure. The first (and perhaps last) value this variable takes on is that of the *expression* passed into the procedure as an actual parameter value. This mechanism is always associated with a precondition, for the value of the expression passed in to initialize a formal parameter variable must be predetermined. Once the statements of the procedure are completed, everything about this variable (both its name and its value) is gone and forgotten.

An identifier preceded by the keyword VAR represents a call by variable. When a parameter is called by variable, the final value assigned to it is passed back to its corresponding actual parameter. This mechanism, used to give a new value to an actual parameter variable, is, at the least, associated with one of the procedure's postconditions. If, furthermore, the actual parameter variable was given a value before the procedure was called, this parameter is also associated with one of the procedure's preconditions. The formal parameter name may be meaningless outside the block, but the final value it takes on survives after the block's statements are completed. The actual parameter associated with a formal parameter called by variable must be variable.

Regardless of which mechanism you use, there must be a second identifier following the colon. This identifier represents a named type (never anonymous!) for the corresponding formal parameter variable(s) in the formal parameter list. This type must match the variable or expression type of the corresponding actual parameter.

The main block and procedure stubs

The advantage gained in using procedural abstraction is that you can postpone the coding details of any given block by writing a procedure call. We will take advantage of this program development tool throughout the remainder of the text. It will allow us to develop one block of code at a time.

The code for the program DoTaxes, using procedures, is given below. Note that we have coded the procedure headers (including documentation) followed by an empty statement. The code for the 4 procedures represent *stubs,* a tool that helps you design source code top-down. The purposes of each procedure for DoTaxes are known, for the headers have been written in complete detail. The means by which these purposes are fulfilled, that is, any necessary declarations within each procedure's block and the statement part for each block, have not yet been filled in.

Stub: a procedure declaration, used as a design technique, consisting of a completed header and an incomplete block.

You use stubs so you can concentrate on the coding details of one block at a time. Even though you are working on the development of just one block, you will never lose sight of the bigger picture (in this case, the main block), for the details of the block that called the procedure have been coded fully. You thus use stubs to allow you to focus on the little picture of developing some 20 lines of code while still keeping your eye on the big picture of implementing a program that may require a few hundred lines of code.

```
PROGRAM DoTaxes(input,output);
   {documentation}
   CONST
      TaxRate = 0.25;              {rate charged to TaxableGrossIncome}
      ExemptionRate = 2000;       {dollar amount for each claimed exemption}
   VAR
      GrossIncome,                {accumulated gross income}
      TaxableGrossIncome,         {accumulated taxable gross income}
      Tax:   real;                {tax on accumulated taxable gross income}
```

```
{*                                                                            *}
PROCEDURE ShowInstructions;
  {out: a set of instructions are displayed}
  BEGIN   END;
{*                                                                            *}
PROCEDURE GetInitialIncomes(VAR GrossIncome,TaxableGrossIncome: real);
  {out:   GrossIncome -- gross income before schedules
   out:   TaxableGrossIncome -- taxable gross income before schedules}
  BEGIN   END;
{*                                                                            *}
PROCEDURE DoSchedules(VAR GrossIncome,TaxableGrossIncome: real);
  {in: GrossIncome -- gross income before schedules
   out: GrossIncome -- gross income after schedules
   in: TaxableGrossIncome -- taxable gross income before schedules
   out: TaxableGrossIncome -- taxable gross income after schedules}
  BEGIN   END;
{*                                                                            *}
PROCEDURE ShowResults(GrossIncome, TaxableGrossIncome,
                                    Tax, NetIncome: real);
  {in: GrossIncome -- computed value of gross income
   in: TaxableGrossIncome -- computed value of taxable gross income
   in: Tax -- computed value of tax
   in: NetIncome -- computed value of net income
   out: all computed values have been displayed}
  BEGIN   END;
{*                                                                            *}
BEGIN    {main block statements}
  ShowInstructions;
  GetInitialIncomes(GrossIncome, TaxableGrossIncome);
  DoSchedules(GrossIncome, TaxableGrossIncome);
  Tax:= TaxableGrossIncome * TaxRate;
  ShowResults(GrossIncome,TaxableGrossIncome,Tax,GrossIncome - Tax)
END.
```

Flow of control

We use the term *flow of control* to describe the sequence in which statements are carried out. Let us describe the flow of control for the first two statements of the main block of DoTaxes. First, the main block calls the procedure ShowInstructions. The flow of control is given to this procedure while the machine executes its statements. Then, control is returned to the main block. When the machine calls GetInitialIncomes, the flow of control is transferred to the statements of that procedure. Once these statements are carried out, the flow of control returns to the main block. We leave it to you as an exercise (Exercise 4) to describe the flow of control for the remaining 3 statements.

Interface analysis

Let us look at the relationship between the procedure calls and the associated headers for each of the stubs of the rewritten program DoTaxes:

I. The procedure ShowInstructions has no parameters and should simply produce display.

II. The procedure `GetInitialIncome` has two actual parameters that represent variables. The procedure should return values to the variables in this parameter list. Therefore the formal parameters are called by variable. Figure 4.4 shows the parameter correspondence between the actual parameters of the procedure call from the main block and the formal parameters of the procedure header as declared.

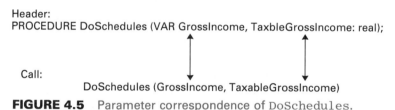

Header:
PROCEDURE GetInitialIncomes (VAR GrossIncome, TaxableGrossIncome: real);

Call:
GetInitialIncomes (GrossIncome, TaxableGrossIncome)

FIGURE 4.4 Parameter correspondence of `GetInitialIncomes`.

III. The procedure `DoSchedules` has actual parameters that represent variables. The procedure should change the values of the variables in the actual parameter list. Therefore, the formal parameters are called by variable. Figure 4.5 shows the parameter correspondences between the procedure call and the procedure header for this procedure.

Header:
PROCEDURE DoSchedules (VAR GrossIncome, TaxbleGrossIncome: real);

Call:
DoSchedules (GrossIncome, TaxableGrossIncome)

FIGURE 4.5 Parameter correspondence of `DoSchedules`.

IV. The procedure `ShowResults` has four actual parameters, each of which is the value of an expression. The procedure fulfills its purpose when it displays the values taken on by these four expressions. Figure 4.6 shows the parameter correspodences between the procedure call and the procedure header for this procedure.

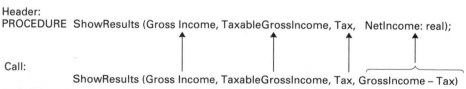

Header:
PROCEDURE ShowResults (Gross Income, TaxableGrossIncome, Tax,   NetIncome: real);

Call:
ShowResults (Gross Income, TaxableGrossIncome, Tax, GrossIncome – Tax)

FIGURE 4.6 Parameter correspondence of `ShowResults`.

Procedure documentation

All procedures we have coded as stubs in the program DoTaxes include documentation. We have given a formalism to our documentation that indicates the preconditions and postconditions for each procedure. A precondition is labelled as `in:` and a postcondition as `out:`. Note how the documentation describes the meaning of the *value* taken on by any given formal parameter variable.

Parameter taxonomy

Each parameter in the formal parameter list of a procedure can be classified as either and *input* parameter, an *output* parameter, or an *input/output* (*i/o*) parameter. This classification is really a description of the effect felt by each parameter of the procedure. We break down the classification as follows:

I.   The value given to a formal parameter variable which is an input parameter will be used but not returned. All variables which are called by value are input parameters. The variables in the formal parameter list of the procedure `ShowResults` are all input parameters.

II.   There is no initial value given to an output parameter. A value is passed out to the actual parameter variable as an initial value for the variable. These parameters are always called by variable. All parameters in the parameter list of the procedure `GetInitialIncomes` are output parameters.

III.   If a variable is passed into a block with one value and returned with a different value, it is an input/output parameter. These parameters are also called by variable. All parameters in the parameter list of the procedure `DoSchedules` are input/output parameters.

Coding Some Procedures

Developing `GetInitial-Incomes`

We still need to code the 4 procedures for the program `DoTaxes`. We will code the 2 procedures `GetInitialIncomes` and `ShowResults`. We leave it to you to develop the code for the procedures `ShowInstructions` and `DoSchedules` as Exercises 6 and 7 at the end of this section.

A procedure is developed the same way that a program is, namely, the process is described first, then coded. The description for the process we have named as the procedure `GetInitialIncomes` is given by the following pseudocode:

keyin GrossIncome
keyin NumberOfExemptions
TaxableGrossIncome ← GrossIncome − NumberOfExemptions ∗ ExemptionRate

The description shows that the procedure has fulfilled its purpose by returning values to the formal parameter variables `GrossIncome` by way of keyboard input and `TaxableGrossIncome` by way of an assignment statement.

In order to fulfill the second purpose, another variable is required, namely `NumberOfExemptions`. This `integer` variable, because its identifier is not found in the formal parameter list, must be declared as a *local variable* to the block of the procedure `GetInitialIncomes`. It is seen as a variable that has a meaning and purpose only within the statement part of the procedure `GetInitialIncomes`. It is therefore unnecessary, and, indeed, ill-advised to declare this variable in the main block.

Local variable: a variable declared as part of a given procedure's block.

Note that this procedure also requires a reference to the global constant ExemptionRate. Strictly speaking, it was incorrect on our part to define this constant in the initial presentation of the main block of the program. The need for defining this constant is only evident after we have described the statement part of the procedure GetInitialIncomes. We confess that we defined Exemption-Rate prematurely so that you would see the complete stub program of DoTaxes without our need to modify its code further.

It is possible to define ExemptionRate as a local constant, but usually this practice is ill-advised. A constant will not change its value regardless of where it may be referenced. If this value is defined in the main block and needs to be changed as part of a program's maintenance, the programmer will not have to hunt for definitions and/or obscure references to it in all the different procedures of a program. He or she can simply change the value at the single place where it is defined, that is in the CONST section of the main block.

The source code for the procedure GetInitialIncomes is shown below. The local variable, NumberOfExemptions, is used to fulfill the purpose of the block. When the flow of control is transfered to GetInitialIncomes, this variable has meaning as an object belonging to the block part of the procedure GetInitialIncomes. After the statements of the block have been executed, this local variable has no meaning nor does the machine supply a location where its value is stored.

This source code can be substituted in place of the original stub we coded for the program DoTaxes.

```
PROCEDURE GetInitialIncomes(VAR GrossIncome, TaxableGrossIncome: real);
   {documentation}
   VAR
      NumberOfExemptions:   {number of claimed exemptions, as read in}
                            integer;
   BEGIN
      write('Enter salary:   ');
      readln(GrossIncome);
      write('Enter number of claimed exemptions:   ');
      TaxableGrossIncome:= GrossIncome - NoOfExemptions*ExemptionRate
   END;
```

The code for the procedure ShowResults is a sequence of display statements showing the values of each input parameter. Proper explanatory text should be included in the display. This code can likewise be substituted in lieu of the stub we initially coded.

```
   PROCEDURE ShowResults(GrossIncome, TaxableGrossIncome,
                                      Tax, NetIncome: real);
      {documentation}
      BEGIN
         writeln('Gross income ....... $', GrossIncome:4:2);
         writeln('TaxableGrossIncome .. $', TaxableGrossIncome:4:2);
```

```
      writeln('Tax ................. $', Tax; 4:2);
      writeln('Net income .......... $', NetIncome:4:2)
   END;
```

Three Fundamental Algorithms

We can categorize 2 of the 4 procedures of DoTaxes as subroutine algorithms. When we describe a subroutine algorithm, a description of the header as well as a description of the statements is necessary. The procedure ShowInstructions, for example, satisfies the description of Algorithm 4.1. We are describing the header with the name DisplayLines.

Algorithm 4.1

{procedure to display lines of text}
PROCEDURE DisplayLines
    display a sequence of literal expressions
{end algorithm}

Use this algorithm if you want the computer to display instructions to some program user. You can also use it to display lines of text where the sequence of writeln statements uses parameters whose values are all constants, anonymous or named.

    Algorithm 4.2, whose header we have named as ReadInValues is described as follows:

Algorithm 4.2

{a procedure to read in values to variables from keyboard input:}
PROCEDURE ReadInValues(all parameters are called by VAR)
    keyin values to all variables in the parameter list
{end description}

There are no relevant preconditions for this algorithm. The values that have been read in to the variables in the parameter list represent the postconditions returned. Use this algorithm when you want initial values read in to variables. You expect to use these values as preconditions for other statements you want to write, hence postconditions are returned by the action of this algorithm.

    The actions of the procedure DisplayResults are described by Algorithm 4.3, to which we have given the name DisplayValues.

Algorithm 4.3

{a procedure to display the values of all variables listed}
PROCEDURE DisplayValues(all parameters are called by value)
    display values of all variables in parameter list
{end description}

The preconditions are that values have been assigned to all the formal parameters. The postcondition is that all these values have been displayed. Use this algorithm when you want the computer to display some results of processing.

EXERCISES

1. The actual parameter list is found in a procedure _____ , and the formal parameter list is found in a procedure _____ .

2. Standard Pascal allows the use of only two reserved words in a procedure header. Which ones?

3. Which of the following class of parameters are associated with preconditions and which are associated with postconditions: input, input/output, output?

4. Give a complete description of the flow of control for the main block of the program DoTaxes, as coded using procedures.

**Practice Your
Analysis Skills**

5. What would happen if the reserved word VAR is deleted from the header of the procedure DoSchedules? Describe what happens in terms of preconditions and postconditions.

**Sharpen Your
Implementation
Skills**

6. Write the code for the procedure ShowInstructions.

7. Write the code for the procedure DoSchedules. Make sure that this procedure does not use more than the 3 (perhaps less) global variables declared in the main block.

**Learn More
About Your
System**

8. Once you have done exercise 7, run the program but comment out the reserved word VAR in the header of DoSchedules. Can you explain the results of the run?

9. Put the reserved VAR before the identifier list in the formal parameter list of ShowResults. Then try to compile the program. Can you explain the result?

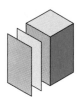

4.2 More About Procedures

We continue the study of procedure by first giving you an example that shows precisely how the machine manages memory for procedures with parameters. We complete our discussion of the syntax and semantics for formal parameter lists, this time focusing on the use and purposes of the comma and the semicolon. After we solve some sample problems, we conclude this section by showing you some program development tools that you can apply specifically to the development and testing of procedures.

Procedure Memory Management

Suppose a procedure with parameters has just been called. Before the computer executes the statements of the procedure, it must manage memory in such a way that all formal parameters and local variables are dealt with. The machine can only execute the statements of the procedure after it has handled the details of memory management first. Let us explore the way the computer takes care of these details.

When a formal parameter is called by variable, the computer uses the identifier as another (local) way to reference the corresponding actual parameter variable. If the two identifiers are different, the formal parameter identifier represents an *alias* to the actual parameter. No new memory is allocated as a result of this mechanism; the same memory location is given another name that can be used as a reference in the statements of the procedure. The effect of any assignment and/or read operation using the formal parameter name is felt in the memory allocated to the actual parameter variable. Once the procedure's statements have been completed, the name of the formal parameter variable is forgotten.

The
call-by-value
mechanism

When a formal parameter is called by value, the computer allocates a memory location to store the value of the actual parameter expression. Once that value has been copied into the named formal parameter variable, the interface between the actual parameter expression and the formal parameter variable is completed. The value taken on by the formal parameter variable may change as the computer carries out the statements of the procedure. This change, however, is felt as a local effect on a local variable. The final value of this variable is not passed out to an alias because there is no alias.

Local variable
declarations

You can declare local variables to allocate still more local memory. As with variables called by value, all variables declared locally within the block are destroyed when the procedure's statements are completed. The difference between a value parameter and a local variable is that the initial value of a local variable is not assigned before the computer starts to execute the statements of the block. You therefore expect a local variable to take on an initial value as a consequence of one of the block's statements.

An example to
illustrate
memory
management

Let us look at how the machine manages memory for the procedure Manipulate, whose code, along with a fragment of code from the main block, is given as Example 4.1. We have chosen this example because it has an input parameter, an output parameter, an i/o parameter, and a local variable. We are going to look at the data areas of the main block and the procedure Manipulate at various points in the execution of Manipulate's statements.

Example 4.1

```
PROCEDURE Manipulate(VIn: integer; VAR VInOut, VOut: integer);
  {An example where VIn's value is used, VInOut's value is changed, and
  VOut's value is set to an initial value}
  VAR
    VLocal:  integer;  {a variable whose value is read in locally}
  BEGIN
    VInOut:= VInOut + VIn;
    readln(VLocal);
    VOut:= VLocal + 1
  END;
    {main block: }
    XInt:= 8;  YInt:= 2; {ZInt not asigned a value}
    Manipulate(YInt + 2, XInt, ZInt);
```

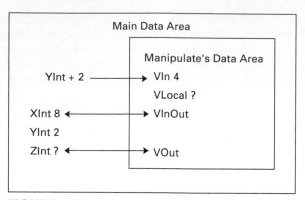

FIGURE 4.7 Program state just after `Manipulate` is called.

The memory set up

Figure 4.7 shows the data areas set up in the main block and in `Manipulate` just before the computer starts to execute the statements of the procedure. From the figure, we see that

1. The value of `Yint + 2`, that is 4, is copied into the local variable `VIn`.
2. The identifiers `XInt` and `VInOut` reference the same variable, `XInt`.
3. The identifiers `ZInt` and `VOut` reference the same variable, `ZInt`.
4. The variable `VLocal` is set up as a local variable of the procedure `Manipulate`.

Just before transfer of control

Suppose the value 20 has been read into `VLocal`, and the computer has just completed the last statement of `Manipulate`. If it has not yet transferred control back to the main block, the data areas look like the drawing of Figure 4.8. The variable `XInt`, as aliased by `VInOut`, has had its value changed by virtue of the first statement in the block. The variable `ZInt` has had its value initially set by virtue of the last statement in the block.

FIGURE 4.8 Program state just before `Manipulate` is exited.

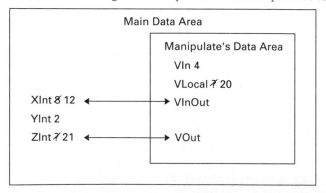

FIGURE 4.9 Program state just after `Manipulate` is exited.

Control transferred

Figure 4.9 shows the picture just after the computer has finished with the procedure `Manipulate`. All variables and local aliases are gone. Only the variable `XInt`, `YInt`, and `ZInt` remain. Two of these three variables, `XInt` and `ZInt`, took on new values as a result of the statements of `Manipulate`.

The comma and the semicolon

The semicolon used in a parameter list separates formal parameter identifiers both by type and by calling mechanism. If one parameter is to be called by value and the other by variable, the two parameters must be separated by a semicolon, even if they are of the same type. Thus, we have used the semicolon between the identifier `integer` and the reserved word VAR in the code of the procedure `Manipulate`.

Suppose, instead, that a procedure requires two value parameters, one of type `integer` and the other of type `char`. The header must be coded as PROCEDURE `UseTwoValues(InInt: integer; InChar: char);` where the semicolon separates the two identifiers of the two different types.

You can use the reserved word VAR more than once in a procedure header. Suppose, for example, you need to write a header with variable calls to two output parameters of type `char` and of type `real`. You would then code PROCEDURE `ReturnTwoVars(VAR OCh: char; VAR ORe: real);`.

The comma separates two identifiers that are of the same type and that are called using the same mechanism. If you want to write a header to return values to two variables of type `char` using the values taken on by two integer expressions, you would code a header that might look like PROCEDURE `UseTwoRet-Two(Int1, Int2: integer; VAR Ch1, Ch2: char);`.

Some Examples

Now that you have all the information you need to know about procedure calls and parameter passing, let us plan and code some more examples where we use procedural abstraction. We will also write the source code for each of these procedures.

Calling the same procedure with different actual parameters

A procedure, once declared, will carry out the same purpose using the same formal parameters and local variables if it is called in some other part of the program. This procedure may be called from two or more different places with different actual parameter values or variables. The following problem, with its coded solution, shows how the aliasing mechanism allows you to code one procedure that works correctly for more than one set of actual parameters.

Example Problem 4.1

The problem statement

Suppose the variables Ch11 and Ch21 have been assigned values. We want to write some code where the values assigned to Ch12 and Ch13 are the next two char values after Ch11 in the ASCII collating sequence. We also want statements to make analogous assignments to the values of the char variables Ch22 and Ch23 with respect to the value of Ch21.

The solution

We can abstract a procedure to solve this problem. The procedure is called twice using the statements

```
AssignNextTwo(Ch11, Ch12, Ch13);
AssignNextTwo(Ch21, Ch22, Ch23);
```

Given initial values for Ch11 and Ch21 as preconditions for the respective calls, the postconditions on Ch12 and Ch13 with respect to Ch11's value are the same as the postconditions on Ch22 and Ch23 with respect to Ch21's value. For example, given that Ch11 is equal to 'A', Ch12 will be equal to 'B' and Ch13 will be equal to 'C'. Then if Ch21 is equal to '1', Ch22 will be equal to '2' and Ch23 will be equal to '3'.

The statements required to achieve the desired postconditions are simple assignments using the succ function. Thus, we obtain the code of the procedure AssignTwo as given below.

```
PROCEDURE AssignNextTwo(Ch1: char; VAR Ch2, Ch3: char);
  {in: Ch1 -- first value in collating sequence of three chars
  out: Ch2 -- second value in the sequence
  out: Ch3 -- third value in the sequence}
  BEGIN
    Ch2:= succ(Ch1);
    Ch3:= succ(Ch2)
  END;  ◆
```

Another example

Let us write another procedure designed such that it can be called from two or more different places in the same program. The procedure we want to code is given in the problem statement of Example Problem 4.2.

Example Problem 4.2

The problem statement

Let us write a procedure that will prompt the user for an integer value, then read in a value to an integer variable. Two calls to this procedure might be coded in the following way:

```
IntReadIn('Enter your present age:  ',Age);
IntReadIn('Enter your first guess:  ',Guess);
```

Two typical interactions resulting from the respective calls might then look like

```
          Enter your present age:   57        {Age ↔ 57}
          Enter your first guess:   42        {Guess ↔ 42}
```

The solution The procedure will have two parameters in its header, a string variable whose value must be displayed, and an `integer` variable whose value must be read in. The first parameter is thus called by value, and the second by variable. In order for the string variable to be a parameter, a string type must be defined in the definitions part of the block. Given this requirement, the code for the solution is as follows:

```
TYPE    {a global definition}
  String60 = STRING[60];     {VAX Pascal:  VARYING[60] of char;}

PROCEDURE IntReadIn(PromptString: String60; VAR Int: integer);
  {in:   PromptString -- value of string to be displayed
  out:   Int -- value read in to Int}
  BEGIN
    write(PromptString);
    readln(Int)
  END;
```

Defining a type In order for this procedure to work, it is necessary to first define the type `String60` using the syntax that is acceptible for the particular dialect of Pascal you are using. Remember that anonymous types are not allowed in the formal parameter list of a procedure declaration. We chose 60 characters to be safe, for we can assume that no prompt string will have as many as 60 characters in it. ◆

Let us write a program using procedural abstraction for the main block. The following case study requires this approach.

CASE STUDY 4.1

A case study An officer at Friendly Savings and Loan wants you to write a promotional program to help a salesperson show a customer how much money he or she can earn over a time period of three years for a given principal and interest rate.

The problem statement The user first enters a principal and interest rate. He or she is then shown the interest and new principal after 1, 2 and 3 years. A typical run of the program might look like

```
          Enter starting principal:  $5000
          Enter interest rate as a percentage: 10.2
          The interest earned for year 1 is $510.00
          The principal after year 1 is $5510.00
          The interest earned for year 2 is $562.02
          The principal after year 2 is $6072.02
          The interest earned for year 3 is $619.35
          The principal after year 3 is $6691.37
```

We can describe the statement part of the main block using the following pseudocode:

> read in values for Principal and Interest rate
> use value of Rate to calculate Interest and Principal for the year
> display value for year 1 of Interest and Principal
> use value of Rate to calculate Interest and Principal for year
> display value for year 2 of Interest and Principal
> use value of Rate to Calculate Interest and Principal for year
> display value for year 3 of Interest and Principal

We can then abstract three procedures from the described actions to write the main block statement as follows:

```
BEGIN
    GetPrincipalAndRate(Principal,Rate);
    CalculateYear(Rate,Interest,Principal);
    ShowForYear(1,Interest,Principal);
    CalculateYear(Rate,Interest,Principal);
    ShowForYear(2,Interest,Principal);
    CalculateYear(Rate,Interest,Principal);
    ShowForYear(3,Interest,Principal);
END.
```

Assertion testing the main block statement   The values returned from the call to the procedure we named `GetPrincipalAndRate` represent the initial principal and the interest rate to be paid. After the first call to `CalculateYear`, the value returned to `Interest` represents the interest earned on the initial value of `Principal` for the given value of `Rate`. The value returned to `Principal` represents the principal in the account after the first year. These values, along with the integer value 1, representing year 1, are then displayed by the action of `ShowForYear`. Thus, the first part of the problem is solved.

The value returned to `Interest` after the second call represents the rate on the initial value of `Principal`, the principal for year 1. The value returned to `Principal` represents the principal after year 2. These values are displayed by the action in the block of `ShowForYear`. The second part of the problem is then solved. The meaning of the values given to `Principal` and `Rate` for the third sequence can be described analogously. The values are also analogously displayed. Thus, the sequence of statements in the main block will be correct if we code the blocks for each of the procedures correctly.

Source code   The program coded as `ShowInterest` represents most of the code required to solve the case study. You are left to code the rest of the block of the procedure `GetPrincipalAndRate` as Exercise 12 at the end of this section.

```
PROGRAM ShowInterest(input,output);
    {The user enters a value for Principal and Rate. Then the Principal
    and Interest after each year is shown for a period of 3 years.}
```

```
VAR
   Principal,  {accumulator variable for principal after each year}
   Interest,   {interest earned on a given principal}
   Rate:       {rate at which interest is earned}
               real;
{*                                                                  *}
PROCEDURE GetPrincipalAndRate(VAR Principal, Rate: real);
   {reads in values to Principal and Rate}
   BEGIN   END;
{*                                                                  *}
PROCEDURE CalculateYear(Rate: real; VAR Interest, Principal: real);
   {uses value of Rate to calculate Interest on initial Principal;
   final Principal is returned as initial Principal plus Interest}
   CONST
      PerCentFactor = 0.01;   {converts Rate to a percentage}
   BEGIN


      Principal:= Principal + Interest
   END;
{*                                                                  *}
PROCEDURE ShowForYear(Year: integer; Interest, Principal: real);
   {displays values of the three parameters}
   BEGIN
      write('The interest earned for year ');
      writeln(Year:1,' is $', Interest:4:2);
      write('The principal after year ');
      writeln(Year:1,' is $',Principal:4:2)
   END;
{*                                                                  *}
BEGIN {insert statements of main block here}   END.
```

Stubs, Drivers and Side-Effects

You have been exposed to a number of *software engineering* tools already. These include: pseudocode, successive refinements, strategy descriptions, desk tracing, structure charts, assertion testing, and procedural abstraction. You will now learn how to use stubs and *drivers,* software engineering tools that apply specifically to the development and testing of procedures.

Software engineering: a term that describes the techniques used in the development, testing, and maintenance of software.

Driver: a short sequence of statements, usually written as the statement of a procedure with no parameters, that is used solely for the purpose of testing a procedure. The driver's sequence first gets values for all input and i/o parameters, then calls the procedure, and then displays the values returned to all i/o and output parameters.

The stubs we have coded so far were empty statements, but they need not be. You can use stubs to signify a general postcondition has been achieved or to simulate the effects returned by the procedure's statements. The following stub for CalculateYear (Case Study 4.1) indicates that the computer has "executed" the procedure:

```
{1}   PROCEDURE CalculateYear(Rate: real; VAR Interest, Principal: real);
          BEGIN
              writeln('Calculate year executed.')
          END;
```

You could likewise write a statement that simulates results returned by the procedure. You can assign two literal values to the two parameters where the stub's code now looks like

```
{2}   PROCEDURE CalculateYear(Rate: real; VAR Interest, Principal: real);
          BEGIN
              INTEREST:= 500.00;   Principal:= 4900;
          END;
```

Finally, you can write a stub where "typical values" are read into the *VAR* parameters. You would code this stub as

```
{3}   PROCEDURE CalculateYear(Rate: real; VAR Interest, Principal: real);
          BEGIN
              write('Enter value for interest:  $');   readln(interest);
              write('Enter value for new principal:   $');   readln(Principal)
          END;
```

Uses for stubs

You may be wondering what purpose these different stubs serve. Remember that a stub represents a part of the program that compiles even though it is incomplete. It can therefore interface with the rest of the program even though its actual statement has not been written.

Suppose you have written most of your program and want to see how it works as a whole. You can simulate on-line testing without strictly going on line with a completed program by writing "fake" assignments to return values to the VAR parameters of the procedures you have not yet written. The stub we coded as {2} is an example where you would use this technique. Perhaps you may want to stimulate values from the keyboard for a number of sample runs. Then use a stub similar to {3}. You may simply want to see if the computer will carry out the actions of a given procedure. Then you would write a procedure similar to stub {1}.

Changing a procedure back to a stub

You can also use any of these stub algorithms on a procedure that has already been written. You can turn the complete procedure back into a stub if you comment out the procedure's statements. Then you can insert a sequence using one of the three suggested stub algorithms. The stub you code depends upon what you want done with it as part of the testing.

This process may not be as easy to implement as we make it seem because many compilers will not allow nested comments. If you have sidebar comments in your source code, then, it is not easy to comment out a block's entire statement with one set of braces.

You can get around this apparent difficulty by using the alternate symbols for comment delimiters, namely, " (*" and "*) ". If you use these alternate delimiters, most compilers will let you comment out the entire text of the procedure, including all sidebar comments that used braces as delimiters.

Drivers

A driver is a very useful device for on-line testing of a procedure. When you write a sequence of statements as a driver for a procedure, you must get values for all input and input/output parameters of the procedure. You then write the statement that calls the procedure using these values. The values returned from the procedure, the input/output variables and the output variables, are then displayed.

The driver algorithm

The sole purpose of a driver is to test some procedure. The less a driver interfaces with the other procedures in the program, the better. Indeed, the best driver is a procedure satisfying the description of Algorithm 4.4.

Algorithm 4.4

{a description of a procedure to drive another procedure:}
PROCEDURE DriveIt
   VAR
      variables for the parameter list of the procedure
   BEGIN {sequence}
      get values for input parameters of the procedure being driven
      call the procedure being driven
      display values returned by the procedure call
   END   {sequence}
{end algorithm}

Note that a driver procedure has no parameter list. All local variables, used simply to test some procedure, are there solely to fulfill the purpose of the driver. A driver, in short, should not pass out values, nor should it normally require that values be passed in.

An example

The procedure named DCalculateYear is a driver coded as a procedure to test the procedure CalculateYear (Case Study 4.1). This driver is simply called from the main block of the program ShowInterest by the statement DCalculateYear. The driver can be declared directly before the statements of the main block.

```
PROCEDURE DCalculateYear;
  VAR
    Rate, Interest, Principal:  real;
  BEGIN
    write('Input real values for Principal and Rate:  ');
    readln(Principal, Rate);
```

```
      CalculateYear(Rate, Interest, Principal);
      writeln('Interest = ',Interest:4:2);
      writeln('Principal = ',Principal:4:2)
    END;
```

Side effects and
modularity

All global variables and global constants can be references by identifiers in any procedure. The practice of referencing a global variable by identifier in a procedure, however, is highly inadvisable, for the procedure would not be self-contained. A well-structured program has procedures that are all self-contained. When all procedures in a program are self-contained, we say that the program is *modular*. All headers are written as good, clean interfaces, where data flow in and out of procedures is clearly shown and easy to understand.

Modularity: a property of a program or a portion of code where all subprograms are self-contained and have no side effects.

Avoid writing code with *side effects*. If an error were found in a program with side effects, it might be very difficult to find the origin of the error because the program's structure is not modular. Fortunately it is easy to guard against side effects: just *do not code them*. You must make sure with every procedure you write that no assignments are made or values read in to variables that are not either declared locally nor found in the parameter list. Be ever diligent, for side effects can be deadly! One side effect buried in thousands of lines of code may take weeks to find and fix.

Side effect: any reference to a variable in the statement part of a subprogram that is neither declared locally nor found in the subprogram's formal parameter list.

Global types

You will usually want to name all types globally, that is, in the TYPE definitions section of the main block. When you follow this practice, the declared variables of the defined type can be used as parameters for any procedure. If, however, you define a type locally, the compiler will not recognize the type name in another procedure's header.

Sometimes, you may find a procedure requires a local variable of some yet undefined type. In this case, it is best to declare the variable locally as a named type and to define the type globally. Then if you find you need to use this type in more than one block, there is no problem.

EXERCISES

Test Your
Understanding

1. Which of each of the mechanisms creates another variable in the data area of a procedure: call-by-value, call-by-variable, local declaration?

2. Which of each of the same three mechanisms will create an alias to a variable outside the procedure's data area?

3. Which of each of the three mechanisms destroys memory representing a variable once the computer finishes the procedure's statements?

4. Indicate which of the following identifiers are best referenced by a local name in a procedure: variable identifier, constant identifier, type identifier?

5. Which of each of the three in Exercise 4 are best referenced as a global name inside a procedure?

6. List four coding algorithms for a procedure stub.

7. Explain why, if possible, a driver is best written without parameters.

Practice Your Analysis Skills

8. Categorize each of the three procedures in Case Study 4.1 into one of the following named algorithms:
   (a) DisplayLines   (b) ReadInValues   (c) DisplayValues   (d) none of them

9. As applied to the procedure `Manipulate`, what values will be returned to XInt, YInt and ZInt for each of the following preconditions?
   (a) XInt $\longleftrightarrow$ 3   YInt $\longleftrightarrow$ 4   ZInt $\longleftrightarrow$ 5   7 read into VLocal
   (b) XInt $\longleftrightarrow$ 10   YInt $\longleftrightarrow$ 0   ZInt $\longleftrightarrow$?   2 read into VLocal

Sharpen Your Implementation Skills

10. Write driver procedures for the procedures `Manipulate` and `AssignNextTwo`.

11. Write a procedure
    (a) `RealReadIn` that uses a prompt to read in a real value to a variable.
    (b) Do the same for the procedure `ChReadIn` to read in a char value to a variable.

12. Write the block for `GetPrincipalAndRate` of Case Study 4.1.

4.3   Making Change: A Case Study in Top-Down Design

So far we have developed programs using procedural abstraction only one level down from the main block. The case study of this section develops procedures beyond the main block's level of abstraction. In other words, calls are made to procedures from other procedures.

CASE STUDY 4-2

The problem statement

Let us write a program that displays the minimum number of coins in quarters, dimes, nickels, and pennies for a value whose input is expressed in cents. Two typical runs might look like:

```
Input cents:   72
Your change is 2 quarters, 2 dimes, 0 nickels and 2 pennies.

Input cents:   55
Your change is 2 quarters, 0 dimes, 1 nickels and 0 pennies.
```

The display will not differentiate between one or more of some coin.

Developing the main block statement

We can describe the sequence of the main block using the pseudocode

keyin Cents   *{read}*
make change   *{process}*
display change   *{display}*

Note that this description is a refinement of the *read, process, display* algorithm.

    Now in addition to the variable Cents, we need variables to represent the number of quarters, dimes, nickels, and pennies. The action of make change will return values to these variables. We can use a *DisplayValues* procedure to show the values of the coins. Thus, the first draft of the main block refines to

keyin value for Cents
MakeChange(Cents, Qs, Ds, Ns, Ps)
ShowCoins(Qs, Ds, Ns, Ps)

    The precondition to the call MakeChange is that the value assigned to Cents represents the amount of money to be changed. The postcondition is that the values assigned to the respective variables Qs, Ds, Ns, and Ps represent the number of quarters, dimes, nickels, and pennies, respectively, in change.

Main block program

    The code for the main block is shown as program ChangeMaker. Its structure chart down to the present level of development is shown in Figure 4.10.

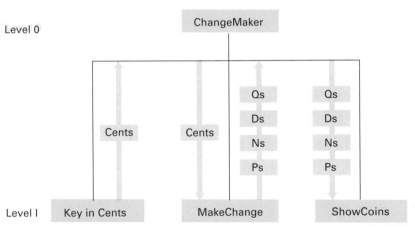

FIGURE 4.10 Structure chart of ChangeMaker through the first level of design.

```
PROGRAM ChangeMaker (input, output) ;
    {The user inputs a value representing cents.  The computer calculates
    and displays the change made with the minimum number of coins.}
    VAR
        Cents,     {the amount of cents to be changed}
        Qs,        {the number of quarters that make up the change}
        Ds,        {the number of dimes that make up the change}
        Ns,        {the number of nickels that make up the change}
        Ps:        {the number of pennies that make up the change}
                   integer;
```

```
{*                                                                    *}
PROCEDURE MakeChange(Cents: integer; VAR Qs, Ds, Ns, Ps: integer);
   {in: Cents -- initial amount of cents to be changed
   out:   Qs, Ds, Ns, Ps -- respective number of quarters, dimes,
          nickels and pennies that make up the change}
   BEGIN    END;
{*                                                                    *}
PROCEDURE ShowCoins(Qs, Ds, Ns, Ps: integer);
   {in: Qs, Ds, Ns, Ps -- number of each coins that makes up change
   out: each formal parameter value is displayed}
   BEGIN    END;
{*                                                                    *}
BEGIN      {main block sequence}
   write('Input cents:   ');
   readln(Cents);
   MakeChange(Cents, Qs, Ds, Ns, Ps);
   ShowCoins(Qs, Ds, Ns, Ps)
END.
```

Developing the actions of MakeChange

We can describe the sequence for MakeChange using the pseudocode

> *find Qs from initial Cents*
> *find Ds from remaining Cents*
> *find Ns from remaining Cents*
> *find Ps from the final value of Cents*

We can refine this sequence by abstracting a procedure GetCoins for the first three *find* actions using

	{Cents ⟷ 72, Qs, Ds, Ns, Ps unknown}
GetCoins(25, Cents, Qs)	*{Cents ⟷ 22, Qs ⟷ 2}*
GetCoins(10, Cents, Ds)	*{Cents ⟷ 2, Ds ⟷ 2}*
GetCoins(5, Cents, Ns)	*{Cents ⟷ 2, Ns ⟷ 0}*
Ps ← Cents	*{Cents ⟷ 2, Ps ⟷ 2}*

The first parameter of the procedure call GetCoins represents the denomination of the coin whose change is required. The third parameter will hold the value of the number of coins contained in the initial value of Cents. The value returned to Cents represents the monetary amount of the change left.

On the right side of the pseudocode, we have provided a sample desk trace of the values given to all the variables when the parameter Cents takes on an initial value of 72. We have assumed the procedure GetCoins will be coded properly. The values passed out to the four variables show that we have a correct solution that solves this specific example, assuming that GetCoins is a correct procedure.

Assertion testing our draft

We can do better if we apply assertion testing to our draft. First, we should state the preconditions that apply to each of the parameters in a call to GetCoins: (1) The first parameter represents the value of the given coin, (2) the second parameter represents the number of cents remaining to change, and (3) the third parameter's value is unassigned.

As postconditions, we have the following: (1) The second parameter's value represents the number of cents left after change has been made for the given coin, and (2) the value returned to the third parameter represents the number of the given coin that makes up part of the change. When we follow through by making assertions related to these conditions on each call to GetCoins, we can say the description we have drafted is logically correct.

The code for the two procedures MakeChange and GetCoins follows:

```
PROCEDURE MakeChange(Cents: integer; VAR Qs, Ds, Ns, Ps: integer);
  BEGIN
    {documentation}
    GetCoins(25, Cents, Qs);
    GetCoins(10, Cents, Ds);
    GetCoins(5, Cents, Ns);
    Ps:= Cents
  END;
```

```
PROCEDURE GetCoins(CoinValue: integer; VAR Cents, Coins; integer);
  {in: CoinValue -- the value of the coin
   in: Cents -- amount of money before change was made
  out: Cents -- amount of money after change was made
  out: Coins -- number of coins to be given as change}
  BEGIN
    Coins:= Cents DIV CoinValue;
    Cents:= Cents - Coins * CoinValue
  END;
```

Structure chart

The structure chart for the program we have developed up to this point is shown in Figure 4.11. This chart does not show that three calls are made to GetCoins from the MakeChange block. Nor does it show how the aliasing mechanism works. It does show that MakeChange requires the GetCoins block as part of its statement. It also shows that the formal parameter CoinValue appears to originate in the MakeChange block and that MakeChange uses the values returned to Coins and Cents. Furthermore, the procedure GetCoins, not being called from the main block, represents a Level II procedure.

Layout considerations

At this point, a very interesting design question arises, namely, "Where should we put the procedure GetCoins?" It belongs to Level II planning and is called from MakeChange. Therefore, we could make GetCoins a local procedure to MakeChange, so that the stub layout for the two procedures look like

```
{*                                                               *}
PROCEDURE MakeChange(Cents; integer; VAR Qs, Ds, Ns, Ps: integer);
  {documentation for MakeChange}
{+                                                               +}
  PROCEDURE GetCoins(CoinValue: integer; VAR Cents, Coins: integer);
    {documentation for GetCoins}
```

```
    BEGIN  {statement for GetCoins}     END;
{+                                                              +}
  BEGIN      {statement for MakeChange}      END;
{*                                                              *}
```

It is also possible to place the procedure declaration for `GetCoins` directly above the declaration for the procedure MakeChange. When this scheme is used, `GetCoins` can be called by any other procedure below it. The stub layout with this scheme is coded as

```
{*                                                              *}
PROCEDURE GetCoins(CoinValue: integer; VAR Cents, Coins: integer);
  {documentation for GetCoins}
  BEGIN    {statement for GetCoins}   END;
{+                                                              +}
PROCEDURE MakeChange(Cents: integer; VAR Qs, Ds, Ns, Ps: integer);
  {documentation for MakeChange}
  BEGIN    {statement for MakeChange}   END;
{*                                                              *}
```

The different separator symbol (+) between `GetCoins` and `MakeChange` indicates that `GetCoins` is used exclusively by `MakeChange`.

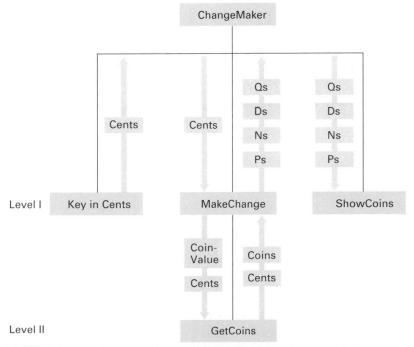

FIGURE 4.11 The complete structure chart for `ChangeMaker`.

If we decide on this second layout, we should place any lower-level procedure above the higher-level one that uses it. Note that if, as in the first layout, we declare GetCoins as a procedure that is local to MakeChange, no statements from the main block can call it. If, however, we declare GetCoins above MakeChange, thus using the second layout, the procedure GetCoins can be called from the main block as well as from MakeChange.

Deciding upon a convention

So which layout will we use? We choose to make each process part of the main block, using the second scheme. We make this choice for the following reasons:

I.   It is easier to read a procedure's statements. Each procedure is read as a self-contained unit with the variable identifiers and the statements close to each other. If we declare local procedures, there will be intervening source code between the variable identifiers and the statement part of the procedure that has the local process.

II.   It is easier to drive any procedure. The code to drive the procedure Get-Coins, for example, is as follows:

```
PROCEDURE DGetCoins;
   {a driver for the procedure GetCoins}
   VAR
      Coins, Cents, CoinValue: integer;   {needed to test GetCoins}
   BEGIN
      readln(Cents,CoinValue);
      GetCoins(CoinValue, Cents, Coins);
      writeln(Coins:1,' ',Cents:1)
   END;
```

Driving local procedures

If we make GetCoins available to the main block, we can simply place this driver directly before the reserved word BEGIN of the main block. We then execute the driver by writing DGetCoins as a statement in the main block.

FIGURE 4.12 Programs state of ChangeMaker just before the final call to GetCoins is exited.

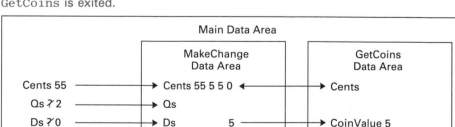

Consider what happens if we opt to use local procedures according to the first layout proposed. We would have to place the driver inside the block of MakeChange. The call to the driver must be made inside MakeChange. Therefore, the main block must call MakeChange first, even if we may just want to test GetCoins.

If we wish to remove any calls to various drivers in different blocks, we need to look for them inside the compound statements of the procedures. Moreover, any driver adds more separating space between the variables and the procedure's statements. The deeper the level of nesting the more complex any of the problems we have just described becomes.

PROGRAM DESIGN RULE 4.1

If you do not nest procedures, then lay out lower level procedures first.

A design rule

The design rule applies to us because we have chosen a format that does not nest procedures. The rule ensures that the programs we code will compile. We will then use different comment separators for different levels of abstraction. Look at the proposed layout scheme with MakeChange in the context of the program Change-Maker again. You will see that we used {*   *} to separate all Level I procedures from each other, but we used {+   +} to separate the Level II procedure Get-Coins from the Level I procedure MakeChange that called it. This scheme shows that GetCoins is a Level II procedure used exclusively by the Level I procedure MakeChange.

Parameter correspondence

Regardless of whether GetCoins is local to MakeChange or not, the computer will make one call to MakeChange and three calls to GetCoins. Each call to GetCoins is done from MakeChange. Each of the 3 calls, moreover, sets up a different process with a different data area.

Figure 4.12 shows the data area after the computer has just completed the statements of the third call to GetCoins. We have assumed that the value entered for Cents was 55. Values have already been assigned to Qs and Ds.

It is interesting to see how each parameter changes values within each block. Look, for example, at what happens to the value of Cents, an identifier used to represent two different variables. In the main data area, its value remains at 55. In the data area of MakeChange, its value was initially 55, but it was decreased via the action on the corresponding VAR parameter of the same name in the GetCoins block.

Source code presentations

The source code for the program ChangeMaker in its entirety is given below. Sometimes, as we have done in this case study, we will present the complete text of the overall program. Most of the time, however, we will develop the source code one block at a time. Usually we will present a program with a fully coded main block statement and procedure stubs. We will document the preconditions and postconditions for each procedure as part of the stub. We will then develop the source code for each of the abstracted procedures.

Once we have developed a procedure's source code, we will present the code the same way the procedure is to be declared in a completed program. It is understood that the completely developed procedure should replace the stub previously given to complete the source code of the main program. Thus, we will present the source code top-down, exactly the way the source code for a program is usually developed.

```
PROGRAM ChangeMaker(input,output);
   {The user inputs a value representing cents.  The computer calculates
   and displays the change made with the minimum number of coins.}
   VAR
      Cents,     {the amount of cents to be changed}
      Qs,        {the number of quarters that make up the change}
      Ds,        {the number of dimes that make up the change}
      Ns,        {the number of nickels that make up the change}
      Ps:        {the number of pennies that make up the change}
                 integer;
   {*                                                                  *}
   PROCEDURE GetCoins(CoinValue: integer; VAR Cents, Coins: integer);
      {in: CoinValue -- the value of the coin
      in: Cents -- amount of money before change was made
      out: Cents -- amount of money after change was made
      out: Coins -- number of coins to be given as change}
   BEGIN
      Coins:= Cents DIV CoinValue;
      Cents:= Cents - Coins * CoinValue
   END;
   {+                                                                  +}
   PROCEDURE MakeChange(Cents: integer; VAR Qs, Ds, Ns, Ps: integer);
      {in: Cents -- amount of initial cents to be changed
      out:   Qs, Ds, Ns, Ps -- respective number of quarters, dimes,
             nickels and pennies that make up the change}
      BEGIN
         GetCoins(25, Cents, Qs);
         GetCoins(10, Cents, Ds);
         GetCoins(5, Cents, Ns);
         Ps:= Cents
      END;
   {*                                                                  *}
   PROCEDURE ShowCoins(Qs, Ds, Ns, Ps: integer);
      {in: Qs, Ds, Ns, Ps -- number of each coin that makes up change
      out: values of the formal parameters are displayed}
      BEGIN
         write('Your change is ');
         write(Qs:1,' quarters, ');
         write(Ds:1,' dimes, ');
         write(Ns:1,' nickels and ');
```

```
      writeln(Ps:1,' pennies.')
   END;
{*                                                                    *}
BEGIN     {main block sequence}
   write('Input cents:    ');
   readln(Cents);
   MakeChange(Cents, Qs, Ds, Ns, Ps);
   ShowCoins(Qs, Ds, Ns, Ps)
END. ◆
```

EXERCISES

**Test Your
Understanding**

1. Explain briefly how assertion testing is done on a procedure.

2. The identifier Cents appears in three blocks. How is it used in each block? Is memory created for a variable in any of the blocks? Which ones? Is an alias created in any of the blocks? Which ones?

3. The identifier Coins appears in two blocks. Repeat Exercise 2, but as it applies to this identifier.

**Practice Your
Analysis Skills**

4. Suppose the initial amount read into Cents is 732. How many of each coin would be returned?

5. Suppose the initial amount read into Cents is 57. Diagram the data area for the three processes (main, MakeChange, and GetCoins) just after the computer completes the statements of GetCoins. Diagram the data area for each of the three calls to Get-Coins.

6. Consider the following source code:

```
PROGRAM Example(output);
   {a driver program for DoIt, which has five different headers, as
   proposed in the exercise}
   VAR
     XInt,YInt,ZInt: integer;
     {*                                                          *}
     PROCEDURE DoIt(  {three formal parameters go here}   );
       {procedure that operates on formal parameters}
       BEGIN
         AInt:= BInt + 2;
         BInt:= 2*CInt;
         CInt:= AInt + BInt
       END;
     {*                                                          *}
     BEGIN
       XInt:= 1;                           {initial assignments}
       YInt:= 3;
       ZInt:= 5;
       DoIt(XInt,YInt,ZInt);               {procedure call}
       writeln(XInt:5,YInt:5,ZInt:5)       {display results returned}
     END.
```

What will be displayed if DoIt's header is?
- **(a)** PROCEDURE DoIt(AInt, BInt, CInt: integer);
- **(b)** PROCEDURE DoIt(VAR AInt, BInt, CInt: integer);
- **(c)** PROCEDURE DoIt(Var CInt, BInt, AInt: integer);
- **(d)** PROCEDURE DoIt(AInt: integer; VAR BInt: integer; CInt: integer);
- **(e)** PROCEDURE DoIt(VAR AInt, BInt: integer; CInt: integer);

Sharpen Your Implementation Skills

7. The following structure chart is given.

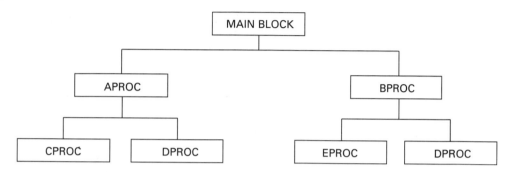

Write a stub program for the main block, where, as suggested, the MAIN BLOCK can call APROC and BPROC, APROC can call CPROC and DPROC, and BPROC can call DPROC and EPROC. When it is run, the program should display

```
Control in main block.
  Control in AProc.
    Control in CProc.
    Control in DProc.
  Control back in AProc.
Control back in main block.
  Control in BProc.
    Control in EProc.
    Control in DProc.
  Control back in BProc.
Control back in main block.
Program terminating.
```

- **(a)** Write the stub in such a way that the procedures are not locally declared.
- **(b)** Write the stub in such a way that the procedures are locally declared.

Program Testing Hints

Procedural abstraction and parameter passing are difficult to master. The only way you will gain facility using these techniques is through continued practice. In the meantime, we give you some hints on how to avoid some of the common mistakes you could make while you work to master the technique of writing structured programs that use procedures.

A List of Common Errors

There are certain syntax errors that, as a beginner, you may be prone to commit. Check your source code to ensure that it contains none of the four errors in the list we have given.

    I.   Do not use field size and precision specifications on a call to procedures other than the standard `write` and `writeln` procedures. A procedure call coded as `ShowIt(XRe:6:4, YInt+2:5)` will not compile.

    II.   In like manner, the formal parameter list only allows one reserved word, VAR. Everything else in a formal parameter list that is not a comma, semicolon, or a colon must be an identifier. You cannot use an anonymous type in a formal parameter list. Thus, a procedure header coded as `PROCEDURE ShowString(AName: STRING[20]);` will not compile, regardless of what dialect of Pascal you may be working in.

    III.   An identifier referring to each formal parameter type must be in the header. A header coded as `PROCEDURE DoIt(XRe;YInt);` will not compile. It must, instead, be coded as `PROCEDURE DoIt(XRe: real; YInt: integer);` in order to compile properly.

    IV.   Make sure you use the reserved word VAR correctly. You must use this word more than once in a header if parameters of different types are called by variable. If, for example, you want to write a procedure that returns values to the three variables `Name`, `Rank`, and `SerialNo`, where the first two are strings and the third is an integer, avoid writing a header such as `PROCEDURE GetInfo(VAR Name, Rank: StringType; SerialNo: integer);`. Remember that the semicolon in the header after the identifier `StringType` separates the variables both by type *and* by parameter-passing mechanism. The code for the correct header is therefore written as `PROCEDURE GetInfo(VAR Name, Rank: StringType; VAR SerialNo: integer);`. The comma indicates that both `Name` and `Rank` are of type `StringType` and that they are also called by variable. The other formal parameter, `SerialNo`, is also called by variable, because it is preceded by the reserved word VAR.

Parameter Passing Errors

Parameter passing is not an easy skill to master. Sometimes you may write a program that runs smoothly and returns the correct results even when there is poor interfacing between actual and formal parameters. We discuss this disturbing phenomenon below, explaining how the program appears "correct," why the program is incorrect, and how to rectify the errors.

Unused value parameters

    You can write a procedure that will return the desired results even if the parameter list does not faithfully represent the actual interface required. This kind of code is difficult to read and maintain. One of the ways you can incorrectly apply value calls is shown in the following example:

```
PROCEDURE DoSomething(IntValue: integer;   {other parameters});
   {documentation and declarations}
   BEGIN
      readln(IntValue);
      {other statements}
   END;
```

If the variable `IntValue` is required as a local variable to the procedure `DoSomething`, the code will "seem correct." It is, nonetheless, very misleading because `IntValue` is in the parameter list. A call by value, remember, sets up a local variable whose value is initialized by an expression external to the block. The value should therefore be used before it is changed. When coded properly, the procedure's statement should first make a reference to this initial value before the value is changed. In our example, the value passed into `IntValue` is not even used, for a new value is immediately read into `IntValue`. It would be equally misleading to

Unused variable parameters

write an assignment to `IntValue` before the value passed in is referenced.
You can likewise write misleading code like the following:

```
PROCEDURE MisuseVar({other parameters};   VAR AnInt: integer);
   BEGIN   {assign and use AnInt locally}      END;
{*
                                                                    *}
BEGIN    {main sequence}
   {other statements}
   MisuseVar( {other parameters}, AnInt)
END.
```

This code is equally misleading, but for a different reason. The computer returns a value to the global variable `AnInt`, but then never uses it, for the program ends. Surely, this action makes no sense. For the present (we will qualify this requirement later), you should use the call by variable mechanism on a variable only if the value returned is used. When a value is returned to a variable, it implies a postcondition of the procedure's action. This postcondition must represent a useful precondition for the next statement or sequence of statements in the program.

Note that is equally absurd to read in a value to `AnInt` directly after the call to `MisuseVar`. It is also wrong to assign a new value to `AnInt` as the first action after the call to `MisuseVar` if the value returned does not make up part of the assignment expression. In both cases, the value returned contributes nothing further to the logic of the program because it is never used.

PROGRAM DESIGN RULE 4.2

Do not use the call-by-value mechanism on a variable if the value passed in is not referenced at least once before the variable takes on a new value.

PROGRAM DESIGN RULE 4.3

Do not use the call-by-variable mechanism if the value returned to the variable is not used at some point in the rest of the program.

Two design errors and their causes

If you follow Program Design Rules 4.2 and 4.3, you can clean up any procedures you code whose parameter lists do not represent a correct interface. Correct application of procedural abstraction and parameter passing is difficult to master, but it can be done with practice. The key to writing a good procedure starts with writing a good interface. There is one fundamental cause behind writing a bad interface—you are focusing on the actions of the procedure before you have dealt with writing the complete header. Ideally, the header is written first and then the actions of the procedure are developed. At first, it is a difficult practice to follow, but you should try to *write the procedure's header before you have thought about the design of the procedure's statements.*

You can say you will do this in your mind, but it is not so easy to do in practice. Yet, if you are aware of the causes that lead to writing parameter lists that confuse, you can guard against the effects. The only way you can achieve the desirable goal of writing clean interfaces is through continued practice. In the meantime, you can apply the two design rules to clean up the code for any procedures you may have written improperly.

PROGRAM DESIGN RULE 4.4

Never reference a variable identifier that does not have local meaning.

Side effects

Perhaps the worst design error of all is a procedure with side effects. A side effect occurs when a reference is made to a global variable identifier inside a procedure's statement. The interface between the procedure and the rest of the program is effectively lost with this kind of code. Data flow is lost, and the program is virtually unreadable.

Never write code with side effects. Even if a procedure is used to return values to only global variables, they should be changed by way of their aliases in a parameter list. When you follow Program Design Rule 4.4, you will make references only to those variables whose identifiers are found either in the parameter list or in the list of local declarations. In other words, you will not write code that has side effects.

An example of bad variable usage

Example 4.2 illustrates bad coding in the extreme. Two major design errors are evident in the source code of AllWrong. In the first place, the meaning and purpose of the formal parameter AInt is completely destroyed by the declaration of the local variable AInt. The local declaration takes precedence over the identifier in the formal parameter list, so that when BadlyUsed is exited, the value displayed for AInt by the final statement in the main block is 2. As far as the program is concerned, AInt did not exist as a formal parameter.

You may be lucky enough to have a compiler that issues a warning or even an error message when two distinct variables belonging to the same block are ambiguously referenced by the same identifier. Other compilers will not give you a warning or an error message, because the two reference mechanisms differ. In this case, the machine will choose which identifier takes precedence. The one that is the "most local" takes precedence, so in this example AInt is seen as a local variable of the procedure BadlyUsed.

The second error is the side effect on the global variable BInt. The procedure contains two assignments to global BInt (locally referenced as CInt), one using the formal parameter name CInt, the other using the global name BInt. The statement causing a problem is the one that references the global identifier BInt instead of its local alias. This statement effectively changes the value of "the local" CInt variable as well as that of "the global" BInt variable. Because they are still referencing the same variable, the value returned by the block's action to BInt via the aliasing mechanism of CInt will be 10 not 5.

Example 4.2

```
PROGRAM AllWrong(output);     {BAD CODE!!!}
  {A driver program illustrating the different ways variables can be
  misused in a procedure call.}
  VAR
    AInt, BInt: integer;   {for illustration}
  {*                                                      *}
  PROCEDURE BadlyUsed(VAR AInt, CInt: integer);
    {Destroys the global meaning of AInt by declaring a local variable
    with the same name; two assignments are made to global BInt, the
    first assignment is a side effect}
    VAR
      AInt: integer;     {formal parameter's purpose is destroyed!}
    BEGIN
      CInt:= CInt + 1;
      BInt:= 2 * CInt;   {side effect!  global reference to BInt}
      AInt:= CInt + 1    {this value is not passed out to global AInt}
    END;
  {*                                                      *}
  BEGIN
    AInt:= 2;
    BInt:= 4;
    BadlyUsed(AInt,BInt);
    writeln(AInt:5,BInt:5)
  END.
```

You can confirm that you have planned and written your procedure well if the block you wrote follows Program Design Rule 4.4. Before you go "on line" with a program, you should check each procedure to see that all references to variable identifiers are either references to a formal parameter or to a local variable. When you plan your procedures well and use procedural abstraction properly, this check should be a mere formality. Side effects will creep in only if you rush off to write your program prematurely without careful planning and checking of the source code.

Procedure Documentation

All procedures are written with a purpose in mind. This purpose is reflected in the parameter list. The value given to each variable in the parameter list is used to fulfill the procedure's purpose. A parameter called by value represents a precondition, whereas one called by variable represents a postcondition. The value passed into a VAR parameter might also represent a precondition, if the variable is an input/output parameter.

PROGRAM DESIGN RULE 4.5

Document each procedure such that it describes the meaning and purpose of each formal parameter.

When a procedure is well-documented, at the very least the meaning given to each value passed into the procedure or returned by the procedure is explained. If you mention each formal parameter in the list by name, describing its purpose as part of the procedure's documentation, you will have followed the design rule.

We gave you a formal way to document each variable in the header that we used in the case studies. You can refer back to the code of the case studies to refresh your memory. Sometimes our documentation for the procedures will be less formal, but we will still adhere to the design rule, regardless.

EXERCISES

Test Your Understanding

1. What is the primary reason a programmer might write a bad header?

2. Define the term "side effect." Explain why it is harmful.

Practice Your Analysis Skills

3. Given that AInt and BInt are integer variables and CRe and DRe are real variables, correct any *syntax* errors in the actual and formal parameter lists for the following:

   (a) header: PROCEDURE DisplayEm(AInt,BInt: integer; CRe: real);
       call: DisplayEm(AInt:5,BInt:10,CRe);
   (b) header: PROCEDURE ChangeEm(VAR AInt,DRe);
       call: ChangeEm(AInt,DRe);

(c) header: PROCEDURE UseSomeChangeOthers(Int: integer; VAR Re: real);

call: UseSomeChangeOthers(5*AInt - BInt, CRe);

(d) header: PROCEDURE UseEm(VAR AInt,BInt: integer; VAR CRe,DRe: real);

call: UseEm(5*AInt,BInt + 1,CRe/DRe,AInt + BInt - CRe);

(e) header: PROCEDURE AddTwo(AInt: integer; VAR BInt: integer);

call: AddTwo(12, AInt);

(f) header: PROCEDURE ChangeAll(VAR AInt, BInt, CRe, DRe);

call: ChangeAll(AInt,BInt,CRe,DRe);

Note that some of the examples may be correct.

4. Correct any logical or syntax errors in the headers for each of the following procedures:

   (a) DoIt's purpose: to use value of BInt and change value of AInt.

   header: PROCEDURE DoIt(VAR AInt, BInt: integer);

   (b) ReturnEm's purpose; to return values to all formal parameters.

   header: PROCEDURE ReturnEm(VAR AInt: integer; BRe: real; Ch: char);

   (c) UseEm's purpose: to use the values of Int1 and Int2 such that they return a value to Ch1.

   header: PROCEDURE UseEm(VAR Ch1:char;VAR Int1:integer; Int2: integer);

5. The following procedure contains variables that are either (1) used properly, (2) have ambiguous references, (3) serve no purpose (i.e., are never used), (4) are improperly called (value instead of VAR or vice versa), or (5) represent side effects. Indicate by identifier which variables are which for the following:

```
PROCEDURE BadStuff(QRe: real; VAR PRe: real; VAR  WInt, QInt: integer);
   VAR
      QRe: real;
      AInt,
      BInt: integer;
   BEGIN
      readln(AInt);
      WInt:= QInt + AInt;
      ZRe:= WInt/QInt;
      PRe:= 7.5 + AInt - QRe;
      CInt:= AInt + 2
   END;
```

Use the statements of BadStuff as a guide to indicate which variable should serve which purpose. The variables you should characterize are identified as PRe, WInt, QInt, QRe, AInt, BInt, ZRe, and CInt.

Sharpen Your Implementation Skills

6. Given the two integer variables AInt and BInt and the two real variables CRe and DRe, write the procedure call and header for the procedure DoIt when the procedure should

   (a) change the values of all four variables

   (b) use the value taken on by AInt and change the values of CRe and DRe

   (c) use the value of the expression AInt+BInt and set an initial value to DRe

(d) change the value of AInt, use the value taken on by BInt, change the value of CRe, and use the value taken on by DRe.

(e) use the values of AInt, BInt, and CRe to assign a value to DRe

REVIEW AND EXERCISES

Every large program uses subroutines that are planned and designed top–down. The design process starts with the *main block,* which calls some subprograms, known as *procedures.* Each procedure call has a *parameter list* that contains *expressions* and *variables.* The values given to these expressions and variables represent a program state that can be termed as required *preconditions* for the procedure call to work. The values returned to the variable parameters represent the *postconditions* returned by the procedure call.

A given procedure call is written such that the *preconditions* are logically correct and the *postconditions* are assumed correct. The details of the procedure are then coded later as a *procedure declaration.* This process of postponing the working out of all details on a given procedure is known as the technique of *procedural abstraction.* When this technique is used properly, any large program can be planned as a program consisting of many independent modules. These modules are interfaced using *formal parameter lists* in such a way that data flow is easy to plan and follow.

When a procedure is called, the computer *manages memory* in this fashion: A parameter called *by value* has the computer initialize the value of the formal parameter variable to the value of the corresponding *actual parameter expression.* When a parameter is called *by variable,* the computer sets up the formal parameter as an identifier *alias* to the *actual parameter variable.* If any *local variables* are declared, the computer sets them up as memory locations, but it does not set initial values to them. The machine then carries out all the actions of the procedure as specified by the statements between the reserved words BEGIN and END. After it has executed the sequence, it destroys all local variables and aliases. Only those values representing calls by variable are returned to the actual parameter variables of the block that called the procedure.

The interface mechanism of parameter lists allows you to use *stubs* and *drivers* to develop and test any given program. A stub is coded as a procedure whose header is complete but whose statement is not completed. It can still interface with the rest of the program, even though its statement is incomplete. You can use stubs effectively to lay out your code in such a way that the details of each abstracted procedure are empty statements that must be filled in. You can likewise use stubs to simulate some postcondition(s) returned by a procedure call.

A *driver,* usually coded as a procedure with only local variables, is a sequence of statements used to test any given procedure. Its pseudocode is easily described: enter any necessary values to fulfill the procedure's preconditions. Call the procedure using these values. Display the postcondition results returned by the procedure call.

If a procedure is written with a parameter list that does not interface well with the rest of the program, the program will be hard to design, read (for another programmer), and maintain. Perhaps the worst code a person can write is a procedure with a *side effect,* a reference to a global variable rather than to its formal parameter alias. Although it is difficult for a beginner to learn good interfacing, there are some checks he or he can make to ensure that good interfacing is carried out in the program.

EXERCISES

Short Answers

1. The parameter list belonging to the statement that is a procedure call is known as the _____ _____ _____ .

2. The parameter list belonging to a procedure's declaration is known as the _____ _____ _____ .

3. Which should be written first, a procedure's header or the details of its statement? Explain.

4. Suppose you have written the procedure call

$$DoIt(AInt + 7, ARe/3);$$

   What can you say about the types and mechanisms that make up the formal parameter list?

5. Is it possible to call the same procedure with different actual parameters? If you can, when would you want to write such a set of calls?

6. Is it possible for a program to run properly if there are side effects? Why are they considered harmful?

7. Under what condition(s) can a call to a procedure be made from within a given procedure?

8. Under what condition(s) is it impossible for the main block to call a declared procedure?

9. Suppose the variables AInt and BInt are of type integer. Given the procedure call coded as DoSomething(AInt+BInt), which of the following will be valid headers?
   (a) PROCEDURE DoSomething(VAR AInt, BInt: integer);
   (b) PROCEDURE DoSomething(AnInt: integer);
   (c) PROCEDURE DoSomething(RealNo: real);
   (d) PROCEDURE DoSomething(VAR AnInt: integer);

10. Write the stub for the procedure, given that its data flow picture is as follows:

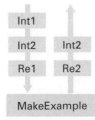

(Note: `Int1` and `Int2` are of type `integer`; `Re1` and `Re2` are of type `real`.)

11. Write the driver sequence for the procedure of Exercise 10. You need not write prompts for the sequence.

12. True or false? The keyword VAR should be found only once in the formal parameter list.

13. A _____ variable in a procedure should be initialized, used, and discarded over the scope of the given procedure's action sequence.

14. A variable called by _____ should return a value to its actual parameter _____ .

15. A variable called by _____ in actuality represents a _____ variable whose value is initialized by the actual parameter expression.

16. True or false? Once the statements of a procedure are completed, all variables that have local meaning to the block are destroyed.

17. True or false? Once the statements of a procedure are completed, all effects of the sequence are gone and forgotten.

Easy Projects   18. Write a procedure whose actions sequence satisfies the description

> *keyin Int1, Int2, Int3*
> *display explanatory string and sum of the three integers*
> *display explanatory string and the product of the three integers*

If the procedure is called, a typical interaction would look like

```
Input three integers:  35  72  50
The sum of the three integers is 157.
The product of the three integers is 1.260000E+05.
```

No data flow is to be returned by this procedure. Once you have written the procedure, write and run a program that calls it a total of three times. Do not declare any global variables in the program; the procedure simply carries out the sequence on three different sets of input data.

19. Write the procedure Savant, as called by

```
Savant(Int1, Int2);
```

The sequence of actions carried out by the procedure results in the display of the five calculated values of the sum, difference, product, `integer` quotient, and `integer` remainder of the two `integer` parameters. Write a main program that is a driver for this procedure. (*Note:* Postcall display is not required for this driver. Why not?)

20. Our party animal Charles C. Charles is at it again. This time, however, rather than having just one guest to greet, he has five of them. Write a program whose main block can be described by

call GreetAGuest five times

where GreetAGuest is a sequence of statements in which Charles introduces himself, requests the guest's name, and then greets the guest by name. (*Hint:* No data flow is necessary here. Why not?)

21. Write a main block program whose sequence is described by

    GetInfo(Name, Age, Height, Weight)
    ShowInfo(Name, Age, Height, Weight)

    The procedure `GetInfo` returns values representing the name, age, height, and weight of a person. Let the name have a maximum of 40 characters in it. Part of the interaction might look like

    ```
    Name:   Phineas T. Barnum
    Age:  52....
    ```

    The procedure `ShowInfo` displays the four values returned by `GetInfo`. The first two lines of display might look like

    ```
    The name is Phineas T. Barnum.
    The age is 52....
    ```

22. The velocity of light is 3×10^8 meters per second. Write a program that solicits a time (in seconds) from the user and displays the distance traveled by light in that amount of time. The program should first display a set of instructions, indicating what is being done and what the user must do. It will then calculate a distance according to the user's input value for time. A typical run would look like

    ```
    This program calculates the distance traveled by light
    for a given time.  If you input the time in seconds, the
    distance traveled in meters will be displayed.

    Enter time:  10.5
    Distance traveled:  3.15000E+09
    ```

    where the main block can be described by

    ShowInstructions
    ShowADistance

    Note that there is no data flow in this program.

23. Write a procedure `FindDAndR` where the computer returns the distance and rate traveled given the initial and final readings on an odometer and the number of hours (expressed as a real number) on the road. A procedure call looks like `FindDAndR(Initial, Final, Hours, Distance, Rate);`, where the values given to the two real variables `Initial` and `Final` represent the two odometer readings. Write the procedure in the context of a small program whose main block sequence is written as a driver for the procedure.

Medium Projects

24. Write a program to make change for a certain number of pence in the old monetary British system. With this system, we have

$$5 \text{ pence} = 1 \text{ shilling}$$

$$1 \text{ crown} = 5 \text{ shillings}$$

The computer should request an amount in pence and express the change in crowns, shillings, and pence. Use the strategies given in the case study.

25. Write a program whose run "sings" a verse of "OldMcDonald Had A Farm." The main block of the program is described by

get animal name and call
display a blank line
sing verse using animal name and call

where at least three procedures need to be written. A typical run of the program is as follows:

```
Enter name:  duck
Enter call:  quack

Old McDonald had a farm.  Eeyi!  Eeyi!  O!
And on this farm he had a duck.  Eeyi!  Eeyi!  O!
With a quack quack here and a quack quack there!
Here a quack, there a quack, everywhere a quack quack!
Old McDonald had a farm.  Eeyi!  Eeyi!  O!
```

Write the program so that the first and last lines of display for the song are executed by a call to the procedure ShowChorus.

26. Write a program where the computer plays a game called "cross-country" that finds the total miles driven and the rate in mph (miles per hour) for three drivers after a given day's cross-country run. A typical machine–user interaction might look like

```
Starting odometer for driver #1:  64381
Finishing odometer for driver #1: 65232
Hours on road for driver #1:  13
Minutes on road for driver #1: 30
-------------------------------------------
Starting odometer for driver #2:  54078
......
-------------------------------------------
Starting odometer for driver #3:  78321
......
XXXXXXXXXXXXXXXXXXXXXXXXXXXXXXXXXXXXXXXXXXXXXX
Driver #1 drove 851 miles in 13.50 hours.  His rate was 63.0 mph.
Driver #2 drove 762 miles in 12.08 hours.  His rate was 63.1 mph.
Driver #3 drove 977 miles in 16.58 hours.  His rate was 58.93 mph.
```

The program requires only six main-block variables, Dist1, Time1, Dist2, Time2,

Dist3, and Time3, to represent the distance and times for the three drivers. (*Hint:* Write a procedure GetDistanceAndTime that returns one of the three distances and times. This procedure should have local variables. Three calls to a second procedure ShowResults will produce the final three lines of display.)

Difficult Projects

27. Professor Teachem wants you to write a program where the computer prints out a single-page answer sheet, according to a given professor's instructions for display. It is assumed that the professor will want to give each question a name string such as "Question #1", "Question #2," and "Question #3." He or she will then have require three subparts to each question, whose first subpart is specified by a character. The other two subparts are the successor values starting from the first character. The main block sequence can be described by

> *ShowFirstInstructions*
> *GetQHeader(Ques1)*
> *GetQHeader(Ques2)*
> *GetQHeader(Ques3)*
> *GetSubQChar(FirstCh)*
> *ShowSecondInstructions*
> *readln   {interrupt for user to set up printer}*
> *PrintSheet(Ques1,Ques2,Ques3,FirstCh)*

where a typical user–machine interraction might look like

```
First question's display:   Part I
Second question's display:   Part II
Third question's display:   Part III
Sub questions start with:    a
PREPARE MACHINE FOR COPY,  THEN HIT RETURN

NAME

SOC SEC NO

Part I
 a)



 b)



 c)

---------------------------------------------------------------
Part II

 a)    . . . . . . . . .
```

28. The Law of Sines is stated as

$$(a/\sin A) = (b/\sin B) = (c/\sin C)$$

where a, b, and c are the sides of the triangle, and A, B, and C are the angles opposite the respective (lowercase) sides. This particular formula is useful for solving triangles in which two angles and the side included between the angles is known (e.g., sides a and b are known and angle C is known). Write a program where the computer requests two angles and the included side and then solves for the other two sides and the area of the triangle. One procedure should be written for user input, a second for the calculations, and

```
Input first angle:     48.87
Input second angle:    55.32
Input common side:     23.63
First angle's side =   20.02
Second angle's side =  18.36
Triangle's area =      178.21
```

Run the program with the given set of values and a set of values of your own choosing. (*Hint:* Recall that the sum of the angles of a triangle is equal to 180 degrees.)

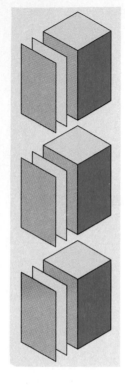

C H A P T E R 5

DECISION-MAKING

OBJECTIVES

After you have read and studied the material of this chapter, you should be able to

- **Write a correct boolean expression using the relational operators**

- **Desk trace a program that uses decision statements**

- **Plan and write correct code using the reserved words** IF, THEN, **and** ELSE

- **Plan and write correct code using the reserved words** CASE **and** OF

- **Apply assertion testing to a program that uses decision statements**

- **Recognize and apply proven algorithms that require decision statements**

- **Determine values for test data such that the program is exhaustively tested**

SUPPOSE YOU ARE WRITING A PROGRAM that simulates the activity at a bank. A user is asked whether the transaction is a deposit or a withdrawal and the amount of the transaction. If the transaction is a withdrawal, its amount is subtracted from the old balance to get a new value for the balance. With a deposit, the new balance is found by adding the amount of the transaction to the old balance. In either case, a decision must first be made to determine whether the new balance is found using addition or subtraction. A decision statement is therefore required.

In this chapter, you will learn how to instruct the computer to execute a statement only if some precondition, coded as an expression, is met. This sort of instruction is the main characteristic of a decision statement. You will also learn how to apply assertion testing on a program that contains decision statements. Finally, you will pick up skills in choosing values for on-line testing and desk-tracing that are particularly useful with algorithms that contain decision statements.

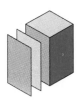

5.1   The IF..THEN..ELSE Statement

In this section, you will first learn how to use the reserved words IF, THEN, and ELSE to implement a decision statement. Then you will see some examples where we develop source code that requires these reserved words for a solution.

IF..THEN..ELSE Syntax and Semantics

A decision statement that uses the reserved words IF, THEN, and/or ELSE requires a *boolean expression* as part of its code. We first show you how to code a boolean expression. Then you will see how to use a boolean expression to plan and code a decision statement.

> **Boolean expression:** expression dependent upon the program state that is written as a condition whose value is either *true* or *false*.

Simple boolean expressions

A simple boolean expression represents a comparison between two expressions of the same type. In Pascal we can write a simple boolean expression to compare two numeric values, two character values, and two string values. The syntax diagram for a simple boolean expression is shown in Figure 5.1. A *relational operator,* as shown in the syntax diagram, is one of the six special symbols given in Table 5.1.

Sample expressions

Suppose, the variables XInt, YInt, Ch1, Ch2, and AString have taken on the values suggested by Figure 5.2. Table 5.2 shows some examples of coded boolean expressions that use the values of Figure 5.2. Note that a boolean expression

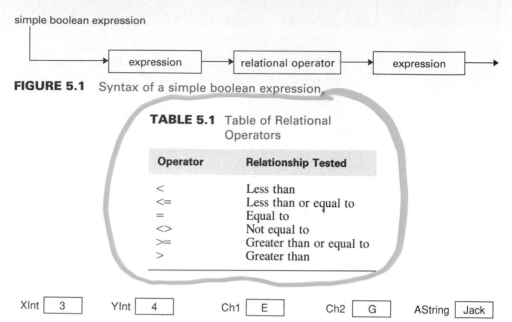

simple boolean expression

expression → relational operator → expression →

FIGURE 5.1 Syntax of a simple boolean expression.

TABLE 5.1 Table of Relational Operators

Operator	Relationship Tested
<	Less than
<=	Less than or equal to
=	Equal to
<>	Not equal to
>=	Greater than or equal to
>	Greater than

XInt 3   YInt 4   Ch1 E   Ch2 G   AString Jack

FIGURE 5.2 Some values assigned to variables.

TABLE 5.2 Showing Examples of Boolean Expressions

Expression	Meaning In Words	Boolean Value
XInt < YInt	3 is less than 4	true
YInt - 3 <= XInt	1 is less than or equal to 3	true
Ch1 = Ch2	'E' is equal to 'G'	false
Ch1 <> Ch2	'E' is not equal to 'G'	true
AString > 'Joe'	'Jack' is greater than 'Joe'	false
succ(Ch1) >= pred (Ch2)	'F' is greater than or equal to 'F'	true

can only take on a value if both expressions that make up the boolean expression have taken on values.

Two examples of decision statements

The syntax diagram for an IF..THEN..ELSE statement is shown in Figure 5.3. When an IF..THEN..ELSE statement is executed, the flow of control depends upon the value of the boolean expression. The statements labelled as {1} and {2} are two examples of decision statements. Note that a value for the integer variable Score is assumed as a precondition.

```
{1} IF Score >= 60 THEN
       writeln('passed')
    ELSE
       writeln('failed');

{2} IF Score >= 60 THEN
       writeln('passed');
```

IF..THEN..ELSE statement

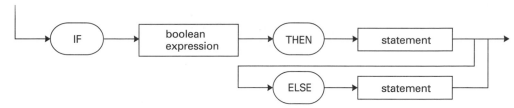

FIGURE 5.3 Syntax of the IF..THEN..ELSE statement.

Each statement's execution

When the computer executes statement {1}, it will display "passed" if the value of Score is greater than or equal to 60. Otherwise, it will display "failed." When the machine executes statement {2}, it displays the character string "passed" if the value of Score is greater than or equal to 60. Otherwise, it does nothing.

Control paths

A decision statement sets up more than one *control path* for the machine to take. When the computer executes an IF..THEN..ELSE statement, there are one of two possible control paths to be taken. One path is to execute the statement(s) associated with the reserved word THEN. The other path is to execute the statement(s) associated with the reserved word ELSE. When the machine carries out an IF..THEN statement, there are also two control paths it can take. One path is to execute the statement associated with the reserved word THEN. The other path is to not execute this statement.

Control path: the sequence, often dependent upon the evaluation of one or more boolean expressions, in which the computer carries out the statements in the source code of a program.

Flowcharts

Figure 5.4 (a) and (b), called *flowcharts*, respectively depict the flow of control for statements {1} and {2}. The figures imply that some previous action assigned a value to Score, thus setting up the necessary precondition for the decision to be carried out.

Pseudocode using IF, THEN, *and* ELSE

A pseudocode description of the IF..THEN..ELSE statement is given as

> {A} *IF the evaluated condition is true THEN*
> *first action*
> *ELSE*
> *alternate action*

We can likewise describe an IF..THEN statement (when the reserved word ELSE is not used) with the pseudocode

> {B} *IF the evaluated condition is true THEN*
> *action*

Let us see how you can use these descriptions to draft and write the source code for a Pascal-compilable IF..THEN..ELSE statement or a Pascal-compilable IF..THEN statement.

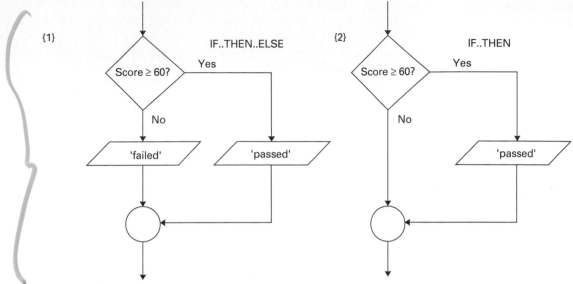

FIGURE 5.4 Flowcharts for fragments (1) and (2).

The words IF, THEN and ELSE used in pseudocode are the same as the corresponding reserved words used in Pascal. In Pascal, the reserved words IF and THEN enclose a boolean expression. In pseudocode, these words enclose a description of a boolean expression. In source code, a statement (often compound) is placed between the reserved words THEN and ELSE. In pseudocode, a description of the statement (perhaps given as a sequence of statements) is placed between these two words. In source code, a second statement follows the reserved`word ELSE. In pseudocode, a description of the statement follows the word ELSE. Finally, in pseudocode, the description of the statement(s) associated with the words THEN and ELSE are always indented.

Assertions for each decision statement

Let us explain how the computer carries out each of the two decision statements we have just described:

If the boolean expression for an IF..THEN..ELSE statement (as described by {A}) is true, the first action, the one associated with the word THEN, is executed. If, instead, the boolean expression evaluates to false, the alternate action, the one associated with the word ELSE, is executed. In either case, exactly one of two actions will always be executed. The action to be executed depends upon the precondition as expressed by the value of the boolean expression. When the computer carries out an IF..THEN..ELSE statement, a postcondition we can always state is that the computer has executed one of the two actions. The action taken depends upon the precondition implied by the value of the boolean expression.

If the boolean expression of an IF..THEN statement (as described by {B}) is true, the machine returns a new postcondition(s) by executing the associated action. If the condition is false, the computer does not execute the associated action, thereby making no change in the program state. The postcondition for an IF..THEN statement, given the precondition that the boolean expression was false, will thus be identical to the precondition just before the decision statement was executed.

The syntax diagram of Figure 5.3 shows that only one statement is associated with the reserved words THEN and ELSE. This one statement, however, can be written as a compound statement, delimited by the reserved words BEGIN and END. Example 5.1 is an illustration of an IF..THEN..ELSE statement where one of two compound statements is executed.

Regardless of the value read into the string variable Name, two lines of display will occur when the computer carries out the coded fragment. If 'Roy G. Biv' is read in, a joyous greeting is given to him. Otherwise, the search for Roy G. Biv continues.

Example 5.1

```
write('May I know your good name? ');
readln(Name);
IF Name = 'Roy G. Biv' THEN
  BEGIN
    writeln('Glad to finally meet you, Roy G. Biv! ');
    writeln('People tell me that you''re quite a bright fellow.')
  END
ELSE
  BEGIN
    writeln('Glad to meet you, ',Name,'.');
    writeln('But tell me, do you know if Roy G. Biv is here?')
  END;
```

PROGRAM DESIGN RULE 5.1

Never precede the reserved word ELSE with a semicolon.

ELSE *Syntax*

You should note that if the reserved word ELSE is preceded by a semicolon, the machine will issue a syntax error message. You can refer back to Figure 5.3 to see why. The figure shows that when the reserved word ELSE is used, two statements are required. The first of these two statements is placed between the reserved words THEN and ELSE. This statement, be it simple or compound, is never terminated by a semicolon.

*Source code
layout*

As you already know, the computer skips over blank lines, blank spaces, and comments in source code. Even though a program with minimum white space will compile, link, and run, a programmer would appreciate a layout of the source program that he or she can read. It is particularly important that source code using decision statements be laid out for easy reading. You should therefore adopt a convention to lay out the source code of decision statements and follow this convention over the entire text of the source program.

We use the following conventions in laying out source code that uses the reserved words IF, THEN and ELSE:

1. The reserved words IF and THEN are placed on the same line.
2. The reserved word ELSE is placed under the associated reserved word IF.
3. The reserved word ELSE, with one important exception, is placed on a line by itself.
4. The statement associated with the reserved word THEN is indented.
5. The statement associated with the reserved word ELSE is indented.
6. The reserved words BEGIN and END associated with a compound statement are placed on lines by themselves.
7. The body of a compound statement is indented with respect to the delimiting reserved words BEGIN and END.

Developing Some Decision Statements

Now that you know the syntax and semantics of Pascal statements that use the reserved words IF, THEN, and ELSE, we are going to solve a few simple coding problems that require these reserved words. Note how we apply the technique of procedural abstraction in each of the examples.

Example Problem 5.1

The problem statement

Let us write a procedure that lets a user choose whether he or she wants to see a display of instructions or not. We will name the procedure ShowOrNot. When the computer is executing the procedure, one of the following two interactions is expected:

```
Do you want to see the instructions?   (Y/N)   Y
    You are to ...{rest of instructions are shown}

Do you want to see the instructions?   (Y/N)   N
{rest of program, skipping display of instructions}
```

The solution

The procedure ShowOrNot will have no parameters, for we can use a local variable to store the reply to the question. The pseudocode to describe the statement part of the procedure is therefore given as

> *keyin Reply*
> *IF Reply = 'Y' THEN*
> *ShowInstructions*

Note that the computer does not call ShowInstructions if any char value other than 'Y' is read in. The code for the solution, with a stub for the procedure ShowInstructions, is given as follows:

```
{*                                                                        *}
PROCEDURE ShowInstructions;
  BEGIN    {sequence of writeln statements}  END;
{+                                                                        +}
PROCEDURE ShowOrNot;
  {Shows instructions if user indicates he or she wants them shown}
  VAR
    Reply: char;    {user's reply to display question}
  BEGIN
    write('Do you want to see the instructions?  (Y/N)  ');
    readln(Reply);
    IF Reply = 'Y' THEN
      ShowInstructions
  END;
{*                                                                        *} ◆
```

Completing a problem   In Case Study 4.2, we did not account for the difference between a single coin and a plural number of coins. Now we will modify the procedure ShowCoins so that   difference between a single and plural number of any given coin is handled in the display. The modification(s) we want to implement are suggested by the code given as Example 5.2.

Example 5.2

```
{*                                                                        *}
PROCEDURE ShowPennies (Ps: integer);
  {in : Ps -- count of pennies
  out: displays value of Ps along with proper string expression}
  BEGIN    END;
{+                  the                                                    +}
PROCEDURE ShowACoin(CoinName: StringType; Coins: integer);
  {in: CoinName -- name of coin;  Coins -- number of the given coin
  out: display indicating singular or plural text}
  BEGIN    END;
{+                                                                        +}
PROCEDURE ShowCoins(Qs, Ds, Ns, Ps: integer);
  BEGIN
    write('Your change is ');
    ShowACoin('quarter', Qs);
    ShowACoin('dime', Ds);
    ShowACoin('nickel', Ns);
    write('and ');
    ShowPennies(Ps);
    writeln(' . ')
  END;
{*                                                                        *}
```

Example Problem 5.2

The problem statement

Let us modify the procedure ShowCoins of the program ChangeMaker using the code suggested by Example 5.2. We want to complete the code for the procedures ShowACoin and ShowPennies. A call to ShowACoin results in a display whose appearance depends upon the actual parameter values. The procedure ShowPennies requires a different abstraction because the plural of "penny" is "pennies" and not "pennys." We can form the plural for the other representative string values by simply displaying an "s" when appropriate.

If we have 81 cents worth of change, for example, the display is

```
Your change is 3 quarters, 0 dimes, 1 nickel, and 1 penny.
```

The solutions

In the case of ShowACoin, we can describe the solution by

> *display Coins, CoinName*
> *IF Coins< > 1 THEN*
>   *display 's, '*   *{display an 's' to indicate plural form}*
> *ELSE*
>   *display ', '*   *{singular form; therefore no 's' is displayed }*

This description codes to the procedure as given.

```
PROCEDURE ShowACoin(CoinName: StringType; Coins: integer);
  {documentation}
  BEGIN
    write(Coins:1,' ',CoinName);
    IF Coins <> 1 THEN
      write('s, ')
    ELSE
      write(', ')
  END;
```

The solution for the source code of ShowPennies is analogously derived.

```
PROCEDURE ShowPennies(Ps: integer);
  {documentation}
  BEGIN
    write(Ps:1,' ');
    IF Ps <> 1 THEN
      write('pennies')
    ELSE
      write('penny')
  END; ◆
```

EXERCISES

Test Your Understanding

1. True or false? The value of a boolean expression depends upon the program state.

2. Describe the relationship between preconditions and postconditions when the computer executes an IF..THEN statement.

3. Repeat Exercise 2, but for an IF..THEN..ELSE statement.

Practice Your Analysis Skills

4. Suppose some variables have taken on the following values:

Int1	$\longleftrightarrow$ 4	Name1	$\longleftrightarrow$ 'George'	Ch1	$\longleftrightarrow$ 'p'
Int2	$\longleftrightarrow$ 7	Name2	$\longleftrightarrow$ 'Bill'	Ch2	$\longleftrightarrow$ 'q'

   How will the computer evaluate the following boolean expressions? (Note: one or two of them may be illegal Pascal.):
   (a) `Name1 < Name2`
   (b) `Int1 + 5 = Int2 + 2`
   (c) `Ch2 + 1 = Ch2`
   (d) `succ(Ch1) >= Ch2`
   (e) `Int2 − Int1 > ord(Ch2) − ord(Ch1)`

5. Consider the statement

   ```
   IF IntA > IntC THEN
      IntA:= IntC
   ELSE
      IntC:= IntA;
   ```

   What are the values assigned to IntA and IntC after its execution if originally?
   (a) IntA $\longleftrightarrow$ 2 and IntC $\longleftrightarrow$ 3
   (b) IntA $\longleftrightarrow$ 7 and IntC $\longleftrightarrow$ 3

Sharpen Your Implementation Skills

6. Write Pascal statements to perform the following decision actions:
   (a) If the value of Re is positive, add 1 to Count and Re to Sum.
   (b) If the value of DataPoint is greater than the value of Large, assign DataPoint to Large.
   (c) If the value of Count is equal to 10, then display the value of the quotient Sum/Count accurate to two decimal places.
   (d) If the value of Present is greater than the value of Previous, then display the character string "up", if it is equal to Previous, then display the string "unchanged", and if it is less than Previous, then display the string "down".
   (e) If the absolute value of the expression (OldX - NewX) is less than 0.0005, display the message "CONVERGENCE HAS OCCURRED"; otherwise add 1 to the variable IterNo.
   (f) If the value of Re is less than zero, then display the value of the square root of −Re followed by the character 'i'; otherwise simply display the square root of Re.
   (g) If the value of Withdrawl is greater than the value of Balance, then display the character string "OVERDRAWN BY" followed by the expression Withdrawl − Balance; otherwise assign the value of the expression Balance − Withdrawl to the variable Balance.

5.2 Case Study: Sorting Three Numbers in Sequence

We have shown you fragments of code and a few procedures that used decision-making statements to carry out their actions. As yet, you have not seen a complete program that uses decision statements. In this section, we develop a program in which decisions are essential for the solution.

CASE STUDY 5.1

The problem statement

Let us solve the following problem: Write a program that reads in three integer values and outputs them in order from lowest to highest. Two different runs of the program might look like

```
Input three integers:  58  72  33
The correct order is:  33  58  72

Input three integers:  88  54  90
The correct order is:  54  88  90
```

Main block

Given the problem statement and two sample runs, we can readily draft the first pseudocode description of the solution as

> *keyin First, Second, Third*
> *obtain the display order*
> *display First, Second, Third*

The action described by *obtain the display order* abstracts to a procedure call we can code as Rearrange (First, Second, Third). The precondition of this procedure call is that the values given to First, Second, and Third represent the order in which the integers were entered. The postcondition is that the values represent the order of the three integers from lowest to highest.

The pseudocode description leads to the code of the stub program Show-In-Order as given. This program represents a correct solution if the code for Rearrange achieves the assumed postcondition.

```
PROGRAM ShowInOrder(input,output);
  {The values of three input integers are read in, then displayed in
  order from lowest to highest.}
  VAR
    First, Second, Third: integer;    {the three integers}
  {*                                                              *}
PROCEDURE Rearrange(VAR First, Second, Third: integer);
```

```
{in: First, Second, Third -- order of entry
 out: First, Second, Third -- numeric order from lowest to highest}
  BEGIN        END;
{*                                                          *}
BEGIN
  write('Input three integers:  ');
  readln(First, Second, Third);
  Rearrange(First, Second, Third);
  write('The correct order is:  ');
  writeln(First:1,'  ', Second:1,'  ', Third:1)
END.
```

Pseudocode for
`Rearrange`

Now we must draft the source code for the procedure `Rearrange`. Our first pseudocode draft for this procedure, using a sequence of three IF statements, is

> IF *First* > *Second THEN*
> > *exchange the values of First and Second*
> IF *First* > *Third THEN*
> > *exchange the values of First and Third*
> IF *Second* > *Third THEN*
> > *exchange the values of Second and Third*

The exchange of two values for the three different variables can be abstracted as three different calls to the same procedure Exchange. The postcondition returned by this procedure is that the values assigned to the two variable parameters have been exchanged. Using this abstraction, we obtain the following refinement:

> IF *First* > *Second THEN*
> > *Exchange (First, Second)*   {assertion First <= Second}
> IF *First* > *Third THEN*
> > *Exchange (First, Third)*   {assertion: First <= Third}
> IF *Second* > *Third THEN*
> > *Exchange (Second, Third)*   {assertion: Second <= Third}

Assertion testing

This refinement is sufficiently detailed that we can code the procedure Re-arrange. Before we code it, however, let us do some assertion testing. As a start, we have shown the assertion we can make after each IF statement is executed to the right of the corresponding statement. Note in particular what happens if the boolean expression for any of the IF statements evaluates to false. The assertion that follows is the same as the implied precondition of the false boolean expression.

Suppose, for example, it is initially true that the value of First is less than or equal to the value of Second. As a result of this condition, the computer carries out the first IF statement by doing nothing further. It is therefore true that First is less than or equal to Second after the statement is executed because the computer did nothing to change the original condition.

After the second decision statement, we can make the assertion that `First` is less than or equal to `Second`, and also that `First` is less than or equal to `Third`. Hence, the value of `First` represents the lowest of the three values once the second IF statement is completed.

The assertion after the third statement is executed leads to the final assertion: `First` is less than or equal to `Second`, and `Second` is less than or equal to `Third`. This assertion represents the desired program state returned by the action of `Rearrange`. Hence, the description of the proposed code for `Rearrange` is logically correct.

The code for `Rearrange` follows. We now need to work on the code for `Exchange`.

```
{*                                                                    *}
PROCEDURE Exchange(VAR Int1, Int2: integer);
   {in:  Int1, Int2 — two values to be exchanged
   out:  Int1, Int2 --old Int1 is new Int2, old Int2 is new Int1}
   BEGIN END;
{+                                                                    +}
PROCEDURE Rearrange(VAR First, Second, Third: integer);
   {insert documentation here}
   BEGIN
     IF First > Second THEN
       Exchange(First, Second);
     IF First > Third THEN
       Exchange(First, Third);
     IF Second > Third THEN
       Exchange(Second, Third)
   END;
{*                                                                    *}
```

Describing Exchange's statement

In order for Exchange to work properly, the values of `Int1` and `Int2` must be preserved. If the first statement of Exchange assigns `Int2`'s value to `Int1`, the initial value of `Int1` is destroyed. Given this condition, the postcondition for Exchange cannot be realized. Hence, we need a local variable, `Temp`, to first store `Int1`'s value before `Int1` can take on `Int2`'s initial value. Having taken this consideration into account, we can describe the sequence for Exchange by the pseudocode

Temp	$\longleftarrow$	*Int1*	{assertion: Temp is equal to Int1's initial value}
Int1	$\longleftarrow$	*Int2*	{assertion: Int1 is equal to Int2's initial value}
Int2	$\longleftarrow$	*Temp*	{assertion: Int2 is equal to Int1's initial value}

We have shown the associated assertion for each assignment statement as a comment to the right of the pseudocoded statement. The last two assertions combine to give us the final assertion. We state this assertion as, "`Int1` is assigned `Int2`'s initial value and `Int2` is assigned `Int1`'s initial value." This final assertion represents the desired postcondition that Exchange should realize. Hence, our descrip-

tion for the statement part of Exchange, is logically correct. The source code for
the procedure Exchange follows:

```
{*                                                                          *}
PROCEDURE Exchange(VAR Int1, Int2: integer);
   {documentation}
   VAR
      Temp:   integer;      {temporary storage for initial value of Int1}
   BEGIN
      Temp:= Int1;
      Int1:= Int2;
      Int2:= Temp
   END;
{+                                                                          +}
```

The complete program   When you substitute the source code for the procedure Exchange in place of
the stub shown with the procedure Rearrange, the code for Rearrange is completed. You can then take this finished procedure and substitute its code in place of
the partially completed procedure declaration for Rearrange in the program
ShowInOrder. Once, you have done that, you have the complete source code for
the program ShowInOrder.

Structure chart   The structure chart for the program ShowInOrder is shown in Figure 5.5.

◆

FIGURE 5.5   Structure chart for ShowInOrder.

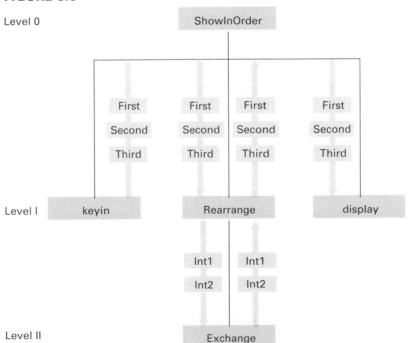

The need to write a sequence that exchanges the values of two variables often arises. Although these variables need not be of type `integer`, they must be of the same type. The required actions to carry out the exchange are the same, however, regardless of the variable type involved. We, therefore, present Algorithm 5.1, an algorithm to exchange the values of two variables:

Algorithm 5.1

{Algorithm to exchange the values of Var1 and Var2:}
Temp ⟵ *Var1*
Var1 ⟵ *Var2*
Var2 ⟵ *Temp*
{end algorithm}

Example 5.3 is the source code for a procedure that exchanges the values of two char variables.

Example 5.3

```
PROCEDURE ExchangeChs(VAR Ch1, Ch2: char);
   {exchanges the values of the char variables Ch1 and Ch2}
   VAR
      Temp: char;
   BEGIN
      Temp:= Ch1;
      Ch1:= Ch2;
      Ch2:= Temp
   END;
```

EXERCISES

**Practice Your
Analysis Skills**

1. Will any exchanges occur if First, Second, and Third are equal?

2. What values are assigned to First, Second, and Third after each statement of Rearrange is executed for each of the following sets of input values?
   (a) 58 72 33   **(b)** 90 85 42   **(c)** 25 32 25

**Sharpen Your
Implementation
Skills**

3. Write a procedure Rearrange that arranges the values of three real variables Re1, Re2, and Re3 so that they are in correct numeric order.

4. Write a procedure StrExchange that exchanges the values of two string variables.

5. Rewrite the procedure Rearrange such that the first action is described by

*IF (Second > Third) THEN
    Exchange(Second, Third);*

The procedure should still return the desired postconditions.

5.3 Nested Decision-Making

A single IF..THEN..ELSE statement will work for a problem that requires, at most, two alternative actions. When you have a problem that implies a choice of more than two actions dependent upon more than one condition, you will need code that requires more than one decision statement.

The case study of the previous section worked out nicely using a sequence of decision statements. Some problems, though, are best solved using an approach where a fixed number of decisions is not predetermined for all possible values. In this section, you will learn how to plan and code a solution to problems of this type.

Example Problem 5.3

The problem statement

Suppose a value has been assigned to the integer variable Age, representing a person's age. Given this value, one of the following messages will be displayed:

1. If the age is under 14, the message "You're too young to work" is displayed.
2. If the age is under 18 but at least 14, the message "You're too young to vote" is displayed.
3. If the age is under 65 but at least 18, the message "You're too young to retire" is displayed.
4. If the age is 65 or over, the message "Enjoy your golden years" is displayed.

Let us write a program fragment to carry out this action.

Drafting a solution

The problem statement implies a choice of more than two control paths dependent upon the value of Age. Hence, we expect our solution to have more than one IF statement. The best way to approach the problem, given the limited tools we have, is to deal with the statement carried out by each IF..THEN..ELSE statement before we code the next one. Using this method of stepwise refinement, we describe the first draft to the solution by

> IF Age < 14 THEN
>   display 'too young to work'
> ELSE
>   display some other message

At this point, we can assert that either an appropriate message is displayed if the Age is under 14, or some other message is displayed. Hence, this description is correct so far.

We can break down the statement described by *display some other message* into a second decision statement that handles the under-18 age bracket:

> *IF Age < 18 THEN*
>   *display 'too young to vote'*
> *ELSE*
>   *display a message about retirement*

This description can be substituted directly after the ELSE word associated with the condition expressed by Age $<$ 14. In order for this path to be taken, the precondition that Age $>$ =14 is true must have been satisfied. After this statement is executed, we can thus assert that either the appropriate message was displayed for all ages under 18 or some other message was displayed.

The display of a retirement message requires yet another decision. We can describe the statement that needs to be carried out, should the computer reach this point in the processing, with the pseudocode

> *IF Age < 65 THEN*
>   *display 'too young to retire'*
> *ELSE*
>   *display 'enjoy golden years'*

This description is placed after the ELSE word associated with the second decision. In order for this statement to be executed, the value of Age must be greater than or equal to 18. The appropriate message for this age value is then displayed.

When we put all the assertions together, we can say that an appropriate message is displayed for all values of Age. Therefore, the proposed fragment, when executed as source code, will result in the correct sequence of actions.

Complete pseudocode and source code

We solved the problem by describing the control paths taken for each decision statement before we went on to specifying the details of each control path. It so happened that some of these paths led to further decisions. When we put all the pseudocode together we get the following complete description to the solution of the problem:

> *IF Age <14 THEN*
>   *display 'too young to work'*
> *ELSE IF Age <18 THEN*
>   *display 'too young to vote'*
> *ELSE IF Age <65 THEN*
>   *display 'too young to retire'*
> *ELSE*
>   *display 'enjoy golden years'*

From the pseudocode description, we obtain the following source code fragment:

```
IF Age < 14 THEN
   writeln('You''re too young to work.')
ELSE IF Age < 18 THEN
```

```
      writeln('You''re too young to vote.')
ELSE IF Age < 65 THEN
      writeln('You''re too young to retire.')
ELSE
      writeln('Enjoy your golden years.');
```

Nested decision algorithms

The control paths for the algorithm we developed are depicted in the flowchart of Figure 5.6. Note how the value of the first condition determines whether the second condition is required for the solution. Likewise, if the second condition is evaluated, it will determine whether the third condition is necessary for the given value of Age. We developed a *nested decision algorithm* and implemented it using nested decision statements to solve the problem. In our example, three IF statements were required for the solution, so the *level of nesting* extended down to a level of 3. ◆

FIGURE 5.6 Flowchart for fragment in Example Program 5.3.

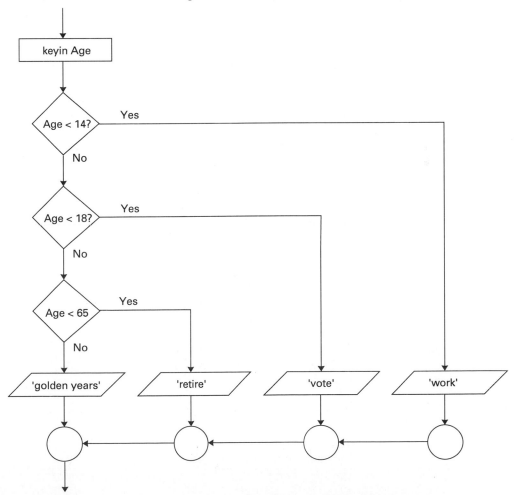

Nested decision algorithm: an algorithm where at least one decision statement is contained by another decision statement.

Level of nesting: as applied to decision algorithms, the maximum number of decision statements that can be carried out in a nested selection algorithm.

The IF-ELSE-IF algorithm

The algorithm we just developed is particularly useful for problems that require one path to be taken as a result of some *ordered* decision process. The decision process is "ordered" because the path taken is the one associated with the first boolean expression that evaluates to true. The values of any subsequent boolean expressions then become irrelevant. If, for example, the value of Age is 17, it is true that Age is both less than 18 and less than 65. However, because the test for less than 18 was applied first, the string "You're too young to vote" rather than the string "You're too young to retire" is displayed.

We call this decision process the *IF-ELSE-IF* algorithm. It has two distinct properties: (1) The order in which the boolean expressions are evaluated is critical, and (2) exactly one of N possible paths is chosen, where the level of nesting is therefore N − 1.

Source code layout of an IF..ELSE..IF statement

We will lay out the source code for an *IF-ELSE-IF* algorithm so that each of the paths taken will appear to be on the same decision level. We do so because *exactly one* path is taken, given an *IF-ELSE-IF* sequence. Even though the level of nesting is N − 1 deep, the statements belonging to one of the N paths will be placed under each other. Moreover, each reserved word ELSE is lined up with the occurrence of the first reserved word IF.

Pseudocode description for IF-ELSE-IF

The *IF-ELSE-IF* algorithm executes the statement associated with the first *true* condition. It executes exactly one of the N prescribed paths. We give you its pseudocode description as Algorithm 5.2.

Algorithm 5.2

{IF-ELSE-IF algorithm where the path taken is determined by the first condition found to be true:}
IF condition 1 THEN
    action 1
ELSE IF condition 2 THEN
    action 2
....
ELSE IF condition M THEN
    action M
....
ELSE IF condition (N − 1) THEN
    action (N − 1)
ELSE
    action N
{end algorithm}

We could have approached Example Problem 5.3 from the other side by first determining whether the value of Age is less than 65. When we take this approach, the first decision statement is described by the pseudocode

> *IF Age < 65 THEN*
>   *display non-golden-year message*
> *ELSE*
>   *display 'enjoy golden years'*

The refinement of *display non-golden-year message* gives us

> *IF Age < 65 THEN*
>   *IF Age < 18 THEN*
>   *display youngster message*
>   *ELSE*
>   *display 'too young to retire'*
> *ELSE*
>   *display 'enjoy golden years'*

The refinement for *display youngster message* leads to the final draft:

> *IF Age < 65 THEN*
>   *IF Age < 18 THEN*
>   *IF Age < 14 THEN*
>   *display 'too young to work'*
>   *ELSE*
>   *display 'too young to vote'*
>   *ELSE*
>   *display 'too young to retire'*
> *ELSE*
>   *display 'enjoy golden years'*

The coded solution to the problem using this approach, is shown as Example 5.4.

Example 5.4

```
IF Age < 65 THEN
  IF Age < 18 THEN
    IF Age < 14 THEN
      writeln('You''re too young to work.')
    ELSE
      writeln('You''re too young to vote.')
  ELSE
    writeln('You''re too young to retire.')
ELSE
  writeln('Enjoy your golden years.');
```

Alternative solutions

The code of Example 5.4 is an equally valid solution to Example Problem 5.3. It also uses nested decisions, but it does not use the *IF-ELSE-IF* algorithm. For this reason, it is perhaps less readable then the first solution. Is there any merit then to this solution? Should we always use the *IF-ELSE-IF* algorithm when appropriate? These are good questions whose answers depend upon other considerations such as readability and efficiency.

Readability vs. efficiency

When two or more decisions are required to solve a problem, many alternate solutions are possible. Let us propose a problem where we can implement a less readable but more efficient sequence of statements as a solution. The second solution will be more efficient than the first one because the machine will make less decisions for some "typical" value when it carries out the second sequence.

CASE STUDY 5.2

The problem statement

Let us write a fragment that according to the value assigned to the variable Score displays one of the following messages:

"unsuccessful and failed" if Score is less than 60
"unsuccessful and passed" if Score is between 60 and 69, inclusive
"successful" if Score is between 70 and 79, inclusive
"successful and very good" if Score is between 80 and 89, inclusive
"successful and distinguished" if Score is above 90

The simplest solution

We can use the *IF-ELSE-IF* algorithm to directly code the sequence which follows. This code represent the most straightforward solution to the problem. It is easy to derive, and the code is easy to read.

```
IF Score < 60 THEN
   writeln('unsuccessful and failed')
ELSE IF Score < 70 THEN
   writeln('unsuccessful and passed')
ELSE IF Score < 80 THEN
   writeln('successful')
ELSE IF Score < 90 THEN
   writeln('successful and very good')
ELSE
   writeln('successful and distinguished');
```

A more efficient, but subtler, solution

Suppose, instead, we want the first decision made around the "midvalue" of 70. Why do so? For starters, we know that every score less than 70 requires the string display "unsuccessful and", and every score greater than 70 results in the string display "successful". Also, our proposed first choice may be closer to some "average" score of 75. Perhaps this approach will give us a solution that is still correct and that also requires less decisions be made.

We can describe the first IF..THEN..ELSE statement by the pseudocode

> IF Score >= 70 THEN
>   display 'successful'
>   further success display
> ELSE
>   display 'unsuccessful and'
>   further unsuccess display

When this statement is executed, we can make the assertion that the computer has either displayed the string "successful" given that the value of Score is greater than or equal to 70, or it has displayed the string "unsuccessful and" given that the value of Score is less than 70. Hence, so far our solution is logically correct.

*The breakdown
of the
"successful"
path*

We can break down the sequence for *further success display* using the pseudocode

> IF Score >= 80 THEN
>   display ' and '
>   further display

As a precondition to this statement's execution, we have that the string "successful" was displayed. If Score was less than 80, there is no further display. Then, the required display for test scores between 70 and 79, inclusive, is correctly done. The fact that the string "and" is displayed for higher test scores is also correct.

The pseudocode for the action *further display* is

> IF Score >= 90 THEN
>   display 'distinguished'
> ELSE
>   display 'very good'

In order for the computer to execute this statement, Score's value must be 80 or greater and the combined string "successful and" must have already been displayed. The remaining strings displayed are correct for scores between 80 and 89 and for scores greater than 90. When we put all the assertions together, we can say that the proposed draft for the statements carried out when Score is greater than or equal to 70 are all correct.

*The
"unsuccess-
ful and" path*

We still need to derive source code for the path taken when Score is less than 70. This *further unsuccess display* sequence can be broken down to another decision that looks like

> IF Score >= 60 THEN
>   display 'passed'
> ELSE
>   display 'failed'

The source code for the solution we just derived is given below. Note that, like the *IF-ELSE-IF* solution, it required that four boolean expressions be evaluated. This solution, however, does not fit the *IF-ELSE-IF* algorithm because there are intervening statements between most of the decision statements. Clearly, it was difficult to derive, and it is also difficult to read. So why even consider it?

```
IF Score >= 70 THEN
  BEGIN                                    {begin 70's or better statement}
    write('successful ');
    IF Score >= 80 THEN
      BEGIN                                {begin 80's or better statement}
        write('and ');
        IF Score >= 90 THEN
          write('distinguished')            {90's or better statement}
        ELSE
          write('very good')
      END                                  {end 80's or better statement}
  END                                      {end 70's or better statement}
ELSE
  BEGIN                                    {begin less than 70's statement}
    write('unsuccessful and ');
    IF Score >= 60 THEN                    {begin 60's or better statement}
      write('passed')
    ELSE
      write('failed')                      {end 60's or better statement}
  END;              {end less than 70's statement; end overall statement}
writeln;                          {now return carriage for line display}
```

Efficiency analysis

A summary of the number of comparisons required of each solution for some given value of Score is shown in Table 5.3. The table shows us that the IF-ELSE-IF approach has the fewest decisions only when the value of Score is less than 60. Therefore, we can say that the second solution is more efficient than the first one, even though the first one is easier to read and hence easier to understand. ◆

Readability vs. efficiency: a trade-off

One solution to the case study is more readable, but the other is more efficient. Which solution, then, should we say is "better?" If we expect frequent

TABLE 5.3 Number of Decisions Made for a Given Value of Score

Score	IF-ELSE-IF	Other Solution
less than 60	1	2
between 60 and 69	2	2
between 70 and 79	3	2
between 80 and 89	4	3
greater than 89	4	3

maintenance work, the first solution is probably better, because a programmer will need to spend less time trying to figure out the source code in order to do maintenance coding. If, however, processing time is critical, the second solution is considered the "better" one.

Any kind of technological discipline has certain trade-offs that are indigenous to the discipline. The issue of readability vs. efficiency is one of those trade-offs indigenous to the discipline of computer science. You will see other examples of this trade-off as you continue your study of this text.

Hints on choosing an algorithm

It is not always easy to develop a part of a program that requires more than one decision. Nonetheless, there are certain standard patterns you can look for to find a suitable algorithm:

I.   If you need to write a sequence that entails an implied choice of 1 of N possible paths, your first consideration should the *IF-ELSE-IF* algorithm. Note that with this algorithm, more than one condition might be `true`. If this scenario should occur, the computer will execute the statement associated with the first condition that evaluates to `true`. Therefore the order in which you write the boolean expressions is critical.

II.   If you see a need for nested decisions but have trouble determining the exact sequence, try using the top-down approach. When you use this method, you describe the sequence for the first (outermost) decision in its entirety. When you have dealt with that decision, you work on the next one, which is a part of the sequence belonging to the outer decision. You continue to work your way inward until you have solved the problem. We used this approach when we drafted the code for the second solution of Case Study 5.2.

III.   Sometimes, a nonnested sequence of decisions will be the correct choice. If you know that the number of decisions that must be made is fixed for any possible circumstance, this approach is most likely the correct one. Case Study 5.1 fell into this catagory, for three comparisons had to be made regardless of the values taken on by the input data.

When this algorithm is used, the order in which decisions are made is also critical. Remember that each action taken as a result of some decision changes the program state and furthermore that each boolean expression to be evaluated depends upon the program state at the time it is evaluated.

Using assertions

You can test your solution after each decision statement by making an assertion. An assertion related to a decision statement must be stated in terms of the precondition(s) associated with the boolean expression. It must also say something about each of the two paths taken, given the value of the boolean expression.

Any assertion associated with an IF..THEN..ELSE statement can be expressed as follows: "Given that the boolean expression is `true`, the changed program state is described by the effect of those statements associated with the reserved word THEN. Given that the boolean expression is `false`, the changed program state is described by the effect of those statements associated with the reserved word ELSE."

EXERCISES

Practice Your Understanding

1. What characterizes a problem that is solvable using an IF-ELSE-IF algorithm?

2. What characterizes a problem that can probably be solved by a nonnested sequence of IF..THEN or IF..THEN..ELSE statements?

3. How do we apply a top–down approach to solve a problem requiring nested decision logic?

Test Your Analysis Skills

4. Prove that the branch on values for (Score < 70) in Case Study 5.2 satisfies the problem statement.

Sharpen Your Implementation Skills

5. Solve the problem for Case Study 5.2 using an *IF-ELSE-IF* algorithm that starts with

```
IF Score >= 90 THEN
   writeln('successful and distinguished')
ELSE IF ...
```

6. Solve the problem for Case Study 5.2 using the "efficient" algorithm but setting up the decision construct with

> *IF Score < 70 THEN*
>   *display strings for unsuccessful scores*
> *ELSE*
>   *display strings for successful scores*

7. Write the fragment that solves Case Study 5.2 using an algorithm that looks like

> *IF Score > 60 THEN*
>   *IF Score > 70 THEN*
>   ...
>   ...
> *ELSE*
>   *display 'unsuccessful and failed'*

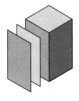

5.4   Solving A Quadratic Equation

Now you have seen program fragments where we have used nested decisions to solve some part of a problem. In this section, we give you a complete program that requires nested decisions for its solution. We will use decision statements to determine whether a given procedure should be called or not. You should note how the boolean expression(s) are used to specify the preconditions on the procedure that is called.

Background information

    A quadratic equation in one unknown is expressed as

$$Ax^2 + Bx + C = 0$$

where *A*, *B*, and *C* are real coefficients. There are two solutions to this equation, as expressed by the two formulas

$$\frac{-B + \sqrt{B^2 - 4AC}}{2A} \quad \text{and} \quad \frac{-B - \sqrt{B^2 - 4AC}}{2A}$$

The quantity $B^2 - 4AC$ is known as the *discriminant*. If this value is real, there are two real roots to the equation. If it is complex, the roots, using the imaginary number "i" are expressed as

$$\frac{-B}{2A} + \frac{\sqrt{-(B^2 - 4AC)}}{2A}i \quad \text{and} \quad \frac{-B}{2A} - \frac{\sqrt{-(B^2 - 4AC)}}{2A}i$$

Note that if $A = B = C = 0$, we do not have a quadratic equation. Instead, we have that $0 = 0$, which is called a "tautology." If A and B are both 0 and C is not 0, we have an "equation" that is actually an incorrect relationship. When $A = 0$, where B and C are not 0, we have an equation with one root. This equation is not quadratic. When A and B are not 0 but C is 0, we have a quadratic equation where one of the roots is 0. This equation is said to have a degenerate root at 0. Finally, when the discriminant is 0, the equation has two roots that are equal.

CASE STUDY 5.3

The problem statement

Let us write a program that displays the solutions to the equation

$$Ax^2 + Bx + C = 0$$

where A, B, and C represent real numbers. The user enters three numbers for A, B, and C. The computer then displays one of the following six messages. The comments in braces do not make up the computer display:

{1} This is not a quadratic equation.   {A = B = C = 0}
    It is a tautology.

{2} This is not a quadratic equation.   {A = B = 0; C <> 0}
    It is not even an equation.

{3} This is not a quadratic equation.   {A = 0; B, C <> 0}
    The linear equation has a root at -2.500

{4} The equation has one degenerate root at 0. {A <> 0; C = 0}
    The other root is at 3.000

{5} The roots are real.   {discriminant is positive}
    Root #1 = 2.400   Root #2 = -1.000

{6} The roots are complex.   {discriminant is negative}
    Root #1 = 7.845 -6.232i   Root #2 = 7.845 + 6.232i

The main block   When we look at the display, we see that after values are entered, either we have an equation that is quadratic or we do not. This condition depends upon the value of *A*. Therefore, we can draft a first pseudocode description of the main block as

> *keyin A, B, C*
> *IF A = 0 THEN*
>   *DisplayNonQuadratic(B, C)*
> *ELSE*
>   *handle quadratic equation*

We can then account for the degenerate root with the refinement

> *IF A = 0 THEN*
>   *DisplayNonQuadratic(B, C)*
> *ELSE IF C = 0 THEN*
>   *DisplayDegenerateQuadratic(A, B)*
> *ELSE*
>   *DisplayTwoRoots(A, B, C)*

        The main block thus requires three procedures. The precondition for a call to `DisplayNonQuadratic` is that A is equal to 0. Because this value is known, it need not be passed on as a parameter of `DisplayNonQuadratic`. The precondition for a call to `DisplayDegenerateQuadratic` is that A is not 0 but C is 0. In this case, it is not necessary for the value of C to be passed into this procedure. Finally, the precondition given that `DisplayTwoRoots` is called is that A and C are not 0.

Structure chart   The structure chart for the program down to this first level is shown in Figure 5.7. We will not code any block statements for this case study while we develop it.

FIGURE 5.7   Partial structure chart for `SolveQuadraticEq`.

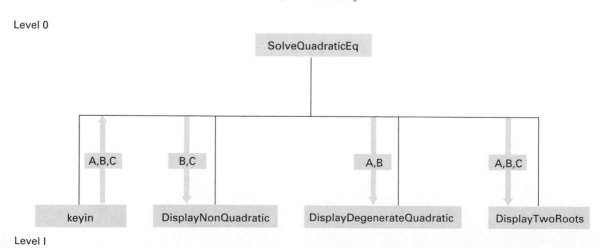

Instead, we will develop the algorithms, then present the source code for the entire program at the end of the section.

The first display of the procedure `DisplayNonQuadratic` is the string "`This is not a quadratic equation.`" Then, depending upon the B and C values, either "`tautology`", "`impossible`", or "`single root`" is displayed. We thus draft the pseudocode for `DisplayNonQuadratic`'s statement as

> *display 'not a quadratic'*
> *IF B = 0 THEN*
>   *display something about nonequation*
> *ELSE*
>   *display root of -C/B*

The display about the nonequation is described by

> *IF C = 0 THEN*
>   *display 'tautology'*
> *ELSE*
>   *display 'not an equation'*

Thus, we can combine the two decisions to get the complete pseudocode description for `DisplayNonQuadratic`'s statement as

> *display 'not a quadratic'*
> *IF B = 0 THEN*
>   *IF C = 0 THEN*
>   *display 'tautology'*
>   *ELSE*
>   *display 'not an equation'*
> *ELSE*
>   *display root of -C/B*

The precondition for entry into the `DisplayDegenerateQuadratic` procedure is that C is 0, A is not 0, and B's value can be anything. If B is also 0, there are two degenerate roots at 0; otherwise there is just one. If we set up a decision on B's value, we have for `DisplayDegenerateQuadratic`:

> *IF B = 0 then*
>   *display 'two degenerate roots at 0'*
> *ELSE*
>   *display 'one degenerate root at 0'*
>   *display 'other root at ', $-B/A$*

Note that the statement associated with the word ELSE will code to a compound statement associated with the reserved word ELSE.

The procedure `DisplayTwoRoots` is called only when A and C are both nonzero, thus implying that the equation has two nondegenerate roots. If we use a local variable to store the value of the discriminant (sqr (B) - 4*A*C), we can draft the description for the procedure's statement as

$$Discrim \leftarrow sqr(B) - 4*A*C$$
$$IF \ Discrim \geq 0 \ THEN$$
$$\quad DisplayRealRoots(A, \ B, \ Discrim)$$
$$ELSE$$
$$\quad DisplayComplexRoots(A, \ B, \ Discrim)$$

From the description, we know we must code calls to the procedures `DisplayRealRoots` and `DisplayComplexRoots`. The quadratic formula includes C's value in the discriminant, so `Discrim`, not C, is the third parameter for both procedures.

Layout considerations

Figure 5.8 shows the structure for the procedure `DisplayTwoRoots`. Because both procedures `DisplayRealRoots` and `DisplayComplexRoots` are called from `DisplayTwoRoots`, we will declare them ahead of `DisplayTwoRoots` in the source code layout.

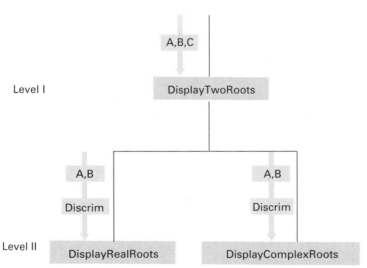

FIGURE 5.8 Structure chart for `DisplayTwoRoots`.

Development of the statement for `DisplayReal-Roots`

The precondition for calling `DisplayRealRoots` is that the value of `Discrim` is greater than or equal to 0. Even when A and C are not equal to zero, one more unusual condition, a double root, is possible. Otherwise, the quadratic formula can simply be applied to A, B, and `Discrim`. Given this thought, we can write the pseudocode for `ShowRealRoots` as

$$FirstTerm \leftarrow -B/(2*A)$$
$$DiscrimTerm \leftarrow sqrt(Discrim)/(2*A)$$
$$IF \ DiscrimTerm = 0 \ THEN$$

> display 'double root at', *FirstTerm*
> *ELSE*
> > display *FirstTerm* + *DiscrimTerm*, *FirstTerm* − *DiscrimTerm*

For the sake of convenience, we have decided to use `FirstTerm` and `DiscrimTerm` as local variables.

The expressions required for `DisplayComplexRoots` are like those required in `DisplayRealRoots`. The fact that `Discrim` is negative, however, means the square root of the negative value of `Discrim` be taken. Moreover, the two terms are not arithmetically combined. The pseudocode for this block is then

Development of the statement for `DisplayComplexRoots`

> *RealTerm* ← −*B*/(2*A)
> *ImTerm* ← *sqrt*(−*Discrim*)/(2*A)
> display *RealTerm*, '+', *ImTerm*, 'i'
> display *RealTerm*, '−', *ImTerm*, 'i'

The entire coded solution to the case study, given all the procedures we developed, is shown by the source code of the program `SolveQuadraticEq`.

```
PROGRAM SolveQuadraticEq(input,output);
  {This program finds and displays the roots of the quadratic equation
  Ax**2 + Bx + C = 0, given that the user has input the A, B, and C
  coefficients.}
  VAR
    A, B, C: real;    {the three coefficients}
  {*                                                              *}
  PROCEDURE DisplayNonQuadratic(B, C: real);
    {procedure to display solutions when A coefficient is 0}
    BEGIN
      writeln('This is not a quadratic equation.');
      IF B = 0 THEN
        IF C = 0 THEN
          writeln('It is a tautology.')
        ELSE
          writeln('It is not even an equation.')
      ELSE
        writeln('The linear equation has a root at ',-C/B:5:3)
    END;
  {*                                                              *}
  PROCEDURE DisplayDegenerateQuadratic(A, B: real);
    {procedure to display solution when A <> 0 but C = 0}
    BEGIN
      IF B = 0 THEN
        writeln('The equation has two degenerate roots at 0.')
      ELSE
        BEGIN
          writeln('The equation has one degenerate root at 0.');
```

SECTION 5-4 SOLVING A QUADRATIC EQUATION **187**

```
                writeln('The other root is at  ',-B/A:5:3)
            END
        END;
{*                                                                              *}
PROCEDURE DisplayRealRoots(A, B, Discrim: real);
    {displays the two real roots to the equation}
    VAR
        FirstTerm,       {-B/2A}
        DiscrimTerm:     {sqrt(Discrim)/2A}
                         real;
    BEGIN
        writeln('The roots are real.');
        FirstTerm:= -B/(2*A);
        DiscrimTerm: = sqrt(Discrim)/(2*A);
        IF DiscrimTerm = 0 THEN
            writeln('The equation has a double root at ',FirstTerm:5:3)
        ELSE
            BEGIN
                write('Root #1 = ',FirstTerm + DiscrimTerm:5:3,'        ');
                writeln('Root #2 = ',FirstTerm - DiscrimTerm:5:3)
            END
    END;
{+                                                                              +}
PROCEDURE DisplayComplexRoots(A, B, Discrim: real);
    {displays the two complex roots to the equation}
    VAR
        ReTerm,          {-B/2A}
        ImTerm:          {sqrt(-Discrim)/2A}
                         real;
    BEGIN
        writeln('The roots are complex.');
        ReTerm:= -B/(2*A);
        ImTerm:= sqrt(-Discrim)/(2*A);
        write('Root #1 = ',ReTerm:5:3,' - ',ImTerm:5:3,'i        ');
        writeln('Root #2 = ',ReTerm:5:3,' + ',ImTerm:5:3,'i')
    END;
{+                                                                              +}

PROCEDURE DisplayTwoRoots(A, B, C: real);
    {displays the two roots, either real or complex, to the equation}
    VAR
        Discrim: real;   {sqr(B) - 4AC}
    BEGIN
        Discrim:= sqr(B) - 4*A*C;
        IF Discrim >= 0 THEN
            DisplayRealRoots(A, B, Discrim)
        ELSE
```

```
        DisplayComplexRoots(A, B, Discrim)
    END;
  {*                                                                    *}
  BEGIN    {main program}
   write('Input coefficients (A,B,C:):  ');
   readln(A, B, C);
    IF A = 0 THEN
       DisplayNonQuadratic(B, C)
    ELSE IF C = 0 THEN
       DisplayDegenerateQuadratic(A, B)
    ELSE
       DisplayTwoRoots(A, B, C)
  END.
```

The guard algorithm

The pseudocode for an algorithm to guard against processing impossible data is given as Algorithm 5.3.

Algorithm 5.3

> *{Algorithm to guard against processing impossible data:}*
> *IF data is impossible to process THEN*
>   *handle the processing separately*
> *ELSE*
>   *process the data as is*
> *{end algorithm}*

The precondition for using this algorithm is that a value or some values have been given to some data. The guard guarantees that preconditions for further correct processing are met.

An alternative form is described by Algorithm 5.4

Algorithm 5.4

> *{Alternate form of guard algorithm:}*
> *IF data can be processed THEN*
>   *process it*
> *ELSE {optional}*
>   *take an alternative action*
> *{end algorithm}*

Usually, the *alternative action* is to display an error message. Regardless of which guard you use, the problem statement will determine whether an alternative action should be taken or not.

Using the algorithms

We applied the first form of the guard algorithm on the main block of the case study when we coded an IF statement controlled by the boolean expression A = 0. This particular statement, which guarded against division by 0, could have been described by the pseudocode

IF A = 0 THEN
    handle cases where A cannot be used as a divisor
ELSE
    use A as a divisor in displaying roots

We used the second form of the guard algorithm as part of the sequence inside `DisplayTwoRoots`. In this case, we guarded against taking the square root of a negative expression. Seen from this viewpoint, we can describe the decision statement in `DisplayTwoRoots` by

IF Discrim >= 0 THEN
    process Discrim in DisplayRealRoots block
ELSE
    process -Discrim in DisplayComplexRoots block

EXERCISES

Test Your Understanding

1. Why did we place `DisplayRealRoots` and `DisplayComplexRoots` before the procedure `DisplayTwoRoots`?

2. State the postcondition returned when a guard algorithm is executed.

3. Is the guard against processing a negative value for `Int` in the following example effective? Why or why not? (*Hint:* Does it guard against keying in a sequence of three nonpositive values?)

    keyin Int
    IF Int $\leq$ 0 THEN
      keyin Int
    process the positive value for Int

Practice Your Analysis Skills

4. (a) State the preconditions at entry into `DisplayRealRoots`.
   (b) State the preconditions at entry into `DisplayComplexRoots`.

5. Draw the structure chart for the program `SolveQuadraticEq`, showing data flow between the different procedures.

6. The program `SolveQuadraticEq` used an additional guard against division by zero in another procedure. Which one? What was the guard statement?

Sharpen Your Implementation Skills

7. Write drivers for `ShowRealRoots` and `ShowComplexRoots`. They should be written as procedures. (Why?)

8. Use a top–down approach to derive the decision statements that represent a guard algorithm whose description is satisfied by

    IF Int lies in the range 1 to 100 THEN
      display 'We can process this value.'
    ELSE
      display 'We cannot process this value.'

5.5 The Case Statement

The CASE statement, like the *IF-ELSE-IF* algorithm, can be applied to a situation where a choice of 1 of *N* paths is implied. When you use this statement, however, only one expression is evaluated, one which is preferably not boolean. The value of the expression determines which path is taken. The CASE statement works best when the proper choice on 1 of *N* possibilities can be determined by the value of a single expression.

A review of the IF-ELSE-IF algorithm

Let us recall the two characteristics of the *IF-ELSE-IF* algorithm: (1) The boolean expressions are evaluated in a given order, and (2) the path taken is on the first boolean condition that evaluates to true. The ideal problem suitable to this algorithm requires that a preference be applied to the order in which conditions are evaluated. These conditions need not be, and usually are not, *mutually exclusive*.

> **Mutually exclusive:** two or more conditions are mutually exclusive when only one of the conditions can be true for any given circumstance.

Syntax and semantics of the CASE statement

The syntax diagram for the CASE statement is shown in Figure 5.9. The expression found between the reserved words CASE and OF is called the *case selector*. Only a relatively limited set of case selector values are expected, because, for all *case labels,* the constants found before each colon can only be of an *ordinal type*. An integer constant such as 8 and a char constant such as 'Q' are both ordinal values. A real constant such as 3.1416 and a string constant such as 'Yes' are not ordinal values. Note also that expressions are not allowed as case labels.

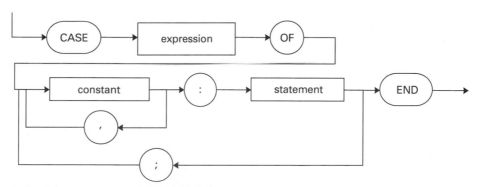

FIGURE 5.9 CASE statement syntax.

> **Ordinal type:** a type where each value, except for the first and last values, have a known next higher value and a known next lower value.

When the computer encounters a CASE statement, it will execute one of the *N* listed statements. The statement executed depends upon the value of the case selector. You can use a CASE statement when a choice of 1 of *N* paths depends upon the value of a single expression that is an ordinal type. Each path is mutually exclusive of all other paths because it depends solely upon the value of the case selector.

An example

The cleanest solution to the problem posed as Case Study 5.2 can be coded using the CASE statement shown in Example 5.5. Note that the case selector is expected to take on only those values between 0 and 10. Moreover, it can take on *only one* of those 11 values at any given time.

Example 5.5

```
CASE Score DIV 10 OF
   0,1,2,
   3,4,5: writeln('unsuccessful and failed');
      6: writeln('unsuccessful and passed');
      7: writeln('successful');
      8: writeln('successful and very good');
   9,10: writeln('successful and distinguished')
   END; {CASE}
```

END documentation

The CASE statement has an unusual syntax property. It terminates with the reserved word END yet has no associated reserved word BEGIN. Most programmers prefer to see a comment after the reserved word END when it is associated with the reserved word CASE. We have therefore adopted this convention with our source code.

Source code layout for the CASE *statement*

Layout conventions for a CASE statement are difficult to formulate because each statement may be associated with a different number of labels. However, some conventions are still possible. In this text, we

1. put the words CASE and END on one line
2. indent all case labels at least two spaces
3. align the associated statements for each list of labels

Another example

Example 5.6 shows the use of the CASE statement with an expression of type char.

Example 5.6

```
CASE LetterGrade OF
   'A': writeln('Excellent');
   'B': writeln('Good');
   'C': writeln('Fair');
   'D': writeln('Poor');
   'F': writeln('Failed')
   END; {CASE}
```

Example Problem 5.4

The problem statement

Your younger brother is interested in geometry. He wants you to write a program that will help him find the areas of geometric figures. He will enter one of three values, R (rectangle), T (triangle), or E (ellipse), to indicate the figure whose area he wants to know. The computer will then prompt him for the figure's dimensions (base and height for the triangle, major and minor axis for the ellipse, and length and width for the rectangle). It uses these values for the dimensions to find and print the figure's area. A typical run of the program for each of the figures (not including anything enclosed by braces) is as follows:

```
{1} Enter figure (R, T, or E): R
    Enter length and width: 7.5  8.2
    The area is 61.5000              {Area = length X width}

{2} Enter figure (R, T, or E):  T
    Enter base and height:  7.1  9.3
    The area is 33.0150              {Area = 1/2 X base X height}

{3} Enter figure (R, T, or E):  E
    Enter major and minor axes:  6.7  5.2
    The area is 109.4533            {Area = Pi X major axis X minor axis}
```

Coding the main block

You can break down the problem the following way:

keyin Figure
keyin Dim1, Dim2 using value of Figure for prompt
find Area using values of Dim1, Dim2 and Figure
display Area

The two middle actions abstract to the two procedure calls ReadDimensions(Figure, Dim1, Dim2) and FindArea(Figure, Dim1, Dim2, Area). The code for the main block is given as the program SolveArea.

```
PROGRAM SolveArea(input, output);
  {The computer solves for the area of a triangle, rectangle or
  ellipse, according to the user's choice.}
  CONST
    Pi = 3.1416;    {needed to find area of ellipse}
  VAR
    Figure: char;   {represents figure chosen by user}
    Dim1, Dim2,     {the two dimensions needed to find figure's area}
    Area:           {the area of the figure}
                real;
  {*                                                              *}
  PROCEDURE ReadDimensions(Figure: char; VAR Dim1, Dim2: real);
    {in: Figure -- the geometric figure chosen by the user
    out: Dim1, Dim2 -- dimensions needed to find area of figure}
    BEGIN  END;
  {*                                                              *}
```

```
PROCEDURE FindArea(Figure: char; Dim1, Dim2: real; VAR Area: real);
  {in:    Figure -- geometric figure chosen by user
   in:    Dim1, Dim2 -- dimensions needed to find area of figure
   out:   Area -- the area of the given figure}
  BEGIN   END;
{*                                                                    *}
BEGIN  {program}
  write('Enter figure (R, T, or E): ');
  readln(Figure);
  ReadDimensions(Figure, Dim1, Dim2);
  FindArea(Figure, Dim1, Dim2, Area);
  writeln('The area is ',Area:6:4)
END.
```

The two block statements

All there is left to code are the statements for ReadDimensions and for FindArea. Both of these require the use of the CASE statement. The source code that makes up the statement part of ReadDimensions is

```
BEGIN
  CASE Figure OF
     'R': write('Enter length and width:   ');
     'T': write('Enter base and height:   ');
     'E': write('Enter major and minor axes:   ')
  END;   {CASE}
  readln(Dim1, Dim2)
END;
```

Likewise, the source code that replaces the stub of FindArea is

```
BEGIN
  CASE Figure OF
     'R': Area:= Dim1 * Dim2;
     'T': Area:= (Dim1 * Dim2)/2;
     'E': Area:= Pi * Dim1 * Dim2
  END {CASE}
END; ◆
```

ELSE and OTHERWISE

There is one major problem with the two CASE statements we wrote, namely, that the value of Figure must be one of the three letters R, T, or E. If Figure does not take on one of these three values, the program will crash at run time.

Many dialects of Pascal get around this kind of difficulty by providing a default path if the case selector does not take on one of the case label values. The machine sets up this path when it recognizes the given reserved word indigenous to the dialect. You should check your user's manual to see if your dialect has this feature.

In Turbo Pascal, the reserved word is ELSE; in VAX Pascal, we have OTHERWISE. The action to be taken, given that the selector did not take on the value of any of the labels, is preceded by this reserved word. For example, in Turbo Pascal, we would use the following CASE statement for ReadDimensions:

```
CASE Figure OF
    'R': write('Enter length and width: ');
    'T': write('Enter base and height: ');
    'E': write('Enter major and minor axes: ')
    ELSE writeln('No such figure exists.')
END;  {CASE}
```

EXERCISES

Test Your Understanding

1. How many expressions need to be evaluated to determine the path taken for a CASE statement?

2. What is the main restriction on the CASE selector expression?

3. What is the main restriction on the CASE labels?

4. What is the main restriction about the CASE statement as a whole?

Sharpen Your Implementation Skills

5. Write a CASE statement that will display the corresponding string representation of the integers 0 through 9. Thus, for instance, if Int (the integer expression) were assigned the value 7, the statement should cause the display of the string 'seven'.

6. At this point, you have six different candidates for a decision algorithm: the single-alternate choice (IF), the double-alternate choice (IF-THEN-ELSE), a sequence of IF statements, the IF-ELSE-IF algorithm, a complex algorithm (derived for each problem), and the CASE statement. Determine which would be the best choice of algorithm for each of the following:

   (a) A statement or sequence that displays the values of two input integers in their proper order.

   (b) A statement or sequence that assigns to a character variable

   the value "M" if an integer variable is greater than 1000

   the value "C" if its value lies between 100 and 999

   the value "X" if the integer's value lies between 10 and 99

   the value "I" if the the integer's value is between 1 and 9

   the value "O" if the variable is nonpositive.

   (c) A statement or sequence that displays

   III if the value assigned to Int is 3

   II if the value assigned to Int is 2

   I if the value assigned to Int is 1

   (d) A statement or sequence that displays the string "odd" if Int's value is odd and "even" if the value is even.

   (e) A statement or sequence that displays: "This way to registration," if the value assigned to Age is greater than or equal to 18 and the value assigned to the char variable Reply is "Y"; "You are not old enough," if the value assigned to Age is less than 18; and "You are not a citizen", if the value assigned to the character variable `Reply` is anything other than "Y". Use the order presented as the preferred order for determining the display.

(f) A statement or sequence that assigns grades as follows:

a grade of "*A*" to a `Score` 85 or greater

a grade of "*B*" to a `Score` between 75 and 84

a grade of "*C*" to a `Score` between 60 and 74

a grade of "*D*" to a `Score` between 50 and 59

a grade of "*F*" to a `Score` below 50

(g) A statement or sequence that adds 5 to `AnInt` if it is positive.

(h) A statement or sequence that displays

"Yes" if `AnInt` equals 5, 6 or 7

"Maybe" if `AnInt` equals 3 or 4

"*No*" if `AnInt` equals to 1 or 2.

(i) A statement or sequence that displays "OK" if the values assigned to the variables `Int1`, `Int2`, and `Int3` are in order from lowest to highest.

7. Write the code for each of the algorithms of exercise 6.

Program Testing Hints

In the first part of this section, we give you a number of common errors associated with decision statements. You should know about these errors in order to avoid committing them. The second part is very important, for it gives you hints on choosing valid test data and planning good test strategies. The techniques we give will help you devise and follow through on a plan for testing a program thoroughly yet sensibly.

Incorrect assignments

Do not use the special symbol : = for the operator = in a boolean expression. The following statement misuses this special symbol:

```
IF XInt := 0  THEN                {ERRONEOUS}
   writeln ('It worked!');
```

Although your intended meaning might be "If `XInt` is assigned the value 0, then," the coded statement is utter nonsense to the compiler. Never use the assignment operator to form any kind of expression.

PROGRAM DESIGN RULE 5.2

Never follow the reserved words THEN or ELSE with a semicolon.

Empty statements

When you put a semicolon after the reserved words THEN or ELSE, your program will compile and link properly, but it will be logically wrong. For example, consider the Pascal code

```
IF XInt > 0 THEN;              {LOGICALLY WRONG}
    Sum: = Sum + XInt;
```

The computer will execute an empty statement associated with the reserved word THEN given that XInt's value is less than 0. It will then always add XInt's value to Sum, regardless of the condition on XInt.

In like manner, even if XInt's value is greater than 0, the computer will always add 1 to Count when it executes the following statement:

```
IF XInt > 0 THEN
    Sum: = Sum + XInt
ELSE;                          {LOGICALLY WRONG}
    Count: = Count + 1;
```

Errors of this sort are very difficult to find, because you can insert an empty statement at any place in the statement part of a block without violating any syntax rules.

PROGRAM DESIGN RULE 5.3

Always use the reserved words BEGIN and END
for code that requires a compound statement.

BEGIN..END errors

Be sure to use the BEGIN and END delimiters on compound statements. In the following statement, the boolean expression controls the execution of only the first writeln statement:

```
IF XRe < 0 THEN
    writeln('This number is imaginary.');          {LOGICALLY WRONG}
    writeln('It's square root is', sqrt(-XRe):5:3, 'i');
```

Regardless of XRe's value, the machine will always execute the second statement. The layout tells you that the programmer intended to use a compound statement, but Pascal syntax rules instruct the machine to *always* execute the second writeln statement. Because the layout looks right, bugs of this sort are also difficult to find.

Testing Methods

Some logical errors

We conclude this section with a discussion of program testing, particularly as it relates to decision statements.

There is often no unique solution to a problem requiring that decisions be made. There are still, however, many incorrect ways to "solve" such a problem. We might have, for example, used the following program fragment as a solution to Example Problem 5.3:

```
IF Age < 14 THEN                              {LOGICALLY WRONG}
    writeln('You''re too young to work.');
IF Age < 18 THEN
    writeln('You''re too young to vote.');
IF Age < 65 THEN
    writeln('You''re too young to retire.')
ELSE
    writeln('Enjoy your golden years.');
```

In this case, any person under 14 years of age will be told in sequence that he or she cannot work, cannot vote, and cannot retire. This code clearly does not solve the problem correctly.

The following fragment likewise represents an incorrect statement for the procedure Rearrange of Case Study 5.1:

```
IF First > Second THEN                {LOGICALLY WRONG}
    Exchange(First,Second)                 8      7      6
ELSE IF First > Third THEN               1ST    2ND    3RD
    Exchange(First,Third)                  7      8      6
ELSE IF Second > Third THEN              6      8      7
    Exchange(Second,Third)                6      7      8
```

Assertion testing   There are fortunately plenty of ways to check whether you have solved the problem correctly. The best method is to make assertions for each statement in a sequence. From this sequence of assertions, you can make a final assertion. If the final assertion satisfies the conditions for the solved problem, you have proven your algorithm is logically correct.

Desk tracing hints   If you feel this method is too "theoretical," you can always desk trace your source code for different values of the variables and expressions just as if you were the CPU. Avoid testing the entire program this way. It is best that you use the "divide-and-conquer method" for testing instead. In other words, desk check each block separately, not the whole program all at once.

PROGRAM DESIGN RULE 5.4

Choose sufficient test data to cover all preconditions for a given sequence that uses decision logic.

Choosing "smart" values   If you go about testing a procedure or program by simply using many data sets haphazardly, you are not testing "smart." Suppose, for example, you try these three sets of data using the proposed erroneous solution for Case Study 5.1:

$$81\ 32\ 95 \qquad 59\ 33\ 62 \qquad 75\ 22\ 89$$

The sets will all return "correct" results, so you may jump to the erroneous conclusion that the program is correct.

What is wrong with this data? For starters, not enough different possibilities were tried. Also, all three sets represent the same precondition (First is greater than Second but less than Third) even though the values of the integers are different. If all integers in the test data are not equal to each other, six different sets of values to cover all the possibilities would be the minimum acceptable number of data sets to apply to the program.

Another example of testing smart

What about test data for Example Problem 5.3? The obvious first candidates are (1) an age value less than 14, (2) an age between 14 and 18, (3) one between 18 and 65, and (4) one greater than 65. You should also test what happens at the specified values of 14, 18, and 65. All these values would seem to represent a sufficient set of test data.

But what about absurd values? What happens when a negative age is read in? What if an age such as 1000 is read in? Does the problem statement require that your code guards against them or not?

On-line testing

Regardless of whether you desk check or apply assertion testing on your algorithms, you will eventually want to perform on-line tests on the program. You can test your program top–down, bottom–up, or use some combination of the two methods.

Top–down testing: on-line testing of the program as an integrated whole, using stubs for those procedures not yet coded or fully tested.

Bottom–up testing: on-line testing of each procedure as a separate logical unit.

No matter which method you choose, be sure to have a clear idea of just how much of the program you are testing. Definitely avoid a testing strategy where the first test is on the whole program with data haphazardly using values that "look typical." The results returned will probably be inconclusive or misleading when such a poor plan is carried out.

PROGRAM DESIGN RULE 5.5

Choose sufficient test data to ensure that every
statement in a program gets executed at least once.

More smart testing

Every decision statement using the reserved words IF, THEN, and ELSE will have two paths that can be taken. When you apply Program Design Rule 5.5, your test data will account for each path in each decision statement. This rule is particularly useful when you are doing some bottom–up testing. If you use procedural abstraction, your statements inside a given procedure should be relatively few in number. If the block you are testing has decision statements, you can apply Program Design Rule 5.5 with relative ease and get a very good idea of any errors that may still be present.

Why test?   On-line testing will not "prove" the program works. Test data are devised and used for the purpose of finding bugs, particularly those where you "mean" one thing but code something else. For example, you may place a semicolon after a THEN or an ELSE. Likewise, you may not delimit an intended compound statement with the reserved words BEGIN and END. On-line testing will help you find errors of this kind.

Will testing help you identify any logical errors? You may feel that if you have shown your program is logically correct, there may not be a need to apply extensive testing. However, *you test programs because that forces you to think of what can go wrong*. One thing that can go wrong is that your assertions are incorrect because you overlooked some significant precondition or postcondition.

When you devise test data, it also forces you to make the program robust. No matter how illogical the input data, the robust program will always run without crashing. A robust program, for example, will always contain guards against division by zero. If such a circumstance occurred at run time, the program should display a message such as "These values will not work", or something similar. Your program users need only deal with problems generated by *their* incorrect data, not by your incorrect program.

EXERCISES

Test Your Understanding

Practice Your Program Analysis Skills

1. List three reasons why on-line testing is important.

2. For what values of Age will the proposed incorrect solution to Example Problem 5.3 work? For what values will the solution not work?

3. List the preconditions on the relationships between First, Second, and Third for which the proposed solution to Case Study 5.1 will work. List the preconditions for which it will not work.

4. Suppose we have the following problem statement: "Write a sequence that will display the message 'too small' if Int is less than 10, 'just right' if Int is between 10 and 25 and 'too large' if Int is greater than 25." A proposed solution is coded as follows:

```
IF Int < 10 THEN
   writeln('Too small');
IF Int <= 25 THEN
   writeln('Just right')
ELSE
   writeln('Too large');
```

   (a) For what values of Int will the computer display a wrong string? Fix the code so that it does solve the problem statement.
   (b) Would you use a CASE statement for this problem? Why or why not?

5. What will be the display if Name does equal 'John' and if it does not equal 'John' for the following:

```
IF Name = 'John' THEN
   writeln('Congratulations, you win.')
ELSE;
   writeln('Sorry, you lose.');
```

Fix the sequence so that it "behaves" properly.

Sharpen Your Implementation Skills

6. **(a)** Write a driver to test the logic of the ShowRealRoots block for Case Study 5.2 of Section 5.4.

   (b) Do the same for the ShowComplexRoots block.

   (c) Do the same for the main program.

   (d) What kind of test data would you propose to use on each block?

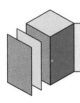

REVIEW AND EXERCISES

The reserved words IF, THEN, and ELSE are used to instruct the computer to choose one path of action over another. The path to be taken is controlled by a *boolean expression*. This coded expression, which depends upon the program state at the time it is evaluated, can be either true or false. If the expression is true, the statement associated with the reserved word THEN is executed. If the expression is false, the statement associated with the reserved word ELSE is carried out. If there is no reserved word ELSE and the expression is false, the computer does nothing further with the IF..THEN statement. Regardless of what happens, the boolean expression defines a *precondition* that determines the actions carried out by the decision statement.

Sometimes more than one decision is needed to solve a problem correctly. When a first decision is required to determine whether a second decision is relevant, we have a decision structure that is *nested*. Each new decision made defines a new *level of nesting*. If a complicated sequence of decisions is required, the best approach is done *top–down,* where the outermost decision is planned and assertion tested first.

A particularly useful algorithm that uses nested decisions is the *IF-ELSE-IF algorithm*. This algorithm follows an ordered sequence of decision making, where the computer executes exactly 1 of *N* predefined paths. The statement executed is the one associated with the first true boolean expression. The CASE statement is useful for solving a problem where 1 of *N* paths is taken that depends upon the single value of a *case selector* expression. The path taken is determined by the value of the particular *case label* to which the case selector evaluates. The statement associated with the selected case label is then carried out.

Regardless of the kind of testing done on a decision statement, all possibilities should be taken into account. When assertion testing is used, all possible postconditions for some given decision must be described. If desk tracing is applied, data should be chosen that tests all possibilities. Likewise, data chosen for on-line testing should guarantee that every statement in the program is executed at least once.

Apply on-line testing on a program with a given strategy in mind. If you plan to do a lot of *bottom–up testing,* write a driver for each procedure to be tested. If you do *top–down testing,* make sure to write good stubs on blocks not yet fully tested. In any case, a program that is planned using procedural abstraction and top-down design is much easier to test than one that is planned poorly with little or no procedural abstraction.

EXERCISES

Short Answers

1. True or false? If a statement is controlled by a boolean expression, that expression represents a precondition for the statement's execution.

2. A boolean expression can take on one of two values: _____ or _____ .

3. True or false? There is no limit to the number of statements that are components of a single compound statement.

4. Name at least two conditions that might be guarded against when processing numeric types.

5. Sometimes a CASE statement is the preferred strategy; sometimes an *IF-ELSE-IF* algorithm is. List the conditions under which the CASE statement algorithm is preferred over the *IF-ELSE-IF* algorithm.

6. List the conditions under which the *IF-ELSE-IF* algorithm is preferred over the CASE statement.

7. How many possible paths of action can actually be taken when a sequence of four IF statements without the ELSE word is executed?

8. How many possible paths of action can actually be taken when an *IF-ELSE-IF* algorithm is used with four different control expressions?

9. What is the logical difference between the two statements

```
IF X > 5 THEN                    IF X > 5 THEN
   writeln('Found');                writeln('Found')
                                 ELSE;
```

10. True or false? Only one of the control expressions will ever be true for the *IF-ELSE-IF* algorithm.

11. True or false? The most efficient sequence is invariably the easiest one to code and maintain.

12. True or false? The following sequence represents a guard strategy:

```
IF XInt <> 0 THEN
   YInt:= YInt DIV XInt;
```

Explain why you answered as you did.

13. Can the CASE statement be used with string expressions? Why or why not?

14. The IF..THEN when used in source code implies that _____ of _____ possible sequences can be carried out, and the IF-THEN-ELSE statement used in source code implies that _____ of _____ possible sequences can be carried out.

15. True or false? On-line testing is a useful technique for finding the syntax errors in a program.

16. True or false? Even the most thorough program testing does not guarantee that a program is correct.

17. What assertion can be made after the following statement has been executed?

```
IF PInt > QInt THEN
  PInt:= QInt
ELSE
  QInt:= PInt;
```

Easy Projects

18. Joseph's Jewelers charge a tax of 5% on all items. If a given item costs over $100, an additional tax of 5% on the amount over $100 is charged to the buyer. Write a program that first reads the price of a purchase, less the tax charged. The total price, including the tax, is then found and displayed.

19. Write a program that reads in three uppercase letters. It sorts and displays the letters in alphabetical order.

20. Write a program that simulates a single transaction at a bank. A value representing a customer's balance is first read in. Then, a letter 'D' for deposit or 'W' for withdrawal, along with a transaction amount, is read in. If the letter 'D' is input, the new balance is calculated and displayed. If the letter 'W' is input and the balance is sufficient, the new balance is calculated and displayed. If the balance is insufficient, an OVERDRAWN message is displayed, a fine of $5 is subtracted from the balance, and the balance is displayed. If any letter other than 'D' or 'W' is entered, the message WE ARE UNABLE TO HANDLE THE TRANSACTION is displayed.

Medium Projects

21. Write a program to set a letter grade for a particular test average on a quiz. You first enter the cut-off scores for 'A', 'B', 'C', and 'D' grades. Then you enter three test scores. The letter grade to be awarded to each score is shown on the next line. A typical run might look like

```
Enter A cut-off:   89
Enter B cut-off:   77
Enter C cut-off:   67
Enter D cut-off:   50
--------------------
Enter test score:   75
The student got C.
--------------------
Enter test score:   89
The student got A.
--------------------
Enter test score:   45
The student got F.
```

22. Write a program where four integers are entered. They are sorted in order from lowest to highest, and the sorted values are then displayed. Solve the problem using a main block sequence that can be described by

> *keyin Int1, Int2, Int3, Int4*
> *OrderFourth(Int1, Int2, Int3, Int4) {assigns highest value to Int4}*
> *SortThree(Int1, Int2, Int3)*
> *display values of Int1, Int2, Int3, Int4*

Note that once you have written the procedure `OrderFourth`, you can use virtually the same logic used in Case Study 5.1 for `SortThree`'s statement.

23. Dr. Rural is a simple country doctor who diagnoses his patients based on four questions. (Sniffles? Headache? Indigestion? Temperature?) A patient with all four symptoms is rushed to the hospital to be operated on, one with three symptoms is sent to the hospital for bed rest, a patient with two symptoms is recommended bed rest for a few days, a patient with one symptom is told to take some aspirin. Finally, a patient with nothing wrong is given a clean bill of health.

    Write a program that behaves as Dr. Rural's assistant. The computer should first display instructions (a few sentences of explanation regarding the input format), then ask the patient's symptoms, and finally display a treatment message. Typical interactions might look like

    ```
    Sniffles?   Y
    Headache?   N
    Indigestion?   N
    Temperature?   Y
    Treatment:   Take a few days of bed rest at home.

    Sniffles?   Y
    Headache?   Y
    Indigestion?   Y
    Temperature?   Y
    Treat:   You are very sick. We will operate immediately!
    ```

24. It's tax time again. Write a program that finds a person's income tax as a percentage of his/her total gross income (TGI). The same user–machine interactions for the program DoTaxes of Chapter 4 should be used. Certain additional features belong to this program, however:
    (a) All exemptions up to the third one are worth $2000 off the TGI, but any additional exemption is worth only $1500.
    (b) A maximum of $3000 capital loss can be taken for any given year.
    (c) The tax schedule is as follows:

TGI	Tax
Under $5000	None
less than $20,000	10%
$20,000 − $40,000	$2000 + 15% of amount over $20,000
$40,000 − $100,000	$5000 + 20% of amount over $40,000
Over $100,000	$17,000 + 30% of amount over $100,000

Difficult Projects

25. Write a program that changes an input `integer` into a Roman numeral representation. Use this program only on values less than 4000. (Why?) Some typical runs:

```
Number:  832
Roman:   DCCCXXXII
Number:  1479
Roman:   MCDLXXIX
```

(*Hint:* The display for thousands should be coded separately. The display for hundreds, tens, and units can be done with a call to the same procedure, using different parameters. After this procedure is exited, the original `integer` value is reduced by the amount that the display string represents. Example: 1479 is used to print `'M'` and 479 is returned; 479 is used to print `'CD'` and 79 is returned; 79 is used to print `'LXX'` and 9 is returned; and 9 is used to print `'IX'`.)

26. A particular brokerage house accepts sell stop and buy stop orders for customer-specified securities. A sell stop order is executed if the price of the security reaches a certain price when the market price is moving down; a buy-stop order is executed if the price of a security reaches a certain price when the market is moving up.

    You are to write a program that simulates a dialog between a client and his broker. The dialog starts when the broker enters a value that represents the opening price of the security his or her client is interested in. The client then enters a buy or sell order for X shares of stock at a given stop price.

    At the end of the trading day, the client calls the broker to find if the order was filled. The broker lets him or her know what the trading range was (day's high and day's low). This value, which the broker just now found time to look up (busy day!), determines whether the client's order is filled. If it is filled, a check is sent to the client (on a sell order) or sent to the broker (on a buy order). This amount is displayed along with the broker's commission, which is a 2% surcharge tacked on the buy order or 2% surcharge taken out of the buy proceeds. Typical runs:

```
Buy or sell?  B
How many shares?  500
Price?  12.25
----------------------
Range?  12.50  13.25
Your order was not filled

{same values as above}
----------------------------
Range?  12.00  13.00
You bought 500 shares at 12.50
It will cost you $6375, which includes $125 for commissions.

{same values, but with a sell order}
----------------------------
Range?  12.00  13.00
You sold 500 shares at 12.50
You will be receiving $6125 where we took out $125 for commissions.
```

27. Write a program that categorizes a triangle and then prints its area. You enter three real values and then the machine executes the sequence described by

```
keyin Side1, Side2, Side3
set sides in ascending order for Side1 to Side3
IF Side3 > sum of other two sides then
   display 'impossible', etc.
ELSE
   process the triangle possibilities
```

The candidate displays for the categories are

1. These values degenerate to a line.   {sum of two sides equals 3rd}
2. This is an equilateral triangle.   {all sides equal}
3. This is an isoceles triangle.   {two of three sides equal}
4. This is a scalar triangle.   {no sides equal}

where some typical runs are

```
Input sides:  16 29 11
This is an impossible triangle

Input sides:  12  6  6
These values degenerate to a line.

Input sides:  6  6  6
This is an equilateral triangle.   Its area is 15.59

Input sides:  5  5  6
This is an isoceles triangle.   Its area is 12.00

Input sides:  1.5  2.0  2.5
   This is a scalar triangle.   Its area is 1.50
```

We refer you back to Exercise 20 at the end of Chapter 3 for the correct formula of the area of a triangle, given the values of the three sides.

C H A P T E R 6

LOOPING

OBJECTIVES

After you have read and studied the material of this
chapter, you should be able to

- Describe the mechanism of the three looping constructs
  of Pascal

- Desk trace the action of source code that has loops in it

- Design correct code for a program that requires one or
  more loops

- Use loop invariants to develop algorithms that require
  a loop

- Apply proven algorithms that use a loop(s) to solve a
  specific problem

- Determine good data to test algorithms and code that
  uses loops.

So far, you have seen code that processed data in groups of threes. You have studied programs that summed up three groups of integers, programs that read in and displayed three characters, programs that put three integers in order, and so forth. Suppose, however, you want a program to find the sum of 5, 10, or even 100 groups of integers. It is ridiculous and tedious to write the same coded sequence 100 times. A problem to add 100 integers is best solved by writing a loop that will make the computer execute the same sequence of actions more than once.

There are many problems you can solve that requires the same sequence of statements to be executed more than once. You can solve this kind of problem by writing a statement to loop repetitively through this sequence. You can, for example, use a loop statement (1) to count the number of positive integer values read in out of a given total number of integer values, (2) to record the highest integer value out of a sequence of integers read in, (3) to display a table showing interest earned over a specified number of years, and so forth. In this chapter you will learn to instruct the computer to loop, that is, to repetitively execute the same sequence of statements more than once.

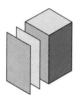

6.1 The WHILE Loop

Of the three *loop statements* in the Pascal language, the statement implemented as the WHILE loop is the most versatile. It is often called the "universal loop," for you can use it to solve any problem requiring a loop. In this section, you will see three coded fragments that use a WHILE loop to solve three specific problems that deal with counting and summing.

Loop statement: a statement whose execution is carried out with the consecutive execution of the same (sequence of) statement(s) more than once.

WHILE statement syntax and mechanism
The syntax diagram for a WHILE statement is shown in Figure 6.1. When the computer carries out this statement, it first evaluates the *loop control expression*. For the WHILE loop, a `true` value for this expression represents the *loop entry condition*. If the loop is entered, the *loop body* is executed as a single *loop pass*. Once the pass is completed, the boolean expression is again evaluated. If it is still `true`, the

FIGURE 6.1 Syntax of the WHILE statement.

WHILE Statement

WHILE → Boolean Expression → DO → Statement →

loop body is executed for another pass. If it is `false`, the *loop exit condition* is achieved, and the computer exits the loop. It will then execute the statement that follows the `WHILE` loop statement.

Loop control expression: an expression (usually boolean) that makes up part of a loop statement. When this expression is of type boolean, its value determines whether the loop entry condition is met or not.

Loop entry condition: a particular condition that must be met for the computer to carry out the statement(s) of the loop body.

Loop body: the part of a loop statement that is the sequence of statements to be executed with one loop pass.

Loop pass or iteration: a single execution of the (sequence of) statement(s) that makes up the loop's body.

Loop exit condition: the condition that must eventually be met so the computer will not carry out another loop pass.

WHILE loop pseudocode

The pseudocode used to describe a `WHILE` loop is written as

$$WHILE \; loop \; control \; expression \; DO$$
$$body$$

The *loop control expression* is pseudocode for a boolean expression. The *body* codes to a Pascal statement, either simple or (usually) compound.

Three Program Fragments

Now that we have defined some terms associated with loops and also given you the Pascal syntax for a `WHILE` loop statement, let us present some examples of source code fragments that use the `WHILE` loop.

The first example

The first example of source code is a fragment that uses a `WHILE` loop to display a table showing the sum of the first five positive integers. The source code for the example is as follows:

Example 6.1

```
Sum:= 0;
Count:= 0;
WHILE Count <> 5 DO
  BEGIN
    Count:= Count + 1;
    Sum:= Sum + Count;
    writeln(Count:5, Sum:5)
  END;
writeln('Finished...');
```

The loop statement for this example is a WHILE loop that starts with the reserved word WHILE and ends with the reserved word END. The loop body is the compound statement delimited by the reserved words BEGIN and END. The loop entry condition is that the value of Count must be inequal to 5. When a loop pass is executed, the computer adds 1 to the variable *Count* and the value taken on by Count to the variable Sum. It then displays these two values. The loop control expression is evaluated at the end of each loop pass. The loop exit condition, the *complementary condition* of the loop entry condition, occurs when Count takes on the value 5.

> **Complementary condition:** given some condition, the condition that is false when the given condition is true and vice versa.

When the computer executes the source code fragment, it will produce the display as shown. Let us walk through each loop pass to show how the computer produces this display.

```
      1       1
      2       3
      3       6
      4      10
      5      15
   Finished...
```

Both Sum and Count are initially set to 0 before the loop entry condition is tested. Then, because Count's value is 0, not 5, the loop is entered. After the loop is entered, Count is assigned the new value of 1. This value is added to the value of Sum. Then the two values are displayed, and the boolean condition is again evaluated.

Because Count's value is 1, not 5, the computer carries out one more loop pass. It sets Count to 2 and Sum to 3, then displays these two values. At the end of the loop body, Count is equal to 2, not 5, so the loop is entered again. Count now takes on the value of 3, Sum is set to 6, and these two values are then displayed. At the completion of this pass, Count is 3, not 5, so the loop is entered once more. Now Count takes on the value 4, Sum takes on the value 10, and these two values are also displayed.

Count is still not equal to 5, so the loop is entered once more. The computer adds 1 to Count, now giving it the value of 5. The exit condition has been achieved, but the body must be completed before the control expression is again evaluated. Hence, Sum takes on the value 15, and the values of Count and Sum are again displayed.

Once the display is carried out, the test for entry is again tried. This time, because Count is equal to 5, the control expression evaluates to false. Hence, the computer exits the loop and executes the writeln statement, thus producing the line display "Finished..."

Even though their values change, the meaning of the variables Count and Sum will be the same with each loop pass. What, then, do the values of these two variables represent? Giving the matter some thought, you realize that the value given to Count represents the number of the loop pass the computer is carrying out. At the end of the loop, this value represents the number of passes executed. The value given to Sum represents the accumulated sum of all values assigned to Count.

These last two sentences are the invariant conditions or *loop invariants* on the variables Count and Sum. Let us now look once more at the problem statement that the source code fragment satisfies: "Write a program fragment that will find and display the count and cumulative sum of the sequence of consecutive integers 1 through 5." Note how the loop invariant and a variable's meaning in the loop body are really the same thing. Both descriptions tell how a variable found in the body of a loop is used to fulfill the loop's purpose.

> **Loop invariant:** a description of a condition, usually a representation of a value taken on by a variable, that is true at the start of a loop, and also true at the completion of each loop pass.

The second example

The next fragment of source code also solves a problem dealing with counting and summing. In this example, the variables Count and Sum likewise take on new values each loop pass, this time dependent upon the value of the last integer read in. If the integer value read in is positive, its value is added to Sum, and 1 is added to Count. If it is nonpositive, the computer exits the loop. This final value read in is not used to assign a new value to Count and Sum. The values that Count and Sum take on at loop exit hence represent the count of positive integers read in and the sum of these integer values.

Example 6.2

```
Count:= 0;
Sum:= 0;
read(Int);
WHILE Int > 0 DO
    BEGIN
        Sum:= Sum + Int;
        Count:= Count + 1;
        read(Int)
    END;
readln;
writeln(Int:1, '    ', Sum:1, '    ', Count:1);
```

Desk tracing the loop

Figure 6.2 shows a desk trace of the program fragment for the following sequence of input values: 7 8 3 −2. Another less formal way to desk trace the loop is given below

Entry ⌐↓

Sum   0̸ 7̸ 1̸5̸ 18
Count 0̸ 1̸ 2̸ 3
Int   7̸ 8̸ 3̸ −2 → *exit: values of −2, 18, and 3 are displayed*

In this trace, each column corresponds to the value taken on by all variables

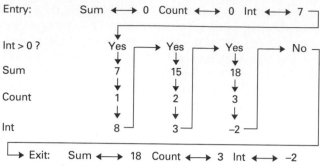

FIGURE 6.2 Desk trace of data for Example 6.2.

for a given loop pass. As a variable takes on a new value, we cross out its old value and write in the new value for the given loop pass. Note how the first column represents the loop entry values, and the last column represents the loop exit values. These last three values are the ones displayed by the writeln statement for the sample test data.

The loop invariants

The three variables in the loop body have the following invariants: The value of Int represents the value of the most recent integer read in from the keyboard. The value of Sum represents the sum of the values of all integers read in, excluding the value of the last one. The value of Count represents the count of the number of integers read in, excluding the last one. If you look again at the desk trace, you can confirm that these invariants are consistent with the sample data of the desk trace.

Making two assertions

The loop for our desk trace is exited when -2 is read into Int. Once the exit event occurs, the values of Sum and Count take on added significance. Respectively, they represent the fact that the sum of the consecutive sequence of positive integers read in was 18 and exactly three positive integers existed in the sequence.

How so? If the loop is entered, the value just read in would have to be positive. Then the loop entry condition is satisfied, so that this value is added to Sum and 1 added to Count. The loop exit condition occurs when the final value read in is not positive. Therefore, this value breaks the sequence of positive values read in. Its value is not added to Sum nor is Count's value incremented by 1.

Regardless of what integers values are read in, at loop exit the value of Sum will represent the cumulative sum of the consecutive positive integers read in. The value of Count will represent the number of positive integer values in the sequence. These two values at loop exit thus represent the solution to the following problem: "Write a fragment that finds the sum and count of a sequence of positive input integers. The process ends when a nonpositive integer is entered."

The third example

In the next example of a source code fragment, 10 integer values are read in. If a value is positive, it is added to the variable Sum. If the value is nonpositive, then the variable Count is incremented by 1. At loop exit, the value assigned to Sum will represent the sum of the positive integers out of the 10 that were read in. The value assigned to Count will represent the count of the number of nonpositive integer values of the 10 that were read in.

The source code for the example we have just described is given as follows:

Example 6.3

```
Sum:= 0;
Count:= 0;
Pass:= 0;
WHILE Pass <> 10 DO
   BEGIN
     Pass:= Pass + 1;
     read(Int);
     IF Int <= 0 THEN
        Count:= Count + 1
     ELSE
        Sum:= Sum + Int
   END;
readln;
writeln(Sum:1,' ',Count:1);
```

Loop invariants

We have the following invariants for each of the variables in the loop body: The value of Pass represents the number of the loop pass that was just executed. The value of Int represents the value of the Passth integer read in. The value of Sum represents the sum of all the positive integers out of the Pass integers that have been read in. The value of Count represents the count of the number of non-positive integers out of the Pass integers that have been read in.

A desk trace

The following is a sample input sequence and a desk trace of the values taken on by the four variables for the given source code fragment:

Entry ⌐

Input:	3	−2	1	5	−8	6	5	−1	1	3
Pass	0	1	2	3	4	5	6	7	8	9	10
Int	1	3	−2	1	3	−8	6	5	−1	1	3
Sum	0	3	3	4	9	9	15	20	20	21	24
Count	0	0	1	1	1	2	2	2	3	3	3	⟶ Exit

You can look at the values taken on by the variables after any loop pass to show that the invariants describe a correct relationship. For example, after Pass 7 we have that 7 values were read in. The seventh value read in was 5. The sum of the positive integers out of these seven values read in was 20. Of these, two values read in were negative.

Three final assertions

The final value assigned to Pass will always be 10 at loop exit. This value represents the fact that 10 integers were read in. The final value assigned to Sum, in our example, 24, represents the sum of all positive integers out of the group of 10 that were read in. The final value assigned to Count, in this case three, represents the count of the number of nonpositive integers that were read in out of the group of 10.

EXERCISES

Test Your Understanding

1. In order for a WHILE loop to be entered, the value of the control expression must be _____ . In order for the WHILE loop to be exited, the value of the control expression must become _____ .

Practice Your Analysis Skills

2. Indicate the values displayed by the source code of Example 6.2 given each of the following sequences of input values:
   (a)   15   35   70   25   −10   30   60   −50   80   90
   (b)   −10   20   30   60   −50   −60   −20   10   20   −50

3. Apply the same sequences for Exercise 2 on the source code of Example 6.3.

4. Indicate the display when the following fragment is executed:

```
Sum: = 0;
Count: = 0;
WHILE Count <> 10 DO
   BEGIN
      Count: = Count + 1;
      Sum: = Sum + 2 * Count;
      writeln(Count: 5,  Sum: 5)
   END;
```

5. Apply the input sequences of Exercise 2 and indicate the resultant display when they are applied on the following fragment:

```
PSum: = 0;   NSum: = 0;
Count: = 0;
WHILE Count <> 10 DO
   BEGIN
      Count: = Count + 1;
      read(Int);
      IF Int < 0 THEN
         NSum: = NSum + Int
      ELSE
         PSum: = PSum + Int
   END;
readln;
writeln(PSum: 5,  NSum: 5);
```

6.2   How Loops Solve Problems

In the previous section, you saw how we used loops to solve three different problems. In this section, we will continue the analysis of the three solutions, this time showing how the specific solutions fall into different categories of standard algorithms that use loops. If you have a problem to solve that requires a loop, perhaps some of the algorithms we present in this section will work as a first draft to your solution.

The Three Parts of a Loop Solution

The pseudocode to a problem that is solved using a loop will usually satisfy the following description:

set necessary initial values	*{set preconditions}*
do the loop processing	*{work towards a solution}*
use values returned by loop	*{use postconditions}*

Neither the first action in the description, *loop initialization*, nor the third action in the description, *loop postprocessing*, is repetitive. The middle action, *execution of the loop body*, is. When the computer carries out this middle action, it executes a sequence of similar events until the exit condition, caused by an event that occurs within the loop body, is met.

Event: a specific statement that, upon being carried out, changes a particular aspect of the program state.

Exit event: an event whose occurrence during the execution of a loop body causes a given loop process to terminate.

Loop initialization: those actions, executed before loop entry, that set up the preconditions for the loop to solve the problem correctly.

Postprocessing: those actions, executed after loop exit, that use the results returned by the loop's actions to complete the solution to the problem.

Loop initializations

The three problems solved in the previous section all require loop initialization statements. In all three examples, the variables Sum and Count are set to 0 before the loop is entered. Sum is assigned the value 0 before loop entry because at that point in the execution of the program fragment no values are yet accumulated into the variable Sum. Count is assigned the value 0 before loop entry because at that point in the execution of the program fragment no events have yet occurred to be counted.

Execution of the loop body

Once the loop is entered, the body is executed repeatedly until the exit event occurs. For a WHILE loop, the exit event occurs at the end of a loop pass when the control expression evaluates to false. At this point, the repetitive part of the problem is "solved." In Examples 6.1 and 6.3, the looping part of the problem was solved after the computer had executed a fixed number of loop passes. In Example 6.2, the loop process was finished when a negative integer value was read in.

Sometimes the actions carried out with each loop pass represent a part of the solution. In Example 6.1, the last action of the loop body was to display the values assigned to Count and Sum, thus producing one more line of the required 5 lines in the tabular display. In the other two examples, the events that occur with each loop pass accumulate values in a variable(s) that works to some final result representing the solution. The values given to Sum and Count after each loop pass for Examples 6.2 and 6.3 used this kind of processing.

Example 6.1 required no postprocessing, for the solution itself was the tabular display. With Examples 6.2 and 6.3, the values of Count and Sum hold the solutions to each problem. These values are displayed after the loops are finished as the required postprocessing that completes the solution for each of the two examples.

Different postprocessing

Sometimes postprocessing requires more than just the display of some solution accumulated by the loop's statements. We could have applied the sequence of Example 6.2 to solve the next problem.

Example Problem 6.1

The problem statement

Write a fragment which will display the average of a consecutive sequence of positive input integers.

The solution

The initialization and loop body of Example 6.2 are sufficient to solve the problem up to the postprocessing part. The postconditions at loop exit on Count and Sum are that Count represents the count of the number of consecutive positive integers read in and Sum represents their sum. The average of these integers is therefore given by the expression Sum/Count as long as Count is not 0.

It is possible, however, that the first number read in is nonpositive, so Count can take on the value of 0. A guard against division by 0 is hence necessary. If we follow the sequence given in Example 6.2 by the source code fragment that follows, we will have solved the problem correctly.

```
{a postloop process for the results returned by Example 6.2.}
  IF Count <> 0 THEN
    writeln('The average of the ',Count:1, 'consecutive '
            'positive integers read in is ',Sum / Count:4:2)
  ELSE
    writeln('The first integer read in was not positive.') ◆
```

Problems that Can be Solved by Loops

Now we will categorize some of the problems that can be solved by loops as "proven algorithms." We will give you both a text description and a pseudocode description of each algorithm. After we present the pseudocode of the algorithm, we will prove it using assertions.

These algorithms are very useful. If you have a problem that can be solved by modifying the pseudocode of a proven algorithm, you have the first draft toward a coded solution. The skill lies in recognizing what proven algorithm, if any, to use. You will develop this skill through study of the text and through continued practice in solving problems.

Assertion testing a loop

Besides giving you the pseudocode descriptions for a number of looping algorithms, we will also prove each of them. Hence, they can be called "proven algorithms." The heart to the proof of an algorithm that uses a loop lies in stating some relevant loop invariants. Recall that an invariant is a condition that is true at the start and end of every loop pass. We might also state that a loop invariant is a postcondition of the previous loop pass and a precondition for the next loop pass. An invariant must therefore hold true just before the loop is entered and just after the loop is exited.

When we apply assertion testing on an algorithm that uses a loop, we first state the loop invariants. The loop initializations must be implemented in a way consistent with the invariant conditions. The invariants, moreover, describe how each loop pass works toward attaining the desired program state that represents a solution at loop exit. At loop exit, we then make further assertions about the program state also in terms of the loop invariants. If the program state they describe represents the desired program state at loop exit, we have shown that the loop represents a logically correct solution to the problem. Let us now look at some proven algorithms:

Sequential Event Counting.   The variable to count events is set to 0 before loop entry. It is incremented by 1 with each loop pass, so that at loop exit its value represents the number of sequential events that had occurred. A loop to count sequential events uses a *counting action* in its body to solve the problem.

> **Event counting:**   a process, often associated with a loop, in which the count of the number of times a specified event occurs is recorded and updated.

> **Event counter:**   the variable used to record the number of specified events in an event-counting process.

The pseudocode description for sequential event counting is given as Algorithm 6.1.

Algorithm 6.1

> {*Sequential-event-counting:*}
> *EventCounter* ← *0*
> *get EventValue*
> *WHILE EventValue represents a countable event DO*
>   *EventCounter* ← *EventCounter* + *1*
>   *get EventValue*
> {*end algorithm*}

Assertion testing Algorithm 6.1   The invariant for *EventValue* is, "The value of *EventValue* represents the value associated with the last event in the sequence." The invariant for the variable *EventCounter* is, "The value of *EventCounter* represents the count of the events that have occurred, excluding the last event." The postloop assertion on *EventValue* is then, "The value of *EventValue* represents the value of the noncountable event that terminated the sequence of countable events. Likewise, the postloop assertion on *EventCounter* is, "The value of *EventCounter* represents the number of events that were counted in sequence."

Using Algorithm 6.1   We used Algorithm 6.1 on Example 6.2 to get a solution. The variables *EventCounter* and *EventValue* of Algorithm 6.1 correspond to the variables Count and Int of the coded program fragment given as Example 6.2.

Selective Event Counting.   With this algorithm, a sequence of events is processed such that the events are selectively counted. The event counter is set to 0 before loop entry. A decision statement is required in the loop body for this algorithm to work properly. The algorithm uses a *conditional counting action* in its body to get a solution.

The pseudocode description for selective event counting is given as Algorithm 6.2.

Algorithm 6.2

> *{Selective Event Counting:}*
> *EventCounter ← 0*
> *WHILE more events to process DO*
>   *get EventValue*
>   *IF EventValue represents a significant event THEN*
>   *EventCounter ← EventCounter + 1*
> *{end algorithm}*

Assertion testing Algorithm 6.2

The invariant for *EventValue* is the same as that of Algorithm 6.1. The invariant for *EventCounter* is, "The value of *EventCounter* represents the count of the number of significant events that have occurred out of the candidate sequence of events." Once the loop is exited, we can make the postloop assertions, "The candidate sequence of events is finished, and the value of *EventCounter* represents the number of significant events that occurred in this sequence."

Using Algorithm 6.2

We used Algorithm 6.2 in Example 6.3 to count the number of nonpositive integers read in, where, again, the analogous variable pairs between pseudocode and source code are (1) *EventCounter* and Count and (2) *EventValue* and Int. In the example of this particular program fragment, a *significant event* occurs when a negative integer is read in. The condition described by *more events to process* codes to the boolean expression Pass <> 10.

Event Accumulation.   We used event accumulation as part of the process for the source code fragments of Examples 6.1 and 6.2. The loop body of both these fragments used a *sum accumulation* process where each event contributed to the final sum returned by the loop's actions.

Accumulation: a process, often associated with a loop, where the old value taken on by an accumulation variable is combined with the value representing the occurrence of a new event to assign a new value to the accumulation variable.

Accumulation variable: a variable used to accumulate values for some specified event.

Algorithm 6.3 describes an algorithm to accumulate a sum over all the events that occur in some well-specified sequence. Each event, furthermore, is represented by a numeric value.

Algorithm 6.3

$$
\begin{aligned}
&\textit{\{Sum accumulation:\}}\\
&\textit{Sum} \leftarrow 0\\
&\textit{WHILE more events to process DO}\\
&\qquad \textit{get EventValue}\\
&\qquad \textit{Sum} \leftarrow \textit{Sum} + \textit{EventValue}\\
&\textit{\{end algorithm\}}
\end{aligned}
$$

Assertion testing Algorithm 6.3

The invariant condition on *EventValue* is the same invariant used with the preceding algorithms. The invariant for *Sum* is, "The value of *Sum* represents the sum of all events whose values have been gotten." When the loop is exited, we can then make the assertions, "The sequence of events is completed, and the value of *Sum* represents the accumulated sum of the events."

Using Algorithm 6.3

In Example 6.1, the action described by *get EventValue* codes to the assignment Count:= Count + 1. The boolean expression whose pseudocode is *more events to process* codes to the entry condition Count <> 5. In Example 6.2, the action described by *getEventValue* codes to read(Int). The condition described by *more events to process* codes to the boolean expression Int > 0.

Selective Event Accumulation. In the case of Example 6.3, we used a decision statement to carry out an accumulation process on selective events. This algorithm used a *conditional accumulation* action in the loop body to get a solution. It is actually a special case of the accumulation process where the description of sum accumulation inside the loop body is given as

$$
\begin{aligned}
&\textit{IF EventValue represents a significant event THEN}\\
&\qquad \textit{Sum} \leftarrow \textit{Sum} + \textit{EventValue}
\end{aligned}
$$

The post-loop assertion on the value of *Sum* for a selective summing algorithm is stated as, "The sum of the significant events which occurred over the loop's sequence of processed events is found in the value of *Sum*." A significant event as it applied to the variable Int in Program Fragment 6.3 was associated with the ELSE path of the IF statement. This significant event was that the value of Int was positive.

Summary comments

We have just described four proven algorithms that are applicable to the solution of four distinct problems. Each algorithm uses a variable to get some event value and another variable to store a value that, at loop exit, represents a solution. The variable used to store this solution value has to be initialized at loop entry to a value representing the fact that no events have yet been processed. Its value at loop exit represents the cumulative effect of the sequence of events carried out with each loop pass. Its value changes with the occurrence of each event, but its purpose does not. This purpose is best expressed as a loop invariant. The invariant condition must hold true for all parts of the loop process in order for the algorithm to be logically correct.

Entry/Exit Algorithms

The algorithms we have presented so far have said little about the loop entry or exit conditions. They concentrated on describing the statements carried out in the loop body. Now let us look at a description of the two loop entry/exit algorithms we used in our examples. Remember that when a loop entry condition is `true`, a sequence of events must be processed to solve the problem. When the loop exit condition becomes `true`, no more events that make up the loop body are required for the solution of the problem.

Executing A Predetermined Number Of Passes. The variable to count loop passes is initialized to 0. The loop entry condition is that the value of this counter not be equal to N, the number of passes desired. As soon as the loop is entered, the loop pass counter is incremented by 1. In order for the algorithm to work, the rest of the loop body should not include statements that change the value of this variable. At the end of the loop, its value represents the number of loop passes that have been executed. The postloop assertion we can therefore make is, "The loop has done N iterations."

The pseudocode description is given as Algorithm 6.4.

Algorithm 6.4

> *{Carrying out N loop passes:}*
> *Pass:= 0;*
> *WHILE Pass < > N DO*
>   *Pass:= Pass + 1*
>   *rest of loop body*   *{Pass is not reassigned a new value!!}*
> *{end algorithm}*

We used Algorithm 6.4 in Examples 6.1 and 6.3. There is a better way to implement this algorithm using a FOR loop. We will show you this form of the algorithm in Section 6.4.

Processing A Sequence Of Events to A Sentinel Event. A value representing a candidate event for processing is obtained and assigned to the variable for holding this value. As long as the event's value does not represent a loop-terminating condition, it is processed in the loop's body. The initial action of the loop body is to process the last event. Then a new event value is gotten and assigned to the event-holding variable. This value is then tested for loop entry. The action of processing the last event, then getting a new event continues until a terminal event is found, thus resulting in the loop's exit.

This algorithm is the one most commonly used with the WHILE statement. We used it in Example 6.2 where the terminating event occurred when a nonpositive value was read in. The algorithm's description is given in the pseudocode of Algorithm 6.5.

Algorithm 6.5

{Processing a sequence of events to a terminating event:}
get EventValue
WHILE EventValue does not represent terminal event DO
process EventValue
get EventValue
{end algorithm}

Assertions

The loop invariants for the algorithm are stated in two sentences: "*EventValue* represents the value of the last event. All events, except for the last one have been processed." The postloop assertion is, "All events except for the last one were processed, and *EventValue* holds the value of the loop-terminating event."

Complementary conditions

If you use Algorithm 6.5, you will need to know the source code to express the loop exit condition. However, the loop entry condition is the boolean expression you must code to apply the algorithm. If you know the expression for the exit condition, you can use it, along with Table 6.1 to code the required loop entry condition.

The entry condition for any loop is the complementary condition of the exit condition. You can code a complement to a given simple boolean expression by replacing the relational operation of the coded expression with its complementary operator. The expressions on either side of the operator are left unchanged. Table 6.1 shows you the six boolean operators and their complements. Table 6.2 shows the complements of the boolean expressions used in the three program fragments.

TABLE 6.1 Boolean Operators and Their Complements

Operator	Complement
$<$	$>=$
$<=$	$>$
$=$	$<>$
$<>$	$=$
$>$	$<=$
$>=$	$<$

TABLE 6.2 Some Boolean Expressions and Their Complements

Expression	Complement
Count $<>$ 5	Count $=$ 5
Int $>$ 0	Int $<=$ 0
Count $<>$ 10	Count $=$ 10
Int $<=$ 0	Int $>$ 0

EXERCISES

1. What are the three parts of a sequence that uses a loop to solve a problem? Are all three parts necessary for every problem?

2. Write down the complementary condition for each of the following boolean expressions:
   (a) Count > 10 **(b)** Sum = 0 **(c)** Sum1 >= Sum2 **(d)** LInt < KInt + 2

3. Determine whether a loop, decision statement, or sequence of statements is required to solve each of the following problems:
   (a) Find the lowest value of 10 integers read in.
   (b) Find the lower value between two integers.
   (c) Exchange the values of variables Int1, Int2, and Int3 such that Int1 will have Int2's initial value, Int2 will have Int3's initial value and Int3 will have Int1's initial value.
   (d) Keep reading input integers from the keyboard until the user guesses the mystery integer.
   (e) Display the string "Fine" if the user inputs the string "OK". Otherwise, do nothing.
   (f) Multiply two numbers if they are both positive; otherwise add them.
   (g) Assign the product of two integer variables to a third variable.
   (h) Search for the first occurance of a particular character that is to be read in.

6.3 Problem-Solving Examples

At this point, we have categorized a number of algorithms, but we have still not solved any problems from an initial problem statement. Now we will, relying heavily on the algorithms presented in the previous section. There are, however, cases where you may be given a problem whose solution is not readily known in terms of a standard algorithm. You can still solve the problem by deriving the required algorithm with an initial description and applying stepwise refinements. We will solve two problems using this method.

When to use a loop

Loops work best on problems that require that a sequence of similar events be processed in a similar manner. This sequence of events must have an exit condition that is an achievable and measurable complement to the loop entry condition. If the solution to a problem can be described in this manner, a loop is a coding strategy to consider.

Loop design questions

Suppose you have decided that a loop is required to solve a problem. In order to implement a solution, you need to find the answer to the following questions:

1. What algorithm should I use?
2. How do I write the entry/exit conditions?
3. What, if any, initialization statements do I write?
4. What statements do I write for the loop body?
5. What, if any, postprocessing statements do I write?

Quite often, if you have answered the first question because you know some standard algorithm, you will know the answers to many of the other questions. For example, if you want to accumulate a sum, you set the variable to 0 before loop entry. Then, for every event to be summed, you simply write code described by *Sum ← Sum + EventValue* as part of the loop body.

If you do not know the answer to the first question, describe what you know about the loop using pseudocode. As you continue to refine the description, you will eventually find the answer to this question.

Example Problem 6.2

The problem statement

Write a program to find and display the average of a sequence of the first 10 *positive* input integers. Any nonpositive integer read in is not included in the average. A typical run might look like

```
40  50  60  -10  -20  90  90  50  -20  50  70  90  -20  80  -70  80  20
The average of the first 10 positive numbers was 58.0
```

The initial draft

We need a process to take the sum of 10 integers, all of which are positive. The actual way to get the positive integers is an issue we will deal with in the second draft. For now, we can combine the algorithm that processes *N* values, Algorithm 6.4, with the sum accumulation algorithm, Algorithm 6.3, to get the description:

> *Sum ← 0*
> *Count ← 0*
> *WHILE Count <> 10 DO*
>   *Count ← Count + 1*
>   *read in a positive value to Int*
>   *Sum ← Sum + Int*
> *readln*
> *display the value of Sum/10*

The refinement

This algorithm is logically correct as long as we can read in a positive value to Int. How do we do this, though? We need to have a process that guarantees that the condition Int > 0 is true when it is completed.

We can look back at Algorithm 6.5 (processing to a sentinel event) to get the right idea. The required process is started by having an initial value read into Int, and then using a WHILE loop whose exit condition is that Int > 0. The pseudocode for this process is

> *read (Int)*
> *WHILE Int <= 0 DO*
>   *read(Int)*

Source code

The program AverageTenPositives is the coded solution to the problem.

```
PROGRAM  AverageTenPositives(input, output);
  {The user enters a sequence of integers where the computer finds and
  displays the average of the first 10 positive integers.}
  VAR
    Sum,        {accumulates sum of positive integers}
    Int,        {used to store value read in}
    Count:      {counts number of integers summed}
                integer;
  BEGIN
    Sum:= 0;
    Count:= 0;
    WHILE Count <> 10 DO
      BEGIN
        Count:= Count + 1;
        read(Int);
        WHILE Int <= 0 DO
          read(Int);
        Sum:= Sum + Int
      END;
    readln;
    write('The average of the first 10 positive numbers was ');
    writeln(Sum/10:3:1)
  END.  ◆
```

A condition-seeking loop

The second WHILE loop in the solution describes an algorithm that seeks out a desired program state. In the problem we solved, as long as values are read into Int that are not positive, the computer keeps reading in values to Int. The loop is exited only when a positive value is read in.

This code is an adoption of an algorithm that seeks out a desired program state. The pseudocode for this algorithm is described by Algorithm 6.6.

Algorithm 6.6

> {*Seek out a desired condition on EventVar:*}
> *get EventVar*
> *WHILE value of EventVar does not represent desired condition DO*
>   *get EventVar*
> {*end algorithm*}

After the computer exits this loop, we can make the assertion, "The value taken on by EventVar represents a desired condition. You can apply this algorithm any time you need to set up preconditions for further processing where the first value obtained may not represent a good precondition that can be processed correctly.

Example Problem 6.3

The problem statement

Let us write a program to display a table showing the sum of the first 50 consecutive integers from 1 to 50. The table should display every fifth sum. The program run looks like

COUNT	SUM
-----	---
5	15
10	55
15	120
20	210
25	325
30	465
35	630
40	820
45	1035
50	1275

First draft

We want the computer to accumulate a sum, one integer at a time, in a manner similar to the actions of Example 6.1. In this case, however, we want every fifth sum rather than every sum to be displayed. Therefore, we can describe the solution with the pseudocode

> *display table headers*
> *Sum ← 0*
> *Count ← 0*
> *WHILE Count <>50 DO*
> *Count ← Count + 1*
> *Sum ← Sum + Count*
> *IF Count is a 5th value THEN*
> *display Count, Sum*

Refining the IF *statement*

Once we find the boolean expression representing the condition *Count is a 5th value*, we have solved the problem. When Count is a fifth value, it means that 5 divides evenly into it. In other words, the boolean expression Count MOD 5 = 0 evaluates to true. This boolean expression is therefore the one we should use.

The solution to this problem is given as the code of ShowSums.

```
PROGRAM ShowSums(output);
  {A table of every 5th sum of the first 50 consecutive integers from 1
  to 50 is displayed.}
  VAR
    Sum,     {accumulates a sum of the first Count integers}
```

```
     Count:      {variable to count processes}
                 integer;

  BEGIN
     writeln('COUNT':10, 'SUM':10);
     writeln('-----':10, '---':10);
     Sum:= 0;
     Count:= 0;
     WHILE Count <> 50 DO
        BEGIN
           Count:= Count + 1;
           Sum:= Sum + Count;
           IF Count MOD 5 = 0 THEN
              writeln(Count:10, Sum:10)
        END
  END.  ◆
```

*Determining an
algorithm*

Sometimes you may not know of a standard algorithm you can use as a first-draft solution to your problem. You still know, however, you need a loop to solve the problem. In this case, you must try to find an algorithm by thinking of how the loop should solve the problem. Usually, you will use at least one variable to get the desired solution. This variable is most likely set to an initial value before the loop is entered. This initial value indicates that no events that make up the sequence of iterations have yet been processed.

Each loop pass is going to carry out at least one event that will affect the value of this variable. The variable's purpose is to record the way the given event contributes to the eventual solution. This purpose should not change each loop pass, but the variable's value probably will.

The purpose can be described by an invariant condition. You can use this condition (1) to determine what should be done for each loop pass and (2) to apply assertion testing on the solution. Once you have a variable with a given purpose, you can draft a solution, applying pseudocode and stepwise refinements.

Example Problem 6.4

*The problem
statement*

Let us write a program to find and display the factorials of the first 10 integers in tabular form. (Recall that a factorial is expressed as $N! = 1 * 2 * 3 * \cdots * (N - 1) * N$). The run of the program looks like

N	N!
1	1
2	2
3	6
4	24

5	120
6	720
7	5040
8	40320
9	362880
10	3628800

The processes
required

We definitely need a variable for counting loop passes. We also want to display every pass. At the end of pass 1, the value 1 is displayed to represent 1! At the end of pass 2, the value 2 is displayed to represent 1 * 2. For pass 3, the display of 6 represents the product 1 * 2 * 3. Therefore, it looks like we need a variable to accumulate a product. Moreover, the value this variable takes on after pass N should represent the value of N!

The accumulation statement is thus described by Prod ← Prod*Count. This variable cannot be initialized to 0, for then the loop invariant would be, "The value of Prod is 0." Clearly, this invariant does not represent a solution! If, however, we initialize Prod to 1, the first product accumulated will be 1 * 1 when Count is equal to 1. Given this initialization, the invariant for the loop will be, "The value of Prod represents the value of Count!" This invariant does describe a correct solution.

Once we have set up these two actions, the problem is just like that of sum accumulation, except that now we are accumulating a product. Hence, the initialization statement before the loop is different, and the assignment statement inside the loop body is different. The accumulation process itself, however, is essentially the same.

The solution to the problem is shown as the program ShowFactorials.

```
PROGRAM ShowFactorials(output);
   {Displays a table of the factorial functions up to 10 factorial.}
   VAR
      Prod,     {product accumulation variable}
      Count:    {variable used to form Count! with Prod}
               integer;
   BEGIN
      writeln('N':15,  'N!':15);
      writeln('-':15,  '--':15);
      Prod:= 1;
      Count:= 0;
      WHILE Count <> 10 DO
         BEGIN
            Count:= Count + 1
            Prod:= Prod * Count;
            writeln(Count:15, Prod:15)
         END
   END.  ◆
```

Every loop, to represent a valid solution to some problem, must have an entry condition and an exit condition. Once a loop is entered, you must be sure that each loop pass represents an attempt to attain an exit condition. You must, therefore, consider the requirements that represent an exit condition for the problem you need to solve. Also, you must be sure you have coded something in the loop body that guarantees the exit condition will eventually be reached.

Perhaps you may not know initially how to determine the entry or exit condition for a problem. If the entry condition is met, the loop is entered. If a loop is entered, it indicates that the same process must be repeated a number of times to solve the problem. Likewise, a loop is exited when no more repetitive processing is required to get a solution. Therefore, the exit condition represents that there is no further need to repeat the process, for some solution condition has been realized. This condition can be expressed as a postloop assertion when the loop is exited.

If you are unsure about coding the entry and exit conditions, you should look at the problem statement again to see how the sequence should start and how it should end. These two conditions together describe the entry/exit conditions for the loop. You can set initial values to variables used for loop entry if you can find the assertion(s) you should make before entry about the problem that must be solved. You can likewise code the loop control expression once you determine what assertion(s) must be made at loop exit to indicate that the problem has been solved.

Example Problem 6.5

The problem statement

Your investment club has just purchased a Pascal program to help make investment decisions. The president of the club wants you to modify the program with a procedure that will read in a sequence of market prices for a specified number of days. The procedure should return the count of the number of days that the price went up and the count of the number of days that it went down for a user-specified period. An unchanged day does not count either as an up day or a down day.

A typical execution, given the call CountDays(10, Ups, Downs) and the following 10 prices: 37.25, 37.50, 38.00, 37.75, 37.50, 38.00, 38.00, 38.25, 38.75, and 38.25 will return Ups ↔ 5 and Downs ↔ 3. The first parameter represents that the prices over the last 10 days should be processed. The variables Ups and Downs, respectively, represent the number of up days and the number of down days for the 10 days.

The stub

The procedure requires that the first parameter be a value call and the other two be VAR calls. The stub for this procedure, without documentation, is thus coded as

```
PROCEDURE CountDays(TotalDays: integer; VAR Ups, Downs: integer);
   BEGIN   END;
```

First draft of the statement

This problem is one we can classify as an event counter. The two counters, Ups and Downs, must be initialized to 0 before the loop is entered. Each loop pass will update one of the two counters depending upon the value of a Previous price and a `Present` price, both local variables. We also expect to use the loop to count the number of values that have been read in. So for our first pseudocode draft, we have

> *initialize Ups and Downs both to 0*
> *intialize values of DayNo, Previous and Present*
> *WHILE DayNo < > TotalDays DO*
>   *DayNo ← DayNo + 1*
>   *update values for Previous and Present*
>   *IF Present < Previous THEN*
>   *Downs ← Downs + 1*
>   *ELSE IF Present > Previous THEN*
>   *Ups ← Ups + 1*

Assertion testing
Now let us check our description. The invariant on `DayNo` is that it represents the day that has just been processed. The value of `Previous` represents the price on `DayNo` −1. The value of `Present` represents the price on `DayNo`. One attempt to update, `Downs` and `Ups` is done per loop pass based on the results of one comparison for each variable. At loop exit, moreover, we can say that the prices for `TotalDays` have been processed. Therefore, it looks like our draft is logically correct. We still need to find initial values for `Previous`, `Present`, and `DayNo`, representing loop entry conditions. Also, we need a description for the updating process on the values of `Previous` and `Present`.

Refinements
If we consider that each loop pass is going to process one more day, only one value should be read in per pass. This value should be read into `Present`. The initial comparison, moreover must be made with day two because an initial value for `Present` must have first been read in. Hence, outside the loop we require the two initializations whose pseudocode is

> *DayNo ← 1*   *{represents count of value to be read in}*
> *read(Present)*   *{represents last value read in}*

Within the loop body, we also want a value read into `Present`. Moreover, the previous value assigned to `Present` must first be assigned to `Previous`. Hence, the way to update the values is described by the pseudocode:

> *Previous ← Present*   *{Previous represents last value read in}*
> *read(Present)*   *{Previous represents next-to-last value read in}*

Assertion testing
We have added assertions as comments to the right of the pseudocode. The assertions are consistent with the semantics we gave to the variables in the first draft. We can also confirm, too, that the loop starts off properly with a comparison of day 1's price with day 2's price. Therefore, these refinements still represent a correct solution.

Source code
The coded solution to this problem is shown as the procedure `CountDays`.

```
PROCEDURE CountDays(TotalDays: integer; VAR Ups, Downs: integer);
  {in:   TotalDays -- the number of prices to be read in and processed}
  out:   Ups -- the number of up days on the market price
         Downs -- the number of down days on the market price}
  VAR
    DayNo:        {the day for which an up or down is being found}
                  integer;
    Previous,     {the price on DayNo - 1}
    Present:      {the price on DayNo}
                  real;

BEGIN
  Ups:= 0;
  Downs:= 0;
  DayNo:= 1;
  read(Present);
WHILE DayNo <> TotalDays DO
  BEGIN
    DayNo:= Day No + 1;
    Previous:= Present;
    read(Present);
    IF Present < Previous THEN
      Downs:= Downs + 1
    ELSE IF Present > Previous THEN
      Ups:= Ups + 1
  END;
  readln        {clear the line}
END;  ◆
```

EXERCISES

Test Your Understanding

1. True or false? It is necessary to know both the loop entry and the loop exit conditions in order to develop the loop body.

2. True or false? A loop invariant's only use is in assertion testing an algorithm that uses a loop.

3. In Example Problem 6.4, we said that if the value of Prod was initialized to 0, the loop invariant would be stated as, "The value of Prod is 0." Briefly explain how this statement is an invariant on Prod for this (faulty) initialization statement.

Practice Your Analysis Skills

4. In the procedure CountDays, what value(s) are returned to Ups and/or Downs if the value passed into TotalDays is 1?

5. Repeat Exercise 4, but this time let TotalDays take on a value of 2.

Learn More About Your System

6. It is important that you know the limits of your machine. Therefore, try running the program ShowFactorials, where the loop control condition is coded as Count <> 50. Can you explain what happened?

7. Repeat Exercise 6, but this time declare the variable `Prod` to be of type `real`. What happened in this case? (*Note:* Make sure to code the display statements so that there are no run-on numbers.)

6.4 The FOR Loop

We have alluded to the FOR loop in Section 6.2. It is a loop that uses a counting action for loop control. When you use a FOR loop, you take care of the details of the loop entry condition, the loop exit condition, and the means of reaching the exit condition with a single line of code. You can use this loop very effectively on an algorithm that uses a counting variable for loop control, where the entry value and the exit value of this variable can be coded as loop control expressions.

FOR statement syntax and semantics

The syntax diagram of the FOR loop statement is shown in Figure 6.3. The variable identifier is the name of the *loop control variable*, the first expression represents the initial value this variable takes on, and the final expression represents the final value it takes on. When the reserved word TO is used, the next value given to the loop control variable is the next higher value it can take on. When the reserved word DOWNTO is used, the value of the loop control variable after each pass is changed to the next lower possible value it can take on.

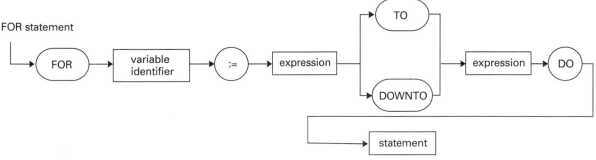

FIGURE 6.3 Syntax of the FOR statement.

Loop control variable: a variable, often associated with the *FOR* loop, whose value determines the loop entry and the loop exit conditions.

FOR loop version of Example 6.1

The FOR loop version of Example 6.1 is shown in the coded fragment given as Example 6.4. The WHILE loop version, Example 6.1 reproduced, is shown on the right. Note that in both cases, the initial value taken on by the loop control variable Count within the loop body is 1. The final value taken on is 5. The value of Count is incremented by 1 each loop pass. In the FOR loop version, this action is carried out because we used the reserved word TO.

Example 6.4

```
{FOR loop counting}              {WHILE loop counting}
Sum:= 0;                         Sum:= 0;
FOR Count:= 1 TO 5  DO           Count:= 0;
  BEGIN                          WHILE Count <> 5 DO
    Sum:= Sum + Count;             BEGIN
    writeln(Count:5, Sum:5)          Count:= Count + 1;
  END;                               Sum:= Sum + Count;
writeln('Finished...');              writeln(Count:5, Sum:5)
                                   END;
                                 writeln('Finished...');
```

We referenced the value of Count, representing the loop pass number being executed, twice in each loop body. You can reference the value of the loop control variable of a FOR loop as often as you need. However, you must *never* write code that assigns or reads in a new value to this variable.

An example that uses DOWNTO

If you use the reserved word DOWNTO in a FOR loop, the value for the loop control variable is set to an upper limit at loop entry. This value is decreased to the next lower value at the start of each loop pass. Example 6.5 and its execution, given below the source code, shows the source code and execution of a FOR loop constructed with the reserved word *DOWNTO*. The logically equivalent WHILE loop version is shown on the right.

Example 6.5

```
FOR Count:= 10 DOWNTO 0 DO       Count:= 11;
  write(Count:3);                WHILE Count <> 0 DO
writeln(' Blastoff!');             BEGIN
                                     Count:= Count - 1;
                                     write(Count:3)
                                   END;
                                 writeln(' Blastoff!');
```

```
    10  9  8  7  6  5  4  3  2  1  0  Blastoff!
```

Using a char *type for loop control*

We have said that the FOR loop uses a counting mechanism. This counting mechanism can be done internally. For example, you can use a variable of type char as a loop control variable of the FOR loop. The internal counting is done through the system's collating sequence for char values. Example 6.6 shows how to display the letters of the alphabet using a FOR loop. We have assumed the machine encodes its char values in ASCII for this example. The analogous WHILE loop that produces the same effect is shown on the right.

Example 6.6

```
FOR Letter:= 'A' to 'Z' DO       Letter:= pred('A'):
  write(Letter);                 WHILE Letter <> 'Z' DO
writeln;                           BEGIN
```

```
                              Letter:= succ(Letter);
                              write(Letter)
                      END;
                  writeln;
```

ABCDEFGHIJKLMNOPQRSTUVWXYZ

Any variable type for which the pred and succ functions are defined can be used as a loop control variable of the FOR statement. Note that real and string variables are not viable candidates as loop control variables of the FOR loop but that integer and char variables are.

Two FOR Loop Algorithms

In this section we present and use two proven algorithms that are readily implemented with the FOR loop.

Carrying out N loop passes

The algorithm to carry out N loop passes using the FOR loop is usually preferred over the WHILE loop implementation. The pseudocode description is given as Algorithm 6.7.

Algorithm 6.7

> *{Carry out N loop passes:}*
> *FOR Count ← TO N DO*
>   *body*
> *{end algorithm}*

The loop invariant for this algorithm is "The value of *Count* represents the number of passes that have been executed," and the postloop assertion is, "A total of *N* loop passes have been executed."

Another FOR loop counting algorithm

There are many problems that require the first one, two or even more events be processed differently from the rest of the N events in a sequence. These initial events must be processed as part of the solution, but they more correctly belong to the initialization part. Example Problem 6.5 was a problem of this type because the price of the first day had to be processed before loop entry. The counting variable in this case took on the value 2 with the first loop pass.

You can implement this algorithm with a FOR loop whose description is given as Algorithm 6.8.

Algorithm 6.8

> *{Process N events, using the first Start-1 events for initialization:}*
> *get and process EventValues 1 through (Start-1)*
> *FOR Count ← Start TO N DO*
>   *get EventValue*
>   *process it*
> *{end algorithm}*

The loop invariant is, "All events through the *Count*th event have been processed." The postloop assertion is likewise, "A total of *N* events have been processed."

If you were to apply this algorithm on Example Problem 6.5 of the last section, the relevant code to carry it out is given as

```
ups:= 0; Downs:= 0;
read(Present);
FOR DayNo:= 2 TO TotalDays DO
  BEGIN
    Previous:= Present;
    read(Present);
    {rest of loop statements}
  END
```

Example Problem 6.6

The problem statement

The Fibonacci numbers are a famous sequence of integers generated the following way: The first two numbers are set to 0 and 1. All other numbers are found by taking the sum of the previous two numbers.

Write a program to generate and display the first N numbers, where the value of N is user-input. A typical run for this program, with 7 numbers per line display, is shown as

```
How many Fibonacci numbers do you want generated?   20
The numbers are:
      0       1       1       2       3       5       8
     13      21      34      55      89     144     233
    377     610     987    1597    2584    4181
```

The main block

We can describe the main block of the solution as

> *InitializeAll(Prev, Pres, N)*
> *display Prev, Pres*
> *FOR Count ← 3 TO N DO*
> * MakeNextNumber(Prev, Pres)*
> * display Pres*
> *clear remaining line display, if necessary*

The solution, with stubs for the two procedures, is then coded as the program MakeFibonacciNumbers.

```
PROGRAM MakeFibonacciNumbers(input, output);
  {The program finds and displays a user-specified count of Fibonacci
  numbers.}
  CONST
    NumbersPerLine = 7;      {total numbers to be shown per line}
    FieldSize = 8;           {reserved field size of 8 for each number}
```

```
VAR
  Prev,    {the previous number found}
  Pres,    {the present number found}
  Count,   {the total numbers generated}
  N:       {the total numbers user wants generated}
           integer;
{*                                                                 *}
PROCEDURE InitializeAll(VAR First, Second, N: integer);
  {out:  First, Second -- values of first and second Fib numbers
   out:  N -- the total count of numbers user wants generated}
  BEGIN   END;
{*                                                                 *}
PROCEDURE MakeNextNumber(VAR Prev, Pres: integer);
  {Generates a new Fibonacci number
   in/out: Prev, Pres -- the previous and present numbers generated}
  BEGIN   END;
{*                                                                 *}
BEGIN
  InitializeAll(Prev, Pres, N);
  write(Prev: FieldSize, Pres: FieldSize);
  FOR Count:= 3 TO N DO
    BEGIN
      MakeNextNumber(Prev, Pres);
      write(Pres: FieldSize);
      IF Count MOD NumbersPerLine = 0 THEN
        writeln
    END;
  IF N MOD NumbersPerLine <> 0 THEN
    writeln
END.
```

Assertion testing

Before the loop is entered, the values given to Prev and Pres respectively represent the first and second numbers generated. Their values have been displayed on one line. The value given to N represents the count of the numbers the user wants generated.

The loop invariants are, "The values given to Prev and Pres represent the values of the (Count −1)th and Countth numbers generated. Count numbers have been displayed on lines in groups of NumbersPerLine. The present line of numbers has Count MOD NumbersPerLine (to be?) displayed." The postloop assertion is, "The first N Fibonacci numbers have either been displayed or will have been displayed when the N MOD NumbersPerLine numbers on the last line are displayed." The final IF statement is necessary to clear the output buffer on some systems.

The procedure MakeNextNumber

The sequence to generate the next number is described by

$Temp \leftarrow Prev + Pres$ {*assertion: Temp is present number generated*}
$Prev \leftarrow Pres$ {*assertion: Prev is previous number generated*}
$Pres \leftarrow Temp$ {*assertion: Pres is present number generated*}

This sequence points out the need for a local variable inside the procedure MakeNextNumber. The code for this procedure follows:

```
PROCEDURE MakeNextNumber (VAR Prev, Pres: integer);
   VAR
     Temp: integer;        {temporary storage for next number}
   BEGIN
     Temp:= Prev + Pres;
     Prev:= Pres;
     Pres:= Temp
   END;  ◆
```

We leave the coding of InitializeAll as Exercise 6 at the end of this section.

Example Problem 6.7

The problem statement Write a fragment to find and display the highest integer value in a sequence of 10 input integers.

The required variables We will need a FOR loop to keep a count of the present number of integer values read in. We will need a variable Int to store this Countth value. We will also need a variable Highest whose value will represent the highest number of the Count numbers that have been read in. When the loop is exited, the value of this variable should represent the highest integer of the 10 that were read in.

Describing the sequence The loop body is described by

$$read(Int)$$
$$IF\ Int > Highest\ THEN$$
$$Highest \leftarrow Int$$

Before the IF statement is executed, the value of Highest, from the previous loop pass, will represent the highest value of all integers read in but the last one. After the IF statement is executed, Highest takes on the value of the highest integer so far read in.

In order for the loop to be valid, an initial value must have been read in to make the first comparison in the loop body possible. In order to be consistent with the loop invariant, this initial value should be stored as the highest value read in of all the 1 values read in. Hence, before loop entry, we should code the two actions

$$read(Int)$$
$$Highest \leftarrow Int$$

From this reasoning, we see that the loop control variable should be initialized to 2, rather than 1. The coded solution to the problem is then given as

```
read(Int);
Highest:= Int;
```

```
FOR Count:= 2 to 10 DO
   BEGIN
      read(Int);
      IF Int > Highest THEN
         Highest:= Int
   END;
readln;
writeln('The highest integer value input was ',Highest:1,'.');
```

Desk trace

A typical sequence and the desk trace of the solution is given below:

Input:	43	58	36	22	60	55	75	89	31	78
Int:	43	58	36	22	60	55	75	89	31	78
Count:	1	2	3	4	5	6	7	8	9	10
Highest:	43	58	58	58	60	60	75	89	89	89

You can confirm that the invariants are all correct for this example by inspection of the values in the desk trace.

Significant event recording

The solution to Example Problem 6.7 used an algorithm to find the most significant event out of a sequence of events. A pseudocode description for this algorithm is given as Algorithm 6.9.

Algorithm 6.9

{*Algorithm to find the most significant event in a sequence of events:*}
get EventValue
MostSignificantEvent ← EventValue
WHILE more events possible DO
   get EventValue
   IF EventValue is more significant than MostSignificantEvent THEN
      MostSignificantEvent ← EventValue
{*end algorithm*}

The invariants are, "*EventValue* represents the value of the last event found, and the value of *MostSignificantEvent* represents the value of the most significant event so far in the sequence." The assertions that can be made at loop exit are, "The sequence of events is completed, and the value of *MostSignificantEvent* is the value of the most significant event that occurred in the sequence." ◆

EXERCISES

Test Your Understanding

1. Suppose we replace the line FOR Count:= 2 TO 10 DO in the solution of Example Problem 6.7 with FOR Count:= 1 TO 9 DO. Will this code solve the problem? If so, what is the meaning of the variable Count in this instance?

2. We used a FOR loop to solve Example Problem 6.7, but then we described the algorithm we used with the WHILE loop construct. Why did we choose a WHILE loop to describe the algorithm?

3. Write down the display for each of the following:

  (a) FOR Count:= 6 DOWNTO 2 DO
        write(3*Count:3);
    writeln;

  (b) FOR Ch:= 'D' TO 'H' DO
        write(Ch);
    writeln;

4. The following program fragments all consist of loops. Indicate for each loop whether (a) counting, (b) accumulating, (c) event recording, or (d) condition seeking is the main purpose of the loop.

  (a) Prod:= 1;
    read(Int);
    WHILE Int > 0 DO
      BEGIN
        Prod:= Prod * Int;
        read(Int)
      END;

  (b) Ct:= 0;
    read(Int);
    WHILE Int > 0 DO
      BEGIN
        Ct:= Ct + 1;
        read(Int)
      END;

  (c) read(Int);
    Low:= Int;
    FOR Count:= 2 TO 15 DO
      BEGIN
        read(Int);
        IF Int < Low THEN
          LOW:= Int;
      END;

  (d) read(Int);
    WHILE Int > 0 DO
      read(Int);

5. State each loop exit condition for the loops of Exercise 4.

6. Write the statement for the procedure InitializeAll of Example Problem 6.5.

6.5 The REPEAT..UNTIL Loop

The third looping statement of Pascal uses the reserved words REPEAT and UNTIL. The body of this particular loop is always executed at least once. This property is the primary characteristic of the REPEAT.. UNTIL statement.

    The syntax diagram for the REPEAT. . UNTIL loop is shown in Figure 6.4. When the computer encounters the reserved word REPEAT, it continues to execute

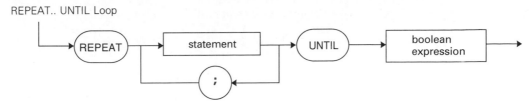

REPEAT.. UNTIL Loop

FIGURE 6.4 Syntax of the REPEAT..UNTIL loop.

the statements of the sequence. Then, when it encounters the reserved word UNTIL, it evaluates the boolean (control) expression. If the expression is `false`, the loop is executed for one more pass. The sequence of statements following the reserved word REPEAT are the ones executed for each loop pass. If the loop control expression evaluates to `true`, the loop is exited, and the statement following the loop is executed.

An example   Example 6.8a represents source code for a typical REPEAT..UNTIL statement. The postloop assertion we can make for this statement is, "The value of Int is positive." The logically equivalent sequence using a WHILE loop is given as Example 6.8b.

Example 6.8a

```
REPEAT
  write('Enter a positive integer:  ');
  readln(Int)
UNTIL Int > 0;
```

Example 6.8b

```
write('Enter a positive integer:  ');
readln(Int);
WHILE Int <= 0 DO
  BEGIN
    write('Enter a positive integer:  ');
    readln(Int)
  END;
```

Pseudocode   The pseudocode description of REPEAT..UNTIL loop is written as

> *REPEAT*
>   *body*
> *UNTIL loop control expression*

The *body* codes to a *sequence* of statements, and the *loop control expression* codes to a *boolean expression*.

WHILE *vs*.   Suppose the body of each of the two loops as described is the same and that
REPEAT..UNTIL   the preconditions are set up such that the WHILE loop is always initially entered:

WHILE more processing DO
body

REPEAT
body
UNTIL no more procesing

Each loop will then return *identical* results.

Note that the loop control expressions are *complements* of each other; that is, when one expression is `true`, the other is `false` and viceversa. The assertion made when both loops are exited is, "There is no more processing." When the control expression for the WHILE loop is `true`, the loop is *entered*. When the control expression for the REPEAT..UNTIL loop is `true`, the loop is *exited*.

Flowcharts

We can compare and contrast these two forms of loop control using flowcharts. Figure 6.5a depicts the action of the WHILE statement and Figure 6.5b that of the REPEAT..UNTIL sequence.

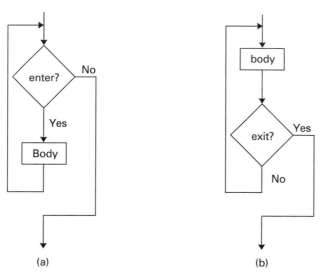

FIGURE 6.5 (a) Flowchart of the WHILE statement and (b) flowchart of the REPEAT..UNTIL sequence.

Summary of the three constructs

Now that you know three ways to loop, you will have to decide which is the best construct to choose. Your choice depends upon the difference between each construct. We can summarize the properties as follows:

I. The entry and exit conditions of the FOR loop are predetermined before loop entry. A single loop control variable, whose value is incremented or decremented by 1 each loop pass, determines the exit condition. References can be made to the value of this variable in the loop body, but its value should not be changed by any actions of the loop body.

II. The sequence of the REPEAT..UNTIL loop is always executed once. The control expression is evaluated for the *first* time *after* a loop pass is completed. If the value of the expression is `true`, the loop is exited.

III. Before the WHILE loop is entered, the control expression is evaluated. If it is true, the loop is entered. As with the REPEAT..UNTIL loop, the control expression is evaluated at the end of a loop pass.

Choosing a construct   You can decide on the best construct to use by the process of elimination. If you know the loop entry/exit can be controlled by a single variable whose value is changed by 1, by its pred, or by its succ with each loop pass, use a FOR loop. If the FOR loop does not work and at least one loop pass must be executed, use the REPEAT..UNTIL loop. If this construct is unsuitable, then use a WHILE loop, which works for any looping problem. If you are initially undecided, draft pseudocode with the WHILE loop, and make a decision after one or more refinements.

A REPEAT..UNTIL seeker   We have already given you an algorithm to seek out a desired program state using the WHILE loop as Algorithm 6.6. The REPEAT..UNTIL version of this algorithm, which is the preferable version, is described by the pseudocode of Algorithm 6.10.

Algorithm 6.10

> *{Seek out a desired condition on EventVar:}*
> **REPEAT**
>   *get EventVar*
> **UNTIL** *value of EventVar represents desired condition*
> *{end algorithm}*

If you know that a precondition on the value of *EventVar* must be satisfied before further processing is done, this algorithm is the best one to use. We used the algorithm on Example 6.8 to ensure that the value read into Int was positive.

Driving a driver   Example 6.9 shows another use for this algorithm. Calls are made to the procedure DriveIt until the program designer is satisfied that the procedure has been sufficiently tested.

Example 6.9

```
REPEAT
  DriveIt;
  write('Do you want to test the procedure again?   (Y/N)  ');
  readln(Ch)
UNTIL Ch = 'N'
```

Using all three loops   In the following case study, we use all 3 looping constructs in one program. Note how we decide which construct is the best one to use.

 CASE STUDY 6.1

The problem statement   J. Q. Public is taking a car trip with his wife and teenage daughter. On this trip, he will stop for fuel, food, or lodging. When the family stops for lodging, they will also have a meal. J. Q. is only willing to spend up to $50 for lodging. If the motel manager says the price is greater than this value, J. Q. will indicate his outrage at the price and look elsewhere.

Let us write a program that simulates this trip. A prompt is given for an action, where either G (gas), F (food), L (lodging), or Q (quit) is entered. When Q is entered, a summary of the trip's expenses are displayed. A typical run is as follows:

```
Welcome to Cross-Country simulator.
When you are prompted for an action, enter G, F, L, or Q.
These actions stand for Gas, Food, Lodging, or Quit.
Input the expenses when you are prompted for costs.
After the journey is over, a summary of the expenses is displayed.

                    Action:  G
                    Price:   15.00

                    Action:    F
                    Food bill for Person #1:  7.50
                    Food bill for Person #2:  6.00
                    Food bill for Person #3:  6.50
                    Total Food Bill = $20.00

                    Action:  G
                    Price:   12.00

                    Action:  L
                    Price for lodging:  70.00
                    Outrageous!  We will look elsewhere.
                    Price for lodging:  45.00
                    Fine, we will stay here.

                    Food Bill for Person #1:  15.50
                    Food Bill for Person #2:  12.75
                    Food Bill for Person #3:  10.25
                    Total Food Bill = $38.50

                    Action:  G
                    Price:   10.00

                    Action:  Q

                    Total Fuel Cost = $37.00
                    Total Food Cost = $58.50
                    Total Lodging Cost = $45.00
                    Total Cost of Trip = $140.50
```

The main block   We require three global variables to accumulate an overall cost for fuel, food, and lodging. These are initialized to 0 before the loop is entered. Because J. Q. is definitely going on the trip, the loop to use in the main block is REPEAT..UNTIL where the loop pseudocode is

> *REPEAT*
> *keyin Action*
> *CASE Action OF*
>   *'G': GetGas (Fuel Bill)*
>   *'F': Eat (FoodBill)*
>   *'L': EatAndSleep (FoodBill, LodgeBill)*
>   *'Q': {empty statement}*
> *UNTIL Action = 'Q'*

The code for the main block is given as the program SimulateCar-Journey. We will develop the code for GetGas, Eat, and EatAndSleep. We leave the coding of the other two procedures as exercises.

```
PROGRAM SimulateCarJourney(input, output);
  {Simulates a car journey, where the user accumulates a fuel bill,
  food bill, and lodging bill. When the journey is completed, the
  cumulative bill for the three items are displayed as well as the
  total cost of the journey.}
  CONST
    PartySize = 3;        {number of people going on the trip}
    MaxLodging = 50.00; {maximum price user will pay for lodging}
  VAR
    FuelBill,        {accumulator variable for fuel bill}
    FoodBill,        {accumulator variable for food bill}
    LodgeBill:       {accumulator variable for lodge bill}
                     real;
    Action: char;   {action taken with each stop of the journey}
  {*                                                              *}
  PROCEDURE ShowDirections;
    BEGIN  {display of directions}       END;
  {*                                                              *}
  PROCEDURE Initialize(VAR FuelBill, FoodBill, LodgeBill: real);
    BEGIN          {initializes all accumulators to 0}
      FuelBill:= 0;  FoodBill:= 0;  LodgeBill:= 0
    END;
  {*                                                              *}
  PROCEDURE GetGas (VAR FuelBill: real);
    {in: FuelBill -- total fuel bill not including bill for this stop
    out: FuelBill -- total fuel bill including bill for this stop}
    BEGIN    END;
  {*                                                              *}
  PROCEDURE Eat(VAR FoodBill: real);
    {in: FoodBill -- total food bill not including bill for this stop
```

```
                                       out: FoodBill -- total food bill including bill for this stop}
       BEGIN     END;
{*                                                                                               *}
    PROCEDURE EatAndSleep(VAR FoodBill, LodgeBill: real);
      {in:  FoodBill -- total food bill not including bill for this stop
       out: FoodBill -- total food bill including bill for this stop
        in: LodgeBill -- total lodge bill not including bill for this stop
       out: LodgeBill -- total lodge bill including bill for this stop}
    BEGIN END;
{*                                                                                               *}
    PROCEDURE ShowCosts(FuelBill, FoodBill, LodgeBill: real);
      {in:  total bills for all three kinds of expenses
       out: values displayed, along with overall cost of trip}
       BEGIN     END;
{*                                                                                               *}
    BEGIN   {main block}
       ShowDirections;
       Initialize(FuelBill, FoodBill, LodgeBill);
       REPEAT
         write('Action:    ');
         readln(Action);
         CASE Action OF
           'G':  GetGas(FuelBill);
           'F':  Eat(FoodBill);
           'L':  EatAndSleep(FoodBill, LodgeBill);
           'Q':  {empty statement}
           END;  {CASE}
         writeln;      {skip a line}
       UNTIL Action = 'Q';
       ShowCosts(FuelBill, FoodBill, LodgeBill)
    END.
```

The code for
GetGas

To code GetGas, we require a variable to read in the value that represents the price for filling the tank. This value is then added to the accumulator variable FuelBill. The code for the procedure, less parameter documentation, is therefore

```
       PROCEDURE GetGas(VAR FuelBill: real);
         VAR

           Cost:   real;   {cost of gas bill for present stop}
         BEGIN
           write('Price:    ');
           readln(Cost);
           FuelBill:= FuelBill + Cost
         END;
```

The code for
Eat

In coding Eat, we require a loop to get each person's food bill. We can use a FOR loop to process each of the PartySize people in the family. A local variable

TotalBill will accumulate the total bill for the party of PartySize members. Once the value for TotalBill is found, it should be added to the accumulator variable FoodBill. The code for this procedure, less parameter documentation, is shown below.

```
PROCEDURE Eat(VAR FoodBill: real);
  VAR
    Bill,          {the bill for one person}
    TotalBill:     {accumulates the food bill for entire party}
                   real;
    Person:        integer;   {the person whose bill is being read in}
  BEGIN
    TotalBill:= 0;
    FOR Person:= 1 To PartySize DO
      BEGIN
        write('Food Bill for Person #', Person:1, ':    ');
        readln(Bill);
        TotalBill:= TotalBill + Bill
      END;
    writeln('Total Food Bill = $', TotalBill:4:2);
    FoodBill:=  FoodBill + TotalBill
  END;
```

The code for EatAndSleep

The pseudocode description for the procedure EatAndSleep is as follows:

> *keyin CostForRoom*
> *WHILE CostForRoom > MaxLodging DO*   {*seek desirable postcondition*}
>   *display outrage message*
>   *keyin CostForRoom*
> *LodgeBill ← LodgeBill + CostForRoom*
> *Eat (FoodBill)*

We are using a WHILE loop to seek the condition CostForRoom <= MaxLodging because the price for lodging at the first motel may be within Mr. Public's budget. He need not express his outrage in this case, so a REPEAT..UNTIL loop is inappropriate. The code we obtain for this procedure is shown below.

```
PROCEDURE EatAndSleep(VAR FoodBill, LodgeBill:  real);
  VAR
    CostForRoom: real;   {candidate bill for a single night's lodging}
  BEGIN
    write('Price for lodging: ');
    readln(CostForRoom);
    WHILE CostForRoom > MaxLodging DO
      BEGIN
        writeln('Outrageous! We will look elsewhere.');
        write('Price for lodging: ');
```

```
        readln(CostForRoom)
    END;
  LodgeBill:= LodgeBill + CostForRoom;
  Eat(FoodBill)
END;   ◆
```

EXERCISES

**Test Your
Understanding**

1. Can you use a FOR loop to count the number of consecutive positive integers read in a sequence? Why or why not?

2. Under what condition is REPEAT..UNTIL preferred over WHILE?

3. Under what condition is WHILE preferred over REPEAT..UNTIL?

4. When is a FOR loop the ideal choice?

**Sharpen Your
Implementation
Skills.**

5. Code the statement for the Initialize block of Case Study 6.1.

6. Code the statement for the ShowCosts block of Case Study 6.1.

7. Suppose J. Q. has two daughters and a wife on the trip. How would you modify the original program to fit this scenario?

6.6   Nested Loops

When one loop statement encloses another loop statement, you have a sequence of statements that makes up a *nested loop*. When the sequence is executed, the outer loop is entered first, then the inner loop. The inner loop is then exited first, followed by the outer loop.

> **Nested loop:**   a loop statement where part of its body is another loop statement.

*Planning a
nested loop
solution*

If you have a problem that requires a nested loop for a solution, the best approach is to plan the outer loop first, then work on the inner loop. We used this approach on Example Problem 6.1, where an inner loop was necessary to get a positive value for processing. In this case, we did not know the solution required an inner loop until the first refinement. Even when you do know you will need a nested loop to solve the problem, this approach is still a good one to follow, regardless.

Example Problem 6.8

*The problem
statement*

Let us write a one-block program that displays the multiplication table from 0 through 9. When the program is run, the display should look like

*	0	1	2	3	4	5	6	7	8	9
0	0	0	0	0	0	0	0	0	0	0
1	0	1	2	3	4	5	6	7	8	9
2	0	2	4	6	8	10	12	14	16	18
3	0	3	6	9	12	15	18	21	24	27
4	0	4	8	12	16	20	24	28	32	36
5	0	5	10	15	20	25	30	35	40	45
6	0	6	12	18	24	30	36	42	48	54
7	0	7	14	21	28	35	42	49	56	63
8	0	8	16	24	32	40	48	56	64	72
9	0	9	18	27	36	45	54	63	72	81

The outer loops We will use two variables for this problem, `Multiplicand` and `Multiplier`. The first line of display tabulates the `Multiplier` values from 0 through 9. Each subsequent line of display shows the product of a fixed `Multiplicand` value times the 10 values `Multiplier` takes on. We can describe the process with the pseudocode

> *display '*'*
> *FOR Multiplier ← 0 TO 9 DO*
>   *display Multiplier*
> *clearline*   *{writeln}*
> *FOR Multiplicand ← 0 TO 9 DO*
>   *display Multiplicand*
>   *display the products on one line*
>   *clearline*   *{writeln}*

Assertions The postcondition for the first loop is, "The values 0 through 9 have been displayed on one line." The postcondition for the second loop is, "Each `Multiplicand` value from 0 through 9 has been displayed on one line. Also, the 10 products of this `Multiplicand` times each `Multiplier` value has been displayed on the same line as the `Multiplicand`." These assertions indicate that we have described a correct solution.

Refinement The action *display the products on one line* codes to a FOR loop using the 10 `Multiplier` values. It is described by

> *FOR Multiplier ← 0 TO 9 DO*
>   *display Multiplicand * Multiplier*

The postloop assertion we can make is, "The products of the `Multiplicand` value and the `Multiplier` values 0 through 9 have been displayed. Hence, this refinement is correct.

Source code From the pseudocode description, we obtain the coded solution as the program `DoTimesTable`.

```
PROGRAM DoTimesTable(output);
  {Displays times tables for integers 0 through 9}
  CONST
    FieldSize = 4;     {field sizes for each value displayed}
  VAR
    Multiplicand,    {loop counter variable for multiplicand values}
    Multiplier:      {loop counter variable for multiplier values}
                     integer;
  BEGIN
    write('*');
    FOR Multiplier:= 0 TO 9 DO
      write (Multiplier: FieldSize);
    writeln;
    FOR Multiplicand:= 0 TO 9 DO
      BEGIN
        write(Multiplicand:1);
        FOR Multiplier:= 0 TO 9 DO
          write(Multiplicand * Multiplier: FieldSize);
        writeln
      END
  END.  ◆
```

Dependent inner loop variables   Quite often you will encounter a problem where the value of the inner loop control variable depends on the value of the outer loop control variable. If you use a top–down approach, where you develop the outer loop first, this sort of problem should not pose serious difficulties, as this next problem demonstrates.

Example Problem 6.9

The problem statement   Your niece wants you to write a small program to display a flag. Three typical display patterns are as follows:

```
*              *              *
**             **             **
***            ***            ***
****                          ****
*****
******
```

She wants the program to prompt her regarding the number of stars to be displayed on the bottom line. Once she inputs this value, the computer skips five lines and then displays the flag she wants.

Development   We can start with the solution description using the pseudocode

> *keyin TotalLines*
> *FOR LineNo ← 1 TO 5 DO   {skips 5 lines}*
> *writeln*

$$\textit{FOR LineNo} <\!\text{--} \textit{ 1 TO TotalLines DO}$$
$$\textit{display a line of stars}$$

Clearly, this initial description represents a correct solution.

If you look at each line, you realize that the number of stars displayed on any given line is equal to the value of LineNO. Hence, the action for *display line of stars* is described by

$$\textit{FOR Stars} \leftarrow \textit{1 TO LineNo DO}$$
$$\textit{display Star}$$
$$\textit{clearline}$$

The identifier Star represents the defined constant '*'. The coded solution to the problem is therefore given as the program ShowFlag as coded.

```
PROGRAM ShowFlag (input, output)
   {A flag of stars is displayed where the user specifies the number of
   stars to be shown on the last line.  The first line has one star in
   it, and each line has one more star in it than the previous line.}
   CONST
     Star = '*';   {the symbol that makes up the flag}
   VAR
     TotalLines,    {the total number of lines to be displayed}
     LineNo,        {counts lines displayed}
     Stars:         {counts number of stars displayed on each line}
                    integer;
   BEGIN
     write('How many stars do you want on the last line?  ');
     readln(TotalLines);
     FOR LineNo:= 1 TO 5 DO      {skips 5 lines}
       writeln;
     FOR LineNo:= 1 TO TotalLines DO
       BEGIN
         FOR Stars:= 1 TO LineNo DO
           write(Star);
         writeln
       END
   END.  ◆
```

EXERCISES

Practice Your Analysis Skills

1. What will be the display for the following segments:

   (a) FOR Outer:= 1 TO 4 DO
           BEGIN
             write(Outer: 1, ': ');

```
                    FOR Inner:= Outer DOWNTO 1 DO
                       write(Inner:1,'   ');
                    writeln;
                 END;
        (b)  FOR Outer:= 'A' TO 'D' DO
                 BEGIN
                    write(Outer: 1, ':   ');
                    FOR Inner:= 1 TO 5 DO
                       write(Inner: 1,'   ');
                    writeln;
                 END;
        (c)  FOR XInt:= 1 TO 3 DO
                 BEGIN
                    FOR YInt:= 2 TO 4 DO
                       BEGIN
                          FOR ZInt:= 3 TO 5 DO
                             write(XInt:1, YInt:1, ZInt:1, '  ');
                          writeln
                       END
                 END;
        (d)  AInt:= 8;
             WHILE AInt > 0 DO
                 BEGIN
                    FOR BInt:= AInt DOWNTO 1 DO
                       write(BInt:3);
                    writeln;
                    AInt:= AInt DIV 2
                 END;
```

2. How many looping structures are required for the following:
   (a) Get the highest and lowest values from a group of 10 integers?
   (b) Find the average for each of three courses where five tests are given in each course?

Program Testing Hints

Even if you write good code, you may sometimes have to do maintenance on code that is not so good. In this section, we give you some "standard" errors that use loops of which you should be aware. Then you can recognize and fix them in other people's code and avoid writing them in your code. We also present some guidelines for choosing data to desk trace and on-line test alogrithms that use loops.

A Compendium of Common Loop Errors

The following discussion will categorize some of the common errors committed with loop statements and loop algorithms. Make sure you do not write code that satisfies any of these descriptions.

PROGRAM DESIGN RULE 6.1

Never follow the reserved word DO with a semicolon.

A misplaced semicolon

Beware of following the reserved word DO with a semicolon. Regardless of what statement is to be executed, this special symbol is incorrectly placed, for the computer will always execute an empty statement rather than the intended sequence. In the following example, if the loop is entered, it will never be exited because the empty statement will not change the program state:

```
WHILE XInt <= 0 DO;  {ERROR!}
    BEGIN {body} END;
```

In the next example, the machine will execute the empty statement *N* times and the statement that is intended as the loop body exactly once:

```
FOR Count:= 1 TO N DO;  {ERROR!}
    BEGIN   {body}   END;
```

PROGRAM DESIGN RULE 6.2

Use the BEGIN..END delimiters with any WHILE or FOR loop whose body consists of more than one statement.

Missing BEGIN END delimiters

When Program Design Rule 6.2 is not followed, endless loops and/or unexecuted statements will likewise result. If, for example, the body of the WHILE loops in the following fragment is entered, the computer will continue to add Int to Sum, regardless of what the user might subsequently do:

```
read(Int);     {ERROR!}
WHILE Int > 0 DO
    Sum:= Sum + Int;
    read(Int);
```

Depending upon what computer you use, this fragment will cause a crash when Sum exceeds maxint, or it will keep adding the same Int to Sum as an endless loop that generates incorrect numbers.

A description of endless loops

Suppose you write a WHILE loop where the loop is entered, but the loop control expression never becomes false. Perhaps, instead, you may write a RE-PEAT..UNTIL loop where the loop control expression never becomes true. In either case, the computer will continue to execute the loop body until the user aborts your program or until some error condition occurs where the computer aborts the program. Regardless of the end result, you will have to find that part of the program that has the endless loop in order to fix it.

If an endless loop has a `writeln` statement in its body, you will see lines upon lines of display. This bug is easy to find. If, however, the faulty loop has no display statements in its body, its execution will appear to halt the computer dead in its tracks. You will find yourself staring at a blinking cursor or a silent printer while the machine continues to execute the body of the endless loop.

Tracer utilities   Many systems for developing Pascal programs come with a tracer utility program. You use it to trace the values taken on by each variable as the computer carries out the statements in the program. If your program development software has this feature, *learn how to use it*. It is very helpful when interactive debugging is required. On the other hand, do not rely so heavily on this utility that you start writing sloppy code. There is no substitute for source code meticulously planned and checked with the verification tools we have given you.

Writing your own tracers   If, however, you are using a system that does not have this utility, you must write your own tracers. Hopefully, you have written modular code with procedures. If so, you can isolate the endless loop by coding a `writeln` statement at the start of each procedure whose statement contains a loop indicating that it was called. Then you code a `writeln` statement just before the reserved word END of the procedure. The following demonstrates this technique:

```
PROCEDURE DoSomething(   {parameter list});
   VAR
      {some local variables}
   BEGIN
{DEBUGGING}   WRITELN('ENTERED DoSomething');
      {procedure's statement}
{DEBUGGING}   WRITELN('EXITING DoSomething')
   END;
```

If all procedures with loops are coded with these tracers, the procedure with the endless loop in it will display that it was entered but it will not display that it was exited.

Note how we laid out these tracers. Once the bug is isolated and fixed, you will want to remove all tracers. If you insert them in such a way that they violate your layout conventions, you will easily see them as eyesores that must be removed from the debugged version of the source program.

Off-by-one errors   Consider the following segment used to find the sum of a sequence of positive integers:

```
Sum: = 0;         {ERROR! }
REPEAT
   read(Int);
   Sum:= Sum + Int
UNTIL Int <= 0;
```

This example illustrates an *off-by-one error* that processes the sentinel value.

> **Off-by-one error:** an error in a program where exactly one more or one less value than the correct number of values is processed.

Semantic context   If the programmer was careless enough to code a fragment like the one just given he or she might choose to "correct" the error by coding the statement Sum:= Sum − Int at loop exit. This sort of debugging practice is as bad as the initial error, for it changes the semantics of Sum. In the loop body, Sum represents the sum of all integers read in. The postloop assignment then changes the meaning such that Sum now represents the sum of all integers read in except for the last one. If you code a program with many "corrections" of this sort, it will be very difficult to read.

Another example   This sequence, to find the sum of the first 100 integers, is also off by one:

```
Sum:= 0;  {ERROR!}
Count:= 1;
REPEAT
  Sum:= Sum + Count;
  Count:= Count + 1
UNTIL Count = 100;
```

A third example   Sometimes you can write code that is off by one because a given statement is executed out of order. For example, we have

```
Sum:= 0;                    {ERROR!}
FOR Count:= 1 TO 100 DO
  BEGIN
    IF Count MOD 5 = 0 THEN
      writeln('The sum of the first ',Count:1, 'integers is ',Sum:1);
{1} Sum:= Sum + Count
  END;
```

When you make an assertion at point {1} in the sequence, you quickly see that the decision statement must go after the variable Sum is updated.

Branch, loop errors   Make sure to use a loop when you want to attain a desired program state. If a number must be positive for further processing, the decision statement in the following example will not do:

```
readln(Int);  {ERROR!}
IF Int <= 0 THEN
  BEGIN
    write('Enter a positive integer:  ')
    readln(Int);
  END;
```

The only assertion we can make is that a second value was read in if the first one was negative. There is nothing in this sequence, however, that guarantees the second value read in is positive.

Loop Testing Techniques

It is important that you choose good test data for code that uses loops. You want to be sure your tests uncover any errors that are present and that they point you to the nature of the error uncovered. You want to choose a sufficient amount of data to ensure thorough testing, but you also want to avoid choosing data that implies redundant testing. The hints you get from this section will help you plan a good testing strategy for the source code you are developing or have developed or for any source code that you must maintain.

PROGRAM DESIGN RULE 6.3

First test loops with small data sets and for the trivial cases.

The small sample rule

Program Design Rule 6.3 is known as "the small sample rule." There is no reason to generate test data for 100 loop passes when you can just as easily find an error with only four or five passes. For example, an off-by-one-error on a summing loop that adds one too few or one too many items will be easier to find with small data sets. Once you are happy your program is working for trivial sets of data, then you can test it with larger data sets.

PROGRAM DESIGN RULE 6.4

Choose test data on loops that check all obvious entry/exit events.

Loop entry/exit checking

On the same note as Program Design Rule 6.3, you should choose values where you expect no loop passes to be executed. Did the computer enter the loop anyway? If not, did the intended postprocessing cause errors? Make sure you are satisfied with the answers to these questions for nonentry conditions.

The next obvious entry/exit condition is with data where you expect just one pass to be carried out. Are the results returned the expected results for this circumstance? If there is a decision statement(s) in your loop body, make sure you choose data to test all paths even with this single data value.

PROGRAM DESIGN RULE 6.5

Choose at least one set of test data on a loop where the first event is significant and at least one set of test data where the final event is significant.

---

*Testing for
off-by-one
errors*

If you have written a program where there is a decision in the loop body, you must make sure the computer carries it out correctly for all possible circumstances. If, for example, you are testing a sequence to find the lowest value in a set of data, make sure you use a test set where the first value obtained is the lowest one. Another test set should be one where the last value obtained is the lowest one.

PROGRAM DESIGN RULE 6.6

Choose "bad" sets of data for testing the loop body.

---

*Pathology
testing*

Suppose your program is to find the sum of all positive integers out of a sequence of 10 integers. One set of test data you are obligated to try is a sequence of integers whose values are all less than or equal to 0. In this case, none of the values read in are accumulated. The flip side of this rule is that you choose one or more data sets where all values are accumulated.

PROGRAM DESIGN RULE 6.7

Choose "normal" sets of data for testing the loop body.

---

*"Normal"
testing*

Do not forget that you wrote your program to work for "normal" data. Make sure then not to get tied up trying to look for all the pathologies when the program may be incorrect for "normal" values. Your initial tests with normal data should of course start with a small sample size.

PROGRAM DESIGN RULE 6.8

Apply assertion testing first.

---

*The two most
important rules*

Program Design Rule 6.8 is the most important rule to apply in your testing. You do not even have to think of generating any on-line test data to apply this rule. Morever, it forces you to think of the meaning and purpose of each variable you have used in the program. Likewise, you will choose test data to check that the assertions you made are correct ones.

The second most important rule is the small sample rule. A loop that should have been exited on the third test value is every bit as endless as the same loop that should have been exited on the three-hundredth value. In the former case, the bug is more easily identified, hence fixed.

Suppose instead that your problem requires a FOR loop to count from 1 to 300? Then you would trivialize the problem with a data set that has three values and set the loop to count from 1 to 3. The same body is still executed, and hence the same bug, if present, will show up.

EXERCISES

Test Your Understanding

1. What is the "rule of small samples" for testing a program with a loop? Why is it such a useful testing rule to know and use?

2. What happens if a semicolon is placed after the reserved word REPEAT?

Practice Your Analysis Skills

3. You want to write a program fragment to process the first 10 input characters that are letters. Assuming you can code a boolean expression for Ch is a letter, what is wrong with the following approach?

> FOR Count ← TO 10 DO
> read (Ch)
> IF Ch is a letter THEN
> process it

How would you fix it?

Sharpen Your Implementation Skills

4. The following source code is supposed to display the average of a sequence of positive input integers. Rewrite it, using more sensible code:

```
Count := -1;
Sum: = 0;
REPEAT
  read(XInt);
  Sum: = Sum + XInt;
  Count: = Count + 1
UNTIL XInt <= 0;
Sum := Sum - XInt;
IF (Count <> 0 ) THEN
  writeln (Sum/Count);
```

5. Will the sequence of Exercise 4 return "correct" results? What, then, is wrong with it as source code?

REVIEW AND EXERCISES

A *loop* is the means by which the computer repeats a sequence of the same actions to process a sequence of similar *events*. In order for a loop to be *entered,* the *loop entry condition* must be satisfied. If it is, the computer executes the sequence of statements that makes up the loop *body* as a single *loop pass.* At the end of the loop pass, a test is made to see if the *loop exit condition,* the *complement* of the loop entry condition, is met. If so, the loop is exited. If not, the computer executes another pass.

There are three constructs in Pascal to implement a loop, namely, the WHILE statement, the FOR statement, and the REPEAT. . UNTIL statement. Each statement has a characteristic entry and exit condition. A WHILE loop is entered if the *control expression* is *true* at the *start of the loop*. When this condition becomes *false* at the end of a loop pass, the WHILE loop is exited. The FOR loop uses a *loop control variable* and a counting action. The number of passes and the values taken on by the loop control variable are *predetermined* before the computer carries out the FOR statement. The REPEAT. . UNTIL loop is *always entered*. When the control expression is *true* at the end of a loop pass, this loop is exited.

Most problems that are solved using a loop require *initilizations* before loop entry and *postprocessing* after loop exit. The initialization statements set up the necessary preconditions for the loop to solve the problem properly. The postprocessing statements use the values accumulated by the loop process to finish the problem.

A *loop invariant* is a description of a condition that is always true at loop entry and after any given loop pass. When a loop is designed well, the invariant for each variable in the loop body is virtually synonymous with a description of the variable's purpose. Thus, invariants are useful tools to apply in designing a loop. Invariants are also very useful tools for assertion testing. If the *postloop assertion(s)*, stated in terms of the invariants, describes a correct program state, then the loop is designed correctly.

There are a number of standard algorithms that can be implemented with loops, namely, *sum accumulators, product accumulators, sequential event counters, selective event counters, significant event recorders*, and *condition seekers*. Likewise, there are certain entry/exit algorithms that can be categorized: *processing events to a sentinel event, doing a process a countable number of times*, and *seeking a precondition for further processing*.

Sometimes a problem uses *nested loops* for its solution. A loop that has two *levels of nesting* consists of an *outer loop* and an *inner loop*, where the outer loop is entered first and the inner loop last. It is usually better to design algorithms that use nested loops by planning the algorithm from the outermost loop inwards.

An *endless loop* is an error condition that occurs when the loop exit condition is never met. An *off-by-one error* occurs when exactly one too few or one too many events have been processed. There are certain coding patterns that will cause one or the other of these two errors. Avoid writing code that satisfies these patterns at all costs.

Data for on-line testing should be chosen to test entry conditions, exit conditions, and the statements of the loop body. The kind of data chosen depends upon the algorithm, where many different conditions indigenous to the particular algorithm should be tested. Regardless of what kind of loop is being tested, however, the earlier tests are best done with *small data sets*, for they can find the obvious errors.

EXERCISES

Short Answers

1. A loop controlled by the reserved words _____ and _____ is always entered regardless of preconditions.

2. A loop controlled by the reserved words _____ and _____ is always exited regardless of the sequence that makes up the loop body.

3. A loop controlled by the reserved words _____ and _____ can be used to solve any kind of coding problem that requires a loop.

4. Under what conditions can an algorithm with an endless loop be correct?

5. A condition that is true after every loop pass is known as a(n) _____ .

6. True or false? If a condition-seeking loop's body is not entered, the program has a bug in it.

7. What does a blinking cursor or a silent printer imply during the course of a program run?

8. A loop strategy, when seen in the context of the rest of the program, has four parts. These parts are the initialization statements, the loop _____ _____ , the loop _____ , and the _____ statements.

9. True or false? The loop body of the outer loop in a nested structure should enclose all logic that deals with the inner loop processing.

10. Match the phrases of column A with the phrases of column B:

Column A	Column B
variable representing solution	requires decision in loop body
loop control variable	a type of assertion
off by one	accumulation variable
significant-event counting	semantic-error condition
initialization	FOR loop counting variable
loop invariant	never exited
endless loop	statements before loop entry

11. A loop used to find the highest value in a sequence of input integers uses an event-_____ algorithm to get a solution.

12. True or false? A loop that is coded correctly will never put the machine into an endless loop condition.

13. A nested loop strategy is described by

$$FOR\ I \leftarrow 1\ TO\ 5\ DO$$
$$FOR\ J \leftarrow 3\ TO\ 7\ DO$$
$$process\ data\ and\ display\ a\ line\ of\ text$$

How many lines of text will be displayed when this strategy is coded?

14. True or false? It is correct to use an IF statement as a guarantee that a given condition is realized.

15. A variable used to accumulate a sum is usually initialized to _____ .

16. A variable used to accumulate a product is usually initialized to _____ .

17. True or false? A variable of type char can be used as the loop control variable of a FOR loop.

Easy Projects

18. Suppose a sentence is terminated by a period. A character that makes up part of the sentence can be anything but a blank. Write a program where the computer reads in the

characters that make up a sentence, then displays the number of characters in the sentence.

19. Write a program that displays the letters of the alphabet where the uppercase letter is shown followed by the lowercase letter. Therefore, the program display is as follows:

AaBbCcDdEeFfGgHhIiJjKkLlMmNnOoPpQqRrSsTtUuVvWwXxYyZz

20. Write a program that displays the addition table from 0 through 9, inclusive. When the program is run, the display looks like

+	0	1	2	3	4	5	6	7	8	9
0 |	0	1	2	3	4	5	6	7	8	9
1 |	1	2	3	4	5	6	7	8	9	10
2 |	2	3	4	5	6	7	8	9	10	11
3 |	3	4	5	6	7	8	9	10	11	12
4 |	4	5	6	7	8	9	10	11	12	13
5 |	5	6	7	8	9	10	11	12	13	14
6 |	6	7	8	9	10	11	12	13	14	15
7 |	7	8	9	10	11	12	13	14	15	16
8 |	8	9	10	11	12	13	14	15	16	17
9 |	9	10	11	12	13	14	15	16	17	18

21. Write a program that displays the integers from 1 to 10 in a table with three columns. The first column is the integer value, the second is the square of the integer, and the third is its cube.

22. You have squares of sheet metal available to you with sides whose values range from 5 to 50 centimeters in 5-centimeter increments. You want to cut out the largest possible circle from each of these squares, and you also want to know how much scrap metal is wasted in each case. Write a program that shows a table with four columns. The first column shows the length of the side, the second shows the area of the given square sheet, the third shows the area of the largest circle that can be cut out (its radius is one-half the length of the square's side), and the fourth column shows the amount of scrap material left over. Each column entry is right-justified 15 spaces, and each numeric value is displayed accurate to four decimal places.

23. Write a program that shows a table of the factorial function 1 to 25 inclusive. Define a value for `maxint` equal to 32767. If the factorial function is less than this value for a given N, display it as an `integer`; otherwise display the value as a `real` number in scientific notation. (*Hint:* Let the product accumulation variable be of type `real`. Use the `round` function, as shown in Appendix D.)

Medium Projects

24. Write a program that finds and displays the average of five input sequences of positive numbers. After a number is entered that breaks the sequence, the rest of the numbers on the line are ignored. Once the user presses the carriage return, the computer displays the average and the number of integers in the group. After the five averages are found and displayed, the computer should then display the count of all numbers processed and their overall average.

25. The value of the exponential function e^x can be found by carrying out the summation

$$1 + \frac{X}{1} + \frac{X^2}{1 \cdot 2} + \frac{X^3}{1 \cdot 2 \cdot 3} + \frac{X^4}{1 \cdot 2 \cdot 3 \cdot 4} + \cdots + \frac{X^N}{1 \cdot 2 \cdots (N-1)(N)}$$

where N is as large a number as necessary to get an accurate answer. Write a program where the computer repeatedly prompts you for a value of X in the range $-10 \le X \le 10$ (use the abs function). Once a good value is entered, the computer finds and displays the approximate value of e^X using the formula. The sum is terminated when the final term takes on an absolute value less than 0.0005. The computer should display the number of terms required to return a result along with the value of the calculated function. You can check your answer by calling the standard *exp* function (see Appendix D).

26. An Armstrong number is an integer consisting of n digits such that the sum of the digits raised to the nth power is equal to the given number. For instance, the number 153 consists of three digits and

$$1^3 + 5^3 + 3^3 = 153.$$

Write a program to find and display the four Armstrong numbers from 10 through 999. (*Hint:* Use a FOR loop for 10 through 99 and one for 100 through 999.)

27. Many numerical formulas exist to calculate approximations for the value of Pi. One of the formulas for calculating a value of Pi is given by

$$\text{Pi}/2 \sim (2/1) \times (2/3) \times (4/3) \times (4/5) \times (6/5) \times (6/7) \times \cdots$$

Write a program to display the value of Pi that has been calculated after the first 2000; 4000; 6000; 8000; 10,000 multiplications.

28. Write a program to read in 10 integers and then display the following:
    (a) The average of the group of numbers.
    (b) The lowest number in the group.
    (c) The highest number in the group.
    (d) The average of the nine lowest numbers in the group.
    (e) The average of the nine highest numbers in the group.

29. Recall that the song "The Twelve Days of Christmas" runs something like this:
    "On the first day of Chrismas, my true love gave to me a partridge in a pear tree.
    "On the second day of Christmas, my true love gave to me two turtle doves and a partridge in a pear tree.
    "On the third day of Christmas, my true love gave to me three French hens, two turtle doves and a partridge in a pear tree. . . ."
    The song continues with the same sequence of gifts plus a new set of gifts whose number corresponds to the day number. This effusive display of generosity continues through the twelfth day of Christmas.
    Write a program that displays the number of gifts received on each day (e.g., one on the first day, three on the second day, six on the third day, etc.) and the overall number of gifts after the third, sixth, ninth, and twelfth days.

Difficult Projects

30. The square root of a number S can be found by repeatedly applying the formula

$$\text{NewValue} = (0.5) \times (\text{OldValue} + S/\text{OldValue})$$

where the NewValue is a better estimate of the square root of S. Once a NewValue has been found, it can then be called the next OldValue and another NewValue can then be found. Eventually, the difference between a given OldValue and the calculated NewValue will differ by a small enough amount that we can say we have found the square root of *S*.

Write a program to carry out this algorithm. You first enter in a positive number (use a guard) whose square root you want. Then you enter a first guess at the square root. From this first guess, the computer will keep generating NewValues until the difference between the OldValue and NewValue is less than 0.0005 (use the abs function to form the boolean expression). The computer should display both the iteration number and the NewValue calculated for each loop pass. (*Note:* Once you have finished the program, it might be interesting to see what happens if a negative value for *S* were input.)

31. The value of the cube root of a number is calculated by starting with two estimates—one too high and one too low. A better estimate for the cube root is found by (Hi + Lo)/2. If this number is too high, it can be used for the new estimate for Hi; if it is too low, it becomes the new estimate for Lo. The process can be repeated until the cube of the estimated root is close enough to the number whose root you are finding.

Write a program to find the cube root of 137 by carrying out the algorithm described. The looping process should stop when the cube of the last estimate is within 0.005 of 137. Let the first Lo estimate be 5 and the first Hi estimate be 6. Have the program show the Hi and Lo estimates before the next estimate is found. Run the program a second time, using the first estimates as 1 and 10.

32. Write a program where the computer simulates the activity of a checking account in the following manner:

Input

The opening balance.

Transactions: a positive number denotes a deposit;

  a negative number denotes a check written;

  a zero input indicates the month's end.

A prompt of "Next transaction: " should be output before a number is read.

Display

The closing balance.

The number of checks written and paid.

The number of checks "bounced" (checks written with an insufficient balance).

The number of deposits made.

If a check bounces, the computer should immediately display the character string "INSUFFICIENT FUNDS" before requesting the next transaction.

33. Your niece was so impressed with the flag program of Example Problem 6.9 that she wants you to write a program for her that will display an arrow made of stars that can point up or down. She specifies how many stars will make up the width of the arrowhead and how many stars should be in the length and width of the shaft. The computer then displays the arrow. If she specifies an even number, the next smaller odd number is used. Include code to ensure that the width of the head is longer than the width of the shaft and that the length of the shaft is at least as long as the width of the shaft. Two sample runs are shown:

```
Direction of arrow (U/D): D        Direction of arrow (U/D): U
Width of head: 7                    Width of head:  7
Length of shaft: 7                  Length of shaft: 5
Too long..                         Width of shaft: 5
Length of shaft: 5                  Too long..
Width of shaft: 3                   Length of shaft: 3
                                    Width of shaft: 1
   ***                                   *
   ***                                  ***
   ***                                 *****
   ***                                *******
   ***                                   *
*******                                  *
 *****                                   *
  ***
   *
```

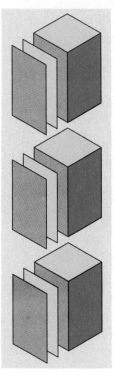

MORE BOOLEAN EXPRESSIONS AND INTRODUCTION TO ARRAYS

OBJECTIVES

After reading and studying the material of the present chapter, you should be able to:

- Write expressions using the reserved words NOT, AND, OR, **and** IN

- Analyze code that uses the reserved words NOT, AND, OR, **and** IN

- Plan, refine, prove, and code algorithms using NOT, AND, OR, **and** IN

- Apply DeMorgan's theorems to analyze and plan programs

- Define a subrange type and declare a subrange variable

- Define a one-dimensional array type and declare a one-dimensional array variable

- Analyze code that uses one-dimensional arrays with integer subscripts

- Plan and code programs that require one-dimensional arrays

- Know and apply standard algorithms that use one-dimensional arrays

IN THIS CHAPTER, you will learn how to use the reserved words NOT, AND, OR, and IN. The word NOT gives you a simple way to complement a boolean expression. The words AND and OR give you the means to write a boolean expression dependent upon the value of more than one candidate condition. When you use IN, you can code a condition that tests whether an expression has taken on one of a candidate set of values.

The rest of the chapter shows you how to implement a solution to a problem requiring many variables (perhaps 100) all of the same type. You can simplify your coding task by defining an array capable of storing the different values. Then you can declare a single variable of this array type. Each of the many variables you need belong to the array variable. The value of one of these variables is readily found or changed with a correct reference to the array variable's name. Thus, you only have to deal with one identifier rather than 100 to solve the problem.

7.1   The Reserved Words NOT, AND, OR, and IN

In this section, you will learn to use the reserved words NOT, AND, OR, and IN, to code boolean expressions. Once you know how to use these words, you will be able to code virtually any condition you can express in pseudocode as a Pascal boolean expression.

boolean literals

You already know that boolean expressions can take on only the two values, false and true. These two values are recognized in source code as standard constants of type boolean. The compiler, for example, will recognize a statement coded as

```
IF (XInt < 0) = true THEN
    writeln('The value is negative');
```

The reserved words NOT, AND, *and* OR

The use of the boolean literal in this statement is unnecessary, but it is still a correct Pascal statement. We will, for the present, use boolean literals to show you how the different reserved words NOT, AND, and OR form boolean expressions.

Tables 7.1, 7.2, and 7.3 are the respective *truth tables* for the reserved words NOT, AND, and OR. The component expressions with these tables are the values taken on by the boolean constants A and B. Table 7.1 shows that the NOT operator complements the given boolean expression. Table 7.2 shows that the component expressions must be true for the AND operation to evaluate to true. Table 7.3 shows that when any component expression is true, the OR operation evaluates to true.

Truth table: a table showing the value taken on by a boolean expression for all of the possible combinations of values taken on by the component boolean expressions.

TABLE 7.1	Truth Table for NOT
A	**NOT A**
false	true
true	false

TABLE 7.2	Truth Table for AND	
A	**B**	**A AND B**
false	false	false
false	true	false
true	false	false
true	true	true

TABLE 7.3	Truth Table for OR	
A	**B**	**A OR B**
false	false	false
false	true	true
true	false	true
true	true	true

Examples of boolean expressions

You can use these three operators to form boolean expressions. In the following example, the computer produces display only if both variables PInt and QInt are equal to 0:

```
IF (PInt = 0) AND (QInt = 0) THEN
   writeln ('Both variables are zero.');
```

Likewise, if either PInt is not 0 or QInt is not 0, the computer produces display when the following statement is executed:

```
IF (PInt <> 0) OR (QInt <> 0) THEN
   writeln ('One or both variables are not zero.');
```

The loop is exited in the following case only when a positive value has been read into the variable PInt:

```
readln(PInt);
WHILE NOT (PInt > 0) DO
   readln(PInt);
writeln('The last value entered was positive.');
```

Syntax rules for forming expressions

Table 7.4 shows why we used parentheses when coding each expression. When parentheses are not used correctly, the program will usually not compile. In the following example, the compiler issues an error message because 0 OR YInt and 0 OR ZInt do not represent valid expressions:

TABLE 7.4 Hierarchy of Applied Operations, from Highest to Lowest

```
(                              )
              NOT
*     /    DIV   MOD    AND
           +     -    OR
<    <=    =    <>    >    >=    IN
```

```
IF XInt = 0 OR YInt = 0 OR ZInt = 0 THEN          {SYNTAX ERROR!!}
   writeln('At least one of the variables is zero.');
```

The sequence will compile properly when you code it as

```
IF (XInt = 0) OR (YInt = 0) OR (ZInt = 0) THEN
   writeln('At least one of the variables is zero.');
```

Likewise, the compiler produces an error message because it does not recognize NOT PInt as a meaningful expression in

```
WHILE NOT PInt > 0 DO          {SYNTAX ERROR!!}
   read(PInt);
```

PROGRAM DESIGN RULE 7.1

If one of the reserved words NOT, AND, or OR is used to form a boolean expression, be sure that all component expressions formed with the relational operators are enclosed by parentheses.

A design rule

Program Design Rule 7.1 tells when syntax rules require that a boolean expression be enclosed in parentheses. The reserved word IN, as seen in Table 7.4, represents another relational operator, whose usage we now discuss.

Set membership test, syntax, and semantics

Figure 7.1 shows the syntax diagram for a test to determine whether the expression on the left-hand side of the IN operator has taken on one of the values implied by the set value expression on the right-hand side of the operator. Figure 7.2

FIGURE 7.1   Syntax diagram to test set membership.

FIGURE 7.2   Syntax diagram for set membership.

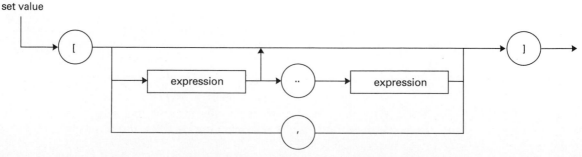

shows that a set's value can be formed from individual values, from an implied range of ordinal values, or from a combination of both of these expressions.

Examples

Some of the common uses of set membership tests are shown in Table 7.5. Suppose, for example, you need to code a statement whose description is given as

IF Ch is a letter of the alphabet THEN
LetterCount ← LetterCount + 1

Using the table, you see that the source code for the given pseudocode is

```
IF Ch IN ['A'..'Z', 'a'..'z'] THEN
    LetterCount:= LetterCount + 1;
```

TABLE 7.5 Some Set Membership Tests

Described Condition	Pascal Source Code Expression
Ch is a digit	Ch IN ['0'..'9']
Ch ends a sentence	Ch IN ['.', '?', '!']
Ch is a letter	Ch IN ['A'..'Z', 'a'..'z']
Ch equals Y, y, N, or n	Ch IN ['Y', 'y', 'N', 'n']
Int is between 0 and 100	Int IN [0..100]

Expressions that will not work

A set membership test can be applied only to expressions that are ordinal types. You cannot test for set membership with `real` types or string types. Also, only a rather small range of values can be applied for set membership tests on `integer` types.

Most systems will allow you to test for membership if the `integer` value lies between 0 and 255. For larger ranges, you would need to code a different expression. Thus, to test whether the `integer` variable Int lies between 0 and 1000, inclusive, the following code will probably not work:

```
IF Int IN [0..1000] THEN              {SYNTAX ERROR!!}
    writeln('The value is in range.');
```

If you use the reserved word AND, however, this statement will work:

```
IF (0 <= Int) AND (Int <= 1000) THEN
    writeln('The value is in range.');
```

Solving Some Problems

Now that we have shown how to form a boolean expression using the reserved words NOT, AND, OR, and IN, let us then develop the code for two problems requiring one or more of these reserved words in their solution.

Example Problem 7.1

The problem statement

Let us write a one-block program that will count the number of letters contained in a sentence. A sentence will end with either a period, question mark, or an exclamation point. After the characters have been read in, the program will display the number of letters in the sentence. A typical run of the program looks like

```
The quick brown fox jumps over the lazy dog.
The sentence had 35 letters in it.
```

Pseudocode description

We need to use a selective event-counting algorithm to solve the problem. Characters are to be read in, and as long as the sentence is not completed, each character is a candidate for counting. We can describe the program with the pseudocode

> *LetterCount ← 0*
> *read in value for Ch*
> *WHILE Ch is not end of sentence DO*
>   *IF Ch is a letter THEN*
>   *LetterCount ← LetterCount + 1*
>   *read in value for Ch*
> *clearline for display   {i.e., readln}*
> *display value of LetterCount*

We can use the reserved words NOT and IN to code the loop control expression as NOT (Ch IN ['.', '?', '!']) and Table 7.5 to code the expression for *Ch is a letter*.

The coded solution is given as the program CountLettersInSentence:

```
PROGRAM CountLettersInSentence(input, output);
  {A sentence is read in where the number of letters in the  sentence is
  counted and displayed.}
  VAR
    LetterCount:  integer;    {used to count letter occurrences}
    Ch: char;                 {stores value of character read in}
  BEGIN
    LetterCount:= 0;
    read(Ch);
    WHILE NOT (Ch IN ['.', '?', '!']) DO
      BEGIN
        IF Ch IN ['A'..'Z', 'a'..'z'] THEN
          LetterCount:= LetterCount + 1;
        read(Ch)
      END;
    readln;
    writeln('The sentence had ', LetterCount:1, ' letters in it.')
  END.
```

Proving the program	The code of `CountLettersInSentence` consists of two proven algorithms, one to selectively count events and the other to process a sequence of events up to the loop exit event. The boolean expression in the loop body correctly represents the occurrence of an event we wish to count. Moreover, the assertion we can make once the loop is exited is that the final value read in ends the sentence. Hence, the program is correct, given the initial problem statement.
On-line testing the program	A test using a sentence with no letters in it should be tried. Also, a test with only uppercase letters and one with only lowercase letters must be tried. A long sentence that runs on for more than one line of text must be tried. Finally, you will find that the test will fail on a sentence containing an embedded real number such as

The world population is now 4.3 billion people.

In order to properly handle this situation, the program must be redesigned. ◆

Example Problem 7.2

The problem statement	Wonderful Widgets Inc. manufactures widgets that can be described by a widget factor, a real number used in quality control, that describes the characteristic of a given widget. Let us write a procedure `TestBatch` that will count the number of good and bad widgets taken from a sample of N widgets coming off a production line. A widget is considered "good" if its widget factor lies in the range *Lower < widget factor < Upper,* where Lower and Upper are passed in as tolerance ratings for a "good" widget. The procedure is called by `TestBatch(Lower, Upper, N, Goods, Bads)`.

Sample data

7.85   7.92   7.71   7.34   8.01   8.12   7.83   7.51   7.22 7.94

Sample calls with the given data

`TestBatch(7.65, 8.00, 10, Goods, Bads)`	returns Goods ↔ 5, Bads ↔ 5
`TestBatch(7.00, 9.00, 6, Goods, Bads)`	returns Goods ↔ 6, Bads ↔ 0
`TestBatch(8.20, 8.70, 10, Goods, Bads)`	returns Goods ↔ 0, Bads ↔ 10
`TestBatch(7.49, 7.99, 8, Goods, Bads)`	returns Goods ↔ 5, Bads ↔ 3

Parameters	The first two parameters, representing tolerances for quality control, are passed into the block as value calls. N, representing the number of widgets to be sampled, is passed in as a value call. Values should be returned to the final two parameters, so they are called by variable.
Describing the block statement	This problem requires that we process N events. Therefore, we can use a FOR loop to solve the problem. The two variables Goods and Bads, which are counting variables, must be initialized to 0 before loop entry. Each loop pass will read in another value for a widget factor and then update one of the counters according to the sequence

> *read(WidgetFactor)*
> *IF WidgetFactor's value represents a good widget THEN*
>   *Goods ← Goods + 1*
> *ELSE*
>   *Bads ← Bads + 1*

The boolean expression in the description of the counter update action codes to (Lower < WidgetFactor) AND (WidgetFactor < Upper). When we put everything together, we get the coded solution to the problem as:

```
PROCEDURE TestBatch(Lower, Upper: real; Size: integer;
                                    VAR Goods, Bads: integer);
 {in: Lower -- lower tolerance limit, exclusive, for a good widget
  in: Upper -- upper tolerance limit, exclusive, for a good widget
  in: Size -- size of sample for quality control test
 out: Goods -- number of widgets in the sample within tolerance range
 out: Bads -- number of widgets in the sample outside tolerance range}
VAR
   Count: integer;        {the particular widget presently being tested}
   WidgetFactor: real;   {widget factor read into the Count_th widget}
BEGIN
   Goods:= 0;
   Bads:= 0;
   FOR Count:= 1 TO Size DO
     BEGIN
        read(WidgetFactor);
        IF (Lower < WidgetFactor) AND (WidgetFactor < Upper) THEN
          Goods:= Goods + 1
        ELSE
          Bads:= Bads + 1
     END
END;
```

Note that the test for a good widget could have been coded just as easily using (WidgetFactor > Lower) AND (WidgetFactor < Upper). We chose to code the expression as we did because it more closely resembles the mathematical expression *Lower < WidgetFactor < Upper*. ◆

EXERCISES

**Test Your
Understanding**

1. If one of the component expressions is _____ , a boolean expression formed with the word AND is always _____ .

2. If one of the component expressions is _____ , a boolean expression formed with the word OR is always _____ .

3. The NOT operator forms the _____ of the operand expression.

4. The expression on the left-hand side of the IN operator must be a(n) _____ type,

and the expression on the right-hand side of the operator is always a(n) _____ expression.

5. Correct the syntax of the following statements, retaining what you feel reflects the intended logic:

(a) IF XInt <= 5 OR YInt = 3 OR (XInt AND YInt = 0) THEN
      WInt:= 0;

(b) IF (5 <= XInt <= 10) OR YInt >= XInt THEN
      WInt:= 0;

(c) IF (5 <= XInt <= 10) OR YInt <= 7 OR YInt >= 10 THEN
      WInt:= 0;

Practice Your Analysis Skills

6. Change the following nested IF sequences to logically equivalent single IF statements:

(a) IF XInt > 0 THEN
    IF XInt < 5 THEN
      YInt:= 0;

(b) IF '0' <= Ch THEN
    IF Ch <= '9' THEN
      writeln('character is numeric');

(c) IF XInt > 0 THEN
    IF XInt < 50 THEN
      IF YInt = 0 THEN
        WInt:= 0;

(d) IF XInt > YInt THEN
    IF YInt > 5 THEN
      WInt:= 0;
    IF YInt > XInt THEN
    IF XInt < 7 THEN
      WInt:= 0;

(e) IF Ch = '+' THEN
    writeln('This is an arithmetic operator.')
  ELSE IF Ch = '−' THEN
    writeln('This is an arithmetic operator.')
  ELSE IF Ch = '*' THEN
    writeln('This is an arithmetic operator.')
  ELSE IF Ch = '/' THEN
    writeln('This is an arithmetic operator.');

Sharpen Your Implementation Skills

7. VAR
  XInt, YInt WInt: integer;
  ZRe: real;
  Ch, Ch1, CH2: char;

Assume the variables have been declared as given. Then write Pascal boolean expressions that are true if the following conditions hold:

(a) XInt is equal to 6, 7, or 8.

(b) XInt is between 10 and 15, inclusive, and YInt is greater than 15.

(c) 6.95 < ZRe < 7.05.

(d) Ch is a lowercase letter.

(e) Ch is neither an uppercase or lowercase vowel (use NOT).

(f) Ch1 and Ch2 are both lowercase letters and Ch1 occurs before Ch2 in the alphabet.

(g) either XInt or YInt are both greater than 10 or they are both equal to 0 or ZRe is positive.

(h) Ch is not a vowel (either uppercase or lowercase).

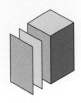

7.2 Common Algorithms Using NOT, AND, and OR

There are a number of algorithms you can categorize whose loop entry or loop exit condition is determined by the value of more than one boolean expression. You need to code these algorithms using the reserved words NOT, AND, and OR. We describe and prove a number of these algorithms in this section.

Complementing an expression

Before we give you some standard algorithms using the new reserved words, it is important that you know how to form the complement of a coded expression. The two DeMorgan theorems, as described in Table 7.6, show how to form the complement of an expression that uses the reserved words AND and OR. You can apply these theorems to determine the loop exit condition if you know the loop entry condition. For example, we have:

1. Loop Entry condition:
       (0 <= Int) AND (Int <= 1000)
    Loop Exit condition:
       (0 > Int) OR (Int > 1000)

2. Loop Entry Condition:
       (S1 >= S2 + S3) OR (S2 >= S1 + S3) OR (S3 >= S1 + S2)
    Loop Exit Condition:
       (S1 < S2+ S3) AND (S2 < S1 + S3) AND (S3 < S1 + S2)

3. Loop Entry Condition:
       (Count <> Max) AND (Int > 0)
    Loop Exit condition:
       (Count = Max) OR (Int <= 0)

TABLE 7.6 DeMorgan's Theorems

Expression	Its Complement
A AND B	NOT A OR NOT B
A OR B	NOT A AND NOT B

Applying the NOT operator

You can likewise apply DeMorgan's theorems to find the logical equivalent of expressions that use the reserved word NOT. For example, we have:

1. Expression:
       NOT ((Count = Max) OR (Int <= 0))
    Equivalent:
       (Count <> Max) AND (Int > 0)

2. Expression:
       NOT ((WidgetFactor < Lower) OR (WidgetFactor > Upper))
    Equivalent:
       (WidgetFactor >= Lower) AND (WidgetFactor <= Upper)

You may need to write code for an algorithm to use a WHILE loop that has one of N possible loop-terminating events. Two forms of this algorithm are described by Algorithms 7.1 and 7.2.

Algorithm 7.1

{*Algorithm using a WHILE loop to process to one of N loop-terminating events:*}
get EventValues
WHILE NOT (Exit1 OR Exit2 OR Exit3 . . . . OR ExitN) DO
    process
    get EventValue(s)
{*end algorithm*}

Algorithm 7.2

{*Algorithm using a WHILE loop to process to one of N loop-terminating events:*}
get EventValue(s)
WHILE NOT Exit1 AND NOT Exit2 AND NOT Exit3 . . . . AND NOT ExitN DO
    process
    get EventValue(s)
{*end algorithm*}

*Proof of the
algorithm*

The loop invariant for this algorithm is, "All *EventValues(s)* have been processed except for those obtained in the last loop pass." The postloop assertions we can make are, "One of the last *EventValues* obtained caused a loop exit condition to become true. All event values obtained except for those in the last loop pass were processed." If we apply DeMorgan's first theorem to Algorithm 7.2, we can likewise describe the postloop assertion as, "At least one of the coded conditions *Exit1*, *Exit2*, *Exit3*, . . . , or *ExitN* is true."

Note that the pseudocode *get EventValue(s)* represents that perhaps more than one variable is given a new value with each loop pass. In order for the algorithm to be satisfied, at least one of the values obtained should change so that one of the loop exit conditions might become true.

REPEAT..UNTIL
version

The REPEAT..UNTIL version of the algorithm to continue a process until one of *N* terminating events occurs is given in the pseudocode description of Algorithm 7.3.

Algorithm 7.3

{*REPEAT..UNTIL loop to process to one of N loop-terminating events:*}
REPEAT
  process
UNTIL Exit1 OR Exit2 OR Exit3 OR . . . . OR ExitN
{*end algorithm*}

*loop, then
decide*

Sometimes you may require an algorithm where the loop has more than one possible terminating event. Each event may require a different path for further processing after the loop exit. In this case, each exit condition is associated with an expression used in a postloop decision. The loop itself serves as the means to set up a precondition for the decision processing. We call this kind of algorithm a *loop, then decide* algorithm.

The pseudocode description of the `loop, then decide` algorithm, using the words WHILE and IF is given as Algorithm 7.4. All the numbered paths in this description code to different sequences of statements.

Algorithm 7.4

{WHILE loop version of loop, then decide algorithm:}
WHILE NOT Exit1 AND NOT Exit2 . . . . AND NOT ExitN DO
   process
IF Exit1 THEN
   path 1
ELSE IF Exit2 THEN
   path 2
ELSE IF . . .
    . . . .
ELSE IF Exit(N–1) THEN
   path (N–1)
ELSE
   path N
{end algorithm}

Let us solve a problem that requires the `loop, then decide` algorithm for its solution. The problem we propose will use the REPEAT..UNTIL form of the algorithm.

Example Problem 7.3

The problem statement

Write a source code fragment to simulate the play of a game of chance. The session of play initiates when the player enters a starting balance. Play continues until the player has either lost the starting balance or doubled its amount. The play of a game is coded as a call to the procedure `PlayAGame(OldBalance, NewBalance)`, where `OldBalance` represents the player's balance before the start of a game and `NewBalance` represents the player's balance after the completion of the game.

The player will want to know his or her balance after each game is completed. In addition, once the session is finished, he or she will want to know the average money won per game or the average money lost per game. Two typical runs are as follows:

```
Enter starting balance:  $10.00
You won.   You now have $14.00.
You lost.  You now have $12.00.
You won.   You now have $18.50.
```

```
You won.   You now have $22.00.
Your average win per game was $3.00.

Enter starting balance:   $15.00
You lost.   You now have $8.00.
You lost.   You now have $3.00.
You won.   You now have $7.00.
You won.   You now have $10.50.
You lost.   You now have $5.50.
You lost.   You now have $3.50.
You lost.   You now have $1.00.
You lost.   You now have −$5.00.
Your average loss per game was $2.50.
```

The fragment's description

We can describe the solution with the pseudocode

keyin StartingBalance
OldBalance ← StartingBalance
GamesPlayed ← 0
REPEAT
  PlayAGame(OldBalance, NewBalance)
  IF New Balance > OldBalance THEN
    display 'won'
  ELSE
    display 'lost'
  OldBalance ← NewBalance   {set up for next game, if necessary}
  display OldBalance
  GamesPlayed ← GamesPlayed + 1
*UNTIL (OldBalance >= 2 * StartingBalance) OR (OldBalance <= 0)*
IF OldBalance <= 0 THEN
  display (StartingBalance − OldBalance)/GamesPlayed   {average losses}
ELSE
  display (OldBalance − StartingBalance)/GamesPlayed   {average wins}

We are using a REPEAT..UNTIL loop because at least one game has to be played for the player to obtain a value for NewBalance.

Proving the logic

Before the loop is entered, the value taken on by OldBalance represents the starting balance. The value returned to NewBalance represents the money the player has after the completion of the game just played. Once, won/loss results have been displayed, OldBalance is assigned the value of NewBalance. Hence, after each loop pass, the value taken on by OldBalance represents the player's updated balance after the play of the last game. The value taken on by GamesPlayed, the games counter, represents the total number of games played. The postloop assertion, "The value of OldBalance is either greater than or equal to twice the value of StartingBalance or less than or equal to 0," fulfills the criterion for finishing the session at the gaming table.

Given the loss condition, the value of the expression coded as (Starting-Balance − OldBalance), represents the amount of money lost. Otherwise, the value of the expression (OldBalance − StartingBalance) represents the money won. Each of these two expressions divided by the value of GamesPlayed respectively represents the average loss per game or the average winnings per game.

Source code

The coded solution to the problem is given below. It is understood that the three variables StartingBalance, OldBalance, and NewBalance are of type real and that the variable GamesPlayed is of type integer.

```
write('Enter starting balance:   $');
readln(StartingBalance);
OldBalance:= StartingBalance;
GamesPlayed:= 0;
REPEAT
  PlayAGame(OldBalance, NewBalance);
  IF NewBalance > OldBalance THEN
    write('You won.   ')
  ELSE
    write('You lost.   ');
  OldBalance:= NewBalance;
  write('You now have   ');
  IF OldBalance < 0 THEN
    write('-');
  writeln('$', abs(OldBalance):4:2);
  GamesPlayed:= GamesPlayed + 1
UNTIL (OldBalance >= 2 * StartingBalance) OR (OldBalance <= 0);
IF OldBalance <= 0 THEN
  BEGIN
    write('Your average loss per game was $');
    writeln( (StartingBalance − OldBalance)/GamesPlayed :4:2)
  END
ELSE
  BEGIN
    write('Your average win per game was $');
    writeln( (OldBalance − StartingBalance)/GamesPlayed :4:2)
  END; ◆
```

Seek N required conditions

There are times when you may need an algorithm to seek that each of N required conditions is met. This algorithm thus seeks out a very specific program state. You will use this algorithm to set up preconditions for further processing. In this case, however, no postloop decision statements are expected, because *all N* conditions have been fulfilled. The idea here is that further processing is impossible *unless* all conditions are fulfilled. The two *WHILE* loop versions of this algorithm can be described by the pseudocode numbered as Algorithm 7.5a and Algorithm 7.5b.

Algorithm 7.5a

{WHILE loop seeking that N required conditions be met:}
get EventValue(s)
WHILE NOT Req1 OR NOT Req2 OR NOT Req3 . . . . OR NOT ReqN DO
    get EventValue(s)
{end algorithm}

Algorithm 7.5b

{WHILE loop seeking that N required conditions be met:}
get EventValue(s)
WHILE NOT (Req1 AND Req2 AND Req3 . . . . AND ReqN) DO
    get EventValue(s)
{end algorithm}

One of the REPEAT..UNTIL versions is described by the pseudocode of

Algorithm 7.6

{REPEAT..UNTIL loop seeking that N required conditions be met:}
REPEAT
    get EventValue(s)
UNTIL Req1 AND Req2 AND Req3 . . . . AND ReqN
{end algorithm}

A typical boolean expression described by *ReqM* represents the *M*th required condition that must be true at loop exit. The postloop assertion for any of these descriptions can be stated as, "All *N* required conditions have been met."

Using the algorithm

We will often use an algorithm to seek that all *N* conditions are fulfilled in the context of a sequence whose pseudocode is described by

    get valid values   *{uses a condition-seeking algorithm}*
    process the values

The action *get valid values* applies a condition-seeking algorithm to guarantee that all *N* conditions specify "validity" are satisfied. The next problem we will solve deals with coding a fragment that seeks a program state dependent upon more than one condition.

Example Problem 7.4

The problem statement

Recall that the sum of any two sides of a triangle must be greater than the length of the third side. Let us write a procedure GetSides which reads in values representing the three sides of a triangle until values representing a valid triangle are entered. A typical run of this procedure will produce the machine–user interaction:

```
Enter three sides of a triangle: 7.82   12.15   1.22
This is not a valid triangle.
Enter three sides of a triangle: 5.55   1.21   3.37
This is not a valid triangle.
Enter three sides of a triangle:  7.18   4.31   5.57
```

Describing the solution
　　　　　The procedure returns values to three parameters representing the three sides of the triangle. We can name these three variables Side1, Side2, and Side3. The pseudocode for the block statement is statisfied by the description

> *keyin Side1, Side2, Side3*
> *WHILE NOT (Side1, Side2, and Side3 represent valid triangle) DO*
> 　　*keyin Side1, Side2, Side3*

The prompt for the *keyin* message inside the loop body is different from the first prompt. In order for the loop to be entered, values indicating an invalid triangle must have been read in. A valid triangle occurs when the sum of any two sides is greater than the length of the third side.

Source code
　　　　　The procedure coded as GetSides is the solution to the problem.

```
PROCEDURE GetSides(VAR Side1, Side2, Side3: real);
   {out: Side1, Side2, Side3 -- length of sides for a valid triangle}
   BEGIN
     write('Enter three sides of a triangle:  ');
     readln(Side1, Side2, Side3);
     WHILE NOT ( (Side1 < Side2 + Side3) AND (Side2 < Side1 + Side3)
                 AND (Side3 < Side1 + Side2) ) DO
       BEGIN
         writeln('This is not a valid triangle.');
         write('Enter three sides of a triangle:  ');
         readln(Side1, Side2, Side3)
       END
   END;
```

The REPEAT..UNTIL version
　　　　　Suppose that if the user enters an improper set of values, the computer simply prompts for another set of values. It does not let the user know the values do not work, but a second prompt indicates that a new set of values is expected. In this case, given the previous numbers, the user-machine interaction looks like

```
Enter three sides of a triangle:  7.82   12.15   1.22
Enter three sides of a triangle:  5.55   1.21   3.37
Enter three sides of a triangle:  7.18   4.31   5.57
```

Using Algorithm 7.6, we then obtain the coded solution as follows:

```
PROCEDURE GetSides(VAR Side1, Side2, Side3: real);
   {out: Side1, Side2, Side3 -- length of sides for a valid triangle}
```

```
BEGIN
  REPEAT
    write('Enter three sides of a triangle:  ');
    readln(Side1, Side2, Side3)
  UNTIL ( (Side1 < Side2 + Side3) AND (Side2 < Side1 + Side3)
            AND (Side3 < Side1 + Side2) )
END; ◆
```

EXERCISES

Test Your Understanding

1. Apply DeMorgan's theorems to find the equivalent boolean expressions without using the reserved word NOT:
   (a) NOT (XInt > YInt) AND NOT((ZInt = 0) OR (Count > 10))
   (b) NOT ((15 < = XInt) AND (XInt <= 25))
   (c) NOT ((Ch1 = ' ') OR (Ch2 <> ' '))
   (d) NOT (XRe > YRe) OR NOT ((0.5 < XRe) AND (XRe < 1.0))

Test Your Analysis Skills

2. What assertion can be made after the following loop is exited:

   ```
   WHILE NOT (Count = 10) AND NOT (XInt = YInt) DO
       BEGIN {some processing}  END;
   ```

3. The following statement has no syntax errors but the semantics represent very bad code. Explain why. (Hint: Make some assertions.)

   ```
   IF (XInt >= 0) AND (YInt > XInt) AND (YInt < 0) THEN
       WInt:= 0;
   ```

Sharpen Your Implementation Skills

4. Write program fragments that do the following:
   (a) Prevent the processing of negative values for the variables XInt and YInt. In other words, the variables must both be positive. The values are read in. Further processing is to be held up until the condition is met.
   (b) Process the variables XInt and YInt only if they are unequal. If they are equal, then the following message is instead displayed:

   UNABLE TO PROCESS.. THE VALUES ARE EQUAL

   No further processing is carried out on XInt and Yint.
   (c) Keep processing XInt and YInt until their values are equal. After this event has occurred, the following message is displayed:

   FINISHED: THE VALUES ARE NOW EQUAL

   You can code the "processing" part of each sequence using the comment {process} in place of the actual code for processing.

5. Write a program fragment that finds the sum of a sequence of input integers until an integer greater than 100 or less than 50 is read in.

6. Write a program fragment to keep reading in integer values until either an integer less than 0 or one greater than 1000 is read in. Once a satisfactory value is read in, if it

is nonpositive, the display "LOW SIDE" is to be shown. If the value read in is greater than 1000, the display "HIGH SIDE" is to be shown.

7.3 Elementary Arrays

Suppose you want to write a program that reads in 10 integers, then displays them in reverse order. You can solve the problem by declaring 10 variables of type integer, but there is a better way. If you have a problem that requires many variables all of the same type, you can define an ARRAY type to implement the solution. Then you declare a variable of this given type where each component of the array variable is another variable. In this section, you will learn some of the basic operations that apply to array types. We will also solve the problem initially posed, using an array that contains 10 integer variables.

Array Syntax and Usage

Before you can use arrays, you need to know the syntax rules for setting up an array variable. Then you need to know the rules that let you manipulate the individual component variables of the array variable. We cover this subject matter in the next few pages. Then we present the solution to the problem we posed in the introduction to this section.

Subrange types   Before you can work with arrays, you need to know about *subrange types*. The syntax diagram to define a subrange type is shown in Figure 7.3. The two constants define the range of values that the associated variable(s) can take on. Correct syntax further requires that the value of the first constant be lower than the value of the second one. The ordinal type used in the subrange definition is known as the *host* type of the defined subrange type.

Subrange type: an ordinal type with a defined lowest value and a defined highest value.

subrange type

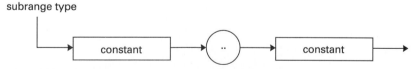

FIGURE 7.3   Syntax diagram for subrange type.

Examples   The source code fragment given as Example 7.1 defines three subrange types, then declares a variable of each type. The definitions specify the values each variable is expected to take on. From the definitions, we see that the variable Date is expected to take on values between 1 and 31, inclusive, the variable Index should take on values only between 1 and 100, inclusive, and the variable Grade is expected to take on values between 'A' and 'F', inclusive.

Example 7.1

```
TYPE
    DateType = 1..31;          {Host type: integer}
    IndexType = 1..100;        {Host type: integer}
    GradeType = 'A'..'F';      {Host type: char}
VAR
    Date: DateType;
    Index: IndexType;
    Grade: GradeType;
```

Range-checking

A subrange type defines the *expected* values the associated variable takes on. Unfortunately, at run time most dialects allow a variable of a given subrange type to take on any out-of-range value of the host type. Many of these dialects, however, give you *range-checking* as a software feature. If you want to use this feature for on-line testing, consult the user's manual of your system for more details.

Range-checking: software to check that each assigned subrange value is in range during the course of the program run.

Scalar and structured variables

The standard Pascal types real, integer and char are all *scalar variables*. An array is a type of variable that we refer to as a *structured variable*. The components of a structured variable can be either scalar or structured variables. Regardless of the component type(s), the value(s) of each component variable of a structured variable can be referenced or changed by means of a predefined *variable-access mechanism*. This mechanism is set up by the compiler when it executes the instruction(s) given in the TYPE definitions section of a block of source code. We are about to present the syntax rules for defining a structured variable that is a *one-dimensional array* type whose *elements* are all scalar types.

Scalar variable: a variable that can take on only one value at any given time.

Structured variable: a variable containing component variables.

Variable access mechanism: the mechanism by which a single component of a structured variable can be manipulated as if it were a single variable.

Array: a structured variable with components all of the same type, whose variable access mechanism consists of one or more subrange expressions.

Element: a component variable of an array.

One-dimensional array: an array whose variable access mechanism consists of a single subrange expression.

Syntax rules

Figure 7.4 is the syntax diagram for defining a one-dimensional array. The subrange type, which can be anonymous, specifies the subrange of allowed values that give access to one of the elements. The *type* following the reserved word OF specifies the variable type that makes up the array's elements.

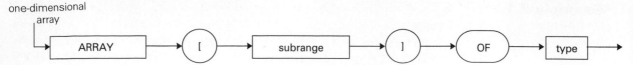

FIGURE 7.4 Syntax definition for a one-dimensional array type.

Figure 7.5 shows the variable access mechanism to one of the elements of a one-dimensional array. The identifier represents a reference to the array variable, and the access expression specifies the particular element being accessed. This expression must take on values within the defined subrange. An access expression using a value that is out of the subrange definition causes a crash with some dialects of Pascal and leads to unpredictable results with all remaining dialects.

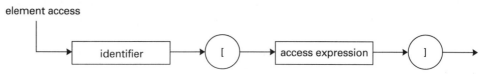

FIGURE 7.5 Accessing an element in a one-dimensional array.

An example   The TYPE and VAR parts of Example 7.2 show how to set up the array variable Reals such that it contains five elements of type real. Figure 7.6 shows a typical appearance of the variable Reals, given that values have been assigned to all the elements. The statements that follow show how the elements of Reals can be individually manipulated as scalar variables of type real.

Reals	[1]	[2]	[3]	[4]	[5]
	6.3	8.1	9.2	5.3	6.5

FIGURE 7.6 Typical appearance of the array Reals.

Example 7.2

```
TYPE
   IndexType = 1..5;
   RealsArray = ARRAY[IndexType] OF real;
VAR
   Reals: RealsArray;
   Index: IndexType;

{statements using the variable Reals:}

{1}   Reals[1]:= 7.5;
{2}   Reals[2]:= Reals[2] + 1;
{3}   Reals[3]:= Reals[1] + Reals[2];
{4}   Index:= 5;
{5}   Reals[Index]:= 0;
{6}   Reals[Index-1]:= Reals[1];
```

The effects of the statements

Figure 7.7 shows how the sequence of statements given in Example 7.2 changes the appearance of Reals from the original appearance given as Figure 7.6. In other words, Figure 7.6 shows the preconditions before the statements of Example 7.2 are carried out and Figure 7.7 shows the postconditions after they are carried out.

Reals	[1]	[2]	[3]	[4]	[5]
	7.5	9.1	16.6	7.5	0.0

FIGURE 7.7 Appearance of Reals after execution of statements.

Note that once the variable access mechanism is applied to any given element of Reals, the element is treated as if it were a real variable. All operations that are defined for a real type can then be applied to the element that is accessed. Note also how statements {4}, {5}, and {6} demonstrate that the variable access mechanism allows *expressions* to be applied to the host type of the access subrange. These examples imply that you can use the value taken on by a variable to gain access to one or more array elements.

Using an array to solve a problem

The solution to the problem of reading in then displaying ten integer values in reserve order is given in the source code of Example 7.3. A typical run of the program is shown below the source code. Note that access to each element is gained using the value taken on by the FOR loop variable.

Example 7.3

```
PROGRAM ReadAndReverse(input, output);
  {10 integer values are read in, then displayed in reverse order}
  TYPE
    SubrangeType = 1..10;
    TenIntsArray = ARRAY[SubrangeType] OF integer;
  VAR
    Ints:  TenIntsArray;         {stores the 10 integers read in}
    Index: SubrangeType;         {the means to access the 10 elements}
  BEGIN
    writeln('Input 10 integers: ');
    FOR Index:= 1 TO 10 DO
      read(Ints[Index]);
    readln;
    writeln('In reverse order, the integers are: ');
    FOR Index:= 10 DOWNTO 1 DO
      write(Ints[Index]:6);
    writeln
  END.

Input 10 integers:
78  95  34  56  80  91  22  31  65  72
In reverse order, the integers are:
    72    65    31    22    91    80    56    34    95    78
```

Array Parameters

*Assignment
compatibility*

Now that you know how to write code that sets up and uses array variables, let us show how array variables work as parameters. We will also show how the parameter-passing mechanism applies to the individual elements of an array.

Consider the following definitions and declarations:

```
TYPE
   FiveIntsArray = ARRAY[1..5] OF integer;
VAR
   Ints, NextInts: FiveIntsArray;
```

Given that `Ints` and `NextInts` are of the same type and assuming that values have been assigned to the elements of `Ints`, the assignment statement coded as `NextInts:= Ints;` is legal Pascal. Two structured variables *of the same type* are assignment-compatible. We point out, however, that the assignment statement is internally carried out by copying the value of each element of `Ints` into each element of `NextInts`. Even though you do not explicitly code a FOR loop, the action carried out by the assignment statement is equivalent *in every way* (not just logically!) to the following sequence:

```
FOR Index:= 1 TO 5 DO
   NextInts[Index]:= Ints[Index];
```

*Making a
nonduplicate
array*

The statement part of Example 7.4 shows how you can use the values of the elements in one array to assign different values to the elements of a second array. The statement for calling the procedure is coded as `MakeNext(Ints, NextInts)` where `Ints` is called by value and `NextInts` is called by VAR.

Example 7.4

```
PROCEDURE MakeNext(Ints: FiveIntsArray; VAR NextInts: FiveIntsArray);
   {A demonstration procedure to show how parameter passing with arrays
   works.  The postcondition returned is that each element of NextInts
   is equal to each elements of Ints plus 3.}
   VAR
      Index: 1..5;     {subrange variable to carry out assignments}
   BEGIN
      FOR Index:= 1 TO 5 DO
         NextInts[Index]:= Ints[Index] + 3
   END;
```

PROGRAM DESIGN RULE 7.2

Do not use operations defined for scalar types on structured variables.

Note in the example that the right-hand side of the assignment operation has an `integer` expression and the left-hand side has an `integer` variable. The following "statement," however, will not work because the "+" operator is incompatible with array types: `NextInts:= Ints + 3`. {WRONG!}

Arrays as parameters

Figure 7.8 shows the data areas for the main block and the procedure MakeNext, given a typical array Ints. The data area is shown just at the point when the computer has assigned a value to `NextInts[3]`.

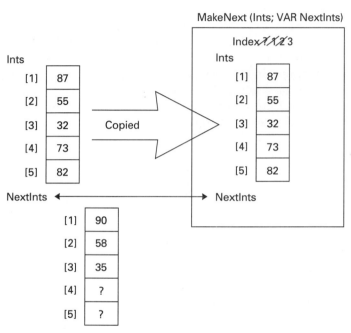

FIGURE 7.8 Data area of `Procedure MakeNext` given typical values of actual parameter `Ints`.

Note that the local variable `Ints`, which belongs in the data area of the procedure `MakeNext`, is copied element by element from the actual parameter variable `Ints` in the main data area. In order to carry out the copy operation, the machine executes a hidden `FOR` loop on all the elements before it begins to execute the block statement. Once the act of copying is completed, the relationship between the actual and the formal parameter variables is finished.

The figure also shows that the local name `NextInts` is the alias for the variable `NextInts` in the main block's data area. No local copy is made, for the aliasing mechanism of the `VAR` call is in effect.

Efficiency considerations

When a procedure is exited, all local structures are destroyed. Thus, a formal parameter call by value on an array will serve to "protect" the values belonging to the elements of the actual parameter. If you want to use the elements of an array as reference values but do not intend to change the values, your initial choice would probably be to pass the actual parameter array into the block using the call-by-value mechanism.

If time or space considerations are critical for your program, it is inadvisable to use the call-by-value mechanism on the reference array. A VAR call is the superior choice on both counts. If run time must be kept down, the computer copies only one starting address that will then allow access to all the elements of the actual parameter structure. Compare this small run-time overhead with the larger time required to execute the hidden FOR loop of a call-by-value action.

If space is a consideration, extra memory is always required to make local copies. Moreover, the effects of this space-extravagant operation are gone and forgotten once the block is exited. For these two reasons, we recommend that you use a VAR call on a large *reference* (not to be changed) structure for most applications.

Arrays elements as parameters

Once an array element is accessed, it is treated as if it were a variable of the element's type. The source code of Example 7.5 shows the use of array elements as actual parameters. In the case of the first call, Ints[1] is copied into Minuend, Ints[2] is copied into Subtrahend, and Ints[3] is aliased as Difference. With the second call, Ints[1] is likewise copied into Minuend, the value of Ints[3] + Ints[4] is copied into Subtrahend, and Ints[5] is aliased as Difference.

Example 7.5

```
PROCEDURE FindDifference(Minuend, Subtrahend: integer;
                                        VAR Difference: integer);
   {returns Difference = Minuend − Subtrahend}
   BEGIN
     Difference:= Minuend − Subtrahend
   END;

{calling the procedure:}

FindDifference(Ints[1], Ints[2], Ints[3]);
FindDifference(Ints[1], Ints[3] + Ints[4], Ints[5]);
```

The following two assignment statements are logically equivalent to the actions carried out by the respective procedure calls:

```
Ints[3]:= Ints[1] - Ints[2];
Ints[5]:= Ints[1] - (Ints[3] + Ints[4]);
```

Exchanging the values of two elements

You can apply procedural abstraction to exchange the values of two elements of an array. Example 7.6 shows how to exchange the values of two elements in an array of integers with a call to the abstracted procedure ExchangeInts. The first call exchanges the elements Ints[1] and Ints[2], and the second call exchanges the elements Ints[M] and Ints[N].

Example 7.6

```
PROCEDURE ExchangeInts(VAR IntA, IntB: integer);
   {IntA takes on IntB's initial value and vice versa}
   VAR
```

```
        Temp: integer;
   BEGIN
     Temp:= IntA;
     IntA:= IntB;
     IntB:= Temp
   END;


ExchangeInts(Ints[1], Ints[2]);
ExchangeInts(Ints[M], Ints[N]);
```

Figure 7.9 shows the data areas just before control returns from the procedure call ExchangeInts(Ints[M], Ints[N]). Note how the variable access mechanism is applied to the elements of Ints and how the aliasing mechanism is applied to the two elements Ints[M] and Ints[N].

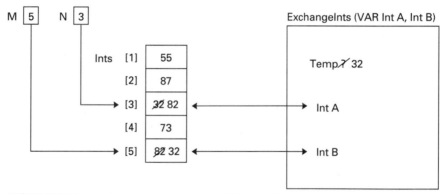

FIGURE 7.9 Data area showing a call to ExchangeInts(Ints[M], Ints[N]).

EXERCISES

Test Your Understanding

1. Indicate which are legal and which are illegal subrange types:
   (a) 2..72   **(b)** 1.8..12.7   **(c)** 1 TO 10   **(d)** 1..10
   (e) −100..100   **(f)** 100..−100   **(g)** 'A'..'Z'   **(h)** ['A'..'Z']
   (i) 'L'..'P'   **(j)** 'P'..'L'

2. Suppose you have defined the type

```
   TYPE
      BigRealsArray = ARRAY[1..1000] OF real;
```

Discuss how the copy mechanism is carried out using each of the following headers:
   (a) PROCEDURE UseReals(VAR Reals: BigRealsArray);
   (b) PROCEDURE UseReals(Reals: BigRealsArray);

3. Suppose a variable Ints has been given these values:

Ints	[1]	[2]	[3]	[4]	[5]	[6]	[7]	[8]	[9]	[10]
	43	26	40	39	20	44	93	72	21	90

From these values and the code of Example 7.6, indicate the display when the following sequence is carried out:

```
ExchangeInts(Ints[3],Ints[7]);
ExchangeInts(Ints[1], Ints[5]);
ExchangeInts(Ints[9], Ints[1]);
FOR Index:= 1 TO 10 DO
   write(Ints[Index]:4);
writeln;
```

4. Indicate what is displayed as a result of the following:

```
TYPE
   SmallArray = ARRAY[1..5] OF integer;
VAR
   SmInts: SmallArray;
   Index: integer;
{*                                                        *}
PROCEDURE ReAssign(VAR SmInts: SmallArray);
   VAR
     Local: SmallArray;
     Index: integer;
   BEGIN
     FOR Index:= 1 TO 5 DO
       IF Index MOD 2 <> 0 THEN
         Local[Index]:= SmInts[Index] DIV 2
       ELSE
         Local[Index]:= 2*SmInts[Index];
     SmInts:= Local
   END;
{*                                                        *}

SmInts[1]:= 78;  SmInts[2]:= 44;  SmInts[3]:= 31;
SmInts[4]:= 19;  SmInts[5]:= 45;
ReAssign(SmInts);
FOR Index:= 1 TO 5 DO
   write(SmInts[Index]:5);
writeln;
```

5. Write the neccessary definitions and declarations for the following:
(a) A structure that stores the prices of five classes of widgets for the company Widgets Inc.
(b) A structure that stores the brand names of the five classes of widgets.
(c) A structure that stores the number of orders on any given day for each of the five widgets.
(d) A structure that stores the names of up to 1000 citizens in a small village.

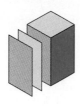

7.4 Some Array-Processing Algorithms

In this section, we give you two of the most common algorithms for array processing. One algorithm is used to read in or assign values to an indefinite number of array elements. We will develop the logic for this algorithm. The other algorithm uses a FOR loop to process elements over a specified subrange.

Assigning values to a subrange of array elements

You will often use an array to store an indefinite number of values for further processing. You may, for example, write a program to read in a list of names until some name to terminate the sequence is input and then use the list as part of some other process. You may want to write code to read in integer values until some negative value is entered. These positive integers, stored as elements in an array, are then used for further processing. Both of these problems require an algorithm to assign values to a subrange of array elements. The algorithm must return two results: the values assigned to the array elements themselves, and a value indicating how many elements have been assigned into.

An initial description

It seems that we can use an algorithm to process values until some terminating event. The actual processing carried out by the loop body is the assignment of another value to an array element. If we name a candiate value for an element Candidate and name the structure AnArray, our initial approach to the problem can be described by

> *get Candidate*
> *WHILE NOT (finished with assignments) DO*
> *   assign Candidate to an element of AnArray*
> *   get Candidate*

We have not included descriptions of specific assignments to the variable AssignedElements in this initial draft. When the loop is exited, the value assigned to this variable will represent the number of elements that have been assigned values.

Getting the exit and entry conditions

Suppose the array is defined as one with an access subrange of *1..MaxElements*. We must be sure that no attempt is made to assign *An Array[MaxElements+1]* ← *Candidate,* for this represents a logical error. Hence, the loop body must be exited if the condition *AssignedElements = MaxElements* becomes true. Likewise, the loop should not be entered again if the last value of Candidate indicates there are no more elements to assign. We can put these two conditions together as a single exit condition that we can express as *(Candidate is sentinel) OR (AssignedElements = MaxElements).*

If this pseudocode represents the exit condition, we must consider how to handle the case where the first candidate obtained is a *sentinel value*. In this case, no elements are assigned, and the loop is not entered. Hence, the initial assignment to AssignedElements before loop entry must be 0.

Sentinel value: a value, often used to terminate a loop, that signifies the end of a given sequence of data.

Assigning the elements

Suppose the first value obtained is not a sentinel value. This first value should be assigned to `AnArray[1]`. Given that the initial assignment outside the loop was *AssignedElements ← 0*, the obvious sequence to carry out the action is described by

$$AssignedElements \leftarrow AssignedElements + 1$$
$$AnArray[AssignedElements] \leftarrow Candidate$$

The complete algorithm

The complete description of the algorithm is given as the pseudocode of Algorithm 7.7. We will give this algorithm the name *partial fill-in* because it assigns values to the elements over part of the definition subrange.

Algorithm 7.7

{the partial fill-in algorithm:}
AssignedElements ← 0
get Candidate
WHILE NOT ((Candidate is sentinel) OR (AssignedElements = MaxElements)) DO
    AssignedElements ← AssignedElements + 1
    AnArray[AssignedElements] ← Candidate
    get Candidate
{end algorithm}

Assertions

The loop invariant for the partial-fill-in algorithm is "The elements over the subrange *1..AssignedElements* have had values assigned to them." The post loop assertion is, "Either the last value obtained represented a sentinel value or all *MaxElements* of *AnArray* have been assigned values." In either case, the algorithm is proven by these assertions.

Using the algorithm

The procedure `GetNames`, coded as Example 7.7, reads in elements to the array `Names` either until a sentinel name of `Zzz` is read in or until `MaxElements` names have been read in and assigned. In order for the example to have meaning, the following variables must have been defined and declared:

```
CONST
  MaxString = 50;     {longest string that can be read in}
  MaxElements = 100;  {total number of names allowed in array of names}
  Sentinel = 'Zzz';   {sentinel name to indicate end of read in}
TYPE
  NameString = STRING[MaxString];     {Turbo; different for other dialects}
  NamesArray = ARRAY[1..MaxElements] OF NameString;
VAR
  TotalNames: integer;
  Names: NamesArray;
```

Example 7.7

```
PROCEDURE GetNames(VAR Names: NamesArray; VAR TotalNames: integer);
 {Values are filled into the array Names until a sentinel name (a global
  constant equal to 'Zzz') is read in or the array is full. The value
  returned to TotalNames indicates how many elements of Names have been
  filled in.}
 VAR
   TempName: NameString;   {candidate array element}
 BEGIN
   TotalNames:= 0;
   write('Name:   ');
   readln(TempName);
   WHILE NOT ( (TempName = Sentinel) OR (TotalNames = MaxElements) ) DO
     BEGIN
       TotalNames:= TotalNames+1;
       Names[TotalNames]:= TempName;
       write('Name:   ');
       readln(TempName)
     END
 END;
```

Comments on semantics

We can describe the loop control expression for Algorithm 7.7 by *NOT (finished OR full)*. The word finished represents a boolean condition where no more elements are to be filled in even though there are still some candidate elements left. The word *full* represents the condition that there are no more elements available to be filled. Note that the loop exit condition can then be described by *finished OR full*.

If we apply DeMorgan's theorem to the control expression, we get an alternate loop control expression *NOT finished AND NOT full*. We could have just as easily used this expression for loop control in the code of Example 7.7. The boolean expression for loop control is then coded as (TempName <> Sentinel) AND (TotalNames <> MaxElements). Applying DeMorgan's theorem to this expression gives us the identical exit condition (TempName = Sentinel) OR (TotalNames = MaxElements). This condition semantically represents the condition described as *finished OR full*.

Processing all assigned elements of an array

Once elements have been assigned to an array structure, they can be processed in many different ways. Algorithm 7.8 uses a FOR loop to process all assigned elements over the subrange *1..TotalElements*.

Algorithm 7.8

{Process all elements over the subrange 1..TotalElements:}
FOR Index ← 1 TO TotalElements DO
*   process AnArray[Index]*
{end algorithm}

Examples   You can use this algorithm for many different applications. For example, we
have the code to

1.   Get the sum over the assigned elements of the array `Ints`:

```
Sum:= 0;
FOR Index:=  1  TO TotalElements DO
   Sum:= Sum + Ints[Index];
```

2.   Assign the value 0 to all the `MaxElements` of `Ints`:

```
FOR Index:= 1 TO MaxElements DO
   Ints[Index]:= 0;
```

3.   Get the count of the number of elements in `Ints` with positive values, the
count of the number of elements equal to 0, and the count of the number of
elements with negative values:

```
Positives:= 0;
Zeroes:= 0;
Negatives:= 0;
FOR Index:= 1 TO TotalElements DO
   IF Ints[Index] > 0 THEN
      Positives:= Positives + 1
   ELSE IF Ints[Index] = 0 THEN
      Zeroes:= Zeroes + 1
   ELSE
      Negatives:= Negatives + 1;
```

4.   Find the index value of the element of `Ints` with the highest value:

```
Highest:= 1;        {candidate first value}
FOR Index:=  2 TO TotalElements DO
   IF Ints[Index] > Ints[Highest] THEN
      Highest:= Index;
```

Note how the last example is a modification of the basic algorithm.

Parallel arrays   You can use Algorithm 7.8 with more than one array variable in the body of
the FOR loop when you have *parallel arrays*. The code given as Example 7.8 declares three parallel arrays, `Names`, `Aves` and `Grades`. Figure 7.10 shows typical
values for the first 8 elements.

> **Parallel arrays:** two or more arrays, not necessarily of the same type, that
> have the same defined access subrange.

Parallel Arrays

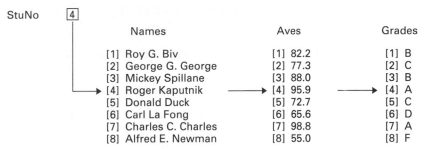

FIGURE 7.10   Parallel arrays.

Example 7.8

```
CONST
  MaxEnroll = 150;
Type
  NameString =  STRING[50];  {Turbo; different in other dialects}
  NamesArray =  ARRAY[1..MaxEnroll] OF NameString;
  RealsArray =  ARRAY[1..MaxEnroll] OF real;
  GradesArray = ARRAY[1..MaxEnroll] OF char;
VAR
  Names: NamesArray;    {stores each student's name}
  Aves:  RealsArray;    {stores each student's average}
  Grades: GradesArray;  {stores each student's letter grade}
  TotalStudents:  integer;  {number of students in the class}
```

Using parallel arrays

Parallel arrays imply a semantic link between different variables by way of the common access mechanism. In our example, three characteristics about the same student (Name, Average, and Grade) can be determined using the same access expression on three different structures. For example, all the information about student 4 (i.e., Roger Kaputnik) can be displayed with the following sequence:

```
StudentNo:= 4;
write(Names[StudentNo],' had an average of ',Aves[StudentNo]:3:1);
writeln(' and received a grade of ',Grades[StudentNo],'.');
```

An algorithm for parallel-array processing

From the figure, we see also that Roy G. Biv had an average of 82.2 and received a "B", George G. George had an average of 77.3 and was awarded a "C," and so forth.

We can describe the algorithm to read in values for the elements of the three arrays over the subrange *1..TotalStudents* by the pseudocode

```
FOR StudentNo ← 1 TO TotalStudents DO
        keyin Names[StudentNo]
        keyin Aves[StudentNo]
        keyin Grades[StudentNo]
```

We will use this algorithm in Section 7.5.

EXERCISES

**Test Your
Understanding**

1. Suppose we can describe a loop entry condition by NOT finished AND NOT found.
   (a) Write down the description of the loop exit condition.
   (b) Write down another description of the loop entry condition, without using the word AND. (Hint: Simply apply NOT to the exit condition found in part (a).)

**Test Your
Analysis Skills**

2. Given the values assigned to the elements of Names, Aves, and Grades in Figure 7.10, what will be the display for the following sequence:

```
Low:= 1;
High:= 1;
FOR Index:= 2 TO 8 DO
   BEGIN
      IF Aves[Index] < Aves[Low] THEN
         Low:= Index;
      IF Aves[Index] > Aves[High] THEN
         High:= Index
   END;
writeln(Names[Low]  ,' -- ',  Aves[Low]:3:1, ' -- ',  Grades[Low]);
writeln(Names[High] ,' -- ',  Aves[High]:3:1, ' -- ',  Grades[High]);
```

3. Given the following code and input stream, indicate what is displayed:

```
FOR Index:= 1 TO 10 DO
   Ints[Index]:= 0;
read(AnInt);
WHILE AnInt > 0 DO
   BEGIN
      IF AnInt <= 10 THEN
         Ints[AnInt]:= Ints[AnInt] + 1;
      read(AnInt)
   END;
readln;
FOR Index:= 1 TO 10 do
   write(Ints[Index]:4);
writeln;

3  4  3  6  3  4  5  1  1  7  9  8  7  10  8  1  4  5  -1
```

Sharpen Your Implementation Skills

4. **(a)** Write a procedure that returns to the variable `Zeros` the count of the number of zeroes assigned to the elements of `Ints`, of type `IntsArray` (capable of storing 10 integer values).

(b) Write a driver to test the procedure.

(c) Indicate the kinds of test arrays you would read into `Ints` using the driver.

7.5 Case Study: Grading an Exam

In this section, we will apply parallel arrays to solve a problem. Note particularly how we use the parameter-passing mechanism in the procedures we develop to solve the problem.

CASE STUDY 7.1

The problem statement

Professor Teachem has just given a 20-question multiple-choice quiz to her class. She wants a program to help her grade test papers. The program is to be executed as follows: First, Teachem enters the number of students in the class. Then she enters the answer key. Next, for each of the students, she enters the name and the answers on the test paper. These answers are compared with the answer key to get a result for a given student's paper. When all test papers have been read in, the results of all students are displayed. A typical line of display for one of the students might look like

```
            Roger Kaputnik had 15 correct answers.
```

The answer key is read in first. Then each student's name and the test answers are read in. The computer displays a column of numbers from 1 to 20 for Teachem to align the answers she enters. Once 20 answers have been read in, Teachem is asked if everything was entered correctly. If she enters Y, the computer prompts for the next set of names and answers; otherwise it attempts to fill in the same information for the same student. A typical set of interactions where Teachem was not satisfied with her first entry sequence might look like

```
Input name:  Roy G. Biv
QuestionNo:  1  2  3  4  5  6  7  8  9  10  11  12  13  14  15  16  17  18  19  20
Answer    :  A  C  D  A  B  B  A  C  A  B   D   C   C   A   A   C   D   B   B   B
Is this OK?  (Y, N) N

Input name:  Roy G. Biv
QuestionNo:  1  2  3  4  5  6  7  8  9  10  11  12  13  14  15  16  17  18  19  20
Answer    :  A  C  D  A  C  B  A  C  A  B   D   C   C   A   A   C   D   B   B   B
Is this OK?  (Y, N) Y
```

First, the number of students in the class must be read in. The students' names and test results, all of which are to be displayed, can be stored in two parallel arrays of name strings and integers, respectively. The answer key (and each student's test paper) can be structured as an array of type char, capable of storing 20 char values. Given these structures, we can describe the action of the main block as

> *display instructions*
> *keyin Enrollment*
> *keyin array element values to AnswerKey*
> *get array element values of Names and Results using AnswerKey*
> *display array element values of Names and Results*

We will abstract all but the second action in the description to procedure calls. Note that the variable AnswerKey is required to assign a value to each element of Results, where Results[StudentNo] represents the number of correct answers on StudentNo's paper. We will need to code a loop for the action to keyin array element values to AnswerKey in case Teachem incorrectly entered values for the answer key.

The main block   The main block for the program with four stub procedures follows. We plan to code everything but ShowInstructions.

```
PROGRAM GradeExam(input,output);
  {A program to grade student test papers on a multiple-choice exam.
  After instructions are displayed, the test key is read in, followed
  by each student's name and test paper. The tests are graded and
  students' names and test results are displayed.}
  CONST
    MaxEnrollment = 150;       {maximum possible enrollment in class}
    TotalQuestions = 20;       {total number of questions on quiz}
  TYPE
    NameString =    STRING[50];  {or whatever works in your dialect}
    NamesArray =    ARRAY[1..MaxEnrollment] OF NameString;
    ResultsArray =  ARRAY[1..MaxEnrollment] OF integer;
    AnswerArray =   ARRAY[1..TotalQuestions] OF char;
  VAR
    Names:        NamesArray;    {stores each student's name}
    Results:      ResultsArray;  {count of each student's correct answers}
    AnswerKey:    AnswerArray;   {contains the answer key to the test}
    Enrollment:   integer;       {total number of students in the class}
    Reply:        char;          {indicates satisfaction with answer key}
  {*                                                                  *}
  PROCEDURE ShowInstructions;
    BEGIN  {displays instructions to user}    END;
  {*                                                                  *}
  PROCEDURE RecordAnswers(VAR ATest: AnswerArray);
    BEGIN  {reads in values to the elements of ATest}    END;
```

```
{*                                                              *}
PROCEDURE GetResults(AnswerKey: AnswerArray; Enrollment: integer;
                     VAR Names: NamesArray;   VAR Results: ResultsArray);
  {reads in Enrollment values to Names and assigns Enrollment values
   to Results using the values assigned to the elements of AnswerKey}
  BEGIN    END;
{*                                                              *}
PROCEDURE DisplayResults(Enrollment: integer; VAR Names: NamesArray;
                                         VAR Results: ResultsArray);
   {displays contents of Enrollment elements of Names and Results}
  BEGIN   END;
{*                                                              *}
BEGIN {main block}
  ShowInstructions;
  write('Enter class enrollment:   ');
  readln(Enrollment);
  REPEAT                              {get satisfactory answer key}
    writeln('Now get answer key...');
    RecordAnswers(AnswerKey);
    write('Are you satisfied?  (Y/N)  ');
    readln(Reply)
  UNTIL Reply IN ['Y', 'y'];         {satisfactory answer key read in}
  GetResults(AnswerKey, Enrollment, Names, Results);
  DisplayResults(Enrollment, Names, Results)
END.
```

*Planning
Record-
Answers*

RecordAnswers should read in values to the elements of ATest. The values read in can either represent a student's paper or the answer key. We expect to use a call to this procedure as part of the statement of GetResults, hence, we give the formal parameter the generic name ATest. We can describe the action of the block by

*display guidelines
read in values for elements of ATest*

We can display the guidelines using a FOR loop. We can likewise use a FOR loop to read in values for the elements of ATest. In this case, however, we want the computer to skip blank characters read in, so we describe the required sequence by

*FOR QuestionNo ← 1 TO TotalQuestions DO
REPEAT
read(Ch)
UNTIL (Ch <> ' ')
ATest [QuestionNo] ← Ch*

The variable Ch is a local variable whose value represents the last character value read in.

The code for RecordAnswers is then written as follows:

```
PROCEDURE RecordAnswers(VAR ATest: AnswerArray);
   {documentation}
   VAR
     QuestionNo: integer;     {represents a given question number}
     Ch: char;                {the last char value read in}
   BEGIN
     write('Question No: ');                    {display answer guide}
     FOR QuestionNo:= 1 TO TotalQuestions DO
       write(QuestionNo:3);
     writeln;
     FOR QuestionNo:= 1 TO TotalQuestions DO    {read in answers}
       BEGIN
         REPEAT
           read(Ch)
         UNTIL Ch <> ' ';
         ATest[QuestionNo]:= Ch
       END;
     readln
   END;
```

Planning
GetResults

The variables Names and Results are parallel arrays, so values can be assigned to the respective elements using the same FOR loop. Before a test can be graded, however, Teachem must be satisfied that the name and test paper read in is satisfactory. Therefore, the sequence for GetResults is described by

FOR StudentNo ← 1 TO Enrollment DO
    REPEAT
        keyin Names [StudentNo]
        RecordAnswers (Student Test)
        keyin Reply   {OK?}
    UNTIL Reply IN ['Y', 'y']
    use Student Test and AnswerKey to assign value to Results [StudentNo]

The variable StudentTest is a local variable of type AnswerArray, representing the test paper of StudentNo. The final action controlled by the FOR loop can be abstracted to a procedure call whose code is GradeTest(StudentTest, AnswerKey, Results[StudentN]), where the value assigned to Results [StudentNo] represents the number of correct answers on the test paper.

```
{*                                                                        *}
PROCEDURE GradeTest(StudentTest, AnswerKey: AnswerArray;
                                  VAR TotalCorrect: integer);
```

```
{the number of answers in the array StudentTest that matches the
answers in the array AnswerKey is passed out to the variable
TotalCorrect}
BEGIN    END;
{+                                                                    +}
PROCEDURE GetResults(AnswerKey: AnswerArray; Enrollment: integer;
                     VAR Names: NamesArray; VAR Results: ResultsArray);
   {documentation}
   VAR
     StudentNo:  integer;    {the number of the student being processed}
     StudentTest: AnswerArray;    {the test paper for student StudentNo}
     Reply: char;           {indicates satisfication with StudentNo values}
   BEGIN
     FOR StudentNo:= 1 TO Enrollment DO
       BEGIN
         REPEAT
           write('Input name:    ');
           readln(Names[StudentNo]);
           RecordAnswers(StudentTest);
           write('Is this OK?  (Y/N) ');
           readln(Reply)
         UNTIL Reply IN ['Y', 'y'];
         GradeTest(StudentTest, AnswerKey, Results[StudentNo])
       END
   END;
  {*                                                                   *}
```

Code for
GetResults

Planning
GradeTest

The source code for GetResults, including the stub for the procedure GradeTest, is given above. Note the parameter correspondence between the actual parameter variable Results[StudentNo] and the formal parameter variable TotalCorrect.

Now let us plan the code for GradeTest. The value assigned to Total-Correct should represent the number of answers on StudentTest that match the answers of AnswerKey. These two are also parallel arrays that can be used in an conditional event-counting algorithm. We plan to count the number of times over the TotalQuestions events that the condition described by the boolean expression StudentTest[QuestionNo] = AnswerKey[QuestionNo] is true. The access expression QuestionNo will also be the loop control variable of the FOR loop that goes from 1 to TotalQuestions. From all these considerations, we obtain the code for the procedure GradeTest as shown.

```
PROCEDURE GradeTest(StudentTest, AnswerKey: AnswerArray;
                                VAR TotalCorrect:integer);
   {documentation}
   VAR
     QuestionNo: integer;    {the number of the question being compared}
```

```
    BEGIN
      TotalCorrect:= 0;
      FOR QuestionNo:= 1 TO TotalQuestions DO
        IF StudentTest[QuestionNo] = AnswerKey[QuestionNo] THEN
          TotalCorrect:= TotalCorrect + 1
    END;
```

The code for
Display-
Results

Because the two variables Names and Results represent parallel arrays, the code for DisplayResults is straightforward and follows:

```
 PROCEDURE DisplayResults(Enrollment: integer; VAR Names: NamesArray;
                                               VAR Results: ResultsArray);
    {documentation}
    VAR
      StudentNo: integer;    {the number of the student being displayed}
    BEGIN
      writeln; writeln; writeln;    {skip some lines}
      FOR StudentNo:= 1 TO Enrollment DO
        BEGIN
          write(Names[StudentNo],' had ');
          writeln(Results[StudentNo]:1,' correct answers.')
        END
    END;
```

PROGRAM DESIGN RULE 7.3

Always use local access variables to array elements.

Access variables

Note that we did not declare any "general-purpose" access variables globally. Even though it would appear "cheaper" to reference StudentNo and QuestionNo globally within each block, this usage is confusing and wrong. Because none of the procedures return values to either variable, neither identifier will appear in any header. Given this premise, these access variables would be referenced as side effects, a coding practice that is strictly taboo. These access variables *served local purposes* and hence needed to be declared locally. ◆

EXERCISES

Test Your Understanding

1. Explain why we did not declare the variables QuestionNo and StudentNo globally, even though they were used in more than one procedure.

2. Note that we used the call-by-variable mechanism on the variables Names and Results

for the procedure `DisplayResults`. No new values were assigned to any elements of the arrays, so why did we use this mechanism?

Practice Your Analysis Skills

3. What would happen if a value greater than `MaxEnrollment` is read into `Enroll-ment`? How would you fix this problem?

Sharpen Your Implementation Skills

4. Write the code to fix the problem as brought out in Exercise 3.

5. The variable `Reply` does not have to be a global variable. Modify the code of `Grade-Exam` in such a way that `Reply` is no longer seen as a global variable. (*Hint:* Replace a sequence of statements by a procedure call and then code the procedure.)

Program Testing Hints

There are certain coding patterns you should recognize that use the words AND, OR, and NOT that "seem correct" at first glance, but that can cause difficulties. Avoid writing code that resembles these patterns. Likewise, we give you some classic ways to misuse arrays in processing. Some code is wrong because it is crash-prone; other code is wrong because it does not conform to accepted practice. You should likewise avoid writing code that mimics these examples.

AND/OR errors   The loop to process a sequence of events until one of the *N* exit events occurs is satisfied by the description

> *WHILE NOT (Exit1 OR Exit2 OR Exit3 OR ... OR ExitN) DO*
> *some process*

This kind of algorithm can be applied to a problem whose wording might be: Process pairs of integers read in until either (1) 10 pairs have been read in, (2) one of the integers is equal to the sentinel value, or (3) the first integer in a pair is greater than the second one. The appropriate WHILE statement, assuming values are properly read in just before the control expression is evaluated, codes to

```
{1}   WHILE NOT ( (Count= 10) OR (First = Sentinel) OR
                   (Second = Sentinel) OR (First > Second)) DO
         BEGIN  {do the processing} END;
```

This loop is duly exited when one of the four conditions becomes `true`. By all means, avoid coding either of these loops:

```
{2} WHILE (Count <>10) OR (First <> Sentinel) OR    {ERRONEOUS CODE!!}
          (Second <> Sentinel OR (First <= Second) DO
       BEGIN {the processing sequence} END;
```

```
{3} WHILE NOT (Count = 10) OR NOT (First = Sentinel) OR {ERRONEOUS CODE!}
          NOT (Second = Sentinel) OR NOT (First > Second) DO
       BEGIN {the processing sequence}     END;
```

Both loops "look correct." However, each one is bug-prone because something is literally lost in the translation from the English statement to the Pascal-coded statement. (What gets lost is the word "not." In English we have, "While Count is not equal to 10 or First or Second is not equal to Sentinel or First is not greater than Second, keep processing.")

Bad logical patterns

As a rule, we can say that the following "algorithm" will not work if processing is to continue until *one* exit condition is met.

WHILE NOT (Exit1) OR NOT (Exit2) .. OR .. OR NOT (ExitN) DO {BAD}
    some process

Indeed, this kind of pattern often characterizes an endless loop. If you apply DeMorgan's second theorem to the control expression, you find that the postloop assertion is, "All of the exit condition expressions that make up the control expression are true."

PROGRAM DESIGN RULE 7.4

Use DeMorgan's theorems in assertion testing.

DeMorgan's theorems and assertion testing

DeMorgan's theorems are very useful in assertion testing. For example, when the keyword WHILE is used, the control expression must be true for the loop to be entered. When you apply a DeMorgan theorem to the control expression of a WHILE loop, you likewise obtain an expression that must be true if the loop is ever to be exited.

You can, in fact, apply one of the DeMorgan theorems to either sequence {2} or sequence {3} that proves the endless loop condition. Applying a DeMogran theorem, you find that the value of the boolean expression (Count = 10) AND (First = Sentinel) AND (Second = Sentinel) AND (First > Second) must be true if either loop is to be exited. However, this expression can never be true, for the last three conditions are mutually exclusive. Hence, the control expressions are guaranteed to put the machine into an endless loop regardless of what event occurs as part of the loop's sequence.

Elements and access expressions

Do not confuse the values of access expressions with the values of the elements themselves. The statement to add 1 to the value of AnArray[Index] is coded as AnArray[Index] := AnArray[Index] + 1. A statement such as AnArray[Index] := AnArray[Index+1] sets the value of the element AnArray[Index] to the value of the element AnArray[Index+1]. The statement AnArray[Index] := AnArray[Index+1] + 1 sets the value of the element AnArray[Index] to the expression found by adding 1 to the value taken on by the element AnArray[Index+1].

Out-of-range values

Every VAX Pascal programmer has at one time or another seen the run-time error message: "Array index value out of range." Users of other dialects might instead see the machine return "garbage" when an access expression with a meaningless value is applied on an array. These bugs occur when a run-time attempt is made to access an element using an expression whose value lies outside the defined sub-range.

The error may be either logical or typographical. Before you determine that the error is logical, however, make sure it is not typographical. When you use an array of integers, it is very easy during an editing session to enter an access expression for an element's value or vice versa. Be on the lookout for this annoying mistake before you conclude you have coded a logical error.

If the error is logical, you may need to code a guard against some unusual event, recode an incorrect access expression or perhaps expand the array subrange. The nature of the bug determines how you should fix the error.

Memory allocation

Often you will not know exactly how many array elements are required to satisfy all run-time possibilities. If you have this kind of problem, try to define all structures so that sufficient memory is allocated. On the other hand, do not set up structures that are clearly too large for the problem. You could push the computer past its capabilities or thoroughly confuse another programmer if you define an array that is clearly too large for the problem.

To determine the "correct" number of elements, look carefully at the problem statement. If you find the problem requires an array to represent information about each student in a given class or to represent a doctor's appointment schedule for a typical day, clearly, an array with 10,000 elements is too large. Likewise, a 10-element or 20-element structure might be too small for either of these applications.

Define a structure with more than enough elements to prevent an index out-of-range error, but do not define a structure unrealistically large. Thus, if the classroom accommodates 50 students and a few more can be "squeezed in," you are probably safe setting up an array with 75 or so elements. If the doctor sees perhaps 25 patients on a busy day, a structure to represent 40 or 50 patients is more than adequate but not too excessive.

PROGRAM DESIGN RULE 7.5

When part of the loop body modifies a variable used in an array access expression, be sure to include code that guards against out-of-range access values.

Poorly constructed loops

Suppose you have coded a "large enough array" for some problem. The elements are initially assigned values from the input file. Regardless of the number of elements AnArray has, do not write code that satisfies the description

$$Count \leftarrow 0$$
$$read(Temp)$$
$$WHILE\ NOT\ Temp = Sentinel\ DO$$
$$\quad Count \leftarrow Count + 1$$
$$\quad AnArray\ [Count] \leftarrow Temp$$
$$\quad read(Temp)$$

You may be fortunate if your users never completely assign values to all the elements, but why tempt fate? You can easily avoid the disaster by coding NOT((Temp = Sentinel) OR (Count = MaxElements)) as the loop exit condition. Then if the array is filled to MaxElements, the user can be informed that no more values can be read in.

The sequence is bug-prone in the first place because the access expression is modified inside the loop body, but no guard against an out-of-range access event was provided. The suggested code provides that guard.

PROGRAM DESIGN RULE 7.6

Do not define two or more identical data types.

Type mismatches

Two named array types that have *identical* definitions are not assignment compatible. The following code wil cause a syntax error due to a type mismatch:

```
TYPE    {BAD CODE!!}
  ArrayAType = ARRAY[1..10]OF integer;
  ArrayBType = ARRAY[1..10]OF integer;
  VAR
    ArrayA: ArrayAType;
{*                                              *}
PROCEDURE DoSomething(VAR AnArray: ArrayBType);
  BEGIN    {statements}    END;
{*                                              *}
......
DoSomeThing(ArrayA);
```

Although it is reasonable to declare two or more variables of the same type, there is never a good reason to define two types in terms of an identical anonymous type.

PROGRAM DESIGN RULE 7.7

If the elements of an array are assigned values only over the subrange 1..UsedElements, pass in the index value UsedElements and code the block to guard against accessing any elements outside this subrange.

Passing element subranges

Whenever you are working with a partially filled array, be sure to pass in the index value of the last assigned element as a value call. Thus, if the procedure DoSomething should process the (assigned) elements of a variable Ints whose type is ARRAY[1..MaxElements] OF integer, call the procedure by coding DoSomething(Ints, UsedElements). Then you must code the block logic so that the unassigned elements of the subrange values UsedElements+1..MaxElements are never accessed. A statement accessing any one of these elements can be seen as a reference to an unassigned variable.

PROGRAM DESIGN RULE 7.8

Do not pass an entire array structure into a procedure when only one or two elements are actually changed or referenced in the statement.

Passing individual elements

Do not pass an entire structure into a procedure when it is not required. For example, the following code is misleading:

```
PROCEDURE Exchange  M,N: Indextype; VAR AnArray: ArrayType);  {BAD}
   VAR
    Temp: ElementType;     {either user or system defined}
   BEGIN
     Temp:= AnArray[M];
     AnArray[M]:= AnArray[N];
     AnArray[N]:= Temp
   END;
Exchange (M, N, AnArray)
```

Instead, you want to code

```
PROCEDURE Exchange(VAR ElementA, ElementB: ElementType);
   VAR
     Temp: ElementType;
   BEGIN
     Temp:= ElementA;
     ElementA:= ElementB;
     ElementB:= Temp
   END;
Exchange(AnArray[M], AnArray[N]);
```

The parameter list in the first call is confusing, because another programmer will think that the entire structure of AnArray is being processed by the action of Exchange. The second call, on the other hand, clearly shows that only two elements are required to carry out the actions of Exchange.

EXERCISES

Test Your Understanding

1. Let A, B, and C represent boolean expressions that are enclosed by parentheses. Write the expression for the loop exit condition if the control expression of a WHILE loop is as follows:

(a) A OR B OR C   (b) NOT(A OR B OR C)

(c) NOT A AND NOT B AND NOT C   (d) NOT (A AND B AND C)

2. Which of each of the control expressions of Exercise 1 will cause an exit: (1) when *only one* of the three component expressions is `true`? and (2) when *all* of the three expressions must be `true`?

3. True of false? A FOR loop used to access array elements whose limits are within range of assigned index values of the array elements will automatically guard against out-of-range access values.

Practice Your Analysis Skills

4. Following each problem statement is code that is poorly written for one reason or another. Indicate what is wrong with the solution:

(a) Problem statement: Process the values XInt and YInt only if both variables are positive, otherwise display the string UNABLE TO PROCESS.

```
IF  (XInt > 0)  OR  (YInt > 0)  THEN
   Process(XInt,YInt)  {procedure call}
ELSE
   writeln('UNABLE TO PROCESS');
```

(b) Problem statement: Write a fragment to keep reading in integer pairs, XPos and YPos, where the values are stored in two arrays, XPath and YPath. The access variable `Tries` also serves as a process counter. Processing is over if one of the following occurs: (1) a total of 10 pairs have been read and stored or (2) a value less then 0 has just been read in for XPos or (3) the most recent pair has values where XPos is greater than YPos.

```
read(XPos, YPos);
Tries:= 1
WHILE NOT( (XPos < 0) OR (XPos > YPos) OR (Tries = 10) ) DO
   BEGIN
      XPath[Tries]:= XPos;
      YPath[Tries]:= YPos;
      Tries:= Tries + 1;
      read(XPos, YPos)
   END;
readln;
```

(c) Problem statement: If the loop of part (b) is exited because 10 pairs have been read in, display the string "WE ARE OUT OF AMMO." If, instead, the loop is exited because XPos is greater than YPos, then display "THE TARGET HAS BEEN HIT." Otherwise display "WE ARE OUT OF RANGE."

```
IF Count = 10 THEN
   writeln('WE ARE OUT OF AMMO');
IF XPos > YPos THEN
   writeln('THE TARGET HAS BEEN HIT')
ELSE
   writeln('WE ARE OUT OF RANGE');
```

(d) Problem statement: Write a guard to prevent processing negative input values of XInt. Assume that the first positive value assigned to XInt must be processed.

```
                    read(XInt);
                    REPEAT
                       IF XInt <= 0 THEN
                          read(XInt)
                    UNTIL XInt >= 0;
                    readln;
                    Process(XInt);
```

(e) Problem statement: Keep reading values for XInt and YInt until they are both positive and not equal to each other. If one of the conditions is not met, display a prompt indicating the kind of input expected.

```
          readln(XInt,YInt);
          IF  (XInt = 0)  OR  (YInt = 0)  THEN
            BEGIN
               write ('Input two positive integers: ');
               readln(XInt,YInt)
            END;
          IF XInt = YInt THEN
            BEGIN
               write('Input two unequal integers: ');
               readln(XInt,YInt)
            END;
          Process(XInt,YInt);
```

(f) Problem statement: Process XInt and YInt only if XInt lies in the range −5 to +10, inclusive, and YInt is positive, otherwise simply do not do any processing.

```
    IF NOT ( (XInt >-5) OR (XInt <=10) OR (YInt > 0) ) THEN
        Process(XInt,YInt);
```

5. Write boolean expressions for the conditions under which
   (a) the action associated with the reserved word ELSE in Exercise 4(a) is carried out
   (b) the loops of Exercises 4(b) and 4(d) are exited
   (c) the statements with each reserved word IF of Exercises 4(c) and 4(e) are not carried out

Sharpen Your Implementation Skills

6. Write the correct code that solves the problem statement of each of the problems of Exercise 4.

REVIEW AND EXERCISES

The reserved word NOT forms the complement of an operand boolean expression. The reserved words AND and OR are used to form a boolean expression whose values depend upon the values of the component expressions. If all component expressions are true, a boolean expression formed using AND will be true; otherwise it will be false. If at least one component expression using the word OR is true, the overall expression is true. Any given boolean expression has an associated *truth table* that shows the expression's value for all possible values of the component expressions.

There are a number of standard algorithms you can apply that use the reserved words NOT, AND, and OR. You can write a loop that is exited if *one of N exit events* is true. Often, you will use this algorithm as part of a loop, then decide algorithm, where the decision after the loop is exited is determined by the particular exit event. You can likewise write a loop where *all N exit events* must be true. This algorithm is useful in achieving a program state that requires that more than one condition be true for further processing to be effective. Regardless of what algorithm you use with these reserved words, the two *DeMorgan theorems* are very useful in analyzing code.

You can use the reserved word IN to test whether an ordinal expression is a *member* of a *set*. The form of the boolean expression using the reserved word IN requires that an *ordinal expression* be on the left-hand side of the operator and that a *set-value expression* be on the right-hand side. The set-value expression contains an implied *membership list* of the test set.

A *structured variable* contains *component variables,* each of whose values can be *accessed*. When a component variable is accessed, it is treated as if it were a single variable separate from the structure. An *array* is a structured variable that contains *elements* all of the same type that can be accessed by *subrange expressions*. A *subrange type,* whose values can be *range checked* at run time, is an ordinal type with a defined lowest and highest value. A subrange type is required as part of the definition of a given array type. All array types, moreover, are programmer-defined.

The arrays we used in this chapter were all *one-dimensional,* that is, only one subrange expression was required to access the elements. All elements, moreover, were *scalar type* variables, for they could only take on one value at any given time.

When an array is called by variable, the formal parameter identifier represents an alias to access all the elements of the actual parameter array variable. If the actual parameter array is called by value, a completely different array variable is *locally copied* inside the data area of the procedure before the computer starts to execute the procedure's statement. This kind of operation is sometimes detrimental to either the *run-time efficiency* or *memory efficiency* of the program.

An element of an array, when associated with a variable parameter, is referenced as an alias inside the given procedure. When associated with a value parameter, however, its value is simply copied as (part of) an expression into the local formal parameter variable.

One array processing algorithm worth knowing is the algorithm to assign values to elements over an indeterminant subrange. When this algorithm is used, a variable to represent the *index value* of the last assigned element is required. If elements greater than this index value are accessed, the program is wrong and could lead to unpredictable results. The algorithm is very important because it guards against an attempt to assign a value to element whose index value is *out-of-range*. Another standard algorithm on arrays uses a FOR loop to process the elements over a predefined subrange (usually 1..Total-ElementsUsed).

When working with complicated boolean expressions, DeMorgan's theorems are invaluable for *assertion testing* your logic. Certain incorrect patterns are easily recognized and hence avoided. One common bug associated with an array is the *access expression out of range*. The causes of this bug are varied, but once found, it is essential that it be fixed.

You should avoid certain coding practices. Do not define two types that are identical in appearance. As always, pass parameters with care, both as entire structures and as individual elements. If you do so, the purpose of the abstraction is clear, and the follow-through when you actually code the procedure will be easier to complete.

EXERCISES

Short Answers

1. True or false? Parentheses are used to form boolean expressions with NOT, AND, and OR solely to increase the readability of one's source code.

2. True or false? The boolean expression Int IN [1..10] is logically equivalent to the boolean expression ((1 <= Int) AND (Int <= 10)).

3. Using DeMorgan's theorem, the equivalent expression to NOT ((AInt = BInt) AND (Count = 10)) using the reserved word OR is _____ .

4. How many simple boolean expressions must evaluate to true in order to exit a REPEAT..UNTIL loop controlled by the expression ((XRe > 0) AND (YRe > 0) AND (ZRe > 0))?

5. Arrays for which the same access expression implies the same semantics are known as _____ arrays.

6. The requirements to access an element's value in an array are an _____ _____ and an _____ _____ .

7. What is the difference between an array element's value and an access expression's value?

8. How many values is the following data type capable of storing?

        ARRAY[101..1000] OF integer;

9. Explain why it makes little sense to declare an array variable as an anonymous global variable.

10. Explain why it makes little sense to declare an integer variable whose purpose is to access the elements of some array as a global variable.

11. Under what circumstances will the compiler accept a reference to an array type variable on the left-hand side of the assignment operator.

12. Arrays are often passed into other blocks using a call-by-variable mechanism even when none of the elements are to be changed. Why?

13. What is the complementary expression to XInt >= 0?

14. Can the IN operator be used with a simple real expressions? Explain your answer.

15. Match the phrases in column A to the corresponding ones in column B:

Column A	Column B
AnArray	scalar variable
AnArray[5]	prevents index out-of-range crashes
guard algorithm	uses boolean expression with component expressions
loop, then decide algorithm	structured variable

16. True or false? If the subranges of elements to be processed is known, the reserved word FOR is used to process the elements.

17. Given the expression NOT((J+K > 5) OR (L = 7)), write down the order in which the operands NOT, +, >, OR, and = are applied.

18. True or false? A real type is a valid host type for a subrange type definition.

Easy Projects

19. The solution to Example Problem 7.1 assumed that the system used the ASCII collating sequence. The program, unfortunately, will not work if your system is EBCDIC. Write the solution to Example Problem 7.1 given that your system uses the EBCDIC collating sequence. (Refer to Appendix A for the EBCDIC collating sequence.)

20. Consider the procedure of Example Problem 7.2. You are to write a program that first reads values into an upper limit and a lower limit for a WidgetFactor. Then the values of 10 widgets are read in and stored. The program should display a table for each widget, showing the sample number, the widget factor and a string "Good" or "Bad" to indicate whether the widget factor falls into the proper range for a good widget or not. From the sample data for the example and with a quality range between 7.65 and 8.00, the table's display for the first five lines looks like

```
   #          Factor          Quality
   1           7.85            Good
   2           7.92            Good
   3           7.71            Good
   4           7.34            Bad
   5           8.01            Bad
```

21. Write a program to read in the values of 20 integers. The average is calculated and then displayed. Then the count of the number of integers above the average and the number of integers below the average is found and displayed. Finally, if one of the counts is at least twice as large as the other count, the string "UnBalanced" should be displayed.

22. Write a program that first reads in integers until a negative number is entered. The values read in are stored in an array. The average over the elements of the array should be found and displayed. Then you enter an integer value, and the computer will display how many elements are greater than this value.

Medium Projects

23. Write a program that finds and calculates the sum of a "noisy" input stream of integers. The stream is noisy because "noise" characters are interspersed between the characters that make up the integers in the stream. The stream ends when a question mark is entered. Two sample runs are

```
rtcb 78@@    th55  32  DCXz**93  21  CCCtvb?
The sum of the integers is 279.
```

The sum of the integers is 620.

24. A parlor game called "Fizz..Fuzz" has the following rules: The players gather in a circle and count off numbers, one per turn. If a number has a 5 in it or is divisible by 5, the player says "Fizz" rather than the number. If a number has a 7 in it or is divisible by 7, the player says "Fuzz." If the number is such that the conditions for both "Fizz" and "Fuzz" are met, the player says "Fizz..Fuzz."

Write a program where the computer plays "Fiz..Fuz" solitaire for the numbers between 1 and 100, displaying the values with 10 numbers per line. The lines of display will look like

```
  1     2     3     4    Fiz     6    Fuz     8     9    Fiz
 11    12    13    Fuz   Fiz    16    Fuz    18    19    Fiz
Fuz    22    23    24    Fiz    26    Fuz   Fuz    29    Fiz
 31    32    33    34    FizFuz  36    Fuz    38    39    Fiz
 41    Fuz   43    44    Fiz    36    Fuz    48    Fiz   Fuz
Fiz    Fiz   Fiz   Fiz   Fiz   FizFuz Fuz  Fuz   Fiz    Fiz   Fiz
 61    62    Fuz   64    Fiz    66    Fuz    68    69    FizFuz
Fuz    Fuz   Fuz   Fuz Fiz Fuz  Fuz          Fuz   Fuz   Fuz   Fiz
 81    82    83    Fuz   Fiz    86    87    88    89    Fiz
Fuz    92    93    94    Fiz    96    Fuz   Fuz    99    Fiz
```

25. The Nils Frills Hotel gives its customers room service 24 hours a day. It has only four "eatables" the customer can order, however, which are (1) crackers and soda for $3.00, (2) eggs for $5.00, (3) a sandwich for $6.00, and (4) pasta for $8.00. These are the normal amounts charged if the customer orders these eatables during "normal hours." If he or she orders an eatable during off hours, the charge is increased an additional dollar for the crackers or eggs and an additional two dollars for the sandwich or pasta. The hotel kitchen, being in business for 24 hours a day, uses a 24-hour clock, where the normal hours for ordering are

1. crackers at "night" between 0000 and 0559

2. eggs in the "morning" between 0600 and 1159

3. sandwiches in the "afternoon" between 1200 and 1759

4. pasta in the "evening" between 1800 and 2400

Write a program that carries out a customer's order and then bills him or her. The customer first enters the time of day as a four-digit integer. He or she is then greeted according to the time of day ("Good morning," etc.). Then, the customer enters a choice of 'C', 'E', 'S', or 'P'. Any other characters are not processed. The bill is displayed according to the billing rules. Typical runs:

```
Hour:   0500
Good evening, your order please? E
That will be $7.00 which includes a $1.00 service charge.

Hour:   1300
Good afternoon, your order please? S
That will be $6.00.
```

26. Write a program to "sing" five verses to the song "Old MacDonald had a farm." First, five animal names and their calls are read in. Then the five verses are displayed. Typically, we have

```
Animal 1's name: cow
Animal 1's call: moo
Animal 2's name: horse
Animal 2's call: neigh

. . . . . . . .


Old MacDonald had a farm! Eeyi, eeyi o!
And on this farm he had a cow. Eeyi, eeyi o!
With a moo, moo here, and a moo, moo there.
Here a moo, there a moo, everywhere a moo, moo.
Old MacDonald had a farm! Eeyi, eeyi, o!


Old MacDonald had a farm! Eeyi, eeyi, o!
And on this farm he had a horse . . . . .
{and so forth}
```

Difficult Projects

27. Many different songs exist that list up to 12 items. Typically, we have the song "Twelve Days of Christmas" or the song "Green Grow the Rushes Grow." Both songs sing a chorus and then count down from the chorus number to one, inserting different "items" as they count. For instance, the third verse of "The Twelve Days of Christmas" might look like

```
On the 3rd day of Christmas, my true love sent to me:       {chorus}
3 french hens, 2 turtle doves, and a partridge in a pear tree. {gifts}
```

Write a program whose main block sequence is described by

> *Initialize(Gifts, Totals)*   *{character strings, counters}*
> *FOR Day ← 1 To 12 DO*
> *SingChorus(Day)*   *{1st, 2nd, 3rd, 4th, 5th, etc.}*
> *SingGifts(Day, Gifts)*
> *AddGifts(Day, Totals)*
> *ShowTotals(Gifts, Totals)*

where the variable `Gifts` is an array of character strings representing the gifts for each day, `Totals` is an array of integers, where each element represents a running total of each gift received, and calls to `SingChorus` and `SingGifts` represent the displays shown by the comments chorus and gifts. `SingGifts` should be coded in such a way that three distinct gifts per line are displayed. Any "remaining" gifts are displayed on the last line. Thus, for the fifth day, we might have

```
On the 5th day of Christmas may true love sent to me:
5 gold rings, 4 calling birds, 3 french hens,
2 turtle doves, and a partridge in a pear tree.
```

where the first line results from a call to SingChorus, and the other two lines are the effect of the call to SingGifts. The call to ShowTotals represents the display of a final verse whose text looks like

```
On all 12 days of Christmas, my true love sent to me:
12 lords a-leaping, 22 fifers fifing, 30 drummers drumming,
36 ladies dancing, 40 maids a-milking, 42 swans a-swimming,
42 geese a-laying, 40 golden rings, 36 calling birds,
30 french hens, 22 turtle doves and 12 partridges in a pear tree.
```

27. The restaurant Veggies Unlimited always has but five dishes on its menu each night. It also has tables that can seat up to six in a party, a fact of which the loyal clientelle of the restaurant are well aware. You are to write a program that simulates the taking of an order at a given table in Veggies Unlimited.

The main block of the program is described as follows:

> *GetMenu(Dishes, Costs)*
> *GetPartySize(Size)*
> *TakeOrders(Orders, Size)*
> *DisplayBill(Orders, Costs, Size)*

The action of GetMenu assigns values to the elements Dishes and Costs. Dishes is an array of strings, describing the dishes' names, and Costs is an array of reals, storing the cost of one of the dishes. GetPartySize returns a value between 1 and 6 (if more than 6, the party size is requested again), representing the customers at a given table. TakeOrders reads in the elements of the array Orders, representing the table's orders. The elements of Orders must take on values from 1 to 5, corresponding to a given dish. DisplayBill then indicates the number of each dish, and the bill total for the party. A typical run is as follows:

```
Enter tonight's menu:
  1:  8.50 Veggies Tempura
  2:  5.75 Meaty Okra
  3:  7.50 Beans Galore
  4:  9.00 Three C's Casserole
  5:  6.50 Steamer Streamers

How many in your party? 3

Your order:  3
Your order:  7
Please order again (1 − 5)
Your order:  2
Your order:  3

Bill
1 Meaty Okra            5.75
2 Beans Galore         15.00
---------------------------
Total                  20.75
```

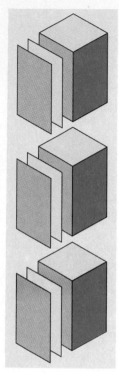

FUNCTIONS, BOOLEAN VARIABLES, AND ENUMERATED TYPES

OBJECTIVES

After reading and studying the material of the present chapter, you should be able to

- Analyze programs that contain programmer-declared functions

- Write the code for a function given the purpose it should fulfill

- Use a call to a function in the correct context

- Plan and code a program that requires the use of functions

- Determine whether a function call or a procedure call is the more appropriate abstraction for a given problem

- Plan and code algorithms where a boolean variable(s) is appropriate

- Plan and code algorithms where an enumerated type(s) is appropriate

- Plan and code functions that return a boolean value

- Plan and code functions that return the value of an enumerated type

WHEN A FUNCTION IS CALLED, it returns a value to be immediately used as part of an expression. In Pascal, you can use the standard functions and also declare and use your own functions. The first step in using your own functions is to abstract a function call. Then, as with procedures, you code the block of the function whose call you have abstracted.

The new variable types you will study in this chapter, the standard `boolean` type and the programmer-defined enumerated type, will make your coding tasks simpler. You should make sure, however, that you use them appropriately, otherwise your code will appear more obscure rather than simpler. Part of the material of this chapter includes a study of what determines "appropriateness" for the use of these types.

8.1 Programmer-Declared Functions

If you need to form a complicated expression, you may want to simplify the appearance of the expression by using a call to a function. The function will have a parameter list of *arguments* that are used to return a value to the function. The function is then used to form the desired expression. In this section, you will learn the syntax rules for declaring your own functions. You will also see a number of examples where we use functions to simplify the coding task.

Argument: an actual parameter of a function call.

A brief review of standard functions

Let us recall some examples from Chapter 3 where we used standard Pascal functions. The following two statements respectively come from the programs `FindHypotenuse` and `RewriteSong`:

```
Hypotenuse:= sqrt( (sqr(Side1) + sqr(Side2) );
Ch12:= succ(Ch11);
```

The first statement contains calls to the standard functions `sqr` and `sqrt`, and the second statement uses a call to the standard function `succ`. Recall that every Pascal dialect has a set of standard functions. Each function is called by an identifier reference and always has a single parameter as its argument. Moreover, the value returned by the call is immediately used in an expression.

Programmer-declared functions

You can declare a function of your own where a call to it returns a single value used in an expression. Like a standard function, one of these functions returns a single value when a reference is made to its identifier. Unlike the functions of standard Pascal, the functions you declare can have as many arguments as you require to get the job done.

Declaration syntax

Figure 8.1 is the syntax diagram for a function declaration. The first identifier represents the function's name, the formal parameter list holds the values

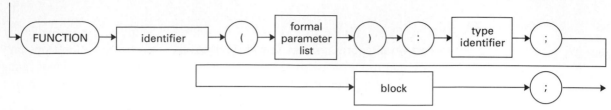

FIGURE 8.1 Syntax for a function declaration.

of the arguments, and the second identifier indicates the type of value returned. The purpose of the block's definitions, declarations, and statements is to assign a value to the function. Any additional code in this block is usually improper and/or superfluous.

Calling syntax   The syntax diagram for a call to a programmer-declared function is shown in Figure 8.2. It should return a value that is immediately used in some expression. Moreover, the actual parameters, representing arguments, are nearly always *expressions* that are called by value.

function call

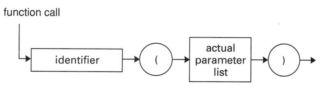

FIGURE 8.2 Syntax for a function call.

An example   The code of Example 8.1 shows a function declaration along with an associated function call. Note the one-to-one correspondence between the arguments and the formal parameter list. The correspondence that applies to the parameter lists of procedure calls also applies to the parameter lists of function calls.

Example 8.1

```
FUNCTION RingArea(OuterRadius, InnerRadius: real): real;
  {the function returns the area of a ring that has a known
  OuterRadius and a known InnerRadius.  Pi is a defined constant.}
  BEGIN
    RingArea:= Pi * sqr(OuterRadius) - Pi * sqr(InnerRadius)
  END;

{using the function RingArea to assign a value to Area:}
write('Enter outer and inner radii:   ');
readln(OuterRadius, InnerRadius);
Area:= RingArea(OuterRadius, InnerRadius);
writeln('The area of the ring is ',Area:4:2);

{typical run:}
Enter outer and inner radii:   6.18   3.75
The area of the ring is 75.81
```

PROGRAM DESIGN RULE 8.1

Write a function such that the last statement executed assigns a value to the function.

The assignment rule

No function is complete without a statement whose description is *identifier ← expression*. The *identifier* references the function's name, and the *expression* represents the value assigned to the function. This statement should virtually always be the last one executed in the statement part of a function declaration.

It is possible to write code where more than one value is assigned to the function over the scope of the block statement. The final value assigned is then the one passed out to the function call. It is our feeling, however, that you will code more readable functions if you follow Program Design Rule 8.1 faithfully.

Another example

We could have coded the function shown in Example 8.2 as part of the solution to Example Problem 5.4. Once values are read into `Figure`, `Dim1`, and `Dim2`, the function can be called as a parameter of `writeln` in the statement `writeln ('The area is ',AreaOfFigure(Figure, Dim1, Dim2): 4: 2);`. Note that the code of Example 8.2 consists of three assignment statements to the function. This code does not violate Program Design Rule 8.1, however, because only *one* assignment is carried out with any given function call.

Example 8.2

```
FUNCTION AreaOfFigure(Figure: char; Dim1, Dim2: real): real;
  {The area of either a triangle ('T'), rectangle ('R'), or an ellipse
  ('E') is returned, given that the values of the two dimensions
  respectively represent a base and height, a length and width, or a
  major and a minor axis. Pi is defined as a global constant.}
  BEGIN
    CASE Figure OF
      'R': AreaOfFigure:= Dim1 * Dim2;
      'T': AreaOfFigure:= (Dim1 * Dim2)/2;
      'E': AreaOfFigure:= Pi * Dim1 * Dim2
    END    {CASE}
  END;   {FUNCTION}
```

Developing Some Functions

In the next series of examples, we develop the code for some functions from an initial problem statement. Note how in each case, we faithfully adhere to Program Design Rule 8.1.

Example Problem 8.1

The problem statement   The formula for the number of combinations of N items taken M at a time is given by the algebraic equation

$$\text{Combinations} = \frac{N!}{(N - M)! \, M!}$$

The symbol "!" represents the factorial function. Let us write the code for the function Combinations that uses a call to the coded function Factorial as part of its solution.

The solution   The straightforward solution to the problem is given as the coded function Combinations. Note that we have used the DIV operation because the value returned must be of type integer. We need to develop the code for the function Factorial.

```
{*                                                                    *}
FUNCTION Factorial (N: integer): integer;
  {Returns the value of N! when N is positive. The function returns
  the value 1 for any nonpositive value of N.}
  BEGIN   END;
{+                                                                    +}
FUNCTION Combinations (N, M: integer): integer
  {returns the number of combinations of N things taken M at a time}
  BEGIN
    Combinations:= Factorial (N) DIV ( Factorial (N - M) * Factorial (M) )
  END;
{*                                                                    *}
```

The function Factorial   The code for the function Factorial is given below. This function requires a product accumulation algorithm to get a value for the call Factorial (N). Note how we have used a local variable Product for the accumulation process and that the assignment labeled as {1} is the statement that returns a value to Factorial (N).

```
    FUNCTION Factorial (N: integer): integer;
      {documentation}
      VAR
        Count,      {counter for the number of products accumulated}
        Product:    {the value of Count!}
                    integer;
      BEGIN
        Product:=  1;
        FOR Count:= 1 TO N DO
          Product:= Product * Count;
  {1}     Factorial:= Product
      END;
```

It might at first seem reasonable to violate Program Design Rule 8.1 and write the statement part of `Factorial` using the source code sequence:

```
        Factorial:= 1;      {WRONG!}
        FOR Count:= 1 TO N DO
{2}        Factorial:= Factorial*Count
```

Unfortunately, this sequence for `Factorial` does not compile because statement {2} uses the function identifier in an expression. This usage represents another call to the function. In order for the expression of statement {2} to be valid, the reference to `Factorial` on the right-hand side of the operator requires an argument.

We dispensed with this apparent coding difficulty when we used the local variable `Product`. The final value accumulated in this variable formed the expression to assign a value to `Factorial`. The variable `Product` was used thus as a *dummy variable*. ◆

Dummy variable: a local variable of a function whose final value will be the expression that returns a value to the function.

PROGRAM DESIGN RULE 8.2

Use a dummy variable to store the value of a candidate result of a function.

You will often use a loop to code a function. One of the variables in the loop body will hold the results of each loop pass through the final pass. The value taken on by this variable at loop exit represents the function's value. If you are writing a function whose algorithm requires that candidate values for the function are found in a sequence of events, it is better that you use a dummy variable to hold the candidate values found. Then when the sequence is finished, the function is assigned the value taken on by the candidate variable.

We solve the problem that follows using a dummy variable to accumulate a product. Once the product is accumulated, we use the value of the dummy variable to return a value to the function.

Example Problem 8.2

Write a function Power that returns the `integer` power of a `real` number. Three calls to the function and the resultant values returned are given as follows:

$$\text{Power}(2.00, \ 4) \leftarrow 16.0$$
$$\text{Power}(2.50, \ 2) \leftarrow 6.25$$
$$\text{Power} \ (2.00, \ -3) \leftarrow 0.125$$

The first argument represents the real number, and the second argument represents the integer power. Note that negative exponents are allowed.

Drafting the solution   We will name the first argument of the formal parameter list XRe and the second argument Exponent. We can easily code the function for positive exponents using a product accumulation algorithm. If we accumulate the product using abs(Exponent) as the exit value for the accumulating FOR loop, we can deal with negative powers in the following way:

> accumulate XRe to the power abs(Exponent) in the variable Product
> IF Exponent >= 0 THEN
>   Power ← Product
> ELSE
>   Power ← 1/Product

Source code   The product accumulation is easily coded, so we readily obtain the source code for the function Power as given.

```
FUNCTION Power(XRe: real; Exponent: integer): real;
   {returns the value of XRe raised to the power of Exponent}
   VAR
      Count:  integer;   {counts the times Product was multiplied by XRe}
      Product:  real;    {the value of XRe raised to the power of Count}
   BEGIN
      Product:= 1;
      FOR Count:= 1 TO abs(Exponent) DO
         Product:= Product * XRe;
      IF Exponent >= 0 THEN
         Power:= Product
      ELSE
         Power:= 1 / Product
   END;  ◆
```

Nonnumeric functions   Lest you get the idea that functions return only numeric results, we give you Example 8.3, a function that returns the uppercase value if the argument passed in is a lowercase letter. Note how the logic ensures that any other char value is passed out unchanged. It is very important that every function you code *always* return some value even if the value is an unchanged argument.

Example 8.3

```
FUNCTION UpperCase(Ch: char): char;
   {returns an uppercase letter given that Ch is a lowercase letter}
   BEGIN
      IF Ch IN ['a'..'z'] THEN
         UpperCase:=  chr( ord(Ch) + ord('A') - ord('a') )
      ELSE
         UpperCase:= Ch
   END;
```

Random Number Generation

There are many coding problems we can pose that require the simulation of *random events*. In order to write a program to simulate random events, you will need a function called a *pseudorandom-number generator* (RNG). Many dialects have a built-in RNG function that you can read about in your user's manual. You can, instead, use the function whose code we will give you to return random `integer` values over a specified subrange in any dialect. We will use this function to simulate a random process for the case study of Section 8.4.

> **Random event:** an event where a sample of many outcomes of the event is predictable but where the outcome of any one event cannot be predicted.
>
> **Pseudorandom-Number Generator:** a function that returns an apparently random number, dependent upon the value of an input `Seed` number.

*The coded
function*

The RNG is given as the coded function `RandomNumber`.

```
FUNCTION RandomNumber(Seed: integer): integer;
  {returns a random number in the subrange 0..Modulus-1}
  CONST
    Modulus = 2187;
    Multiplier = 10;
    Increment = 10891;
  BEGIN
    RandomNumber:= (Multiplier*Seed + Increment) MOD Modulus
  END;
```

You may wonder where these strange constants come from. Number theory shows that the following sequence of code will return the 2187 different possible values to Seed before the numbers start to repeat themselves:

```
                    readln(Seed);
                    Seed:= abs(Seed MOD Modulus);
                    FOR Count:= 1 TO Modulus DO
                        Seed:= RandomNumber(Seed);
```

*The property of
"randomness"*

This function is not completely random. As Exercise 19 at the end of the chapter shows, the numbers generated alternate between oddness and evenness for all 2187 calls. This property, completely predictable, certainly does not characterize randomness! The magnitudes of the values returned for all 2187 calls, however, are distributed in a random fashion over the subrange interval *0..2186*.

*Using the
function*

This function is extremely useful in the simulation of a random process such as rolling a single die. We will use the RNG we have just coded to solve this problem in our next example.

Example Problem 8.3

The problem statement

Write a procedure GetOneRoll that uses the RNG to simulate the roll of a single die. The procedure is called by GetOneRoll(Seed, Roll) where the parameter Seed is input/output and the parameter Roll is output. The two parameters respectively represent the changed value of Seed due to the use of the RNG and the simulated roll of a single die.

Breaking up the subrange interval

The RNG is supposed to return numbers randomly in the subrange $0..2186$. We can use this fact to divide the subrange up into six even intervals. A given value lying within a specified interval will represent a particular roll of a single die. The suggested assignment intervals are shown in Table 8.1. We are using these numbers because the value of the expression 2187 DIV 6 is 364. In this way, the numbers in the subrange $0..2183$ are broken up into six evenly divided intervals. (see Figure 8.3)

TABLE 8-1   Assignment Intervals Using The Function Random Number

Interval	Roll
0– 363	1
364– 727	2
728–1091	3
1092–1455	4
1456–1819	5
1820–2183	6

Roll		1		2		3		4		5		6	
Seed	0	—	363	—	727	—	1091	—	1455	—	1819	—	2183

FIGURE 8.3   Assignments to VAR Roll using value of Seed

Coding the solution

Once the values returned from the RNG have been broken up into six evenly divided intervals, the code to return a value to Roll is straightforward. We can apply the DIV operator to a value in the subrange $0..2183$ as returned by a call to RandomNumber to get the following pseudocode description:

> *get Seed value less than 2184*
> *Roll ← Seed DIV 364 + 1*

We obtain a Seed value less than 2184 using an event-seeking algorithm. The coded solution to the procedure GetOneRoll is then given as follows:

```
PROCEDURE GetOneRoll(VAR Seed, Roll: integer);
   {i/o: Seed -- value used/returned by RNG function
    out: Roll -- value of roll returned to single die}
   CONST
```

```
        HighestPermissibleRandomNumber = 2183;
        RollInterval = 364;
     BEGIN
       REPEAT
          Seed:= RandomNumber (Seed);
       UNTIL Seed <= HighestPermissibleRandomNumber;
       Roll:= Seed DIV RollInterval + 1
     END;
```

On-line testing   This particular procedure is best tested with a large number of rolls starting with different seed values. Although perhaps 1000 trials would indicate a fairer test, we applied the following driver to simulate 120 rolls. Two sample runs, with the distribution of values returned, follow directly after the code for the driver:

```
        write('Input a seed value: ');
        readln(Seed);
        Seed:= abs(Seed) MOD 2187;  {gets valid subrange}
        FOR TrialNo:= 1 TO 120 DO
          BEGIN
            GetOneRoll(Seed, Roll);
            write(Roll:2);
            IF TrialNo MOD 20 = 0 THEN
              writeln
          END;
```

```
Input a seed value:   101
 3  3  6  3  4  4  4  2  6  4  2  6  5  4  4  6  3  1  1  4    {1s -- 20}
 1  3  6  5  6  4  1  1  5  3  5  5  5  4  2  2  6  5  5  5    {2s -- 19}
 5  2  5  3  5  2  6  2  1  1  6  2  6  4  5  4  2  5  5  1    {3s -- 19}
 6  5  5  4  3  4  5  6  3  1  6  2  6  5  2  1  2  1  4  3    {4s -- 17}
 1  3  2  2  5  6  2  2  2  3  2  2  3  5  6  4  3  3  6  4    {5s -- 25}
 4  1  1  3  3  6  6  5  1  1  1  5  1  3  5  5  6  1  1  3    {6s -- 20}

Input a seed value:   1585
 2  2  4  1  2  4  4  1  2  5  1  1  4  1  2  2  2  6  4  2    {1s -- 19}
 6  4  3  2  2  4  1  5  5  2  5  1  5  4  3  4  2  5  5  3    {2s -- 21}
 1  3  3  3  2  6  6  4  3  3  3  3  6  3  1  3  6  4  6  5    {3s -- 22}
 5  4  6  4  2  3  2  6  3  3  5  4  3  3  2  1  2  3  4  1    {4s -- 22}
 5  4  6  4  3  6  5  6  5  2  1  5  1  6  6  3  4  6  6  6    {5s -- 17}
 1  6  6  1  3  4  2  1  1  4  2  2  5  5  1  1  4  4  3  5    {6s -- 19}
```

The results returned by the two calls to the driver are as expected. The number of different rolls for each of the 120 trials is close to 20. Moreover, there are no out-of-range results such as having a value less than 1 or a value greater than 6 returned for any given trial.

The ultimate test   The procedure's validity rests on the validity of the RNG. The RNG itself is best tested with a driver to see that the numbers do distribute themselves randomly for a large (but not exhaustive) number of trials. Likewise, the other 2186 numbers should be generated before the initial value of Seed is returned. You will learn the necessary skills for on-line testing of this kind when you study the material in Section 10.1.

EXERCISES

Test Your Understanding

1. What is the last statement that should be executed in a function's block?

2. What is a dummy variable and how is it used?

Practice Your Analysis Skills

3. Suppose Ints is an array of type IntsArray, consisting of 10 integers. You want to code the function IntsSum to return the sum over all the elements. Indicate what is wrong with the following code:

```
FUNCTION IntsSum(Ints: IntsArray): integer;
  VAR
    Index: integer;
  BEGIN
    IntsSum:= 0;
    FOR Index:= 1 TO 10 DO
      IntsSum:= IntsSum + Ints[Index]
  END;
```

Sharpen Your Implementation Skills

4. Write code for the following functions:
   (a) SphereVolume to return the volume of a sphere, given its radius.
   (b) Lower to return the value of the lower of two integers.
   (c) LowerCase to return a lowercase letter, if the value passed into the block is a char representing an uppercase letter.
   (d) RectVolume to return the volume of a rectangular solid, given its length, width and height.

5. Write the code for the function IntSum that will make it a valid function.

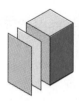

8.2 Boolean Variables and Boolean Functions

You have been using boolean expressions since Chapter 5. Even though the Pascal language allows boolean variables, you have not yet had to use them. In this section, we show some effective uses of these variables. We also show a number of examples where your logic can be clarified by a call to a boolean function.

Boolean Variables Syntax and Semantics

To start off this section's discussion, we first declare some boolean variables then use them in fragments of source code. Our purpose in this initial discussion is simply to show how boolean variables can be used in Pascal source code. We will cover their effective usage in the next subsection.

Boolean variable declarations

A *boolean variable* belongs to a standard Pascal type that can take on the values of `true` or `false`. These standard variable types are declared the usual way, that is, typically by

```
VAR
      Sample, BadCount: integer;
      TooLow, TooHigh, BadValue, BadBatch: boolean;
```

We have included two `integer` variables `Sample` and `BadCount` in the sample declaration because we will refer to them in the examples that follow.

Assignment statements

A value can be assigned to a `boolean` variable using the assignment operator. The expression on the right-hand side must be of type `boolean`. For example, we can initialize the boolean variable `BadBatch` to `false` using the statement

$\{1\}$ `BadBatch:= false;`

Then, let us say a value for `Sample` is obtained. Next we can set a value to the `boolean` variables `TooLow` and `TooHigh` with the respective statements:

$\{2\}$ `TooLow:= Sample < 5;`
$\{3\}$ `TooHigh:= Sample > 15;`

The variable `TooLow` takes on the value `true` if `Sample` is less than 5. Otherwise it takes on the value `false`. The variable `TooHigh` is likewise assigned the value `true` if `Sample`'s value is greater than 15. Otherwise it is assigned the value `false`.

Using boolean variables

The value taken on by a `boolean` variable can be used in a context where a `boolean` expression is required. We might, for example, use the values of `TooLow` or `TooHigh` in either of the two statements

```
   (* get value for Sample, then insert statements {2} and {3} *)
{4}   IF TooHigh OR TooLow THEN
         BadCount:= BadCount + 1;
```

```
   (* get value for Sample, then insert statements {2} and {3} *)
{5}   WHILE TooLow OR TooHigh DO
         BEGIN
           (* get value for Sample, then insert statements {2} and {3}; *)
         END;
```

In statement $\{4\}$, the counter variable `BadCount` is incremented by 1 if either variable `TooHigh` or `TooLow` is `true`. In statement $\{5\}$, the loop is not exited until the condition *NOT TooLow AND NOT TooHigh* is attained.

Another assignment statement

The value(s) taken on by a `boolean` variable(s) can be used to assign a value to another `boolean` variable. For example, we can assign a new value to the variable `BadBatch` using the statement

$\{6\}$ BadBatch:= TooLow OR TooHigh;

In this statement BadBatch is set to true if either the value of TooLow or the value of TooHigh is presently true. Otherwise it takes on the value of false.

Flag variables   A boolean variable is generally used in a program as a *flag variable*. In statements $\{2\}$, $\{3\}$ and $\{6\}$, the variables TooLow and TooHigh recorded events. In statements $\{4\}$ and $\{5\}$, the variables were used to control a statement. Statement $\{1\}$ set a flag variable in the context that the sequence of events to follow will represent a batch that is assumed "good." If, in the course of processing, the batch is found to be bad, the variable BadBatch is set to true as in statement $\{6\}$.

> **Flag variable:** A boolean variable used to record an event, then to control one or more loop or decision statements.

The Effective Use of Boolean Variables

When used effectively, boolean variables can simplify certain coding tasks. When used ineffectively (see Section 8.5), they can clutter up source code unnecessarily. The examples which follow show some of the ways you can use flag variables in an effective manner.

A flag input parameter   You can pass a boolean expression into a procedure to set up a control path. Suppose, for example, you want the procedure SortTwo to return the postcondition *Int1* $<=$ *Int2*. You can achieve the desired postcondition with the procedure call SortTwo(Int1, Int2, (Int1 > Int2)). The last expression is a boolean input parameter. The code for the procedure, using a boolean variable as an input parameter, is given below.

```
PROCEDURE SortTwo(VAR Int1, Int2: integer; MakeExchange: boolean);
   {exchanges the values of Int1 and Int2 if MakeExchange is true.}
   BEGIN
     IF MakeExchange THEN
        ExchangeInts(Int1, Int2)
   END;
```

Note that the call SortTwo(Int1, Int2, (Int1 < Int2)) will carry out an exchange that attains the complementary postcondition.

Using flags effectively   A flag variable is assigned a value that represents something about the program state. Once it is set, its value is used in another part of the program to control the flow of logic. It thus appears to serve a dual purpose, rather than just one purpose. This dual usage seems to violate a fundamental principal of good programming.

A boolean variable's value, however, should depend upon the occurrence (or absence) of only *one* specified event that makes up the overall program state. The value of the boolean variable should therefore have only one meaning over the scope of the block where it is declared. As the block's statements are executed, the event's occurrence or absence is recorded in the flag variable. At some further point in the execution of the block's statements, the flag's value is used to control the execution of a loop or decision statement.

Flag-controlled loops

You can use a `boolean` variable to control a loop entry or exit condition. When the loop is exited, the flag's value is examined. The flag variable, then, is used in two control expressions. However, the value it takes on still represents the occurrence of just one specified event. This special form of the *loop, then decide* algorithm is described by the pseudocode of Algorithm 8.1.

Algorithm 8.1

> *{Loop, then decide, using a Flag variable:}*
> *Flag ← false*
> *WHILE NOT Flag AND NOT (other exit condition) DO*
>   *processing that, among other actions, might set the flag*
> *IF Flag THEN*
>   *execute further processing*
> *{end algorithm}*

The postloop assertion we can make is, "Either the value of *Flag* is *true* or the other exit condition is *true*." After the decision is executed, we can in addition assert, "*Further processing*" was carried out, given that the loop was exited because *Flag* was *true*. The loop invariant depends upon the particular problem that is being solved.

In the following example, we use a flag variable (1) to flag an error condition and (2) to assign a value to another variable dependent upon the presence or absence of the error condition.

Example Problem 8.4

The problem statement

Now Professor Teachem wants you to write a procedure that returns the average on an exam given to N students. She does not trust her assistant's typing abilities, so she would like the procedure to return an absurd value (0, for example) if her assistant enters an invalid test score. A valid average is returned if all scores are valid.

The professor gives all her students 5 points credit on the exam for spelling their name correctly. The maximum grade she will give on any exam is 100. If the following data is entered for 10 students, the procedure will return a value to Average of 74.2:

| 85 | 72 | 63 | 44 | 78 | 92 | 91 | 72 | 57 | 88 |

The next set of data for 10 students has an invalid entry for the eighth student, so the value returned to Average is 0:

| 85 | 72 | 63 | 44 | 78 | 92 | 91 | 2 | 57 | 88 |

Drafting the solution

Clearly, the loop body should sum valid test scores. If a test score is invalid, there is no reason to continue the sum. We can use a flag variable to draft the pseudocode for loop control as follows:

$$Sum \leftarrow 0$$
$$Count \leftarrow 0$$
$$InvalidScore \leftarrow false$$

WHILE NOT InvalidScore AND NOT (Count = N) DO
　read (Score)
　IF (Score < 5) OR (Score > 100) THEN
　　InvalidScore ← true
　ELSE
　　Sum ← Sum + Score
　　Count ← Count + 1

The loop invariant for this description is, "If InvalidScore is true, the last value read in was not a valid score." Note that this condition leads to a loop exit. The other part of the invariant is, "If InvalidScore is false, the value of Sum represents the sum of the Count valid scores read in.

The pseudocode for the decision statement at loop exit is then described by

IF InvalidScore THEN
　Average ← 0
ELSE
　Average ← Sum/Count

After this statement is executed, we can assert that given an invalid score, the value returned to Average is 0, otherwise the value returned is the average of the Count valid scores read in.

Source code

The coded solution to the problem is given as the procedure GetClassAverage.

```
PROCEDURE GetClassAverage(N: integer; VAR Average: real);
   {If the N integers read in are all in range, Average is returned as
   the average of the integers. If one of the integers read in is
   out-of-range, Average is returned as 0.}
   VAR
      Score,            {the last score read in}
      Count,            {the number of valid scores read in}
      Sum:              {the sum of the valid scores read in}
                        integer;
      InvalidScore:     {true if last score read in is invalid}
                        boolean;
   BEGIN
      Sum:= 0;
      Count:= 0;
      InvalidScore:= false;
      WHILE NOT InvalidScore AND NOT (Count = N) DO
         BEGIN
```

```
          read(Score);
          IF (Score < 5) OR (Score > 100) THEN
            InvalidScore:= true
          ELSE
            BEGIN
              Sum:= Sum + Score;
              Count:= Count + 1
            END
      END;
    readln;
    IF InvalidScore THEN
      Average:= 0
    ELSE
      Average:= Sum/N
  END;  ◆
```

Boolean Functions

You can use `boolean` functions in expressions quite effectively to hide some complicated control expressions. In the following pages you will see a number of examples where we use this technique.

One-statement boolean functions
Given a meaningful name, the use of a one-statement `boolean` function can hide a very complicated control expression. The decision statement in Example 8.4 is controlled by the value returned to the `boolean` function `InOrder`. Likewise, the WHILE loop in Example 8.5 is controlled by the value returned with the call to the `boolean` function `BadTriangle`. In both examples, some complicated expressions are effectively hidden in the statement part of a `boolean` function.

Example 8.4

```
    FUNCTION InOrder(X1, X2, X3: real): boolean;
      {returns true if X1 <= X2 <= X3}
      BEGIN
        InOrder:= (X1 <= X2) AND (X2 <= X3)
      END;

    {usage: }
    IF NOT InOrder(X1, X2, X3) THEN     {true when X1 <= X2 <= X3}
      OrderThem(X1, X2, X3);
```

Example 8.5

```
  FUNCTION BadTriangle(Side1, Side2, Side3: real): boolean;
    {returns true if the value of one of the three parameters is greater
    than the sum of other two}
    BEGIN
      BadTriangle:= (Side1 > Side2 + Side3) OR (Side2 > Side1 + Side3)
                    OR (Side3 > Side1 + Side2)
    END;
```

```
{usage: }
readln(Side1, Side2, Side3);
WHILE BadTriangle(Side1, Side2, Side3) DO
  readln(Side1, Side2, Side3);
```

Arrays as parameters of function calls

A function should return a single value that is immediately used in an expression. The implication, given this premise, is that the arguments of the function should all be value calls. If, however, a large reference array is passed into the block, it is better, for the sake of efficient code, to call the structure by variable. In the following example problem, we will use this technique.

Example Problem 8.5

The problem statement

Samantha Smart and Josephine Joker are the two best students in CS1. They work together on their projects and always receive "A" grades. Josephine, however, is a bit of a practical joker. To keep Samantha on her toes, she sometimes gives Samantha bad values for data, claiming they are good.

The latest project requires the use of an array of integers with about 500 elements, sorted in order from lowest to highest. When an array is sorted in this order, the following condition must hold true for each *Index* value: *AnArray[Index-1]* <= *AnArray[Index]* <= *AnArray[Index+1]*. It is assumed that all access expressions are in range given this condition.

Samantha suspects the Josephine is up to her tricks again with the values of Ints, an array with TotalElements assigned to the integer elements of type IntsArray. Although the elements are supposed to be sorted, Samantha wants to be sure. She plans to write the boolean function SortedArray, which is called in the context of

> IF *SortedArray(Ints, TotalElements)* THEN
> do the rest of the project

Let us write the code for this function along with her.

The initial draft

We can use a flag-controlled loop, where the flag's value at loop exit is used to assign a value to the function. In terms of the loop body and postprocess, we have

> *StillSorted ← true*
> *WHILE more comparisons required AND StillSorted DO*
> *   make another comparison that attempts to set StillSorted to false*
> *SortedArray ← StillSorted*

The comparison statement

We want the computer to compare the values of all adjacent elements. The loop invariant is set up where the value assigned to the access variable Index should represent the last element compared. StillSorted should likewise be true if all elements compared, including the last one, satisfy the condition for a sorted array. Finally, we want the computer to set up the next comparison if the last one indicates the array is "still sorted."

Given these considerations, we find that the decision statement inside the loop is coded as

```
IF Ints[Index] > Ints[Index+1] THEN
    StillSorted:= false
ELSE
    Index:= Index + 1
```

Entry/exit conditions

The first comparison made must be between elements 1 and 2. Hence, the loop is entered when Index equals 1. The decision statement shows us that the last comparison is between TotalElements-1 and TotalElements given that StillSorted was not set to false. If these two elements are in order, Index will take on the value of TotalElements. Hence, the exit condition, the complementary condition to the loop entry condition, is given by the expression Index = TotalElements. The expression described by *more comparison required* therefore codes to Index <> TotalElements.

Source code

When we put everything together, we obtain the source code for the boolean function SortedArray as shown.

```
FUNCTION SortedArray(VAR Ints: IntsArray;
                     TotalElements: integer): boolean;
  {returns true if the elements of Ints from 1..TotalElements are
  sorted in order from lowest to highest}
  VAR
    Index:            {index value of present element being compared}
                      integer;
    StillSorted:      {true if elements in 1..Index are sorted}
                      boolean;
  BEGIN
    Index:= 1;
    StillSorted:= true;
    WHILE (Index <> TotalElements) AND StillSorted DO
      IF Ints[Index] > Ints[Index+1] THEN
        StillSorted:= false
      ELSE
        Index:= Index + 1;
    SortedArray:= StillSorted
  END;
```

Another coded solution

You can often code boolean functions where the value of the function is initialized before the sequence of events is processed. Any given event in the sequence then sets the function to its complement. Example 8.6 uses this strategy to obtain a solution for SortedArray.

Example 8.6

```
FUNCTION SortedArray(VAR Ints: IntsArray;
                     TotalElements: integer): boolean;
{documentation}
VAR
   Index:  integer;  {the index value of element being compared}
BEGIN
   SortedArray:= true;
   FOR Index:= 1 TO TotalElements-1 DO
     IF Ints[Index] > Ints[Index+1] THEN
       SortedArray:= false
END;
```

We prefer not to use this technique, even though the source code looks simpler. First of all, it is contrary to Program Design Rule 8.1. Obviously, this design rule need not be followed to produce correct code in every instance. If the rule is followed, though, the coding style for all functions will be consistent. In most situations, moreover, the first value assigned to a function will also be the last one.

On a different note, if the array is unsorted, more comparisons will be made than required with the solution coded as Example 8.6. As soon as an element is found out of order with the code of the first solution, no further comparisons are made. ◆

EXERCISES

Test Your Understanding

1. True or false? A boolean variable's ultimate purpose in any given block is to control part of the flow of logic.

2. True or false? A call to a boolean function cannot be used in a control expression for a loop or a decision statement.

Practice Your Analysis Skills

3.
```
PROCEDURE ModestCalcs(Add1, Subtract2: boolean; VAR XInt: integer);
   BEGIN
      IF Add1 THEN
         XInt:= XInt + 1;
      IF Subtract2 THEN
         XInt:= XInt - 2;
      IF NOT (Add1 OR Subtract2) THEN
         XInt:= 2*XInt
   END;
```

Given the procedure ModestCalcs and the precondition that XInt is five, what value will be returned to XInt as a result of each of the following calls?
   (a) ModestCalcs(false, false, XInt);
   (b) ModestCalcs(false, true, XInt);
   (c) ModestCalcs(true, false, XInt);
   (d) ModestCalcs(true, true, XInt);

4. Write the following boolean functions:
   (a) Correct, a function that returns the value of true if a guess at some unknown integer value is correct or not.
   (b) IsDigit, a function that returns the value of true if a character variable is a digit.
   (c) OrderedPair, a function that returns the value true if the first of the two numbers in the formal parameter list is less than the second.
   (d) LessThanOneHundred, a function that returns the value true if the sum of the N elements of Ints is less than 100.

8.3 Enumerated Types

Suppose you want to write a program that requires a variable to represent one of the colors of the spectrum. You may instead need to write a program that requires a variable to represent a day of the week or a month of the year. The Pascal language allows you to define a type that represents the value of a color, a day of the week, or a month of the year. This programmer-defined type is known as an *enumerated type*.

Enumerated type: an ordered set of programmer-defined values.

Enumerated type syntax and semantics

The syntax diagram for defining an enumerated is shown in Figure 8.4. The first identifier names the type, and the identifier list specifies the values that variables of the defined type can take on. If you want to define an enumerated type for some colors, for example, you would code

```
TYPE
   ColorType = (NullColor, Red, Green, Blue);
VAR
   Color: ColorType;
```

The variable Color, given the source code, can take on only one of four distinct values. These values are the identifier literals found in the definition for Color-Type.

Assignment statements

When you assign a value to a variable whose type is enumerated, you must use one of the identifiers in the list that defines the type. *Do not use a string value!*

FIGURE 8.4 Syntax for an enumerated type definition.

enumerated type definition

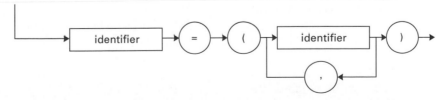

The first two assignment statements shown below are correct, but the third statement will cause a syntax error:

```
Color:= Green;
Color:= succ(Color);   {Color ⟵ Blue}
Color:= 'Red';         {SYNTAX ERROR!}
```

The functions
ord, pred and
succ

The standard Pascal functions `ord`, `pred` and `succ` will work on enumerated types. Indeed, the types are "enumerated" because the `ord` function forces an order on them where `ord` of the lowest value in the identifier list of defined values is equal to 0. This property of ordering allows you to use an enumerated type as a loop control variable of a FOR loop.

Example 8.7 shows how we can use the variable `Color` of type `ColorType` as the loop control variable of a FOR loop. The results of the source code execution of the FOR loop is shown below the coded fragment.

Example 8.7

```
FOR Color:= Red TO Blue DO
   write(ord(Color):5);
writeln;
```

```
    1      2      3
```

It is valid to code assignment statements like `Color:= succ(Color)` and `Color:= pred(Color)` as long as an attempt is not made to find the `succ` of the largest value or the `pred` of the smallest value. Given the values of `ColorType`, an error will result if you try to code `pred(NullColor)` or `succ(Blue)`. Neither of these values is defined, hence they do not exist.

Read in and
display

Most dialects of Pascal, unfortunately, will not allow read in or display statements such as `readln(Color)` or `writeln(Color)` on enumerated types. Therefore, you will need to write procedures to specifically carry out either of these operations. If you want to read in or display the "value" of an enumerated type, the logical approach is to represent it as a string variable.

Example 8.8 shows the approach you should take when you want to display the "value" of an enumerated type that will work for any given dialect. Note that the CASE statement works for an enumerated type variable because it is an ordinal type.

Example 8.8

```
PROCEDURE OutColor(Color: ColorType);
   {in: Color -- the value of the ColorType to be displayed
   out: the corresponding string expression for Color is displayed}
   BEGIN
     CASE Color OF
       Red: write('red ');
       Green: write('green ');
```

```
    Blue: write('blue ')
    END   {CASE}
END;
```

Example 8.9 shows the required code for reading in a value to `Color`. Note that there is *no prompt* for this procedure. The prompt is deliberately omitted to allow for more flexibility in coding. The user may be prompted to "Enter a color:" or to "Enter your favorite color:" or given some other different prompting string.

Example 8.9

```
PROCEDURE RdLnColor(VAR Color: ColorType);
  {Returns a value to Color, dependent upon the value of the character
  read in.}
  VAR
    Ch: char;         {a single char value read in}
  BEGIN
    readln(Ch);
    Ch:= UpperCase(Ch);       {coded as Example 8.3}
    IF Ch IN ['R', 'G', 'B'] THEN
      CASE Ch OF
        'R':  Color:= Red;
        'G':  Color:= Green;
        'B':  Color:= Blue
      END   {CASE}
    ELSE
      Color:= NullColor
END;
```

Null values
Note in the example how we used the value `NullColor`. It is usually a good idea to define an enumerated type with a "null" value to handle possible error conditions. An error condition can then be identified using a `boolean` function as coded in Example 8.10. Example 8.11 shows a fragment of source code that uses the function `ValidColor` in a guard loop that guarantees correct keyboard entry for assigning a value to the variable `Color`.

Example 8.10

```
FUNCTION ValidColor(Color: ColorType): boolean;
  {returns true if Color <> NullColor}
  BEGIN
    ValidColor:= Color <> NullColor
  END;
```

Example 8.11

```
REPEAT
  write('Enter a color (Red, Green, or Blue):  ');
  RdLnColor(Color)
UNTIL ValidColor(Color);
```

Enumerated types and clear source code

In the early years of programming, there were no languages that had enumerated types. Days of the week, months of the year, colors of the rainbow, and any other ordinal types had to be implemented as `integer` variables. This kind of abstraction led to confusing code that required additional documentation to clear up the confusion.

In Pascal, such inelegant code is not necessary because we can use enumerated types. In the next problem, we define an enumerated type to represent the days of the week, thus giving us source code that is easy to understand.

Example Problem 8.6

The problem statement

Write a program to display a calendar for some given month. The user is prompted for the number of days in the month and the first day of the month. Once a valid set of values is entered, the computer displays the calendar for the month. A typical run might look like

```
Enter number of days in the month:  3 0
Enter number of days in the month:  30
Enter first day of the month:   Tesdey
Enter first day of the month:   Tuesday
```

SUN	MON	TUE	WED	THU	FRI	SAT
		1	2	3	4	5
6	7	8	9	10	11	12
13	14	15	16	17	18	19
20	21	22	23	24	25	26
27	28	29	30			

The main block

The main block can be described in terms of three procedure calls as follows:

> *GetInfo(TotalDays, DayOne)*
> *ShowHeader*
> *ShowDays(TotalDays, DayOne)*

The postconditions returned by the first procedure is that `TotalDays`, of type `integer`, and `DayOne`, of enumerated type `DayType`, have both taken on valid values. The trivial postcondition returned by `ShowHeader` is that the calendar header has been displayed. The postcondition of the third procedure call is that the days of the month have been displayed in calendar form. Let us now develop the code for the first and third procedures.

Developing the code for `GetInfo`

The pseudocode for the procedure `GetInfo` is described by

> *REPEAT*
>   *keyin TotalDays*
> *UNTIL TotalDays IN [28..31]*
> *REPEAT*

show prompt
RdLnDay (DayOne)
UNTIL ValidDay (DayOne)

The code for the procedure RdLnDay is similar to the code of the procedure RdLn-Color (Example 8.9). In this case, however, two char values must be read in. Therefore, the code for the IF..ELSE..IF decision statement starts off as

IF (Ch1 = 'S') AND (Ch2 = 'U') THEN
  DayOne:= Sun
ELSE
  assign some other value to DayOne

Before this statement is started, moreover, the two variables Ch1 and Ch2 will have been converted from lowercase (if entered as such) to uppercase by means of the function UpperCase (Example 8.3). The procedure also requires a call to the function ValidDay, coded as a boolean one-liner. We will present the code for the overall program when we finish developing all the pseudocode.

*Developing
ShowDays*

The header for the procedure ShowDays uses a call by value on the two formal parameter variables TotalDays and Today. The variable Today, initialized as DayOne then passed into ShowDays, is used as a local variable to represent the value of the given day being displayed. We can then describe the required sequence for this block with the pseudocode:

write 1, using the value of Today to determine indentation
FOR Date ← 2 TO TotalDays DO
  Today ← NextDay (Today)
  write Date
  IF Today = Sat THEN
    writeln
writeln

The value of 1, representing the first day of the month is indented a total of ord (Today) * Spaces, where Spaces is a defined constant to represent the number of spaces between each of the columns on the calendar.

The function NextDay should return the succ of the input parameter Day unless the value of Day is Sat. Then, the function should return the value Sun. We can use a decision statement to carry out this action.

Source code

The coded solution to the problem is given as the program ShowMonthCalendar.

```
PROGRAM ShowMonthCalendar (input, output);
   {A calendar for a month specified by the number of days it contains
   and by the first day of the month is displayed.}
   CONST
     Spaces = 8;      {number of spaces between each column of calendar}
   TYPE
```

```
      DayType =  (NullDay, Sun, Mon, Tue, Wed, Thu, Fri, Sat);
   VAR
     TotalDays:  integer;   {specified number of days in month}
     DayOne: DayType;       {specified first day of month}
   {*                                                                    *}
   FUNCTION ValidDay(Day: DayType): boolean;
     {returns true if Day <> NullDay}
     BEGIN
       ValidDay:= Day <> NullDay
     End;
{+                                                                        +}
FUNCTION UpperCase(Ch: char): char;
  {If Ch is lowercase letter, function returns uppercase equivalent;
  otherwise value of Ch is returned unchanged}
  BEGIN
    IF Ch IN ['a'..'z'] THEN
      UpperCase:= chr ( ord(Ch) + ord('A') - ord('a') )
    ELSE
      UpperCase:= Ch
  END;
{X                                                                        X}
  PROCEDURE RdLnDay(VAR Day: DayType);
  {assigns a value to Day, using value of two chars read in; the user
  can enter in two lowercase char values for the days}
  VAR
    Ch1, Ch2: char;    {first and second char values read in}
  BEGIN
    readln(Ch1, Ch2);
    Ch1:= UpperCase(Ch1);
    Ch2:= UpperCase(Ch2);
    IF (Ch1 = 'S') AND (Ch2 = 'U') THEN
      Day:= Sun
    ELSE IF (Ch1 = 'M') AND (Ch2 = 'O') THEN
      Day:= Mon
    ELSE IF (Ch1 = 'T') AND (Ch2 = 'U') THEN
      Day:= Tue
    ELSE IF (Ch1 = 'W') AND (Ch2 = 'E') THEN
      Day:= Wed
    ELSE IF (Ch1 = 'T') AND (Ch2 = 'H') THEN
      Day:= Thu
    ELSE IF (Ch1 = 'F') AND (Ch2 = 'R') THEN
      Day:= Fri
    ELSE IF (Ch1 = 'S') AND (Ch2 = 'A') THEN
      Day:= Sat
    ELSE
      Day:= NullDay
  END;
```

```
{+                                                                      +}
PROCEDURE GetInfo(VAR TotalDays: integer; VAR DayOne: DayType);
   {reads in valid values for TotalDays and DayOne}
   BEGIN
     REPEAT
       write('Enter number of days in the month:  ');
       readln(TotalDays)
     UNTIL TotalDays IN [28..31];
     REPEAT
       write('Enter first day of the month:  ');
       RdLnDay(DayOne)
     UNTIL ValidDay(DayOne)
   END;
{*                                                                      *}
PROCEDURE ShowHeader;
   {displays header for calendar}
   BEGIN
     write('SUN': Spaces, 'MON': Spaces, 'TUE': Spaces, 'WED': Spaces);
     writeln('THU': Spaces, 'FRI': Spaces, 'SAT': Spaces);
     writeln
  END;
{*                                                                      *}
FUNCTION NextDay(Day: DayType): DayType;
   {returns the day following the day represented by the value of the
   input parameter}
   BEGIN
     IF Day <> Sat THEN
       NextDay:= succ(Day)
     ELSE
       NextDay:= Sun
  END;
{+                                                                      +}
PROCEDURE ShowDays(TotalDays: integer; Today: DayType);
   {displays the days of the month in calendar form from 1 to TotalDays
   the value passed into Today represents the first day of the month}
   VAR
     Date: integer;    {the date whose value is displayed each loop pass}
   BEGIN
     write(1: ord(Today) * Spaces);   {displays first date}
     IF Today = Sat THEN              {clear line for Sat}
       writeln;
     FOR Date:= 2 TO TotalDays DO
       BEGIN
         Today:= NextDay(Today);
         write(Date: Spaces);
         IF Today = Sat THEN
           writeln
```

```
      END;
    writeln
  END;
{*                                                              *}
BEGIN  {main block}
  GetInfo(TotalDays, DayOne);
  ShowHeader;
  ShowDays(TotalDays, DayOne)
END.  ◆
```

EXERCISES

Test Your Understanding

1. Why is it advisable to define a null value for an enumerated type?

2. True or false? Standard Pascal allows enumerated type values to be read in as a simple read or readln operation.

3. TYPE
       MonthType = (NullMonth, Jan, Feb, Mar, Apr, May, Jun,
                                Jul, Aug, Sep, Oct, Nov, Dec);
   VAR
     Month: MonthType;

   From the definitions and declarations, indicate what value is assigned to Month after each statement of the following sequence:

```
            Month:= NullMonth;
            Month:= succ(succ(Month));
            Month:= pred(succ(succ(Month)));
            Month:= Jul;
            Month:= pred(pred(succ(Month)));
            Month:= succ(Dec);
```

Practice Your Analysis Skills

4. State the loop invariant on the variable Today in the procedure ShowDays. The invariant should be stated in terms of the value of the loop control variable.

Sharpen Your Implementation Skills

5. The procedure RdLnDay can also be coded using CASE statements. Write the procedure using CASE statements where you can assume that ELSE or OTHERWISE works as a reserved word that is used with the CASE statement.

6. Given MonthType of Exercise 3, write the following functions:
   (a) NextMonth, a function that returns the next month of the argument.
   (b) PrevMonth, a function that returns the previous month of the argument.
   (c) ValidMonth a function that returns true if the value of Month is one of the "valid" values.

8.4   The Game of Snakes and Ladders

You have seen how to write functions and then used this skill to simulate the roll of a die. You have also done some work with arrays. In the case study of this section, we bring both skills together to simulate the play of the children's game of Snakes And Ladders.

CASE STUDY 8.1

*The problem
statement*

The game of Snakes And Ladders is played on a game board consisting of consecutive numbered squares. A player rolls the dice and advances his or her token by the number rolled. Sometimes the player's token may land on the head of a "snake." In this case, the token is moved back to the square marked as the snake's "tail." In other cases, the token may land on a square that marks the "foot of a ladder." Then the token is moved up the ladder to its "top rung." The players roll the dice in turn. The first player to get his or her token on the last square wins the game.

We are going to write a program that plays "solitaire" Snakes And Ladders. First, the player sets up a game board of 50 squares, where a combination of up to 10 snakes and/or ladders is allowed on the board. Then the player rolls a die, rather than a pair of dice, to move the token over the board according to the value of the simulated roll. The computer keeps track of the number of rolls required to complete the game. When the game is over, this result is displayed.

The player enters up to 10 pairs of numbers that lie in the subrange *1..50*. The first number read in represents the starting position for a snake or a ladder, and the second number read in is the ending position. When the starting position is less than the ending position, we have a ladder. Otherwise, we have a snake. If either of these two numbers has already been assigned as a starting position for a snake or a ladder, the pair is not used. When a number is read in that is out of the board's subrange, it indicates that the set up of the game board is completed.

*Playing the
game*

After the board is set up, the player hits the "Enter" key, and the die is "rolled." The new position of the token is displayed, along with information regarding whether the player has fallen down a snake or climbed a ladder. Play continues until the token is on square 50. Then the number of rolls required to complete the game is displayed.

A typical run of the program, where comments in braces are not part of the display, is as follows:

```
   Welcome to Snakes And Ladders, Pascal style. First you will
set up the board, by entering up to 10 pairs of integers between
1 and 50.  If you enter an integer out of this range, the board
is considered complete. Once you have set up the board, it is
displayed.  Then actual play starts!  Roll the die simply by
pressing the ENTER key.

Set up the board, by entering pairs of numbers:
   8   24   42   28   12   35   17   35   46   15   30    5   11   27    0   50
```

```
Board:
   1    2    3    4    5    6    7   24    9   10        {ladder on 8}
  27   35   13   14   15   16   35   18   19   20        {ladders on 11, 12, and 17}
  21   22   23   24   25   26   27   28   29    5        {snake on 30}
  31   32   33   34   35   36   37   38   39   40
  41   28   43   44   45   15   47   48   49   50        {snakes on 42 and 46}
```

```
Enter a good luck number:   101                     {seed for RNG}

Roll:   3
You are on square 3.
Roll:   3
You are on square 6.
Roll:   6
You landed on square 12 and took a ladder to square 35.
Roll:   3
You are on square 38.
Roll:   4
You landed on square 42 and took a snake to square 28.
Roll:   4
You are on square 32.
Roll:   4
You are on square 36.
Roll:   2
You are on square 38.
Roll:   6
You are on square 44.
Roll:   4
You are on square 48.
Roll:   2
You are on square 50.
You completed the game in 11 moves.
```

The main block

The source code of the main block is given as the program PlaySnakes-AndLadders. We are using a one-dimensional array to simulate the game board. The code for the procedure Instruct is straightforward, and we will not develop it. We will develop the code for the procedures MakeBoard and PlayGame. This time we will not show the code for either procedure until we have developed it completely.

```
PROGRAM PlaySnakesAndLadders(input, output);
  {Simulates the game of Snakes and Ladders where one die is used, and
  the player sets up the game board.  The game is set up for solitaire
  play.}
  CONST
    LastSquare = 50;          {total number of squares on board}
  TYPE
    BoardType = ARRAY[1..LastSquare] OF integer;
  VAR
    GameBoard: BoardType;     {the game board}
    Moves: integer;           {moves required to finish game}
  {*                                                                    *}
  PROCEDURE Instruct;
    BEGIN   {display instructions about game}   END;
```

```
{*                                                                          *}
PROCEDURE MakeBoard(VAR GameBoard: BoardType);
  {sets up gameboard from user input}
   BEGIN   END;
{*                                                                          *}
PROCEDURE PlayGame(VAR GameBoard: BoardType; VAR Moves: integer);
   {the game is simulated; the number of Moves required to complete
   the game on the given GameBoard is returned by the procedure}
   BEGIN   END;
{*                                                                          *}
BEGIN
  Instruct;
  writeln;
  MakeBoard(GameBoard);
  writeln;
  Moves:= 0;
  PlayGame(GameBoard, Moves);
  writeln;
  writeln('You completed the game in ',Moves:1,' moves.')
END.
```

The first draft for MakeBoard   The first action to carry out in the procedure MakeBoard is to initialize the board by setting all squares equal to their own value. Once that action is completed, values are solicited for snakes or ladders. Because a maximum of 10 snakes and/or ladders is allowed, we need to use a loop that counts the number of snakes and ladders placed on the game board. Also a value read into a pair could cause the process to terminate, so we need to use a boolean flag StillMaking. This variable is initialized to true before the integer pairs are read in. The flag variable is then set to false if an integer value is read in that is off the board. The draft for these actions, including prompts and displays is described by the pseudocode

> FOR Square ← 1 TO LastSquare DO   {initialize GameBoard}
>   GameBoard[Square] ← Square
> Count ← 0   {initialize loop control variables}
> StillMaking ← true
> display prompt
> read(Before, After)   {get first candidate squares}
> WHILE (Count <> 10) AND StillMaking DO
>   IF either Before or After is off the board THEN
>   StillMaking ← false
>   ELSE
>   IF NOT (Before or After already starts a snake or a ladder) THEN
>   GameBoard[Before] ← After
>   Count ← Count + 1
>   read(Before, After)
> ShowBoard(GameBoard)   {display GameBoard}

We use Square as a loop counting variable of the FOR loop. The variables Before and After represent the candidate squares for a snake or a ladder.

Assertion testing the draft

After the FOR loop is executed, all squares on the board are set to their own values. The invariants of the WHILE loop are: (1) the elements assigned to Board represent the partially constructed game board, (2) Count represents the number of snakes and ladders placed on the game board, (3) StillMaking represents a condition indicating whether or not the board is still being built, and (4) Before and After represent the last candidate values read in. Note that these invariant conditions are all satisfied at loop entry, as they should be.

An assertion we can make on the values of Before and After used with the decision statement is, "Given that one of the two values is off the board, the value of StillMaking is false, otherwise these values represent candidates for a snake or a ladder. If the latter path is taken, we can further assert, "Given that GameBoard[Before] and GameBoard[After] do not represent the starting position of another snake or ladder, the value of GameBoard[Before] is set to After." Put more simply, we can say the action carried out is to put a new snake or ladder on the board. Note that if the one of values read into the first pair is off the board, no snakes or ladders are placed.

The postloop assertion we can make is, "Either 10 snakes/ladders were placed on the board or an integer representing a value off the board was read in." This assertion meets the condition required for filling in the board. The loop invariants, moreover, ensure that GameBoard was properly filled in.

Refining the decision statements

We can refine the boolean expression associated with the first decision statement by abstracting two calls to the boolean function OffBoard. The pseudocode described as *either Before or After is off the board* then codes to the expression OffBoard(Before) OR OffBoard(After). We can likewise abstract a boolean function AlreadySet and use it to get the code for the control expression of the second decision statement as NOT(AlreadySet (GameBoard[Before], Before) OR AlreadySet(GameBoard[After], After)). The function returns true if the two integer arguments are equal. Thus a snake or ladder cannot be changed nor can one snake or ladder terminate at the start of another snake or ladder.

Source code

The source code for the procedure MakeBoard is shown below. We leave the coding of ShowBoard as Exercise 5 at the end of this section.

```
{*                                                                    *}
FUNCTION OffBoard(Square: integer): boolean;
  {returns true if Square is out of subrange 1..LastSquare}
  BEGIN
    OffBoard:= NOT (Square IN [1..LastSquare])
  END;
{+                                                                    +}
FUNCTION AlreadySet(PresentSquare, NextSquare: integer): boolean;
  {returns true if NextSquare <> PresentSquare}
  BEGIN
    AlreadySet:= NextSquare <> PresentSquare
  END;
```

```
{+                                                                        +}
PROCEDURE ShowBoard(VAR GameBoard: BoardType);
  {display of GameBoard, 10 squares per line}
  BEGIN    END;
{+                                                                        +}
PROCEDURE MakeBoard(VAR GameBoard: BoardType);
  {sets up GameBoard with snakes and ladders}
  VAR
    Square,    {loop counter for initializing GameBoard}
    Before,    {candidate initial position for snake or ladder}
    After,     {candidate final position for snake or ladder}
    Count:     {number of snakes and ladders put on GameBoard}
               integer;
    StillMaking:    {if true, GameBoard is still being built}
                boolean;
  BEGIN
    FOR Square:= 1 TO LastSquare DO        {initializes GameBoard}
      GameBoard[Square]:= Square;
    Count:= 0;   StillMaking:= true;
    writeln('Set up the board by entering pairs of numbers:');
    read(Before, After);
    WHILE (Count <> 10) AND StillMaking DO
      IF OffBoard(Before) OR OffBoard(After) THEN
        StillMaking:= false
      ELSE
        BEGIN
          IF NOT ( AlreadySet(GameBoard[Before], Before) OR
                   AlreadySet(GameBoard[After], After) ) THEN
            BEGIN
              GameBoard[Before]:= After;
              Count:= Count + 1;
            END;
          read(Before, After)
        END;
    readln;   ShowBoard(GameBoard)
  END;
{*                                                                        *}
```

Structure chart   The structure chart for the program, including all blocks we have developed up to this point is shown as Figure 8.5.

The pseudocode for the statement part of PlayGame is described as follows:

Developing
PlayGame

    keyin valid Seed
    PresentSquare ← 0
    WHILE PresentSquare <> LastSquare DO
        MakeMove(GameBoard, Seed, PresentSquare)
        Moves ← Moves + 1

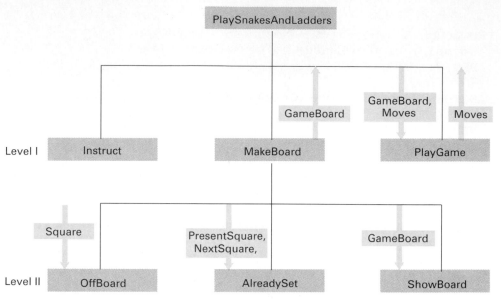

FIGURE 8.5 Structure chart of Case Study 8.1.

The variable Seed is required for the RNG that we coded in Section 8.1. We can get a valid value for Seed from the candidate value read in with the assignment Seed: = abs(Seed) MOD Modulus where Modulus is defined as the same constant (2187) in two different blocks. The variable PresentSquare represents the present position on which the token is placed. We leave the assertion testing of this block as Exercise 4 at the end of the section.

Drafting
MakeMove
 The preconditions for the call to the procedure MakeMove are that (1) GameBoard has been set, (2) Seed's value represents the last value returned by the RNG, and (3) PresentSquare represents the square the token is currently on. The postconditions returned are the same as the preconditions, except that another move has been made and recorded. Hence, the parameters Seed and PresentSquare are input/output parameters. The pseudocode for MakeMove is then given as follows:

> *GetOneRoll(Seed, Roll)*
> *display Roll*
> *TempSquare ← PresentSquare + Roll*   {*candidate next square*}
> *IF TempSquare < = LastSquare THEN*   {*still on the board*}
> *NextSquare ← GameBoard [TempSquare]* {*take possible snake or ladder*}
> *DisplayMoveInfo(TempSquare, NextSquare)*
> *PresentSquare ← NextSquare*

Local variables
 The procedure requires three local variables, Roll, TempSquare, and NextSquare that respectively represent (1) the roll of the die, (2) the square to which the token is moved as a result of the roll, and (3) the square to which the token is moved as a result of the value of the gameboard's square.

Assertions
 The value of TempSquare represents the square to which the token is

moved as long as this value is not off the board. Thus, the token is advanced to TempSquare from PresentSquare, using the value of Roll. The decision statement makes sure that the token is not moved off the board. If TempSquare's value is off the board (as represented by a value greater than LastSquare), the token is not moved at all.

Given that TempSquare does not represent a position off the board, the token is "moved" to this position. A new value is then assigned to PresentSquare, using the value of GameBoard[TempSquare]. When this path is taken, we must make three assertions, one for each statement associated with the actions carried out.

Source code

These three assertions are: (1) The value of NextSquare represents the square to which the token is moved from TempSquare. The token will fall down a snake, climb up a ladder, or not move to another square. Only the values of TempSquare and NextSquare are necessary to know which of the three actions is taken. (2) Information about one of these three moves has been displayed. (3) The new square on which the token rests is assigned to the variable PresentSquare.

The source code for the procedure PlayGame is given below. Note that we used a VAR call on GameBoard in the procedure MakeMove. We did so for the sake of writing more efficient code. The code for the function RandomNumber and for the procedure GetOneRoll is identical to the code we developed in Section 8.1, so we need not reproduce it here. We leave the coding of DisplayMoveInfo to Exercise 7 at the end of the section.

```
{*                                                              *}
FUNCTION RandomNumber (Seed: integer): integer;
  BEGIN {RNG function, required by GetOneRoll} END;
{#                                                              #}
PROCEDURE GetOneRoll(VAR Seed, Roll: integer);
  BEGIN {procedure to simulate roll of a die} END;
{X                                                              X}
PROCEDURE DisplayMoveInfo(TempSquare, NextSquare: integer);
  {displays move information; if TempSquare <> NextSquare the
  information is about a snake or a ladder}
  BEGIN  {statement}  END;
{X                                                              X}
PROCEDURE MakeMove(VAR GameBoard: BoardType;
                   VAR Seed, PresentSquare: integer);
  {moves token from PresentSquare to new value of PresentSquare, using
  the GameBoard to figure out next position; the Seed's value, used to
  generate a new random number, is changed by the call to GetOneRoll}
  VAR
    Roll,         {roll of die used to make move}
    TempSquare,   {square moved to as result of roll}
    NextSquare:   {square moved to from TempSquare on GameBoard}
                  integer;
  BEGIN
    GetOneRoll(Seed,Roll);
```

```
      write('Roll: ', Roll);
      readln;              {pause for player to press ENTER}
      TempSquare:= PresentSquare + Roll;
      IF TempSquare <= LastSquare THEN
        BEGIN
          NextSquare: = GameBoard[TempSquare];
          DisplayMoveInfo(TempSquare, NextSquare);
          PresentSquare:= NextSquare
        END
    END;
{+                                                                           +}
PROCEDURE PlayGame(VAR GameBoard: BoardType; VAR Moves: integer);
    {documentation}
    CONST
      Modulus = 2187;    {same as Modulus for function RandomNumber}
    VAR
      Seed,              {required for call to RandomNumber}
      PresentSquare,     {square token is on after Moves rolls of die}
                         integer;
  BEGIN
    write('Enter a good luck number: ');
    readln(Seed);
    Seed: = abs(Seed) MOD Modulus; {makes "workable" seed value}
    PresentSquare: = 0;
    WHILE PresentSquare <> LastSquare DO
      BEGIN
        MakeMove(GameBoard, Seed, PresentSquare);
        Moves: = Moves + 1
      END
  END;
{ *                                                                          *}
```

Structure chart
The structure chart of Figure 8.6 shows the development of the Level I procedure PlayGame.

Some on-line testing
Due to the interconnectedness between the blocks, the problem of testing this program is an interesting one. You can first test the procedure MakeBoard by commenting out all other statements in the main block. You should then choose test data that (1) return a board with no snakes or ladders, (2) return a board with 10 snakes, (3) return a board with 10 ladders, (4) return a board with a combination of 10 snakes and ladders, and (5) return a "typical" board with more than 0 but less than 10 snakes and/or ladders. Certainly, some test values should be made up for which a snake or ladder should not be placed. A typical board with, perhaps 4 snakes and 4 ladders should then be built to apply to the next tests.

MakeMove is a critical block to test. It can be tested once a GameBoard has been set up. A driver should be coded for this procedure where the created GameBoard is passed into the block, and any kind of Seed value is used. The driver should read in a value(s) for PresentSquare.

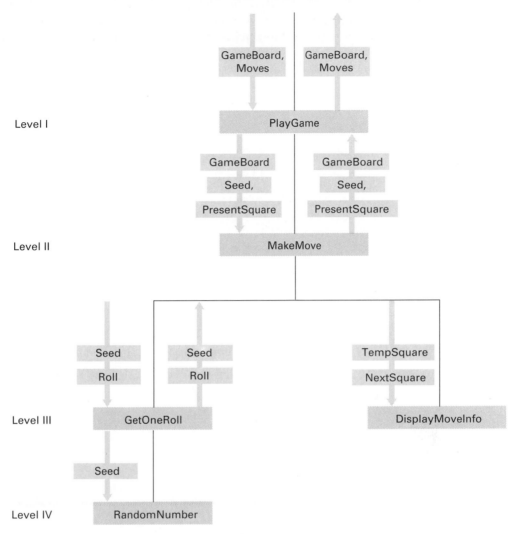

FIGURE 8.6 Structure chart for procedure PlayGame.

Along with this driver, you should comment out the statement part of GetOneRoll and substitute a statement to solicit a roll value to be read in. The driver for MakeMove and the stub for GetOneRoll can be used together to test rolls from any given position on the board that will land the token on a snake, on a ladder, or on some squares that are neither snakes nor ladders. Sufficient data should be chosen to test every snake and ladder at least once. If you test MakeMove for every snake and ladder with an adequate GameBoard (at least 4 snakes and 4 ladders), you will have in the process adequately tested DisplayMoveInfo.

Once MakeMove has been tested, perhaps 3 or 4 test points at most are necessary for PlayGame. One test should be made where the token is on a square such that the next roll might put the token off the board. Another test should be made using data where the move finishes the game. Finally one or two tests should be made to ensure that the move counting is correct. You will implement a number of these tests if (when) you do Exercises 8 and 9 at the end of the section. ◆

EXERCISES

Test Your Understanding

1. Why did we use a VAR call on GameBoard in all the blocks?

2. Is the test strategy we proposed closer to top-down testing or bottom-up testing?

3. Why are no stubs or drivers necessary to test MakeBoard?

Practice Your Analysis Skills

4. Draw the GameBoard for each of the following sets of data:
   - **(a)** 20 47 38 22 25 20 10 47 50 32 16 8
   - **(b)** 10 35 42 28 41 15 21 37 39 46 17 36 12 43
     44 13 38 6 25 16 17 48 0 50
   - **(c)** 12 28 42 17 34 12 17 47 49 28 49 43 0 50
   - **(d)** 10 50 21 39 41 28 −1 0

5. Assertion test the code of the PlayGame block.

Sharpen Your Implementation Skills

6. Write the procedure ShowBoard.

7. Write the procedure DisplayMoveInfo.

8. Write the driver to the procedure MakeMove and the stub to the procedure GetOneRoll such that the proposed test strategy on MakeMove is properly carried out.

9. What changes would you make on the code of PlayGame to test the block for the conditions we proposed? Would you keep these changes as part of the block's logic?

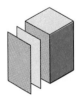

Program Testing Hints

In this section we present some common errors and bad practices to avoid when designing programs that require functions and/or boolean variables.

PROGRAM DESIGN RULE 8.3

Never use the reserved word VAR in a function header to change the value of a formal parameter's alias.

Function arguments

Although it is possible to use a VAR parameter in a function header, you should *never* use a VAR call with scalar types. Remember that a function is always written with just one purpose in mind: to return a value to a function call. This value is not meant to be saved; rather, it is used in forming an expression. When some variable in the function's argument list takes on another value as a direct result of the function call, the result is unexpected. This sort of code represents a side effect, not due to a global reference, but due to a change in the value of a variable that makes up the function's parameter list.

Procedure or function?

Note that we coded a *procedure* to simulate the single roll of a die. It would have been wrong to code a function that simulates a roll using the header FUNC-TION Roll(VAR Seed: integer): integer; because the value of Seed is also changed. If you think you want to abstract a function but find that two or more values must be returned by the action of the function, then *abstract a procedure instead.*

Superfluous boolean flags

Usually you use a boolean flag to record the occurrence of some event. Later on in the program, this flag's value makes up part of an expression that determines the control path for a loop or decision statement. "Later on," however, rarely refers to the next statement. The boolean variable Finished as used in the source code fragment of Example 8.12 is completely unnecessary and complicating. The logically equivalent fragment given as Example 8.13 represents a better solution to the problem.

Example 8.12

```
read(AnInt);
Finished:= AnInt <= 0;  {BAD PROGRAMMING STYLE}
WHILE NOT Finished DO
  BEGIN
    {process the value of AnInt as part of the loop body}
    read(AnInt);
    Finished:= AnInt <= 0
  END;
```

Example 8.13

```
read(AnInt);
WHILE AnInt > 0 DO
  BEGIN
    {process the value of AnInt as part of the loop body}
    read(AntInt)
  END;
```

Initializations

If you are using a boolean variable to flag an event that occurs within the body of a loop, make sure that you set the variable to its complementary value outside the loop. Part of the loop body's purpose is to set a new value to the flag variable, should the sought-for event occur. In order to set a *new* value, an assumed condition must be specified with an initial assignment to the flag variable. If a boolean variable is not initialized before loop entry, there are many computers that will automatically give it some initial value (often false).

The good news about not setting a boolean variable to some initial value is that it can take on only one of two values anyway. The bad news is that perhaps 50% of the references to this value may be wrong. Moreover, because any reference is usually found in an expression that controls the action of a loop or decision statement, there is plenty of opportunity for the source code to return incorrect results.

This news is very bad! It is better that you initialize the values of all boolean variables before you reference them in expressions.

If you are using a boolean variable to flag an event that you assume does not initially occur, you must "record" the absence of the event by setting an initial value to the flag. Then if (when) the sought-for event occurs, the flag is set to the complement of the initial value.

PROGRAM DESIGN RULE 8.4

Always use an IF statement to flag an event that occurs inside the body of a loop.

---

*Flag setting
inside a loop*

Never use a simple assignment statement to set a flag inside the body of a loop. If you do, the flag variable is set one loop pass, but the events in the next loop pass might set it back to its original value. Example 8.14, whose code looks so simple and "elegant," is wrong because the function's value depends solely upon the relationship between Ints[TotalElements-1] and Ints[TotalElements].

If you make some assertions, you will see why. The invariant for the assignment to the function SortedArray is stated as, "Given that Ints[Index] is greater than Ints[Index+1], the value of SortedArray is *false*. Otherwise, its value is true.

Example 8.14

```
FUNCTION SortedArray(VAR Ints: IntsArray;
                     TotalElements: integer): boolean; {BAD CODE}
   {the function gets set one pass, then perhaps reset the next one}
   VAR
      Index: integer;
   BEGIN
      SortedArray:= true;
      FOR Index:= 1 TO TotalElements-1 DO
         SortedArray:= Ints[Index] > Ints[Index+1]
   END;
```

It is equally unfortunate if you code the loop body with the fragment of Example 8.15. Note that this fragment is logically equivalent to the statement that makes up the loop body of Example 8.14. You can *keep* a flag variable set in the body of a loop only with a decision statement where one of the paths sets the flag to a boolean literal.

Example 8.15

```
IF Ints[Index] > Ints[Index+1] THEN
   SortedArray:= false
```

```
      ELSE
         SortedArray:= true
```

Program Design Rule 8.4 does not preclude the use of an IF..THEN..ELSE statement inside a loop body where the action associated with one of the two paths is to flag a boolean variable. If, for example, your program requires an IF..THEN..ELSE statement that uses a flag-controlled loop, by all means write the IF..THEN..ELSE statement. Just make sure, however, that only one of the two paths of this statement sets the flag variable to the boolean literal that is the complement of the flag's initial value.

The grammar of choosing identifier names

Think back to all the procedures we have written. They all dealt with actions. They *did something*. All variables we used until the material of this chapter represented *things*. A function likewise often represents the value of some *event* that you can classify as a *thing*. When we used boolean variables and functions, however, they invariably represented some given *condition*.

You can choose identifier names that are consistent both with the rules of English grammar and with the rules of Pascal syntax. How so? In English *verbs* do things. Thus, you should try to use verbs for procedure identifiers. In English, *nouns* are things, and in Pascal constants, variables, and nonboolean functions also represent the values taken on by *things*. Hence, you want to use nouns as identifiers for constants, nonboolean variables, and nonboolean functions. Finally, in the English language, *adjectives* often describe conditions. Therefore, your code will be easier to understand if you choose *adjectives* or *descriptive phrases* (e.g., *IsPositive*) for the names of boolean variables and functions.

EXERCISES

Test Your Understanding

1. When is it possible to use the reserved word VAR in the formal parameter list of a function?

2. Under what conditions is it ill-advised to use the reserved word VAR in the formal parameter list of a function declaration?

Practice Your Analysis Skills

3. Consider the following:

```
{the fragment returns false if and only if one of the elements in
AnArray is less than 0}
NoNegatives:= true;
FOR Count:= 1 TO 5 DO
  IF AnArray[Count] < 0 THEN
    NoNegatives:= false
  ELSE
    NoNegatives:= true;
```

AnArray	[1]	[2]	[3]	[4]	[5]
	5	3	-2	6	4

What value will be assigned to NoNegatives given the values of the elements of AnArray? What is the loop invariant for the variable NoNegatives?

4. A function to flag that some invalid value is an element in AnArray might be coded as follows:

```
FUNCTION Invalid(VAR AnArray: ArrayType; Lower, Upper: integer;
                          AssignedElements: integer): boolean;
{Returns true if one of the elements in 1..AssignedElements of AnArray
is less than Lower or greater than Upper}
VAR
   Index: integer;
BEGIN
   Invalid:= false;
   FOR Index:= 1 TO TotalElements DO
       IF (AnArray[Index] < Lower) OR (AnArray[Index] > Upper) THEN
          Invalid:= true
   END;
```

Is this function correct? Why or why not?

Sharpen Your Implementation Skills

5. Rewrite logically equivalent code for the following sequence such that it does not use `boolean` variables:

```
BadValue:= XInt > 5;
IF BadValue THEN
   REPEAT
      readln(XInt);
      GoodValue:= XInt <= 5
   UNTIL GoodValue;
```

6. Recode Example 8.14 so that a local flag variable is used and so that only one assignment is made to the function.

7. Rewrite the sequence given as Exercise 3 so that it executes according to the programmer's intentions.

8. Recode the function of Exercise 4 so that only one assignment will be (correctly) made to `Invalid`.

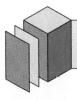

REVIEW AND EXERCISES

If your program requires one or more complicated expressions, you can abstract a *function call* that returns a single value using actual parameters that make up its *argument list*. A function is declared with one purpose in mind: to return a value of a specified type that is immediately used in an expression of which the function call is a part.

The last statement executed in the block of a function declaration should be an assignment statement. The function identifier is found on the left-hand side of the assignment operator. The right-hand side has an expression representing the *func-*

tion's value. Sometimes, especially when a loop is required, it is necessary to use a *dummy variable* to accumulate *candidate values* of the function. The final value this dummy variable takes on is the value assigned to the function as the last statement of the block.

A *pseudorandom-number generator* is a very useful function to simulate a sequence of *random events*. No single random event can be predicted, but the result of the execution of many random events is highly predictable. A pseudorandom-number generator (RNG) is often coded as a function requiring a single argument called the *seed* value. Each call to the RNG returns a new number as long as the seed value is different.

A *boolean variable* can take on only the values *true* or *false*. They are best used as *flags,* variables that record something about the program state in one part of the program and that are used to control a decision or a loop statement(s) in another part of the program. As with all other variables, the meaning of the value taken on by the flag variable should be consistent over the scope of the block in which the variable is declared.

Boolean variables, when used properly, can add an elegance to one's code. A boolean expression, for example, can be passed into a procedure where the formal parameter is a boolean variable. This variable might serve as a flag in carrying out a decision statement. Boolean variables are also useful in implementing a *loop, then decide* algorithm. A boolean variable used in this context serves as part of the control expression of a *flag-controlled* loop. One of the possible conditions causing an exit would be the setting of the flag. The value taken on by the flag, regardless of whether it caused the exit or not, is used in the decision statement after the loop is exited.

Boolean functions represent an excellent programming device to hide some very complicated control logic. Quite often such functions are coded as short, often one-statement, blocks. If the function is given a good name, another programmer can easily understand its purpose and thus not have to try to evaluate a complicated-looking boolean expression.

It is also possible to simplify a program by defining an *enumerated type*. The definition consists of a list of identifiers that represent the values that any variable of this type is allowed to take on. An enumerated type is an *ordinal* type because the functions ord, pred, and succ are all defined. Only pred of the first value and succ of the last value are undefined.

Unfortunately, the standard *read/display* procedures will not work with enumerated types for most dialects. This difficulty is easily surmounted by coding *read/ display* procedures that use string literals to represent the values for the enumerated types. It is a good practice to define the *NullValue* for any given enumerated type to handle error conditions. Conventionally, a call to the ord function using the null value as an argument is 0. The value returned by a call of ord to the first "legal" defined value is then 1.

Although VAR calls are allowed as function arguments, *never* use a VAR call on an argument that is a scalar variable. You want to use a VAR call with a structured variable solely for the sake of making the code efficient. A "function" that returns more than one value is misleading and dangerous code that causes unexpected *side effects*. Avoid coding functions that return more than one value at all costs.

Do not use a `boolean` variable if a *single* `boolean` expression can accomplish the same purpose. A flag variable should be set in one part and then examined in another part of the program. Or once set, its value is examined more than once.

It is imperative, moreover, to *initialize a flag* (s) whose value(s) represents the occurrence of a sought-for event in a sequence of candidate events. This initialization to a *boolean literal* represents the fact that the sought-for event did not occur. It is imperative, too, that when the event occurs, the flag is set, and (unless the problem statement does not require it) *remains set* for all subsequent events. You can ensure that this act is properly carried out in a loop body by setting the flag to the *complement* of its initial value with an IF statement.

EXERCISES

Short Answers

1. What is meant by the term "dummy variable?"

2. What is a flag variable? How and why might it be useful?

3. The last statement executed in a function's block should always perform what action?

4. True or false? The call-by-variable mechanism is not allowed in the formal parameter list for a function.

5. True or false? There are times when it is recommended that you use a call by variable with an argument of a function that is a scalar type.

6. True or false? Liberal use of `boolean` variables will always simplify the logic of one's program.

7. Can a function return an array? Why or why not?

8. True or false? A function can be coded in such a way that its execution can return new values to one or more of its arguments.

9. True or false? A function should often be coded in such a way that its execution can return new values to one or more of its arguments.

10. True or false? Regardless of the variable type, it is best to call arguments of a function by value.

11. Do these two statements realize the same effect?

> `ABool:= X > 10;`   `IF (X > 10) THEN`
> `                             ABool:= true;`

Explain your answer.

12. Do these two statements realize the same effect?

> `ABool:= (X > 10) OR ABool;`   `IF (X > 10) THEN`
> `                                        ABool:= true;`

Explain your answer.

13. Why do we sometimes define a "null value" for an enumerated type?

14. When a random-number generator is used in a program, what two purposes does the seed variable serve?

15. Match the phrase in column A with the phrase in column B:

Column A	Column B
subrange type	candidate value
integer	possible host for a subrange type
dummy variable	required for arrays
flag-controlled loop	uses boolean variable
programmer-defined	enumerated type

16. Suppose a WHILE loop control expression is given as NOT ((Index = 0) OR Found). Write down the expression for the exit condition.

17. Write an expression logically equivalent to the control expression of Exercise 16 that does not have the word OR in it.

18. Classify each of the following identifier names as characterizing a procedure, a variable other than boolean, or a boolean variable: Finished, ExamineValues, LastOne, FindOne, Executed, OneLetter.

Easy Projects

19. Write a program that does the following:
  (a) First, it reads in a value to Seed and then uses the RNG to generate and store 500 numbers in an array.
  (b) Use this array as an argument of the *boolean* function AlternatesOddAndEven, that returns true if the numbers generated alternate between oddness and evenness.
  (c) Drives the function three times, generating three different arrays. If you coded it correctly, the function should always evaluate to true.

20. (a) Use the RNG to write a procedure GenerateRange that will generate random numbers uniformly in the interval 200 to 499, inclusive. *Note: Each call* to this procedure *must* return a result. *Do not* write a procedure that simply keeps calling the RNG until an in-range value is returned.
  (b) Test this procedure with a procedure CheckValidity that returns true to the boolean variable Valid if perhaps 600 numbers generated lie within the specified intervals.
  (c) Then write a procedure CountIntervals that will count the number of values in the 200s, those in the 300s, and those in the 400s for 600 trials. Approximately 200 of each value should be returned by the procedure.

The main block of the program consists of calls to each of the three procedures.

21. (a) Write a procedure to simulate the rolling of a pair of dice. Then test the procedure as follows.
  (b) The expected value, given many different trials for a pair of dice, is that a 7 will be the average roll. Write a program to simulate the rolling of a pair of dice 500 times for five different initial Seed values that are read in. Have the computer find and display the average of each of the five groups of the 500 trials.

22. Write a program that assigns 100 values to the elements of an array using the RNG. Once values have been read in, write a procedure that will display the 100 array elements, 10 per line. You can use a field size of 6 to ensure there is sufficient space. Then using the array both as data and as the means to confirm correctness, write functions that will do the following:

(a) Return the index value of the lowest element in the array.

(b) Count how many elements lie within a specified subrange (say, 100 to 800) for the 100 elements.

(c) Return the boolean value `true` to the function `HasZero` if one of the elements generated is equal to `0`.

The main block of the program simply generates the array and then drives each of the three functions.

Medium Projects

23. Write a program that simulates the play of a game between two players. The rules are as follows:

Each player rolls a pair of dice. Whoever gets the higher roll wins a "point." If both players roll the same number, no points are awarded and the turn is a "draw." The first player to get 5 points wins. You are free to write the display as you wish, but make sure the game follows the logical rules as outlined.

24. Write a program to test that 2187 random numbers in the RNG are generated before the initial seed value is again generated. Use an `ARRAY [0..2186]` of boolean variables for loop control. All 2187 flags in this array `AlreadyGenerated` are set to `false` before the RNG is called. Each time a number is generated, the corresponding flag is set to `true`. The value of the next number generated is compared with the corresponding boolean flag, so that the loop control expression is `NOT AlreadyGenerated AND (TotalGenerated <> 2187)`.

Regardless of what seed you start with, the loop should always be exited only after 2187 numbers have been generated. In other words, the test should indicate that the generator is valid. In order to truly test the program, make up an RNG for which `Multiplier` and `Modulus` are even numbers. In this case, the generator will be invalid.

25. Write a program that uses the algorithm of the Sieve of Eratosthesnes to find and store all the prime numbers in the integer subrange 2..100. The program displays the number of primes in the subrange along with the values of all these prime numbers.

The algorithm works the following way: All numbers in the candidate subrange are considered prime. Then multiples of the first number (i. e., 2) are eliminated from the candidate subrange, although 2 is still considered to be a prime number. Once these numbers are eliminated, the next prime candidate is considered (i.e., 3). All multiples of 3 are then eliminated. As per the algorithm, the next candidate will be 5 (because 4 was eliminated). Once the Sieve has been applied on 5, the next candidate will be 7 (6 was eliminated using the value of 2 on the sieve.) The process continues until all numbers in the candidate subrange have been tried. At that point, the prime numbers are displayed.

The results of the program run should produce the display:

```
There are 26 prime numbers in the subrange. They are as follows:
    2    3    5    7   11   13   17   19   23   29
   31   37   41   43   47   53   57   59   61   67
   71   73   79   83   89   97
```

(*Hint:* Use an array of `boolean` elements to represent the candidates. All the elements are initialized to `true`, and when a candidate is eliminated, its value is set to `false`. After the sieve has been applied, the index values of all those elements still equal to `true` are the prime numbers.)

26. Modify the program `SnakesAndLadders` so that after a game board is entered, 200 games are played. Only an initial seed value to start the first game need be entered. No further input and output is necessary until all 200 games have been played. Once the games are completed, the computer should display the following:

(a) the average number of moves per game

(b) the number of moves required for the longest game

(c) the number of moves required for the shortest game

27. Write a program where the computer reads in integers until a value of 0 is read in or 100 integers are read in. The integers are stored in an array `Ints` capable of holding 100 integer values. The rest of your main block is to display the values of functions that return the following:

(a) the count of the number of positive integers read in

(b) the count of the highest consecutive run of positive integers read in

(c) the value of the last positive integer read in

(d) the value of the first positive integer read in. (If no positive integers were read in, a value of −1 is forced on the function.)

(e) the value of the *N*th integer read in. The value for *N* is also read in once the array elements have been assigned. If less than *N* integers were assigned, the value of `maxint` is forced on the function.

(f) the count of the number of negative integers read in

(g) the value of the highest-magnitude integer (the integer with the largest absolute value), be it positive or negative.

Difficult Projects

28. The 10 male students in Mr. Digits' tenth-grade gym class all want to play on a team. In order to sort things out, Mr. Digits decided to take a head count of who should play what. He decided that, in order to be eligible for any team, a student must have a GPA above 2.75. He then decided that (1) wrestlers must weigh between 105 and 200 pounds, (2) basketball players must be at least 72 inches tall but not weigh more than 230 pounds, (3) football players must be over 67 inches tall and weigh at least 170 pounds, and (4) that tennis players cannot weigh more than 190 pounds.

Mr. Digits will ask each member of the class in turn for his GPA, height, and weight. From these values, he determines which sport each student can play. After Mr. Digits takes his survey, he recaps the results by telling the class how many eligible athletes there are for each sport.

You are to write a program to simulate what Mr. Digits does. Some typical interactions between Mr. Digits and his students are

```
Your GPA? 2.82
Height? 71
Weight? 185
You are eligible for football and tennis.

Your GPA? 2.32
You are not eligible for any sport.

{GPA ↔ 3.32, Height ↔ 75, Weight ↔ 167}
You are eligible for wrestling, football, and tennis.

{GPA ↔ 3.56, Height ↔ 72, Weight ↔ 185}
You are eligible for all four sports.
{GPA ↔ 3.32, Height ↔ 56, Weight ↔ 125}
You are eligible for wrestling.
```

(*Hint:* Use parallel arrays of strings and booleans to enable the different strings of "You are eligible . . ." to be displayed.)

29. Write a program that simulates the quality control in a widgets line. Twenty-five widgets are turned out per day, each having a particular widget factor, that is represented as an integer value. A widget that is "normal" is considered to be "bad" in this case, for these particular widgets are unique works of art. You are to determine whether a given day's batch is good or bad according to the following criteria:
    (a) If five or more widgets have widget factors whose values lie within the subrange -50..50, the batch is considered bad.
    (b) If the widget factor increased over a streak of at least five widgets coming off the production line, the batch is also considered bad.
    (c) Likewise, if the widget factor decreased over a stretch of five widgets out of the 25, the batch is rejected.
    (d) If more than 17 widgets have a factor that is positive, the batch is rejected.
    (e) If more than 17 widgets have a factor that is negative, the batch is rejected.

    The 25 widget values are read in, then tested. If a given batch is rejected, the program should display the reason why. If a given batch is acceptable, the program should display the fact of acceptablity. (*Hint:* The easiest way to solve the problem is to read in the values for the widgets, then code some functions.)

TEXT FILES AND MORE STRING PROCESSING

OBJECTIVES

After reading and studying the material of the present chapter, you should be able to

- Write programs that read and process data contained in a text file

- Write programs that create text files containing processed data

- Explain the operation of the standard Pascal procedures and functions that apply to text files

- Analyze source programs that use text files for processing

- Build string variables using the concatenation operator

- Correctly apply string variables to text-file processing

Unless you have been working with a system that uses batch mode, so far all the programs you have written used internally generated data or data read in from the keyboard. Furthermore, the results of any given program run were always displayed on the output device.

In this chapter, you will learn how to write programs that read data from and write data to external files. This kind of processing has many advantages: (1) A lot of data can be processed with very few keystrokes by the user. (2) The same data can be read in and used more than once. (3) The results of a program run can be permanently stored in a data file.

You will also learn more about string manipulations. In particular, you will learn how to write programs that can read in more than one string value from a line of text. You will also learn about the length function as it applies to string expressions. Finally you will learn how to access and change the individual characters of a string variable.

9.1 Basic Text-File Operations

In this section, we present the standard operations that apply to text files. We also show some of the minor differences in the way different Pascal dialects handle text files.

Text File Interfacing

The program header contains a file parameter list that gives a program access to *external files*. Unlike the parameter list of a procedure or function, a program requires additional code to complete the interface with an external file(s). Even though very little additional source code is required to complete the interface, it differs from dialect to dialect.

> **External file:** a file stored in secondary memory that is created and used by more than one program.

Text files

Every file you have edited as a Pascal source program is an external file containing readable text. Any one of these files can be processed in another program as a *text file*. A program file, when processed by another Pascal program as a text file, is treated as if it were a data file rather than as a program file.

Text files generally do not contain source code. A typical file may contain text representing the names, addresses, and telephone numbers of your friends. Clearly, this file cannot compile as a Pascal source program! Its contents, however, can be read and processed by some other Pascal program. We will work mainly with these kinds of data files in the material of this chapter.

Text file: a standard data type that represents an external file whose contents are always human-readable characters.

File variable

Every external file has a *directory name*. You can use the directory name to compile a Pascal source program with the correct system command. You can likewise use a directory name to display the contents of a text file using the proper system command (e.g. PRINT in DOS, TYPE in VAX). You cannot, however, use the directory name to access the file's components in a Pascal program. Most dialects require that you use a *file variable* in the program header's parameter list for each directory file that is processed. Then you declare the file variable as a text file in the declarations part of the main block.

Directory name: the name by which a file is known in the operating system's environment.

File variable: a variable used in accessing the components of an external file.

An example

Example 9.1 shows a stub where PurpleCow will be the file variable for the program. The example represents sufficient code to complete the interface between the file variable and the directory file in standard Pascal. In this example, the file variable's name is the same as the directory name. It is not necessary that this relationship hold for every file-processing program you write.

Example 9.1

```
PROGRAM EchoFile(output, PurpleCow);
  {The stub for a program that will display the contents of the
  external text file PurpleCow.  In this case, the file variable and
  directory name are the same.}
VAR
  PurpleCow: text;
  Ch: char;      {used to hold a char value read in from PurpleCow}
BEGIN
  {statements}
END.
```

Opening a file

Before the contents of an external file can be accessed in a program, the file must be *opened*. Once the external file is opened, the file variable identifier is the means by which the computer reads from or writes into the external file.

Opening a file: a source code process that associates an external file with a file variable.

Source code to open a file

Different dialects require different code to open a file. In a dialect such as VAX Pascal, if you use a file variable whose name is the same as the external data file, the standard Pascal process of opening the file is complete. The machine sets up a data area where the file variable and the directory name are the same by default.

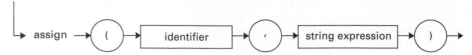

the assign procedure

FIGURE 9.1 Syntax of the assign procedure (Turbo Pascal).

Turbo Pascal, however, does not support this mechanism, even if you intend to make the two names the same. In this dialect, you must not only declare a text file variable but must also write a call to the Turbo Pascal `assign` procedure. This procedure has two parameters, a file variable identifier and a string expression (see Figure 9.1). The string expression is the directory name of the external file.

If you use the code of Example 9.1 in Turbo Pascal, the contents of `PurpleCow` are opened to the file variable of the same name only if you code the statement `assign(PurpleCow, 'PurpleCow.dat')` directly after the reserved word `BEGIN`.

Reading the Contents of a File

In Standard Pascal, a file can either be read from or written into but not both read from and written into simultaneously. All programs we present in this text will assume this mechanism. Once a file is opened, it must be prepared either for reading or writing. Let us look at the required code to prepare a file for reading in standard Pascal and some of the dialects.

The reset *procedure*
The `reset` procedure in standard Pascal prepares a file to be read from. The syntax diagram for a successful call to the `reset` procedure is shown in Figure 9.2. When the computer carries out this statement, the *file window* is placed at the start of the file. Just after a text file is reset, the window is on the first character in the file. In most dialects (VAX Pascal and Turbo Pascal, included), a directory file is first opened to some file variable, then the `reset` procedure is invoked using the file variable as the parameter.

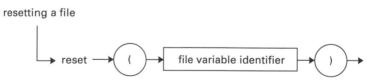

resetting a file

FIGURE 9.2 Syntax for a call to reset procedure (standard Pascal).

> **File window:** a software device that represents the candidate file component for the next read operation.

In Apple Pascal (including MacIntosh), an external file is *opened for reading* using the `reset` procedure with two parameters, the file variable and a string expression that represents the file's directory name (see Figure 9.3). In order for the file `PurpleCow.dat` to be read from in Apple Pascal, you must write the state-

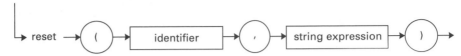

FIGURE 9.3 Syntax of the reset procedure (Apple Pascal).

ment reset(PurpleCow, 'PurpleCow.dat') directly after the reserved word BEGIN of Example 9.1.

Summary of the three dialects

Examples 9.2(a), 9.2(b), and 9.2(c) show the necessary code before data can be read in from the directory file PurpleCow.dat by means of the file variable PurpleCow for the three dialects. If you are using a dialect that is different from these three, either consult your user's manual or have your instructor tell you the required source code. Once the file has been prepared for reading, the source code to read in text from the external file via the file variable will be the same regardless of the Pascal dialect.

Example 9.2(a)

```
{VAX Pascal preparation to read text from PurpleCow.dat:}
reset(PurpleCow);        {also standard Pascal}
```

Example 9.2(b)

```
{Turbo Pascal preparation to read text from PurpleCow.dat:}
assign(PurpleCow, 'PurpleCow.dat');
reset(PurpleCow);
```

Example 9.2(c)

```
{Apple Pascal preparation to read text from PurpleCow.dat:}
reset(PurpleCow, 'PurpleCow.dat');
```

The appearance of a text file

In addition to readable text, all text files contain some *<eoln>* (end-of-line) characters and a final *<eof>* (end-of-file) character. We cannot read these characters, but the computer can. The appearance of the text file PurpleCow.dat, as the computer sees it, is shown in Figure 9.4. If you were to get a directory listing of this file, the computer would print it out as shown in Figure 9.5. Figure 9.6 shows the general appearance of any text file.

The <eoln> character marks the end of a given line of text. The <eof> character marks the end of the sequence of characters that make up the text of the file. Both of these characters are necessary to evaluate a call to either standard Pascal functions eoln or eof. Both of these functions have meaning for all dialects of Pascal.

The standard eoln *and* eof *functions*

The number of characters in a text file will differ from line to line. Likewise, the number of lines in any given text file will differ from file to file. If you want to write a program that processes a *line* of characters, you will need to use the boolean function eoln to determine when the line has no more characters on it. Likewise,

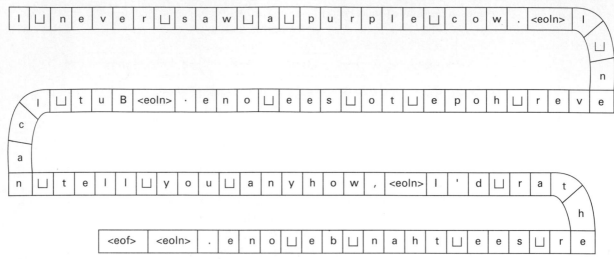

FIGURE 9.4 Actual appearance of the text file PurpleCow. dat.

I never saw a purple cow.
I never hope to see one.
But I can tell you anyhow,
I'd rather see than be one.

FIGURE 9.5 Printed appearance of PurpleCow. dat.

text file appearance

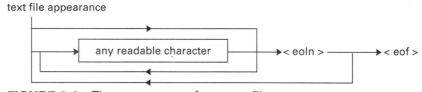

FIGURE 9.6 The appearance of any text file.

when you want to process an entire text file, you will need to use the eof function to indicate when there are no more lines or characters to be processed.

Table 9.1 summarizes the characteristics of both of these standard functions. Each function's argument is a file variable, representing the file window. The value of the function is determined by the status of the file window.

When a read or readln statement is carried out, the window moves for-

TABLE 9.1 The eoln and eof Functions

Function Call	Argument Type	Result
eoln(FVar)	text file variable	Returns true if next character in the file window is <eoln>
eof(FVar)	any file variable	Returns true if next character in the file window is <eof>

ward. Note that the window always *looks ahead* to the next character, the candidate first character to be read in with the next `read` or `readln` statement.

Some examples   Figure 9.7 shows the program state as it relates to the file window of `PurpleCow` directly after the procedure `reset(PurpleCow)` has been executed. In this case, the function call `eoln(PurpleCow)` will return the value `false`. Figure 9.8 shows the state when all characters on the first line have been read in, but `readln(PurpleCow)` has not yet been executed. In this case, the function call `eoln(PurpleCow)` returns `true`. Finally, Figure 9.9 shows the file window when the function call `eof(PurpleCow)` returns `true`. At this point in the program execution, all characters except for the <eof> character have been processed.

A complete example   Example 9.3 is the complete source code that will display the contents of `PurpleCow.dat` using standard Pascal. When this program is run, the contents of the file as given in Figure 9.4 will be displayed such that they look like Figure 9.5.

FIGURE 9.7   Window on `PurpleCow.dat` after reset.

FIGURE 9.8   Window on `PurpleCow.dat` after all characters on first line are read in.

FIGURE 9.9   Window on `PurpleCow.dat` after all characters but <eof> have been processed.

Example 9.3

```
PROGRAM EchoFile(output, PurpleCow);
   {The source code for the program EchoFile that displays the contents
   of the file PurpleCow.  This particular program will run properly for
   a dialect that supports standard Pascal's treatment of files.}
   VAR
      PurpleCow: text; {the file to be read from}
```

```
  Ch: char;          {the value of the last character read in}
BEGIN
  reset(PurpleCow);
  WHILE NOT eof(PurpleCow) DO
    BEGIN
      WHILE NOT eoln(PurpleCow) DO
        BEGIN
          read(PurpleCow, Ch);
          write(Ch)
        END;
      readln(PurpleCow);
      writeln
    END
END.
```

Figure 9.10 shows the status of the text file variable PurpleCow and the char variable Ch for the first three inner loop passes after the file has been reset. Note how the file window looks ahead to the next character. Note, too, that it is moved ahead when a file component has been read in.

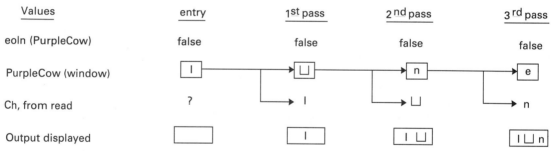

FIGURE 9.10   Status after first three inner loop passes of EchoFile.

When EchoFile is executed, the function call eoln(PurpleCow) will have evaluated to true four times. The function call itself does not move the window forward. When the expression eoln(PurpleCow) evaluates to true, the inner loop is exited, and the readln(PurpleCow) statement is then executed. After the writeln statement is executed, the window, as represented by the file variable PurpleCow, is examined to see if it holds the <eof> character. Four out of the five times this function is called, it does not, so the inner loop is entered again, and the next line processed.

read *and*
readln

When the standard input file is used, literal values are read in from the keyboard. The file variable in this case is, by default, the input file. When an external file is read from, its file variable identifier is the first one in the parameter list for a read or a readln statement. All the other parameters in the list are the variables to which literal values are read in from the file.

Writing the Contents of a Text File

In order to prepare a file for writing, you must write code that calls different, but analogous, procedures to those that prepare a file for reading. Let us look at the code required to write a text file from a Pascal source program. Once again, we will include different dialects in our discussion.

Writing to a text file

You prepare a file for writing using the standard `rewrite` procedure. The syntax diagram for a successful call to this procedure in standard Pascal is shown as Figure 9.11. This call works in most dialects. In Apple Pascal, an external file is *opened for writing* using `rewrite` with the same two parameters that work for `reset` in any dialect of Apple Pascal. The syntax diagram for this dialect is shown in Figure 9.12.

rewriting a file

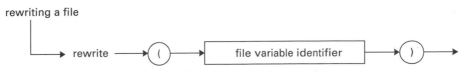

FIGURE 9.11   Syntax for a call to the `rewrite` procedure.

the rewrite procedure (Apple Pascal)

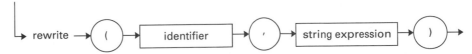

FIGURE 9.12   Syntax of the rewrite procedure (Apple Pascal).

Regardless of the dialect, the postcondition returned by a call to `rewrite` is that the file variable is associated with an external file that does not have any characters in it. The external file is therefore visualized as a "blank piece of paper" on which characters will be written.

An example

Example 9.4 shows the stub for copying the contents of `PurpleCow.dat` into another file `DupePurpleCow.dat`. We are assuming that this program will read in a string of characters from each line of `PurpleCow.dat`, then write out this string into the file `DupePurpleCow.dat`. You must insert code to define a string containing up to 80 characters that works for your particular dialect.

When put in the main block sequence of statements, the program fragments given below the main program stub that are shown as Examples 9.5(a), 9.5(b), and 9.5(c) will prepare `DupePurpleCow.dat`, a directory file, for writing (respectively) in the VAX Pascal, Turbo Pascal, or an Apple Pascal dialect. In each example, the name of the file variables are `PurpleCow` and `DupePurpleCow`.

Example 9.4

```
PROGRAM MakeDuplicateFile(output, PurpleCow, DupePurpleCow);
  {A stub for a program that will duplicate the contents of the file
PurpleCow into DupePurpleCow. In this case character strings will be
read in from PurpleCow, then written into DupePurpleCow.}
  TYPE
    String80 =  {INSERT DEFINITION TO WORK FOR GIVEN DIALECT};
  VAR
    PurpleCow,         {represents file being read from}
    DupePurpleCow:     {represents file being written into}
                       text;
    LineString: String80;  {line of text read in and copied}
  BEGIN
    {statements}
  END.
```

Example 9.5(a)

```
        {preparing DupePurpleCow for writing in VAX Pascal:}
        rewrite(DupePurpleCow);
```

Example 9.5(b)

```
        {preparing DupePurpleCow for writing in Turbo Pascal:}
        assign (DupePurpleCow, 'DupePurpleCow.dat');
        rewrite(DupePurpleCow);
```

Example 9.5(c)

```
        {preparing DupePurpleCow for writing in Apple Pascal:}
        rewrite(DupePurpleCow, 'DupePurpleCow.dat');
```

write *and*
writeln

Once a file has been prepared for writing, values are written into it using a call to either the standard write or the standard writeln procedure. The file variable should be the first parameter. The values of the expressions in the parameter list are then written as literal expressions into the associated external text file.

Example 9.6 shows the required main block statement to duplicate the file PurpleCow.dat as DupePurpleCow.dat in Turbo Pascal. Note that in this case a line, as represented by a string variable, is read in from PurpleCow and copied into DupePurpleCow. The final statement of the program is important, for it lets the user know the file has been duplicated.

Example 9.6

```
  BEGIN  {main block statement for Example 9.4, Turbo Pascal dialect}
    assign(PurpleCow, 'PurpleCow.dat');
    reset(PurpleCow);
```

```
assign(DupePurpleCow, 'DupePurpleCow.dat');
rewrite(DupePurpleCow);
WHILE NOT eof(PurpleCow) DO
  BEGIN
    readln(PurpleCow, LineString);
    writeln(DupePurpleCow, LineString)
  END;
close(PurpleCow);
close(DupePurpleCow);
writeln('The file has been duplicated.')
END.
```

The close
procedure

In most dialects of Pascal, the close procedure breaks the interface between the file variable and the directory file. Its single actual parameter is the file variable. You *must* close any Turbo Pascal file after it has been written into, otherwise some of the text may be lost in main memory.

Apple Pascal requires two parameters for its close procedure, the file variable identifier and a second identifier to indicate whether the file is to be saved in the directory or not. When you want the file saved, you should use the identifier lock. If the code of Example 9.6 were applied in Apple Pascal, the sequence of close statements are coded as follows:

```
close(PurpleCow, lock);
close(DupePurpleCow, lock);
```

EXERCISES

Test Your Understanding

1. Even when a text file is "blank," it still has some characters in it. Describe the *exact* appearance of a blank text file.

2. True or false? The eoln and eof functions are handled differently with different dialects.

3. True or false? The procedures for opening a file vary from dialect to dialect.

4. State the difference between a file variable and a directory file. How are they related to each other in a program?

Sharpen Your Implementation Skills

5. Rewrite the program EchoFile where a string variable is used to produce identical results as the original program.

6. Write and run Example 9.3 so that it works in the Pascal dialect you are using. Mark down the differences in code between the given program and the one you wrote.

7. Repeat Exercise 6, but apply it to Example(s) 9.4 and 9.6.

8. Write a short program to count the number of nonblank characters in the file PurpleCow.

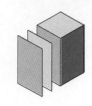

9.2 Some Text-File-Processing Algorithms

More about file variables

In this section, we give some common algorithms to process text files. We also solve some example problems that use one or more of these algorithms for their solution.

A file being read from is said to be in the *read mode*. Likewise, a file being written into is in the *write mode*. The associated file variable for each mode has a distinctly different appearance.

When a text file is in the read mode, the file variable represents a window on the next character to be read in from the associated directory file. The execution of any read or readln, besides reading in one or more values to the variables in the parameter list, moves the window forward.

When a text file is in the write mode, the file variable represents a buffer that holds a line of text. A write statement simply adds or concatenates characters to the buffer. A writeln statement with parameters first adds characters to the buffer, then sends the buffer contents as text to be written into the associated directory file. The computer appends the <eoln> marker at the end of this text. The buffer itself is then set to a blank line that fills up with characters that will eventually be written into the file as the next line of text.

PROGRAM DESIGN RULE 9.1

Always use the call-by-variable mechanism on a file variable parameter.

File parameter passing

Every read or readln statement applied to a file variable moves the window forward. Any write or writeln statement adds characters to the file buffer. Regardless of which mode the file is in, its variable will be changed by any action done on the file. Therefore, when used as a parameter, a file variable is always aliased rather than copied.

A generic copy procedure

Example 9.7 is the code for a procedure to copy the unread contents remaining in the file associated with the actual parameter of InFile into the file associated with the actual parameter of OutFile. This procedure is remarkably useful when you consider that the input file is an eligible actual parameter for InFile and that the output file is an eligible actual parameter for OutFile.

Example 9.7

```
PROCEDURE CopyFile(VAR InFile, OutFile: text);
  {in: Infile has been prepared for reading; OutFile, for writing.
  out: all contents of InFile have been copied into OutFile}
  VAR
    Ch: char;    {char value read in from InFile}
```

```
      BEGIN
        WHILE NOT eof(InFile) DO
          BEGIN
            WHILE NOT eoln(InFile) DO
              BEGIN
                read(InFile, Ch);
                write(OutFile,Ch)
              END;
            readln(InFile);
            writeln(OutFile)
          END
      END;
```

Example 9.8 shows how to use the CopyFile procedure to display the contents of a file. Note that the output file is the actual parameter for OutFile. In most dialects, this standard file is always rewritten.

Example 9.8

```
PROGRAM EchoFileII(PurpleCow, output);
  {Same results as Example 9.3, but this time done using the CopyFile
  procedure.}
  VAR
    PurpleCow: text;      {file to be echoed on output device}
  {*                                                                    *}
  PROCEDURE CopyFile(VAR InFile, OutFile: text);
    BEGIN    {code for CopyFile goes here}    END;
  {*                                                                    *}
  BEGIN
    reset(PurpleCow);
    CopyFile(PurpleCow, output);
  END.
```

The program given as Example 9.9, with a sample run shown below it, uses the procedure CopyFile to create a file from the keyboard. Dependent upon your dialect, you may need to add one or two lines of code to make the example work on your machine. (See Exercise 7 at the end of the section).

Example 9.9

```
PROGRAM MakeAndDisplayJunk(input, output, Junk);
  {Creates a text file from the keyboard into Junk.dat.  Then displays
  the contents of the text file Junk.dat}
  VAR
    Junk: text;   {file created from keyboard input}
    Reply: char;  {reply to question asked}
```

```
{*                                                                        *}
PROCEDURE DisplayInstructions;
  BEGIN {informs user to press <CNTRL-Z> when finished}   END;
{*                                                                        *}
PROCEDURE CopyFile(VAR InFile, OutFile: text);
  BEGIN {code for CopyFile goes here}    END;
{*                                                              *}
BEGIN
  rewrite(Junk);
  CopyFile(input, Junk);
  reset(input);                         {necessary for some dialects}
  write('Copy done.  Would you like to see the file? (Y,N)    ');
  readln(Reply);
  IF Reply IN ['Y', 'y'] THEN
    BEGIN
      writeln;         {skips a line for display}
      reset(Junk);
      CopyFile(Junk, output)
    END;
END.
```

```
Enter contents of Junk file. Press <CONTROL-Z> when finished.
Well, hello there.
Okay, goodbye.
^Z
Copy done, would you like to see the file?  (Y, N) Y

Well, hello there.
Okay, goodbye.
```

<CONTROL-Z>
and the input
file

Another use for
the procedure
CopyFile

In virtually all dialects, the <eof> marker is represented from the keyboard by pressing the <CTRL> key and Z simultaneously. This input sequence is often referred to as "CONTROL-Z." Once this character is entered, many dialects require that the input file be reset before further text can be read from the keyboard. The dialect we used to run Example 9.9 (VAX Pascal) required this statement. Other dialects do not require the statement, and, in fact, will issue an error message at run time when the computer attempts to reset the input file.

You can use the procedure CopyFile to copy the contents of more than one file into another file, as the following problem demonstrates.

Example Problem 9.1

The problem statement

Let us say the contents of file CinqAnsApres.dat are as follows:

> Ah yes, I wrote the Purple Cow.
> I'm sorry now, I wrote it.

But I can tell you anyhow,
I'll thank you not to quote it!

We want to write a program that uses the contents of PurpleCow.dat and the contents of CinqAnsApre.dat to create the file, PoetsLament.dat, whose contents will be

I never saw a purple cow.
I never hope to see one.
But I can tell you anyhow,
I'd rather see than be one.

Ah yes, I wrote the Purple Cow.
I'm sorry now, I wrote it.
But I can tell you anyhow,
I'll thank you not to quote it!

Source code   The solution to the problem, using the CopyFile procedure, is given as the program CreateLamentation.

```
PROGRAM CreateLamentation(output, PurpleCow, CinqAnsApre, PoetsLament);
  {Contents of PurpleCow and CinqAnsApre are copied into the file
  PoetsLament.}
  VAR
    PurpleCow,        {first source file}
    CinqAnsApre,      {second source file}
    PoetsLament:      {destination file}
                      text;
  {*                                                                        *}
  PROCEDURE CopyFile(VAR InFile, OutFile: text);
    BEGIN    {insert statement of CopyFile}   END;
  {*                                                                        *}
  BEGIN
    rewrite(PoetsLament);
    reset(PurpleCow);
    CopyFile(PurpleCow, PoetsLament);
    writeln(PoetsLament);    {skip line between two poems}
    reset(CinqAnsApre);
    CopyFile(CinqAnsApre, PoetsLament);
    writeln('Process completed.')
  END.  ◆
```

Often as a user, you will want to specify the file(s) to be processed in a program. In order to solve this problem, you will need an algorithm to read in a direc-

Specifying a directory file from the keyboard

tory name and then open a file variable using the specified name. We can describe the algorithm as a procedure with two output parameters. Its pseudocode is given as Algorithm 9.1.

Algorithm 9.1

> *{Linking a file variable to an external file whose name is read in:}*
> *PROCEDURE LinkReadIn(VAR FileName: StringType; VAR AFile: text);*
> *keyin FileName*
> *open AFile to the directory file specified by FileName*
> *{end algorithm}*

The implementation for this algorithm depends upon the procedure to open a file variable to a directory file. In Turbo Pascal, for example, we have the code

```
PROCEDURE LinkReadIn(VAR FileName: StringType; VAR AFile: text);
  {Turbo Pascal version; the file variable AFile is opened to the
  directory file whose name is the value of FileName.}
  BEGIN
    write('Enter name of file to be processed:  ');
    readln(FileName);
    assign(AFile, FileName)
  END;
```

In Apple Pascal, the `assign` statement is replaced by `reset` or `rewrite`, using the same parameter list.

VAX Pascal

VAX Pascal has a procedure named open that allows you to open a specified directory file to a file variable. The syntax diagram for a call to this procedure is shown in Figure 9.13. The string expression represents the name of the directory file. If a file is to be read from, the identifier `old` is required as a third parameter to indicate that the file is already in the directory. No third parameter is required if the file is not yet in the directory.

The implementation of `LinkReadIn` to open a file that is already on the user's disk, given the VAX Pascal dialect, is coded as follows:

```
PROCEDURE LinkReadIn(VAR FileName: StringType; VAR AFile: text);
  {VAX Pascal implementation of LinkReadIn algorithm, given that the
  directory file had already been created}
```

FIGURE 9.13 Syntax of the VAX Pascal open procedure.

opening a directory file in VAX Pascal

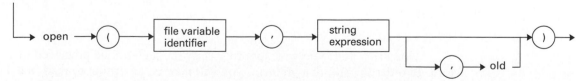

```
BEGIN
  write('Enter name of file to be processed:   ');
  readln(FileName);
  open(AFile, FileName, old)
END;
```

Some Algorithms Using the Eoln Function

In the remainder of this section, we present the description of some algorithms that require a call to the `eoln` function for their successful execution. All of these algorithms can be implemented using the same source code, independent of the particular dialect you are using.

The `eoln` *default*

The default file for the `eoln` function, as with the `read` or `readln` procedure, is the `input` file. Although the algorithms we are about to describe use file variables, you should understand that they can be applied to programs that read in values from the keyboard. Hence, if you apply any one of these algorithms to the `input` file, you need not include a file parameter with `eoln`, `read`, or `readln`.

Processing a line of text

Suppose you want to process a line from a text file, character by character. The algorithm you require to solve this problem uses a WHILE loop controlled by a call to the `eoln` function. When the <eoln> character is identified, the processing is completed. The pseudocode for this important algorithm is described as Algorithm 9.2.

Algorithm 9.2

{Algorithm to process a line of text, character by character:}
WHILE NOT eoln(AFile) DO
    read(AFile, Ch)
    process Ch
readln(AFile)
{end algorithm}

At loop exit, we can make the assertions: "All characters on the present line were read in, and the next candidate character for reading is the *<eoln>* marker." The postloop *readln* statement clears the line for the next sequence of input values. If this action were not included in the algorithm, the first character read in from the "new" line would be a blank, for the computer will read in the *<eoln>* marker as a blank.

Semantics

Note that the first action carried out at loop entry is to read in a character value. This action is consistent with the semantics of the algorithm, that can be described by the pseudocode

WHILE there is another character on the line to process DO
    read in the value and process it
clearline {readln}

The following problem applies Algorithm 9.2 for its solution. We will use the default `input` file to code the solution to the problem.

Example Problem 9.2

The problem
statement

Write a program fragment to count the number of nonblank characters read in from the keyboard. After the line has been read in, the count should be displayed. A sample run of the fragment might look like:

```
The quick brown fox jumps over the lazy dog.
The number of nonblank characters on the line was 36.
```

The solution

We can apply Algorithm 9.2 and an event counter to get the code

```
Count:= 0;
WHILE NOT eoln DO
  BEGIN
    read(Ch);
    IF Ch <> ' ' THEN
      Count:= Count + 1
  END;
readln;
write('The number of nonblank characters on the line was ');
writeln(Count:1, '.');  ◆
```

A guard against
reading eoln

Sometimes you may require that a character value be read in as long as the next character is not *<eoln>*. If the next character is *<eoln>*, the computer should force an assignment on the character variable (usually a blank). It should not read the *<eoln>* character, but rather leave the *eoln* condition unchanged. You can achieve this action by implementing code that satisfies the description given as Algorithm 9.3.

Algorithm 9.3

{Reading in a char value as long as it is not <eoln>:}
IF NOT eoln(AFile) THEN
    read(AFile, Ch)
ELSE   {forced assignment is optional, depending upon problem}
    Ch ← ' '
{end algorithm}

Skipping blanks

You may likewise want the computer to read and skip blanks until either a nonblank character is read in or *<eoln>* is identified. The pseudocode for this event-seeking action is described by Algorithm 9.4.

Algorithm 9.4

> *{Return the first nonblank char read in or the <eoln> condition:}*
> *Ch ← ' '   {forces loop entry}*
> *WHILE (Ch = ' ') AND NOT eoln(AFile) DO*
> *   read(AFile, Ch)*
> *{end algorithm}*

The post-loop assertion we can make is, "Either *Ch* is not a blank value or the next character to be read is *<eoln>*."

Using the algorithms

We will apply both of these algorithms when we solve the case studies presented in Section 9.4. Before we use the algorithms, however, we will present some string-processing algorithms in Section 9.3.

EXERCISES

Test Your Understanding

1. State the differences between a file variable associated with a file in *read* mode and a file variable associated with a file in *write* mode.

2. True or false? A file parameter is always called by variable.

3. What value is returned to *Ch* for Algorithm 9.4, given that the next character to be read is *<eoln>*?

Practice Your Analysis Skills

4. Assume the file PoetsLament.dat contains the nine lines of text as given in Example Problem 9.1. Given this text and the fact that the procedure CopyFile is available, write down the display for each of the following fragments:

   (a) reset(PoetsLament);
   CopyFile(PoetsLament, output);

   (b) reset(PoetsLament);
   FOR Count1:= 1 to 5 do
      readln(PoetsLament);
   CopyFile(PoetsLament, output);

   (c) reset(PoetsLament);
   WHILE NOT eof(PoetsLament) DO
      IF eoln(PoetsLament) then
        readln(PoetsLament)
      ELSE
        BEGIN
          WHILE NOT eoln(PoetsLament) DO
            BEGIN
              read(PoetsLament,Ch);
              write(Ch)
            END;
          readln(PoetsLament);
          writeln
        END;

   (d) FOR Count1:= 1 TO 3 DO
      BEGIN
        reset(PoetsLament);

```
          FOR Count2:= 1 TO Count1 DO
            BEGIN
              WHILE NOT eoln(PoetsLament) DO
                BEGIN
                  read(PoetsLament, Ch);
                  write(Ch)
                END;
              readln(PoetsLament);
              writeln
            END
        END;
```

Sharpen Your Implementation Skills

5. Modify the procedure CopyFile so that all blank lines from InFile are not copied into OutFile.

6. Write a small program to display the count of the number of blank lines in a text file. (Hint: Do any character values need to be read in?)

Learn More About Your System

7. Try to run Example 9.9 on your system as it stands. If there is a problem, modify the code accordingly. (Hint: On VAX Pascal, you must call reset(input) at the correct place; in Turbo Pascal, you will need to write a call to the assign procedure. In some dialects, you may need to close the file after writing and open it again for reading.)

9.3 Some String Operations

So far, your ability to write code that uses string variables is quite limited. In this section, you will learn some more operations that you can apply on string variables. The additional operations we present belong to the extension of ANSI Pascal that allows for string variables. The functions and operations you will see, moreover, are implemented in most dialects using the same special symbols and identifiers. If they do not work for your dialect, consult your user's manual for the proper special symbols and/or identifiers.

The length *function*

Every dialect of Pascal that supports strings has the length function. This function, whose argument is a string expression, returns an integer value that represents the number of characters in the expression. The following example, whose execution follows the three lines of code, shows how you can use this function to center the character string 'BANK STATEMENT' on an 80-character line:

```
DisplayString:= 'BANK STATEMENT';
Spaces:= (80 - length(DisplayString)) DIV 2;
writeln(' ':Spaces, DisplayString);
```

                         BANKSTATEMENT

The expression (80 - length(DisplayString)) represents the count of the number of blank characters that will make up the line display. When this value is divided by 2, we obtain the number of characters that should be indented before the string is displayed.

Concatenation

Most dialects of Pascal (including Turbo Pascal and VAX Pascal) use the concatenation operator, a plus sign, to chain two or more string expressions together to

TABLE 9.2 Some Concatenated String Expressions

Concatenation Expression	Expression's Value
'Roy ' + 'G. ' + 'Biv'	'Roy G. Biv'
'pre-' + 'condition'	'pre-condition'
'WHILE' +'..' + 'DO' + ' loop'	'WHILE..DO loop'

form another string expression. The characters in this new expression consist of the chain of characters that make up the other component expressions.

Table 9.2 shows three examples where component string literals are concatenated together to form a single string value.

Other implementations
If your dialect does not implement concatenation with this special symbol (e.g., MacIntosh Pascal), it will have a standard function to carry out the operation. The identifier for this function is, more than likely, `Concat`. Thus, in MacIntosh Pascal, the final expression of Table 9.2 is obtained with the code `Concat('WHILE', '..', 'DO', ' loop')`.

Accessing individual characters
Each character in a string variable can be referenced by position using code identical to that of referencing an array element. Suppose, for example, the variable `AString` has taken on the value `'recieve'` (a misspelled word). The values of `AString[4]` and `AString[5]` need to be changed. The spelling of the variable `AString` is therefore readily corrected with the coded sequence.

```
AString[4]:= 'e';
AString[5]:= 'i';
```

Making all characters in a string uppercase
You can take advantage of this particular mechanism to implement some very useful operations. Suppose, for example, you want to change all lowercase letters in a string expression to uppercase. The source code given as Example 9.10 shows how you can implement a procedure to carry out this operation.

Example 9.10

```
{*                                                              *}
FUNCTION UpperCase(Ch: char): char;
  {if Ch is lowercase letter, the function returns an equivalent
  uppercase letter, otherwise it returns Ch unchanged}
  BEGIN
    IF Ch IN ['a' .. 'z'] THEN
      UpperCase:= chr( ord(Ch) + ord('A') - ord('a') )
    ELSE
      UpperCase:= Ch
  END;
{+                                                              +}
PROCEDURE MakeCaps (VAR AString: StringType);
  {changes all lowercase letters in AString to uppercase letters}
  VAR
    Position: integer;   {accesses a character in AString}
```

```
BEGIN
  FOR Position:= 1 TO length(AString) DO
    AString[Position]:= UpperCase(AString[Position])
END;
{*                                                              *}
```

An Algorithm to Read in a String Value

It is possible to read in more than one string value from a line of text if (1) you know what characters the string is allowed to contain or (2) know what character signifies the end of the string value. We are going to develop an algorithm to read in a string value, stopping the process with the reading in of a sentinel character.

The null string
The algorithm requires that characters be read in and concatenated onto a string variable. An initial string with no characters in it is required to start the process. This string literal (but not a char literal) is expressed by two apostrophes (' ') with no space between them. This special string value, called the *null string*, is found in every dialect that supports string types.

Null string: a string value with a length of 0 that contains no characters.

The problem
Suppose we have text consisting of names and numbers. We want to read each name into a string variable but also want to ensure that numbers are not read in as names. In order for the process to be successful, a sentinel character must be associated with each name so that subsequent characters are used to read in numbers. For example, a line that uses the symbol ' ^ ' as a sentinel character might look like

```
Roy G. Biv^  80  70  90<eoln>
```

The value returned when the string variable is read in would be 'Roy G. Biv' where the final character read in is ' ^ '.

Development
We can develop the algorithm quite simply if we assume that (1) the *eoln* condition is not critical and (2) the length of allowed characters will not be exceeded. Given these rather arbitrary assumptions, the algorithm concatenates values to a sentinel character into a string variable initialized to the null string. The pseud-code description is given as Algorithm 9.5.

Algorithm 9.5

> {*Reading in values to AString up to a sentinel char:*}
> *AString ← '' {initialize to null string}*
> *read(AFile, Ch)*
> *WHILE CH < > SentinelChar DO*
>   *AString ← AString + Ch*
>   *read(AFile, Ch)*
> {*end algorithm*}

The loop invariant for the algorithm is, "All characters but the last one read in make up the characters in *AString*." The assertion at loop exit is, "The value of *AString* represents the sequence of characters read in excluding the final sentinel character."

Adapting the algorithm

The description of Algorithm 9.5 works as long as there is no danger of (1) either attempting to concatenate more than the maximum number of characters in *AString* or (2) reading in the <*eoln*> character. Suppose, however, that *AString* can only take on *MaxLength* characters. If an attempt is made to concatenate the *MaxLength*+1th character onto *AString,* the program will crash. Let us suppose further that there is a chance of accidentally reading in <*eoln*>. Taking these possibilities into account, we realize that we must guard against further concatenation if one of these two events occurs. Therefore, inside the loop body, we must substitute the following guard for the *read(AFile, Ch)* statement:

IF NOT eoln(AFile) AND NOT (length(AString) = MaxLength) THEN
    read(AFile, Ch)
ELSE
    Ch ← SentinelChar

It is also necessary to guard against reading in <eoln> before loop entry. The description for this guard is given by Algorithm 9.3.

Source code

The solution to the problem just posed is given in the code of Example 9.11. We will refer to this important example a number of times throughout the remainder of the text.

Example 9.11

```
PROCEDURE GetString (Sentinel: char; VAR AString: StringType;
                                      VAR InFile: text);
   {char values are read into AString from InFile until one of three
   events occurs: (1) the Sentinel character is read in from InFile, (2)
   the number of characters accumulated in AString is MaxLength, or (3)
   the next character to be read is the <eoln> marker.}
   VAR
     Ch: char;     {holds char value read in from InFile}
   BEGIN
     AString:= '';    {initialize to null string}
     IF NOT eoln(InFile) THEN
       read(InFile, Ch)
     ELSE
       Ch:= Sentinel;
     WHILE  (Ch <> Sentinel) DO
       BEGIN
         AString:= AString + Ch;
         IF NOT eoln(InFile) AND (length(AString) <> MaxLength) THEN
           read(InFile, Ch)
```

```
          ELSE
            Ch:= Sentinel
        END
    END;
```

EXERCISES

**Test Your
Understanding**

1. What type of argument is required for the `length` function and what type of value does it return?

2. What is the value returned by `length('')`?

**Practice Your
Analysis Skills**

3. Assume that the string variables `AString` and `BString` can hold up to 40 characters. Assume further that `Ch` is of type `char`, and `Pos` is of type `integer`. Indicate the display that results from the following fragments:

(a)
```
AString:= 'Johnny B. Goode';
writeln(length(AString));
```

(b)
```
AString:= 'Jack';
BString:= 'Gillian';
writeln('12345678901234567890');
write(' ':10 - length(AString), AString);
writeln(' ':10 - length(BString), BString);
```

(c)
```
AString:= 'Joseph Roger Ingram';
BString:= '';
Pos:= 1;
Ch:= AString[Pos];
WHILE CH <> ' ' DO
  BEGIN
     BString:= Ch;
     Pos:= Pos + 1;
     Ch:= AString[Pos]
  END;
writeln(BString);
```

(d)
```
AString:= 'E. E. Cummings';
FOR Pos:= 1 TO length(AString) DO
  BEGIN
     Ch:= AString[Pos];
     IF Ch IN ['A'..'Z'] THEN
       BEGIN
          Ch:= chr( ord(Ch) + ord('a') - ord('A') );
          AString[Pos]:= Ch
       END
  END;
writeln(AString);
```

9.4 Three Short Case Studies

So far you have seen programs to process `text` files that read in values to `char` and string variables. In this section, we develop some programs that read in numeric values along with string values. In the interest of not getting too far off course, we are assuming a dialect of Pascal for which strings are defined using the reserved word STRING. Except for the last program, we will assume that the file variables are opened to any directory files by the default mechanism.

Mixing types

For the first case study, we will develop a program that reads in `integer`, `real` and string types from a single line of text. Each line of text has an assumed appearance, and the coded solution to the problem relies on this assumed appearance.

CASE STUDY 9.1

The problem statement

The text file Checks contains the checking account activity of Mr. Namor Nemo. Each line of the text has three pieces of information on it: (1) the check number, (2) the payee, and (3) the amount of the check. Two lines of this file might look like:

```
741    ^Dagwood Bumpstead^   43.71<eoln>
740    ^Condo Community Corporation^   856.50<eoln>
```

Namor wants you to write a program for him that displays a table of the account activity for a given month. After the table is displayed, a summary of the number of checks written and the dollar amount paid on these checks is displayed. Given that the first line is simply a guide for the table, the first four lines of the tabular display should look like

```
{    5    10   15   20   25   30   35   40   45   50   55   60   65   70}
  CHECK NO.        PAYEE                                        AMOUNT
  ---------        -----                                        ------
      741          Dagwood Bumpstead                             43.71
      740          Condo Community Corporation                  856.50
```

The check number requires 5 spaces of right-justified display, the payee string should be allowed 40 spaces of left-justified display, and a check amount as high as $9,999,999.99 can be shown as a `real` number that is right-justified. If Namor only wrote two checks for the month (as given by the two sample lines), the summary line of display looks like

```
    CHECKS WRITTEN = 2        MONTHLY TOTAL = $900.21
```

The main block

We can draft a description of the main block as follows:

> *Initialize (TotalChecks, TotalPaid, Checks)*
> *DisplayHeaders*
> *WHILE NOT eof (Checks) DO*
>   *DisplayAndUpdate(TotalChecks, TotalPaid, Checks)*
> *writeln   {skip a line between table and totals}*
> *ShowTotals(TotalChecks, TotalPaid)*

The procedure `Initialize` assigns 0 to TotalChecks and TotalPaid, then prepares the file Checks for reading. `DisplayHeaders` simply displays the first two lines of the table. `DisplayAndUpdate` reads in a line of text, and displays the information contained on this line. It also updates the counting variable TotalChecks and the summing variable TotalPaid. `ShowTotals` displays the values taken on by these two variables after all information has been processed.

Assertion testing

The loop invariant about the display part of `DisplayAndUpdate` is, "The lines that have been displayed show the information about all checks read in." The loop invariant describing the purpose of TotalChecks is, "The value of TotalChecks represents the count of the number of checks read in." Finally, the loop invariant regarding TotalPaid is, "The value assigned to TotalPaid represents the total amount of money paid for the check amounts that have been read in." When the loop is exited, all lines have been read, and hence all checks have been processed. All these assertions prove the draft of the main block to be logically correct.

The code for the main block of the program is given below. We must still develop the code for the procedure `DisplayAndUpdate`.

```
PROGRAM ProcessMonthsChecks(output, Checks);
 {Displays a table about the checking activity for the month, as read in
  from the text file Checks. Also displays the total number of checks
  written and the total amount paid.}
 CONST
    Sentinel = '^';    {sentinel char to delimit NameType expression}
 TYPE
    NameType = {INSERT DEFINITION FOR A STRING WITH UP TO 40 CHARS};
 VAR
    Checks:    text;       {contains information about checks written}
    TotalChecks: integer;  {number of lines read in from Checks}
    TotalPaid:  real;      {sum of real numbers read in from Checks}
 {*                                                                    *}
    PROCEDURE Initialize(VAR TotalChecks: integer; VAR TotalPaid: real;
                                              VAR Checks: text);

    {sets counting variable TotalChecks to 0, summing variable
    TotalPaid to 0, and prepares Checks file for reading}
    BEGIN
      TotalChecks:= 0;
      TotalPaid:= 0;
      reset(Checks)
    END;
 {*                                                                    *}
 PROCEDURE DisplayHeaders;
   {displays headers for table}
   BEGIN
     writeln('CHECK NO', 'PAYEE': 11, 'AMOUNT': 46);
     writeln('--------', '-----': 11, '------': 46)
   END;
```

```
{*                                                                      *}
PROCEDURE DisplayAndUpdate(VAR TotalChecks:  integer;
                           VAR TotalPaid: real; VAR Checks: text);
  {displays information on present line read in from Checks; adds 1 to
  TotalChecks and the check amount read in to TotalPaid}
  BEGIN   END;
{*                                                                      *}
PROCEDURE ShowTotals(TotalChecks: integer;  TotalPaid: real);
  {displays the values assigned to the two amounts}
  BEGIN
    write('CHECKS WRITTEN = ', TotalChecks: 1, '       ');
    writeln('MONTHLY TOTAL = $', TotalPaid: 4: 2)
  END;
{*                                                                      *}
  BEGIN
    Initialize(TotalChecks, TotalPaid, Checks); DisplayHeaders;
    WHILE NOT eof(Checks) DO
    DisplayAndUpdate(TotalChecks, TotalPaid, Checks);
  writeln;     {one blank line before summary}
  ShowTotals(TotalChecks, TotalPaid)
END.
```

*Developing
DisplayAnd-
Update*
We can describe the required sequence for `DisplayAndUpdate` using the `read`, `process`, `display` algorithm as follows:

> *read in values for CheckNo, Payee and CheckAmount from Checks*
> *TotalChecks ← TotalChecks + 1*
> *TotalPaid ← TotalPaid + CheckAmount*
> *display the values of CheckNo, Payee and CheckAmount on output line*

The variables CheckNo, of type `integer`, Payee, of type `NameType`, and CheckAmount, of type `real`, are local variables.

Read in values
The pseudocode to *read in values* refines to the following description:

> *read(Checks, CheckNo)*
> *Ch ← ' '*
> *WHILE Ch = ' ' DO*
>   *read(Checks, Ch)*   *{Postcondition: Ch = Sentinel}*
> *GetPayee(Sentinel, Payee, Checks)*
> *readln(Checks, CheckAmount)*

The WHILE loop skips over blank characters. It is assumed that the file was prepared with a very specific format, so the WHILE loop is assumed to terminate when the value of '^' is read into Ch. When we code GetPayee, we will further assume that 40 characters or less make up the payee's name. In short, we are assuming a "good file" whose text contains valid character strings for all read-in operations.

The value of CheckNo is displayed with a field size of 5, and the value of CheckAmount with a field size of 10 and a precision of 2. The other 40 characters make up the left-justified display for Payee. The left-justified display sequence is described by

display Payee
display 40 − length(Payee) trailing blanks

From the given descriptions, we obtain the code for DisplayAndUpdate as

```
{*                                                              *}
PROCEDURE GetPayee(Sentinel: char; VAR.Payee: NameType;
                                     VAR Checks: text);
  {reads in characters to string variable Payee from the file Checks
  until the Sentinel character is read in}
  VAR
    Ch: char;  {represents value of char read in from Checks}
  BEGIN
    Payee:= '';
    read(Checks, Ch);
    WHILE (Ch <> Sentinel) DO
      BEGIN
        Payee:= Payee + Ch;
        read(Checks,  Ch)
      END
  END;
{+                                                              +}
PROCEDURE DisplayAndUpdate(VAR TotalChecks: integer;
                           VAR TotalPaid: integer; VAR Checks: text);
  {documentation}
  CONST
    SpacesForPayee = 40; {field size for left-justified payee display}
  VAR
    CheckNo: integer;     {check number read in from Checks}
    Payee: NameType;      {Payee string read in from Checks}
    CheckAmount: real;    {check amount value read in from Checks}
    Ch: char;             {candidate Ch value for non-blank}
  BEGIN
    read(Checks, CheckNo);
    Ch:= ' ';
    WHILE Ch = ' ' DO
      read(Checks, Ch);
    GetPayee(Sentinel, Payee, Checks);
    readln(Checks, CheckAmount); TotalChecks:= TotalChecks + 1
    TotalPaid:= TotalPaid + CheckAmount; write(CheckNo:5);
```

```
        write(Payee, ' ': SpacesForPayee - length(Payee));
        writeln(CheckAmount: 10:2)
      END;
{*                                                                        *} ◆
```

Processing a known number of lines

If the number of lines to be processed is known in advance, the loop control for reading in a sequence of values can be coded with a FOR loop. After each loop pass, one more line of text has been read in. The next case study is an example of this kind of problem.

CASE STUDY 9.2

The problem statement

A class with *N* students in it has taken a total of *M* tests. Both *N* and *M* are written as integer values on the first line of the directory file Results.dat. Each subsequent line has a single student's name on it and the scores he or she received on the *M* tests.

Let us write a program that displays the results showing each student's name and test average. A sample run, showing the first three lines of the file and the first two lines of display, is as follows:

```
20   4<eoln>
Roy G. Biv^   75    85    90    80<eoln>
Dagwood Bumpstead^   90    90   100   100<eoln>

Roy G. Biv had an average of 82.50 on the 4 tests.
Dagwood Bumpstead had an average of 95.00 on the 4 tests.
```

For the file in the given example, a total of 20 lines will be displayed of which the first two are shown.

Drafting the main block

We can readily draft the main block of the program using the pseudocode description

> *Initialize(Results, TotalStudents, TotalTests)*
> *FOR StudentNo ← 1 TO TotalStudents DO*
> *ShowAStudent(TotalTests, Results)*

Source code

The procedure Initialize prepares Results for reading, then reads in the values for TotalStudents and TotalTests from the first line of the file.

The solution to this program, which is quite straightforward, is given in the source code for the program DoTests. Note that each line display can be carried out with local variables inside the ShowAStudent block.

```
PROGRAM DoTests(output, Results);
  {The program reads in students' names and scores from Results. It
  then displays each student's name and average.}
```

```
CONST
  Sentinel = '^'; {sentinel character for name string}
TYPE
  NameType = {INSERT DEFINITION FOR A STRING WITH UP TO 40 CHARS};
VAR
  Results: text; {contains all the student information}
  StudentNo,      {the number of the student being processed}
  TotalStudents,  {total number of students in class}
  TotalTests:     {total number of tests they took}
                  integer;
{*                                                                  *}
PROCEDURE Initialize(VAR Results: text;
                     VAR TotalStudents, TotalTests: integer);
  {The block prepares Results for reading and gets initial values for
  TotalStus and TotalTests.}
  BEGIN
    reset(Results);
    readln(Results, TotalStudents, TotalTests)
  END;
{*                                                                  *}
PROCEDURE GetName(Sentinel: char; VAR Name: NameType;
                                  VAR Results: text);
  {The logic is identical to that of the GetPayee block in the
  previous case study.}
  BEGIN   END;
{+                                                                  +}
PROCEDURE ShowAStudent(TotalTests: integer; VAR Results: text);
  {Reads in and echoes a Name. Then reads in TotalTests scores and
  displays their average, along with accompanying text.}
  VAR
    Sum,        {sum of TestCount Scores read in}
    TestCount,  {count of test scores read in}
    Score:      {last test score read in}
                integer;
    Name:       {the student's name}
                NameType;
  BEGIN
    GetName(Sentinel, Name, Results);
    Sum:= 0;
    FOR TestCount:= 1 TO TotalTests DO
      BEGIN
        read(Results, Score);
        Sum:= Sum + Score
      END;
    readln(Results);                   {no more data on the line}
    write(Name, ' had an average of ');
    writeln(Sum/TotalTests:4:2, ' on the ', TotalTests:1, ' tests.')
```

```
    END;
{*                                                                    *}
BEGIN
    Initialize(Results, TotalStudents, TotalTests);
    FOR StudentNo:= 1 TO TotalStudents DO
        ShowAStudent(TotalTests, Results)
END. ◆
```

*Changing a
file's appearance*

The final case study uses the contents of one file to produce a second file with a different appearance. If you are using a dialect that does not have an interactive debugging utility, you may want to use this program after you have completed the on-line testing part of the program(s) you have developed.

CASE STUDY 9.3

*The problem
statement*

Suppose your system does not have a tracer utility program. The source program you wrote needed some debugging tracers, which you have coded and "flagged" at the start of each line with the comment string {D}. Now you would like to remove all these tracers with another program. An example of some lines of text that you might want to remove from this file are:

```
{D}  FOR COUNT:= 1 TO 50 DO
{D}     BEGIN
{D}        WRITE(ANARRAY[COUNT]:5,' ');
{D}        IF COUNT MOD 10 = 0 THEN
{D}           WRITELN
{D}     END;
```

*Describing a
solution*

The solution is quite simple. All lines not beginning with the flag string are simply copied "as is" into the new file; all lines beginning with the flag string are skipped over and not copied. A typical interaction between user and machine for this program might look like

```
Remove diagnostic tracers from?    Update.pas
Edited file's new name?  UpdateII.pas
The file is being created...
The job is done.
```

The two lines of display let you know that the program is finished with a "clean" source program.

*Main block
description*

The contents of one file are copied into another, but first both files must be opened. We can describe the main block for the program with the pseudocode

> *OpenFiles(InFile, OutFile)*
> *WHILE NOT eof(InFile) DO*
> *CreateLine(InFile, OutFile)*
> *close(InFile)*
> *close(OutFile)*

CreateLine will either copy or not copy a line of InFile into OutFile, dependent upon whether the line is a diagnostic line of code or not.

Source code   Most of the code is given below as the program RemoveDiagnostic-Lines. The only significant code we need to develop is the block statement for the procedure CreateLine.

```
PROGRAM RemoveDiagnosticLines(input, output, InFile, OutFile);
  {Creates a new version of a named file, where lines beginning with
  the DiagSentinel are not copied into the new version.}
  CONST
    DiagSentinel= '{D}'; {indicates that a line should not be copied}
  TYPE
    StringType= {INSERT DEFINITION FOR STRING WITH UP TO 80 CHARS};
  VAR
    InFile,          {file to be copied from}
    OutFile:         {file to get InFile's contents}
                     text;
  {*                                                                *}
  PROCEDURE LinkReadIn(VAR FileName: StringType; VAR AFile: text);
    BEGIN  {statements for LinkReadIn that work in your dialect} END;
  {+                                                                +}
  PROCEDURE OpenFiles(VAR InFile, OutFile: text);
    {uses LinkReadIn for both files, then resets InFile and rewrites
    OutFile}
    VAR
      FileName: StringType;            {name of each file to be prepared}
    BEGIN
      write('Remove diagnostic tracers from?  ');
      LinkReadIn(FileName, InFile);
      write('Edited file''s new name?  ');
      LinkReadIn(fileName, OutFile);
      reset(InFile);
      rcwritc(OutFile)
    END;
  {*                                                                *}
  PROCEDURE CreateLine(VAR InFile, OutFile: text);
    BEGIN  {copies a nonflagged line of InFile into OutFile} END;
  {*                                                                *}
  BEGIN
    OpenFiles(InFile, OutFile);
    writeln('The file is being created...');
```

```
      WHILE NOT eof(InFile) DO
         CreateLine(InFile,OutFile);
      close(InFile);
      close(OutFile);
      writeln('The job is done.')
   END.
```

Drafting
CreateLine
We can describe the statement for CreateLine as follows:

> *GetString(' ', First, InFile)*
> *readln(InFile, Remainder)*
> *IF First <> DiagSentinel THEN*
>   *writeln(OutFile, First + ' ' + Remainder)*

GetString assigns the first string on a given line of InFile to the string variable First. The string terminates with a blank character. We assume that the diagnostic flag string will always begin as the first character on a line of text. Thus, any leading blanks or blank lines will return the null string to the variable First. The variable Remainder represents the remaining string characters on the line of text. Note that GetString will not execute readln(InFile) under any circumstances. The rest of the line to be read in is done only after GetString is executed.

Source code
From the description, we arrive at the following code for CreateLine:

```
{*                                                              *}
PROCEDURE GetString(Blank: char; VAR OutString: StringType;
                                        VAR InFile: text);
   {Returns a string of nonblank characters to OutString as read from
   InFile, if the line begins with a nonblank character.  A forced
   sentinel occurs if eoln(InFile) returns a value of true.}
   VAR
      Ch: char;   {char value read in from InFile}
   BEGIN
      OutString:= '';
      IF NOT eoln(InFile) THEN
         read(InFile, Ch)
      ELSE
         Ch:= Blank;
      WHILE Ch <> Blank DO
         BEGIN
          OutString:= OutString + Ch;
          IF NOT eoln(InFile) THEN
             read(InFile, Ch)
          ELSE
             Ch:= Blank
         END
   END;
```

```
{+                                                                   +}
PROCEDURE CreateLine(VAR InFile, OutFile: text);
  {copies a line of Infile into OutFile as long as the line is not a
  tracer line for debugging}
  VAR
    First,          {first string; checked to see if it equals DiagSentinel}
    Remainder:      {remaining characters on the line}
                    StringType;
  BEGIN
    GetString(' ', First, InFile);
    readln(InFile, Remainder);
    IF First <> DiagSentinel THEN
    writeln(OutFile,First + ' ' + Remainder)
  END;
{*                                                                   *}
```

Note that we had to check for eoln(InFile) inside the GetString block and force a sentinel value on Ch to get out of the loop if the function call returns true. Note, too, that readln is done in only one block. Moreover, this block was set up to process *one line* of text, so the semantics are consistent with the actual code. ◆

EXERCISES

Test Your Understanding

1. Indicate which lines are written into the output text file when RemoveDiagnostic-Lines is applied to

```
FOR No:= 1 TO 10 DO
  BEGIN
    IF Unsatisfactory(Upper, Lower, Sample[No]) THEN
       Count:= Count + 1;
{D} IF DEBUGGING THEN
{D}    WRITELN('COUNT = ', COUNT: 1)
    END;
```

Practice Your Analysis Skills

2. It is important that the contents of a given text file match the appearance assumed in the statements of the program. If the appearance does not match, problems can occur. Indicate what will occur with the program given as the solution to Case Study 9.1 if two sequential lines of text in Checks.dat appear as follows:

   (a) 5 ^Richerd Robin N. Rippenemov 10000.00<eoln>
         6 ^Larson E. Flubditupbad^ 10000.00<eoln>

   (b) 723 ^Gabel T. Vee^ 35.00 ^^
         721 ^Telly Visors, Inc.^ 75.00<eoln>
         722 ^Condo Community Corporation ^ 856.50<eoln>

   (c) 162 ^Phoolan T. Public^ 10000.00<eoln>
         163 ^Larson E. Flubditupbad^ 10000.00<eoln>

3. Repeat Exercises 2, this time applying the program DoTests to the text file Results.dat given that TotalTests ↔ 3:

(a) Fred Smith 70 80 90<eoln>
Joe Jones^ 65 75 85<eoln>
(b) Josephine Smith^ 75 85 95 55<eoln>
Maxine Blum^50 70 60<eoln>
(c) Jubilation Thaddeus Cornpone 50 90 82<eoln>
Maximilliam Phineas Barnumby^ 98 97 100<eoln>

Sharpen Your Implementation Skills

4. Modify the program DoTests to skip a line after the last student display, then display the name and average of the student with the highest average in the class. The display might typically be

Albert Einstein had the highest average of 97.25.

Program Testing Hints

In this section, we give some of the errors to guard against when working with text files. Programs that process files incorrectly can have catastrophic consequences, like not processing some of the data in the file. In addition to pointing out common errors, we give some hints in choosing test data for your file-processing programs.

PROGRAM DESIGN RULE 9.2

Use a file variable, never the directory name, to access the contents of a file.

Opening files

Before any text file can be used in a program, it must be opened to a file variable. Program Design Rule 9.2 reminds you of this fact. Remember that the code to open a file differs with each dialect, so be sure to use the code that is correct for your dialect of Pascal if the default mechanism is not in effect.

Closing files

If you use a procedure to open a file variable to some directory file, you must use the close procedure with the file variable as the parameter once the program is finished with the file. If you do not use close, the results at run time will be unpredictable, particularly if the file is being written into. In personal computers, text that should have been written into the file often gets lost if the file is not properly closed.

If a file variable was opened by default in a dialect that allows this mechanism, you need not be concerned with this coding detail. Since the machine opened the file by default, it will likewise close the file by default just before the program ends.

Differences in dialects

Different dialects open and close files using different syntax. Sometimes these differences go beyond simply coding the proper identifier to open or close a file.

Suppose, for example, you are used to working in Turbo Pascal and find yourself coding a program in VAX Pascal. You need to open the file variable `AFile` to a directory file that is read into the string variable `FileName`. Experience with Turbo Pascal might lead you to code the sequence

```
open(AFile, FileName);
reset(AFile);
```

Each time you run the program, however, the computer processes an empty file because the procedure call without the identifier `old` simply creates a new directory file. In order for an existing file to be read from in VAX Pascal, you must code `open(AFile, FileName, old)`, where the parameter `old` indicates that a file already in the directory will be opened.

Reading past <eof>

If the computer attempts to read in values past the <eof> marker, the program will crash at run time. You must be sure, then, that your code will never cause this error condition.

PROGRAM DESIGN RULE 9.3

Avoid using the `eoln` or the `eof` function with the REPEAT..UNTIL loop

---

REPEAT..UNTIL and file processing

A REPEAT.. UNTIL sequence works best for algorithms that satisfy the description "process then look." The value returned by a call to `eof` or `eoln` is associated with the next character *to be read in*. These functions work best for algorithms described by the phrase "look then process." Thus, using `eof` or `eoln` with the REPEAT.. UNTIL construct is dangerous.

For example, the following sequence will crash when applied to an empty file:

```
REPEAT     {BAD CODE!}
  REPEAT
    read(AFile, Something);
    {process Something}
  UNTIL eoln(AFile);
  readln(AFile)
UNTIL eof(AFile);
```

Even when the file is not empty, blank lines of text could lead to unfortunate results. Suppose the computer has just read in and processed the last character on the line previous to the empty line. When the computer executes the `readln` statement after the inner loop exit, the window will contain the <eoln> marker for the next blank line. This value is read in as a blank character rather than used as a control character.

PROGRAM DESIGN RULE 9.4

When values are to be read in from a file, always follow an `eoln` test
with a `read` statement when `false` is returned. An `eoln` test that returns `true` is usually (but not always) immediately followed by `readln`.

Another kind of
`eoln` *error*

When values are read in from a file, the `eoln` test evaluates the condition of
whether or not there are more values to be processed. If so, the next action that
should be taken is to read in another value; if not, the next action to be taken is to
clear the line so that a new line can be processed. If you do not follow the program
design rule, your code might process one-too-many or one-too-few values, as in the
following example:

```
read(Ch);                         {BAD CODE!   OFF-BY-ONE! }
WHILE NOT eoln DO
  BEGIN
    {process Ch};
    read(Ch)
  END;
readln;
```

This code will lead to an off-by-one error because the last character read in will not
be processed. Instead, the loop is exited.

The reason for
a forced sentinel
algorithm

Suppose you want a loop to process either a line of data or a sequence that
terminates if one of the values read in represents some sentinel condition. Avoid
coding an algorithm whose description is

> *read(AFile, AValue)*
> *WHILE NOT eoln(AFile) AND NOT (AValue represents sentinel condition) DO*
> *process AValue*
> *read(AFile, AValue)*

The loop will work fine if the exit occurs because the sentinel condition is
`true`. If, however, the loop is exited because the <eoln> marker was identified,
the last value read in is not processed. An off-by-one error that processes one-too-
few values is the result.

Do not fix this problem by changing the algorithm to

> *WHILE NOT eoln(AFile, AValue) AND NOT (AValue at sentinel condition) DO*
> *read(AFile, AValue)*
> *process AValue*

Unfortunately, this sequence will process any sentinel value that is read in if the loop is exited due to the sentinel condition. In this case, the off-by-one error occurs when one-too-many values are processed.

The reason neither algorithm works is becuase the loop bodies differ so radically for the algorithm to process to a sentinel condition versus the algorithm to process a line of text. When values are read in and processed until some sentinel value, the read operation is done just *before* loop exit; if a line of values is to be processed, the read operation is done just *after* loop entry.

The correct algorithm to apply if the two conditions are to be combined is, therefore,

> *IF NOT eoln(AFile) THEN*
>   *read(AFile, AValue)*
> *ELSE*
>   *AValue ← representative sentinel value*
> *WHILE NOT (AValue at sentinel condition) DO*
>   *process AValue*
>   *IF NOT EOLN(AFile) THEN*
>   *read(AFile, AValue)*
>   *ELSE*
>   *AValue ← representative sentinel value*

Blank characters   Extra blank characters inconveniently written into a file can cause plenty of difficulties. Suppose, for example, you have edited a text file where two lines of it look like

```
75    92    57 <eoln>
55    86   92   35   72<eoln>
```

You want the computer to process a line of integers using code such as

```
WHILE NOT eoln(IntsFile) DO
  BEGIN
    read(IntsFile, AnInt);
    {process AnInt}
  END;
readln(IntsFile);
```

Instead of processing two lines with three and four integers on them, the computer will process one line with seven integers on it. When 57 is read in to AnInt, the character following the '7' is a blank, not <*eoln*>. Hence, the loop is not exited, and the value 55 is read in from the next line.

Test Data For Files

When you devise data for on-line testing of source code that processes files, there are certain tests you must include, regardless of the particulars of the program.

Other tests depend upon the particular appearance of the file and on the statements of the program. The hints that follow will help you determine the kind and amount of data that go into a text file for on-line testing.

Blanks of all sorts

We have covered three classic examples of files that can cause problems, namely, files that are empty, files that have blank lines, and files that have extra blank characters. If there is a chance that your program might process files with these problems, make sure the source code handles these possibilities adequately. Also, make sure to test your program with these kinds of "extraordinary" files.

Criticizing the case studies

Programs whose statements assume something about a file's appearance can cause errors. If you refer back to the code for the case studies in Section 9.4, you will find that there are plenty of "nearly correct" data files whose contents can crash the first two programs. A text file used with Case Study 9.1 that is missing a string delimiter for one of the payees will lead to erroneous results and a possible crash. Any program whose statements assume something about the length of a file (number of lines, number of values stored, etc.) can lead to errors. If only 19 lines follow the first line of the data file used in Case Study 9.2, the program will crash when the machine attempts to read values past $<eof>$. Just one less test score on any given line could also lead to major problems.

Unfortunately, if we "user-proof" every program we present, the code would become prohibitively long and obscure. In the interest of "staying on course," we will often ignore this issue of robustness to keep the attention focused on other aspects of the problem. The robustness issue though, should never be forgotten, particularly if you are writing code for a naive end user.

Creating robust files

When a text file is used, it will often have data representing `integer` values, `real` values, and string values mixed together. When you write a program to read data from this kind of file, you expect the file to be written with a certain "format." The programs of the first two case studies in the previous section assumed a given format for the file *as a precondition*. If either actual file's appearance did not match the assumed appearance, the program would not have run properly.

How do you guard against these difficulties? You should ensure that the program to create the data file does it properly. You, therefore, must write the file creation program so that the assumed format is achieved. This appproach is the simplest and best one to follow. If, however, you can make no such assumptions because you did not write the program that created the file, you will need to write code that guards against reading in data that does not follow the expected format.

Using the system editor to create files

If you are creating text files using the system editor, make sure you enter all data *properly*. It is a definite convenience to build data files directly from the system editor. Make sure you do not cause *great inconvenience* when a program runs poorly because data was improperly entered into the text file.

Choosing test data

When writing programs that handle data files, there are certain factors to consider:

I.   *The count of data values*. Test your program using insufficient data and too much data as it applies to the problem statement. If your program reads from a file, test it with an empty file. If your program processes character strings, see how it handles strings with irrelevant or unnecessary characters. How does it work with trailing blanks on a line of text? The first example represents testing with insufficient data (an empty file). The second one represents testing with too much data (trailing blanks).

It is also useful to test the program (or block) with one value, with an average number of values, and, if counters are involved, with exactly one more value than the program or block was designed to handle. You use this latter test to check for off-by-one errors that you may have coded.

If string variables are used, test the program with null strings, strings with one character in them, strings with a typical length, strings with one less than the maximum allowed length, and strings with exactly the allowed length. Also, test your guards using data that represent too long a string.

II. *Subrange values, access values, and access expressions.* Is the program supposed to process only a subrange of values, such as the letters of the alphabet? Test it with data that lies at both extremes of the subrange and also with data outside of it. Should integer values be between 0 and 100? Test the program using these extreme values and some out-of-range values. Also try some "normal" values.

III. *Values undefined by the problem statement.* Suppose you want to write a program that processes only positive numbers. Will it crash when you run it with negative numbers? Or (worse still) will it yield incorrect results? Test the program with at least one negative value, perhaps more. If your program is to take an average of values read in from an input stream, what happens when no values are entered? Suppose your program should count the number of nonblank characters in a file. What kind of a count do you get with files that have sequences of blank characters or blank lines?

Rethinking the "solved" problem

In order to determine relevant test data, you can always go back to the problem statement. Knowledge of precisely what the program should do will often give the terms under which (1) the count of values is insufficient or excessive, (2) the values read in are out of range or not, and (3) those values that cannot be processed. Considering the requirements for the solution will often lead you to determine those exceptional events that can cause problems when the program handles them improperly.

Sane testing

Making up test data for a program can bring out the compulsive worst in any of us. Remember the rule of small samples, particularly when testing programs that process files. Also, do not apply excessive testing when it is not required. If, for example, a procedure initializes five variables using a sequence of assignment operations, you need only check the header to see that it passes all these initial values out of the block. If you must drive it, only one call to the driver is necessary.

It is a good rule of thumb to remember that the larger the program, the more sense it makes to do bottom–up testing, at least on some procedures. You certainly do not want to complete the overall program and discover you have to debug the main block top–down because you have no idea of which procedures are correct. When applying bottom–up testing, moreover, apply the preconditions and postconditions intelligently. Test data applied to one procedure may be irrelevant with respect to another procedure that has a different set of preconditions.

EXERCISES

Test Your
Understanding

1. True or false? A correct and complete assertion about the exit condition from the loop that uses a forced sentinel for <eoln> is as follows: "Either the last *AValue* read in was a sentinel value or the next char value to be read in is <eoln>.

Practice Your
Analysis Skills

2. Henrietta Hackerd believes that the following application will not cause problems as a line processor:

```
IF NOT eoln(InFile) THEN
  REPEAT
    read(InFile, Ch);
    {process Ch}
  UNTIL eoln(InFile)
ELSE
{perhaps display some message about the blank line};
 readln(InFile);
```

Is she correct or incorrect with her code? Explain your answer using assertions.

3. The program DoTests (Case Study 9.2) can easily lead to bad results if a file improperly formatted is used.
   (a) What kind of error will result if there are less lines than TotalStudents would indicate?
   (b) What kind of error will result if there are less test scores on any given line?

4. You want to devise test data on a procedure that fills in an array capable of storing strings up to MaxLength. Also, the array is capable of storing MaxElements (perhaps 1000) strings.
   (a) What are the different kinds of strings you would use for testing the procedure?
   (b) You can also test the filling logic of the procedure by considering the number of elements you wish to put into the array. How many different tests with respect to the number of elements can you devise? (*Note:* We are interested in efficiency. If MaxElements happens to be 1000, for example, you would not try it out with first 0 elements, then 1 element, then 2 elements, etc.)
   (c) Which tests, (a) or (b), would you apply first?

Sharpen Your
Implementation
Skills

5. (a) Rewrite DoTests with code that will guard against the event described in Exercise 3(a). When it is known that there are less students than expected, have the computer display a message indicating how many students are missing with a display such as

    WARNING: THE FILE IS MISSING THE SCORES OF 2 STUDENTS

   (b) If a particular student took less tests than was warranted, DoTests could also crash. Modify the program to guard against this possibility. After the display of those students with complete tests, have the computer print out the names of those students who need to take more tests. (*Hint:* Use an array of strings to store the students' names.)

6. You want to answer Henrietta's argument (Exercise 2) with a WHILE loop that does what her REPEAT.. UNTIL loop does. Fortunately, you can do it with almost identical code using the IF and WHILE statements. Write a fragment logically equivalent to Henrietta's code, but use the reserved words IF and WHILE.

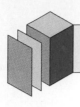

REVIEW AND EXERCISES

In Pascal, the contents of an *external file* are made available to a program by means of a *file variable*. Each dialect has a different way to *open* a *directory file* to the file variable. Once the file has been opened, the code to process the data in the file via a reference to the file variable will be the same, regardless of the Pascal dialect. If a directory file consists of readable text, it can be opened to a file variable of type *text* and processed as a structured variable in a program.

When a file has been prepared for reading, it is said to be in the *read mode*. Regardless of the dialect, a file is prepared for reading by a call to the reset procedure. A file variable in the read mode represents a *window* into the actual file on disk. This window contains the next eligible character to be read in. The two standard boolean functions eoln and eof will return true if the file parameter has the <eoln> *marker* or the <eof> *marker* in its window, respectively. As components are read from the file, the file window is moved forward.

A file that has been prepared for writing, using the call to the standard rewrite procedure, sets up the file variable to act as a *buffer* capable of holding a single line of text. A write operation adds more characters to the buffer; a writeln adds characters to the buffer and then sends the contents to the associated directory file. The buffer is then cleared for the next sequence of calls to the write procedure.

Regardless of whether the file is in the read or write mode, the file variable should always be called by VAR in a formal parameter list. It is possible to use the standard input and output files as actual parameters for file-handling procedures. When a file variable is not a parameter of the call to eoln or eof, the default file parameter is the input file. Moreover, when no file variable is specified as a parameter of the read or readln statement, the file is the input file by default. In like manner, when no file variable is present with a write or a writeln statement, the default file parameter is the output file.

Most dialects of Pascal use the plus sign (+) as a *concatenation operator* for building strings. Virtually all dialects also have the length function, whose argument is a string expression that returns an integer value representing the number of characters in the operand expression. An algorithm to read in values to a string variable from part of a line of text requires that the variable first be initialized to the *null string*. This particular string value represents a string that has a length of 0 and contains no characters. The algorithm also requires a *sentinel* character to *delimit* the text that makes up the string literal.

Certain coding techniques are virtually standard when it comes to processing files. If a file has not been *opened by default*, it must be closed with a call to the close procedure. If this procedure is not called, unpredictable results may occur. In particular, some text that should have been written into the file may be left over in the buffer if the file is not closed.

Remember that the eof and eoln functions *look ahead* to the next character. These functions are best applied on algorithms whose logic satisfies the description "look, then read" rather than on algorithms described by "read, then look." Thus, you should avoid using these two functions to control REPEAT.. UNTIL statements. It is also wise to follow any call to eoln that returns false by a statement that reads in a value from the associated file.

Blank characters, blank lines, and blank files can be particularly troublesome if not handled properly. If there is a possibility that the file being read from has any of these three characteristics, the program must have code that handles this kind of data.

Most programs that read data from text files are planned with the assumption that the text file has a certain appearance. If, for some reason, the file does not have this appearance, the program run will result in errors. It is, therefore, important that the program that created the file be coded in such a way that the assumed appearance is not violated.

There are three considerations regarding the choice of test data for a file-processing program: (1) the number of components that have been read in and processed, (2) the values read in that can represent subrange values and/or access values, and (3) the values read in that cannot be processed. Depending upon the specifications of the problem statement, one or more of these factors will be important for determining test data.

It is important to remember that the input and output files are legitimate actual parameters for file variables. Therefore, they can be used to generate test data for processes that read in values from files. They can likewise be used to display results that will be written into an actual file when the output parameter is replaced by a file variable.

EXERCISES

Short Answers

1. Before an external file can be accessed for either reading or writing, it must be _____ to a _____ _____ .

2. Before a file can be read from, it must be _____ .

3. Before a file can be written into, it must be _____ .

4. True or false? Standard Pascal allows a file to be read from and written into during the same time in the program run.

5. If a program header has file names in it, where else should these identifiers appear in the source code?

6. True or false? Only values for character variables can be read from a text file.

7. What is the cause of the error message, "Get attempted after end-of-file?"

8. Under what circumstances can the same file be written into and then read from within the same program?

9. True or false? The process of bottom–up design entails coding a procedure's statement before coding its header.

10. True or false? A programmer need not be concerned with blank spaces and blank lines in his or her coding because the machine fills in any necessary logic.

11. What is meant by the term "null string?" How is this value used?

12. What is the value of length('Hi there, guy!')?

13. What is the logical appearance of a file variable associated with a file that has just been reset?

14. What is the logical appearance of a file variable associated with a file that has just been rewritten?

15. Suppose the first line of the associated InFile is blank. How will the computer handle the execution of the following procedure?

```
PROCEDURE GetTotal (VAR InFile: text; VAR Total: integer);
   BEGIN
     reset(InFile);
     readln(InFile, Total)
   END;
```

16. In Exercise 15, what appearance of the file could cause a crash at run time? Be specific.

17. Assume the file variable OutFile has been rewritten. Will the following compile? Explain.

```
PROCEDURE PutTotal(OutFile: text; Total: integer);
   BEGIN
      writeln(OutFile, Total)
   END;
```

18. Suppose the text file Ints contains character strings that represent only integer values. The procedure CopyFile, given as Example 9.7, is available. Will the following sequence faithfully display the contents of Ints? Why or why not?

```
reset(Ints);
CopyFile(Ints, output);
```

Easy Projects

19. Use your system editor to create the following file of integer values:

```
75   90   80   60<eoln>
70   80   90   90<eoln>
60   50   70   80<eoln>
70   70   80   80<eoln><eof>
```

Write a program to read and process these four lines of integers, producing the output:

```
Sum #1 =   305
Sum #2 =   330
Sum #3 =   260
Sum #4 =   300
-------------
Total   = 1195
```

Write the program with the foreknowledge that the file contains four lines of four integers. You can name the file anything you wish.

20. Write a program that uses the RNG of Chapter 8 to generate 100 `integer` values that are written in the text file `Integers.dat`. There are to be 10 integers per line. Then write a second program that uses the file contents to do the following:

(a) Find and display the largest, smallest, and `integer` sum of the integers on each line.

(b) Find and display the overall largest, smallest, and `integer` sum of the 100 integers in the file.

A typical display for line 5 might look like:

```
Line 5:   Smallest -- 32 Largest -- 2058 Sum -- 11833
```

The summary display typically should look like

```
File:     Smallest -- 8 Largest -- 2185 Sum -- 107864
```

21. Write a program that counts the number of times a user-specified word, consisting solely of letters, is found in a specified text file. The comparisons between the specified word and each candidate word read in from the file should be case-insensitive. The main block is described by

> *read in file name and open FileVar to file name*
> *read in SearchWord*
> *CountOccurrences(SearchWord, Occurrences, FileVar)*
> *display value of Occurrences*

22. Write a program to create a new file consisting of the contents of an indifinite number of user-specified files. The contents of each specified file are appended to the new file. A typical interaction that copies `NewJersey.dat` into `AllRecs.dat` and then appends the contents of `NewYork.dat` and `Conn.dat` into `AllRecs.dat` looks like

```
Input name of combined file: AllRecs
Input name of file #1: NewJersey
The contents of NewJersey have been copied into AllRecs.
Are you finished? No
Input name of file #2: NewYork
The contents of NewYork have been copied into AllRecs.
Are you finished? No
Input name of file #3: Conn
The contents of Conn have been copied into AllRecs.
Are you finished? Yes
```

You can do this program with just *two* file variables. Test your program by first creating some files with three or four lines in them and using them as the external files.

Medium Projects

23. Write a program `FileStats` that finds and displays the count of the number of words, the number of blank lines, the number of lines, the number of nonblank characters, and the longest word contained in a text file. A "word" begins with a nonblank character and ends with at least one blank character or an end-of-line marker. Your program should account for more than one trailing blank after some words. As an example of what constitutes a word, the following line contains nine words:

```
The quick brown fox    jumps    over the lazy dog.<eoln>
```

You can test the program with any file you wish. You should try testing it with at least one empty file, with a file containing some blank lines, and with a file that contains trailing blanks between words.

24. Write another program to get a different set of statistics from a text file's contents. This program should find and display the following:
    (a) The number of sentences in the file. A sentence is formed when a character string ends with "?", ".", or "!" (Should real numbers present a problem with this definition? What about abbreviations? Is there a way you can handle them? *Suggestion:* Look at the next word.)
    (b) The number of questions asked in the text.
    (c) The number of "nonwords" in the text. A "nonword" consists of a character string with no vowels in it.

25. Write a program CensorFile that will read in the contents of an uncensored file and write them into the censored file. The censored file should contain **** for any four-letter words that were read in. As an example, an uncensored line of text and the censored lines is

<pre>
        The quick brown fox jumps over the lazy dog.
        The quick brown fox jumps **** the **** dog.
</pre>

Difficult Projects

26. Write a program to simulate the billing action at a college bookstore. The store policy is that no customer may purchase any more than five titles at any given time. If between 20 and 50 of a given title are purchased, the customer is allowed a 25% discount; if over 50 of a given book is purchased, the customer is allowed a 50% discount. The title, number of books, and price of each book are read in. Once a sales order is completed, the summary is displayed as a neat table. A typical run is as follows:

<pre>
Title: Advanced Flower Arranging
Amount and Cost: 40 22.50
Title: Varieties of Celery
Amount and Cost: 100   10.00
Title: The Super Soybean
Amount and Cost: 20 55.00
Title: @@@@@   {sentinel string}

AMOUNT   TITLE   PER BOOK   TOTAL COST
  #40   Advanced Flower Arranging   22.50   675.00
  @100   Varieties of Celery   10.00   500.00
   20   The Super Soybean   55.00   825.00

                                             Total Bill $2000.00
</pre>

The field sizes in the summary display should be properly aligned. The characters "#" and "@" preceding the number of books represent the 25% and 50% discounts on each order. Note that the final total is properly aligned with the column costs. (*Hint:* Use parallel array structures to solve the problem.)

27. Write a program to print form letters using the contents of three text files. The first file, Addressee, contains the names and addresses of those people to whom the form letter is being sent, the second file, UserInfo, contains the name and address of the sender,

and the third file contains the body of the letter. The letter is to have the following format:

```
{lines showing addressee's name/address}
                            {lines showing user's name/address}

Dear {addressee's name},
   {letter's body}


                                    Truly yours,
                                    {user's name}
```

Appropriate characters should be used to separate one address from the next in the Addressee file. Write the program so that the letter has a line length of 70, and the left margin is 4 spaces. The user's name/address strings should be set up so that the last character on the longest line is on the seventieth space.

28. Write a program `StoreArrow` that behaves as an interactive graphics package that writes an arrow into a text file specified by the user as per (a) orientation, (b) base size, (c) rectangle dimensions, and (d) message. The main block's code looks like

```
{main block}
BEGIN
  REPEAT
    GetOrientation(Orientation);
    GetBaseSize(BaseSize);
    GetDimensions(Length, Width);
    GetMessage(Message);
    GetIndentation(Spaces);
    IF Possible(BaseSize, Message) THEN
      BEGIN
        ShowArrow(Orientation, Spaces, BaseSize, Length, Width, Message);
        GetReply(Satisfied)
      END
    ELSE
      BEGIN
        writeln('Message too big. You need a bigger arrowhead.');
        Satisfied:= 'N'
      END
  UNTIL Satisfied = 'Y';
  GetFileName(FName);
  StoreArrow(FName, Orientation, Spaces, BaseSize, Length, Width, Message)
END.
```

A typical interaction is as follows:

```
How should the arrow be oriented?  U    {only U or D will work}
How many stars in the base of the arrow?   15
Enter length and width of shaft:   4  9
Enter Message (each word is one line):  THIS SIDE UP
```

```
            *
           ***
          *****
         *******
        ***THIS**
       ****SIDE***
      ******UP*****
     **************
        *********
        *********
        *********
        *********
```
Are you satised?   Y
Enter file name the arrow should be printed in: Caution.dat

Test some impossible arrows for this program (*Example:* With a base size of 6, the message "HANDLE" "WITH" "CARE" cannot be output to insufficient size for "HANDLE".)

29. Write a program, CheckBlockDocs, to have the computer check your source code headers for documentation. The program should search for the three reserved words PROGRAM, PROCEDURE, and FUNCTION, and then determine whether there is a comment immediately following the header. The precondition for this program to work is that the source code file will compile properly and that the comment begins on the next line of text after the header. Once the file is completely read, the program should display the names of all those processes that require documentation. (*Hint*: Use the syntax rules of Pascal to determine the end of a header. Once the header is ended, the next nonblank character should be "{" if the PROGRAM, PROCEDURE, or FUNCTION was properly documented.

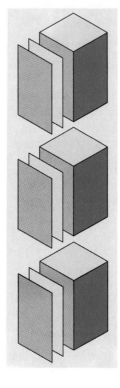

C H A P T E R

MORE ONE-DIMENSIONAL ARRAYS

OBJECTIVES

After reading and studying the material in the present chapter, you should be able to

- Write programs with arrays whose elements are accessed using noninteger expressions

- Analyze programs using arrays whose elements are accessed using noninteger expressions

- Discuss the advantages of using a sorted array in a problem

- Recognize and use the bubble sort, insertion sort, and selection sort algorithms

- Describe the characteristics of a search algorithm

- Use the linear search and binary search algorithms in programs

- Explain what is meant by an algorithm's "big-Oh" and apply elementary big-Oh analysis on a given algorithm

IN THIS CHAPTER, you will learn additional ways to use arrays in implementing solutions. The first section shows how to use any ordinal type as the host subrange for elemental access. This feature of Pascal allows you to solve certain classes of problems, such as counting classifiable events or building look-up tables, quite easily.

You will also learn some sorting and searching algorithms. A sorted array is arranged such that the elements and the index values of an array are in order from lowest to highest. A search through an array finds the index value of a given element whose value is being sought.

We will use the searching and sorting algorithms as the basis for presenting the topic of algorithm efficiency, known as "big-Oh." This software engineering concept gives you a criterion by which you can compare two algorithms that solve the same problem using different logic.

10.1   Arrays with Host Subranges Other than Integer

In Chapter 7 material, we used only integer subranges to access array elements. Pascal, however, allows any ordinal type to be a subrange that accesses the elements of an array. You can take advantage of this fact to implement array structures that solve problems clearly and ingeniously. The case studies of this section show you two such applications.

An array of counters

You are already familiar with the kind of problem that uses a counting algorithm for its solution. You initialize an event-counting variable to 0, then increment it by 1 each time an event occurs. Now let us suppose you require an algorithm to count the occurrences of many similar, yet distinctly different, events.

You can solve this problem by implementing an array of counters, where each element of the array counts a specific event. All elements are set to 0 before the counting process starts. When a particular countable event occurs, the proper array element is then incremented by 1. We apply this implementation strategy for the case study that follows.

CASE STUDY 10.1

The problem statement

Let us write a program that counts the number of times each letter of the alphabet is read in from a text file. Part of a typical program run might look like

```
This program counts the number of times each letter occurred in the
file you specify.  Input file name:  FatherWilliam.dat

The letter occurrences in the file FatherWilliam.dat were:
```

```
A's -- 14
B's -- 1
. . . . . . . .
Y's -- 10
Z's -- 0
```

The contents of the text file FatherWilliam.dat, as used in the program run looks like

```
"You are old, Father William," the young man said, <eoln>
"And your hair has become very white.<eoln>
And yet you incessantly stand on your head<eoln>
Do you think at your age this is right?"<eoln><eof>
```

A solution variable We will use an array variable LetterCount to count the occurrences of each letter read in from the text file. The elements of the array are of type integer, and the index subrange is 'a'..'z'. The index value for each element, a lowercase letter, represents the letter whose occurrence count is being accumulated in the particular array element.

Figures 10.1 and 10.2 show the precondition, postcondition values for each of the elements of the array LetterCount before and after the characters of the specified file are read in. The array LetterCount is then envisioned as an array of counters where each element accumulates a count of the number of times the corresponding letter was read in from the file.

Implementing the array We will assume the ASCII collating sequence. The array of counters can then be set up using the following source code:

```
TYPE
  CounterArray = ARRAY ['a'..'z'] OF integer;
VAR
  LetterCount:  {element -- number of times referenced letter occurred}
            CounterArray;
```

Efficiency considerations We are using a lowercase subrange rather than an uppercase subrange as a matter of efficiency. The problem statement requires that the program be case-insensitive with respect to the letters read in. We do, however, expect more lowercase letters to occur in the text. When an uppercase letter occurs, in order for it to be counted, its value must be converted to its lowercase equivalent. If we choose to use 'A'..'Z' as the access subrange, far more conversions from lowercase to uppercase values are necessary.

The main block description We can describe the main block sequence with the pseudocode

> *LinkReadIn(FileName, AFile)*
> *reset(AFile)*
> *ZeroCounters(LetterCount)*
> *CountOccurrences(AFile, LetterCount)*
> *close(AFile)*
> *ShowOccurrences(FileName, LetterCount)*

LetterCount				LetterCount		
['a']	0			['a']	14	
['b']	0			['b']	1	
['c']	0			['c']	2	
['d']	0			['d']	7	
['e']	0			['e']	11	
['f ']	0			['f ']	1	
['g']	0			['g']	3	
['h']	0			['h']	9	
['i']	0			['i']	10	
['j']	0			['j']	0	
['k']	0			['k']	1	
['l']	0			['l']	4	
['m']	0			['m']	3	
['n']	0			['n']	9	
['o']	0			['o']	11	
['p']	0			['p']	0	
['q']	0			['q']	0	
['r']	0			['r']	8	
['s']	0			['s']	7	
['t']	0			['t']	10	
['u']	0			['u']	7	
['v']	0			['v']	1	
['w']	0			['w']	2	
['x']	0			['x']	0	
['y']	0			['y']	10	
['z']	0			['z']	0	

FIGURE 10.1 The initialized counting array.

FIGURE 10.2 The counting array after counting letter occurrences.

Assertion testing

LinkReadIn opens the directory file represented by the value of File-Name to the file variable AFile. The action of ZeroCounters sets the 26 elements of LetterCount to 0, indicating that so far no letters were read from the file. The postcondition returned by CountOccurrences is that the value of any given element of LetterCount represents the number of times the corresponding letter was read in from the file. When the file name and the values of the 26 elements of LetterCount are displayed by the action of ShowOccurrences, the problem is solved.

Source code

Most of the source code for the program is shown below. We still must develop the code for the procedure CountOccurrences.

```
PROGRAM CountLetters(input, output, AFile);
  {This program counts and displays the total number of times  each
  letter of the alphabet occurred in a file whose directory name was
  read in and opened to AFile.}
  TYPE
```

```
  CounterArray = ARRAY ['a'..'z'] OF integer;
  NameString = {INSERT DEFINITION FOR STRING OF UP TO 20 CHARS HERE};
VAR
  AFile: text;        {file variable from which letters are counted}
  LetterCount: CounterArray;  {stores occurrences for each letter}
  FileName: NameString;      {represents name of the directory file}
{*                                                                  *}
PROCEDURE LinkReadIn (VAR FileName: NameString; VAR AFile: text);
  BEGIN  {use your system's open procedure}  END;
{*                                                                  *}
PROCEDURE ZeroCounters (VAR LetterCount: CounterArray);
  {out:  All elements of LetterCount are set to 0}
  VAR
    OneLetter: 'a'..'z';   {each element in turn is zeroed}
  BEGIN
    FOR OneLetter:= 'a' TO 'z' DO
      LetterCount[OneLetter]:= 0
  END;
{*                                                                  *}
PROCEDURE CountOccurrences(VAR LetterCount: CounterArray;
                                        VAR AFile:text);
  {in: all elements of LetterCount are 0, AFile was reset
   out: values of LetterCount represent number of occurrences for
        each letter read in from AFile; eof(AFile) is true}
  VAR
    Ch: char;      {a character read in from AFile}
  BEGIN  {statements}  END;
{*                                                                  *}
PROCEDURE ShowOccurrences(FileName: NameString;
                           LetterCount: CounterArray);
  {Displays the directory name and number of occurrences for each of
   the letters as read in from the named directory file.}
  VAR
    OneLetter: 'a'..'z'; {access variable to each of counter elements}
    DisplayLetter: 'A'..'Z';       {used to display uppercase letters}
    Offset: integer;       {used to form expression for DisplayLetter}
  BEGIN
    Offset:= ord('A') - ord('a');
    write('The letter occurrences in the file ');
    writeln(FileName, ' were:  ');
    writeln;
    FOR OneLetter:= 'a' TO 'z' DO
      BEGIN
        DisplayLetter:= chr(ord(OneLetter) + Offset);   {change to uc}
        write(' ':24,DisplayLetter,'''s -- ');
        writeln(LetterCount[OneLetter]:1)
      END
```

```
      END;
   {*                                                              *}
   BEGIN
      LinkReadIn(FileName, AFile);
      reset(AFile);
      ZeroCounters(LetterCount);
      CountOccurrences(LetterCount, AFile);
      close(AFile);
      ShowOccurrences(FileName, LetterCount)
   END.
```

Developing the statement for Count Occurrences

When control passes from CounterOccurrences, all characters in AFile with the exception of the <eof> marker will have been processed. It is optional whether or not to read in or skip <eoln> because the solution only requires character-by-character processing. As a matter of simplicity, we will choose to read in all char values except <eof>. Therefore, no check for the *eoln* condition is necessary.

The loop invariant we require is that the value taken on by each element of LetterCount represents the number of times each letter was read from AFile, up to and including the last candidate value read in. Thus each loop pass must update or attempt to update one of the letter counters. We therefore obtain the following pseudocode description for the block statement.

> *WHILE NOT eof(AFile) DO*
> *read(AFile, Ch)*
> *IF Ch is a letter THEN*
> *add 1 to proper element of LetterCount*

After each loop pass, we can assert that the value taken on by each element LetterCount represents the number of times each letter occurred. When the loop is exited, all values except the final <eof> character will have been read in. Hence, this sequence is correct.

Further refinements

Ch is a letter codes to Ch IN ['A'..'Z', 'a'..'z'] where we must "shape" Ch's value if it lies in the subrange 'A'..'Z'. We can solve both problems by applying a sequence whose pseudocode is

> *IF Ch IN ['A'..'Z'] THEN*
> *convert Ch to lowercase*
> *IF Ch IN ['a'..'z'] THEN*
> *Letters[Ch] ← Letters [Ch] + 1*

The assertion we can make after the first decision is that if Ch was read in as a letter of the alphabet, it is now lowercase. After the second decision we can assert that if Ch is a letter, the corresponding letter counter, LetterCount[Ch], is incremented by 1. Hence the sequence is correct.

Source code

The code for the procedure CountOccurrences, given the pseudocode descriptions, is as follows:

```
PROCEDURE CountOccurrences (VAR LetterCount: CounterArray; VAR AFile: text);
  {documentation}
  VAR
    Offset:  integer:   {used to change lower case to upper case letter}
    Ch:  char;          {last character read in from AFile}
  BEGIN
    Offset:= ord('a') - ord('A');
    WHILE NOT eof(AFile) DO
      BEGIN
        read(AFile,Ch);
        IF Ch IN ['A'..'Z'] THEN           {change u.c. to l.c.}
          Ch:= chr( ord(Ch) + Offset );
        IF Ch IN ['a'..'z'] THEN             {update count of letter}
          LetterCount[Ch]:= LetterCount[Ch]  + 1
      END
END;  ◆
```

Enumerated types as access subranges

An enumerated type is an ordinal data type. Therefore, Pascal will let you use two values from an enumerated type to form an access subrange to the elements of an array. In the next case study, we implement an array that uses an enumerated type as the host type for an access subrange. The array itself represents a conversion array used to change dollars into an equivalent monetary amount in a foreign currency.

CASE STUDY 10.2

The problem statement

Let us simulate the day's activity at a foreign exchange bank capable of exchanging money in the following currencies: U.S. dollar, Australian dollar, British pound, Canadian dollar, Deutsch mark, Swiss franc, and Japanese yen. The simulation is carried out as follows:

The daily exchange rate in terms of U.S. dollars is read in for each currency at the start of the day. Then, during the rest of the day, customers bring in currency from one country to be exchanged for an equivalent amount of another country's currency. Customers keep coming until the bank closes for the day.

A typical run of part of the program might look like:

```
Good morning!  Enter the exchange rates for the day:
Dollars to Australian dollars:  1.3249
Dollars to British Pounds:  0.6196
Dollars to Canadian Dollars:  1.1525
Dollars to German Marks:  1.6113
Dollars to Swiss Francs:  1.3645
Dollars to Japanese Yen:  141.85
Thank you!  Have a nice day!
```

```
Are we finished for the day?  N        {is it the end of the day?}
Currency to be converted:  Japanese Yen
Currency to convert to:  British Pound
Conversion is from Japanese Yen to British Pounds.
Input amount: 10000
10000.00 Japanese Yen converts to 43.75 British Pounds.
.........
Are we finished for the day? Y
```

An array implementation We can use an array like the one shown in Figure 10.3 to store currency exchange rate information. The values stored represent the rate of exchange of one U.S. Dollar to any one of the other currencies. The code for this implementation is given below.

```
TYPE
   MoneyType = (NilMoney, USDollar, AustralianDollar, BritishPound,
                CanadianDollar, GermanMark, SwissFranc, JapaneseYen);
   ConversionArray = ARRAY[USDollar..JapaneseYen] OF real;
VAR
     DollarsTo: ConversionArray;    {dollar exchange rates for the day}
```

DollarsTo [USDollar]	1.000
[AustralianDollar]	1.3249
[BritishPound]	0.6196
[CanadianDollar]	1.1525
[GermanMark]	1.6113
[SwissFranc]	1.3645
[JapaneseYen]	141.8500

FIGURE 10.3 An array for money conversion.

Main block sequence We can describe the main block statement by the pseudocode

keyin values for DollarsTo
REPEAT
  keyin InCurrency, OutCurrency
  display InCurrency, OutCurrency
  keyin InAmount
  OutAmount ← In Amount*DollarsTo[OutCurrency]/DollarsTo[InCurrency]
  displayInCurrency, InAmount, OutCurrency, OutAmount
  keyin Reply
UNTIL Reply indicates finished processing

We are using REPEAT..UNTIL because we expect at least one exchange to be made. The variable InCurrency is of type MoneyType and its value represents the particular currency to be exchanged. The value of OutCurrency, also of type MoneyType, represents the name of the currency InCurrency will be converted to. The value of InAmount represents the InCurrency amount of money to be exchanged. The value of OutAmount represents the equivalent amount of money in OutCurrency.

Main block procedures

When we apply procedural abstraction to the actions in the main block, we get the refined pseudocode description

> *GetRates(DollarsTo)*
> *REPEAT*
>   *GetCurrencies(InCurrency, OutCurrency)*
>   *keyin InAmount*
>   *OutAmount ← InAmount*DollarsTo[OutCurrency]/DollarsTo[InCurrency]*
>   *DisplayConversionInfo(InCurrency, OutCurrency, InAmount, OutAmount)*
>   *keyin Reply*
> *UNTIL Reply IN ['Y', 'y']*

Values are read into the elements of DollarsTo from the call to GetRates. Values are read into the variables InCurrency and OutCurrency by the action of the statements in GetCurrencies. All information about the exchange is shown by the sequence of DisplayConversionInfo.

Source code

Part of the coded solution to the problem is given as the program SimulateExchangeBank. We plan to develop all the procedures for this program. The coded statement for the procedure DisplayConversionInfo is trivial, so we are presenting it as a completely coded procedure without discussing its development. Note that we expect ShowCurrency to be called from more than one procedure. Hence, we have put its stub before the stub for all other procedures.

```
PROGRAM SimulateExchangeBank(input, output);
   {This program simulates the day's activity at a foreign exchange
   bank.  The conversion rates from dollars into 6 different foreign
   currencies are first read in. Then exchanges are made in these
   currencies until the bank's business is done for the day.}
   TYPE
      MoneyType = (NilMoney, USDollar, AustralianDollar, BritishPound,
                   CanadianDollar, GermanMark, SwissFranc, JapaneseYen);
      ConversionArray = ARRAY[USDollar..JapaneseYen] OF real;
   VAR
      DollarsTo:     {dollar exchange rates for the day}
                     ConversionArray;
      InCurrency,    {currency type to be changed from, as read in}
      OutCurrency:   {currency type to be changed into, as read in}
                     MoneyType;
      InAmount,      {amount of InCurrency money to be converted}
```

```
      OutAmount:     {amount InCurrency money is worth in OutCurrency}
                     real;
      Reply: char; {holds reply to question "Are we finished?"}
{*                                                                           *}
PROCEDURE ShowCurrency(ACurrency: MoneyType);
  {out: displays string indicating value of ACurrency}
  BEGIN        END;
{*                                                                           *}
PROCEDURE GetRates(VAR DollarsTo: ConversionArray);
    {out: elements of DollarsTo represents day's dollar exchange rates}
  BEGIN        END;
{*                                                                           *}
PROCEDURE GetCurrencies(VAR InCurrency, OutCurrency: MoneyType);
    {out: values are read in from keyboard to InCurrency and OutCurrency}
  BEGIN        END;
{*                                                                           *}
PROCEDURE DisplayConversionInfo(InCurrency, OutCurrency: MoneyType;
                                          InAmount, OutAmount: real);
    {out: displays conversion information, using all parameters in list}
  BEGIN
    write(InAmount:4:2, ' ');
    ShowCurrency(InCurrency);
    write(' converts to ');
    write(OutAmount:4:2, ' ');
    ShowCurrency(OutCurrency);
    writeln
  END;
{*                                                                           *}
BEGIN
  GetRates(DollarsTo);
  REPEAT
    GetCurrencies(InCurrency, OutCurrency);
    write('Input amount: ');
    readln(InAmount);
    OutAmount =InAmount*DollarsTo[OutCurrency]/DollarsTo[InCurrency];
    DisplayConversionInfo(InCurrency, OutCurrency, InAmount, OutAmount);
    write('Are we finished for the day? ');
    readln(Reply)
  UNTIL Reply IN ['Y', 'y']
END.
```

Coding
GetRates

The procedure GetRates simply assigns values to the elements of DollarsTo. We can use a FOR loop to read in values to the elements, where the loop
control variable is of type MoneyType. The pseudocode description to assign values to the elements of DollarsTo is then

DollarsTo[USDollar] ← 1.000
FOR Currency ← AustralianDollar TO JapaneseYen DO
  ShowCurrency(Currency)   {prompt for user to key in correct rate}
  readln(DollarsTo[Currency])

Currency is a local variable of type MoneyType. From the description, we obtain the source code for GetRates as follows:

```
PROCEDURE GetRates(VAR DollarsTo: ConversionArray);
  {documentation}
  VAR
    Currency: MoneyType;   {access variable to elements of DollarsTo}
  BEGIN
    DollarsTo[USDollar]:= 1.0000;
    writeln('Good morning!  Enter the exchange rates for the day:  ');
    FOR Currency:= AustralianDollar TO JapaneseYen DO
      BEGIN
        write('DollarsTo: '); ShowCurrency(Currency);
        write(':    ');
        readln(DollarsTo[Currency])
      END;
    writeln('Thank you!  Have a nice day!')
  END;
```

Developing Get-Currencies   The procedure GetCurrencies, which returns values to InCurrency and OutCurrency, requires user input. It is possible to read in an improper entry, so a guard loop is required to ensure that the values read in correctly represent the two currencies. We can then describe the block's sequence as follows:

REPEAT
  keyin CurrencyCh
UNTIL Valid(CurrencyCh)
InCurrency ← Denomination(CurrencyCh)
REPEAT
  keyin CurrencyCh
UNTIL Valid(CurrencyCh)
OutCurrency ← Denomination(CurrencyCh)
display string values for currencies

The variable CurrencyCh is a local variable of type char. It must take on one of the following values: 'U', 'A', 'B', 'C', 'D', 'S', or 'J'. The boolean function Valid returns true if one of these values is entered. The function Denomination then uses this char value to return a value of type MoneyType. This value is assigned either to InCurrency or OutCurrency.

Source code   The source code for the procedure GetCurrencies, including the auxiliary functions is then coded as shown.

```
{*                                                                    *}
FUNCTION Valid(CurrencyCh: char): boolean;
  {returns true if character entered represents first letter of one of
  the currencies}
  BEGIN
    Valid:= CurrencyCh IN ['U', 'A', 'B', 'C', 'D', 'S', 'J']
  END;
{+                                                                    +}
FUNCTION Denomination(CurrencyCh: char): MoneyType;
  {returns a valid money type as represented by value ofCurrencyCh}
  BEGIN
    CASE CurrencyCh OF
      'U': Denomination:= USDollar;
      'A': Denomination:= AustralianDollar;
      'B': Denomination:= BritishPound;
      'C': Denomination:= CanadianDollar;
      'D': Denomination:= DeutschMark;
      'S': Denomination:= SwissFranc;
      'J': Denomination:= JapaneseYen
    END    {CASE}
  END;
{+                                                                    +}
PROCEDURE GetCurrencies(VAR InCurrency, OutCurrency: MoneyType);
  {documentation}
  VAR
    CurrencyCh: char;   {read in; represents a given type of currency}
  BEGIN
    REPEAT
      write('Currency to be converted:    ');
      readln(CurrencyCh)
    UNTIL Valid(CurrencyCh);
    InCurrency:= Demomination(CurrencyCh);
    REPEAT
      write('Currency to convert to:    ');
      readln(CurrencyCh)
    UNTIL Valid(CurrencyCh);
    OutCurrency:= Denomination(CurrencyCh);
    write('Conversion is from ');
    ShowCurrency(InCurrency);
    write(' to ');
    ShowCurrency(OutCurrency);
    writeln('.')
  END;
{*                                                                    *}
```

EXERCISES

Test Your
Understanding

1. Will the program CountLetters work for a system that uses EBCDIC? Explain.

2. Is it possible to write the program SimulateExchangeBank without using an array? How many variables would be required? Can the exchange rates be read in with a FOR loop in this case?

Practice Your
Analysis Skills

3. In the program SimulateExchangeBank, what would happen if the user entered in the string 'japanese yen' when prompted for a currency to exchange?

4. Consider the following:

```
TYPE
    DayType = (NilDay, Sun, Mon, Tue, Wed, Thu, Fri, Sat);
    JobType = (None, Shipping, Receiving, Inventories, Maintenance);
    WeeksWork = ARRAY[Sun..Sat] OF JobType;
VAR
    AWeek: WeeksWork;
```

   (a) How many elements will AWeek have?
   (b) What does the variable AWeek represent?
   (c) What will an element of AWeek represent?

5. Consider the following:

```
TYPE
    RangeArray = ARRAY[0..10] OF integer;
VAR
    Distribution: RangeArray;
    AScore,
    AValue: integer;

{part of a coded sequence:}
AValue:= AScore DIV 10;
Distribution[AValue]:= Distribution[AValue] + 1;
{end sequence}
```

   (a) Assume that the coded sequence is part of a program that uses the three variables. Redefine the two scalar variables AScore and AValue so that they are subrange types whose values are consistent with the intended semantics of the variable Distribution.
   (b) Given the coded sequence, briefly describe what you feel is the purpose served by each of these variables.

Sharpen Your
Implementation
Skills

6. Suppose we had decided to define CounterType in the program CountLetters as

```
TYPE
    CounterType = ARRAY['A'..'Z'] OF integer;
```

   Indicate any changes that would have to be made in the code of the program.

7. Write the code for the procedure ShowCurrency. It should display two words such as "Australian dollar" or "British pound."

8. Rewrite the main block statement for the program `SimulateExchangeBank` using a WHILE loop instead of a REPEAT..UNTIL loop.

9. We want to write a program where the machine counts the occurrences for both upper-case letters and for lowercase letters as found in a text file. Define and declare the objects for this program.

10. Write a procedure to display the values stored in the variable AWeek. (You will need to write an auxiliary procedure to display string values for the enumerated types.)

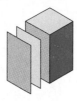

10.2   The Linear Search Algorithm

Searching is a common problem that is applied on array variables. An array search algorithm requires that some *SearchValue*, a possible value one of the array elements can take on, be specified. The array's elements are examined systematically in an attempt to find an *Index* value such that the condition *AnArray[Index]* = *SearchValue* is *true*. Either this event will occur or there will be no more candidate elements left to examine. In this section, we discuss the characteristics of all array search algorithms and derive the code for two forms of the linear search algorithm.

Describing the search algorithm   The search algorithm we are going to describe is implemented using a loop. Each loop pass represents an attempt to find the match between an array element's value and the SearchValue. If a match is found, the search is completed; if not, a new element is tried. If and when all possible elements have been tried and no match found, the search is completed without success.

The pseudocode presentation of this description is given as Algorithm 10.1.

Algorithm 10.1

> {*The array search algorithm:*}
> *Index ← initial probe value*
> *Found ← false*
> *WHILE NOT finished AND NOT Found DO*
>   *IF TheArray[Index] = SearchValue THEN*
>   *Found ← true*
>   *ELSE*
>   *Index ← next probe value, using old Index value*
> *IF NOT Found THEN*
>   *Index ← 0*
> {*end algorithm*}

Requirements of the algorithm   This pseudocode description can be applied as a starting point for deriving the source code for a search through an array. The comparison between an element of *TheArray* and *SearchValue* is known as a *probe*. Any search algorithm derived from this pseudocode description should have a systematic way to determine the initial probe value and all subsequent probe values.

Note that there are two loop control conditions: *finished* and *Found*. The probe values must be chosen in such a way that the *finished* condition becomes *true* if none of the elements is equal to *SearchValue*. If this property is not fulfilled, the search algorithm is invalid, for the exit condition will never be achieved. The assertion we can make at loop exit is then, "Either (1) the search is finished and no element of *TheArray* is equal to *SearchValue* or (2) the search was successful and the value of *TheArray[Index]* is equal to *SearchValue*."

The loop body itself should reduce the number of candidate elements if an unsuccessful probe occurs. Certainly, at the very least, an unsuccessful probe value for a given loop pass represents an element that can be eliminated. All previous probe values used in previous loop passes should have also been eliminated from the list of candidates. If we find a systematic way to eliminate candidate elements, we can state the loop invariant for the search as, "Either the *Index* value with a match has been found or the number of candidates has been reduced by (..something..)." The wording of "something" depends upon the way we code the expression that represents the next probe value.

The linear search algorithm

An obvious approach that solves the search problem is to develop an algorithm that starts at either the highest or lowest element in the candidate subrange of values as the initial probe. Each loop pass will eliminate exactly one candidate. The next probe is then either the next lower or next higher *Index* value. Thus, the candidates are eliminated one by one until either a match is found or all candidates are exhausted. If we start with the highest candidate element and work our way down to the Index value 0, our refinement of Algorithm 10.1 becomes Algorithm 10.2, one form of the linear search algorithm.

Algorithm 10.2

{*Linear search algorithm with boolean flag variable:*}
Index ← *TotalElements*
Found ← *false*
WHILE NOT (Index = 0) AND NOT Found DO
    IF (TheArray[Index] = *SearchValue) THEN*
        Found ← *true*
    ELSE
        Index ← *Index* − *1*
{*end algorithm*}

By starting out with the highest element as the initial candidate and working our way down, we do not need to code a postloop decision statement if *SearchValue* is not found as an element of *TheArray*. The condition *Index = 0* represents the *finished* condition, and it also represents the conventional value to indicate a failed search.

Loop invariants

One invariant for this particular form of the search algorithm is, "The elements in the subrange expression *Index + 1..TotalElements* do not contain *Search-*

Value, but *TheArray[Index]* might." At loop exit, if *Index* is *0*, clearly none of the elements contains *SearchValue*. If the value is not *0*, the event that *Found* is *true* causes the loop exit. The *boolean* variable *Found* is set to this value due to the fact that the the *boolean* expression *TheArray[Index]* = *SearchValue* became *true* with the last probe. Hence the value of *Index* represents the index value of the element whose value matches *SearchValue*.

Note that another invariant for this algorithm is, "The candidate subrange of elements that can still contain *SearchValue* is *1..Index*." This invariant says something about the remaining candidate subrange where a match could be found. An invariant that says something about the implied process of elimination is stated by, "Either an element equal to *SearchValue* value has been found or the number of candidates has been reduced by 1." The fact that exactly one candidate is eliminated per loop pass makes this a *linear search algorithm*.

> **Linear search algorithm:** any search algorithm that eliminates exactly one candidate from the search with each probe.

Example Problem 10.1

The problem statement

Let us take the structured variable Names of type NamesArray, as used in Case Study 7.1, and write a function NameIndex to return the index value of the array element in Names that matches the value of SearchName, a variable of type NameString. We can use this function in the context of a source code sequence such as

```
Index:= NameIndex(Name, Enrollment, SearchName);
IF Index <> 0 THEN
  BEGIN
    write(SearchName, ' got ',Result[Index]:1);
    writeln(' correct answers on the quiz.')
  END
ELSE
  writeln(SearchName,' did not take the quiz.');
```

Source code

The source code for the function, using Algorithm 10.2, is given as

```
FUNCTION NameIndex(VAR Names: NamesArray; Enrollment: integer;
                              SearchName: NameString): integer;
  {in: Names[1]..Names[Enrollment] have been assigned values
   in: SearchName has been assigned a value
  out: the value returned to NameIndex is such that Names[NameIndex]
       is equal to SearchName; if 0 is returned, no match was found}
  VAR
    Probe: integer;    {candidate value for NameIndex}
    Found: boolean;    {variable to flag found condition}
  BEGIN
    Probe:= Enrollment;
```

```
      WHILE NOT(Probe = 0)  AND NOT Found DO
         IF Names[Probe] = SearchName THEN
            Found:= true
         ELSE
            Probe:= Probe-1;
      NameIndex:= Probe
   END;
```

Note that we passed in the reference structure Names using a VAR call for the sake of efficiency. ◆

Example Problem 10.2

The problem statement

If we look at the solution to Example Problem 10.1, we see that a failed search will always return the value 0. No probe value below 0 will be tried. Given this information, we might find a clever way to eliminate the boolean variable and still have a clear algorithm. We can do so by defining the access subrange for Names as 0..MaxEnroll. The array element Names[0] can then be used as a sentinel element.

> **Sentinel element:** an array element whose value, when accessed, flags a sentinel condition.

The algorithm description

Before the search loop is entered, the value of Names[0] is set to Search-Name. The initial probe is still with Names[Enrollment], but now the loop control expression is described by *Names[Probe] <> SearchName*. If Probe is equal to 0 when the match occurs, the loop will be exited where all candidates in the subrange *1..Enrollment* have been tried. Hence, the match with the sentinel element indicates a failed search.

Source code

The source code solution to this problem is given as the function NameIndex. Note how much simpler it is when compared with the previous implement of the function NameIndex, the solution to Example Problem 10.1. This solution is also more efficient because the computer evaluates less expressions per loop pass.

```
FUNCTION NameIndex(VAR Names: NamesArray; Enrollment: integer;
                             SearchName: NameString): integer;
   {the same function as before, but this time with Names [0] as a
   sentinal element}
   VAR
      Probe: integer;    {candidate value for NameIndex}
   BEGIN
      Names[0]:= SearchName;
      Probe:= Enrollment;
      WHILE Names[Probe] <> SearchName DO
         Probe:= Probe-1;
      Names[0]:= ''       {set sentinel element back to null string}
      NameIndex:= Probe
   END;
```

Note how we deal with the sentinel element. Only those elements in the sub-range 1..Enrollment are assumed to have meaning outside the block. Hence, we are assuming a precondition that Names[0] is passed into the function as a null string. We therefore will pass it out of the block with the same value, thus eliminating the remote possibility of coding a side effect. The element Names[0] is changed over the statement part of the function but then changed back to its original value before the last statement of the function. ◆

Properties of all array search algorithms

We will develop some more array search algorithms, starting with Algorithm 10.1 as our first draft. Regardless of the kind of search algorithm you choose to use or develop, it should have the following properties: (1) Each loop starts with an implied candidate subrange of index values. This precondition implies that the element must lie within the candidate subrange. (2) Each loop pass either reduces the candidate subrange or results in a successful probe. (3) Given a failed probe, the new candidate subrange will always be expressed as some function of the index value of the probe. (4) The next probe should be a function of the index value of the previous probe.

EXERCISES

Test Your Understanding

1. Write the boolean expression for loop control of the generic search algorithm without using the word *AND*.

2. What is meant by the term "sentinel element?"

3. Explain how you would use the function NameIndex to return the index value(s) of all array elements containing the name 'Smith'. Note that you cannot modify the function but that you can write code to call it more than once.

Sharpen Your Implementation Skills

4. Suppose we have the following structure:

```
TYPE
   IntsArray = ARRAY[1..100] OF integer;
VAR
   Ints: IntsArray;
```

Assume there are no duplicate elements in the array. Write a linear search function to return the index value of the array element in Ints equal to the search value of Int. Start the search with the first probe as the hundredth element. You can assume all 100 elements have been assigned values.

5. Write the linear search function on the structure of Exercise 4 such that the first probe is on element 1 rather than on element 100.

6. You can just as easily apply the linear search algorithm to seek out a condition rather than a given value. Write the function AllPositive, which returns true if all the elements of Ints are positive. (*Hint:* Your code should search for a nonpositive element. If the search fails, the value returned to AllPositive is true.)

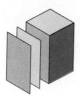

10.3 Sorting

A sorted array has the elements arranged such that one of the following two relationships holds for all assigned array elements: *AnArray[Index]* <= *AnArray [Index + 1]* or *AnArray[Index]* >= *AnArray[Index + 1]*. In the first case, the elements are sorted in *ascending order*, and in the second case, they are sorted in *descending order*. Sorted arrays are quite useful, as you will see, for many search problems. In this section, we present three sorting algorithms.

Background Information

Before we look at the algorithms, let us first choose a structure that we can use to demonstrate the properties of each algorithm. We will also specify the problem by coding a procedure header that returns a sorted array. We also present the initial draft for the first two algorithms, namely the bubble sort algorithm and the selection sort algorithm.

The structure to sort   The algorithms we will discuss are applicable to any kind of an array whose elements can be ordered. The number of elements for any of the three algorithms to work, moreover, is limited only by the storage capabilities of the computer. Nevertheless, for the sake of simplicity, let us pose a sorting problem using a list of only five integer elements that make up the array variable *Ints*. We have chosen such a small structure to make it easier for us to desk trace the source code for each of the three algorithms. Thus, we are applying the rule of small samples.

Implementing the structure   The structure is implemented using the code

```
CONST
   LastElement = 5;
TYPE
   IntArray = ARRAY[1..LastElement] OF integer;
VAR
   Ints: IntArray;
```

Specifying the problem   Each of the procedures we are going to develop has the same header. The stub for the procedures is coded as

```
PROCEDURE SortIt(VAR Ints: IntArray);
   {in: the elements of Ints are assigned but in no particular order
   out: the elements of Ints are in ascending order}
   BEGIN   END;
```

We will derive three different statements for SortIt, each of which will return the desired postcondition of a sorted list.

A generalized sorting algorithm

Perhaps the simplest way to sort an array would be to use the following approach:

> FOR Sorted ← 1 TO LastElement-1 DO
> exchange elements in the subrange Sorted..LastElement

The loop invariant we want to achieve can be stated as, "The elements in the subrange *1..Sorted + 1* are in order." We are free to "assume" that before the loop is entered, *Sorted* is equal to 0, so, initially, the invariant holds with the tautology that the elements in the subrange *1..1* are sorted. We will use this approach when we implement the statement part of the bubble sort and selection sort algorithms.

The algorithm's mechanism

How does the invariant apply to each loop pass? If the elements in the subrange *1..Sorted* are in their final positions, it means that the elements in the remaining subrange *Sorted + 1..LastElement* are all greater than *Ints[Sorted]*. Therefore the subrange over which all elements are sorted is *1..Sorted + 1* rather than *1..Sorted*. This invariant suggests Figure 10.4 where the array is divided into a sorted part that grows and an unsorted part that diminishes in size with each loop pass.

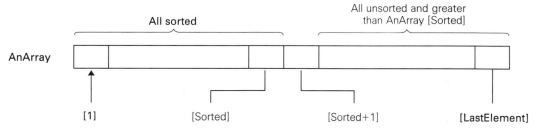

FIGURE 10.4 The invariant for some sorting algorithms.

The Bubble Sort Algorithm

The first of the three sorting algorithms we present is the Bubble Sort Algorithm. Of the three algorithms, it is the least efficient.

Pseudocode

The bubble sort algorithm requires two nested loops in order to be successfully carried out. We have already given the pseudocode description for the outer loop. The algorithm exchanges elements using an inner loop statement described by the pseudocode

> FOR Index ← LastElement−1 DOWNTO Sorted DO
> IF Ints[Index] > Ints[Index+1] THEN
> ExchangeInts(Ints[Index],Ints[Index+1])
> {invariant: Ints[Index] is the lowest element of all array elements in
> the subrange Index..LastElement}
>
> {postloop assertion: Ints[Sorted] is less than all other elements in
> the subrange Sorted+1..LastElement}

Note how the postloop assertion of the inner loop satisfies the invariant we proposed for the outer loop.

Source code   When we put both descriptions together, we obtain the source code for the procedure BubbleSort as shown.

```
{*                                                                    *}
PROCEDURE ExchangeInts(VAR Int1, Int2: integer);
  BEGIN    {exchanges the values of Int1 and Int2}    END;
{+                                                                    +}
PROCEDURE BubbleSort(VAR Ints: IntArray);
  {A version of the bubble sort algorithm applied to an array of
  integers.}
  VAR
    Sorted,    {index value of last element put in its proper place}
    Index:     {used to compare/exchange Ints[Index] and Ints[Index+1}
           1..LastElement;
  BEGIN
    FOR Sorted:= 1 TO LastElement-1 DO
      FOR Index:= LastElement-1 DOWNTO Sorted DO
        IF Ints[Index] > Ints[Index+1] THEN
          ExchangeInts(Ints[Index], Ints[Index+1])
  END;
{*                                                                    *}
```

The code for the procedure ExchangeInts, you may recall, was developed as part of Case Study 5.1. Notice how convenient it is to apply the call by VAR mechanism on any two elements of Ints to carry out the exchange of the two elements.

A desk trace   Figures 10.5 and 10.6 show the desk trace for the first two outer loop passes of the bubble sort algorithm, given the following initial values for the elements of Ints: 87, 90, 63, 86 and 72. The two traces confirm the correctness of the invari-

FIGURE 10.5   Bubble sort of the first outer loop pass with Sorted = 1.

	Ints [1]	[2]	[3]	[4]	[5]
initially:	87	90	63	86	72
Index ← 4	87	90	63	72	86
Index ← 3	87	90	63	72	86
Index ← 2	87	63	90	72	86
Index ← 1	63	87	90	72	86

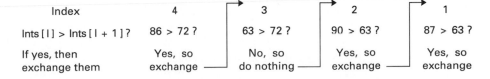

Index	4	3	2	1
Ints[I] > Ints[I + 1]?	86 > 72 ?	63 > 72 ?	90 > 63 ?	87 > 63 ?
If yes, then exchange them	Yes, so exchange	No, so do nothing	Yes, so exchange	Yes, so exchange

Assertion: array sorted over subrange 1..2

Ints	[1]	[2]	[3]	[4]	[5]
initially:	63	87	90	72	86
Index ← 4	63	87	90	72	86
Index ← 3	63	87	72	90	86
Index ← 2	63	72	87	90	86

Index	4	3	2
Ints [I] > Ints [I + 1] ?	72 > 86?	90 > 72 ?	87 > 72 ?
If yes, then exchange them	No, so do nothing	Yes, so exchange	Yes, so exchange

Assertion: array sorted over subrange 1 . . 3

FIGURE 10.6 Bubble sort of the second outer loop pass with Sorted = 2.

ants we have made regarding the logical mechanism of the algorithm. The bubble sort algorithm gets its name because the lowest element in the unsorted part of the array appears to "rise like a bubble" through the action of the inner loop passes. When the inner loop is exited, this value has bubbled up to its final position as Ints[Sorted].

The Selection Sort Algorithm

The bubble sort algorithm is woefully inefficient because of all the exchanges made in the body of the inner loop. The selection sort algorithm, which uses the same outer loop as the bubble sort, is more efficient because only one exchange is made per loop pass. The number of comparisons, however, is exactly the same.

Pseudocode description   The pseudocode for the selection sort algorithm is as follows:

> FOR Sorted ← 1 TO LastElement–1 DO
> Lowest ← index value of lowest element in subrange Sorted..LastElement
> ExchangeInts(Ints[Sorted], Ints[Lowest])

Source code   The value gotten for the variable Lowest is found using a *most significant event recorder*. The source code is then given as the procedure SelectionSort.

```
{*                                                                        *}
PROCEDURE ExchangeInts(VAR Int1, Int2: integer)
  BEGIN  {interchanges the two values}    END;
{+                                                                        +}
PROCEDURE SelectionSort(VAR Ints: IntArray);
  {the selection sort algorithm on Ints}
  VAR
    Sorted,   {index value of last element put in its proper place}
```

```
      Index,     {inner loop control variable and candidate for Lowest}
      Lowest:    {index value for lowest element in subrange Sorted..LastElement}
                 1..LastElement;
   BEGIN
      FOR Sorted:= 1 TO LastElement-1 DO
        BEGIN
          {logic to assign value to Lowest}
          Lowest:= Sorted;
          FOR Index:= Sorted+1 TO LastElement DO
            IF Ints[Index] < Ints[Lowest] THEN
              Lowest:= Index;
          {postloop assertion: Lowest is index value of lowest element
          in the subrange Sorted..LastElement}
          ExchangeInts(Ints[Lowest], Ints[Sorted])
        END
   END;
```

Desk trace of the selection sort algorithm

The appearance of an array whose elements were initially 87 90 63 86 72 is shown after each outer loop pass of the selection sort algorithm as Figure 10.7. Note that here too the desk trace confirms the invariants and assertions we have made about the logical mechanism of the algorithm.

initial   Ints [1][2][3][4][5]
                 | 87 | 90 | 63 | 86 | 72 |

Sorted = 1 Ints [1][2][3][4][5]
                  | 63 | 90 | 87 | 86 | 72 |

Sorted = 2 Ints [1][2][3][4][5]
                  | 63 | 72 | 87 | 86 | 90 |

Sorted = 3 Ints [1][2][3][4][5]
                  | 63 | 72 | 86 | 87 | 90 |

Sorted = 4 Ints [1][2][3][4][5]
                  | 63 | 72 | 86 | 87 | 90 |

FIGURE 10.7 Appearance of Ints after each outer loop pass of the selection sort algorithm.

The Insertion Sort Algorithm

The insertion sort algorithm is the most intuitively appealing of the three algorithms, because it is similar to the way you might sort a deck of cards. Suppose you start off with a partially sorted deck. Given this precondition, you would take the next card and insert it into its proper place. Having inserted this card, the place to find the following card is found, and that card is inserted. After all cards are properly inserted, the deck is sorted. When we implement this process as source code, we have the insertion sort algorithm.

Pseudocode description

In developing the algorithm, let us start with the assumption that the first element is "sorted." Given this assumption, we must put the second element in order with respect to the first element. Then, the third element must be placed in order with respect to the first two elements. The outer loop to implement this algorithm is therefore described by

> FOR NextPlace ← 2 TO LastElement DO
>   *shift all elements greater than AnArray[NextPlace] up by one position*
>   *put AnArray[NextPlace] into its proper position*

Figure 10.8 suggests the mechanism of the algorithm. The elements over the subrange *1..NextPlace-1* have been put in order. All elements greater than the position found for *AnArray[NextPlace]* must be moved up so that *AnArray[NextPlace]* can be placed properly. The remaining elements over the subrange *NextPlace + 1..LastElement* still need to be sorted. The invariant we wish to achieve is thus stated as, "The elements over the subrange *1..NextPlace* are in order."

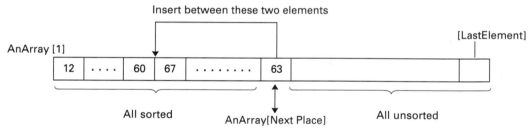

FIGURE 10.8 The mechanism of the insertion sort algorithm.

Refinements

In order to shift each element up by one position, we require an inner loop. We can apply a linear search until we find an element of *AnArray* less than *AnArray [NextPlace]*. The search for the candidate index *Position* is then described by the pseudocode

> Temp ← Ints[NextPlace] {*preserve value of Ints[NextPlace]*}
> Position ← NextPlace-1
> WHILE Ints[Position] > Temp DO
>   Ints[Position+1] ← Ints[Position]
>   Position ← Position-1

The postloop assertion we can make is then, "*Ints[Position]* is less than or equal to *Temp*, the initial value of *Ints[NextPlace]*." We can also say that all elements in the subrange *Position + 1..NextPlace* have been shifted up one place from their original positions. Thus, it looks like this approach will work.

Suppose, however, that *Temp* is less than all the elements that have been sorted? In this case, the approach will lead to a crash when an attempt is made to access *Ints[0]*. We can get around this difficulty, however, by defining the array subrange to go from 0 to 5 and then using *Ints[0]* as a sentinel element. This element is set to the value of *Ints[NextPlace]* before the inner loop is entered. At loop exit, we then set the value of this sentinel element to *Ints[Position + 1]*.

Source code   If we define the array subrange to go from 0..LastElement, we obtain the source code InsertionSort as shown.

```
PROCEDURE InsertionSort(VAR Ints: IntsArray);
  VAR
    NextPlace,      {index value of element to be put in proper place}
    Position:       {Position+1 is candidate position for Ints[NextPlace]}
                    0..LastElement;
  BEGIN
    FOR NextPlace:= 2 TO LastElement DO
      BEGIN
        Ints[0]:= Ints[NextPlace];      {assign sentinel element}
        Position:= NextPlace-1;
        WHILE Ints[Position] > Ints[0] DO {Now Ints[0] is element to place}
          BEGIN
            Ints[Position+1]:= Ints[Position];
            Position:= Position-1
          END;
        Ints[Position+1]:= Ints[0]
      END
  END;
```

Desk trace   A desk trace showing the appearance of Ints after each outer loop pass of the insertion sort algorithm is given as Figure 10.9.

FIGURE 10.9 Appearance of Ints after each outer loop pass of the insertion sort algorithm.

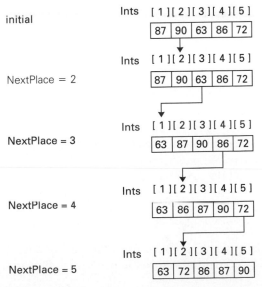

EXERCISES

Test Your
Understanding

1. Suppose all the elements of Ints have the same value. How many calls to Ex-changeInts are made with the bubble sort algorithm? How many calls are made with the selection sort algorithm?

2. Suppose all elements of Ints are initially in order from highest to lowest. For example, they might initially have been assigned values in the order 97, 86, 75, 64, and 50. Repeat Exercise 1 for this array.

Practice Your
Analysis Skills

3. Sketch the appearance of Ints after each outer loop pass when the bubble sort algorithm is applied to an original array whose elements were assigned values in the order 74, 32, 87, 66, 82.

4. Repeat Exercise 3, but this time apply the selection sort algorithm.

5. Repeat Exercise 3, this time applying the insertion sort algorithm.

Sharpen Your
Implementation
Skills

6. Write the bubble sort algorithm so that it sorts the elements of Ints in descending order, i.e., Ints[1] contains the highest value and Ints[LastElement] contains the lowest value.

7. Write the selection sort algorithm so that it sorts Ints in descending order.

8. The bubble sort algorithm can be written so that the highest element is in its final position after each loop pass. The outer loop is coded as

$$FOR\ Sorted \leftarrow LastElement\ DOWNTO\ 2\ DO$$
$$exchange\ adjacent\ elements\ if\ out\ of\ order$$

The loop invariant for this loop is, "The elements in the subrange from *Sorted-1* to *LastElement* are in order from lowest to highest." Write the bubble sort using this approach to sort the elements in ascending order.

9. The selection sort algorithm can be written with the same outer loop as the one suggested by Exercise 8. In this case, the assertion made after the inner loop is exited will be, "The element *Ints[Sorted]* is larger than all other elements of *Ints* contained in the access subrange *1* to *Sorted-1*." Write the selection sort algorithm using this approach to sort the elements of *Ints* in ascending order.

10.4 The Binary Search Algorithm

The *binary search* is a very efficient algorithm that can be applied to a sorted array. It is so efficient because half of the elements in the candidate subrange are eliminated with each loop pass. We present two versions of this algorithm: one that uses a boolean flag variable and the other that does not.

Binary search: any search algorithm that eliminates half the candidates from the search with a given probe.

Searching
through a sorted
list

Let us consider a search problem from the human angle. If you have an un-sorted list of some 10,000 names, you would need some time to hunt through the list to find a given name. In fact, you would probably require less time to find a name in a sorted list of even 5,000,000 names. Thus, a search is definitely easier if the list is sorted. It is for this reason that the names in a telephone book are sorted alphabetically.

As it is with the human problem, so it is with the machine problem. If an array has 10,000 unsorted names, the computer may need to probe all 10,000 elements using the linear search algorithm before a result is found. The binary search algorithm needs only 14 probes at the most when the array contains 10,000 names. The algorithm will work, however, only if the list is sorted. Given this precondition, it can set a probe as the middle element in the candidate subrange, then get a new candidate subrange over the lower or upper half of the original subrange if there is no match.

Developing the Binary Search Algorithm

We have established the fact that the binary search works only if the array elements are sorted. Let us now describe and develop the algorithm, keeping in mind that the elements of the array being searched are in ordered from lowest element to highest element.

Describing the algorithm

Suppose the array *Names* has 10,000 elements in it. It is sorted such that *Names[1]* occurs first in the alphabet and *Names[10000]* occurs last. The candidate subrange in which the *SearchName* may be found consists initially of those elements over the subrange *1..10000*. If we are to eliminate half the elements with the first probe, the obvious choice must be *Names[5000]* as our initial probe.

If *Names[5000]* is less than *SearchName*, all those elements in the subrange *1..5000* are eliminated. The candidate subrange for the next probe must be *5001..10000*. If instead, *Names[5000]* is greater than *SearchName*, the candidate subrange must be *1..4999*. The elements from *5000..10000* can be eliminated for the next probe.

If our candidate subrange is *1..4999*, the next probe must be *Names[2500]*. Given this probe, the next candidate subrange will be *1..2499* or *2501..4999*. If instead, the candidate subrange was *5001..10000*, the next probe is *7500*. Depending upon the results of the probe, the next candidate subrange is *5001..7499* or *7501..10000*.

This process of subrange halving continues until either there is no more subrange of candidate values or *Names[Probe]* = *SearchName*. The first condition describes a *finished* search, where the element is not present, and the second condition described a search with a successful result. We can use this latter event to set the boolean variable *Found* to *true*, as we did in Algorithm 10.1 (the generic search algorithm). Recall that with this algorithm, the loop is exited when the variable *Found* is set to *true*.

Drafting a solution

In order to solve the problem, it looks like we will need three variables to represent index values. The two variables *Lo* and *Hi* can define the candidate subrange after each loop pass. We will need a third variable, *Mid*, equal to the value of the expression *(Lo + Hi) DIV 2*, to set the probe for the next loop pass. If *Names[Mid]* = *SearchName*, the flag variable *Found* is set to *true*. If

Names[Mid] < *SearchName*, the next candidate subrange must be *Mid + 1..Hi*. If the probe value is greater than the search name, the candidate subrange will be *Lo..Mid-1*.

Pseudocode

Let us write the pseudocode for the binary search algorithm using Algorithm 10.1. The variable *AnArray* has elements assigned over the subrange *1..TotalElements*. The value whose index is being sought we will call *SearchValue*. The description of the binary search algorithm we can derive from Algorithm 10.1 is given as follows:

```
Lo ← 1
Hi ← TotalElements
Found ← false
WHILE NOT finished AND NOT Found DO
    Mid ← (Lo + Hi) DIV 2
    IF AnArray[Mid] = SearchValue THEN
        Found ← true
    ELSE IF AnArray[Mid] < SearchValue THEN
        Lo ← Mid+1
    ELSE
        Hi ← Mid-1
assign IndexValue to Mid if Found or to 0 if not Found
```

*The finished
condition*

We need to determine an expression for the *finished* condition, indicating a failed search. In order to find a valid expression, let us envision a scenario that leads to a failed search. Suppose, we have just two candidates left. The condition described by *Lo + 1 = Hi* is therefore *true*. Given this scenario, the variable *Mid* must be set to *Lo*.

Suppose, then, that the expression *AnArray[Mid]* < *SearchValue* evaluates to *false*. The value assigned to *Hi* will then be *Mid-1* (i.e., *Lo-1*) so that the candidate subrange is equal to *Lo..Lo-1*. Therefore, because there is no candidate subrange (*Lo > Hi* is *true*), the search is finished.

We have chosen only one scenario, but other possibilities could occur. For example, if there are two elements left and the expression *AnArray[Mid]* < *SearchValue* is *true*, the candidate subrange becomes *Lo..Lo*. Clearly, one of the two expressions *AnArray[Mid]* = *SearchValue* or *Lo > Hi* will be *true* after the next loop pass. No matter what scenario you may choose, the *finished* condition can always be described by *Lo > Hi* where the candidate "subrange" is *Lo..Lo-1*. Hence the code to represent the condition *NOT finished* must be *Lo <= Hi*, the complement of the *finished* condition.

*Complete
pseudocode*

Now that we have an expression for *finished*, we can present the pseudocode for the binary search as Algorithm 10.3.

Algorithm 10.3

```
{Binary search algorithm, using boolean flag:}
Lo ← 1
Hi ← TotalElements
```

$$Found \leftarrow false$$
$$WHILE\ (Lo <= Hi)\ AND\ NOT\ Found\ DO$$
$$Mid \leftarrow (Lo + Hi)\ DIV\ 2$$
$$IF\ AnArray[Mid] = SeachValue\ THEN$$
$$Found \leftarrow true$$
$$ELSE\ IF\ AnArray[Mid] < SearchValue\ THEN$$
$$Lo \leftarrow Mid+1$$
$$ELSE$$
$$Hi \leftarrow Mid\text{-}1$$
$$IF\ Found\ THEN$$
$$IndexValue \leftarrow Mid$$
$$ELSE$$
$$IndexValue \leftarrow 0$$
$$\{end\ algorithm\}$$

Implemention of the algorithm
The source code given as Example 10.1 is an implementation of Algorithm 10.3. The search is for a given name through an array of sorted names. Note how counterproductive it is to call the array Names by value. In doing so, we are killing the efficiency of the algorithm because the machine requires MaxElements (perhaps 10,000) hidden loop passes to copy all elements locally. Only then is the search algorithm, which requires at most 14 loop passes, applied.

Example 10.1

```
FUNCTION NameIndex(VAR Names: NamesArray; SearchName: StringType;
                                  TotalElements: integer): integer;
  {the binary search algorithm, using a boolean flag variable to
  indicate a found condition}
  VAR
    Lo,         {specifies lowest index value in candidate subrange}
    Hi,         {specifies highest index value in candidate subrange}
    Mid:        {index value of a probe determined by subrange values}
                integer;
    Found:      {flags a found condition}
                boolean;
  BEGIN
    Lo:= 1;                                     {initialize locals:}
    Hi:= TotalElements;
    Found:= false;
    WHILE (Lo <= Hi) AND NOT Found DO   {finished occurs with Lo > Hi}
      BEGIN
        Mid:= (Lo + Hi) DIV 2;            {get probe index value}
        IF Names[Mid] = SearchName THEN        {set flag if found}
          Found:= true
        ELSE                             {set next candidate subrange:}
          IF Names[Mid] < SearchName THEN
            Lo:= Mid+1
```

```
      ELSE
          Hi:= Mid-1              {candidate subrange: Lo..Mid-1}
      END
    IF Found THEN    {assign value to NameIndex using Found condition:}
      NameIndex:= Mid    {return successful search value}
    ELSE
      NameIndex:= 0        {return predefined failed search value}
  END;
```

Eliminating the Boolean Variable

We eliminated the boolean variable when we coded the linear search algorithm. Let us derive an algorithm to eliminate the boolean variable Found in the binary search. Then we will examine some of the properties of this form of the binary search algorithm.

A pseudocode draft

If we can successfully eliminate the boolean variable, we expect the pseudocode description of the algorithm to be as follows:

> *Lo ← 1*
> *Hi ← TotalElements*
> *WHILE Lo <= Hi DO*
>   *Mid ← (Lo + Hi) div 2*
>   *IF AnArray[Mid] < SearchValue THEN*
>   *Lo ← Mid+1*
>   *ELSE*
>   *Hi ← Mid-1*
> *IF AnArray[index expression] = SearchValue THEN*
>   *IndexValue ← index expression*
> *ELSE*
>   *Index ← 0*

This description assumes that the algorithm gives us an index expression where the relationship *AnArray[index expression] = SearchValue* returns *true* when the loop is exited if *SearchValue* is an element of *AnArray*. Our problem is to find the value of the index expression.

A loop invariant

If we assume the loop does work toward returning some final solution, we might be able to find an invariant relationship we can use to get the value of the index expression. Because we have eliminated the comparison of *AnArray[Mid]* with *SearchValue*, let us choose our invariant so that it is expressed in terms of *Lo* and *Hi*. We will try to find an invariant relationship by making assertions that apply to each path taken by the decision statement inside the loop.

Suppose the first path is taken for a given loop pass. Because the relationship *AnArray[Mid] < SearchValue* is *true*, we can say that, due to the assignment operation, the relationship *AnArray[Lo-1] < SearchValue* must also be *true*. If the other path is taken, this relationship will *still be true because Lo* is not assigned a new value.

Now let us suppose instead that the second path was taken. In this case, we can say *AnArray[Mid]* >= *SearchValue* is *true*. This condition implies, by the action of the assignment statement, that the relationship *SearchValue* <= *AnArray[Hi + 1]* must be true. The relationship will likewise hold *true* if the first path is taken.

We can combine these two relationships to get the invariant relationship *AnArray[Lo-1]* < *SearchValue* <= *AnArray[Hi + 1]*. From the invariant, we see that when the loop is exited, the value that should be returned to *IndexValue* must be *Hi + 1* or *SearchValue* is not an element in the array.

Another viewpoint

When the loop is exited, the relationship *Lo* > *Hi* also holds *true*. If you think about it a bit, you realize that the interval-halving process guarantees that the condition *Lo* = *Hi + 1* will be *true* when the loop is exited. Now let us suppose that at some point in the processing, the condition *AnArray[Mid]* = *SearchValue* becomes *true*. In the original version of the algorithm, the machine will exit the loop, but for this modified version it does not. Given this condition, the "candidate subrange" becomes *Lo..Mid-1*, where *Hi* is set to *Mid-1* for that pass.

With this run-time event, the machine returns a "candidate subrange" from *Lo* to *Hi* where *Hi* is the index value of the element one less than the one being sought. With no duplicate names in the array, this value of *Hi* will be the same for each loop pass, so that the condition expressed as *AnArray[Mid]* < *SearchValue* will always return *true*. Therefore the machine works its way down to the condition where *Lo* > *Hi* becomes *true*, and the element is found in *AnArray[Lo]* = *AnArray[Hi + 1]* or not at all.

Algorithm description

With these thoughts in mind, we can describe this form of the binary search with the pseudocode given as Algorithm 10.4. The first decision statement after loop exit is necessary as a guard against the possibility that *Lo* was assigned a final value of *TotalElements + 1*. (How)?

Algorithm 10.4

```
{Binary search algorithm where boolean flag is not used:}
    Lo ← 1
    Hi ← TotalElements
    WHILE Lo <= Hi DO
        Mid ← (Lo + Hi) DIV 2
        IF AnArray[Mid] < SearchValue THEN
            Lo ← Mid+1
        ELSE
            Hi ← Mid-1
    IF Lo <= TotalElements THEN      {guard out-of-range value of Lo}
        IF AnArray[Lo] = SearchValue THEN
            IndexValue ← Lo
        ELSE
            IndexValue ← 0
    ELSE
        IndexValue ← 0
{end algorithm}
```

Using Algorithm 10.4

You may wonder if this analysis is worth all the effort, particularly when the post-loop assignment logic is so complex. At the very least, this form of the binary search algorithm should be documented well enough to avoid confusing another programmer. It would seem simpler to just code the clearer version, the one that uses Found. But then we have not yet discussed the issue of duplicate elements.

Duplicate elements and Algorithm 10.4

If the array contains no duplicate elements, the use of the boolean flag is justified for the sake of simpler code. When duplicate values are present, however, the alternate form of the binary search algorithm is an 'attractive choice. We can prove this statement by considering the implications of the invariant condition *AnArray[Lo-1] < SearchValue*. If the condition *AnArray[Lo] = SearchValue* is also *true*, it means that the value of *Lo* represents the index value of the lowest index in *AnArray* equal to *SearchValue*.

We cannot make the same claim if we apply Algorithm 10.3. To prove our claim, let us first express the subrange of elements that match *SearchValue* as *M..N*. Thus we have that *AnArray[M]* and *AnArray[N]* are equal to *SearchValue*. Likewise, the other elements lying within the given subrange will be equal to *SearchValue*. Algorithm 10.3 guarantees only that *AnArray[Mid] = SearchValue* if such an element exists. Given the condition of duplicate elements, the only guarantee on the value of *Mid* we can make is that *M <= Mid <= N*. We cannot pinpoint *Mid* to any one element in the subrange.

Using the property

We can use the property of Algorithm 10.4 to solve the next problem, one where an array of names might contain duplicate names. We are only going to code part of the solution to the problem, leaving the full implementation details as exercises.

Example Problem 10.3

Suppose we have an array of names that can have duplicate elements. We want to write a procedure to return LowestMatch and HighestMatch, the variables we have previously called M and N. If there is no match, then LowestMatch and HighestMatch will both be given the value 0.

Pseudocode description

We can write the function BinLowest using Algorithm 10.4 to return the lowest element in the subrange that matches the search value, if one exists. A call to the function BinHighest, an analogous function to BinLowest that returns the index value of the highest element in Names that matches the value of Search-Name, is used to find the value of HighestMatch. We therefore can describe the statement for the procedure we want to implement using

$$LowestMatch \leftarrow BinLowest(Names, TotalElements, SearchName)$$
$$HighestMatch \leftarrow BinHighest(Names, TotalElements, SearchName)$$

Source code

The source code for the procedure GetSubrange that returns values to LowestMatch and HighestMatch is given below. We leave the implementation details for BinLowest and BinHighest as Exercises 8 and 9 at the end of this section.

```
{*                                                                    *}
FUNCTION BinLowest (VAR Names: NamesArray; TotalElements: integer;
                                SearchName:NameString): integer;
  BEGIN {insert implementation of Algorithm 10.4 here} END;
{+                                                                    +}
FUNCTION BinHighest (VAR Names: NamesArray; TotalElements: integer;
                                SearchName: NameString): integer;
  {returns the highest index value of the element in Names that matches
  SearchName using the binary search algorithm.
  BEGIN {statement}   END;
{+                                                                    +}
PROCEDURE GetSubrange (VAR Names: NamesArray; TotalElements: integer;
      SearchName: NameString; VAR LowestMatch, HighestMatch: integer);
  {returns values to LowestMatch and HighestMatch such that LowestMatch
  is the element with the lowest index value in Names that matches
  SearchValue and HighestMatch is the element with the highest index
  value that matches SearchName. TotalElements represents the total
  number of elements in Names that have been assigned values. If there
  is no match, the value 0 is returned to both variables}
  BEGIN
     LowestMatch:= BinLowest (Names, TotalElements, SearchName);
     HighestMatch:= BinHighest (Names, TotalElements, SearchName)
  END;
{*                                                                    *}
```

EXERCISES

Test Your Understanding

1. Suppose the binary search algorithm is applied on an unsorted array. Which of the following possibilities is the most likely outcome: (a) an endless loop, (b) a failed search, (c) an incorrect value is returned, or (d) a correct value is returned.

2. Some of the events listed in Exercise 1 will never occur. List those events that will not occur, regardless of the condition of the array.

3. Specify the condition under which the variable *Lo* will be assigned the final value of *TotalElements + 1*.

Practice Your Analysis Skills

4. Suppose Names is sorted and has elements assigned over the subrange *1..50*. Let us apply the binary search that uses the boolean variable Found to this structure. Indicate the values taken on by Lo and Hi with each loop pass, given the following:
   (a) the value of the search name is the value of the twenty-fifth element.
   (b) the value of the search name is the value of the tenth element.
   (c) the value of the search name is the value of the forty-seventh element.
   (d) Name [10] < SearchName < Names [11] (failed search).
   (e) Names [24] < SearchName < Names [25] (failed search).
   (f) SearchName < Names [1] (failed search).
   (g) Names [50] < SearchName (failed search).

5. Apply the same conditions of Exercise 4, except this time use the binary search algorithm in which the flag variable Found is not used.

6. Another form of the loop action for the binary search can be described by the pseudocode

$$Lo \leftarrow 1$$
$$Hi \leftarrow TotElements$$
$$WHILE\ Lo <= Hi\ DO$$
$$\quad Mid \leftarrow (Lo + Hi)\ DIV\ 2$$
$$\quad IF\ AnArray[Mid] > SearchValue\ THEN$$
$$\quad\quad Hi \leftarrow Mid - 1$$
$$\quad ELSE$$
$$\quad\quad Lo \leftarrow Mid + 1$$

    (a)   What is the loop invariant for this form of the binary search?
    (b)   If the search is successful, what value should be returned to IndexValue?

Sharpen Your Implementation Skills

7. Another version of the binary search algorithm that still halves the search interval can be coded using the REPEAT..UNTIL construct. Write the block statement for the binary search using this construct such that everything required of the block is the same as the two versions we presented. Use a boolean flag in this version.

8. Write the source code for the function BinLowest of Example Problem 10.3.

9. Derive and write the source code for the function BinHighest of Example Problem 10.3. (Hint: Do Exercise 6 from this section first).

10.5 Efficiency Analysis

We say that the binary search algorithm is more efficient than the linear search algorithm because it requires less time to find a name if the list is very large. The reason it is more efficient is that less loop passes are made to find an element. Efficiency can be expressed in a more precise manner than "more efficient" or "less efficient" using big-Oh notation. In this section, we discuss how an algorithm's big-Oh (often referred to simply as its "O") describes its efficiency.

Estimating Run Times

Generally, the more data there is to process, the longer the required run time to carry out the process. But how dependent is the run time on the value of N, the count of data values that are (or may be) processed? As the forthcoming analysis shows, the answer to this question depends upon the nature of the algorithm as well as the size of N.

Processing time for linear search algorithm

Let us consider how long it might take for the linear search to return a solution, given that *AnArray* has N elements. We will say that it takes approximate K_l microseconds to set up initial conditions for the loop to be entered. Then we can say that each loop pass takes about k_l microseconds to be carried out. Given that there are N elements in the array, we can further say that on the average it will require $N/2$ loop passes to find the index value of a given element. We can express the time taken to return a result as T_l, so that we have the equation

$$T_l \approx k_l' * N + K_l \tag{10.1}$$

We have simplified the relationship by saying k_l' is approximately equal to $k_l/2$. Thus, the constant $\frac{1}{2}$ is absorbed in the factor k_l'. We can further simplify Equation (10.1) by saying that the term $k_l' * N$ is very much greater than the term K. Hence, an even simpler expression for the approximate run time is given by Equation (10.2):

$$T_l \approx k_l' * N \tag{10.2}$$

Processing time for binary search algorithm

The binary search will require considerably less than N loop passes to find the index value of *AnArray* that matches the value of *SearchValue*. Thus, Equation (10.2) does not represent the correct approximation for the run time required to carry out the binary search algorithm.

How many loop passes are required given N elements? Consider that each loop pass divides the candidate subrange by 2. After two loop passes, the candidate subrange is reduced by a factor of 4 from the original subrange; after three loop passes, it is reduced by a factor of 8. In the worst case, after Y loop passes, the candidate subrange will have been reduced by a factor of N, indicating that either an index was found or the search had failed. But how do we find Y?

If you look at the numbers, you realize that we are looking for a relationship between Y and N expressed by Equation (10.3):

$$2^Y \approx N \tag{10.3}$$

We can solve this equation simply by taking the logarithm to the base 2 of both sides. Then we have Equation (10.4):

$$Y \approx \log_2(N) \tag{10.4}$$

Now that we know the approximate number of loop passes required to solve the problem with the binary search, we can apply the same analysis we used with the linear search to arrive at Equation (10.5).

$$T_b \approx k_b' * \log_2(N) \tag{10.5}$$

In this case, k_b' is different from k_l'. Because the loop body of the binary search is more complicated than that of the linear search, we expect that k_b' is considerably greater than k_l'.

Big-Oh Notation

Now that you can find an algebraic expression for the run time of an algorithm, let us define its big-Oh. This property is expressed as a function of N and serves as a good criterion to compare the efficiency of two different algorithms. In addition to giving a working definition, we present a table of the big-Oh for some of the most widely used algorithms.

Equations (10.2) and (10.5) represent the approximate run times given N elements in *AnArray* and a certain amount of time, k_l' or k_b', per loop pass. The run time required for the computer to carry out a given algorithm, A, can be expressed in a form similar to Equations (10.2) and (10.5) as Equation (10.6)

$$T_A \approx k_A * f(N) \tag{10.6}$$

where k_A is a proportionality constant, usually representing the time cost of a single loop pass, and $f(N)$ is a function of N.

Computer scientists call this function the algorithm's *big-Oh* or sometimes simply its O. We use this abbreviation because it represents an *o*rder of magnitude measure for the algorithm's efficiency. We formally represent the efficiency of the linear search as $O(N)$ and that of the binary search as $O(\log_2(N))$. The linear search is said to be an "O of N" algorithm, and the binary search is an "O of log of N" algorithm.

Table 10.1 shows a list of the big-Oh for many of the algorithms you will encounter. The table is laid out in order of efficiency from the most to the least efficient.

TABLE 10.1 Showing Different O's for Different Algorithms

Efficiency	Comments
$O(1)$	A nonloop approach
$O(\log_2(N))$	Binary search algorithm; halves search interval each loop pass
$O(N)$	Any single "for" loop; the linear search algorithm
$O(N\log_2(N))$	The fastest sorting algorithms; in particular, the "quick sort"
$O(N^2)$	Two nested "for" loops; many sorting algorithms

The binary search with its $O(\log_2(N))$ is more efficient than the linear search, an $O(N)$ algorithm. Thus, it is the preferred algorithm to use on a large *sorted* list. However, if the list is small, the linear search is preferred because the loop body is simpler to execute.

We stated earlier that the cost per loop pass of the binary search is much greater than that of the linear search even though the binary search is more efficient. Given this premise, you would expect some N value below which the linear search takes less time to execute than the binary search. In other words, there exists some N (call it N') for which the following approximate equation is satisfied:

$$T_b(N') \approx T_l(N')$$

What is this value of N'? It depends upon your machine, but usually an N' of about 20 objects is accepted as the cross-over point.

Using Big-Oh For Further Analysis

Even if you do not know the values of all proportionality constants, you can still estimate the effect on run time when you change the number of items to be processed. You can also use big-Oh analysis effectively to let you know if or when you should implement a very costly process.

Proportionality relationships

The big-Oh of an algorithm gives an estimate of the run-time cost if the number of data values to process increases or decreases by a given factor. Suppose, for example, it takes T seconds for the linear search to work with N elements. How long will this search take if we double the number of elements?

We can use the big-Oh of the algorithm to get the proportion suggested by Equation (10.7), where T' represents the new run time.

$$\frac{T'}{T} = \frac{k_l * (2N)}{k_l * (N)} \tag{10.7}$$

Inspection of the equation shows that if we double the number of elements in the linear search algorithm, we will double the run time for the algorithm to return a result.

We can likewise use the big-Oh notation of the binary search algorithm with the same kind of analysis. Suppose rather than doubling the number of elements that we *square* the number of elements. Let us calculate this run-time increase. The relationship to apply is suggested by Equation (10.8).

$$\frac{T'}{T} = \frac{k_b * \log_2(N^2)}{k_b * \log_2(N)} = \frac{k_b * 2 \log_2(N)}{k_b * \log_2(N)} \tag{10.8}$$

When we solve this equation, we find that squaring the number of elements only increases the run time by a factor of 2. Surely this result also drives home the fact that the binary search algorithm is more efficient than the linear search algorithm.

The three sorting algorithms

The bubble, selection sort, and insertion sort algorithms, using nested FOR loops for their solutions, are $O(N^2)$ algorithms. Even though the selection sort and insertion sort are more efficient than the bubble sort, they still have the same big-Oh. For example, if you double the number of array elements, you will quadruple the run time required to complete either of the three sorts. If you triple the number of elements, you increase the run time ninefold, and so forth.

The significance of big-Oh

Usually, an algorithm's big-Oh is considered the most important measure of its efficiency. We can hence say that the three sorting algorithms are equally efficient because they are all $O(N^2)$ algorithms. Therefore, the selection sort and insertion sort algorithms represent only a marginal improvement over the bubble sort algorithm. A "better" sorting algorithm (of which there are many) must have a big-Oh better than $O(N^2)$ to represent a significant improvement over the sorting algorithms of this chapter.

Big-Oh as it relates to parameter passing

If you use the binary search algorithm and pass the reference array in by value, you might as well use the linear search algorithm. How so? When you use the value call, you are imposing an $O(N)$ process (element-by-element copy into a local variable) on an $O(\log_2(N))$ algorithm. The big-Oh for the overall process is then $O(N)$ because we can express the overall efficiency by $O(N + \log_2(N))$. The element-by-element copy process, which is $O(N)$ and the less efficient of the two processes, dominates.

If you use the call-by-variable mechanism, you will be imposing an $O(1)$ process (copying a single address) on the big-Oh of the binary search algorithm. The big-Oh of the entire process is, therefore, $O(1 + \log_2(N))$. The less efficient process, the big-Oh of the binary search, contributes the dominating term in this case. Hence, the overall process is on the order of $O(\log_2(N))$, as desired.

EXERCISES

Test Your Understanding

1. What is the big-Oh of an algorithm requiring three nested FOR loops?

2. Suppose A is an array with M elements and B is an array with N elements. The elements in both structures are of the same type. Show the following:
   (a) If an $O(N^2)$ algorithm is applied to both structures, the ratio of the time taken to complete the algorithm on structure A versus structure B is M^2/N^2.
   (b) If an $O(N)$ algorithm is applied to both structures, the ratio of time taken to complete the algorithm on structure A versus structure B is M/N.
   (c) If an $O(1)$ $(O(N^0))$ algorithm is applied to both structures, the amount of time taken to complete the algorithm as applied to either structure is virtually the same.

3. Given *AnArray* with 1000 elements. Both algorithm A, which is $O(N)$, and algorithm B, which is $O(N^2)$, require T seconds of run time for completion when applied on *AnArray*. If the number of elements in *AnArray* is increased to 5000, how long will it now take for the two algorithms to run?

4. A one-dimensional array is passed into the block for a linear search algorithm using call-by-value mechanism. What is the big-Oh of the overall process?

Program Testing Hints

Whenever you work with arrays, you must make sure that all access expressions will be in range at run time. On sorting algorithms, you must be sure your sort works correctly for all possible sets of unsorted data. When you write a search algorithm, you should choose test data that appear to exhaust all possibilities. In this section, we discuss these issues, mainly as they apply to on-line testing.

PROGRAM DESIGN RULE 10.1

Write a guard loop any time an access expression is solicited from the program user.

Make sure you guard against access expression errors when access values are solicited from the keyboard. Suppose, for example, you have written a program that uses an array to count letter ocurrences. The program allows for the user to periodically check the number of times a particular letter(s) has occurred in the text.

Avoid writing code such as the following:

```
write('Input the letter whose occurrence count you want to see:   ');
readln(Letter);
writeln('It occurred ',LetterCount[Letter]:1,' times in the text.');
```

In this case, the user will have to guess whether an uppercase or lowercase letter is appropriate. It would be better if you code both (1) a more enlightening prompt to let the user know the expected case and (2) a guard to ensure that the value assigned to Letter is in range. (See Exercise 8.)

PROGRAM DESIGN RULE 10.2

Verify that all coded access expressions are in range.

In both the bubble sort and selection sort algorithms, we coded a statement that required access to AnArray[Index + 1]. The precondition for this access mechanism to work is that Index be less than MaxElements. Other algorithms may use more complicated access expressions. You should, in these cases, check the preconditions to make sure that they guarantee legal access for all cases.

Consider, for example, the following fragment:

```
TYPE
    ArrayType = ARRAY[Lower..Upper] OF SomeType;
VAR
    AnArray: ArrayType;

{typical access may be to AnArray[some expression]}
```

Program Design Rule 10.2 requires that every time an element of AnArray is accessed via *some expression,* you must confirm that the relationship *Lower <= some expression <= Upper* holds *true* for all possibilities that may occur at run time.

The rule of small samples applies here. You do not simply want to try a 100-element array on an algorithm and hope it works. Remember, the idea of testing is not just to show that an algorithm is incorrect, but, if incorrect, to show how it is incorrect so you can fix it.

By now you know that loop entry and loop exit events are always critical. With the sorting algorithms of this chapter, the first element is sorted just after loop entry and the last element is sorted just before loop exit. You should therefore test arrays where the extreme elements (first and last) are properly placed and where they must be exchanged with at least one other element.

Other extreme cases that must be tested are arrays in reverse order and arrays already in order. The first test checks that all required operations in this worst-case scenario are properly carried out to put the array in order. The second test checks that no operation is carried out that improperly rearranges one or more elements.

You should try at least two tests with duplicate elements. One of the tests might have two or more duplicate elements adjacent to each other, and the other test might have them distributed widely apart. Naturally, if the algorithm works, they should end up adjacent to each other.

Once you have covered the special cases, you must always test the sorting algorithm with one or two "typical" arrays. You certainly need not attempt to exhaust all possibilities. Even if the array has just five elements, there are 120 different ways they can be arranged. Once you are sure the algorithm works with small arrays, you should test it with one or two arrays of the size intended when the program is put on line.

Test data for searching algorithms

Before you determine different search values, you should first make up a test array for the search. Make the elements of the test array take on the kind of values that are expected. If the problem allows for duplicate values, you must use two different test arrays: one with duplicate values and the other without. If you are testing with the linear search algorithm, one pair of duplicate values should be separated and another pair adjacent to each other. If you are testing the binary search algorithm, make sure the test array is sorted. If duplicate values are allowed, set up an array with at least one set of duplicate values, perhaps more. You can choose to have three or more values that are the same for at least one group of elements.

Once you have a test array, you must be sure to account for (1) successful searches on nonduplicate elements, (2) successful searches on duplicate elements, (3) failed searches, and (4) extreme elements for failed and successful searches. Table 10.2 summarizes test data you should choose with a known successful outcome, and Table 10.3 shows test data you should apply that will give you a known failed search. Both tables are written with the binary search algorithm in mind.

Readability vs. efficiency

Of the different search algorithms you have seen, which is the "best" one? All computer scientists would insist that the binary search algorithm, which is $O(\log_2(N))$, is better than the linear search, which is $O(N)$, given that the array is sorted. The binary search algorithm, however, is a bit more complicated than the linear search, so its source code is somewhat harder to understand. If we use a boolean flag variable Found, however, the code still looks fairly straightforward.

TABLE 10.2 Test Data to Apply on the Binary Search Algorithm That Will Return a Successful Search

(1) the first array element
(2) the last array element
(3) some nonduplicate elements between the first and last elements
(4) some duplicate elements you have chosen

TABLE 10.3 Test Data to Apply on the Binary Search Algorithm That Will Return a Failed Search

---

(1) a value below the value of the first element
(2) a value above the value of the last element
(3) one or more typical values between these extremes

The issue of which is the best search algorithm becomes somewhat less clear-cut when we consider the version of the binary search that does not use the boolean flag variable. This version, although seemingly obscure, is more efficient than the first one because less boolean expressions are evaluated per loop pass. Moreover, it has the additional attractive property of finding the lowest element in an array with duplicate elements. So then which version is better?

There is no simple answer to this question. When you have to decide between two competing algorithms that both work but that have different big-Ohs, you should choose the more efficient one. If two algorithms have the same big-Oh, your choice should be based on both human and machine factors. Sometimes the cost of using a slightly less efficient algorithm may be greater in the long run, especially if the program is maintained frequently.

Suppose, for example, a block statement with clever but obscure code saves a few hours of run time over a year's period of being on line. If the statement is so "clever" that the person maintaining the code requires "a few more hours" to decipher the logic, it may be better to use the less-efficient but clearer version.

This trade-off between readability and efficiency sometimes requires a very difficult judgment call on your part. If you apply big-Oh analysis, you can get an expression to compare two competing algorithms with respect to machine time. Unfortunately, there is no ready expression you can apply to determine a program's "readability." Human time spent on off-line maintenance work cannot be measured so easily.

EXERCISES

Test Your Understanding

1. True or false? Both the linear search and the binary search can be applied to the array of Figure 10.10.

2. True or false? Both the linear search and the binary search can be applied to the array of Figure 10.11.

Practice Your Analysis Skills

3. Indicate which value(s) could cause errors in the following form of the linear search algorithm through Names.

```
FUNCTION NameIndex(VAR Names: NamesArray; Enrollment: integer;
                                    SearchName: NameString): integer;
  {documentation}
  VAR
    Probe: integer;
    Found: boolean;
```

Names [1]	Adams	Names [1]	Vreeland
[2]	Archibald	[2]	Nelson
[3]	Davis	[3]	McGillicutty
[4]	Davis	[4]	Griffin
[5]	Egbert	[5]	Thomasin
[6]	Griffin	[6]	Jones
[7]	Griffin	[7]	Segal
[8]	Griffin	[8]	Davis
[9]	Jones	[9]	Egbert
[10]	Klein	[10]	Archibald
[11]	McGillicutty	[11]	Griffin
[12]	Nelson	[12]	Rodger
[13]	Rodger	[13]	Young
[14]	Rodgers	[14]	Adams
[15]	Segal	[15]	Klein
[16]	Thomasin	[16]	Davis
[17]	Vreeland	[17]	Rodger
[18]	Williams	[18]	Griffin
[19]	Young	[19]	Davis

FIGURE 10.10   **FIGURE 10.11**

```
BEGIN
  Probe:= 1;
  Found:= false;
  WHILE NOT(Index = Enrollment) AND NOT Found DO
    IF Names[Probe] = SearchName THEN
      Found:= true
    ELSE
      Probe:= Probe + 1;
  NameIndex:= Probe
END;
```

4. Consider the following function:

```
FUNCTION NoNegatives
        (VAR AnArray: IntsArray; LastElement: integer): boolean;
 {Returns true if none of the elements of AnArray in 1..LastElement
 is negative}
VAR
  Index: integer;    {index to present element of AnArray being accessed}
BEGIN
  NoNegatives:= true;
  FOR Index:= 1 TO LastElement DO
    IF AnArray[Index] < 0 THEN
      NoNegatives:= false
    ELSE
      NoNegatives:= true
END;
```

    (a) What value will be assigned to NoNegatives given that LastElement is equal to 5 and the values assigned to the elements of AnArray are as follows?

```
            AnArray   [1]      [2]      [3]      [4]      [5]
                       5        3       -2        6        4
```

(b) What is the loop invariant on the value given to NoNegatives?

5. A function to flag that some invalid value is an element of AnArray might be coded using

```
FUNCTION Invalid(VAR AnArray: ArrayType; Lower, Upper: integer;
                              LastElement: integer): boolean;
  {If one of the elements of AnArray in the subrange 1..LastElement has
  a value either less than Lower or greater than Upper, Invalid returns
  true}
  VAR
    Index: integer;   {index to present element in AnArray being accessed}
  BEGIN
    Invalid:= false;
    FOR Index:= 1 TO LastElement DO
      IF (AnArray[Index] < Lower) OR (AnArray[Index] > Upper) THEN
          Invalid:= true
  END;
```

Is this function correct? Explain using assertions.

Sharpen Your Implementation Skills

6. Rewrite the function of Exercise 4 so that it is correct.

7. Rewrite the function of Exercise 5 so that only one assignment is made to Invalid.

8. Rewrite the example given at the start of the section so that both (1) a more enlightening prompt is displayed and (2) a guard to ensure the proper postcondition is coded.

Practice Your Program Testing Skills

9. Use Tables 10.2 and 10.3 to determine test values on the elements of Names as shown in Figure 10.10. Indicate values of SearchName that represent good test values using Names.

10. What test values would represent an exhaustive set of values for a search with Figure 10.10? Is exhaustive testing appropriate on very large structures (say, 10,000 elements)? Why or why not?

11. The array Names should be sorted and not contain duplicate names. Write how Names of Figure 10.10 should appear given this requirement.

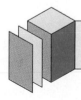

REVIEW AND EXERCISES

It is possible to define a one-dimensional array whose host type for the access subrange is not of type integer. You can use this capability to implement an *array of counters,* an *array of conversion values,* an *array of flag values,* an *array to encode or decode values,* and so forth. Many problems can be solved quite ingeniously by taking advantage of this feature of the Pascal language.

The problem to *search* for a particular element in an array is well-studied. Usually, a given search algorithm is coded as a function that returns the *index value* of the first array element *probe* whose value matches the *search* value. If no matches are found in the entire structure, the value returned to the function is, by convention, 0. This situation flags a *failed search*. If a nonzero index value is returned, it indicates a *successful search*.

A good search algorithm has the following properties: (1) One probe is made per loop pass. (2) Either the probe returns a successful match or a new probe is chosen. (3) The new probe's value depends upon the old probe's value and the *candidate subrange*. (4) If a probe fails, the candidate subrange is reduced in size. (5) The postloop assertion must always be, "Either a match has been found and the index value is known or all possibilities for a match have been exhausted." Typically, this exit condition is known as *finished or Found*.

The *linear search algorithm* eliminates one candidate element per loop pass. It is possible to code this algorithm with a *sentinel element*, initialized to the search value. If the match is found with the sentinel element, it indicates a failed search. A correct linear search algorithm needs no preconditions except a well-defined candidate subrange in order for it to work properly.

The *binary search algorithm* eliminates half the candidate elements with each looppass. It thus reduces the size of the candidate subrange by half. In order for this algorithm to work, however, the elements of the array must be sorted. It is possible to eliminate the boolean flag variable with this algorithm also, although the code is somewhat more difficult to read. A sentinel element is inappropriate for this algorithm.

A sorting algorithm does not change the actual values of the array elements, but it rearranges them so that the elements are in either *ascending order* or *descending order*. As the computer carries out the sorting algorithm, more elements are put in order, and less elements are out of order with each loop pass. After the final loop pass of the outermost loop, all elements are in order.

Any given algorithm is characterized by its *big-Oh*. An algorithm's big-Oh is expressed as a function of N, the number of variables that are to be processed. Typical functions are $O(N^2)$ for many sorting algorithms, $O(N)$ for the linear search algorithm, $O(\log_2(N))$ for the binary search algorithm, and $O(1)$ for all algorithms that do not require repetitive processing. The function used to express a big-Oh applies to the equation $T \approx k * f(N)$, where T represents the time required for the algorithm to be completed, k represents the time cost per loop pass, and $f(N)$, the algorithm's big-Oh, is a function of N.

Make sure that all array *access expressions* are *in range* for all possible values they can take on at run time. You can make sure they are in range with some good assertion testing. You can likewise desk check each access expression to make sure all values fall within the defined subrange(s).

When testing a search algorithm, be sure to choose an array of test data for a search that reflects the characteristics of the structure to be used in the program. If duplicate elements are allowed, you absolutely must include some in your test array. If a binary search is to be tested, make sure the array is sorted.

When you choose test values for the actual search, be sure to test that the algorithm correctly finds the first and last elements in the structure. Besides these two extreme values, you should also try "typical" values that return a successful search. Do not forget to test extreme values for which the search fails. Thus, a search for an element less than the smallest one and a search for an element greater than the largest one must be tried. Be sure, also, to test typical "middle" values for which the search fails. Finally, if duplicate values are allowed, make sure to test a search for some of these values. If your search algorithm is to return the lowest or highest index in the subrange of duplicate values, this test will determine whether this aspect of the algorithm is correct or not.

When two competing algorithms can be applied and the big-Ohs are different, you should always choose the algorithm with the best big-Oh. Usually, the more efficient algorithm will be coded such that it employs a "trick" to gain run-time efficiency. If both algorithms have the same big-Oh, you will have to decide whether clarity of code or run-time efficiency is the main issue. If the more efficient code is too obscure and the program must be maintained frequently, the somewhat less efficient but more readable algorithm may be the better choice.

EXERCISES

Short Answers

1. An algorithm with $O(1)$ is the (most, least) efficient kind of algorithm.

2. If it takes 50 microseconds to process 250 values with an algorithm of $O(N)$, how long will it require to process 1000 values using the same algorithm?

3. Repeat Exercise 2, but assume an algorithm of $O(N^2)$.

4. A precondition required in order for the binary search algorithm to work is that the list be _____ .

5. The linear search algorithm is preferred over the binary search algorithm when the list is either _____ or _____ .

6. Does standard Pascal allow values for enumerated types to be read from the keyboard?

7. What is the big-Oh of an algorithm that displays the values of a one-dimensional array?

8. True or false? If the binary search algorithm is used when the array is called by value, the overall process has an efficiency of $O(N)$.

9. The following unsorted array is given.

A[1]	A[2]	A[3]	A[4]	A[5]
37	92	15	45	78

How will its appearance change after the first outer loop pass if the selection sort is applied to it?

10. Repeat Exercise 9 for the bubble sort algorithm.

11. True or false? An expression used to gain access to one of the elements of an array always has implied semantics, regardless of how the array is used.

12. Suppose you have a sorted list that contains duplicate names. Explain why the binary search algorithm without the boolean variable Found is the better of the two versions to use on this structure.

13. Suppose the time required for the computer to complete an algorithm is given by the equation

$$T = k * f(N) + K$$

   (a) Indicate what $k, f(N)$, and K represent.
   (b) Which of these three quantities is used to express an algorithm's big-Oh?

14. Indicate the big-Oh for each of the following processes: linear search, bubble sort, selection sort, any call by variable, call by value on a scalar object, call by value on an array, binary search with a flag variable, and binary search algorithm without a flag variable.

15. What would be the big-Oh for the following two looping processes:
   (a) *FOR I ← 1 TO N DO*
           FOR J ← 1 TO N DO
               some O(1) process
   (b) *FOR I ← 1 TO N DO*
           some O(1) process
       FOR J ← 1 TO N DO
           some O(1) process

16. After each loop pass of a search algorithm, one of two actions is taken. What are they?

17. True or false? Arrays can only be sorted in ascending order.

Easy Projects

18. The solution to Case Study 10.1 will not work if you are on a system that uses the EBCDIC collating sequence rather than the ASCII sequence. First, consult Appendix A to see how the EBCDIC collating sequence is set up. Then write a program that will work for either the ASCII or the EBCDIC collating sequence. (*Hint:* You will need three array variables.)

19. Two very interesting statistics related to sorting algorithms are the number of compares made and the number of exchanges done. You are to write a program that takes these statistics for the three sorting algorithms. In order to do so, you must write the following procedures:
   (a) Generate, a procedure that uses the RNG to generate and store in an array a specified amount of random integers. The array variable is the output parameter, and the two input parameters are the initial seed value and the count of the numbers to be generated.
   (b) CountBubbleSort, a procedure that carries out the bubble sort algorithm while also keeping a count of the number of comparisons done and the number of exchanges made.
   (c) CountSelectionSort, a procedure that does the same thing with the selection sort algorithm.
   (d) CountInsertion Sort, a procedure that does the same thing using the insertion sort algorithm.
       The main program should generate perhaps generate 100 random numbers and then get the statistics for the bubble sort algorithm. It should generate the same 100 random numbers and get selection sort statistics. Finally, the same 100 numbers are again generated to get insertion sort statistics. Then all sets of statistics are displayed.

20. Repeat Exercise 2 but this time solely for the insertion sort algorithm. This time, set up and run the program so that an average number of compares and exchanges is found for 25 different arrays.

21. Use the random-number generator to generate and store 100 numbers in the array variable Ints such that all numbers lie in the subrange 1..25. Have the values displayed on 10 lines of output. Then write a procedure ShowIndices that displays the *index values* of the elements in Ints equal to the search value. A typical call to display the index values equal to 25 is coded as ShowIndices(Ints, 25). The main block of the program should first set up Ints, display the elements of Ints, and then drive the procedure ShowIndices three times with values read in from the keyboard.

Medium
Projects

22. Use the random-number generator and a sorting algorithm to generate and store 100 elements into Ints, a sorted array where the values of the elements can lie in the subrange 1..25. Then use a form of the linear search algorithm to code a procedure Return-Subrange that will return the lower and upper subrange values of all elements of Ints whose values are equal to SearchValue. The procedure is typically called by ReturnSubrange(Ints, SearchValue, Lower, Upper), where Ints[Lower] and Ints[Upper] are both equal to SearchValue. As the problem is stated, you know that Ints[Lower-1] and Ints[Upper+1] are not equal to SearchValue. If there is no subrange, have the procedure return the values of 0 and 0 to Lower and Upper. Once the array is built, the main block should call this procedure three times where SearchValue is read in from the keyboard.

23. You are to use the computer to stimulate the play of a game of solitaire with the following rules:

Integers between 1 and 50 are generated and stored into Game, an array capable of holding 50 integer values. The elements are assigned values in sequence from Game[1] to Game[50] using the RNG. Exactly 50 integers are to be generated, and no integer is to be returned twice.

You must use an array of booleans to keep track of the numbers generated. If a number is returned that was previously generated, have the computer return the next higher number. Thus, if 28 is returned and had already been generated, an attempt is made to assign 29 to an element of Game. If 29 was also generated, the computer will see if 30 was assigned, and so forth. Obviously, if 50 were already assigned, an attempt is made to assign 1 and not 51.

The integer values in Game are then checked to see how many of the 50 integers are in their "proper place." If an integer is in its proper place (e.g., on the Nth loop pass, the value of Game[N] is N), a running counter IntsInPlace is incremented by 1. The object of the game is for IntsInPlace to be as small a number as possible. After the values are checked, the value of IntsInPlace is displayed.

The game is played 10 times where the values of Game for the first two games along with the value IntsInPlace are to be displayed. For all 10 games, the highest, lowest, and average value(s) of IntsInPlace are to be displayed. *Example:* Given the following values of Games:

12	46	32	15	9	5	22	50	27	10
39	45	36	6	24	16	26	18	37	1
33	21	23	7	44	48	13	20	4	11
31	42	47	29	30	17	43	34	14	2
41	35	19	8	25	40	3	38	49	28

IntsInPlace $\leftarrow$ 7 (as shown by the underscored integers).

24. You are to write a program that generates cryptograms using the RNG. First, encoder and decoder arrays are built and the encoded elements are found using an RNG. Both arrays Encoder and Decoder contain characters in the subrange 'a'..'z', where the access subrange is also `'a'..'z'`. If, for example, `Encoder['a'] ↔ 'p'`, it means that the letter `'a'` encodes into `'p'`. The corresponding element in the `Decoder` array is `Decoder['p'] ↔ 'a'`.

Once the encoder and decoder arrays are built, a file of text to be encoded is read in character by character and written into another file where the characters have been encoded. The contents of the encoded file are then displayed. Next, this file is again read in and decoded character by character. The decoded values are displayed as characters that are read in from the encoded file.

The main block is described by the following pseudocode:

> *assign values to encoder array using RNG*
> *generate decoder array from encoder array*
> *display Encoder and Decoder arrays*
> *read contents of FileA, encoding it into FileB*
> *display contents of FileB*
> *read FileB again, this time displaying the contents as decoded*

Most of the logic is straightforward, except for the action that assigns values to the encoder array. The values are assigned using the algorithm that follows.

The RNG values returned are divided up into 26 "even" intervals. You will use these intervals to assign encoded letters according to the following sequence:

> *FOR letter ← 'A' to 'Z' do*
>   *get Coder {letter between 'A'..'Z' using RNG}*
>   *WHILE (Coder value has already been used) DO*
>   *Coder ← succ(Coder) {when Coder = 'Z', wrap around to 'A'}*
>   *Encoder [Letter] ← Coder*

You should use an array of booleans to indicate that a "Coder has already been used."

Difficult Projects

25. Write a program `SortMerge` whose run will result in the following actions:
    (a) The creation of two files, `FileA.dat` and `FileB.dat`, of unsorted integers using the RNG. You (the user) indicate the number of values to be stored in each file at run time. A sentinel value of `maxint` is used to indicate the end of each file.
    (b) The reading and sorting of the contents of `FileA` into the array `FileAPrime`.
    (c) The reading and sorting of the contents of `FileB` into the array `FileBPrime`.
    (d) The merging of the contents of `FileAPrime` and `FileBPrime` into `FileC.dat`, such that it is sorted and has `maxint` to indicate the end of the file.
    (e) The display of the contents of `FileA.dat`, `FileB.dat`, and `FileC.dat`. The run need not generate lots of numbers; perhaps 25 or so in each file will do. Do not use more file variables than are required.

26. Write a program to censor words in a text file, where the censored words are found in the file `BadWords.dat`. Each line of text in this file contains a word that must be censored from the other text file. The number of words to be censored from any given file is expected to be no more than 20 and could be considerably less. Words that are candidates for censorship are stored in the array of strings `Censor`. A word that is censored will be replaced by a string of "***", where the number of stars in the string will be the number of letters in the censored word. The main block sequence for the program is described by

> *reset(BadWords)*

assign elements of Censor, using contents of BadWords
alphabetically sort Censor
open and reset SomeFile
create OtherFile, the censored version of SomeFile, using Censor
display Censor's elements and the contents of both files

The program should censor any words that are to be censored, regardless of whether they consist of all uppercase letters, all lowercase letters, or a combination of the two. (*Hint:* The words in `Censor` should be all of one case, and the comparison word should be of one case.) Note that alphabetizing `Censor` increases the efficiency of the search for censorship of a given test word.

27. Each commuter van in the Vancee Vans fleet can seat up to 15 people. Suppose a given route serviced by Vancee Vans has N stops and the route originates at the 0th stop. You are to write a program that simulates the pickup and discharge actions taken from the point of origin (stop 0) to the final destination (stop N) for the van route.

The action of the main block sequence is described the following way:

Initialize(Departs, N, TotPassengers)
FOR Stop ← 1 TO N-1 DO
    Discharge(TotPassengers, Departs, Stop)
    IF TotPassenger < MaxPassengers THEN
       PickUp(Departs, TotPassengers)
Discharge(TotPassengers, Departs, N)

The array element *Departs[M]* represents the count of the number of passengers getting off at stop M. The action of the procedure *Discharge* should be obvious from the sample run. If no passengers are getting off a full van, the machine displays a "no room" message.

If more passengers are waiting for the van than there are available seats, the computer issues a "no more room" message to the remaining passengers. Otherwise all passengers waiting are let on the van. Before getting on the van, each passenger is asked the number of the stop (whose value must be greater than the present stop, but not greater than $N + 1$) where he or she is getting off. If an out-of-range number is entered, the passenger does not get on, otherwise he or she does. From the value entered, the count of passengers getting off at the designated stop is incremented by 1, and the value of `TotPassengers` is incremented by 1. Typical run:

```
Enter total number of stops:   5
Enter number of passengers:   14
Enter destination:   2
Enter destination:   7
We have no stops for that destination.   {passenger not let on}
Enter destination:   1
{13 passengers with: 3 passengers getting off at stop 1, 2 getting off
at 2, 0 getting off at 3, 5 getting off at 4, 3 getting off at 5}
----------
3 passengers were let off at stop 1
Enter number of passengers:   7
Enter destination:   2
Enter destination:   2
Enter destination:   6
We have no stops for that destination.
```

```
Enter destination:   4
Enter destination:   5
Enter destination:   4
Sorry, the van is full.
---------
4 passengers were let off at stop 2.
Enter number of passengers:   4
Enter destination:   5
Enter destination:   5
Enter destination:   4
Enter destination:   5
----------
0 passengers were let off at stop 3.
Sorry, the van is full.
----------
8 passengers were let off at stop 4.
Enter number of passengers:   3
Enter destination:   5
Enter destination:   5
Enter destination:   5
----------
10 passengers were let off at stop 5.
```

C H A P T E R 11

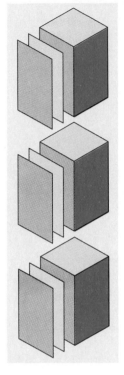

MULTIDIMENSIONAL ARRAYS

OBJECTIVES

After reading and studying the material of the present chapter, you should be able to

- Define and declare multidimensional arrays, using proper syntax

- Develop programs that require the use of multidimensional arrays

- Correctly apply proven algorithms that use two-dimensional arrays

- Compare the relative merits of using a multidimensional array versus parallel arrays to solve a problem

- Use one-dimensional and multidimensional arrays together to solve a problem

- Discuss the memory costs of using large multidimensional arrays in a program

YOUR PROFESSOR'S GRADEBOOK HAS MANY ROWS OF NUM-
BERS IN IT. Each row represents a given student's test results. We could also
say the book contains columns of numbers. Each column represents the class results on a given test. Any row-by-column value, moreover, represents the score
a given student (row number) received on a given test (column number).

You have seen other two-dimensional objects in everyday life that hold
values. For example, the row-by-column positions on a chess board can be occupied by a given chess piece. Rows of numbers divided into 12 columns might
indicate the sales records of sales personnel for a particular company over the
past year.

You can implement any of these row-by-column structures in Pascal as an
array variable requiring two access expressions. In this chapter, you will learn
how to implement these structures for problems that require them.

11.1   Two-Dimensional Array Syntax and Semantics

In this section you will learn the syntax rules that apply to the implementation of
two-dimensional arrays. There are many different situations for which this type of
structured variable is appropriate. This section discusses three circumstances where
the two-dimensional array is the appropriate structure to use.

*Multi-
dimensional
arrays*

The syntax diagram to define any kind of array is shown in Figure 11.1. Note
that more than one subrange can be used in the definition syntax. An array defined
with more than one access subrange is known as a *multidimensional array*. If an array is defined in terms of two subranges, it has a *dimensionality* of 2. The defining
subranges can be of different types, but the array elements themselves are all of the
same type.

> **Multidimensional array:**   an array defined such that more than one expres-
> sion is required to access an element.

> **Dimensionality of an array:**   the number of subrange expressions required
> to access an element.

FIGURE 11.1   Syntax for defining an array of any dimensionality.

array definition

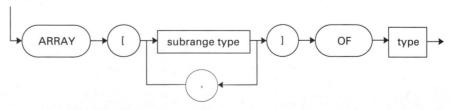

Access syntax rules

The syntax diagram to access an element of an array for any given dimensionality is shown in Figure 11.2. The access expressions must agree one to one with each subrange host type, otherwise there is a syntax error.

Using Integer Subscripts

Let us write a source code fragment that represents a teacher's grade book. We will use a two-dimensional array for the implementation. Then we will consider the semantics implied by the structure.

Source code

We want the array to have an appearance suggested by Figure 11.3. The required code to implement this structure is as follows:

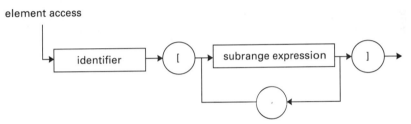

element access

FIGURE 11.2 Syntax diagram to access an array element.

Results	1]	2]	3]	4]	5]	6]	7]	8]
[1,	72	65	80	83				
[2,	78	70	89	86	U			
[3,	54	60	75	71				
[4,	90	60	34	55		N		
[5,	72	86	94	88				
⋮	⋮	⋮	⋮	⋮		U		
[M,	75	63	82	82			S	
⋮	⋮	⋮	⋮	⋮				
[N,	90	98	91	94			E	
⋮	⋮	⋮	⋮	⋮				
[36,	45	63	60	65			D	
[50,	U	N	U	S	E	D		

Total Students 36

TotalTests 4

FIGURE 11.3 The array variable Results.

```
CONST
   MaxStus = 50;      {total allowed students in a class}
   MaxTests = 8;      {maximum number of tests any professor might give}
TYPE
   StuNoType = 1..MaxStus;      {access subrange for a student's results}
   TestNoType = 1..MaxTests;    {access subrange for a test's results}
   ResArray = ARRAY[StuNoType, TestNoType] OF integer;
VAR
   TotalStudents,         {total number of students in class}
   TotalTests: integer;   {total number of tests given to class}
   Results: ResArray;     {results of all students on all tests}
```

Semantics

The first access expression on an element of Results represents a particular student, and the second access expression represents a particular test. For example, the variable Results[5, 3], which is equal to 94, suggests that student five scored a 94 on test three.

Note how Figure 11.3 suggests that some of the elements do not have values assigned to them. The structure is capable of storing the results for 50 students on eight tests, but all the elements may not necessarily be used. Even though 400 integer values can be stored in Results (50×8), a total of 36×4 elements are actually used. In this case, the population of the given class was 36, and the teacher elected to give them a total of 4 tests.

Using two-dimensional arrays

The elements across any given row of Results can be envisioned as a one-dimensional array parallel to any other "row array" of MaxTests elements. Figure 11.4, for example, shows how the Mth and Nth rows of Results can represent test results for student M and for student N. Results[M, 3], for example, represents the score student M received on test 3. So does the element MsTests[3]. Likewise, Results[N, 3] and NsTests[3] represent the test score for student N on test 3.

The elements down any column in Results can likewise represent parallel arrays, each containing MaxStus elements. Refer to Figure 11.5 for the one-dimensional arrays that are equivalent to the column values for the first and second columns of Results. The figure shows that the elements Results[5, 1] and

FIGURE 11.4 The one-dimensional array equivalent for students *M* and *N* from Results.

	[1]	[2]	[3]	[4]	[5]	[6]	[7]	[8]	
MsTests	75	63	82	82	UNUSED				(Mth row of Results)

Total Tests 4

	[1]	[2]	[3]	[4]	[5]	[6]	[7]	[8]	
NsTests	90	98	91	94	UNUSED				(Nth row of Results)

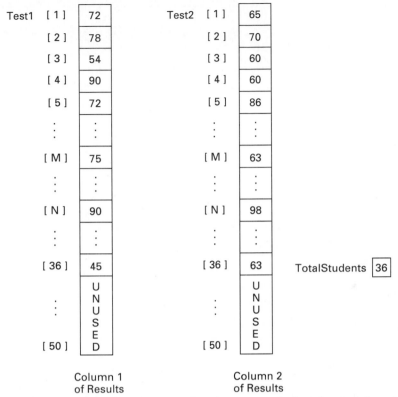

Test1 [1] 72   Test2 [1] 65
      [2] 78   [2] 70
      [3] 54   [3] 60
      [4] 90   [4] 60
      [5] 72   [5] 86
        ⋮   ⋮
      [M] 75   [M] 63
        ⋮   ⋮
      [N] 90   [N] 98
        ⋮   ⋮
      [36] 45   [36] 63   TotalStudents 36
           U   U
           N   N
        ⋮ U   ⋮   U
           S   S
           E   E
      [50] D   [50] D

        Column 1   Column 2
        of Results   of Results

FIGURE 11.5 The one-dimensional array equivalent for test 1 and test 2 from `Results`.

`Test1[5]` both represent the score student number 5 got on test 1. In like manner, `Results[5, 2]` and `Test2[5]` represent the score the same student 5 received on test 2.

Two-dimensional versus parallel arrays

You will often use two-dimensional arrays to exploit the implied semantics of parallel arrays in the solution of a problem. If you want to find the average of student *M*, for example, you simply write code to average the scores over row *M* of `Results`. Likewise, if you want to find the class average on test 1, you write code to take the average over the scores in column 1 of the array `Results`.

In the next section, you will learn some algorithms that apply specifically to two-dimensional arrays. These algorithms work because a two-dimensional array takes on the implied semantics of parallel arrays. All elements, though, must be of the same type, a property that detracts from this structure's apparent usefulness. The elements of two-dimensional arrays, however, take on the semantics of parallel arrays for two totally different access mechanisms. This property makes the two-dimensional array an attractive choice for problems when all implied parallel structures contain elements of the same type.

PROGRAM DESIGN RULE 11.1

Always access the elements of a multidimensional array using access expressions coded in the order in which they were defined.

PROGRAM DESIGN RULE 11.2

Always assign values to all variables used in forming the access expressions before applying the expressions to any given array.

*Two program
design rules*

If you use a two-dimensional array in processing, you must always remember to follow both Program Design Rules. The access order to any given element is always the same regardless of the logic used to set up the access expressions. Moreover, all expressions must take on an actual value before an element can be accessed.

*Applying the
rules*

Example 11.1 shows how both of these design rules apply. The value assigned to TestNo was assigned outside the block first. The value of StudentNo is then assigned inside the block by loop control. Nevertheless, each element of Results is accessed first by student number and then by test number. Regardless of the assignment order, the access variables both have values. This precondition ensures proper access to the integer variable Results[StudentNo, TestNo].

Example 11.1

```
FUNCTION ClassAverage
        (VAR Results: ResArray; TestNo, TotalStudents: integer): real;
  {returns the class average on TestNo for the TotalStudents in the
  class.  Results contains the test results for all students on all
  tests.}
VAR
  StudentNo,    {the present student whose score is being accessed}
  ScoreSum:     {the sum of the test scores for 1..StudentNo students}
            integer;
BEGIN
  ScoreSum:= 0;
  FOR StudentNo:= 1 TO TotalStudents DO
    ScoreSum:= ScoreSum + Results[StudentNo, TestNo];
  ClassAverage:= ScoreSum/TotalStudents
END;
```

Failure to follow Program Design Rule 11.1 will usually result in a syntax-error message. Even if the program compiles, the semantics would be misapplied, and the program would definitely be wrong. Failure to follow Program Design Rule 11.2 will usually result in a run-time crash due to an out-of-range index value. On some machines, however, a default assignment value may be applied to the access expression. This event will most commonly occur with the value of 0 when the access type is an `integer`. If you have defined a subrange such that the access value of 0 is allowed, the computer may access the zeroth row or column more times than it should.

Subscripts with Other Ordinal Types

As long as the access subranges are ordinal types, they can be of any type required to solve the problem. The host types to access the elements of a multidimensional array need not even be of the same type, as the next two examples illustrate.

*An array of
strings*

We can use a two-dimensional array variable `Villagers` to store the names of the citizens in six different villages. The appearance of the array is suggested by Figure 11.6. Each column defines the population of a different village. If an element is not used, its value is the null string. Note that although this structure is capable of holding 6000 character strings, all elements are not used. In fact, because each village has a different population, the number of column elements with values filled in will differ from one column to the next.

Source code

The code to implement the two-dimensional array `Villagers` is given in the following fragment:

```
CONST
  MaxCitizens = 1000;
TYPE
  StringType = STRING[50];   {use your dialect's syntax here}
  CitizenSubrange = 1..MaxCitizens;
  NamesOfVillages = (NilVillage, Brownesville, Fairtown, Pleasantville,
                     Smallville, Tinseltown, Wayoutsville);

                                          OF StringType;
VAR
  Villagers: NamesArray;
```

*Variable access
semantics*

The row values in this case represent a given citizen's "number." From the array definition, you can see that there is no inherent relationship between citizen M in one village and citizen M in another village. Thus, `Villagers[319, Fairtown]`, whose value is `'Sandy Hobart'`, has no relationship to `Villagers[319, Tinseltown]` whose value is `'Roy Biv'`.

You can set up a program that uses this structure where the names in each village are arranged in some order. For example, the element Vil-

Villagers	Brownesville]	Fairtown]	Pleasantville]	Smallville]	Tinseltown]	Wayoutsville]
[1,	Joe Blowe	Jason Chasten	Jackson Andrews	Mac Nife	Sally Silly	Jack Ripper
[2,	Geraldine Go	Helen Poole	George Boole	Sam Samuel	Josie Boyce	Beth Bethe
. . .	. . .	. . .	. . .	. . .	. . .	. . .
[319,	J.J. Jones	Sandy Hobart	Bugsy Moran	Mata Hari	Roy Biv	Alice Towers
. . .	. . .	N	. . .	. . .	. . .	. . .
[422,	Sharon Rose	U	Richard Hertz	Suzanne Yee	Westley East	Earl Lorde
. . .	. . .	L	N	. . .	. . .	. . .
			U			
[515,	Peaches Jamm	L	L	Brook Babble	Jane Plane	Eastly West
. . .	. . .		L	. .	N	. .
			L		U	
[628,	Jill Bowen			Sunny Daye	L	Gus Trick
	N	S		. .	L	. .
	U	T	S			
[732,	L	R	T	William Till	S	Sol I. Terry
	L		R	. .	T	N
		I				U
	S		I		R	L
	T	N			I	L
[849,	R	G	N	N. Owen Letfe	N	S
	I		G		G	T
	N	S		NULL	S	R
	G		S			I
	S			Strings		N
[1000,						G
						S

FIGURE 11.6 The structured variable `Villagers`.

lagers [1, Brownesville] might represent the name of the mayor of Brownesville or this village's eldest citizen. In the latter case, 'Jill Bowen', the 628th citizen of Brownsville, might then be the youngest citizen. With Villagers, it is easier to envision algorithms that operate down a column of elements rather than across a row of elements.

A structure for a game board

You can implement a chessboard, as suggested by Figure 11.7, using the code given as Example 11.2. Row access is defined by the anonymous subrange 'A'..'H' and column access by the subrange '1'..'8'. The chess pieces themselves will take on the *char* values K, k, Q, q, R, r, N, n, B, b, P, p, and X where the upper case characters represent the white player's pieces and the lower case characters represent the black player's. The char value 'X' represents an unoccupied space.

ChessBoard

	1]	2]	3]	4]	5]	6]	7]	8]
[H,	R	N	B	Q	K	B	N	R
[G	P	P	P	P	P	P	P	P
[F,	X	X	X	X	X	X	X	X
[E,	X	X	X	X	X	X	X	X
[D,	X	X	X	X	X	X	X	X
[C,	X	X	X	X	X	X	X	X
[B,	P	P	P	P	P	P	P	P
[A,	r	n	b	q	k	b	n	r

FIGURE 11.7 The array variable ChessBoard.

Example 11.2

```
TYPE
    GameBoardType: ARRAY['A'..'H', '1'..'8'] OF char;
VAR
    ChessBoard: GameBoardType;
```

The appearance of ChessBoard at the start of a game is shown in the figure. We see, for example, that the value of ChessBoard['B', '7'] is 'p', indicating that a black pawn is on this square. As additional examples we have that the white queen occupies row 'H' and column '4', and that the square designated by row 'D' and column '4' is presently unoccupied.

Access expression semantics

When you implement a game board, the type of processing on the array elements depends upon the rules of the game. On a chessboard, for example, a queen can move up or down a row, up or down a column, or up or down one of the two diagonals. If you set up some chess-playing program, you need plenty of operations that apply specifically to the game of chess. Depending upon the chess piece, operations can be applied in directions other than just along the row or column values.

EXERCISES

Test Your Understanding

1. Explain briefly why the variable `Results`, as given in the first example, will usually have unassigned elements when used in a program.

2. If the variable `ChessBoard` of Example 11.2 is used in a program, will it ever have unassigned elements? Explain your answer.

Test Your Analysis Skills

3. Explain in one sentence why the access subrange for the second dimension of `Villagers` did not start with `NilVillage`.

4. State the loop invariant on the variable `ScoreSum` as it is used in Example 11.1.

Sharpen Your Implementation Skills

5. Define and declare structures for each of the following:
   (a) A variable to store the names of the students for the four different courses a professor teaches for a given semester. Up to 50 students are allowed in each class.
   (b) A variable to store the names of the students for one given course that a professor teaches for a given semester.
   (c) A variable to store the averages of each of the `TotalStudents` students in a given class.
   (d) A variable to store the results of test M for each of the `TotalStudents` students in a given class.
   (e) A variable to store the progress of a tic-tac-toe game.
   (f) A variable to store the number of games won by each team from each of the other teams in a bowling league that has 8 teams.
   (g) A variable to store the coefficients of a set of five linear equations with five unknown quantitites. (Hint: How many coefficients are there? How did you know the answer to this question?) Note that some of the structures may not require two-dimensional arrays.

6. Do any of the structures of Exercise 5 represent a parallel array to one or more of the structures given in the text? If so, which ones? Do any of them represent parallel structures between the different parts of Exercise 5? If so, which ones?

7. Using the array `Results`, write a function that does the following:
   (a) Returns the highest overall average of all the students.
   (b) Returns the lowest test score on the third test given.

11.2 Two-Dimensional Array-Processing Algorithms

We have already said that the elements across a given row or down a given column are logically equivalent to a one-dimensional array. The two-dimensional array can thus be envisioned as a structure containing parallel arrays in both the row and the column directions. The algorithms we present in this section are based on this particular vision of a two-dimensional array variable.

A sample structure

Before you see the algorithms, let us implement a structured variable on which we can apply them. The variable we will use, `Sales`, is shown in Figure 11.8. It represents the sales records at Wonderful Widgets Inc. Any given element represents the number of one of the five models a given representative sold for the last month. The row access values represent a given sales representative's number.

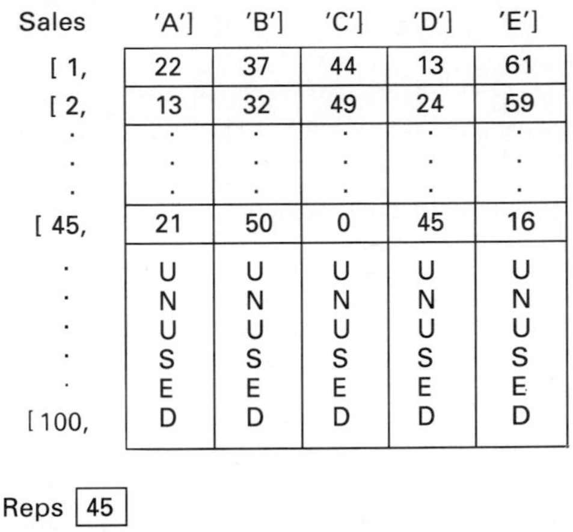

Sales	'A']	'B']	'C']	'D']	'E']
[1,	22	37	44	13	61
[2,	13	32	49	24	59
.	.	.	.	.	.
.	.	.	.	.	.
.	.	.	.	.	.
[45,	21	50	0	45	16
.	UNUSED	UNUSED	UNUSED	UNUSED	UNUSED
[100,					

Total Reps 45

FIGURE 11.8 The array variable Sales.

The column access values ('A' through 'E') represent one of the five widget models available for sale.

    The figure shows, for example, that sales representative 1 sold 22 model A widgets over the last month, sales representative 2 sold 59 model E widgets, and so forth. The value of TotalReps represents the total number of sales representatives in the company for the month the report was put together. The implementation for the variable of Figure 11.8 is given as

```
CONST
  MaxReps = 100;      {maximum number of possible sales reps}
TYPE
  RepType = 1..MaxReps;
  ModelType = 'A'..'E';
  SalesArray = ARRAY[RepType, ModelType] OF integer;
VAR
  Sales: SalesArray;   {number of models each rep sold}
  TotalReps: RepType;  {total reps in sales force}
```

Four Useful Algorithms

The array Sales has implied semantics both across a single row and down a single column. The nature of these semantics suggest four standard algorithms, namely (1) row-by-column processing, (2) column-by-row processing, (3) single-row processing, and (4) single-column processing. We will describe these four algorithms in turn, then use the array Sales to implement each of them.

Row-By-Column Processing. A row-by-column processor uses nested FOR loops, where the row access variable is assigned a value first. The description of the algorithm is given in the pseudocode of Algorithm 11.1.

Algorithm 11.1

{Row-by-column processing of a two-dimensional array:}
FOR RowIndex ← FirstRow TO LastRow DO
FOR ColumnIndex ← FirstColumn TO Last Column DO
process AnArray[RowIndex, ColumnIndex]
{end algorithm}

Using the
algorithm

Suppose the text file `SalesFile` (which is also a file variable) contains all integer values. The first line of the file contains the number of sales reps in the sales force. Each of the subsequent `TotalReps` lines in the file contains five integer values. Line *M + 1*, for example, represents the sales record for sales rep *M*. The five integers on this line represent the number of sales the representative had for the models `'A'` through `'E'`. We want to write a procedure `ReadSalesFile` that reads in values to the elements of `Sales` using the lines of `SalesFile`.

The code for `ReadSalesFile` is shown as Example 11.3. Figure 11.9 shows the access order for the row-by-column processing as it applies to the statement of `ReadSalesFile`. A row-by-column processor is the correct algorithm to use because each line of the file represents a sales rep's record of sales, just like a row in the structure `Sales`.

Example 11.3

```
PROCEDURE ReadSalesFile(VAR TotalReps: RepType; VAR Sales: SalesArray;
                                        VAR SalesFile: text);
   {assigns the elements of Sales, row by column, over the row subrange
   1..TotalReps.  TotalReps is first read in from SalesFile, then each
   line read in is used to assign values to another row of Sales.}
   VAR
      SalesRep: RepType;    {present rep whose sales are being read in}
      Model:  ModelType;    {the sales of the widget model being read in}
   BEGIN
      reset(SalesFile);
      readln(SalesFile, TotalReps);
      FOR SalesRep:= 1 TO TotalReps DO
        BEGIN    {process a row}
          FOR Model:= 'A' TO 'E' DO {process over column subrange:}
            read(SalesFile, Sales[SalesRep,Model]);
          readln(SalesFile)
        END
   END;
```

Column-By-Row Processing. A column-by-row processor uses nested FOR loops, where the column access variable is assigned the first value. The pseudocode for this algorithm as it applies to a generic `AnArray` is given in the description of Algorithm 11.2.

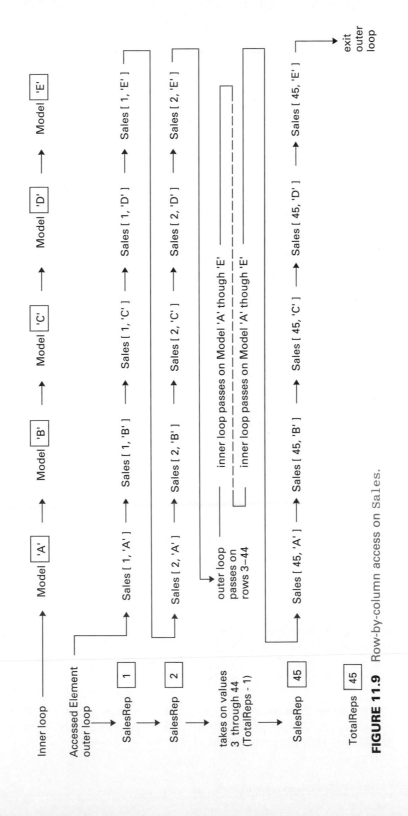

FIGURE 11.9 Row-by-column access on Sales.

Algorithm 11.2

{Column-by-Row processing of a two-dimensional array}
FOR ColumnIndex ← FirstColumn TO LastColumn DO
   FOR RowIndex ← FirstRow TO LastRow DO
      process AnArray[RowIndex, ColumnIndex]
{end algorithm}

Using the algorithm
    Suppose the elements of Sales have taken on values. Let us write a procedure ShowSalesByModel to display the number of overall sales for each of the five models. The computer will find the sum over the column elements and then display this value. It will carry out this process five times for each of the five columns. Thus, a column-by-row processor is the relevant algorithm to apply on the statement of this procedure.

    The access order to each of the elements using the column-by-row processor on the array Sales is shown as Figure 11.10. The code for the procedure ShowSalesByModel is given as Example 11.4, with a typical run shown below the source code.

Example 11.4

```
PROCEDURE ShowSalesByModel(VAR Sales: SalesArray; TotalReps: RepType);
   {uses the values of the elements of Sales to display the total number
   of each of the models sold by all TotalReps sales people}
   VAR
      SalesRep: RepType;    {sales rep reference variable}
      Model: ModelType;     {present model whose sales are being summed}
      Sum: integer;         {sum over 1..SalesRep of Sales for given Model}
   BEGIN
      FOR Model:= 'A' TO 'E' DO               {process a column}
         BEGIN
            Sum:= 0;
            FOR SalesRep:= 1 TO TotalReps DO    {process a row}
               Sum:= Sum + Sales[SalesRep, Model];
            writeln('The total sales for Model ',Model,' was ',Sum:1,'.')
         END
   END;
```

```
The total sales for Model A was 1342.
The total sales for Model B was 987.
The total sales for Model C was 1385.
The total sales for Model D was 1032.
The total sales for Model E was 877.
```

Single-Row Processing. Sometimes you may want to process the elements across a single row of a two-dimensional variable. The pseudocode for this algorithm is shown as Algorithm 11.3.

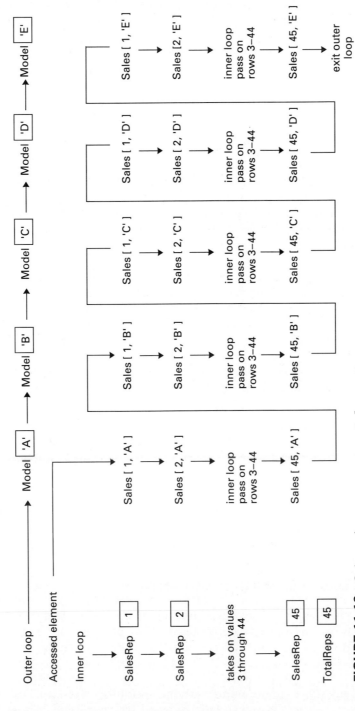

FIGURE 11.10 Column-by-row access on Sales.

Algorithm 11.3

> *{Single-row processor on a two-dimensional array:}*
> *get value for RowIndex*
> *FOR ColumnIndex ← FirstColumn TO LastColumn DO*
>   *process AnArray[RowIndex, ColumnIndex]*
> *{end algorithm}*

Using the
algorithm

Suppose we have also declared another array `Prices` using the code

```
TYPE
   PricesArray = ARRAY[ModelType] OF real;
VAR
   Prices: PricesArray;   {prices for each model}
```

The value of any given element of `Prices` represents the cost for the given (in-dexed) model. Let us use this array and the array `Sales` to write a function `RepsRevenues` that returns the revenues earned by a given sales representative for the month.

We require a row processor on the elements of `Sales`. The value of the row access expression, representing a given sales rep, is passed into the block. A sum of money earned is accumulated over the column subrange of a particular row of `Sales`. Each column element of the selected "row array" of `Sales` is multiplied by the associated element of `Prices` to get a dollar amount for the number of widgets sold.

Figure 11.11 shows the access mechanism used on the *M*th row of sales, and the source code for the function is shown as Example 11.5.

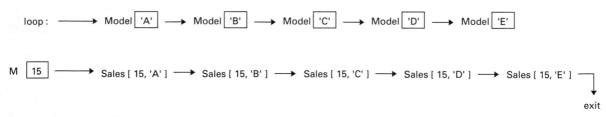

FIGURE 11.11 Single-row access on `Sales`.

Example 11.5

```
FUNCTION RepsRevenues(VAR Sales: SalesArray; VAR Prices: PricesArray;
                                  SalesRep: RepType): real;
 {uses the array Sales that represents all rep's sales records and the
  array Prices whose elements represent the prices of each widget model
  to return the dollar amount of revenues brought in by a given
  SalesRep}
 VAR
   Model:  ModelType;    {the model whose numbers are being summed}
   Sum: real;            {sum variable used to return value to function}
```

```
BEGIN
  Sum:= 0;
  FOR Model:= 'A' TO 'E' DO
    Sum:= Sum + Sales[SalesRep, Model] * Prices[Model];
  RepsRevenues:= Sum
END;
```

Single-Column Processing. We can likewise use a single-column processor on a two-dimensional array. The description for this algorithm on a generic two-dimensional AnArray is given in the pseudocode of Algorithm 11.4.

Algorithm 11.4

{Single-column processor on two-dimensional array:}
get ColumnIndex
FOR RowIndex ← FirstRow TO LastRow DO
    process AnArray[RowIndex, ColumnIndex]
{end algorithm}

Using the
algorithm

Let us write a function that returns the number of the sales representative who sold the most of a specified model. We can use this function, for example, to display the number of the sales rep who sold the most model C widgets with the code

```
write('The sales rep who sold the most C widgets was ');
writeln(BestRep(Sales, 'C', TotalReps):1, '.');
```

FIGURE 11.12 Single-column access on Sales.

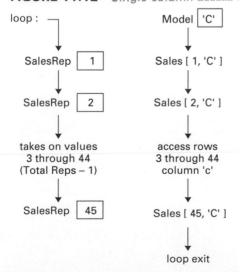

The required access mechanism for this function's statement is shown as Figure 11.12. We can use a most-significant-event-processing algorithm to find the row value of the element in column 'C' that has the highest value. The code for this function is shown as Example 11.6.

Example 11.6

```
FUNCTION BestRep(VAR Sales: SalesArray; Model: ModelType;
                                        TotalReps: RepType): RepType;
  {uses Sales to find the number of the sales rep out of all TotalReps
  sales reps who sold the most widgets of the given Model}
  VAR
    SalesRep,       {present rep whose sales is compared with PresentBest}
    PresentBest: RepType;  {candidate for BestRep}
  BEGIN
    PresentBest:= 1;        {initial candidate}
    FOR SalesRep:= 2 TO TotalReps DO
      IF Sales[SalesRep, Model] > Sales[PresentBest, Model] THEN
        PresentBest:= SalesRep;
    BestRep:= PresentBest
  END;
```

EXERCISES

Test Your Understanding

1. True or false? With column-by-row processing, the outer loop control variable is the column access variable.

2. True or false? With column-by-row processing, the first variable in the access expression to an element is the column access variable.

Practice Your Analysis Skills

3. Suppose we have defined and declared the following:

```
TYPE
  SmallSubrange = 1..4;
  SmallArray = ARRAY[SmallSubrange, SmallSubrange] OF integer;
VAR
  AnArray: SmallArray;
  I,J,K,L: SmallSubrange
  AValue : integer;
```

and that the appearance of AnArray is suggested by

7	12	15	10
19	15	2	18
13	20	16	9
11	15	14	15

What will be displayed by each of the following fragments of code?

(a)
```
FOR I:= 1 TO 4 DO
   FOR J:= 1 TO 4 DO
      write(AnArray[I,J]:3);
writeln;
```

(b)
```
FOR J:= 1 TO 4 DO
   FOR I:= 1 TO 4 DO
      write(AnArray[I,J]:3);
writeln;
```

(c)
```
K:= 3; AValue:= 0;
FOR J:= 1 TO 4 DO
   AValue:= AValue + AnArray[K,J]);
writeln(AValue:1);
```

(d)
```
K:= 1; L:= 2;
FOR I:= 2 TO 4 DO
   IF AnArray[I,L] > AnArray[K,L] THEN
      K:= I;
writeln(AnArray[K,L]:1);
```

(e)
```
AValue:= 0;
FOR K:= 1 TO 4 DO
   AValue:= AValue + AnArray[K,K];
writeln(AValue:1);
```

(f)
```
K:= 1, L:= 1;
FOR I:= 1 TO 4 DO
   FOR J:= 1 TO 4 DO
      IF AnArray[I,J] > AnArray[K,L] THEN
         BEGIN
            K:= I;
            L:= J
         END;
writeln(AnArray[K,L]:1);
```

4. Describe in one sentence what is accomplished by each of the fragments presented in Exercise 3. Also catagorize the looping strategy in each case.

Sharpen Your Implementation Skills

5. Given the variable Sales, write a procedure GetMostSales that returns: (a) the index value of the sales rep who sold the most models (all five models) and (b) the total number of models (again, all five) sold by this rep.

6. Write a procedure using both Sales and Prices, GetHighestRevenue, that returns: (a) the index value of the sales rep who generated the most revenue and (b) the amount of revenue generated.

7. Given the variable Results from Section 11.1, indicate which of the four algorithms is required for a function that returns:
   (a) the highest overall average of all the students
   (b) the lowest test score for the class on the Nth test given
   (c) the test number of the worst test taken by the Mth student

(d) a count of the number of perfect test papers written for all the tests given (a perfect paper is represented by a score of 100)

(e) the count of the number of students who failed the *N*th test. A failing grade is one for which a given score is below the value taken on by the formal parameter `PassingGrade`.

8. Write the code for each of the functions of Exercise 7.

11.3   Case Study: Processing a Payroll File

The case study of this section requires the use of arrays for its solution where one of the arrays is two-dimensional. We will use some of the ready-made algorithms given in the previous section to solve the problem posed as this case study.

CASE STUDY 11.1

The problem statement

The text file `PayrollInfo.dat` contains all numeric values. The first line of the file has a single integer on it representing the number of employees on a company's payroll. Each of the remaining lines of text contains payroll information about one of the employees. Any of these remaining lines has eight real numbers on it. The first seven numbers represent the hours an employee worked for each day of the week, beginning with the hours on Sunday. The last number represents the hourly rate at which the employee is paid.

If an employee works on Sunday, he or she is paid twice their normal pay rate for the hours worked. They receive 1.5 times their normal hourly rate for each hour worked on Saturday. On Monday through Friday, the employee is paid his or her regular pay rate for each hour worked.

The company president wants you to write a program that reads in the file's contents and then displays: (1) the size of the paycheck each of the employees should receive, (2) the total payroll for the week, (3) the number of employee hours worked for each of the seven days of the week.

A typical run of the program for a given `PayrollInfo` file is given along with a sample `PayRollInfo.dat` file as follows:

```
PayRollInfo.dat's contents

    4
    0.00   8.00   8.00   8.00   8.00   8.00   4.00   15.00
    0.00   7.50   9.00   7.50  10.00   0.00   8.00   12.00
    8.00   0.00   0.00   8.00   8.00   8.00   0.00   10.00
    0.00   8.00   8.00   8.00   7.00   9.00   0.00   20.00
```

Run:

Paychecks:
    Employee 1 receives a check for $690.00
    Employee 2 receives a check for $552.00
    Employee 3 receives a check for $400.00
    Employee 4 receives a check for $800.00
The total weekly payroll is $2442.00

Hours worked by all employees:
    Sunday   8.00
    Monday   23.50
    Tuesday   25.00
    Wednesday   31.50
    Thursday   33.00
    Friday   25.00
    Saturday   12.00

The main block   We can describe the main block of the program as follows:

prepare PayRollInfo file for reading
ReadFile(TotalEmployees, Hours, PayRates, PayRollInfo)
ShowPayroll(TotalEmployees, Hours, PayRates)
ShowHoursWorked(Hours)

When the computer executes the procedure ReadFile, it first reads in a value to TotalEmployees and then fills in the elements of the two array variables Hours and PayRates. The appearance of these two variables using the data from the sample file is shown in Figure 11.13. Each element of Hours represents the number of hours a given employee worked on a given day. Each element of

FIGURE 11.13 The structured variables Hours and PayRates.

Hours	Sun]	Mon]	Tue]	Wed]	Thu]	Fri]	Sat]	PayRates	
[1,	0.00	8.00	8.00	8.00	8.00	8.00	4.00	[1]	15.00
[2,	0.00	7.50	9.00	7.50	10.50	0.00	8.00	[2]	12.00
[3,	8.00	0.00	0.00	8.00	8.00	8.00	0.00	[3]	10.00
[4,	0.00	8.00	8.00	8.00	7.00	9.00	0.00	[4]	20.00
[5,	UNUSED	UNUSED	UNUSED	UNUSED	UNUSED	UNUSED	UNUSED		UNUSED
.									
.									
.									
[25,								[25]	

Total Employees [4]

Max Employees [25]

PayRates represents the hourly pay rate a given employee earns. All information about checks paid out to employees is displayed by the action of the ShowPayRoll block. The number of employee-hours worked for the seven days is shown when the computer executes the procedure ShowHoursWorked.

Source code

The source code layout for the main block is given as the program ProcessWorkWeek. We are assuming a Pascal dialect where the file variable is opened to a directory file by default.

```
PROGRAM ProcessWorkWeek(output, PayrollInfo);
   {Information about the company's operation over the past week is read
   in from PayrollInfo. The dollar amount for the checks written to each
   employee and the total amount paid out is displayed. Also, the number
   of employee hours worked for each day of the week is displayed }
   CONST
     MaxEmployees = 25;    {maximum possible workers company will employ}
   TYPE
     DayType = (NilDay, Sun, Mon, Tue, Wed, Thu, Fri, Sat);
     WorkArray = ARRAY[1..MaxEmployees, Sun..Sat] OF real;
     RatesArray = ARRAY[1..MaxEmployees] OF real;
   VAR
     PayrollInfo: text;         {contains payroll information}
     Hours: WorkArray;          {hours worked by each employee for each day}
     PayRates: RatesArray;      {hourly wages for each employee}
     TotalEmployees: integer;   {number of employees working over last week}
   { *                                                                    *}
   PROCEDURE ReadFile(VAR TotalEmployees: integer; VAR Hours: WorkArray;
                      VAR PayRates: RatesArray; VAR PayrollInfo: text);
     {Values are read into TotalEmployees and the elements of Hours and
     PayRates from the PayRollInfo file.}
     BEGIN    END;
   { *                                                                    *}
   PROCEDURE ShowPayroll(TotalEmployees: integer; VAR Hours: WorkArray;
                                        VAR PayRates: RatesArray);
     {displays amount of check written out to each employee and total
     amount of checks paid}
   { *                                                                    *}
   PROCEDURE ShowHoursWorked(VAR Hours: WorkArray);
     {display employee hours worked for each day of the week}
     BEGIN    END;
   { *                                                                    *}
   BEGIN
     reset(PayRollInfo);
     ReadFile(TotalEmployees, Hours, PayRates, PayRollInfo);
     ShowPayRoll(TotalEmployees, Hours, PayRates);
     writeln; writeln; {skip 2 lines}
     ShowHoursWorked(Hours)
   END.
```

The value read into the variable TotalEmployees indicates the number of lines of eight real values the file contains. Each row will represent an employee's number. The first seven numbers on the row represent the hours worked Sunday through Saturday for the given employee. The last number represents the pay rate for the same employee. Therefore, we can describe the way the lines are read in after the first one with the pseudocode

> *FOR Employee ← 1 TO TotalEmployees DO*
>   *read in values for Hours[Employee, Sun..Sat] from PayRollInfo*
>   *readln(PayRollInfo, PayRates[Employee])*

This description leads directly to the source code for the procedure ReadFile. We have used a row-by-column processor to fill in the elements of Hours, but we can also use the outer loop counter to assign a value to the proper element of PayRates.

```
PROCEDURE ReadFile(VAR TotalEmployees: integer; VAR Hours: WorkArray;
                   VAR PayRates: RatesArray; VAR PayrollInfo: text);
   {documentation}
   VAR
      Employee:    {number of employee whose data is being read in}
                   integer;
      Day:         {present Day information being read into Hours}
                   DayType;
   BEGIN
      readln(PayRollInfo, TotalEmployees);
      FOR Employee:= 1 TO TotalEmployees DO
         BEGIN
            FOR Day:= Sun TO Sat DO
               read(PayRollInfo, Hours[Employee, Day]);
               readln(PayRollInfo, PayRates[Employee])
         END
   END;
```

To code ShowPayroll, each employee's salary for the week must be found and displayed. This salary must also be added to a sum accumulation variable whose value is displayed once all employees have been processed. We can describe the required sequence with the pseudocode

> *TotalPayroll ← 0*
> *FOR Employee ← 1 TO TotalEmployees DO*
>   *OneCheck ← PayCheck(Hours, PayRates[Employee], Employee)*
>   *display Employee, OneCheck*
>   *TotalPayroll ← TotalPayroll + OneCheck*
> *display TotalPayroll*

The function PayCheck returns the size of the check that the given Employee should receive. Note that we can pass in a *single element* (PayRates[Employee]) of an array into the function, but that the syntax of Pascal prohibits us from passing a row of elements from Hours. In order to access the correct elements of Hours, we must pass in the value of Employee to the function.

Source code The source code for the procedure ShowPayRoll is given below. Note that we used a modified form of a row processor for the code of the function Pay-Check.

```
{*                                                                        *}
FUNCTION PayCheck(VAR Hours: WorkArray; PayRate: real;
                                        Employee: integer): real;
   {uses the Employee row of Hours and the PayRate representing hourly
   wages to calculate the given Employee's check for the week}
   VAR
     Day: DayType;    {present day whose work hours are being referenced}
     Sum: real;       {accumulates sum of pay for each day}
   BEGIN
     Sum:= 2 * PayRate * Hours[Employee, Sun];          {get Sun's pay}
     FOR Day:= Mon TO Fri DO                          {add weekdays' pay}
        Sum:= + PayRate * Hours[Employee, Day];
     Sum:= Sum + 1.5 * PayRate * Hours[Employee, Sat];  {add Sat's pay}
     PayCheck:= Sum
   END;
{+                                                                        +}
PROCEDURE ShowPayroll(TotalEmployees: integer; VAR Hours: WorkArray;
                                        VAR PayRates: RatesArray);
   {documentation}
   VAR
     Employee:      {the number of the employee being processed}
                    integer;
     OneCheck,      {the paycheck the given Employee will receive}
     TotalPayroll:  {accumulates sum of all employee's checks}
                    real;
   BEGIN
     TotalPayroll:= 0;
     writeln('Paychecks: ');
     FOR Employee:= 1 TO TotalEmployees DO
       BEGIN
         OneCheck:= PayCheck(Hours, PayRates[Employee], Employee);
         write(' Employee ',Employee:1,' receives a check for $');
         writeln(OneCheck:4:2);
         TotalPayroll:= TotalPayroll + OneCheck
       END;
```

```
    writeln('The total weekly payroll is $',TotalPayroll:4:2)
  END;
{*                                                                    *}
```

Drafting
ShowHours-
Worked

To code ShowHoursWorked, we need to sum up the hours over a single column to get the number of employee hours worked for a given day. To display each of the 7 days in turn, we need code to take 7 sums. Hence, a column-by-row processor is appropriate for this block. Therefore, we have the description

> *FOR Day ← Sun TO Sat DO*
> *TotalHours ← 0*
> *FOR Employee ← 1 TO TotalEmployees DO*
> *TotalHours ← TotalHours + Hours[Employee, Day]*
> *display string representing value of Day, TotalHours*

We will need to code an auxiliary block for the display of the "string representing value of day." This block, ShowDay, is easily coded using a CASE statement.

Source code

Given all these considerations, we obtain the source code for the procedure ShowHoursWorked as shown.

```
{*                                                                    *}
PROCEDURE ShowDay(Day: DayType);
  {displays string representing value of Day}
  BEGIN
    CASE Day OF
      Sun: write('Sunday    ');
      Mon: write('Monday    ');
      Tue: write('Tuesday   ');
      Wed: write('Wednesday ');
      Thu: write('Thursday  ');
      Fri: write('Friday    ');
      Sat: write('Saturday  ')
    END {CASE}
  END;
{+                                                                    +}
PROCEDURE ShowHoursWorked(VAR Hours: WorkArray);
  {documentation}
  VAR
    TotalHours: real;    {accumulates hours worked for each day}
    Day: DayType;        {present day whose hours are being summed}
    Employee: integer;   {used to get each employee's work for a day}
  BEGIN
    writeln('Hours worked by all employees:');
    FOR Day:= Sun TO Sat DO
```

```
  BEGIN
    TotalHours:= 0;
    FOR Employee:= 1 TO TotalEmployees DO
      TotalHours:= TotalHours + Hours[Employee, Day];
    ShowDay(Day);
    writeln(TotalHours:4:2)
  END
END;
```
{ *   *} ◆

EXERCISES

**Test Your
Understanding**

1. Suppose the first line of the file PayRollInfo.dat still contains the number of employees who worked for the week. Each subsequent line, except for the last one, contains the hours each of the TotalEmployees worked for Sunday through Saturday. The last line contains the pay rates for each employee. Write down the appearance of the text file, given the same data but with the format suggested.

2. Suppose the array Hours is still of type WorkArray. What kind of processor is required to fill in the elements given the text file's appearance suggested by Exercise 1?

3. For the text file of Exercise 1, would the code for ShowPayroll and ShowHoursWorked have to be changed? Explain your answer.

4. Why was Hours called by VAR in the procedure ReadFile? Why was Hours called by VAR in the function PayCheck?

**Practice Your
Analysis Skills**

5. State the loop invariant on the variable TotalHours for the inner loop of the procedure ShowHoursWorked.

6. State the loop invariant for the variable TotalPayroll as seen in the procedure ShowPayroll.

**Sharpen Your
Implementation
Skills**

7. Write the code for the procedure ReadFile, given that the file has the appearance of Exercise 1.

8. Modify the procedure ShowHoursWorked to also display the total hours worked by all employees for the entire week. The final line displayed, given the sample file of the case study would be

```
The total hours worked for the week was 158.0
```

11.4 Array Variables that Use Three or More Access Expressions

In Pascal, you can implement a single array structure that has three or more dimensions. You can also implement a structure that is an array whose elements are in turn arrays. In this section we present an example of each kind of implementation.

Three-Dimensional Arrays

The array variable

Once you understand how to use two-dimensional array variables, it is relatively easy to apply the same skills on array variables with more than two dimensions. First, we will present the source code implementation of a three-dimensional array variable. Then we will show how to use this variable in the implementation of some procedures and functions.

The company Wonderful Widgets has expanded to Widgets Galore. Now there are enough sales representatives in the company that management has decided to divide up the sales force into districts. Each district should have a maximum of 100 sales reps, and there will be up to 20 districts. The company still manufactures the same five widget models A through E.

If we wish to use an array to hold the sales records of each representative in each district for each model, we will need to implement a three-dimensional array for the variable *Sales* as given by the source code of Example 11.7.

Example 11.7

```
TYPE
  RepType = 1..MaxReps;      {MaxReps = 100}
  DistType = 1..MaxDists;    {MaxDists = 20}
  ModelType = 'A'..'E';
  SalesArray = ARRAY[DistType, RepType, ModelType] OF integer;
  RepsArray = ARRAY[DistType] OF RepType;
VAR
  Sales: SalesArray;         {models sold by all reps in all districts}
  TotalReps: RepsArray;      {total reps in any given district}
  TotalDistricts: integer;   {total number of districts}
```

Semantics of the structure

The appearance of the variables used in Example 11.7 is shown in Figure 11.14. Note that three access expressions are required on each element of Sales. The mechanism is straightforward. For example, to display the number of sales of model 'B' sold by sales rep 3 in district 7, you would code the statement writeln(Sales[7, 3, 'B']).

Each district will probably have a different number of sales reps in it, so we will also use the one-dimensional array TotalReps. Each element will hold the number of sales reps in the given district. A generalized subrange "expression" to access all the elements of Sales for some given District will then look like 1..TotalReps[District].

Using the structures

There are many different algorithms that we can apply on the array Sales. Because three dimensions are involved, access to any element of Sales always requires three expressions. Naturally, we can use nested loops when required. We can, moreover, nest loops involving access variables down to three levels because we have three access dimensions.

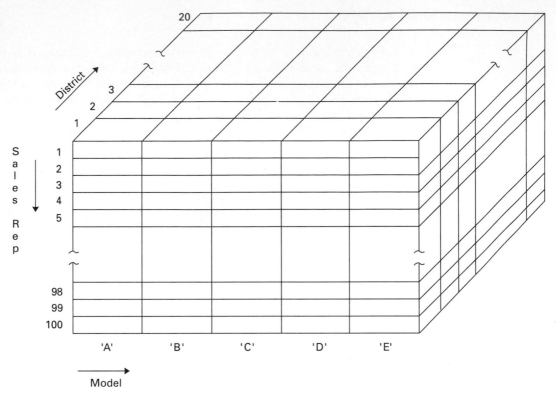

FIGURE 11.14 The three-dimensional array variable `Sales`.

Three nested loops

The source code of Example 11.8, a function that finds the total number of all widgets sold, requires three nested loops to sum over all the elements of the array `Sales`. Note how we use each element of `TotalReps` to set the limits for the `SalesRep` loop.

Example 11.8

```
FUNCTION TotalSold(VAR Sales: SalesArray;
        VAR TotalReps: RepsArray; TotalDistricts: integer): integer;
  {returns total number of all  widgets sold, using Sales, the records
  in all districts for all reps and all models. The variable TotalReps
  contains the count of the number of reps in each district, and
  TotalDistricts represents the number of sales districts}
  VAR
    District: DistType;   {access variable to Sales for the districts}
    SalesRep: RepType;    {access variable to Sales for sales reps}
    Model: ModelType;     {access variable to Sales for the models}
    PartialSum: integer;  {sum accumulation variable}
```

```
BEGIN
  PartialSum:= 0;
  FOR District:= 1 TO TotalDistricts DO
    FOR SalesRep:= 1 TO TotalReps[District] DO
      FOR Model:= 'A' TO 'E' DO
        PartialSum:= PartialSum + Sales[District,SalesRep,Model];
  TotalSold:= PartialSum
END;
```

Two nested
loops
We can also pose a problem where one of the three access expressions will be kept constant. Access is then gained to all the relevant assigned elements of Sales using two variable expressions for the other two dimensions. Usually, a problem of this kind can be solved with two nested FOR loops.

Example 11.9 shows the source code for a function that finds the total overall sales of a given model. Note that in this case a sum is taken over all the districts and sales reps for the model. Hence, the two nested FOR loops are over the specified subranges for District and SalesRep as they apply to the company's sales force.

Example 11.9

```
FUNCTION TotalModelSales(Model: ModelType; VAR Sales: SalesArray;
        VAR TotalReps: RepsArray; TotalDistricts:integer): integer;
  {documentation}
  VAR
    District: DistType;    {access variable to Sales for Districts}
    SalesRep: RepType;     {access variable to Sales for sales reps}
    TotalSales: integer;   {sum accumulation variable}
  BEGIN
      TotalSales:= 0;
      FOR District:= 1 TO TotalDistricts DO
        FOR SalesRep:= 1 TO TotalReps[District] DO
          TotalSales:= TotalSales + Sales[District, SalesRep, Model]
      TotalModelSales:= TotalSales
    END;
```

One-loop
algorithms
There are also algorithms we can apply that require access to the elements over just one of the subranges of Sales. In this case, the access expressions for the other two dimensions are held constant. The source code of Example 11.10 shows one usage of this kind of algorithm.

Example 11.10

```
FUNCTION TotalRepSales (VAR Sales: SalesArray; District: DistType;
                                    SalesRep: RepType): integer;
   {uses the values of Sales to return the count of the number of all 5
   models sold by a given SalesRep in a given District}
   VAR
      Model: ModelType;  {access variable to element of Sales}
      Total: integer;    {accumulation variable for models sold}
   BEGIN
      Total:= 0;
      FOR Model:= 'A' TO 'E' DO
         Total:= Total + Sales[District, SalesRep, Model];
      TotalRepSales:= Total
   END;
```

Another example of a one-loop algorithm is shown in the code of Example 11.11. A call to this function is shown in the statement below the function declaration. Note that the value for the `integer` input parameter `TotalReps` is passed into the function as the array element `TotalReps[District]`, where a value has been assigned to the variable `District`.

Example 11.11

```
FUNCTION ModelSales (VAR Sales: SalesArray; District: DistType;
                     Model: ModelType; TotalReps: RepType): integer;
   {uses Sales to return the total number of a given Model sold in a
   given District that has TotalReps sales representatives in it}
   VAR
      SalesRep: RepType;   {access variable to element of Sales}
      Total: integer;      {accumulation variable to count models sold}
   BEGIN
      Total:= 0;
      FOR SalesRep:= 1 TO TotalReps DO
         Total:= Total + Sales[District, SalesRep, Model]
   END;

write('The sales for model ',Model, in district ',District:1,' are ');
writeln(ModelSales(Sales, District, Model, TotalReps[District]):1,'.')
```

An Array of Arrays

It is possible to declare an array where each of its elements are also arrays. Suppose we want to write a program that simulates a chess game. We have already given a two-dimensional structure to implement a chessboard, but now we want a structure that holds the appearance of the chessboard after each move is made.

In order to store the history of a chess game, we must declare a one-dimensional array of chessboards, thus giving a structure that is an array of arrays. The definitions and declarations for this structure are given in the code of Example 11.12. We are assuming that the chess game will not go on for more than 200 moves.

Example 11.12

```
CONST
  MaxMoves = 200;
TYPE
  GameBoardType = ARRAY['A'..'H', '1'..'8'] OF char;
  GameHistoryArray = ARRAY[0..MaxMoves] OF GameBoardType;
VAR
  ChessMatch: GameHistoryArray;
  MoveNo: integer;     {from 0..200}
```

Parameter passing

The advantage gained by choosing this form of implementation is that we can use an element of ChessMatch as a parameter for a procedure. If, for example, we code the procedure GetMove, we would pass in two array elements of Chess-Match, one representing the present board and the other representing the next board. The procedure call and matching stub are shown in the code of Example 11.13.

Example 11.13

```
PROCEDURE GetMove(VAR PresentBoard, NextBoard: GameBoardType);
  {in: PresentBoard -- chess board before move is made
  out: NextBoard -- chess board after move is made}
  BEGIN   END;

GetMove(ChessMatch[MoveNo], ChessMatch[MoveNo+1]);
MoveNo:= MoveNo + 1;
```

Accessing the elements

The rules of access to one of the squares on one of the boards is straightforward. Example 11.14 shows the source code to display the course of the game at move MoveNo.

Example 11.14

```
FOR Row:= 'A' TO 'H' DO
  BEGIN
    FOR Column:= '1' TO '8' DO
      write(ChessMatch[MoveNo][Row, Column]:3);
    writeln
  END;
```

The array ChessMatch, being an array of two-dimensional arrays, can also be envisioned as a three-dimensional array. Indeed, most dialects of Pascal will allow the write statement of Example 11.14 to be coded as write(Chess-Match[MoveNo, Row, Column]:3); just as if we had initially declared the structure to be a three-dimensional array.

Most likely, however, we would code neither this statement nor the statement of Example 11.14. We set up the structure as an array of arrays so that we could use ChessMatch[MoveNo] as a parameter of one or more main block procedures. Within the procedure statements themselves, access would be done on the two-dimensional structure representing the chess board at a given point in the game.

EXERCISES

Test Your Understanding

1. How many elements does the array Sales have?

2. State the advantage of declaring a structure as an array of arrays.

Practice Your Analysis Skills

3. Suppose we have defined/declared the following:

```
TYPE
   ThreeDArray = ARRAY[1..3, 1..3, 1..3] OF integer;
VAR
   AnArray: ThreeDArray;
   I, J, K: integer;
   AnInt: integer;
```

The code and input sequence to assign values to the elements of an array is as follows:

```
FOR I:= 1 TO 3 DO
   BEGIN
      FOR J:= 1 TO 3 DO
         FOR K:= 1 TO 3 DO
            read(AnArray[I,J,K]);
      readln
   END;
```

14	3	11	6	15	8	11	3	2<eoln>
10	13	12	5	9	3	1	12	6<eoln>
16	20	1	17	5	4	14	19	15<eoln>

From the given source code fragement and the input sequence, indicate the values displayed for each of the following fragments:

(a) FOR I:= 1 TO 3 DO
         FOR K:= 1 TO 3 DO
            write(AnArray[I, 2, K]:3);
      writeln;

(b)
```
FOR K:= 1 TO 3 DO
   write(AnArray[2, 2, K]:3);
writeln;
```
(c)
```
AnInt:= 0;
FOR J:= 1 TO 3 DO
  FOR K:= 1 TO 3 DO
     AnInt:= AnInt + AnArray[1, J, K];
writeln(AnInt:1);
```
(d)
```
AnInt:= AnArray[1, 2, 1];
FOR I:= 1 TO 3 DO
  FOR K:= 1 TO 3 DO
     IF AnArray[I, 2, K] < AnInt THEN
        AnInt:= AnArray[I, 2, K];
writeln(AnInt:1);
```
(e)
```
AnInt:= 0;
FOR I:= 1 TO 3 DO
   AnInt:=AnInt + AnArray[I, I, I];
writeln(AnInt:1);
```

4. Give a one or two-sentence description that catagorizes each of the fragments of code in Exercise 3.

Sharpen Your Implementation Skills

5. For each of the following, assume that values have been assigned to the elements of Sales and the elements of TotalReps:
   (a) Write a procedure BestRep that returns the SalesRep number and the District number of the sales rep who sold the most overall models.
   (b) Write a function MostPopular that returns the model with the most sales over all the districts of Widgets Galore.
   (c) Write a function BestDistrict that returns the District number that sold the most of a given model type.
   (d) Explain why part (a) requires a procedure but parts (b) and (c) can be coded using functions.

Program Testing Hints

At various points in the text, we have stated the maxim, "Know the properties of the machine." In this section, we effectively restate the maxim by warning you that memory allocation is finite and that you cannot declare very large arrays without the real chance you could crash the program. We also remind you that a good program has consistent semantics, in this case as they apply to array definitions, declarations, and access expressions.

Memory Allocation

Memory that can be allocated to carry out a program is limited. You should be aware of this fact, particularly when you are writing programs that deal with multi-dimensional arrays.

Remember that regardless of what machine you have, there are limits both to the size of memory and the count of the number of discrete variables that can be allocated. Most of the time, the compiler will let you know when you have pushed it past the limit. Example 11.15 shows the source code of a program that causes an error on the VAX system at compilation time. The error message follows the source code.

Example 11.15

```
PROGRAM TestAllocation(output);
   {The program will not compile because the system recognizes the
   excessive requirements on memory allocation.}
   TYPE
     LArrayType = ARRAY[1..1000,1..1000,1..1000] OF integer;
   VAR
     AnArray: LArrayType;
   BEGIN
     writeln('We did it!')
   END.
```

```
00005    0    0    LArrayType = ARRAY[1..1000,1..1000,1..1000] OF integer;
                                   1
(1) Size exceeds MAXINT bits
PASCAL completed with 1 diagnostic
```

How much memory?

The error message itself tells us that the VAX machine will allocate a total of maxint bits to any given program for any given structure or combination of structures. Indeed, with this knowledge, we might investigate just how large a structure (or group of structures) we can build.

Given that the value of maxint on the VAX system is approximately 2.1E+09 and that a VAX integer is represented by 32 bits, we expect that the following definition will work because memory allocated will be 2.0E+09 bits ($250 \times 500 \times 500 \times 32 = 2.0\text{E}+09$):

```
TYPE
   LArrayType = ARRAY[1..250, 1..500, 1..500] OF integer;
```

When we substituted this definition into Example 11.15, the computer compiled the program successfully.

The syntax error message of the example leads us to believe that the VAX compiler will not permit the usage of two such arrays. We can test our suspicions by coding Example 11.16. The compilation error message, which follows the source code, proves our suspicions to be correct.

Example 11.16

```
PROGRAM TestAllocation(output);
   {Gives error message when we attempt to allocate 2 large arrays;
   compiles when we comment out the allocation of one of the arrays.}
   TYPE
      LArrayType = ARRAY[1..250, 1..500, 1..500] OF integer;
   VAR
      ArrayA,
      ArrayB: LArrayType;
   BEGIN
      writeln('We did it!)
   END.
```

```
00008    0    0    ArrayB: LArrayType;
                        1
(1) Allocation of ArrayB causes automatic storage to exceed MAXINT bits
PASCAL completed with 1 diagnostic
```

Solving memory problems

These programs illustrate that the computer is a *physical* machine that carries out *physical* actions in the *physical* world. And everything in the physical world is limited by both time and space. In this case, we must deal with space limitations. (In these examples, the problem is due more to the limitations on the computer's ability to count. It externally appears to manifest as a "space problem.") How, then, do you solve a problem if you find the coded solution requires too much memory? Can the problem be solved at all?

The simplest solution, given the error messages we have shown, is to allocate a smaller structure. If the problem can still be solved, you are out of trouble. If, however, you need "all the memory you can get your hands on," try to restate the problem in such a way that it severely reduces the memory requirements. If this method fails or is simply not feasible, you are forced to use external memory (i.e., files) in some clever way so that you can get around the allocation restrictions.

Dimensionality and capacity

One- and two-dimensional arrays will not cause allocation difficulties unless each array element contains a very large structure or the access subranges are excessively large. When you write a program that requires arrays with three or more dimensions, you should be aware that memory allocation can be a problem even for modest access subranges (e.g., $1..500$).

As a rule of thumb, we can say that adding one more dimension to an array structure multiplies the requirements by a factor of N, given that the defining subranges can take on approximately N distinct values. Consider, for example, the following definition that uses "only" 5 dimensions where each access subrange can take on "only" 1 of 100 values:

```
TYPE
   MDimArray = ARRAY [1..100,1..100,1..100,1..100,1..100] OF boolean;
```

Even though each element stores "only" 1 bit, a *boolean* value, an array of type *MDimArray* requires that the computer access 1E+10 addresses. This access requirement is too large for most machines to be able to handle internally. It is possible, nevertheless, to store this much data "externally" in a file. The entire file's contents, however, cannot be read in and used in a single structure.

Access Order Semantics

There are many applications where you may need to access all the elements of a multidimensional array. As you have already seen, the order in which values are assigned to access expressions defines the particular algorithm that is used to process the array. A different sequence of assignments to the necessary access expressions often implies a different problem is being solved. We illustrate these points with some examples.

A sample structure   We are going to illustrate our point using source code that implements three different arrays. This code is given as Example 11.17.

Example 11.17

```
TYPE
    SquareArray = ARRAY[1..50, 1..50] OF integer;
    SumArray = ARRAY[1..50] OF integer;
VAR
    AMatrix: SquareArray;
    RowSums,        {sum over 50 rows of AMatrix}
    ColumnSums:     {sum over 50 columns of AMatrix}
                    SumArray;
```

Finding row sums and column sums   The procedures to fill in the elements of RowSums and the elements of ColumnSums, given that values have been assigned to the elements of AMatrix, are shown as Example 11.18 and 11.19, respectively.

Example 11.18

```
PROCEDURE FillRowSums(VAR AMatrix: SquareArray; VAR RowSums: SumArray);
   {in: AMatrix -- all elements have been assigned
    out: RowSums -- all elements have been assigned where RowSums[N]
                    represents the sum over the Nth row of the elements
                    of AMatrix}
   VAR
     Row, Column: 1..50;   {array access variables}
   BEGIN
     FOR Row:= 1 TO 50 DO
       BEGIN
         RowSums[Row]:= 0;
         FOR Column:= 1 TO 50 DO
            RowSums[Row]:= RowSums[Row] + AMatrix[Row, Column]
       END
   END;
```

Example 11.19

```
PROCEDURE FillColumnSums(VAR AMatrix: SquareArray;
                                       VAR ColumnSums: SumArray);
   {in:  AMatrix -- all elements have been assigned
   out:  ColumnSums -- all elements have been assigned where
                        ColumnSums[N] represents the sum over the Nth
                        column of the elements of AMatrix}
VAR
   Row, Column: 1..50;   {array access variables}
BEGIN
   FOR Column:= 1 TO 50 DO
     BEGIN
       ColumnSums[Column]:= 0;
       FOR Row:= 1 TO 50 DO
          ColumnSums[Column]:= ColumnSums[Column] + AMatrix[Row, Column]
     END
END;
```

Comments

These examples once again show that the order in which the access expressions are found determines whether row sums or column sums are being calculated. The fact that you are generally used to thinking of a two-dimensional table as being in a row-by-column format should not in the least deter you from coding the problem you wish to solve. Thus, in the latter case, the outer loop must be the column access variable, but *the array elements are still accessed in the fixed order in which the structure was defined.*

EXERCISES

Test Your Understanding

1. Assume that you have a machine that requires 8 bits to store a char value and 32 bits to store an integer value. We then have the following definitions:

```
TYPE
    IntsArray = ARRAY[1..100, 1..100] OF integer;
    LineString = STRING[80];
    PageType = ARRAY[1..60] OF LineString;
```

Indicate how many bits of memory and how many addresses are required to allocate sufficient memory for the following declarations:

(a) VAR
        Ints1, Ints2: IntsArray;
(b) VAR
        SmallManuscript: ARRAY[1..10] OF PageType;
(c) VAR
        IntsA: IntsArray;
        ALine: LineString;
        APage: PageType;

2. Assume your system is capable of allocating 15,000 addresses for all its arrays. Which of the following could cause difficulties:

(a) global declaration:

```
TYPE
   ThreeDArray = ARRAY[1..100, 1..100, 1..10] OF integer;
VAR
   AnArray: ThreeDArray;
```

(b)

```
PROGRAM Arrays(input,output);
   TYPE
     ModestArray = ARRAY[1..7000] OF real;
   VAR
     AnArray: ModestArray;
   {*                                                    *}
   PROCEDURE Process(VAR AnArray: ModestArray);
     VAR
        Temp1, Temp2: ModestArray;
     BEGIN  {stub}  END;
   {*                                                    *}
   BEGIN {main}
     Process(AnArray);
     {other statements}
   END.
```

(c)

```
PROGRAM ArraysII(input,output);
   TYPE
     ModestArray = ARRAY[1..50, 1..100] OF real;
   VAR
     AnArray, OtherArray: ModestArray;
   {*                                                    *}
   PROCEDURE Process(VAR AnArray, OtherArray: ModestArray);
     VAR
        Temp: ARRAY[1..1000] OF real;
     BEGIN  {stub}  END;
   {*                                                    *}
   BEGIN
     Process(AnArray,OtherArray);
     {other statements}
   END.
```

3. Explain your answers to each part of Exercise 2.

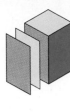

REVIEW AND EXERCISES

A *multidimensional array* requires more than one expression to access a single element. The number of required access expressions makes up the array variable's *dimensionality*. An array variable that is multidimensional should virtually always be declared as a named type, otherwise it cannot be used as a parameter of a procedure. Hence, these structures are defined as types first and then declared as variables.

The different host subranges need not be of the same type. As with one-dimensional arrays, however, they must all be ordinal types. The array elements themselves are always of the same type.

The two-dimensional array is particularly useful for implementations that require row-by-column storage of data. When used in this manner, four standard processing algorithms, namely, *row-by-column processing, column-by-row processing, single-row processing,* and *single-column processing,* all have meaning.

These four algorithms are useful because you can envision a two-dimensional array along either the row or the column directions as parallel arrays of one dimension. This choice of implementation is attractive because the arrays in the structure are parallel over two semantically different dimensions rather than over just one dimension. You can, if the problem requires it, also define a one-dimensional array containing elements of a different type that are parallel to either the row or column elements of the two-dimensional structure.

It is common practice to use a two-dimensional array as an implementation of a game board. Perhaps one, two, or even all four "standard" row/column processing algorithms will work on the game board. The operations carried out on this structured variable ultimately depend upon the rules of the game. For example, if you are implementing a chessboard, procedures to process elements along some diagonal (queen, king, pawn, and bishop moves) will definitely be necessary.

Pascal allows you to define an array with more than two dimensions. You can likewise declare a structure to be an *array of arrays,* where effectively more dimensions are added with each "ARRAY OF" definition. This particular implementation strategy is useful if you want to pass part of the overall multidimensional structure as a parameter for one or more procedures.

You should always exercise due caution in declaring very large arrays or arrays with "many" (three or more) dimensions, for you may exceed the limits of your computer. A good rule of thumb to apply is that each new dimension added to an array, given that each subrange expression has approximately N ordinal values, multiplies the number of elements in the structure by a factor of N.

It is also essential that you remember to code the access expressions to any array element according to the order in which you defined them. Access along different directions (row or column, for example) is determined solely by the order in which values are assigned to the access expression variables. The means of gaining access to an element of an array that is multidimensional must *never* change, regardless of the algorithm you are applying to the multidimensional variable.

EXERCISES

Short Answers

1. You are given AnArray that is anonymously declared as

   AnArray: ARRAY[1..30, 1..40, 'A' ..'E'] OF integer;

   (a) You want to write code that accesses all the elements. How many loop structures are required?
   (b) How many elements does AnArray contain?

2. Explain why, when an access value is solicited from the keyboard, it is dangerous to write a program without some guard algorithm.

3. True or false? An identifier representing a multidimensional array can never appear on the left-hand side of the assignment operator.

4. Suppose you want to write a procedure that assigns the values of the column elements in a given row of a two-dimensional array into a one-dimensional array. What algorithm would you use?

5. You want to process only the diagonal elements (AnArray[1,1], AnArray[2,2], etc.) of a two-dimensional $N \times N$ array named AnArray. Describe the algorithm using pseudocode.

6. How many loops are required to subtract a constant value from all the elements in a two-dimensional array of integers? Why is a single assignment statement impossible?

7. An algorithm to process some elements in a two-dimensional array structure is described by

   > FOR I ← LowI TO HiI DO
   > FOR J ← LowJ TO HiJ DO
   > process AnArray[I,J]

   Under what circumstance(s) does the algorithm reduce to (a) a single-row processor, (b) a single-column processor, or (c) a single-element processor?

8. True or false? The two multidimensional arrays Array1 and Array2 must have the same dimensionality in order for them to be considered parallel arrays.

9. True or false? The two multidimensional arrays Array1 and Array2 must have elements of the same type in order for them to be considered parallel arrays.

10. Suppose we have each of the following definitions:

    TYPE
       ArrayAType = ARRAY[1..20, 1..50, 'A' ..'J'] OF char;
       ArrayBType = ARRAY[1..3, 1..3, 1..3, 1..3, 1..3] OF integer;
       ArrayCType = ARRAY[1..10000, 1..10000] OF real;

    Write down the dimensionality and number of elements belonging to each of the three array types.

11. Suppose the structure AnArray contains 100 elements in it, where the access subranges are 1..10 and 1..10. The appearance of the original structure is to be modified. How many more variables would AnArray contain if the following occurred?

(a) It were changed to a three-dimensional variable whose access subranges are *1..10,* *1..10,* and *'A' ..'F'*.

(b) The access subrange for the row dimension is changed to 1..15.

12. Suppose the variable `ArrayA` is defined to be of type `ArrayAType` as seen from Exercise 10, part (a). Explain why the following code is incorrect:

```
FOR Ch:= 'A' TO 'F' DO
  FOR Row:= 1 TO 10 DO
    FOR Col:= 1 TO 10 DO
      Process(ArrayA[Ch,Row,Coll]);
```

Correct the code so that it has no errors, where the programmer's intentions are still achieved.

13. Would the following code work, given the suggested structure of Exercise 10, part (a)? Explain.

```
FOR Ch:= 'A' TO 'F' DO
  FOR Row:= 1 TO 10 DO
    FOR Col:= 1 TO 20 DO
      Process(AnArray[Row, Col, Ch]);
```

14. Given the definitions and declarations:

```
TYPE
  ArrayType = ARRAY[1..500, 'A'..'M'] OF integer;
  OtherArrayType: ARRAY['A'..'M'] OF integer;
VAR
  AnArray: ArrayType;
  AnotherArray: OtherArrayType;
```

Sketch the appearances of `AnArray` and `AnotherArray`.

15. Refer to Exercise 14. Assume that all the elements of `AnArray` have had values assigned to them. Write the pseudocode description that represents a solution to the following problems:

(a) Return the sum over the Chth column of `AnArray` to the Chth element of `AnotherArray`.

(b) Return the value of the lowest element in the Jth row of `AnArray` to the variable `LowestLetter`.

(c) Return the count of all the elements in `AnArray` whose value is zero to the variable `Zeroes`.

(d) Return the count of the number of values in the Jth row of `AnArray` whose values match the corresponding elements of `AnotherArray`.

16. Suppose we define/declare the array `AThirdArray` as

```
TYPE
  ThirdArrayType = ARRAY[1..500] OF OtherArrayType;
VAR
  AThirdArray: ThirdArrayType;
```

where we make reference to the structures of Exercise 14. True or false? The following boolean expression represents valid syntax, given that subrange values are satisfied: (AThirdArray[Int][Ch] = AnArray[Int, Ch]).

17. What advantage might be gained to define an array of arrays?

Easy Projects

18. Write a program that reads in five lines containing five integer values into 5 × 5 two-dimensional array variable First. Use the values of these elements to create another two-dimensional array variable Second, where the relationship between the elements is First[I, J] = Second[J, I]. Then display the elements of Second as five lines of text containing five integers per line. Typical First and Second array variables might look like

```
16  23  45  32  60     16  22  42  12  99
22  73  98  12  50     23  73  17  39  56
42  17  65  69  87     45  98  65  80  77
12  39  80  55  29     32  12  69  55  58
99  56  77  58  76     60  50  87  29  76
```

19. Define the array ManyReals to be a 25 × 25 array containing real types. Then write a program whose main block is described by the pseudocode

> GetDimensions(LastRow, LastColumn)
> MatRead(LastRow, LastColumn, ManyReals)
> Sum ← MatSum(ManyReals)
> MaxReal ← AbsHighest(ManyReals)
> Zeroes ← ZeroCount(ManyReals)
> display Sum, MaxReal, Zeroes

where (a) GetDimensions reads in values to LastRow and LastColumn such that they are both values in the subrange 1..25. (b) MatRead reads in values to elements of ManyReals. The read in is done row by column for the row, column subranges of 1..LastRow and 1..LastColumn. The remaining elements are all assigned the value 0. (c) The function MatSum returns the sum over the elements. (d) The function AbsHighest returns the value of the element having the largest absolute value. (e) The function Zeroes returns the count of the number of elements whose value was 0. A typical run follows:

```
Enter row and column subranges:   3   5
Enter 3 rows of 5 numbers:
-50.6    -45.1    62.7    88.9    0
 78.3     66.0    77.3   -92.7   12
-78.7     20.7    74.9   -86     23.5
The sum over the elements is 151.2
The value of the highest absolute element is -92.7
The number of zero elements is 611.
```

20. (a) Redo Exercise 2 using more efficient code for the three functions. The values passed into each of the functions should also include the parameters LastRow and LastColumn.

   (b) The execution of the call MatRead(25, 25, ManyReals) is quite tedious for the user. Replace the MatRead procedure with the MatAssign procedure, which uses the RNG of Example 8.7. The procedure is called by MatAssign (LastRow, LastCol, Multiplier, Offset, ManyReals). The initial value for Seed is read in from this block. The value given to the element of ManyReals comes from the expression Seed * Multiplier + OffSet, where Multiplier and Offset are real numbers read in from GetDimensions.

(c) Test MatAssign using the call MatAssign(25, 25, 0.1, -109.3, ManyReals) and then finish the rest of the program. Explain why the sum over the elements is so close to zero and why there are no zero elements.

21. Write a program to read in five lines of six integers into the array variable SomeInts. (You define the structure for SomeInts.) Use SomeInts to assign values to two one-dimensional arrays RowSums and ColumnSums whose elements represent the row and column sums over SomeInts, respectively. You must likewise define the dimensions for these two arrays. Finally, write three short functions that find the sum over the elements of RowSums, ColumnSums, and SomeInts. Are you surprised with the results?

Medium Projects

22. The array Results, as described by Figure 11.3, is used as a data structure in which you are to write the following procedures and functions:

(a) The procedure FillClass. This procedure reads in values to TotalStudents, TotalTests, and Results from a text file. The first line contains values for the two integer variables, and the remaining TotalStudents lines contains TotalTests integer values, values read in row by column to the elements of Results.

(b) The function TestAverage. This function returns the class average on a given test. Determine what parameters are required for this function to work.

(c) The function BestScore. This function returns the number of the student who got the best score on a given test.

(d) The procedure GetStudentNos. This procedure returns an array StudentNos of student numbers whose test results fell in the range Lower..Upper for a specified test number. It is typically called by GetStuNos (Results, TotalStudents, Lower, Upper, Elements, StudentNos); where Elements represents the count of the number of students whose tests scores fell in the specified sub-range.

(e) The function StudentAverage. This function returns the average of a given student in the class. The average is found by taking a straight average of the Total-Tests for the specified student.

(f) The function HighestAverage. This function returns the student number with the highest average over all the tests given. The average to be returned is a simple straight average over the TotalTests.

(g) Write a main block sequence to drive all procedures and functions.

23. Recall Case Study 7.1 from Chapter 7. Use the ideas from this case study to write a program that does the following:

First, it reads in a line of text from a file of 10 char values (blanks are skipped) that represent the answer key to a quiz containing 10 questions. These values are to be stored in the array Key.

Then it reads in 20 lines of 10 char values, where a given line represents a student's paper. These values are used to fill in the array CorrectAnswers, a 20 × 10 array of booleans. A value of *true* for CorrectAnswers [M, N] represents the fact that student *M* answered question *N* correctly.

Use the values of this array of booleans to write functions that find the following:

(a) The number of correct answers on the best test paper. (If 10 correct answers are found, the function can terminate early.)

(b) The number of correct answers on the worst test paper.

(c) The number of the "easiest" question (the question with the most correct answers)

(d) The number of the "hardest" question.

The main block of the program displays the values given to the functions.

24. Redo the part of Exercise 23 that gets values for the elements of CorrectAnswers. Then use the array CorrectAnswers to write the following procedures:

(a) ShowNs, a procedure to display the numbers of those students who got exactly N answers correct on the test.

(b) ShowEasies, a procedure to display those question numbers that no fewer than M students answered correctly. M is passed in as a parameter.

(c) ShowHards, a procedure to display the question numbers that no more than M students answered correctly.

(d) ShowHighsAndLows, a procedure to display the numbers of those students who got the best and the worst grades.

Besides filling in the elements of CorrectAnswers, the main block consists of a call to each of the four procedures. If you answered Exercise 23, you might want to use some of the functions you coded.

25. Write a program to drive the following functions that apply to a 5 × 5 array of integer values:

(a) Sum, a function that finds the sum over all the elements.

(b) DiagSum, a function that finds the sum over the diagonal elements (elements for which the row and column subrange values are equal).

(c) IsUpperTragonal, a function that is true if the array satisfies the definition of an upper-triangular matrix. The definition is satisified if all array elements that physically appear below the diagonal elements (assuming a row-by-column display) are equal to 0.

(d) IsSymmetric, a function that is true if for all elements the relationship AnArray[I,J] = AnArray[J,I] holds true.

(e) IsSkewSymmetric, a function that is true if the relationship AnArray[I,J] = -AnArray[I,J] for all elements.

The driver first reads in values from the keyboard and then displays the results of the calls to each of the five functions.

26. The PGA (Professional Golfers Association) has four major tournaments: (1) the Masters, (2) the U.S. Open, (3) the British Open, and (4) the PGA.

The names of the top five finishers in the four major tournaments over the years 1993, 1994, and 1995 are stored in the file Finishers.dat, with one name per line of text. The first 20 lines contain the tournament results for 1993; the next 20, the results for 1994; and the last 20, the results for 1995. The first five lines contain the first five finishers in the 1993 Masters, lines 6 through 10 contain the names of the five finishers in the 1993 U.S. Open, and so forth.

Write a program that reads in these values and then uses them to do the following:

(a) Display the first place finishers for each tournament on four lines according to the format

Tournament	1993	1994	1995
Master's	Joe Toppro	Samuel Longball	Harry Shortgame
US Open	Samuel Longball	Peter Putter	Henry Niblick
British Open	Reggie English	Gregory Parfour	Harry Shortgame
PGA	Harry Shortgame	James Darkhorse	Bobbie Birdie

Code the program where the longest name will have at most 20 characters in it.

(b) Display the top five finishers for a specified tournament in a specified year. The year and tournament are read in from the keyboard. A character (M, U, B, P, or Q) followed by an integer is read in to determine the tournament results for display. When Q is read in, calls to the display routine are finished. Typically, we have

```
Tournament:  M93
Top 5 finishers for 1993 Masters:
    (1)  Joe Toppro
    (2)  Jerry Braber
    (3)  Joe Links
    (4)  Samuel Longball
    (5)  Harry Shortgame
Tournament:  Q90
```

(c) Display the names of all players who finished in the top five of one of the majors for the three years. Do not display duplicate names. The display should have three names per line in tabular form, as follows:

```
Joe Toppro         Jerry Braber       Joe Links
Samuel Longball    Harry Shortgame    Nedland Amateur
```

27. Write a program that simulates the play of a game of Tic-Tac-Toe. Some of the definitions and variables required for the program are given as

```
TYPE
    PlayerType = (None, X, O);
    TTTBoard = ARRAY[1..3, 1..3] OF PlayerType;
VAR
    GameBoard: TTTBoard;
    Player,
    Winner: PlayerType;
```

The main block of the program is described by

```
MakeNewBoard(GameBoard)
Player ← X
MovesMade ← 0
REPEAT
  ShowBoard(GameBoard)
  GetMove(Row, Col)
  IF ValidMove(Board, Row, Col) THEN
    place mark on GameBoard
    MovesMade ← MovesMade + 1
  Player ← NextPlayer(Player)
  Winner ← WinningPlayer(GameBoard)
UNTIL (Winner <> None) OR (MovesMade = 9)
IF Winner <> None THEN
  display Winner
ELSE
  display 'game tied'
ShowBoard(GameBoard)
```

where (1) MakeNewBoard sets all elements of GameBoard to None, (2) GetMove reads in values to Row and Column, (3) ValidMove is true if Row and Column are in range and GameBoard[Row, Column] equals None, (4) *place mark on board* puts the given player's mark on the Row, Column position, (5) Nextplayer returns X given 0 and 0 given X. WinningPlayer returns None if the game has no winner.

Difficult Projects

28. A text file League.dat contains the names and win/loss results of the Crazy Keglers bowling league. The league consists of eight teams and a total of six matches is played against each of the teams. The first eight lines of text contain the names of each team, and the remaining lines contain the number of wins each team had against each of the other teams. Thus, the file might look like

```
Bogota Bears
Englewood Eagles
Fort Lee Fanatics
Hackensack Honchos
Leonia Lions
Palisades Park Pirates
Teaneck Titans
Tenafly Tigers
0   3   4   2   1   2   5   3     {ex: Bears won 3 vs. Eagles, etc.}
2   0   2   2   4   2   4   2     {ex: Eagles won 2 vs. Tigers}
1   3   0   5   2   3   3   2     {ex: Fanatics won 5 vs. Honchos}
3   3   0   0   5   3   3   5     {ex: Honchos won 5 vs. Tigers}
4   1   3   0   0   2   2   3
3   3   2   2   3   0   5   2
0   1   2   2   3   0   0   4
2   3   3   0   2   3   1   0
```

You are to write a program that reads in the information to some array variables and then uses these variables to display information about the teams. The team names are read in as elements of two one-dimensional arrays, Places and Names. The last word (e.g., Bears, Fanatics) makes up an element of Names, and the other word(s) (e.g., Bogota, Fort Lee) makes up an element of Places. The eight lines of integers are then read into the 8 × 8 array, Standings.

Once values have been read in, the program should display the standings in the following tabular form:

TEAM	WINS	LOSSES	WINS/GAMES
Hackensack	22	13	0.629
Bogota	20	15	0.571
Palisades Park	20	15	0.571
Fort Lee	19	16	0.543
Englewood	18	17	0.514
Leonia	15	20	0.429
Teaneck	14	21	0.400
Tenafly	12	23	0.343

Next, the program reads in a character value followed by a space and then a string value on one line. A second string value is read in from the second line. The character value must be W, L or Q, and the two string values read in must represent the name or place of two bowling teams. If Q is read in, the program terminates. When W is read in, the program displays the number of wins the first team had over the second team. When L is read in, the number of losses the first team suffered at the hands of the second team is displayed. If an invalid entry is read in, the computer displays a line indicating that the entry was invalid. A typical execution of this part of the program is as follows:

```
Enter choice and first team:  W Leonia
Enter second team:  Hackensack
The Leonia Lions won 0 games playing against the Hackensack Honchos.

Enter Choice and first team:  X FortLee
Invalid entry

Enter choice and first team:  L Fort Lee
Enter second team: Bears
The Fort Lee Fanatics lost 4 games playing against the Bogota Bears.

Enter choice and first team:  W Pirates
Enter second team: Penguins
Invalid entry

Enter choice and first team:  Q
```

29. A distance table showing the relative distance between various cities and towns can be constructed from the file Distances.dat whose appearance is

```
    7
Smallville@Metropolis@Gotham City@Necropolis@Ur@La Croix Sud@Perigee
    0     75    150   6666    375    450     62<eoln>
   75      0     89   6666    420    475     56<eoln>
  150     89      0   6666    352    433     45<eoln>
 6666   6666   6666      0   6666   6666   6666<eoln>
  375    420    352   6666      0    128    110<eoln>
  450    475    433   6666    128      0    140<eoln>
   62     56     45   3333    110    140      0<eoln>   <eof>
```

The first integer on the first line represents the number of places (TotalPlaces) that make up the table. The second line represents the TotalPlaces different names to be assigned the elements of Places, an array of strings. The seven rows of seven integer values represent the distances between the places, which are assigned to the array Table. As the file stands, Table[5, 1] and Table[1, 5] must both be assigned the value 128, representing the distance between Smallville (also, Places[1]) and Ur (likewise, Places[5]). You are to use this file to write a program that does the following:

First, it reads in values to TotalPlaces, Places, and Table. It should return a value to the boolean function ValidFile if (1) the diagonal elements of Table are all equal to 0, (2) Table is a symmetric array (Table[I, J] = Table[J, I] for all elements), and (3) the file has Total-Places lines of integers with TotalPlaces integer values on them. If this function returns *false,* the program should halt with an error message, otherwise further processing is done.

Next, the distance table is displayed in a form similar to

	S m a	M e t	G o t	N e c	U r	L a	P e r
Sma |	0	75	.150	6666	375	450	62
Met |	75	0	89	6666	420	475	56
Got |	150	89	0	6666	352	433	45
Nec |	6666	6666	6666	0	6666	6666	6666
Ur |	375	420	352	6666	0	128	110
La |	450	475	433	6666	128	0	140
Per |	62	56	45	3333	110	140	0

Use a field size of 7 to separate the integers.

Then an itinerary is read in from the keyboard, where any of the TotalPlaces places can make up part of the itinerary. The same place may be visited more than once in the itinerary, and up to 20 places may be visited. One place is read in per line. If an invalid place is read in, the computer diplays "Invalid entry," and no further processing is done. The itinerary is completed when a blank line is read in. The final display is the total number of miles traveled for the given itinerary. Two sample runs of this part of the program are

```
Starting point:   Ur
Enter place:   Metropolis
Enter place:   Gotham City
Enter place:   Perigee
Enter place:   Metropolis
Enter place:   La Croix
Enter place:   Ur
Enter place:
The total distance travelled is 1213 miles.

Starting point:   Ur
Enter place:   New York City
Invalid entry.
```

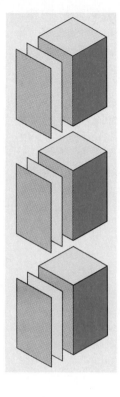

RECORDS AND ARRAYS OF RECORDS

OBJECTIVES

After reading and studying the material of this chapter, you should be able to

- Define and declare RECORD type variables using correct Pascal syntax

- Correctly select the desired field variable of a record variable

- Implement hierarchical record structures for a program solution

- Implement and use an array of records for a program solution

- Use proven algorithms to solve problems dealing with arrays of records

- Determine when a record is a good or bad choice for implementation of a solution

YOU CAN DESCRIBE CHARACTERISTICS ABOUT A SINGLE PER-
SON that make up an inhomogeneous mixture of data types. A person has a
name, represented by a string type; an age, represented by an `integer` type; an
address, represented by a number of string types; a height, represented by a `real`
type, and so forth. In this chapter you will learn how to group all of these characteristics about one person into a single data structure known as a RECORD.

Up to this point, if you wanted to implement an "array of people," you would
need to use parallel arrays to hold the values of the different characteristics about
each person. This implementation technique is clumsy at best. You will learn, from
the material of this chapter, that the more attractive alternative is to implement an
array of records. Each element in the array will contain a record about a person with
a name, age, address, and so forth. This more natural approach is far less clumsy
and bug-prone than the implementation of parallel arrays.

12.1   Records: Syntax and Semantics

In this section, you will learn about the syntax rules for defining, declaring, and using variables that are *record* types. We begin the discussion with an example showing the implementation of three different record types as coded in the definitions and
declarations part of a block. The rest of the section consists of examples that use
these variables in the statement part of a block.

> **Record:** a structured type whose components, which may be of different
> types, are accessed by name.

Defining and Declaring Records

Let us pose a problem that requires a record variable for its solution. Having posed
the problem, we then present the syntax rules for defining and declaring record variable types. Then we solve the problem posed by writing the source code to implement the desired variable. We wind up the subsection by presenting one of the ways
to access a component variable of a given record variable.

*An example
where a record
variable is
appropriate*

A record variable holds component variables that may differ by type. If you
have an implementation problem requiring a variable of this type, you should use a
record. Suppose, for example, you need a variable to hold information about a person's name (first, middle, and last), age, and birthdate (month, date, and year). The
variable you need is suggested by the picture of Figure 12.1.

Definition syntax

The syntax diagram for defining a record (of a named type) is shown in
Figure 12.2. The *field list* contains the identifiers for the *field variables* that can be
accessed through a reference to the associated record variable. A satisfactory syntax
diagram of a field list is shown in Figure 12.3. Note how closely it resembles the
syntax diagram for variable declarations found in the VAR section of a block.

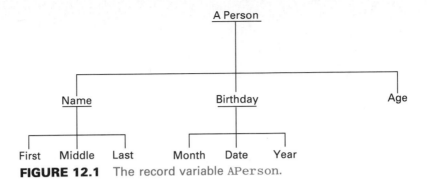

FIGURE 12.1 The record variable APerson.

record definition

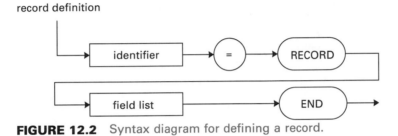

FIGURE 12.2 Syntax diagram for defining a record.

field list

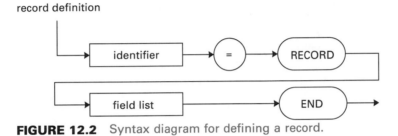

FIGURE 12.3 Syntax diagram for a field list.

Field list: a list of the identifiers and types that make up the component variables of a record.

Field variable: one of the named component variables in a record.

Source code

The source code implementation for the problem we wish to solve is given as Example 12.1. In addition to the variable APerson, we include the variables Today, ABirthday, and AName. We will refer to all four variables in the examples that follow.

Example 12.1

```
TYPE
  DateType = RECORD
    Month,        {or a subrange 1..12}
    Date,         {or a subrange 1..31}
    Year: integer
  END; {DateType}

  String20 = {INSERT DEFINITION OF STRING WITH UP TO 20 CHARS IN IT};
  NameType = RECORD
    First,
    Middle,
    Last: String20;
  END;  {NameType}

  PersonRecord = RECORD
    Name: NameType;
    Birthday: DateType;
    Age: integer
  END;  {PersonRecord}
VAR
  Today,
  ABirthday: DateType;
  AName: NameType;
  APerson: PersonRecord;
```

Describing each variable

The variable APerson of type PersonRecord contains three field variables: Name of type NameType, Birthday of type DateType, and Age of type integer. The variables Today and ABirthday, of type DateType, contain the three field variables Date, Month and Year, all of type integer. The variable AName contains the three field variables First, Middle, and Last, all of type String20.

Access syntax for field variables

We say that a particular field variable of a record variable is *selected*. Figure 12.4 shows how to use a *field selector* to select one of the field variables in a record. The first variable of the field selector, which can be coded as an identifier, as an element of an array, or even as another field variable, is a record variable. The second variable, which can likewise be an identifier, an array element or a record variable, is the field variable being accessed. Note that although the field selector is an *expres-*

FIGURE 12.4 Syntax diagram for field selection.

field selection

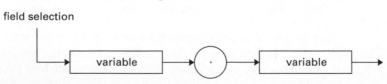

sion, its "value" is represented by a *variable name*. This value selects the named field variable of the record variable.

> **Field selector:** an expression, made up of a record variable, a period, and a field variable, used to select a named field variable of a named record variable.

Using Record Variables in Statements

Once a field variable has been selected, it is treated as if it were a variable distinct from the record variable that contains it. The coded examples that follow use the variables of Example 12.1 to demonstrate how to use field selector expressions in statements that make up legal Pascal source code.

Three examples

The following statement displays the value of the field variable Age (of type integer) that belongs to the record variable APerson. The display, given that APerson.Age↔25, follows the program fragment.

```
writeln('This person is ',APerson.Age:1,' years old.')
This person is 25 years old.
```

The next fragment shows a sequence to assign values to the fields of the variable Today as read in from the keyboard. A typical execution follows the code. The boolean function ValidDate returns true if the values read into Month and Date are in range. Note that you can use a RECORD type variable as a parameter of a procedure or function call.

```
REPEAT
  write('Input today''s date (1..12, 1..31, Year):  ');
  readln(Today.Month, Today.Date, Today.Year)
UNTIL ValidDate(Today);

Input today's date (1..12, 1..31, Year):  7  21  1991
```

The boolean function ValidDate, as abstracted, requires a record variable (TheDate) of type DateType as its input parameter. The fields of the variable TheDate are then selected in such a way that they return a value to the function ValidDate. The source code for the function ValidDate is given below. Note that TheDate.Month and TheDate.Date, being of type integer, can be used with the reserved word IN.

```
FUNCTION ValidDate(TheDate: DateType): boolean;
  {returns true if the Month and Date fields are in range}
  BEGIN
    ValidDate:= (TheDate.Month IN [1..12]) AND (TheDate.Date IN [1..31])
  END;
```

You can use a field variable of a record variable as a parameter of a procedure or function call. A call to the procedure GetFullName, as shown in the source code that follows, uses the variable APerson. Name as one of its parameters. The statement of the procedure, moreover, uses three successive calls to the procedure GetWord (See Example 9.3), where each of the three fields of TheName are used as actual parameters of GetWord. A typical run of the fragment is given below the source code.

```
PROCEDURE GetFullName(VAR TheName: NameType; VAR InFile: text);
   {This procedure assigns values to the three fields of TheName as read
   in from the contents of InFile. It uses calls to GetWord, a
   procedure that returns values to the string variable, given that the
   sentinel character is passed in as a blank.}
   BEGIN
      GetWord(' ', TheName.First, InFile);
      GetWord(' ', TheName.Middle, InFile);
      GetWord(' ', TheName.Last, InFile);
   END;

write('Input name: ');
GetFullName(APerson.Name, input);
readln(input);
```

```
Input name: Patrick Aloysius Brady
```

Note that, according to the syntax of Pascal, the formal parameter variable TheName matches the actual parameter variable APerson. Name by type. Likewise, the formal parameter variable for the procedure GetWord that corresponds to the actual parameter variables TheName.First, TheName.Middle, and TheName.Last should be of type String20 in order for the syntax to be correct.

Two more
examples
The procedure GetDate reads in values to the fields of the formal parameter variable ADate of type DateType. This procedure is coded with the assumption that the next sequence of characters to be read from InFile correctly represents three integer values. Hence, no guards are coded because we have assumed the text in the file was properly written in.

```
PROCEDURE GetDate(VAR ADate: DateType; VAR InFile: text);
   {reads values into the fields of ADate from the text file AFile}
   BEGIN
      read(InFile, ADate.Month);
      read(InFile, ADate.Date);
      read(InFile, ADate.Year)
   END;
```

The following fragment shows how calls to the procedure GetFullName and GetDate can be used to read in values to six of the seven variables that make up the structure of the variable APerson:

```
GetFullName(APerson.Name, InFile);
readln(InFile);                {assumes birthday is on next line of text}
GetDate(APerson.BirthDay, InFile);
```

Field Variables and Expressions

An example

As with array elements that are accessed, when a field variable is selected, it is treated in the context of the statement as if it were a (nonstructured) variable of the defined type. The following examples show how to use field variables in forming expressions. They also show how to write assignment statements that use record variables and/or field variables.

The next fragment of code illustrates a number of aspects of Pascal syntax. First, it shows how the values taken on by the field variables can also be referenced in expressions. It also shows that field variables can be found on the left hand side of the assignment operator. Finally, it shows that the same access rule using a field selector expression applies no matter how "deep" the levels of record definition are. Thus the expression APerson.Birthday selects the Birthday field of APerson. Because this field is also a record variable, its field variables are referenced using the same expression syntax, namely a reference to the record variable, followed by a period, followed by a field variable identifier.

```
IF (Today.Month = APerson.Birthday.Month) AND
        (Today.Date = APerson.Birthday.Date) THEN
   BEGIN
     APerson.Age:= Today.Year - APerson.BirthDay.Year;
     writeln('Happy birthday!');
     writeln('How does it feel to be ',APerson.Age:1,' years old?')
   END;
```

Comparing two record variables

Even though both variables Today and ABirthday represent single calendar dates, each variable contains three field variables. The pseudocode that follows does not code directly to equivalent Pascal source code because the boolean equality operator can only work on scalar or string expressions in most dialects. (Apple Pascal, however, does allow the use of the two relational operators = and <> to form boolean expressions between two structured variables of the same type.)

> *IF Today = Birthday THEN*
> *display congratulatory message on becoming a parent*

In most dialects, then this "statement" will not compile:

```
IF Today = ABirthday THEN      {SYNTAX ERROR!}
  writeln('Congratulations on the birth of a new offspring');
```

The pseudocode expression that compares two record variables is correctly implemented as a function that carries out a comparison between all the component field variables. Example 12.2 shows the required source code to deliver the desired congratulatory message.

Example 12.2

```
FUNCTION EqualDates(FirstDate, SecondDate: DateType): boolean;
  {returns true if the three fields of both dates are the same}
  BEGIN
    EqualDates:= (FirstDate.Month = SecondDate.Month) AND
                 (FirstDate.Date = SecondDate.Date) AND
                 (FirstDate.Year = SecondDate.Year)
  END;

IF EqualDates(Today, ABirthday) THEN
  writeln('Congratulations on the birth of a new offspring!');
```

Another example

If you are writing a search procedure that looks for a match between a candidate name and a search name, the correct source code to carry out the comparison is given as Example 12.3.

Example 12.3

```
FUNCTION EqualNames(Name1, Name2: NameType): boolean;
  {returns true if the first, middle, and last names are all equal}
  BEGIN
    EqualNames:= (Name1.First = Name2.First) AND
                 (Name1.Middle = Name2.Middle) AND
                 (Name1.Last = Name2.Last)
  END;

IF EqualNames(CandidateName, SearchName) THEN
  Found:= true
ELSE
  {other code};
```

The assignment rule for record types

It is possible to copy the contents of one record variable into another using the assignment operator if both variables are of the same type. Thus, both of the following statements represent legal Pascal:

```
BirthDay:= Today;
AName:= APerson.Name;
```

EXERCISES

Test Your Understanding

1. State how the components of a record variable differ from the components of an array variable.

What does the selection expression(s) to a field in a record variable represent? What does the access expression(s) to one of the elements in an array represent?

Practice Your Analysis Skills

Consider the following fragment:

```
TYPE
   String3 = STRING[3];
   String4 = STRING[4];

   NumberType = RECORD
     AreaCode,
     Exchange: String3
     FourDigits: String4
   END;

VAR
   MyNumber,
   MyFriendsNumber:   NumberType;
```

(a) Draw a picture of the variable MyNumber.

(b) Indicate which of the following statements or sequences have syntax errors:
  (i) MyNumber:= MyFriendsNumber;
  (ii) IF MyNumber = MyFriendsNumber THEN
       writeln('We live at the same address.');
  (iii) IF MyNumber.AreaCode = MyFriendsNumber.AreaCode THEN
       writeln('We live in the same state.');
  (iv) write(' My friend''s telephone is ');
       write(MyFriendsNumber.AreaCode);
       writeln(MyFriendsNumber.Exchange.FourDigits);
  (v) write('My telephone number is (', MyNumber.AreaCode, ')');
       writeln(MyNumber.Exchange, '-', MyNumber.FourDigits);

4. Suppose the telephone number represented by MyNumber is (218) 555–8818 and that represented by MyFriendsNumber is (218) 555–7233. Write down the display for each correct sequence of Exercise 3.

Sharpen Your Implementation Skills

5. Correct any of the errors in the code of Exercise 3(b), so the intended code is properly executed.

6. Propose an implementation (with CONST and TYPE definitions) for the following variables (note that not all implementations are records):
  (a) AccNo, a variable whose appearance looks like 10 decimal digits. No arithmetic operations are required for this variable.
  (b) Stats, a variable that stores numeric information about a person's age, weight to the nearest pound, and height to the nearest inch.
  (c) Board, a variable that holds the present status of an 8 × 8 checkerboard. A given square is either unoccupied, or occupied by a black or a red checker.
  (d) Account, a variable containing an account number, the customer's name (first, middle, and last), and the customer's balance.
  (e) Occurred, an event-recording variable that holds information about whether or not a particular random number in the subrange 0..Modulus-1 has been returned by a random number generator.

(f) `PriceInfo`, a variable that contains the highest price and the lowest price of a given stock over the last 52-week period. It should also contain the value of the present price of the stock.

(g) `StockInfo`, a variable containing `PriceInfo`, the name of the company (a string of chars), the trading symbol (another string of chars), and the company's earnings for the last year.

(h) `ClosingPrices`, a variable containing the closing price on Dec 31 for a given stock over the last 10 years.

7. Using the respective variables you declared in Exercise 6, write program fragments that will result in the display of
   (a) the value assigned to `AccNo`.
   (b) the values associated with the variable `Stats`.
   (c) the present status of the 8 × 8 checkerboard.
   (d) a particular customer's account number, name (first, middle, then last) and balance.
   (e) the count of the numbers in the candidate subrange that have not yet been returned by the RNG.
   (f) the 52-week low, 52-week high and last quoted price of the given stock.
   (g) the stock symbol and the earnings for the last year of the given stock.
   (h) the average closing price on Dec. 31 of the stock, as taken over the last 10 years.
   You can define or declare any additional variables you feel are necessary to solve each problem.

12.2 The WITH Statement and Hierarchical Records

When using a period as a field selector, you need to mention the record variable by name. If you are selecting all the fields to a given variable, this requirement can make your coding task quite tedious. An attractive alternative is to use the WITH statement. When you use this statement, you can select as many field variables of the record variable that you require with just one identifier reference to the record variable.

The WITH statement

The WITH statement lets you select more than one field of a record variable using just one reference to the record variable's name. Figure 12.5 shows the syntax diagram of this statement. The comma allows you to code a shorthand for nested

FIGURE 12.5 Syntax diagram for the WITH statement.
WITH statement

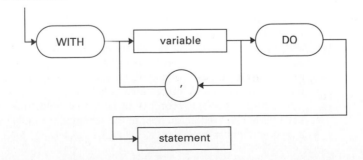

WITH statements, a topic that we will take up shortly. The pseudocode description of the WITH statement is written as

WITH the referenced record variable(s) DO
access any field(s) of the record variable by identifier

Scope of reference

When you use a WITH statement, you increase the *scope of reference* (or simply, *scope*) for the field variables of the referenced record variable. When you use a period, the scope of reference exists only for the given field variable and only for the given reference. In short, there is no extended scope when a period is used, only a single reference.

Scope: the extent of source code over which a reference to a predefined or predeclared identifier(s) has meaning.

Two examples

Examples 12.4 and 12.5 apply the WITH statement to the two variables TheName and ADate, respectively. The scope of reference for the variable TheName in Example 12.4 extends over the three statements between the BEGIN and END delimiters of the WITH TheName DO statement. Likewise, in Example 12.5 the scope of ADate extends over the three statements between the reserved words BEGIN and END for the WITH ADate DO statement.

Example 12.4

```
PROCEDURE GetFullName(VAR TheName: NameType; VAR InFile: text);
  {Logically equivalent to the procedure GetFullName as coded in
  Section 12.1.  The WITH statement obviates the need to reference
  TheName three times.}
  BEGIN
    WITH TheName DO
      BEGIN
        GetWord(' ',First, InFile);
        GetWord(' ',Middle, InFile);
        GetWord(' ',Last, InFile)
      END
  END;
```

Example 12.5

```
PROCEDURE GetDate(VAR ADate: DateType; VAR InFile: text);
  {Equivalent to the procedure GetDate as coded in Section 12.1
  Because of the WITH statement, only one reference to the variable
  ADate is required}
  BEGIN
    WITH ADate DO
      BEGIN
        read(InFile, Month);
        read(InFile, Date);
        read(InFile, Year)
      END
  END;
```

Nested WITH Statements

The variable APerson coded as Example 12.1 in Section 12.1, has a *hierarchical record structure*. A structured variable that is hierarchical has record variables nested within record variables. This sort of structure implies that you can use nested WITH statements to select one (or more) of the field variables of a record variable that is in turn a field variable of another record variable. The next set of examples shows how to implement both explicit and implicit nested WITH statements to select field variables in a hierarchical structure.

Hierarchical record structure: a structure where at least one of the field variables is also a record variable.

An example
The fragment that follows shows how to use explicit nested WITH statements to display the Name fields of the variable APerson. A typical result of the statements's execution (Name.First↔'Roy', Name.Middle↔'Green.', Name.Last↔'Biv') is given below the source code.

```
write('And the winner is  ....   ');
WITH APerson DO
  WITH Name DO
    writeln(First,' ',Middle,' ',Last,'!');

And the winner is  ....   Roy Green Biv!
```

Implicit nesting
Pascal lets you use a comma in an implicit way to code nested WITH statements. You can, for example, write code that carries out the same action as the previous fragment using

```
WITH APerson, Name DO
  writeln('And the winner is  ....   ',First,' ',Middle,' ',Last,'!');
```

The following example (where a sample run is given below the source code) shows that you can have variables on the same level of hierarchy in the *variable list* of the WITH statement.

```
WITH APerson, Name, Birthday DO
  BEGIN
    write(First, ' ', Middle, ' ', Last, ' was born on ');
    writeln(Month:1, '/', Date:1, '/', Year:1,'.');
    writeln('He or she is now ', Age:1, ' years old.')
  END;

Roy Green Biv was born on 5/21/48.
He or she is now 44 years old.
```

Variable list of a WITH statement: the record variables found between the reserved words WITH and DO.

There is a very simple rule to determine whether a given variable list will work for a particular WITH statement. If the proposed statement using a comma(s) can be changed to explicit nested WITH statements, the single WITH statement that has a variable list will work. Thus, the variable list of the previous fragment successfully compiles because the following statement will also compile:

```
WITH APerson DO
   WITH Name DO
      WITH BirthDay DO
         BEGIN  {execute same sequence}  END;
```

In like manner, this fragment will also work:

```
WITH APerson, Birthday, Name DO
   BEGIN {execute same sequence}  END;
```

The following code, however, will not work because the rule requires that the variables be selected according to the hierarchical order in which they were defined:

```
WITH Name, APerson, BirthDay DO      {COMPILATION ERROR!}
   BEGIN  {execute same sequence}  END;
```

Variables on the same hierarchical level may be placed in any order in the variable list, but any record variable(s) that contains another record variable(s) must be placed ahead of the variable(s) it contains.

We mentioned in the previous section that it is possible to have any type of variable as a field of a record. We have seen hierarchical records where the field variables are other records. It is also possible to have an array variable as a field variable of a record variable. The problem we are about to pose requires this kind of implementation for its solution.

Example Problem 12.1

Let us implement a structured variable AStudent with the following fields: (1) a Name field consisting of a First, Middle, and Last name, (2) a SocSecNo field consisting of nine characters representing the student's social security number (or student ID number), (3) a Status field, consisting of a string variable that represents the student's status (Freshman, Sophomore, Junior, or Senior), (4) a Tests field, consisting of an array that stores the results of the three quizzes and final exam, and (5) an Average field consisting of the student's average on the quizzes and the final exam. The hierarchical structure for the variable AStudent is suggested by Figure 12.6. Figure 12.7 shows a typical variable with values assigned to all the fields.

The source code for implementation of the record variable AStudent is as follows:

```
CONST
   TotalTests = 4;    {three quizzes plus a final}
```

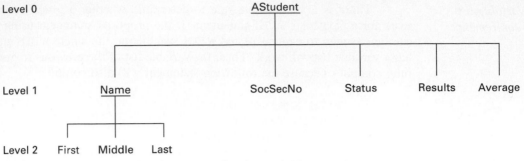

FIGURE 12.6 Hierarchical structure for the variable AStudent.

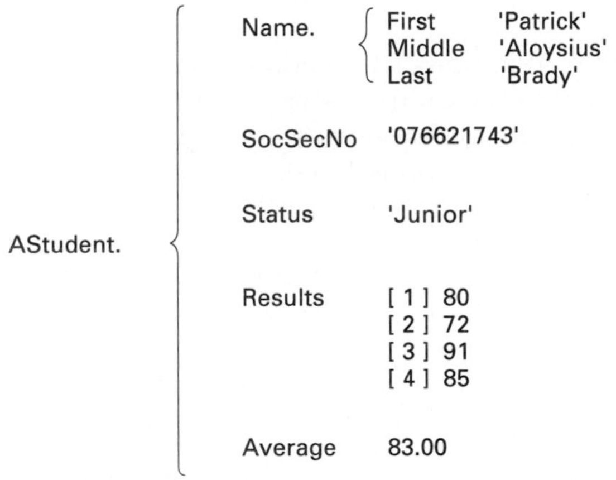

AStudent.
{
Name.
{
First   'Patrick'
Middle   'Aloysius'
Last   'Brady'

SocSecNo   '076621743'

Status   'Junior'

Results   [1] 80
            [2] 72
            [3] 91
            [4] 85

Average   83.00
}

FIGURE 12.7 Typical assignments to the field variables of AStudent.

```
TYPE
  String25 = {STRING TYPE CAPABLE OF HOLDING UP TO 25 CHARACTERS};
  SSNoType = {STRING TYPE CAPABLE OF HOLDING UP TO 9 CHARACTERS};
  ResArray = ARRAY[1..TotalTests] OF integer;        {holds test results}

  NameType = RECORD
    First,
    Middle,
    Last: String25
  END;   {NameType}

  StuRecord = RECORD
    Name: NameType;          {the student's name}
    SocSecNo: SSNoType;      {his/her social security number}
    Status: String25;        {frosh, soph, jr or sr}
    Results: ResArray;       {three test results + final}
    Average: real            {weighted average of three tests and final}
  END;   {StuRecord}

VAR
  AStudent: StuRecord;
```

Note that all 5 field variables of the record type StuRecord are named types. We chose to implement StuRecord in this manner so that any of the field variables can be used as an actual parameter to a procedure call. (Remember that the corresponding formal parameter requires an identifier for its type specification.) ◆

Using
AStudent

Let us now develop the code that reads in the values to the variable AStudent from the contents of a text file.

Example Problem 12.2

The problem
statement

Suppose a text file StudentRecords.dat contains the values for all the fields of AStudent (except for Average) on two lines of text. The first line contains the student's name, and the second line contains the ID number (Social Security number), the Status, and the 4 test grades. Let us write the procedure FillStudentRecord. It reads the two lines from the text file and fills in the fields of AStudent. The Average is found by weighing the quiz results as 50% and the final exam (the last integer read in) as 50%. Two typical lines of text are as follows:

```
Patrick Aloysius Brady<eoln>
076621743Junior    80    72    91    86<eoln>
```

Source code

The source code that follows is the solution to the problem.

```
{*                                                              *}
FUNCTION TestAverage(Results: ResArray): real;
  {returns a value based on the following scheme: 50% of the average
  of the first 3 elements and 50% of the last element}
  VAR
    TestNo;   {reference to test result presently being accessed}
    Sum:      {accumulation variable for sum of tests}
              integer;
  BEGIN
    Sum:= 0;
    FOR TestNo:= 1 TO TotalTests-1 DO
      Sum:= Sum + Results[TestNo];
    TestAverage:= 0.5 * Sum/(TotalTests - 1) + 0.5 * Results[TotalTests]
  END;
{+                                                              +}
PROCEDURE FillStudentRecord(VAR AStudent: StuRecord; VAR InFile: text);
  {Fills in the fields of AStudent by reading in two lines of text from
  InFile; also calls the function TestAverage to assign a value to the
  field variable Average.}
  VAR
    TestNo: integer;     {access variable to elements of Results}
  BEGIN
    WITH AStudent, Name DO        {access to all fields by name reference}
```

```
      BEGIN
        GetWord(' ',First, InFile);
        GetWord(' ',Middle, InFile);
        GetWord(' ',Last, InFile);
        readln(InFile);
        read(InFile,SocSecNo);                      {9 characters are read in}
        GetWord(' ',Status, InFile);
        FOR TestNo:= 1 TO TotalTests DO
          read(InFile,Results[TestNo]);
        readln(InFile);
        Average:= TestAverage(Results)
      END
    END;
{*                                                                         *}
```

Variable access and selection
Note from the source code that all fields on Level I of the hierarchy chart (see Figure 12.6) can be selected via the reference to the variable AStudent in the variable list of the WITH statement. The First, Middle, and Last fields of the record variable AStudent.Name can also be selected because the variable list contains a reference to the identifier Name. Note too how each element of AStudent.Results can be accessed using the usual subrange expression. It is also noteworthy to look at the statement Average:= TestAverage(Results). In this case, two field variables are used in completely different contexts as part of the same statement. ◆

The WITH Statement and Coding Style

Although the WITH statement can simplify your coding tasks, you must use this statement with care to avoid writing unclear source code. The reason for this possible difficulty is that the WITH statement, in extending the scope of reference of a record variable, also hides the hierarchical structure of the variable. It may therefore be unclear whether a variable reference in the body of a WITH statement is a field variable or a global reference.

Hidden referencing
You should be aware that variable identifiers not associated with the record variable can still be referenced in the body of a WITH statement. In coding Fill-StudentRecord, for example, we reference the variable TestNo in the body of the WITH statement. No problem arises, though, because TestNo is visible as a locally declared variable.

There is nothing in the code of FillStudentRecord, however, to clearly indicate that the identifiers First, Middle and Last are fields of the record variable AStudent.Name. Indeed, this "hiding" mechanism applies to all the identifiers that are field variables of either AStudent or of AStudent.Name. The WITH statement can just as easily contain references to global variables that may be mistaken as field variables of the record variable!

"Correct" usage
If we never use the WITH statement in our programs, our code will never have this potential problem. On the other hand, writing selection expressions to the

field variables of a record is much less clumsy using the WITH statement. Is there a happy medium we can exercise to help us decide when WITH is appropriate?

Unfortunately, there is no good answer to this question. Usually, you will use the WITH statement to keep selection expressions simple. If, however, you plan to select only one or at most two fields of a record variable in only one or two statements of a given block, it is better that you use the period rather than a WITH statement. Also, if there is even a remote chance that a coded sequence can be misunderstood due to ambiguities in referencing, you should probably select all field variables using the period.

EXERCISES

Test Your Understanding

1. What is meant by the term "hierarchical record structure?"

2. Can the variable list of a WITH statement contain unrelated variables? (Hint: Consider how a variable list applies to the WITH statement.)

Example 12.6

```
TYPE
  String50 = {STRING TYPE CAPABLE OF HOLDING UP TO 50 CHARACTERS};
  LicenseType = (None, Novice, Technician, General, Advanced, Extra);
  StateType = {STRING TYPE CAPABLE OF HOLDING UP TO 2 CHARACTERS};
  ZipType = {STRING TYPE CAPABLE OF HOLDING UP TO 5 CHARACTERS};

  PNameType = RECORD
    First,   {member's first name}
    Middle,  {member's middle name}
    Last:    {member's last name}
            String50
  END;   {PNameType}

  CityRecord = RECORD
    CityName, {name of city}
    Street,   {name of street}
    No:       {house number, including letters, dashes, etc.}
            String50
  END;   {CityRecord}

  AddressRecord = RECORD
    City: CityRecord;
    State: StateType;
    ZipCode: ZipType
  END;   {AddressRecord}
```

```
MemberRecord = RECORD
    Call: String50;            {member's call letters, if licensed}
    Class: LicenseType;        {class of operator privileges}
    PName: PNameType;          {the member's name}
    Address: AddressRecord     {the member's address}
END;      {MemberRecord}

VAR
    Member: MemberRecord;
```

Practice Your Analysis Skills

Use the code of Example 12.6 to answer the following questions:

3. How many levels of records are there in the variable Member?

4. Indicate the field variables that can be directly accessed by identifier reference for each of the following WITH statements:

   (a) WITH Member, Address DO
         BEGIN {statements} END;

   (b) WITH Member.PName DO
         BEGIN {statements} END;

   (c) WITH Member.Address DO
         BEGIN {statements} END;

   (d) WITH Member.Address,City DO
         BEGIN {statements} END;

5. Draw the hierarchical structure for the variable Member. (You will need a big sheet of paper!)

6. Suppose an additional Address field, as shown in Example 12.6, is added as another field to StuRecord, the solution to Example Problem 12.1. Given that AStudent is a variable of type StuRecord, indicate which field variables can be directly referenced by identifier using each of the following WITH statements:

   (a) WITH AStudent DO
         BEGIN {statements} END;

   (b) WITH AStudent.Address DO
         BEGIN {statements} END;

   (c) WITH AStudent, Address DO
         BEGIN {statements} END;

   (d) WITH AStudent, Name DO
         BEGIN {statements} END;

Sharpen Your Implementation Skills

7. Write the WITH statement that allows selection of all the fields of Member (Example 12.6) by name.

8. Use the code of Example 12.7 for this exercise.

Example 12.7

```
TYPE
    String20 = {STRING TYPE THAT CAN HAVE UP TO 20 CHARACTERS IN IT};
    NameType = RECORD
        First, Middle, Last: String20
    END;      {NameType}

    RankType = (Private, PFC, Corporal, Sergeant, Lieutenant);
    SNType = {STRING TYPE THAT CAN HAVE UP TO 12 DIGITS IN IT};

    SoldierRecord = RECORD
        Name: NameType;
```

```
      Rank: RankType;
      SerialNumber: SNType
   END;    {SoldierRecord}

VAR
   PlatoonMember:   SoldierRecord;
```

Assume that the variable PlatoonMember has had values assigned to all its fields. Write a statement or sequence of statements that does the following:

(a) Displays the platoon member's name in the order: last name, first name, and middle initial. A comma is displayed between the middle and first names and a period is displayed after the middle initial. As an example, the display of the name "John Quincy Adams" is

```
                    Adams, John Q.
```

(b) Displays the platoon member's rank followed by his or her full name. Assume you can use the procedure ShowRank whose header is coded as PROCEDURE ShowRank(Rank: RankType);. A typical display is

```
              Corporal John Quincy Adams
```

(c) Assigns the value of true to the boolean function IsOfficer if the platoon member's rank is Lieutenant.

(d) Assigns the value of true to the boolean variable IsNCO if the platoon member's rank is PFC, Corporal, or Sergeant.

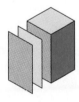

12.3 Arrays of Records

As we mentioned in the chapter introduction, an array of records represents an attractive alternative to parallel arrays. The array elements of this structure are inhomogeneous field variables that are, nonetheless, related to each other. In this section, we first implement code to read in the elements to an array of records. Then we develop and code algorithms that can be applied to the array variable.

Reading in the structure

Let us suppose the text file StudentsRecords.dat has an integer value on its first line that represents the number of students in the class. The remaining lines of text contain information about all the students, where two lines of text contain the information about each student. We will use the procedure FillStudentRecord to assign values to the fields of each element in the array.

Figure 12.8 shows the structured variable we plan to implement. Figure 12.9 shows a typical appearance of the file StudentsRecords.dat. The source code required to implement the structure and read in values is given as the program UseClassRecords. In the rest of the section, we will deal with deriving the code for some of the procedures and functions that use this structure. A call to any of these procedures and/or functions can simply be substituted in the place indicated.

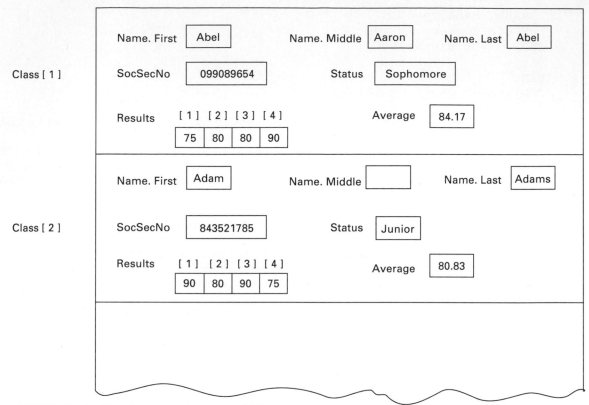

FIGURE 12.8 The first two elements of Class.

```
PROGRAM UseClassRecords(input, output, StudentsRecords);
   {This program first reads in values to an array of records.  It then
   uses the array for further processing.  The procedures and functions
   to be coded illustrate some of the many ways this particular array of
   records can be processed.}
   CONST
      TotalTests = 4;      {three quizzes plus a final}
      MaxClass = 150;      {largest possible class size}
   TYPE
      {insert all types required to define StuRecord here; also insert
      StuRecord definition}
```

FIGURE 12.9 A typical appearance of the text file StudentsRecords. dat.

82<eoln>
Abel Aaron Able<eoln>
099089654 Sophomore 75 80 80 90<eoln>
Adam   Adams<eoln>
843 521785 Junior   90 80 90 75<eoln>
{ 158 lines of text about 79 other students }
Joseph George Zorba<eoln>
374875129 Freshman   60 50 55 65<eoln> <eof>

```pascal
  IndexType = 0..MaxClass;        {0th value will be used for a sentinelelement}
  ClassArray = ARRAY[IndexType] OF StuRecord;
VAR
  Class: ClassArray;          {the array of student's records}
  Enrollment: IndexType;      {number of students enrolled in class}
  StudentsRecords: text;      {contains information about each student}
{*                                                                      *}
PROCEDURE FillStudentRecord(VAR AStudent: StuRecord;
                                      VAR InFile: text);
  BEGIN
    {fill in all the details from solution to Example Problem 12.2}
  END;
{+                                                                      +}
PROCEDURE FillAClass(VAR Enrollment: IndexType;
          VAR Class: ClassArray;  VAR StudentsRecords: text);
  {A value is read into Enrollment from StudentsRecords.  Then values
  are assigned to the elements of Class as read in from the file over
  the subrange 1..Enrollment}
  VAR
    Index: IndexType;      {present record variable being read in}
  BEGIN
    readln(StudentsRecords, Enrollment);
    FOR Index:= 1 TO Enrollment DO
      FillStudentRecord(Class[Index], StudentsRecords)
  END;
{*                                                                      *}
{PROCEDURES AND FUNCTIONS WE WILL DEVELOP IN THIS SECTION GO HERE}
{*                                                                      *}
BEGIN
  reset(StudentsRecords);
  FillAClass(Enrollment, Class, StudentsRecords);
  {calls to procedures and functions we will code as examples}
```

Reusing algorithms

Once the elements of Class are read in, you can devise many different ways to use the structure. For example, you can write procedures to (1) find and display the name of the student with the highest average, (2) find and display a given student's test scores, (3) find and display the names of those students whose average was greater than 85, and so forth.

As you study the examples, be aware of the way we impose proven algorithms on the elements of Class. A specific problem involving an array of records often depends on the values of only one or two field variables for each of the elements. Once you know the field variable(s) to select, you can determine what algorithm applies to a given *array of the field variable's type* that solves the specific problem. You can then apply the algorithm to the field variable(s), making sure to follow the selection rules for the variable(s) whose value(s) you need.

Suppose you want to write a function that finds the index value of the student with the highest class average. The algorithm to use is one that finds the index value of the highest element in an array of real numbers. Therefore, you simply use this algorithm and apply the necessary comparison logic on the field variable `Average` of each element of the array variable `Class`.

Semantics of an index variable

When you are working with an array of records, the value of the index to a given record "says it all." Once a record is referenced by its index value, all fields can be accessed. If you require code to "pull" a record, you need to write a search function or procedure that returns an index value or an array of index values. If you are using a function, you require a variable to store the value returned by the call to the function. Therefore, some of the procedures we code will require a local variable `Index` to store the value returned by a search function.

Using an Array of Records

Now let us write some procedures and functions that use the variable `Class`. The precondition for each example to work is that values have been assigned to all variables of all elements in `Class` over the subrange `1..Enrollment`.

Example Problem 12.3

The problem statement

Let us write a procedure `ShowTests` that finds and displays the test results of a given student in the class. The only parameters for the procedure are `Class` and `Enrollment`. The student's full name is read in (first, middle, and last) and then the test results are displayed for the student if he or she is in the class. A typical run looks like

```
Enter full name:   Jublation Thaddeus Cornpone
Jublation Thaddeus Cornpone scored 70, 80, and 85 on the quizzes.
The final exam grade was 82.
```

Drafting the solution

The solution requires code to read in the student's name. Next, a search for this name through the array of records is required. If the name is found, the test scores are displayed; otherwise a message indicating the student is not in the class should be displayed. We can describe these actions with the pseudocode

> *display prompt*
> *GetFullName(StudentName, input)*   {*Example 12.4*}
> *Index ← ARecord(Class, Enrollment, StudentName)*
> *IF Index <> 0 THEN*
>   *display Class[Index]. Name and elements of Class [Index]. Results*
> *ELSE*
>   *display 'not in class' message*

Refinements

We have already written the procedure `GetFullName`, so there is no need to develop it again. The function `ARecord` is a search function that returns a nonzero value if the fields of StudentName match the fields of Class[Index].Name. The variables Index and StudentName are declared locally.

Source code   Given the pseudocode description and the narrative description of the necessary refinements, we obtain the procedure ShowTests as the source code for the solution.

```
{*                                                                        *}
PROCEDURE GetWord(Sentinel: char; VAR Word: String25; VAR InFile: text);
  BEGIN {insert code of Example 9.3}   END;
{X                                                                        X}
PROCEDURE GetFullName(VAR TheName: NameType; VAR InFile: text);
  BEGIN {insert code of Procedure Example 12.4} END;
{+                                                                        +}
FUNCTION ARecord(VAR Class: ClassArray; Enrollment: IndexType;
                                SearchName: NameType): IndexType;
  {linear search function to be coded}
  BEGIN   END;
{+                                                                        +}
PROCEDURE ShowTests(VAR Class: ClassArray; Enrollment: IndexType);
  {This procedure outputs the quiz and final exam results for a student
  in the class as specified by user input.}
  VAR
    Index: IndexType;      {holds index value of element with StudentName}
    StudentName: NameType;        {name of student whose record is sought}
    TestNo: integer;          {access variable to Class[Index].Results}
  BEGIN
    write('Enter full name: ');
    GetFullName(StudentName, input);
    readln(input);
    Index:= ARecord(Class,Enrollment, StudentName);    {search function}
    IF Index  <> 0 THEN                          {the student was found}
      BEGIN
        WITH Class[Index], Name DO                 {displays information}
          BEGIN
            write(First,' ',Middle,' ',Last,' scored ');
            FOR TestNo:= 1 TO (TotalTests-2) DO
              write(Results[TestNo]:2,', ');
            writeln('and ',Results[TotalTests-1]:2,' on the quizzes.');
            write('The final exam grade was ');
            writeln(Results[TotalTests]:2,'.')
          END {WITH}
      END {IF part of decision statement}
    ELSE                                        {the sudent was not found}
      writeln('There is no student in the class with that name.')
  END; {ShowTests}
{*                                                                        *}
```

The WITH *statement, revisited*	The code of ShowTests is one more example showing how selection rules are applied to the elements of an array of records. Note how the WITH statement gives access to all nonrecord fields on the first hierarchical level of Class[Index] and the use of the comma gives access to all the fields of Name, a lower-level record variable of Class[Index].
Structure chart	The structure chart for the procedure ShowTests is given in Figure 12.10. In order to code this procedure in its entirety, many other procedures and functions must be coded. One of them, the linear search function ARecord, is the next problem we will solve. ◆

Example Problem 12.4

The problem statement	Let us write the code for the function ARecord. To keep matters simple, we are going to develop this function using the linear search algorithm with a sentinel element to indicate a failed search.
The initial draft	The pseudocode description for this function is as follows:

> *Class[0]. Name ← SearchName*   *{set sentinel element}*
> *Probe ← Enrollment*
> *WHILE Class[Probe].Name <> SearchName DO*

FIGURE 12.10   Structure chart for the procedure ShowTests.

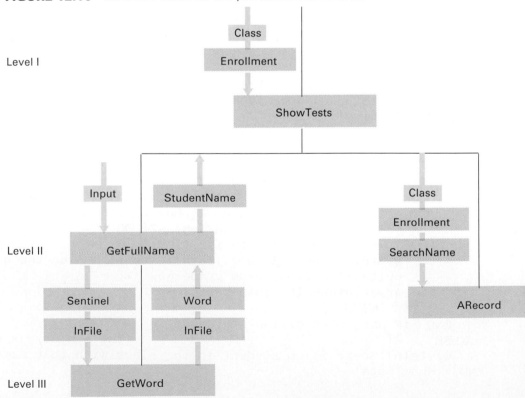

$$Probe \leftarrow Probe - 1$$
$$ARecord \leftarrow Probe$$

Source code

We have used a proven algorithm for our first draft. The `boolean` "expression" to compare the two names, however, requires that all fields match. We have already coded this `boolean` function as Example 12.3, that is, the function `EqualNames`. We can therefore code the function `ARecord` without the need for further refinements.

```
{+                                                                          +}
FUNCTION EqualNames(Name1, Name2: NameType): boolean;
  BEGIN {insert code of Example 12.3}  END;
{X                                                                          X}
FUNCTION ARecord(VAR Class: ClassArray; Enrollment: IndexType;
                                SearchName: NameType): IndexType;
  {the linear search function for a complete name match between
  Class[Index].Name and SearchName; the elements of Class have been assigned
  over the subrange 1..Enrollment; if no match is found, the value
  returned to ARecord is 0.}
  VAR
    Probe: IndexType;   {index value of element being probed}
  BEGIN
    Class[0].Name:= SearchName;   {set sentinel record}
    Probe:= Enrollment;
    WHILE NOT EqualNames(Class[Probe].Name, SearchName) DO
      Probe:= Probe - 1;
    ARecord:= Probe
  END;
{+                                                                          +} ◆
```

Getting the highest average

The next problem first finds the array element of the student with the highest average. Once this index is found, it is used to reference and display the student's name as well as the student's average.

Example Problem 12.5

The problem statement

Let us write a procedure to display the name and average of the student in the class who had the highest average. The procedure's parameters are likewise `Class` and `Enrollment`. When the procedure is executed, the display might look like

```
Joseph Izzie Smart had the highest test average of 98.75.
```

The solution

We simply need to write a function that returns the index value of the student with the highest average. The function itself uses a proven algorithm to find the index value of the highest element in an array of real numbers. Once the index value is found, we use it to display the Name and Average fields of the array element. The source code solution to the problem is given as the procedure ShowHighest.

```
{*                                                                    *}
FUNCTION BestAve(VAR Class: ClassArray;
                          Enrollment: IndexType): IndexType;
  {returns the index value of the element in Class whose Average field
  is the highest. The search is over the elements in the subrange
  1..Enrollment}
  VAR
    TempHighest,  {index value of best average over subrange 1..Index}
    Index:        {candidate index for BestAve}
                  IndexType;
  BEGIN
    TempHighest:= 1;
    FOR Index:= 2 TO Enrollment DO
      IF Class[Index].Average > Class[TempHighest].Average THEN
        TempHighest:= Index;
    BestAve:= TempHighest
  END;
{+                                                                    +}
PROCEDURE ShowHighest(VAR Class: ClassArray; Enrollment: IndexType);
  {displays the name and average of the student with the highest
  Average field in Class over the subrange 1..Enrollment}
  VAR
    HighIndex:  {holds index value of element with the highest average}
                IndexType;
  BEGIN
    HighIndex:= BestAve(Class, Enrollment);
    WITH Class[HighIndex], Name DO
      BEGIN
        write(First, ' ',Middle,' ',Last);
        writeln(' had the highest test average of ',Average:4:2)
      END
  END;
{*                                                                    *} ◆
```

Event-counting   The next problem we possess uses an event-counter on one of the field variables for each element of Class.

Example Problem 12.6

The problem statement   Let us write a procedure ShowEnrollmentByStatus to display the enrollment breakdown by class status. When the procedure is executed, the display, given that there are 82 students in the class, might look like

The class has 22 freshmen, 15 sophomores, 33 juniors, and 12 seniors.

The solution   We can apply an event-counting algorithm on the Status field of each element of Class. The solution is quite straightforward, so we present the code directly as shown.

```
PROCEDURE ShowEnrollmentByStatus(VAR Class: ClassArray;
                                     Enrollment: IndexType);
{displays the count of the freshmen, sophomores, juniors, and seniors
in the class}
VAR
  Index: IndexType;          {access variable to element of Class}
  Frosh, Sophs, Jrs, Srs:    {counters for each status level}
                             integer;
  BEGIN
    Frosh:= 0;
    Sophs:= 0;
    Jrs:= 0;
    Srs:= 0;
    FOR Index:= 1 TO Enrollment DO
      WITH Class[Index] DO
        IF Status = 'Freshman' THEN
          Frosh:= Frosh + 1
        ELSE IF Status = 'Sophomore' THEN
          Sophs:= Sophs + 1
        ELSE IF Status = 'Junior' THEN
          Jrs:= Jrs + 1
        ELSE If Status = 'Senior' THEN
          Srs:= Srs + 1;
      writeln('The class has ', Frosh:1, ' freshmen, ', Sophs:1,
              ' sophomores, ', Jrs:1,' juniors, and ', Srs:1, ' seniors,')
END; ◆
```

One last   The final example we will develop is a procedure that uses a combination of
problem   event counting and event recording (actually event displaying) to get the job done.

Example Problem 12.7

The problem   Unfortunately, some students missed the final exam and have to make it up. Suppose
statement   that any student who missed the final was given a temporary grade for his or her
Results[4] test of 0. Let us write a procedure ShowMissedFinal that displays
the names of those students who missed the final. It also displays the count of the
number of students who missed the final. A typical run looks like

```
The following students missed the final:
Joseph Lewis Doakes
```

```
Gerald Thomas Fox
Sanford Dunne Misted
Gillian Isadore Tardy
Willie William Williams
A total of 5 students missed the final.
```

The source code   The solution to the problem is straightforward. The array elements from `1..Enrollment` must be processed. If the value of the expression `Class[Index].Result[TotalTests]` is equal to 0, the associated name is displayed, and this event is counted. The source code solution to the problem is given as the procedure `ShowMissedFinal`.

```
PROCEDURE ShowMissedFinal(VAR Class: ClassArray;
                              Enrollment: IndexType);
{Displays the names of those students whose result on the
last test (the final) is 0. Also displays the count of the students
who missed the final}
VAR
   Index: IndexType;       {element access variable}
   TotalMissed: integer;   {count of those who missed final}
BEGIN
   writeln('The following students missed the final:');
   TotalMissed:= 0;
   FOR Index:= 1 TO Enrollment DO
     WITH Class[Index], Name DO
       IF Results[TotalTests] = 0 THEN
         BEGIN
           writeln(First,' ', Middle,' ',Last);
           TotalMissed:= TotalMissed + 1
         END;
   writeln('A total of ',TotalMissed:1, ' students missed the final.')
END;  ◆
```

EXERCISES

Test Your Understanding

1. Indicate which field variable(s) of the elements of `Class` you would have to access to do the following:
   (a) Find the index value of the student who got the highest score on the third quiz.
   (b) Count the number of freshman who passed the course, given that a passing grade required an average of 60.
   (c) Sort the array elements in order according to the social security number.
   (d) Sort the array elements in order according to the last name.

Practice Your Analysis Skills

2. Given the following additional definition:

```
IndexArray = ARRAY[1..MaxClass] OF IndexType;
```

After the following procedure has been executed, what do the elements of the array SomeIndices represent?

```
PROCEDURE GetArray(VAR Class: ClassArray; Enrollment: IndexType;
                   VAR SomeIndices: IndexArray; VAR TotalAssigned: integer);
   VAR
     LocalIndex: IndexType;
   BEGIN
   TotalAssigned:= 0;
   FOR LocalIndex:= 1 TO Enrollment DO
     IF Class[LocalIndex].Average >= 85.00 THEN
       BEGIN
         TotalAssigned:= TotalAssigned+1;
         SomeIndices[TotalAssigned]:= LocalIndex
       END
   END;
```

Sharpen Your Implementation Skills

3. Write a procedure ShowNames to display the names associated with the elements of the array SomeIndices of Exercise 2. Make sure that all relevant parameters are passed into the block and that all irrelevant parameters are not.

4. Write a function to find the index value of the sophomore with the highest average. If there are no sophomores in the class, the function should return the value 0.

5. Modify the code of the procedure GetClass so that it is called by GetClass(InOrder, Enrollment, Class, StudentsRecords) where InOrder is a boolean variable that is true if the values read in are alphabetically sorted by the student's last names. Write the procedure in such a way to compare first names if duplicate last names are found.

6. Write a procedure to sort the array Class by last name using the selection sort algorithm. Your procedure should account for the possibility of the same two last names.

7. Write the binary search algorithm that finds the index value of a student with a given SearchName (all 3 fields must match).

8. Write a procedure to display the name and score of the student who got the highest grade on the final exam. The display should look like

   Joseph Izzie Smart got the high score of 97 on the final exam.

9. Write the code for a different implementation of StuRecord. This implementation should contain three fields: (1) Personal, (2) Status, and (3) CourseInfo. All these fields are records. Personal contains (1) the student's name, (2) address and (3) IDNo. Status contains (1) the student's QPA (average for all the courses he/she has taken), (2) total number of credit hours taken and (3) the class the student is in (frosh, soph, etc.). CourseInfo contains (1) the total number of courses taken, (2) each course's name (3) each course's number, (4) the year the given course was taken, (5) the grade the student received (a letter grade) in the course and (6) the number of credit hours in the course. (Hint: You may want to use an array of records as part of the implementation for CourseInfo.)

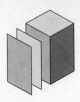

Program Testing Hints

It is just as important to choose a workable data structure to solve a problem as it is to write the statements that correctly solve the problem. Besides presenting the bugs you must avoid when working with records, we also give some hints to help you choose a relevant variable types(s) to solve a problem.

Choosing a Structure

Now you can use one-dimensional arrays, multidimensional arrays, and records to implement a solution to a problem. Your choices, which you will make quite early in the process of developing a solution, are critical in obtaining a correct and efficient solution. Let us look at the important considerations involved in deciding on a data structure(s).

Some criteria
The first step in deciding on a structure is careful analysis of the problem statement. If the problem is clearly stated, you know what your coded solution "should do." Even though you have not yet decided upon some structures, you at least have an idea of the operations that must be carried out. You can use some of these defining operations as a starting point to determine the candidate structure(s) or variable(s) that make up the best choice(s). In short, you do a small feasibility study.

To help you choose the best candidate(s), you should ask the following questions about each candidate:

1. Can I implement the required operations easily?
2. Will the operations use efficient algorithms?
3. Will the implementation be easy to understand?
4. Will the implementation be easy to document?

PROGRAM DESIGN RULE 12.1

Know the access rules for any candidate structure that is being considered as a solution to the problem.

The fundamental requirement
The first criterion you should apply on any candidate structure is ease of implementation. In order to get an idea of what is effective and simple, you should know how the selection and access rules apply to the component variables for each candidate structure. If you can code the necessary operations such that there is easy and efficient access and/or selection to each component variable, the structure is probably a good one. If not, try a new candidate structure(s). You should *under no circumstances* charge ahead using some structure(s) you "hope" will work.

The other criteria
Once you have determined that a particular structure works, you should then consider the efficiency issue. It is, for example, certainly feasible for the computer to

search for a particular record in a sequential file, but does it make sense if your program requires many searches? It is far more efficient to read the contents into an array variable if memory allocation is not a problem.

The final two criteria complement each other. If the logical implementation is understandable, the program is easily maintained. Obscure logic and inadequate or (worse still) misleading documentation will add up to plenty of wasted time and money spent on program maintenance.

PROGRAM DESIGN RULE 12.2

Choose a data type that solves the problem in the simplest possible way.

Applying Program Design Rule 12.2

The simplest choice that solves the problem is usually the best choice. Suppose, for example, you need to write a program that counts the number of occurrences of a certain character in a text file. A simple integer variable can serve as a counter with this application. Suppose, instead, the problem is to count the number of occurrences of all the letters of the alphabet. Then you are better off using an array of counters rather than 26 scalar counter variables. Finally, if you need to process the student enrollment in CS101, it is easier to work with an array of records rather than with a large number of parallel arrays.

Arrays vs. records

Sometimes a structure that is apparently easier to implement might nonetheless represent a poor semantic choice. When we chose to implement a structure capable of holding a person's name, we decided to use a record with three field variables of the same type. You might make a case, however, for an implementation suggested by Example 12.8. With this choice, you can use a FOR loop to access the components of a person's name, as shown by the source code of the procedure GetFullName that follows the definitions and declarations.

Example 12.8

```
TYPE        {POOR SEMANTIC CHOICE!!}
  String20 = {STRING TYPE THAT CAN HOLD UP TO 20 CHARACTERS};
  NameElement = (First, Middle, Last);
  NameType = ARRAY[First..Last] OF String20;
VAR
  AName: NameType;

PROCEDURE GetFullName(VAR AName: NameType; VAR InFile: text);
  VAR
    NameAccess: NameElement;
  BEGIN
    FOR NameAccess:= First TO Last DO
      GetWord(' ', AName[NameAccess], InFile)
  END;
```

Although the access logic is easy to code, the implementation of Name as an array type represents a poor choice. Why? Let us consider the implications of using an array as a candidate structure:

1. An array represents an ordered set of elements all of the same type.
2. The values given to any two elements have virtually the same meaning.

The difference in meaning is found completely in the value of the access expression(s) rather than in each element's value.

Let us recall some of the ways we used an array: An element of Results represented a score by a given student on a given test. An element of ChessBoard represented a space on which a given token was placed. An element of Class held information about a given student. Each example applied an array type to three distinctly different uses. Yet in each case there was no radical difference in the meaning of the value of any given element. Thus, 95 is a valid score for any student on any test, the black queen can be on any of the 64 squares of a chessboard, and an element of Class can contain information about any student.

We cannot make the same statement about a person's three names. From the time people started naming children, the difference between a first name and a last name was quite clear. There is no strong argument we can make in favor of saying that a last name can just as well be a first name for any given person. Hence we chose a record with three different fields of the same type. The implication is that each field variable takes on a meaning very different from the other two field variables.

Sometimes your initial choice may not appear as good as it first seemed. Should this circumstance become obvious, do not compound the error by continuing to use an obviously bad choice. Well-chosen structures can facilitate the rest of the design and implementation process. Poorly chosen structures can lead to severe coding difficulties that only get worse with each refinement. Therefore, do not be afraid to abandon a candidate structure if you find *early on* that it will not work as well as you first thought it would.

Errors Related to Record Variable Syntax and Semantics

Now let us discuss some of the common errors to be avoided when you are developing code dealing with variables that are of some record type.

There are certain errors using records that the compiler will always catch. For example, the following code, which attempts to access the Indexth element of the variable Class is missing a subscript expression:

```
Index:= {some value from some expression};
WITH Class DO                              {SYNTAX ERROR!!}
   BEGIN
      {statements}
   END;
```

You can fix this error by replacing Class with Class[Index].

The compiler will also catch an attempt at boolean operations on structured variables. Thus, given that `Class[Index].Name` and `SearchName` are both of type `NameType`, the boolean "expression" used in the following example is likewise a syntax error:

```
IF Class[Index].Name = SampleName THEN     {SYNTAX ERROR!}
   BEGIN  {do something with Class[Index]}   END;
```

Although this error is readily found at compilation time, you may have planned a good deal of your program based on the assumption that boolean operators will work on the candidate structured variables. Having made this wrong assumption, you may then have developed many lines of source code that prove to be incorrect. When you get the error message(s) at compilation time, you may suddenly feel that your reasons for choosing some of the structures you did were invalid. Remember to use feasibility preplanning!

In most cases, you can readily fix the errors, but you may have to write more code that you had not initially planned on writing. You can, for instance, fix the error of the present example using a call to the function `EqualNames` (Example 12.3) to get

```
IF EqualNames(Class[Index].Name, SampleName) THEN
   BEGIN {do something with Class[Index]} END;
```

In this case, the simple `boolean` expression that you assumed would work requires instead that you code a complete `boolean` function.

An uncodable "algorithm"

You can never use a loop control variable in a FOR statement to sequentially access each field in a record variable. Thus the following "pseudocode" description does not code to anything legal in Pascal:

```
FOR FieldVar ← FirstField TO LastField DO     {BAD IDEA!!!}
    manipulate ARecord.AFieldVar
```

The FOR loop changes the *value* of a *single variable* with each loop pass. The period represents a *selection mechanism* using a record variable to one of a number of *different variables*. The value of the variable selected may not even change. Do not even consider an "algorithm" that uses a loop to access the different field variables of a record, for it makes no sense.

Errors with special symbols

It is unfortunate that the comma and period not only look alike, but that they are adjacent to each other on the keyboard. The following two statements differ by only one special symbol, but the selection mechanism to the field variables is very different:

```
WITH Class[Index].Name DO
   BEGIN  {statements}   END;
```

```
WITH Class[Index],Name DO
   BEGIN   {statements}    END;
```

In the first case, only the field variables of the record variable Class[Index].Name can be selected directly by identifier reference. In the second case, all nonrecord fields of Class[Index] can be selected by identifier reference, and additionally all fields of Class[Index].Name can be selected by identifier reference. Be particularly careful to enter the correct symbol when you edit programs that use both the period and the comma to select fields of a record.

Note that when you use the period, the field variables of all record variables but the specified one are *excluded* from being selected. Thus, if the variable list of a WITH statement is Class[Index].Name, only the field variables of the record variable Class[Index].Name can be referenced directly by identifier.

On the other hand, when you use a comma, all field variables belonging to the record variables that make up the variable list can be selected by identifier reference. Thus, the variable list of a WITH statement coded as Class[Index],Name allows selection to all fields of the record variable Class[Index] by identifier reference. Additionally, selection by identifier reference to all fields of the record variable Class[Index].Name is possible.

Incorrect access expressions
Suppose you want the computer to display the Name fields of all the elements of Class. Be careful not to write code such as the following:

```
WITH Class[Index], Name DO
   FOR Index:= 1 TO Enrollment DO
      writeln(First, ' ',Middle, ' ' ,Last);
```

This fragment will always lead to a run-time error. When the machine executes its sequence, it will either issue an index-out-of-range message or display the same name a total of Enrollment times. The reason for either error is that the record Class[Index] is accessed before the loop control variable Index takes on its first value. If the value of Index associated with the WITH statement is out of range, a run-time crash will occur. If this value, however, is in range, the same name is displayed Enrollment times.

Fixing the error
The problem requires access to all the elements in the array Class. We defined each element of Class as a record. Hence, we must first access the record as an array element. Therefore, we must assign a value to the loop control variable before writing the WITH statement. Hence, the correct code for the sequence is

```
FOR Index:= 1 TO Enrollment DO
   WITH Class[Index], Name DO
      writeln(First, ' ',Middle, ' ',Last);
```

The WITH statement, again
Remember that the WITH statement adds scope to the field identifiers of each record variable in the variable list. This property makes it less tedious for you to select the field variables of the associated record variables. Unfortunately, this statement also hides the relationship between the variables in the list itself and also the relationship between the field variables that are referenced.

An example of ambiguity
Suppose a particular program has the following statement in it:

```
WITH Dealer, Automobile, Model DO
   BEGIN
```

```
          {references to variables Discount, Cost, Location, InStock}
     END;
```

The variable list does not necessarily mean the records were set up with a hierarchical structure that has `Automobile` as a field of `Dealer` and `Model` as a field of `Automobile`. `Automobile` and `Dealer` could, for example, be completely separate records. Likewise, `Discount` could refer to a given dealer's discount, the discount on a given make of automobile, or a discount for a given model.

Suggestions

There are no clear-cut rules to follow when you plan and code `WITH` statements. If you adopt certain conventions, however, your code will be easier to understand. It is best, for example, to use variable lists that select variables in the hierarchical structure of just *one* record variable. If you feel you must reference the fields of two unrelated variables as part of the body of the same `WITH` statement, clarify this usage with a sidebar comment after the reserved word DO.

A detachable TYPE and VAR section

Many programs rely heavily on records to get the job done. In solving a problem that requires records, you will often pass record variables as parameters to different procedures. These procedures will reference the field variables in their statements. If you use the `WITH` statement inside these blocks, you may find yourself continually scrolling to the start of the program to check the identifier references you want to make to the field variables.

You need not submit yourself to this inconvenience, if you provide sufficient white space between the global TYPE and VAR sections and the PROCEDURE and FUNCTION declarations. You can simply get a printout of this part of the program, and tear it off so you can refer to it as you develop the rest of your code. An illustration of this technique is shown in the source code (incomplete) of Example 12.9.

Example 12.9

```
TYPE
   {some type definitions};
   SomeRec = RECORD
      {a record with many field variables}
   END;
   {other type definitions};
VAR
   {some variable declarations};
   ARec:  SomeRec;
   {other variable declarations}




{*                                                                *}
PROCEDURE  {the rest of the program ...};
```

EXERCISES

Test Your Understanding

1. State the main disadvantage of using a `WITH` statement in a program.

2. State the main advantage of using a `WITH` statement in a program.

3. Consider the structured variable Class, as coded in the program UseClassRecords (Section 12.3). Indicate what is wrong with the following statement:

```
WITH Class[1], Class[5] DO
    writeln('The average is ',Average:4:2);
```

4. Given the same structure used in Exercise 3, determine if anything is wrong with the following statement:

```
WITH Class[Index].Name DO
    writeln(First,' ',Last,' had an average of ',Average:4:2);
```

If so, indicate what is wrong and fix it.

5. Indicate what is wrong with the following implementation:

```
TYPE
    String20 = {STRING TYPE CAPABLE OF HOLDING UP TO 20 CHARACTERS};
    NameRecord = RECORD
        First, Middle, Last: String20
    END;    {NameRecord}

    CityRecord = RECORD
        Name,
        State: StringType;
    END;    {CityRecord}

    PersonRecord = RECORD
        Name: NameRecord;
        City: CityRecord
    END;    {PersonRecord}
```

Fix the erroneous code.

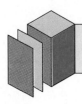

REVIEW AND EXERCISES

A variable that is a *record type* has component variables that are accessed by *name*. A record type is defined by a *field list* containing the identifiers to the *field variables* that make up the components of the defined RECORD. A particular field variable is selected by means of a *field-selector expression*. The value of this expression is the name of one of the field variables. A field selector is formed with a reference to a record variable, the special symbol that is a period, and a reference to one of the field variables.

A field variable can be a scalar variable, an array variable, or another record variable. Once it is selected with a proper expression, all syntax rules that apply to the field variable's type can be applied to the particular field variable.

Two record variables of the same type are assignment-compatible. In standard Pascal, however, boolean expressions will not work on two record variables as a whole, even if they are assignment compatible. The values of both variables must be compared field by field in order to establish that they have taken on equal values for all fields.

You can use the WITH statement to select more than one field variable of a given record variable. Therefore, we say that the WITH statement *extends the scope* of the record variable's reference mechanism. It is also possible to use the comma as a special symbol in forming a *variable list* of record variables whose field variables you want to select. Variable lists are extremely handy when it comes to selecting field variables of *hierarchical records*. A record variable is hierarchical if at least one of its fields is also a record variable.

An attractive alternative to a structure containing parallel arrays of different types is an *array of records*. Many of the algorithms that apply to single-array structures can be used on the field variables(s) of an array-of-records structure. Once you determine which field variable(s) is the relevant one for a given problem, you can apply a proven algorithm to the necessary field variable(s) required for the solution of the problem.

The selection of the best structure(s) is part of the process involved in finding the solution to a given problem. The factors you must consider in making this important decision are (1) the ease of implementation, (2) the efficiency of all proposed algorithms and (3) the readability of the source code (of which documentation is an important part).

It is possible to have one or two false starts. If a candidate structure is found less than ideal when you start to implement the required source code, do not be afraid to abandon it and start over. You should try nonetheless to avoid these false starts, if at all possible. Good feasibility preplanning based on knowledge of the allowed operations for each structure will help you quite a bit in this process. Do not even start the implementation process with the "hope" that your idea will work.

Be careful during your editing session that you do not make typographical errors with the period and the comma. Even if you are careful, check all selection expressions of your source code at least twice, for these two symbols that look so much alike can cause errors due to the different ways each one is applied. Also be careful when you use the WITH statement. This reserved word effectively hides the relationship (1) among the variables in the variable list and (2) between the record variables and their field variables. If you feel that its usage makes your code less readable, it would be better that you use field-selector expressions with the period instead.

EXERCISES

Short Answers

1. Explain why it is a bad programming practice to use anonymous types on the field variables with an array of records.

2. True or false? The index value of an element in an array of records contains virtually all the information you need about a given record. Explain your answer.

3. Can a field variable of an element in an array of records be another array of records? Give an example of a variable that might require such a structure.

4. You want to build a structure to describe certain characteristics about a person. The characteristics are (1) his or her height, (2) weight, and (3) age, all expressed as integer values. Which makes more sense to use: an array of three integers or a record with three fields? Why? Draw the appearance of the structure you decide upon.

5. A FOR loop can always be used to access the elements of any given array, but it can never be used to access the fields of a given record. Explain the reason for this statement. Your explanation should refer to the syntax diagrams for the two structures.

6. True or false? An access expression is always required for the machine to display the value of a scalar field variable. Explain.

7. Suppose the following statement compiles for a given program:

```
WITH Student[N], Course[2], Professor, Name DO
    BEGIN  {statement}  END;
```

   (a) What is the minimum number of levels of hierarchy possible for the given statement?
   (b) What is the maximum number of levels of hierarchy suggested by the statement? For all the remaining questions, assume that the structure has the maximum number of hierarchical levels.
   (c) Assuming that each level has some nonrecord fields, how many levels of access are realized by the given statement?
   (d) What can you say about the appearance of the variable Student?
   (e) What can you say about the appearance of the variable Course?
   (f) What can you say about the appearance of the variable Professor?
   (g) The construct between the WITH and DO is known as a _____ _____ .

8. The word _____ increases the _____ of _____ to the field variables for a given record variable.

9. The same word in Exercise 8 also hides the association between the variables in the _____ _____ and the _____ _____ .

10. Suppose all the commas in the statement of Exercise 7 were changed to periods. How many levels of hierarchical structures are accessible with this construct? Which levels?

11. True or false? A variable selection expression can sometimes take on a scalar value. Explain.

12. Is it possible to assign the value(s) taken on by one record variable to another record variable using only the assignment operator? If so, under what circumstances.

13. Can a single array of records be sorted in order according to the values taken on by two distinct field variables? Why or why not?

14. Under what circumstances will the boolean operator for equality work with two record variables?

Easy Projects

15. The roster for course CS101 at LearnIt U. is in file CS101.dat, where the names are sorted alphabetically by last name. The first line of the file contains the number of students in the class, and all subsequent lines contain the following information about each student: (1) status indicated by Fr, So, Jr, and Sr, (2) the ID number, and (3) the student's name. Information about each student is on one line of text, where the first four lines of text might look like

```
57
Fr 888989098 Roy Green Biv
Jr 111111212 Robert William Browne
Fr 745454545 Kent Jonathon Clark
```

Professors at LearnIt U. like their class rosters given to them as four tables, one for the freshmen, one for the sophomores, and so forth. You are to write a program that reads in the information about each student and then displays the four tables. The start of the freshman table, given the previous file, is shown as

```
FRESHMEN
  ID No           Name
  -- --           ----
  888989098       Roy Green Biv
  745454545       Kent Jonathon Clark
```

16. Linguists Inc. has a list of at most 100 people who speak foreign languages and can be used as interpreters. The information about any given linguist is found on a line of the text file Interpreters.dat that contains the interpreter's name (terminated by a carat) and the languages he or she speaks (terminated by a carat). Each interpreter is capable of speaking up to five different languages. A typical entry on the file looks like

```
Albert Allemand^ French^ German^ Italian^ Russian^ English<eoln>
```

You are to write a program that reads in the values from the file and then provides a list of names to a client seeking an interpreter capable of speaking two languages as specified by the input. The program ends when the characters Q Q are entered (both languages are "Q"). A typical run is as follows:

```
Enter languages:  German English
The following names qualify:
  Albert Allemand
  Josephine Grant
  Rolf Gustavsen
  Tina MacIntosh

Enter languages:  Q Q
The program is terminated.
```

17. The semester is completed in CS101 and each student's name and average is stored in file CS101R.dat. The first line of the file contains the number of students who completed the course (sat for all the exams and hence has an average), and each subsequent line contains a student's name and his or her average. Three typical lines are as follows:

```
Albert Average^  78.25
Brenda Bright^   95.00
Dudley Dunce^    58.00
```

Write a program that reads the information in the file CS101R.dat, finds the class average, and then displays as OUTSTANDING the names of all those students whose average was at least 15 points above the class average, as AVERAGE the names of all students greater than 15 points below the average but less 15 points above the average, and as POOR the names of all students who scored at least 15 points lower than the class average. The final line of display is the class average. A typical run (given the three lines in the file) is shown as

```
            OUTSTANDING STUDENTS:
              Brenda Bright
              . . . . . . . . . .
            AVERAGE STUDENTS:
              Albert Average

              . . . . . . . . . .
            POOR STUDENTS:
              Dudley Dunce
              . . . . . . . . . .


       The class average was 76.87.
```

18. The Brighton Bombers are a Little League team with 15 members. The record of each team member is stored in the file TeamRecord.dat, where each line of the file has the player's name (terminated by a carat), the number of times he was at bat, the number of hits he got, and the number of runs he scored. The file is sorted in order of the player's last name, where the first two lines might look like

```
       Charlie Braxton^ 20   3    2<eoln>
       Billy Estler^  27  16   13<eoln>
```

Write a program that uses the information from the file to print a table showing each player's name, the batting average accurate to three places (hits divided by at bats), and the runs scored. The table should be ordered such that the player with the best average is first in the table and the one with the worst average is last. If, for example, Estler has the best average and Braxton the worst, the display will look like

```
       Player's Name              Average      Runs
       -------------              -------      ----
       Billy Estler                0.592        13
       {other 13 players --------------------------}
       Charlie Braxton             0.150         2
```

19. A file Match.dat contains the results of a wrestling meet at Smallville High School. There are ten different weight classes divided up according to the weight classes 103, 112, 120, 129, 135, 145, 154, 165, 177, and heavyweight. Each match has three rounds, for which points are scored.

     Each line of the file contains (1) the wrestler's name, a string of up to 40 characters, (2) the wrestler's weight class, and (3) the results of each of the rounds against his opponent, shown as three pairs of numbers, where the points for a given wrestler and the opponent are scored per round.

     Examples: Junior Hulk Hodges, in the 154-pound class won his match by pinning his opponent in the third round. His opponent scored 4 points in the first round and Hulk scored 0. In the second round, Hulk scored 6 points to his opponent's 4. Then in the third round, his opponent had scored no further points when Hulk pinned him. This scenario is reflected by the entry

```
       Junior Hulk Hodges^ 154 0 4 6 4 99 0<eoln>
```

Write a program that reads in the contents of the file Match.dat and then displays the team members by weight class and name in tabular form. Next, it lists those members who won by a pin, those who won by points, those who lost by points, and those who lost by a pin. If a given match is won on points (no pin, but one wrestler scored more points than his opponent), a team wins 3 points on the meet; if a given match is won by a pin (as represented by 99 points in a round), the team is awarded 5 meet points. Finally, the program displays the number of points scored by Smallville High and the number of points scored by its opponent.

20. Mr. Digits, the coach at Smallville High, has just learned that the school has a data file HealthInfo.dat of all its students, where each line contains the following information about one student: (1) the student's name, (2) sex (M or F), (3) height in inches, and (4) weight in pounds.

He wants to use this information in recruiting possible team members for some of the different sports. Write a program to help him in his recruiting efforts, where Digits will specify a sex, a height range, and a weight range. The computer will display the names of all those students of the desired sex whose heights and weights are in range. Mr. Digits may keep asking for lists of students until he enters Q (quit) when the machine prompts him for the sex of the students(s). If Digits enters anything other than M of F for this prompt, the machine will prompt again. Typical interactions are

```
Sex: M
Height range (low first, then high in inches): 67 75
Weight range (low first, then high in inches): 130 195
Qualified students:
  Jack Adams
  William Bartholemew
  .....
Sex: Q
```

Two typical lines of the file are

```
Jack Adams^ M   70   165<eoln>
William Bartholemew^   M   74   191 < eoln>
```

The information from the file is first read into an array of records. Then Digits will enter his requests. To read in values, set up the data structure so that it can hold up to 1000 students in memory. The reading in is stopped when <eof> is reached. (You do not, of course, need anywhere near that number of lines in the file to test your program.)

Difficult Projects

21. The *Literary Giant* is a small literary magazine with a list of very loyal customers. The magazine uses a computer to update its customer list, where information about each customer is stored in the text file OCustomerInfo.dat. The first line contains the customer's number, followed by the customer's name, and ending with the number of months left in the subscription. The file is sorted by customer number in order from lowest to highest number. The numbers can take on values from 1 to 500, inclusive. The remaining lines contain address information. A single blank line separates one customer from the next. The final line of the file is, likewise, a blank line of text followed by <eof>.

You are to write a program that reads this information into an array of records representing the old customers. As it reads numbers in, it checks them off in the variable Used, an array containing boolean variables with an access subrange from 1..500. This array indicates that a particular customer number is already "used."

Then the program reads in entries for new customers. The values read in are sorted according to customer number. A new file `NCustomerInfo.dat` is then written, where the old and new customer records are combined in such a way that the updated file is still in order according to customer number.

New customer information is gotten the following way: The subscription size is over a 12-month period. The customer's name and lines representing the customer's address information are read in. The final line is read in as a blank line. The program generates the customer number by calling an RNG as a starting point of a linear search for an unused number in the subrange `1..500`. This information is then inserted into its proper place in the array of records representing the new customers. The list of new customers is considered complete when a null string is read in given a prompt for the customer's name. Allow up to 500 customer records to be read in (in other words, your array of records has the subrange `1..500`) from either file.

Typical entries on disk are

```
175 ^Nicolas Santa^   11
North Pole
Iceberg 783
Arctic Ocean

179 ^Joseph L. Liteburn^   2
{and other information}
```

Typical interactions for update are

```
Enter name:  Jason Chasten<eoln>
Enter address information, as it should appear on the envelope. Terminate
entry with a blank line:
789 Glaxonic Drive<eoln>
Short Branch, NJ 00000<eoln>

Enter name: <eoln>
Files updating...
Program terminated with updated file information on NCustomers.dat
```

22. Assume the same information is available on `OCustomer.dat` that we used in Exercise 21. You are to write a program that reads in the information into an array of records just as before. Now, however, an array of `booleans` is not required, for this time the program processes changes of addresses and issues renewal notices. These operations are carried out in the following way.

First, the computer addresses mailing labels to customers whose subscriptions end in less than 3 months. The number of blank lines between each mailing label is 3. Next, it processes any change of addresses. These values are read in from the keyboard, where the user specifies whether the search key is a name (entry value of 1; requires a linear search) or a customer number (entry value of 2; can use a binary search). The array is searched, and if the name or number is found, the user enters the new address, which replaces the old one. The address field of the array element is then changed.

When all updates are finished, enter 3. The information in the updated array is then copied into the text file `UCustomers.dat`. Typical interactions are

```
Update by (enter 1, for Name, 2 for Number, 3 to quite);  1
Name:   Joseph L. Smith
Enter new address, exactly as it should appear on the envelope:
985 Sunnyside Drive
Out There, Tx  00000

Update by (enter 1 for Name, 2 for Number, 3 for quit):  2
Number:  341
The name is Lionel Leonine
Enter new address, exactly as it should appear on the envelope:
Cage 3
Smallville Zoo
Smallville, NY 00000

Update by (enter 1 for Name, 2 for Number, 3 for quit):  3
File being updated...
Updated information is now found in the file named UCustomers.dat.
```

23. Each warehouse of Wonderful Widgets has an inventory of the five widgets (models A through E) that is shipped out to the retailers who order the widgets. The inventory for the widgets is found in five lines of the file Inventories.dat, where each line has four numbers on it: (1) an integer representing the number of widgets in stock, (2) an integer representing the minimum allowable quantity of widgets in stock before more have to be reordered, (3) an integer representing the size of the reorder quantity, and (4) a real number representing the wholesale cost per widget charged to the customer who ordered some widgets.

   The orders for the day are found in another file Orders.dat, where each line contains the name of the customer with an order, the number of widgets ordered, and the model of the widget ordered. You are to write a program that uses these two files to simulate the invoicing and inventory updating at the warehouse.

   First, the values of Inventories.dat are read in and stored. The initial number of widgets in stock is displayed. Next, a line from Orders.dat is read in, and if a sufficient number of widgets is on hand, a two-line invoice is displayed. The first line contains the name "Wonderful Widgets" and the name of the company being billed. The second line indicates the number of widgets ordered, the model ordered, and the total bill. The filling of this order decreases the number of widgets on hand. If an order cannot be filled, it is stored in an array containing back orders. At the end of the day, the sum of the revenues generated, the present widget inventories, reorder information, and back orders are displayed.

   Typical line of Orders.dat is

```
        Sal's Widgets Shop^   100   E<eoln>
```

   Typical displays are

```
Bill FROM Wonderful Widgets TO Sal's Widget Shop
100 Model E widgets ...... $2000.00    {suppose Model E is for $20.00}

REVENUES FOR THE DAY .... $25,500.00
```

REORDERS
  Model A 5000   {5000 is reorder quantity for Model A}
  Model C 1000   {1000 is reorder quantity for Model C}

ORDERS DUE
  The General Store . . . . 2000 Model A widgets
  Bond's Widget House. . . . 550 Model C widgets

WIDGETS IN STOCK
  Model A 1500
  Model B 900
  Model C 450
  Model D 835
  Model E 2350

DATA ABSTRACTION

OBJECTIVES

After reading and studying the material of the present chapter, you should be able to

- Explain what is meant by the terms "data abstraction" and "abstract data type"

- List the categories of operations that apply to an abstract data type

- Implement the code for an abstract data type using records and arrays

- Write a client program that uses one or more abstract data types

- Describe the logical properties of the stack and queue abstract data types

- Write client programs that specifically require a stack or a queue as part of their solution

Aɴʏ ᴅᴀᴛᴀ ᴛʏᴘᴇ ʏᴏᴜ ᴜѕᴇ ɪɴ ᴀ ᴘʀᴏɢʀᴀᴍ can be described in terms of the values it can take on and the operations that can be applied to it. An `integer`, for example, is a data type that can take on values between `-(maxint +1)` to `maxint`. If a program requires an `integer` variable(s) or expression(s), all operations found in the system library can be applied to the variable(s) or expression(s) of type `integer` required in the program.

In this chapter, you will learn a formal method for implementing your own *abstract data types (ADTs)*. As with the standard Pascal types, an ADT is defined in terms of the values it can be take on and the operations that can be applied to it. Once its appearance has been defined and its operations implemented, it can be stored in a file that is part of your own personal library of ADTs. If you then have a program(s) that requires the use of an ADT found in your library, you can declare a variable(s) of the given type and apply any operations belonging to this type that are needed for the execution of the program.

13.1 Abstract Data Types

In this section, you will get an overview of the properties of an *abstract data type (ADT)*. As our first example, we intend to implement complex numbers, a data type that does not exist in standard Pascal. In keeping with the spirit of data abstraction, we will not implement the details of any of the operations. We will, however, present the code for the ADT in such a way that a programmer who wishes to use the abstraction can apply the operations without having to know anything about the details that deal with the implementation of the operations.

> **Abstract data type:** one defined in terms of both its logical appearance and the operations that can be applied to it.

Data abstraction

Recall that a complex number consists of two numeric parts, one representing a real part and the other representing an imaginary part. In your high school algebra class, you may have expressed this number by the definition $Z = X + Yi$, where X and Y are real numbers, and i represents the imaginary factor $\sqrt{-1}$. Recall further that you can add, subtract, multiply, and divide two of these numbers. You can also determine the value of the number's real and imaginary parts, as well as its absolute value or magnitude.

We will implement the ADT `ComplexNo`, by first defining the type `ComplexNo` to be a RECORD containing two field variables `XRe` and `YIm`. These two variables, respectively, represent the real and imaginary parts of an abstract complex number variable. We will then code headers for the procedures and functions using variables(s) of type `ComplexNo` to perform these arithmetic operations. When we code the headers, we will use the syntax of standard Pascal in such a way that the statements to carry out the operations are separated from the associated headers. By doing so, we are employing the technique of *data abstraction*.

Data abstraction: the separation of the logical meaning of the operations in an ADT from the implementation details.

Units and programs

Each of the ADTs we will implement in this chapter make up source code that can be copied into a file as an ADT *unit*. The ADT unit is not a program, but its operations can be used by *client programs*. Suppose, for example, you are developing a program requiring variables that represent complex numbers. If your directory contains a unit for a complex number type, you can use the code implemented in the unit to apply to the complex number arithmetic required in the client program.

ADT unit: a file containing the TYPE definition and defining operations of an ADT.

Client program: a program that uses an ADT for one or more of its variables.

ADT Interfacing

Ideally, the client user of an ADT should only see that part of a unit containing the identifiers representing the abstract type and those representing the abstract operations. In particular, he or she would prefer to see a list of headers for the operations that are separate from the implementation details that make up the statement part of each operation.

The FORWARD *directive*

Standard Pascal allows you to code the header of a procedure or function, then forward-reference its statement using the FORWARD directive. The syntax diagram showing the proper usage of this directive is given in Figure 13.1(a) for procedures and in Figure 13.1(b) for functions.

When the compiler encounters a header with the FORWARD directive, it looks further down the block for a matching header that contains the procedure's or function's compound statement. This second header must satisfy the syntax of Figure 13.2(a) for a procedure and Figure 13.2(b) for a function.

The FORWARD directive separates the header of a proceudure or function from its statement. At run time, the machine uses the parameters of the first header to carry out the (compound) statement found after the second header. Note that there is *no parameter list* with this second header. Usually, however, it is wise to include the parameter list as a comment.

The ComplexNo unit

The code given as Example 13.1 shows how you can use the FORWARD directive in standard Pascal to separate the headers of all the operations contained in a unit from the statements that carry out the operations.

Example 13.1

```
{              INTERFACE PART OF ADT COMPLEXNO                    }
{This unit contains the operations for an ADT of type ComplexNo.  The
operations that belong to the unit are the procedures MakeComp,
AddComp, SubtrComp, MultComp, and DivComp.  The functions that make up
the unit are RealPart, ImaginaryPart, and Magnitude.}
```

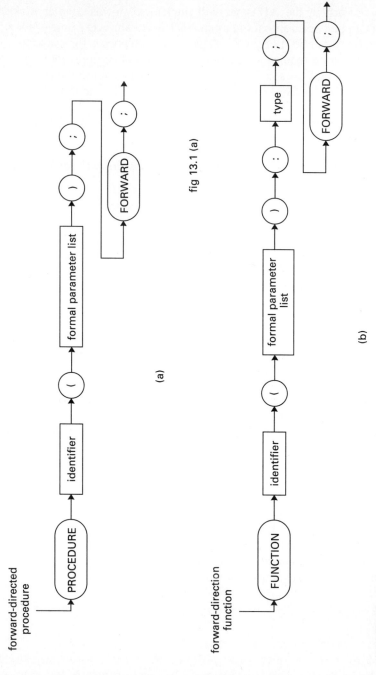

fig 13.1 (a)

(a)

(b)

FIGURE 13.1 Using the FORWARD directive with (a) a procedure and (b) a function.

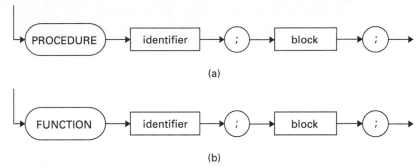

(a)

(b)

FIGURE 13.2 Matching a header to a FORWARD-directed (a) procedure and (b) function.

```
TYPE
  ComplexNo = RECORD
    XRe, YIm: real
  END;
{                          THE OPERATIONS                          }
PROCEDURE MakeComp(XPart, YPart: real;
                        VAR CNumber: ComplexNo);          FORWARD;
  {assigns the value of XPart to the real part of CNumber and the value
  of YPart to the imaginary part of CNumber}
{+                                                               +}
FUNCTION RealPart(CNumber: ComplexNo): real;              FORWARD;
  {assigns the real part of function CNumber to the function RealPart}
{+                                                               +}
FUNCTION ImaginaryPart(CNumber: ComplexNo): real;        FORWARD;
  {assigns the imaginary part of CNumber to the function ImaginaryPart}
{+                                                               +}
FUNCTION Magnitude(CNumber: ComplexNo): real;            FORWARD;
  {assigns the absolute magnitude of CNumber to the function Magnitude}
{+                                                               +}
PROCEDURE AddComp(Term1, Term2: ComplexNo;
                           VAR Sum: ComplexNo);           FORWARD;
  {assigns the value of (Term1 + Term2) to Sum}
{+                                                               +}
PROCEDURE SubtrComp(Term1, Term2: ComplexNo;
                           VAR Difference: ComplexNo);    FORWARD;
  {assigns the value of (Term1 - Term2) to Difference}
{+                                                               +}
PROCEDURE MultComp(Factor1, Factor2: ComplexNo;
                           VAR Product: ComplexNo);       FORWARD;
  {assigns the value of (Factor1 * Factor2) to Product}
{+                                                               +}
PROCEDURE DivComp(Factor1, Factor2: ComplexNo;
                           VAR Quotient: ComplexNo);      FORWARD;
  {assigns the value of Factor1/Factor2 to Quotient}
```

```
{*                    IMPLEMENTATION PART OF ADT COMPLEXNO                    *}
PROCEDURE MakeComp      {XPart, YPart: real; VAR CNumber: ComplexNo};
  BEGIN   END;
{+                                                                            +}
FUNCTION RealPart    {(CNumber: ComplexNo): real};
  BEGIN    END;
{+                                                                            +}
FUNCTION ImaginaryPart   {(CNumber: ComplexNo) real};
  BEGIN    END;
{+                                                                            +}
FUNCTION Magnitude   {(CNumber: ComplexNo): real};
  BEGIN    END;
{+                                                                            +}
PROCEDURE AddComp {Term1, Term2: ComplexNo; VAR Sum: ComplexNo};
  BEGIN    END;
{+                                                                            +}
PROCEDURE SubtrComp {Term1, Term2: ComplexNo;
                                 VAR Difference: ComplexNo};
  BEGIN    END;
{+                                                                            +}
PROCEDURE MultComp {Factor1, Factor2: ComplexNo;
                                 VAR Product: ComplexNo};
  BEGIN    END;
{+                                                                            +}
PROCEDURE DivComp {Factor1, Factor2: ComplexNo;
                        VAR Quotient; ComplexNo};
  BEGIN    END;
{*                    END COMPLEXNO IMPLEMENTATIONS                    *}
```

Interface and implementation sections

The first part of the ComplexNo unit contains everything the client programmer needs to know about the unit to use it effectively in a client program. This part is called the *interface section*. The part of the unit we have coded as stubs contains the statements of the FORWARD-directed headers. This part of the unit, whose details need not be seen by the client, makes up the *implementation section* of the ComplexNo unit.

Interface section: the part of an abstract unit containing the definitions and headers that are meant to be referenced in a client program.

Implementation section: the part of an abstract unit that contains the source code to carry out the abstract operations. This part of the unit should be hidden as much as possible from the client user.

In the interest of using standard Pascal, we will code all our ADTs in a manner similar to the code we used in Example 13.1. When used in a client program, the code for the unit is then copied directly into the text of the client program. All operations in the unit thus become available to the client program.

It is important to supply *clear* and *complete* documentation for each operation in the interface section of a unit. If a client programmer is considering whether a particular unit can be used in a client program, he or she can tell from the documentation whether the unit contains the operations that the client program requires.

Separately compiled units

Many Pascal compilers (e.g., Turbo Pascal, VAX Pascal, UCSD Pascal) allow separately compiled units. If you are working in a dialect that has this feature, you can use the reserved words of the dialect to give the client program a direct interface to the unit. There is no need with this feature to copy the unit's source code into the client program (see Appendix I). None of the headers is even seen in the client program, but they can be referenced by identifier just as if they were directly copied into the text of the program.

Using an Abstract Unit

Regardless of how the unit is put together, the client program uses the type definition in the interface section to declare the required ADT variable(s). Once these have been declared, all abstract operations of the unit can be applied to the variable(s).

Declaring some complex number variables

If you copy the code of Example 13.1 directly into a program requiring the three complex number variables XComp, YComp, and Sum, you need to insert the following declarations after the TYPE definitions and before the function/procedure declarations:

```
VAR
    XComp, YComp, Sum: ComplexNo;
```

Suppose XComp represents the complex number $a + bi$, YComp represents the number $c + di$, and Sum represents the number $e + fi$, where a, b, c, d, e, and f are real numbers, and i represents $\sqrt{-1}$. The following table shows the correspondence between the field variables of the ComplexNo type variables and the actual numbers they represent:

Actual number	Pascal variable
a	XComp.XRe
b	XComp.YIm
c	YComp.XRe
d	YComp.YIm
e	Sum.XRe
f	Sum.YIm

Although the table shows you how the numbers are represented, you should not make references to the field variables in a client program.

Reading in values

The ADT unit itself does not contain any *read* or *display* operations. As a client user, you can use the ComplexNo unit to implement these operations any way you see fit. You can, for example, read in a value to the variable XComp using two real variables (XPart and YPart) and the MakeComp operation. The following fragment shows the required code to read a value into the variable XComp from the keyboard:

```
write('Enter real part, then imaginary part:   ');
readln(XPart, YPart);
MakeComp(XPart, YPart, XComp);
```

Displaying values

You can display the value of XComp neatly and accurately to two decimal places using the code that follows. Two typical displays follow the required fragment of code.

```
XPart:= RealPart(XComp);
YPart:= ImaginaryPart(XComp);
write('The value of X is ', XPart:4:2);
IF YPart >= 0 THEN          {include the + sign for nonnegative values}
   write(' + ')
ELSE
   write(' - ');
writeln(abs(YPart):4:2, 'i');

The value of X is 7.82 + 4.75i
The value of X is -2.37 - 4.55i
```

Some other operations

You can use MakeComp to assign the value $8.32 - 7.86i$ to the variable YComp by coding the statement MakeComp(8.32, -7.86, YComp). If XComp and YComp have taken on values, their sum can be assigned to the variable Sum using a call to AddComp coded as AddComp(XComp, YComp, Sum).

Classifying the Operations of an ADT

When you implement your own ADTs, it is important that you be able to classify the operations required for the abstraction. We give you a taxonomy you can apply to any ADT you wish to code as a check to be sure that the unit is *complete*. A complete unit does not need additional operations for it to be of use to any client program you may wish to code.

The three categories of operations

When you put together an abstract unit, you should be able to fit each of the operations into three distinct categories: *constructors, selectors,* and *predicates.* The characteristics of each category are as follows:

I. A *constructor* changes or initializes the value(s) of an abstract variable. The ComplexNo ADT has the following constructions: MakeComp, AddComp, SubtrComp, MultComp, and DivComp.

A *primitive constructor* assigns a value(s) to an abstract variable without using the value(s) of other abstract variables of the same type. In other words, a primitive constructor has no input or input/output parameters of the given abstract type. The single parameter of the abstract type in a primitive constructor is an output parameter. All parameters other than the one output parameter are input parameters used to assign a value or appearance to the abstract variable whose alias is the output parameter.

Every ADT requires *at least one* (and often no more than one) primitive constructor so the client program can set an initial value(s) to an abstract variable(s). You can use the primitive constructor MakeComp, for example, either to read in values or assign values to the fields of a given ComplexNo variable.

A nonprimitive constructor has at least one input parameter whose type is the same as the type of the abstract variable returned by the operation. These constructors assign a value to an ADT variable dependent upon values assigned to one or more input variables of the same type. All constructors other than MakeComp in the ComplexNo unit are nonprimitive constructors. For example, a value is returned to the variable Sum of type ComplexNo by using the value assigned to Term1 and Term2, two input parameters also of type ComplexNo.

II.   A *selector* returns some information about an input ADT variable to some result parameter. Often, you can code a selector as a function. The result parameter is the function's value. The three functions RealPart, Imaginary-Part, and Magnitude of the unit ComplexNo are all selector functions.

A *primitive selector,* such as RealPart or ImaginaryPart, is a function or procedure that returns the value(s) of one of the abstract variable's components. Every unit requires primitive selectors; otherwise the client cannot display the value(s) of the abstract variable(s). A nonprimitive selector (e.g., Magnitude) returns a result that is not one of the components of the abstract variable but that nevertheless represents information useful to a client program.

III.   A *predicate* is a boolean function that returns information about the value or status of the abstract variable. We did not require any predicate operations in the ComplexNo unit, but we will implement these operations in the Queue and Stack units we plan to code in Sections 13.4 and 13.5.

Designing a complete unit

If an ADT unit is complete, the client program need only reference (1) the type identifier for the ADT in declaring some abstract variables and (2) any identifier that is the name of an operation belonging to the ADT unit. All the details of the ADT's implementation should remain hidden. The client should never feel a need (1) to access the individual components of an ADT variable, (2) to change the logic of the operations of the unit, or (3) to add more operations because the defining set of operations in the ADT unit is incomplete.

What operations are required for all units, regardless of their type, to be complete? First, any ADT unit should definitely have one (and usually not more than one) primitive constructor. Then values can be read in and assigned to the ADT variables. It should also have primitive selectors in order to display values or write them into files. The remaining nonprimitive constructors, selectors, and any necessary predicates are determined by the specifics of the required operations for the given unit.

EXERCISES

Test Your Understanding

1. Are the standard types of the Pascal language abstract data types? Why or why not?

2. What is the relationship between a client program and an ADT?

3. What are the three classes of operations that belong to an ADT? What purpose does each accomplish?

Practice Your Analysis Skills

4. Assume that the variables XComp, YComp, and ZComp are all of type ComplexNo. Indicate the values assigned to the variable ZComp (expressed as a complex number, not as a record variable) after each of the following sequences:

   (a) MakeComp(1.5, 2.0, XComp); MakeComp(2.5, -1.0, YComp);
   MultComp(XComp, YComp, ZComp);

   (b) MakeComp(1.0, -3.0, XComp);
   MakeComp(1, 0, ZComp);
   FOR Count:= 1 TO 3 DO
       MultComp(XComp, ZComp, ZComp);

   (c) MakeComp(2.0, 3.0, XComp); MakeComp(4.0, 1.0, YComp);
   IF Magnitude(XComp) > Magnitude(YComp) THEN
       ZComp:= XComp
   ELSE
       ZComp:= YComp;

Sharpen Your Implementation Skills

5. Write a statement to assign the value 0 to the variable Sum of type ComplexNo.

6. Write a sequence of statements to display the value of the variable XComp, where both parts are displayed accurately to four decimal places.

13.2 The ADT ComplexNo

We complete our discussion of the ComplexNo ADT by first drafting and coding a small client program. Then we develop the code for the (FORWARD-directed) implementation section of the unit.

A Client Program

Before we deal with implementing the operations of the ComplexNo unit, let us first derive the code for a simple client program.

Example Problem 13.1

The problem statement

Let us write a program to solve for X in the equation

$$AX + B = C$$

The numbers A, B, and C are all read in as complex numbers. For the sake of simplicity, we assume that the number A is not read in as 0. A typical run of the program then looks like

This program solves the equation AX + B = C, where all three
coefficients must be keyed in as complex numbers. At the prompt for
each coefficient, you are to key in the real part of the coefficient
first, then the imaginary part. Then press the carriage return.

```
Enter coefficient for A (real part first):   4.00  -3.00
Enter coefficient for B (real part first):  -2.00   1.50
Enter coefficient for C (real part first):   5.00  -0.50
```

The root of the equation is 1.36 + 0.52 i

The solution   Because A, B, and C are complex numbers, we can apply the operations belonging to the ComplexNo unit to solve the problem. We can assume that the operations are copied from a directory file containing the unit into our client program.
    Values are read into variables A, B, and C with the help of the abstract oper-
ation MakeComp. Then the operations SubtrComp and DivComp are applied
to find the value of the expression $(C - B)/A$, whose value is assigned to the variable X. The value of X is displayed with the help of the functions RealPart and
ImaginaryPart.
    The code for the client program follows. We leave the coding of the proce-
dures GetCoefficients and ShowRoot as Exercises 6 and 7, respectively, at
the end of this section.

```
PROGRAM SolveIt(input, output);
  {The coefficients to the equation AX + B = C are read in as complex
  numbers.  The equation is solved for X, and the root displayed.}
  TYPE
              {INSERT COMPLEXNO TYPE DEFINITION HERE}
    {This definition is copied from the file containing the unit
    ComplexNo as given in the code of Example 13.1};

  VAR
    A,B,C,                  {the three coefficients}
    X: ComplexNo;           {the complex root}

  {*                      ADT ComplexNo                              *}
        {INSERT ALL OPERATIONS FROM COMPLEXNO UNIT HERE}
    {The procedures and functions belonging to the unit ComplexNo are
    copied and inserted here.}
  {*                    END ADT ComplexNo                            *}

  PROCEDURE ShowInstructions;
  {informs user about expected keyin/display sequence}
  BEGIN    END;
  {*                                                                 *}
  PROCEDURE GetCoefficients(VAR A, B, C: ComplexNo);
    {reads in values to A, B, and C}
    BEGIN    END;
```

```
{*                                                                              *}
PROCEDURE SolveEquation(A, B, C: ComplexNo; VAR X: ComplexNo);
  {Applies the formula, X = (C - B)/A, using the operations of the
  unit.  Note the requirement for the local variable  CMinusB as
  storage for the result of the operation C - B.}
  VAR
    CMinusB: ComplexNo;    {value of C - B}
  BEGIN
    SubtrComp(C, B, CMinusB);
    DivComp(CMinusB, A, X)
  END;
{*                                                                              *}
PROCEDURE ShowRoot(X: ComplexNo);
    {displays the value of X, along with other text}
    BEGIN    END;
{*                                                                              *}
BEGIN
  ShowInstructions;
  GetCoefficients(A, B, C);
  SolveEquation(A, B, C, X);
  ShowRoot(X)
END.
```

Structure chart   The structure chart for the program is given in Figure 13.3. Note how the figure implies that all blocks using the ComplexNo unit "see" the unit as a whole rather than as many individual operations. Each procedure uses the operations of the unit to carry out its particular purpose. ◆

FIGURE 13.3   Structure chart for the program SolveIt.

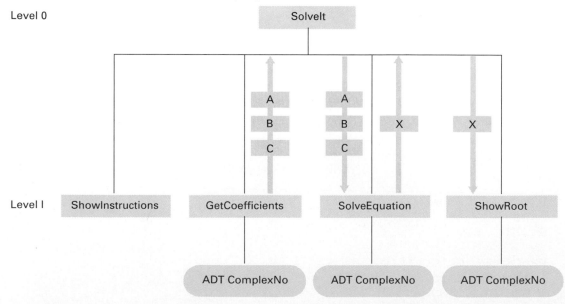

Developing the Implementation Section

The primitives

Having shown how to use the abstract unit ComplexNo in a client program, let us now code the operations. We assume they have been FORWARD-directed, so each header has the parameter lists commented out.

The code for the primitive constructor MakeComp simply assigns XPart to CNumber.XRe and YPart to CNumber.YIm. The value of CNumber.XRe is returned to the primitive selector function RealPart. Finally, the value of CNumber.YIm is returned to the primitive selector ImaginaryPart. The following is source code for these three primitives.

```
PROCEDURE MakeComp {XPart, YPart: real; VAR CNumber: ComplexNo};
  BEGIN
    CNumber.XRe:= XPart;
    CNumber.YIm:= YPart
  END;

FUNCTION RealPart {(CNumber: ComplexNo): real};
  BEGIN
    RealPart:= CNumber.XRe
  END;

FUNCTION ImaginaryPart {(CNumber: ComplexNo): real};
  BEGIN
    ImaginaryPart:= CNumber.YIm
  END;
```

*Coding
Magnitude*

Recall from high school algebra that the absolute value of a complex number is the square root of the sum of the squares of the real part and the imaginary part. When we express this arithmetic relationship in Pascal, we obtain the one-line function Magnitude.

```
FUNCTION Magnitude {(CNumber: ComplexNo): real};
  BEGIN
    Magnitude:= sqrt(sqr(CNumber.XRe) + sqr(CNumber.YIm))
  END;
```

*Developing
AddComp and
SubtrComp*

The real part of the sum of two complex numbers is equal to the sum of each number's real part. Likewise, the imaginary part of the sum is equal to the sum of each number's imaginary part. In like manner, the real part of the difference between two complex numbers is equal to the difference of the two real parts. The imaginary part of the difference between the two numbers is equal to the difference between the two imaginary parts. From these descriptions, we obtain the code for the operations AddComp and SubtrComp.

```
PROCEDURE AddComp {Term1, Term2: ComplexNo; VAR Sum: ComplexNo};
  BEGIN
```

```
        WITH Sum DO
          BEGIN
            XRe:= Term1.XRe + Term2.XRe;
            YIm:= Term1.YIm + Term2.YIm
          END
      END;

    PROCEDURE SubtrComp {Term1, Term2: ComplexNo;
                                        VAR Difference: ComplexNo};
        BEGIN
          WITH Difference DO
            BEGIN
              XRe:= Term1.XRe - Term2.XRe;
              YIm:= Terml.YIm - Term2.YIm
            END
        END;
```

MultComp

Recall that the algebraic expression for the product of the complex numbers $a + bi$ and $c + di$ is $(ac - bd) + (ad + bc)i$. We can use this relationship to write the source code of MultComp.

```
    PROCEDURE MultComp{Factor1, Factor2: ComplexNo;
                                        VAR Product: ComplexNo};
        BEGIN
          WITH Product DO
            BEGIN
              XRe:= Factor1.XRe * Factor2.XRe -
                    Factor1.YIm * Factor2.YIm;
              YIm:= Factor1.XRe * Factor2.YIm +
                    Factor2.XRe * Factor1.YIm
            END
        END;
```

DivComp

The algebraic expression for the quotient of the complex numbers $a + bi$ and $c + di$ is written as

$$\frac{(ac + bd) + (bc - ad)i}{c^2 + d^2}$$

This expression leads to the code of DivComp:

```
    PROCEDURE DivComp{Factor1, Factor2: ComplexNo;
                                        VAR Quotient: Complex No};
      VAR
        Divisor: real;   {equals square of magnitude of Factor2}
      BEGIN
        Divisor:= sqr(Factor2.XRe) + sqr(Factor2.YIm);
```

```
        WITH Quotient DO
          BEGIN
            XRe:= (Factor1.XRe * Factor2.XRe +
                   Factor1.YIm * Factor2.YIm) / Divisor;
            YIm:= (Factor1.YIm * Factor2.XRe -
                   Factor1.XRe * Factor2.YIm) / Divisor
          END
      END;
```

EXERCISES

Test Your Understanding

Sharpen Your Implementation Skills

1. If you test the ADT for different values, one of the operations will fail for a given complex number pair. Which operation will fail, and for what pair of XRe and YIm values?

2. Write a program fragment to divide the value of the complex number ZComp by 5. (*Hint:* Use an auxiliary complex variable.)

3. Modify the logic of the operation found in Exercise 1 so that the display IMPOSSI-BLE OPERATION will be the result instead of a program crash.

4. Write three boolean functions, (1) PureReal, (2) PureIm, and (3) Mixed, using the relevant operations that are part of the ADT ComplexNo. The functions, respectively, return true when the arguments represent (1) a pure real number, (2) a pure imaginary number, and (3) a number whose real part or imaginary part does not vanish.

5. In electrical circuit applications, impedance is expressed as a complex number. Two impedances can be combined to return a resultant impedance. If $Z1$ and $Z2$ represent two impedances, they can be combined in series, where the resultant impedance *ZSeries* is found by the value of $Z1 + Z2$. They can likewise be connected in parallel, where the resultant impedence *ZParallel* is found by the value of $(Z1 * Z2)/(Z1 + Z2)$. Write two client procedures, GetTwoSeries and GetTwoParallel, that assign respective values to ZSeries and ZParallel.

6. Write the code for the procedure GetCoefficients as given in Example Problem 13.1.

7. Write the code for the procedure ShowRoot as given in Example Poblem 13.1.

13.3 The Queue ADT

A queue is an ADT that takes on the properties of a line of people waiting to be served. Its appearance changes either when an item is added to its rear or deleted from its front. These two operations, both nonprimitive constructors, imply that the number of items in the queue changes over the course of a program run. For this reason, the queue abstraction is classified as a *dynamic data type*.

> **Dynamic data type:** one for which the number of components in the data type changes over the course of a program run.

The logical description of a queue

We can describe a queue in terms of its head, its tail, and the items in the queue. For ease of implementation, we also include a variable to represent the count of the number of items on queue at any given time as part of its definition. The head and tail respectively reference the beginning and end of the queue. The items themselves are the actual values contained by the queue. A typical queue with three components in it (say, the components are all character strings that represent a last name) is shown in Figure 13.4.

Queue dynamics

The queue structure is defined such that items are added only to the tail and deleted only from the head. If, for example, the name "Jones" is added to the queue of Figure 13.4, the queue's appearance is described by Figure 13.5(a). If, on the other hand, a name is deleted from the queue of Figure 13.4, its appearance is described by Figure 13.5(b). These two operations, AddQueue and DeleteQueue, define the essence of the queue ADT.

The Head *and* Tail *abstractions*

The two variables Head and Tail represent "logical values," where the next candidate to be removed from the queue is the Head item, and a new item is added to the queue after the Tail item. The actual values taken on by Head and Tail are *not important at all* to the client programmer. Indeed, we can go one step further and say that the fact of their existence is *of no concern whatsoever* to the client. The only thing the client needs to know is that (1) when an item is added to the queue, there may be other items ahead of it, (2) when an item is deleted from the queue, there may be other items still on queue, and (3) the first item added to a queue is the first item to be deleted from the queue.

From this last description, we sometimes say that a queue uses a *FIFO* discipline to maintain its logical appearance. This term is an acronym for the four words "first in, first out."

FIGURE 13.4 Appearance of a queue.

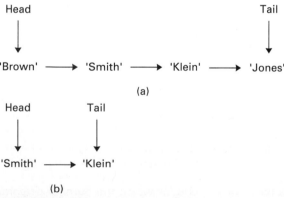

FIGURE 13.5 (a) Adding 'Jones' to queue of Figure 13.4 (b) Deleting head item from queue of Figure 13.4.

The pseudocode for the interface part of the queue ADT is

CONST
    MaxQueue = a number that represents the maximum number of items
        allowed on queue
    NullItem = a value to indicate that there is nothing on queue
TYPE
    ItemType = type of item contained in the queue
    QueueType = implementation of the queue ADT as a structured type
PROCEDURE *MakeQueue(VAR Queue: QueueType)*
    {returns Queue such that it has no items on it}
PROCEDURE *AddQueue(Item: ItemType; VAR Queue: QueueType)*
    *{adds an item onto the queue as long as the queue is not full; if the
    queue is full, the operation is not carried out, and an error message
    is displayed}*
PROCEDURE *DeleteQueue(VAR Queue: QueueType)*
    *{deletes an item from the queue; if the queue is already empty, the
    operation is not carried out, and an error message is displayed}*
FUNCTION *FirstOnQueue(Queue: QueueType): ItemType*
    *{assigns the value of the Item at the head of the queue to the
    function; if the queue is empty the value NullItem is assigned; if
    the queue's items are structured variables, this selector function
    codes to a procedure}*
FUNCTION *QCount(Queue: QueueType): integer*
    {assigns the value of the number of items on queue to QCount}
FUNCTION *QEmpty(Queue: QueueType): boolean*
    {this predicate function returns true if there are on items on queue}
FUNCTION *QFull(Queue: QueueType): boolean*
    *{this predicate function returns true if no more items can be added
    to the queue}*

Note that our description allows for any kind of item on the queue. It can contain numbers, strings, or even records. The constant NullItem, if appropriate, is used to return a value to FirstOnQueue when the queue is empty. For example, a queue with strings will have the null string defined as its NullItem.

For the queue of strings shown as Figure 13.5(a), a call to the function QEmpty returns the value of false. Unless MaxQueue is defined as 4, a call to QFull would also return the value of false. A call to QCount returns the integer value 4. A call to FirstOnQueue, which we will code as a procedure, returns the value 'Smith'. The header for this operation is coded as PROCEDURE FirstOn-Queue(Queue: QueueType; VAR Item: ItemType);. When the queue consists of structured variables, it is necessary to code a procedure rather than a function for FirstOnQueue. (*Note:* Many dialects allow this operation to be coded as a function.)

A Client Program

Let us write a client program that requires a queue consisting of character strings. We assume all definitions and declarations given in the pseudocode are available for the client program's usage. The `ItemType` for this queue is a string of up to 20 characters (`STRING[20]`), and the `NullItem` is defined as the null string.

CASE STUDY 13.1

The problem statement

The ticket agents for Spacey, Stacey, and The Cadets have an unusual way of doing business. Any given agent will start a queue, unannounced, with the idea of selling a certain number of tickets. The agent's policy is to allow queues of people with a maximum size of three, otherwise they will feel hassled. Each person in the queue must buy *exactly* two tickets. When all tickets are sold, anybody left standing in the queue is out of luck. Let us write a program that simulates an agent's way of selling tickets.

A program run

The total number of tickets to be sold by the agent is read in, always as an even number. Then the user enters one of the following three actions: A (Add), S (Sell), R (Recap). When A is entered and the queue is not too big, a name is requested and put on queue. When S is entered, the first person on the queue is congratulated and sold two tickets. If the queue is empty when S is read in, the computer displays a string where the agent appears to be hawking the tickets. If, when all tickets are sold, there are still customers on the queue, they are told with regrets that tickets have been sold out. Finally, when R is entered, the number of tickets sold, the size of the queue, and the number of tickets remaining to sell are displayed.

A typical run of the program might look like

```
How many tickets to sell?  14
Spacey, Stacey tickets here!  Come and get them!
Action:   A
Name:  Jones
Please get in line, Jones.
Action: A
Name:  Smith
Please get in line, Smith.
Action: S
Congratulations, Jones, you are going to the concert.
Action: A
Name: Klein
Please get in line, Klein.
Action: R
2 tickets have been sold, and the size of the queue is 2.
12 tickets are left for sale.
```

```
Action:  A
Name:  Williams
Please get in line, Williams.
Action:  A
We're too hassled.  Please come back later.
Action:  A
We're too hassled.  Please come back later.
Action:  S
Congratulations, Smith, you are going to the concert.
Action:  S
Congratulations, Klein, you are going to the concert.
Action:  R
6 tickets have been sold, and the size of the queue is 1.
8 tickets are left for sale.
Action:  S
Congratulations, Williams, you are going to the concert.
Action:  S
Spacey, Stacey tickets here! Come and get them!
Action:  A
Name:  Meyers
Please get in line, Meyers.
Action:  A
Name:  Powers
Please get in line, Powers.
Action:  S
Congratulations, Meyers, you are going to the concert.
Action:  A
Name:  Coe
Please get in line, Coe.
Action:  A
Name:  Davis
Please get in line, Davis.
Action:  S
Congratulations, Powers, you are going to the concert.
Action:  A
Name:  Adams
Please get in line, Adams.
Action:  S
Congratulations, Coe, you are going to the concert.
Sorry, Davis, we're all sold out.
Sorry, Adams, we're all sold out.
```

Describing the main block

The description for the actions executed in the main block is given by the pseudocode

Initialize (Queue, ToSell)
TotalSold ← 0

display hawk string
WHILE ToSell > 0 DO
    keyin Action
    IF Action IN ['A', 'a', 'S', 's', 'R', 'r'] THEN
      CASE Action OF
        'A', 'a': IncreaseQueue(Queue)
        'S', 's': MakeSale(Queue, TotalSold, ToSell)
        'R', 'r': display TotalSold, ToSell, QCount(Queue)
DisplayRegrets(Queue)

The procedure `Initialize` sets up an empty queue and reads in a value to the variable `ToSell`, representing the number of tickets to be sold. Only an even number of tickets can be sold, so if the number read in is odd, 1 is subtracted from this value. The procedure `IncreaseQueue` adds a name to the queue as long as the queue size is less than 3. If the queue is not empty, the procedure `MakeSale` deletes an item from the queue, adds 2 to `TotalSold`, and subtracts 2 from `ToSell`. After each sale is made, `ToSell`, an even number, is reduced by 2. Hence, the exit condition of the loop in the main block can be achieved. Finally, `DisplayRegrets` deletes names until the queue is empty, displaying regrets to each person who was not sold two tickets.

Source code

The following source code is for the main block's statement and for the procedures `Initialize` and `Recap`. We still need to develop the code for the procedures `IncreaseQueue`, `MakeSale`, and `DisplayRegrets`.

```
PROGRAM TicketSeller(input, output);
  {Simulates a queue for buying a limited number of tickets.  The queue
  is finished when all tickets are sold.}
  CONST
    MaxSize = 3;    {maximum allowable queue size for this program}
    HawkString = 'Spacey, Stacy tickets here!  Come and get them!';
  {                                                                    }
  {            INSERT QUEUETYPE DEFINITIONS HERE                       }
  {                                                                    }
  {                                                                    }
  VAR
    Queue: QueueType;       {the queue of ticket buyers}
    TotalSold,              {running count of tickets sold}
    ToSell: integer;        {total number of tickets to be sold}
    Action: char;           {menu item to be selected}
  {*                                                                  *}
  {            INSERT QUEUETYPE OPERATIONS HERE                        }
  {*                                                                  *}
  PROCEDURE Initialize(VAR Queue: QueueType; VAR ToSell: integer);
    {Starts the queue and reads in an even value to ToSell.}
    BEGIN
      MakeQueue(Queue);
      write('How many tickets to sell?  ');
```

```
      readln(ToSell);
      ToSell:= abs(ToSell);   {guards against negative numbers}
      IF ToSell MOD 2 <> 0 THEN
        ToSell:= ToSell - 1
   END;
{*                                                                *}
PROCEDURE IncreaseQueue(VAR Queue: QueueType);
   {adds a prospective ticket buyer to the queue}
   BEGIN    END;
{*                                                                *}
PROCEDURE MakeSale(VAR Queue: QueueType;
                          VAR TotalSold, ToSell: integer);
   {deletes a buyer from Queue; increments TotalSold by 2 and
   decrements ToSell by 2}
   BEGIN    END;
{*                                                                *}
PROCEDURE Recap(TotalSold, ToSell, OnQueue: integer);
   {displays the values passed into the three formal parameters}
BEGIN
   write(TotalSold:1,' tickets have been sold, and ');
   writeln('the size of the queue is ', OnQueue:1, '.');
   writeln(ToSell:1, ' tickets are left for sale.')
END;
{*                                                                *}
PROCEDURE DisplayRegrets(Queue: QueueType);
   {empties the queue, displaying regrets to each name left on the
   queue that they were not sold any tickets}
   BEGIN    END;
{*                                                                *}
BEGIN
   Initialize(Queue, ToSell);
   TotalSold:= 0;
   writeln(HawkString);
   WHILE ToSell > 0 DO
     BEGIN
       write('Action:   ');
       readln(Action);
       IF Action IN ['A', 'a', 'S', 's', 'R', 'r'] THEN
         CASE Action OF
            'A', 'a': IncreaseQueue(Queue);
            'S', 's': MakeSale(Queue, TotalSold, ToSell);
            'R', 'r': Recap(TotalSold, ToSell, QSize(Queue))
            END {CASE}
     END;
   DisplayRegrets(Queue)
END.
```

As long as the queue size is not equal to MaxSize, a name can be added to the queue. The procedure IncreaseQueue requires the function QCount as well as the procedure AddQueue in order to work properly. It likewise needs the local variable Name of type ItemType to represent the value of the item added to the queue. The code for the procedure is

```
PROCEDURE IncreaseQueue(VAR Queue: QueueType);
  {documentation}
  VAR
    Name: ItemType;    {name to be added to queue}
  BEGIN
    IF QCount(Queue) < MaxSize THEN
      BEGIN
        write('Name:    ');
        readln(Name);
        writeln('Please get in line, ', Name, '.');
        AddQueue(Name, Queue)
      END
    ELSE
      writeln('We''re too hassled.  Please come back later.')
  END;
```

We can describe the action for MakeSale by the pseudocode

> *IF NOT QEmpty(Queue) THEN*
>   *FirstOnQueue(Queue, Name)*
>   *TotalSold ← TotalSold + 2*
>   *ToSell ← ToSell − 2*
>   *display congratulatory message using value of Name*
>   *DeleteQueue(Queue)*
> *ELSE*
>   *display HawkString*

We see that we need to use three of the operations in the ADT QueueType for the code of MakeSale. We likewise need a local variable Name of type ItemType. From the pseudocode, we obtain the source code for MakeSale as shown.

```
PROCEDURE MakeSale(VAR Queue: QueueType;
                                VAR TotalSold, ToSell: integer);
  {documentation}
  VAR
    Name: ItemType;    {name of person sold the pair of tickets}
  BEGIN
    IF NOT QEmpty(Queue) then
      BEGIN
        FirstOnQueue(Queue, Name);
        TotalSold:= TotalSold + 2;
        ToSell:= ToSell - 2;
        write('Congratulations, ',Name);
```

```
            writeln(',  you are going to the concert. ');
            DeleteQueue(Queue)
         END
      ELSE
         writeln(HawkString)
   END;
```

Developing
`Display-`
`Regrets`

The pseudocode for the procedure `DisplayRegrets` is given as

> *WHILE NOT QEmpty(Queue) DO*
> *FirstOnQueue(Queue, Name)*
> *display regret string using value of Name*
> *DeleteQueue(Queue)*

Thus, we obtain the source code for `DisplayRegrets`.

```
PROCEDURE DisplayRegrets(Queue:  QueueType);
   {documentation}
   VAR
      Name: ItemType; {holds name of person to whom regret is directed}
   BEGIN
      WHILE NOT QEmpty(Queue) DO
         BEGIN
            FirstOnQueue(Queue, Name);
            writeln('Sorry, ',Name, ', we"re all sold out. ');
            Delete Queue(Queue)
         END
   END;
```

FIGURE 13.6 Structure chart for the program `TicketSeller`.

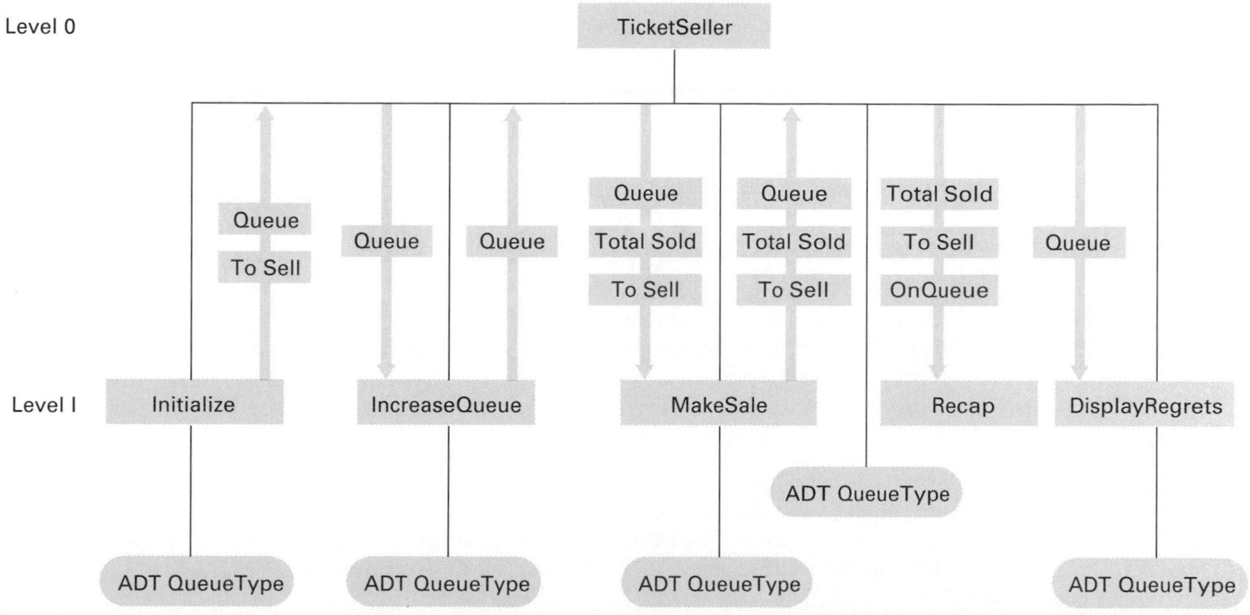

The structure chart

The structure chart for the program is shown in Figure 13.6. Once again, the oval in the chart represents an ADT. The chart shows that all blocks except Recap require at least one of the operations of the ADT QueueType. ◆

EXERCISES

Test Your Understanding

1. Categorize each of the queue operations: constructor, selector, or predicate.

2. If MaxQueue is either 50 or 5, will the agents feel less hassled in this case? Why or why not?

3. Suppose MaxQueue is reduced to 2. Would the agents feel less hassled in this instance?

4. Let MaxQueue be defined as 5. A given variable Queue at a particular time looks like

Sketch the queue's appearance after each operation in the sequence:

```
DeleteQueue(Queue);
AddQueue('Truman', Queue);
AddQueue('Adams', Queue);
AddQueue('Burr', Queue);
DeleteQueue(Queue);
DeleteQueue(Queue);
DeleteQueue(Queue);
AddQueue('Roosevelt', Queue);
```

5. Suppose instead we want to create a queue that will hold user account numbers. We want the queue to be capable of holding up to 10 users where the account number is an integer value from 1 to 500. From the pseudocode description, what parts of the queue source code would need to be modified?

Sharpen Your Implementation Skills

6. Write a client procedure ShowQueue. The postcondition of a call to this procedure is that all items on queue have been displayed (perhaps five items per line), but the queue itself has not been changed. (*Hint:* Use a call by value.)

7. Write a client function QPosition with two arguments, a name and the queue. The function is to return the position on queue of the person whose name is passed into the function. Note that once again the queue should not be changed by a call to this function. With the initial queue of Exercise 4, the values given to the calls QPosition('Tyler', Queue), QPosition('Lincoln', Queue), and QPosition('Fillmore', Queue) are 4, 2, and 0, respectively. The last value is 0 because Fillmore is not on queue.

8. Write a client procedure ShowQLast that assigns the name and queue position of the last person on queue. In the initial queue of Exercise 4, the call ShowQLast(Name, Position, Queue) assigns 'Tyler' and 4, respectively. The original queue should not be destroyed by this operation.

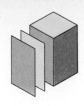

13.4   Implementation of the Queue ADT

We have already given you a client program that uses the QueueType ADT. In this section, we give you the details for implementing the operations of QueueType. Although a queue can contain items of any type, in order to code a complete ADT, we specify the queue as containing items that represent character strings.

Implementing the queue's appearance

In order to implement a queue, first, we need a structure capable of holding more than one item, where each item is of the same type. The logical choice of structure to hold the items is therefore an array. We have likewise said that we need two variables to reference the first and last items on queue. These variables, whose values will change over the course of the program run, can be array index values. Finally, we can use an `integer` variable to represent the count of the number of strings in the queue.

Now we see that we need four variables, an array, two array index variables, and an `integer` to define the components of QueueType. The abstract variable Queue must hold the values given to these different variables in one structure. Given this requirement, the best structure to use is a record.

Source code

From all these considerations, we obtain the source code for the unit that follows. We must now develop the code for each of the stubs in the implementation part of the unit.

```
{                    INTERFACE PART OF QUEUE ADT                        }
{This abstraction is for a queue of string variables. The queue is
capable of holding up to 100 string variables in it at any given time.
The constant NullItem, a null string, is the value given to the
procedure call FirstOnQueue when the queue is empty.}
CONST
  MaxQueue = 100;    {maximum number of items queue can hold}
  NullItem = '';     {null string for this queue of strings}
TYPE
  ItemType = {STRING TYPE CAPABLE OF HOLDING UP TO 20 CHARACTERS};
  QueueType = RECORD
    Head,                  {reference to first item on queue}
    Tail: 1..MaxQueue;     {reference to last item on queue}
    InUse: 0..MaxQueue;    {count of number of items on queue}
    Items: ARRAY[1..MaxQueue] OF ItemType   {holds items on the queue}
  END;
{                        THE OPERATIONS                                  }
PROCEDURE MakeQueue(VAR Queue: QueueType);                    FORWARD;
  {initializes the queue to empty}
{*                                                                      *}
PROCEDURE AddQueue(Item: ItemType; VAR Queue: QueueType);  FORWARD;
  {if Queue is not full, adds Item; if Queue is full, prints error
  message}
{*                                                                      *}
PROCEDURE DeleteQueue(VAR Queue: QueueType);                  FORWARD;
```

```
{if Queue is not empty, deletes first Item; if Queue is empty, prints
error message}
{*                                                                    *}
PROCEDURE FirstOnQueue(VAR Queue: QueueType;
                                        VAR Item: ItemType);      FORWARD;
  {if queue is not empty, assigns value of first item on queue to Item;
   if queue is empty, assigns NullItem to Item}
{*                                                                    *}
FUNCTION QCount(VAR Queue: QueueType): integer;          FORWARD;
   {assigns number of items on Queue to QueueCount}
{*                                                                    *}
FUNCTION QEmpty(VAR Queue: QueueType): boolean;          FORWARD;
   {true if no items on Queue}
{*                                                                    *}
FUNCTION QFull(VAR Queue: QueueType): boolean;           FORWARD;
   {true if no more items can be added to Queue}


{*                   IMPLEMENTATION PART OF QUEUE ADT               *}
PROCEDURE MakeQueue{VAR Queue: QueueType};
   BEGIN    END;
{*                                                                    *}
PROCEDURE AddQueue{Item: ItemType; VAR Queue: QueueType};
   BEGIN    END;
{*                                                                    *}
PROCEDURE DeleteQueue{VAR Queue: QueueType};
   BEGIN    END;
{*                                                                    *}
PROCEDURE FirstOnQueue{VAR Queue: QueueType; VAR Item: ItemType};
   BEGIN    END;
{*                                                                    *}
FUNCTION QCount{(VAR Queue: QueueType): integer};
   BEGIN    END;
{*                                                                    *}
FUNCTION QEmpty{(VAR Queue: QueueType): boolean};
   BEGIN    END;
{*                                                                    *}
FUNCTION QFull{(VAR Queue: QueueType): boolean};
   BEGIN    END;
{*                          END QUEUE ADT                            *}
```

Efficiency considerations   Note that we have used a VAR call for the variable Queue in all formal parameter lists for all operations. We are using this mechanism so that all operations are the most efficient. The statement part of each operation, as you will presently see, has an efficiency of O(1). Why, then, should we ruin this efficiency by using the O(N) process of copying the array structure Queue.Items into each block with a value call?

The selector function QCount and the predicate functions QEmpty and QFull are all one-line functions. The source code for each of these functions is given as follows:

```
FUNCTION QCount{ (VAR Queue: QueueType): integer};
  BEGIN
    QCount:= Queue.InUse
  END;

FUNCTION QEmpty{ (VAR Queue: QueueType): boolean};
  BEGIN
    QueueEmpty:= (Queue.InUse = 0)
  END;

FUNCTION QFull{(VAR Queue: QueueType): boolean};
  BEGIN
    QFull:= (Queue.InUse = MaxQueue)
  END;
```

The selector procedure FirstOnQueue requires a check first to see if the queue is empty. If not, the value of Queue.Items[Head] is assigned to *Item*, otherwise the null string (NullItem) is assigned.

```
PROCEDURE FirstOnQueue{VAR Queue: QueueType; VAR Item: ItemType};
  BEGIN
    WITH Queue DO
      IF InUse <> 0 THEN
        Item:= Items[Head]
      ELSE
        Item:= NullItem
  END;
```

The AddQueue, DeleteQueue, and MakeQueue Operations

Now we must derive the source code for the AddQueue, DeleteQueue, and MakeQueue operations. Before we code them, however, we must first determine how to represent the queue's Head and Tail values.

The key to implementing the constructor operations is determined by the way we use the field variables Head and Tail. The logical first choice for maintaining the queue is to employ the built-in array index order on the relative positions of the items on queue. If, for example, Head is set to SomeValue, the item on queue following the Head item is referenced by the expression SomeValue+1. Given an infinite access subrange and that InUse items are on queue, Tail's value will be equal to SomeValue+InUse-1. The proposed implementation is shown in Figure

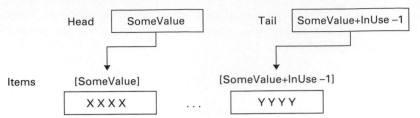

FIGURE 13.7 A queue where the condition `Tail` > Head is always true.

13.7. With this (unrealizable) implementation strategy, we can describe the sequence to add an item to the queue with the pseudocode

> *WITH Queue DO*
> *Tail ← Tail+1*
> *Items[Tail] ← Item*
> *InUse ← InUse + 1*

We likewise describe the deletion operation by

> *WITH Queue DO*
> *Head ← Head+1*
> *InUse ← InUse − 1*

Wrap-around

Unfortunately, the actual array has an access subrange limited by 1..MaxQueue. Even with this finite queue, the proposed statements for Add-Queue and DeleteQueue work until the value of `Tail` is equal to MaxQueue. Then a difficulty occurs due to an apparent lack of available memory locations for more items.

We can resolve this difficulty, given that some items have already been deleted, by setting `Tail` to 1 when we add the next item. This implementation, sometimes referred to as the "circular queue," is shown by Figure 13.8.

We can readily achieve the wrap-around logic when we code the assignment to `Tail` as `Tail:= Tail MOD MaxQueue + 1`. When `Tail` is less than MaxQueue, it is simply incremented by 1, and when `Tail` is equal to MaxQueue, its new value becomes 1.

A question of efficiency

A very astute question you might ask at this point is, "So what?" Why not just delete an item from the queue by moving up all the items? Then we would have no problems with MaxQueue unless the queue is full. In this case, it is impossible to

FIGURE 13.8 A circular queue where Items[1] follows Items[MaxQueue].

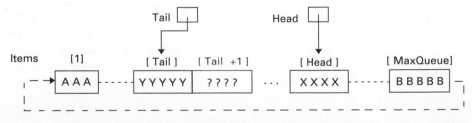

add a new item, regardless. Moreover, we will not even need a variable for Head, because the head of the queue will always be the first element of Queue.Items."

The objection is a reasonable one, until you consider the issue of efficiency. If you use this approach, the DeleteQueue operation has an efficiency of O(N) because $N - 1$ loop passes (for the $N - 1$ array elements) are required to move the items forward. The AddQueue operation will still have an efficiency of O(1).

Note that if we use the circular queue, the index value of some element in Queue.Items does not usually represent the item's position in the queue. This departure from the "logical choice" makes the code somewhat less readable. However, we more than compensate for this difficulty when we replace an O(N) algorithm with an O(1) algorithm.

Coding
AddQueue

Before we add an item to the queue, we must guard against adding an item to a full queue. As the documentation indicates, an error message is displayed if the queue is full. Taking this event into account and using the wrap-around logic of the circular queue gives us the source code for the AddQueue operations as shown.

```
PROCEDURE AddQueue{Item: ItemType; VAR Queue: QueueType};
  BEGIN
    WITH Queue DO
      IF InUse <> MaxQueue THEN
        BEGIN
          Tail:= Tail MOD MaxQueue + 1;    {set Tail}
          Items[Tail]:= Item;              {put on the item}
          InUse:= InUse + 1                {add 1 to InUse}
        END
      ELSE
        writeln('ERROR:  QUEUE IS FULL AT THIS POINT.')
  END;
```

Coding
DeleteQueue

The operation to delete an item requires that we check for an empty queue. If the queue is not empty, we can delete an item; otherwise the computer should display an error message. The source code for the delete operation is then as shown.

```
PROCEDURE DeleteQueue{VAR Queue: QueueType};
  BEGIN
    WITH Queue DO
      IF InUse <> 0 THEN
        BEGIN
          Head:= Head MOD MaxQueue + 1;  {move Head forward}
          InUse:= InUse - 1              {decrement InUse by 1}
        END
      ELSE
        writeln ('ERROR:  QUEUE IS EMPTY AT THIS POINT.')
  END;
```

Note that we can move Head forward with the same logic we used to move Tail forward. The fact that we can move either the Head or the Tail forward with the same assignment logic attests to the semantic consistency of the implementation.

The simplest way to start the queue would be to set the values of Head to 1, Tail to MaxQueue, and InUse to 0. Then we get the code for MakeQueue as shown.

```
PROCEDURE MakeQueue{VAR Queue:  QueueType};
   BEGIN
     WITH Queue DO
       BEGIN
         Head:= 1;
         Tail:= MaxQueue;
         InUse:= 0
       END
   END;
```

Starkness and Indivisibility

There are some questions you may have regarding the way we implemented the queue ADT. Why, for example, did we delete an item from the queue without returning its value as part of the process? Why, too, are all field variables belonging to the record QueueType anonymous? These are astute and important questions that we will now answer.

Starkness

Once a person standing on a queue has been served, he or she leaves the queue. You may wonder, then, why we did not choose to code the header for the operation DeleteQueue as PROCEDURE DeleteQueue(VAR Queue: QueueType; VAR Item: ItemType);. We deliberately avoided coding the proposed header to ensure that the abstraction consists solely of "pure" operations that only do one thing. Every operation in the unit is solely a constructor, a selector, or a predicate. The alternate operation we just proposed for DeleteQueue, on the other hand, is both a constructor and a selector.

If you develop an ADT with "pure" operations, it will be stark, but it can still be complete. Indeed, the issue of ensuring completeness is easier if you opt to code pure operations. When you adopt this design strategy, you can focus on coding only those operations that are *absolutely required* for the complete unit.

The client programmer, in using the ADT, likewise knows that each operation does only one thing. This starkness property frees clients from having to deal with unnecessary extraneous variables that might be a part of some "combination" operation.

Anonymous-type field variables

We chose to declare all field variables as anonymous types to make it difficult for a client to use any one of them as a parameter. The more your code discourages the client from individually accessing the ADT components, the better. If a client writes code that tampers with the component variables directly, he or she may destroy the logic of the ADT structure.

Suppose, for example, the client program directly accesses and changes the value of Head without changing the value of InUse. If this operation were carried out, the remaining calls to the other operations in the ADT would all yield incorrect results. Thus, the more pains you take to ensure that the client sees the abstraction as an indivisible unit, the more difficult you make it for the client to tamper with its internal logic.

Ideally, the client should not be allowed to access any of the components that make up the abstract type. It is impossible to achieve this ideal in the Pascal language, but the closer you come to achieving it with your code, the better your abstraction will be.

Error Handling

An ADT is a unit separate from a regular program that other programmers use. Being human, any client user may write code that incorrectly uses one or more of the abstract operations in the unit. You must be aware of this fact and ensure that your code handles all possible errors correctly.

Purity and starkness

If you have coded a unit with pure operations, it should be a relatively easy task for you to determine the error conditions that you must guard against. For our implementation of the queue, errors can occur if a client program tries (1) to add an item to a queue that is already full, (2) to delete an item from a queue that is already empty, or (3) to get the value of the first item from an empty queue.

In the interest of keeping the unit as stark as possible, we chose to handle errors for the AddQueue and DeleteQueue operations with display messages. Note that the client program will not crash if the ADT is used improperly because we made sure all possible error conditions were handled. Note further that we handled the error condition of FirstOnQueue by returning the value of NullItem. We are virtually obligated to write this code, for a selector demands that *some* value be given to the selected component. Regardless of how error conditions are handled, the client must be informed in the documentation as to how these exceptional cases are handled.

Flagging an error

Suppose that the problem statement to implement the queue requires you to flag errors, passing them out to a boolean variable. If you are required to handle errors in this manner, the code for the two constructors must begin with the headers

```
PROCEDURE AddQueue(Item: ItemType; VAR Done: boolean; VAR Queue: QueueType);
PROCEDURE DeleteQueue(VAR Done: boolean; VAR Queue: QueueType);
```

The statement for each of these operations then requires that Done takes on the value of true if the operation is successfully carried out or the value of false if the operation cannot be done. If you use this form of the abstraction, you will need to declare and use a boolean variable to complete the parameter list for both headers.

How should you handle errors in abstract units? It depends upon the problem statement and/or the requirements of the client user. Regardless of how they are handled, you must be sure to guard against them in your source code. Similarly, you must indicate how they are handled in the documentation.

EXERCISES

Test Your
Understanding

1. Suppose we want to implement a queue of integer values. How much code needs to be changed in the queue of names we implemented? Is it necessary to change the code of any of the forward-referenced procedures and functions?

2. If we were to use the call-by-value mechanism with the Queue variable for all the selector and predicate operations, what would be their O? Explain.

Practice Your
Analysis Skills

3. Suppose we choose to implement the queue as an array of strings. We would then use the following definitions:

```
CONST
   MaxQueue = 100;
   NullItem = '';
TYPE
   ItemType = STRING[50];
   QueueType = ARRAY[1..MaxQueue] OF ItemType;
```

A queue with five items in it would then be represented such that the first item is stored in Queue[1], the last item in Queue[5], and the values in Queue[6] through Queue[MaxQueue] are all set to NullItem. Given this implementation strategy, do any of the original headers of the ADT QueueType need to be changed?

4. Suppose we choose to implement our ADT QueueType according to the approach suggested by Exercise 3. Which statements need to recoded? What will be the O for each of the operations? (Assume that Queue is passed in as a variable call.)

Sharpen Your
Implementation
Skills

5. Modify the implementation of AddQueue and DeleteQueue so that values are given to the boolean variable Done for each invocation. The value true is assigned if the operation was successfully carried out, otherwise false is assigned.

6. Will any of the functions for the suggested implementation strategy of Exercise 3 still code to one-liners? Which ones? Write the code for them.

7. Write the code for the statements of those functions suggested by Exercise 3 that are not one-liners.

8. Write the code for the constructor operations using the implementation suggested by Exercise 3.

13.5   The Stack ADT

In this section, you will learn about the operation of the stack, another abstract data type. Like the queue, this type is also dynamic. It is a particularly useful abstraction for solving problems related specifically to computer science applications.

Stack dynamics

   The stack, like the queue, has two nonprimitive constructor operations: one to add an item to the stack and the other to delete an item from the stack. These two operations are described by the acronym *LIFO*, meaning "last in, first out." The acronym indicates that the last item added to the stack is the candidate item to be deleted from the stack. When an item is added to the stack, we say that it is *pushed* on the stack's *top*. An item is removed from the stack's top by a call to the *pop* operation.

Figures 13.9(a) to 13.9(d) show how push and pop operations apply to a stack that contains items of type char. Figure 13.9(a) shows a stack with the char value 'a' on its top. If the next constructor to be executed on the stack is a pop, this value is popped off the stack's top. Figure 13.9(b), however, shows the next operation to be a push of the char value 'b'. It is then this particular value that becomes the new candidate for a pop operation.

Figure 13.9(c) shows the stack's appearance when this character is popped as the next operation. The candidate to be popped, as per the stack discipline, is again 'a'. This character is popped off the top of the stack by the action shown in Figure 13.9(d).

Coding the stack ADT interface
The source code for the interface part of a stack of char values is given as Example 13.2.

Example 13.2

```
{                    INTERFACE PART OF STACK ADT                    }
{This abstraction is for a stack capable of holding up to MaxStack
characters.}
CONST
  MaxStack = 80; {capable of holding a line of char types}
TYPE
  ItemType = char;
  StackType = RECORD
    Top: 0..MaxStack;
```

FIGURE 13.9 (a) Stack with 'a' on top, (b) after pushing 'b' on the stack, (c) after popping (b)'s stack, and (d) after popping (c)'s stack.

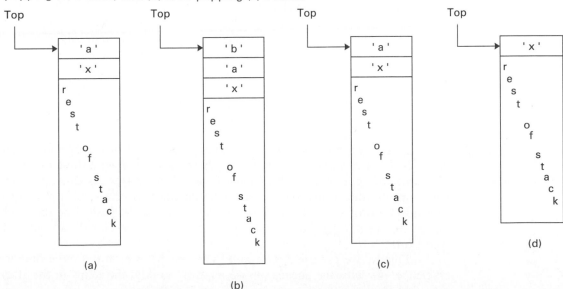

```
    Items: ARRAY[1..MaxStack] OF ItemType
  END;
{                          THE OPERATIONS                                }
PROCEDURE MakeStack(VAR Stack: StackType);                  FORWARD;
  {sets up an initial stack with no items on it}
{+                                                                      +}
PROCEDURE Push(Item: ItemType; VAR Stack: StackType);      FORWARD;
  {if the stack is not full, this operation adds an item to the top;
   if the stack is full, an error message is displayed}
{+                                                                      +}
PROCEDURE Pop(VAR Stack: StackType);                        FORWARD;
  {if the stack is not empty, pops an item off the top of the stack;
   if the stack is empty, an error message is displayed}
{+                                                                      +}
FUNCTION StackTop(VAR Stack: StackType): ItemType;          FORWARD;
  {if the stack is not empty, assigns the value of the item on the
   stack's top to the function; if the stack is empty, assigns the
   NullItem, in this case chr(0), the null character}
{+                                                                      +}
FUNCTION StackEmpty(VAR Stack: StackType): boolean;         FORWARD;
  {if the stack is empty, the value of true is assigned to the
   function, otherwise the value false is assigned}
{+                                                                      +}
FUNCTION StackFull(VAR Stack: StackType): boolean;          FORWARD;
  {if the stack is full, the value of true is assigned to the function,
   otherwise the value false is assigned}
{+                                                                      +}
```

Comments about the abstraction

The field variable Top references the item on the top of the stack. When Stack.Top takes on the value 0, the stack is empty. Note that we have chosen the field variables Top and Items to be anonymous types. This choice discourages the client from using either of these variables as parameters in some client procedure.

We also chose to define ItemType even though our stack consists of items that contain standard char values. We made this implementation choice for the sake of flexibility. We can, for example, modify the code to implement a stack of integers simply by redefining ItemType. The only other small modification we would have to make is to define a value as an error condition if a call is made to StackTop with an empty stack.

In keeping with our implementation strategy, all of the operations done on the stack are with variables of type ItemType rather than with those of type char. This type, being a defined alias for the standard char type, is assignment-compatible with all other char types. The value obtained off the stack's top can be assigned to a char variable, and a char value can also be pushed on the stack even though the stack is defined as containing variables of type ItemType rather than of type char.

Finally, we are using the call-by-VAR mechanism on the three functions for efficiency. As with the queue, we use an array to hold the items in the stack. All three functions have O(N) if the variable `Stack` is passed in by value. Passing it in by VAR, however, gives the three functions an efficiency of O(1).

Using the Stack ADT

We said in the introduction to this section that a stack is an incredibly useful abstraction. Let us show how versatile this abstraction is by solving two problems using a stack of characters. Note how apparently unrelated the two problems are, yet a stack can be used in the solution of both of them.

Example Problem 13.2

Let us use the stack of characters to write a small program that reads in a line of text and then displays the characters on the line in reverse. A typical run of the program is

```
The quick brown fox jumps over the lazy dog.<eoln>
.god yzal eht revo spmuj xof nworb kciuq ehT<eoln>
```

Describing the solution
       Clearly, the last character read in should be the first one that is displayed. Likewise, the first character read in should be the last one displayed. This description suggests a structure to hold characters for display using a LIFO discipline. A stack of characters is thus called for. The pseudocode description for the program is given as

> *MakeStack(ChStack)*   *{initializes an empty stack}*
> *WHILE NOT eoln DO*
>   *read(Ch)*
>   *push Ch onto ChStack*
> *readln*
> *WHILE ChStack is not empty DO*
>   *display value of Ch on stack's top*
>   *pop Ch value on top of ChStack*
> *writeln*

Using the ADT and the pseudocode description, we obtain the source code for the program `ReverseALine`.

```
PROGRAM ReverseALine(input, output);
  {The program uses a stack of characters to read in a line of text and
  then displays it in reverse.}
  TYPE
    {INSERT ALL DEFINITIONS ASSOCIATED WITH THE STACKTYPE ADT HERE}

  VAR
    ChStack: StackType;
```

```
  Ch: char;      {candidate item pushed on and popped off ChStack}
  {INSERT ALL OPERATIONS ASSOCIATED WITH THE STACK ADT HERE}
BEGIN
  MakeStack(ChStack);
  WHILE NOT eoln DO
    BEGIN
      read(Ch);
      Push(Ch, ChStack)
    END;
  readln;
  WHILE NOT StackEmpty(ChStack) DO
    BEGIN
      Ch:= StackTop(ChStack);
      Pop(ChStack);
      write(Ch)
    END;
  writeln
END.  ◆
```

In Example Problem 13.2, items continued to be pushed on the stack until it was time to initialize the sequence to pop all items. In the following problem, the choice of whether to push or pop is determined by the events that occur when the source code is being executed.

Example Problem 13.3

The problem statement

Write a function to verify that a string of characters representing a line of text is balanced with respect to the parentheses, braces, and brackets it contains. The line is balanced if the left-hand symbol, that is (, {, or [, is matched by its corresponding right-hand symbol,), }, or]. The line is unbalanced if either a right-hand symbol occurs before its corresponding left-hand symbol or if there are some unpaired left-hand symbols. The following shows three examples of a balanced line and three examples of an unbalanced line.

Balanced Line	Unbalanced Line
{ AnArray[1] }	Re:= sqrt((sqr(ARe) + sqr(BRe)
(3 + 2)/ AnArray[1][4] {!}	{unpaired comment
(1 + (1/A[1] + (1/A[(2 + 1)])))	{ (A[4,3] + B[5,1] }

The header for the `boolean` function `BalancedLine` is then coded as FUNCTION `BalancedLine(ALine: LineString): boolean;`, where a variable of type `LineString` is capable of holding up to 80 characters.

The solution　　　　　If you look at the lines that are balanced, you will notice that any left-hand delimiter can enclose another balanced expression. The braces in the first expression, for example, enclose a set of square brackets. You can deduce then that once an expression is started and a left-hand symbol intervenes, the expression must be completed first. A LIFO method to store these symbols for comparison is suggested by this analysis, so let us use a stack whose items are of type char to develop the source code for the solution.

A pseudocode　　　　The pseudocode for the solution is as follows:
description

> *MakeStack(ChStack)*
> *StillBalanced* ← *true*
> *FOR Position* ← *1 TO length(ALine) DO*
> 　　*Ch* ← *ALine[Position]*
> 　　*IF Ch is a left-handed delimiter THEN*
> 　　　*Push(Ch, ChStack)*
> 　　*ELSE IF Ch is a right-handed delimiter THEN*
> 　　　*IF NOT Matched(StackTop(ChStack), Ch) THEN*
> 　　　　*StillBalanced* ← *false*
> 　　　　*Pop(ChStack)*
> *BalancedLine* ← *StillBalanced AND StackEmpty(ChStack)*

Required local　　　　The FOR loop checks all characters in ALine to determine whether the line
variables　　　is balanced or not. The local variable Position represents the index value of the present char in ALine being examined. Ch is a convenient variable for storing the value of ALine[Position]. StillBalanced is initialized to true and should remain true as long as the characters in the index subrange *1..Position* of ALine still make up a potentially balanced line. It should take on the value of false and remain false for all remaining loop passes if ALine[Position] is found to be a mismatched right-hand delimiter. The local variable ChStack contains the still unmatched left-hand delimiters of ALine found in the index subrange 1..Position. The function Matched returns true if the right-hand delimiter Ch matches the left-hand delimiter that is the top item of ChStack.

Assertion testing　　　　At the end of each loop pass, the value on the top of ChStack is the candidate left-hand delimiter to be matched. If Ch is not a delimiter, the status of the flag variable StillBalanced does not change, nor is the stack pushed or popped. If Ch is a left-hand delimiter, it is pushed on the stack, for it is the new candidate delimiter to be compared for a match. If Ch is a right-hand delimiter, its value must be compared with the value on top of ChStack. If there is a proper match, the value of the flag variable StillBalanced does not change. If there is a mismatch, StillBalanced is set to false, indicating an unbalanced line.

　　　　When the loop is exited, the value of StillBalanced indicates whether or not all right-hand delimiters in the index subrange *1..length(ALine)* were matched by left-hand delimiters. Regardless of the status of the flag variable, if the stack is not empty, it means that some of the characters in ALine are left-hand delimiters that have no right-hand delimiters to match up with. Given this condition or the condition that `StillBalanced` is `false`, the value returned to the `boolean` function must be `false`, indicating an unbalanced expression. If, however, `StillBalanced` is `true` and the stack is empty, all left-hand delimiters were matched by right-hand delimiters, so the function properly returns the value `true`.

Source code

We have proven that our pseudocode description for the function `BalancedLine` is correct. Therefore, we present the source code for `BalancedLine` as follows:

```
{*                                                                          *}
FUNCTION Matched(LeftCh, RightCh: char): boolean;
   {returns true if LeftCh and RightCh make up a matching pair of
   delimiters}
   BEGIN
     Matched:= (LeftCh = '{') AND (RightCh = '}') OR
               (LeftCh = '[') AND (RightCh = ']') OR
               (LeftCh = '(') AND (RightCh = ')')
   END;
{+                                                                          +}
FUNCTION BalancedLine(ALine: LineString): boolean;
   {returns true if the left-hand and right-hand delimiting characters
   present in the variable Line are matched}
   VAR
     Position: 1..80;   {access to present char on ALine being processed}
     Ch: char;          {value of present char on ALine being processed}
     StillBalanced: boolean; {true if chars in 1..Position are balanced}
     ChStack: StackType;     {stack containing left chars to be balanced}
   BEGIN
     MakeStack(ChStack);
     StillBalanced:= true;
     FOR Position:= 1 TO length(ALine) DO
       BEGIN
         Ch:= ALine[Position];
         IF Ch IN ['{', '[', '('] THEN
           Push(Ch, ChStack)
         ELSE IF Ch IN ['}', ']', ')'] THEN
           BEGIN
             IF NOT Matched(StackTop(ChStack), Ch) THEN
               StillBalanced:= false;
             Pop(ChStack)
           END
       END
     BalancedLine:= StillBalanced AND StackEmpty(ChStack)
   END;
{*                                                                      *} ◆
```

Implementing the Stack ADT

We have looked at two client examples that used the stack ADT. Now let us complete our discussion of the stack by coding the implementation section of the unit. As usual, we assume that all operations were FORWARD-referenced in the interface section.

The one-liners

The procedure MakeStack simply sets Stack.Top to 0, indicating that no items are on the initial stack. The functions StackEmpty and StackFull return true, respectively, when Stack.Top is 0 and Stack.Top is equal to MaxStack. The code for these three operations is therefore:

```
PROCEDURE MakeStack{VAR Stack: StackType};
  BEGIN
    Stack.Top:= 0
  END;

FUNCTION StackEmpty{(VAR Stack: StackType): boolean};
  BEGIN
    StackEmpty:= (Stack.Top = 0)
  END;

FUNCTION StackFull{(VAR Stack: StackType): boolean}:
  BEGIN
    StackFull:= (Stack.Top = MaxStack)
  END;
```

The function StackTop

If the stack is empty, the null character (whose value is chr(0)) should be returned as an error condition, otherwise the item on the stack top is returned. Therefore, we obtain the code for StackTop as

```
FUNCTION StackTop{(VAR Stack: StackType): ItemType};
  BEGIN
    WITH Stack DO
      IF Top = 0 THEN
        StackTop:= chr(0)
      ELSE
        StackTop:= Items[Top]
  END;
```

The Push operation

In the proposed implementation, if the client program attempts to push an item on the stack when it is already full, the computer does not carry out the operation and it displays an error message. Otherwise the top of the stack is moved up and the item's value is assigned to the element Stack.Items[Top]. A precall, postcall picture of the Push operation as it might apply to a stack containing char items is given in Figures 13.10(a) and 13.10(b).

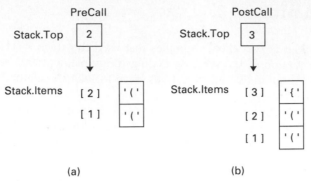

(a)   (b)

FIGURE 13.10   (a) Before and (b) after pushing '{' on the stack.

The source code for the Push operation is as follows:

```
PROCEDURE Push {Item: ItemType; VAR Stack: StackType};
   BEGIN
     WITH Stack DO
       IF Top <> MaxStack THEN
         BEGIN
           Top: = Top + 1;
           Items[Top]: = Item
         END
       ELSE
         writeln('ERROR:   ATTEMPTED PUSH OPERATION ON A FULL STACK')
   END;
```

The Pop
operation

Figure 13.11(a) and 13.11(b) show the precall, postcall picture we want to obtain for a Pop operation.

Once again, we need to write code that informs the client if an attempt is made to pop an item off an empty stack. The code for the Pop operation, taking into account the error message, is

FIGURE 13.11   (a) Before and (b) after popping an Item.

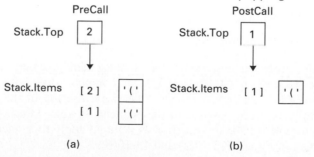

(a)   (b)

```
PROCEDURE Pop{VAR Stack: StackType};
  BEGIN
    WITH Stack DO
      IF Top <> 0 THEN
        Top:= Top - 1
      ELSE
        writeln('ERROR:   ATTEMPTED POP OPERATION ON AN EMPTY STACK')
  END;
```

Other Uses for Stacks

We have given you two examples of client programs that required a stack of char values. We can, however, pose many client programs that require the use of stacks containing items other than character values. Case Study 17.1 in Chapter 17, for example, shows how you can use a stack of numeric values to evaluate an arithmetic expression.

You will likewise see in Chapter 15 how the computer uses a stack to execute a program. Suppose, for example, the computer is executing a sequence of statements that belong to procedure A. If one of the statements is a call to procedure B, procedure A is interrupted, and the statements of procedure B are executed. Only when procedure B is completed will the machine resume its execution of the statements in procedure A. Thus, the last procedure called is the first procedure completed. Hence, a mechanism that uses a LIFO discipline, that is to say a stack, is the way the computer manages the execution of the processes that make up a Pascal program.

EXERCISES

Test Your Understanding

1. What does the acronym LIFO stand for? Which part of the abbreviation is associated with a push operation and which part is associated with a pop operation?

2. Briefly explain why we used a call by VAR for all of the stack operations, including the selectors and the predicates.

3. Suppose we had decided to solve Example Problem 13.2 by pushing both left-hand and right-hand parentheses, braces, and brackets on the stack. Now the popping of the stack is not done until the whole line is read in. Once all the characters have been read in, the stack is used to determine whether the expression is matched or not. Does this approach work? Explain why or why not.

Practice Your Analysis Skills

4. The table associated with Example Problem 13.2 shows three balanced expressions and three unbalanced expressions. Show how the ChStack would appear after each push or pop operation for the different examples when the statements of the solution are carried out.

5. Suppose no parentheses, brackets, or braces are found in the variable LineString. What value is returned to the function BalancedLine for this input data?

6. You want to implement a stack of `integer` values. Write down the changes you would have to make on the code given in Example 13.2 to have an abstract unit of this type.

7. The clients of Example 13.2 want a "stack dump" if an attempt is made to push an item on a full stack. A stack dump displays the contents of the stack. Modify the Pop operation in the stack ADT so that the client gets the desired stack dump. You can assume that if an error condition occurs, the rest of the program will be meaningless, so the contents of the stack need not be saved by the stack dump.

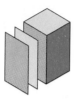

Program Testing Hints

A client should be able to use an ADT unit without having to disturb any of the implementation details that make up the abstraction. In this section, we give you some hints that will ensure the client does not have to know or modify any of the implementation details of an ADT.

PROGRAM DESIGN RULE 13.1

Do not access any of the components that make up an ADT in the source code of a client program.

Information hiding

The hallmark of a good ADT is information hiding. Whoever wishes to use an abstract unit (including yourself) should not have any need to disturb the components that make up the ADT variable(s). Once you write code in a client program that tampers with the components of the abstraction, you cannot be sure from that point onward that the operations in the ADT will function properly. An unspoken precondition for a call to any given operation is that all manipulations on a variable of the abstract type have been carried out using only the operations defined for the type.

Unfortunately, these "illegal" operations usually do not violate the syntax rules of most dialects of Pascal. Tampering is therefore possible in the same way that side effects are. Your code, however, should always use the abstraction *as if* its component variables were all inaccessible.

PROGRAM DESIGN RULE 13.2

If you find it impossible to write a client program without accessing one or more components of an ADT, then modify the ADT by writing the required additional operations.

Suppose you find you must write code that accesses the variable components of an ADT variable in order to solve a given coding problem. Do you violate Program Design Rule 13.1? Absolutely not. Instead, you apply Program Design Rule 13.2.

No matter how well you put together an ADT, you may later feel that it requires one or more add-on operations. If the code for the operation(s) must access the hidden components of the ADT, you have no choice in the matter, for your first implementation was probably incomplete. If, however, you find that no additional selectors or constructors are required at the primitive level, you should consider again whether the extra operation(s) are necessary.

If you can envision many client programs that will use this candidate add-on operation, then you probably should include it in the abstract unit. Avoid, however, making the ADT too unwieldy. Few clients would be willing to read through the headers of some hundred-odd operations that make up an ADT.

An add-on example

Many clients may need to compare two complex numbers for "equality." They can code a function `NearlyEqual` that returns `true` if the real and imaginary fields differ by some specified "small value." To make their coding task simpler, you might consider coding `NearlyEqual` as an add-on predicate function. Its code follows:

```
FUNCTION NearlyEqual(No1, No2: ComplexNo; Criterion: real): boolean;
  {returns true if the difference between the respective parts of the two
  numbers is less than the value of Criterion}
  BEGIN
    NearlyEqual:= (abs(No1.XRe - No2.XRe) < Criterion) AND
                  (abs(No1.YIm - No2.YIm) < Criterion)

  END;
```

Testing an ADT

Remember that an ADT is set of operations that many client programs will use. When you test each operation, keep this notion in the back of your mind. You must make sure your abstraction handles all possibilities that may come up. In particular, make sure you thoroughly test all error conditions for the different operations.

Unless you are testing the primitive selectors, be sure to use test data consistent with the abstraction. In testing the constructor operations of the queue, you must use the test variable `Queue` exactly the way you intend the client to use it. If you are testing the `DeleteQueue` operation, for example, build the queue with an initial call to `MakeQueue` followed by calls to `AddQueue`.

Useful tools for testing

When you have put an ADT together, you will not want the client to see any of its components directly. However, when you are testing the ADT, you will certainly want to have direct access to all its components. Thus, for example, the client should not be able to see the values assigned to `Queue.Head`, `Queue.Tail`, or any of the elements of `Queue.Items`. You will want to see them, though, so you can study the effects of each coded operation.

If you have tracer utilities available in your dialect of Pascal, you will not have to code procedures that access each of the different components directly. If you do not have this feature, you will need to code these required operations. An example of two of the operations you may require to test the queue ADT might be the following:

```
PROCEDURE ShowHead(VAR Queue: QueueType);
   {displays the value of Head}
   BEGIN
     writeln('The value of Head is now  ',Queue.Head)
   END;


PROCEDURE ShowOneItem(VAR Queue: QueueType; Index: integer);
   {shows the item Queue.Items[Index]}
   BEGIN
     write(Queue.Items[Index])
   END;
```

You may also want to write a procedure to show the value of Queue.Tail and even one to show *all* items on the queue. Clearly, none of these operations is intended to be of use to the client.

Laying out test routines
The best place to put these testing routines is below the implementations section of the ADT. Obviously, their headers should not be a part of the interface section. The operations are placed last in the unit to keep them away from the client's eyes. You may even want to comment out all these operations once you have finished with your on-line testing. It is a good idea, however, not to delete them, for they may prove useful if you require maintenance work on the ADT.

Choosing test data
Absolutely all error conditions must be tested for all operations. When you are working with the queue, for example, you will want to try to delete an item from an empty queue as well as add an item to a full queue. The queue can become empty in two ways: (1) if it is initially empty and (2) if it becomes empty after items have been deleted from it.

If you are testing for error conditions, you can certainly apply the rule of small samples for the add operations. In your testing, you can define the queue to be capable of holding only four or five items. Error handling is more easily tested in this case.

The wrap-around operation as it applies to both the add and delete operations of the circular queue should also be tested. When Queue.Tail is equal to MaxQueue, will the next QueueAdd operation change this value to 1? Will the item added be put at Queue.Items[1]? Likewise, when Queue.Head is equal to MaxQueue, will the item be deleted properly? Suppose Queue.Head is MaxQueue and there is only one item on queue. Will this operation work properly when it is applied?

You must also remember that the queue is a dynamic ADT. Thus, you should apply some combination operations such as adding two items and then deleting one item. You might try this combination with three sets of data. Then, you might try deleting two items and adding one item for three sets of data. Do you eventually get an empty queue? Does the queue become empty when it should?

Make the queue empty a number of times and full a number of times with your tests. If all operations are carried out successfully for different values of Head and Tail, the chances are your code is correct. Do not forget, too, to test the code with add and delete combinations where the queue is only partially full. Again, if some simple combinations work, the chances are good that your code is correct.

Assertion testing   We remind you once again that you should apply assertion testing before you do any on-line testing. As with programs, you should feel confident that the operations you have coded for the ADT are logically correct before you start the editing and on-line testing phase of development.

EXERCISES

**Test Your
Understanding**

1. Why are all maintenance operations coded after the implementation section of a unit? Why are their headers not found in the interface section?

2. Explain why it is useful to keep the maintenance operations as part of the unit's code even after the unit has been fully developed.

**Sharpen Your
Implementation
Skills**

3. Write the maintenance procedures to display the values of Tail and InUse for the queue ADT.

4. Write the maintenance procedure to display all items on the queue. How does the operation differ from one where the client user codes a client procedure to display the queue's items?

5. Repeat Exercise 4, but code the operations as they apply to the stack ADT.

6. Outline a testing strategy for the stack ADT.

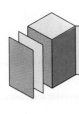

REVIEW AND EXERCISES

An *abstract data type*, also called an *ADT*, is expressed in terms of a logical appearance and some defining operations. It is coded and tested as a *unit* that a *client program* can then use. When you use an ADT in a client program, you first declare one or more variables of the abstract type. Then you can use the defining operations of the ADT on the required variables to solve the problem. When you use the abstract operations in the ADT without knowledge of their implementation details, you are applying the technique of *data abstraction* to solve the problem.

Many dialects of Pascal allow *separately compiled units* that are meant to be used in client programs. With the proper reserved words, the unit can be interfaced with the client program. Most units are set up so that the operations are coded in an *interface section* as procedure and function headers. The client programmer will not even have to look at the *implementation section,* which contains the details of the defined operations. If your system does not have this feature, you can still separate the header from the implementation details using the standard Pascal FORWARD directive.

The operations in a *complete unit* fall into three distinct categories: *constructors, selectors,* and *predicates.* A constructor changes or initializes the associated abstract variable. If the constructor does not change or use other variables of the same abstract type to carry out the operation, it is called a *primitive constructor.* A *selector,* often coded as a function, returns information about the present state of an abstract variable. A *primitive selector* is an operation that directly accesses an individual component of the abstract variable. A *predicate* is a special class of selector that is a `boolean` function.

A problem statement to build an ADT describes the *capabilities* of the abstract type. A client program will use these capabilities to carry out a sequence of actions the same way any other program does. A good design goal in putting together an ADT is to code it with only pure constructors, pure selectors, and pure predicates. The abstraction, which will appear quite *stark* with these pure operations, is both easier to test and easier to use.

Good documentation is a must for any ADT. The client user should know what to expect for every conceivable circumstance with each of the defined operations. In particular, *error-handling* information should be included in the documentation. An *error condition* occurs if an operation is called that cannot be carried out due to one or more preconditions that apply to the abstract variable. All error conditions must be handled properly to prevent the client program from crashing as a result of misapplying the operations of the ADT.

The *queue* and the *stack* are *dynamic ADT*s, that is, data types whose number of components is expected to change over the course of a program run. Both can be implemented using a RECORD type where an ARRAY holds the *items* that make up either abstraction. An acronym used to describe the add/delete operations of a queue is *FIFO,* which means "first in, first out." The first item added to a queue is the first one to be deleted from the queue. The acronym used to describe the stack *push* and *pop* operations is *LIFO,* for "last in, first out." If you can, it is a good design technique to define an `ItemType` as one of the items belonging to a dynamic ADT. For example, you may have coded a stack of `char` values and put it on file as an abstract unit. If you had defined `ItemType` to be `char`, you can readily code a stack of *numeric* values just by redefining `ItemType` to be `real` or `integer`, then using the operations you have already coded. The only operation you may need to modify is `StackTop` such that it handles the error condition of returning a value on an empty stack properly.

When you are testing an ADT, be sure that you test all possible error conditions. You should also apply combination testing of the different operations in different sequences, just as if you were a client. Remember that once the ADT goes on line, the clients will use it without looking at the implementation details, so it must be correct.

EXERCISES

Short Answers

1. Why did we declare anonymous variables types in the field lists of the ADTs we coded?

2. Define the three terms *constructor, selector,* and *predicate.*

3. When we coded the Stack ADT, we chose to define the items as type `ItemType` even

though they were the standard type char. Why did we implement the stack of char values in this fashion?

4. What is the difference between an incomplete unit and an incorrect one? What kinds of problems would a client programmer have with each?

5. If, as a client programmer, you feel a particular unit is incomplete, how do you deal with the problem?

6. What would cause you to suspect that a unit is incorrect? How would you deal with that problem?

7. The ADT QueueType did not give the client user direct access to some of the fields to a variable of QueueType (e.g., Queue.Head). Why not?

8. Under what circumstances would you want to write code to gain access to a field variable such as Queue.Head? Should the client programmer(s) know about this operation? Why or why not?

9. We introduced the word FORWARD in this chapter so that you can write code separating the header from the statement. Why would you want to write such code? Would you use this word in the same context in a client program?

10. If an array is used in the implementation of a dynamic ADT, at least some of the fields of the abstraction require variables to access the array elements. Why?

11. The stack discipline is maintained using *FIFO* processing, and the queue discipline is maintained using *LIFO* processing. What do these two acronyms stand for?

12. Why did we use VAR calls on all queue and stack operations, even those that were selectors?

13. What is the difference between a problem statement that begins with "Write a program that . . ." and a problem statement that begins with "Write an ADT that . . ."?

14. We want to write a procedure SumN to read in and sum the values of N complex numbers. List the operations from the ComplexNo ADT that are required by this procedure.

15. Write the statement to assign the value $7 + 2i$ to the complex variable ZComp using the operations of the ComplexNo ADT.

Easy Projects

16. Use the ComplexNo ADT to write a client program that reads in 10 complex numbers into an array. The average of the 10 numbers is to be found and displayed. Likewise, the number with the largest magnitude and the one with the smallest magnitude are to be found and displayed.

17. Write a client program to solve the following simultaneous equations consisting of complex numbers:

$$AX + BY = C$$

$$DX + EY = F$$

The main block for the program is described by

> *GetNumbers(A, B, C, D, E, F)*   {*values read into 6 coefficients*}
> *Solve(A, B, C, D, E, F, X, Y)*   {*X and Y solved*}
> *ShowAnswers(X, Y)*   {*X and Y displayed*}

18. It is possible to use the stack ADT to implement a queue ADT. The appearance of a queue of characters, for example, can be achieved using

```
TYPE
  ItemType = char;
  CharsQueue = RECORD
    Stack1,
    Stack2: StackType      {stack of chars used in Section 13.5}
END;
```

Use this code and the stack implementation of Section 13.5 to code the operations of CharsQueue. Write all operations except for the selector QCount using the suggested implementation strategy.

19. Use a stack of characters to evaluate two separate integers read in from the keyboard. The digits making up each integer are to be read in and pushed on the char stack. Once a number is completed (as signified by a blank or <eoln>), the characters are popped from the stack to get a value for the number. The LIFO mechanism is useful, because the least significant digit will be on top of the stack and the most significant will be the last item on the stack. After a digit is evaluated and then popped, the next digit on the stack represents the next higher power of 10.

The program is to evaluate two integers and then print their sum. A sample run is

```
Enter two numbers:    532    625
Their sum is 1157.
```

Note that you simply sum up the *two* digits to indicate that the stack to convert digits works. The main block of the program is described by

> *GetNumber(FirstNumber)*
> *GetNumber(SecondNumber)*
> *display FirstNumber + SecondNumber*

The procedure GetNumber reads in char values to build the stack and then uses the stack to evaluate the "number" read in.

20. A problem similar to Exercise 4 is to have the computer read in a sequence of characters expressing a number in a base different from base 10. Write a program that first reads in the number base (any integer from 2 through 9) and then reads in a number in that base. It uses a stack to convert this number to its base-10 equivalent. The last line of display shows the equivalent decimal (base-10) number. We can describe the main block by:

> *keyin Base*
> *BuildStack(ChStack)*
> *Int ← ItsValue(ChStack, Base)*
> *display Int*

A typical run is

```
Enter base:   4
Enter number 302
Its decimal equivalent value is 50.
```

21. Write a client program that sets up a stack called `Opstack` such that only the following values are allowed on the variable `OpStack`:

A, S, M, D, X

The computer first reads in a line of text representing the push and pop operations it should perform on `OpStack`. In addition to A, S, M, and D, the two character values + and − are legal for the line of text read in. The computer then processes each of the characters in the string as follows: When a plus sign is encountered, the next char value is pushed on `OpStack`. When a minus sign is encountered, the char value on the top of the stack is popped.

   Before the push operation is performed, the computer should display one of five character sequences: "`Add started..`," "`Subtract started..`," "`Multiply started..`," "`Divide started..`," or "`Illegal operation...`" If the computer displays the latter string, it should follow it with the display "`process halted`" and no further display. When a character is to be popped off the stack, just before it is popped, one of the following four strings is displayed: "`Add completed,`" "`Subtract completed,`" "`Multiply completed,`" and "`Divide completed.`" Finally, if all characters in the input string have been processed and `OpStack` is not empty, the computer should display the string "`Incomplete expression.`" If, instead, the stack is empty, the display is "`Expression evaluated.`"

   Sample runs are

```
+M+A-+S--<eoln>
Multiply started..
Add started..
Add completed.
Subtract started..
Subtract completed.
Multiply completed.
Expression evaluated.

+C+M--<eoln>
Illegal operation -- process halted.

+M+D-<eoln>
Add started..
Divide started..
Divide completed.
Incomplete expression.
```

22. Change the StackType ADT of Section 13.5 to a stack of real values and then use the stack to evaluate a math expression using reverse Polish notation (RPN). A line of text representing the RPN expression is read in and evaluated. The four operators allowed in the expression are +, −, *, and /. Real number operands, expressed using decimal notation, are the other legal characters on the input line.

   An RPN expression uses *postfix notation*, where the two numeric operands precede the operation to be applied to them. For example, the RPN expression 7 8 3 * + 15 - is evaluated step by step as 24 7 + 15 -, then 31 15 -, and finally 16. You can solve the problem by pushing operands on the stack until an operator is read in. Then the values of the first two operands are found, and they are also popped off the stack. The operation is applied to these two operands, and the result is then pushed back on the stack. After the final operation is applied, the stack should contain a single numeric value, otherwise the RPN expression is unbalanced. Typical runs are

```
75  15  /  3  +  8  2  -  /<eoln>
Value = 2.00


14.2  12.5  3.7  8.6  +  -  +  2  *<eoln>
Value = 28.80
```

23. Build a rational number ADT using the following implementation for its appearance:

```
TYPE
  RationalNo = RECORD
    Num,                    {numerator}
    Den: integer   {denominator}
  END;
```

If, for example, ANo of type `RationalNo` is equal to 3/7, its fields will have the values ANo.Num ↔ 3 and ANo.Den ↔ 7.

The ADT is defined in terms of the following operations:

`RatAssign`, the primitive operation to assign values to the Num and Den fields.

`Reduce`, an operation that returns the operand as an equivalent ratio reduced to its lowest terms. (*Hint:* Find the greater common divisor (GCD) between Num and Den. Then use this value to reduce the fraction. You can find the GCD between `Int1` and `Int2`, where as preconditions `Int1` > `Int2` and `Int2` > 0 using

> *REPEAT*
>   *Rem ← Int1 MOD Int2*
>   *Int1 ← Int2*
>   *Int2 ← Rem*
> *UNTIL (Int2 = 0)*
>   {*Postcondition: Int1 is the GCD of the initial* Int1 *and* Int2 *integers*}

`RatAdd`, a constructor that returns the sum of the two operands, reduced to lowest terms.

`RatSubtr`, a constructor that returns the difference of the two operands, reduced to lowest terms.

`RatMult`, a constructor that returns the product of the two operands, reduced to lowest terms.

`RatDiv`, a constructor that returns the quotient of the two operands, reduced to lowest terms.

`RatInvert`, a constructor that returns the inverted ratio of the input operand.

`RatNum`, a primitive selector that returns the value of ANo.Num.

`RatDen`, a primitive selector that returns the value of ANo.Den.

`RatReal`, a selector that returns the real numeric value as represented by the ratio.

`RatEqual`, a predicate that returns true if the two operands represent the same ratio.

`RatGreaterThan`, a predicate that returns true if the first operand represents a ratio greater than the second operand.

24. You are to use the queue ADT to code a form of a priority queue. A priority queue adds items first in, and still deletes them first out, but, dependent upon some priority rule(s). The priority in this problem is defined as two memberships, class A and class B. A queue variable will contain an account number, implemented as a string of three digits, and a membership class, implemented as a single char value. For simplicity, the queue type will be able to hold up to 5 members.

Priority is given to class A members. The first class A member on the queue is deleted. If there are no class A members on queue, a class B member is deleted.

(a) Define a record structure PQueueType for this queue. (*Hint:* PQueueType will contain two defined queues. QSize will contain the count of the items on both queues, and is capable of taking on values from 0 to 5.)

(b) The priority queue will have the following constructors:

PQAdd: add an item to the queue.

PQDelete: delete an item from the queue according to the priority rules.

MakePQueue: set up an empty PQueueType variable.

Write the code for the constructors. (*Hint:* An attempt is made to delete an item from the A queue first.)

(c) Next write the selectors:

PQSize, which returns the membership size.

PQFirstNo, which returns the account number of the first item on queue.

PQFirstClass, which returns the membership class of the first item on queue.

(d) Next write the predicates PQFull and PQEmpty.

(e) Test the queue using a client program described as follows:

MakePQueue(PQueue)
keyin Command
WHILE NOT Finished(Command) DO {Finished is true when Command is 'F'}
    CASE UpperCh(Command) OF
        'S' : ShowPQueue(PQueue)
        'A' : keyin Item.Class, Item.No
            IF NOT PQFull(PQueue) THEN
                PQueueAdd(Item, PQueue)
            ELSE
                display 'not carried out'
        'D' : IF NOT PQEmpty(PQueue) THEN
                PQueueDelete(PQueue)
            ELSE
                display 'not carried out'
        'S' : display PQSize(PQueue)
        'H' : display PQFirstClass(PQueue), PQFirstNo(PQueue)
DeleteAll(PQueue)

The procedure ShowPQueue displays the contents of the priority queue *using the ADT* (i.e., as a client procedure), where the class type followed by the account number is displayed for each item on queue. The procedure DeleteAll deletes the items one by one, displaying the item that is first just before it is deleted.

25. Implement another kind of priority queue where a given item is known by its account number and its priority number. The items are arranged on the priority queue in such a way that the item with the lowest priority number is placed first and the item with the highest priority number is placed last. You can call this ADT PQType.

Implement the usual constructors, selectors, and predicates for a queue of this type. Besides the PQSize selector, the other two selectors are PQFirstAccNo and PQFirstPriNo, which respectively select the values of the AccNo and the PriNo (priority number) of the first item on queue. (*Hint:* PQueueAdd should *insert* an item into the queue according to the value of its PriNo field. It is thus an $O(N)$ operation.)

Apply the same client program used in Exercise 24 to test the operations of the ADT.

Difficult Projects

26. The rows and seats at The Exclusive Theater go from row A to row J and seats 1 through 15. The ADT TheaterSeats can thus be implemented by using the following abstraction:

```
CONST
   NullItem = '';              {used to represent an empty seat}
TYPE
   ItemType = STRING[50];      {represents a name}
   TheaterSeats = RECORD
      Seating:  ARRAY['A'..'J', 1..15] OF ItemType;
      Cost:  ARRAY['A'..'J'] OF real
   END;
```

(a) The constructor operations on a variable of type TheaterSeats are

EmptyTheater: sets up the theater such that all seats are empty.

SetRow: sets the *cost* of a seat in a given *row* to a given real value.

Reserve: sets a given seat (known by a *row* and a *column* value) to a given Name of type ItemType.

Cancel: sets a given seat to the value of NullItem.

The selectors on a variable of this type are

Occupant: returns the value of the Name occupying a given seat.

SeatCost: returns the cost for a given seat.

The one predicate is

SeatEmpty: returns the value true if a given seat is empty.

Write the code for the ADT TheaterSeats.

(b) Use ADT TheaterSeats in a client program described by

> EmptyTheater(Exclusive)
> fill in Cost field of Exclusive from keyboard input
> keyin Action
> WHILE NOT Finished(Action) OR SoldOut (Exclusive) DO
>   process Action
>   keyin Action

The actions that can occur represent procedure calls whose code is

BuyTickets(Row, First, Last, Done, Exclusive): buys tickets in a given row over First..Last subrange, representing seat numbers. Carries out the operation and returns true to Done only if all given seats are initially available.

ReturnTickets(Row, First, Last, Name, Done, Exclusive): cancels tickets over a given row, seat subrange if named for all seats. Carries out the operation and returns true to Done only if all specified seats match the specified Name value.

RowsShow(Exclusive, TotalSeats, MaxCost): displays the rows over which a *sequence* of TotalSeats empty seats is available at less than or equal to the value of MaxCost.

PricesShow(Exclusive): displays the costs of the different tickets available.

TotalAvailableShow(Exclusive, MaxCost): displays the total number of seats available less than or equal to MaxCost.

The actions are respectively entered by B, C, R, P, I, and F where F indicates the Finished condition. If any of the other actions are read in, the computer prompts the user for the given input parameter values to the procedure call.

27. You are to implement a "priority set," where there is a membership of three classes: A, B, or C. The set can contain a maximum of 10 members of any class in it. Each member in the set is known by a class and a number. Class A members are deleted from the set the least number of times, and class C members are deleted the most number of times.

   The members are deleted according to the value of a deletion counter, initialized to 0 when the set is first made empty. It is incremented by 1 with each deletion. If, when the deletion is completed, it takes on an odd value, the order in which an attempted deletion is made is class C first, class B second, and class A last. If its value is divisible by 6, the deletion is attempted in the order A, B, and C. If its value is an even number not divisible by 6, the preferred deletion order is B, C, and A.

   (a) The set has the following constructors:

   MakePSetEmpty: return a PSetType variable that has no members in it.

   PSetAdd: any member who applies is added to the set. If the set is full, a PSetAdd operation forces a PSetDelete operation.

   PSetDelete: deletes a member according to the value of the deletion counter. The rules have already been given.

   The sct has the following selectors:

   TotalMembers: shows the total number of members in the set.

   NextMemberToGo: returns the number of the next member to be deleted from the set.

   NextClassToGo: returns the class type due next for deletion.

   It is completed with the following predicates:

   FullPSet: returns true if the set has MaxMembers in it (10).

   EmptyPSet: returns true if the set has no members in it.

   Implement the ADT PSetType. (*Hint:* Use three different queues to represent different membership classes. A given member is added to the set by being added to the given queue class. Then when a PSetDelete operation is carried out, the queue from which a member is deleted can be determined by the value of the deletion counter.)

   (b) Write a client program to test this priority set. It is described by the pseudocode

```
           MakePSet(PSet)
           keyin Command
           WHILE NOT Finished(Command) DO      {Finished is true when Command is 'F'}
             CASE UpperCh(Command) OF
               'S' : ShowPSet(PSet)
               'A' : IF NOT FullPSet(PSet) THEN
                       keyin Item.Class, Item.No
                       PSetAdd(Item, PSet)
                     ELSE
                       display 'not carried out'
               'D' : IF NOT PSetEmpty(PSet) THEN
                       PSetDelete(PSet)
                     ELSE
                       display 'not carried out'
               'M' : display TotalMembers(PSet)
               'H' : display NextClassToGo(PSet), NextMemberToGo(PSet)
         DeleteAll(PSet)
```

ShowPSet uses the PSetType ADT to display the order in which the set members are to be deleted. (*Hint:* Call PSet by value and then you can delete members from this PSet without destroying the original PSet passed into the block.) DeleteAll uses the same logic as ShowPSet, but this time PSet is passed in by variable.

SETS
AND STRINGS

OBJECTIVES

After reading and studying the material of the present chapter, you should
be able to:

- Properly define and declare variables that are set types

- Correctly apply set operations to form set expressions

- Know and correctly use the boolean operations that
  apply to set expressions

- Use set variables and set expressions correctly in solving
  problems where they are relevant

- Know and use operations that belong to string types

- Use the abstract string operations of our ADT and your
  dialect to solve problems requiring string variables

Y**OU HAVE ALREADY USED SETS** on the right-hand side of the IN operator in tests for set membership. This boolean test is easy to code and understand.
You often use these expressions because other candidate boolean expressions are
more difficult and clumsier to code. In this chapter, you will learn to use set variables and to code boolean expressions that apply the relational operators to two set
expressions. When you use set variables and/or set expressions to solve a coding
problem, you will often find your code has an elegance and simplicity that would be
missing had you tried another implementation without using set types.

You will also learn quite a bit more about string operations. We have chosen
to present the strings used in this chapter in the form of an ADT implementation
that will work for all dialects of Pascal. The operations in the ADT we will implement are, for the most part, standard to systems that use string types. Hence, the
skills you pick up in using our ADT can be applied to the string operations that belong to your dialect of Pascal.

14.1   Set Variables and More Set Expressions

You have already had some exposure to sets. In Chapter 7, you learned how to form
a set membership expression to make up part of a boolean expression. So far, this
has been the only way you have used sets.

In this section, you will learn quite a bit more about sets. You will learn how
to declare one or more set variables whose membership can change over the course
of a program run. You will also see how to use set operators to combine two or more
operand set expressions to form a resultant set expression. Finally, you will see how
to form a boolean expression with one of the six relational operators to compare the
membership of two set expressions.

Set values
Every set expression implies a *set value*. Consider, for example, the following
set expressions and the set value implied by each expression:

$\{1\}$ ['A', 'E', 'I', 'O', 'U', '0'..'9']
$\{2\}$ ['A', 'E', 'U' '0'.. '9', 'I', 'O']
$\{3\}$ [2, 4, 6, 8]
$\{4\}$ [4, 2, 8, 6]

The expressions labeled $\{1\}$ and $\{2\}$, which are equivalent, represent a set value with
a membership of all uppercase vowels and the 10 decimal digits. The expressions labeled $\{3\}$ and $\{4\}$ represent set values containing the first four even numbers. Note
that the order of listed members is immaterial to a set's value; only the actual values
in the set's membership list determines the set's value.

Set value: the membership of a set as implied by a set expression.

Set variables and set types

In the introduction to this section, we said Pascal allows you to declare *set variables*. As you already know, before you can declare a variable, you must have a definition of its type. A given set type is always programmer-defined. The syntax for a set type is described by Figure 14.1.

Set variable: a variable that takes on the value of a set expression.

Base types, universal sets, and empty sets

The syntax diagram implies that a set variable can contain members only of the type belonging to the set's definition. This type is called the set's *base type,* or *host type.* Most of the time, you will code the base type as a subrange type (usually named).

Base type: an ordinal type that defines all possible members that a set variable can take on.

Usually, a dialect's compiler will allow the collating sequence of characters as a base type. Therefore, a type coded as SET OF char is, for the most part, legal Pascal. No compiler, however, will allow you to define SET OF integer, for there is a limit to the size of the *universal set* for any set type you want to define.

Universal set: a set value whose membership contains all the values in the defined base type.

The maximum allowed membership size of a universal set differs with each dialect. Most dialects allow base sets with up to 256 possible values. Besides the universal set, there is one other important set value you should know, namely, the *empty set,* or *null set.* Every set, regardless of its base type, has the empty set as one of its possible values.

Empty set: a set value that has no members in it.

An example

The code of Example 14.1 defines IntSet to have the subrange 1..100 (BaseInts) as its base type. The three variables Universal, SomeInts, and NullInts are all of type IntSet. The statements below the declarations respectively assign (1) the universal set of IntSet to Universal, (2) the set of numbers divisible by 10 from 1 to 100 to SomeInts, and (3) the empty set to NullInts.

Example 14.1

```
TYPE
   BaseInts = 1..100;
   IntSet = SET OF BaseInts;
```

FIGURE 14.1   Syntax diagram for defining a set type.

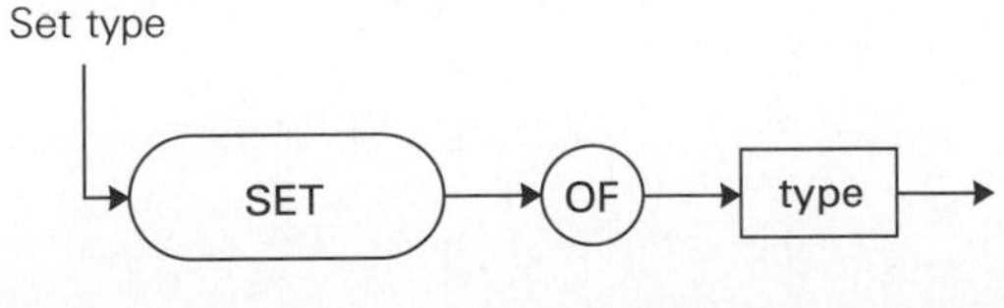

Set type

```
VAR
    Universal, SomeInts, NullInts: IntSet;

    Universal:= [1..100];
    SomeInts:= [10, 20, 30, 40, 50, 60, 70, 80, 90, 100];
    NullInts:= [];   {empty set}
```

An Application for Set Variables

Set "constants" Suppose you are writing a text-processing program. You want the computer to read in char values and then to take action dependent upon whether the value read in is a letter, digit, or special mark. You can use set variables for the required membership tests to make your code easier to read.

Suppose we are planning to write a text-processing program. We know that we will be processing characters, each of which might represent a letter, a digit, or an end of sentence. A test to see if Ch represents a letter might be coded using Ch IN ['A'..'Z', 'a'..'z'], but we prefer the more meaningful expression Ch IN Letters, where Letters is a set whose value remains constant over the scope of the program. The variable Letters, as well as Digits and SentenceEnders, can be declared as a set variable, assigned its initial value, and then referenced *globally* wherever its value is required in a membership test.

Implementation The implementation of these three set values is given in the code of Example 14.2. Note that these three set variables, being virtual constants, are referenced globally over the remainder of the program.

Example 14.2

```
TYPE
  CharSet = SET OF char;
{...MORE CODE...}
VAR
  {THE FOLLOWING SET VARIABLES WILL BE USED AS GLOBAL "CONSTANTS"}
  Letters,           {Value assigned:   ['A'..'Z', 'a'..'z']}
  Digits,            {Value assigned:   ['0'..'9']}
  SentenceEnders:    {Value assigned:   ['.', '!', '?']}
                     CharSet;
{...MORE CODE...}
{*                                                                    *}
PROCEDURE MakeTestSets(VAR Letters, Digits, SentenceEnders: CharSet);
  {sets values to the set constants Letters, Digits and SentenceEnders}
  BEGIN
    Letters:= ['A'..'Z', 'a'..'z'];
    Digits:= ['0'..'9'];
    SentenceEnders:=['.', '!', '?']
  END;
{*                                                                    *}
```

Anonymous expressions or set variables?

Are the extra lines of code required to define a set type, declare a set variable, and then initialize it to some "constant value" worth the extra trouble of having a "named" set value for membership tests? If you intend to use this value only once or twice in a program, perhaps an anonymous set expression would be better. If, however, the program requires that the same set expression be used quite frequently, it would probably be worth the extra lines of code.

These "set constants" (which, incidentally, can be defined as actual constants in Turbo Pascal) are best assigned their intial values in a procedure whose code is laid out just below the main block's variable declarations. The procedure's documentation should stress the fact that the values assigned to these variables will be kept constant throughout the course of the program run, and, hence, the set identifiers can be referenced as global identifiers without leading to harmful side effects.

Example Problem 14.1

The problem statement

Let us write a procedure GetWord that assigns a value to the variable Word, a string of characters that are alphabetic, by reading in char values from the text file InFile. The procedure also returns LastCh, the char value read in that breaks the string-building sequence. If <eoln> is the next value to be read in, LastCh is returned as a blank, and the computer does not execute readln(InFile). The procedure is called by GetWord(Word, LastCh, InFile), where Letters is referenced as a global value.

The solution

The problem is straightforward. Values read into Ch are concatenated onto Word as long as they represent letters of the alphabet. A guard to prevent reading <eoln> from AFile is also required. The solution is coded as the procedure Get-Word, using the procedure ReadInCh as a guard.

```
{*                                                              *}
PROCEDURE ReadInCh(VAR Ch: char; VAR InFile: text);
  {reads in a char value if the next char is not <eoln>; otherwise it
  forces a blank char value on Ch}
  BEGIN
    IF NOT eoln(InFile) THEN
      read(InFile, Ch)
    ELSE
      Ch:= ' '
  END;
{+                                                              +}
PROCEDURE GetWord(VAR Word: StringType; VAR LastCh: char;
                                        VAR InFile: text);
  {This procedure reads in a value to Word from InFile where all char
  values in Word must be in Letters.  The final value assigned to
  LastCh represents the first char value read in which is not in
  Letters.  A forced sentinel of a blank is given to LastCh if <eoln>
  is the next character to be read in.}
```

```
BEGIN
  Word:= '';      {initialize Word to NullString}
  ReadInCh(LastCh, InFile);
  WHILE LastCh IN Letters DO
    BEGIN
      Word:= Word + Ch;
      ReadInCh(LastCh, InFile)
    END
END;
{*                                                                    *}
```
◆

Set Operations and Expressions

A set type definition specifies the values a set variable might take on. In this section, you will learn how to code set expressions so that they can be used to modify or change the values(s) of a set variable(s).

Set operators and operations

Table 14.1 shows the three operators that can be applied to two or more set expressions. A set formed by the *union* of two sets contains the members of both sets, a set formed by the *intersection* of two sets contains only those members common to both sets, and a set formed by the *difference* of two sets contains only those members in the first set that are not in the second set.

TABLE 14.1 Set Operators Used in Forming Set Expressions

Operator	Operation
+	set union
*	set intersection
−	set difference

Table 14.2 has two examples of each of the three set operations. Inspection of the table shows that (1) the union of two sets returns a set whose membership is larger than the operand sets, (2) the intersection of two sets forms a set whose membership is smaller than the operand sets, and (3) the difference between two sets forms a set whose membership is smaller than the membership of the first operand set.

Enumerated types as base sets

You can use an enumerated type as the base set for one or more set variables you may need in a program. In Example 14.3, we use set variables to represent vegetables available at some vegetable market. We will use AllVegs to hold the value of the universal set of vegetables, as per the assignment of statement {1}. Joes and Sams will represent the vegetables available at each of the two vegetable stands. Statements {2} and {3} assign values to these two variables. Inspection of the set values used in each assignment shows that both stands have eight vegetables for sale. As yet, no value(s) has been assigned to Veggies.

TABLE 14.2 Some Set Expressions

Set Expression	Resultant Set Value
['A'..'C'] + ['1'..'3']	['A'..'C', '1'..'3']
[1, 3, 5] + [2, 4, 6]	[1..6]
['A'..'J'] * ['B'..'D', 'H'..'L']	['B'..'D', 'H'..'J']
[1..9] * [3..12]	[3..9]
['A'..'J'] − ['B'..'D', 'H'..'L']	['A'..'E'..'G']
[1..9] − [3..12]	[1, 2]

Example 14.3

```
TYPE
   VegType = (Broccoli, Carrots, Celery, Corn, Cukes, Lettuce,
              Onions, Peas, Potatoes, Squash, Tomatoes, Yams);
   VegSet = SET OF VegType;
VAR
   Joes,      {vegetables carried at Joe's market}
   Sams,      {vegetables carried at Sam's market}
   AllVegs,   {will be initialized to the universal set}
   Veggies:   {used to store information about Joe's and Sam's}
              VegSet;

   AllVegs:= [Broccoli..Yams];
   Joes:= [Carrots..Corn, Lettuce, Peas, Squash..Yams];
   Sams:= [Broccoli..Lettuce, Tomatoes, Yams]
```

Semantics of set operations

Set operations are useful for the implied semantics of the set expressions that they form. Table 14.3 shows some examples of assignment statements to Veggies using the values assigned in Example 14.3. The meaning taken on by Veggies for each assignment statement is shown at the bottom of the table.

Relational operators and set expressions

If two set expressions represent sets of the same type, you can apply one of the six relational operators to compare the memberships of the two expressions. Suppose we have two variables, SetA and SetB, of the same set type. Table 14.4 shows you the meaning and usage of the six relational operators as they apply to the two set expressions SetA and SetB.

The first two expressions, respectively, test for *equality* and *inequality* between SetA and SetB. The second two expressions test whether SetA is a *subset* of SetB and whether SetA is a *proper subset* of SetB. The final two expressions test whether SetA is a *superset* of SetB and whether SetA is a *proper superset* of SetB. The definitions of the terms *subset, proper subset, superset,* and *proper superset* can be inferred from the table.

Examples

Given the values of Joes and Sams as presented in Example 14.3, all of the following expressions are true:

```
{1} [Onions, Potatoes] * (Sams + Joes) = []
{2} Sams <> Joes
```

TABLE 14.3 Assigning Set Values to Veggies

Assignment Statements	Veggie's Value
{1} Veggies:= Joes + Sams;	[Broccoli..Lettuce,Peas,Squash..Yams]
{2} Veggies:= Joes*Sams;	[Carrots..Corn,Lettuce,Tomatoes,Yams]
{3} Veggies:= AllSet − Joes;	[Broccoli,Cukes,Onions,Potatoes]
{4} Veggies:= AllSet − Sams;	[Onions..Squash]
{5} Veggies:= AllSet − Joes − Sams;	[Onions, Potatoes]
{6} Veggies:= Joes − Sams;	[Peas, Squash]
{7} Veggies:= Sams − Joes;	[Broccoli, Cukes]

Meanings

{1} all the vegetables available between the two markets;
{2} the only vegetables available at both markets;
{3} the vegetables not available at Joe's;
{4} the vegetables not available at Sam's;
{5} the vegetables not available at either market;
{6} the vegetables available at Joe's but not at Sam's;
{7} the vegetables available at Sam's but not at Joe's.

TABLE 14.4 Applying the Six Relational Operators on Set Expressions

Expression	True When
SetA = SetB	The set memberships are identically equal
SetA <> SetB	One of the sets has at least one member not in the other set
SetA <= SetB	All of SetA's membership is found in SetB
SetA < SetB	All of SetA's membership is found in SetB and SetB has a larger membership count than SetA
SetA >= SetB	All of SetA's membership contains the membership of SetB
SetA > SetB	All of SetA's membership contains SetB's membership and SetA has a larger membership count than SetB

```
{3} [Carrots, Lettuce, Tomatoes] < Sams
{4} Joes <= AllVegs
{5} Sams + Joes + [Onions, Potatoes] >= AllVegs
{6} AllVegs > Sams + Joes
```

Meanings   The fact that each of the boolean expressions are true means something. The meanings implied by each expression are as follows:

1. Neither onions nor potatoes are found at Sam's or at Joe's.
2. Sam's and Joe's do not stock exactly the same vegetables.
3. Carrots, lettuce, and tomatoes are all stocked at Sam's.
4. Joe's does not have more vegetables than the universal set.
5. The vegetables at Sam's and Joe's in addition to onions and potatoes contain at least all of the same vegetables found in the universal set.

6. There are more kinds of vegetables in the universal set of 12 than there are at Sam's and Joe's combined.

EXERCISES

Test Your Understanding

1. Is the following code possible on all systems?

   ```
   TYPE
      ThousandsSet = SET OF 1000..2000;
   VAR
        TSet: ThousandsSet;
   ```

   Explain your answer.

2. Given three set variables, ASet, BSet and CSet, all of the same type, and the boolean variable ABool, indicate which coded sequences will *always* assign true to ABool:
   (a) CSet:= ASet + BSet;
      ABool:= (CSet < ASet) AND (CSet < BSet);
   (b) CSet:= ASet + BSet;
      ABool:= (CSet >= ASet) AND (CSet >= BSet);
   (c) CSet:= ASet*BSet;
      ABool:= (CSet <= ASet) AND (CSet <= BSet);
   (d) CSet:= ASet*BSet;
      ABool:= (CSet > ASet) AND (CSet > BSet);
   (e) CSet:= ASet - BSet;
      ABool:= (CSet <= ASet);
   (f) CSet:= ASet - BSet;
      ABool:= (CSet <= BSet);
   (g) CSet:= ASet - BSet;
      ABool:= (CSet*BSet = []);

3. Assume that we have the variables ASet and BSet whose universal set is ['0'..'9']. State the implied conditions about the values taken on by the members of ASet and BSet such that the following boolean expressions will evaluate to true:
   (a) (ASet - BSet) = ASet
   (b) (ASet*BSet) = []
   (c) (ASet*BSet) = (ASet + BSet)
   (d) (ASet + ['8'] = BSet) AND (ASet < BSet)
   (e) (ASet < BSet) AND (ASet = ['0'..'6'])
   (f) (BSet*ASet = []) AND (ASet > ['0'..'8'])
   (g) (ASet + BSet = ['0'..'9']) AND (BSet = ['0'..'2','4','5', '7','8'])

   Note that some of these expressions imply one or more conditions about possible members and that other expressions imply specific values are included or excluded from each set's membership.

Practice Your Analysis Skills

4. The following definitions and declarations are given:

   ```
   TYPE
       ColorType = (Red,Orange,Yellow,Green,Blue,Indigo,Violet);
       ColorSet = SET OF ColorType;
   ```

```
VAR
    Palette: ColorType;
```

Write down the membership taken on by `Palette` after the execution of each statement in the sequence:

```
Palette:= [Red..Blue,Violet];
Palette:= Palette - [Yellow..Blue];
Palette:= Palette + [Indigo];
Palette:= Palette + [Red..Yellow];
Palette:= Palette - [Red..Violet];
```

Sharpen Your Implementation Skills

5. **(a)** Write a statement that assigns the universal set to `Palette`.
   (b) What is the characteristic of the set expression that makes it the universal set of `ColorSet`?
   (c) Write a statement that assigns the null set to `Palette`.
   (d) What are two characteristics of the null set value?

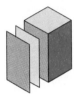

14.2   Some Set-Processing Algorithms

In this section, you will learn three very useful algorithms that require the use of set variables for their application. The case study uses all three algorithms for its solution.

Event accumulation
You can use a set variable to record the occurrence of a set of events in some defined candidate event set over some repetitive processing event. The set variable is used as a cumulative recorder of the events that have occurred. Algorithm 14.1 is a description of this kind of process. You can apply this algorithm, for example, to record the numbers in the subrange `1..100` that were returned with perhaps 50 calls to some RNG process.

Algorithm 14.1

> *{Accumulate events from an initial null set:}*
> *EAccumulator ← []   {accumulator variable initialized to null set}*
> *WHILE more events can occur DO*
> *   get EventValue*
> *   IF EventValue lies in the universal set of EAccumulator THEN*
> *   EAccumulator ← EAccumulator + [EventValue]*
> *{end algorithm}*

The loop invariant can be stated as, "The members of EAccumulator represent the possible events in the predefined universal set that have occurred so far during the processing sequence." Once the sequence to get values for candidate events is finished, the members of EAccumulator represent all those events out of the candidate set that occurred *at least once* during the sequence.

Event deletion
Let us say, instead, that you want to know the numbers over the subrange `1..100` that did not occur with perhaps 500 trials of the RNG. In this case, you would want to use an approach described by Algorithm 14.2.

Algorithm 14.2

> *{Record events that did not occur over a sequence:}*
> *NERecorder ← [{universal set of candidate events}]*
> *WHILE more events can occur DO*
>   *get EventValue*
>   *IF Event Value lies in the universal set of candidate events THEN*
>   *NERecorder ← NERecorder − [EventValue]*
> *{end algorithm}*

We can state the loop invariant for Algorithm 14.2 as, "The members of NERecorder represent the possible events that have *not* occurred so far in the processing sequence." When the loop is exited, the members of NERecorder represent those events that did not occur over the entire sequence of events carried out during the process in which candidate event values were gotten. The variable in this case serves as a *non-event recorder*.

Sets and arrays of booleans

Each algorithm has its analog in one of the two boolean flag-setting algorithms of Chapter 8. Algorithm 14.1 is analogous to the algorithm that initializes the single boolean flag to false, then sets it to true if the sought-for event occurs. Algorithm 14.2 is analogous to the algorithm that initializes the boolean flag to true and then sets it to false if the event occurs.

We can envision a set variable as an abstraction capable of flagging more than one event, that is, an array of boolean variables. When the set variable is initialized to the null set, all the flags that make up the set are effectively initialized to a value of false. When a set variable is initialized to its universal set, all the flags that make up the set are effectively initialized to true. When a one-member set is added to a set variable, the corresponding flag is effectively set to true. Likewise, when a one-member set is subtracted from a set variable, the corresponding flag that represents the event is effectively set to false.

Algorithm 14.1 describes an accumulation process that starts off with a set of flags that are all false. During the loop execution, true values are accumulated as events occur. Algorithm 14.2 initiates the processing with a set of flags whose values are all true. Any event that occurs effectively sets its corresponding flag variable to false.

Process all set members

Once either sequence is finished, the implied flags of the set variable will be used in some other process. Regardless of which algorithm was applied to get a set value, the membership of the set implies flags that are all set to true. One postloop algorithm we can use is given as Algorithm 14.3. You use this algorithm to process all the members present in the set variable SomeSet.

Algorithm 14.3

> *{Process all members in SomeSet:}*
> *FOR CandidateMember ← LowestValue TO HighestValue DO*
>   *IF CandidateMember IN SomeSet THEN*
>   *process CandidateMember*
> *{end algorithm}*

The precondition for this algorithm to be of any use is that SomeSet has been assigned some meaningful set value. The base type for the variable SomeSet is expressed by the subrange LowestValue..HighestValue.

Using the algorithms

The following case study uses the three algorithms we have just presented. Note that the problem requires the completion of Algorithms 14.1 and 14.2 before Algorithm 14.3 can be carried out. Note further that the first two algorithms can be carried out within the body of the same loop, but Algorithm 14.3 must be applied twice using two different loops.

Case Study 14.1

The problem statement

Write a program that displays all those uppercase letters contained in a text file and all those lowercase letters not contained in the file. If we run this program using the text of the file PurpleCow.dat (see Section 9.1), the display will be

```
Uppercase letters present:  B I
Lowercase letters absent:   f g i j k m q x z
```

The main block and required variables

We will need two set variables for this problem, one to accumulate uppercase letters in an initial null set and the other to delete lowercase letters from an initial universal set. The main block statement is then described by the pseudocode

> *Initialize(LowerCaseSet, UpperCaseSet, PurpleCow)*
> *RecordInformation(LowerCaseSet, UpperCaseSet, PurpleCow)*
> *DisplayInformation(LowerCaseSet, UpperCaseSet)*

The procedure Initialize assigns the universal set containing all lowercase characters to the variable LowerCaseSet, assigns the null set to the variable UpperCaseSet, and resets the file variable PurpleCow. The procedure RecordInformation reads in Ch values from the file, deleting any Ch value from the LowerCaseSet, and adding any uppercase value to UpperCaseSet. When all characters from the file have been read in and processed, the procedure DisplayInformation displays the membership values of both sets.

Part of the coded solution to the problem is given in the source code of the program ShowCharacters. We have coded the main block and the procedure Initialize. We still must develop the code for the two procedures RecordInformation and DisplayInformation.

```
PROGRAM ShowCharacters(output,PurpleCow);
   {This program displays all uppercase letters that are found in the
   text file PurpleCow.  Furthermore, it displays all lowercase letters
   not found in the text.}
   TYPE
      LCSetType = SET OF 'a'..'z';
      UCSetType = SET OF 'A'..'Z';
```

```
VAR
  PurpleCow: text;          {the sample text file}
  LowerCaseSet: LCSetType;  {recorder for l.c. nonoccurrences}
  UpperCaseSet: UCSetType;  {recorder for u.c. occurrences}
{*                                                              *}
PROCEDURE Initialize(VAR LowerCaseSet: LCSetType;
           VAR UpperCaseSet: UCSetType; VAR PurpleCow: text);
  {resets PurpleCow, initializes LowerCaseSet to universal set and
   UpperCaseSet to null set}
  BEGIN
    reset(PurpleCow);
    LowerCaseSet:= ['a'..'z'];
    UpperCaseSet:= []
  END;
{*                                                              *}
PROCEDURE RecordInformation(VAR LowerCaseSet: LCSetType;
           VAR UpperCaseSet: UCSetType;  VAR PurpleCow: text);
{character-by-character processing of all the characters in PurpleCow
any uppercase Ch value read in is added to UpperCaseSet
any lowercase Ch value read in is deleted from LowerCaseSet}
BEGIN   END ;
{*                                                              *}
PROCEDURE DisplayInformation(LowerCaseSet: LCSetType;
                                    UpperCaseSet: UCSetType);
  {the membership of LowerCaseSet and UpperCaseSet is displayed}
  BEGIN   END;
{*                                                              *}
BEGIN
    Initialize(LowerCaseSet, UpperCaseSet, PurpleCow);
    RecordInformation(LowerCaseSet, UpperCaseSet, PurpleCow);
    DisplayInformation(LowerCaseSet, UpperCaseSet)
END.
```

Developing
Record-
Information
        Any char value read in from the file is a candidate value to be added to UpperCaseSet or subtracted from LowerCaseSet. Hence in writing Record-Information, we can use the same processing loop that reads in one candidate value per loop pass. Line processing is not necessary for this block, so an <eoln> character can simply be read in as a blank. Thus, only one loop controlled by eof(PurpleCow) is required. The first draft for the pseudocode description of the block is therefore described by

> *WHILE NOT eof(PurpleCow) DO*
>   *read(PurpleCow,Ch)*
>   *IF Ch is a letter THEN*
>   *add it or subtract it from the appropriate set variable*

The decision logic then refines to

$$IF \; Ch \; IN \; ['a'..'z'] \; THEN$$
$$LowerCaseSet \leftarrow LowerCaseSet - [Ch]$$
$$ELSE \; IF \; Ch \; IN \; ['A'..'Z'] \; THEN$$
$$UpperCaseSet \leftarrow UpperCaseSet + [Ch]$$

Source code   Note that multiple occurrences have no effect on the values of the two set variables. Once a first occurrence has been subtracted from LowerCaseSet, further subtractions of the same value will not change the value of LowerCaseSet. We can say the same thing about adding a Ch member to the variable Upper-CaseSet. The code for RecordInformation is as shown.

```
PROCEDURE RecordInformation(VAR LowerCaseSet: LCSetType;
        VAR UpperCaseSet: UCSetType; VAR PurpleCow: text);
  {documentation}
  VAR
    Ch: char;    {value of character read in from PurpleCow}
  BEGIN
    WHILE NOT eof(PurpleCow) DO
      BEGIN
        read(PurpleCow,Ch);
        IF Ch IN ['a'..'z'] THEN
          LowerCaseSet:= LowerCaseSet - [Ch]    {delete a member}
        ELSE IF Ch IN ['A'..'Z'] THEN
          UpperCaseSet:= UpperCaseSet + [Ch]    {add a member}
      END
  END;
```

Developing
Display-
Information   The sequence for DisplayInformation is described by the pseudocode

$$display \; members \; of \; LowerCaseSet$$
$$display \; members \; of \; UpperCaseSet$$

The membership of each set must be displayed using two separate loops, for the defining base types are different. Using Algorithm 14.3, our refinement of the first draft is given as

display explanatory text { 'Uppercase letters present: '}
FOR Ch←'A' TO 'Z' DO
  IF Ch IN UpperCaseSet THEN
    write(Ch)
  writeln
display explanatory text { 'Lowercase letters absent: '}
FOR Ch←'a' TO 'z' DO
  IF Ch IN LowerCaseSet THEN
    write(Ch)
  writeln

Although two separate loops are required, we can use a common loop control variable of type char without ambiguity. From the descriptions, we obtain the code:

```
PROCEDURE DisplayInformation(LowerCaseSet: LCSetType;
                            UpperCaseSet: UCSetType);
  {documentation}
  VAR
    Ch: char;    {loop control variable for both display loops}
    BEGIN
      write('Uppercase letters present:   ');
      FOR Ch:= 'A' TO 'Z' DO
        IF Ch IN UpperCaseSet THEN
          write(Ch);
      writeln;
      write('Lowercase letters absent:    ');
      FOR Ch:= 'a' TO 'z' DO
        IF Ch IN LowerCaseSet THEN
          write(Ch);
      writeln
    END; ◆
```

EXERCISES

Test Your Understanding

1. You have a problem that requires the use of a set variable. If, before loop entry, you initialize the variable to the null set, what purpose is it probably serving?

2. Suppose, instead, you initialize the set variable to the universal set. Would you expect a set addition operation or a set subtraction operation to be a part of the loop's body? Explain.

3. We can propose an algorithm to "accumulate" non-events with the description:

> *EAccumulator ← []*
> *WHILE events are possible DO*
> *   get event value*
> *   EAccumulator ← EAccumulator + [event value]*
> *EAccumulator ← [{universal set}] − EAccumulator*

Will this description produce the desired result after the final assingment statement's execution? If it does, what is wrong with the algorithm? (*Hint:* Consider the semantics.)

Practice Your Analysis Skills

4. Given the following,

```
TYPE
  CityType = (NilCity,Bos,NYC,Phil,Cleve,Atl,Rchmnd,Chi,StL,Minn,KC,Dal,SF);
  CitySet = SET OF CityType;
VAR
  City: CityType;
  Present,
  Missing: CitySet;
```

indicate the display as a result of the sequences:

(a)
```
Present:= [];
FOR City:= Bos TO Cleve DO
  Present:= Present + [City];
Present:= Present + [Chi] + [Minn];
Missing:= [Bos..SF];
Missing:= Missing - Present;

FOR City:= Bos TO SF DO
  IF City IN Present THEN
    write(ord(City):5);
writeln;
FOR City:= Bos TO SF DO
  IF City IN Missing THEN
    write(ord(City):5);
writeln;
```

(b)
```
Missing:= [Bos..SF];
Missing:= Missing - [Dal] - [KC];
FOR City:= SF DOWNTO Chi DO
  Missing:= Missing - City;

FOR City:= Bos TO SF DO
  IF City IN Missing THEN
    write(ord(City):5);
writeln;
```

(c)
```
Present:= [];
FOR City:= Bos TO SF DO
  IF ord(City) MOD 3 = 0 THEN
    Present:= Present + City;
FOR City:= Phil TO Minn DO
  Present:= Present + [City];

FOR City:= Bos TO SF DO
  IF NOT (City IN Present) THEN
    write(ord(City):5);
writeln;
```

5. Each FOR loop in Exercise 4 can be classified as a loop that (a) accumulates members in a set, (b) deletes members from a set, or (c) processes all members in a set. Categorize the actions of each of the FOR loops in Exercise 4.

14.3 Using Set Values and Boolean Expressions

In this section, we solve some problems using boolean expressions formed from set expressions. As you will see, the solution to a problem of this type often depends upon finding the one relational operator that is the key to solving the whole problem.

How to "think sets"

As you saw from the previous section, we can use a set variable to accumulate members in an initial empty set or to delete members from an initial universal set. The memberships of either kind of set may be examined at various points during the course of a program run. On some occasions, the value of one of these sets may be compared with the value of some *test set* (e.g., the set of alphabetic characters). The value for the test set is usually initialized before the accumulation or deletion process starts. There are also problems that can be solved when the results found in two sets that accumulate or delete events are logically combined to represent a significant processing event.

The use of set expressions lends an aura of elegance to the solution logic. Very often the heart of the solution to a problem lies in finding the *single* suitable set operation that solves the problem. Once the key operation is determined, the problem of logically combining the sets has been solved.

Example Problem 14.2

The problem statement

Let us write a quick-and-dirty spell checker that reads a "word" and then determines whether the word has at least one vowel in it. If it does not, further processing (e.g., immediate display, storage in a file containing all the misspelled words, storage as an element in an array containing all the misspelled words) on the word is to be done. We can use a get-then-check sequence whose pseudocode is given as

> *GetAWord(Word, ChSet, SomeFile)*
> *IF VowelMissing(VowelSet, ChSet) THEN*
> *Process(Word)*

`SomeFile` is a text file from which words are read in, `VowelSet` is the value of an initialized test set (all the vowel characters), and the elements of `ChSet` represent the characters found in the variable `Word`. `VowelMissing` will then be the (elegantly coded) `boolean` function that, if it returns the value of `true`, indicates that the variable `Word` does not have a vowel in it. Let us code the function, `VowelMissing`, leaving the coding of `GetAWord` as Exercise 2 at the end of this section.

The solution

As a precondition for `GetAWord` and `VowelMissing` to work, we have assumed that the following code has been executed:

```
TYPE
   ChSetType = SET OF char;
VAR
   WordSet, VowelSet: ChSetType;
{initializing VowelSet:}
VowelSet:= ['A', 'E', 'I', 'O', 'U', 'a', 'e', 'i', 'o', 'u'];
```

What operations(s) should we use with `VowelSet`, the test set, and `WordSet` to return the representative value to the `boolean` function? We can use the intersection of `VowelSet` and `WordSet`. If the value of the resultant set is the null set, then it is true that WordSet contains no vowels. Hence, we obtain the code for the one-line function VowelMissing as shown.

```
FUNCTION VowelMissing(VowelSet, WordSet: ChSetType): boolean;
  {returns true if WordSet has no vowels in it}
  BEGIN
    VowelMissing:= (VowelSet*WordSet = [])
  END;  ◆
```

Example Problem 14.3

The problem statement

Let us, instead, write a function NoConsonants that returns the value true if the word read in (and, hence, membership letters accumulated in WordSet) has no consonants in it. A local variable ConSet can serve as a set for comparison with WordSet. If VowelSet has been initialized, the value of ConSet is assigned using *ConSet ← [all letters] − VowelSet*. If the intersection of ConSet and WordSet returns the null set, we know that no consonants were read into Word. The code for NoConsonants is then

```
FUNCTION NoConsonants(VowelSet, WordSet: ChSetType): boolean;
  {returns true if WordSet has no consonants in it}
  VAR
    ConSet: ChSetType;   {used to form the test set of consonants}
  BEGIN
    ConSet:= ['a'..'z', 'A'..'Z'] - VowelSet;
    NoConsonants:= (ConSet*WordSet = [])
  END;  ◆
```

Example Problem 14.4

The problem statement

The boolean expressions representing subset or superset relationships can be used with excellent results for certain problems. Suppose, for example, there are 15 officers in Fly-By-Night Enterprises. The officers meet at least twice a week, although often not all of them can attend. If, however, a vote is to be taken, a "quorum" is necessary. The by-laws of Fly-By-Night Enterprises define a quorum as

(a) more than half the officers are present and
(b) either (1) the president and secretary are in attendance or
(2) the president and the treasurer are in attendance or
(3) the senior vice-president, the secretary, and the treasurer are in attendance

Our problem is to write a function Quorum, to determine given an attendance list, whether a vote can be taken at one of the officers' meetings.

The function we want to write is described in the context of the pseudocode

> GetAttendeesAndCount({attendance list}, Attendees, TotalPresent)
> IF Quorum(Attendees, TotalPresent) THEN
>   take votes

`Attendees` is a set variable whose membership represents the titles of the officers at the meeting and `TotalPresent` is an `integer` variable whose value represents the head count of all those officers attending the meeting. The `boolean` function `Quorum` returns `true` if the meeting makes up a quorum according to the by-laws of the company.

Structure chart

The structure chart for the given sequence is shown in Figure 14.2. The procedure `GetAttendeesAndCount` assigns values to the two set variables, `Attendees` and `TotalPresent`, using the meeting's attendance list. We leave the coding of this block as Exercise 3 at the end of the section.

Required variables

The variables required for the part of the problem we are presently solving are given in the following fragment:

```
TYPE
  OfficerType = (Pres, Secty, Treas, SenVP, VPSales, VPMarketing
                 VPProductDevelopment, VPPersonnel, VPPlant, PlantMgr);
  SetOfAttendees = SET OF OfficerType;
VAR
  Attendees: SetOfAttendees;     {set describing ranking officers present}
  TotalPresent: integer;         {head count of officers present}
```

The stub for the boolean function `Quorum`, consistent with the sequence we have already drafted and with included documentation, is given as follows:

```
FUNCTION Quorum(Attendees: SetOfAttendees;
                          TotalPresent: integer): boolean;
  {in: Attendees--set representing officers at meeting
   in: TotalPresent--head count of officers in attendance
   out: true is assigned to Quorum if
                   (put in by-laws as shown above)}
  BEGIN    END;
```

FIGURE 14.2 Structure chart for Example Problem 14.2.

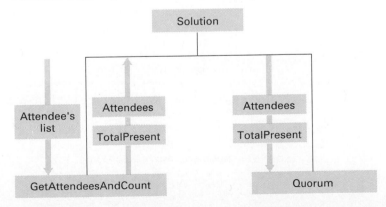

The problem statement tells us what operations need to be coded. If more than half the officers are present, the value of the boolean expression Total-Present > TotalOfficers DIV 2) must be true. This expression's value is used as part of the logic of the function Quorum. TotalOfficers is a global constant.

Also, the three comparison sets [Pres, Secty], [Pres, Treas], and [SenVP, Secty, Treas] must satisfy some set relationship with Attendees. With a little bit of thought, we realize that the "one-liner" relationship we seek is that of a subset. If, for example, the coded expression ([Pres, Treas] < Attendees) is true, we have the fact that the President and the Treasurer were two of the attendees at the meeting.

Now that we know the boolean relationships we need, we can code the function's statement:

```
BEGIN
   Quorum:= (TotalPresent > TotalOfficers DIV 2) AND
            ( ([Pres, Secty] < Attendees)  OR
              ([Pres, Treas] < Attendees) OR
              ([SenVP, Secty, Treas] < Attendees) )
END;  ◆
```

EXERCISES

1. Let us define the following:

```
TYPE
   IntSet = SET OF 0..9;
VAR
   SetA, SetB: IntSet;
   Int: integer;
```

Using these definitions, indicate the display for each of the following fragments of code:

(a) SetA:= [2, 4, 6];   SetB:= [1, 3, 5];
```
IF SetA * SetB = [] THEN
   writeln('Nothing in common')
ELSE
   writeln('The sets overlap.');
```

(b) SetA:= [1..4];   SetB:= [2..3];
```
IF SetA > SetB THEN
   writeln('A contains B')
ELSE
   writeln('there is a different relationship');
```

(c) SetA:= [1, 5, 9];   SetB:= [2, 4, 8];
```
IF SetA + SetB > [1..6] THEN
   write('All members accounted for')
ELSE
   FOR Int:= 1 TO 6 DO
```

```
        IF NOT(Int IN (SetA + SetB)) THEN
            write(Int:4,' ');
    writeln;
```

2. Write the statement for the procedure GetAWord, as used in Example Problem 14.2. The computer is to assign a value to Word from a nonblank sequence of characters read in from SomeFile. Once a blank is read in or < eoln > identified, Word and ChSet will have taken on the values passed out of the block.

3. Write the statement for GetAttendeesAndCount. The main loop for this block can be described by

> *initialize variables*
> *keyin Code*
> *WHILE Code <> 0 DO*
> > *Officer ← OffcerName(Code)*
> > *execute other statements*
> > *keyin Code*

The coded values represent the officer's particular title. Thus, a President is coded as 1, a Secretary as 2, a Treasurer as 3, etc. You will need to write a function OffcerName using the value of Code.

4. All the officers in Fly-By-Night Enterprises except for the Plant Managers are unique. Sometimes, a nonmember posing as an officer will try to crash the meeting. Recode GetAttendeesAndCount such that if more than one of any given officer except for Plant Manager is read in, the set returned to Attendees is the null set, indicating an invalid Attendees list.

5. Dr. Jones is an old country doctor with just 5 recommendations to his patients: (0) go home—you are hale and hearty, (1) take aspirin, (2) take pain killer, (3) take virus killer, and (4) go to the hospital. He also recognizes only 4 classes of symptoms: sniffles, fever, muscleache, and headache. His recommendations are predictable: with 3 or more symptoms, the patient must go to the hospital, with a headache and backache, the patient takes the pain killer, with sniffles and fever, the patient takes the virus killer, and with all other symptoms, the patient takes aspirin. With none of these symptoms, the patient is declared "hale and hearty." Write a function Recommendation whose header looks like

```
    FUNCTION Recommendation(Symptoms: SickSet): integer;
```

where the value returned represents the number of the recommendation and SickSet describes the symptoms of type SympType defined as

```
    SympType = (Sniffles, Fever, Headache, Muscleache);
```

6. Write a procedure GetSymptoms to read in a value for Symptoms. The computer reads in nonblank char values on a line of input to assign a membership to the variable Symptoms. The four letters S, F, H, and M represent one of the symptoms. Any other characters read in from the input line are simply ignored. For example, a typical interaction, where the value given to Symptoms is [Sniffles,Headache] will be

```
    Enter symptoms (S, F, H, M): S H<eoln>
```

7. Write the procedure ShowSymptoms that displays the membership list of Symptoms. For example, the call ShowSymptoms([Headache, Sniffles]) would result in the display

sniffles headache

8. Detroit City auto dealers can supply their customers with cars of any color from the following: Red, Green, Canary, Blue, Silver, Black, and Pink. Customers also know that cars can have the following colors: Orange, Yellow, Violet, White, and Grey. If it is in stock, a customer can order his or her car to have either a single color or two colors. Set up the data types and write the boolean function Available whose header looks like FUNCTION Available(Choice, InStock: ColorSet): boolean;, where Choice is the choice of colors (one or two) the customer wants for his or her dream car, and InStock represents the colors Detroit City dealers have in stock.

9. Write the code to assign values to the two input parameters of the function Available. One of the procedures should read in values, and the other procedure should assign a fixed value to a set variable.

14.4 A Portable String Unit

We have been using string variables since Chapter 3, downplaying the fact that each dialect implements strings differently. Virtually all dialects include strings as an ADT, but the operations and identifiers differ from dialect to dialect. We are going to code the ADT unit StringADT as a portable abstraction, that is, it will be compatible with every dialect of Pascal.

The unit's appearance

A string is known by its character sequence and its length. We define the data type StringADT as a record variable with two fields: (1) an array of characters where the subscripting implies a sequence, and (2) an integer whose value represents the string's length. Because we are using an array, we also need to define the subrange 1..MaxLength, where MaxLength defines the maximum number of characters a StringADT variable can take on.

Primitive constructors

We include the following primitive constructors in the ADT unit:

NullString: returns a string with no characters in it.

ConvertSysString: changes a given system's string to the equivalent string of type StringADT.

ReadString: reads in a string value from a specified file up to but not including a specified sentinel character.

ReadlnString: reads in a string value from a line of a specified file.

We include NullString as an operation so the client can accumulate char values into an initial null string variable. The procedure call ConvertSysString('Pascal', AName) returns the value 'Pascal' to AName, a variable of type StringADT. We require this operation to set an abstract string variable to a string constant. This operation is the only one that differs from one dialect to the next. Because character strings are usually read from files (including the *input* file), we are treating `ReadString` and `ReadlnString` as primitive constructors.

We must include the following two functions as primitive selectors:

`ACh`: returns the value of the client-specified *N* th character in the specified string.

`StrLength`: returns the length of the specified string.

No other primitive selectors are necessary, but the unit also requires the selector operations:

`WriteString`: writes the value of the string into the specified file.

`WriteLnString`: writes the value of the string into the specified file and then writes <eoln> into the file.

Note that one of the "specified" files can be the standard `output` file. We are including these two selector operations in the unit because they are so widely used by client programs.

One more useful selector, `StartPos`, is described by

`StartPos`: returns the starting position of a specified substring in a specified operand string.

A client may want to compare two string values for a search operation or for alphabetizing. Thus, we include the following predicate operations:

`StrEqual`: returns `true` if the operand strings have the same characters and length.

`StrLessThan`: returns `true` if the first string operand is alphabetically before the second string operand.

The remaining constructor operations that a client might find useful are as follows:

`ChConcat`: concatenates, or links, a single character onto the input/output string variable.

`StrConcat`: concatenates two operand strings into an output string variable.

`StrExtract`: copies a string of a specified length from a specified beginning position of an operand string into an output string variable.

`StrRemove`: removes a specified number of characters starting at a specified position from the input/output string variable.

`StrInsert`: inserts a given operand string into a specified position of the input/output string variable.

The interface section of the string unit follows. Note how our documentation includes information about exception handling. We will code the implementation details for the unit in Section 14.6 of this chapter.

```
{               INTERFACE PART OF STRING ADT                        }
{The abstraction is a portable unit of type StringADT.  Use type
StringADT to carry out all operations.  Only use SysString for the

CONST
  MaxLength = 80;       {maximum allowable length of string}
TYPE
  SysString = STRING [MaxLength]; {or "string type" for your system}
  StringADT = RECORD
    Chars: ARRAY[1..MaxLength] OF char;
    Len: 0..MaxLength
   END;
{*                        THE OPERATIONS                           *}
PROCEDURE NullString(VAR OutStr: StringADT);                 FORWARD;
   {assigns a string with no characters in it}
{*                                                                 *}
PROCEDURE ConvertSysString(StrValue: SysString;
                                VAR OutStr: StringADT);     FORWARD;
   {assigns the value of StrValue to the parameter OutStr}
{*                                                                 *}
PROCEDURE ReadString(Sentinel: char; VAR OutStr: StringADT;
                                VAR InFile: text);          FORWARD;
   {assigns the characters read in from Infile up to but not including the
   Sentinel char value into OutStr. If <eoln> occurs, the characters up
   to, but not including <eoln> are assigned and further reading ends.}
{*                                                                 *}
PROCEDURE ReadlnString(VAR OutStr: StringADT; VAR InFile: text);
                                                            FORWARD;
   {assigns the characters read in from a line of InFile into OutStr. The
   line is then cleared.}
{*                                                                 *}
PROCEDURE WriteString(InStr: StringADT: VAR OutFile: text);   FORWARD;
   {writes the characters of InStr to OutFile}
{*                                                                 *}
PROCEDURE WritelnString(InStr: StringADT; VAR OutFile: text);   FORWARD;
   {writes characters of InStr to OutFile as a line of text}
{*                                                                 *}
FUNCTION StrLength(InStr: StringADT): integer;               FORWARD;
   {returns the length of InStr}
{*                                                                 *}
FUNCTION ACh(InStr: StringADT; Position: integer): char;     FORWARD
   {returns the value of the Position_th char of InStr. The null
   character chr(0) is returned if Position exceeds InStr's length}
{*                                                                 *}
FUNCTION StrEqual(InStr1, InStr2: StringADT): boolean;       FORWARD;
```

        {returns true if InStr1 and InStr2 are equal to each other}
{*   *}
    FUNCTION StrLessThan(InStr1, InStr2: StringADT): boolean;   FORWARD;
        {returns true if InStr1 is alphabetically before InStr2. This
        function is case-insensitive, but it can only return meaningful
        results if both strings contain only alphabetic characters.}
{*   *}
    PROCEDURE ChConcat(Ch: char; VAR InOutStr: StringADT);   FORWARD;
        {concatenates Ch onto InOutStr. If InOutStr will be too long, it is
        returned unchanged.}
{*   *}
    PROCEDURE StrConcat(InStr1, InStr2, StringADT; VAR OutStr: StringADT);
                                                                     FORWARD;

        {assigns the concatenation of InStr1 and InStr2 to OutStr. If the
        length of the resultant string is greater than MaxLength, the
        remaining characters in InStr are not concatenated}
{*   *}
    PROCEDURE StrExtract(InStr: StringADT; Start, TotalChs: integer;
                                        VAR OutStr: StringADT);   FORWARD;
        {assigns a substring of length TotalChs extracted from InStr
        beginning with the Start_th character to OutStr. If Start is greater
        than InStr's length, a null string is returned. If InStr has an
        insufficient number of characters, all characters beginning at the
        Start_th position are returned, and the length of OutStr is less than
        TotalChs.}
{*   *}
    PROCEDURE StrRemove(Start, TotalChs: integer; VAR InOutStr: StringADT);
                                                                     FORWARD;

        {TotalChs characters are removed from InOutStr beginning with the
        Start_th character. If Start is greater than the initial length of
        InOutStr, InOutStr is returned unchanged. If InOutStr contains an
        insufficient number of characters, it is returned with characters
        truncated from the Start_th position.}
{*   *}
    PROCEDURE StrInsert(InStr: StringADT; Start: integer;
                                        VAR InOutStr: StringADT);   FORWARD;
        {Inserts InStr into InOutStr at the Start_th character position. If
        Start exceeds the length of InOutStr, InStr is simply concatenated.
        If the resultant string will be too long, InOutStr is truncated at
        MaxLength.}
{*   *}
    FUNCTION StartPos(SubStr, SearchStr: StringADT): integer;   FORWARD;
        {returns the character position of the first occurrence of SubStr in
        SearchStr. If SubStr is not found in SearchStr, 0 is returned}
{*   *}

Examples of the Operations

Let us show how each operation might be applied. If we assume that the variables `String1` and `String2` of type `StringADT` have been declared, we have

I.

```
NullString(String1);
ConvertSysString('@@@@@@@@@@', String2);
WritelnString(String2, output);
WritelnString(String1, output);
ChConcat('A', String1);
WritelnString(String1, output);
WritelnString(String2, output);
```

The sequence of I. results in the display:

```
@@@@@@@@@@

A
@@@@@@@@@@
```

The blank line is due to a `writeln` display of the null string.

II. The {a} coded sequence applied to the {b} sample input produces the {c} results:

```
{a}  ReadString(' ', String1, input);
     ReadlnString(String2, input);
{b}  The quick brown fox jumps.<eoln>
{c}  String1↔'The'
     String2↔'quick brown fox jumps.')
```

III. Given the preceding `String1`'s and `String2`'s values, the {a} operation achieves the {b} result:

```
{a}  StrConcat(String1, String2, String1);
{b}  String1↔'The quick brown fox jumps.'
```

IV. Given `String1`'s value, the effect of the {a} statement is the {b} result:

```
{a}  StrRemove(4, 5, String1);
{b}  String1↔'The brown fox jumps.'
```

V. Given `String1`'s value, the {a} sequence gives the {b} result:

{a} ConvertSysString('quick ', String2);
     StrInsert(String2, 5, String1);

{b} String1↔'The quick brown fox jumps.'

VI.   Then, we can assign the value 'fox' to String2 using

StrExtract(String1, 17, 3, String2);

VII. The value 17 is returned to Int with the function call

Int:= StartPos(String2, String1);

VIII. The value returned to Ch will be 'f' with the function call

Ch:= ACh(String1, 17);

IX.   The integer value of 26 is displayed using

writeln(StrLength(String1):1);

X.   A display results with the execution of

IF NOT StrEqual(String1, String2) THEN
    writeln('The strings are not equal.');

XI.   Finally, we also get a display with the following:

IF StrLessThan(String2, String1) THEN
    writeln('String2 is alphabetically before String.');

EXERCISES

Test Your Understanding

1. Which parts of StringADT depend upon the dialect being used? Name the identifiers associated with these parts.

2. Categorize each of the constructors of StringADT as (a) primitive, (b) one that changes the value of a string variable, and (c) one that assigns a value to an unassigned variable using other string expressions.

3. Why was it unnecessary to write the predicate function StrGreaterThan?

Practice Your Analysis Skills

4. Suppose you have the variable Strings, an array capable of storing 5 elements of type StringADT.
   (a) Write the named definition for this variable type.
   (b) How many characters of memory are used for the array Strings?
   (c) Write down the code for the initial string assignments

String[1] ← 'John Doe and String[2] ← 'Richard Roe'

(d) Given the assignments of Part (c), what will be the effect of the following sequence (indicate the values of any elements that were changed by the operation):

```
StrExtract(Strings[1], 1, 5, Strings[3]);
StrExtract(Strings[2], 9, 3, Strings[4]);
StrConcat(Strings[3], Strings[4], Strings[5]);
StrRemove(6, 3, Strings[1]);
StrInsert(Strings[1], 1, Strings[2]);
StrRemove(6, 8, Strings[2]);
IF StrEqual(Strings[2], Strings[5]) THEN
   writeln('The results are as expected.');
```

5. **(a)** What value will be returned to ACh if the Null string is the operand String?

   (b) What will AString 's appearance be after the following sequence is executed:

```
NullString(AString);
FOR Count:= 1 TO 15 DO
   ChConcat('*', AString);
```

   (c) Given the value of AString for part (b), how will the machine respond to the sequence

```
write('{');
WriteString(AString, output);
writeln('}');
```

6. Given the variable Strings of Exercise 4, another variable AString of type StringADT, and the variable Pos of type integer, indicate the result of the following sequence of operations:

```
ConvertSysString('"The time has come,"', Strings[1]);
ConvertSysString('the carpenter said,', Strings[2]);
StrConcat(String[1], String[2], AString);
WritelnString(AString, output);
ConvertSysString('carpenter', Strings[3]);
Pos:= StartPos(String[3], AString);
IF Pos <> 0 THEN
   StrRemove(Pos, StrLength(String[3]), AString);
WritelnString(AString, output);
ConvertSysString('walrus', Strings[4]);
StrInsert(Strings[4],Pos, AString);
WritelnString(AString, output);
```

Sharpen Your Implementation Skills

7. Write a procedure MakeSeparator that writes a separator line in a specified file. The first character should be "{" and the last character should be "}". The 68 characters between the two delimiters consist of the character that is a parameter of the procedure call. For example, the call MakeSeparator('@', output); will result in the line display

{@@}

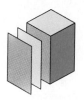

14.5 Case Study: Preparing an Acceptance Card

In this section, we will code a client program for StringADT. Note that you can use the operations that belong to your system's implementation of strings to solve the same problem.

CASE STUDY 14.2

The problem statement

Dancer D. Dancer, that social butterfly with the flying feet, wants you to write a program that displays centered acceptance/regret cards for the dances to which he is invited. He is to enter his text, and the machine displays a card with centered text. The card should have borders such that it appears to be 14 lines long and 40 spaces wide. As a sample run of the program, we have

```
Dancer D. Dancer
accepts with pleasure
your kind invitation to attend
the annual gala dance
at
the Crystal Cotillion Lounge
on
December 30, 1991
@@@@@
```

```
 ----------------------------------------
|                                        |
|                                        |
|            Dancer D. Dancer            |
|         accepts with pleasure          |
|     your kind invitation to attend     |
|          the annual gala dance         |
|                   at                   |
|       the Crystal Cotillion Lounge     |
|                   on                   |
|           December 30, 1991            |
|                                        |
|                                        |
|                                        |
 ----------------------------------------
```

Initial draft and stub

Dancer is to "cut along the dotted lines" once the machine has displayed the card. We can readily describe the main block sequence with the pseudocode

partial fill-in TotalLines of the array TextLines
skip 5 lines {i.e. 5 "writeln" statements}

$$PrepareCard(TextLines, TotalLines, CardLines)$$
$$DisplayCard(CardLines)$$

TextLines is an array of strings containing the text of the card. Each element in the array contains a line of text. TotalLines is the total number of lines of text, and CardLines holds exactly 14 strings that contain the actual appearance of each line of the card. From this description, we obtain the stub program that follows:

```
PROGRAM MakeCard(input, output);
  {reads up to 10 lines of text and echoes them, centered between the
  borders}
  CONST
    Blanks      =     '|                                        |';
    Borders     =     '------------------------------------------';
    CLines = 14;       {lines on entire card, not including borders}
    LineLength = 40;  {length of card, not including border chars}
    MaxLines = 10;    {maximum number of text lines}
  TYPE
    {INSERT STRING ADT DEFINITIONS HERE}
    LinesArray = ARRAY[1..MaxLines] OF StringADT;
  VAR
    TextLines,    {contains nonblank lines of text to be displayed}
    CardLines:    {contains all 14 lines of card to be displayed}
              LinesArray;
    TotalLines: integer;   {total number of nonblank lines in card}
{*                                                                    *}
{              INSERT THE STRING ADT OPERATIONS HERE                  }
{*                                                                    *}
PROCEDURE GetText(VAR TextLines: LinesArray;
                              VAR TotalLines: integer);
  {fills in TextLines of nonblank text from keyboard input; assigns
  value to TotalLines indicating number of "nonblank" lines to be
  displayed}
  BEGIN    END;
{*                                                                    *}
PROCEDURE PrepareCard(TextLines: LinesArray; TotalLines: integer;
                              VAR CardLines: LinesArray);
  {prepares 14-lines card for display into the variable CardLines,
  using the values assigned to the TotalLines elements of TextLines}
  BEGIN    END;
{*                                                                    *}
PROCEDURE DisplayCard(CardLines: LinesArray)
  {displays the card, with all lines centered}
  BEGIN    END;
{*                                                                    *}
  BEGIN
    GetText(TextLines, TotalLines);
```

```
      writeln; writeln; writeln; writeln; writeln;
      PrepareCard(TextLines, TotalLines, CardLines);
      DisplayCard(CardLines)
   END.
```

Coding
GetText
In GetText, a local variable is necessary to hold a value for the sentinel string. We can then apply a partial fill-in algorithm on the array TextLines, where values are assigned to the elements using ReadlnString to get the source code as shown.

```
PROCEDURE GetText(VAR TextLines: LinesArray; VAR TotalLines: integer);
   {documentation}
   VAR
      Sentinel,          {holds the value of the "sentinel line"}
      Temp: StringADT;   {candidate for array element}
   BEGIN
      ConvertSysString('@@@@@', Sentinel);
      TotalLines:= 0;
      ReadlnString(Temp, input);
      WHILE NOT(TotalLines = MaxLines)AND NOT StrEqual(Temp, Sentinel) DO
         BEGIN
            TotalLines:= TotalLines + 1;
            TextLines[TotalLines]:= Temp;
            ReadlnString(Temp)
         END
   END;
```

Coding
DisplayCard
Borders should be displayed above and below the card lines. The card lines themselves are displayed using WritelnString for each line. We then arrive at the following code for the procedure DisplayCard:

```
PROCEDURE DisplayCard(Lines: LinesArray);
   {line-by-line display of CardLines lines in the card}
   VAR
      LineNo: 1..CLines;   {array index value for Lines}
   BEGIN
      writeln(output, Border);
      FOR LineNo:= 1 TO CLines DO
         WritelnString(Lines[LineNo], output);
      writeln(output, Border)
   END;
```

Developing
PrepareCard
The pseudocode for PrepareCard is given as follows:

> *assign lines of blanks to upper part of card*
> *center and assign lines to text part of card*
> *assign remaining blanks to lower part of card*

We can refine the first action in the initial description with

$$ConvertSysString(Blanks, BlanksString)$$
$$UpperBlankLines \leftarrow BlankLineCount(TotalLines)$$
$$FOR\ LineNo \leftarrow 1\ TO\ UpperBlankLines$$
$$CardLines[LineNo] \leftarrow BlanksString$$

The local variable `BlanksString` is of type `StringADT`, whose value is the `StringADT` equivalent to the global string constant `Blanks`. `BlankLineCount` represents a call to a function that returns the number of blank lines to be displayed in the upper part of the card. `LineNo` is a local variable used to assign elements to the variable `CardLines`.

We can refine the sequence to center the lines of text using the pseudocode

$$NoTextLines \leftarrow 0$$
$$FOR\ LineNo \leftarrow UpperBlankLines+1\ TO\ UpperBlankLines+TotalLines\ DO$$
$$NoTextLine \leftarrow NoTextLine + 1$$
$$CenterALine(TextLines[NoTextLine], CardLines[LineNo])$$
$$NoTextLine \leftarrow NoTextLine + 1$$

`CenterALine` is a procedure that "shapes" a given text line so that it is centered with borders (the char value ' | ').

Finally, the refinement of the last action in the initial description is given by the pseudocode

$$FOR\ LineNo \leftarrow UpperBlankLines+TotalLines+1\ TO\ CLines\ DO$$
$$CardLines[LineNo] \leftarrow BlanksString$$

Structure chart

We will present the source code for `PrepareCard` along with the code for the function `BlankLineCount` and the procedure `CenterALine` once we have developed the latter two blocks. The complete structure chart that includes all blocks to be developed from the `PrepareCard` block is shown as Figure 14.3.

Developing
`BlankLine-`
`Count`

Half of the `CLines` that are not actual text should be displayed above the lines of text as "blank lines," and the other half should be displayed below the lines of text as "blank lines." If there is an odd number of blank lines to display, the upper part of the card gets the extra blank line. The pseudocode for `BlankLineCount` is, therefore, described by

$$BLines \leftarrow (CLines - TotalLines)\ DIV\ 2$$
$$IF\ odd(CLines - TotalLines)\ THEN$$
$$BlankLineCount \leftarrow BLines + 1$$
$$ELSE$$
$$BlankLineCount \leftarrow BLines$$

The expression *(CLines - TotalLines)* represents the total number of blank lines to be displayed. The standard function odd returns the value of true for the given integer argument. The decision statement, therefore, handles the setting of the extra blank line to the upper part of the card.

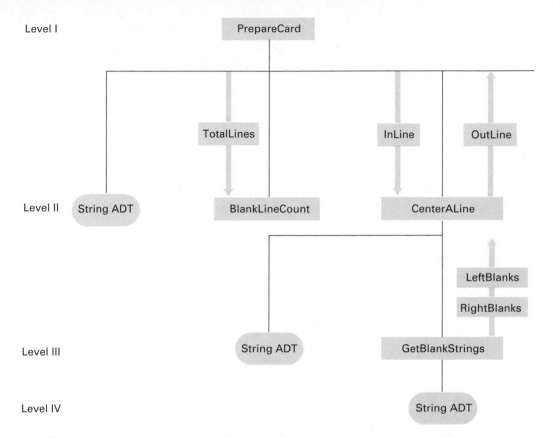

Level I — PrepareCard

TotalLines — InLine — OutLine

Level II — String ADT — BlankLineCount — CenterALine

LeftBlanks — RightBlanks

Level III — String ADT — GetBlankStrings

Level IV — String ADT

FIGURE 14.3 Structure chart for the procedure PrepareCard.

Developing
CenterALine

The procedure header for CenterALine is coded as PROCEDURE CenterALine(InLine: StringADT; VAR OutLine: StringADT);, where TextLines[NoTextLine] is copied into InLine, and CardLines[LineNo] has OutLine as its alias.

Our first pseudocode draft for the statement of CenterALine is described by

> *OutLine ← '|'*
> *OutLine ← OutLine + string of left-side blanks*
> *OutLine ← OutLine + InLine*
> *OutLine ← OutLine + string of right-side blanks*
> *OutLine ← OutLine + '|'*

where, using the unit, the first, third, and fifth actions code to

> *ConvertSysString('|', OutLine)*
> *StrConcat(OutLine, InLine, OutLine)*
> *ChConcat('|', OutLine)*

The second and fourth actions can be coded using

$$StrConcat(OutLine,\ LBlanks,\ OutLine);$$
$$StrConcat(OutLine,\ RBlanks,\ OutLine);$$

LBlanks and RBlanks represent local string variables consisting solely of blank characters.

The number of blank characters in each of these strings depends upon the number of characters in InLine. We thus abstract the procedure call Get-BlankStrings(StrLength(InLine), LBlanks, RBlanks). CenterA-Line first calls this procedure to get values for LBlanks and RBlanks before starting the concatenation operations.

Drafting the code for GetBlank-Strings

The header for GetBlankStrings is coded as

```
PROCEDURE GetBlankStrings(TotalChars: integer;
                          VAR LBlanks, RBlanks: StringADT);
```

If there is an odd number of blanks, the variable LBlanks may have one more blank in it than RBlanks. The logic for determining the number of blank characters is similar to that used in developing BlankLineCount. The pseudocode for this block is readily given as

$$TotalRightBlanks \leftarrow (LineLength\ -\ TotalChars)\ DIV\ 2$$
$$NullString(RBlanks)$$
$$FOR\ BlankCount \leftarrow 1\ TO\ TotalRightBlanks\ DO$$
$$\quad ChConcat('\ ',\ RBlanks)$$
$$LBlanks \leftarrow RBlanks$$
$$IF\ odd(LineLength\ -\ TotalChars)\ THEN$$
$$\quad ChConcat\ ('\ ',\ LBlanks)$$

RBlanks is formed by concatenating TotalRightsBlanks blank characters onto the initial null string value. The variables TotalRightBlanks and BlankCount are local variables of type integer.

Source code for PrepareCard

Now that we have described the block statement for PrepareCard as well as the code for all its auxiliary procedures, we can present the source code that makes up the remainder of the text in this section.

```
{*                                                                    *}
FUNCTION BlankLineCount(TotalLines: integer): integer;
  {returns number of blank upper lines using value of TotalLines that
  represents the number of nonblank lines to be displayed}
  VAR
    BLines: integer;     {candidate variable for UpperBlankLines}
  BEGIN
    BLines:= (CLines - TotalLines) DIV 2;
    IF odd(CLines - TotalLines) THEN
      BlankLineCount:= BLines + 1
```

```
     ELSE
        BlankLineCount:= BLines
END;
{+                                                                          +}
PROCEDURE GetBlankStrings(TotalChars: integer;
                          VAR LBlanks, RBlanks: StringADT);
   {uses the value of TotalChars, representing the number of nonblank
   characters for display to assign values to LBlanks and RBlanks,
   strings consisting solely of blank characters to be displayed on
   either side of the nonblank text}
   VAR
      TotalRightBlanks,    {number of right-side blanks on text line}
      BlankCount:          {loop counter for char concatenating blanks}
                           integer;
   BEGIN
      TotalRightBlanks:= (LineLength - TotalChars) DIV 2;
      NullString(RBlanks);
      FOR BlankCount:= 1 TO TotalRightBlanks DO
        ChConcat(' ', RBlanks);
      LBlanks:= RBlanks;
      IF odd(LineLength - TotalChars) THEN
        ChConcat(' ', LBlanks)
   END;
{-                                                                          -}
PROCEDURE CenterALine(InLine: StringADT; VAR OutLine: StringADT);
   {centers InLine with leading and trailing blanks into OutLine}
   VAR
      LBlanks,    {string of blanks before text of OutLine}
      RBlanks:    {string of blanks after text of OutLine}
                  StringADT;
   BEGIN
      GetBlankStrings(StrLength(InLine), LBlanks, RBlanks);
      ConvertSysString('|', OutLine);
      StrConcat(OutLine, LBlanks, OutLine);
      StrConcat(OutLine, InLine, OutLine);
      StrConcat(OutLine, RBlanks, OutLine);
      ChConcat('|', OutLine)
   END;
{+                                                                          +}
PROCEDURE PrepareCard(TextLines: LinesArray; TotalLines: integer;
                      VAR CardLines: LinesArray);
   {documentation}
   VAR
      BlanksString:   StringADT;        {a blank line with borders}
      LineNo,                           {references one of CLines on the card}
      NoTextLine,                       {reference to a nonblank line of text}
```

```
UpperBlankLines:    {number of blanks lines above text part}
                    integer;
BEGIN
   ConvertSysString(Blanks, BlanksString);
   UpperBlankLines:= BlankLineCount(TotalLines);
   FOR LineNo:= 1 TO UpperBlankLines DO
     CardLines[LineNo]:= BlanksString;
   NoTextLine:= 0;
   FOR LineNo:= UpperBlankLines+1 TO UpperBlankLines+TotalLines DO
     BEGIN
        NoTextLine:= NoTextLine + 1;
        CenterLine(TextLines[NoTextLine], CardLines[LineNo])
     END;
   FOR LineNo:= UpperBlankLines+TotalLines+1 TO CLines DO
     CardLines[LineNo]:= BlanksString
END;
{*                                                                    *}  ◆
```

EXERCISES

Test Your Understanding

1. In the procedure `DisplayCard`, we did not use `WritelnString` to display the borders of the card. Why not?

2. Suppose instead we were to write the contents of the card to an external file. Would it be necessary to use `WritelnString` for the card's borders in this case?

Sharpen Your Implementation Skills

3. Using the string ADT, write a function `Occurrences` that returns the number of times a particular substring occurred in a given candidate string. Write a driver to test this function.

4. Write a procedure `CutAndPaste` that searches a `Candidate` string for one or more substrings containing the `CutStr` value. If `CutStr` is found, it is cut and replaced with `Replacestr`. If the cut string is not found or the candidate string will have too many characters, the action is not carried out.

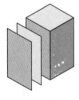

14.6   Implementation of `StringADT`

In this section, we code most of the operations of `StringADT`. We leave writing the rest of the operations to you as Exercises 3 and 4 at the end of this section. In each case, we are going to code the parameter lists as comments because all procedures and functions are FORWARD-directed.

Where to start

We need to test all procedures and functions belonging to the unit. Many of the constructors and all of the predicates require test strings for input values. All constructors, moreover, return a value to some output or input/output string variable. Thus, we need to have reliable code to both generate and display string values. If we develop the `ReadString`, `ReadlnString`, and `ConvertSysString` operations first, we are then able to read in values and assign values to string variables. If we also develop the `WriteString` and `WritelnString` operations, we can display the value taken on by a given string variable. Thus, we must code these operations first, so we can use them for on-line testing of the remaining operations in the unit.

Developing
ReadString

The computer should fill in the elements of the Chars field until either (1) a value of Ch equal to the value of Sentinel has been read in, (2) <eoln> has been identified, or (3) the length of OutString is MaxChars. We can describe the action of the block with

> *WITH OutString DO*
>   *Len ← 0*
>   *ReadCh(Sentinel, Len, Ch, InFile)*
>   *WHILE Ch <> Sentinel DO*
>   *Len ← Len + 1*
>   *Chars[Len] ← Ch*
>   *ReadCh(Sentinel, Len, Ch, InFile)*

This procedure is logically identical to the procedure we developed as Example Problem 9.3 in Chapter 9. ReadCh forces a sentinel condition if either OutString.Len = MaxLength or eoln(InFile) returns true. Otherwise a char value is read into Ch from InFile. The procedure ReadCh acts as a guard against either reading in <eoln> to Ch or reading in the one too may Ch values from InFile.

The descriptions for ReadString lead to the code for the procedures as shown.

```
{*                                                                    *}
PROCEDURE ReadCh(Sentinel: char; PresentLength: integer; VAR Ch: char;
                                          VAR InFile: text) ;
   {forces a sentinel value if PresentLength is equal to MaxLength or if
   eoln(InFile) is true; otherwise reads in a char value from InFile
   into Ch}
   BEGIN
     IF NOT(eoln(InFile) OR (PresentLength = MaxLength)) THEN
        read(InFile,Ch)
     ELSE
        Ch:= Sentinel
   END;
{+                                                                    +}
PROCEDURE ReadString {Sentinel: char; VAR OutStr: StringADT;
                                          VAR InFile: text};
   VAR
     Ch: char; {holds char value read in from AFile}
   BEGIN
     WITH OutStr DO
        BEGIN
          Len:= 0;
          ReadCh(Sentinel, Ch, Len, InFile)
```

```
        WHILE Ch < > Sentinel DO
            BEGIN
                Len: = Len + 1;
                Chars[Len]: = Ch;
                ReadCh(Sentinel, Ch, Len, InFile)
            END
        END
    END;
{*                                                                    *} ◆
```

The code for
ReadlnString

The code for the operation ReadlnString is shown below. Note that, as we have coded it, if the loop is exited because InString's length exceeds MaxLength, the remaining text is lost. The client should be told of this effect in the interface part of the unit.

```
    PROCEDURE ReadlnString {VAR OutStr: StringADT; VAR InFile: text} ;
        VAR
            Ch: = char;  {Ch value read in from InFile}
        BEGIN
            WITH InString DO
                BEGIN
                    Len: = 0;
                    WHILE NOT eoln(InFile) AND NOT(Len = MaxLength) DO
                        BEGIN
                            read(InFile, Ch);
                            Len: = Len + 1;
                            Chars[Len]: = Ch
                        END
                END;
            readln(InFile)
        END;
```

The code for
WriteString
and Writeln-
String

The code for WriteString simply requires a FOR loop. WritelnString calls WriteString and then executes writeln(OutFile). Note from the code how the NullString value is easily handled by the action of the FOR loop. The loop is clearly not entered if InStr.Len is equal to 0.

```
    PROCEDURE WriteString {InStr: StringADT; VAR OutFile: text} ;
        VAR
            Position: integer;  {used to access elements of Chars field}
        BEGIN
            WITH InStr DO
                FOR Position: = 1 TO Len DO
                    write(OutFile, Chars[Position])
        END;
```

```
PROCEDURE WritelnString {InStr; StringADT; VAR OutFile: text} ;
  BEGIN
    WriteString(InStr, OutFile);
    writeln(OutFile)
  END;
```

NullString's
code

NullString is written as a one-line statement that assigns OutStr.Len to 0:

```
        PROCEDURE NullString {VAR OutStr: StringADT}
          BEGIN
            OutStr.Len:= 0
          END;
```

The code for
ConvertSys-
String

Every dialect has primitive selectors to return a given character in a string and to return the string's length. Most dialects access a given character using the same syntax for access to an array element. Moreover, most dialects have the standard function length. We have used both of these features to code Convert-SysString as shown. Note that SysString's definition is the only part of the unit that depends upon a particular dialect.

```
PROCEDURE ConvertSysString {StrValue: SysString; VAR OutStr: StringADT} ;

  VAR
    Position: 1..MaxLength;      {access to char in StrValue}
  BEGIN
    WITH OutStr DO
      BEGIN
        Len:= length(StrValue);
        FOR Position:= 1 TO Len DO
          Chars[Position]:= StrValue[Position]
      END
  END;
```

The two
primitive
selectors

Both primitive selectors are easily coded. You should note, however, that we must guard against returning a value to ACh for a character that does not exist in InStr.

```
  FUNCTION StrLength {(InStr: StringADT): integer};
    BEGIN
      StrLength:= InStr.Len
    END;


  FUNCTION ACh {(InStr: StringADT; Position: integer): char};
    BEGIN
      IF Position > InStr.Len THEN
        ACh:= chr(0)              {returns null char as error condition}
```

```
      ELSE
        ACh:= InStr.Chars[Position]
    END;
```

Clearly, two strings are not equal if their lengths are different. If the lengths are equal, a linear search for a mismatch can be used. Therefore, we can describe the code for `StrEqual` with the pseudocode

> IF *InStr1.Len* <> *InStr2.Len THEN*   {*initialize StillEqual flag*}
>   *StillEqual* ← *false*
> *ELSE*
>   *StillEqual* ← *true*
>   *attempt to set StillEqual to false using a search for a mismatch*
> *StrEqual* ← *StillEqual*

We can then describe the search for a mismatch by the pseudocode

> *TotalChars* ← *InStr1.Len*   {*convenient local variable*}
> *Pos* ←1
> *WHILE NOT(Pos > TotalChars) AND StillEqual DO*   {*search for mismatch*}
>   *IF LowerCase(InStr1.Chars[Pos])* <> *LowerCase(InStr2.Chars[Pos]) THEN*
>   *StillEqual* ← *false*
>   *ELSE*
>   *Pos* ← *Pos + 1*

Note that the search is *finished* if all characters have been checked. A mismatch is *found* if two characters at the same position do not have the same value. The function `LowerCase` changes any uppercase letter to lowercase to make the logic case insensitive. The local variable `StillEqual` is `false` either if there is a character mismatch or if the lengths do not agree. Hence, the description is logically correct.

From the pseudocode descriptions, we obtain the source code for `StrEqual` as follows:

```
{*                                                                      *}
FUNCTION LowerCase(Ch: char): char;
  BEGIN
    IF Ch IN ['A'..'Z'] THEN
      LowerCase:= chr( ord(Ch) + ord('a') - ord('A') )
    ELSE
      LowerCase:= Ch
  END;
{+
FUNCTION StrEqual {(InStr1,   InStr2: StringADT): boolean} ;
  VAR
    Pos,                        {access to chars of InStr1 and InStr2}
    TotalChars: integer;        {length of the two strings}
    StillEqual: boolean;        {flags character mismatch}
```

```
BEGIN
  IF InStr1.Len <> InStr2.Len THEN
    StillEqual:= false
  ELSE
    StillEqual:= true;
  TotalChars:= InStr1.Len;
  Pos:= 1;
  WHILE NOT(Pos > TotalChars) AND StillEqual DO
    IF LowerCase(InStr1.Chars[Pos]) <> LowerCase(InStr2.Chars[Pos]) THEN
      StillEqual:= false
    ELSE
      Pos:= Pos + 1;
  StrEqual:= StillEqual
END;
```

Coding
StrLessThan

The algorithm for StrLessThan requires another linear search where a mismatch is again sought. The *finished* expression is described by *(Pos > InStr1.Len) OR (Pos > InStr2.Len)* because the comparison strings may be of different length. The postloop assignment logic is tricky, for either Pos is greater than the length of one of the two operand strings or there has been a mismatch. The description for the postloop process is thus described by the pseudocode

IF (Pos > InStr1.Len) AND (Pos <= InStr2.Len) THEN
    StrLessThan ← true
ELSE IF (Pos <= InStr1.Len) AND (Pos > InStr2.Len) THEN
    StrLessThan ← false
ELSE IF (InStr1.Chars[Pos] < InStr2.Chars[Pos]) then
    StrLessThan ← true
ELSE
    StrLessThan ← false

The coding of the function is left to you as Exercise 4 at the end of the section.

Coding
ChConcat

A guard against concatenating too many characters should be included in the statement of ChConcat. If another char value can be concatenated, the value of InOutStr.Len is increased by 1 and Chars[Len] is set to Ch. The required code is, therefore,

```
PROCEDURE ChConct {Ch: char; VAR InOutStr; StringADT} ;
  BEGIN
    WITH InOutStr DO
      IF Len < MaxLength THEN
        BEGIN
          Len:= Len + 1;
          Chars[Len]:= Ch
        END
  END;
```

The logic to code `StrConcat` is fairly easy to figure out. The first part of `OutStr` is simply set to `InStr1`. The remaining characters are then added using a partial fill-in algorithm on the array field variable `OutStr.Chars`. The candidate characters come from the elements of `InStr2.Chars`. From the description, we obtain the code as given.

```
PROCEDURE StrConcat {InStr1, InStr2: StringADT; VAR OutStr: StringADT};
   VAR
      PosStr2: integer;   {access to the characters of InStr2}
   BEGIN
      OutStr:= InStr1;      {assign first part of resultant string}
      PosStr2:= 0;
      WITH OutStr DO
         WHILE NOT(PosStr2 = InStr2.Len) AND NOT(Len = MaxChars) DO
            BEGIN
               PosStr2:= PosStr2 + 1;
               Len:= Len + 1;
               Chars[Len]:= InStr2.Chars[PosStr2]
            END
   END;
```

The pseudocode description for the operation `StrExtract` is

> *WITH OutStr DO*
>   *get value of Len*
>   *InStrPos ← Start*
>   *FOR OutStrPos ← 1 TO Len DO*
>   *Chars[OutStrPos] ← InStr.Chars[InStrPos]*
>   *InStrPos ← InStrPos + 1*

The value of `OutStr.Len` depends upon the length of `InStr`. Let us develop the action to carry out *get value of Len* using successive refinements.

If `Start` is greater than `InStr.Len`, `OutStr` is returned as a null string. This action can be accomplished by setting `OutStr.Len` to 0. Thus, the FOR loop is not entered, so that we can describe the logic of *get value of Len* by

> *IF Start > InStr.Len THEN*
>   *Len ← 0*
> *ELSE*
>   *assign nonzero value to Len*

If the ELSE path is taken, we can make an assertion that the subrange expression *Start..InStr.Len* represents the candidate subrange from which the values of `InStr.Chars` can be obtained. The total number of characters contained by `InStr.Chars` in this subrange is represented by the coded `integer` expression `InStr.Len + 1 - Start`. If `TotalChs` is greater than this value, the number of characters that can be returned is represented by this `integer` expression.

Hence, this value is assigned to `OutStr.Len`. Therefore, the action associated, with the ELSE path is described by

$$IF\ TotalChs > InStr.Len + 1 - Start\ THEN$$
$$Len \leftarrow InStr.Len + 1 - Start$$
$$ELSE \qquad \{enough\ chars\ are\ in\ InStr\}$$
$$Len \leftarrow TotalChs$$

Putting everything together, we arrive at the code as given.

```
PROCEDURE StrExtract    {InStr: StringADT; Start, TotalChs: integer;
                                          VAR OutStr: StringADT};
  VAR
    InStrPos,    {access to a character in InStr}
    OutStrPos:   {access to a character in OutStr}
              integer;
  BEGIN
    WITH OutStr DO
      BEGIN
        IF Start > InStr.Len THEN      {get value for OutStr.Len}
          Len:= 0
        ELSE IF TotalChs > InStr.Len + 1 - Start THEN
          Len:= InStr.Len + 1 - Start
        ELSE
          Len:= TotalChs;
        InStrPos:= Start;                   {get first char in InStr}
        FOR OutStrPos:= 1 TO Len DO         {char-by-char assignment}
          BEGIN
            Chars[OutStrPos]:= InStr.Chars[InStrPos];
            InStrPos:= InStrPos + 1
          END
      END
END;
```

Code for
StrRemove

Once we have the code for `StrConcat` and `StrExtract`, `StrRemove` is easy to implement. If exceptions do not occur, the substrings before the starting position and following the final position are extracted and then concatenated. The exception where `Start` is greater than the `InOutStr.Len` should be handled by the logic

$$IF\ NOT(Start > InOutStr.Len)\ THEN$$
$$remove\ chars\ from\ InOutStr$$

If the control expression is `false`, `InOutStr` is not changed. Thus, we obtain the code for `StrRemove` as follows:

```
PROCEDURE StrRemove {Start, TotalChs: integer; VAR InOutStr:  StringADT};
  {documentation}
```

```
PredString,      {substring of InOutStr before characters to be removed}
SuccString:      {substring of InOutStr after characters to be removed}
                 StringADT;
BEGIN
  IF NOT(Start > InOutStr.Len) THEN
    BEGIN
      StrExtract(InOutStr, 1, Start-1, PredString);
      StrExtract(InOutStr, Start + TotalChs, InOutStr.Len, SuccString);
      StrConcat(PredString, SuccString, InOutStr)
    END
END;
```

Coding
`StrInsert`

The operation `StrInsert` can also be coded using the `StrExtract` and `StrConcat` operations. We leave the coding of this block as Exercise 3 at the end of the section. You should note that all exceptions are handled by the logic of the `StrExtract` and `StrConcat` operations.

Coding
`StartPos`

We can also use the other operations we coded to simplify the logic of `StartPos`. We can use a linear search where the *found* condition occurs if a substring extracted from the `SearchStr` operand matches the `SubStr` operand string. We describe this logic with the pseudocode

$SLen \leftarrow SubStr.Len$
$Found \leftarrow false$
$Pos \leftarrow 1$
$WHILE\ NOT\ (SearchStr.Len + 1 - Pos > SLen)\ AND\ NOT\ Found\ DO$
 $StrExtract(SearchStr, Pos, SLen, CandStr)$
 $IF\ StrEqual(CandStr, SubStr)\ THEN$
  $Found \leftarrow true$
 $ELSE$
  $Pos \leftarrow Pos + 1$
$IF\ Found\ THEN$
 $StartPos \leftarrow Pos$
$ELSE$
 $StartPos \leftarrow 0$

The variable `CandStr` serves as a local candidate string for comparison, and `SLen` holds the value of the search substring's length. The search is finished if there are less characters remaining in the `SearchString` for a match with the `SLen` characters in `SubString`. The code for the function is therefore:

```
{*                                                                    *}
FUNCTION StartPos {(SubStr, SearchStr: StringADT): integer} ;
  VAR
    SLen,           {number of characters in SubStr and hence in CandStr}
    Pos:            {candidate position value for StartPos}
                    integer;
```

```
  Found:           {flag variable for search}
                   boolean;
  CandStr:         {candidate string to be compared with SubStr}
                   StringADT;
BEGIN
  SLen:= SubStr.Len;
  Found:= false;
  Pos:= 1;
  WHILE NOT (SearchStr.Len + 1 - Pos > SLen) AND NOT Found DO
    BEGIN
      StrExtract(SearchStr, Pos, SLen, CandStr);
      IF StrEqual(CandStr, SearchStr) THEN
        Found:= true
      ELSE
        Pos:= Pos + 1
    END;
  IF Found THEN
    StartPos:= Pos
  ELSE
    StartPos:= 0
END;
```

EXERCISES

Test Your Analysis Skills

1. State the invariant for the loop of StrConcat.

2. State the invariant for the loop of StrExtract.

Sharpen Your Implementation Skills

3. Write the code for the constructor operation StrInsert.

4. Write the code for the predicate operation StrLessThan.

5. Write the code for another (derived) predicate function StrGreaterThan that returns true if the first operand string value alphabetically occurs after the second operand string value. A precondition of the function is that both operand strings consist solely of letters. The function should be case-insensitive. (*Hint:* Use the other predicate functions.)

Program Testing Hints

When appropriate, set variables can greatly simplify your coding tasks. If, however, you use sets inappropriately or apply the incorrect syntax rules with them, they can lead to coding disasters. In this section, we present some of the common mistakes dealing with these types so you can avoid making them.

PROGRAM DESIGN RULE 14.1

Never enclose a set variable identifier by brackets.

Using brackets correctly

Never nest set expressions nor use brackets to enclose a set variable. Both uses imply an expression representing a "set of sets," a logical structure that makes no sense. If, for example, you wish to add a member representing the value Ch to ChSet, the statement is coded as `ChSet:= ChSet + [Ch]` and *never* as `ChSet:= [ChSet] + [Ch].` {BAD!}

PROGRAM DESIGN RULE 14.2

All set expressions other than those represented by set variables should be enclosed by brackets.

The expression coded as `[Ch]` represents the value of a set with exactly one member in it. Whatever value Ch takes on, it should *always* be enclosed by brackets if it is used in a set expression. Thus, a single member can *never* be added to a set using the "code" `ChSet:= ChSet + Ch.` {WRONG!}

Using the IN *operator correctly*

The IN operator tests whether a *scalar value* is a member of some test set. The operand on the left-hand side of the word IN always represents some scalar value that is a possible member of the test set. To test whether the character `'X'` is the ChSet, you should, therefore, use

```
IF 'X' IN ChSet THEN
    writeln('X is a member');
```

A set expression is never found on the left-hand side of this operator. The following "statement" is, therefore, wrong:

```
IF ['X'] IN ChSet THEN          {WRONG}
    writeln('X is a member');
```

Read and display restrictions

It is impossible to read in a set value directly from the keyboard or from any other text file. The character (or coded value) must be read in first before it can be expressed as a one-member set. The statement coded as `read([Ch])` is wrong under any conditions. (Indeed, what base set is being referred to?) If a one-member set is to be read from the keyboard to satisfy the pseudocode description `keyin([Ch])`, it must be refined to the sequence

> *keyin Ch*
> *SetVar ← [Ch]*

There is, likewise, no simple statement that directly codes to *display SetVar*. If you want the machine to display all the members of *SetVar,* you must code a sequence that satisfies the description

FOR *MemberValue* ← *LowestMember* TO *HighestMember* DO
  IF *MemberValue* IN *SetVar* THEN
    display MemberValue

Semantic mix-ups

Be aware of the differences between the relational operators as they apply to set expressions. Consider, for example, the following:

```
{1}  'A' IN ChSet
{2}  ['A'] = ChSet
{3}  ['A'] < ChSet
{4}  ['A'] <= ChSet
```

Only two of the four expressions are logically equal to each other, namely, expressions {1} and {4}. Expression {1} tests whether a scalar expression is contained in the membership of ChSet. Expression {4} tests whether the single-member set ['A'] is a subset of ChSet. The expressions are logically equivalent because they both evaluate to true when (1) the *single* value 'A' is in ChSet and (2) no further restrictions are placed on the value of ChSet.

So how do expressions {2} and {3} imply restrictions? Expression {2} requires that ChSet be identically equally to ['A']. ChSet must, therefore, have *exactly* one member in it to evaluate as true. Expression {3} requires that 'A' be in ChSet and that ChSet has at least two members in it.

Base set size

Every dialect has a limit to the number of members in its base set. The number of allowed members is considerably less than maxint. Indeed, most systems allow set variables capable of having a maximum of 256 members. For this reason, the following definition does not work:

```
TYPE  {UNWORKABLE! }
   IntSet = SET OF integer;
```

You can use an integer set if you define a small enough subrange for the base set. For example, the following works for most dialects:

```
TYPE
   MaxMember = 63;
   IntSetType = SET OF 0..MaxMember;
VAR
   IntSet: IntSetType;
   AMember: 0..MaxMember;
```

Given these declarations, the coded statement IntSet:= IntSet + [AMember*2] is perfectly legal provided that the value of the expression inside the brackets lies in the subrange 0..MaxMember.

If you need larger integer base sets than your system provides, you can always use an ADT implementation such as

```
TYPE
   MaxMember = 2186;
   IntSetType = ARRAY[0..MaxMember] OF boolean;
VAR
   SetVar: IntSetType;
```

An integer value is then a member of `SetVar` if the value of `SetVar[Int]` is equal to `true`. Unfortunately, you must write all the abstract operations that correspond to the set operations of standard Pascal. Once you have written the ADT unit, however, it can be used again and again.

Appropriateness   If you are considering sets to implement part of a solution, make sure the problem you want to solve is relevant for set variables. If the occurrence or absence of individual events in an event set dictates some of the control logic, set variables make good sense. If, however, your problem requires that some kind of *event counting* of one or more events dictates the control logic, set variables are woefully inadequate. They can only differentiate between no occurrences of an event and one *or* more occurrences.

Before you start planning logic with sets, ask yourself whether the proposed control structures depend solely upon the presence or absence of one or more *separate* events that comprise an *event set*. Do not consider sets if the proposed control structures are based on the number of occurrences of a *single* event or even on a number of occurrences of different events in an event set.

EXERCISES

Test Your Understanding

1. Given the following definitions and declarations:

```
TYPE
   CharSet = SET OF char;
VAR
   UpCase,
   LowCase,
   ChSet: CharSet;
   Ch: char;
   Correct: boolean;
```

Correct the syntax for each of the following:

```
UpCase:= [A..Z];
LowCase:= 'a'..'z';
Correct:= Ch IN [LowCase];
NOT Correct:= Ch IN UpCase;
ChSet:= '';
Chset:= ChSet + UpCase - ['A' 'E' 'I' 'O' 'U'];
```

2. You want to implement a sequence that accumulates members in ChSet from a line of keyed-in text. Correct the following sequence so that it does what it should:

```
WHILE NOT eoln DO
   BEGIN(Ch);
      read(Ch);
      ChSet:= [Ch]
   END;
```

3. Simplify the following expressions, using the proper set operations:
   (a) ('A' IN ChSet) AND ('E' IN ChSet) AND ('I' IN ChSet)
   (b) ('A' IN ChSet) OR ('E' IN ChSet) OR ('I' In ChSet)

4. Determine whether set variables can be of use or not for the following kinds of problems:
   (a) Write a function to count how many blonde, blue-eyed models are employed in the Ace Modeling Agency.
   (b) Write a procedure that, among other actions, counts how many times a number greater than 1000 was keyed in from a group of 100 numbers.
   (c) Write a function Won that determines whether a lottery player picked the six winning letters on a pick-six (letters) lottery.
   (d) Write a function CountNames that returns the number of people with a given first name in an array of name records.
   (e) Write a function FinishedShopping that returns the value true if a spice store has the spices you need as specified from their catalog.
   (f) Write a function GoodBouquet that returns a value of *true* if a florist has the flowers available for one of three different proposed flower arrangements, for example, (1) carnations, daisies, and chrysanthemums, (2) zinneas and snapdragons, and (3) roses, violets, and irises. Assume the florist has a catalog indicating the different flowers he or she might stock.
   (g) Write a function NumberofBouquets that counts the number of possible "good" bouquets from the three candidate bouquets.

REVIEW AND EXERCISES

A *set expression* represents a *set value* containing *members* that make up the expression. Two set expressions can be used as operands to form a third set expression that represents a *union, intersection,* or *difference* of the two sets. The union (+) of two sets contains the combined membership of both operand sets. The intersection (*) of two sets contains only those members common to both sets. The difference (-) of two sets contains only those members in the first set that are not in the second set.

It is possible to define a *set type* whose memebrship consists of ordinal values. The subrange of all possibles members that can exist in the set make up the set's *base type*. Once a set type has been defined, it is possible to declare one or more *set variables* of that type. A set variable or expression whose membership contains all the values of the base type is known as a *universal set* of that type. A set variable or expression that has no members in it is known as *null set* or *empty set*.

The six relational operators that work on scalar types can also work on set types. Two set expressions (SetA and SetB) are *equal* (=) when they have identical members. The two expressions are *unequal* (<>) when their memberships differ. SetA is a *subset* (<=) of SetB when all members found in SetA are also in SetB. SetA is a *proper subset* (<) of SetB when all members of SetA are found in SetB, and SetB also has more members than SetA. SetA is a *superset* (>=) of SetB when its membership contains all of SetB's members. SetA is a *proper superset* (>) of SetB when its membership contains all of SetB's members and other additional members.

A common algorithm used to *accumulate set members* initializes the membership-accumulating variable to the null set. Any event that occurs during the event-processing sequence that can be represented as a set member is added to the variable's membership using the set union operation. Once the accumulation process is over, all events that occurred during the process are found in the set variable's membership.

Another algorithm using a set variable starts off by initializing it to the universal set. Any given event that subsequently occurs is deleted from the set variable's membership using the set difference operation. Once the event processing is over, all events that had not occurred are found in the set variable's membership.

A third algorithm that processes all members of some set variable can be implemented with a FOR loop. The limits of the loop are the lower and uppr values of the base type. Each member in the set is processed using the control variable's value and the boolean expression for a set membership test.

The relational boolean expressions that can be used with set values are very useful for solving problems that deal with sets. Quite often, the key to coding the correct algorithm lies in finding the correct relational operation to apply to the two set expressions. Many times a given set variable with a value accumulated over some given process is compared with some *test set* value. The test set's value is often assigned to a variable as a fixed value that will not change over the rest of the program or process.

Although set variables lend an elegance to source code when used appropriately, they have their limitations. The size of a universal set's membership, for example, is quite modest with most dialects, usually 255 or 256. If you require set operations for larger membership values, the *standard* set type will not work. You can, however, get around this difficulty by coding a set ADT using an array of booleans to represent a set variable. This implementation can work with memberships as large as the available memory to carry out the program or process.

Sets are appropriate for counting algorithms only when the number of members in the set is to be counted. If you require an algorithm to count the same event more than once over a sequence, set variables will not be particularly useful in solving the problem. If, however, you require an algorithm to record the occurrences of different but similar events, set variables are probably a good implementation choice.

Many dialects of Pascal use string variables and string expressions. Dialects that have this feature will also have some abstract operations that work with strings. In particular, most dialects have *concatenation* (StrConcat), *substring search* (StartPos), *substring removal* (StrRemove), *substring copy* (StrExtract), as well as other operations. You can use the features of your dialect that have these operations to work with string variables and expressions.

If you are working with a dialect that does not have strings, you can use the stringADT unit given in Section 14.6 of the chapter. If you likewise work with many dialects and prefer dealing only with one "standard" string type, you can use the StringADT we developed in this chapter, for, being written in standard Pascal, it is easily interfaced with any other Pascal dialect.

EXERCISES

Short Answers

1. Suppose the variables ASet, BSet, CSet, and VowelSet are all of type SET OF char. Does the following coded statement work?

   ```
   IF OK(ASet*BSet, ASet-CSet, VowelSet) THEN
      BEGIN  {statement}  END;
   ```

2. If the statement for Exercise 1 does work, write the header for the function. If it does not work, write down any additional code to make it work and then write the header for the function.

3. Will the following statement work for any given set type?

   ```
   SomeSet:= [];
   ```

   Explain your answer.

4. Explain how to implement a statement described by the pseudocode

   SomeSet ← its base set

5. Given that the expression (ASet <= BSet) is true, answer the following questions:
   (a) Can BSet be equal to the null set? If so, under what conditions?
   (b) What can be said about the number of members ASet has in terms of the number of members BSet has?

6. Suppose that the expression (ASet < BSet) is true. Given this condition, answer the following:
   (a) If the expression (Ch IN ASet) is true, will the expression (Ch In BSet) be true?
   (b) If the expression (Ch IN BSet) is true, will the expression (Ch IN ASet) be true?
   (c) What can be said about the number of members ASet has in terms of the number of members BSet has?

7. **(a)** Why would you want to initialize a set variable to the null set?
   (b) Why would you want to initialize a set variable to the universal set?
   (c) Why would you want to initialize a set variable to some "constant" value?

8. Suppose ChSet is a variable of type SET OF char. Write the coded Pascal statement to:
   (a) accumulate the value Ch into ChSet
   (b) accumulate the members of the set Vowels into ChSet
   (c) accumulate the characters over the subrange LoCh..HiCh into ChSet

(d) delete a single character Ch from ChSet's membership

(e) delete the characters in the subrange LoCh..HiCh from ChSet's membership

(f) delete all characters in ChSet except possibly those in the subrange LoCh..HiCh

9. Match the phrases and expressions in column A with the corresponding ones in column B:

Column A	Column B
"	predicate
+	<
=	null string
[]	same membership
superset	null set
StrEqual	set union
proper subset	>=

10. What is the advantage gained in using StringADT of this chapter rather than a given dialect's string implementations?

11. What is the major disadvantage of using the StringADT rather than a given dialect's strings?

12. How would you classify the operation WriteString: constructor or selector? Explain.

13. Suppose the StringADT only had the one predicate function StrEqual. Would the unit be complete? Explain.

14. How would you use the operations of StringADT to read in values from the keyboard?

15. You want to code a driver to test a client procedure you have coded using the StringADT. What operations would you need to use from the ADT for the driver's statement?

Easy Projects

16. Many dialects have the capabilities of converting a string value to a numeric value and vice-versa. You are to write and test an extension to StringADT that has the following four operations:

IntValue is a function where the computer converts an input IntString of type StringADT ito its equivalent integer value. If some of the characters in IntString are not digits, the computer returns maxint as an error condition.

RealValue is a function where an IntString representing a real number *decimal* (not scientific notation) is an input string. The function returns the equivalent real value. If the string does not represent a real number, the function should return maxint.

IntConvert is a procedure to convert an integer value into its equivalent StringADT representation.

RealConvert is an analogous function to IntConvert where the function converts a real argument to its representative StringADT value. A second integer argument Precision is required to determine how many digits are found after the decimal point.

The code for this extension must be written as a set of client procedures and functions to StringADT.

17. Extend the StringADT with an "alphabetic processor" whose four operations are as follows:

MakeCaps: an output string is assigned where all the lowercase letters in the operand string are changed to uppercase letters.

MakeLowers: an output string is assigned where all the uppercase letters in the operand string are changed to lowercase letters.

MakeLettersOnly: an output string is assigned where all characters that are not letters or spaces in the operand string are deleted.

AllLetters: a function that returns the value true if the operand string consists only of letters and spaces.

The three procedures each return a new string; none of the operations destroys the original operand string, use only those operations that already belong to the StringADT to code the alphabetic processor. Write and test the code for this extension.

18. Use the StringADT to redo Exercise 9.25 at the end of Chapter 9.

Medium Projects

19. Use the StringADT to redo Exercise 10.27 at the end of Chapter 10.

20. The state lottery lets players choose 10 numbers out of a subrange from 1..100 on a ticket. There are three classes of winners in the lottery: (1) those for whom the numbers on their tickets match at least four of the eight winning numbers are "small winners," (2) those for whom the numbers on their tickets match at least six of the eight numbers are "medium winners," and (3) those for whom all numbers match are "grand winners."

    Write a program where the computer simulates 25 players in the lottery using a random-number generator. The generator should return numbers in the interval 1..100. Each of these tickets should be stored in a 25-element array. Once the tickets have been generated, you are to input eight integer values representing the winning ticket. Once these values are entered, the computer displays the numbers of the players who are winners, along with the set value that made up the winning tickets.
    (*Note:* It will be difficult to test this program unless you know the player's tickets ahead of time. Therefore, you should also code a procedure to display each of the 25 tickets. You can use these values to input winning ticket numbers that guarantee winners for the given tickets generated.)

21. Recruitment for summer employment at Tech U has started again. You are to write a program that helps a prospective employer find some students. The file Students, containing all the necessary information about each student, is first read into an array of records. The first line of the file contains the number of students who applied for summer employment, and all other lines contain information about each student, one student per line. Each line has the student's name, his or her GPA, the number of years completed, and the major. Five typical lines from Students might look like

```
Sam J. Sneed^  2.77  3  EE<eoln>
J. J. John^  3.55  2  ME<eoln>
Reed Richards^  3.75  2  CS<eoln>
Henrietta Hackerd^  2.42  4  CS<eoln>
Mac N. Tosh^  2.62  1  ET<eoln>
```

A prospective employer can request a minimum GPA, a minimum number of years completed, and a list of majors (two uppercase letters) he or she wants for employment over the summer. The information about each eligible student is displayed to the recruiter. A typical interaction, given the five students in the file, might look like

```
GPA cut-off:  2.70<eoln>
Minimum years completed:  2<eoln>
Majors:  EE  CS<eoln>


Sam J. Sneed  2.77  Junior  EE
Reed Richards  3.75  Sophomore  CS
```

The following majors are available: EE, IE, CE, ME, CS, LS, ET, and CT. Have at least 20 students in the file Students to choose from, and run the program with at least five recruiters.

Difficult Projects 22. In order to graduate as a CS major at Comp U, a student must take the following 10 courses: C101, C102, C210, C220, C225, C240, C315, C335, C340, and C370. The prerequisites for the courses are as follows: C102 requires that C101 was completed. Any C200 or C300 course requires that C101 and C102 were taken. C240 requires that C210 was completed and that C225 is a corequisite. C225 requires that C210 be completed. C315 requires that C220 and C325 were completed. C340 requires C220, C225, and C335 as prerequisites. C315 requires completion of C210 first. Finally, to take C370, a student must have completed C340.

You are to write an advisement program that reads in courses the user has taken up to this point. The computer then displays the courses that are remaining along with the possible courses that can be taken. (*Hint*: Set up an array of sets for checking prerequisites.)

Examples:

```
Courses taken?  C101 C102 C210<eoln>
You need to take C220 C225 C240 C315 C335 C340 C370
The courses open to you are C220 C225 C315


Courses taken?  <eoln>
You need to take C101 C102 C210 C220 C240 C315 C335 C340 C370
The courses open to you are C101
```

23. We suggested that if you have too many items in a base set, you can use an array of booleans to implement a set type. Build an IntSetType ADT using the suggested implementation technique. In order to simplify the testing of the ADT, allow the set membership to be over the subrange 1..100.

Then use the abstraction in a client program to test that the RNG in Chapter 8 does indeed generate numbers in the subrange 0..2186 without repeating itself. You can adopt IntsADT to the problem at hand by extending the subrange to 0..5000. As numbers are generated over the 2187 trials, they are added to the test set. None of the numbers generated should be in the set [2187..5000].

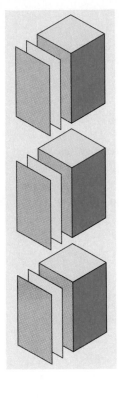

C H A P T E R 15

RECURSION

OBJECTIVES

After reading and studying the material of the present chapter, you should be able to

- Explain how the mechanism of recursion works

- Write the code for an algorithm that requires a repetitive process using recursion

- Use mathematical induction to prove that a recursive algorithm is logically correct

- Desk trace recursive code by drawing a tree of the process

- Apply good on-line testing techniques for a recursive process

I**F YOU CAN SOLVE A PROBLEM USING A LOOP,** you can likewise solve it using recursion. When you use recursion, you instruct the computer to carry out a sequence of statements more than once, just as if it were executing a loop. Before finishing one repetitive sequence, however, it may interrupt that sequence to start another one. When the machine executes a loop, it completes the loop body in its entirety before it executes another loop pass. When the computer recurses, it interrupts one process to start and complete another version of the same process.

If we already have one mechanism by which the computer carries out a repetitive process, you may wonder why we need to devise another mechanism. In actuality, we do not. However, there are some algorithms whose solution makes more sense when done recursively. Searching, for example, is more naturally envisioned as a recursive process. Other algorithms, such as the merge–sort algorithm, are much harder to derive and understand when they are planned and coded iteratively.

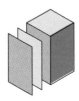

15.1   Solving Problems Recursively

When you solve a problem by recursion, you find more than one solution to the same kind of problem. The second, third, and subsequent problems that you solve are necessary for finding the solution to the initial problem. These solutions, whose results are used to solve a "larger" problem, make up smaller versions of the original problem. In this section, you will see how to implement this mechanism on a computer to solve a given problem.

An ancient process

People used recursion as a process for solving problems centuries before the birth of Christ. The first example problem we will solve is attributed to Euclid who lived around the third century B.C. Needless to say, he did not have a computer to execute the algorithm he derived!

Example Problem 15.1

The problem statement

Let us write a function GCD to find the greatest common divisor between two integers. The GCD of two integers is defined as the largest integer value that divides evenly into both integers. We solve this problem using a *recursive algorithm*.

> **Recursive algorithm:**   an algorithm where the solution is found in terms of the solution to smaller versions of the same problem.

Euclid's algorithm

Before we solve the problem as a coded Pascal function, let us derive the algorithm the way Euclid did. He used a geometric model for solving the problem, and applied recursive reasoning on this model to obtain a way for finding the GCD of two integers.

Figure 15.1 shows the geometric model Euclid used, where each segment is of some "unit" length. He envisioned the problem as one of finding a line represented by X that can divide evenly into two line segments AB and AC, where AC is the larger segment. Thus, X is of length xU, where U is the unit length, and x is an integer value. Similarly, AB is of length pxU and AC of length $(px + qx)U$, where p and q are integer values.

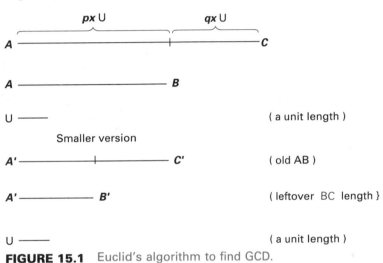

FIGURE 15.1   Euclid's algorithm to find GCD.

From this initial problem, Euclid reasoned that X will also divide evenly into AB, as represented by the integer value px, and BC, as represented by the integer value qx. Note that the length of the line segment BC is the integer remainder of AC divided by AB. The new problem to find the GCD of AB and BC represented a problem with smaller numbers such that its solution is also a solution to the original problem.

He used similar reasoning on this smaller problem, replacing the old AC with the smaller segment AB and the old AB with the smaller segment BC. Eventually, the problem to solve reduces to one where AC is divided evenly by AB. The AB of this line segment represents a solution to the problem. Note that when a solution is found, the length of the remaining segment BC is 0.

Drafting a solution

Now we are going to apply this algorithm to coding a function GCD, which is typically called by `writeln(GCD(M, N):1);`, where M and N are `integer` values. We derive the code with the assumed precondition that M is greater than N. The stub for the function is coded as

```
FUNCTION GCD(M, N: integer): integer;
   {returns the GCD between M and N}
   BEGIN    END;
```

Let us apply Euclid's algorithm, this time using pseudocode to derive a solution.

The pseudocode for the solution is given by

> IF the M and/or N values represent a known solution THEN
>   GCD ← value of a known solution
> ELSE
>   GCD ← GCD(N, M MOD N)

Note that the next call to GCD uses the lower of the two integers as the new value for M and the integer remainder of the two integers as the new lower value. Each subsequent call to GCD represents a reduction in the "size" of the problem to be solved. Eventually, the problem is reduced to one with a known solution, as determined by the values of M and N. As the pseudocode shows, this known solution is also a solution to the larger versions of the same problem that were solved. The "largest" version of the problem was the original call to the function GCD.

Base cases

The pseudocode for the GCD function requires that the problem eventually reduces to one for which a known solution exists. Further reduction of the problem is unnecessary. A solution of this kind represents a *base case*, or *stopping case*, of the recursive algorithm. It is not possible to implement a recursive solution to a problem unless there are well-defined condition(s) that can be used to find the base case(s) that exist for the problem.

Base case: a solution to a recursive algorithm for which further recursive calls are unnecessary. Every recursive algorithm requires at least one base case in order to be valid.

In the case of the GCD problem, we can say that the base case occurs when the variable N is equal to 0. This base case is reached when the value passed into N from the previous call is 0. Given that N is 0, GCD is assigned the value M. Note that this value came from the expression M MOD N in the next larger version of the problem. This higher value of M is therefore divisible by the higher value of N as implied by the base case condition.

Source code

The coded solution to the problem is given as the function GCD.

```
FUNCTION GCD(M, N: integer): integer;
  {documentation}
  BEGIN
    IF N = 0 THEN
      GCD:= M
    ELSE
      GCD:= GCD(N, M MOD N)
  END;
```

Desk tracing the GCD algorithm

A desk trace of the solution to the problem GCD(66, 48) is shown in Figure 15.2. The figure represents that point in the sequence where the solution to a base case has been found. The solid lines show a trace of actions the machine has already executed, and the dotted lines show actions the machine has not yet executed.

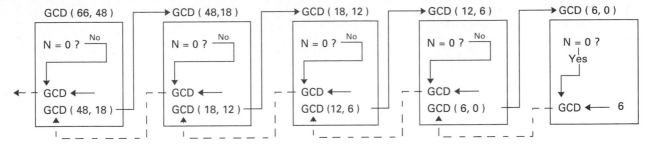

FIGURE 15.2 Tracing the solution of GCD(66, 48) to the base case.

The initial call leads to the recursive call GCD(48, 18). This particular problem cannot be solved until the solution to the problem GCD(18, 12) is found. But this problem requires the solution of GCD(12, 6), which further requires the solution of GCD(6, 0). This problem represents a base case with a known solution, namely, 6. This value is about to be returned as the solution to the problem GCD(12, 6). The solution to this problem, moreover, is the solution to the problem GCD(18, 12), which in turn is the solution to GCD(48, 18). The solution to this last problem is the solution of the problem initially posed, namely, GCD(66, 48).

The run-time stack

When the computer executes a call to procedure or function A, it must first carry out all the statements belonging to A before it can resume the statements in the block that made the call to A. If subprogram A in turn calls procedure or function B, the statements belonging to B must be completed before the computer can resume execution of the statements that make up A. The *last* procedure or function called is, hence, the *first* one to be completed. The computer executes all Pascal programs in this manner.

The mechanism for managing procedure and function calls works using a LIFO discipline, thus suggesting a stack. The subprogram on top of this *run-time stack* is the one the computer is presently executing. The subprogram that is on top of the stack once the given subprogram is finished is the one that called the given subprogram.

> **Run-time stack:** the software means by which the computer maintains the LIFO discipline required to process the procedures and functions in a program.

Desk-tracing the function GCD

Figure 15.2 represents a picture of the run-time stack after the computer has pushed the calls GCD(66, 48), GCD(48, 18), GCD(18, 12), GCD(12, 6), and GCD(6, 0) on it. The GCD(6, 0) problem, having been solved, is about to be popped off the run-time stack. When the value 6 is returned to the function GCD(12, 6), the function representing the base case is popped.

Then the solution for GCD(12, 6), that is, 6, is passed out to the function GCD(18, 12) and the former function is popped. This value of 6 also represents the solution to GCD(18, 12). The value 6 is likewise returned to GCD(48, 18), and then GCD(18, 12) is duly popped. The picture of the run-time stack at this point in the processing is shown as Figure 15.3. All that remains is for the final two

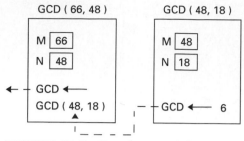

FIGURE 15.3 Run-time stack for GCD(66, 48) after the computer has found GCD(18, 12).

functions to be popped, where the value of 6 is returned to the call GCD(66, 48) before that function is popped. When this final function is popped, 6 is returned and the problem is solved. ◆

Accumulation and recursion

In the preceding example, we developed a recursive algorithm that found the solution to a trivial problem, then returned the solution unchanged to larger versions of the same problem. In the next example, we use recursion in a cumulative process to solve some initial "large" problem. The logical mechanism first solves ever smaller versions of the original problem as part of the recursive process. As each solution is found, it is accumulated into the solution of a larger version of the same problem. Eventually all solutions are accumulated in such a way that they make up the solution of the initial problem.

Example Problem 15.2

The problem statement
The solution

Let us write a function that finds the value of the variable XRe raised to the power of N, where N is a nonnegative integer value. The solution is to be coded recursively.

We can derive the solution by recognizing that the value of X^N can be defined by

$$X^N = \begin{cases} 1, & \text{given that } N = 0 \\ X * X^{N-1}, & \text{given that } N > 0. \end{cases}$$

The definition when N is 0 represents the base case for the desired algorithm, and the definition when N is greater than 0 is recursive. The function PowerOfN is the coded solution to the problem.

```
FUNCTION PowerOfN(XRe: real; N: integer): integer;
   {the function returns the value of XRe raised to the Nth power; N
   must be a nonnegative value}
   BEGIN
      IF N = 0 THEN
         PowerOfN:= 1
      ELSE
         PowerOfN:= XRe * PowerOfN(XRe, N-1)
   END;  ◆
```

Figure 15.4(a) shows the appearance of that part of the run-time stack used to return a value to the function call PowerOfN(0.9,3) just after the function has been called. Figure 15.4(b) shows the run-time stack at the time the base case value has just been found. Figure 15.4(c) shows the run-time stack just after the computer has returned the solution of PowerOfN(0.9,1) to the PowerOfN(0.9,2) function call. Figure 15.4(d) shows the stack at the moment the computer will find the value of PowerOfN(0.9,3).

FIGURE 15.4 (a) Initial run-time stack for call PowerOfN(0.9, 3), (b) run-time stack for PowerOfN(0.9, 3) at the moment the base case is found, (c) run-time stack just after PowerOfN(0.9, 1) has been returned, and (d) run-time stack just before PowerOfN(0.9, 3) is returned.

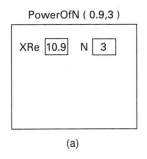

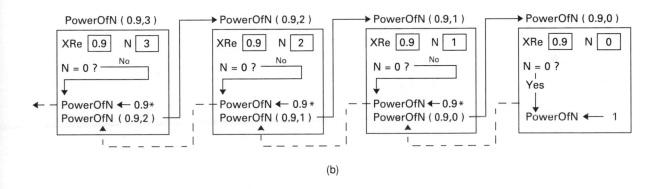

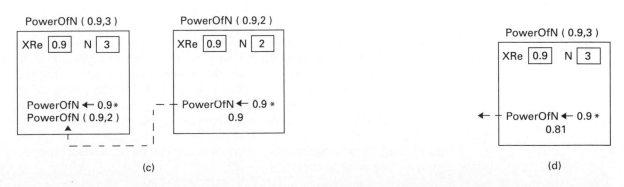

EXERCISES

Test Your Understanding

1. Explain in one sentence why every recursive algorithm requires a base case.

2. What would happen to a program if the computer starts a recursive process where the base case will never be attained?

3. True or false? The value returned to the call GCD(M, N) not only represents the GCD of M and N, but also the GCD of all the other problems solved by recursive calls. *Briefly* explain your answer.

Practice Your Analysis Skills

4. Sketch the data areas set up until the base case is reached when the call GCD(384, 216) is carried out.

5a. Will the function PowerOfN work for negative values of XRe? Show the values returned by each recursive call from the original call of PowerOfN(-0.9, 4).

5b. Will the call PowerOfN(0.9, -3) work without error? Explain your answer.

Sharpen Your Implementation Skills

6. Modify the GCD function such that an initial call where M is less than N returns the GCD of the two numbers.

7. Modify the GCD function further so that it works for negative as well as positive numbers. For example, all of the following: GCD(26,-4), GCD(-26,-4), and GCD(-26,4) will return the value 2 as the GCD. (*Hint:* Set all arguments positive as the first action of the GCD block. Try doing this problem in two ways: (a) set the values positive recursively and (b) set the values positive as part of a nonrecursive sequence in the block.)

8. Modify the function PowerOfN so that it works for negative values of N. (*Hint:* Use division by the XRe value when N is negative. Then make the recursive call with the parameter value N+1.)

15.2 How Recursion Works

When you first encounter recursion, it seems quite strange. You see a decision statement and a process that calls itself to make the computer carry out this process repetitively. Yet there are no looping statements involved. In this section, we dispel the mystery by describing the logical mechanism behind a recursive process.

Pseudocode description of a recursive process

  The variables in a parameter list specify a particular problem for the computer to solve. If the value parameters for two calls to a given subprogram differ, most likely different results are returned. The computer will have found results for each subprogram, but the different results mean a different *specific* problem was solved in each case.

  A recursive algorithm must be started with an initial call to a procedure or function that calls itself. Once this call is made, the computer carries out a sequence where the process calls itself until a base case is reached. Once the base case is reached, the interrupted processes are completed in turn, using the LIFO mechanism of the run-time stack. When the last process, representing the initial call is completed, the problem is solved.

  Algorithm 15.1 is the pseduocode description you can use to develop any recursive algorithm you want to code.

Algorithm 15.1

{the generic algorithm for a recursive process:}
{precondition: a given set of values specifies a given problem}
IF the parameters passed in indicate a base case THEN
    solve the problem
ELSE
    use the values passed in to set up a smaller version of the problem
    CALL THE PROCEDURE OR FUNCTION TO SOLVE A SMALLER PROBLEM
    use the values returned to solve the present problem
{postcondition: the problem has been solved for the given set of
values}

call the procedure or function to solve a problem
{end algorithm}

We have put the recursive call in capital letters and also included preconditions and postconditions as documentation of the pseudocode description.

The logical mechanism

The pseudocode shows us that an initial call to the recursive process is required. The parameters belonging to this initial call represent the problem to be solved using recursion as the repetition mechanism. Note how the parameters passed into any given block represent a particular problem, not necessarily the original one posed, that must be solved.

When control exits any given process, the given problem has been solved. In the interim, smaller versions of the same problem were solved. All of these solutions returned are applied to the solution of a larger (eventually, the original) problem. The method of "divide and conquer" is thus used with recursive algorithms where it is the machine that does the dividing and conquering.

Given the initial call, we can state the initial precondition as, "The set of values in the parameter list specifies the problem to be solved." The postcondition returned when the statements belonging to the initial call are completed can be stated as, "The initial problem has been solved."

Looping vs. recursion

When the computer executes the body of a loop, it performs a given *uninterrupted* sequence of statement from start to finish for each loop pass. This repetitive action is all done within the same process. The machine stops the repetitive processing once the loop exit condition is achieved. Postprocessing is then done on the results accumulated over the sequence of loop passes.

When the computer carries out a recursive process, it partially executes it and interrupts itself to start a new version of the same process. When a version of the process is set up that signals a base case, the associated actions to handle this case are carried out. Within this process, the computer does not make a recursive call. The overall recursive process, however, is far from finished. Indeed, the statements done after control returns to a particular process are as critical to the success of the algorithm as those done before the machine calls another process.

A recursive algorithm is finished only when the final recursing process is popped from the run-time stack. In other words, control must have been relinquished completely from the recursing block before a recursive sequence is considered "finished."

In order to be able to write a recursive solution to a problem, your algorithm must satisfy the following requirements:

1. There are one or more known base cases whose solution(s) can be trivially found.
2. All other problems can be solved in terms of correctly expressed smaller versions of the same problem.
3. The actions applied to the solution(s) of a smaller problem(s) always result in a corect solution to the larger problem.
4. Regardless of how large the original problem is, one or more base cases must have been found and solved in the process of solving the initial problem.

If your description to solve a problem recursively lacks one of these four requirements, it is definitely not going to work.

Mathematical induction and recursion

You can prove a recursive algorithm by *mathematical induction* if you can show that (1) the solutions to *all* base cases are correct, and (2) if the values returned by the smaller version(s) of the problem are correct, the results returned are combined in such a way to represent a correct solution to the larger problem.

We can "prove this proof" for some problem requiring N recursive calls with the following reasoning: Suppose (1) the base case(s) is correct, and (2) the $(N - 1)$th nonbase case calls will combine in such a way that the Nth call is also correct. Given these two correct cases, the algorithm will work for all possibilities, regardless of how large or small N may be.

Applying mathematical induction

We can prove that the function PowerOfN works for all nonnegative powers because

1. $X\text{Re}^0 = 1$, regardless of $X\text{Re}$'s value and
2. $X\text{Re}^N = X * X\text{Re}^{N-1}$ if $N > 0$, regardless of $X\text{Re}$'s value.

The base case is correct, the Nth call is correct given that the $(N - 1)$th call is correct, and repeated calls to PowerOfN reduce the problem to its base case. Therefore, PowerOfN is correct by mathematical induction.

We can also prove Euclid's algorithm correct by induction, although this proof is a bit more complicated. We have: (1) The integer N, regardless of its value, divides evenly into 0, so the base case is correct. (2) Given M and N, let us assume that N (which becomes M') and M MOD N (which is N') are both divisible by the *GCD* X. We must show that the original M and N are also be divisible by X.

Clearly, N, which is equal to M', is divisible by X. The original value for M would have to be equal to the expression $kN + N'$, where k is an integer, because N' represents the integer remainder of M/N. But both N' and N are divisible by X. Hence, because k is an integer, the original M must also be divisible by X. Therefore, the algorithm is correct.

Completeness

If you are attempting to prove a recursive algorithm, make sure your solution is *complete*. In order for a solution to be complete, it must work for some defined universe of values. As we coded it, the function PowerOfN is not a complete solution with respect to all the integer values that N can take on. If you want the solution to work for all integer values of N, you must include code to handle the case where N is passed in as a negative value.

If you assume any integer value as a precondition on N and apply the coded solution of Example Problem 15.2, a negative value of N passed into the PowerOfN block will never reduce to 0. Indeed, the machine will keep calling PowerOfN where abs(N) gets bigger and bigger. Consequently, the run-time stack will get bigger and bigger. This situation, an error condition analogous to an endless loop, is known as an *infinite stack*.

> **Infinite stack:** an error condition that occurs with recursive algorithms where the base case for one or more initiated recursive calls is never achieved.

When you draft a solution to a recursive algorithm, make sure you have found all possible base cases and handled them properly. If there is more than one possible base case, you can apply an *IF-ELSE-IF* algorithm to handle them first. When the machine has checked all base cases, it will carry out the statements associated with the rest of the remaining ELSE (or IF-ELSE) reserved word(s) that contain the recursive call(s).

A nonnumeric example

Just because our first two examples used numeric processing, you should not feel that recursion works only with problems that process numbers. In the following example, we use recursion to solve a file-processing problem.

Example Problem 15.3

The problem statement

Let us write a program ReverseLines that displays the lines of text in a file in reverse order. A run of the program using the contents of PurpleCow.dat (see Chapter 9, Section 9.1) as a default file variable looks like

```
I'd rather see than be one.
But I can tell you anyhow,
I never hope to see one.
I never saw a purple cow.
```

The main block

We can describe the main block statement using

reset (PurpleCow)
ShowReversedLines(PurpleCow)

We will write the code for the procedure ShowReversedLines using recursion to get the solution. We plan to take advantage of the LIFO mechanism of the run-time stack so that the first line of text read in will be the last line of text displayed. The single statement for the procedure ShowReversedLines will be a call to the procedure StoreDisplay, a recursive process. The code for the main block is given as the program ReverseLines, where we must write the code for the procedure StoreDisplay.

```
PROGRAM ReverseLines (PurpleCow, output);
  {This program reverses the display of the lines in the text file
  PurpleCow using a recursion strategy.}
  VAR
    PurpleCow: text;
  {*                                                              *}
  PROCEDURE StoreDisplay (VAR PurpleCow: text);
    {A recursive block, set up in such a way that the last line read in
    will be the first line displayed}
    BEGIN    END;
  {+                                                              +}
  PROCEDURE ShowReversedLines (VAR PurpleCow: text);
    {This procedure contains the initial call to the recursive block
    StoreDisplay.}
    BEGIN
      StoreDisplay (PurpleCow)
    END;
  {*                                                              *}
  BEGIN
    reset (PurpleCow);
    ShowReversedLines (PurpleCow)
  END.
```

Writing
`StoreDisplay`
The computer should read in a line of text and then hold it until it has read in and displayed lines of text that follow the one read in. The base case occurs when there are no more lines of text to be read in. When the base case occurs, the computer does nothing. We can use this description to draft the pseudocode for the solution as

> IF NOT eof(PurpleCow) THEN
> readln(PurpleCow, ALine)
> StoreDisplay(PurpleCow)
> writeln(ALine)

The variable `ALine` is a local variable that holds the contents of the line of the text file read in.

Proving the
algorithm
The base case where there is no line of text to be displayed correctly results in no action. Next we will assume that all lines read in following some Nth line have been displayed in reverse order. From the pseudocode, we see that the Nth line read in is not displayed until `StoreDisplay` has been executed for all subsequent lines. Therefore, this line's text is displayed only after all other lines read in were displayed. Hence, the algorithm is correct.

Source code
The code for `StoreDisplay` is then

```
PROCEDURE StoreDisplay (VAR PurpleCow: text);
  {documentation}
  VAR
```

```
      ALine: {STRING CAPABLE OF HOLDING 80 CHARACTERS};
   BEGIN
     IF NOT eof(PurpleCow) THEN
       BEGIN
         readln(PurpleCow, ALine);
         StoreDisplay(PurpleCow);
         writeln(ALine)
       END
   END; ◆
```

The recursive stack of `StoreDisplay`

Figure 15.5 shows the stack containing the values of the local variable ALine for the recursive calls made to StoreDisplay. The <eof> marker has just been identified, and the computer is about to pop this data area off the stack by executing an empty statement. It must then complete each process on the stack in turn by first displaying the char values contained in the different local variables of ALine.

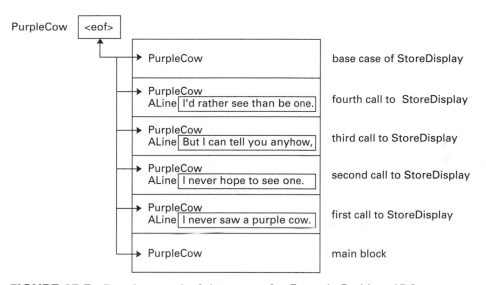

FIGURE 15.5 Run-time-stack of data areas for Example Problem 15.3.

EXERCISES

Test Your Understanding

1. What action(s) occurs with a push operation on the run-time stack?

2. What actions occur with a pop operation on the run-time stack?

3. True or false? The computer uses a run-time stack only when it executes recursive processes.

Practice Your Analysis Skills

4. Suppose the file PurpleCow has been reset and the following code is applied to it:

```
PROCEDURE Display(VAR PurpleCow: text);
  VAR
```

```
      ALine: STRING[80];
    BEGIN
      IF NOT eof(PurpleCow) THEN
        BEGIN
          readln(PurpleCow, ALine);
          writeln(PurpleCow);
          Display(PurpleCow)
        END
    END;

    Display(PurpleCow);        {initial call to recursive process}
```

Write down the resultant display when the computer executes the code.

5. Sketch the run-time stack for the code of Exercise 4 the moment the base case has been found. Why does `StoreDisplay` of Example Problem 15.3 result in different output from `Display`?

Sharpen Your Implementation Skills

6. Write a program, `ReverseChars`, whose run displays the characters on each line of a text file backwards. Use a recursive procedure `ReverseEm` to reverse a single line of text. The following shows a text file and a run. The file's contents:

```
        Greetings.<eoln>
        Hello to you, too.<eoln><eof>
```

The run of `ReverseChars`:

```
          .sgniteerG
          .oot ,uoy ot olleH
```

15.3 More Examples of Recursion

In this section, you will see some more examples of recursive functions. You will also see some examples of recursive procedures where each procedure processes one or more events that are accumulated into a variable whose final value is the solution to the problem. Pay close attention to how we use the parameter-passing mechanism for the examples that use an accumulation variable.

Product and sum accumulation

We have already solved the two problems we are about to pose by iteration. Now we are going to solve them by recursion. The first problem requires a product-accumulation process for its solution, and the second problem requires a sum-accumulation process.

Example Problem 15.4

The problem statement

Recall that the factorial function is defined by

$$\{1\} \quad N! = N*(N-1)*(N-2)* * *(2)*(1)$$
$$\{2\} \quad 0! = 1$$

This definition works for any nonnegative value of N. Let us write the code that finds Factorial(N) recursively.

The solution   We can use the second definition as a base case, and the relationship $N! = N * (N - 1)!$ to get the coded function Factorial as shown.

```
FUNCTION Factorial(N: integer): integer;
   {returns the value of N! using recursion}
   BEGIN
     IF N = 0 THEN
       Factorial:= 1
     ELSE
       Factorial:= N*Factorial(N-1)
   END;  ◆
```

Example Problem 15.5

The problem   Let us now write a recursive function to find the sum of the first N positive integers.
statement   In this case, the base case and recursive relationship is given as follows:

1. The sum of the first 0 integers is 0.
2. The sum of the first N integers is equal to the sum of N plus the sum of the first $N - 1$ integers.

The solution   The coded solution for this problem, using recursion, is given as the function SumOfFirstNIntegers.

```
FUNCTION SumOfFirstNIntegers(N: integer): integer;
  {a recursive function to find the sum of the first N nonnegative
  integers}
  BEGIN
    IF N = 0 THEN
      SumOfFirstNIntegers:= 0
    ELSE
      SumOfFirstNIntegers:= N + SumOfFirstNIntegers(N-1)
  END;  ◆
```

VAR *parameters*   We have said previously that if a problem can be solved using iteration, it can likewise be solved using recursion. As you already know, loops are often used to accumulate values into one or more *variables* that represent solutions. When you apply recursion as the accumulation process into some variable(s), you must ensure that the accumulated value(s) is passed from process to process. The value taken on by the variable in one recursive process, moreover, should not be destroyed within any other recursive process. Hence, it must be passed from block to block using a call by VAR mechanism.

Example Problem 15.6

Let us write a recursive procedure that returns the value of the sum of the first *N* positive integers. In the process of finding this value, it also displays every *M*th partial sum. Let us name the procedure ShowSums, where a typical call and run is as follows:

```
ShowSums(15, 4, Sum);
writeln('The sum of the first 15 integers is ',Sum:1);

Output follows:
The sum of the first 4 integers is 10.
The sum of the first 8 integers is 36.
The sum of the first 12 integers is 78.
The sum of the first 15 integers is 120.
```

The code for the header, along with preconditions and postconditions, is written as

```
PROCEDURE ShowSums(N, M: integer; VAR Sum: integer);
   {in: N -- used to give Sum the value of 1 + 2 + .. + N-1 + N
    in: M -- used to determine whether Sum's value is displayed
   out: Sum -- the value of the sum 1 + 2 + .. + N-1 + N
   out: Sum's value is displayed if it is an M_th sum}
   BEGIN   END;
```

We need to find a block statement that uses recursion to satisfy the preconditions and postconditions of the problem.

The first draft

The base case occurs when N is equal to 0. The value assigned to Sum for this case is 0. We can apply Algorithm 15.1 in our initial draft to get the pseudocode

> *IF N = 0 THEN*
>   *display message*
>   *Sum ← 0*
> *ELSE*
>   *{statements}*
>   *ShowSums(N−1, M, Sum)*
>   *{statements}*

We have handled the base case and know that each recursive call means that the next smaller sum must be found. Now let us deal with finding the next smaller sum.

Drafting the statements for the recursive cases

Given some N and the call ShowSums(N-1, M, Sum), the problem ShowSums will have been solved for all calls up to finding the solution of ShowSums for the value N. Hence, the value of Sum represents the sum of $1 + .. + N-1$ when control is returned from the call to ShowSums using the value $N-1$. Therefore, the necessary assignment of *Sum ← Sum + N* must be made only after Sum has taken on the value of $1 + .. + N-1$. Then after this assignment is executed, Sum's value represents the sum of the first N integers. If N is divisible by

M, this value is displayed. Thus, the statements following the return from the recursive call are given by

$$Sum \leftarrow Sum + N$$
$$IF \ N \ MOD \ M = 0 \ THEN$$
$$display \ N, \ Sum$$

Source code   The coded solution is given as the procedure ShowSums.

```
PROCEDURE ShowSums(N, M: integer; VAR Sum: integer);
  {documentation}
  BEGIN
    IF N = 0 THEN
      BEGIN
        writeln('Output follows:');
        Sum:= 0
      END
    ELSE
      BEGIN
        ShowSums(N-1, M, Sum);
        Sum:= Sum + N;
        IF N MOD M = 0 THEN
          writeln('The sum of the first ',N:1, ' integers is ',Sum:1, '.')
      END
  END;  ◆
```

Assigning array   As the next example shows, you can write source code to read in values to
elements   the elements of an array using a recursive process. Pay particular attention to the
way we deal with the issue of parameter passing in deriving the code for this solution.

Example Problem 15.7

The problem   Let us write a recursive procedure FillIn that assigns positive values to the ele-
statement   ments of Ints, an array of integers, over the subrange 1..TotalAssigned. Each of the
TotalAssigned integer values are read in from the keyboard. If Total-
Assigned is less than MaxElements, then TotalAssigned positive values
were read in and assigned, but the last value read in was not positive.

The procedure is called by FillIn(MaxElements, TotalAssigned,
Ints), where the code for the recursive stub is

```
PROCEDURE FillIn(Left: integer;
               VAR TotalAssigned: integer; VAR Ints: IntsArray);
  {in: Left -- count of elements left that can be assigned a value
```

```
out: TotalAssigned -- count of elements that were assigned values
out: Ints -- the elements over 1..TotalAssigned that were assigned values}
  BEGIN    END;
```

Drafting a solution

There are two bases cases here, one externally determined by the value of Left and the other internally determined by a value read into Temp, a local variable of type integer. We can describe the handling of the base cases and draft the recursive call with the pseudocode description

IF Left = 0 THEN   *{no more candidates are possible}*
   handle base case #1
ELSE   *{another candidate value can be read in}*
  read(Temp)
  IF Temp <= 0 THEN
   handle base case #2   *{the last value read in is not positive}*
  ELSE
   prerecursion statements
   FillIn(Left-1, TotalAssigned, Ints)
   postrecursion statements

The variable Temp represents a candidate value to be assigned to an element of Ints. Note that a nonpositive value read into Temp stops the recursive calling.

Second draft

Let us deal with handling the base cases in the next draft. If we look at the postconditions returned by FillIn, we see that the elements of Ints have been assigned values over the subrange *1..TotalAssigned*. Moreover, the value read into Temp is still an unassigned candidate. Thus, the required postrecursion statements are described by

$$TotalAssigned \leftarrow TotalAssigned + 1$$
$$Ints[TotalAssigned] \leftarrow Temp$$

Handling the base cases

Note that if a recursive call is made, it implies that values will have been assigned to the elements of Ints over the access subrange *1..TotalAssigned*. If one of the two base cases occurs, no recursive calls are made, and, hence, no values are assigned to any elements of Ints. Thus, in either case, TotalAssigned must be given the value of 0. For the first base case, we should additionally have the computer display a message indicating that there are no more values that can be read in.

Source code

We have filled in enough of the logic that we can write the code for the procedure. It is given as follows:

```
PROCEDURE FillIn(Left: integer;
                 VAR TotalAssigned: integer; VAR Ints: IntsArray);
   {documentation}
   VAR
     Temp:  integer;   {element for Ints or a process terminator}
   BEGIN
     IF left = 0 THEN
```

```
        BEGIN
          readln;    {clear input line}
          writeln('No more values can be read in.');
          TotalAssigned:= 0
        END
      ELSE
      BEGIN
        read(Temp);
        IF Temp <= 0 THEN
          TotalAssigned:= 0
        ELSE
          BEGIN
            FillIn(Left-1, TotalAssigned, Ints);
            TotalAssigned:= TotalAssigned+1;
            Ints[TotalAssigned]:= Temp
          END
      END
    END;  ◆
```

Some Useful Hints

As you already know from other applications, improper use of the parameter-passing mechanism leads to buggy source code. When you use recursion to solve a problem, you should, more than ever, be careful about the way you pass parameters.

Also, the order in which statements are executed can determine the success or failure of an algorithm. It is important that you know whether statements belonging to the recursive part of the algorithm be executed before or after the recursive call. To make your coding task easier, we give you a few hints on how to deal with these two important issues.

Parameter Passing Hints

1. Generally, use a value call on any parameter that is required to determine whether a base case has occurred.

2. If the recursive process is supposed to accumulate values in some variable, the variable is called by VAR. A change made on it in any one block is thus felt in all other recursing blocks. Without this mechanism in place, a value cannot be accumulated in the variable from process to process.

3. Use a local variable when its value is *initially* set by a statement within the recursing process. This value is stored and used over the statements of just one process. Do not forget that a value assigned to one of these variables before the recursive call(s) is always reinstated when control returns from the recursive call.

Hints on Placing Statements Belonging to the Recursive Part

1. If a statement or sequence is used to reduce the size of the problem, it should definitely precede the recursive call.

2. If the statement or sequence requires the results of a recursive call, it is placed after the call. We could just as easily say that if the statement or sequence should be postponed while a smaller problem is being solved, it should definitely be placed after the call.

EXERCISES

Practice Your Analysis Skills

1. Draw the appearance of the array Ints after the following process has been executed:

```
PROCEDURE FillIn(Left: integer; VAR Ints: IntsArray);
  VAR
    Temp: integer;
  BEGIN
    IF Left < > 0 THEN
      BEGIN
        FillIn(Left-1, Ints);
        read(Temp);
        Ints[Left]:= Temp
      END
  END;

FillIn(4, Ints);  readln;

Sample data input:
52   78   44   91   75<eoln>
```

2. Repeat Exercise 1, except this time the compound statement of the IF statement is coded as

```
BEGIN
  read(Temp);
  FillIn(Left-1, Ints);
  Ints[Left]:= Temp
END
```

Sharpen Your Implementation Skills

3. Rewrite the function Factorial as a procedure ShowFactorials called by Show-Factorials(N, M, Factorial);, where every Mth factorial is displayed. The value returned to Factorial, representing the value of N!, is to be displayed once the recursive process is completed.

4. A permutation of N items taken from a set of M possible items represents an ordered sample. The number of different permutations of N items taken M at a time is found by the product $M * (M-1) * (M-2) \cdots$, where N multiplications are done. Write the recursive function Permutations. If N is greater than M, the function should return the value of 0.

5. A combination of M items taken for a set of N possible items represents an unordered sample. The number of combinations of a possible N items taken M at a time is found by the formula

$$(\text{permutations of } M \text{ items taken } N \text{ at a time})/N!$$

Use calls to the two recursive functions Permutations and Factorial to write a function Combinations as called by Combinations(M, N).

6. Write the function Combinations as a one-block recursive function. No calls should be made either to Permutations or Factorial. (*Hint:* Use an integer quotient to find each factor in the accumulated product.)

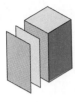

15.4   Desk Tracing Recursive Code

So far, you have seen coded solutions to problems that used *linear recursion* where a maximum of only one recursive call is made for any given block. In this section, you will see an algorithm that is *nonlinearly recursive*. In this case, more than one recursive call is made per block.

It is difficult to desk trace an algorithm that makes more than one recursive call in a block if you do not use a *stack-history tree*. In this section, you will learn how to trace recursive logic by sketching a stack-history tree.

> **Stack-history tree**:   a diagram that shows the history of the run-time stack at any given time.

A simple example

In order to show how to build a stack history tree, we need a sample process. The program given as Example 15.1, although it consists mainly of stubs, is complete enough to illustrate how you apply this source code analysis technique.

Example 15.1

```
PROGRAM TreeExample(output);
  {a program used to demonstrate how a stack-history tree is built}
  {*                                                                    *}
  PROCEDURE C(N: integer);
    BEGIN
      IF N > 0 THEN
        C(N-1)
    END;
  {*                                                                    *}
  PROCEDURE B;
    BEGIN
      C(1)
    END;
  {*                                                                    *}
  PROCEDURE A;
    BEGIN
      B
    END;
  {*                                                                    *}
```

```
BEGIN
   A;
   C(1);
   writeln('Finished')
END.
```

An example of a stack-history tree

If we "walk through" the source code of Example 15.1 and number each event that represents a call to or a return from a procedure, we obtain the description

1. main calls A
2. A calls B
3. B calls C(1)
4. C(1) calls C(0)
5. C(0) returns to C(1)
6. C(1) returns to B
7. B returns to A
8. A returns to main
9. main calls C(1)
10. C(1) calls C(0)
11. C(0) returns to C(1)
12. C(1) returns to main
13. main calls writeln('Finished')
14. writeln('Finished') returns to main.

Figure 15.6 shows the tree that depicts the history of the run-time stack for this sample program.

Tree-building rules

You can build a tree to depict the history of the run-time stack by following these rules:

I. Every tree must have a main root from which all branches originate. This principal root will always represent some initial process. In our present example, the main root represents the main block's process.

II. The tree consists of *nodes* that represent the processes that were on the run-time stack at any given time. Each node should be labeled to represent *exactly one* process. Usually, a header identifier or some reasonable abbreviation of it suffices. If you are drawing a tree that has recursive calls, you should also include the significant values taken on by the parameters. For example, Figure 15.6 has two C nodes, C(1) and C(0).

III. A branch of the tree (solid line) shows the call-return path between any two processes. The calling process is always placed above the called one. Thus, A is shown above B, B is shown above C(1), and C(1) is shown above C(0). Also, if a given node has more than one branch, an earlier call is always shown to the left of the later call. Thus, A is shown to the left of C(1) and C(1) is shown to the left of writeln.

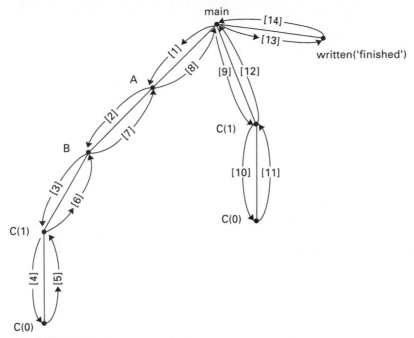

FIGURE 15.6 Tree showing the run-time stack of Example 15.1.

IV.   The arrows showing the call and return operations are unnecessary, for a move down the tree will always indicate a push and a move up the tree will always represent a pop. Furthermore, every node (representing a given process) is "visited" (pushed and popped) exactly once, and no given process is popped until all the processes it has called have been popped.

Fibonacci numbers

A sequence for which the next number is found by taking the sum of the previous two numbers defines a Fibonacci sequence. We can define a way to generate Fibonacci numbers recursively with

$$(N >= 2): \quad Fib(N) \leftarrow Fib(N-2) + Fib(N-1)$$
$$(N = 1): \quad Fib(N) \leftarrow 1$$
$$(N = 0): \quad Fib(N) \leftarrow 0$$

We can use this definition to code the Fibonacci function shown as Example 15.2. We use the function of this example to show how recursive algorithms can be desk traced using stack-history trees.

Example 15.2

```
FUNCTION Fibonacci(N: integer): integer;
  {returns the N_th Fibonacci number, given that the first two numbers
  are 0 and 1}
  BEGIN
```

```
IF N = 1 THEN
   Fibonacci:= 0
ELSE IF N = 2 THEN
   Fibonacci:= 1
ELSE
   Fibonacci:= Fibonacci(N-2) + Fibonacci(N-1)
END;
```

This function uses *nonlinear recursion* to find a Fibonacci number. It would be hopeless to do a desk trace of the function without trees, even with an initial N as small as 6 or 7. Using trees, the task is laborious but straightforward, even for relatively large values of N.

Linear recursion: a term used to describe a recursive algorithm where at most one recursive call is carried out as part of the execution of a single recursive process.

Nonlinear recursion: a term used to describe a recursive algorithm where more than one recursive call can be carried out as part of the execution of a single recursive process.

Building some trees

The tree for the call Fibonacci(3) is shown in Figure 15.7. It describes the following actions:

1. some block calls *F(3)*
2. *F(3)* calls *F(1)*
3. *F(1)* returns to *F(3)*
4. *F(3)* calls *F(2)*
5. *F(2)* returns to *F(3)*
6. *F(3)* returns control to the calling block

FIGURE 15.7 Tree for Fibonacci(3).

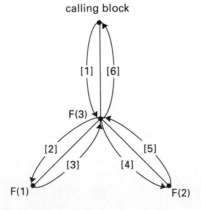

The tree for a call to Fibonacci (4) is shown as Figure 15.8. This time we have not used arrows to show pushes and pops. Clearly, the figure shows that the machine needs to create (push) and destroy (pop) five separate processes in order to find Fibonacci (4). In words, we have "*F(4)* is pushed; *F(2)* is pushed from *F(4)* and immediately popped; *F(3)* is pushed from *F(4)*; *F(1)* is pushed from *F(3)* and immediately popped; *F(2)* is pushed from *F(3)* and immediately popped; *F(3)* (whose value is now known) is popped and its value returned to *F(4)*; and *F(4)* is popped, returning a value to the calling block."

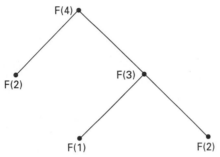

FIGURE 15.8 Tree for Fibonacci (4).

Finally, Figure 15.9 shows Fibonacci (6)'s tree, a process where the machine executes a total of 15 pushes and pops.

Efficiency of Fibonacci   If you look at the trees of Figures 15.7, 15.8, and 15.9, it appears that as *N* increases, the number of recursive calls to the function dramatically increases. Indeed, the call Fibonacci (20) adds up to 13,529 pushes and pops of the run-time stack. If you think that such a number sounds horribly inefficient, you are correct, for it can be shown that the efficiency of this function is approximately $O(1.61^N)$.[1] Let us determine just how many pushes and pops are required using the computer to count the processes.

Example Problem 15.8

Let us write a driver to count the number of calls made to find Fibonacci (20). Although it is not normally recommended, we must code the function including the VAR parameter Calls in the header because we want to count the number of calls made to the function Fibonacci. We expect to use the driver in the context of

> *display Fibonacci(20, Calls)*
> *display Calls*

[1] Kruse, Robert L., *Data Stuctures and Program Design,* 2nd Ed., p. 512. Prentice Hall, Englewood Cliffs.

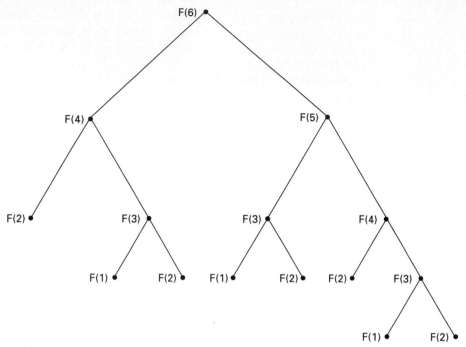

FIGURE 15.9 Tree for `Fibonacci(6)`.

The code for the driver is straightforward, so we can present the solution as the program `CountCalls`. The program run is given below the source code. We have written the program to show the number of calls made to find the first through fifth Fibonacci numbers so you can get an idea of how quickly this function becomes computationally costly.

```
PROGRAM CountCalls(output);
  {displays the number of calls made to the recursive function
  Fibonacci  for different values of N.}
  VAR
    Calls,      {count of number of calls made to the function}
    No:         {used as a loop counter to find results of F(1) thru F(5)}
            integer;
  {*                                                                      *}
  FUNCTION Fibonacci(N: integer; VAR Calls: integer): integer;
    {The recursive function used to count calls for any given initial
    N.  The side effect on the variable Calls is deliberate.}
    BEGIN
      Calls:= Calls + 1;   {counts that another call was made}
      IF N = 1 THEN
        Fibonacci:= 0
```

```
        ELSE If N = 2 THEN
          Fibonacci:= 1
        ELSE
          Fibonacci:= Fibonacci(N-2) + Fibonacci(N-1)
      END;
  {*                                                              *}
  BEGIN
    FOR No:= 1 TO 5 DO          {display and check for first five numbers}
      BEGIN
        Calls:= 0;
        write('No ', No:1,':   ',Fibonacci(No, Call):1,'    ');
        writeln('CALLS = ',Calls:1)
      END;
    Calls:= 0;
    write('No 20:   ',Fibonacci(20, Calls);
    writeln('CALLS =   ',Calls:1)
  END.
```

```
                    No 1:   0    CALLS = 1
                    No 2:   1    CALLS = 1
                    No 3:   1    CALLS = 3
                    No 4:   2    CALLS = 5
                    No 5:   3    CALLS = 9
                    No 20: 4181     CALLS = 13529
```

*Why
Fibonacci is
inefficient*

Look again at the tree for calculating Fibonacci(6). It shows that the function Fibonacci(4) was calculated twice *as two apparently separate problems* during the run. Indeed, Fibonacci(3) was found three separate times, Fibonacci(2) five times, and Fibonacci(1) three times.

The situation gets even worse when larger numbers are found. For example, to find Fibonacci(10) using the recursive function, the machine needs to solve for Fibonacci(8) two separate times, Fibonacci(7) three separate times, Fibonacci(6) five separate times, Fibonacci(5) eight separate times, and so forth.

All these apparently separate evaluations represents a lot of duplicate processing, whose results, once used by the machine, are discarded. Thus, the same problem is solved, "forgotten," and then solved again in another process. It is this characteristic of the function that ultimate makes it so inefficient. ◆

*A more efficient
algorithm*

Can we make the process of finding the Nth Fibonacci number more efficient? It is possible if we code an iterative solution. But what about deriving a more efficient recursive solution? Such an algorithm is also possible, but we can no longer code Fibonacci as a function.

Example Problem 15.9

The problem
statement

In theory, once a Fibonacci number has been found, it should simply be referenced to find higher numbers. Given this hypothesis, we should be able to write an algorithm that will be O(*N*), where each repetitive process finds the value of Fibonacci (N) only once. Let us devise a recursive algorithm to find the *N*th Fibonacci number using recursive processing.

Using an array

We can speed things up considerably by using virtually the same recursive algorithm, but, instead, using it in a procedure to assign values to the elements of FibNos, an array of integers whose elements are accessed by the subrange 1..MaxFib. When we apply this approach, each time a new Fibonacci number is found, it is stored as an element of FibNos. Once the value of any given element is found, its value can be accessed in the other processes. Hence, the same problem need not be solved again and again.

The procedure is initially called by the statement SetFibNo (N, FibNos), where the corresponding header of the recursive block looks like PROCEDURE SetFibNo (N: integer; VAR FibNos: FibArray). The purpose of the block is to set the value of the element FibNos [N] using recursive logic.

Coding
SetFibNo

The base case occurs when N equals 2 at which point the machine should assign *FibNos[1]* ← *0* and *FibNos[2]* ← *1*. (Recall that we need to know *two* numbers in order to set a Fibonacci number.) We also need a statement such as SetFibNo (N-1, FibNos); for the recursive call. Finally, we need to code a statement described by *FibNos[N]* ← *FibNos[N − 2] + FibNos[N − 1]* that is carried out after the computer has assigned values to FibNos [N-2] and FibNos [N-1]. The statement for SetFibNo is thus described by the pseudocode

$$
\begin{aligned}
&IF\ N = 2\ THEN \\
&\quad FibNos[2] \leftarrow 1 \\
&\quad FibNos[1] \leftarrow 0 \\
&ELSE \\
&\quad SetFibNo(FibNos,N\text{-}1) \\
&\quad FibNos[N] \leftarrow FibNos[N - 2] + FibNos[N - 1]
\end{aligned}
$$

Source code

From the description, we obtain the source code for SetFibNo as

```
PROCEDURE SetFibNo (N: integer; VAR FibNos: FibArray);
   {in: N -- the element of FibNos to be given a value
    out: FibNos -- the elements over the subrange 1..N are given
                   Fibonacci number values}
BEGIN
   IF N = 2 THEN
     BEGIN
       FibNos [2] := 1;
       FibNos [1] := 0
     END
   ELSE
```

```
        BEGIN
          SetFibNo (N-1, FibNos);
          FibNos[N]:= FibNos[N-2] + FibNos[N-1]
        END
    END;  ◆
```

EXERCISES

Test Your Understanding

1. Is the function `Fibonacci` linearly recursive? What about the procedure `SetFibNos`? Explain your answers.

2. Draw the recursion tree for `Fibonacci(7)`.

3. Draw the recursion tree for the call `SetFibNo(7, FibNos)`.

Sharpen Your Implementation Skills

4. The function to find the combination of M things taken N at a time can be expressed by the recursive relationships:

$$C(M, 0) = 1$$

$$C(M, M) = 1$$

$$C(M, N) = C(M - 1, N) + C(M - 1, N - 1)$$

Write a recursive function to find the combination of M items taken N at a time and test it for M = 10 and N = 4. (Answer for test values is 210.)

5. Draw the recursion tree for `Combinations(5, 3)`. Is the function linearly recursive or not?

6. You can improve on the efficiency of the recursive function in Exercise 4 by coding a procedure `SetCombos` and storing values computed into an array `Combos`. How many dimensions should this array have?

7. Write the code for the procedure suggested by Exercise 6 and use it to find C(10, 4).

8. Draw the recursion tree for the call `SetCombos(5, 3, Combos)`, where the final value found as an element of `Combos` represents M = 5 and N = 3.

15.5 Searching Recursively

If you recall the properties of search algorithms that use loops, it would seem that recursion, which works because a problem is reduced in size with each recursive call, would seem the more natural strategy to adopt. In this section, we present the generic search algorithm as it applies to recursion and use it to solve problems that require some kind of searching logic.

The recursive form of the search algorithm   A search function requires an array and a key value for the search. This function, as usual, returns the index value of that element that matches the value of the search key (`Key`). If values have been assigned to the elements in `AnArray` over the subrange *1..TotalElements,* the recursive form of the search function is described by Algorithm 15.2.

Algorithm 15.2

{Recursive search through AnArray:}
FUNCTION Index(VAR AnArray; Key; {subrange parameter(s)}): IndexType
   IF finished THEN   *{boolean expression formed from subrange vars}*
     Index ← 0   *{returns null index}*
   ELSE
     get Candidate   *{next index value to test; a local reference var}*
   IF AnArray[Candidate] = Key THEN   *{Found}*
     Index ← Candidate
   ELSE   *{keep searching}*
     revise a subrange value(s), thus reducing the candidate subrange
     Index ← Index(AnArray, Key, {revised subrange values})

AnIndex ← Index(AnArray, Key, {expressions representing an initial subrange})
{end algorithm}

The required parameters to represent the candidate subrange for both the initial call and the recursive calls are determined by the kind of search algorithm (linear or binary) we wish to write.

In the algorithm's description, the *Candidate* index value is found using the value(s) in the parameter list. The *revised subrange values* are formed using the *Candidate* value and one (or more) of the initial subrange values passed into the function. These expressions (although sometimes there is only one expression) always imply a reduction in the size of the candidate subrange with the next recursive call.

Characteristics of recursive searching

Before we derive the recursive forms of the linear and binary search algorithms, let us list some properties that characterize the code for a recursive search algorithm:

1. The array passed into the recursing block is called by VAR, for it is too costly to copy an entire array into each new process.

2. A recursive call always implies a reduction in the subrange of candidate elements. Therefore, at least one value parameter representing a subrange of elements is found in the header. The corresponding actual parameter expression(s) is a function of some local candidate subrange. This expression, whose value must represent a reduction in the size of the candidate subrange, is found and passed into the next search process.

3. The *finished* condition is expressed in terms of the candidate subrange parameter(s). This condition represents the base case when there is no candidate subrange left to probe.

4. The other base case is the *found* condition when *AnArray[Candidate]* matches the value of *Key*.

The linear search

If we plan to use a linear search algorithm, we can envision calling the search function using Linear(AnArray, Key, TotalElements), where values have been assigned to the elements over the subrange *1..TotalElements*. The formal parameter corresponding to this header is N, where the implication is that the candidate subrange must be *1..N*. If N is passed into Linear as 0, the search is finished, otherwise N's value serves as the candidate probe. Let us apply the algorithm to solve the next problem.

Example Problem 15.10

The problem statement

Suppose we have the structured variable People of type VillageType, an array of records with values assigned over the subrange *1..Population*. One of its fields, SocSecNo of type SSNType, will be the key field for a linear search. A typical call to this function, named Linear, is coded as Index:= Linear(People, KeyNo, Population) where KeyNo represents the value of the Social Security number field for the record being sought. The function is to be coded recursively.

Source code

Using Algorithm 15.2, we arrive at the code for Linear as follows:

```
FUNCTION Linear(VAR People: VillageType; KeyNo: SSNType;
                                        N: integer): integer;
   {An example of a recursive linear search.}
   BEGIN
     IF N = 0 THEN        {finished}
       Linear:= 0
     ELSE IF People[N].SocSecNo = KeyNo THEN      {N is candidate index}
       Linear:= N
     ELSE
       Linear:= Linear(People, KeyNo, N-1)
   END;  ◆
```

The binary search

When we use the binary search algorithm, we require two parameters, Lo and Hi, to represent a candidate subrange. The candidate probe value is obtained from the expression (Lo + Hi) DIV 2. This value can be stored in a local variable Mid. The same *finished* condition used in the itcrative version, that is Lo > Hi, indicates a failed search array. Given that the variable AnArray has values assigned to the elements over the subrange *1..TotalElements*, the initial call to this function is coded as Binary(AnArray, Key, 1, TotalElements). The pseudocode description for the recursive form of the binary search is given as Algorithm 15.3.

Algorithm 15.3

{recursive form of binary search algorithm:}
FUNCTION Binary(VAR AnArray; Key; Lo, Hi): IndexType
    IF Lo > Hi THEN   *{finished condition}*
      Binary ← 0
    ELSE   *{else keep looking:}*
      Mid ← (Lo + Hi) DIV 2   *{1. get candidate index}*
      IF AnArray[Mid] = Key THEN   *{2. if Found terminal condition then}*
      Binary ← Mid   *{return Mid to Binary}*

$$ELSE\ IF\ AnArray[Mid] < Key\ THEN \quad \{else\ not\ found,\ so:\}$$
$$Binary \leftarrow Binary(AnArray,\ Key,\ Mid+1,\ Hi) \quad \{try\ again\ with\}$$
$$ELSE \quad\quad\quad\quad\quad\quad\quad\quad\quad\quad\quad\quad\quad\quad \{a\ smaller\ subrange\}$$
$$Binary \leftarrow Binary(AnArray,\ Key,\ Lo,\ Mid\text{-}1)$$

$$Index \leftarrow Binary(AnArray,\ Key,\ 1,\ LastElement)$$
$$\{end\ algorithm\}$$

Using the
algorithm
Let us apply this algorithm to the same problem we posed as Example Problem 15.10. In this case, however, we are assuming an array of records sorted by SocSecNo. Hence, we can apply the binary search for this problem.

Example Problem 15.11

The problem
and its solution
Suppose the array of records People is sorted by social security number. Let us write a binary search function, initially called by Index:= Binary(People, KeyNo, 1, Population), that returns the index value of the element in People whose SocSecNo matches the value of KeyNo. If no such record exists, the value returned is 0.

Source code
From Algorithm 15.3, we directly obtain the source code for the function Binary as

```
FUNCTION Binary(VAR People: VillageType; KeyNo: SSNType;
                                    Lo, Hi: integer): integer;
  {The recursive version of the binary search algorithm.}
  VAR
    Mid: integer;    {local candidate index}
  BEGIN
    IF Lo > Hi THEN                            {check finished condition}
      Binary:= 0
    ELSE                                              {not finished, so}
      BEGIN
        Mid:= (Lo + Hi) DIV 2;                  {get candidate index and}
        IF People[Mid].SocSecNo = KeyNo THEN   {check found condition}
          Binary:= Mid
        ELSE                                          {not found, so}
          IF People[Mid].SocSecNo < KeyNo THEN      {try again with}
          Binary:= Binary(People, KeyNo, Mid+1, Hi) {smaller subrange}
        ELSE
          Binary:= Binary(People, KeyNo, Lo, Mid-1)
      END
END; ◆
```

A recursive
boolean function
We can use a form of the generic search algorithm to solve any problem for which a search is implied. Consider, for example, the function Sorted used in the context of a statement such as

```
           IF Sorted(AnArray, TotalElements) THEN
             BEGIN {some sequence}   END;
```

We can adopt the recursive form of the linear search to solve the problem. In this case, the search is for an element out of order.

Example Problem 15.12

The problem statement

Write a recursive function `Sorted` that returns `true` if the elements of `AnArray`, an array of integers with values assigned over the subrange *1..TotalElements,* are in ascending order.

The solution

The machine is to search for an element that is out of order over a candidate subrange, initially *1..TotalElements.* If the candidate subrange has been reduced to a single element, no further comparisons are required. The search is finished with no element out of order, so `true` is returned to `Sorted`.

If the expression (`AnArray[N-1]` > `AnArray[N]`) evaluates to `true`, a condition indicating the elements are not in order is *found.* Then the value `false` is returned to the function. Should neither condition hold `true`, the search subrange is reduced by 1, and another attempt is made to return a value to `Sorted`.

Source code

The coded solution to the problem is given as the function `Sorted`.

```
FUNCTION Sorted(VAR AnArray: IntsArray; N: integer): boolean;
  {A recursive function that checks whether an array of integers is
  sorted.}
BEGIN
    IF N = 1 THEN              {sorted, no more comparisons possible, so}
      Sorted:= true           {return a value of true}
    ELSE IF AnArray[N-1] > AnArray[N] THEN   {not sorted, so}
      Sorted:= false                         {return a value of false}
    ELSE                                      {not finished or found, so}
      Sorted:= Sorted(AnArray, N-1)      {try again with smaller subrange}
  END;  ◆
```

Another use for the search algorithm

If you want to write a function that returns the index value of the lowest element in an array of integers, you need an algorithm that examines each element in turn. You can modify the recursive form of the linear search to get the code for this function. A function to return the index value of the lowest element is given as Example 15.3, where the first call to the function follows the code.

Example 15.3

```
FUNCTION Lowest(VAR AnArray: IntsArray; Candidate, N: integer): integer;
  BEGIN
    IF N = 0 THEN
      Lowest:= Candidate
```

```
    ELSE IF AnArray[N] < AnArray[Candidate] THEN
      Lowest:= Lowest(AnArray, N, N-1)
    ELSE
      Lowest:= Lowest(AnArray, Candidate, N-1)
  END;

Index:= Lowest(AnArray, TotalElements, TotalElements-1);
```

Explaining the
semantics

An assumed candidate for the index whose elements have the lowest value is required for the algorithm to work. The initial call uses `AnArray[TotalElements]` as the candidate lowest value. The recursive process uses `Candidate` to represent the index value of the lowest element in the subrange $N+1..TotalElements$. If the value of the probe `AnArray[N]` is found to be smaller than the present candidate index value, this probe is passed in as the new candidate index value for the next comparison with element `AnArray[N-1]`.

Eventually, the *finished* condition is reached. When this condition is achieved, the value of `Candidate` represents the index value of the lowest element in the subrange $1..TotalElements$. We can use the value 1 rather than 0 (N's last value) for the subrange because no comparison to find a new candidate is done in this final process.

EXERCISES

Test Your
Understanding

1. Given the four functions we wrote in this section, which of them, when executed, does the following:
   (a) Might terminate before the entire subrange of elements is processed?
   (b) Definitely requires that the entire subrange of elements be processed?

2. What is the O for each of the four functions?

3. Suppose the binary search function were applied to an unsorted array. What would be the more likely outcome: a failed search or an infinite stack? Explain your answer in one or two sentences.

Sharpen Your
Implementation
Skills

4. Write a recursive function to return the index value of the highest element in the subrange *1..TotalElements*.

5. Write the call and the procedure `GetLoAndHi` that uses a recursive algorithm to find the index value of the lowest and highest elements in an array of integers. (*Hint:* Initialize candidate values before the procedure call.)

6. The function `Binary` that we wrote will cause difficulties if there are duplicate elements. Suppose you are using the binary search to seek out a match for a name in a large array of last names. You want the function to return the lowest index value in the array `Names` that matches the name you are seeking. Write the code for this form of the binary search algorithm. (*Hint:* Don't seek a match and don't return the value of *Mid* when finished.)

15.6 The Merge–Sort Algorithm

There are a number of sorting algorithms that are implemented using recursion. One of these is the merge–sort algorithm. Its efficiency is $O(N \log_2(N))$, thus more efficient than the $O(N^2)$ algorithms derived in Chapter 10. The merge–sort algorithm is efficient because (1) each recursive call reduces the sorting problem by a factor of 2 and (2) no duplicate processing is done within any of the different processes that are recursively called.

CASE STUDY 15.1

Let us derive the code for the merge-sort algorithm.

Partition sorting

The algorithm depends upon a "partitioning" process by which a given array (or array subrange) is partitioned as two subarrays with smaller subranges. This technique of "partitioning" is a property of virtually any sorting algorithm whose efficiency is better than $O(N^2)$. For this reason, these "better-than-$O(N^2)$ sorting algorithms" (some of which are not recursive) are classified as "partition–sort" algorithms.

Merge–sort's pseudocode

The initial pseudocode draft for the merge–sort algorithm is as follows:

> {Merge–sort algorithm:}
> PROCEDURE SortIt(Lo, Hi: IndexType; VAR AnArray: ArrayType);
>   use input index values to divide AnArray into lower and upper subarrays
>   IF the lower subarray index values imply a sortable subrange THEN
>   SortIt ({index parameters representing lower subarray}, AnArray)
>   IF the upper subarray index values imply a sortable subrange THEN
>   SortIt ({index parameters representing upper subarray}, AnArray)
>   merge the two sorted subarrays over the subrange of AnArray
>
> SortIt (1, TotalElements, AnArray)
> {end algorithm}

The initial call to `SortIt` indicates the elements of `AnArray` are to be sorted over the subrange *1..TotalElements*. The header for `SortIt` indicates that the problem is to sort the array elements over the subrange *Lo..Hi*.

Refinements and code

We can use a local variable `Mid` to divide the subrange into the two "subarrays" that are first sorted then merged. The base cases will occur for either subarray when it has only one element in it. When this event occurs, the subarray is trivially "sorted" and no more recursive calls are necessary.

Note that the two base cases can occur within the same `SortIt` process. Should this event occur, the trivial merge of two adjacent array elements is done.

On the other hand, if *lower index value* < *upper index value* holds true for either of the two subranges, there is more than one element in the subarray. This condition does not describe the base case of a subarray with one element in it. Given this condition, then, the subarray needs to be sorted. From these thoughts, we obtain the following refinement of the original algorithm:

$$Mid \leftarrow (Lo + Hi) \text{ DIV } 2 \quad \{divides \ array \ in \ half\}$$
IF Lo < Mid THEN   *{lower subarray is "sortable" if true}*
     SortIt(Lo, Mid, AnArray)
IF Mid+1 < Hi THEN   *{upper subarray is "sortable" if true}*
     SortIt(Mid+1, Hi, AnArray)
Merge(Lo, Mid, Hi, AnArray)

Source code   From the algorithm, we obtain the source code given below. We still need to write the procedure Merge.

```
{*                                                              *}
PROCEDURE Merge(Lo, Mid, Hi: integer; VAR AnArray: ArrayType);
  {in: AnArray[Lo]..AnArray[Mid] are in ascending order
   in: AnArray[Mid+1]..AnArray[Hi] are in ascending order
  out: AnArray[Lo]..AnArray[Hi] are in ascending order}
  BEGIN  END;
{+                                                              +}
PROCEDURE SortIt(Lo, Hi: integer; VAR AnArray: ArrayType);
  {A recursive algorithm to sort the elements of AnArray over the
  subrange Lo..Hi. It divides AnArray into two subarrays with
  specified subranges. The elements over each of these subranges are
  sorted and then merged.}
  VAR
    Mid: integer;  {used to divide the array}
  BEGIN
    Mid:= (Lo + Hi) DIV 2;
    IF Lo < Mid THEN
      SortIt(Lo, Mid, AnArray);
    IF Mid+1 < Hi THEN
      SortIt(Mid+1, Hi, AnArray);
    Merge(Lo, Mid, Hi, AnArray)
  END;
{*                                                              *}
```

Building a tree   Let us look at the tree to sort an array (or subarray) where the elements *1..8* have assigned values. Using parentheses to show the values taken on by Lo and Hi and bracketing the value of each local Mid value, we obtain the tree shown by Figure 15.10.

Walking through   In the example, the root node is represented by the process where Lo is 1 and
the example   Hi is 8, so that Mid is assigned the value 4. The first recursive call from the root

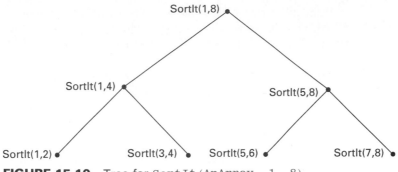

FIGURE 15.10 Tree for SortIt(AnArray, 1, 8).

node of SortIt(1,8) is then to SortIt(1,4), where AnArray is understood as the array parameter. This push on the run-time stack is shown by the left-hand branch of the main root.

SortIt(1,4) then breaks the problem into the two smaller problems, SortIt(1,2) and SortIt(3,4). These results are found and then merged. The end result when SortIt(1,4) returns control to SortIt(1,8) is that the elements over the subrange *1..4* are in order.

Next, the call within SortIt(1,8) is made to SortIt(5,8). In like manner, the actions executed in SortIt(5,8) break the problem down into smaller subranges. Eventually, SortIt(5,8) returns control to the SortIt(1,8) process, having accomplished the task of putting the elements over the subrange *5..8* in order.

The final step left is to merge the sorted elements of AnArray[1] through AnArray[4] with the sorted elements of AnArray[5] through AnArray[8]. When this merge is completed, the elements of AnArray[1] through AnArray[8] are sorted, and the root process is popped off the run-time stack.

Checking a base case

The tree shows that we have four base cases for which we can check the mechanism. Let us pick the process we have labeled as SortIt(5,6). Within this environment, Mid ↔ 5. Then, because the boolean expressions (Lo < Mid) and (Mid+1 < Hi) are both false, further subdivisions will not be made. Hence, the merge will be called with Merge(5, 5, 6, AnArray) representing a call from SortIt to merge the sorted array subrange *5..5* with the other sorted subrange of *6..6*. When Merge is exited, the smaller of the two elements will be assigned to the element AnArray[5] and the larger to AnArray[6]. SortIt(5,6) is then exited, returning the sorted subarray to the calling process SortIt(5,8).

Desk tracing a recursive algorithm

Sometimes you may find it helpful to desk trace a recursive algorithm. If the recursion process is nonlinear, you will need to use a tree for your desk trace. Remember the rule of small samples. The number of branches on the tree can become quite large even when just two recursive calls are made from a process. Also remember that the different parameter values determine the process on top of the stack at any given time. Therefore, be sure to label all necessary value parameters by their actual values.

Remember that a desk trace is used to find possible errors in your code. Therefore, you should be sensitive to certain events when you desk trace a recursive algorithm. Thus, you should do the following.

1. Check that all the branches from the main root reduce the problem and that the results returned represent solutions that are indeed useful to the larger problem. If this check is correct, the branches that result in the recursive calls are probably correct.

2. Check some of the cases that lead to a base case. If they return valid solutions to the trivialized problem, the logic that handles the base case(s) is probably correct.

We keep using the phrase "probably correct" because smaller problems solved correctly with correct handling of base cases implies that larger problems will be solved correctly. The very nature of the recursion mechanism allows you to jump to these conclusions, for you are applying the principles of mathematical induction to a specific problem.

*Writing a tracer
stub*

Given our partial solution, we can use a modified stub for Merge to confirm that the proper subranges are merged. We give you a stub to test the SortIt block with a sample run as follows:

```
PROCEDURE Merge(Lo, Mid, Hi: integer; VAR AnArray: ArrayType);
  {Stub to check subrange parameters passed into block.}
  BEGIN
    write('MERGING subrange (', Lo:1, '..', Mid:1, ')');
    writeln('WITH subrange  (',Mid+1:1, '..', Hi:1, ')');
    writeln('SORTED SUBRANGE:  ',Lo:1,'..', Hi:1);
  END;

{as driven by:}

SortIt(1,8,AnArray);
writeln('ALGORITHM COMPLETED');

{Resultant display:}

MERGING subrange  (1..1) WITH subrange  (2..2)
SORTED  SUBRANGE:   1..2
MERGING subrange  (3..3) WITH subrange  (4..4)
SORTED  SUBRANGE:   3..4
MERGING subrange  (1..2) WITH subrange  (3..4)
SORTED  SUBRANGE:   1..4
MERGING subrange  (5..5) WITH subrange  (6..6)
SORTED  SUBRANGE:   5..6
MERGING subrange  (7..7) WITH subrange  (8..8)
SORTED  SUBRANGE:   7..8
```

```
MERGING subrange (5..6) WITH subrange (7..8)
SORTED SUBRANGE:   5..8
MERGING subrange (1..4) WITH subrange (5..8)
SORTED SUBRANGE:   1..8
ALGORITHM COMPLETED
```

Developing
Merge

The best way to develop code for `Merge` is to use a local array `Temp` of type `ArrayType`. We can then describe the solution to the `Merge` problem as follows:

> *FOR Index ← Lo TO Hi DO*
>   *assign Temp[Index] from candidate subarray element(s)*
> *FOR Index ← Lo TO Hi DO*
>   *AnArray[Index] ← Temp[Index]*

If the elements assigned to `Temp` correctly come from the elements of the subarray *AnArray[Lo]..AnArray[Hi]* such that the values are assigned in ascending order, we have described a correct algorithm. We now need to work on developing the body of the first FOR loop.

Developing the
first loop

In order to ensure that the correct array element from `AnArray` is assigned to `Temp[Index]`, we need two variables representing the candidate index values from the two subarrays *AnArray[Lo]..AnArray[Mid]* and *AnArray[Mid + 1]..AnArray[Hi]*. The first candidate values given to these variables, which we will name `Index1` and `Index2`, must be the values `Lo` and `Mid+1`. Hence, the assignments *Index1 ← Lo* and *Index2 ← Mid+1* are required before the first loop is entered.

The invariant condition on `Index1` and `Index2` is that `AnArray[Index1]` and `AnArray[Index2]` are the candidate values to be assigned to the element `Temp[Index]`. Once `Temp[Index]` has been assigned a value, a new candidate must be assigned for the next loop pass. This action is accomplished by adding 1 to the index value referencing the subarray whose element was assigned to `Temp[Index]`. Thus, within the loop body one of the two candidate index values is going to be incremented each loop pass. Therefore, we would expect to see some code within the loop body described by

```
IF AnArray[Index1] < AnArray[Index2] THEN
   Update(AnArray, Index1, Temp[Index])
ELSE
   Update(AnArray, Index2, Temp[Index])
```

The `Update` procedure assigns the `Temp[Index]` its proper value, and adds 1 to the candidate index value, the second parameter of the procedure.

A look at the
procedure
Merge so far

We can summarize what we have developed so far with the pseudocode

> *Index1 ← Lo*
> *Index2 ← Mid+1*
> *FOR Index ← Lo TO Hi DO*

$$IF \ AnArray[Index1] < AnArray[Index2] \ THEN$$
$$Update(AnArray, \ Index1, \ Temp[Index])$$
$$ELSE$$
$$Update(AnArray, \ Index2, \ Temp[Index])$$

One more refinement
We are not yet ready to code Merge, however, because our draft is still incomplete. Within the loop body, one of the two subarrays will run out of candidates before the other one. We must account for this event or we may end up assigning an incorrect element to Temp [Index] from a "subarray element" that does not exist. Thus, the decision statement in the loop body requires a guard before two elements are compared. Hence, the decision statement inside the loop is modified to

IF subarray1 has no more candidates THEN
Update(AnArray, Index2, Temp[Index])
ELSE IF subarray2 has no more candidates THEN
Update(AnArray, Index1, Temp[Index])
ELSE
use the decision statement of the previous draft

The candidates from *subarray1* will have run out when Index1 becomes greater than Mid, and the candidates from *subarray2* will have run out when Index2 becomes greater than Hi. We thus need to use a nested *IF..ELSE..IF* algorithm for the body of the first loop in order to code a correct Merge algorithm.

Source code
Now we are ready to code Merge. Its source code, including the code of the procedure Update is as follows:

```
{*                                                                           *}
PROCEDURE Update(VAR AnArray: ArrayType; VAR CandidateIndex: integer;
                VAR NewElement: ElementType);
  {in: AnArray -- reference array for element AnArray[CandidateIndex]
   in: CandidateIndex -- index of element in AnArray to be assigned
  out: CandidateIndex -- next candidate index in AnArray for merge
  out: NewElement -- element of Temp assigned value of AnArray element}
  BEGIN
    NewElement:= AnArray[CandidateIndex];
    CandidateIndex:= CandidateIndex + 1
  END;
{+                                                                           +}
PROCEDURE Merge(Lo, Mid, Hi: integer; VAR AnArray: ArrayType);
  {documentation}
  VAR
    Temp:      {storage for elements over Lo..Hi subrange}
               ArrayType;
    Index,     {loop index variable to carry out merge}
    Index1,    {candidate for merge from Lo..Mid subrange}
    Index2:    {candidate for merge from Mid+1..Hi subrange}
               integer;
```

```
BEGIN
  Index1:= Lo;
  Index2:= Mid+1;
  FOR Index:= Lo TO Hi DO
    IF Index1 > Mid THEN
      Update(AnArray, Index2, Temp[Index])
    ELSE IF Index2 > Hi THEN
      Update(AnArray, Index1, Temp[Index])
    ELSE IF AnArray[Index1] < AnArray[Index2] THEN
      Update(AnArray, Index1, Temp[Index])
    ELSE
      Update(AnArray, Index2, Temp[Index]);
  FOR Index:= Lo TO Hi DO
    AnArray[Index]:= Temp[Index]
  END;
{*                                                              *}  ◆
```

EXERCISES

Test Your Understanding

1. Draw the recursion tree for the call SortIt(AnArray,53,94).

2. How many trivial cases will have been solved when the machine returns AnArray sorted over the subrange *53..94?*

3. If the initial subrange to sort is *1..TotalElements,* would a call to sort over subrange *1..0* ever occur? Explain your answer.

4. The final action in the Merge procedure appears to assign the elements of Temp to AnArray. Suppose, instead of the second FOR loop, that we substitute the statement AnArray:= Temp. Why is this code erroneous?

Practice Your Analysis Skills

5. The merge–sort algorithm is time-efficient, but it is not space-efficient, due to the presence of the local array variable Temp in the Merge procedure. A trivial merge of two elements, for example, still uses Temp, which contains MaxElements (say, 10,000) elements. You are to see if this requirement for extra memory constitutes a major problem by answering the following questions:
   (a) Given 10,000 elements to sort, how many SortIt blocks are on the run-time stack when the machine is trivially sorting two elements?
   (b) If the machine is trivially sorting two elements, how many Merge blocks are on the run-time stack?
   (c) How many 10,000-element arrays (both local and global), therefore, are required for the algorithm?
   (d) Is it possible to improve on this space cost overhead? Explain.

Program Testing Hints

In this section, we give some ways to check that the logic of your code is correct for a recursive process. We also give hints on choosing test data and on coding statements for on-line tracing of recursive processes.

Checks on Your Source Code

Every recursive procedure or function has certain characteristics that are always the same. When you check the code for these characteristics, you are guarding against the possibility of coding a faulty recursive process.

PROGRAM DESIGN RULE 15.1

When planning a recursive algorithm, make sure to include all base cases.

Missing base cases

Any recursive process must eventually reduce to a base case. Moreover, each call should ensure that the computer works its way down to a base case. Without this mechanism in place, the process will never stop calling itself. For example, an attempt to find N! with the following code will cause an error condition:

```
FUNCTION Factorial(N: integer): integer;
   {ERROR:   BASE CASE MISSING}
   BEGIN
      Factorial:= N*Factorial(N-1)
   END;
```

An enormous run-time stack is created and a crash will eventually occur either due to a *stack overflow condition* or an integer overflow condition. In other words, either the stack will be too big or abs (N) will be too big.

Stack overflow condition: a run-time error where so many processes are on the run-time stack that the computer has insufficient memory to allocate for further processing.

Not achieving the base case

If the function Factorial, written as the solution to Example Problem 15.4, were initially called with a negative value of N, the computer would pass larger and larger values of abs (N) into each recursive call. The base case of N equal to 0 will never be achieved. This condition will cause an error either due to an integer overflow or a stack overflow condition.

Solving the problem

Let us say that N! is undefined when N is a negative number. In this case, we can flag the error condition where N is negative by passing out maxint to Factorial. If we choose to write Factorial this way, its statement must be changed to the following:

```
BEGIN
   IF N < 0 THEN                    {base case:   incorrect initial N}
      Factorial:= maxint
```

```
    ELSE IF N = 0 THEN          {base case: definition of 0!}
       Factorial:= 1
    ELSE
       Factorial:= N*Factorial(N-1)
END;
```

Statement order

In the light of this solution, we could say that the initial problem was coded incorrectly because it *overlooked* the base case where N might be negative. In order for the function to be correct for all values of N, the base case where N is less than 0 had to be dealt with.

We remind you once more that a statement for a recursive process can be divided into the following five parts:

1. Those statements executed at the start of a new process.
2. Those statements executed when a base case is met.
3. Those statements executed before another recursive call is made.
4. Any recursive call that is made.
5. Those statements executed after the recursive call has been made.

A statement placed out of sequence, particularly with respect to parts 3 and 5, can lead to results that are incomprehensible. A buggy recursive sequence illustrates the classic situation of a problem gone awry by the GIGO (garbage-in, garbage-out) mechanism.

Suppose one statement is incorrectly placed. This incorrect statement will either set up incorrect preconditions for the recursive call or misuse the results returned by a recursive call. Either the conditions required to solve a problem correctly were not met or the incorrect result(s) was passed on as a "correct" solution to another problem. In either case, the error gets worse and worse as more and more incorrect results are generated. It takes little imagination to see how such a negative feedback mechanism can lead to incomprehensible results, even when tracer logic is inserted in the block.

Defensive planning

Before you are ready to go "on line" with some recursive process, check that each statement in the block is correctly placed. Keep in mind the following characteristics about each of the parts of a recursive process:

Statements placed in part 1 will be executed each time a call is made. Use a statement here to check for some terminal condition or to show processes as they are called. Statements placed at this point *are executed with every recursive call*.

Statements belonging to part 2 most often assign values to parameters that represent a trivial solution to the problem. There are times when other actions may be required. For example, the statement write('Display follows: ') might be used as part of the base case condition's sequence if all display is postponed until the base case condition is found.

Do not mix up the statements of parts 1 and 2. When the following example of ShowSums is run, the string 'Display follows' will be shown $N + 1$ times instead of just once:

```
PROCEDURE ShowSums(N, ShowEvery: integer; VAR Sum: integer);
  BEGIN
    write('Display follows:  ');
    IF N = 0 THEN
      Sum:= 0
    ELSE
    BEGIN
      {other statements}
    END
  END;
```

Statements placed at part 3 are used to set up the conditions that will help solve a smaller version of the problem. Likewise, statements placed in part 5 should use the results of the smaller problem(s) solved to return a solution to the larger problem. If any statements placed in these two parts do not, on close scrutiny, appear to be fulfilling such "timely" purposes, regard them with suspicion.

Choosing Test Data

When you test a recursive process, there are some data values you must always choose to test particular conditions. Make sure not to forget them. Also, remember to choose data in such a way that if there is an error, it can easily be found. If you follow the rule of small samples to test recursive processes, you have a much better chance of finding an error quickly.

Base cases   Be sure to test each base case condition. You do not need to test every base case (all 10,000 base cases of a merge sort?), but you do want to check each coded condition. Also make sure that the correct actions are done with each base case.

Before you actually put the code on line, take one last look to ensure that you have included all base cases in the algorithm. If you have missed some, we hope that when you test your program with nontrivial data, the results returned will indicate that the machine is well on its way to creating an infinite stack. If, for example, the cursor blinks "forever" while your program is running, you may want to interrupt it so you can write a line of code to count processes. If you find your stack size is becoming very large, chances are that you missed some terminal condition.

Revisiting the   Once you have determined that the base cases work, test the recursive code
rule of small   in such a way that the run-time stack will stay small. You would not, for example,
samples   first test Fibonacci or Factorial with numbers that are expected to generate 20 process stacks. You can identify bugs just as easily when the maximum size of the stack is 3, 4, or 5 as opposed to 20, 25, or 30. Indeed, it is far easier to find an error with a small stack because GIGO is in effect when faulty logic is applied to a recursive process.

When you are sure that the code is correct for small problems, then you can test it with larger problems. In this case, you can be more certain that the larger problems will be done correctly because the correct results of the smaller problems solved will lead to correct results for the larger problems to be solved.

On-Line Tracing of Recursive Code

If your dialect does not have a tracer utility and your code has a bug in it, you will have to insert your own tracer statements to find the bug. Sometimes you may want to get further information about your code even if your system does have a tracer utility. The following hints should help you write any necessary tracer statements such that they help rather than hinder the dubugging process.

Writing tracer statements

If you have a bug in your recursive process, you may want to insert some WRITELN statements to trace the logic. *Don't compound the problem of debugging by misplacing your tracer statements.* If you do so, you will probably never finish your program, for confusion will reign supreme.

There are two obvious places to put tracer WRITELN statements: directly after the first BEGIN or directly before the final END. A WRITELN placed at the beginning of the sequence of block statements can be used to display the values passed into the block. By implication, the display of these values indicates the version of the problem *to be solved*. A WRITELN placed at the end of the statement sequence usually displays the results returned by a problem that *has been solved*.

Counting processes

If you want to count pushes or pops, do not pass the counting variables in by value. The simplest way to count the processes is to declare the counters as global variables and reference them as side effects. You should also increment the counters in their proper places. PUSHES is incremented as soon as the block is entered and POPS is incremented just before the block is exited.

You may also want the machine to count and display other statistics, such as the number of recursive processes on the stack. Regardless of what you wish to do, remember that a tracer variable or expression related to some process count is best referenced in only one of two places—at the start of the block or at the end of the block.

Displaying process numbers

Often, you may want to count processes. If you want to count both pushes and pops, be sure to *label* the number of each push and/or pop. A suggested push/pop counter for some recursive process might be written as follows:

```
BEGIN    {recursive block's statement}
   PUSHES:= PUSHES + 1;   {increment first!}
   WRITELN('PUSH #', PUSHES:1,':  ');
      {rest of statements}
   POPS:= POPS + 1;
   WRITELN('POP #',POPS:1,':  ')
END;
```

Auxiliary variables

If you want to see the values returned by the partial solutions of a call to a recursive function, you can use a local variable to display the valuc returned to a function. You can then assign the value of this "candidate" variable to the function itself. If, for example, you want a display of the values of all calls to the function PowerOfN, you could code

```
FUNCTION PowerOfN(XRe: real, N: integer): real;
  VAR
    SOLN: REAL;    {local solution variable}
  BEGIN
    IF N - 0 THEN
      SOLN:= 1
    ELSE
      SOLN:= XRe * PowerOfN(XRe, N-1);
    {ASSERTION:  The value of SOLN represents the value of XRe**N.}
    WRITELN('XRE**N = ',SOLN:8:6);
    PowerOfN:= SOLN
  END;
```

The logic of the recursive function is not changed because the local variable SOLN is used for display purposes only. Once you are sure your function is working properly, you can eliminate the final two statements and use the expression XRe*PowerOfN(XRe, N-1) instead of SOLN.

EXERCISES

Test Your Understanding

1. When the factorial function is coded without accounting for the terminal condition, the bug will probably not result in an integer overflow of the value of Factorial. Why not?

Practice Your Analysis Skills

2. Suppose you wrote one of the following (incorrect) statements for the recursive procedure StoreDisplay (Example Problem 15.3):

    (a)
```
    BEGIN
        IF NOT eof(SomeFile) THEN
          BEGIN
            StoreDisplay(SomeFile);
            readln(SomeFile, ALine);
            writeln(Aline)
          END
    END;
```
    (b)
```
    BEGIN
        IF NOT eof(SomeFile) THEN
          BEGIN
            readln(SomeFile, ALine);
            writeln(ALine);
            StoreDisplay(SomeFile)
          END
    END;
```

    Indicate what would be the effect of each of these two statements if they are applied to the following text file:

    Hi there!<eoln>
    Goodbye!<eoln><eof>

3. Write the function `Fibonacci` so that you can trace all the partial solutions. In other words, the call `XInt:= Fibonacci(4);` should result in the display

```
Fib(2) = 1
Fib(1) = 0
Fib(2) = 1
Fib(3) = 2
Fib(4) = 3
```

4. Now write the function `Factorial` so that you can trace the partial solutions in the same manner as you did for `Fibonacci` in exercise 3.

5. Another interesting statistic that can be obtained from `Fibonacci` is the stack size at any given time. Drive the function `Fibonacci` in such a way that the stack size is displayed with each push. You can use side effects on the function for this display. Test your logic with a call to `Fibonacci(10)`. (The largest stack should have 9 processes on it.)

6. There are other ways we can define the value of `Factorial(N)` when N is less than zero. One way would be to simply ignore the sign of N. Thus, given that N is less than 0, we can say that `Factorial(N)` is equal to `Factorial(-N)`. Write the code for the function `Factorial` so that it satisfies this definition.

REVIEW AND EXERCISES

When a problem is solved using *recursion,* the computer does part of a process, then interrupts itself to start a smaller version of the same process. This smaller version is started by making a *recursive call* to the original process, but with different values for the parameters. Eventually, a *base case* is reached and recursive calling is stopped. The base case is solved, and control returns to the previous unfinished process that called the base case.

Perhaps no more recursive calls are made after the one base case occurs or perhaps more recursive calls are necessary. If more recursive calls are made, another base case eventually must be reached. Regardless of the problem, however, all recursive calls must be reduced to some base case, and all problems posed by recursive calls must be solved in order for the original problem to return a solution(s).

In order for a *recursive algorithm* to work, there must be at least one trivial version(s) of the problem with known solution(s) that code to a base case(s). Each recursive call must, in some way, reduce the problem so that a base case is eventually reached. Finally, all correct solutions returned from previous calls must be combined in such a way to return a correct solution to any one given call.

Recursive algorithms are proven by *mathematical induction.* The base cases must be shown to be (1) correct and (2) exhaustive. Next it is assumed that all previous calls to a recursive algorithm are correct. Given this premise, the recursive algorithm is shown to be correct if the results returned by the previous call(s) are combined in such a way that they return a correct solution to the present call.

Recursion works because the computer carries out processes using a *run-time stack*. This LIFO mechanism is the means by which the computer manages the sub-routines of a program. Given that the source code is written in Pascal, a run-time stack is used to manage the execution of all subroutines, regardless of whether the machine is carrying out a recursive process or not.

Desk-tracing recursive code is a bit more tedious than desk tracing other kinds of code, but it is still straightforward. It is done by drawing a *stack-history tree*, where a *node* indicates a particular process, a *branch* repesents a call-return path, a move down the tree is a *push* (call to another process), and a move up the tree is a *pop* (return from a given process). The *root node* on the tree starts the trace from an initial process.

The problem of searching for a particular element in an array is naturally adaptive to recursive algorithms. Certain ground rules, however, must be followed: (1) The array containing the candidates is passed into a recursive block using the call-by-VAR mechanism. (2) The parameters of the recursive search process will consist of the array, a key value being sought, and values that imply a subrange of candidates. (3) Any given process will either return a value to the search (a *found* condition), stop the calling with a *finished* condition, or make a recursive call with an implied reduction in the candidate subrange.

Linear recursion is a process where at most one recursive call is made within each process. *Nonlinear recusion* describes a process where more than one recursive call may be made within the same process. It is particularly important a process using nonlinear recursion does not carry out *duplicate processing* in different parts of the program run. This kind of recursive process is usually very inefficient.

Debugging a recursive algorithm may at first seem difficult, but there are certain rules and preliminary checks to make that will simplify the task. First of all, all base cases should be checked for validity. Second, it is important to confirm that any call made will eventually reduce to a base case. If not, the recursive equivalent to an infinite loop, that is, an *infinite stack,* will be the incorrect result when the machine executes the code.

There are essentially four parts to a recursive algorithm: (1) the testing and handling of base cases, (2) processing before the recursive call(s) is made, (3) the recursive call(s), and (4) processing after control returns from the recursive call(s). Each statement in a recursive algorithm should be examined carefully to see that it is placed properly.

When choosing test data for some recursive algorithm, remember the rule of small samples. A recursive algorithm that is faulty can only get worse with each new call, for erroneous "solutions" beget even more erroneous "solutions." If the maximum size of the run-time stack has 10 faulty recursive processes on it, for example, there is far less chance of finding the error by on-line testing than if its maximum size will be 3 or 4.

It is likewise important that all display statements used for debugging are inserted in the proper places with clear display messages. If placed improperly, these tracers might further obscure the error by adding unintentional errors due to faulty tracing. The tracers must likewise indicate *what* process is being shown as well as the values that make up the particular process.

EXERCISES

Short Answers

1. What is the difference between linear and nonlinear recursion?

2. What is the significance of statements placed after the recursive call has been made within a recursive block?

3. What is meant by an "endless stack"? What coding error could cause this result?

4. Why is the recursive form of coding the Fibonacci function so inefficient?

5. Suppose you want the computer to read and display a line of text *in order* using a recursive strategy. Is it possible? If so, write the pseudocode for the block statement.

6. What happens if a display statement is the first statement to be executed in a recursive block? When would you want to put such a statement there?

7. True or false? Exactly the same number of pushes and pops will have been done on the run-time stack for any given program, recursive or otherwise. Explain your answer.

8. Explain briefly why trees are useful in tracing the action of a recursive strategy. Are they of any use in tracing iterative strategies?

9. Consider the following description of a recursive algorithm:

> *{Point A}*
> *IF trivial problem THEN*
>   *{Point B}*
>   *return solution*
> *ELSE*
>   *{Point C}*
>   *set up smaller problem(s)*
>   *{Point D}*
>   *MAKE RECURSIVE CALL(S)*
>   *{Point E}*
>   *combine result(s) of smaller solution(s)*
>   *{Point F}*

We have labeled different points in the description. You want to code some WRITELN statements to study the mechanism. At what point would you place a WRITELN sequence to do the following:

(a) Test whether the algorithm handles terminal conditions properly.

(b) Test whether the run-time stack is too large. In this case, you will need a counting variable. At what point should 1 be added to this variable? At what point should 1 be subtracted from this variable?

(c) Indicate that the machine must solve a smaller version of a given problem.

10. Match the phrase in Column A with the corresponding phrase in Column B.

Column A	Column B
Infinite stack	Aid in tracing recursive algorithm
Pop	No base case occurs
Smaller problem posed	More than one recursive call per block
Result of buggy recursive code	Push
Recursion tree	Proving a recursive algorithm
Nonlinear recursion	GIGO
Mathematical induction	Solution returned

11. Why does it make more sense to use a call-by-VAR mechanism on the array reference structure when a recursive search algorithm is used?

12. If arrays were not passed in by VAR for a recursive search algorithm, what would be the effect on the run-time cost of the algorithm? What about the memory cost?

13. Which (if any) of the following uses nonlinear recursion for its solution: (a) the merge-sort algorithm, (b) the recursive form of the binary search algorithm, (c) the recursive form of the linear search algorithm, (d) the Fibonacci function, and (e) the procedure SetFibNo.

14. When debugging a recursive algorithm, it makes little sense to look beyond the first two or three recursive calls. Why?

15. Suppose you want to hide the details of the recursive logic of SortIt (the merge–sort algorithm) from the block that requires that AnArray be sorted. This "naive" block will call the sorting algorithm by

```
Sort(AnArray,TotalElements);
```

Given this requirement and that the code for SortIt and MergeTwo is known, how would you code the Sort block?

Easy Projects
16. "If you can solve a problem iteratively, you can also solve it recursively." To (partially) prove this claim, write recursive algorithms to solve each of the following problems:
    (a) Write a function Highest that returns the index value of the highest element in Ints over the subrange 1..MaxEl.
    (b) Write a procedure GetProduct to read in N real numbers from InFile and assign the product of the N numbers to the variable Product.
    (c) Write a procedure GetCount that returns to Count the count of the number of times the char value Ch was read in from a line of InFile.
    (d) Write the function Matched that returns the value of true if Str1 equals Str2, where these input parameters represent character strings.

17. A palindrome is a word or sequence of characters that appears the same in both the forward and reverse directions. For example, we have words such as "noon", "tot", "radar," etc. Write a function that uses recursion to determine whether a string of characters (each character in the string should be accessible, naturally) is a palindrome or not.

18. Write a program to evaluate and display a 10 × 10 table showing the values of the following function for the two integer parameters X and Y:

```
F(X, Y) = Y,                                 if X = 0
F(X, Y) = X,                                 if Y = 0
F(X, Y) = X,                                 if X = Y
F(X, Y) = F(X-1, Y) + F(X, Y-1),  in all other cases
```

The main block is described by

$$FOR\ X \leftarrow 0\ TO\ 10\ DO$$
$$FOR\ Y \leftarrow 0\ TO\ 10\ DO$$
$$GetSolution(Solns,\ X,\ Y)$$
$$ShowSolns(Solns)$$

The action of the ShowSolns block should display only the solutions over the *X* and *Y* subranges of *1..10*.

19. Write a main block program to drive a procedure that converts a decimal integer to its equivalent representation in a base *N* system. The procedure is called by GetDigits(Int, Base, DString);, where Int is the base 10 integer Base is given the value *N*, and *N* must lie in the subrange 2..16. DString is a string of characters representing the equivalent number in the base *N* system. Two typical runs are

```
Input number and base-N value: 72    8
In base-8, the number 72 is 110.

Input number and base-N value: 200    12
In base-12, the number 200 is 148.
```

(*Hint:* If you convert an integer in our decimal number system to its equivalent representation in a base *N* system, you find the least significant digit first and the most significant digit last. The display rules, however, require that the most significant digit be shown first. Given these two facts, a logical approach to solving the problem would be to build a string of characters using the call to a recursive procedure AssignDigit.

Medium Projects

20. Write a recursive sorting procedure using the selection sort algorithm. Each call puts the *N*th element in order, where initially *N* is equal to 100 (the total number of elements to be sorted). The computer finds the element in *1..N* that is the highest value and then exchanges it with the *N*th element. (The search for this highest element can likewise be recursive.) The action sequence of the recursive process has the computer find the index value of the lowest element in the subrange Lo..Hi. (This sequence need not be recursive.) It will then make a recursive call to Sort using N-1 to imply a sort over the subrange 1..N-1.

   Test this procedure using an RNG to fill in an array of 100 integers. Then have the computer sort the array. The sorting procedure should be called from the main block in such a way that the recursive logic is completely hidden.

21. The quicksort algorithm invented by C. A. Hoare is another form of a partition sort algorithm that uses recursion. A typical process, given a candidate subrange Lo..Hi to sort, is carried out with logic that partitions the array about the value of a "pivot" element. All elements higher than the pivot value will have index values higher than the pivot value's index. Likewise all elements lower than the pivot value will have lower index values than the pivot element's index. Both of these partitions are then sorted.

The "pivot value" around which the partition is built will be `AnArray[Lo]`. A FOR loop where the computer counts from Lo+1 to Hi is the means by which the partition is built. The initial element found lower than `AnArray[Lo]` is exchanged with the element `AnArray[Lo+1]`. The next element found lower than `AnArray[Lo]` is exchanged with the element at `AnArray[Lo+2]`. The loop body also keeps a running account of the last element to be exchanged at position LastExchange. Once the loop is exited, all elements in the subrange *Lo..LastExchange* will be less than `AnArray[Lo]` and all elements in the subrange *LastExchange + 1..Hi* will be greater than `AnArray[Lo]`. The final step within the `Partition` procedure is to have the computer exchange the elements `AnArray[Lo]` and `AnArray[LastExchange]`.

Write and use the procedure `Partition`, and also write the code for `QuickSort`, whose description is given as

> IF there is a subrange to sort THEN
>   Partition(Lo, Hi, Pivot, AnArray)   {Pivot is alias of LastExchange}
>   sort AnArray over the subrange Low..Pivot-1
>   sort AnArray over the subrange Pivot+1..Hi

Test the quicksort algorithm with an array of 100 integers. You can generate these integers randomly. Write the procedure so that the client is "naive" about the recursive process. In other words, a call to sort the array is made by `Sort(TotalElements, AnArray);`, where `TotalElements` represents the index value of the last element.

22. Write a program, using recursion, where the computer will read and reverse display everything in a text file. In other words, the very last character on the very last line should be the first character to be displayed, and the final character to be displayed is the first character on the first line. An example of text file contents and the result of the program run is as follows:

```
        Greetings.<eoln>
        Hello to you, too.<eoln>
        Well, goodbye.<eoln>
        Yeah, goodbye.<eoln><eof>
.eybdoog ,haeY
.eybdoog ,lleW
.oot ,uoy ot olleH
.sgniteerG
```

Do not use any subscripting to solve the problem. (*Hint:* Write one recursive procedure to get, store, and display one line of text. The line of text is returned from another recursive procedure to get, store, and build a single line from the characters read.)

Difficult Projects

23. The integer operations +, −, *, DIV, MOD, and ** (exponentiation) can be written as recursive functions that use only calls to succ, pred, and the defining functions to achieve all six operations. You are to write these six functions whose respective names are `IntSum`, `IntSub`, `IntMult`, `IntQuot`, `IntRem`, and `IntPower`. Each function has two parameters, XInt and YInt, that are passed into the function as `integer` expressions. You are to write these six functions as an ADT unit. Some hints on implementing these functions are given as follows:

The recursive call to Sum, using the XInt and YInt values, is described by `IntSum ← succ(IntSum(XInt, pred(YInt)))` with the stopping case where `IntSum` is given the value of XInt when YInt is 0. The `IntSum` function works because the computer adds 1 to the value of IntSum's result each time it calls IntSum with the predecessor of YInt's value.

Each function call to IntProd returns the value of the IntSum of XInt added to the product of XInt and the predececessor of YInt. The stopping case occurs when the value of YInt is 0.

Each call to IntPower returns the IntProd of XInt multiplied by XInt raised to the power of pred(YInt).

The IntSub function's code is similar to the IntSum's except that the pred function is used in place of the succ function. Similar analogies can be drawn for the division functions.

Assume that only positive values are used for these functions. Test IntPower with small numbers (such as IntPower(4, 3)), for this function takes a long time to execute.

24. Ackerman's function, defined in terms of two integers M and N, is a famous function used to test how well a given computer handles recursive processing. It is defined the following way:

$$Ack(0,N) = N + 1, \qquad\qquad \text{if } N >= 0$$
$$Ack(M,0) = Ack(M - 1, 1), \qquad \text{if } M > 0$$
$$Ack(M,N) = Ack(M - 1, Ack(M, N - 1)), \qquad \text{for M and N both greater than 0.}$$

Believe it or not, this function taxes the machine "to the limit" even for such apparently modest values as Ack(4,2).

You are to write a program to display the values of all Ackerman functions that can be evaluated for M and N over the subranges 0..4. A function is considered to be "impossible" if the stack size gets as large as 100. Should this occur, have the computer halt the evaluation and return a value of -1 to the function. The main block sequence is described by

> *CONST*
> *MaxStackSize = 100*
>
> *FOR M ← 0 TO 4 DO*
>   *FOR N ← 0 TO 4 DO*
>   *StopIt ← false*
>   *XInt ← Ack(M, N, StopIt, MaxStackSize)*
>   *display M,N, and XInt*
>   *clearline*

StopIt is set to true if PossibleCalls, the fourth parameter of the function Ack, is 0. This latter parameter is reduced by 1 with each recursive call, indicating the number of calls possible before the run-time stack is deemed too large. The boolean parameter StopIt is called by VAR in Ack, and is thus set in every process from the root node on down for Ack's stack. In this processwide base case, the value passed out to all calls of Ack is given as -1, thus eventually returning -1 to XInt, the initial call.

25. There are many boolean functions you can code that describe some single property of a square ($N \times N$) numeric array. All of these functions are to be coded using recursion. Assume you have a test array Square, a 5×5 matrix of type integer. When one of these functions is called, Square is the sole parameter passed into the function call, and it is understood that it is a 5×5 array. Therefore, the recursive logic is to be hidden from the calling block to each of these functions. You are then to write the code for the

following:

(a) The boolean function `Zero` that returns `true` if all the elements are equal to 0.

(b) The boolean function `Identity` that returns `true` if all the elements of `Square`, where `I` is equal to `J`, are equal to 0 and if all those elements `Square[I, I]` (i.e., those elements with `I` and `J` equal) are set to 1.

(c) The boolean function `Diagonal` that returns `true` if all elements of `Square`, where `I` is not equal to `J`, are equal to 0. All `Square[I, I]` elements can take on any value.

(d) The boolean function `UpperTriangle` that is `true` if `Square[I, J]` elements where `I` is less than `J` are 0.

(e) The boolean function `LowerTriangle` that is `true` if all `Square[I, J]` elements where `I` is greater than `J` are zero.

(f) The boolean function `Symmetric` that is `true` if the condition `Square[I, J] = Square[J, I]` is true for all elements.

(g) The boolean function `SkewSymmetric` that is `true` if the condition of `Square[I, J] = -Square[I, J]` is true for all elements.

26. The determinant of a 2 × 2 array of real numbers is found by the expression

$$Det \leftarrow A[1,1] * A[2,2] - A[1,2] * A[2,1]$$

where A is the array. The determinant of a 3 × 3 array of real numbers is found by

$$
\begin{aligned}
Det \leftarrow &A[1,1] * Det(2 \times 2 \text{ array formed from rows 2 and 3}) \\
&-A[2,1] * Det(2 \times 2 \text{ array formed from rows 1 and 3}) \\
&+A[3,1] * Det(2 \times 2 \text{ array formed from rows 1 and 2})
\end{aligned}
$$

Likewise, the determinant of a 4 × 4 array is found by

$$
\begin{aligned}
Det \leftarrow &A[1,1] * Det(3 \times 3 \text{ array formed from rows 2,3,4}) \\
&-A[2,1] * Det(3 \times 3 \text{ array formed from rows 1,3,4}) \\
&+A[3,1] * Det(3 \times 3 \text{ array formed from rows 1,2,4}) \\
&-A[4,1] * Det(3 \times 3 \text{ array formed from rows 1,2,3})
\end{aligned}
$$

The same algorithm can be applied on an $N \times N$ array, where the sum of N products are found using the column 1 elements and determinants on $(N-1) \times (N-1)$ arrays. Each of the elements of the $(N-1) \times (N-1)$ array B used in the product expressed as $A[M, 1] * Det(B)$ can be formed in the following manner:

$$
\begin{aligned}
B[J,K-1] &\leftarrow A[J,K], \text{ when } J < M \\
B[J-1,K-1] &\leftarrow A[J,K], \text{ when } J > M
\end{aligned}
$$

Write a program that drives the function `Det`. This function can return the determinant of a square array whose dimensions go as high as 10 × 10. The function is typically called by

```
write('The value of the determinant is ')'
writeln(Det(A, N):4:2);
```

A represents the array for which values have been assigned over the row and column subranges `1..N`. In this case, the user knows the function is recursive because `N` is in the parameter list.

BINARY FILES AND POINTERS

OBJECTIVES

After reading and studying the material of the present chapter, you should be able to

- Explain the difference between a binary file and a text file

- Write programs that use binary files

- Define what is meant by a pointer variable

- Know the difference between a static variable and a dynamic variable

- Correctly apply the standard Pascal new and dispose procedures on dynamic variables

- Write programs that use pointer variables in such a way that they cut down on a program's memory requirements

IN PASCAL, YOU CAN IMPLEMENT PROGRAMS that use files whose components are types other than char values. You can, for example, have a file of integers, a file of strings, or, indeed, a file of records. The one requirement is that the components of any given file must all contain values of the same defined type.

The Pascal language also allows you to allocate and deallocate memory for variables within the statement part of a block. Variables of this nature are known as *dynamic* variables. Memory is given to a dynamic variable through reference to another type of variable known as a *pointer*. Pointers, whose values are addresses in memory, are given their name because they *point* to the location where data assigned to a dynamic variable are stored.

16.1 Binary File Usage

In this section, you will be introduced to *binary files*. These files are also called *non-text files,* for the data in them is packed in such a way that the component values are not represented by human-readable text. The components of a binary file must all be of the same type, be they numeric values, string values, records, or even arrays. A binary file gets its name because the computer stores all its components as a packed sequence of 0s and 1s; that is, a packed sequence of binary digits.

> **Binary file:** a file whose programmer-defined components are all of the same type. The contents of these files are not represented as text.

Syntax Rules

Defining a file

An example

A binary file variable in a program is best declared as a reference to a named type. The standard operations that apply to binary files have syntax rules different from the analogous operations done on text files.

Figure 16.1 shows the syntax for defining a binary file containing components of a given type. The identifier is a reference name for variable declarations, and the type box specifies the components the file is to hold.

Example 16.1 is the stub for a program that uses three files variables, each of which serves as a reference to a directory file whose components consist of data types that differ from the ones contained in the other two files. Each component of the directory file referenced by Ints must be an integer value, each component

FIGURE 16.1 Syntax for defining a binary file.

named file type

identifier → = → FILE → OF → type →

of the directory file referenced by Reals must be stored as a real value, and the directory file referenced by the file variable Names must only contain records of type NameType.

Example 16.1

```
PROGRAM UseFiles(output,Ints,Reals,Names);
   {Showing different file types}
   TYPE
      String30 = {STRING TYPE CAPABLE OF HOLDING UP TO 30 CHARS}
      NameType = RECORD
         First,
         Middle,
         Last: String30
      END;
      IntsFile = FILE OF integer;
      RealsFile = FILE OF real;
      NamesFile = FILE OF NameType;
   VAR
      Ints: IntsFile;          {values in file are all integers}
      Reals: RealsFile;        {values in file are all reals}
      Names: NamesFile;        {values in file are all of NameType}
   {*                                                                  *}
   BEGIN   END.
```

Preparing files for reading   The usual operations for file preparation apply the same way to binary files as they do to text files. Thus, the following sequence of statments prepares the three files of Example 16.1 for reading:

$$reset(Ints);$$
$$reset(Reals);$$
$$rcset(Names);$$

Once a binary file has been reset, it can be read from. In this case, the read procedure and the eof function can be applied to any of the three files.

Preparing files for writing   If, on the other hand, you want the program to write component values into the three respective files, you would use the rewrite procedure to code

$$rewrite(Ints);$$
$$rewrite(Reals);$$
$$rewrite(Names);$$

If these actions were carried out on the three file variables, the write procedure is applicable on any of the three file variables.

File variables   If a file is prepared for reading, the file variable represents a window into the next component to be read in from the file. Regardless of the type of components a file contains, the <eof> marker follows the last component. For this reason, the function eof (SomeFile) will work on any type of file, be it binary or text.

Names.dat

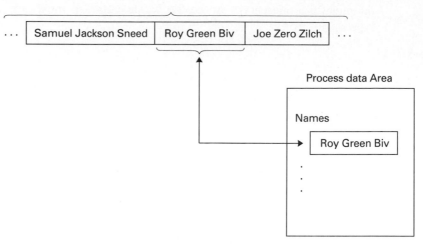

FIGURE 16.2 Relationship between a directory file and the file variable for Names.dat (directory file) and Names (file variable).

Some examples of read *operations*

Figure 16.2 shows a typical appearance of the directory file Names.dat, where the last name read in using the file variable identifier Names was the name Samuel Jackson Sneed. The next name to be read in (all three fields of the record NameType) is the name stored as Roy Green Biv. This record value is the one presently in the window of the file variable Names.

The next time the computer executes the statement read (Names, AName), values would be assigned to the fields of AName as

$$AName.First \leftrightarrow 'Roy'$$
$$AName.Middle \leftrightarrow 'Green'$$
$$AName.Last \leftrightarrow 'Biv'$$

After this read operation is carried out, the window moves forward, and the next candidate value to be read in from Names is Joe Zero Zilch.

It is also possible to read in more than one file component with a single read operation. If, for example, you want the computer to read in values from Reals to the three real variables Re1, Re2, and Re3, you would simply code the statement read(Reals, Re1, Re2, Re3).

Eof {VALID} and eoln *{ERROR}*

You can use the eof function on any file variable that has been prepared for reading. For example, the following sequence will read in and "process" each component integer value from the file Ints:

```
reset(Ints);
WHILE NOT eof(Ints) DO
  BEGIN
    read(Ints, AnInt);
    Process(AnInt)                {uses AnInt's value in the procedure Process}
  END;
```

The components of a binary file are not laid out in any format except that component values of the specified type follow each other up to the <eof> marker. There are *no lines* or <eoln> markers in a binary file. Thus, a call to the standard Pascal function `eoln` using a binary file variable will result in a syntax error.

Write operations

You can write component values into a binary file, as long as the file has been prepared for writing. For example, we have

```
write(Ints, AnInt, 3*AnInt);
write(Reals, Re1, 3.1416);
write(Names, AName);
write(Names, Name1, Name2);
```

The first two statements indicate that expressions can be used if (and only if) the file contains a component type that can be coded as a *single* expression. The third statement works because the variable AName is of type NameType, the component type for the file `Names`. The last statement indicates that more than one component can be written into a file using the `write` procedure, even when the component represents a structured type.

Illegal `write` *statements*

Individual components of a structured variable *cannot* be written into a file containing values belonging to a structured type. Thus, the "statement" `write (Names, AName.First, AName.Middle, AName.Last)` {WRONG!} will not compile because the variables AName.First, AName.Middle, and AName.Last are of type String30 and not of type NameType. We point out once again that a binary file contains no lines. Hence, the standard procedure `writeln` does not work on a binary file for the same reason the procedure `readln` does not work.

Some Common Algorithms

In the remainder of this section, you will learn some proven algorithms applicable specifically to problems that require the processing of binary files.

Copying a file

Suppose AFile and BFile are both files of SomeType whose components are of type ComponentType. Algorithm 16.1 is a description of the algorithm to copy AFile into BFile, given that AFile was reset and BFile was rewritten.

Algorithm 16.1

{Algorithm to copy binary AFile components into binary BFile:}
WHILE NOT eof(AFile) DO
    read(AFile, AComponent)
    write(AFile, AComponent)
{end algorithm}

Example 16.2 is an implementation of this algorithm.

Example 16.2

```
PROCEDURE CopyFile(VAR OutNames, OutNames: NamesFile);
   {copies the components of AFile into Bfile}
   VAR
      AName: NameType;
   BEGIN
      WHILE NOT eof(InNames) DO
         BEGIN
            read(InNames, AName);
            write(OutNames, AName)
         END
   END;
```

Writing in components from keyboard input

Note that even if the components are record values containing 20 or more fields, the action of copying one component variable from one file into another is still the same. If values have been given to all the parts of a structured variable that can be a component of a file, it can be written into the file with a single write operation. Likewise, an entire variable, including all values assigned to all components, can be read in to a given variable using a single read operation.

Algorithm 16.2 describes how to write a single record component into a file of records. The values for the fields of the record are read in from keyboard input.

Algorithm 16.2

{Algorithm to read in fields from the keyboard, then write these fields into a file containing the record components:}
WITH RecordVar DO
   keyin values for the fields
write(Outfile, RecordVar)
{end algorithm}

An application of the algorithm is shown in the code of the procedure WriteAName.

```
PROCEDURE WriteAName(VAR OutFile: NamesFile);
   {reads in component name values from keyboard, then writes the
   component NameType into OutFile}
   VAR
      AName: NameType;   {holds values for component being written}
   BEGIN
      WITH AName DO         {keyin the three fields of Name}
         BEGIN
            write('First name: ');
            readln(First);
            write('Middle name (<CR> for none):  ');
            readln(Middle);
```

```
            write('Last name:    ');
            readln(Last)
        END;   {WITH}
      write(Outfile, AName)   {write AName to Outfile}
    END;
```

Filling in an
array of records

Let us recall the array of records example from the program coded in Section 12.3 (UseClassRecords). Suppose, then, we have the following definitions and declarations:

```
CONST
    MaxStus = 150;
  TYPE
    StuRecord = RECORD
      {fields of StuRecord from Example Problem 12.1 in Section 12.2}
    END;   {StuRecord}
    ClassArray = ARRAY[1..MaxStus] OF StuRecord;
    StuRecFile = FILE OF StuRecord;
  VAR
    InFile: StuRecFile;
    AClass; ClassArray;
    TotalStudents: integer;
```

Example 16.3 fills in the elements of AClass using the idea suggested by Algorithm 16.2 and the proven algorithm to fill in the elements of an array over the subrange *1..TotalElements*. We coded the procedure under the assumption that the file was originally created with less than MaxStus components in it. Therefore, we have dispensed with coding a guard against an out-of-range value for TotalStudents.

Example 16.3

```
PROCEDURE FillClass(VAR AClass: ClassArray; VAR TotalStudents: integer;
                                         VAR InFile: StuRecFile);
  {fills in elements of AClass where it is assumed that there are less
  than MaxStus records in AFile}
  VAR
    AStudent: StuRecord;  {record for one student on file}
  BEGIN
    TotalStudents:= 0;
    reset(InFile);
    WHILE NOT eof(InFile) DO
      BEGIN
        TotalStudents:= TotalStudents + 1;
        read(InFile, AStudent);
        AClass[TotalStudents]:= AStudent
      END
  END;
```

EXERCISES

1. Explain why the `readln` and `writeln` operations are not applicable to binary files.

2. Can the following algorithm be implemented on a file of any type?

> *read(AFile, TotalComps)*
> *FOR Count ← 1 TO TotalComps DO*
> *read(AFile, AComp)*
> *Process(AComp)*

If so, what type of components must `AFile` have?

3. Write a short program to read in integers from the keyboard and write their values into a file `Ints`, a `FILE OF integer`. The program is to write only positive values into the file. Thus, any nonpositive value read in ends the process of writing into the file.

4. Now write a short program to read and echo the contents of the file `Ints`. Have the progam display five integers per line. Also it should count the number of integers stored in the file, displaying this count after the last integer has been read and its value displayed.

5. Modify the procedure `FillClass` so that if the number of records in the file is greater than `MaxStus` (use a smaller number than 150), the machine displays the names of those students left over in the format:

```
CLASS IS FILLED
THE FOLLOWING STUDENTS ARE TO BE PLACED IN ANOTHER SECTION:
Jack Jacob Schmidt
Charlie Edgar Jones
. . .
```

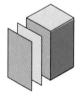

16.2   File Updating

A directory file is created and then can be used and/or changed by more than one program. When this file's components are records, it is easy to conceive of one or more programs that may require the use of some but not all of the fields of each component. The case study that follows is an example of this kind of program.

CASE STUDY 16.1

The problem statement

The Fall 1992 semester is finished, and the results for the course CS101 are stored in the directory file `CS101F92.dat`. The file's records are sorted by student name. These records are to be merged with the records of the directory file `CS101S.dat`, also sorted by student name. This second file is the master file containing the records of all students, in order by name, who have taken the CS101 course from its inception up through the spring term of the present year. The destination file for the update is `CS101F.dat` the master file for all student records in CS101 through the fall term of the present year 1992. This new directory file should likewise be sorted by name.

The records of CS101F.dat and CS101S.dat are almost the same as those of CS101F92.dat, except that they have an extra field variable Term, which is a string type. Its value (e.g., 'F92') indicates the particular term a given student took the course.

The user-machine interaction for the program run looks like

```
Input course: CS101
Input term ("S" or "F"): F
Input year (two-digit number): 92
The update is completed.
```

The final line of display occurs after the contents of CS101F92.dat have been merged with CS101S.dat into CS101F.dat.

The main block　　　The file names are to be read in from the keyboard, so we need to code a procedure that opens a file variable to a directory name. We have chosen to use the Turbo Pascal assign procedure for this operation. If you are working with a different dialect, you will need to use that dialect's procedure for linking a file variable to a directory file.

The program UpdateMerge, as given, is the source code for the solution. We still must develop the code for the procedure Merge.

```
PROGRAM UpdateMerge(input, output, Semester, OldMaster, NewMaster);
   {the file contents in a specified Semester file are merged with the
   contents of OldMaster into the file NewMaster. Each file is sorted by
   name, last name first.}
   TYPE
      {insert String25, SSNoType and StuRecord, defined as before}
      MStuRecord = RECORD
         Term: String25;      {the additional field in MasterFile}
         Info: StuRecord      {includes Name and SocSecNo fields}
      END;
      StuRecFile = FILE OF StuRecord;
      MStuRecFile = FILE OF MStuRecord;
   VAR
      TheTerm:      {represents term just ended}
                    String25;
      Semester:     {file containing records for term just ended}
                    StuRecFile;
      OldMaster,    {master file of records up through previous term}
      NewMaster:    {master file to include present term}
                    MStuRecFile;
{*                                                                     *}
   PROCEDURE AssignFiles(VAR TheTerm: String25;
         VAR Semester: StuRecFile; VAR OldMaster, NewMaster: MStuRecFile);
      {The value for TheTerm is read in from the keyboard; the file
```

variables Semester, OldMaster, and NewMaster are opened. OldMaster and Semester are prepared for reading, and NewMaster is prepared for writing. The names for the files are found from the string values keyed in. For the sake of simplicity, we have not written any guards, thus assuming the user will key in a correct sequence of characters for the string variables.}

```
    VAR
       CourseName,     {name of the course}
       SpringOrFall,   {term of the course}
       Year:           {year of the course}
                       String25;
    {*                                                       *}
  BEGIN
    write('Input course: ');
    readln(CourseName);                              {e.g., CS101}
    write('Input term ("S" or "F"):   ');
    readln(SpringOrFall);                            {e.g., S}
    write('Input year (two-digit number):   ');
    readln(Year);                                    {e.g., 92}
    TheTerm:= SpringOrFall + Year;                   {e.g., S92}
    assign(Semester, CourseName + TheTerm + '.dat');{e.g., CS101S92.dat}
    IF SpringOrFall .= 'S' THEN
       assign(OldMaster, CourseName + 'F' + '.dat')
    ELSE
       assign(OldMaster, CourseName + 'S' + '.dat');
    assign(NewMaster, CourseName + SpringOrFall + '.dat');
    reset(OldMaster);
    reset(Semester);
    rewrite(NewMaster)
  END;
{*                                                           *}
PROCEDURE Merge(TheTerm: String25; VAR Semester: StuRecFile;
                       VAR OldMaster, NewMaster: MStuRecFile);
```

{merges the contents of OldMaster and Semester into NewMaster by order of student names. If two students have identical names, the one with the lower IDNo is written first.}

```
    VAR
       AStu:       {record variable read in from Semester}
                   StuRecord;
       MStu1,      {record variable read in from OldMaster}
       MStu2:      {record variable made from AStu and TheTerm}
                   MStuRecord;
  BEGIN   END;
{*                                                           *}
BEGIN
  AssignFiles(TheTerm, Semester, OldMaster, NewMaster);
```

```
    Merge(TheTerm, Semester, OldMaster, NewMaster);
    writeln('The update is completed.')
END.
```

The initial draft and first refinement of Merge
Our initial description of the actions we want carried out by Merge is given in the pseudocode

> get MStu1 record from OldMaster
> get MStu2 record from Semester
> WHILE not finished with either file DO
> > write record with "smaller" name into NewMaster
> > get another record from the proper file {OldMaster or Semester}
> copy last MStu1 and MStu2 records into NewMaster
> copy records from unfinished file into NewMaster

We can then write the two *get* operations as the respective procedure calls

> GetMasterRec(MStu1, OldMaster)
> GetSemesterRec(TheTerm, MStu2, Semester)

The procedure GetSemesterRec fills in all fields of MStu2. Hence AStu is not needed. The value of TheTerm is required to assign a value to the Term field of MStu2. These procedures are also going to be used when we draft the code for the *get* part of the loop body. If the "proper" file is OldMaster, the call is made to GetMasterRec. If Semester is the "proper" file, the call is made to GetSemesterRec.

The next refinement
Both *get* procedures must check the eof condition before a record is read in. If there are no records to be read in, no action is taken and the recognized eof condition is passed out with no action taken. Using this assumption, we can code the loop control condition of the WHILE loop as the boolean expression NOT eof(OldMaster) AND NOT eof(Semester).

Each *get* procedure first checks the eof conditions before reading in a value to the record variable. Hence, before the loop is entered, an attempt is made to read in records from both files, and before another loop pass is started, an attempt is likewise made to read from one of the two files. Thus given an eof condition for the candidate file, no record is read in and the loop is properly exited when one of the two files runs out of records.

From the fact the eof condition is true for one of the two files at loop exit, we can code a sequence after the loop using the three procedure calls

> CopyLastTwo(MStu1, MStu2, NewMaster)
> CopyOldMasterRecs(OldMaster, NewMaster)
> CopySemesterRecs(The Term, Semester, NewMaster)

Why is there no decision logic after the loop is exited? It is not required if both *copy* procedures check for <eof> before reading in the first record from the file. Thus, no further action is taken for the file that is empty, and the remaining records are copied from the file that has not yet been completely read.

Now we must draft the sequence for the loop body. The record written into `NewMaster` is the one with the alphabetically first name of the record variables `MStu1` and `MStu2`, as obtained from `OldMaster` and `Semester`, respectively. The "proper" file to read for a new record is the one whose record was just written into `NewMaster`. Thus, the body of the loop is described by the decision statement

> *IF Stu1GoesFirst(MStu1.Info, MStu2.Info) THEN*
>   *write(NewMaster, MStu1)*
>   *GetMasterRec(MStu1, OldMaster)*
> *ELSE*
>   *write(NewMaster, MStu2)*
>   *GetSemesterRec(TheTerm, MStu2, Semester)*

`Stu1GoesFirst` is a boolean function that returns `true` if `MStu1` should be written before `MStu2`.

Putting everything together, we get the overall description for `Merge`'s statement as

> *GetMasterRec(MStu1, OldMaster)*
> *GetSemesterRec(TheTerm, MStu2, Semester)*
> *WHILE NOT eof(OldMaster) AND NOT eof(Semester) DO*
>   *IF Stu1GoesFirst(MStu1.Info, MStu2.Info) THEN*
>   *write(NewMaster, MStu1)*
>   *GetMasterRec(MStu1, OldMaster)*
>   *ELSE*
>   *write(NewMaster, MStu2)*
>   *GetSemesterRec(TheTerm, MStu2, Semester)*
> *CopyLastTwo(MStu1, MStu2, NewMaster)*
> *CopyOldMasterRecs(OldMaster, NewMaster)*
> *CopySemesterRecs(TheTerm, Semester, NewMaster)*
> *close all files*

Let us present the code for the `Merge` procedure in its entirety after we have developed the function `Stu1GoesFirst`. We will also develop the code for the two procedures `GetSemesterRec` and `CopySemesterRecs`.

The header for the function `Stu1GoesFirst` is given as `FUNCTION Stu1GoesFirst(Stu1, Stu2: StuRecord): boolean;`. The value `true` is returned if `Stu1` should be written out ahead of `Stu2`. The decision of which goes first is made according to the order: last name, first name, middle name, and Social Security number. If, for example, the last names are the same and the first names differ, the one with the first name that is alphabetically first must be written first. If all three names are the same, the Social Security number is used to determine which name goes first.

It sounds like the algorithm we require is an `IF-ELSE-IF` algorithm that follows a specified decision order. We thus describe the function's statement with the pseudocode

$$IF\ Stu1.Name.Last <> Stu2.Name.Last\ THEN \qquad \{check\ last\ name\}$$
$$Stu1GoesFirst \leftarrow Stu1.Name.Last < Stu2.Name.Last$$
$$ELSE\ IF\ Stu1.Name.First <> Stu2.Name.First\ THEN \qquad \{check\ first\ name\}$$
$$Stu1GoesFirst \leftarrow Stu1.Name.First < Stu2.Name.First$$
$$ELSE\ IF\ Stu1.Name.Middle <> Stu2.Name.Middle\ THEN \qquad \{check\ middle\ name\}$$
$$Stu1GoesFirst \leftarrow Stu1.Name.Middle < Stu2.Name.Middle$$
$$ELSE \qquad \{all\ names\ match,\ so\ use\ SocSecNo\}$$
$$Stu1GoesFirst \leftarrow Stu1.SocSecNo < Stu2.SocSecNo$$

The first mismatch that occurs determines which record variable must be copied into the file linked to NewMaster.

Describing
GetSemester
Rec *and*
CopySemester
Recs

Using a guard against reading in <eof>, we can describe the required statement for GetSemesterRec as

$$IF\ NOT\ eof(Semester)\ THEN$$
$$read(Semester,\ MStu.Info)$$
$$MStu.Term \leftarrow TheTerm$$

Coding Merge

The statement for CopySemesterRecs is analogously described with a WHILE-NOT-eof loop.

We can put all pseudocode descriptions together to get the code for Merge as given. We leave the coding of the statements for GetMasterRec and CopyOld-MasterRecs as Exercises 4 and 5 at the end of the section.

```
{*                                                                    *}
PROCEDURE GetMasterRec(VAR MStu: MStuRecord; VAR OldMaster:MStuRecFile);
  {reads and returns a value to MStu if not eof(OldMaster}
  BEGIN   END;
{+                                                                    +}
PROCEDURE GetSemesterRec(TheTerm: StringType; VAR MStu: MStuRecord;
                                           VAR Semester: StuRecFile);
  {reads in MStu.Info from Semester and assigns MStu.Term using value
  of TheTerm. If eof is true, no action is taken}
  BEGIN
    IF NOT eof(Semester) THEN
      BEGIN
        read(Semester, MStu.Info);
        MStu.Term:= TheTerm
      END
  END;
{+                                                                    +}
FUNCTION Stu1GoesFirst(Stu1, Stu2: StuRecord): boolean;
  {returns true if Stu1 should be written before Stu2}
```

```
    BEGIN
      IF Stu1.Name.Last <> Stu2.Name.Last THEN
        Stu1GoesFirst:= Stu1.Name.Last < Stu2.Name.Last
      ELSE IF Stu1.Name.First <> Stu2.Name.First THEN
        Stu1GoesFirst:= Stu1.Name.First < Stu2.Name.First
      ELSE IF Stu1.Name.Middle <> Stu2.Name.Middle THEN
        Stu1GoesFirst:= Stu1.Name.Middle < Stu2.Name.Middle
      ELSE
        Stu1GoesFirst:= Stu1.SocSecNo < Stu2.SocSecNo
    END;
{+                                                                    +}
PROCEDURE CopyOldMasterRecs(VAR OldMaster, NewMaster: MStuRecFile);
  {The remaining contents of OldMaster are copied into NewMaster}
  BEGIN  END;
{+                                                                    +}
PROCEDURE CopyLastTwo(MStu1, MStu2: MStuRecord;
                                VAR NewMaster: MStuRecFile);
  BEGIN{copy MStu1, MStu2 in correct order into NewMaster} END;
{+                                                                    +}
PROCEDURE CopySemesterRecs(TheTerm: String25;
              VAR Semester: StuRecFile; VAR NewMaster: MStuRecFile);
  {copies remaining information in Semester file to NewMaster file}
  VAR
      MStu: MStuRecord;   {holds record to be written into NewMaster}
  BEGIN
    WHILE NOT eof(Semester) DO
      BEGIN
        read(Semester, MStu.Info);
        MStu.Term:= TheTerm;
        write(NewMaster, MStu)
      END
  END;
{+                                                                    +}
PROCEDURE Merge(TheTerm: String25; VAR Semester: StuRecFile;
                        VAR OldMaster, NewMaster: MStuRecFile);

  {documentation}
  VAR
    MStu1,    {MStuRec read in from OldMaster}
    MStu2:    {MStuRec read in/assigned from Semester}
              MStuRecord;
  BEGIN
    GetMasterRec(MStu1, OldMaster);
    GetSemesterRec(TheTerm, MStu2, Semester);
    WHILE NOT eof(OldMaster) AND NOT eof(Semester) DO
      IF Stu1GoesFirst(MStu1.Info, MStu2.Info) THEN
        BEGIN
          write(NewMaster, MStu1);
```

```
              GetMasterRec(MStu1, OldMaster)
          END
        ELSE
          BEGIN
            write(NewMaster, MStu2);
            GetSemesterRec(TheTerm, MStu2, Semester)
          END;
        CopyLastTwo(MStu1, MStu2, NewMaster)
        CopyOldMasterRecs(OldMaster, NewMaster);
        CopySemesterRecs(TheTerm, Semester, NewMaster);
        close(Semester);
        close(OldMaster);
        close(NewMaster)
      END;
    {*                                                                    *}
```

The merge algorithm

The program we coded "merged" two files whose contents were slightly different. Suppose, instead, the files InFile1 and InFile2 have records of identical types. They are both sorted by a field we can call Key. Algorithm 16.3 describes a merge for two sorted binary files containing identical component records.

Algorithm 16.3

> *{algorithm to merge two sorted binary files:}*
> *GetRec(Rec1, InFile1) {get first record from each file}*
> *GetRec(Rec2, InFile2)*
> *WHILE NOT eof(InFile1) AND NOT eof(InFile2) DO*
>   *IF Rec1. Key < Rec2.Key THEN {copy record with lower Key}*
>   *write(OutFile, Rec1)   {and get next record}*
>   *GetRec(Rec1, InFile1)*
>   *ELSE*
>   *write(OutFile, Rec2)*
>   *GetRec(Rec2, InFile2)*
> *CopyLastTwo(Rec1, Rec2, OutFile)*
> *CopyRemainder(InFile1, OutFile)*
> *CopyRemainder(InFile2, OutFile)*
> *close all files*
> *{end algorithm}* ◆

EXERCISES

Test Your Understanding

1. Why is it necessary to close each of the file variables at the particular places in the program?

2. Does it make sense to merge two files with different record components? Explain.

Sharpen Your Implementation Skills

3. Suppose the records were sorted by SocSecNo field instead. Briefly explain what changes would need to be made in the source code of UpdateMerge.

4. Write the code for the procedure `GetMasterRec`.

5. Write the code for the procedure `CopyMRecRemainder`.

6. Write the code for the procedure `CopyLastTwo`.

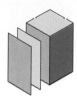

16.3 Pointers

Up to this point, you have only seen programs where the memory allocated to all variables over the scope of a block is set up before the block statement is executed. The memory for all local variables, moreover, is automatically deallocated as soon as the machine completes the block statement. This kind of memory allocation is known as *static allocation.* In this section, you will learn how to write programs where memory is allocated and/or deallocated from the statement part of a block. This kind of memory allocation is known as *dynamic allocation.*

> **Static allocation:** the means by which memory is automatically allocated to a declared process from the identifiers in the parameter list and from the identifiers representing local variables and constants. This memory is automatically deallocated when the process is finished.

> **Dynamic allocation:** the means by which memory is allocated and/or deallocated from the statement part of a process. This memory usually does not exist before the statements are carried out and may well exist after the process is finished.

What is a Pointer?

A *pointer* is a data type that can take on the value of a machine address. You use a *pointer variable* to allocate memory to a *dynamic variable* from the statement part of a block. The memory given to this variable need not have existed before the machine started to execute the block's statements. A dynamic variable, moreover, is *anonymous,* because its value(s) can be accessed only by means of a reference to an associated pointer variable. Once created, a dynamic variable must likewise be deallocated by one of the statements in the procedure's block.

> **Pointer variable:** a variable type whose value represents an address. It is the means both for creating a dynamic variable and for accessing the value(s) contained in the dynamic variable.

> **Dynamic variable:** a variable to which memory is allocated or deallocated during the execution of the statement part of a process.

Pointer Syntax and Dynamic Variables

Now let us discuss the syntax rules that apply to pointer types. The discussion covers how to define a pointer type and how to allocate and deallocate dynamic variables using pointer variables.

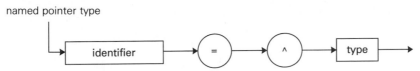

named pointer type

FIGURE 16.3 Syntax for defining a pointer data type.

Definition/
declaration
syntax
An example

The syntax diagram for defining a pointer type is shown in Figure 16.3. The identifier is the name of the pointer type, and the type box indicates the data type of the dynamic variable associated with the defined pointer type.

The following example shows how you can define some pointer types and declare some associated pointer variable(s) in a program:

```
TYPE
   DateType = RECORD
      Month:  1..12;
      Date: 1..31;
      Year: integer
      END;
   DatePtr = ^DateType;
   IntPtr = ^integer;
VAR
   Today: DatePtr;
   IntAPtr, IntBPtr: IntPtr;
```

It is important to note that the pointer variable Today does not take on the three values of the field variables of DateType. Nor do the pointer variables IntAPtr, and IntBPtr take on integer values. The three variables take on the values of addresses once memory has been allocated to them by the standard procedure new.

The procedure
new

The standard procedure new is the means by which memory for a dynamic variable is allocated. A call to this procedure requires one parameter that must be a variable of a pointer type. The postcondition returned by the call is that memory has been allocated to a dynamic variable. You can then use the pointer variable as an identifier to access the value(s) stored in the allocated location.

Using new

Using the three pointer variables, we can create memory for them from the statement part of the block with the code

```
new(Today);
new(IntAPtr);
new(IntBPtr);
```

The before-after pictures showing the execution of these statements is given in Figures 16.4(a) and 16.4(b). Note that initially the values of each of the three variables are undetermined. After the call new(Today) is carried out, an address to hold the value(s) of a variable of type DateType is allocated. No values, however, are yet assigned to the fields of this anonymous variable. Likewise, the calls new(IntAPtr) and new(IntBPtr) create memory for two anonymous integer variables. Values are likewise not yet assigned to these two variables.

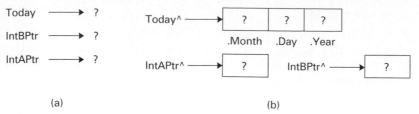

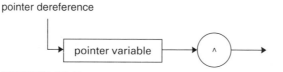

FIGURE 16.4 Memory given to `Today`, `IntAPtr`, and `IntBPtr` (a) before calls to new, and (b) after three calls to new.

Dereferencing

Figure 16.5 is the syntax diagram that shows how the value of a dynamic variable can be referenced or changed. Once a dynamic variable has been created by the new procedure, the computer can carry out a *dereferencing operation* on the pointer variable. The carat is known in Pascal as a *dereferencing operator*. From the syntax diagram for a variable (see Appendix F), we can see that Figure 16.5 represents a variable. Because a variable of a dereferencing operation is anonymous, it can only be used in the statement part of a block. We call this variable a *dereferenced variable*.

pointer dereference

```
  ┌──────────────────┐      ╭───╮
  │ pointer variable │─────▶│ ^ │─────▶
  └──────────────────┘      ╰───╯
```

FIGURE 16.5 Syntax to dereference a dynamic variable.

> **dereferencing operation:** the means by which the value of a dynamic variable is used or changed in the statement part of a program. This operation is carried out on a pointer variable using the dereferencing operator. In order for it to be successfully carried out, memory must have been allocated to the pointer variable used in the operation.

> **dereferencing operator:** in Pascal, a carat. The operator that, when used with a pointer variable, makes up a statement to carry out a dereferencing operation.

> **dereferenced variable:** the dynamic variable that is dereferenced when the dereferencing operation is carried out on a pointer variable.

Examples

For any given pointer variable, there is only one dereferencing operation. This operation can only be applied on a pointer variable that has had memory allocated to it. The dereferencing operations that apply to the three pointer variables of our example are respectively represented by the source code `Today^`, `IntAPtr^` and `IntBPtr^`. The dereferenced variables that can be used in statements are likewise `Today^`, `IntAPtr^`, and `IntBPtr^`.

The dereferenced variable `Today^` represents a record variable with 3 fields. These three fields can be selected either using a period or a WITH statement. Because the three fields represent integer types, the operations that apply to integers also apply to the field variables of the record variable Today^. These field variables are coded in the statement part of a program as Today^.Month, Today^.Date, and Today.^Year. The scope over which selection to the three field variables is extended can be carried out by a WITH statement whose code is

```
WITH Today^ DO
    BEGIN  {references to Month, Date, and Year possible}  END;
```

These statements all work because the pointer variable Today *points to* the dynamic variable Today^. The operations that apply to a *named* record variable of type DateType can be applied to the *anonymous* variable Today^ because this variable is also of type DateType.

The pointer variables IntAPtr and IntBPtr respectively point to the anonymous integer variables IntAPtr^ and IntBPtr^. An integer value can be assigned or read in to either anonymous variable, and you can use either variable correctly in the statement part of a program to represent an integer value.

Do not confuse the pointer variable with the variable it points to. Consider, for example, the two variables IntAPtr and IntAPtr^. IntAPtr's value is a machine address. This address contains an integer value for the variable IntAPtr^. The operations that apply to the pointer variable IntAPtr are different from those applying to the integer variable IntAPtr^. An integer value cannot be assigned to IntAPtr nor can you use IntAPtr to form an integer expression.

Some statements   Suppose memory has been allocated to IntAPtr^, IntBPtr^ and Today^, using the sequence of new statements we coded previously. Figure 16.6 shows the effects of the sequence of source code statements that follows. The interaction to read in values to the field variables of Today^ as shown in the figure follows the sequence of source code statements.

```
IntAPtr^:= 5;
IntBPtr^:= 7;
write('Enter a date (month, date, year):  ');
WITH Today^ DO
    readln(Month, Date, Year);

Enter a date (month, date, year): 12  25  1992
```

FIGURE 16.6 Values assigned to IntAPtr^, IntBPtr^, and Today^.

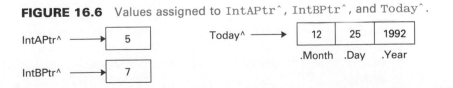

Operations on Pointer Variables and Dynamic Variables

The only operators that can work on pointers variables are the assignment operator and the two boolean operators = and <>. When an assignment operation on a pointer variable is carried out, the address of the pointer variable on the left-hand side of the operator is changed to the address represented by the pointer expression on the right-hand side of the operator. In the following discussion, we show how these operations apply both to the pointer variables and the dynamic variables they point to.

Boolean operations   The boolean expression `IntAPtr = IntBPtr` is true only if the two pointers point to the same dynamic variable. Note that `IntAPtr^` and `IntBPtr^` can be two different variables whose values are equal. Given this scenario, the boolean expression `IntAPtr^ = IntBPtr^` is true, and likewise the boolean expression `IntAPtr <> IntBPtr` is also true.

An example   Suppose `IntAPtr^` and `IntBPtr^` have taken on the values described by Figure 16.6. The effect of the statement `IntAPtr^ := IntBPtr^` is shown in Figure 16.7. If the assignment statement is carried out so that a partial description of the program state is given by Figure 16.7, the computer will display two lines of text when it executes the following code:

```
IF (IntA^ = IntB^) AND (IntA <> IntB) THEN
  BEGIN
    writeln('The two pointer variables are different.');
    writeln('The values of the variables pointed to are equal.')
  END;
```

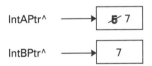

FIGURE 16.7   Effect of `IntAPtr^ := IntBPtr^` given the precondition of Figure 16.6.

Pointer variable assignment statements   Suppose the program state is initially described by Figure 16.7. Then the statement `IntBPtr := IntAPtr` is carried out. Figure 16.8 describes the postcondition after this assignment statement is carried out. Given the new state, the computer will produce display when it executes the statement

```
IF IntAPtr = IntBPtr THEN
  writeln('The two pointers are pointing to the same variable.');
```

Note that the memory given to the original address of `IntBPtr` is not destroyed by the action of the assignment statement. One of the unfortunate effects of the assignment statement is that the memory originally dereferenced by `IntBPtr^` is now *garbage*.

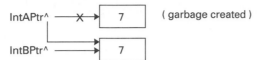

FIGURE 16.8 Effect of `IntAPtr^ := IntBPtr^` given the precondition of Figure 16.7.

Garbage: a dynamic variable still existing in memory that can no longer be dereferenced. This effect occurs if no pointer variable holds the value of the dynamic variable's address.

The harmful effects of garbage

Consider the situation represented by Figure 16.8 as it applies to the definition of garbage. If an anonymous variable exists in memory that can no longer be dereferenced, it is useless. Given that the memory available to you as a program user is finite, you can see the harmful effects of garbage creation. If too many garbage variables are created during the course of a program run, the program will crash because further memory to carry out the program instructions is no longer available. Therefore, you must avoid garbage creation in the statement part of any source code sequence at all costs.

The procedure `dispose`

If, for some reason, you want to assign the memory value of `IntAPtr` to the pointer variable `IntBPtr` and memory has been allocated to `IntBPtr`, you avoid creating garbage by first freeing the memory allocated to `IntBPtr` so that it can be used for other processing. You accomplish this desirable effect with a call to the standard procedure `dispose`. The parameter of this procedure, like that of the procedure `new`, is a pointer variable. A call to `dispose` is successfully carried out only if memory has been allocated to the pointer variable. Given this required precondition, the postcondition returned by the call to the procedure is that the memory of the parameter variable has been freed for further usage.

A source code example

Suppose you want to assign `IntAPtr`'s value to `IntBPtr`. Suppose further that `IntBPtr` has had memory allocated to it. If you do not want to create garbage in the assignment process, you must write the following code:

```
dispose(IntBPtr);
IntBPtr := IntAPtr;
```

When these two statements are carried out, the memory given to `IntBPtr` is first deallocated. Then, the value of `IntAPtr` is (safely) assigned to `IntBPtr` without the harmful effect of garbage creation.

The run-time heap

When a call to the procedure new is carried out, the computer takes memory off the *run-time heap* and allocates it to the pointer variable. When a call to the procedure `dispose` is carried out, the computer returns the memory allocated back to the run-time heap.

Run-time heap: the memory available for allocation to an object or process at any given time in the course of a program run.

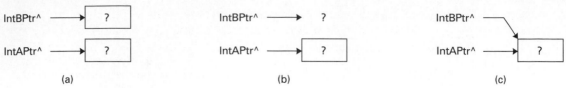

(a)   (b)   (c)

FIGURE 16.9 Assigning `IntBPtr` to `IntAPtr` with the precondition that memory was first allocated to `IntBPtr`: (a) precondition, (b) `dispose(IntBPtr)`, and (c) `IntBPtr:= IntAPtr`.

More pictures   ·Let us consider how the program state changes with each statement of the previous source code sequence. Figure 16.9(a) shows the program state when `IntAPtr` and `IntBPtr` contain different address values. After the statement `dispose(IntBPtr)` is executed, the program state is described by Figure 16.9(b). The run-time heap is slightly larger because the memory originally allocated to the pointer variable `IntBPtr` has been added to the heap. Figure 16.9(c) shows the effect of the statement `IntBPtr:= IntAPtr` on the program state. Note that new memory is not taken off the run-time heap to carry out this last assignment statement.

Assignments to   The last assignment statement shows that it is possible to assign memory to a
pointer pointer variable without the need to call the procedure new. For example, the fol-
variables lowing sequence, given the precondition that memory has not been allocated to either pointer variable, is legal and will achieve the same program state described by
Figure 16.9(c):

```
new(IntAPtr);
IntAPtr^:= 12;
IntBPtr:= IntAPtr;
```

As with all assignments, the statement will work properly only if the expression on the right-hand side of the assignment operator has taken on some value. This
value, with one important exception, can only be to an address of a dynamic variable that already exists in memory. After an assignment statement is carried out, the
pointer variable on the left-hand side of the operator points to the same dynamic
variable pointed to by the pointer variable that makes up the expression on the right-
The value NIL hand side of the operator.

There is one value a pointer variable can take on that does not represent the
address of a dynamic variable. We refer to the value represented by the reserved
word NIL. This value can be assigned to a pointer variable of any defined type.
When a pointer variable is assigned NIL, it cannot be used to dereference a dynamic
variable. A typical statement to assign the NIL value is coded as `IntAPtr:= NIL`.

Memory is not taken from nor added to the run-time heap to carry out a NIL
assignment to a pointer variable. We generally use the NIL value to represent the
fact that memory has not yet been allocated to some dynamic variable. Then we can
use this value in a boolean expression such as `IntAPtr = NIL` or To-

day <> NIL to test whether memory has been allocated to a dynamic variable or not. We point out that the NIL value must be explicitly assigned to a pointer variable in order to guarantee that a value of true is returned to the first expression and one of false is returned to the second expression. In other words, you should not assume that the NIL value is assigned to a declared pointer variable by default.

Garbage disposal and NIL assignments

It is important to also note that an assignment of the NIL value to a pointer variable does not automatically dispose of the memory previously allocated. When memory is previously allocated to some pointer variable, it must be disposed of before an assignment to NIL is made. Otherwise, garbage might be created. Therefore, if your program had previously allocated memory to the variable IntAPtr, and you want IntAPtr to take on the value NIL, you can avoid creating garbage only if you code the sequence:

```
dispose(IntAPtr);
IntAPtr:= NIL;
```

Suppose memory has been allocated to the pointer variable IntAPtr and the dispose statement is not carried out before an assignment to NIL is made. In this case, the dynamic variable previously dereferenced by IntAPtr^ belongs neither to the run-time heap nor to the memory of some process on the run-time stack. It is lost for the rest of the program run as unavailable garbage.

EXERCISES

Test Your Understanding

1. We showed you a statement that assigned the value NIL to the variable IntBPtr of type IntPtr. Given that this statement is possible, can you likewise code the statement Today:= NIL where Today is of type DatePtr? Explain your answer.

2. Discuss briefly the difference between IntAPtr and IntAPtr^.

3. Given that IntA and IntB are of type IntPtr, which of the following boolean expressions represent valid syntax?

   (a) IntAPtr <> IntBPtr   **(d)** IntAPtr^ = IntBPtr^
   (b) IntAPtr < IntBPtr   **(e)** IntAPtr^ < IntBPtr^
   (c) IntAPtr = NIL   **(f)** IntAPtr^ = NIL

Practice Your Analysis Skills

4. Suppose you have the following definitions and declarations:

```
TYPE
    IntPtr = ^integer;
VAR
    IntAPtr, IntBPtr: IntPtr;
```

Assuming that the statements new(IntAPtr) and new(IntBPtr) have been executed, indicate what will be displayed for each of the following (sometimes an error message will be the result):

   (a)
```
IntAPtr^:= 7;
IntBPtr:= IntAPtr;
writeln(IntAPtr^:1, ' ', IntBPtr^:1);
```

(b) {same assignments as above and}
IntAPtr^ := IntAPtr^ + 2;
writeln(IntAPtr^:1, ' ', IntBPtr^:1);

(c) IntAPtr^ := 7;
{assume here that new(BPtr) was not executed}
IntBPtr := IntAPtr;
writeln(IntAPtr^:1, ' ', IntBPtr^:1);

(d) IntAPtr^ := 5;
IntBPtr := IntAPtr;
writeln(IntAPtr:1, ' ', IntBPtr:1);

(e) IntPtr^ := 5;
IntBPtr^ := IntAPtr^;
writeln(IntAPtr^:1, ' ', IntBPtr^:1);

(f) {same as the assignment sequence of (e) and}
IntBPtr^ := 2 * IntAPtr^;
writeln(APtr^:1, ' ', IntBPtr^:1);

(g) IntAPtr := 5;
IntBPtr := IntAPtr;
writeln(IntAPtr:1, ' ', IntBPtr:1)

16.4 Arrays of Pointers

In the previous section, we said it was possible to assign memory to a pointer variable without the need to call the procedure *new*. This capability allows us to write code where two different pointer variables can point to the same dynamic variable. You can, for certain programs, use this property to cut down on the memory requirements of a source program. The solution to the case study of this section is an example of one of these kinds of programs.

CASE STUDY 16.2

The problem statement

You work in the software publishing company User's Friend, Inc., and your boss has given you an overnight project. You are given a file of type ClientsFile where the file contains components of type ClientRecord. A record of this type has a Name field, a ClientNo field, and an Information field.

The Name field contains the customer's first, middle, and last names. The file, as represented by the file variable ClientsOnFile, has components that are sorted in order according to the values contained in the Name field of each Client-Record. ClientNo is a string variable that always contains five characters. Each char value in the string must be a digit, so the range of values possible for ClientNo is '00000' to '99999'. The value of '00000' is known never to be given out as a customer number so it can be used as a sentinel value. The contents of the Information field are irrelevant to the problem.

The definitions and declarations you must work with are as follows:

```
CONST
  MaxClients = 1000;

TYPE
  String20 = STRING[20];
  String5 = STRING[5];
  NameType = RECORD
    First,
    Middle,
    Last: String20
  END;

  ClientRecord = RECORD
    Name: NameType;
    CustomerNo: String5;
    {other fields}
  END;

  ClientsFile = FILE OF ClientRecord;
  ClientPointer = ^ClientRecord;
  PointerArray = ARRAY[0..MaxClients] OF ClientPointer;

VAR
  ClientsOnFile: ClientsFile;
  ByName,
  ByNo: PointerArray;
  TotalClients: integer;
```

Your boss wants you to write a procedure `GetClients` that reads in values from `ClientsOnFile` to set up two arrays of pointers, `ByName` and `ByNo`. The dynamic variables pointed to by each array element of `ByName` are to be sorted by their Name field. The dynamic variables pointed to by the elements of `ByNo` are to be sorted in order of the `CustomerNo` field.

The software to search through `ByName` using the binary search has already been coded. As part of your work, the boss wants you also to code the binary search function through the array `ByNo`. This function returns the pointer to the dynamic variable whose `CustomerNo` field matches the value of `SearchNo`. If the search fails to find a match, the function returns the NIL pointer.

The logical appearance of the two arrays

Figure 16.10 shows how three typical elements in the two arrays are set up. `ByName[1]` points to the record with the last name in the client list that is alphabetically first, `ByName[Mid]` points to the first probe value for the binary search by name fields, and `ByName[TotalClients]` points to the record of the alphabetically last name. `ByNo[K]`, the record containing the lowest of the three `CustomerNo` fields, points to the same record variable as `ByName[Last]`. `ByNo[L]` points to the same record variable as `ByName[1]` because its `CustomerNo` field is greater than the one pointed to by `ByNo[K]`. Finally, `ByNo[M]` points to the record variable that has the highest `CustomerNo` field.

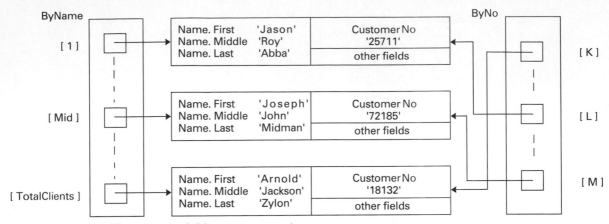

FIGURE 16.10 The array variables ByName and ByNo.

Planning the procedure   The stub for the procedure, GetClients is written as follows:

```
PROCEDURE GetClients(VAR ByName, ByNo: PointerArray;
        VAR TotalClients: integer; VAR ClientsOnFile: ClientsFile);
{in:  ClientsOnFile -- has been linked to an external file
out:  ClientsOnFile -- entire contents read in and assigned
out:  ByName -- pointers to contents of Clients, sorted by Name
out:  ByNo -- pointers to contents of Clients, sorted by CustomerNo
out:  TotalClients -- count of records read in and assigned}
BEGIN    END;
```

The procedure you need to write can use a partial fill-in algorithm for both arrays. Your boss says that you can assume there are less than 1000 client records in the file, so you need not write a guard against an array index value out of range. Having been relieved of this problem, your initial description will look like

> *reset(ClientsOnFile)*
> *TotalClients ← 0*
> *new(ByNo[0])*   {sets up sentinel for Insert procedure}
> *ByNo[0]ˆ.CustomerNo:= '00000'*
> *WHILE NOT eof(ClientsOnFile) DO*
>   *new(Clients)*   {assigns memory to read in next record}
>   *read(ClientsOnFile, AClientˆ)*
>   *TotalClients ← TotalClients + 1*
>   *ByName[TotalClients] ← AClient*
>   *Insert(AClient, TotalClients, ByNo)*
> *close(ClientsOnFile)*

The variable AClientˆ is a record read in from ClientsOnFile that is assigned to ByName[TotalClients] each loop pass using the partial fill-in algorithm. The procedure Insert has the precondition that the elements of ByNo are sorted by CustomerNo over the subrange *1..TotalClients-1*. The values stored in this array point to the previous `TotalClients-1` records read in. The postcondition returned is that the values in ByNo point to the previous `TotalClients` records read in and that they are sorted by CustomerNo field over the subrange *1..TotalClients*. The procedure returns this postcondition by inserting the variable `AClient` into its proper place in the array ByNo. You plan to to use the record variable `ByNo[0]ˆ` as a sentinel record for the `Insert` procedure. Thus you allocate memory for the pointer variable `ByNo[0]`. You then assign the sentinel value of `'00000'` to the `CustomerNo` field of the variable `ByNo[0]ˆ`.

Source code

From the pseudocode, you obtain the source code for `GetClients` as

```
{*                                                                    *}
PROCEDURE Insert(NewElement: ClientPointer; Candidate: integer;
                                VAR ByNo: PointerArray);
   {in: NewElement -- element to be added to ByNo
    in: Candidate -- candidate position to insert NewElement
    in: ByNo -- sorted without NewElement in array
   out: ByNo -- sorted with NewElement included in array}
   BEGIN   END;
{+                                                                    +}
PROCEDURE GetClients(VAR ByName, ByNo: PointerArray;
         VAR TotalClients: integer; VAR ClientsOnFile: ClientsFile);
   {documentation}
   VAR
     AClient:   {AClientˆ is the record read in from ClientsOnFile}
                ClientPointer;
   BEGIN
     reset(ClientsOnFile);
     TotalClients:= 0;
     new(ByNo[0]);
     ByNo[0]ˆ.CustomerNo:= '00000';
     WHILE NOT eof(ClientsOnFile) DO
       BEGIN
         new(AClient);
         read(ClientsOnFile, AClientˆ);
         TotalClients:= TotalClients + 1;
         ByName[TotalClients]:= AClient;
         Insert(AClient, TotalClients, ByNo)
       END;
     close(ClientsOnFile)
   END;
```

Planning the code for `Insert`

Given the sentinel element `ByNo[0]`, you arrive at the following pseudocode description for the procedure `Insert`:

> *WHILE (ByNo[Candidate-1]ˆ.CustomerNo > NewElementˆ.CustomerNo) DO*
>   *ByNo[Candidate] ← ByNo[Candidate-1]*   *{put element in order}*
>   *Candidate ← Candidate - 1*   *{get new candidate}*
> *ByNo[Candidate] ← NewElement* *{insert NewElement into its correct place}*

After each loop pass, it is true that all elements in the subrange *Candidate+1..TotalClients* point to dynamic variables whose CustomerNo fields are all greater than the value of NewElement^.CustomerNo. The elements over this subrange, moreover, remain sorted. When the loop is exited, it is true that the value of ByNo[Candidate-1]^.CustomerNo is less than the value of NewElement^.CustomerNo, assuming no duplicate CustomerNo values. Hence, it is correct to place NewElement^.CustomerNo into the position of Candidate.

Source code
The source code for the procedure Insert is as shown.

```
PROCEDURE Insert(NewElement: ClientPointer; Candidate: integer;
                                    VAR ByNo: PointerArray);
{documentation}
BEGIN
  WHILE (ByNo[Candidate-1]^.CustomerNo > NewElement^.CustomerNo) DO
    BEGIN
      ByNo[Candidate]:= ByNo[Candidate-1];         {move element up}
      Candidate:= Candidate - 1                     {get new candidate}
    END;
  ByNo[Candidate]:= NewElement                      {insert NewElement}
END;
```

Writing the binary search function
Let us apply the recursive version of the binary search algorithm to write the code for the function NumberSearch. This function is supposed to return a pointer, not an index value, so we must be sure to code the statement NumberSearch:= ByNo[Mid] if the search is a success. In the case of a failed search, the assignment is NumberSearch:= NIL. The code for the function is then quite easy to implement, and so we have

```
FUNCTION NumberSearch(VAR ByNo: PointerArray; TheNumber: String5;
                              Lo, Hi: integer): ClientPointer;
VAR
  Probe: integer;        {candidate probe value}
BEGIN
  IF Lo > Hi THEN
    NumberSearch:= NIL
  ELSE
    BEGIN
      Probe:= (Lo + Hi) DIV 2;
      IF ByNo[Probe]^.CustomerNo = TheNumber THEN
        NumberSearch:= ByNo[Probe]
      ELSE IF ByNo[Probe]^.CustomerNo < TheNumber THEN
        NumberSearch:= NumberSearch(ByNo, TheNumber, Probe+1, Hi)
      ELSE
        NumberSearch:= NumberSearch(ByNo, TheNumber, Lo, Probe-1)
    END
END;  ◆
```

EXERCISES

Test Your Understanding

1. How many records have to be read in from the statement part of GetClients before we can definitely say that the final value has been assigned to each of the following elements?

   (a) ByName [1]   **(d)** ByNo [1]
   (b) ByName [5]   **(e)** ByNo [5]
   (c) ByName [TotalClients]   **(f)** ByNo [TotalClients]

2. Suppose the first five records were read in as follows:

   ```
   Lord Jeffrey Amherst   34109
   Andrew Jackson Andrews   87412
   James Baylor Bailey   08649
   Raymond Earl Bartleson   18887
   Joseph Edison Browne   56718
   ```

   Draw the appearance of the two arrays ByName and ByNo just after the fifth loop pass in GetClients has been carried out.

Sharpen Your Implementation Skills

3. Given the array ByNo, write a procedure MakeClientsII that will create a file, referenced by file variable ClientsII, whose components are of type ClientRecord arranged by order of account number from lowest to highest.

4. Write the code for the binary search function NameSearch. This function returns the pointer to the dynamic variable whose Name field matches the value of SearchName. Assume the elements are sorted in order of last name, first name, and middle name. All three name fields must match. If no such match is found, the NIL value is returned.

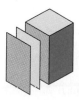

Program Testing Hints

This section contains suggestions to help you test programs that involve the use of binary files and/or pointer variables. When pointers are used as parameters, some very subtle effects occur. A good deal of this section discusses the effects on an actual parameter that is a pointer when the formal parameter is called by VAR and when it is called by value.

Text Files vs. Binary Files

Some errors dealing with file processing can be committed the same way using either a binary file or a text file. Other errors may occur if you confuse the operations that apply to binary files with those that apply only to text files. Let us look at both kinds of errors.

Common patterns to avoid

        Some patterns that are dangerous to use with text files are equally dangerous to use with binary files. For example, regardless of the file type, you should avoid using REPEAT..UNTIL in the following context:

```
        reset(SomeFile)
        REPEAT                                    {DANGEROUS!}
            read(SomeFile, SomeComponent)
            process SomeComponent
        UNTIL eof(SomeFile)
```

If you insist on using REPEAT..UNTIL for reading in values, it is safe to enter the loop as long as you guard against an attempt to read an empty file. Thus, the following algorithm using REPEAT..UNTIL is safe:

```
        reset(SomeFile)
        IF NOT eof(SomeFile) THEN              {guard against empty file}
            REPEAT
                read(SomeFile, SomeComponent)
                process SomeComponent
            UNTIL eof(SomeFile)
```

Make sure not to code reset or rewrite inside a file-processing loop. The following example shows a fragment of source code that processes the first component of SomeFile endlessly:

```
        WHILE NOT eof (SomeFile) DO
          BEGIN
            reset (SomeFile);        {BAD! }
            read (SomeFile, SomeComponent);
            Process (SomeComponent)
          END;
```

Remember that a file variable's value *always* changes, regardless of whether it is used in a read or write procedure. Hence, always call formal parameter identifiers representing file variables by VAR and never by value. Finally, remember that the standard procedures readln and writeln and the standard function *eoln* are operations that work only with text files and never with binary files.

PROGRAM DESIGN RULE 16.1

Make sure that all variables read in or written to a binary file are the same data type as the file's components.

Parameter list requirements

Even though text files store homogeneous values that are all of type char, the human-readable characters they store can represent the values of different data types. Hence, you will often have different variable types in the actual parameter list of read, readln or write, writeln statements.

Do not forget, however, that values stored in binary files are all of the same type. When using `read` or `write` on binary files, the actual parameters must contain only variables whose type matches the data type stored in the file. If, for example, the binary file contains records as components, the parameter list for any `read` or `write` statement must contain only variables that are of the corresponding record type. Remember, too, that the record's field variables cannot be read in or written as individual variables.

Data entry and display

It is simple to code a program that writes component values to or reads component values from an external binary file. A single binary file may be processed, and hence have its component values altered, by more than one program. Text processing may not be necessary for most of these programs.

Nonetheless, do not forget that there must always be a program to create the original file, usually from data entry at the keyboard. When you develop this program, do not forget to display the required prompts and code the required guards to ensure that proper data are read in from the keyboard. Likewise, there will always be one other program that displays some or all of the contents of the processed file. Do not forget to take the necessary analogous steps in this program to ensure that the processed data are displayed both neatly and legibly.

Testing Strategies

Devising test data for programs that process files containing hundreds of component record types each with 20 field variables may seem like an impossible task. You can, however, simplify the task by following some of the suggestions given in this subsection.

Displaying results

Even though the problem statement for a file-processing program may not require any display, you should write one or more procedures to display values read in from or written out to the file or files. A typical header for display, given the `MergeUpdate` program of Section 16.2 might be coded as PROCE-DURE SHOWMREC(ASTU: MSTURECORD); . We are using uppercase letters to indicate that the procedure is a development tool and not part of the finished program.

Is it necessary to display all the fields? Not really. Only the ones relevant to the problem statement need be displayed. For example, in the program `MergeUpdate`, it is only necessary to display the Name fields and perhaps the IDNo field of each record.

The rule of small samples, revisited

When generating test data, you can again use the "rule of small samples" on file-processing programs. Even though the actual program may process perhaps 500 records, you can test it quite well using as little as 20, 10, or even 2 records. Remember that obvious bugs can be found with a very small sample size.

Devising test data

You should think carefully about the kind of test files to use. First, think of what can possibly go wrong and devise data to see how your program handles it. Besides the usual empty file testing, you might consider files with exactly one component in them. Then try files with an odd and an even number of components in them. These are quick-and-dirty tests that depend solely upon the number of components in the file.

Besides devising tests based on component counts, you need to generate test data using typical values taken on by the file's components. You can simplify this task considerably by generating data that assign values into only those field variables relevant to the problem statement. In the MergeUpdate program, you can use test files where values are assigned only to the Name and IDNo fields of each record. If your system will not allow unassigned field variables to be written into a test file, you can assign the same dummy values to all the remaining fields of each component record contained in the file.

Counting processed components

If you are not careful with your logic, you might develop a program that writes too many or too few records into the destination file. Without some kind of auxiliary variables, bugs such as these may be very difficult to find if a large number of components are processed. You can defensively code against these problems if you include some auxiliary counting variables in your source code.

What should these variables count? Certainly it is important to count the number of records read in from a source file or written to a destination file. Likewise, all events significant to the processing logic should be counted. Then, once all files have been processed, the values of these counters are displayed and checked to see if they indicate that more or less than the expected number of records were processed.

An example

As part of the development process of MergeUpdate, we could have declared the following counters:

```
VAR
    SRECS,      {number of records read from Semester file}
    ORECS,      {number of records read from OldMaster}
    NRECS:      {number of records written into NewMaster}
                integer;
    Semester: StuRecFile;
    OldMaster,
    NewMaster: MStuRecFile;
```

These variables are initialized to 0 at the start of the program. Then, the respective read operations and write operations on any of the files are coded using

```
read(Semester, MStu.Info);
SRECS:= SRECS + 1;

read(OldMaster, MStu);
ORECS:= ORECS + 1;

write(NewMaster, MStu);
NRECS:= NRECS + 1;
```

Once the merging is completed, the last statement of the main block is coded as

```
IF  SRECS + ORECS = NRECS THEN
    writeln('THE FILE COUNT APPEARS CORRECT')
```

```
       ELSE IF SRECS + ORECS > NRECS THEN
         writeln('SOME OF THE FILES READ IN WERE NOT MERGED')
       ELSE
         writeln('SOME DUPLICATE FILES SEEM TO HAVE BEEN MERGED')
```

Saneness, revisited   Given all these global counters that need to be initialized and incremented in the proper places, you might wonder whether the extra coding is worth all the effort. It depends upon the nature of the problem. If the number of records being processed is small, you can check your logic by comparing the files' contents before and after processing. In this case, you still need to write some programs that display the contents of the files involved.

   If, however, the program processes hundreds or even thousands of records, by all means use counters. Given 5000 records to process, a program that skips 50 records or causes 50 duplicate records to be created (a customer may be billed twice in cases such as these) is 99% correct. That percentage, however, is certainly not good enough. Defensive coding to process such large files is virtually mandatory. The mishandling of records might be detected if an anomoly is found with one of the counters. Once this error is found, it can be dealt with.

Pointer Parameters

The same rules of parameter passing apply to pointers as they do to other variables. Thus, when a pointer is called by value, a local copy of its value, an address, is made. When a pointer is called by variable, a local alias to the actual parameter variable is made. Because pointers represent addresses, however, you must exercise special care with your code, as the following examples illustrate.

Pointers as value parameters   Let us use the coded fragment of Example 16.4 to show how the statement part of a procedure changes the program state when a pointer variable is passed in as a value call. The different block statements for the procedure ValCall are to be inserted for each example listed after the source code of the example.

Example 16.4

```
TYPE                           {definitions/declarations used in examples}
  IntPtr = ^integer;
VAR
  AnIntPtr: IntPtr;

PROCEDURE ValCall(XPtr: IntPtr);        {procedure used in examples}
  BEGIN
    {INSERT STATEMENT(S) HERE}
  END;

new(AnInt);                             {sequence used in examples}
AnIntPtr^:= 5;
ValCall(AnIntPtr);
writeln(AnIntPtr^:1);
```

1. `XPtr^:= 7`

    If the block's statement assigns a new value to `XPtr^`, this effect is passed out to `AnIntPtr^`. Hence, the value displayed will be 7 and not 5. The reason for this result is that the *address* passed out of the block remains the same, but the value contained in the address changes. Indeed, a value call using a pointer variable is equivalent to a call by variable on the object pointed to (i.e. `XPtr^`). Its value(s) can be changed by the block's action *and felt* once the block is exited.

2. `dispose(XPtr)`

    This statement deallocates the address `XPtr`. This address, copied into the block, is also the address of `AnIntPtr`. It is clear that a reference to `XPtr^`, once this statement is carried out, has no meaning. Likewise, any reference to `AnIntPtr^`, once `CallVal` is exited has no meaning because the address has been deallocated. Hence, we cannot predict what value is displayed.

3. `dispose(XPtr);`
    `new(XPtr);`

    In this case, the original `XPtr` whose value was `AnIntPtr` is still deallocated. Hence, the display once `CallVal` is exited is unpredictable. Moreover, the memory allocated by `new(XPtr)` is lost as garbage once the block is exited.

4. `XPtr:= NIL`

    This statement reassigns a value to `XPtr`. Now `XPtr` and `AnIntPtr` have different values. When `ValCall` is exited, `XPtr`'s NIL value is gone and the value of `AnInt^Ptr`, that is 5, will be displayed. In this case, moreover, no garbage is created by the reassignment to the NIL pointer.

5. `new(XPtr);`
    `XPtr^:= 7;`
    `writeln(XPtr^:1);`

    Here a new address is allocated to the variable that originally had the value of `AnIntPtr`. When followed by `XPtr^:= 7`, the effect is only felt over the scope of the `ValCall` block. Within the scope of `ValCall`, the effect of `writeln(XPtr^)` is the display of the value 7. Because `XPtr` and `AnIntPtr` now represent different variables, the value displayed when the block is exited will be 5, the value initially given to `AnIntPtr^`. Moreover, the memory given to `XPtr` is lost once the block is exited. Because `XPtr` is not locally disposed of, the value given to it via the new statement is lost as garbage.

Pointers as VAR parameter We will use the code of Example 16.5 to show the effects of the same sequence of statements previously given. In this case, as the source code shows, the pointer variable is passed in as a call by VAR

Example 16.5

```
PROCEDURE VarCall(VAR XPtr: IntPtr);        {example with VAR calls}
   BEGIN
```

```
        {INSERT  STATEMENT(S)  HERE}
   END;

new(AnIntPtr);                              {the sequence using VarCall}
AnIntPtr^:=5;
VarCall(AnIntPtr);
writeln(AnIntPtr^:1);
```

1. XPtr^:= 7
    The effects are the same for either parameter-passing mechanism in this case
    because the effective statement due to the aliasing mechanism is An-
    IntPtr^:= 7. Hence 7 is again displayed.

2. dispose(XPtr)
    Here, too, nothing is different, so the value displayed is unpredictable. Note
    that memory given to the variable AnIntPtr is disposed of by this action.

3. dispose(XPtr);
    new(XPtr)
    In this case, the value is likewise unpredictable because no value has been as-
    signed into the newly allocated address of AnIntPtr. Unlike the sequence
    when used on a call by value, no garbage is created by this action.

4. XPtr:= NIL
    Here AnIntPtr is assigned the value NIL. Therefore, when the block is ex-
    ited, the display is unpredictable (on some systems you get a run-time crash
    with the error message "REFERENCE TO NIL POINTER"). Moreover, be-
    cause AnIntPtr is reassigned a new value, the old address that contained the
    integer value 5 becomes garbage.

5. new(XPtr);
    XPtr^:= 7;
    writeln(XPtr^:1)
    The statement new(XPtr) causes the original value of AnIntPtr, whose
    address contains the integer value 5, to become garbage. The value 7 is dis-
    played twice, once by the action of writeln(XPtr^:1) in VarCall and
    then by the action of writeln(AnIntPtr^:1) when control returns from
    VarCall.

EXERCISES

**Test Your
Understanding**

1. Assume it is possible to have a file type for which the following source code fragment
    works:

    ```
    read(AFile, AValue)
    WHILE AValue <> Sentinel DO
      BEGIN
        Process(AValue, {other parameters}
        read(AFile,AValue);
      END;
    ```

    (a) Given this assumption, what further assumptions can be implied about the appear-
    ance of the file component read into the variable AValue?

(b) If more than one type of file works for part (a), do the empty files for the different types resemble each other in any way? How?

2. Given that AFile is a binary file, AnInt is of type integer, and AReal is of type real, does the statement read (AFile, AnInt, AReal); work or not? Explain.

3. Suppose we have defined/declared the following:

```
TYPE
    RecType = RECORD
        AnInt: integer;
        AReal: real
    END;
    RecFile = FILE OF RecType;
VAR
    AFile: RecFile;
    ARec,
    BRec: RecType;
```

Which of the following statements works?

(a) readln(AFile, ARec);
(b) write(AFile, ARec.AnInt);
(c) write(AFile, ARec.AnInt, ARec.AReal);
(d) read(AFile, ARec);
(e) write(AFile, ARec, BRec);
(f) read(AFile, ARec, ARec, BRec);

Explain your reasons for each answer.

Practice Your Analysis Skills

4. What is the effect of statement (f) in Exercise 3? Does this statement make any sense? Explain.

5. Suppose, instead you were to code write (AFile, ARec, ARec, BRec). Does this statement serve any pupose? Describe the purpose, if any.

6. Suppose we have the following definitions/declarations:

```
TYPE
    String20 = STRING[20];
    Str20Ptr = ^String20;
VAR
    AStr, BStr: Str20Ptr;
```

Draw pictures showing the allocated memory and the contents of any variables for each of the following sequences:

(a) new(AStr);
new(BStr);
AStr^:= 'Billy';
BStr:= AStr;

(b) new(AStr);
new(BStr);
AStr^:= 'Billy';
BStr^:= AStr^;

7. Which of the two sequences of Exercise 6 is garbage-prone? If one of the new statements is removed from this sequence, it would no longer be garbage-prone. What statement must be removed?

8. Suppose the sequence of Exercise 6(b) is used as the block statement for each of the following procedures whose headers are respectively:
   (a) PROCEDURE VarCalls(VAR AStr, BStr: Str20Ptr);
   (b) PROCEDURE ValCalls(AStr, BStr: Str20Ptr);
   One of the headers results in a clean execution, but the other header will cause garbage. Which one? How much garbage is created?

9. Suppose the following statement is added after the sequence of statements in Exercise 6(a):

$$BStr\char94 := AStr\char94 + \text{' The Kid'}$$

   What value is contained in the variable AStr^?

10. Repeat Exercise 9, but this time the statement is placed after the sequence of Exercise 6(b).

Sharpen Your Implementation Skills

11. Suppose you were to use the code of Exercise 1. One of two possible events will cause a loop exit condition: either (1) a sentinel value is read in or (2) the eof condition on AFile is reached. Modify the code of Exercise 1 to account for the possibility of the second condition.

REVIEW AND EXERCISES

A *binary file* is defined in the TYPE definitions section of a block using the two reserved words FILE OF. The type of components contained in the file make up the rest of the definition. Unlike the components of a text file, the components of a binary file are usually not human-readable.

A call to the standard procedure reset prepares a binary file for reading. Likewise, a file is prepared for writing using the standard procedure rewrite. The read procedure reads in a component value(s) from the file into a variable(s) whose type is the same as the file's components. In like manner, a component value(s) is written into a binary file using the write procedure. The first parameter of a call to either procedure must be a file variable. The remaining parameters must be of the same type as the file's components.

There are no <eoln> markers in binary files, so a call to the procedures readln, writeln, or to the function eoln will cause a syntax error if used with binary file parameters. The eof function, however, is defined for any type of file and returns true if there are no more component values to be read in from the file.

A binary file of records is a particularly convenient data type for read and write operations. An entire record can be read into a record variable of the same type as the file components using a single call to the read procedure. Similarly, one call to the write procedure can write a record variable into a binary file of the given record type.

Any one program need not use all the fields in the record variable, even though all values are read in when a read statement is executed. The relevant field variables for the particular program can be selected, while the other variables, although read in, are ignored. Because of this property, many diverse programs might use the contents of one given binary file of records, selecting the values of the relevant field variables for each record variable read in.

A *pointer type,* defined using a *carat* followed by a (defined or anonymous) data type, takes on the value of an address that in turn holds the value(s) of a *dynamic variable.* A dynamic variable is *anonymous,* for it is not declared and it cannot be referenced directly by an identifier. The dynamic variable's type is the type associated with the pointer definition.

Memory is *allocated* to a pointer variable using a call to the procedure new. This procedure has a single actual parameter that must be a *pointer variable.* A call to new assigns an address, previously found on the *run-time heap* of unused memory, to the pointer variable. The pointer variable then is said to *point* to the allocated dynamic variable of the defined type. This variable is *dereferenced* using a reference to its associated pointer variable and a carat. This operation is known as *dereferencing,* and the carat is the *deference operator* for standard Pascal.

There are very few operations in addition to dereferencing that can be applied directly to a pointer variable. Two pointer variables or expressions can be compared for equality or inequality using the boolean operators = and <>. A pointer variable can also take on the value of another pointer variable or a pointer expression using the assignment operator (: =). A value that can be assigned to a pointer variable of any type is NIL, a reserved word representing an "address" that cannot be used to dereference a dynamic variable. A pointer variable can likewise be a parameter of a call to the procedure new or to the procedure dispose.

When a pointer variable is a parameter of the standard procedure dispose, the memory allocated is thrown back on the run-time heap. Memory previously allocated is thus *deallocated.* The dispose procedure is necessary if you want to avoid the phenomenon of *garbage creation.* When memory is allocated to a dynamic variable that has no pointer to dereference it, this variable can serve no further purpose in a program. Because it still takes up memory, it is called *garbage.* If enough garbage is created at run time, the program crashes because the computer does not have sufficient memory to finish carrying out the program's instructions.

When memory given to a pointer variable has been deallocated, an attempt to dereference the pointer variable causes unpredictable results. Likewise, if a pointer variable has taken on the value NIL, an attempt to dereference an associated dynamic variable will lead to unpredictable results. A pointer variable can be assigned the value NIL at any time. In order for dispose to be carried out successfully, however, memory must have initially been allocated to the pointer variable.

In testing the logic of a program that uses binary files, it is often necessary to see what values have been read in from a file or are written out to a file. Thus, even though display may not be necessary in the actual program, it may be necessary when on-line testing is done. Therefore, you may have to write some procedures to display a value(s) taken on by each of the file's components. Writing test files for program testing is further complicated by the fact that another program must create the file(s).

If a pointer variable is called by value, the address passed into the block is a local copy of the actual parameter address. This address does not change, but its contents may. In other words, a call by value using a pointer variable is the same as the call by variable on the dynamic variable that is the dereference of the pointer variable. If the dereferenced variable's value(s) is changed by the procedure, this effect is passed out of the block. Moreover, if memory is deallocated, this effect, too, is passed out of the block.

EXERCISES

Short Answers

1. **(a)** State the major advantage of using binary files over text files.
   (b) State the major disadvantage.

2. Answer true or false for the following:
   (a) The eof function works on files of any type.
   (b) The eoln function works on files of any type.
   (c) Under absolutely no circumstances can the same file be read from and written into in the same program.
   (d) A given file variable can be linked to only one file throughout the course of a program run.

3. Is it possible to have more than one file parameter for any of the following procedures: reset, rewrite, read, and write?

4. Suppose Ints is a FILE OF integer. Given that the file has been prepared for writing, does the following statement work? Explain.

   write(Ints, 7 + 3, 15 MOD 4);

5. Suppose *Ints* has been prepared for reading. If Int1 and Int2 are two integer variables, is the following statement acceptible?

   read(Ints, Int1, Int2)

6. If Ints has been prepared for reading, do any of these statements make sense?
   (a) read(Ints, 7 + 3, 15 MOD 4);
   (b) readln(Ints, Int1, Int2);
   (c) write(Ints, Int1)
   Explain your reasons for each answer.

7. True or false? A given file variable can be linked to two different files containing components of different types during the course of the same program run.

8. Is the following declaration possible?

   VAR
       ArFile: FILE OF ARRAY[1..10] OF integer;

   If so, is it good code? Explain your answers.

9. Match the phrases and expressions in column A with the corresponding ones in column B:

COLUMN A	COLUMN B
dynamic variable	sorted components
text file	can be assigned to any pointer variable
NIL	eof
pointer variable	eoln
new	an address
file merging	easy input/output operations
any file	dynamic memory allocation
binary file	anonymous

10. What is meant by the term "garbage?" Why is it considered harmful? Name some of the ways it can be created.

11. What is the actual value of a pointer variable? Can this value be used in input/output statements?

12. Assume that memory has not been allocated to either APtr or BPtr (both of type ˆ integer). Does the following sequence work?

```
new(APtr);
APtr^:= 7;
BPtr:= APtr;
writeln(BPtr^);
```

Write down what is displayed and explain how it works, or explain why it does not work.

13. Let the same assumptions be made as in the previous exercise. This time, however, the sequence is

```
new(APtr);
APtr^:= 7;
BPtr^:= APtr^ + 1;
writeln(BPtr^);
```

Answer the same questions posed in exercise 12.

14. Repeat Exercise 12 for this sequence:

```
new(APtr);
APtr^:= 7;
BPtr:= APtr;
writeln(BPtr);
```

15. How is an array of pointers useful? When would you use such a structure as the preferred choice of structure over an array of records?

16. True or false? The statement APtr:= NIL works for all pointer variables regardless of the type of variable APtr ˆ might represent.

17. Which of the 6 relational operators works when the values of two pointer variables of the same are compared?

18. Assume that initially memory has not been allocated to either `APtr` or `BPtr`, both pointer variables of the same type. Given this precondition, indicate which of the following sequences are garbage prone:

(a) `new(APtr);`
    `new(APtr);`

(b) `new(APtr);`
    `new(BPtr);`
    `BPtr: = APtr;`

(c) `new(APtr);`
    `BPtr: = APtr;`

Explain your answer for each case.

Easy Programs

19. Suppose one file of records `Men.dat` contains the names of men, sorted in order by last name, and a second file of records `Women.dat` contains the names of women, sorted in order by last name. Write a program to merge the two files into a third file of records, `People.dat`, sorted in order by last name. A given record in this file should contain both the person's name and the person's sex.

Create the two files for your program (you can enter the names as sorted values) with about 10–20 names in each file. Run the program and then read and display the record contents of the file `People.dat`.

20. Suppose we have three files of integers, `Ints1`, `Ints2`, and `Ints3`, where the contents of each file is sorted in order from lowest to highest. Write a program to merge the contents of the three files into a single file `Ints.dat`. Use an algorithm where `Ints1` and `Ints2` are merged into a file `TempInts`. Then the contents of `TempInts` is merged with `Ints3` into `Ints`.

Create the three sample files such that each one contains about 20 integers, then run the program. Finally, display the contents of the new file `Ints`.

21. Groups of data have been taken and stored in a file of real numbers called `Results.dat`. Each group of data consists of positive real numbers, where the end of a group is marked by the value 0. Up to 25 data points can be found in one group of data. An undefined number of groups of data exist in the file, where the end of the last group is marked by <eof>.

Write a program that creates a new file which contains a records to represent each group. One record contains the real numbers in the group and a count of the number of data values in the group. Thus, a record is defined by

```
TYPE
   DataArray = ARRAY[1..25] OF real;
   DateRecord = RECORD
      Data: DataArray;
      Points: integer
   END;
```

Create a file that contains perhaps five groups of data with between 5 to 10 numbers per group. Run the program. Next write a small program to read in and display each group, one group per line of display.

22. A file of records contains peoples' names, sorted in alphabetical order, and their ages. Write a program to read in the contents of the file where two arrays of pointers are set up. One array points to records that are sorted by name, and the second array points to records that are sorted by age. Once, the file has been completely read in (make the file contain no more than 100 records, so each array can have up to 100 elements), display the contents of both arrays. Set up the sorting algorithm for the array sorted by age so that the first element if two people are of the same age is the one representing the person who is alphabetically first.

23. Repeat Exercise 20 again, except this time use an algorithm that initially has all three files merged into Ints at once. Divide the problem into one that calls a procedure to merge the contents of all three files. As soon as one file runs out of data, execute a call from the main block to a procedure that merges the contents of the two remaining files. Once one of these remaining files runs out of memory, execute a call to a procedure to copy the file with integers remaining directly into Ints.

24. Software Services, Inc. stores billing information about its customers in a file of records named Accounts. dat. Each record contains the customer's name, a string of up to 40 characters, the date the bill is due (month, day, and year), and the amount of the bill. You are to write a program that first reads in today's date (input as three integer values). Then it reads in records and generates a report that displays three lists: (1) bills due, (2) bills overdue, and (3) bills long overdue. Each table should display the customer's name, the bill's due date, and the bill's amount.

   A bill is considered due if today is the same date or later than the due date but not so late that it is the next month and the date is greater than or equal to the date field of the due date. A bill is overdue if it is the next month and the date is greater than or equal to the date field of the due date. A bill is long overdue if it is two months later and the date is greater than or equal to the date field of the due date.

   (Example: If the due date is 5/7/92, the bill becomes overdue on 6/7/92 and long overdue on 7/7/92.)

25. A particular bank that deals strictly in cash uses five files for processing: Yesterdays, Todays, Deposits, Withdrawls, and Overdrawns. Each file contains records that have an account number and a real (dollar) amount. All files are sorted by account number, a six-digit sequence of characters. The dollar amount of each record in Yesterday contains the customer's balance before updating, and the amount in Today is the balance after updating. The dollar amount of each record in Deposits contains the amount of a deposit the customer made, and the dollar amount in Withdrawls holds the amount of money the customer withdrew. If, upon updating, a customer's account takes on a negative balance, the dollar amount in the field of an Overdrawns record contains the amount of money the account is overdrawn. This file is not updated; it is simply created as the day's transactions are handled.

   Write a program where the computer updates all customer accounts for a given day. The balances from the old account are updated and written into Todays using the values stored in the Yesterdays, Deposits and Withdrawls files. Overdrawns is created as a new file where the records of all overdrawn customers is stored.

26. An external sorting problem is one that requires that a very large file of unsorted components (called BFile) be sorted into another file (called AFile). If the number of components in BFile is too large to sort internally (using CPU memory with arrays), you can get around this difficulty with the following algorithm:

```
reset(BFile)
WHILE NOT eof(BFile) DO
    Prepare(TFile, RFile)
    FillIn(AnArray, TotComponents, BFile)
    Sort(TotComponents, AnArray)
    Merge(AnArray, TFile, RFile)
```

RFile's contents will have been sorted when the loop is exited.

   Assume your machine is capable of sorting 100 file components internally. Then AnArray is be an ARRAY [1..100] of components whose values are filled in by reading components of BFile. The final call to FillIn only partially fills in AnArray, thus returning a value to TotComponents of less than 100. All other calls to FillIn will assign all 100 elements of AnArray. These array components are sorted after the FillIn procedure is exited. Then AnArray's elements are merged with TFile's components into RFile.

The Prepare procedure interchanges the roles of the two actual files through the mechanism of the file variables. Thus after one loop pass RFile will have been written into with 100 more components (coming from the elements of AnArray) than TFile. Clearly, TFile will have been read from. The next loop pass is started by making the old RFile variable assume the role of TFile. The old TFile variable is to be the new RFile variable. Thus, the external sort can be coded with only three file variables and an internally sorted array.

Generate numbers (integers) for BFile using the RNG. Generate perhaps 525 numbers to test that FillIn will return a correct partial fill in for the final loop pass. You can test that the file is sorted by writing a function Sorted (Yes, the file RFile can be called by variable because the *whole file* is to be read) as called by

```
IF Sorted(AFile) THEN
    writeln('The algorithm is successful,)
ELSE
    writeln('There is a bug somewhere.');
```

27. It's election time and you have been hired to write a program that processes votes. The first rule of the election is that a candidate must win by a majority of votes. The second rule is that if no candidate wins, the candidate with the least votes is eliminated when four or less candidates are running. When five or more candidates are running, the two lowest candidates are eliminated in a round of voting.

The computer is to use three files of records:

(1) Candidates, where each record is described by

```
TYPE
  CandRec = record
    Name: STRING[25];   {First and Last names -- you code this record}
    Symbol: 'A'..'J'  {corresponding vote representation in Votes file}
  END;
```

(2) Survivors, a file containing the survivors as CandRec components, where the active symbol subrange ('A'..'J' or less) is reduced by 2 if there were initially 5 or more candidates or reduced by 1 if there were 4 or less.

(3) Votes, a file of characters that contains the characters in the active subrange. These characters represent votes. Their values are used to tally up votes in an array of counters.

The program you must write is described by

> *partial-fill-in(Cands) using the file Candidates*
> *tally votes to Cands using the file Votes*
> *display tally and percentages using values of elements of Cands*
> *eliminate elements from Cands returning smaller active subrange*
> *IF Win(Cands, TotalVotes) THEN*
>   *declare winner*
> *ELSE*
>   *write new file Survivors using elements of Cands*

Cands is an array of records with each element described by

```
TYPE
   CandsRec = record
      VoteCount: integer:        {count of votes}
      CandName: NameType
   END;
```

and referenced by CSymbol, the active subrange.

28. Write a program to get values into the initial Candidates file and to get values for the Votes file. Setting the initial Candidates file is easy. You simply need to write a sequence described by:

> *keyin(TotCands)*
> *FOR Symbol ← 'A' TO Last(TotCands) DO*
>   *keyin(Name)*
>   *write(Candidates,Name,Symbol)*

To set the Votes file, you are to use a random-number generator that divides the subrange of possible values into TotCands subranges. These values are used to return a Symbol in the active subrange. This symbol represents a vote for a particular candidate. You need a procedure to divide the candidate subranges into intervals according to user (i.e., program designer and tester) specifications. (You may, for example, have four candidates, where A gets 25% of vote, B gets 40%, C gets 10%, and D gets 25%). The code to generate the values for Votes is then described by:

> *keyin(TotVoters)*
> *keyin(TotCands)*
> *keyin percentage values and set Returns*
> *rewrite(Votes)*
> *set initial RNum*
> *FOR Count ← 1 TO TotVoters DO*
>   *RNum ← Random(RNum)*
>   *write(Votes, AVote(RNum,Returns))* {AVote returns a char value}

Returns is an array of reals that divides the interval into subranges such that a given number returned can represent a particular vote for a candidate. (e.g., Values less than Reals[1], the first 25% of the RNG interval, represents a vote for 'A', values between Reals[1] and Reals[2], the 25% to 65% interval, represents a vote for 'B', and so forth).

Test the program with some different percentage values and tally up the votes for each candidate. None of the percentages should be off by more than 5% (and probably, given enough votes, 1% or 2% is a better figure).

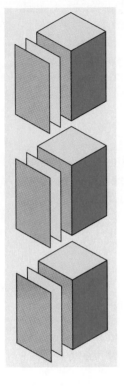

LINKED LISTS WITH POINTERS

OBJECTIVES

After reading and studying the material of the present chapter, you should be able to

- Explain what is meant by the term linked list

- Implement a queue ADT and a stack ADT using pointers to create the required linked lists

- Solve problems that use the dynamic-variable implementation of a queue or stack ADT

- Implement a general-purpose linked list ADT

- Use a general-purpose linked list ADT in the solution of problems that require such a structure

- Identify some of the pitfalls to avoid when implementing and/or using linked lists consisting of dynamic variables

YOU HAVE ALREADY LEARNED how to implement a queue or a stack using an array to hold the items. In this chapter, you will learn how to implement both of these ADTs using dynamic variables. This approach is the natural route to take, for both ADTs are dynamic structures. Thus, when an item is added to a queue or stack, memory for the variable is allocated, and when an item is deleted from the queue or stack, the candidate variable for deletion is deallocated.

Not all linked lists need be queues or stacks. Sometimes you may require a structure where it is necessary to add or delete an item in the middle of the list. You may likewise need to search for a particular item in the list or display the contents of the list. You will learn to write the code to implement these operations where the linked list is created and changed using pointers and dynamic variables.

17.1   Linked List Nodes

A *linear linked list* is a structured variable in which each item in the structure holds an addressed reference (a pointer variable) to the next item. One item, a component of the structure, is known as a *node*. All nodes of a list implemented in this manner are dynamic variables. In this section, we present a set of node primitives that are applicable on the nodes of a linear linked list of any type, be it a queue, stack, or some other list where each item is linked to a "next" item.

> **Linear linked list:**   a collection of dynamic record variables (items) linked together by pointers. The single pointer variable that is a field of an item points to the next item in the structure.
>
> **Node:**   a variable that is an item in a linked structure.

Implementing a Linked List

Before we discuss the operations that apply to the nodes of a linked list, we first present the source code to implement one of these nodes. Then we show the appearance of a typical list. We also show how to access any node using the field variables of other nodes.

The primitive component variable

A node in a linear linked list is a dynamic record variable where one of its fields is a pointer to the next node. This field is called the node's *link field*. The other field(s) containing specific information about a given node makes up the *data field(s)*. A node pointed to by another node also contains a data field(s) and a single link field that in turn points to the next node. In this way, component nodes of the same type are linked together to form the structured data type that makes up a linear linked list.

Link field(s): the field variable(s) of a node that points to another node.

Data field(s): the field variable(s) of a node that contains information about the particular node.

A source code example

Suppose we want to build a linked list of names. Each name consists of a string variable containing up to 20 characters. This string variable is the node's data field. The other field variable is the link field. The appearance of a typical node variable, APtr^, a dereference of the pointer variable APtr, is shown in Figure 17.1. The data field of the node, APtr^.Item, contains the name Beth, and the link field APtr^.Next points to another node whose data field contains the name Tom.

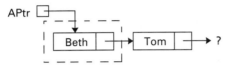

FIGURE 17.1 The node variable APtr^.

Implementation of APtr

The implementation of a dynamic variable to represent a node in the list and the pointer variable APtr, the means to dereference this node, is given in the following source code:

```
CONST
  NullItem = '';    {used to flag error conditions in source code}
TYPE
  ItemType = {STRING TYPE CAPABLE OF HOLDING UP TO 20 CHARACTERS}
  LNodePtr = ^LNodeType;   {pointer to a list's node}
  LNodeType = RECORD       {the definition of a node}
    Item: ItemType;        {data field, in this case containing a name}
    Next: LNodePtr         {link field}
  END;
VAR
  APtr: LNodePtr;
```

Some observations regarding the source code

We point out that the node variable itself, of type LNodeType, is anonymous. Hence, a node variable is not part of the declaration to implement a linked list. Note also that the identifier LNodePtr is defined before the dynamic record LNodeType. When you are implementing a structured type that contains link fields, you must first define the pointer type before you define the node type. This single exception to the usual referencing rules of Pascal is the one time you must use an identifier reference to a type that is defined after the reference is made.

A typical list

Figure 17.2 shows the appearance of a typical linked list that starts with the node variable APtr^. Note that the Next field of the last node in the list is the NIL pointer. It is common practice to use the NIL pointer value to indicate the end of a sequence of links. We have adopted this convention for all ADTs we will implement that use dynamic variables with link fields.

APtr

| Beth | → | Tom | → | Dick | → | Harry | → | Alice |

FIGURE 17.2 A linked list pointed to by `APtr^`.

Dereferencing expressions

Table 17.1 shows how to dereference each variable in the linked list of Figure 17.2. The first variable, whose `Item` field is `Beth`, is pointed to by the variable `APtr`. The value contained in the `Item` field of this node is found using the dereferencing expression `APtr^.Item`. The dereference value of `APtr^.Next^` is the node variable of the node following this first node. Figure 17.2 and Table 17.1 both show that the value of the `Item` field of this node is `Tom`. This value is dereferenced by the source code `APtr^.Next^.Item`. The table further shows expressions to dereference the nodes containing the names `Dick`, `Harry`, and `Alice`. After Alice's node, there are no more nodes. This fact is evidenced by the NIL value of `APtr^.Next^.Next^.Next^.Next^.Next`.

TABLE 17.1 Values Starting from `APtr^`

Variable	Value
`APtr^.Item`	Beth
`APtr^.Next^.Item`	Tom
`APtr^.Next^.Next^.Item`	Dick
`APtr^.Next^.Next^.Next^.Item`	Harry
`APtr^.Next^.Next^.Next^.Next^.Item`	Alice
`Aptr^.Next^.Next^.Next^.Next^.Next`	NIL

Node Primitives

Regardless of the kind of linear linked list you wish to create, there are some primitive operations that can be applied to any node in the list. These primitives will allow you to dereference any node in the list and also to implement the operations for a specific kind of linear list such as queue or a stack. We will use these primitives for all linked lists that we implement in this chapter.

The operations

There are only four operations in this primitive set. One operation creates a new node with a value(s) assigned to the data field(s) and the NIL value assigned to the link field. The other constructor operation disposes of a node given the precondition that it exists as a dynamic variable. The two selector operations respectively select the data field(s) of a node and the pointer to the next node.

Interface source code

The headers for these operations (that we will FORWARD direct) are coded as follows:

```
{*         INTERFACE PART OF LINEAR LIST NODE OPERATIONS            *}
{The following operations can be applied to any node that makes up a
linear linked list. These primitives are therefore useful in
```

implementing a queue, stack, or any other kind of specific linear linked list.}
{+   +}
PROCEDURE MakeNode(AnItem: ItemType; VAR Node: LNodePtr);   FORWARD;
  {Primitive Constructor: creates new Node, then assigns AnItem to its
  data field and NIL to its link field. This node constructor is used
  in the constructor operations that build linear linked lists.}
{+   +}
PROCEDURE KillNode(VAR Node: LNodePtr);   FORWARD;
  {Constructor: if Node is not NIL, disposes of memory allocated to
  Node, then sets Node to NIL}
{+   +}
PROCEDURE ItemValue(Node: LNodePtr; VAR AnItem: ItemType);   FORWARD;
  {Primitive selector: returns value of AnItem for a given Node:
  returns NullItem if Node's value is NIL, indicating the start of an
  empty list. This "primitive" procedure can be further broken to a
  function or a group of functions. If AnItem is a scalar variable,
  the procedure codes directly to a function. If AnItem is structured,
  a group of functions to access each component variable is
  appropriate.}
{+   +}
FUNCTION NextNode(Node: LNodePtr): LNodeType;   FORWARD;
  {returns the node in the list following the one whose value is Node;
  the implication is that Node represents some given node in the list
  and NextNode represents the rest of the list following Node; if
  Node's value is NIL, NextNode is returned as NIL, indicating that the
  rest of an empty list is an empty list}
{*   THE OPERATIONS   *}
{FORWARD-directed headers and statements go here}

Implementations   The source code for implementing each operation is easily found from the specifications given in the interface part's documentation. We have:

```
PROCEDURE MakeNode{AnItem: ItemType; VAR Node: LNodePtr};
  BEGIN
    new(Node);
    Node^.Item:= AnItem;
    Node^.Next:= NIL
  END;

PROCEDURE KillNode{VAR Node: LNodePtr}
  BEGIN
    IF Node <> NIL THEN
      BEGIN
        dispose(Node);
        Node:= NIL
      END
  END;
```

```
PROCEDURE ItemValue {Node: LNodePtr; VAR AnItem: ItemType};
   BEGIN
     IF Node <> NIL THEN
       AnItem:= Node^.Item
     ELSE
       An Item:= NullItem
   END;

FUNCTION NextNode { (Node: LNodePtr): LNodePtr};
   BEGIN
     IF Node <> NIL THEN
       NextNode:= Node^.Next
     ELSE
       NextNode:= NIL
   END;
```

Showing a list　　　　　We have made the claim that these node primitives allow you to dereference any node in the list. This claim is true as long as there is a variable that points to the first node in the list. The example problem shows how to use these primitives to display the list's contents.

Example Problem 17.1

The problem statement　　　　Given a particular variable APtr (suppose APtr is pointing to Beth's node in Figure 17.2), write a procedure ShowList that displays the values of all the items on the list starting with the value of the item contained in the node pointed to by APtr. Use only the node primitives for this procedure.

The recursive solution　　　　Perhaps the most elegant solution is a recursive one whose pseudocode description is as follows:

> *PROCEDURE ShowList(APtr)*
> *ItemValue(APtr, AName)*
> *IF AName <> NullItem THEN*
> *display AName*
> *ShowList(NextNode(APtr))*

AName is a local variable, and the initial call to this procedure is coded as ShowList(APtr).

The trivial proof of this solution is that (1) an empty list (no items on it) will display nothing, (2) a list that is not empty displays the value of AName, the selected data field of the node variable APtr^, followed by the rest of the items on the list, and (3) the list of items to be displayed eventually reduces to a null list.

Source code　　　　The source code for the recursive solution is then given as

```
PROCEDURE ShowList(APtr: LNodePtr);
  {as long as the value of APtr indicates that there is a list, the
```

value of the item at APtr is displayed, followed by the values of the remaining items in the list}
```
VAR
  AName:   ItemType;    {the value of the name pointed to by APtr}
BEGIN
  ItemValue(APtr, AName);
  IF AName <> NullItem THEN
    BEGIN
      writeln(AName);
      ShowList(NextNode(APtr))
    END
END;
```

An iterative solution
The iterative solution to the problem is equally straightforward. As long as APtr is not NIL, its data field is displayed and the value of the next node is then assigned to APtr. The source code to implement this description is then

```
PROCEDURE ShowList(APtr: LNodePtr);
  {each item in the list is displayed, starting with the node pointed
  to by APtr}
VAR
  AName:   ItemType;    {the value of the name pointed to by APtr}
BEGIN
  ItemValue(Aptr, AName);
  WHILE AName <> NullItem DO
    BEGIN
      writeln(AName);
      APtr:= NextNode(APtr);
      ItemValue(APtr, AName)
    END
END;  ◆
```

EXERCISES

Test Your Understanding

1. Can a component in a linked list be a scalar variable? Explain why or why not.

2. Is there a theoretical limit to the number of nodes that can be found in a linked list? Explain your answer.

3. Is there a practical limit to the number of nodes that can be found in a linked list? Explain.

Practice Your Analysis Skills

4. Suppose we implement a linked list of integers and define NullItem to be equal to maxint. A list with the following appearance is then constructed, where a value has been assigned to APtr:

Int Ptr ☐

28 → 75 → 32 → 63 → 98 → 82 → 66

Indicate the display for each of the following segments of code:

(a) `ItemValue(IntPtr, AnInt);`
   `writeln(AnInt:1);`

(b) `ItemValue(NextNode(IntPtr), AnInt);`
   `writeln(AnInt:1);`

(c) `ItemValue(NextNode(NextNode(IntPtr)), AnInt);`
   `writeln(AnInt:1);`

(d) `FOR NodeCt:= 2 TO 5 DO`
   `    IntPtr:= NextNode(IntPtr);`
   `ItemValue(IntPtr, AnInt);`
   `writeln(AnInt:1);`

(e) `FOR NodeCt:= 2 to 10 DO`
   `    IntPtr:= NextNode(IntPtr);`
   `ItemValue(IntPtr, AnInt);`
   `writeln(AnInt:1)`

Sharpen Your Implementation Skills

5. Write the source code for the TYPE section that makes the list of Exercise 4 possible.

6. Write `ItemValue` as a primitive selector function, rather than as a procedure, for the linked list of integers. Use a `NullItem` value of `maxint`. Two examples, using `Item-Value` and the list given in Exercise 4 are:

```
writeln('The first value is ', ItemValue(IntPtr):1, '.');
writeln('The second value is ',ItemValue(NextNode(IntPtr)):1, '.');

The first value is 19.
The second value is 87.
```

7. Write the function `NthInt` that returns the Nth integer in the list where the call `NthInt(IntPtr, 1)` returns the first integer in the list, `NthInt(IntPtr, 2)` returns the second integer in the list, and so forth.

17.2 The Queue as a Linked List

In this section, we implement the ADT QType. This unit is a linked list implemented such that its defining operations make it a queue. There are two important nodes in this abstraction, namely Head and Tail. These two nodes are required to implement the AddQueue and DeleteQueue operations.

A queue's appearance

Figure 17.3 shows how the linked list of Figure 17.2 can be made into a queue. The candidate node for deletion, as dereferenced by Head^, is the one whose Name field is equal to Beth. If any item is to be added to the queue, it must be added after the node whose Name field is Alice. The queue structure we implement as suggested by Figure 17.3, has three fields: (1) ItemsOnQueue of type integer, whose value represents the count of the items on queue, (2) Head, of

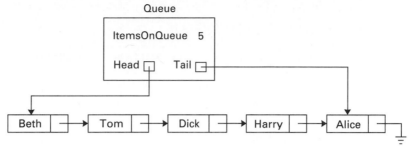

Queue

ItemsOnQueue   5

Head ☐   Tail ☐

| Beth | → | Tom | → | Dick | → | Harry | → | Alice | → |

FIGURE 17.3   The variable Queue.

type LNodePtr, the pointer to the first item on queue, and (3) Tail, of type LNodePtr, the pointer to the last item on queue.

The Operations

The operations for the ADT QType are almost the same ones we devised in Section 13.2. We do not, however, need the predicate function QFull because there is no theoretical limit to the size of the queue when we use dynamic variables. To make our implementation task simpler, we will include the four node operations, MakeNode, KillNode, ItemValue, and NextNode, as part of the unit.

The interface section

The source code for the interface section of the ADT QType is shown below. Note that we are coding the selector FirstOnQueue as a function that returns a pointer value. This selector function works, regardless of the type of items found on the queue. It provides the means of finding all information contained in that first node. A client can assign the value to a pointer variable, then use the variable and the node primitives to get information about the node's data field(s).

```
{*                     INTERFACE PART OF QTYPE ADT                          *}
{A queue ADT of strings using a linked list for its implementation}
CONST
  NullItem = '';                  {indicates null node or error condition}
TYPE
  LNodePtr = ^LNodeType;        {pointer to a node}
  ItemType = {STRING TYPE CAPABLE OF HOLDING UP TO 20 CHARACTERS}
  LNodeType = RECORD            {a node's definition}
    Item: ItemType;             {data field}
    Next: LNodePtr              {link field}
  END;
  QType = RECORD                {the queue abstraction}
    ItemsOnQueue: integer;
    Head,
    Tail: LNodePtr
  END;
{*                     THE NODE OPERATIONS                                  *}
PROCEDURE MakeNode(AnItem: ItemType; VAR Node: LNodePtr);      FORWARD;
```

```
{+                                                                              +}
PROCEDURE KillNode(VAR Node: LNodePtr);                          FORWARD;
{+                                                                              +}
PROCEDURE ItemValue(Node: LNodePtr; VAR AnItem: ItemType);      FORWARD;
{+                                                                              +}
FUNCTION NextNode(Node: LNodePtr): LNodePtr;                     FORWARD;
{documentation for all node operations given in Section 17.1}
{*                      THE QUEUE OPERATIONS                                *}
PROCEDURE MakeQueue(VAR Queue: QType);                           FORWARD;
    {sets up initial queue}
{+                                                                              +}
PROCEDURE AddQueue(AnItem: ItemType; VAR Queue: QType);          FORWARD;
    {adds Item to Queue}
{+                                                                              +}
PROCEDURE DeleteQueue(VAR Queue: QType);                         FORWARD;
    {if Queue is not empty, deletes first Item; if Queue is empty, does
    nothing}
{+                                                                              +}
FUNCTION FirstOnQueue(Queue: QType): LNodePtr;                   FORWARD;
    {if queue is not empty, returns the node representing the first item
    on queue; if queue is empty, returns NIL to function}
{+                                                                              +}
FUNCTION QCount(Queue: QType): integer;                          FORWARD;
    {assigns number of items on Queue to QueueCount}
{+                                                                              +}
FUNCTION QEmpty(Queue: QType): boolean;                          FORWARD;
    {true if no items on Queue}
{*                  IMPLEMENTATION PART OF QUEUE ADT                        *}
{FORWARD-directed headers and statements go here}
```

We have already written the code for the node operations. Let us write the code to implement the remaining operations of the ADT QType, those operations that are associated with the list as a whole.

Coding
MakeQueue
Source code

A queue with no items on it should have both Head and Tail pointing to NIL. Likewise, the value of the ItemsOnQueue field should be set to 0.

The source code to implement these initilizations is as shown. Because the procedure is FORWARD-directed, we are coding the formal parameter list as a comment.

```
PROCEDURE MakeQueue {VAR Queue: QType};
    {documentation}
BEGIN
  WITH Queue DO
    BEGIN
      ItemsOnQueue:= 0;
      Head:= NIL;
```

```
            Tail:= NIL
         END
      END;
```

Writing the
three functions
Before we write the code for the other two constructors, let us code the two primitive selector functions and the predicate function. They all require just one-line statements. We have:

```
FUNCTION FirstOnQueue { (Queue: QType): LNodePtr };
   BEGIN
      FirstOnQueue:= Queue.Head
   END;

FUNCTION QCount { (Queue: QType): integer };
   BEGIN
      QCount:= Queue.ItemsOnQueue
   END;

FUNCTION QEmpty { (Queue: QType): boolean };
   BEGIN
      QEmpty:= Queue.Head = NIL
   END;
```

Deriving
AddQueue
Adding a node containing the value of AnItem to the queue first requires a call to the node constructor MakeNode. This node, with its Next field set to NIL, is then added to the queue after the Tail^ node. Tail's value is then assigned to this new node. The pseudocode for the constructor operation AddQueue is thus described by

> *MakeNode(AnItem, Temp)* {*Temp points to the new node*}
> *WITH Queue DO*
>   *link the Temp node to the rest of the queue*
>   *Tail ← Temp*
>   *ItemsOnQueue ← ItemsOnQueue + 1*

The variable Temp is a local variable of type LNodePtr. Even though it is locally declared and locally created, its value as well as the locally created dynamic variable survives beyond the statements of the AddQueue block.

Linking Temp *to*
the queue
If the queue is not empty, we can directly link the node using the assignment Tail^.Next:= Temp. This scenario is shown in Figures 17.4(a, and 17.4(b). If the queue is empty, however, the values assigned to the queue's Head and Tail are initially both NIL. Given this precondition, a queue with one item on it is created with the assignment Head:= Temp. Then Tail is set to Head's value. The postcondition when an item is added to an empty queue is suggested by Figure 17.4(c). The pseudocode to link Temp to the rest of the queue is therefore described by

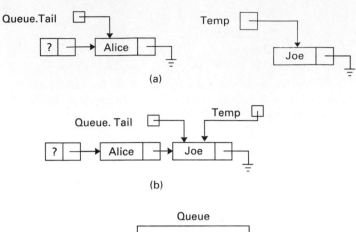

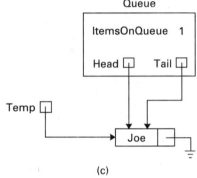

FIGURE 17.4 (a) Before Temp^ is added to Queue, (b) after Temp^ is added to Queue, and (c) after Temp^ is added to an empty Queue.

$$
\begin{aligned}
&IF\ Head = NIL\ THEN\\
&\quad Head \leftarrow Temp\\
&ELSE\\
&\quad Tail \leftarrow Temp\char94.Next
\end{aligned}
$$

Source code   From the pseudocode descriptions, we readily obtain the source code for Add Queue as shown.

```
PROCEDURE AddQueue {AnItem: ItemType; VAR Queue: Qtype);
  VAR
    Temp: LNodePtr;     {points to new node to be added to queue}
  BEGIN
    MakeNode(AnItem, Temp);
    WITH Queue DO       {add Temp to Queue}
      BEGIN
        IF Head = NIL THEN
          Head:= Temp
        ELSE
          Tail^.Next:= Temp;
```

```
        Tail:= Temp;
        ItemsOnQueue:= ItemsOnQueue + 1
    END
END;
```

If the queue has items on it, the postcondition returned by the action of
`DeleteQueue` is that the original head node has been deleted, and a new head
node has been assigned. Once the old head node is taken off queue, its value is of no
further use, for it no longer belongs to the queue. Therefore, it must be disposed of.

What if an attempt is made to delete a node from a queue that has no items
on it? In this case, let us code the operation such that the computer does nothing.

From this discussion, we arrive at the first draft for the `DeleteQueue` operation using the following description:

> *Temp ← Queue.Head*
> *IF Temp <> NIL THEN*
>   *WITH Queue DO*
>   *assign a new value to Head*
>   *KillNode(Temp)*
>   *ItemsOnQueue ← ItemsOnQueue − 1*

In this case, the local variable `Temp` is used to store the value of a pointer to a candidate node for deallocation.

Given that the queue is not empty, the new value for `Head` is set by coding
`Head:= Temp^.Next`. This statement will maintain the logical appearance of the
queue if there is more than one item on queue. What happens, though, if there is exactly one item on queue? The precondition to describe a 1-item queue is that both
`Head` and `Tail` point to the same node. Given this precondition, the value of `Head`
is properly set to `NIL` by the assignment statement, but the value of `Tail` (also the
value of `Temp`) is simply disposed of. Because `Head` and `Tail` are two different
variables, `Tail` is not automatically set to `NIL` when `Head` is set to `NIL`.

According to the convention we adopted when we coded `MakeQueue`, if 1
item is on the queue and it is deleted, the value of `Tail` must also be set to `NIL`.
Otherwise, we have not satisfactorily set up an empty queue. Hence, the pseudocode
for assigning a new value to `Head` (and perhaps `Tail`) is given by

> *Head ← Temp^.Next*
> *IF Head = NIL THEN*   *{occurs when queue consists of just one node}*
>   *Tail ← NIL*

From the pseudocode descriptions, we get the source code for `Delete-`
`Queue` as shown.

```
PROCEDURE DeleteQueue {VAR Queue: QType};
  VAR
    Temp: LNodePtr;      {points to candidate node for deletion}
```

```
BEGIN
   Temp:= Queue.Head;
   IF Temp <> NIL THEN            {check for empty queue first}
      WITH Queue DO               {change the queue's appearance}
         BEGIN
            Head:= Temp^.Next;    {move Head to next node}
            IF Head = NIL THEN    {check for a queue with only one node}
               Tail:= NIL;
            dispose(Temp);        {node's link removed, so dispose of it}
            ItemsOnQueue:= ItemsOnQueue - 1
         END
END;
```

Using the Node Primitives

If you want to write code that requires access to more than just the first node of a queue, you can apply the node primitives to achieve this objective. The best feature of these primitives is that any node in a linked list is accessible through the selector primitives. When these selectors are used, as in the next problem, the overall structure itself does not change even though nodes beyond the first one are dereferenced.

Example Problem 17.2

The problem statement

Let us write a function QPos that returns the queue position of a given Item. If the item is not present, the value returned is 0. Suppose, for example, we want to find the position of Harry in our sample queue of Figure 17.3. We can find Harry's position on the queue with the function call writeln('The queue position is ', QPos(Queue, 'Harry'):1, '.'). The result of the writeln statement, given the sample queue, is the display

The queue position is 4.

The solution

We can use the linear search algorithm on the queue to good effect. Each node, starting with the first node in the queue, is probed until either a match is found or there are no more items on the queue. The source code for the function QPos using the proven algorithm (linear search) is shown below.

```
FUNCTION QPos(Queue: QType; SearchItem: ItemType): integer;
   {documentation}
   VAR
      CandNode: LNodePtr;     {the candidate node}
      CandItem: ItemType;     {value of Item at candidate node}
      CandPos:  integer;      {position in queue of candidate node}
   BEGIN
      CandNode:= FirstOnQueue(Queue);    {initialization for first probe}
      ItemValue(CandNode, CandItem);
```

```
      CandPos:= 1;
      WHILE (CandItem <> NullItem) AND (CandItem <> SearchItem) DO
        BEGIN
            CandNode:= NextNode(CandNode);        {loop body sets up next probe}
            ItemValue(CandNode, CandItem);
            CandPos:= CandPos + 1
        END;
      IF CandItem = SearchItem THEN              {found condition}
        QPos:= CandPos
      ELSE                                       {finished condition}
        QPos:= 0
   END;
```

Note that the *finished* condition is reached if CandItem takes on the value of NullItem, indicating the end of the list. The *found* condition obviously occurs if CandItem is equal to the value of SearchItem. ◆

EXERCISES

Test Your Understanding

1. True or false? All queue operations can still be implemented if the field variable Items-OnQueue is eliminated from the QType definition.

2. If you answered true to Exercise 1, which operations in the ADT require a new implementation? If you answered false, list the operations in the ADT that cannot be carried out without the use of ItemsOnQueue.

3. True or false? All queue operations can still be implemented if the field variable Tail is eliminated from the QType definition.

4. Answer the question analogous to Exercise 2 as it applies to Exercise 3.

5. True or false? All queue operations can still be implemented if the field variable Head is eliminated from the QType definition.

6. Answer the question analogous to Exercise 2 as it applies to Exercise 5.

Practice Your Analysis Skills

7. Consider the code of the function QPos. What value does CandPos take on as a post-condition if SearchItem is not found on queue?

8. Consider the following sequence of code:

```
              MakeQueue(Names);
              AddQueue('Reddy', Names);
              AddQueue('Perez', Names);
              ItemValue(FirstOnQueue(Names), AName);
              GiveService(AName);
              DeleteQueue(Names);
              AddQueue('Kelly', Names);
              AddQueue('Forte', Names);
              ItemValue(FirstOnQueue(Names), AName);
              GiveService(AName);
              DeleteQueue(Names);
```

```
              AddQueue('Smith', Names);
              ItemValue(FirstOnQueue(Names), AName);
              GiveService(AName);
              DeleteQueue(Names);
```

The procedure `GiveService` uses the value of AName to "serve" that person.
(a) Write down the names of the people who have been served.
(b) How large was the queue at its largest size?
(c) How many people are presently on queue?
(d) Write down the queue's appearance at the end of the given sequence.

9. Will this code work for the statement part of AddQueue?

```
           BEGIN
             WITH Queue DO
               BEGIN      .
                 IF Head = NIL THEN
                   BEGIN
                     MakeNode(AnItem, Head);
                     Tail:= Head
                   END
                 ELSE
                   BEGIN
        {1}          MakeNode(AnItem, Tail^.Next);
                     Tail:= NextNode(Tail)
                   END;
                 ItemsOnQueue:= ItemsOnQueue + 1
               END    {WITH}
           END;   {AddQueue}
```

Explain how it works or why it does not work.

10. Repeat Exercise 9, except change the statement labelled as {1} to MakeNode(An-Item, NextNode(Tail))

Sharpen Your Implementation Skills

11. The sequence in Exercise 8 that calls `ItemValue`, `GiveService`, `DeleteQueue` can be coded as a procedure. Write the code for this procedure `ServeOne`. Write the code both for the call to the procedure and the procedure declaration.

12. Suppose the variables `Tail` and `ItemsOnQueue` are eliminated from the definition of QType. Given that these two variables are eliminated, write the code required to implement the function QCount.

13. Repeat Exercise 12, but this time implement the procedure AddQueue.

17.3   The Stack as a Linked List

A stack ADT is also a special kind of linked list. In this section, we implement a stack of integer values. We then use this stack in a client program to evaluate arithmetic integer expressions.

Example Problem 17.3

The problem statement

Implement an ADT as a stack of integers. The ADT is to have the following operations: (1) MakeStack, the primitive constructor that creates an empty stack, (2) Push, the constructor to push an integer value on the stack, (3) Pop, the constructor to pop an integer value off the top of the stack, (4) TopItem, a primitive selector that returns the value of the integer on top of the stack, and (5) StackEmpty, a predicate that returns true if no integers are on the stack. If an attempt is made to pop an empty stack, no action is carried out. The value returned when TopItem is called with an empty stack will be maxint, a value used to represent a "null integer."

The interface part

The stack ADT is trivially defined as the pointer to the top item. We then have the following source code for the interface part of the ADT StkType:

```
{*                  INTERFACE PART OF STKTYPE ADT                    *}
CONST
  NullItem = maxint;
TYPE
  StkPtr = ^StkNode;
  ItemType = integer;
  StkNode = RECORD
    Item: ItemType;
    Next: StkPtr
  END;
  StkType = RECORD        {the definition for a StkType variable}
    Top: StkPtr
  END;
{*                       THE OPERATIONS                              *}
PROCEDURE MakeNode(AnItem: ItemType; VAR ANode: StkPtr);      FORWARD;
  {same procedure as MakeNode in Section 17.1}
{+                                                                  +}
PROCEDURE KillNode(VAR ANode: StkPtr);                        FORWARD;
  {same procedure as KillNode in Section 17.1}
{+                                                                  +}
PROCEDURE MakeStack(VAR Stack: StkType);                      FORWARD;
  {sets up an empty stack}
{+                                                                  +}
PROCEDURE Push(AnItem: ItemType; VAR Stack: StkType);         FORWARD;
  {pushes the value of AnItem onto the Stack}
{+                                                                  +}
PROCEDURE Pop(VAR Stack: StkType);                            FORWARD;
  {pops the top item off Stack; if the stack is empty, no action is
  carried out}
{+                                                                  +}
FUNCTION TopItem(Stack: StkType): ItemType;                   FORWARD;
```

```
  {returns the value of the item on the top of Stack
  ; if the stack is empty, the value of NullItem is returned }
{+                                                                              +}
FUNCTION StackEmpty(Stack: StkType): boolean;                    FORWARD;
  {returns true if there are no items on the stack}
{*                           IMPLEMENTATION PART                              *}
{FORWARD-directed headers and statements for all operations go here}
```

Note how we have defined StkType as a RECORD with just one field. We chose this implementation strategy to hide the stack's Top from the client. Only the operations in the ADT itself will directly reference the value of Top.

Coding
MakeStack

The code for MakeStack, a one-line statement, follows. Note that, as usual, we are using the NIL pointer value to indicate the end of the linked list.

```
PROCEDURE MakeStack{VAR Stack: StkType};
  BEGIN
    Stack.Top:= NIL
  END;
```

Coding
TopItem

The code for the selector TopItem is also trivial. We must be sure, however, to guard against an attempt to dereference the NIL value if the stack is empty. The code for this selector is then:

```
FUNCTION TopItem {(Stack: StkType): ItemType)};
  BEGIN
    WITH Stack DO
      IF Top <> NIL THEN
        TopItem:= Top^.Item
      ELSE
        TopItem:= NullItem
  END;
```

Coding
StackEmpty

The one-line function StackEmpty trivially codes to the following:

```
FUNCTION StackEmpty{ (Stack: StkType): boolean};
  BEGIN
    StackEmpty:= Stack.Top = NIL
  END;
```

Coding Push

If we want to Push the integer value 7 on a stack already containing the integers 5 and 2, the precondition and postcondition pictures are shown respectively as Figures 17.5(a) and 17.5(b). These pictures suggest that the source code for pushing an item onto a stack is given by

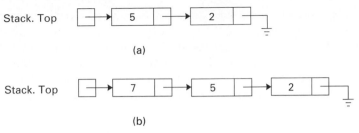

FIGURE 17.5 (a) A typical stack of integers and (b) after pushing 7 on the stack.

```
PROCEDURE Push{AnItem: ItemType; VAR Stack: StkType};
  VAR
    Temp: StkPtr;
  BEGIN
    MakeNode(AnItem, Temp);        {create Temp with AnItem data field}
    Temp^.Next:= Stack.Top;        {assign link field to present Stack's top}
    Stack.Top:= Temp               {set Stack's Top to Temp}
  END;
```

Figures 17.6(a) through 17.6(c) show how each action of Push works toward the desired postcondition of Figure 17.5(b). Clearly, this procedure is correct for any kind of stack that was not initially empty. If the stack was initially empty, moreover, Temp's link is to the NIL pointer, the previous value of Stack.Top.

FIGURE 17.6 (a) After execution of MakeNode(7, Temp), (b) after execution of Temp^.Next:= Stack.Top, and (c) after execution of Stack.Top:= Temp.

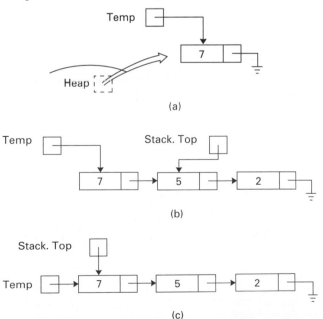

Thus we correctly get a stack with one item on it. Hence, the code is correct, given all possible preconditions.

Coding Pop

To pop an item from the stack, we must first check that the stack is not initially empty. If it is, no action is to be taken. If it is not, the value of the stack's Top is assigned to a pointer variable Temp and the stack's Top is assigned the value of Temp^.Next. Then Temp is deallocated. This description codes to the following:

```
PROCEDURE Pop{VAR Stack: StkType};
   VAR
      Temp: StkPtr;          {candidate node for disposal}
   BEGIN
      WITH Stack DO
         IF Top <> NIL THEN
            BEGIN
               Temp:= Top;
               Top:= Temp^.Next;
               KillNode(Temp)
            END;
   END;
```

Figures 17.7(a) through 17.7(c) show the actions carried out if a stack that initially has the values 7, 5, and 2 on it is popped. ◆

FIGURE 17.7 (a) Stack after Temp:= Top, (b) stack after Top:= Temp^.Next, and (c) memory after KillNode(Temp),

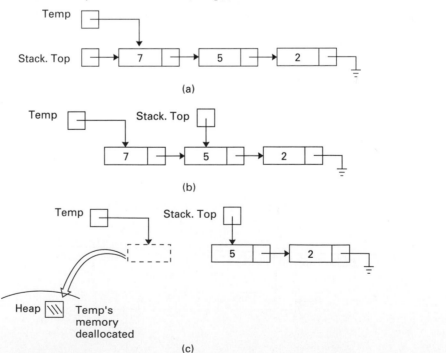

A Reverse Polish Calculator

In 1951, the Polish mathematician Jan Lukasiewicz proved that parentheses are not necessary when arithmetic expressions are written either in postfix or prefix notation. These two notations are often referred to as the reverse Polish notation (RPN) and the Polish notation (PN) in honor of Lukasiewicz's nationality. In the case study that follows, we will write a program to evaluate an integer expression written in RPN.

Reverse Polish expressions

Any operation applied to an arithmetic expression written in RPN requires that two operands precede it. Each RPN operation is applied to the two operands directly preceding an operator. Thus, the RPN expression written as 7 2 – evaluates to the infix notation expression 7 – 2. Infix notation, where the operator is placed between two operands, is the way we usually write arithmetic expressions. Therefore, the value of the RPN expression 7 2 – is equal to the value of the infix expression 7 – 2, that is 5.

Reverse Polish expressions may be formed using more than one operation, but the same rule for evaluating the expression applies. For example, the RPN expression 6 5 3 + * is equivalent to the expression 6 8 *, because the two preceding operands associated with the addition operation were 5 and 3. The whole expression then evaluates to 48.

Let us find the value of a more complicated expression such as 7 3 5 + * 3 1 + /. The first operator + is preceded by the operands 3 and 5, so the expression reduces to 7 8 * 3 1 + /. Now we have the two operands 7 and 8 for the multiplication operation, so the simplified expression to evaluate is 56 3 1 + /. Addition is then applied to the operands 3 and 1 to get the expression 56 4 /. Finally, division is applied to the two operands 56 and 4, thus giving us the value 14.

CASE STUDY 17.1

The problem statement

Let us write a program to evaluate an integer expression written in RPN. The character / is read as a DIV operation and the character \ is read as a MOD operation. The RPN expression is read in on a single line of text, and its value is printed out on the next line. Two typical runs of the program are given as

```
7 3 5 + * 3 1 + /<eoln>      {input RPN expression}
14                           {its value, found and displayed}

8 6 1 - \ 4 + <eoln>         {input RPN expression}
7                            {its value, found and displayed}
```

A model for the solution

Consider how RPN works. When an operation is to be applied, the last two values (either read in or evaluated from other operations) found before an operator are the operands. This order of application suggests a structure that uses a LIFO discipline, for the last operands obtained are the first ones used. Therefore, we expect to solve the problem using a stack of integer values. The top two integers on the stack become the operands when an operator is encountered. The result of the operation is then pushed on the stack, thus becoming an operand for the next operation.

A walk-through of the solution mechanism

Let us apply the proposed mechanism on the sample expression 8 6 1 − \ 4 +. If an integer value is read in, it is pushed on the integer stack. If an operator is read in, the last two integer values pushed on the stack are returned and popped off the stack, the expression is evaluated, and the result is pushed on the stack. Once all operations have been carried out, the value of the original RPN expression will be the top item on the stack. Given this algorithm description, we have the following walk-through on our sample expression:

1. Initially the stack is empty. Then the integer value 8 is read in and pushed on the stack, giving it the appearance of Figure 17.8(a).
2. Next 6 is read in and pushed on the stack, thereby giving it the appearance of Figure 7.8(b).
3. Then 1 is read in and pushed, so the stack now appears as Figure 17.8(c).
4. The operator \ is read in. The value 1 is returned and popped, the value 6 is returned and popped, the operation 6 − 1 is applied, and then the result, 5, is pushed on the stack. The appearance is given as Figure 17.8(d).
5. The operator \ is read in. The value 5 is returned and then popped. Likewise 8 is returned and then popped. The operation 8 MOD 5 is applied and then pushed on the stack. The stack's appearance now is shown by Figure 17.8(e).
6. Next 4 is read in and pushed on the stack, resulting in Figure 17.8(f).
7. Finally, + is read in. 4 is returned and then popped, 3 is returned and then popped, and the operation 3 + 4 is applied and then pushed. The stack's appearance, shown in Figure 17.8(g), has one integer on it equal to the value of the original RPN expression.

Pseudocode of the solution

From the description and walk-through, we can describe the solution to the problem using the pseudocode

```
MakeStack(IntStack)
WHILE NOT eoln DO
    SkipBlanks(Ch)
    IF Ch is a digit THEN
        GetInteger(Ch, Int)
        Push(Int, IntStack)
    ELSE IF Ch is an operator THEN
        ApplyOperation(Ch, IntStack)
    ELSE IF NOT eoln THEN        {an illegal character was read in}
        Push(NullItem, IntStack)
    readln
    ShowValue(IntStack)
```

The postcondition returned by SkipBlanks is that either (1) the last Ch value read in is not blank, (2) the eoln condition is true, or (3) both conditions

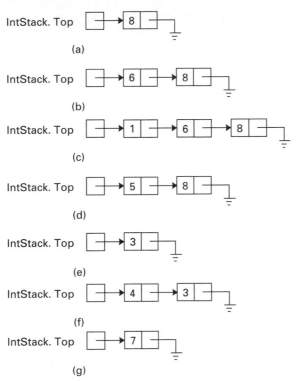

IntStack. Top → 8

(a)

IntStack. Top → 6 → 8

(b)

IntStack. Top → 1 → 6 → 8

(c)

IntStack. Top → 5 → 8

(d)

IntStack. Top → 3

(e)

IntStack. Top → 4 → 3

(f)

IntStack. Top → 7

(g)

FIGURE 17.8 (a) Stack's appearance after '8' is read in and processed, (b) stack after '6' is read in and processed, (c) stack after '1' is read in and processed, (d) stack after '−' is read in and processed, (e) stack after '\' is read in and processed, (f) stack after '4' is read in and processed, and (g) stack after '+' is read in and processed.

are true. The postcondition returned by GetInt is that the value given to Int is the integer value of the sequence of digit characters read in. If the sequence is terminated with a character other than a blank or <eoln>, the value of NullItem is returned, thus indicating an error condition. The postcondition returned by the call to ApplyOperation is that IntStack has been changed, where the value on top of the stack represents the result of the last applied operation.

Source code   The source code, in which we have left space to copy in all the ADT identifiers, is given as the program RPNCalculator.

```
PROGRAM RPNCalculator(input, output);
   {An integer expression in RPN is read in on one line of text, and the
   expression's value is displayed on the second line of text.}

                {INSERT ALL STKTYPE ADT DEFINITIONS HERE}
   VAR
      IntStack: StkType;      {stack used to evaluate RPN expression}
      Ch: char;               {value of last char read in}
      Int: integer;           {value of last integer converted from chars}
```

```
                    {INSERT ALL STKTYPE ADT OPERATIONS HERE}
{*                                                                        *}
PROCEDURE SkipBlanks(VAR Ch: char);
   {documentation}
   BEGIN
     Ch:= ' ';        {forces loop entry}
     WHILE (Ch = ' ') AND NOT eoln DO
       read(Ch)
   END;
{*                                                                        *}
PROCEDURE GetInteger(Ch: char; VAR Int: ItemType);
   {documentation}
   BEGIN
     Int:= 0;                             {initialize Int to 0}
     WHILE Ch IN ['0'..'9'] DO            {accumulate an integer value}
       BEGIN
         Int:= 10 * Int + ord(Ch) - ord('0');
         IF NOT eoln THEN                 {force a blank, given eoln}
           read(Ch)
         ELSE
           Ch:= ' '
       END;
       IF Ch <> ' ' THEN         {return error if last Ch is not blank}
         Int:= NullItem
     END;
   {*                                                                     *}
PROCEDURE ApplyOperation(Operator: char; VAR IntStack: StkType);
   {documentation}
   BEGIN    END;
{*                                                                        *}
PROCEDURE ShowValue(IntStack: StkType);
   {displays value of top item on stack if no error condition; if error
   condition, displays error message}
   BEGIN    END;
{*                                                                        *}
BEGIN    {main block}
   MakeStack(IntStack);
   WHILE NOT eoln DO                          {process line with expression}
     BEGIN
       SkipBlanks(Ch);
       IF Ch IN ['0'..'9'] THEN                  {get integer and push it}
         BEGIN
           GetInteger(Ch, Int);
           Push(Int, IntStack)
         END
       ELSE IF Ch IN ['+','-','*','/','\'] THEN  {apply operation of Ch}
         ApplyOperation(Ch, IntStack)
```

```
    ELSE IF NOT eoln THEN            {undefined Ch value was read in}
        Push(NullItem, IntStack)
    END;
  readln;                            {clear line for display}
  ShowValue(IntStack)
END.
```

Developing
`Apply-`
`Operation`
The code for the procedure `ApplyOperation` is straightforward as long as we guard against any error conditions. An error condition occurs if (1) the stack does not initially have two operands on it or (2) an error condition had previously occurred. In the latter case, the top item on the stack should already be set to `NullItem`. Given this scenario, we can initially draft the solution for the statement of `ApplyOperation` as

> *Operand2* ← *TopItem(IntStack)*
> *Pop(IntStack)*
> *Operand1* ← *TopItem(IntStack)*
> *Pop(IntStack)*
> *IF (Operand2 = NullItem) OR (Operand1 = NullItem) THEN*
>   *Push(NullItem, IntStack)*
> *ELSE*
>   *Result* ← *function of Operator and two operands*
>   *Push(Result, IntStack)*

The variables `Operand1`, `Operand2` and `Result` (of the single applied operation) are all local `integer` variables. A value can be assigned to `Result` using a CASE statement.

Source code
Taking all considerations into account, we obtain the code for `ApplyOperation` as shown.

```
PROCEDURE ApplyOperation(Operator; char; VAR IntStack: StkType);
  {documentation}
  VAR
    Operand1, Operand2,       {the top two items on the stack}
    Result: integer;          {result of the applied operation}
  BEGIN
    Operand2:= TopItem(IntStack);
    Pop(IntStack);
    Operand1:= TopItem(IntStack);
    Pop(IntStack);
    IF (Operand2 = NullItem) OR (Operand1 = NullItem) THEN {error check}
      Push(NullItem, IntStack)
    ELSE
      BEGIN
        CASE Operator OF
          '+': Result:= Operand1 + Operand2;
          '-': Result:= Operand1 - Operand2;
```

```
        '*': Result:= Operand1 * Operand2;
        '/': Result:= Operand1 DIV Operand2;
        '\': Result:= Operand1 MOD Operand2
     END; {CASE}
     Push(Result, IntStack)
   END    {ELSE}
END;      {PROCEDURE}
```

Developing
ShowValue

The procedure ShowValue is easily coded if there are no error conditions. We must, however, account for any error conditions that may occur. If, before <eoln> is typed in an error condition is found, NullItem is pushed on the stack. Once this initial value is pushed, the source code of ApplyOperation guarantees that the value NullItem is always the top item on the stack.

A second error might occur if there are too many operands on the stack when the <eoln> character is keyed in. In this case, there are too many operands and not enough operators to correctly evaluate the RPN expression. When we take both possibilities into account, we arrive at the source code for ShowValue as given.

```
PROCEDURE ShowValue(IntStack: StkType);
  {documentation}
  VAR
    Result: integer;       {candidate value of RPN expression}
  BEGIN
    Result:= TopItem(IntStack);
    Pop(IntStack);          {IntStack should now be empty}
    IF (Result = NullItem) OR NOT StackEmpty(IntStack) THEN
      writeln('The expression was ill-formed.')
    ELSE
      writeln(Result:1)
  END; ◆
```

EXERCISES

Test Your
Understanding

1. Why is it unnecessary to have a variable that points to the "bottom" of the stack?

2. Given the defining operations of the ADT StkType, is there any way to display the contents on the stack without changing the stack's appearance?

3. Evaluate the following RPN expressions (some are ill-formed):
   (a) 12 2 4 + /
   (b) 16 3 - 2
   (c)   5 8 + 7 3 - \
   (d) 18 4 - 7 2 +
   (e) 12 5 3 + \ 2 3 + *
   (f) 15 17 8 6 + - /
   (g)   7 3 2 - + * 6 +

Practice Your
Analysis Skills

4. What value is displayed if the user enters a blank line when the program RPNCalculator is run? Explain your answer.

5. Suppose, instead, the user enters a single integer value on the input line. What expression value is displayed?

6. While an RPN expression is being evaluated, one of three error conditions can occur: (1) an insufficient number of operands has been read in, (2) too many operands have been read in, (3) an illegal character has been read in. A fourth condition where no error has occurred so far is also possible. Propose a mechanism to keep track of the error status of the RPNCalculator. (Hint: Define/declare another variable.)

7. Modify the coded statements of RPNCalculator so that a given error event is recorded as soon as it occurs. Make sure the evaluation process stops as soon as an error occurs.

8. Recode the statement for ShowValue so that the appropriate error message is displayed if an error does occur.

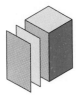

17.4   Generalized Lists

You have already seen primitive operations that apply to the nodes of a linked list. We have also shown implementations of the special linked lists known as the queue and stack. In this section, we solve the problem of implementing a generalized list ADT where any given node in the list can be added or deleted. We then use some of the operations of this abstraction in the case study, a problem to implement another kind of linked list ADT known as an ordered list.

The ADT ListType

The queue and the stack are linked list ADTs where the add and delete operations are always carried out on the same node(s) in the structure. Now we are going to implement a linked list where either operation can be carried out aat any node in the structure. The node to be added or deleted, however, must always be at some specified place in the list. Given this requirement, we find that both operations need an additional parameter, a pointer to one of the list's nodes that specifies the point at which the list is to be changed.

Example Problem 17.4

The problem statement

Using the node primitives, write the implementation for the ADT ListType, a linked list where a node may be added or deleted at any specified place in the list. The defining operations of the abstraction are the 4 node primitives, the primitive constructor MakeList that returns an empty list, the primitive selector FirstNode that returns the pointer to the first node in the list, the predicate function EmptyList, and the two constructors InsertNode and DeleteNode. One of the parameters for these last two operations is the pointer variable PrevNodePtr. If a node is to be inserted, it should follow the item pointed to by PrevNodePtr. If a node is to be deleted, it is the one that follows the item pointed to by PrevNodePtr.

Coding the
interface part

From the specifications of the ADT, we obtain the source code for the interface part of the abstraction as shown.

```
{                      INTERFACE PART OF LIST ADT                          }
{This unit consists of a generic linked list where an item on the list
can be added or deleted at any place in the list. The unit contains
primitive operations that apply to the nodes of the list as well as
operations that apply to the list as whole.}
{*                      THE APPEARANCE                                   *}
CONST
  NullItem = {AN ITEMTYPE VALUE THAT FLAGS AN ERROR CONDITION};
TYPE
  ItemType = {DEFINITION OF THE TYPE OF ITEMS THAT MAKE UP LIST};
  LNodePtr = ^LNodeType;   {points to a list's node}
  LNodeType = RECORD        {a list's node}
    Item: ItemType;
    Next: LNodePtr
  END;
  ListType = RECORD         {definition of the list itself}
    First: LNodePtr
  END;
{*                      THE OPERATIONS                                   *}
{*                                                                       *}
{          INSERT NODE PRIMITIVES FROM SECTION 17.1 HERE                 }
{*                                                                       *}
PROCEDURE MakeList(VAR AList: ListType);                       FORWARD;
  {initializes an empty list}
{*                                                                       *}
PROCEDURE InsertNode(AnItem: ItemType; PrevNodePtr: LNodePtr;
                              VAR AList: ListType);            FORWARD;
  {inserts a node in the list whose data field is AnItem. The node is
  the one following PrevNodePtr^. When PrevNodePtr is NIL, the value
  AnItem is to be inserted as the first item in the list}
{*                                                                       *}
PROCEDURE DeleteNode(PrevNodePtr: LNodePtr;
                  VAR AList: ListType);                        FORWARD;
  {deletes the node in the list following PrevNodePtr^; if PrevNodePtr
  is NIL, the first node is deleted; if the list is empty, no action is
  taken}
{*                                                                       *}
FUNCTION FirstNode(AList: ListType): LNodePtr;                 FORWARD;
  {returns the pointer variable to the first node on the list}
{*                                                                       *}
FUNCTION EmptyList(AList: ListType): boolean;                 FORWARD;
  {returns true if the list is empty}
{                      END INTERFACE SECTION                             }
{*                                                                       *}
{FORWARD-directed headers and statements of implementation section}
```

The parameter `PrevNodePtr` is required for both the insertion and the deletion operations. In the case of the insertion operation, it points to the node after which the new node is to be inserted. In the case of the deletion operation, the node *pointed to* from `PrevNodePtr^` is the candidate for deletion. In both instances, if the operation is successfully carried out, the `Next` field of `PrevNodePtr^` will have changed its value.

Even though one of the field variables of `PrevNodePtr^` is changed, the pointer variable `PrevNodePtr` is still passed into both constructors using a call by value. We can justify this blatant side effect with the argument that `AList`, the parameter representing the entire structure, is passed into both constructor operations as a VAR call. This mechanism indicates that one of the components of the linked list variable `AList`, hence `AList` itself, is changed by `InsertNode` and `DeleteNode`. The client can then see `PrevNodePtr` as the pointer to the node after which the original list changes its appearance. It is understood that the value of `PrevNodePtr` for either operation is found in a client process (a program or some procedure belonging to another unit).

The source code to implement `MakeList`, `FirstNode`, and `EmptyList` is as shown.

```
PROCEDURE MakeList{VAR AList: ListType};
   BEGIN
      AList.First:= NIL
   END;

FUNCTION FirstNode{(AList: ListType): LNodePtr};
   BEGIN
      FirstNode:= AList.First
   END;

FUNCTION EmptyList{(AList: ListType): boolean};
   BEGIN
      EmptyList:= AList.First = NIL
   END;
```

In order to insert a node into the list, a new node is first constructed with a call to the node primitive `MakeNode`. After the call to `MakeNode`, the link from the new node to the node that follows `PrevNodePtr^` is constructed. Only then is it safe to to link `PrevNodePtr^` to the new node.

This strategy works if the node to be inserted is not a candidate for the first node in the list. If the node is to be the new first node, the link from it to `AList.First^` must be assigned first. Then it is safe to assign a new value to the pointer variable `AList.First`. Given these considerations, we arrive at the following code for the procedure `InsertNode`:

```
PROCEDURE InsertNode{AnItem: ItemType; PrevNodePtr: LNodePtr;
                                       VAR AList: ListType};

   VAR
```

```
   Temp: LNodePtr;     {the variable that points to the new node}
BEGIN
   MakeNode(AnItem, Temp);
   IF PrevNodePtr = NIL THEN     {Temp will be the new AList.First node}
     BEGIN
        Temp^.Next:= AList.First;
        AList.First:= Temp
     END
   ELSE
     BEGIN
        Temp^.Next:= PrevNodePtr^.Next;
        PrevNodePtr^.Next:= Temp
     END
END;
```

Pictures

Figures 17.9(a) through 17.9(c) show how the procedure InsertNode is carried out when a node is inserted somewhere in the middle of AList. The pictures to show how the procedure works when PrevNodePtr is passed in as a NIL value are identical to the pictures you would draw for the Push operation on a stack.

Developing
DeleteNode

In order to delete a node from the linked list, we must guard against any attempt to dereference a NIL pointer. The first guard is applied to the value of Prev-NodePtr. When this value is NIL, the first node in the list is to be deleted. Thus, our first pseudocode draft for DeleteNode is described by

> IF PrevNodePtr <> NIL THEN
>   Temp ← PrevNodePtr^.Next   {set candidate for deletion}
> ELSE
>   Temp ← AList.First
> delete Temp from the list

Delete Temp
from the list

There is also the possibility that the client program may try to delete the (non-existent) node following the last node in the list. In this case, the value assigned to Temp by the action of the first path of the decision statement will be NIL. A client may likewise attempt to delete the first node from an empty list. Then, the value assigned to Temp will be NIL by virtue of the the second path of the decision statement.

Whether either path is taken, there is a definite chance that the postcondition returned by the first decision is that Temp was set to NIL. Should this event occur, it represents the fact that there is no node to delete. Hence, the action described as *delete Temp from the list* refines to a decision statement described by

> IF Temp <> NIL THEN
>   set new link
>   KillNode(Temp)

When an attempt is made to delete a non-existing node, the statements of

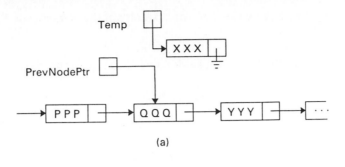

(a)

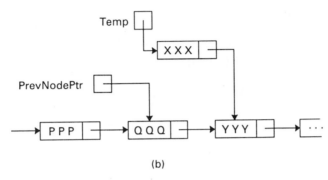

(b)

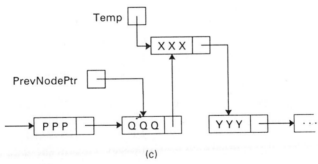

(c)

FIGURE 17.9 (a) Postconditions after `MakeNode('XXX', Temp)`, (b) postconditions after `Temp^.Next:= PrevNodePtr^.Next`, and (c) postconditions after `PrevNodePtr^.Next.= Temp`.

`DeleteNode` do not change the list (recall that `KillNode` guards against disposing the NIL pointer). We must be sure that the interface documentation informs the client user that no action is taken if the link field of `PrevNodePtr` is to a node that does not exist.

Set new link   The pseudocode for *set new link* is then described by

> IF *PrevNodePtr* <> *NIL THEN*
>   *PrevNodePtr^.Next* ← *Temp^.Next* {*new link set in middle of list*}
> *ELSE*
>   *First* ← *Temp^.Next* {*new first link is set*}

From the final two refinements, we obtain the source code for *DeleteNode* as shown.

```
PROCEDURE DeleteNode{PrevNodePtr: LNodePtr; VAR AList: ListType};
  VAR
    Temp: LNodePtr;       {points to candidate node for deletion}
  BEGIN
    IF PrevNodePtr <> NIL THEN        {check for AList.First}
      Temp:= PrevNodePtr^.Next
    ELSE                              {AList.First is candidate}
      Temp:= AList.First;
    IF Temp <> NIL THEN              {check that candidate node exists}
      IF PrevNodePtr <> NIL THEN     {check again for AList.First}
        PrevNodePtr^.Next:= Temp^.Next
      ELSE
        AList.First:= Temp^.Next;
    KillNode(Temp)
  END;  ◆
```

An Ordered List ADT

The List ADT is an extremely useful abstraction. Its operations can be used to implement virtually all ADTs that require a linear linked list. For example, a stack implementation is accomplished using a `PrevNodePtr` value of `NIL` for the `InsertNode` and `DeleteNode` operations. A queue can likewise be implemented, although `AddQueue` becomes an $O(N)$ process without the `Tail` node to reference the last node in the list.

An ordered list

The following case study uses the operations of the List ADT to implement an ADT that is an ordered list of integers. We define this list in such a way that its first node has the lowest integer value. All nodes that follow any given node in the list have integer values greater than the integer value in the data field (`Item`) of the given node.

CASE STUDY 17.2

The problem statement

Use any of the operations in the ADT `ListType` to build an ADT `OListType` of integers. The ADT is to contain the following operations:

three node primitives (`MakeONode`, `NextONode`, `ONodesValue`).
`MakeOList`: initializes `OList` to an empty list.
`LowestONode`: returns pointer to the node with the lowest integer value.
`EmptyOList`: returns `true` if the ordered list is empty.
`AddOItem`: inserts an integer item into its proper position in the ordered

list; if the item is already present, the operation is not carried out, and a value of false is returned to a boolean flag variable Done.

DeleteOItem: deletes a specified integer value from the list; if the integer value is not in the list, a value of false is returned to the boolean flag variable Done.

ShowOList: displays the contents of the variable OList of type OListType in order from the lowest to the highest integer value.

Using the ADT ListType

If we can use the operations that belong to the ADT ListType, there is very little code we will need to develop. If we simply copy the identifiers and operations we need for the ADT OListType, we should include the following definitions:

```
TYPE
   OListPtr = LNodePtr;
   OListType = ListType;
```

These definitions make all the operations of the ADT ListType compatible with the ADT OListType we are developing.

The first six operations

The first six operations, given the availability of the operations from the ADT ListType are trivial to implement, for they are the same ones used in the ADT List-Type. The (FORWARD-directed) source code to implements four of the six operations, namely, MakeONode, NextONode, MakeOList, and LowestNode, is as follows:

```
PROCEDURE MakeONode  {AnItem: ItemType; VAR ONode: OListPtr}
   BEGIN
      MakeNode(AnItem, OList)
   END;

FUNCTION NextONode  {(ONode: OListPtr): OListPtr};
   BEGIN
      NextONode:= NextNode(ONode)
   END;

PROCEDURE MakeOList  {VAR OList: OListType};
   BEGIN
      MakeList(OList)
   END;

FUNCTION LowestNode  {(OList: OListType): OListPtr};
   BEGIN
      LowestNode:= FirstNode(OList)
   END;
```

Developing ShowOList

The implementation for ShowOList is also trivial. The variable OList is the single parameter for the procedure. We can use a loop whose pseudocode is given as

$$TempNodePtr \leftarrow LowestNode(OList)$$
$$WHILE\ ONodesValue(TempNodePtr) <> NullItem\ DO$$
$$display\ ONodesValue(TempNodePtr)$$
$$TempNodePtr \leftarrow NextONode(TempNodePtr)$$

We can state the loop invariant as, "The integer values for each node from the first node to the node just before TempNodePtr have had their values displayed." The postloop assertion is, "TempNodePtr is the sentinel node indicating the end of the list." Therefore at loop exit, the entire ordered list has been displayed, and hence the description is correct.

Source code   The source code for the (FORWARD-directed) procedure ShowOList is

```
PROCEDURE ShowOList {VAR OList: OListType};
  VAR
    TempNodePtr: OListPtr;        {points to candidate node for display}
  BEGIN
    TempNodePtr:= LowestNode(OList);
    WHILE ONodesValue(TempNodePtr) <> NullItem DO
      BEGIN
        writeln(ONodesValue(TempNodePtr):1);
        TempNodePtr:= NextONode(TempNodePtr)
      END
  END;
```

Developing
AddOItem   The first statement of AddOItem should find a value for the pointer variable PrevNodePtr. The properties of the list require that the value of NodesValue(PrevNodePtr) be less than the value of AnItem. If the value of the node following PrevNodePtr^ is equal to AnItem, a new node is not inserted, and Done is returned as false. Otherwise, the node is inserted, and Done is returned as true. Hence, we obtain the pseudocode description

$$PrevNodePtr \leftarrow Search(OList, AnItem)$$
$$IF\ ONodesValue(NextONode(PrevNodePtr)) = AnItem\ THEN$$
$$Done \leftarrow false$$
$$ELSE$$
$$InsertNode(AnItem, PrevNodePtr, OList)$$
$$Done \leftarrow true$$

Search, a function that we also use in the statement part of DeleteOItem, returns the pointer to the last node in the list whose data field is less than the value of AnItem. We will develop the code for this function after we have developed the code for DeleteOItem.

Source code   From the pseudocode descriptions, we obtain the (FORWARD-directed) source code for the procedure AddOItem as given.

```
PROCEDURE AddOItem {AnItem: ItemType; VAR OList: OListType;
                                        VAR Done: boolean};
  VAR
    PrevNodePtr: OListPtr; {points to node that precedes AnItem's node}
  BEGIN
    PrevNodePtr:= Search(OList, AnItem);
    IF ONodesValue(NextNode(PrevNodePtr)) = AnItem THEN
      Done:= false              {duplicate item, insertion not done}
    ELSE
      BEGIN
        InsertNode(AnItem, PrevNodePtr, OList);
        Done:= true       {insertion of non-duplicate item is done}
      END
  END;
```

Developing
DeleteOItem
Given the Search function, we can draft the description for the action carried out by the procedure DeleteOItem as

> *PrevNodePtr ← Search(OList, AnItem)*
> *IF PrevNodePtr = NIL THEN* {AnItem may be first node's value}
>   *ProbeNodePtr ← LowestNode(OList)*
> *ELSE*
>   *ProbeNodePtr ← NextONode(PrevNodePtr)*
> *IF ONodesValue(ProbeNodePtr) = AnItem THEN*
>   *DeleteNode(PrevNodePtr, OList)*
>   *Done ← true*
> *ELSE*
>   *Done ← false*

Assertions
Let us show that this pseudocode description fulfills the block's purpose using assertions. After the call to Search, PrevNodePtr points to the node whose data field contains the highest value less than the value of AnItem. After the first decision, ProbeNode points to the candidate node in the list for deletion. If this node's data field matches the value of AnItem, it is deleted from the list with the call to DeleteNode. Otherwise, no node is deleted.

Source code
The pseudocode description gives us the following source code:

```
PROCEDURE DeleteOItem {AnItem: ItemType; VAR OList: OListType;
                                        VAR Done: boolean};
  VAR
    PrevNodePtr,      {points to node before candidate node for deletion}
    ProbeNodePtr: OListPtr;    {points to candidate node for deletion}
  BEGIN
    PrevNodePtr:= Search(OList, AnItem);
    IF PrevNodePtr = NIL THEN
```

SECTION 17-4   GENERALIZED LISTS   **791**

```
              ProbeNodePtr:= LowestNode(OList)
          ELSE
              ProbeNodePtr:= NextONode(PrevNodePtr);
          IF ONodesValue(ProbeNodePtr) = AnItem THEN
              BEGIN
                  DeleteNode(PrevNodePtr, AnItem);
                  Done:= true
              END
          ELSE
              Done:= false
      END;
```

Developing
the auxiliary
function
`Search`

Now let us develop the function `Search`. It is quite possible that the search returns NIL. This event can occur either if the list is empty or if `AnItem` is less than or equal to the integer value of the lowest node. If neither of these two cases occur, a search for a candidate node that is not the first node in the list must be carried out. And so we obtain the following pseudocode:

> *IF EmptyOList(OList) THEN*
>   *CandNode ← NIL*   *{empty list condition}*
> *ELSE IF AnItem < ONodesValue(LowestNode(OList)) THEN*
>   *CandNode ← NIL*   *{AnItem < first node's data value}*
> *ELSE*
>   *search through list for CandNode*
> *Search ← CandNode*

The postcondition returned by the search through the list is that the data field of the node following CandNode must have a value greater than or equal to `AnItem`. The condition-seeking loop we wish to code is then described by

> *CandNode ← LowestNode(OList)*   *{first candidate node}*
> *WHILE AnItem < ONodesValue(NextONode(CandNode)) DO*
>   *CandNode ← NextONode(CandNode)*

The loop is exited when the node following CandNode is greater than or equal to the value of `AnItem`. Hence, CandNode must be the last node in the last whose data field contains an integer value lower than the value of `AnItem`.

Source code From the pseudocode descriptions, we obtain the source code for the function `Search` as given.

```
FUNCTION Search(AnItem: ItemType; OList: OListType): OListPtr;
    {returns pointer to the highest node whose data field is less than
    the value of AnItem.  If there are no lower nodes or the list is
    empty, the value NIL is returned}
    VAR
        CandNode: OListPtr;    {candidate node for Search}
```

```
    BEGIN
      If EmptyOList(OList) THEN
        CandNode:= NIL                {AnItem's node will be first on list}
      ELSE IF AnItem < ONodesValue(LowestNode(OList)) THEN
        CandNode:= NIL                {likewise, but list is not empty}
      ELSE
        BEGIN                    {list is not empty, search for CandNode}
          CandNode:= LowestNode(OList);
          WHILE AnItem > ONodesValue(NextONode(CandNode)) DO
            CandNode:= NextONode(CandNode)
        END;
      Search:= CandNode
    END; ◆
```

EXERCISES

Test Your Understanding

1. What is the difference between the two types OListType and OListPtr?

2. True or false? The two identifiers ONodePtr and LNodePtr refer to the same data type. Explain.

3. Explain in one sentence how the call InsertNode(AnItem, NIL, AList) is logically equivalent to the push operation of a stack.

Practice Your Analysis Skills

4. Given that OList initially has the appearance:

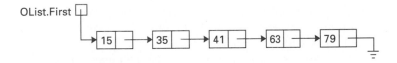

OList.First

Sketch the appearance of OList after each of the following statements in the given sequence has been carried out:

```
                    AddOItem(72, OList, Done);
                    AddOItem(41, OList, Done);
                    DeleteOItem(55, OList, Done);
                    DeleteOItem(41, OList, Done);
                    AddOItem(8, OList, Done);
```

Sharpen Your Implementation Skills

5. Write a procedure KillList that has the single input parameter AList of type List-Type. The procedure is supposed to return AList as an empty list where no garbage is created in the process. (*Note*: You cannot simply write a call to MakeList, for this one-line statement creates garbage.)

6. Write the code for ChangeNodesValue, a procedure that will change the Item field of a node in AList. The procedure can only use the operations belonging to List-Type. The code for calling the procedure is written as ChangeNodesValue(An-Item, PrevNodePtr, AList) where NextNode(PrevNodePtr) is the node

whose data field is to be changed, AnItem is the new value for this node, and AList is the list variable.

7. Suppose the items in AList are integers. Write a procedure, using ChangeNodes-Value, to add 5 to each node in the list.

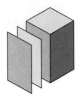

Program Testing Hints

When you use pointers, you must check your logic thoroughly before compiling the source code. An error with pointers is particularly difficult to find, for there is no way to distinguish one anonymous variable from another in a linked list except in terms of the defined ADT operations! We also recommend that you develop the ADT so a client user need not deal with the low-level details of manipulating pointer variables in his or her program. In this section we give you guidelines that will (1) help you avoid pointer errors and (2) help you develop client-friendly units.

Coding the Headers of a Linked List ADT

An ADT consists of operations defined by their headers. Let us first consider the issues of developing the headers for a unit that uses dynamic variables.

Why pointers?

The best ADT you can implement with pointers is one where a client process does not ever have to dereference a pointer variable. Do not forget that your ultimate purpose is to free a client user from low-level implementation details. A well-coded unit is (1) complete and correct and (2) a unit where the client does not have to deal with any low-level pointer operations other than the exceptional boolean operation that deals with NIL pointer values.

Pointers, representing machine addresses, are data types that require coding at the lowest possible level in Pascal. Errors with pointers can be subtle and are often difficult to isolate. Therefore why develop a unit where a client still needs to deal with operations that can lead to coding headaches?

A development philosophy

If pointers are such a hassle, you may ask, why bother to use them at all? You use them for the sake of versatility. Remember that a pointer can be defined to point to any type of variable you wish (even another pointer). An abstraction virtually impossible to implement with the other constructs of Pascal is often very easy to implement with pointers.

Required definitions

When you design a dynamic ADT that uses links, keep in mind that you must define two data types, one type that defines a component node variable and the other type that defines the data structure as a whole. Both types should be defined as records. The type that defines a node must have (1) a data field variable(s) and (2) a link field variable(s). The type that defines the structure must have at least one field variable that points to a node. This pointer, along with the defined selector operations for the component nodes, should allow the client to access any component node. The problem statement may require more pointers (e.g., the Tail pointer for type QType) and/or other additional field variables for the structure.

ADT operations

Just as you are required to define two data types when you set up a linked list ADT, you must define two sets of operations. The first set consists of a constructor to make a new node and one to kill a node that is of no further use. There should also be primitive selectors to each of the field variables of a node. These operations can be used for virtually all kinds of ADTs you may want to implement that have nodes with link fields. The second set of operations is the constructors, selectors, and predicates that are unique to the type of abstract structure you want to implement.

Parameter lists for the operations

Use a value call on a pointer variable when you want to dereference it. If a link in a given node is to be changed by an add or a delete operation, the usual convention is to pass in the node by value and the identifier representing the overall structure by VAR.

A call by VAR implies that a new value (address) is assigned to a pointer variable. If this action is your intention, you *must* use the call-by-VAR mechanism. It is mandatory that you use this mechanism on a pointer variable when you want to initialize or change the appearance of a linked structure.

Statements with Pointer Variables

There are some absolute rules that apply to the way pointers can be used in the statement part of a block. This section summarizes these rules and discusses some of the consequences that may occur if or when one of the rules is broken.

Assignment statements

An assignment statement to a pointer variable requires that the expression on the right-hand side of the operator be either a pointer expression of the same type or the standard constant NIL. *Memory is neither allocated nor deallocated by an assignment statement.* The only postcondition of the assignment statement APtr: = BPtr is that APtr and BPtr represent the same address. Thus, garbage is created if memory to APtr had been allocated and not disposed of prior to the assignment statement. Remember, too, that the statement APtr: = NIL does not deallocate the memory originally dereferenced by APtr^. If memory was originally allocated, this kind of statement also creates garbage.

PROGRAM DESIGN RULE 17.1

Dispose of dynamic variables as soon as they are of no further use.

PROGRAM DESIGN RULE 17.2

Use the standard procedures new and dispose sparingly.

Using new *and*
dispose

The simplest defense against garbage creation is to follow Program Design Rule 17.1. Be sure, however, that you are disposing of a variable that already exists. On some systems (e.g., Turbo Pascal), the call dispose(APtr) crashes the program at run time if no value had been allocated to APtr^.

You manage memory best when you create new variables as soon as they are required and deallocate old ones as soon as they are no longer needed. When you are writing an ADT that is a linked list, you expect that a call to add a link invokes the procedure new at some place in its sequence. Likewise, a call to delete a node invokes the procedure dispose should the operation be carried out.

The fewer operations that directly call the procedures new and dispose, the easier it is to manage memory. We do not mean to say that a given ADT should have exactly one way to add an item and/or just one way to delete an item. A deque, for example, an ADT we have not implemented in this chapter, has two delete operations, namely, to delete an item from its top and to delete an item from its bottom. Thus, there are two procedures that must ultimately call dispose. The actual call to dispose, however, is done in one place, namely, from KillNode. Likewise, if there are two or more places where an item can be added to an ADT, there is only one place in the unit, that is, MakeNode, where the call is actually made.

More about
Program Design
Rule 17.2

Why follow a rule such as Program Design Rule 17.2? For starters, it marks those places in your code where known preconditions must be met and known postconditions are returned as they relate to the creation or deletion of a node. Thus, for example, you know a value(s) must have been assigned to AnItem before MakeNode is called and that an additional node with a data field (perhaps partially) filled in is returned.

Suppose, perhaps, you suspect problems with memory management (e.g., garbage creation). You may then want to test the unit with calls to its add and/or delete operations, periodically displaying the count of anonymous variables that exist. You know that within each operation you must increment or decrement the "live nodes" counter after each call to MakeNode or KillNode.

PROGRAM DESIGN RULE 17.3

Never attempt a dereference on a NIL pointer value.

Referencing
pointer values

Program Design Rule 17.3 reminds you never to use the dereference APtr^ once the pointer variable APtr has been assigned the value NIL. An attempted dereference of a NIL value always results in an error of some kind. In VAX Pascal, it leads to a run-time crash with the error message "Reference to nil pointer." In Turbo Pascal, the erroneous dereference does not cause a crash, but it does lead to unpredictable results.

You likewise should not dereference APtr when memory has not yet been allocated. In VAX Pascal, the program crashes with the error message "Access violation error." In Turbo Pascal, the machine simply halts. Different results occur with different dialects, but an attempt to dereference a pointer that has not been allocated memory always cause an error condition.

Using the NIL
value

You can use NIL to form boolean expressions with the equality or inequality operator. Thus, both coded expressions APtr <> NIL and APtr = NIL work. None of the other relational operators work, however. You cannot, for example, use < to represent a condition such as "is ahead of." You must, instead, write an explicit function ('Joe' is ahead of 'John' in the queue) to apply this kind of operation.

The Dynamic Operations of an ADT

We conclude this section with some hints on how to implement the constructor operations of a dynamic ADT that, if followed, help ensure that the source code of the units you write is both correct and complete.

Operations that
are always
required

If you are developing an ADT that represents some kind of linked list, there are certain operations you should always code. First of all, virtually every unit should have an empty structure constructor. It should likewise have a predicate to test for an empty structure. A deletion operation should always guard against an attempt to delete a node from an empty structure.

The add/delete
operations

Pay close attention to the order in which links are made or broken. The correct statements done in an incorrect sequence causes bugs. You are usually safe if you add a new record to the structure by coding a sequence that satisfies the description given as Algorithm 17.1.

Algorithm 17.1

> {*Add a candidate node to a linked structure:*}
> *assign values to the data field(s) of CandNode^*
> *assign link(s) from CandNode^ to the structure*
> *assign links from the structure to CandNode^*
> {*end algorithm*}

In order to remove a node or record correctly, all links to the removal candidate must first be reassigned. The final action is the disposal of the candidate node. For deletion, then, a safe strategy is described by Algorithm 17.2.

Algorithm 17.2

> {*Delete a candidate from a linked structure:*}
> *set new links bypassing CandNode*
> *dispose(CandNode)*
> {*end algorithm*}

Drawing
pictures

Every procedure has preconditions and postconditions that you must be able to state. When you are coding a procedure that changes a dynamic structure, *draw the preconditions and postconditions as pictures* if you are not sure of the correct sequence of statements. As you step through the block sequence, draw each picture to show how the structure changes. The practice helps ensure that your code works toward its desired goal.

On-line testing   When devising tests on linked lists, be sure that empty structures are handled properly under all circumstances. See how the machine handles an attempt to delete a record from an empty structure, given an initial empty structure. Use test data that builds a non-empty structure and then keeps deleting items from it until an empty structure is returned. Will the structure be seen as empty in this case?

If you are still not satisfied, you might try some combinations of your own choosing. You might, for example, key in a sequence of two add operations for one delete operation, repeating this sequence three times. You might then follow it with a sequence that adds only one item and then deletes two items. You repeat this sequence 4 times. If you are working with a linear list, these simple strategies are usually more than adequate in helping you ferret out bugs. It is by no means required that you make 100 calls to each operation.

PROGRAM DESIGN RULE 17.4

Always write a procedure to display the values of the data field(s) for any dynamic variable(s).

Display and testing   In standard Pascal, it is impossible to display a pointer's value. This fact alone makes software implemented with pointers "harder" to read and debug. Therefore, it is mandatory for you to include a procedure that displays some (if not all) data fields of a dynamic variable, using a pointer's value as the single input parameter. You might as well develop these procedures even before you start testing, for most assuredly the first piece of code you may require as a testing aid is a display of the fields contained in the variable APtr˄.

Conventionality   One final word about working with pointers: *be conventional*. It is not worth it to find some clever new way to create a linked list. There are enough ways to use the basic queue on other structures that preclude the need for you to be "clever." Linked lists and operations using linked lists are best expressed in pictures. Unfortunately, program documentation can only be expressed in words. If your program uses identifiers such as Head and Tail or Front and Rear for a queue implementation, a programmer need not waste time trying to figure out that you have simply coded some queue ADT.

There are certain other ways you can be conventional. Make sure you define an empty queue such that Head and Tail are both NIL. Also, do not forget the defining identifiers. The purpose of a pointer variable of type QueuePtr that points to either QueueRec or, better yet, QueueNode is easy to fathom. Nobody reading such source code will get confused by these names.

EXERCISES

Test Your Understanding

1. Suppose a client is using a linked list ADT of some given type. At one point in the program, it is necessary to execute a call to the new procedure in order to create another link. What does this requirement say about the ADT the client is using?

2. In devising a linked list ADT, at least two record types need to be defined. What do each of these definitions represent?

3. Suppose the computer has just executed the statement APtr:= NIL. Indicate which of the following statements is in error:
   (a) IF APtr = NIL THEN
      writeln(APtr^.Item);
   (b) IF APtr = NIL THEN
      writeln('There are no more items in the list.');
   (c) IF APtr > NIL THEN
      writeln('There are still some items in the list.');
   (d) IF APtr <> NIL THEN
      writeln('There are still some items in the list.');

4. Under what circumstances does the statement APtr:= NIL create garbage?

Practice Your Analysis Skills

5. A record pointed to by Temp is to be added directly after the record pointed to by Present in a linear linked list. Sketch the appearance of the list after the following sequence is executed:

    Present^.Next:= Temp;
    Temp^.Next:= Present^.Next

Sharpen Your Implementation Skills

6. Correct the code of Exercise 5 so that the sequence is properly carried out.

7. Write the code for the procedure ShowNode, a procedure to display the value of the scalar variable Item whose value is pointed to by ANodePtr, a node in a linked list. You can use any of the ListType ADT operations.

REVIEW AND EXERCISES

A *linked list* is a structured variable whose components are *nodes*. Each node is a dynamic variable with at least two fields: a *data field,* containing information, and a *link* field pointing to the next node in the list. Regardless of how items are added to or deleted from a linked list, it is useful to implement some *node operations* as part of a linked list ADT. The operations that should always be included are (1) an operation to allocate memory to a node, then assign value(s) to the data field(s); (2) an operation to dispose of a node, returning the value of NIL to the pointer variable; (3) an operation to return the value(s) of each of the data fields in a node; and (4) an operation to return the pointer to the next node in the list.

When a queue is implemented as an ADT, it should include the four node operations as part of the unit. The type definition for the queue must have a pointer to the Head node and one to the Tail node. Any other fields, such as one to count the items on queue, are optional. The usual operations to construct an empty queue, add an item to or delete an item from the queue, test for an empty queue, and select the first item on the queue should be included as part of the operation set.

The stack can also be implemented as a type of linked list. Besides the four node operations, the operations that must be included to make up a stack ADT are (1) an initialization to an empty stack, (2) push, (3) pop, (4) return the top item on the stack, and (5) check for an empty stack.

The queue and stack are special forms of a more generic linked list type that we implemented in Section 17.4. The add/delete operations for this type are InsertNode and DeleteNode, both of which require a value for PrevNodePtr. This parameter, passed in by value, either points to the place where a node is to be inserted, or it points to the node directly ahead of the note to be deleted. AList, a pointer variable that represents the structure, is always passed in as a VAR call, for the structure is changed by the successful execution of InsertNode and DeleteNode.

If you are not careful with your logic, pointers and dynamic variables present special difficulties. A pointer's value cannot be displayed, and a dynamic variable's value(s) can only be found using a dereference of a pointer variable. The value taken on by any pointer variable, moreover, is implemented solely through the programmer's logic, be it good or bad. Given this premise, we recommend that you implement an ADT with pointers so that a user of the ADT does not need to deal with any pointer dereferences in his or her source code. Put more simply, he or she should not have to use the carat (^) once in the source code of a client process.

Certain operations are common and/or useful to all linear lists. The four node operations given in Section 17.1, for example, should be included in all ADTs that use linear lists. An operation to create an empty list, one to check for an empty list, and one to return the first node in the list are other standard operations. The add and delete operations, on the other hand, will differ from list to list.

When implementing an ADT as a linked list, you may often want to draw pictures to check your work. First, you should sketch pictures that illustrate the preconditions and postconditions. Then, starting from the precondition sketch, draw a picture to show the effect of each statement in the operation you are implementing. The final statement's picture should give you one identical to the sketch of the postcondition you want the source code to achieve.

EXERCISES

Short Answers

1. What are the characteristics of a linked list?

2. True or false? A function to find the Nth node in a linked list is an O(1) algorithm.

3. What is the difference between a data field and a link field? To what kind of variable do each of these terms apply?

4. Suppose the variable `APtr` is the only means to access an anonymous linked list. Explain why the single statement `dispose(APtr)` creates garbage.

5. What is the meaning of the `Next` field of one of the variables in a linked list?

6. Let `APtr^` be a node in a linked list. What, then, does it mean when the boolean expression `APtr^.Next = NIL` is true?

7. Write the code for the expression of Exercise 6 as a client would write it using the primitive node operations.

8. Suppose `APtr`'s data field (`Item`) contains a single integer value. Write the code to display the value of `APtr^.Item` using the primitive node operations.

9. In `QType`, we wrote the selector function `FirstOnQueue` as part of the unit. Why did we not also write a selector `LastOnQueue`?

10. We wish to display the value of the last item on queue. Does the following statement work?

$$\texttt{writeln(Queue.Tail\textasciicircum.Item)}$$

11. If the statement of Exercise 10 does not work, explain why not. If it does work, explain why, in the light of the material of Section 17.2, this statement represents bad code.

12. Why is the predicate function `FullQueue` unnecessary for a queue ADT implemented with pointers?

13. True or false?
    (a) The ADT `QType` cannot be implemented if the field variable `ItemsOnQueue` is not a part of QType's definition.
    (b) The ADT `QType` cannot be implemented if the field variable `Tail` is not a part of QType's definition.
    (c) The ADT `QType` cannot be implemented if the field variable `Head` is not a part of QType's definition.

14. The following linked list is given.
    What value is displayed by the statement `writeln(APtr^.Next^.Next^.Item)`?

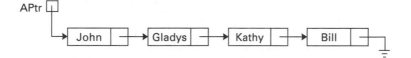

15. Under what circumstances is it correct to reference one of the field variables of the NIL pointer?

16. The variable `AList` of type `ListType` has 20 items on it. Explain why the call `MakeList(AList)` is a bad idea given these circumstances.

17. What would have to be done with `AList` to set up the required preconditions such that the call to `MakeList(AList)` in Exercise 16 is not harmful?

Easy Projects 18. Use only the operations of the ADT ListType, as given in Section 17.4, to implement a stack of integers. The operations that make up the stack were given in Section 17.3.

19. Use only the operations of the ADT ListType, as given in Section 17.4, to implement a queue of Names (last names only). The operations to make up the queue were given in Section 17.2.

20. Polish notation, also discovered by Lukasiewicz, has the operator come first followed by two operands to form expressions. Thus, the expression / * + 3 5 7 + 3 1, using only integer operands, reduces to the following: / * 8 7 + 3 1. This expression, in turn, becomes / 56 + 3 1, which then becomes / 56 4, and finally we get 14. Write a program, using a stack of integers, to read in and evaluate an integer expression (using the same operators as the case study) written in Polish notation.

21. Implement and use a stack of characters with pointers and then write the code to solve Example Problem 13.2 in the text.

Medium Projects

22. A priority queue is a type of queue where items are deleted from a queue according to some preferred ordering. One kind of priority queue can be implemented where a node of the queue is defined as

```
PQueuePtr = ^PQueueNode;
PQueueNode = RECORD
   Item: ItemType;
   PriorityNo: integer;   {determines where item is placed in queue}
   Next: PQueuePtr
END;
```

The priority queue structure is maintained in such a way that the item with the lowest priority number of all items added to the queue is at the head of the queue. The highest priority number is the last item in the queue.

Write an ADT unit to implement the priority queue. You can use the operations of the ListType ADT for this queue. The usual node primitives should be included in the unit (although a selector for the PriorityNo is not a required operation). The usual queue operations (MakePQueue, PQAdd, PQDelete, PQueueFirst, and EmptyPQueue) should also be a part of the unit. Implement the unit so that the priority queue contains names.

23. You are to write another unit that represents a different kind of priority queue. The priority here is given to class membership, where a given item is an A or a B member. Members are deleted from the queue based on a cycle of 3. A class B member is deleted for every third delete operation, and a class A member is deleted for all other calls to the PQDelete operation.

If there are no class A members on queue when it is time for a class A deletion, a member is deleted from the class B queue. Should it be time for a class B deletion, and no members are on the B queue, an attempt is made to delete a member from the class A queue.

You can use many of the definitions and operations for the QType ADT in this problem. We suggest the following additional definitions required to make the priority queue:

```
ItemType = RECORD
   Class:   char;   {'A' or 'B'}
   Name: String20
END;
```

```
PQueueType = RECORD
  ItemsDeleted: integer;   {determines who goes next}
  QueueA,
  QueueB: QType
END;
```

You can use the operations of QType and the basic node operations for a linear linked list as part of the unit. Note that `ItemsDeleted` is initialized to 0 by the operation MakePQueue. This particular field is incremented by 1 each time an item is successfully deleted. When you test the unit, make sure to enter in the member's class of priority in addition to his or her name.

24. A Ring ADT is a linked list that has no first item in it, but where one item points to the next one. The structure is a list that closes in on itself, as shown in the following figure:

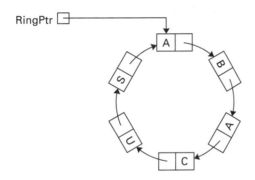

One variable `RingPtr` is the means to gain access to the list. If a node is to be added to or deleted from the ring, the candidate is the node following the one pointed to by `RingPtr`.

Using the operations of ListType, implement the code for the ADT RingType. For the sake of simplicity, have the ring contain `integer` items. Besides the usual node primitives, the five operations for this ADT are MakeRing (makes an empty ring), AddRing, DeleteRing, RingNode (a selector that returns a pointer value, and EmptyRing. In addition to implementing these operations, write the client procedure ShowRing that displays the contents of the ring.

25. The node for a double-linked list has two link fields: one that points to the Next node, and the other that points to the Previous node. A typical node in this structure thus looks like

Prev   Next

The DLinkedList ADT thus has two nodes, a First node and a Last node. Write down the definition for a node of a double-linked list and the operations for the node primitives. Next, given a double-linked list, write the client procedure ShowFromFirst that displays the list starting from the First node. The last item displayed is the one pointed to by Last. Also write the client procedure ShowFromLast that displays the list starting with the Last item. With this procedure, the last item displayed is the one pointed to by First.

26. Write the code for the operations of the ADT described in Exercise 25. The ADT has the following constructors: MakeDList (makes an empty list), InsertBefore (inserts item before node passed in), InsertAfter (inserts node following node passed in), and DeleteNode (deletes node pointed to). It has the two selectors, FirstNode and LastNode, that return pointer values. The one predicate is EmptyDList. We point out that the node before First, like the node after Last, is always NIL. Be sure to also include the primitive node operations.

Difficult Projects

27. A deque is a double-linked list (see Exercise 25) where an item can be added either ahead of the first item or after the last item. Likewise, either the first item or the last item can be deleted from a deque. You are to use the code suggested by Exercise 25 to implement an ADT DequeType. The unit is to have the following constructors: MakeDeque, AddFirst, AddLast, DeleteFirst, and DeleteLast. It should likewise have the selectors FirstNode and LastNode, which return pointer values. Finally, it should have the one predicate EmptyDeque.

28. A palindrome is a sequence of items that looks the same whether it is listed forward or backward. If we allow for case-insensitivity and only include letters in our list of palindrome candidates, the following are all palindromes: (1) Otto, (2) Anna, (3) Madam, I'm Adam, (4) A man, a plan, a canal, Panama. Use the deque ADT of Exercise 27 to write a client program that reads in a sequence of letters and then determines whether it is a palindrome or not. Sample runs:

```
Able was I, 'ere I saw Elba.
The sequence is a palindrome.

Able was I.
The sequence is not a palindrome.
```

29. You can use the LinkedList ADT to construct an ADT that handles strings, just like the ADT we implemented in Section 14.6. Write a unit StringType using a linked list of char values. Rather than using an array to hold the characters in the string, you are to use a linked list. Test the unit with the operations we gave as examples just before the exercise set of Section 14.4.

C H A P T E R *18*

BINARY TREES

OBJECTIVES

After reading and studying the contents of this chapter, you should be able to

- Define the term "binary tree" and all those terms that describe the characteristics of a binary tree

- Describe the characteristics of binary search tree (BST) ADT

- Implement an ADT that is a binary search tree, using dynamic variables

- Use the BST abstraction as part of the solution to a client program where such a structure is applicable

- Define the term "expression tree"

- Build and use an expression tree as part of the solution to a problem

- Explain the difference between LNR, NLR, and LRN traversals

- Use the correct tree traversal algorithm(s) to solve a given problem

WE HAVE USED THE TREE STRUCTURE quite extensively in the presentation of various topics throughout the text. You have seen trees used as an aid in (1) designing a program top–down, (2) depicting a hierarchical record structure, and (3) desk tracing a recursive algorithm. So far we have used trees as a tool in software design and software analysis. Now you will see how to implement a tree as a data structure.

The chapter discusses two kinds of trees: search trees and expression trees. A search tree stores data in such a way that information about a given node can be retrieved very quickly. Moreover, the operations for addition and/ or deletion of nodes on the tree are very efficient. An expression tree holds information in its nodes in such a way that the tree as a whole represents the value of an expression. A proper traversal of the tree, where all nodes are visited, returns the value of the expression that the tree represents.

18.1   The Nodes of a Binary Search Tree

In Pascal, you can define ADTs whose nodes require more than one link field. In this section, we discuss the properties of the *binary search tree* (BST), an ADT whose nodes require two link fields. A search for a node in a structured variable that is a binary search tree is usually very efficient, as we shall explain.

The Defining Terms

A *tree,* like all other data structures, has a defined appearance. It is a structure, that, like a linked list, contains component variables that are nodes. Unlike a linked list, each node of a tree contains two or more variables that serve as links to other nodes. Let us start off our discussion of trees by first defining a number of terms.

> **Tree:**   a hierarchical data structure constructed from a single node known as the *root node* (also *root*).

> **Root node:**   the first node of a tree structure. All other nodes in the structure ultimately tie back to an initial link from the root node.

Binary trees   Figure 18.1 shows the appearance of a typical node in a *binary tree*. It has two link fields, one pointing to the root node of a *subtree* of nodes that are all positioned "left" of the given node, the other pointing to the root node of a subtree of nodes that are all positioned "right" of the given node.

> **Binary tree:**   a tree where each node has exactly two field variables that are links.

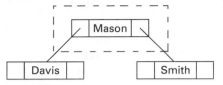

FIGURE 18.1 A node of a binary tree.

Subtree of a node: a node pointed to by the link field of a given node. It defines the root node of a tree structure smaller than the original tree.

Figure 18.2 shows the appearance of a typical binary tree. We have used the node depicted in Figure 18.1 as the root node for this tree. The root node contains the name Mason. The left link of this root node points to the left subtree, whose root node contains the name Holmes. The right link points to the right subtree whose root node contains the name Smith.

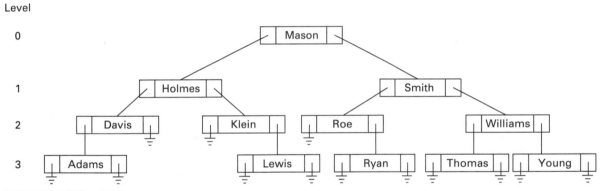

FIGURE 18.2 A binary tree.

More subtrees

The definition of a subtree applies to any node on the tree. For example, the left subtree of the root node contains the name Holmes. This subtree, whose root is the Holmes node, has 5 nodes. The left subtree of the node containing Holmes is the node containing the name Davis. The left subtree for the Davis node contains the name Adams. Its right subtree, pointing to NIL, is empty. Both subtrees whose root node contains Adams are empty.

The right subtree for the Holmes node holds the name Klein. The left subtree of the Klein node is empty, but the node for its right subtree contains the name Lewis. Both subtrees of the Lewis node are empty.

Trees and subtrees

The definition of a tree is recursive. Any node on a tree whose address is not NIL contains other nodes that form subtrees. Each of these nodes also satisfies the definition of a tree, for it is the root node of all the subtrees that its link fields point to. Every node not referenced by the NIL pointer, then, can be seen as a root node that starts another tree.

When a node on a tree is pointed to from the link field of another node, we more commonly refer to this node as the root node of a subtree. This more precise

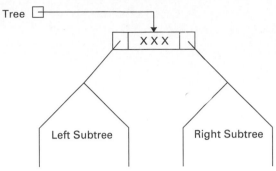

Tree

x x x

Left Subtree   Right Subtree

FIGURE 18.3   Description of a binary tree.

definition allows us to specify a tree variable in terms of its single root node, the node through which access is gained to all other nodes in the structure.

Figure 18.3 shows the general appearance of a binary tree. The pointer variable `Tree` points to the root node of the binary tree. This pointer variable, dereferenced by `Tree`, is used to represent the anonymous variable that is the binary tree. The dereference `Tree^` then represents the variable that is the root node of the tree.

Empty trees and subtrees

Refer back to Figure 18.2 again. The figure shows that there are many links in the structure that point to NIL. The NIL pointer defines a tree or a subtree that does not contain nodes. This kind of tree (subtree) is known as an *empty tree (subtree)*. Every tree structure, regardless of the number of nodes it contains, will always contain some empty subtrees.

Empty tree (subtree):   a tree (subtree) that contains no nodes.

Other definitions

The nodes that form the subtrees of a given node are called its *children*. The node above any given node on a tree is its *parent*. The unique sequence of nodes to be visited before a given node is found is known as the *path* to the node. The number of nodes, excluding the root node, that makes up the path to a particular node defines the node's *level*. If two nodes are on the same level and have the same parent node, they are known as *siblings*. The maximum number of levels belonging to a given tree is known as its *height*. Finally, any node on the same level as the tree's height is a *leaf*, a node where both its subtrees are empty.

Applying the definitions

From the tree of Figure 18.2, we see that the node containing Roe is the left child of the node containing `Smith`. Thus, Roe's parent is `Smith`. Also, Roe has one sibling, namely `Williams`. Moreover, both Roe and `Williams` are on level 2 of the tree. The overall tree itself has a height of 3. The nodes containing the names Adams, Lewis, Ryan, Thomas, and Young are all leaves.

Paths

Let us use Figure 18.2 to look at the paths to some of the nodes. The path to the node that contains the name Davis for the tree shown in the figure starts with the root node that contains the name Mason. From this node, the left subtree is taken to the node containing the name Holmes. The left subtree of the Holmes node leads to the node that contains the name Davis.

The path to the node Thomas likewise starts with the root node. The right subtree of the root node is taken in this case, leading to the node that contains

Smith. When the right subtree of the Smith node is taken, it leads to the node that contains the name Williams. When the left subtree of the Williams node is taken, the node being sought, the one that contains the name Thomas, is found as a level-3 node.

The binary search tree

We have described the paths to two different nodes on the tree given in Figure 18.2. We can say that each path describes a search for a given node on the *binary search tree* that Figure 18.2 depicts. The first path describes a search for the node whose *key field* contains the name Davis. The second path describes a search for the node whose key field contains the name Thomas.

> **Binary search tree:** a binary tree where, for each node, (1) its left subtree contains only nodes whose key field is of a lower value than the node's, and (2) its right subtree contains only nodes whose key field is of a higher value than the node's. A search for a node on a BST is usually very efficient.

> **Key field:** as used in a search tree, the field of a node variable that imposes an order on the tree structure. It is also the field used when a given node is probed for a match with some search value.

Paths and probes

The binary search tree is modelled after the binary search algorithm. The key value of each node on the tree can be envisioned as a probe. If a match is not found between the key field of the probe and the search value, a new probe is made on the root node of either the left or the right subtree. When the probe's key is greater than the search value, the new probe is the root node of the left subtree. Hence, all nodes in the right subtree, whose key fields are all greater than the probe's, are eliminated from the candidate of nodes. When the probe's key is less than the search value, the next probe is on the root node of the right subtree.

Successful and unsuccessful searches

A successful search occurs when a match between the specified search value and the key field of a node on the tree is found. In Figure 18.2, the searches for a Davis node and for a Thomas are both successful. An unsuccessful search terminates on an empty tree. Suppose, for example, we want to see if a node containing the name Norton is on the tree. Let us look at the probe values.

Norton is alphabetically after Mason, and so the right subtree is probed. Because Norton comes alphabetically before Smith, the next probe is to the left subtree. Norton is likewise less than Roe. Hence, the left subtree of the Roe node is probed. This subtree is empty, so we conclude that the name Norton is not in the binary search tree of Figure 18.2.

Node Definitions and Operations

We have described the characteristics of a BST in great detail. Now let us define and implement the source code for a node and the operations that can be applied to a node (dereferenced by a pointer variable) on a BST.

Defining a node

A node on a tree has three important fields, a Key field whose value determines a node's place in the tree and the two link fields Left and Right. A node may also contain one or more additional data fields. The source code to define a node on a BST is therefore given as

```
CONST
  NullKey = {some value for a Key to indicate a node that is NIL};
  NullInfo = {if possible to implement, the "info" in a NIL node};
TYPE
  KItemType =    {a data type for which relational operators apply};
  InfoType =     {a data type for all nonkey data fields};
  BSTPtr = ^BSTNode;       {the usual pointer definition}
  BSTNode = RECORD         {a node on the BST}
    Key: KItemType;        {the Key field of the node}
    Info: InfoType;        {data fields other than the Key field}
    Left,                  {subtree where all nodes are less than Key}
    Right:                 {subtree where all nodes are greater than Key}
            BSTPtr
  END;
```

It may not be possible to define a value or set of values for NullInfo, but it is essential to define a value for NullKey. These null values will be used to return a value to the selector operations when the input parameter is a pointer whose value is NIL.

The node operations
From our definitions, we see that we need to implement the following node operations: MakeTNode, KillTNode, GetNodesKey, GetNodesInfo, NodesLeftTree, and NodesRightTree. The first operation constructs a new node, and the second operation disposes of a node and sets the pointer variable to NIL. The other four operations select one of the four fields of the dereferenced pointer to a node.

Source code
If we use the FORWARD directive to implement the interface part of these node primitives, we obtain the following source code:

```
{*                  INTERFACE PART OF BST NODE PRIMITIVES                    *}
PROCEDURE MakeTNode(KeyValue: KItemType; TheInfo: InfoType;
                                    VAR TNode: BSTPtr);            FORWARD;
  {allocates memory to TNode and sets Key and Info fields; sets the
  pointers to the left and right subtrees equal to NIL}
{+                                                                          +}
PROCEDURE KillTNode(VAR TNode: BSTPtr);                           FORWARD;
  {dispose of TNode's memory, then sets TNode to NIL}
{+                                                                          +}
PROCEDURE GetNodesKey(TNode: BSTPtr; VAR TheKey: KItemType);      FORWARD;
  {returns the Key field of the node pointed by TNode; if TNode is NIL,
  returns the value NullKey}
{+                                                                          +}
PROCEDURE GetNodesInfo(TNode: BSTPtr; VAR TheInfo: InfoType);     FORWARD;
  {returns the information contained in the node pointed to by TNode;
  if TNode is NIL, returns the value(s) NullInfo}
{+                                                                          +}
FUNCTION NodesLeftTree(TNode: BSTPtr): BSTPtr;                    FORWARD;
```

{returns the pointer to the left subtree of TNode; if TNode is NIL,
returns NIL}
{+   +}
FUNCTION NodesRightTree(TNode: BSTPtr): BSTPtr;   FORWARD;
  {returns the pointer to the right subtree of TNode; if TNode is NIL,
  returns NIL}
{*   *}

Implementations   The source code to implement each of the (FORWARD-directed) node operations is given below. It is understood that all these node primitives are included in
the operations for the ADT BSTType, the binary search tree abstraction whose
source code we present and develop in Sections 18.2 and 18.3.

```
PROCEDURE MakeTNode {KeyValue: KItemType; TheInfo: InfoType;
                                          VAR TNode: BSTPtr};
  BEGIN
    new(TNode);
    WITH TNode^ DO
      BEGIN
        Key:= KeyValue;
        Info:= TheInfo;
        Left:= NIL;
        Right:= NIL
      END
  END;


PROCEDURE KillTNode {VAR TNode: BSTPtr};
  BEGIN
    IF TNode <> NIL THEN      {guard against disposal of NIL pointer}
      BEGIN
        dispose(TNode);
        TNode:= NIL
      END
  END;


PROCEDURE GetNodesKey {TNode: BSTPtr; VAR TheKey: KItemType};
  BEGIN
    IF TNode <> NIL THEN      {guard against dereference of NIL}
      TheKey:= TNode^.Key
    ELSE
      TheKey:= NullKey
  END;


PROCEDURE GetNodesInfo  {TNode: BSTPtr; VAR TheInfo: InfoType};
  BEGIN
    IF TNode <> NIL THEN      {guard against dereference of NIL}
      TheInfo:= TNode^.Info
```

```
    ELSE
      TheInfo:= NullInfo
  END;

  FUNCTION NodesLeftTree { (TNode: BSTPtr): BSTPtr };
    BEGIN
      IF TNode <> NIL THEN    {guard against dereference of NIL}
        NodesLeftTree:= TNode^.Left
      ELSE
        NodesLeftTree:= NIL
    END;

  FUNCTION NodesRightTree { (TNode: BSTPtr): BSTPtr };
    BEGIN
      IF TNode <> NIL THEN    {guard against dereference of NIL}
        NodesRightTree:= TNode^.Right
      ELSE
        NodesRightTree:= NIL
    END;
```

An algorithm
for selecting
a node's field

In this section and in the previous chapter, we implemented some primitive selector operations to the fields of a node in a linked structure. If you look at all these selectors, you will see that we always guarded against selecting a field of a NIL pointer. In each case, if the pointer value passed in is NIL, some Null value (NullInfo if Info is being selected, NullKey if the Key field is being selected, and NIL if a link field is being selected) is returned. Otherwise, the value assigned to the field is returned.

Algorithm 18.1 describes the code for this primitive selector operation. If the field selected is not a structured variable, you should code a function rather than a procedure.

Algorithm 18.1

{Selecting a field from a node in a linked structure:}
PROCEDURE GetNodeField(ANode: NodePtr; VAR FieldVar: FieldType)
*   IF ANode <> NIL THEN*
*   FieldVar ← ANode^.(variable identifier of field selected)*
*   ELSE*
*   FieldVar ← NullValue*
{end algorithm}

Search Efficiencies

A BST is an ordered structure, constructed (we hope) in such a way that a search through it is very efficient. There are, however, many different ways a tree containing the same nodes can be put together. You might thus expect the effcency of a search through a particular BST to depend upon the way the tree was constructed.

Level

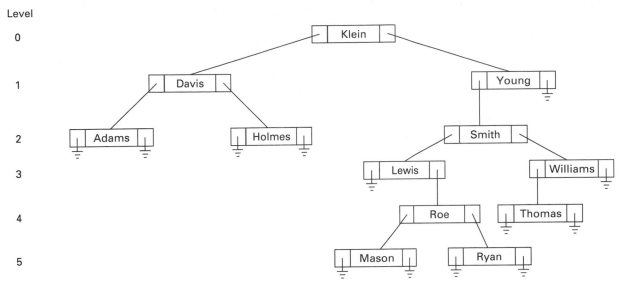

FIGURE 18.4 A BST with the same data as the BST of Figure 18.2.

Equivalent trees

Consider Figure 18.4. Clearly, it satisfies the definition of a BST. If you look at the tree of Figure 18.2 again, you will see that its nodes contain the same names. Thus, a client program that searches for a node containing a given name on either tree will return the same end results. These trees, although internally very different, will return the same search results because they are both binary search trees with nodes containing the same names.

Although a search or an ordered display will return identical results to a client program that uses either tree, the trees of Figure 18.2 and 18.4 are decidedly different. The path to the node Thomas using the tree of Figure 18.2, for example, is found by way of the nodes Mason, Smith, and Williams. Given the tree of Figure 18.4, the path to Thomas is through the nodes Klein, Young, Smith, and Williams.

Adding nodes

If the two trees produce identical search results, why are they so different internally? To answer this question, let us consider how each tree might have been constructed from a client program. First of all, you should remember that a BST, constructed with dynamic variables, is a dynamic variable in which nodes are created as they are needed. A node added to an already existing tree, moreover, has just one unique place for it to be added to the tree. Given these characteristics, it is easy to see how two BST's can become "equivalent" yet so internally different. It all depends upon the order in which the nodes are added to the tree.

The tree of Figure 18.2, for example, might have been constructed from data obtained in the following order: Mason, Holmes, Klein, Smith, Roe, Lewis, Davis, Williams, Adams, Ryan, Thomas, and Young. Note that Mason, the first node to be made, is the root node. The tree of Figure 18.4 could have been built from data entered in this order: Klein, Young, Davis, Adams, Smith, Holmes, Lewis, Roe, Mason, Ryan, Williams, and Thomas. Here, Klein, the first value obtained, is the root node for the entire tree.

Balanced vs. unbalanced trees

Of the two sample trees, the one described by Figure 18.2 is a more efficient structure for a search because it is *balanced*. A tree is balanced if the level of all the leaves is either equal to the tree's height or equal to 1 less than the tree's height. The tree given in Figure 18.4 is not balanced, for its height is 5. The nodes containing Adams and Holmes, both leaves for this tree, are on level 2. We therefore call this tree *unbalanced*.

The efficiency of searching a balanced BST

Suppose we have a balanced BST with M levels. Because the tree is balanced, we know it is holding at least $2^M + 1$ records but not as many as $2^{(M+1)}$ records. If we assume a nearly full balanced tree, we have a structure with $N \approx 2^{M+1}$ records. As there are $M+1$ levels to search through, the worst-case results for a search requires at most $M+1$ probes. Given approximately 2^{M+1} records, we can say that the search for a node in a balanced BST has an efficiency of $O(\log_2(N))$.

FIGURE 18.5 A worst-case binary search tree (BST).

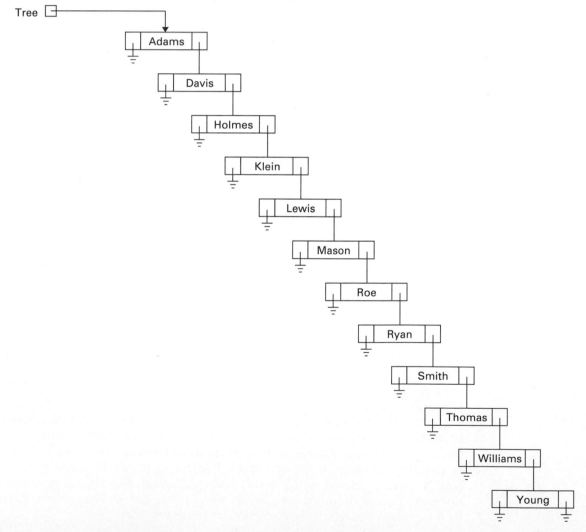

The worst thing that can happen in constructing a BST from a client program is to add the nodes in complete forward or complete reverse order. Such a tree would be of height N, have only one leaf, have all its other nodes with only one assigned child and require that on the average at least half the nodes are searched to return a result. This worst-case tree requires an average of $N/2$ probes to return search results. Hence, a search through this worst-case tree has an efficiency of $O(N)$. If the machine inadvertently constructs this kind of tree, we might as well have used a linear list as the search structure. A worst-case tree, given the nodes of Figures 18.2 and 18.4, is shown as Figure 18.5.

An "average" BST is built from an unordered, apparently random, node-entry sequence. For example, values returned from an RNG and used to build integer nodes on a BST gives us an average BST. It can be shown in more advanced texts that a search for a node through this structure is worse than a search done on a balanced BST by a factor of approximately 1.39.[1] Thus, although an average BST represents a less efficient structure, a search done using it still has an effective efficiency of $O(\log_2(N))$, for it is worse than the best-case possibility by the constant factor 1.39, a value that is functionally independent of N's value.

A balanced BST is a more efficient structure to use than an average tree. However, the operations for keeping the tree balanced is a bit beyond the scope of this text. Thus, we intend to implement operations that do not entail keeping the BST balanced. Hence, we are assuming that the nodes on this structure are added and/or deleted in random fashion.

EXERCISES

Use Figure 18.4 to answer the following questions:

1. List the nodes that are leaves.

2. Which of the following pairs of nodes are siblings?
   (a) Davis and Young
   (b) Holmes and Smith
   (c) Klein and Young
   (d) Lewis and Williams
   (e) Roe and Thomas
   (f) Mason and Ryan

3. How many nodes are in the left and right subtrees of
   (a) the node Klein
   (b) the node Holmes
   (c) the node Smith
   (d) the node Roe

4. Write down the nodes that are the left and right children for each of the nodes given in Exercise 3.

Again, use Figure 18.4 for these questions. Assume that a single node Root has been declared and that the call NodesKey(Root, AName) returns the value 'Klein' to AName. You can also assume that NullKey is equal to ' ', i.e. the null string.

5. What value is returned to the variable AName for each of the following operations:
   (a) GetNodesKey(NodesLeftTree(Root), AName);
   (b) GetNodesKey(NodesLeftTree(NodesLeftTree(Root)), AName);

[1] Kruse, Robert L., *Data Structures And Program Design*, p. 343. Prentice Hall, New Jersey.

(c) GetNodesKey(NodesLeftTree(NodesLeftTree
(NodesLeftTree(Root))), AName);
(d) GetNodesKey(NodesRightTree(Nodes LeftTree(Root)), AName);
(e) GetNodesKey(NodesRightTree(NodesRightTree(Root)), AName);
(f) GetNodesKey(NodesRightTree(NodesLeftTree
(NodesRightTree(Root))), AName);

**Sharpen Your
Synthesis Skills**

6. Assume that Root points to the first node in a BST. Write the code for the function Leftmost. The function returns the variable that points to the leftmost node on a BST that is not NIL. For example, given the tree of Figure 18.4, the following sequence will result in the display of the name Adams:

GetNodesKey(Leftmost(Root), AName);
writeln(AName);

Assume that you can use the value NIL in this procedure. (*Hint:* Write a loop to access Left nodes until NIL is returned.)

7. Suppose the BST we wish to implement consists only of names, as given by the examples of Figure 18.2 and 18.4. Write down the required definitions in order for the BST Node operations headers to be consistent with the BST of names.

18.2 The Binary Search Tree Operations

We have already presented the source code for implementing the nodes and primitive node operations of a BST. In this section, we present the interface part of the BST operations. We conclude the section with two short client procedures that use the operations of a BST.

The Interface Section

We have given you the first part of the interface section for a BST with the node definitions and the node operations. Now we will define the rest of the BST as a structured type with all associated operations that can be applied to a variable of this type.

*A variable of
type* BSTType

We have stated that any given node on a BST points to two other nodes. These two nodes can be seen as dynamic record variables. They can likewise be seen as the root nodes of two different subtrees. This definition is very convenient, for many client processes that use a BST are most readily implemented with a recursive algorithm. A BST variable (a pointer to the root node of a BST that also represents a BST variable) is passed into one of these blocks, the root node (perhaps) is processed, then a subtree is passed into the next block as a recursive call.

If we wish, we can define the BSTType as a pointer to a node. In order to write clearer code, however, we can go one step better by defining the type BST-

Type = BSTPtr. Both identifiers then define a variable that is the pointer to a node on a BST. A variable of type BSTType, however, will be used to represent an entire tree or subtree, whereas a variable of type BSTPtr will represent the pointer to a single node on the BST.

Why two names for one type?

At first, it seems a bit odd to define an alias for a named type, but we do so to differentiate between a reference to a pointer variable that points to (hence represents) a node and a pointer variable that points to (hence represents) an entire tree.

Let us consider the function SearchTNode of the BST, for example. It searches through the tree to find a match between the key value passed in and a node on the tree containing this key value. The result of the search is returned as a pointer to a node. The tree variable itself, however, is also expressed as the same pointer type, one that points to the root node of the tree. We choose the two different identifiers for the same pointer type to clarify the difference between the two references in a parameter list. The identifier BSTPtr is associated with a node on the tree, while BSTType represents an entire tree (subtree) structure.

The headers for the operations

The source code for the interface part of the ADT BST is given below. It is understood that the node primitives are also included in the FORWARD-directed set of operations.

```
{*                INTERFACE PART OF BST OPERATIONS              *}
PROCEDURE MakeTree(VAR Tree: BSTType);                    FORWARD;
  {sets Tree node to Nil, indicating an empty tree}
{+                                                              +}
PROCEDURE AddTNode(KeyValue: KItemType; TheInfo: InfoType;
                   VAR Tree: BSTType; VAR Done: boolean;   FORWARD;
  {adds a node to the tree such that it keeps the logical structure of
  the BST with respect to KeyValue; if KeyValue matches the key
  field of one of the nodes, the node is not added and Done is returned
  as false, otherwise Done is returned as true}
{+                                                              +}
PROCEDURE DeleteTNode(KeyValue: KItemType;
                VAR Tree: BSTType; VAR Done: boolean);  FORWARD;
  {deletes the node from the tree whose Key field matches the value of
  KeyValue; if there is no such node, Done returns false; if, however,
  the item is deleted, Done returns true}
{+                                                              +}
FUNCTION SearchTNode(Tree: BSTType; KeyValue: KItemType): BSTPtr;
                                                          FORWARD;
  {if the Key field of one of the nodes in Tree matches KeyValue, the
  value of this node is returned to SearchTNode; if there is no match,
  the NIL value is returned}
{+                                                              +}
FUNCTION EmptyTree(Tree: BSTType): boolean;            FORWARD;
  {returns true if the value of Tree represents an empty tree}
{*                END INTERFACE PART OF BST                     *}
```

Client Processes

Before we implement the BST operations, let us first develop some client processes. The first process we will develop is a procedure to build a BST of last names from keyboard input. The second process is a procedure to display the contents of the BST in alphabetic order.

The ADT definitions

Before we are ready to pose some problems, we need to define a BST on which to apply the problems. Let us use a structure that is a BST of last names. The value(s) of the `Info` field are immaterial to the procedures we are coding. We are setting up a dummy field variable for `Info` so that the client processes are compatible with the parameter lists of the defining operations of the BSTType.

Source code

The required definitions and declarations for the structure we are using is given in the source code that follows.

```
CONST
  NullKey = '';
  NullInfo = '';   {dummy value for implementation purposes}
TYPE
  KItemType = {STRING TYPE CAPABLE OF HOLDING UP TO 30 CHARACTERS};
  InfoType = {STRING TYPE CAPABLE OF HOLDING UP TO 30 CHARACTERS};
  BSTPtr = ^BSTNode;      {definition for a node on the tree}
  BSTNode = RECORD        {a dynamic variable type that is a node}
    Key: KItemType;       {Key field of the node}
    Info: InfoType;       {dummy field}
    Left,      {root node of subtree with nodes less than Key's value}
    Right:     {root node of subtree with nodes greater than Key's value}
          BSTPtr
  END;
  BSTType = BSTPtr;       {definition for a tree variable}
VAR
  NameTree: BSTType;
```

Client processes

Now that we have some defining operations and have declared the variable `NameTree`, let us solve some problems. For the first problem, we will build a name tree from keyboard input.

Example Problem 18.1

The problem statement

Let us write a procedure to build a BST of last names, suggestive of Figures 18.2 and 18.4. The building process is finished when the user enters a blank line. This value is read in as the value `NullKey` (i.e. a null string). A typical run that builds the tree as shown in Figure 18.2 looks like:

```
          Enter name:  Mason
          Enter name:  Holmes
          Enter name:  Klein
```

```
Enter name:    Smith
Enter name:    Roe
Enter name:    Lewis
Enter name:    Davis
Enter name:    Williams
Enter name:    Adams
Enter name:    Ryan
Enter name:    Thomas
Enter name:    Young
Enter name:
The tree of names has been built.
```

Parameter lists   A typical call to this procedure is coded as BuildNameTree(NameTree), where the variable NameTree is of type BSTType, indicating that this pointer to the root node also represents the overall tree structure. The procedure header is then coded as PROCEDURE BuildNameTree(VAR NameTree: BSTType);

The solution   Given the defining operations, the code for the procedure is straightforward. First, an empty tree is created. Then nodes are added to the tree until the null string is read in, indicating the end of the building process. We thus have the pseudocode description:

> *MakeTree(NameTree)*
> *keyin LastName*
> *WHILE LastName <> NullKey DO*
>   *AddTNode(LastName, NullInfo, NameTree, Success)*
>   *IF NOT Success THEN*
>   *display message that LastName is already on the tree*
>   *keyin LastName*
> *display finished message*

The local variable Success is required to indicate if an attempt is made to add a duplicate name to the tree. Clearly, the variable LastName is of type KItemType. *Source code*   The source code for the procedure is as shown.

```
PROCEDURE BuildNameTree(VAR NameTree: BSTType);
  {out: NameTree -- a BST whose nodes contain the names read in}
  VAR
    LastName: KItemType;    {the last name value read in}
    Success: boolean;       {true if LastName value added to NTree}
  BEGIN
    MakeTree(NameTree);
    write('Enter name:  ');
    readln(LastName);
    WHILE LastName <> NullKey DO
      BEGIN
        AddTNode(LastName, NullInfo, NameTree, Success);
```

```
        IF NOT Success THEN
          writeln(LastName,' is already on the tree.');
        write('Enter name:   ');
        readln(LastName)
      END;
   writeln('The tree of names has been built.')
  END;  ◆
```

Traversals　　　　The next problem requires that we develop an algorithm to display each node on the tree. This kind of processing is known as a *traversal*. In this section, we develop a traversal algorithm to solve the next problem. In Section 18.4, we present some other traversal algorithms that can be used to solve other kinds of problems.

> **Traversal:**　an algorithm performed on a structured variable with links such that a process is carried out on every node that does not represent an empty subtree.

Example Problem 18.2

The problem statement　　　Write a procedure ShowTree that displays the names contained in NameTree in alphabetical order. The call to the procedure is coded as ShowTree(NamesTree). If this procedure is applied to the trees of Figure 18.1 or Figure 18.4, the display looks like

Adams
Davis
Holmes
Klein
Lewis
Mason
Roe
Ryan
Smith
Thomas
Williams
Young

A recursive process　　　If we consider that the traversal must begin at the root node of the tree (i.e. NameTree), we can describe the required sequence of actions with the pseudocode

> *display the Key field of all nodes on the left subtree of NameTree*
> *display the Key field contained in NameTree^, the root node*
> *display the Key field of all nodes on the right subtree of NameTree*

If we use the example of Figure 18.2, the pseudocode implies that we expect all nodes to the left of Mason (i.e. Adams, Davis, Holmes, Klein, and Lewis) to be displayed before the name Mason is. Likewise, the names Roe, Ryan, Smith, Thomas, and Young must be displayed after Mason. Given that the procedure to display the entire tree is initially called by ShowTree (NameTree), the nodes to the left of the root node should be displayed with the call ShowTree (NodesLeftTree (NameTree)). In like manner, the nodes right of the root node can be displayed using the call ShowTree (NodesRight-Tree (NameTree)).

From this reasoning, we see that the psudocode sequence required for ShowTree codes to the following:

```
ShowTree(NodesLeftTree(NameTree));
GetNodesKey(NameTree, LastName);
writeln(LastName);
ShowTree(NodesRightTree(NameTree))
```

The base case

The code we have drafted for ShowTree makes sense, except that we have described a recursive process that, as yet, has no base case. In order for the code to work, we must find a base case, a way for the machine to stop calling ShowTree recursively. We therefore need to find a base case.

Under what circumstances is it ill-advised to call ShowTree again? If you think about it, it makes little sense to display a tree's contents if the tree is empty. Moreover, an empty tree means that there is nothing to display even at the root node, whose value is NIL. This case appears to be the base case we are looking for, so we can describe ShowTree's statement with the pseudocode

IF NOT EmptyTree(NameTree) THEN
execute sequence already described

Proving the algorithm

Clearly if NameTree is empty, no recursive calling is done, and the correct action of no display is carried out. Suppose NameTree represents a leaf. When the recursive call is made to display the keys belonging to the left subtree, nothing is displayed, for this tree is empty. The value of the key contained in this leaf node is then displayed. Then nothing is displayed as a result of the recursive call to display the contents of the empty right subtree.

If NameTree has two nodes where the left subtree is not empty, the value contained in the root node of this subtree is displayed first as a tree that consists of a single leaf. Then the value in the root node of the main tree is displayed. No display occurs as a result of the empty right subtree. If, instead, a two-node tree has an empty left subtree, the root node's key is displayed, followed by a display of the value contained in the leaf that is the right node.

Suppose NameTree has three nodes where the left subtree and right subtree are both leaves. The value contained in the left leaf is displayed first, followed by the value in the root node, and then by the value in the right leaf. We have thus proven that the display works for trivial cases where the tree contains from 0 to 3 nodes.

We have proven some trivial cases, but will our proposed strategy work for a large tree? If we have a nontrivial tree, we know that all keys in the left subtree are displayed before the root's key. Following the display of the root's key, we know that the keys in the nodes to the right of the root node are then displayed. Regardless of how the tree is constructed, each recursive process eventually reduces to one of the trivial cases we have just proven correct. Therefore, the overall process, regardless of the size of the tree, works.

Source code   From the pseudocode and proof of correctness, we obtain the source code for the procedure ShowTree as given.

```
PROCEDURE ShowTree(NameTree: BSTType);
  {in order tree traversal where the key value in each node is
  displayed}
  VAR
    NodesKey: KItemType;
  BEGIN
    IF NOT EmptyTree(NameTree) THEN
      BEGIN
        ShowTree(NodesLeftTree(NameTree));
        GetNodesKey(NameTree, NodesKey);
        writeln(NodesKey);
        ShowTree(NodesRightTree(NameTree))
      END
  END; ◆
```

EXERCISES

Test Your Understanding

1. True or false? The base cases occurs only once for the procedure ShowTree, regardless of the tree's size.

2. Describe the tree's appearance if, during execution of the procedure BuildTree, the names were read in alphabetically.

3. Given the case described by Exercise 2, which of the two recursive calls in ShowTree always results in no display?

4. Suppose the header of BuildTree is coded as

   PROCEDURE BuildTree(NameTree: BSTType);

   What are the run-time consequences of the value call? Why is it ill-advised to code BuildTree with this header?

5. Suppose the header of ShowTree is coded as

   PROCEDURE ShowTree(VAR NameTree: BSTType);

   What are the run-time consequences of the VAR call? Why is it ill-advised to code ShowTree with this header?

Practice Your Analysis Skills

6. Draw the appearance of each BST, given the following sequences of names as read in during the execution of BuildTree:
   (a) Smith, Roe, Mason, Davis, Klein, Holmes, Young.

(b) Roe, Mason, Davis, Klein, Young, Holmes, Smith.
(c) Mason, Holmes, Davis, Klein, Smith, Roe, Young.
(d) Young, Smith, Roe, Mason, Klein, Holmes, Davis.
(e) Young, Roe, Mason, Smith, Holmes, Klein, Davis.

7. Describe what is displayed when the following procedure is executed:

```
PROCEDURE MysteryShow(NameTree: BSTType);
  VAR
    NodesKey: KItemType;
  BEGIN
    IF NOT EmptyTree(NameTree) THEN
      BEGIN
        MysteryShow(NodesRightTree(NameTree));
        GetNodesKey(NameTree, NodesKey);
        writeln(NodesKey);
        MysteryShow(NodesLeftTree(NameTree))
      END
  END;
```

18.3 Implementation of the Binary Search Tree

In this section, we implement the operations of the BST. Once again, we will code the headers for the operations in such a way that we assume they are FORWARD-directed.

The two one-liners

The primitive constructor, MakeTree, returns an empty BST tree. The source code for this primitive constructor is

```
PROCEDURE MakeTree {VAR Tree: BSTType};
  BEGIN
    Tree:= NIL
  END;
```

Note that, once again, an empty structure that consists of nodes and link fields is represented by the NIL value.

Clearly, given the definition of an empty tree, the predicate function that returns *true* if Tree is empty codes to

```
FUNCTION EmptyTree {(Tree: BSTType): boolean};
  BEGIN
    EmptyTree:= Tree = NIL
  END;
```

BST node semantics

Let us recall the requirements of a search algorithm. First of all, there is a candidate structure containing components that can be probed. A given component is probed when the value of its key field is compared with the value of some search key. If there is a match, no further probes are made. If there is no match, a new component in the candidate structure is probed. The new probe is chosen in such a way that it reduces the number of components in the structure that are candidates for a match. If there is no component in the structure that matches the search key, the sequence of probes executed eventually reduces the number of possible candidates for a match to 0.

The binary search tree is modelled after the binary search algorithm. The tree contains candidate values in each node that might match some key value. Initially all nodes on the tree are candidates for a match. The root node contains a key whose value is used for the first probe. If a match occurs with the first probe, the search is finished. If no match occurs, the key value of the root node will be either less than or greater than the search key. If the root's key is less than the search key, the candidates for a match lie in the right subtree. Otherwise they lie in the left subtree.

Regardless of which subtree contains the candidates that remain (note that one subtree is eliminated with each probe), the first probe for the remaining candidates will be a child of the level 0 root node. The other child is the root node for a subtree of candidates that can be eliminated from the search. If a mismatch occurs at level 1 as well, either the left or right subtree of this level 1 node will contain the remaining candidates. Thus, another subtree (on level 2) is chosen that (1) represents the remaining candidates whose key might match the search keys and (2) whose root node contains the key field for the next probe.

Drafting
`SearchTNode`

We can apply the recursive algorithm for a binary search to obtain the pseudocode draft for the function `SearchTNode`. The pseudocode for the function is as follows:

```
FUNCTION SearchTNode(Tree; KeyValue): BSTPtr
    IF EmptyTree(Tree) THEN
        SearchTNode ← NIL              {no more candidates left}
    ELSE
        GetNodesKey(Tree, TheKey)      {get probe value}
        IF TheKey = KeyValue THEN      {successful search so}
            SearchTNode ← Tree         {return the node}
        ELSE IF KeyValue < TheKey      {look to left subtree for probe}
            SearchTNode ← SearchTNode(NodesLeftTree(Tree), KeyValue)
        ELSE                           {look to right subtree for probe}
            SearchTNode ← SearchTNode(NodesRightTree(Tree), KeyValue)
```

The function requires a local variable `TheKey` to hold the value of the key field for the node that is being probed. Note that the variable `Tree` represents both a subtree and a node. The fact that `BSTPtr` and `BSTType` are identical types means that we can use `Tree`'s value to assign a value to the function `SearchTNode` if the search is successful. We can likewise use `Tree` as a parameter of the selectors `GetNodesKey`, `NodesLeftTree`, and `NodesRightTree`. The values returned by calls to the last two functions can, furthermore, be passed into `SearchTNode`.

Source code

The source code for implementing the function `SearchTNode` is shown below.

```
FUNCTION SearchTNode {(Tree: BSTType; KeyValue: KItemType): BSTPtr};
  {documentation}
  VAR
    TheKey: KItemType;      {holds key value of probe}
  BEGIN
    IF EmptyTree(Tree) THEN      {no candidates left, so return NIL}
      SearchTNode:= NIL
    ELSE                              {candidate still remaining}
      BEGIN
        GetNodesKey(Tree, TheKey);     {get probe value}
        IF TheKey = KeyValue THEN  {match found}
          SearchTNode:= Tree
        ELSE IF KeyValue < TheKey   {look to left subtree for probe}
          SearchTNode:= SearchTNode(NodesLeftTree(Tree),KeyValue)
        ELSE                             {look to right subtree for probe}
          SearchTNode:= SearchTNode(NodesRightTree(Tree),KeyValue)
      END
  END;
```

The precondition and postcondition pictures for AddTNode

In order to add a node to the tree, we must first determine if a node on the tree that has the key field already exists. If so, the node is not added. If not, we must find a candidate position for the node to be added. This position should have a parent node and should return a NIL pointer value.

Suppose, for example, the name Stone is added to the tree of Figure 18.2. The value returned of the Parent node has the key field Thomas. This scenario is shown in Figure 18.6. The value Stone will then be the key field of the left child of the Thomas node.

FIGURE 18.6 Preconditions for inserting the name 'Stone' into the BST of Figure 18.1.

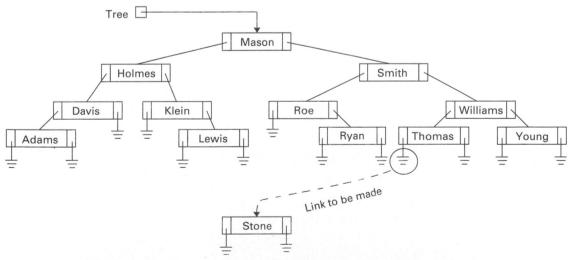

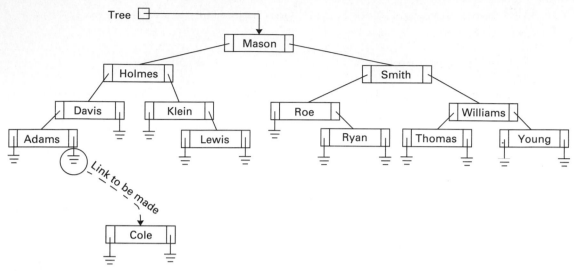

FIGURE 18.7 Preconditions for inserting the name `'Cole'` into the BST of Figure 18.1.

Suppose, instead, the name Cole is added to the tree. Its parent will be the node containing the name Adams. Thus, Cole is added as the right child of the Adams node. This situation is depicted by Figure 18.7.

An auxiliary procedure Search

Regardless of whether a node is added successfully or not, it seems that we need to code an auxillary procedure Search. This procedure should return values to two pointer variables: (1) TNode, a pointer to the node matching the key whose value is to be added, if such a node exists, and (2) Parent, a pointer to the node that is the parent of this first node. If there is no match, the value returned to the TNode is NIL. Unless the tree is empty, the value returned to Parent, the second node, is not NIL.

When Search is called and NIL is returned to the two pointer variables, it means a root node has to be constructed for an empty tree. If NIL is returned to TNode and a value other than NIL is returned to Parent, a node should be added as a child to Parent. If the value returned to TNode is not NIL, a new node should not be added to the tree for there is a node whose key field matches the key field of the node to be added.

Developing AddTNode

Given the requirements of AddTNode, our first draft for this operation is described by the pseudocode

> *Search(Tree, KeyValue, TNode, Parent)*
> *IF NOT EmptyTree(TNode) THEN* {true if KeyValue is a node on the tree}
>   *Done ← false*
> *ELSE*   {KeyValue is not yet a node on the tree}
>   *make and add a new node as a child of Parent*
>   *Done ← true*

Refinements

MakeTNode(KeyValue, TheInfo, SomeNode) where SomeNode is a pointer to the node created in MakeTNode. The value returned to Parent by the procedure Search will determine the link field of Parent that is the third parameter of the call to MakeTNode.

If Parent is returned as NIL, the item is found in the root node of a previously empty tree. Hence, the call MakeTNode(KeyValue, TheInfo, Tree) is appropriate. Otherwise, the value of the parent's key determines whether the third parameter of MakeTNode is Parentˆ.Left or Parentˆ.Right. The first two parameters are always KeyValue and TheInfo.

Source code
From these descriptions, we obtain the source code as given.

```
{*                                                                      *}
PROCEDURE Search(Tree: BSTType; KeyValue: KItemType;
                                VAR TNode, Parent: BSTPtr);
  {in: KeyValue -- key whose match is being sought of nodes in Tree
       Tree -- the BSTType variable
  out: TNode -- node where the match is or will be found
       Parent -- node that is or will be the parent of the matched node}
    BEGIN    END;
{*                                                                      *}
PROCEDURE AddTNode {KeyValue: KItemType; TheInfo: InfoType;
                               VAR Tree: BSTType; VAR Done: boolean};
  VAR
    TNode,       {should be NIL for node to be added to Tree}
    Parent:      {the parent of the candidate node to be added}
              BSTPtr;
    ParentsKey:  {key field of the Parentˆ node}
              KItemType;
  BEGIN
    Search(Tree, KeyValue, TNode, Parent);
    IF NOT EmptyTree(TNode) THEN        {node is already on the tree}
      Done:= false
    ELSE
      BEGIN
        IF EmptyTree(Parent) THEN     {new node will be root of tree}
          MakeTNode(KeyValue, TheInfo, Tree)
        ELSE
          BEGIN
            GetNodesKey(Parent, ParentsKey);
            IF ParentsKey > KeyValue THEN   {new node is left child}
              MakeTNode(KeyValue, TheInfo, Parentˆ.Left)
            ELSE                            {new node is right child}
              MakeTNode(KeyValue, TheInfo, Parentˆ.Right)
          END;
        Done:= true
      END
  END;
```

About the procedure `Search`

The procedure `Search` is a useful auxiliary procedure both for `AddTNode` and `DeleteTNode`. In fact, had we not first coded `SearchTNode`, we would find that we can trivially code the function `SearchTNode` using a call to the procedure `Search` (see Exercise 10).

Developing the procedure `Search`

The source code for `Search` can be implemented if we find an algorithm to obtain the path to a particular node on the tree. If the node does not exist, the value returned to TNode is NIL. If the node does exist, the value returned is not NIL. In any case, the value returned to the variable `Parent` is the next-to-last node on the path to the node being sought. The search is thus for two nodes rather than one.

Let us write the initial draft for the procedure `Search` using an algorithm that is similar to the generic array search algorithm. The initial probe for TNode is the root, and the initial candidate for `Parent` is NIL. Recall that loop control for the generic search algorithm is described by the condition *NOT finished AND NOT found*. With each mismatch, the old TNode value becomes the new candidate for `Parent`, and a new value for TNode is found. From these considerations, we obtain the pseudocode description for the statement of `Search` as

> *Parent ← NIL {the root node has no parent}*
> *TNode ← Tree {the root node is first probe}*
> *GetNodesKey (TNode, NodesKey)*
> *WHILE (more nodes to probe) AND (no match found) DO*
>   *Parent ← TNode   {this TNode is parent node of next probe}*
>   *TNode ← proper subtree, given KeyValue*
>   *GetNodesKey(TNode, NodesKey)*

Refinements

The *proper subtree* to represent the new value for TNode is gotten from the description

> *IF NodesKey > KeyValue THEN*
>   *TNode ← left subtree's root*
> *ELSE*
>   *TNode ← right subtree's root*

The respective subtrees are assigned to TNode with calls to the node primitives `NodesLeftTree` and `NodesRightTree`. There are more nodes to probe if TNode's value does not represent an empty tree. Finally, the source code for the expression *no match found* is `NodesKey <> KeyValue`.

Source code

From all considerations, we obtain the source code for `Search` as

```
PROCEDURE Search(Tree: BSTType; KeyValue: KItemType;
                             VAR TNode, Parent: BSTPtr);
  VAR
    NodesKey: KItemType;   {holds key field value of node being probed}
  BEGIN
    Parent:= NIL;                            {Parent of root is NIL}
    TNode:= Tree;                         {root is first node to probe}
    GetNodesKey(TNode, NodesKey);       {get key value for comparison}
```

```
    WHILE NOT EmptyTree(TNode) AND (NodesKey <> KeyValue) DO
      BEGIN
        Parent:= TNode;         {mismatch, so TNode is a Parent candidate}
        IF NodesKey > KeyValue THEN    {candidates are in left subtree}
          TNode:= NodesLeftTree(TNode)
        ELSE                              {candidates are in right subtree}
          TNode:= NodesRightTree(TNode);
        GetNodesKey(TNode, NodesKey)    {get key value for comparison}
      END
  END;
```

Note that even with a failed search, the final call to GetNodesKey will return the value NullKey rather than attempt an access to one of the "fields" of the NIL pointer.

Planning
DeleteTNode We can use the procedure Search to code DeleteTNode as well. The initial description for the statement of DeleteTNode is given as

> *Search(Tree, KeyValue, Candidate, Parent)*
> *GetNodesKey(Candidate, CandsKey)*
> *IF CandsKey <> KeyValue THEN*
>   *Done ← false*
> *ELSE*
>   *rearrange values on Tree for Candidate removal*
>   *KillTNode(Candidate)*
>   *Done ← true*

If KeyValue is on the tree, the value of the key field of Candidate^ equals Key-Value. Given this condition, the Candidate node, whose value may be changed by the action of *rearrange values on Tree,* is killed and Done is set to true.

The initial draft describes a correct process. If *rearrange values on Tree* is drafted correctly, the following postconditions should be returned: (1) there is no node in Tree with the value of KeyValue, and (2) the Candidate for disposal points to a node that can be deallocated such that the remaining nodes still make up a BST. This latter condition implies that (1) the nodes whose keys are not equal to KeyValue are left on Tree, and (2) these nodes are linked such that Tree is still a BST.

Node disposal
when
Candidate
has an empty
subtree

If Candidate has a parent node, there is more than one node on the tree, and hence, at the very minimum, the link to Candidate from its parent must be bypassed. This operation will return a correct Tree if either the left or right subtree of Candidate is empty. These two scenarios are shown as Figure 18.8(a) and 18.8(b), respectively.

Both figures indicate that one of Parent's children is equal to Candidate, a postcondition returned by the call to Search. The correct link is made with a call to the procedure LinkParent, so that the pseudocode *rearrange values on Tree* refines to the following description:

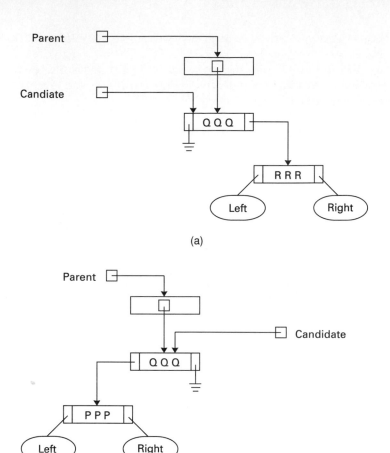

(a)

(b)

FIGURE 18.8 Precondition before call to `LinkParent` when `Candidate` has (a) empty left subtree and (b) empty right subtree.

If EmptyTree(NodesLeftTree(Candidate)) THEN
  LinkParent(Candidate, NodesRightTree(Candidate), Parent, Tree)
ELSE If EmptyTree(NodesRightTree(Candidate)) THEN
  LinkParent(Candidate, NodesLeftTree(Candidate), Parent, Tree)
ELSE
  refine further   *{neither subtree of Candidate is empty}*

The parameter list for `LinkParent`

The header for `LinkParent` is coded as

```
PROCEDURE LinkParent(OldChild, NewChild, Parent: BSTPtr;
                                    VAR Tree: BSTType)
```

The first parameter of `LinkParent` represents the old child of `Parent`, the second parameter represents the new child for the parent node, and the third parameter is the node whose link field will be assigned the value of `NewChild`. `Tree` is passed into the LinkParent block as a VAR call because the statement of Link-Parent will change its structure. A successful call to LinkParent, given an empty left subtree from the Candidate node, will return the postcondition shown as Figure 18.9(a). Given an empty right subtree, the postcondition is described by Figure 18.9(b).

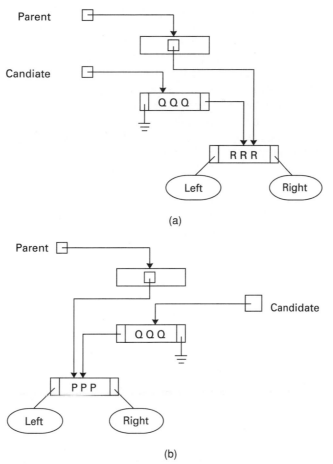

(a)

(b)

FIGURE 18.9 Postcondition returned by LinkParent when Candidate has (a) empty left subtree and (b) empty right subtree.

Developing
LinkParent

When we drew Figures 18.8(a) and 18.8(b), we assumed that Parent was not returned from Search as NIL. If, however, it is given the value NIL, the root node, whose value is equal to the value of Tree, must be deleted. Given this condition, Tree must take on the value of NewChild. Otherwise, the subtree of Parent that is equal to OldChild must be assigned the value of NewChild. Thus, the statement for LinkParent is described by

> *IF Parent = NIL THEN*   {*new root must be assigned*}
> *Tree ← NewChild*

ELSE IF OldChild = NodesLeftTree(Parent) THEN
    Parent^.Left ← NewChild
ELSE
    Parent^.Right ← NewChild

Making refine further into a procedure

    If neither subtree of `Candidate` is empty, a new candidate node for deletion must be found. The data in the old candidate node, moreover, should be removed from the `Tree`. Finally, the tree must retain its structure as a BST. We can simplify the appearance of the `DeleteTNode` block if we code *refine further* as the procedure call `GetNewCandidate`. This procedure will use the values of `KeyValue` and `Candidate` to return a different value to `Candidate`, thereby changing the appearance of `Tree`. The procedure is coded as `GetNewCandidate(Key-Value, Candidate, Tree)` where the first parameter is a value call and the other two parameters are VAR calls.

The required statements for `GetNew-Candidate`

    Let us assume the initial candidate node with two subtrees will not be deleted. A candidate node for deletion will then be a node where one of the subtrees is empty, for we have already solved this problem. Which node must go then? A good choice would be the leftmost node in the right subtree of `Candidate`.

    This node, the new `Candidate` for disposal, holds the lowest key in the subtree. Its `Info` and `Key` fields field can be copied into the `Info` and `Key` fields of the original candidate node (`OldCandidate`), thus preserving the node's information in the tree. Once this value is copied, it is guaranteed that all nodes in the left subtree of `OldCandidate` will have keys with lower values and all nodes in its right subtree will have keys with higher values. Before removing `Candidate`, however, one of the nodes in its `Parent` must be linked to its right subtree. Then the structure will still be a BST, and it will be safe to remove `Candidate` from it.

Pseudocode

    From the verbal description, we find the pseudocode for the statement of `GetNewCandidate` to be

        OldCandidate ← Candidate   {*preserve the old value of Candidate*}
        Search(NodesRightTree(OldCandidate), KeyValue, Dummy, Candidate)
        OldCandidate^.Info ← Candidate^.Info
        OldCandidate^.Key ← Candidate^.Key
        GetNodesKey(Candidate, CandsKey)
        Search(NodesRightTree(OldCandidate), CandsKey, Dummy, Parent)
        If Parent = NIL THEN {*OldCandidate is Parent of Candidate*}
          LinkParent(Candidate, NodesRightTree(Candidate), OldCandidate, Tree)
        ELSE
          LinkParent(Candidate, NodesRightTree(Candidate), Parent, Tree)

    The first call to `Search` returns `Candidate` as the node whose key has the lowest value in the right subtree. The second call to `Search` returns the parent node of `Candidate` to `Parent`. Then `LinkParent` is called using either `OldCandidate` or `Parent` as the third parameter.

Source code

    The source code for the procedure `DeleteTNode`, including all auxiliary procedures other than `Search`, is given below. As usual, we are coding `DeleteTNode` as a FORWARD-directed procedure.

```
{*                                                                        *}
PROCEDURE LinkParent(OldChild, NewChild, Parent: BSTPtr;
                                          VAR Tree: BSTType);

  BEGIN
    IF Parent = NIL THEN        {replacement is to Tree's root node}
      Tree:= NewChild
    ELSE IF OldChild = NodesLeftTree(Parent) THEN
      Parent^.Left: = NewChild {replacement is to Parent's left child}
    ELSE
      Parent^.Right:= NewChild {replacement is to Parent's right child}
  END;
PROCEDURE GetNewCandidate(KeyValue: KItemType; VAR Candidate: BSTPtr; +}
                                          VAR Tree: BSTType);
  VAR
    Dummy,              {dummy parameter for call to Search}
    Parent,             {parent node to new value for candidate}
    OldCandidate:       {original Candidate, its Info field is reassigned}
                        BSTPtr;
    CandsKey:           {key field of new candidate}
                        KItemType;
  BEGIN
    OldCandidate:= Candidate;
    Search(NodesRightTree(OldCandidate), KeyValue, Dummy, Candidate);
    OldCandidate^.Info:= Candidate^.Info;
    OldCandidate^.Key:= Candidate^.Key;
    GetNodesKey(Candidate, CandsKey);
    Search(NodesRightTree(OldCandidate), CandsKey, Dummy, Parent);
    IF Parent = NIL THEN
      LinkParent(Candidate, NodesRightTree(Candidate), OldCandidate, Tree)
    ELSE
      LinkParent(Candidate, NodesRightTree(Candidate), Parent, Tree)
  END;
{+                                                                        +}
PROCEDURE DeleteTNode {KeyValue: KItemType; VAR Tree: BSTType;
                                          VAR Done: boolean}            ;
  VAR
    Candidate,          {pointer to candidate node for deletion}
    Parent:             {pointer to parent of the candidate node}
                        BSTPtr);
    CandsKey:           {key value stored in the candidate node}
                        KItemType;
  BEGIN
    Search(Tree, KeyValue, Candidate, Parent);
    GetNodesKey(Candidate, CandsKey);
    IF CandsKey <> KeyValue THEN       {node to delete is not in tree}
      Done:= false
```

```
    ELSE
      BEGIN
        IF EmptyTree(NodesLeftTree(Candidate)) THEN
          LinkParent(Candidate, NodesRightTree(Candidate), Parent, Tree)
        ELSE IF EmptyTree(NodesRightTree(Candidate)) THEN
          LinkParent(Candidate, NodesLeftTree(Candidate), Parent, Tree)
        ELSE
          GetNewCandidate(KeyValue, Candidate, Tree);
        KillTNode(Candidate);
        Done:= true
      END
  END;
```

EXERCISES

Test Your
Understanding

1. Under what condition(s) will the Search procedure return NIL to both Parent and TNode?

2. The loop control expression for a search algorithm is described as NOT finished AND NOT found. What expression describes the finished condition and what expression describes the found condition for the loop coded inside Search?

3. Will Search still be correct if we change the control expression of the WHILE loop to (NodesKey <> NullKey) AND (NodesKey <> KeyValue)? Explain your answer.

4. In GetNew Candidate, the first call to Search returns NIL to Dummy and the second call returns the value of Candidate to Dummy. Explain why.

5. Why is it incorrect to call MakeTNode from the procedure AddTNode using Make-TNode(KeyValue, TheInfo, NodesLeftTree(Parent))? How will the computer respond to this call?

Practice Your
Analysis Skills

6. Suppose an initial tree is built by the following sequence of names: Smith Jones Jacobsen Kelly Williams Mix Lincoln Vroom Young Thomas Todd West
Sketch the tree.

7. Let the following sequence of operations be done on the tree of Exercise 6:

```
        AddNode('Melman', NullInfo, Tree, Success);
        DeleteTNode('Thomas', NullInfo, Tree, Success);
        DeleteTNode('Smith', NullInfo, Tree, Success);
        AddTNode('Coe', NullInfo, Tree, Success);
        AddTNode('Jones', NullInfo, Tree, Success');
        DeleteTNode('Lincoln', NullInfo, Tree, Success);
```

Draw the tree's appearance after each operation is carried out.

Sharpen Your
Implementation
Skills

8. Suppose a node with a given key is to have its Info field changed. Its key field should not be changed. Write the code for the procedure ChangeNodesInfo(KeyValue, NewInfo, Tree) using only the tree and node operations we coded. (*Hint:* Use DeleteTNode and AddTNode.)

9. Use the operations of the BST abstraction to write a statement that returns the rightmost node in the left subtree of STree, a node whose key value is equal to AKey, to the BSTPtr variable RightMost.

10. Write the code for the function SearchTNode, using the auxiliary procedure Search.

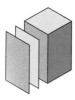

18.4 Traversal Algorithms

In Section 18.2, we developed an algorithm to carry out an in order display of the nodes contained in a BST. We used a strategy where the left subtree of each node was visited first, then the node, and then the right subtree. In this section, you will learn the other two ways to traverse a binary tree. The case study uses these two traversal algorithms to first build and then evaluate a tree that represents an arithmetic expression.

The Three Traversal Algorithms

The three algorithms for traversing a binary tree are *in order* (*LNR*), *preorder* (*NLR*), and *Postorder* (*LRN*). All three traversal algorithms are recursive. The stopping case for each algorithm occurs when an attempt is made to traverse an empty tree.

In order traversal (LNR):   a traversal of a binary tree where the left subtree is visited first, then the root node, and finally the right subtree.

Preorder traversal (NLR):   a traversal of a binary tree where the root node is visited first, then the left subtree, and finally the right subtree.

Postorder traversal (LRN):   a traversal of a binary tree where the left subtree is visited first, then the right subtree, and finally the root node.

Pseudocode descriptions

The pseudocode descriptions for the three algorithms are as follows:

Algorithm 18.2

```
{In order traversal of a binary tree:}
PROCEDURE Traverse(Root)
   IF Root <> NIL THEN
      Traverse(Root^.Left)              {visit all nodes of left subtree}
      Visit(Root)
      Traverse(Root^.Right)             {visit all nodes of right subtree}

   Traverse(Tree)
   {end algorithm}
```

Algorithm 18.3

{Preorder traversal of a binary tree:}
PROCEDURE Traverse(Root)
  IF Root <> NIL THEN
    Visit(Root)
    Traverse(Root^.Left)   *{visit all nodes of left subtree}*
    Traverse(Root^.Right)   *{visit all nodes of right subtree}*

Traverse(Tree)
{end algorithm}

Algorithm 18.4

{Postorder traversal of a binary tree:}
PROCEDURE Traverse(Root)
  IF Root <> NIL THEN
    Traverse(Root^.Left)   *{visit all nodes of left subtree}*
    Traverse(Root^.Right)   *{visit all nodes of right subtree}*
    Visit(Root)

Traverse(Tree)
{end algorithm}

The procedure Visit uses the value(s) pointed to by Root to carry out some action. To keep each description as general as possible, we have used an explicit expression for the left and right subtrees rather than a call to some node selector function.

Using one of the algorithms

If you want to kill a binary tree without creating garbage, the simplest solution is to use a postorder traversal algorithm. Each node visited is deleted. We formalize the application of the algorithm with the Example Problem that follows.

Example Problem 18.3

The problem statement

Using the primitive node operations given in Section 18.1, write a procedure Kill-Tree that disposes of all nodes on a BST, returning an empty tree.

The solution

The idea is to destroy the tree without creating any garbage. The simplest solution is to use a postorder traversal, disposing of each root node that is visited. Figure 18.10 shows the order in which each node is destroyed, given the 12-node tree of Figure 18.2. The algorithm works because the last node to be deallocated on any tree is the root node, so no links are prematurely broken.

Source code

The source code for the procedure, using postorder traversal, is as shown.

```
PROCEDURE KillTree(VAR Tree: BSTType);
   {returns an empty BST with proper disposal of all nodes}
   BEGIN
     IF NOT EmptyTree(Tree) THEN
```

```
BEGIN
  KillTree(NodesLeftTree(Tree));
  KillTree(NodesRightTree(Tree));
  KillTNode(Tree)
END
END; ◆
```

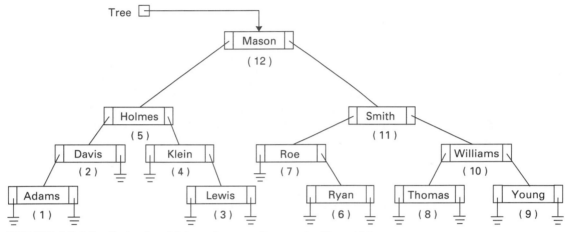

FIGURE 18.10 Order in which nodes are disposed of by `KillTree(Tree)`.

Expression Trees

The arithmetic operations to add, subtract, multiply, and divide all require one operation and two operands. Any expression formed using only these four operations always requires two operands for the application of each operation. This fact suggests the possibility of storing the value of an expression in a structure known as a *binary expression tree*.

> **Binary expression tree:** a binary tree representing an expression made up of binary operators and operand values. Each node in the tree is either an operator with two children or an operand value with no children.

A typical expression tree

Any given arithmetic expression whose operands are all known values is unique. This property suggests that any expression has a unique expression tree. Figure 18.11, for example, shows the tree that represents the integer expression (5 * 3) DIV (4 - 1). (We are using the slash to represent the integer DIV operator.)

Note how each of the 7 nodes on the tree also represents the value of an expression. The four nodes on the bottom simply represent operand values that are integer literals. The node containing '*' is the root node for the subtree that represents the expression 5 * 3. Likewise, the node containing '-' represents the expression 4 - 1. The node containing '/' (the operator DIV) represents the overall expression.

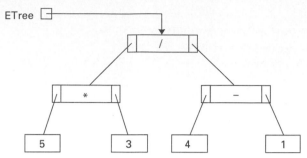

ETree

/

* −

5 3 4 1

FIGURE 18.11 A binary expression tree of integer operations.

Polish notation

Recall from Chapter 17 that an arithmetic expression written in RPN does not require parentheses. In RPN, the operator follows the two operands. It is also possible to write an expression in Polish notation (PN) where the operator *precedes* the operands. Our sample expression, for example, is written in PN as / * 5 3 − 4 1, where we have used the slash to indicate the DIV operation as it applies to integer values. By applying the rules for evaluation in PN, the original expression is equivalent to / 15 − 4 1. This expression then becomes /15 3, and the final application gives us the value 5. We plan to use Polish notation and two of the three traversal algorithms to solve the problem posed by the case study.

CASE STUDY 18.1

The problem statement

Let us write a program to evaluate an integer expression written in Polish notation using an expression tree. As the expression is read in, the computer will build an expression tree. The expression terminates with the input of the <eoln> character. Then the computer evaluates and prints the value of the expression by traversing the expression tree.

In order to make the coding simpler, we will assume that (1) each integer operand is a single-digit positive integer, (2) the DIV operation is represented by a slash and the MOD operation is represented by a backslash (\), and (3) all PN expressions read in are well-formed.

Sample runs

Given these assumptions, we have the following three typical runs:

```
/ * 5 3 - 4 1<eoln>                    {  (5*3) DIV (4-1)  }
The value of the expression is 5.

\ + * 6 3 2 - 9 1<eoln>               {  (6*3+2) MOD (9-1)  }
The value of the expression is 4.

/ + * * 3 8 8 * 2 8 + * 6 8 4<eoln>   {  (3*8*8 + 2*8) DIV (6*8 + 4)  }
The value of the expression is 4.
```

Before the <eoln> is pressed, the computer is building the expression. Then the computer displays the string constant 'The value of the expression is'.

In each sample run, the display of the `integer` value on the second line results from a call to the function `TreesValue(Root)`, a postorder traversal algorithm that evaluates the expression tree.

A solution structure

The simplifications permit us to use the following source code for the implementation of the variable `ETree`:

```
TYPE
  NodePtr = ^ExpressionNode;
  ExpressionNode = RECORD
    Token: char;        {either an operator or a char value in '0'..'9'}
    Operand1,           {points to expression implied by left subtree}
    Operand2:           {points to expression implied by right subtree}
          NodePtr
  END;
VAR
  ETree:  NodePtr;
```

If the value of Token is a digit, it represents an `integer` value. Given one of these values, the other two fields, representing operands, are left unassigned. If Token represents an operator, values must be assigned to `Operand1` and `Operand2`.

Coding the main block

The source code for the main block of the program, `EvaluateTree`, is given below.

```
PROGRAM EvaluateTree(input, output);
  {The program first builds an expression tree from user input.  The
  expression to be evaluated must be entered in PN.  The tree is built
  using an NLR (preorder) traversal algorithm.  Once the tree is built,
  it is evaluated using LRN (postorder) traversal.}
  TYPE
    NodePtr = ^ExpressionNode;
    ExpressionNode = RECORD
      Token: char;        {either an operator or char in '0'..'9'}
      Operand1,           {points to left expression subtree}
      Operand2:           {points to right expression subtree}
            NodePtr
      END;
  VAR
    ETree: NodePtr;
  {*                                                                *}
  PROCEDURE MakeTree(ETree: NodePtr);
    {builds tree from input PN expression using code suggestive of NLR
    traversal}
    BEGIN  {        }  END;
  {*                                                                *}
  FUNCTION TreesValue(ETree: NodePtr): integer;
    {returns value of tree using LRN node traversal}
```

```
   BEGIN    {         }   END;
{*                                                                      *}
BEGIN
  new(ETree);
  MakeTree(ETree);
  readln;                        {clear input line for display}
  write('The value of the expression is ');
  writeln(TreesValue(ETree):1)
END.
```

The variable ETree points to the root node of the expression. Memory must be allocated to this variable before the call to the procecure MakeTree. It is essential that ETree be passed into this procedure as a value call, for it must still point to the root node of the entire tree when MakeTree is exited.

Before we derive the code for MakeTree and TreesValue, let us appeal to your intuition regarding the documentation we have included. If the expression is read in using PN, an operator precedes the two expressions it requires. The logical choice in building the tree, then, would be to build the root node first and then the two subtrees representing the operands. The tree is thus built using preorder traversal.

In order to evaluate an expression that uses an operation, the values of the two operands must be known first. The suggested approach here is thus an LRN traversal, where the operand values implied by the left and right nodes must be found before the operation can be applied.

Drafting MakeTree's sequence   When a character value Ch is read in, it represents either an operator or a single-digit number. Either of these values is assigned to the Token field of the expression being pointed to. If the token represents an operator, it means that a left and right subtree must be built. Any blank character read in is skipped. When <eoln> is identified, the value returned to Ch is a blank, signifying that no more nodes are to be added to the tree. From this prose description, we can describe the required sequence of MakeTree with the pseudocode

> *SkipBlanks(Ch)*   {*returns blank when eoln function is true*}
> *IF Ch <> ' ' THEN*
>   *WITH ETree^ DO*
>   *Token ← Ch*
>   *IF Token is an operator THEN*
>   *make left subtree*
>   *make right subtree*

The boolean expression *Token is an operator* is readily coded using a set membership expression. The two subtrees are made using recursive calls to Make-Tree. We can describe either *make subtree* sequence with the pseudocode

> *new(Subtree)*   {*Subtree is either Operand1 or Operand2*}
> *MakeTree(Subtree)*

The source code for `SkipBlanks` is straightforward. Thus, we can use the pseudocode descriptions we have drafted to obtain the source code for the procedure `MakeTree` as shown.

```
{*                                                                          *}
PROCEDURE SkipBlanks(VAR Ch: char);
  {Skips all blank characters from keyboard input. The procedure
  returns a blank character to Ch only if eoln evaluates to true.}
  BEGIN
    Ch:= ' '; {for loop entry}
    WHILE NOT eoln AND (Ch = ' ') DO
    read(Ch)
  END;
{+                                                                          +}
PROCEDURE MakeTree(ETree: NodePtr);
  {An expression tree is created from keyboard input with Root as the
  root node. Subtrees whose token values represent an integer value
  will have no values assigned to the fields Operand1 and Operand2.}
  VAR
    Ch: char;        {candidate for Token field}
  BEGIN
    SkipBlanks(Ch);
    IF Ch <> ' ' THEN                          {not at eoln, so more to build}
      WITH ETree^ DO
        BEGIN
          Token:= Ch;                          {set Token value of present root}
          IF Token IN ['*','/','\','+','-']  THEN          {operator so}
            BEGIN
              new(Operand1);                              {make left subtree}
              MakeTree(Operand1);
              new(Operand2);                              {make right subtree}
              MakeTree(Operand2)
            END
        END
  END;
{*                                                                          *}
```

Suppose a given node on an expression tree is an operator. In order to evaluate the expression implied by this node, the value of each of the two operand subtrees must be found first. The root's operation is then applied to the two values returned from the subtrees. Given a node that is an operator, we can then find the tree's value using code that satisfies the description

LeftOperand ← evaluation of left subtree expression
RightOperand ← evaluation of right subtree expression
Trees Value ← application of operation to left and right operands

Note that we have just described the sequence for LRN traversal, excluding any required actions for the base case.

The base case for the LRN traversal in this problem occurs when a node represents a simple numeric operand. This case is handled with a call to the function `NumericValue`, using Token as the single parameter. The pseudocode for `TreesValue`, therefore, is given as

> *WITH ETree^ DO*
>   *IF Token represents an integer literal THEN*
>   *TreesValue ← NumericValue(Token)*
>   *ELSE*
>   *LeftOperand ← TreesValue(Operand1)* {*get left operand expression*}
>   *RightOperand ← TreesValue(Operand2)* {*get right operand expression*}
>   *TreesValue ← ExpressionValue(LeftOperand, RightOperand, Token)*

The function `ExpressionValue` uses the two operands and the token to return a value to the representative binary expression.

The source code for the functions `ExpressionValue` and `Numeric-Value` is readily found. The source code for the function `TreesValue` is therefore given as shown.

```
{*                                                                  *}
FUNCTION ExpressionValue(Operand1, Operand2: integer;
                                    Operator: char): integer;
{returns value to numeric operation where Operand1 and Operand2
represent numeric operands and Operator represents the operation to be
applied}
 BEGIN
   CASE Operator OF
      '*': ExpressionValue:= Operand1 * Operand2;
      '/': ExpressionValue:= Operand1 DIV Operand2;
      '\': ExpressionValue:= Operand1 MOD Operand2;
      '+': ExpressionValue:= Operand1 + Operand2;
      '-': ExpressionValue:= Operand1 - Operand2
   END   {CASE}
 END;
{+                                                                  +}
FUNCTION NumericValue(Ch: char): integer;
  {returns integer number represented by value of Ch}
  BEGIN
    NumericValue:= ord(Ch) - ord('0')
  END;
{+                                                                  +}
FUNCTION TreesValue(ETree: NodePtr): integer;
  {documentation}
  VAR
```

```
      LeftOperand,          {first of the two operands}
      RightOperand: integer; {other operand}
  BEGIN
    WITH ETree^ DO
      IF Token IN ['0'..'9'] THEN
        TreesValue:= NumericValue(Token)
      ELSE
        BEGIN
          LeftOperand:= TreesValue(Operand1);
          RightOperand:= TreesValue(Operand2);
          TreesValue:= ExpressionValue(LeftOperand, RightOperand, Token)
        END
  END;
{*                                                                  *} ◆
```

EXERCISES

Test Your Understanding

1. Will an in-order traversal work for the procedure KillTree? Assume that a visit to a node is a call to KillTNode. Explain your answer.

2. True or false? It is possible to build a binary tree using either an LRN or an LNR traversal strategy. Explain your answer.

3. Why is it so much easier to build an expression tree when data is entered using Polish notation?

4. Any traversal out of order on a given tree makes up a "nonsense" traversal. Thus either a preorder or postorder traversal on any BST is a nonsense traversal. Write down the LRN and NLR nonsense traversals that display the values in the nodes of the BSTs shown in Figures 18.1 and 18.4. Should the display be the same in each case? Why is the display the same for an LNR traversal even though the trees are different?

5. Suppose a traversal described by RNL is implemented for a BST. Does this traversal represent nonsense? Explain.

Practice Your Analysis Skills

6. Draw the expression tree and evaluate it for the following sequences:
   (a) 7 3 *
   (b) - * 5 2 3
   (c) / + 6 4 - 6 4
   (d) + - * 7 2 / 9 3 5
   (e) * 8 / \ \ / 9 3 2 2 - 5 3
   (f) / + * * 3 8 8 * 2 8 + * 6 8 4

Program Testing Hints

If the nodes of an ADT have two links, there are clearly more ways you can err in coding the abstract operations required to solve the problem. In this section, we give hints to help (1) keep the design and logic errors down to a minimum (we hope to zero), (2) choose test data in such a way that each operation is thoroughly tested, and

(3) avoid (or recognize and correct) some of the common errors dealing with tree manipulations.

Summarizing the implementation strategy for BST

Note how our implementation strategy for the BST unit follows the practices recommended in the previous chapter. First, we implemented some node operations. One operation creates a new node and fills in the data fields, the other operation kills a node. The selectors to the link fields give a client access to all nodes in the list, and selectors are coded for all data fields. The link fields of a new node are set to *NIL*, a node just killed is returned as the NIL value, and each selector guards against the possibility of NIL as a parameter.

FIGURE 18.12 The leftmost node of the subtree SRoot.

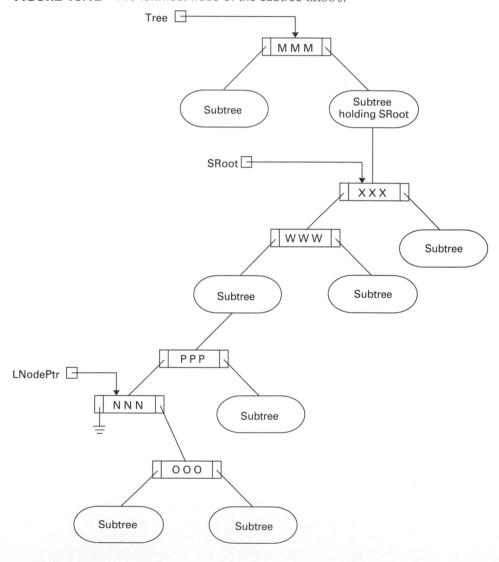

Next, we did the tree operations, using the node operations when possible. All operations, both node and tree, are "pure," that is, they only do a single construction, selection, or predication. Because the key field plays prominently in the definition of a BST structure, we include a Key field as a separate field variable from the fields of Info. Each operation is coded to preserve the logical integrity of a BST. Finally, although the unit has few operations, they still are sufficient to make the unit complete.

Desk tracing

We remind you once again to draw pictures when you are planning operations that use linked variables. It is particularly useful to draw the precondition and postcondition pictures for some operation you want to implement. If the problem is very tricky, you may want to draw a picture for each operation in the implementation logic as it is carried out. This technique is an invaluable aid in desk tracing pointer operations.

How much to draw?

Note that with a large structure, you should not have to draw *every* node to see what is happening. Simply use the logical properties of the structure to draw the picture you need. For example, if you want to show the leftmost node (lowest value) in a subtree, Figure 18.12 is certainly adequate. Tree represents the tree structure, SRoot is the subtree whose leftmost node you need to find and LNodePtr^ is the leftmost node.

This picture works regardless of whether Tree has 5, 50, 500, or even 5000 nodes, as long as SRoot^ itself is not the leftmost node. If it is, you must draw another picture to take this case into account. Even though you should not have to draw every node on a tree, you should, if necessary, be able to draw a picture to cover each case that represents a viable precondition for some operation you wish to implement.

Testing Strategies

In practice, exhaustive testing is hopeless even with a BST that has just 10 nodes (there are 20! different trees that can be built with these nodes). In theory, exhaustive testing can be achieved if you choose your test data carefully. Simply choosing good values, however, does not guarantee "smart testing." There are other practices you must follow to help you identify any errors that may show up during the process of testing.

PROGRAM DESIGN RULE 18.1

The number of combinations to ensure exhaustive testing for links to the NIL pointer from any given node is two to the power of the number of link fields.

Program Design Rule 18.1 tells you how many different empty tree cases (2^2) you must consider if you are to test all NIL cases from the root node of a nonempty subtree of a binary tree. The rule helps you remember that each of the two links from a node in a BST can be set to NIL or point to another subtree. Your testing (both logical and on-line) must, therefore, take four cases into account, namely (1) a leaf node, (2) a node with an empty left subtree, (3) a node with an empty right subtree, and (4) a node where neither subtree is empty.

The same sort of strategies for testing (both on-line and off) applies to binary trees as they do to linear structures. First, test the operations using an empty tree. Then use some very simple (1, 2 and 3 nodes) nonempty trees. Program Design Rule 18.1 helps ensure that the testing on these "near trivial" cases is exhaustive. The rule reminds you to test how each operation handles (1) a tree with just one node, (2) a tree with a left subtree that has one node and an empty right subtree, (3) a tree with an empty left subtree and one node for its right subtree, and (4) a tree with one node for its left subtree and one for its right subtree.

Once you feel that the trivial cases work, you can get venturesome. Before you start, it might be a good idea to write a driver menu for addition, deletion, searching and display, and traversal of the tree. You can then use this menu to test the operations with further operations.

You will still want to work "small." Build a tree with perhaps seven nodes and then apply some delete operations. Certainly, you must try to add a node that is already part of the tree and likewise try to delete a node that is not part of the tree. Here you are looking for that "random" error caused by some case you may have overlooked in coding.

Write down the operations on a piece of paper as you apply them. Also, be sure to call the traversal procedure after every third or fourth operation. Put a star next to the last operation called if the traversal produces the expected results. That way if the traversal produces unexpected results, you have a sequence of operations that led to the error.

Certain patterns using the "four possibilities" rule for a BST must be tested to ensure that all cases are covered. You should, for example, apply DeleteTNode to (1) a leaf, (2) nodes with one empty subtree, (3) a node with no empty subtree whose right subtree has an empty left subtree, and (4) the same scenario as (3) but one whose left subtree is not empty. Each of these patterns is determined by applying Program Design Rule 18.1.

It goes without saying that you apply the saneness approach to testing. You do not need a large tree to find problems with source code. Moreover, a small tree allows you to *draw a picture* after each operation. Then you will know the key value of the node to delete when applying the tests for the different possibilities. Without these pictures, you do not really know what is happening when you run across a bug.

As soon as you find a bug, moreover, *stop further testing*. The fact that there is a bug means that the test variable you are using no longer satisfies the properties of the abstraction you are trying to implement. The next thing to do is either rebuild a structure that you know is correct and try to reproduce the bug or log off and try to fix the bug. Do not, under any circumstances, apply a testing strategy that supports GIGO operations, for you will gain no further information about the error you are trying to identify and fix.

Some Final Words

Pointers are tricky, but also lots of fun. Do not be discouraged with your initial errors. Just recheck the semantics of the source code, apply more testing, and (above all) draw more pictures. Remember, too, that experience is the best teacher. The more you practice using dynamic variables and pointers, the better you will become with them.

Pointer semantics

Pointers give you a "semantic blank check" for any ADT you wish to implement because you can define a pointer to point to any kind of structure that Pascal allows. This property is both a blessing and a curse. It is a blessing because you can build virtually any structure that is possible to build with pointers. It is a curse because you can make a semantic mess with pointers to such an extent that your code becomes unreadable.

As you work with any given pointer variable, then, always keep its purpose in mind. Remember that when you apply assertion testing to a proposed algorithm, you are actually checking the algorithm for semantic consistency. The *Left* field of some node on a BST, for example, must always, point to a node whose key field is smaller. Regardless of how you change the tree's appearance with add and/or delete operations, this property must be true for all nodes on the tree that are not empty.

A word about experimentation

Avoid using the machine to experiment with *algorithms* you need to code in the hope that they will work. By all means, experiment to see how your machine handles some "unusual" operations with pointers. You do these experiments, however, solely to find out the properties of the machine and never as a hope that "perhaps this idea will work." Clarity of thought and a logical follow-through with your code will save hours of unnecessary work that come with the hit-or-miss approach.

The best debugging strategy

Because you cannot see pointer values, bugs caused by misusing pointers can be very difficult to find. Prevention of bugs using sound logic is the best "debugging" strategy. Test and retest the logic of the source code before putting it into the machine. You will find that there is nothing more satisfying than having those procedures using pointers work on the first try

On practice

Regardless of what your personal experiences may be, do not be discouraged. It takes a good deal of practice to gain facility with pointers. Moreover, each bug you find and fix will give you that much more experience using these types. Practice may not make perfect (What is "the perfect program?"), but it will get you fairly close.

EXERCISES

Test Your Understanding

1. How many NIL cases should be considered for a node with 3 link fields?

2. List all the different possibilities for your answer to Exercise 1.

3. State two reasons why errors with pointers are more difficult to deal with than errors made with other variable types.

4. How do we desk trace a sequence of code that uses link variables?

5. You are given a BST and want to work with the rightmost node in a given subtree. Draw the picture of the tree using Tree^ as the root node, SRoot^ as the subtree whose rightmost node you want, and RNode^ as the rightmost node of SRoot^.

Practice Your Analysis Skills

6. Suppose we change the header of AddTNode to the following:

```
PROCEDURE AddTNode(AnItem: ItemType; Tree: BSTType; VAR Done: boolean);
```

The statement part of AddTNode remains unchanged. This code works for all but one very important circumstance. What is the one precondition that will result in an incorrect postcondition with this header?

7. In the BST procedure LinkParent, a test is made to see if Parent is equal to the NIL pointer. What can you say about the tree's appearance (clearly, the root node is to be deleted) if the test returns true? (*Hint*: Study the preconditions for each call to LinkParent.)

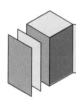

REVIEW AND EXERCISES

A *tree* is a structured variable containing nodes that can all be accessed by way of the *root* node. A *binary* tree, starting with the single root node on *level 0,* contains some data and two link variables that point to a *left child* node and a *right child* node. These two *level 1* nodes, *siblings* of the single root node that represents the tree, are in turn root nodes for the left and right *subtrees*. Each node on a subtree likewise contains a data field and two link fields to its children.

At some point in this structure, there is a node that points to an *empty* subtree. An empty subtree, by convention, is assigned the NIL value. A *leaf* on a tree is a node where both its children represent empty subtrees. A lowest level node on a tree that is not empty is always a leaf. During the course of a program run, a tree's appearance may change. The lowest level on the tree during any given time that has no subtrees defines the tree's *height* at that time.

The *binary search tree* is an ADT where one of the fields holds a *key value* used to define the tree's logical structure. The left subtree of any node on a BST contains only (1) nodes with key values less than the key value of the subtree's root node and/or (2) empty subtrees. The right subtree contains only nodes whose key value is greater than the root node's and/or empty subtrees. The BST is a structure such that there is just one unique *path* to any given node that exists in the tree. The nodes on the path to this one node are *visited* in a manner that mimics the binary search algorithm.

The minimum set of node operations to guarantee that all information held in the BST is accessible are selectors to the data fields of a single node and selectors to the left and right subtrees of a single node. A NIL input value is dealt with by returning a predefined *null value* to a given data field selector. A NIL value is returned to either link selector when the input pointer value is NIL. To complete the set of node operations, we have (1) the primitive constructor that creates a node with values assigned to the data fields and whose subtrees are empty, and (2) a constructor that disposes of the input node variable and returns it as a NIL value.

There is, as usual, a set of operations applicable to the BST variable as a whole. The add constructor for a BST type variable adds a node, given some data that includes a key value, in such a way that the BST property is kept. Likewise, the delete constructor removes a node with a key value that matches the value specified in such a way that the integrity of the BST variable is maintained. The search function is a selector to the node whose key value matches the input key's. If there is no match, NIL is returned. Finally, the unit has a primitive constructor that assigns an empty tree to a BST variable and a predicate to test whether the input BST variable is an empty tree.

A *traversal* of a tree is a process that visits all nodes on a tree, performing some kind of operation on (using the values in) the node visited. The BST traversal algorithm, which visits the nodes in order from lowest to highest key value, is an *inorder* or *LNR* traversal. When this traversal is carried out, all nodes in the left subtree are visited first, then the root node is visited, and finally all nodes in the right subtree are visited.

There are two other traversal algorithms that can be applied meaningfully to tree variables of other types, namely, *preorder* traversal (NLR) and *postorder* traversal (LRN). With preorder traversal, the root node is visited first, followed by visits to all nodes in the left subtree, and then all nodes in the right subtree. In the case of postorder traversal, the left and right subtrees are visited before the root node.

A *binary expression tree* contains nodes that either represent *binary operators* or simple operand values. Each node on the tree represents a unique expression. The single expression held in the tree starts at the root node. Each node, being an expression, also has an implied value. This value is the value of the expression formed that starts with the root node of the expression subtree.

When an expression is written in *Polish notation,* it is easy to build a binary expression tree using the preorder traversal algorithm. Each node visited is first created and then its left and right subtrees are created. The tree is evaluated using postorder traversal, for the operand values found in each subtree must be evaluated before the operation of the root node can be applied.

It is a good idea to draw pictures when planning, desk tracing, or testing code that deals with link variables. A good strategy to aid in the development of a particularly tricky operation is to draw a picture to represent the preconditions and one to represent the postconditions. Often you will want to draw a picture for each statement belonging to the sequence that works toward the desired postcondition(s) as well.

The first tests done on the operations of an ADT with links should be on the type's null (empty) value. Then an ADT with a single node should be tested. Next simple structures should be created (with as many nodes on them as there are pointers from the first node) and tests applied to them.

If all operations on small-sized variables containing some three or so nodes work, "random" tests using a somewhat larger variable (perhaps 10 nodes) should be tried. As soon as some test fails, it is a good idea not to keep using the test variable, for its logical appearance is no longer correct. It would be better instead to find the code that caused the error and/or try to reproduce the error condition.

If an empty structure is defined, the number of tests to be applied at a given node that deals with empty structures is 2^N, where N is the number of link fields in a node variable. Regardless of where the node may be in the structure, all 2^N possibilities must be tested and proven correct. Thus, for example, if a node is to be deleted in a BST, the four cases that must be tested are (1) a leaf, (2) a node with an empty left subtree, (3) a node with an empty right subtree, and (4) a node where neither subtree is empty. As you build a tree to apply each of these *pattern tests,* it is essential to draw pictures to ensure which of the four kinds of nodes is being tested.

EXERCISES

Short Answers

1. What is the difference between a binary tree and any other tree?

2. The first node visited on a path to any given node in a tree is always the _____ .

3. True or false? A binary tree that is not empty always contains other binary trees.

4. What does the NIL value represent when it assigned to a variable of type BSTType (as defined in Section 18.2)?

5. What does the NIL value represent when it is assigned to a variable of type BSTPtr (as defined in Section 18.1)?

6. What value should be returned by the call NodesLeftTree(NIL)?

7. Under what circumstances does a binary tree structure degenerate to a linked list? Illustrate with an example where the tree has five nodes.

8. Does preorder traversal of a BST make any sense? Why or why not?

9. Does in-order traversal of a BST make any sense? Why or why not?

10. Suppose a traversal of a BST is to be carried out. How many stopping cases have occurred if the tree has (a) 0 nodes, (b) 1 node, (c) 2 nodes, (d) 3 nodes, and (e) N nodes?

11. Given a balanced BST with approximately 2048 nodes. Suppose a particular record is being sought and three probes have been made. Assuming the record was not found on the third probe, how many candidates have been eliminated from the structure after the third probe?

12. True or false? The node pointed to after the third probe in Exercise 11 represents the root node of the subtree that contains the remaining candidates. Explain why you answered as you did.

13. Given a BST with its root node. What is the big-Oh for each of the following processes?
    (a) Displaying the fields of the root node.
    (b) Returning the result of a search for a given key.
    (c) Traversing the structure in order.
    (d) A function that returns the height of the tree.
    (e) A function that returns the lowest level at which a leaf is found.

14. Suppose an ADT is constructed where each node has four link fields. How many different logical combinations of NIL and not-NIL links are possible?

15. The BST variable ATree is not empty, but you wish to make it empty as part of a program. Why is it incorrect to simply code the call MakeTree(ATree)? How should you use the operations of the BST unit to return an empty tree?

16. What is the value of the PN expression $*$ $+$ $-$ 7 2 $-$ 8 4 6?

17. Draw the expression tree formed from the PN expression given in Exercise 16.

Easy Projects

18. The treesort algorithm is yet another algorithm to sort an array. This particular sort is described by the pseudocode.

> *{TreeSort algorithm:}*
> *build tree using the elements of AnArray*
> *in-order traverse the tree, assigning the elements to AnArray in order*
> *{end algorithm}*

Write and test the tree sort algorithm on an array containing 200 integer elements with a main-block sequence whose pseudocode is described by

> *fill-in AnArray of 200 elements using a RNG*
> *TreeSort(AnArray)*
> *IF Sorted(AnArray) then*
>   *writeln('The algorithm works.')*
> *ELSE*
>   *writeln('The algorithm fails.')*

`Sorted` is a boolean function that returns `true` if `AnArray` is sorted.

19. Write a main block program to test the BST unit. As recommended in the section on program testing, the block should first call `MakeTree` and then continue to select one of the following operations from a menu: Add (node), Delete (node), Search for (node), Traverse (tree) in order, Kill (tree), and Quit (program). When `Add` or `Delete` is called, the key value is read in and the result of the operation (success or failure) is displayed. When `SearchNode` is called, the key value is read in and the search result (found or not) is displayed. `Traversal` of the name tree (make names have only up to 10 characters in them) should display five names per line. `Kill`, after deleting all nodes, displays a message that the tree is now empty. `Quit` simply halts the program.

20. **(a)** The operation to delete a node where both its subtrees are not empty can be implemented by finding the rightmost node in the left subtree, copying its information into the initial candidate, and then killing that node. Change the implementation of `DeleteTNode` so that this algorithm is used.

    (b) Test the BST unit as implemented using the same approach as suggested in Exercise 19. Start the tree with about 10 nodes and then apply about 7 or 8 `AddTNode`, `DeleteTNode`, and `SearchTNode` operations. Set up the initial tree so that each of the deletion possibilities can be tested.

21. Write the auxiliary procedure `Search` using recursion rather than iteration. (*Hint:* The best approach is to set an initial value to the variable `Parent` before making a recursive call. Then both candidates `Parent` and `TNode` are updated with each new call until either a match is found or there are no more candidate nodes.)

22. Modify the case study in Section 18.4 (`EvaluateTree`) so that integer values with more than one digit can be read in as operands. Let integer values within the range 0–9999 be possible. (*Hint:* Change the Token field into a string variable `Tokens`. `TreesValue` can then check the first char value of `Tokens` to determine whether an operation must be applied or the integer value represented by `Tokens` must be found.)

23. You are to develop the code for some functions that use the traversal algorithm to get a solution. You need not use a big tree to test each function; a tree of integers with between 10 to 20 nodes should suffice for the following functions:

    (a) Write a function that finds and returns the height of the test tree. (*Hint:* Use a counter that is incremented for each move down the tree and decremented for each move back up the tree. Consider what in a traversal constitutes a move "down" and what constitutes a move "up." The candidate value for height and the move counter must be initialized before the traversal procedure is called.)

    (b) Write a function that returns the count of the number of level N nodes on the tree. (*Note:* The solution-finding mechanism need not look past any node found at level N.)

    (c) Write a function that returns the count of the number of leaves on the tree.

    (d) Write a function(s) that returns the number of nodes where (1) only the left subtree is empty and (2) only the right subtree is empty.

    (e) Write a function that returns the number of nodes on the tree having two nonempty subtrees.

    Note that some functions themselves are not necessarily recursive, but a traversal algorithm is required to accumulate the value that is returned to the function.

24. (a) Write a procedure that returns a linked list pointed to by `First`, representing the path taken on the BST to a given node.

    (b) Write a procedure `GetLevNPaths` that fills in an array of linked lists where each list contains the nodes to reach one of the level N nodes on the tree. All non-empty `LevelN` nodes should be filled in. If, for example, we have a balanced tree with 16 nodes, we would expect four array elements to be assigned values to `Paths` if the procedure were called by `GetLevNPaths(Paths, Root, 2);`, where `Paths` is an array of linked lists.

25. It is possible to build two BSTs containing the same records with different keys. Suppose, for example, a particular account can be looked up either by `AccNo` or by `Name`. A given record with a name field and an account number field can be added to one BST whose key field is the name and to a second BST whose key field is the account number.

    (a) Write a program that reads perhaps 50 records from a file into an array of records (the array is for testing). Each record contains a name (last name only—duplicate names not allowed for simplicity) and an account number. Add each record to the BST sorted by name and the BST sorted by account number.

    (b) Next use the array of records to eliminate every fifth record in the array from each tree. Follow this action with a search through each tree in turn for each of the 50 records. If the search is successful for any element whose index is divisible by 5, have the computer print out an error message. If the search is unsuccessful for any other records, have the computer likewise print out an error message. Once all elements have been tested, the computer should print out "TESTING FINISHED."

    (c) Wind up the testing with a traversal of each tree, displaying the key values at each node.

26. A BST can be used to record and count the occurrences of the words in a given text file. The program can be described by

    link-keyin(AFile)   {*link to user-specified file name*}
    initialize WordTree
    WHILE NOT eof(AFile) DO

GetWord(AWord, AFile)
look for AWord on WordTree
IF AWord is found on WordTree THEN
    increment occurrences counter by 1
ELSE
    add AWord to WordTree, setting occurrences counter to 1
traverse WordTree, displaying words and number of occurrences

A "word" is considered to be a string of characters that are alphabetic. The word tree itself contains words using only lowercase letters, so any characters read in that are uppercase letters are changed to lowercase by the action of `GetWord`.

A node of `WordTree` has an integer field along with the field to represent a typical word's value. Write the word tree traversal so that each node, once visited, is deleted. Thus, after the traversal, `WordTree` should be empty.

Difficult Projects

27. Suppose you have `AnArray` that is sorted. You want to devise an algorithm that takes the elements of this sorted array and builds a BST that does not degenerate to a linear list. A quick-and-dirty algorithm that returns a "random" tree would use an RNG to determine which element in `AnArray` is to be the next element added to the BST.

    (a) Write an algorithm to create a BST from the sorted `AnArray` using an RNG to return numbers between 1 and 50 (Example Problem 8.3). The number returned represents the index value of the next element to go on the BST. If the candidate element has already been selected, it is clearly skipped, and the RNG is called again.

    After perhaps half of the elements have been added, assume that a random enough tree has been built to add the remaining elements in sequence. Thus, a FOR loop through the 50 array elements is applied, where an attempt is made to add each element to the tree. Clearly, half of these attempts will be unsuccessful.

    (b) Once the tree has been built, you are to test the success of this algorithm by writing the procedure `TestTree` that uses `AnArray` and `Tree` to determine (1) if any of the 50 elements in `AnArray` is missing from the tree and (2) the number of nodes at different levels in the tree. This information can be obtained by (1) using a boolean variable `Missing` set to `true` if one of the array elements is missing and (2) using an array of counters `Levels` where the index value represents the level and the element's value represents the number of nodes on that level.

    Note that a different procedure from `SearchTNode` must be coded. You can still, however, use only the abstract operations of the ADT to assign values to `Levels`. Just in case the tree is degenerate, set up the access subrange for the elements of levels to go from 1 to 50.

    (c) Write a procedure to display the number of nodes at the different levels. As soon as an element is found to be 0, further display is not required (Why?).

28. Develop a structure using a BST of `Last` names that contains `First` and `Last` names. Implement the tree such that duplicate last names can be found. A search returns a node only if both names match. If a name is to be deleted, both name fields must match, and *all* names that match must be deleted. (Note that if there is only one `First` name node for a given `Last` name, *two* nodes must be deleted. If, however, there is more than one node in the linked list of first names, then probably just the node from the linked list is deleted.) Likewise, any node to be added is always added regardless of duplicate last name (or, for that matter, first name) nodes.

    Each node on the tree contains two fields: (1) a field containing the last name key, and (2) a pointer to the first record in a linked list containing the `First` names of all records with the given `Last` name. Let the list of `First` names be a sorted linear list.

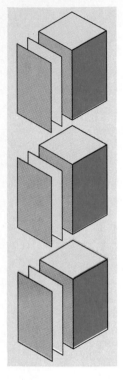

RESERVED WORDS AND STANDARD IDENTIFIERS

Reserved Words

AND	DOWNTO	IF	OR	THEN
ARRAY	ELSE	IN	PACKED	TO
BEGIN	END	LABEL	PROCEDURE	TYPE
CASE	FILE	MOD	PROGRAM	UNTIL
CONST	FOR	NIL	RECORD	VAR
DIV	FUNCTION	NOT	REPEAT	VARYING†
DO	GOTO	OF	SET	WHILE
			STRING*	WITH

*Turbo Pascal reserved word.
†VAX Pascal reserved word.

Standard Identifiers

Constants:

false   true   maxint

Types:

boolean	char	integer	real	text

Files:

crt*	input	lst*	output

*Turbo Pascal standard file identifier.

Functions:

abs	arctan	chr	cos	eof	eoln
exp	length*	ln	odd	ord	pred
round	sin	sqr	sqrt	succ	trunc

*VAX Pascal and Turbo Pascal standard function.

Procedures:

assign*	dispose	get	new	open†	pack
page	put	read	readln	reset	rewrite
unpack	write	writeln			

*Turbo Pascal standard procedure.
†VAX Pascal standard procedure.

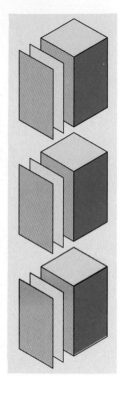

TABLE
OF OPERATORS

Operator	Operation	Operand(s) Type	Result Type
:=	Assignment	Any type other than a file	Same as type on left-hand side of operator
Arithmetic operations:			
+ (unary)	Identity	Numeric	Same as operand
− (unary)	Sign inversion	Numeric	Same as operand
+	Addition	Numeric	Numeric and real, unless both operands are of type integer
−	Subtraction	Numeric	Same as addition
*	Multiplication	Numeric	Same as addition
DIV	Integer division	Integer	Integer
MOD	Remainder of integer division	Integer	Integer
/	Real division	Numeric	Real
Relational operations:			
=	Equal to	Ordinal, real, string, set, or pointer	Boolean
<>	Not equal to	Same as "equal to"	Boolean

Operator	Operation	Operand(s) Type	Result Type
<	Less than	Ordinal, string, or real	Boolean
	Subset	Set	Boolean
<=	Less than or equal to	Ordinal, string, or real	Boolean
	Proper subset	Set	Boolean
>	Greater than	Ordinal, string, or real	Boolean
	Superset	Set	Boolean
>=	Greater than or equal to	Ordinal, string, or real	Boolean
	Proper superset	Set	Boolean
IN	Set membership	First operand is ordinal; second is a set type	Boolean
Logical:			
NOT	Negation	Boolean	Boolean
AND	Conjunction	Boolean	Boolean
OR	Disjunction	Boolean	Boolean
Set:			
+	Set union	Any set type	Same set type as operand
*	Set intersection	Any set type	Same as set union
−	Set subtraction	Any set type	Same as set union

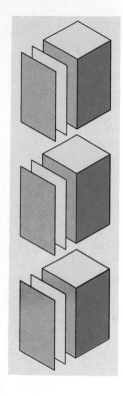

HIERARCHY
OF OPERATOR
APPLICATIONS

$$(\quad)$$
$$NOT$$
$$AND \quad * \quad / \quad DIV \quad MOD$$
$$OR \quad + \quad -$$
$$< \quad <= \quad = \quad <> \quad >= \quad > \quad IN$$

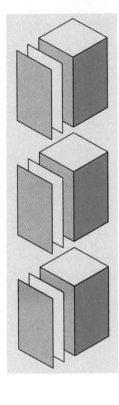

TABLE OF STANDARD FUNCTIONS

Name	Value Returned	Argument Type	Result Type
abs	Absolute value of argument	Numeric	Same as argument
exp	*e* (2.71828) raised to power of the argument	Numeric	Real
ln	Logarithm to base *e* of argument	Numeric	Real
sqr	Square of the argument	Numeric	Same as argument
sqrt	Square root of the argument	Numeric	Real
round	Nearest integer value of argument	Real	Integer
trunc	Integer part of argument	Real	Integer
arctan	Inverse tangent of argument	Numeric	Real (in radians)
sin	Sine of argument	Numeric (in radians)	Real
cos	Cosine of argument	Numeric (in radians)	Real
chr	Character whose ordinal number is the argument	Integer	Char
length*	Number of characters that make up argument string	String	Integer
odd	*True* if argument is odd number; otherwise returns *false*	Integer	Boolean
ord	Ordinal number of argument	Ordinal	Integer

Name	Value Returned	Argument Type	Result Type
pred	Returns predecessor of argument	Ordinal	Ordinal
succ	Returns successor of argument	Ordinal	Ordinal
eoln	Returns *true* if next char value to be read in file is end-of-line; otherwise returns *false*	Text file	Boolean
eof	Returns *true* if no more components to be read or obtained exist in the file	File of any type	Boolean

*VAX Pascal and Turbo Pascal standard function.

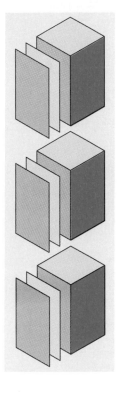

TABLE OF STANDARD PROCEDURES

Procedure Call	Action Carried Out
assign(FileVar,StrExpression)*	The actual file on disk whose name is the same as the string expression's is linked to the associated FileVar, a file variable.
close(FileVar)	The actual file on disk that was linked to the file variable FileVar is delinked.
dispose(APtr)	Memory allocated to the pointer variable APtr is thrown back on the heap, and the reference APtr$^\wedge$ is meaningless.
get(FileVar)	The file pointer to FileVar is advanced to the next component, and the value of the component obtained is assigned to FileVar$^\wedge$.
new(APtr)	Memory is taken from the heap and assigned to the associated pointer variable APtr. A reference to the object APtr$^\wedge$ is then possible.
open(FileVar,StrExpression)†	Same as the assign procedure, except applied to VAX Pascal.
pack(UArray,I,PArray)	The elements of the unpacked array, UArray, starting from position I, are stored into the elements of the packed array, PArray.

Procedure Call	Action Carried Out
page(TextFileVar)	A new page is started on the printer for the associated TextFileVar components that are in the process of being displayed.
put(FileVar)	The current contents of FileVar$^\wedge$ are appended to the associated actual file.
read(FileVar,variables)	The data in the file associated with FileVar are read into the variables listed.
readln(TextFileVar,variables)	The data in the text file on disk associated with TextFileVar are read into the variables listed, where further characters on the last line read from are skipped.
reset(FileVar)	The file on disk associated with the FileVar is prepared for reading, where the first component in the file is the first candidate value to be read.
rewrite(FileVar)	The file on disk associated with FileVar is prepared for writing, where the first component is written at the beginning of the file.
unpack(PArray,I,UArray)	The elements in the packed array variable, PArray, starting with the first element, are copied into the array variable, UArray, starting with element I.
write(FileVar, values)	The data values specified in the list are written into the actual file on disk associated with the file variable FileVar.
writeln(TextFileVar, values)	The data values specified in the list are written as a line of text into the actual file on disk associated with the text file variable TextFileVar.

*Turbo Pascal standard procedure
†VAX Pascal standard procedure

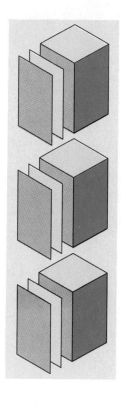

PASCAL SYNTAX DIAGRAMS

Identifiers

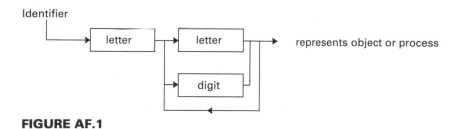

FIGURE AF.1

Processes

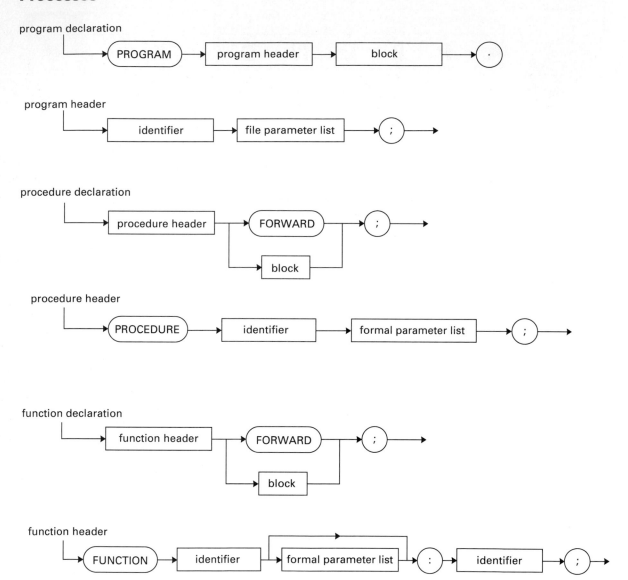

FIGURE AF.2

block

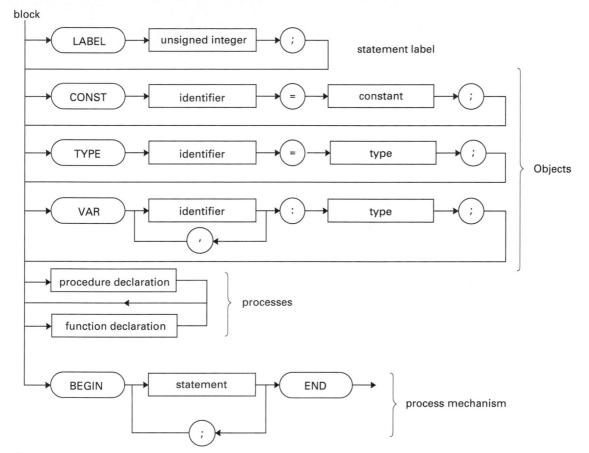

FIGURE AF.3

Parameter Lists

file parameter list

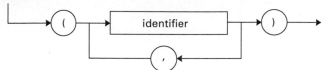

actual parameter list

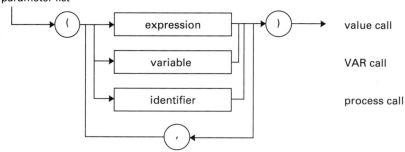

formal parameter list

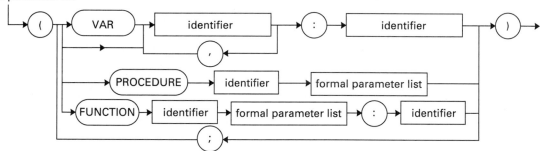

FIGURE AF.4

Objects

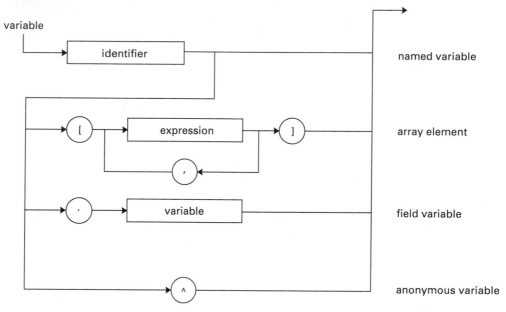

named variable

array element

field variable

anonymous variable

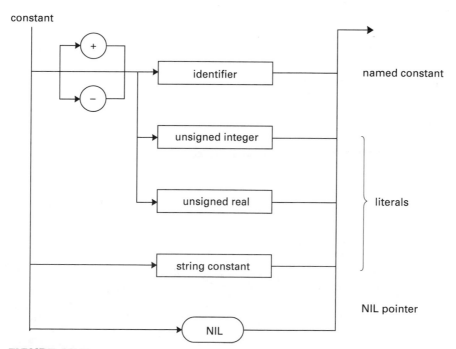

named constant

literals

NIL pointer

FIGURE AF.5

Literals

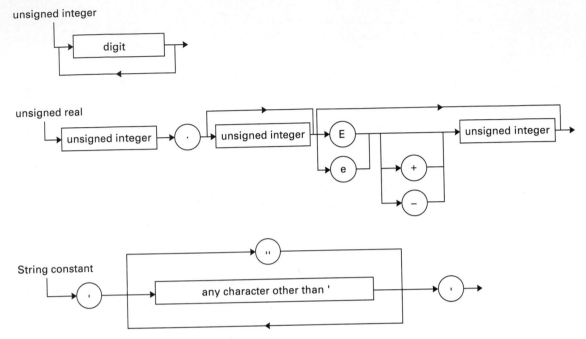

FIGURE AF.6

Object Types

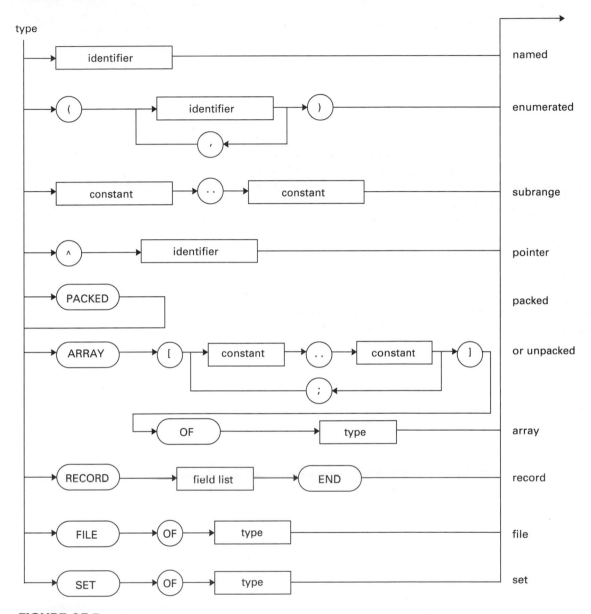

FIGURE AF.7

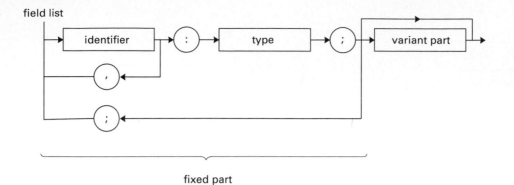

fixed part

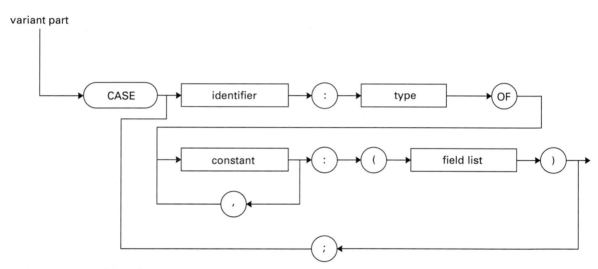

FIGURE AF.7 *(Cont.)*

Statement

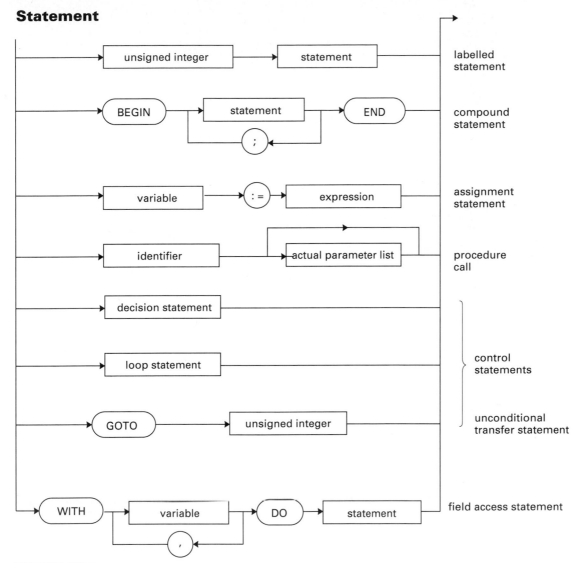

FIGURE AF.8

Decision Statement

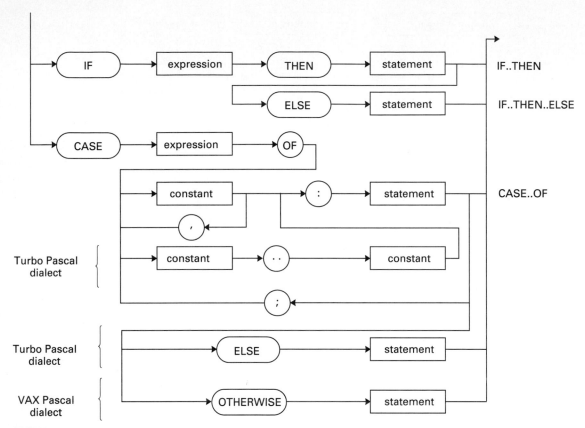

FIGURE AF.9

Loop Statement

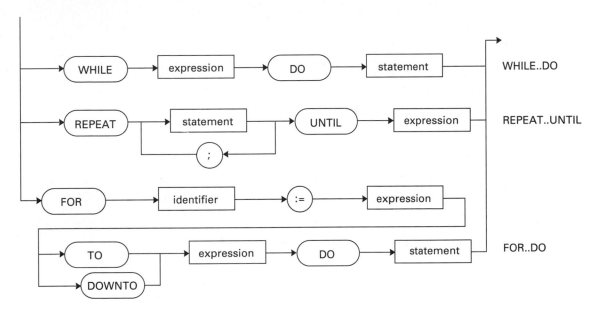

FIGURE AF.10

Expressions

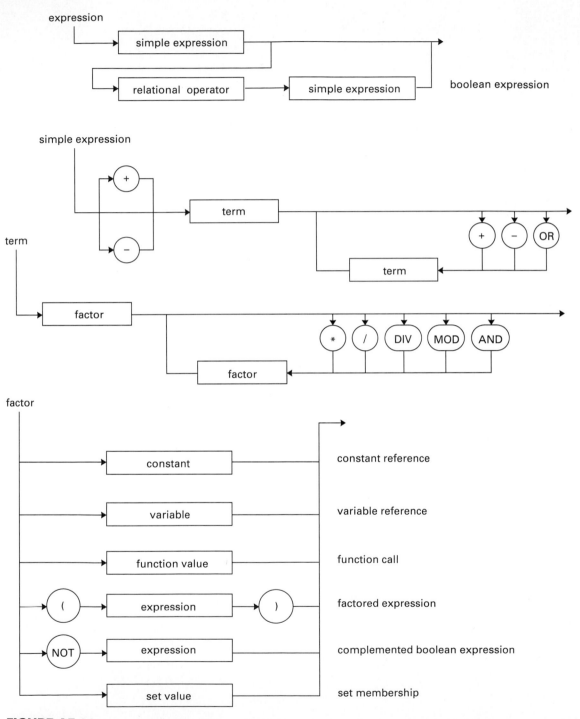

FIGURE AF.11

function value

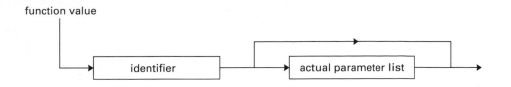

Set value

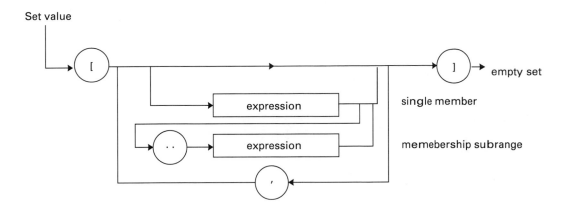

empty set

single member

memebership subrange

relational operator

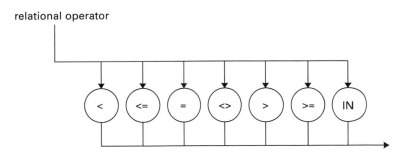

FIGURE AF.11 *(Cont.)*

A P P E N D I X *G*

PSEUDOCODE DESCRIPTIONS OF PROVEN ALGORITHMS

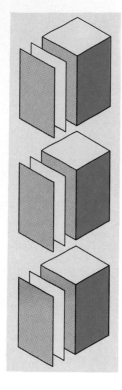

Algorithm	Ref. Page

4.2   *123*
{*read in values*}
   PROCEDURE *ReadInValues(all parameters called by VAR)*
     keyin values to all variables in the parameter list
{*end algorithm*}

4.3   *123*
{*display values*}
   PROCEDURE *DisplayValues(all parameters are called by value)*
     display values of all variables in parameter list
{*end algorithm*}

4.4   *133*
{*drving a procedure*}
   PROCEDURE *DriveIt*
    VAR
      variables for parameter list of procedure to drive
    {*statements:*}   *172*
      get values for input parameters of the procedure being driven
      call the procedure being driven
      display values returned by the procedure call
{*end algorithm*}

5.1
{*exchange values*}
   Temp ⟵ *Var1*
   Var1 ⟵ *Var2*
   Var2 ⟵ *Temp*
{*end algorithm*}

5.2   *176*
{*the IF..ELSE..IF algorithm*}
   IF *condition 1* THEN
    action 1
   ELSE IF *condition 2* THEN
    action 2

   ....

   ELSE IF *condition M* THEN
    action M

   ....

   ELSE IF *condition (N-1)* THEN
    action (N-1)
   ELSE
    action N
{*end algorithm*}

5.3   *189*
{*the guard algorithm*}
   IF *data are impossible to process* THEN
    handle the processing differently
   ELSE
    process data as intended
{*end algorithm*}

5.4   *189*
{*alternative form of guard algorithm*}

Algorithm	Ref. Page

IF data can be processed THEN
    process data as intended
ELSE   {optional}
    handle the processing differently
{end algorithm}	

6.1
{sequential event counting}
   EventCounter ⟵ 0
   get EventValue
   WHILE EventValue represents a countable event DO
      EventCounter ⟵ EventCounter + 1
      get EVentValue
{end algorithm}
	217

6.2
{selective event counting}
   EventCounter ⟵ 0
   WHILE more candidate events to process DO
      get EventValue
      IF EventValue represents a countable event THEN
         EventCounter ⟵ EventCounter + 1
{end algorithm}
	218

6.3
{sum accumulation}
   Sum ⟵ 0
   WHILE more events to process DO
      get EventValue
      Sum ⟵ Sum + EventValue
{end algorithm}
	219

6.3(a)
{sum accumulation of significant events}
   Sum ⟵ 0
   WHILE more events to process DO
      get EventValue
      IF EventValue represents a significant event THEN
         Sum ⟵ Sum + EventValue
{end algorithm}
	219

6.4
{do a process N times, using WHILE loop}
   Pass ⟵ 0
   WHILE Pass <> N DO
      Pass ⟵ Pass + 1
      rest of loop body   {Pass is not assigned a new value here}
{end algorithm}
	220

6.5
{process to a terminal event}
   get EventValue
   WHILE EventValue does not represent terminal event DO
      process EventValue
      get EventValue
{end algorithm}
	221

PROCEDURE SolveIt(parameters representing size of problem, {others})
  IF parameters passed in indicate a base case THEN
    solve the problem
  ELSE
    use values passed in to set up smaller version of the problem
    SolveIt(parameters representing smaller problem, {others})
    use values returned to solve present problem

SolveIt(parameters representing initial problem, {others})
{end algorithm}

{recursive search through elements of AnArray}
  FUNCTION Index(VAR AnArray; Key; {subrange parameter(s)}): IndexType
    IF subrange has vanished THEN
      Index ⟵ 0
    ELSE
      get Candidate probe from subrange parameter(s)
      IF AnArray[Candidate] = Key THEN
        Index ⟵ Candidate
      ELSE
        revise a subrange value(s) that reduces candidate subrange
        Index ⟵ Index(AnArray, Key, {revised subrange parameters})

IndexVar ⟵ Index(AnArray, Key, {parameters for initial subrange})
{end algorithm}

{recursive form of binary search through AnArray}
  FUNCTION Binary(VAR AnArray; Key; Lo, Hi): Index Type
    IF Lo > Hi THEN
      Binary ⟵ 0
    ELSE
      Mid ⟵ (Lo + Hi) DIV 2
      IF AnArray[Mid] = Key THEN
        Binary ⟵ Mid
      ELSE IF ANArray[Mid] < Key THEN
        Binary ⟵ Binary(AnArray, Key, Mid+1, Hi)
      ELSE
        Binary ⟵ Binary(AnArray, Key, Lo, Mid-1)

IndexVar ⟵ Binary(AnArray, Key, 1, LastElement)
{end algorithm}

{copy A file's components into B file's}
  WHILE NOT eof(AFile) DO
    read(AFile, AComponent)
    write(BFile, AComponent)
{end algorithm}

{read in, then write a record var into OutFile}
  WITH RecordVar DO
    keyin values for the field variables of RecordVar
  write(OutFile, RecordVar)
{end algorithm}

{two-file merge for sorted files of records}

GetRecord(Rec1, InFile1)   {*GetRecord guards against reading <eof>*}
GetRecord(Rec2, InFile2)
WHILE NOT eof(InFile1) AND NOT eof(InFile2) DO
  IF Rec1.Key < Rec2.Key THEN
    write(OutFile, Rec1)
    GetRecord(Rec1, InFile1)
  ELSE
    write(OutFile, Rec2)
    GetRecord(Rec2, InFile2)
CopyLastTwo(Rec), Rec2, OutFile)
CopyRemainingRecords(InFile1, OutFile)   {*no action with <eof>*}
CopyRemainingRecords(InFile2, OutFile)
{*end algorithm*}

17.1   797
{*add candidate node to linked structure*}
  assign value(s) to data field(s) of CandNode$^\wedge$
  assign link(s) from CandNode$^\wedge$ to the structure
  assign link(s) from the structure to CandNode$^\wedge$
{*end algorithm*}

17.2   797
{*delete candidate node from linked structure*}
  set new links in the structure that bypass CandNode$^\wedge$
  dispose(CandNode)
{*end algorithm*}

18.1   812
{*primitive field selector for a node in a linked structure ADT*}
  PROCEDURE GetNodesField(ANode: NodePointer; VAR FieldVar: FieldType)
    IF Node <> NIL THEN
      FieldVar ⟵ ANode$^\wedge$.{variable identifier of field selected}
    ELSE
      FieldVar ⟵ NullValue
{*end algorithm*}
{*Note: Algorithm 18.1 often codes to a function*}

18.2   835
{*inorder traversal of binary tree*}
  PROCEDURE Traverse(Root: TreeType)
    IF Root <> NIL THEN
      Traverse(Root$^\wedge$.Left)
      Visit(Root)
      Traverse(Root$^\wedge$.Right)

  Traverse(Tree)
{*end algorithm*}

18.3   836
{*preorder traversal of binary tree*}
  PROCEDURE Traverse(Root: TreeType)
    IF Root <> NIL THEN
      Visit(Root)
      Traverse(Root$^\wedge$.Left)
      Traverse(Root$^\wedge$.Right)

  Traverse(Tree)
{*end algorithm*}

Algorithm	Ref. Page
18.4	*836*

{postorder traversal of binary tree}
    PROCEDURE Traverse(Root: TreeType)
      IF Root <> NIL THEN
        Traverse(Root$^\wedge$.Left)
        Traverse(Root$^\wedge$.Right)
        Visit(Root)

    Traverse(Tree)
{end algorithm}

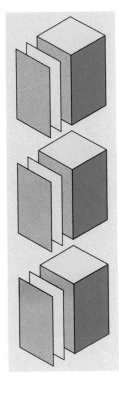

COMPENDIUM OF CODING RULES

The following table is a compendium of coding rules by chapter. When a coding rule is first presented in the text, it is given a number such as Coding Rule 12.2. The first of the two numbers represents the chapter number, and the second is the number in which the rule was presented in the given chapter. In the compendium, this same rule is listed under Chapter 12 as Rule 2. Each listed rule is followed by a brief reason that explains how or why the rule serves as an aid in planning and/or writing good source code.

Chapter 2

Rule	Reason
1. When you use a sequence of `write` statements to display a line of text, make sure to end the line display with a `writeln` statement.	Clears buffer for next line display.
2. Code any real literal with at least one digit before the decimal point.	Helps in avoiding syntax error.
3. Always precede a series of `read` statements or a single `readln` statement with a `write` or `writeln` statement that describes the input expected by both format and type.	Lets user know required form of input data.
4. Make all identifiers self-documenting.	Makes code more readable.

Rule	Reason
5. Correct the earlier syntax errors first.	Requirement for some dialects. For others, makes debugging easier.
6. Learn how your system handles `write` and `writeln` statements for every data type.	Makes it easier to code display statements that produce neat and readable display.

Chapter 3

Rule	Reason
1. Write code that is semantically consistent.	Makes code easier to read and modify.

Chapter 4

Rule	Reason
1. Lay out lower-level procedures first.	Syntax requirement when nested procedures are not used in source code. If nesting of procedures is done, this rule has no meaning.
2. Do not use the call by value mechanism on a variable if the value passed in is not referenced at least once before the variable takes on a new value.	If not followed, the initial value passed in is never used. At best, this practice makes source code difficult to understand.
3. Do not use the call by variable mechanism if the value returned to the variable is not used at some point in the rest of the program.	This rule may be relaxed with structured variables, but it always applies to scalar variables. If not followed, the final value passed out to the variable is never used. At best, this practice makes source code difficult to understand.
4. Document each procedure such that it describes the meaning and purpose of each formal parameter.	The logical flow of all data in and out of a block is then documented. This practice thus makes source code more readable.

Chapter 5

Rule	Reason
1. Never precede the reserved word ELSE with a semicolon.	Helps in avoiding syntax errors.
2. Never follow the reserved words THEN or ELSE with a semicolon.	Avoids error due to execution of an unintentionally coded empty statement.
3. Always use the reserved words BEGIN and END for code that requires a compound statement.	Must be followed to code a correct compound statement.

Rule	Reason
4. Choose sufficient test data to cover all preconditions for a given sequence that uses decision logic.	Tests every path of a decision statement at least once.
5. Choose sufficient test data to ensure that every statement in a program gets executed at least once.	A restatement of Rule 4, this time one that applies to the statement part of any block of code.

Chapter 6

Rule	Reason
1. Never follow the reserved word DO with a semicolon.	Avoids execution of an unintentionally coded empty statement.
2. Use the BEGIN. . END delimiters with any WHILE or FOR loop whose body consists of more than one statement.	Ensures that all statements required in the loop body are executed. We can likewise say the intended compound statement that makes up the loop body is properly coded.
3. First test loops with small data sets and for the trivial cases.	The "rule of small samples." Simplifies debugging part of programming.
4. Choose test data on loops that check all obvious entry/exit events.	Helps ensure exhaustive testing.
5. Choose at least one set of test data on a loop where the first event is significant and at least one set of test data where the final event is significant.	Helps ensure exhaustive testing.
6. Choose "bad" sets of data for testing the loop body.	Helps ensure exhaustive testing and forces the programmer to write code that guards against bad data.
7. Choose "normal" sets of data for testing the loop body.	Helps ensure exhaustive testing.
8. Apply assertion testing first.	Helps in developing correct logic that leads to source code with consistent semantics.

Chapter 7

Rule	Reason
1. If one of the reserved words NOT, AND, or OR is used to form a boolean expression, be sure that all component expressions formed with the relational operators are enclosed by parentheses.	Helps in avoiding syntax errors.
2. Do not use operations defined for scalar types on structured variables.	Helps in avoiding syntax errors and keeps one from writing poorly designed code.

Rule	Reason
3. Always use local access variables to array elements.	Prevents the use of too many global variables. Helps ensure that access variables are properly applied in access expressions.
4. Use DeMorgan's theorems in assertion testing.	Helps in the understanding of complicated control expressions.
5. When part of the loop body modifies a variable used in an array access expression, be sure to include code that guards against out-of-range access values.	Makes more robust source code.
6. Do not define two or more identical data types.	Helps in avoiding possible syntax errors. Definitely makes source code easier to understand.
7. If the elements of an array are assigned values only over the subrange *1..UsedElements*, pass in the index value `UsedElements` and code the block to guard against accessing any elements outside this subrange.	Makes more robust source code. Also makes code easier to understand.
8. Do not pass an entire array structure into a procedure when only one or two elements are actually changed or referenced in the statement.	At the very least, makes source code easier to understand.

Chapter 8

Rule	Reason
1. Write a function such that the last statement executed assigns a value to the function.	At the very least, makes source code easier to understand. Quite often required to avoid a syntax error.
2. Use a dummy variable to store the value of a candidate result of a function.	At the very least, makes source code easier to understand. For accumulation and/or recording functions that are not recursive, this rule is usually helpful in avoiding syntax errors.
3. Never use the reserved word VAR in a function header to change the value of a formal parameter's alias.	Avoids the side effect of having the function return more than one result.
4. Always use an IF statement to flag an event that occurs inside the body of a loop.	Guarantees that the flag remains set and does not accidentally get set back to its original value by an event that should not reset the flag.

Chapter 9

Rule	Reason
1. Always use a call by VAR on a file variable parameter.	Helps in avoiding syntax errors.
2. Use a file variable, never the directory name, to access the contents of a file.	Helps in avoiding syntax errors.
3. Avoid using the eoln or the eof function with the REPEAT..UNTIL loop.	REPEAT..UNTIL's mechanism of "execute, then test" does not match the look-ahead mechanism of the eoln and eof functions. The WHILE loop, whose mechanism is "test, then execute" better suits the use of these boolean functions.
4. When values are to be read in from a file, always follow an eoln test with a read statement if false is returned. An eoln test that returns true must be followed by readln before the next call to read.	Helps make code more readable and also guards against possible coding errors.

Chapter 10

Rule	Reason
1. Write a guard loop any time an array access expression is solicited from the program user.	Helps in avoiding run-time errors.
2. Verify that all coded access expressions are in-range.	Helps in avoiding run-time errors and helps give source code consistent semantics.

Chapter 11

Rule	Reason
1. Always access the elements of a multi-dimensional array using access expressions coded in the order in which they were defined.	Helps in avoiding syntax errors. Also helps one in planning clear source code.
2. Always assign values to all variables used in forming the access expressions before applying the expressions to any given array.	Helps in avoiding syntax errors and/or run-time errors.

Chapter 12

Rule	Reason
1. Know the access rules for any candidate structure that is being considered as a solution to the problem.	Helps in designing correct and efficient code.
2. Choose a data type that solves the problem in the simplest possible way.	Helps in the planning and writing of correct and understandable code.

Chapter 13

Rule	Reason
1. Do not access any of the components that make up an ADT in the source code of a client program.	Guarantees the integrity and correct usage of the unit ADT.
2. If you find it impossible to code a client program without accessing one or more components of an ADT, then modify the ADT by coding the required additional operations.	Guarantees the integrity of the ADT, both in the client program that is presently using it and in further client programs that will use it.

Chapter 14

Rule	Reason
1. Never enclose a set variable identifier by brackets.	Helps in avoiding syntax errors.
2. All set expressions other than those represented by set variables should be enclosed by brackets.	Helps in avoiding syntax errors.

Chapter 15

Rule	Reason
1. When planning a recursive algorithm, make sure to include all base cases.	Helps ensure the development of a logically correct recursive algorithm.

Chapter 16

Rule	Reason
1. Make sure that all variables read in or written to a binary file are the same data type as the file's components.	Helps in avoiding syntax errors and in writing correct code.

Chapter 17

Rule	Reason
1. Dispose of dynamic variables as soon as they are of no further use.	Prevents garbage creation.
2. Use calls to the procedures new and dispose sparingly.	Simplifies the programmer's ability to manage memory in a source program.
3. Never attempt a dereference on a NIL pointer value.	Helps in avoiding syntax and/or run-time errors. Also helps one plan source code more carefully.
4. Always write a procedure to display the values of the data field(s) for any dynamic variable(s).	Required for on-line testing and debugging.

Chapter 18

Rule	Reason
1. The number of combinations to ensure exhaustive testing for links to the NIL pointer from any given node is two to the power of the number of link fields.	Helps ensure exhaustive testing.

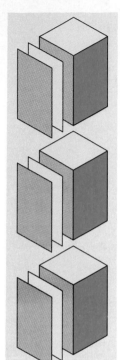

ADDITIONAL FEATURES OF PASCAL

Although we have given you most of the constructs of standard Pascal in the main body of the text, there are some we have omitted. These include the GOTO statement, packed arrays, the standard procedures get and put, variant records, and the use of functions or procedures as formal parameters. Some of these constructs are quite useful. For example, you can use a packed array of characters if you want to implement a variable that always has a fixed number of characters in it. Other constructs, such as the GOTO statement, should be avoided whenever possible.

We are also including the important topic of separately compiled modules in this appendix. Although this feature, like strings, is not a part of standard Pascal, it is found in most dialects. Of the topics covered in the appendix, you will find this one the most useful, for you can build a library of ADT units consisting of source code modules. These modules are compiled and tested separately from any client program that may use them.

When a unit is fully written and debugged, we say that it can be *exported* to any client program that requires it. The client program that uses the unit is then said to *import* it. Once a unit is imported, it is possible for the client program to reference any identifier found in the interface part of the unit. As you already know, this interface contains the identifiers for the objects and processes that make up an abstract data type.

GOTO

The GOTO statement has a long history, for it is found in the instruction set of many other high-level languages such as FORTRAN, BASIC, COBOL, and so forth. When this statement is carried out, it unconditionally transfers control to a specified *labelled statement* in the source code. Although GOTO is part of a standard Pascal, we recommend that you never use it in your source code, for it obscures the logical flow of the program.

Labelled statement: a statement specified by a label.

Labels

Any GOTO statement requires that a label be specified in the LABEL declarations section of a block. This section, which is optional, comes before the CONST definitions section. The syntax diagram for a label declaration(s) is shown as Figure AI.1. Once a label has been declared, it can be used to code a labelled statement. The syntax diagram for a labelled statement is shown as Figure AI.2.

GOTO syntax and execution

The syntax diagram for a GOTO statement is shown in Figure AI.3. When the computer encounters this statement in source code, it transfers control to the statement with the associated label.

Label Declarations

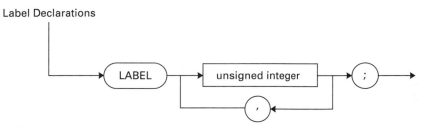

FIGURE AI.1 LABEL declarations.

Labelled statement

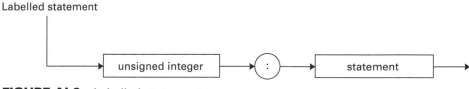

FIGURE AI.2 Labelled statement.

The GOTO statement

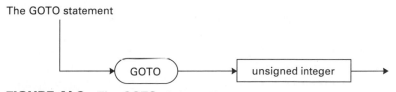

FIGURE AI.3 The GOTO statement.

The mechanism of the GOTO statement using labels can be seen by the following example (of nonsense):

```
PROGRAM MachineProtest(input, output);
  {Shows the mechanism of labels and GOTO's. Also how not to write
  source code!}
  LABEL
    59, 69, 79, 89, 99;
  BEGIN
59: {here it comes!}
    GOTO 69;
89: writeln('made me execute!');
    GOTO 99;
79: write('you have ever ');
    GOTO 89;
69: write('This is the worst program ');
    GOTO 79;
99: {empty statement}
  END.
```

When the program is run, the computer displays the following text:

```
This is the worst program you have ever made me execute!
```

Why is GOTO *bad?*   The source code of the program MachineProtest should indicate the problems that occur if you pepper your program with too many GOTO statements. The main problem deals with the logical flow of control. If control is unconditionally transferred from some other part of the program to a labelled statement, it is difficult to determine the preconditions that existed just before the transfer was carried out. From the labelled statement onward, it is then not possible to know the program state. Once you do not know the program state, you have, for all intents and purposes, lost intellectual control of the program.

When you cannot use GOTO   There are some built-in restrictions dealing with the GOTO statement to help ensure that source code with these statements is still somewhat readable. In order to avoid ambiguous label references, no two statements can have the same label. No compiler, moreover, will accept a GOTO statement that transfers control into the body of a loop or decision statement. Finally, a GOTO statement will not transfer control beyond the scope of the block in which the statement is coded. This last restriction severely limits the extent of confusion you can create when you use many GOTO statements in a program.

Our final say on the matter   Despite the mitigating effects of these Pascal language restrictions, we recommend that you avoid writing source code with GOTO statements. Any fragment of source code written using a GOTO statement can always be recoded differently. Therefore, not only is source code with GOTO statements confusing, it is also unnecessary, for clearer code is always possible.

Packed Arrays

In standard Pascal you can declare a structured variable(s) that is a *packed type*. It is possible to implement string-like variables with packed arrays of characters, thus sticking to standard Pascal. This method of string implementation is clumsy, however, for an array variable, packed or not, cannot take on a varying number of elements. You are therefore usually better off using your dialect's way of implementing strings, because a string variable can take on a varying number of characters.

On those occasions when you want to implement a string that always contains the same number of characters, you do have a better choice, namely, the packed array of characters. We give some examples in the following text that show you when it is appropriate to define/declare a variable(s) that is of type PACKED ARRAY OF CHAR. A variable of this type can then be treated as a string variable with a fixed number of characters in it.

Packed types: structured types where the computer stores values such that they take up a minimum amount of storage.

PACKED ARRAY syntax

The syntax diagram for defining a 1-dimensional packed array is shown in Figure AI.4. Like other array types, a variable of a packed array type has individual elements whose values can be accessed by (in-range) subrange expressions. Hence, the usual rules that apply to accessing an element of an array also applies to accessing an element of a packed array.

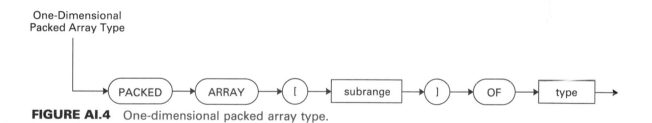

One-Dimensional Packed Array Type

FIGURE AI.4 One-dimensional packed array type.

Packed arrays and read/write *statements*

Packed array types differ from regular array types in one important application: the *read/write* statements of Pascal treats these variables as string types if the variable reference(s) in the parameter list is not accompanied by an access expression. In other words, all elements of the packed array variable can be read in or displayed by simply using just the variable identifier in a read or write statement. No loops are required to access the individual elements; indeed no access expression to the elements is necessary. It is this feature that makes packed array types an attractive choice when we want to implement a string variable(s) that has a fixed amount of characters.

An example

Suppose we have defined/declared the following:

```
TYPE
   AccNoType = PACKED ARRAY[1..5] OF char;
   SSNoType = PACKED ARRAY[1..9] OF char;
VAR
   AccNo: AccNoType;
   SocSecNo: SSNoType;
```

The next sequence of statements, with a sample run given below the sequence, shows an example where you can treat the variables AccNo and SocSecNo like string types. In each case, you know that a fixed number of characters is to be read in or displayed for each variable.

```
write('Enter the account number:  ');
readln(AccNo);
write('Enter the social security number:  ');
readln(SocSecNo);
write('The account number and social number are ');
writeln(AccNo, 'and ',SocSecNo, '.');
```

```
Enter the account number:  13865
Enter the social security number:  999989909
The account number and social number are 13865 and 999989909.
```

The Procedures GET and PUT

In Pascal, a file variable is actually a pointer to a buffer in the CPU that is linked to an external file. When a file is in read mode, then, you can write source code to examine the contents of the file window without having to read a value into some other variable. All you need do is apply the dereferencing operator (a carat) on the file variable. You can likewise put contents into the output buffer of a file variable without actually writing some expression into the file. Again, this action is possible by using a dereference on the file buffer variable.

Both of these characteristics of Pascal seem but useless features unless there is some means to move the file pointer forward or to send the contents of the buffer variable to the file. They are not useless features, however, because Pascal has two standard procedures to carry out the operations, named get and put. A call to the procedure get moves the file window to the next component without reading the previous value into a variable. A call to the procedure put writes the contents of the dereferenced file buffer variable into the associated file without the need for a coded expression as a parameter. In this section, we will briefly study how you can use these two procedures in lieu of the other standard procedures read and write.

get and put
syntax

We have already described the mechanics carried out by the call to either of the standard procedures get and put. The syntax diagram for a successful call to either procedure is shown in Figure AI.5. In order for the procedure get to be carried out successfully, the file must be in read mode and <eof> cannot be the next

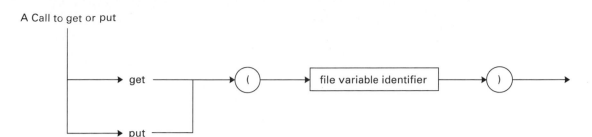

A Call to get or put

FIGURE AI.5 A call to get or put.

component. The procedure put is carried out successfully when the file is write mode.

Equivalence to read and write statements

Suppose the value presently in the file window IntsA has already been processed. We want to get the next (integer) component in the file referenced by the file variable IntsA and assign it to the integer variable Int1. We can carry out this operation with the following sequence of source code:

```
get(IntsA);     {put next component of external file in the file window}
Int1:= IntsA^; {assign dereference of the file window to Ints1}
```

This sequence is completely equivalent to the single statement coded as read(IntsA, Int1).

The source code to put the value assigned to the variable Int1 into an external file referenced by the file variable IntsB is coded as

```
IntsB^:= Int1; {assign Int1 to the dereference of the file variable IntB}
put(IntB);      {put the contents of the buffer into the external file}
```

It is completely equivalent to the statement coded as write(IntsB, Int1).

A complete example

Let us write a procedure that copies the contents of an external file referenced by FileA into an external file referenced by FileB. We will assume both files are of type SomeFileType that contain components of type SomeVarType. The source code for the procedure CopyFile, given these identifiers, is then coded as follows:

```
PROCEDURE CopyFile(Var FileA, FileB: SomeFileType);
  {copies contents of FileA into FileB, using the procedures get and
  put.}
  BEGIN
    reset(IntsA);
    rewrite(IntsB);
    WHILE NOT eof(IntsA) DO
      BEGIN
        get(IntsA);           {get component from file}
        IntsB^:= IntsA^;      {copy in buffer into out buffer}
```

```
            put(IntsB)              {put component into file}
      END
   END;
```

Note that we do not need to declare a local variable of type SomeVarType, for we can use dereferences to the two anonymous variables FileAˆ and FileBˆ to carry out the required operations.

Why use get *and* put?

If the procedures read and write are available, then why does Pascal also have the procedures get and put? Apparently, the developers of Turbo Pascal asked this same question and decided that it has no good answer. Hence, they chose not to incorporate these two procedures in the Turbo Pascal dialect.

If your dialect supports get and put, you may find that using these two procedures saves on run-time costs. When read is carried out, for example, the contents from the file are first put into the file buffer variable. Then the contents of the file buffer variable must be copied into the named variable(s) of the read statement that receives the file contents. This second copy operation takes time.

Suppose you are writing a program where all file components must be examined but very few components are required to be read in. In this case, you can use a call to the procedure get to look at the value(s) of each component. If the component's value(s) needs to be assigned to a variable for further processing, the additional copy operation can be carried out as an assignment statement.

CopyFile
using read *and*
write

Note that the loop body of the procedure CopyFile as we coded it is more efficient than an equivalent loop body whose source code, along with clarifying documentation, is written as

```
BEGIN
   read(IntsA, AnInt);   {get component into buffer, copy buffer into AnInt}
   write(IntsB, AnInt)   {copy AnInt into buffer, put AnInt into file}
END;
```

The additional copy operation necessary for each read statement makes this procedure somewhat less efficient than the first one we coded.

Variant Records

Quite often the need arises to implement a record type where different field variables are required for different circumstances. You can solve this problem of implementation by writing the source code for a *variant record type*. A record of this type contains two parts: the *fixed part* and the *variant part*. The fixed part consists of field variables that will be the same, regardless of the program state. These variables can always be selected in the statement part of a block. The variant part contains different groups of field variables, of which only the variables of one group have meaning at any given time. The value of the *tag field variable* determines which of the different variant groups has meaning. The only variables that can be selected from the variant part of a record variable in the statement part of a block are those belonging to the group of field variables that presently has meaning.

Variant record: a record type defined such that it has a fixed part and a variant part.

Fixed part: those field variables of a record that are the same, regardless of the value of the tag field variable.

Variant part: those field variables of a record that vary according to the value taken on by the tag field variable.

Tag field variable: the single (ordinal) field variable found in all variant records that determines which variables in the variant part can presently be selected in the statement part of a block.

Variant record syntax   The variant part of a field list is optional. If it is used, this part of the record type is placed after the fixed part. The syntax diagram for a variant record type is shown as Figure AI.6. The syntax diagram for the variant part is shown as Figure AI.7.

The first identifier of Figure AI.7 represents the tag field variable, the type box represents the variable type of the tag field variable, and the constants represent the different values that can be taken on by the tag field variable. The variables en-

Variant Record Type Definition

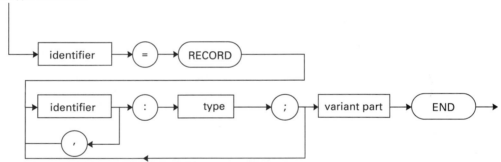

FIGURE AI.6   Variant RECORD type definition.

FIGURE AI.7   Variant part.

variant part

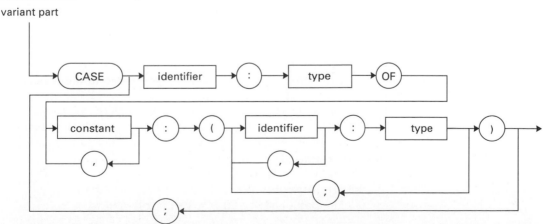

closed by each set of parentheses are the different variable groups whose field variables can be selected given that the tag field variable has taken on the associated value.

An example   Let us write the source code to implement the record variable APerson of type PersonType. The variable will have fields that contain the person's (1) name, (2) age, (3) height, (4) weight, and (5) sex as its fixed part. The tag field variable will represent the person's marital status. If the person is married, let us include field variables to represent the spouse's name and the number of children in the family. If the person is divorced or single, only one boolean variable, indicating whether the person lives alone or not, is required.

Source code   The source code to implement the variable APerson is given as Example A1.

Example A1

```
TYPE
  NameString = {STRING CAPABLE OF HOLDING UP TO 50 CHARACTERS}
  SexType = (Male, Female);
  MSType = (Single, Married, Divorced);
  PersonType = RECORD
    Name: NameString;
    Age,
    Height,
    Weight: integer;
    Sex: SexType;
    {tag field follows:}
    CASE MaritalStatus: MSType OF:
      Single,
      Divorced: (LivesAlone: boolean);
      Married:  (SpouseName: NameString; NumberOfKids: integer)
  END; {PersonType}
VAR
  APerson: PersonType;
```

Selecting field variables in the variant part   There is no difference in the syntax for selecting field variables in the variant part and field variables in the fixed part of a record. If, for example, APerson is married, the statement whose source code is written as writeln(APerson. SpouseName) will display the value taken on by the field variable SpouseName. If the person is single or divorced, there is no value assigned to the field variable SpouseName. Given this precondition, an attempt to select the field variable SpouseName will either cause an error message or lead to unpredictable results at run time.

Before you write statements that select the value(s) in the variant part, you are well-advised to write a guard against selecting a meaningless field variable. A better statement, given that the value of APerson.MaritalStatus is not yet known, is written using the following source code:

```
WITH APerson DO
  IF MaritalStatus = Married THEN
```

```
            writeln(SpouseName)
        ELSE
            writeln('The person is not married.');
```

Selecting the *correct variants*

Suppose you want to write a procedure that displays the marital status of a person. It should also display the values of the variant field list. The procedure is to be called by ShowMaritalInfo(APerson); where APerson is a record of PersonType.

The block statement is readily coded using a CASE statement whose control expression is the value of MaritalStatus. The source code for this procedure is given as Example A2.

Example A2

```
    PROCEDURE ShowMaritalInfo(APerson: PersonType);
      {displays information related to the person's marital status}
      BEGIN
        WITH APerson DO
          CASE MaritalStatus OF
            Married:  ShowMarriedInfo(APerson);
            Divorced,
            Single:  ShowInfo(APerson)
          END {CASE}
    END;
```

The source code for the two procedures ShowMarriedInfo and ShowInfo is given as Examples A3 and A4.

Example A3

```
  PROCEDURE ShowMarriedInfo(APerson: PersonType);
    {displays fact that person is married, the spouse's name and number
    of children}
    BEGIN
      WITH APerson DO
        BEGIN
          writeln(Name, ' is married.');
          writeln('The spouse''s name is ', SpouseName, '.');
          writeln('They have ', NumberOfKids: 1, ' children.')
        END
    END;
```

Example A4

```
 PROCEDURE ShowInfo(APerson: PersonType);
   {displays that person is single and whether or not he or she is living
   alone}

   BEGIN
     WITH APerson DO
```

```
      BEGIN
        write(Name, ' is ');
        CASE MaritalStatus OF
          Single:  writeln('single.');
          Divorced: writeln('divorced.')
        END;  {CASE}
        IF Sex = Male THEN
          write('He ')
        ELSE
          write('She ');
        IF LivingAlone THEN
          writeln('lives alone.')
        ELSE
          writeln('is not living alone.')
      END  {WITH}
   END;
```

Functions and Procedures As Formal Parameters

In certain cases, Pascal allows you to use procedures and/or functions as parameters. When you apply this mechanism, the corresponding formal parameter represents an alias to a user-declared process. When the aliased process is called in the statement part of the coded procedure or function, the actual process, whose identifier is found in the actual parameter list, is called.

Syntax rules   The syntax diagram for a procedure or function header that has a procedure or function as a formal parameter is shown in Figure AI.8. The corresponding actual parameter that represents the coded process must simply be a reference to the process (procedure or function) identifier. A process can be used as an actual parameter for another process only if there are no VAR parameters for the candidate process parameter. Also, only user-declared procedures or functions can be coded as actual parameters of procedures or functions. The example program that follows shows an application of this mechanism where a function is used as a parameter of a procedure.

Example Problem A1

The problem statement   Suppose we have written the code for three different functions, Poly1, Poly2, and Poly3. They are all numeric functions that depend upon the value of a single real variable. We want the computer to display in tabular form the values of each of these functions in increments of 0.1 over the real-number interval 1.0 to 2.5, inclusive.

Let us write a procedure ShowValues that is capable of displaying the values taken on by any function that has one real input parameter over a specified numeric interval. We can then call this procedure three times, using Poly1, Poly2, and Poly3 as different actual parameters. The other parameters, 1.0, 2.5, and 0.1 will be the same for each procedure call. The call to display the values over the spe-

(a) PROCEDURE

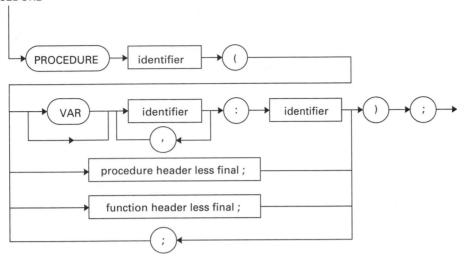

(b) Function

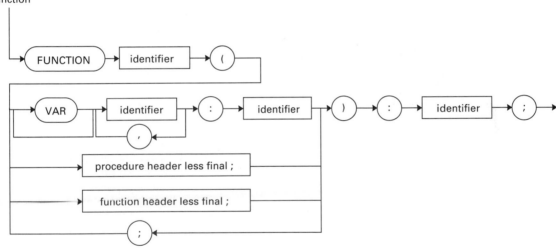

FIGURE AI.8 Header for (a) PROCEDURE or (b) FUNCTION that has a procedure or function as a parameter(s).

cified intervals for the function Poly1, for example, is coded as ShowValues (1.0, 2.5, 0.1, Poly1).

The solution   The source code solution to the problem is given as follows:

```
PROCEDURE ShowValues (LowPoint, HighPoint, Increment: real;
                      FUNCTION AFunc (XValue: real): real);

  VAR
    XRe: real;    {argument of the function}
  BEGIN
    writeln('XVALUE':10, 'F(X) VALUE':10);
```

```
        writeln('------':10,  '----------':10);
     XRe:= LowPoint;
     WHILE XRe <= HighPoint DO
        BEGIN
           writeln(XRe:10:4, AFunc(XRe):10:4;     {calls aliased function}
           XRe:= XRe + Increment
        END
   END;  ◆
```

If we desire to display the tables for each function and skip three lines between tabular display, the fragment of code to drive ShowValues is given as:

```
writeln('Poly1 Table:')
writeln;
ShowValues(1.0, 2.5, 0.1, Poly1);
writeln; writeln; writeln;
writeln('Poly 2 Table:');
writenln;
ShowValues(1.0, 2.5, 0.1, Poly2);
writeln; writeln; writeln;
writeln('Poly3 Table:');
writeln;
ShowValues(1.0, 2.5, 0.1, Poly3);
```

Separately Compiled Modules

Starting with the material of chapter 13, we have given numerous examples dealing with the implementation of ADTs. Each implementation, however, assumed the source code would be copied into the main block of a client program. In the material that follows, we show how to implement a unit that is separately compiled. Given the proper reserved words and an identifier reference to the particular unit, a client program can use all the identifiers that make up the interface part of the ADT unit.

Although standard Pascal does not include this capability as part of the language, most dialects allow separate compilation of modules as one of its features. These modules are meant to be coded and tested as ADT units that make up part of a programmer's library of abstract data types. Much of what you learned in the main text still applies to these units, as you shall see.

Turbo Pascal units
We have chosen to discuss the way units are written in the Turbo Pascal dialect. Many other dialects, such as Microsoft Quick Pascal, Apple Pascal, UCSD Pascal, and so forth use virtually the same syntax for setting up and using separately compiled units. As you read on, you will find that much of the material is not new, for we have modelled the ADT source code in the main text after the way they are written in Turbo Pascal. Thus, a Turbo Pascal unit has an interface section and an implementation section. The procedures and functions in the interface section are only headers; the implementation details are found in the implementation section of the unit.

Rather than present a number of syntax diagrams, we will instead show the source code layout for a Turbo Pascal unit, using the reserved words that are required for all Turbo Pascal units. These words are UNIT, INTERFACE, IMPLE-MENTATION, BEGIN, and END. The source code layout, using these reserved words, must then appear as follows:

```
UNIT {SomeName};      {unit is given a particular name}
  {documentation}
  {*                                                        *}
  INTERFACE  {section}
  {CONST, TYPE and VAR declarations that the client is allowed to
  reference};
  {PROCEDURE and FUNCTION headers that the client is allowed to
  reference};
  {*                                                        *}
  IMPLEMENTATION  {section}
  {CONST, TYPE and VAR declarations that are private; the client cannot
  reference them};
  {PROCEDURE and FUNCTIONS declarations that are private; the client is
  not allowed to reference them};
  {PROCEDURE and FUNCTIONS declarations that the client is allowed to
  reference; their headers match those in the interface section};
  {*                                                        *}
  BEGIN  {optional sequence of statements}
  {sequence of statements that might be required to initialize the unit
  for client program usage}
  END.
```

Explanations

The reserved word UNIT establishes the fact that the given source code is a Turbo Pascal unit. Every unit has to be named by identifier, so that it can be referenced in a client program(s). The next reserved word, INTERFACE, contains all the definitions and declarations for all identifiers that can be referenced in a client program that uses the imported unit. Note that there are absolutely no Pascal statements in this section.

The first part of the IMPLEMENTATION section contains the definition and/or declarations for any private identifiers that are visible only to the source code that makes up the unit. Most of the time, these private declarations will be the procedures and/or functions that are auxiliary to the implementation details of an operation that is visible (exportable) to a client. Following the private identifiers is the source code (header included) for all procedures and functions found in the INTER-FACE section. The details of this part of the unit are also private to the unit.

A unit statement is optional. This statement should not solve any specific problem other than to set up the unit so it can be used by a client program. Most of the time, a unit statement is not necessary, so the unit's code is completed with an empty statement enclosed by the reserved words BEGIN and END. The reserved word END is then followed by a period.

Example A5 shows some of the source code for the ADT unit ComplexNo. It is the Turbo Pascal implementation of the ADT ComplexNo that we described, used, then implemented in Sections 13.1 and 13.2.

Example A5

```
UNIT ADTComplexNo;
  {documentation}
  {*                                                                    *}
  INTERFACE    {section}
    {THE ADT DEFINITION:}
    TYPE
      ComplexNo = RECORD
        XRe, YIm: real
      END;
  {                        THE OPERATIONS                               }
  PROCEDURE MakeComplex(XPart, YPart: real;VAR CNumber: ComplexNo);
  {documentation explaining the operation}
  {+                                                                    +}
  FUNCTION RealPart(CNumber: ComplexNo): real;
  {documentation explaining the function}
  {+                                                                    +}
  {INSERT THE HEADERS FOR ALL OTHER OPERATIONS HERE}
  {*                                                                    *}
  IMPLEMENTATION    {section}
  {+                                                                    +}
  PROCEDURE MakeComplex(XPart, YPart: real; VAR CNumber: ComplexNo);
    BEGIN
      CNumber.XRe:= XPart;
      CNumber.YRe:= YPart
    END;
  {+                                                                    +}
  FUNCTION RealPart(CNumber: ComplexNo): real;
  BEGIN
    RealPart:= CNumber.XRe
  END;
  {+                                                                    +}
  {INSERT IMPLEMENTATION DETAILS FOR ALL OTHER OPERATIONS HERE}
  {*                                                                    *}
  BEGIN    {no itialization statements required}
  END.
```

Compiling a unit   Once the source code for a unit has been coded, it must be compiled. In Turbo Pascal, you must compile the unit *on disk*. In order to compile it on disk, you must go to the COMPILE options menu and select DISK compilation (as opposed to MEMORY compilation). Then, the unit can interface with a client program.

Turbo Pascal USES clause

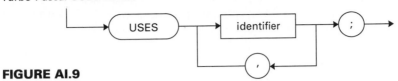

FIGURE AI.9

Using a unit
The unit's name is ADTComplexNo. If you want to use the unit in a client program, you must write a USES clause that includes the identifier name for the unit(s) you want to use. This clause must be coded directly after the program header. The syntax diagram for the USES clause in Turbo Pascal is shown in Figure AI.9.

A client program example
Let us recode Example 13.1 as given in Section 13.2. Recall that the program is to solve for the value of X in the equation $AX + B = C$, where A, B, and C are all complex numbers. The values of the coefficients A, B, and C are to be read in from the keyboard.

Source code
Part of the source code for the program, SolveIt, the solution as coded in Turbo Pascal, is shown below. This time we are assuming that the unit ADTComplexNo has compiled successfully on disk. We could just as well have said that we are assuming the unit ADTComplexNo exists in our library of Turbo Pascal units.

```
PROGRAM SolveIt(input, output);
  {documentation}
  USES
    ADTComplexNo;   {imports the unit into the source program}
  VAR
    A,B,C,              {the three coefficients}
    X: ComplexNo;       {the complex root}
{*                                                                  *}
PROCEDURE ShowInstructions;
  {documentation}
  BEGIN {insert statements as coded in example}     END;
{*                                                                  *}
PROCEDURE GetCoefficients(VAR A, B, C: ComplexNo);
  {documentation}
  BEGIN   {insert statements as coded in example}     END;
{*                                                                  *}
PROCEDURE SolveEquation(A, B, C: ComplexNo; VAR X: ComplexNo);
  {documentation}
  VAR
    CMinusB: ComplexNo;
  BEGIN
    SubtrComp(C, B, CMinusB);
    DivComp(CMinusB, A, X)
  END;
{*                                                                  *}
PROCEDURE ShowRoot(X: ComplexNo);
```

```
     {displays the value of X, along with other text}
     BEGIN  {insert statements as coded in example}  END;
  {*                                                                    *}
  BEGIN
    ShowInstructions;
    GetCoefficients(A, B ,C);
    SolveEquation(A, B, C, X);
    ShowRoot(X)
  END.
```

VAX Pascal

The source code as given in our example will work for many other dialects of Pascal with little or no changes because the reserved words are the same. In particular, it will work in Microsoft Quick Pascal, UCSD Pascal, and the different dialects of Apple Pascal. It will not work in VAX Pascal because this dialect uses different reserved words.

VAX Pascal modules

In VAX Pascal, the reserved words to code a module (VAX jargon for a unit) are MODULE, ENVIRONMENT, and END. A VAX Pascal module is coded such that it contains identifiers that a client program can use. There is no interface or implementation section to a VAX Pascal module; all identifiers that are defined and/or declared can be referenced in a client program. A VAX Pascal module never has an initialization statement. Once the last procedure or function has been declared, the source code of the module ends with the reserved word END followed by a period.

Although there is no formal interface section in a VAX Pascal module, it is better to separate the procedure and function headers from the implementation details. Therefore, we recommend that you make your own interface section of FOR-WARD-directed processes just as we did in the main part of the text. The required headers for interfacing are then up front, and the implementation details are hidden in the "implementation section" that follows the headers coded with the reserved word FORWARD.

Syntax

Figure AI.10 shows the syntax diagram for a VAX Pascal module that is coded as an ADT. The string constant enclosed by the parentheses is the directory name of the module. This name does not include the file's extension (such as ".pas", ".exe", ".dat", and so forth). This directory name is matched with the name (also coded as a string constant) in the client program to create the interface between the module(s) and the program.

An example

Part of the source code for the module ADTComplexNo, coded in VAX Pascal, is given as follows:

```
[ENVIRONMENT ('ADTComplexNo')]
MODULE ADTComplexNo;
  {                   INTERFACE PART OF ADT COMPLEXNO                   }
  {documentation}
  TYPE
    ComplexNo = RECORD
      XRe, YIm: real
    END;
  {*                        THE OPERATIONS                             *}
```

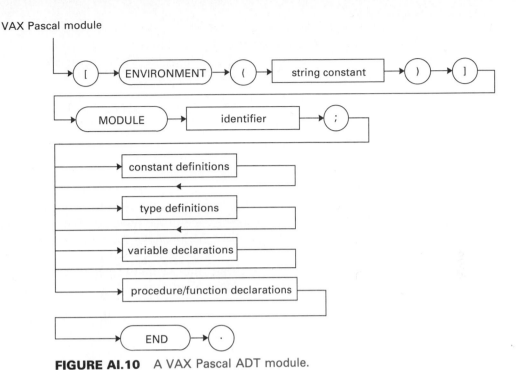

VAX Pascal module

FIGURE AI.10 A VAX Pascal ADT module.

```
PROCEDURE MakeComplex(XPart, YPart: real;
                           VAR CNumber: ComplexNo);               FORWARD;
{documentation}
{+                                                                           +}
FUNCTION RealPart(CNumber: ComplexNo): real;               FORWARD;
{documentation}
{+                                                                           +}
{INSERT OTHER HEADERS FOR FORWARD-DIRECTING ALL STATEMENTS HERE}
{*            IMPLEMENTATION PART OF ADT COMPLEXNO                       *}
PROCEDURE MakeComplex {XPart, YPart: real; VAR CNumber: ComplexNo};
  BEGIN
    CNumber.XRe:= XPart;
    CNumber.YIm:= YPart
  END;
{+                                                                           +}
FUNCTION RealPart {(CNumber: ComplexNo): real};
  BEGIN
    RealPart:= CNumber.XRe
  END;
{+                                                                           +}
{INSERT CODE FOR IMPLEMENTING ALL OTHER OPERATIONS HERE}
END.    {MODULE}
```

VAX Pascal client program

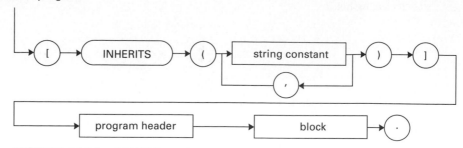

FIGURE AI.11   A VAX Pascal client program.

*The client
program in VAX*
    A client program in VAX Pascal uses the reserved word INHERITS to link the ADT module(s) with the source code of the program. The syntax diagram for a client program in VAX Pascal that.inherits one or more modules is given in Figure AI.11.

An example
    We can use the same example from section 13.2 to obtain the source code for the client program SolveIt in VAX Pascal as

```
[INHERITS ('ADTComplexNo')]    {VAX importation of module ADTComplexNo}
PROGRAM SolveIt(input, output);
  VAR
    A,B,C,              {the three coefficients}
    X: ComplexNo;       {the complex root}
  {*                                                              *}
  PROCEDURE ShowInstructions;
    {documentation}
    BEGIN {insert statements as coded in example}    END;
  {*                                                              *}
  PROCEDURE GetCoefficients(VAR A, B, C: ComplexNo);
    {documentation}
    BEGIN   {insert statements as coded in example}    END;
  {*                                                              *}
  PROCEDURE SolveEquation(A, B, C: ComplexNo; VAR X: ComplexNo);
    {documentation}
    VAR
      CMinusB: ComplexNo;
    BEGIN
      SubtrComp(C, B, CMinusB);
      DivComp(CMinusB, A, X)
    END;
  {*                                                              *}
  PROCEDURE ShowRoot(X: ComplexNo);
    {displays the value of X, along with other text}
    BEGIN {insert statements as coded in example}    END;
  {*                                                              *}
  BEGIN
    ShowInstructions;
```

```
     GetCoefficients(A,  B  ,C);
     SolveEquation(A,  B,  C,  X);
     ShowRoot(X)
  END.
```

Compilation and linking

Both the module ADTComplexNo and the client program SolveIt are compiled the usual way, that is, with the respective commands pascal ADTComplexNo and pascal SolveIt. In order to run properly, however, they must be linked together using the same link command. For this program, the command is written as link SolveIt, ADTComplexNo. In VAX Pascal, you must always link the client program to all modules by naming the client program first, then all the different modules it uses. Each source code file name is separated by a comma.

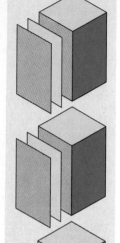

ANSWERS TO SELECTED EXERCISES

Section 1.1

2. **(1)** Primary memory is volatile, and secondary memory is not.
   (2) A primary memory device is not easily removed from the rest of the system, whereas a secondary memory device, such as a floppy disk, is.

4. A *program file* stores program instructions to the computer. A *data file* stores data to be processed by some program.

Section 1.2

1. false

3. No. Even though there is ANSI Pascal, there are many dialects.

Section 1.3

3. The editor and the compiler   4. Syntax error, run-time crash, semantic error
5. false

Section 1.4

1. An object holds one or more data values in a computer's memory, and a process is a sequence of instructions to be carried out by the computer.

4. `writeln`, `write`, `readln`, and `sqr`

6. named constant—`Pi`; anonymous constant—`'First, enter the radius: '`

7. false   8. false

Section 1.5

1. true **2.** header, declarations, statement **3.** CONST **4.** VAR
6. It assigns the value of the expression on the right-hand side of the assignment operator to the variable on the left-hand side of the operator.
8. by a pair of braces or by the symbol pair (* *)

Chapter 1 Review Exercises

1. object **4.** identifier **7.** syntax **9.** CPU **14.** 0s and 1s
15. program header, interface

Section 2.1

1. **(a)** valid **(c)** invalid **(e)** invalid **(h)** valid
2. **(a)** user-defined identifier **(c)** reserved word **(h)** none of the three

Section 2.2

1. display field size **2.** decimal precision
3. Writeln clears the display line, but write lets more characters be displayed on the line.
4. **(a)** 13.0 **(e)** 1.0 **(f)** 17.0 **(g)** 68.0 **(j)** 2 **(k)** 16.0 **(l)** 1.0
6. **(a)** 417045.89

Section 2.3

1. No, once a constant's value is defined, it cannot be changed.
3. **(a)** assigns two values **(c)** assigns two values **(i)** crashes
5. **(b)** Ch1 ⟷ 'X' Ch2 ⟷ '⊔' **(d)** Ch1 ⟷ '1' Ch2 ⟷ '5'

Section 2.4

1. They both must be of the same type.
3. **(a)** No **(b)** Yes **(c)** No **(d)** Yes **(e)** Yes **(f)** No
5.

```
PROGRAM DoExercise(input, output); {or any other program identifier}
  VAR
    Int1, Int2: integer;
    Ch: char;
    Re: real;
  BEGIN
    {insert statement of Exercise 2 here}
  END.
```

Section 2.5

1. A text file contains characters that are all human-readable. Yes.

Chapter 2 Programs Testing Hints

1. Maxint, for a given dialect of Pascal, is the highest possible integer value that can be expressed in that dialect.

Chapter 2 Review

1. PROGRAM, BEGIN, END **3.** Comments help make source code more readable.
5. 2.0, real **7.** true **9.** read, readln **11.** true **12.** true

Section 3.1

1. desk-tracing, assertion testing, on-line testing. Desk-tracing and assertion testing can be done as soon as a process is described, but on-line testing requires that the source code has compiled.

4. After `readln(Ch1, Ch2, Ch3)` the variables Ch1, Ch2 and Ch3 represent the first, second, and third char values read in.
   After `readln(Score)`, the value Score represents the score read in.
   After the `write, writeln` sequence the values of Ch1, Ch2, and Ch3 and the integer quotient of Score and 1000 have been displayed.

5. Define the constant Hundred = 100, change the arithmetic expression to Score DIV Hundred and display one less "0".

Section 3.2

1. A categorized algorithm can be applied as a ready-made initial draft for many diverse problems that, nonetheless, can be described in terms of the one algorithm. When many categorized algorithms are available, there are many candidate algorithms that can represent the initial draft to the solution of a specified problem. These algorithm thus make up a "software toolchest" that can be applied to solving a specific problem.

2. `write, readln` **3.** `read, process, display`

6. ```
write('Enter an integer and a real value: ');
readln(Int1, Re1);
```

## Section 3.3

1. Pascal does not have a standard type to represent a string variable.

3. The argument of a function must be known before the function can be evaluated. The inner function call, which is an argument of the other function call, must therefore be evaluated first.

4. `Ch:= chr( ord(Ch) + ord('a') - ord('A') );`

## Section 3.4

1. false

2. Yes; after `readln`'s the values read into each of the three variables represent Schedule B, Schedule D, and Schedule A variables, respectively. After the first assignment statement, GrossIncome will be the original GrossIncome after adjustments for Schedules B and D. After the second assignment, TaxableGrossIncome will represent the original TaxableGrossIncome after adjustments for Schedules B, D, and A.

4. Declare another variable of type real named CorporateIncome. Then after the Schedule B sequence, add the code:

```
write('Enter corporate gain (+) or loss (-):   ');
readln(CorporateIncome);
TaxableIncome:= TaxableIncome + CorporateIncome;
TaxableGrossIncome:= TaxableGrossIncome + CorporateIncome;
```
```

Chapter 3 Program Testing Hints

1. **(a)** Code second statement as: `Prod:= Int1 * Int2 * Int3;`
   (c) Code second statement as: `Ave:= (Int1 + Int2 + Int3) / 3;`

Chapter 3 Review

1. true   **2.** successive refinements
4. The variable `Int1` is serving more than one purpose.
6. an incorrect assignment statement   **7.** `'Y'`   **8.** 50   **10.** chr
11. false   **12.** true   **13.** `'G'`

Section 4.1

1. call, header   **2.** PROCEDURE and VAR
3. Associated with preconditions: input, input/output; associated with postconditions: output, input/output
5. The values would be returned unchanged. Preconditions: `GrossIncome` and `TaxableGrossIncome` represent values before doing schedules. Postconditions: none, because there are no VAR calls.
6.

```
PROCEDURE ShowInstructions;
  {documentation}
  BEGIN
    writeln('Welcome to Tax Helper, the easy and carefree way to do ');
    writeln('your taxes.  Enter all values in dollars amounts when ');
    writeln('prompted.  If you have suffered a capital loss, enter ');
    writeln('a negative value.  All other entries are positive.')
END;
```

Section 4.2

1. call-by-value and local declarations   **2.** call-by-variable
5. constant identifier and type identifier   **6.** (1) an empty statement (2) display that a procedure has been executed (3) values assigned as anonymous constants to all VAR parameters (4) values read in from keyboard to all VAR parameters.
9. **(a)** XInt ↔ 9 **(b)** YInt ↔ 4 **(c)** ZInt ↔ 8
10.
```
        PROCEDURE DManipulate;
            VAR
                XInt, {input parameter}
                YInt, {input/output parameter}
                ZInt: {output parameter}
                        integer;
            BEGIN
                write('Input values for XInt and YInt:  ');
                readln(XInt, YInt);
                Manipulate(XInt, YInt, ZInt);
                writeln('YInt = ',YInt:1,'   ZInt = ',ZInt:1)
            END;
```

12.

```
PROCEDURE GetPrincipalAndRate(VAR Principal, Rate: real);
  {documentation}
  BEGIN
    write('Enter starting principal:  $');
    readln(Principal);
    write('Enter interest rate as a percentage:  ');
    readln(Rate)
  END;
```

Section 4.3

2. In main block, Cents represents the amount of money to be made into change. In MakeChange, Cents is copied in and represents same purpose as in main block. In GetCoins, Cents is value to be changed for given coin, then value remaining to be changed for remaining coins. Memory is created for Cents in main block and MakeChange. Cents is an alias in GetCoins.

4. 29 quarters, 1 nickel, and 2 pennies

6. **(a)** 1 3 5 **(b)** 5 10 15 **(c)** 5 2 7

Chapter 4 Program Testing Hints

1. planning and coding the statements before doing the header

2. a reference to a variable identifier not seen in the header. A side effect is harmful because it obscures the data flow between a procedure call and the procedure's actions.

3. (c) and (e) are correct

4. **(a)** PROCEDURE DoIt(BInt: integer; VAR AInt: integer);

5. PRe used properly; WInt used properly; QInt improper call QRe ambiguous reference; AInt used properly; BInt never used ZRe side effect; CInt side effect

6. **(b)**   call: DoIt(AInt, CRe, DRe);
      header: PROCEDURE DoIt(AInt: integer; VAR CRe, DRe: real);
   (c)   call: DoIt(AInt + BInt, DRe);
      header: PROCEDURE DoIt(XInt: integer; VAR DRe: real);

Chapter 4 Review

1. actual parameter list   4. first parameter is of type integer; second parameter is of type real; both are called by value

5. Yes, when the same subprogram is needed in more than one place in the execution sequence of a program.

7. Either if the first procedure is nested inside the second one or the first procedure has been declared ahead of the second one.

9. (b) and (c) are valid headers   12. false   13. local   17. false

Section 5.1

1. true   2. Given that the boolean expression is true, the associated statement is executed, otherwise no further action is carried out.

4. **(a)** false **(b)** true **(c)** illegal

5. `IF sqr(B) − 4*A*C > 0 THEN`
   `    writeln('REAL')`

```
        ELSE IF sqr(B) - 4*A*C = 0 THEN
          writeln('DOUBLE')
        ELSE
          writeln('IMAGINARY');
```

6. **(a)**
```
     IF Re > 0 THEN
         BEGIN
           Count:= Count + 1;
           Sum:= Sum + Re
         END;
```

   (e)
```
     IF abs(OldX - NewX) < 0.0005 THEN
         writeln('CONVERGENCE HAS OCCURRED')
     ELSE
         IterNo:= IterNo + 1;
```

   (g)
```
     IF Withdrawl > Balance THEN
         writeln('OVERDRAWN BY ',Withdrawl - Balance)
     ELSE
         Balance:= Balance - Withdrawl;
```

Section 5.2

1. no 2. (c) 25 32 25; 25 32 25; 25 25 32

4.
```
   PROCEDURE StrExchange(VAR Str1, Str2: StringType);
     VAR
       Temp: StringType;
     BEGIN
       Temp:= Str1;
       Str1:= Str2;
       Str2:= Temp
     END;
```

5. block statement:

```
   BEGIN
     IF Second > Third THEN
       Exchange(Second, Third);
     IF First > Third THEN
       Exhange(First, Third);
     IF First > Second THEN
       Exchange(First, Second)
   END;
```

Section 5.3

1. Exactly one of *N* possible paths is to be taken. The order in which paths are considered is critical.

3. Describe and prove the first decision that must be made. Then describe and prove the next decision(s), given the result of the first decision. Continue the development process until all necessary decisions have been described and acted upon.

5.
```
   IF Score >= 90) THEN
     writeln('successful and distinguished')
   ELSE IF Score >= 80 THEN
     writeln('successful and very good')
```

```
ELSE IF Score >= 70 then
   writeln('successful')
ELSE IF Score >= 60 THEN
   writeln('unsuccessful and passed')
ELSE
   writeln('unsuccessful and failed');
```

Section 5.4

2. Given that the data can be processed, it is processed. Optional: otherwise some error-handling sequence, such as a message display, is carried out.

3. No, because the only assertion that can be made given that the first value read into Int is nonpositive is that another value is read into Int. This second value read in can also be nonpositive.

4. **(a)** A and C are not zero, and Discrim is nonnegative.

7.
```
PROCEDURE DriveDisplayRealRoots;
VAR
   A, B, Discrim: real;
BEGIN
   write('Enter nonzero value for A:   ')
   readln(A);
   write('Enter nonzero value for B:   ')
   readln(B);
   write('Enter nonnegative value for Discrim:  ');
   readln(Discrim);
   IF A = 0 THEN
      writeln('CANNOT CALL PROCEDURE')
   ELSE IF B = 0 THEN
      writeln('CANNOT CALL PROCEDURE')
   ELSE IF Discrim < 0 THEN
      writeln('CANNOT CALL PROCEDURE')
   ELSE
      DisplayRealRoots(A, B, Discrim)
END;
```

Section 5.5

1. one   3. They must be constants.

5.
```
CASE Int OF
   0: write('zero');
   1: write('one');
   2: write('two');
   3: write('three');
   4: write('four');
   5: write('five');
   6: write('six');
   7: write('seven');
   8: write('eight');
   9: write('nine')
END;   {CASE}
```

7. **(a)**
```
readln(Int1, Int2);
   IF Int1 < Int2 THEN
      writeln(Int1:1,' ',Int2:1)
   ELSE
      writeln(Int2:1,' ',Int1:1);
```
(c)
```
CASE Int OF
   3: write('III');
   2: write('II');
   1: write('I')
END;    {CASE}
```
(e)
```
readln(Age);
IF Age >= 18 THEN
   BEGIN
     write('Are you a citizen?  ');
     readln(Answer);
     IF Answer = 'Y' THEN
        writeln('This way to registration')
     ELSE
        writeln('You are not a citizen.')
   END
ELSE
   writeln('You are not old enough.');
```
(g)
```
IF Int > 0 THEN
   Int:= Int + 5;
```

Chapter 5   Program Testing Hints

1. Helps find errors; forces one to think of what can go wrong; forces one to write robust code.

2. It will "work" for any value of Age greater than or equal to 18.

4.
```
IF Int < 10 THEN
   writeln('too small')
ELSE IF Int <= 25 THEN
   writeln('just right')
ELSE
   writeln('too large');
```
   (b) A case statement is not viable because (1) it requires too many labels and (2) nothing is explicitly stated about the problem for negative or very large positive values. Thus, ambiguous "otherwise" conditions would result.

6. Main block values: Choose A = 0 and A <> 0 values along with any B and C values; when A <> 0, choose C = 0 and any B values; choose A and C values <> 0 and any B values.
   ShowRealRoots values: must have A <> 0, C <> 0. Test with Discrim equal to 0 and also with Discrim not equal to 0.

Chapter 5   Review

1. true   3. true   4. division by zero and square root of negative number   7. 4   8. 1
9. No logical difference exists.   10. false
14. 1 of 2 (where second path does nothing), 1 of 2   15. false

Section 6.1

1. true, false   2. (b) 0,   0   3. (b) 140,   5   5. 140,   −190

Section 6.2

1. initialization, loop body, postprocess, no   2. (a) Count <= 10
2. (b) Sum <> 0   3. (a) loop (e) decision (g) sequence of statements

Section 6.3

1. false   2. false   3. Zero times any number is always zero.   4. both 0
5. one of the two values is 1, the other is 0

Section 6.4

2. The algorithm is not an entry-exit algorithm; it is a recording algorithm whose usage does not depend on the number of items to process.
3. (a) 18 15 12 9 6 (b) DEFGH 5. (a), (b), (d) Int <= 0

Section 6.5

2. when at least one loop pass is required
4. when the loop is controlled by one variable whose type is ordinal, whose entry-exit values are predetermined and whose value for the next pass is the pred or succ of the value for the present loop pass.
6. {statement}
```
BEGIN
   writeln('Total Fuel Cost = $', GasBill:4:2);
   writeln('Total Food Cost = $', FoodBill:4:2);
   writeln('Total Lodging Cost = $', LodgeBill:4:2);
   write('Total Cost of Trip = $');
   writeln(GasBill + FoodBill + LodgeBill:4:2)
END;
```
7. Set the value of the constant PartySize to 4 rather than to 3. Realistically speaking, a new value should be set for MaxLodging.

Section 6.6

1. (b)

A:	1	2	3	4	5	(c)	123	124	125
B:	1	2	3	4	5		133	134	135
C:	1	2	3	4	5		143	144	145
D:	1	2	3	4	5		223	224	225
							233	234	235
							243	244	245
							323	324	325
							333	334	335
							343	344	345

Chapter 6   Program Testing Hints

1. Choose test data with few data values first. The rule is useful because obvious errors can be found with the need for very little testing.

3. The counter is incremented, regardless of whether Ch is a letter or not. Use a WHILE loop and increment the Count only if a letter is read in.

5. Yes, bad semantics on the variables Count and Sum

Chapter 6 Review

1. REPEAT   UNTIL   **4.** under no conditions   **6.** false

8. exit condition, body, postprocessing   **11.** counting   **13.** 25   **15.** 0   **16.** 1

9. Either one more or one less loop passes than required for a *correct* solution has been executed. Off-by-one errors are not considered a decision-making phenomenon because a decision is executed exactly once. Thus, there is no such event as N−1 or N+1 decision-making "passes."

10. solution variable ↔ accumulation variable;
loop control variable ↔ FOR loop counting variable
solution condition ↔ guard loop strategy
off-by-one ↔ semantic error condition
special-event counting ↔ requires decision in loop body
initialization ↔ actions executed before loop entry
loop invariant ↔ a type of assertion
endless loop ↔ never exited

12. true   **14.** false   **16.** 1

Section 7.1

1. false, false   **2.** true, true   **3.** complement   **4.** ordinal, set

6. **(a)** IF XInt IN [1..4] THEN
      YInt:= 0;
  (d) IF ((XInt > YInt) AND (YInt > 5)) OR
      ((YInt > XInt) AND (XInt < 7)) THEN
     WInt:= 0;
  (e) IF Ch IN ['+', '−', '*', '/'] THEN
     writeln('This is an arithmetic operator.');

7. **(a)** XInt IN [6..8]
  (c) (6.95 < ZRe) AND (ZRe < 7.05)
  (f) (Ch1 IN ['a'..'z']) AND (Ch2 IN ['a'..'z']) AND (Ch1 < Ch2)

Section 7.2

1. **(b)** (XInt < 15) OR (XInt > 25)
  (c) (Ch1 <> ' ') AND (Ch2 = ' ')

3. The three expressions are mutually exclusive; therefore the control expression for the IF statement will never return true, regardless of the values of XInt and YInt.

4. **(a)** REPEAT
     write('Input two positive integer values: ');
     readln(XInt, YInt)
    UNTIL (XInt > 0) AND (YInt > 0);
  (b) IF (XInt <> YInt) THEN
     Process(XInt, YInt)
    ELSE
     writeln('UNABLE TO PROCESS..THE VALUES ARE EQUAL');

```
    6.  REPEAT
          read(Int)
        UNTIL (Int < 0) OR (Int > 1000);
        readln;
        IF (Int < 0) THEN
          writeln('LOW SIDE')
        ELSE
          writeln('HIGH SIDE');
```

Section 7.3

1. **(a)** legal **(b)** illegal **(c)** illegal **(d)** legal
2. **(a)** only a single starting address is copied
   (b) all 1000 elements are copied into a local array variable
4. 39 88 15 38 22
5. **(a)**
```
TYPE
  RealsArray = ARRAY[1..5] OF real;
VAR
  Prices: RealsArray;    {contains prices of each of 5 widgets}
```
(c)
```
TYPE
  IntsArray = ARRAY[1..5] OF integer;
VAR
  Orders: IntsArray;    {counts orders for each of 5 widgets}
```

Section 7.4

2. Alfred E. Newman — 55.0 — F
   Charles C. Charles — 98.8 — A
4. **(a)**
```
     PROCEDURE CountZeroes(Ints: IntsArray; VAR Zeroes: integer);
       VAR
         Index: integer;
       BEGIN
         ZCount:= 0;
         FOR Index:= 1 TO 10 DO
           IF Ints[Index] = 0 THEN
             ZCount:= ZCount + 1
       END;
```
(b)
```
   PROCEDURE DriveCZeroes;
     VAR
       Ints: IntsArray;
       Index,
       ZCount: integer;
     BEGIN
       writeln('Key in 10 integers, some of which are equal to 0:');
       FOR Index:= 1 TO 10 DO
         read(Ints[Index]);
       readln;
```

```
        CountZeroes(Ints, ZCount);
        writeln('The array has ',ZCount:1,' zeroes in it.')
    END;
```

(c) Definites: one with all zeroes, one with no zeroes, one with some zeroes;
Possibles: one where the first element is 0, one where the last element is 0.

Section 7.5

1. The process of accessing the elements was locally carried out; hence, local variables are declared in each block that carries out the process.

2. It is more efficient; no local copy of the array variable is made.

Chapter 7   Program Testing Hints

1. **(c)** A OR B OR C **(d)** A AND B AND C   **3.** true

4. **(a)** Processing is carried out only if one variable is positive.
   (c) When Count = 10, instead of just one message, two are displayed.
   (d) It works, but the logic is confusing.

6. **(a)**
```
    IF (XInt > 0) AND (YInt > 0) THEN
        Process(XInt, YInt)
    ELSE
        writeln('UNABLE TO PROCESS');
```
   (c)
```
    IF Count = 10 THEN
        writeln('WE ARE OUT OF AMMO')
    ELSE IF XPos > YPos THEN
        writeln('THE TARGET HAS BEEN HIT')
    ELSE
        writeln('WE ARE OUT OF RANGE');
```
   (d)
```
    REPEAT
        read(XInt)
    UNTIL XInt >= 0;
    readln;
    Process(XInt);
```

Chapter 7   Review

1. false   **3.** (AInt   BInt) OR (Count <> 10)   **4.** 3   **5.** parallel
9. then it cannot be used as a parameter
11. when the expression on the right-hand side represents an array variable of the same type
14. No, the IN operator works only with ordinal types.   **17.** +, >, =, OR, NOT

Section 8.1

1. an assignment statement that returns a value to the function
3. The function is "called" with no parameter list.
4. **(a)**
```
    FUNCTION SphereVolume(Radius: real): real;
        BEGIN    {Pi is defined constant}
            SphereVolume:= (4/3)*Pi*sqr(Radius)*Radius
        END;
```

(b)
```
FUNCTION Lower(Int1, Int2: integer): integer;
    BEGIN
        IF Int1 < Int2 THEN
            Lower:= Int1
        ELSE
            Lower:= Int2
    END;
```

5.
```
FUNCTION IntsSum(Ints: IntsArray): integer;
    VAR
        Index; integer;
    BEGIN
        Sum:= 0;
        FOR Index:= 1 TO 10 DO
            Sum:= Sum + Ints[Index];
        IntsSum:= Sum
    END;
```

Section 8.2

1. true   2. false   3. **(a)** 10   **(b)** 6

4. **(a)**
```
FUNCTION Correct(Guess, IntsValue: integer): boolean;
    BEGIN
        Correct:= Guess = IntsValue
    END;
```

(c)
```
FUNCTION OrderedPair(Int1, Int2: integer): boolean;
    BEGIN
        OrderedPair:= Int1 < Int2
    END;
```

Section 8.3

1. to handle any error conditions with input/output   2. false

6. **(a)**
```
FUNCTION NextMonth(InMonth: MonthType): MonthType;
        {assumes valid InMonth value}
    BEGIN
        IF InMonth = Dec THEN
            NextMonth:= Jan
        ELSE
            NextMonth:= succ(InMonth)
    END;
```

(c)
```
FUNCTION ValidMonth(InMonth: MonthType): boolean;
    BEGIN
        ValidMonth:= InMonth <> NullMonth
    END;
```

Section 8.4

2. closer to bottom-up testing because lower-level procedures are tested first.

3. There is no input; only output that is generated from values solicited from the keyboard.

4. **(a)** Ladders: 20 to 47, 10 to 47   Snakes: 38 to 22, 25 to 20
   (d) no Snakes or Ladders

6.  ```
    PROCEDURE ShowBoard(VAR GameBoard: BoardType);
      VAR
        SquareNo: 1..LastSquare;
      BEGIN
        FOR SquareNo:= 1 to 50 DO
          BEGIN
            write(GameBoard[SquareNo]:4);
            IF SquareNo MOD 10 = 0 THEN
              writeln
          END
      END;
    ```

Chapter 8 Program Testing Hints

1. it is always possible   2. When it is a scalar variable or (worse) when its value is changed by the statements of the function.

4. Yes, because once the function is set true by the condition being sought, it remains true for all loop passes.

5.  ```
    IF XInt > 5 THEN
      REPEAT
        readln(XInt)
      UNTIL XInt <= 5;
    ```

8.  ```
    FUNCTION Invalid(VAR AnArray: ArrayType; Lower, Upper: integer;
                                   AssignedElements: integer): boolean;
      VAR
        StillValid: boolean:
        Index: integer;
      BEGIN
        StillValid:= true;
        FOR Index:= 1 TO AssignedElements DO
          IF (AnArray[Index] < Lower) OR (AnArray[Index > Higher} THEN
            StillValid:= false;
        Invalid:= NOT StillValid
      END;
    ```

Chapter 8 Review

2. A boolean variable to flag a change in the program state. This variable can be used in a control expression at any point in the sequence of statements that makes up the program.

4. false   5. false   6. false   7. No, because an array contains more than one value.

8. true   9. false   10. false (not always)

12. No, the first assignment depends upon a previous value assigned to ABool; the second assignment assigns a value to ABool regardless of its previous value.

14. To hold the value returned by a call to RNG and to help generate another value from the RNG.

18. boolean, procedure, variable, procedure, boolean, variable.
    ```

Section 9.1

1. A blank text file has exactly two characters in it. The first character is the <eoln> marker. The second character is the <eof> marker.
2. false 3. true
4. A file variable is the means to access a directory file in a Pascal program. A directory file is a file that is found in secondary memory. A file variable is the means by which access is gained to the contents of a directory file during the course of a program run.
8.

```
PROGRAM ChCount(output, PurpleCow);   {standard Pascal}
  VAR
    Ch: char;                {holds char value read in}
    Blanks: integer;         {counter variable for blank char values}
  BEGIN
    reset(PurpleCow);
    Blanks:= 0;
    WHILE NOT eof(PurpleCow) DO
      BEGIN
        WHILE NOT eoln(PurpleCow) DO
          BEGIN
            read(PurpleCow,Ch);
            IF Ch = ' ' THEN
              Blanks:= Blanks + 1
          END;
        readln(PurpleCow)
      END;
      writeln('The number of non-blank characters was ',Blanks:1, '.')
  END.
```

Section 9.2

1. A file variable in the read mode is seen as a window to the next item in the file being read from. A file variable in the write mode (for a text file) is seen as a buffer to hold characters that are eventually written into the associated directory file.

4. **(b)** Ah yes, I wrote the Purple Cow.
  I'm sorry now, I wrote it.
  But I will tell you anyhow,
  I'll thank you not to quote it!

  (d) Ah yes, I wrote the Purple Cow.
  Ah yes, I wrote the Purple Cow.
  I'm sorry now, I wrote it.
  Ah yes, I wrote the Purple Cow.
  I'm sorry now, I wrote it.
  But I will tell you anyhow,

Section 9.3

1. some defined string type, integer 2. 0 3. **(a)** 15 **(d)** e.e. cummings

Section 9.4

1. FOR No:= 1 TO 10 DO

```
    BEGIN
      IF Unsatisfactory(Upper, Lower, Sample[No]) THEN
        Count:= Count + 1;
    END;
```

2. **(a)** Crash, too many characters for Payee variable read in on first line **(b)** no information about check 721 is read in **(c)** will run properly

Chapter 9   Program Testing Hints

2. Yes, because the decision statement serves as a guard against reading in the first character if it is the <eoln> marker.

3. **(a)** attempt to read past <eof> **(b)** reading in a letter when a digit (for an integer value) is expected

4. **(b)** 0 elements, 1 element, some in-between numbers of elements, 999 elements, 1000 elements, 1001 elements

5. **(a)**
Write the main block statement as follows:
```
BEGIN
  Initialize(Results, TotalStudents,TotalTests);
  StudentNo:= 0;
  WHILE NOT eof(Results) AND NOT(StudentNo = TotalStudents) DO
    ShowAStudent(TotalTests, Results);
  IF StudentNo < TotalStudents THEN
    BEGIN
      write('WARNING:  THE CLASS IS MISSING THE SCORES OF ');
      writeln(TotalStudents − StudentNo: 1,' STUDENTS')
    END
END.
```

6.
```
IF NOT eoln(InFile) THEN
  WHILE NOT eoln(InFile) DO
    BEGIN
      read(InFile, Ch);
      {process Ch}
    END
ELSE
  {display error condition message};
readln(InFile);
```

Chapter 9   Review

1. opened, file variable   3. rewritten   5. as declared variables   6. false   9. false

11. a string with no characters in it; possibly as a sentinel value, always to initialize a character accumulation into a string variable

14. an empty file   16. the first nonblank character is not a digit or an empty file

17. No, the file variable is called by value.

Section 10.1

1. No, because the subranges 'A'..'Z' and 'a'..'z' in EBCDIC do not contain values that represent only letters of the alphabet.

3. No currency is read in; another prompt for input is displayed.

4. **(a)** 7 **(c)** the department in which a person worked for a given day

6. all subranges are from 'A'..'Z' to access elements of Letters; in CountOccur-rences, any lowercase Ch is changed to uppercase; there is no need for Offset and DisplayLetter variables in ShowOccurrences, and a simple FOR loop to access the array elements is all that is needed

7. ShowCurrency's statement:

```
BEGIN
   CASE ACurrency OF
      USDollar:              write('American dollars');
      AustralianDollar:      write('Australian dollars');
      BritishPound:          write('British pounds');
      CanadianDollar:        write('Canadian dollars');
      GermanMark:            write('German marks');
      SwissFranc:            write('Swiss francs');
      JapaneseYen:           write('Japanese yen');
      END    {CASE}
END;
```

Section 10.2

1. *NOT (finished OR Found)*

3. Call NameIndex and get one value for the Index to 'Smith'. Store this value as an array of indices (say, FoundIndices[1]), then call NameIndex where the search starts with element FoundIndices[1]−1. When (if) another match is found, store this index in FoundIndices[2], then start the search with element FoundIndices[2]−1. Continue the process until no more matches are found.

6.
```
FUNCTION AllPositive(VAR Ints: IntsArray; TotEls: integer): boolean;
  VAR
    StillPositive: boolean;
    Index: integer;
  BEGIN
    StillPositive:= true;
    Index:= TotEls;
    WHILE (Index <> 0) AND StillPositive DO
      IF Ints[Index] <= 0 THEN
        StillPositive:= false
      ELSE
        Index:= Index−1;
    AllPositive:= StillPositive
  END;
```

Section 10.3

2. 9 4

4. 32 74 87 66 82; 32 66 87 74 82; 32 66 74 87 82; 32 66 74 82 87

8. statement for this form of the bubble sort algorithm:

```
    BEGIN
      FOR Sorted:= LastElement DOWNTO 2 DO
        FOR Index:= 2 TO LastElement DO
          IF Ints[Index] < Ints[Index-1] THEN
            ExchangeInts(Ints[Index], Ints[Index-1])
    END;
```

Section 10.4

1. a failed search

4. **(a)** Lo = 1, Hi = 50, found on first probe
   (b) Lo = 1, Hi = 50, Lo = 1, Hi = 24; Lo = 1, Hi = 11;
       Lo = 7, Hi = 11; Lo = 10, Hi = 11, found on this probe
   (d) Lo = 1, Hi = 50, Lo = 1, Hi = 24; Lo = 1, Hi = 11;
       Lo = 7, Hi = 11; Lo = 10, Hi = 11; Lo = 11, Hi = 10, fails
   (g) Lo = 1, Hi = 50, Lo = 26, Hi = 50; Lo = 39, Hi = 50;
       Lo = 45, Hi = 50; Lo = 48, Hi = 50, Lo = 50, Hi = 50;
       Lo = 51, Hi = 50, fails

6. **(a)** *Names[Lo-1]* <= *SearchName* < *Names[Hi+1]*
   (b) either *Names[Lo-1]* or *Names[Hi]*, for they both represent equivalent values

Section 10.5

1. O(N³)   3. B—25 T secs   4. O(N)

Chapter 10   Program Testing Hints

1. true   **2.** false   **4. (a)** true   **(b)** Given that `AnArray[Index]` is less than 0,
   `NoNegatives` is `false`, otherwise it is `true`.

8.
```
REPEAT
    write('enter letter (lowercase) whose occurrence count you want: ');
  readln(Letter);
UNTIL Letter IN ['a'..'z'];
```

10. Aaron, Adams, Griffin, Ryan, Thomasin, Young, Zacherly

Chapter 10   Review

1. most   **3.** 800 microseconds   **5.** unsorted or small   **7.** O(N)

9. 15   92   37   45   78   **11.** true

13. K—overhead to set up and finish the process; f(N)—function of N, usually represent-
    ing number of repetitive processes carried out; k—run-time cost for carrying out one
    repetitive process

15. **(a)** O(N²) **(b)** O(N)   **17.** false

Section 11.1

1. There will usually be less than `MaxStus` students in a class, and the professor will usually give less than `MaxTests` quizzes.

2. No, a chessboard must always have eight rows and eight columns on it.

5. **(a)**

```
CONST
  TotalClasses = 4;
  MaxInClass = 50;
TYPE
  NameType = STRING[40];        {or whatever works in another dialect}
  NamesArray = ARRAY[1..TotalClasses, 1..MaxInClass] OF NameType;
VAR
  Names: NamesArray;
              (b)
CONST
  MaxInClass = 50;
TYPE
  NameType = STRING[40];        {or whatever works in another dialect}
  NamesArray = ARRAY[1..MaxInClass] OF NameType;
VAR
  Names: NamesArray;
            (c)   CONST
                    MaxInClass = 50;
                  TYPE
                    AvesArray = ARRAY[1..MaxInClass] OF real;
                  VAR
                    StuAves: AvesArray;
                    TotalStudents: integer;    {1..50}
          7.
          FUNCTION BestAverage(VAR Results: ResArray;
                  TotalStudents, TotalTests: integer): real;
            VAR
              BestTemp,              {candidate for BestAverage}
              Sum: real;             {sum of test scores for a given student}
              StuNo,                 {access to a particular student}
              TestNo: integer;       {access to a particular test}
            BEGIN
              BestTemp:= 0;
              FOR StuNo:= 1 TO TotalStudents DO
                BEGIN
                  Sum:= 0;
                  FOR TestNo:= 1 TO TotalTests DO
                    Sum:= Sum + Results[StuNo, TestNo];
                  IF BestTemp > Sum/TotalTests THEN
                    BestTemp:= Sum/TotalTests
                END;
              BestAverage:= BestTemp
            END;
```

Section 11.2

1. true   2. false   3. (c) 58 (e) 53
4. (c) sum of row 3 elements (e) sum of diagonal elements
7. (a) row-by-column processing (c) single-row processing (e) single-column processing

8. **(a)** refer to Exercise 7 of previous section

(c)
```
FUNCTION WorstTest(VAR Results: ResArray;
                        M, TotalTests: integer): integer;
    VAR
      TempWorst,
      TestNo: integer;
    BEGIN
      TempWorst:= 1;
      FOR TestNo:= 2 TO TotalTests DO
        IF Results[M, TestNo] < Results[M, TempWorst] THEN
          TempWorst:= M;
      WorstTest:= TempWorst
    END;
```

(e)
```
FUNCTION TotalFailed(VAR Results: ResArray;
            TotalStudents, N, PassingGrade: integer): integer;
  VAR
    StuNo,                    {access to one student's test score}
    CountSoFar: integer;   {accumulates count of failing students}
  BEGIN
    CountSoFar:= 0;
    FOR StuNo:= 1 TO TotalStudents DO
      IF Results[StuNo, N] < PassingGrade THEN
        CountSoFar:= CountSoFar + 1;
    TotalFailed:= CountSoFar
  END;
```

Section 11.3

1. 4

0.00	0.00	8.00	0.00
8.00	7.50	0.00	8.00
8.00	9.00	0.00	8.00
8.00	7.50	8.00	8.00
8.00	10.00	8.00	7.00
8.00	0.00	8.00	9.00
4.00	8.00	0.00	0.00
15.00	12.00	10.00	20.00

2. The values must be read in using column-by-row processing.

4. It is more efficient to simply pass in a reference array by VAR.

6. The value of TotalPayRoll represents the total payroll for the first Employee workers paid.

Section 11.4

1. 10,000 **3. (b)** 5 9 3 **(c)** 73 **(e)** 38

4. **(b)** display all K elements for fixed I, J access expressions
   (c) sum over all elements for fixed access on I dimension
   (e) sum over the diagonal elements

5. **(d)** Two values are returned for part (a) but only one for parts (b) and (c).

Chapter 11   Program Testing Hints

1. **(a)** 640,000 **(b)** 384,000 **(c)** 359,040

Chapter 11   Review

1. **(a)** 3 **(b)** 6000 **3.** false **4.** a single-row processor

7. **(a)** when *LoI* = *HiI* **(b)** when *LoJ* = *HiJ* **(c)** when both equalities hold

8. true **9.** false **11.** **(a)** 500 more **(b)** 50 more

13. Yes, the syntax to access one of the elements is correct.

15. **(a)** *Sum ← 0*
    FOR Index ← 1 TO 500 DO
        Sum ← Sum + AnArray[Index, Ch]
    AnotherArray[Ch] ← Sum

  (c) *Zeroes ← 0*
    FOR Index ← 1 TO 500 DO
      FOR Ch ← 'A' TO 'M' DO
        IF AnArray[Index, Ch] = 0 THEN
          Zeroes ← Zeroes + 1

16. true

Section 12.1

2. a variable identifier; a subrange expression **3.** **(b)** ii, iv

4. (v) My telephone number is (218)555-8818

6. **(a)** CONST
```
        TotalDigits = 10;
     TYPE
        AccNoType = STRING[10];   {or PACKED ARRAY[1..10] OF char}
     VAR
        AccNo: AccNoType;
```
  (b) TYPE
```
        StatsRecord = RECORD
          Age, Height, Weight: integer
        END;
     VAR
        Stats: StatsRecord;
```
  (d) TYPE
```
        NameString = STRING[20];
        NameRecord = RECORD
          First, Middle, Last: NameString
        END;
        AccRecord = RECORD
          AccNo: AccNoType;     {see Answer 6(a)}
          Name: NameRecord;
          Balance: real
        END;
     VAR
        Account: AccRecord;
```
  (f) TYPE
```
        PricesRecord = RECORD
```

```
                    Hi, Lo, Last: real
                 END;
               VAR
                 PriceInfo: PricesRecord;
```

7. **(a)** `writeln(AccNo);`

   (b) `WITH Stats DO`
   ```
         writeln('AGE = ', Age:1,'    HEIGHT = ',Height:1,
                     '   WEIGHT = 'Weight:1);
   ```

   (d) `WITH Account, Name DO`
   ```
         BEGIN
           writeln('The account number is ', AccNo, '.');
           writeln('The name is ', First, ' ', Middle, ' ', Last, '.');
           writeln('The balance is $', Balance:4:2)
         END;
   ```

   (f) `WITH PriceInfo DO`
   ```
         writeln('HIGH = ', Hi:4:2,'    LOW = ', Lo:4:2,
                     '    LAST = ', Last:4:2);
   ```

Section 12.2

1. A hierarchical record structure is a record type such that at least one record in the structure contains another record type.

4. **(a)** `Call, Class, State,` and `ZipCode`
   (d) `CityName, Street, No, State,` and `ZipCode`

6. **(b)** `State` and `ZipCode`
   (c) `SocSecNo, Status, Results, Average, State,` and `ZipCode`

7. `WITH Member, PName, Address, City DO    BEGIN  {statements}    END;`

8. **(a)** `WITH PlatoonMember.Name DO`
   ```
              writeln(Last,', ',First,' ',Middle[1],'.');
   ```
   (c) `FUNCTION IsOfficer(Rank: RankType): boolean;`
   ```
         BEGIN
           IsOfficer:= Rank = Lieutenant
         END;
   ```
   as called in the context of
   ```
         IF IsOfficer(PlatoonMember.Rank) THEN
           {statement};
   ```

Section 12.3

1. **(a)** `Results[3]` **(b)** `Average` and `Status` **(c)** `SocSecNo`
   6.

```
{*                                                                *}
PROCEDURE ExchangeTwoRecs(VAR RecA, RecB: StuRecord);
  VAR
    Temp: StuRecord;
  BEGIN
    Temp:= RecA;
    RecA:= RecB;
    RecB:= Temp
  END;
```

```
{+                                                                              +}
    PROCEDURE SortClass(Enrollment: integer; VAR Class: ClassArray);
      VAR
        Sorted,
        Index,
        Lowest:  1..MaxStus;
      BEGIN
        FOR Sorted:= 1 to (Enrollment − 1) do
          BEGIN
            Lowest:= Sorted;
            FOR Index:= Sorted+1 TO Enrollment DO
              IF Class[Index].Name.Last < Class[Lowest].Name.Last THEN
                Lowest:= Index;
            Exchange(Class[Lowest],Class[Sorted])
            END
      END;
{*                                                                              *}
```

8.

```
PROCEDURE ShowHighestFinal(VAR Class: ClassArray; Enrollment: IndexType);
  VAR
    Index,
    HiIndex: IndexType;
  BEGIN
    HiIndex:= 1;
    FOR Index:= 2 TO Enrollment DO
      IF Class[Index].Results[TotalTests] >
         Class[HiIndex].Results[TotalTests]   THEN
        HiIndex:= Index;
    WITH Class[HiIndex], Name DO
      BEGIN
        write(First, ' ', Middle, ' ', Last, ' got the high score of ');
        writeln(Results[TotalTests]:1, ' on the final exam.')
      END
  END;
```

9.
```
      TYPE
        {define NameType, AddressRecord, SSNoType as before}
        PersonRecord = RECORD
          Name: NameType;
          Address: AddressRecord;   {Example 12.6}
          IDNo: SSNoType
        END;

        StatusRecord = RECORD
          QPA: real;
          HrsCompleted: integer;
          ClassLevel: String40  {e.g. 'Junior'}
        END;

        CourseRecord = RECORD
          CourseName,
          CourseNo: String40;
```

```
      YearTaken,
      CreditHrs: integer;
      Grade: char
   END;

   CourseArray = ARRAY[1..50] OF CourseRecord;

   InfoCourseRecord = RECORD
     TotalCourses: integer;
     Courses: CourseArray
   END;

   StuRecord = RECORD
     Personal: PersonRecord;
     Status: StatusRecord;
     CourseInfo: InfoCourseRecord
   END;

 VAR
   AStudent: StuRecord;
```

Chapter 12   Program Testing Hints

1. In the context of a single block of code, one cannot distinguish between a reference due to field selection and a reference that is due to a global variable.
2. The selection expressions are less clumsy to code.
4. Replace the period by a comma.

Chapter 12   Review

1. None of these anonymous fields can be passed into other blocks as parameters.
3. Yes, it would make sense. Suppose, for example we have customer accounts that make up one array of records. Each field in this array could represent the checks written out or the deposits made. Both of these types can be coded as records. There may be problems with memory, however, if too many elements are given to the field variables.
4. Use a record with three fields to emphasize that the only semantic relationship between the three fields is that they represent the characteristics of the same person.

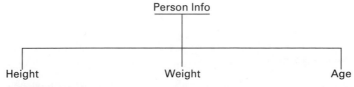

FIGURE AJ.1

7. **(a)** One level where access is made to the fields of four completely different records. This type of code, however, is very obscuring. Most likely, 4 levels are being accessed.
   (b) 4 **(c)** 4 **(d)** an array of records where the structure is hierarchical

(e) an array of records where the structure is hierarchical

(f) a hierarchical record structure (g) a record structure

10. 1, the one that contains the professor's name

11. False, it can only be an identifier that represents a particular field variable

Section 13.1

1. Yes, because they all have a defined logical appearance and a set of defining operations that work on the specified type.

2. A client program declares a variable(s) of the given abstract type, then uses the defining operations on the variable(s) of the given type.

4. (b) the cube of $1 - 3i$, that is $-26 + 18i$

5. MakeComp(0, 0, Sum)

Section 13.2

1. The DivComp operation will fail when the value of the Factor2 is equal to the complex number $0 + i0$, i.e. Factor2.XRe $\leftrightarrow$ 0.0 and Factor2.YIm $\leftrightarrow$ 0.0.

4.
```
FUNCTION PureReal(ANumber: ComplexNo): boolean;
  BEGIN
    PureReal:= (ANumber.XRe <> 0) AND (ANumber.YIm = 0)
  END;

FUNCTION PureIm(ANumber: ComplexNo): boolean;
  BEGIN
    PureIm:= (ANumber.XRe = 0) AND(ANumber.YIm <> 0)
  END;

FUNCTION Mixed(ANumber: ComplexNo): boolean;
  BEGIN
    Mixed:= (ANumber.XRe <> 0) AND (ANumber.YIm <> 0)
  END;
```

5.
```
PROCEDURE GetTwoParallel(Z1, Z2: ComplexNo; VAR ZParallel: Comple
  VAR
    Prod,
    Sum: ComplexNo;
  BEGIN
    MultComp(Z1, Z2, Prod);
    AddComp(Z1, Z2, Sum);
    DivComp(Prod, Sum, ZParallel)
  END;
```

Section 13.3

3. Yes because only 2 people rather than 3 are allowed on queue at any given time.

4. Head: Lincoln, Tail: Tyler; Queue: Lincoln Jackson Tyler
Head: Lincoln, Tail: Truman; Queue: Lincoln Jackson Tyler Truman
Head: Lincoln, Tail: Adams; Queue: Lincoln Jackson Tyler Truman Adams
queue is unchanged, Burr cannot be added because queue is full
Head: Jackson, Tail: Adams; Queue: Jackson Tyler Truman Adams
Head: Tyler, Tail: Adams; Queue: Tyler Truman Adams

Head: Truman, Tail: Adams; Queue: Truman Adams
Head: Truman, Tail: Roosevelt; Queue: Truman Adams Roosevelt

7.
```
FUNCTION QPosition(SearchName: ItemType; Queue: QueueType): integer;
  VAR
    CandPos: integer;
    CandName: ItemType;
    Found: boolean;
  BEGIN
    Found:= false;
    CandPos:= 1;
    WHILE NOT QueueEmpty(Queue) AND NOT Found DO
      BEGIN
        FirstOnQueue(Queue, CandName);
        IF CandName = SearchName THEN
          Found:= true
        ELSE
          CandPos:= CandPos + 1;
        DeleteQueue(Queue)
      END
    IF Found THEN
      QPosition:= CandPos
    ELSE
      QPosition:= 0
  END;
```

Section 13.4

1. Define NullItem = maxint; and ItemType = integer; no other changes are necessary.
2. All operations would O(N), the cost of making a local copy of an array.   3. No
4. All of them; all operations will be O(1), except for DeleteQueue, which would be O(N).   6. Yes, the function QEmpty and QFull.

```
FUNCTION QEmpty(Queue: QueueType): boolean;
  BEGIN
    QEmpty:= Queue[1] = ''
  END;
```

```
FUNCTION QFull(Queue: QueueType): boolean;
  BEGIN
    QFull:= Queue[MaxQueue] <> ''
  END;
```

Section 13.5

1. last in, first out; last in   2. so all operations are O(1)   3. No

Chapter 13   Program Testing Hints

1. To separate them from the operations that are actually required for the implementation of the ADT. The client has absolutely no use for the maintenance operations; only the ADT designer requires them.

2. so they can be used again if modifications on the ADT become necessary

3.
```
PROCEDURE ShowTail(VAR Queue: QueueType);
  BEGIN
    writeln('The value of tail is ', Queue.Tail:1)
  END;

PROCEDURE ShowInUse(VAR Queue: QueueType);
  BEGIN
    writeln('The value of InUse is ', Queue.InUse:1)
  END;
```

Chapter 13 Review

1. So that none of the components of the ADT can be used as parameters. This wrongly applied usage can destroy the integrity of the ADT.

4. An incomplete unit is missing some operations, but the operations present may be correctly coded. An incorrect unit may have a complete set of operations, but some of them are incorrectly coded.

8. when doing some on-line testing of the queue ADT; no, because the value of Head is part of the queue's implementation, not part of its interface.

9. to separate the interface part from the implementation part of an ADT; absolutely not

13. The first is a problem statement for a program or a client program, and the second is a problem statement for the implementation of an ADT.

14. MakeComp and AddComp

Section 14.1

1. No, the subrange is too large.

3. (a) Either ASet or BSet is the null set.
   (d) The membership of ASET and BSet is the same, except that BSet contains the additional member ['8'].
   (f) BSet is the null set.

5. (a) Palette:= [Red..Violet]
   (b) It contains all possible members of ColorSet.
   (c) Palette:= []; (d) It contains no members of ColorSet.

Section 14.2

1. accumulating members from an initial null set.

3. Yes. The problem with this strategy is that the meaning of the set variable changes over the course of the algorithm's execution. Until the final statement, EAccumulator's value represents the membership of all values that occurred during the sequence of events. With the final statement, the value of EAccumulator represents the membership of all values that did not occur during the sequence of events.

4. (c) 1 2 10 11

Section 14.3

1. (a) Nothing in common (b) A contains B (c) 3 6

5. {* *}
```
    FUNCTION TotalSymptoms(Symptoms: SickSet): integer;
      VAR
        Count: integer;
        Complaint: SympType;
      BEGIN
        Count:= 0;
        FOR Complaint:= Sniffles TO Muscleache DO
          IF Complaint IN Symptoms THEN
            Count:= Count + 1;
        TotalSymptoms:= Count
      END;
```
{+ +}
```
    FUNCTION Recommendation(Symptoms: SickSet): integer;
      BEGIN
        CASE TotalSymptoms(SickSet) OF
          0:   Recommendation:= 0;
          1:   Recommendation:= 1;
          2:   IF Symptoms = [Headache, Muscleache] THEN
                 Recommendation:= 2
               ELSE IF Symptoms = [Sniffles, Fever]) THEN
                 Recommendation:= 3
               ELSE
                 Recommendation:= 1;
          3,4: Recommendation:=4
        END {CASE}
      END;
```
{* *}

8.
```
   TYPE
      ColorType = (Red, Green, Canary, Blue, Silver, Black,
                   Pink, Orange, Yellow, Violet, White, Grey);
      ColorSet = SET OF ColorType;
   VAR
     Choice, InStock: ColorSet;

   FUNCTION Available(Choice, InStock: ColorSet): boolean;
     BEGIN
       Available:= Choice <= InStock
     END;
```

as called in the context of

```
IF Available(Choice, InStock + [Red..Pink]) THEN   {statement}
```

Section 14.4

1. the TYPE definition for SysString
3. It can be derived as a function using the two functions StrEqual and StrLessThan.

4. **(d)** String[3] ⟷ 'John '
   String[4] ⟷ 'Roe'
   String[5] ⟷ 'John Roe'
   String[1] ⟷ 'John '
   String[2] ⟷ 'John Richard Roe'
   String[2] ⟷ 'John Roe'
   display will occur because the strings are equal

5. **(a)** the null char value   **(b)** ***************   **(c)** {***************}

Section 14.5

3. FUNCTION Occurrences(SubStar,CandStr: StringADT): integer;
```
   VAR
     Pos,              {returned by call to StarPos}
     RemLen,     {length of SubStr}
     Count: integer;
   BEGIN
     RemLen:= StrLength(SubString) - 1;
     Count:= 0;
     Pos:= StartPos(SubStr, CandStr);
     WHILE (Pos <> 0) DO
       BEGIN
         Count:= Count + 1;
         StrRemove(1, Pos+RemLen, CandStr);
         Pos:= StartPos(SubStr, CandStr)
       END;
     Occurrences:= Count
   END;
```

Section 14.6

2. The Chars field of OutStr has had values assigned over the subrange 1..OutStrPos as taken from the Chars field of InStr over the corresponding subrange Start..Start + InStrPos − 1.

3.
```
PROCEDURE StrInsert{InStr: StringADT; Start: integer;
                                      VAR InOutStr: StringADT};
  VAR
    PredString, SuccString: StringADT;
  BEGIN
    StrExtract(InOutStr, 1, Start-1, PredString);
    StrExtract(InOutStr, Start, PredString.Len+1-Start, SuccString);
    StrConcat(PredString, InStr, InOutStr);
    Concat(InOutStr, SuccString, InOutStr)
  END;
```

Chapter 14   Program Testing Hints

1. ```
   UpCase:= ['A'..'Z'];
   LowCase:= ['a'..'z'];
   Correct:= Ch IN LowCase;
   Correct:= NOT(Ch IN UpCase);
   ```
   ```

```
        ChSet:= [];
        ChSet:= ChSet + UpCase - ['A', 'E', 'I', 'O', 'U']
```

3. **(a)** `['A', 'E', 'I'] <= ChSet` **(b)** `['A','E','I'] * ChSet <> []`

4. **(a)** No **(d)** No **(e)** Yes **(f)** Yes

Chapter 14   Review

1. Yes   **3.** Yes, because the null set is defined for any set type.

5. **(a)** Yes, if `ASet` is also a null set.
   (b) `ASet` does not have more members than `BSet`.

7. **(a)** To record specific events that occurred during a particular sequence.
   (b) To record specific events that did not occur during a given sequence.

8. **(a)** `ChSet:= ChSet + [Ch];` **(b)** `ChSet:= ChSet + Vowels;`
   (e) `ChSet:= ChSet - [LoCh..HiCh];`

10. It can be used in any dialect of Pascal.

11. All string "constants" have to be converted into compatible `StringADT` type variables in order to work with other strings.

13. No, it requires another function to determine which of two strings is alphabetically ahead of the other.

14. Use `ReadStr` or `ReadlnStr` with the standard file `input` as the file variable.

Section 15.1

3. True; the algorithm is of that sort where the solution to the smaller problem also represents a solution to a larger problem.

5. No. The computer "goes the wrong way" with each recursive call. The first few calls have the values of N go from -3 to -4 to -5 to -6, and so forth. The trivial problem where N is 0 will never be achieved when N is a negative value because $(N - 1)$ is passed into each successive block. Hence, the computer builds an "infinite stack."

7. block statement:

```
BEGIN
  IF  (M < 0)  OR  (N > 0)  THEN
    GCD:= GCD(abs(M),  abs(N))
  ELSE IF  M < N THEN
    GCD:= GCD(N,  M)
  ELSE IF  N = 0 THEN
    GCD:= M
  ELSE
    GCD:= GCD(N,  N MOD N)
END;
```

Section 15.2

1. A new data area is set up, and the sequence of statements belonging to the process pushed is carried out.

2. The data area of the process on top of the run-time stack is returned back to memory available for further processing because there are no more process statements to be carried out.

6.

```pascal
PROGRAM ReverseChars(output, AFile);
  {Uses the LinkKeyIn procedure}
  VAR
    AFile: text;
  {*                                                                    *}
PROCEDURE LinkKeyIn(var AFile: text);
  BEGIN {insert sequence here; local string variable required}  END;
{*                                                                      *}
PROCEDURE GetStoreDisplay(VAR AFile; text);
  {procedure that uses recursion to reverse display chars on a single
  line of text}
  VAR
    Ch: char;
  BEGIN
    IF NOT eoln(AFile) THEN
      BEGIN
        read(AFile, Ch);
        GetStoreDisplay(AFile);
        write(Ch)
      END
    ELSE
      readln(AFile)
  END;
{+                                                                      +}
PROCEDURE ReverseALine(var AFile: text);
  {makes the initial call to the recursive procedure GetStoreDisplay}
  BEGIN
    GetStoreDisplay(AFile)
  END;
{*                                                                      *}
BEGIN
  LinkKeyIn(AFile);
  reset(AFile);
  WHILE NOT eof(AFile) DO
    ReverseALine(AFile);
  close(AFile)
END.
```

Section 15.3

1. Ints[1] ⟷ 52; Ints[2] ⟷ 78; Ints[3] ⟷ 44; Ints[4] ⟷ 91
2. Ints[1] ⟷ 91; Ints[2] ⟷ 44; Ints[3] ⟷ 78; Ints[4] ⟷ 52
4.  ```pascal
    FUNCTION Permutations(M, N: integer): integer;
        BEGIN
            IF M < N THEN
          Permutations:= 0
            ELSE IF N = 1 THEN
          Permutations:= M
            ELSE
            Permutations:= M * Permutations(M - 1, N - 1)
        END;
    ```
    ```

Section 15.4

1. The function Fibonacci is not linearly recursive because more than one recursive call is possibly within a single process. The procedure SetFibNos is linearly recursive because at most only one recursive call is made to the procedure within the processing environment of another SetFibNos procedure.

3. See Figures AJ-2 and AJ-3 for Exercises 3 and 4 below.

Set (7)

Set (,6)

Set (5)

Set (4)

Set (3)

FIGURE AJ.2 Exercise 3 in Section 15.4   Set (1)

4.
```
FUNCTION Combinations (M, N: integer): integer;
    BEGIN
        IF M < N) THEN
            Combinations:= 1
        ELSE IF M = N THEN
            Combinations:= 1
        ELSE
            Combinations:= Combinations (M-1, N) + Combinations (M-1, N-1)
    END;
```

5.

C(5,3)

C(4,3)   C(4,2)

C(3,3)   C(3,2)   C(3,2)   C(3,1)

C(2,2)   C(2,1)   C(2,2)   C(2,1)   C(2,1)   C(2,0)

C(1,1)   C(1,0)   C(1,1)   C(1,0)   C(1,1)   C(1,0)

FIGURE AJ.3 Exercise 5 in Section 15.4

Section 15.5

1. **(a)** Linear and Binary **(b)** Lowest and Sorted
2. Binary is $O(\log_2(N))$; all others are $O(N)$
5. PROCEDURE GetLoAndHi (Probe: integer; VAR Ints; IntsArray;
   VAR Lo, Hi: integer);

```
    BEGIN
      IF Probe <> 0 THEN
        IF Ints[Probe] < Ints[Lo] THEN
          Lo:= Probe
        ELSE IF Ints[Probe] < Ints[Hi] THEN
          Hi:= Probe;
        GetLoAndHi(Probe-1, Ints, Lo, Hi)
    END;


    Lo:= TotalElements;
    Hi:= TotalElements;
    GetLoAndHi(TotalElements-1, Ints, Lo, Hi);
```

Section 15.6

2. 42
3. It will never occur because if the initial call is over the subrange
   1..TotalElements where TotalElements is greater than 1, the precondition
   for the relationship between Lo and Hi is that Lo must always be less than or equal to
   Hi.
5. **(a)** 14 **(b)** 1 **(c)** 2
   (d) No, it is not possible because the local array for Merge is absolutely necessary. If
   Temp is passed into each block using a VAR call, the algorithm simply will not
   work.

Chapter 15 Program Testing Hints

2. **(a)** An endless stack would be built as a result of this code. The computer will keep
   calling GetStoreDisplay with the file pointer's never advancing to the next
   line.
3. FUNCTION Fibonacci (N: integer): integer;

```
    VAR
       Temp: integer;
    BEGIN
      IF N IN [1, 2] then
        Temp:= N - 1
      ELSE
        Temp:= Fibonacci(N-2) + Fibonacci(N-1);
      writeln('Fib(', N:1 ,') = ', Temp:1);
      Fibonacci:= Temp
    END;
```

Chapter 15 Review

1. A linear recursive process makes at the most one recursive call per process. A nonlinear recursive process may make more than one recursive call per process.

4. The recursive code for the Fibonacci function is so inefficient because it solves the same problem more than once in different processes.

6. Text is displayed every time the computer makes a recursive call to the given process. Such code may be placed at that point in a process for the purpose of tracing the mechanism of a recursive algorithm.

7. True. A push on the stack represents a call to a procedure or function, and a pop off the stack represents the completion of a procedure or function. Because every procedure or function called must be completed when a program runs successfully to completion, the same number of pushes and pops on the run-time stack must have occurred.

9. **(a)** at point B **(b)** add 1 at point A and subtract 1 at point F

11. It is more efficient both with respect to run time and memory allocation.

13. (a) and (d)

15. Write it as a one-block statement that makes the call `SortIt(1, TotalElements, AnArray)`.

Section 16.1

1. `Readln` is illegal with binary files because no binary file contains the <eoln> marker. The `writeln` statement does not work because the <eoln> marker cannot be written into a binary file.

2. No. It can be implemented only if the file has `integer` components.

3.
```
PROGRAM MakeInts(input, output, Ints);
   {default linking mechanism assumed}
   VAR
      Ints:FILE OF integer;
      AnInt: integer;
   BEGIN
      rewrite(Ints);
      writeln('Enter integers, ending sequence with negative value:')
      read(AnInt);
      WHILE AnInt > 0 DO
        BEGIN
           write(Ints, AnInt);
           read(AnInt)
        END;
      readln;
      writeln('The file has been created.');
   END.
```

Section 16.2

1. The procedure `close` should be executed to free up any file variable so that it can be opened to another external file as soon as a given link with the previous directory file is no longer required. If a program requires access to many different external files all of the same type, this practice keeps the number of global file variables to a minimum. Also, if a given file is written into and the file variable is not closed, the contents contained in the actual file may not be complete. This error-prone event will occur regardless of the rest of the statements in the program.

3. The `boolean` function `Stu1GoesFirst` is called as

```
IF Stu1GoesFirst(MStu1.Info.SocSecNo, MStu2.Info.SecSocNo) THEN
  {statements}
```

The function itself is coded as the one-liner:

```
FUNCTION Stu1GoesFirst(SSNo1, SSNo2: SSNoType): boolean;
  BEGIN
    Stu1GoesFirst:= SSNo1 < SSNo2
  END;
```

Section 16.3

1. Yes, because the NIL value is defined for any pointer variable.
3. (a), (c), (d), and (e) are all valid   4. (a) 7 7   (d) error message   (f) 5   10

Section 16.4

2. ByNo[1] points to 'Bailey', ByNo[2] points to 'Bartleson', ByNo[3] points to 'Amherst', ByNo[4] points to 'Browne', and ByNo[5] points to 'Andrews'

Chapter 16   Program Testing Hints

1. **(a)** AValue cannot be a structured variable unless it is a string variable.
   (b) They all have an identical appearance, for the single <eof> marker is all that any empty binary file contains.
3. **(a)** Does not work because <eoln> is not a component of a binary file.
   (e) Works because more than one component can be read in from a binary file.
4. It effectively skips over the first record, and reads in values for the record variables from the second and third components of AFile.
5. Yes. In this case two records are written as duplicate components into AFile as the values taken on by the fields of ARec. The values taken on by BRec are written as a non-duplicate component into AFile.
7. sequence **(a)** The statement new(BStr) should be removed.
9. Billy The Kid   **10.** Billy

Chapter 16   Review

2. **(a)** True **(b)** False **(c)** False **(d)** False   **3.** No   **4.** Yes, the expressions being writ-
7.   ten are both integer
8. False

   Yes, but it represents bad code because the file components cannot be used as parame-
11. ters in a program.
12. a machine address no

    The first statement allocates memory to APtr. The next statement assigns the value 7 to APtr^. The third statement sets up a configuration where APtr^ and BPtr^ are dereferences to the same dynamic variable. The final statement displays the value as-
15. signed to the dereferenced variable.

    Less memory can be used to hold information in structures that otherwise have to be implemented as duplicate arrays of records. Use an array of pointers when the implementation with two or more arrays of records will contain identical information. The records themselves may be arranged in a different order with each array.

18. (a) and (b)

Section 17.1

1. No. It must be a record variable where one of the field variable is the link field.
3. Yes. If the list is large enough (it must have *very* many items), the machine can run out of memory. **4. (a)** 75 **(d)** 98 **(e)** maxint's value
5. CONST
    NullItem = maxint;
  TYPE
    ItemType = integer;
  {all other code is the same as in the text}

Section 17.2

1. True   **2.** The function QCount would need to be recorded as an $O(N)$ function.
5. False.
6. Virtually no operation would have meaning if this variable were eliminated from the field list of QType. For starters, there is no means by which the list that makes up the queue can be accessed.
7. one more than the number of items on queue
10. No, because a function call returns a value and never a variable. In this case, an attempt is made to pass an address value into a VAR parameter.

13. PROCEDURE ADDQueue{Item: ItemType; VAR Queue: QType};
    VAR
      PrevNode,
      Temp: LNodePtr;
    BEGIN
      MakeNode(Item, Temp);
      IF Queue.Head = NIL THEN
        Queue.Head:= Temp
      ELSE
        BEGIN
          PrevNode:= Queue.Head;
          WHILE NextNode(PrevNode) <> NIL DO
            PrevNode:= NextNode(PrevNode);
          PrevNode^.Next:= Temp
        END
    END;

Section 17.3

2. No, because there is only a function to return the pointer to the top node on the stack.
3. **(a)** 2   **(c)** 1   **(g)** ill-formed
4. An error message is displayed because an attempt is made to pop an item from an empty stack.
5. the value of the integer read in

Section 17.4

1. `OListType` defines an ordered list type, consisting of many nodes, and `OListPtr` defines a pointer that points to a single `OList` node.

4.
```
15   35   41   63   72   79      no change        no change
15   35   63   72   79       8   15   35   63   72   79
```

5.
```
PROCEDURE KillList(VAR AList: ListType);
  VAR
    TempPtr,    {points to candidate node for deletion}
    NextPtr:    {points to node that follows TempPtr^}
                LNodePtr;
  BEGIN
    TempPtr:= AList.First;
    WHILE TempPtr <> NIL DO
      BEGIN
        NextPtr:= NextNode(TempPtr);
        KillNode(TempPtr);
        TempPtr:= NextPtr
      END;
  END;
```

6.
```
PROCEDURE ChangeNodesValue(AnItem: ItemType;
                    PrevNodePtr: LNodePtr; VAR AList: ListType);
  BEGIN
    DeleteNode(PrevNodePtr, AList);
    InsertNode(AnItem, PrevNodePtr, AList)
  END;
```

Chapter 17   Program Testing Hints

1. The unit is incomplete. At the very least, it is missing a node primitive.
2. a node of the structure and the structure itself
5. The structure is broken because `Present` points to `Temp`, but `Temp` then points back to `Present`. All nodes following `Present` in the initial structure are no longer accessible. Hence, part of the list is lost as garbage.

Chapter 17   Review

2. False: N loop passes must be executed to find the Nth node.
4. All the nodes beyond `APtr^` are no longer accessible because the pointer address `APtr^.Next` was thrown back on the run-time heap by `dispose(APtr)`.
6. `APtr^` is the last node in the list.   7. `NextNode(APtr) = NIL`
9. The last item in a queue is not meant to be directly accessible to a client program.
12. In theory, the size of the queue is limitless because dynamic variables can keep being created and added to the queue.
13. **(a)** false **(b)** false **(c)** true   14. Kathy   15. under no circumstances

Section 18.1

1. Adams, Holmes, Mason, Ryan, Thomas

3. **(a)** left — 3, right — 8 **(c)** left —4, right — 2
4. **(a)** left — Davis, right — Young **5. (a)** Davis **(c)** null string **(f)** Williams
6.
```
FUNCTION Leftmost (Root: BSTPtr): BSTPtr;
  VAR
    Candidate: BSTPtr;
  BEGIN
    IF EmptyTree(Root) THEN
      Candidate:= NIL
    ELSE
      Candidate:= Root;
    WHILE NodesLeftTree(Candidate) <> NIL DO
      Candidate:= NodesLeftTree(Candidate);
    Leftmost:= Candidate
  END;
```

Section 18.2

1. false **3.** ShowTree(NodesLeftTree(NameTree)).
4. Garbage, if the computer does not issue an error message. The means to reference the tree structure is not passed out of the block.

6.

FIGURE AJ.4

Section 18.3

1. an empty tree
3. Yes, because when TNode is equal to NIL, the value returned by the call to NodesKey is NullKey.
4. The node containing KeyValue is the parent of the subtree being searched. Hence, no match will be found. The search is being done using the Key field of the node variable Candidate.

6.

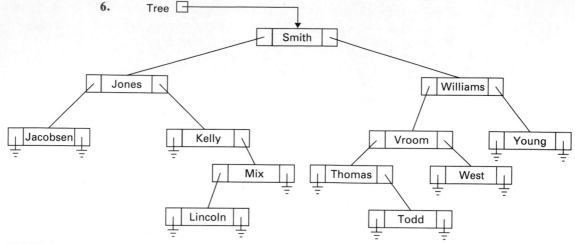

FIGURE AJ.5

7. final tree

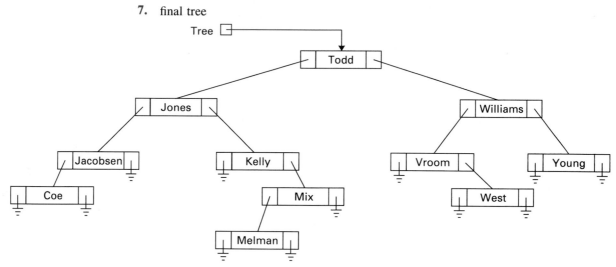

FIGURE AJ.6

8.

```
PROCEDURE ChangeNodesInfo(KeyValue: KItemType; NewInfo: InfoType;
                                    VAR Tree: BSTType);
  VAR
    Success: boolean;   {returns true if node with KeyValue exists}
  BEGIN
    DeleteTNode(KeyValue, Tree, Success);
    IF Success THEN
      AddTNode(KeyValue, NewInfo, Tree, Success)
    ELSE
      writeln('There is no such node on the tree.')
  END;
```

10.
```
FUNCTION SearchTNode{(Tree: BSTType; KeyValue: KItemType): BSTPtr;
    VAR
        Dummy,        {required dummy variable for parameter of Search}
        Candidate:  {candidate value for the function}
                    BSTPtr;
    BEGIN
        Search(Tree, KeyValue, Candidate, Dummy);
        SearchTNode:= Candidate
    END;
```

Section 18.4

2. False, a node must be created before its links can be built.

3. The values are read in such that the preorder traversal can be used to build the tree. The node is created first using this algorithm. Any operator precedes the two operands, hence the node containing its value is created before the operand nodes are.

4. The display is not the same for the nonsense traversals because the two trees are constructed differently even though their nodes contain the same information fields. The display for LNR traversals must be the same because of the logical natuer of a BST.

6. **(a)** nothing, machine needs further input **(b)** 7 **(c)** 5 **(d)** 16 **(e)** 4

Chapter 18   Program Testing Hints

1. 8

3. Their values are not readily displayed, and they are assigned values based completely on the programmer's logic, be it good or bad.

4. draw pictures   **6.** a tree that is initially empty

Chapter 18   Review

1. Every node on the binary tree has exactly two link fields; other trees may have more link fields for each node.

2. root node   **6.** NIL

7. when the tree is built where node values are added in ordcr   Example: Young, Williams, Levy, Jimenez, Adams

9. Yes, the nodes are visited in alphabetic order.

10. **(a)** 1 **(b)** 2 **(c)** 3 **(d)** 4 **(e)** N + 1   **11.** 1792

12. True, because of the way the BST is constructed.   **14.** 16

15. It creates garbage. A postorder traversal where each node is killed as it is visited solves the problem without creating any garbage.

16. 54

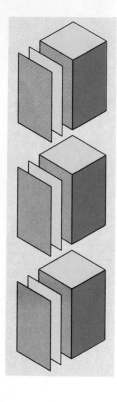

INDEX

G

Garbage, 732–33, 746–47
Get, 898–900
Global constant, 115, 122
Global procedure, 138–41
Global type, 134
Global variable, 115, 147–48
GOTO, 894–96
  harmfulness of using, 896
Guard against:
  dereference of NIL pointer, 786
  processing bad data, 189–90
  reading <eoln>, 378
  reading <eof>, 725

H

Hardware, 2
    system, 3
    faulty, 5
Hard disk, 9
Header:
  function, 316
  as part of a process, 25
  procedure, 116
  program, 36
Heap, run-time, 733–35
Hoare, C. A. R., 709

I

Identifier, 22
  choosing names for, 61, 353
  standard, 22
  syntax for, 37
IF..THEN..ELSE, 159–64
IMPLEMENTATION, 907
Import, 894
IN, 264, 268
  and subrange expressions, 266–68
Information hiding, 592
INHERITS, 912
Initialization:
  counting variable, 217–18
  product-accumulation variable, 227
  recording variable, 237
  set-accumulation variable, 614–15
  sum-accumulation variable, 219
  variables in general, 71
Input device, 3
Input, 36
INTERFACE, 907
Insertion sort, 431–33
Interface, 25
  with periperal devices, 67
  procedure header as, 116
  program to external file, 362–64
  program header as, 25–26
  section of an ADT, 553, 908
Income tax preparation, 97–102
IF-ELSE-IF algorithm, 176

K

Key field. *See* binary search tree, key field
Keyin, 87

L

LABEL, 895–96
Language:
  assembly, 12
  command, 15
  high-level, 12
  machine, 12
  programming, 10
Layout conventions for source code, 61–63,
    138–40, 163–64, 176, 186, 192
Length, 380
Level of nested decisions, 176
Level of top-down design, 135, 138–40
LIFO, 582
Line processor, 377
Linear search. *See* search, linear
Linked list, 758
  linear, 758
LinkReadIn, 376
ListType, 783–88
  interface section, 784
  implementation section, 785–88
Literal, 23, 51
  boolean, 264
  char, 50, 58
  integer, 43
  real, 24, 44
  string, 24, 40–41
Local procedure, 138–41
Local variable, 121, 125, 147–48
Logging on, 15
  protocol for, 15
Loop body, 209–10
Loop control expression, 209
  finding, 221
  for REPEAT..UNTIL loop, 239
  for WHILE loop, 209
Loop control variable, 231, 248
  FOR loop, 231
Loop design considerations, 222, 240–41
Loop entry condition(s), 209
  examples, 210–12
  finding, 228
  FOR statement, 231
Loop exit condition(s), 209
  examples, 210–12
  finding, 221, 228
  FOR statement, 231
Loop, flag-controlled, 327–28, 330–31
Loop initialization, 215. *See also* loop entry
    condition
Loop invariant, 210–12
  finding, 226–27
Loop iteration. *See* loop pass.
Loop pass, 209–13
Loop testing. *See* assertion testing, choosing
    test data

U

UNIT, 907
uppercase and reserved words, 36
USES, 62, 907

V

VAR, 49, 62–63, 117–20
  with file variables, 372
  with function calls, 350
Variable, 23
  access, 300
  accumulation, 219
  anonymous, 728, 730–31
  boolean, 324–28
  char, 50–51
  counting, 217–18
  declaration of, 49–51
  dereferenced, 730
  dummy, 319–20
  dynamic, 714, 728
  event-recording, 237
  field, 508–9, 513–14
  file, 65, 363, 714
  flag, 326–28
  global, 115
  integer, 49–51

  local, 121
  loop-control,
  node vs. ADT,
  pointer, 714, 72   23
  probe, 424–25,
  record, 508
  real, 49–51
  set, 606
  string, 88–90
  structured, 281
Variable list of WITH statement, 518–19
VAX, as multiuser system, 15

W

WHILE, 208–14
  examples, 209, 211, 213, 232, 239–40
  vs. FOR, 232
  vs. REPEAT. . UNTIL, 239–40
  syntax, 208
Wirth, Dr. Nicholas, 13
WITH, 516
  and coding style, 522–23
Wrap-around of array elements, 578
Write, 28, 39–40, 45–48, 367, 372–73, 717
Writeln, 28, 39–40, 45–48, 367, 373–77,
    717